# Pub Guide
# 2011

AA Lifestyle Guides

The RED LION

14th edition September 2010.
© AA Media Limited 2010.

Assessments of AA inspected establishments are based on the experience of the Hotel and Restaurant Inspectors on the occasion(s) of their visit(s) and therefore descriptions given in this guide necessarily contain an element of subjective opinion which may not reflect or dictate a reader's own opinion on another occasion. See pages 6–7 for a clear explanation of how, based on our Inspectors' inspection experiences, establishments are graded. If the meal or meals experienced by an Inspector or Inspectors during an inspection fall between award levels the restaurant concerned may be awarded the lower of any award levels considered applicable.

AA Media Limited strives to ensure accuracy of the information in this guide at the time of printing. Nevertheless, the Publisher cannot be held responsible for any errors or omissions, or for changes in the details given in this guide, or for the consequences of any reliance on the information provided by the same. This does not affect your statutory rights. Due to the constantly evolving nature of the subject matter the information is subject to change. AA Media Limited will gratefully receive any advice from our readers of any necessary updated information.

Please contact:
Advertising Sales Department: advertisingsales@theAA.com
Editorial Department: lifestyleguides@theAA.com
AA Hotel Scheme Enquiries: 01256 844455

Web site addresses are included in some entries and specified by the respective establishment. Such web sites are not under the control of AA Media Limited and as such AA Media Limited has no control over them and will not accept any responsibility or liability in respect of any and all matters whatsoever relating to such web sites including access, content, material and functionality. By including the addresses of third party Web Sites the AA does not intend to solicit business or offer any security to any person in any country, directly or indirectly.

AA Media Limited would like to thank the following photographers, companies and picture libraries for their assistance in the preparation of this book.
Abbreviations for the picture credits are as follows: (t) top; (b) bottom; (l) left; (r) right; (c) centre; (AA) AA World Travel Library.
Front Cover (t) The Durham Ox; (bl) The Bridge Inn; (br) Rose & Crown;
Back Cover (l) The Bugle; (c) The Seven Stars (r) The Anchor.
Every effort has been made to trace the copyright holders, and we apologise in advance for any accidental errors. We would be happy to apply any corrections in the following edition of this publication.
Photographs in the gazetteer provided by the establishments.

Typeset/Repro: Keenes Repro Ltd, London.
Printed and bound by Graficas Estella, Spain.

Directory compiled by the AA Lifestyle Guides Department and managed in the Librios Information Management System and generated from the AA establishment database system.

Pub descriptions have been contributed by the following team of writers: Phil Bryant, Neil Coates, David Foster, David Halford, David Hancock, Mark Taylor and Jenny White.

Published by AA Publishing, a trading name of AA Media Limited, whose registered office is Fanum House, Basing View, Basingstoke RG21 4EA. Registered number 06112600.
A CIP catalogue for this book is available from the British Library.
ISBN: 978-0-7495-6681-4
A04315

Maps prepared by the Mapping Services Department of AA Publishing.

Maps © AA Media Limited 2010.

This product includes mapping data licensed from Ordnance Survey® with the permission of the Controller of Her Majesty's Stationery Office.
© Crown copyright 2010.
All rights reserved.
Licence number 100021153.

Information on National Parks in England provided by the Countryside Agency (Natural England).

Information on National Parks in Scotland provided by Scottish Natural Heritage.

Information on National Parks in Wales provided by The Countryside Council for Wales.

# Contents

# How to Use the Guide

## 1 LOCATION

**Guide order** Pubs are listed alphabetically by name (ignoring The) under their village or town. Towns and villages are listed alphabetically within their county (a county map appears at the back of the guide). The guide has entries for England, Channel Islands, Isle of Man, Scotland and Wales in that order. Some village pubs prefer to be initially located under the nearest town, in which case the village name is included in the address and directions.

**Pick of the Pubs** Over 600 of the best pubs in Britain have been selected by the editor and inspectors and these are highlighted. They have longer, more detailed descriptions and a tinted background. Over 200 of these have a full page entry and two photographs.

## 2 MAP REFERENCE

The map reference number denotes the map page number in the atlas section at the back of the book and (except for London maps) the National Grid reference. The London map references help locate their position on the Central and Greater London maps.

## 3 ESTABLISHMENT NAME AND SYMBOLS

See Key to symbols in the panel on page 5.

## 4 ADDRESS AND POSTCODE DETAILS

This gives the street name and the postcode, and if necessary the name of the village is included (see 1 above). This may be up to five miles from the named location.

☎ **Telephone number,** 🖹 **fax number, e-mail and websites:** Wherever possible we have included an e-mail address.

## 5 DIRECTIONS

Directions are given only when they have been supplied by the proprietor.

## 6 DESCRIPTION

Description of the pub and food.

## 7 OPEN

Indicates the hours and dates when the establishment is open and closed.

## 8 BAR MEALS

Indicates the times and days when proprietors tell us bar food can be ordered, and the average price of a main

---

**1**  **3**  **4**  **14**  **5**  **2**

**CHINLEY**  Map 16 SK08

**Old Hall Inn** ★★★★ INN ♛ NEW

Whitehough SK23 6EJ ☎ 01663 750529
e-mail: info@old-hall-inn.co.uk
dir: *From Chapel-en-le-Frith take B5470 W. Right into Whitehough Head Ln. 0.8m to inn*

Smack in the heart of prime walking country, with Kinder Scout, Mam Tor and Stanage Edge all within easy reach, this family-run, 16th-century traditional pub adjoins Whitehough Hall and offers an impressive choice of ciders and local cask ales (Thornbridge, Abbeydale, Storm), alongside daily menus that make good use of local produce, and comfortable en suite bedrooms. Typical dishes range from steak and kidney pudding and ham, egg and chips to Chatsworth venison with redcurrant and port sauce, and roast leg of lamb. Classic puddings include sticky toffee pudding.

**Open** all day all wk **Bar Meals** L served Mon-Sat 12-2, Sun 12-7.30 booking required D served Mon-Thu 5-9 Fri-Sat 5-9.30 Sun 12-7.30 booking required Av main course £9 **Restaurant** L served Mon-Sat 12-2, Sun 12-7.30 booking required D served Mon-Thu 5-9 Fri-Sat 5-9.30 Sun 12-7.30 booking required Av 3 course à la carte fr £18 ⊕ FREE HOUSE ◀ Marstons, Thornbridge, Phoenix, Abbeydale, Storm Ö Thatchers, Sheppy's, Westons. ♛ 12 **Facilities** Children's menu Children's portions Dogs allowed Garden Parking **Rooms** 4

**6**

**8**

**7**  **9**  **11**  **10**  **12**

---

course as supplied by the proprietor. Please be aware that last orders could vary by up to 30 minutes.

### 9 RESTAURANT

Indicates the times and days when proprietors tell us food can be ordered from the restaurant. The average cost of a 3-course à la carte meal and a 3- or 4-course fixed-price menu are shown as supplied by the proprietor. Last orders may be approximately 30 minutes before the times stated.

### 10 BREWERY AND COMPANY

⊕ **The barrel symbol** indicates the name of the Brewery to which the pub is tied, or the Company that owns it. A free house is where the pub is independently owned and run.

◧ **The beer tankard symbol** indicates the principal beers sold by the pub. Up to five cask or hand-pulled beers are listed. Many pubs have a much greater selection, with several guest beers each week.

Ŏ **The apple symbol** indicates that real cider is available and listed.

♆ **The wine glass symbol** followed by a number indicates the number of wines sold by the glass.

### 11 FACILITIES

Indicates if a pub has a children's menu, children's portions, a garden, allows dogs on the premises, offers parking and has a children's play area. For further information please phone the pub.

### 12 ROOMS

Only accommodation that has been AA inspected and rated is indicated, with the number of en suite bedrooms listed. Many pubs have rooms, but we only indicate those that are AA rated.

### 13 NOTES

As so many establishments take one or more of the major credit cards we only indicate if a pub does not take cards.

### 14 AA STARS/DESIGNATORS

AA Stars (and designators as appropriate) are shown at the beginning of an entry. The AA, in partnership with the national tourist bodies (VisitBritain, VisitScotland and VisitWales) has introduced new Quality Standards for inspected accommodation. See pages 6-7 for details of AA ratings.

| KEY TO SYMBOLS | |
|---|---|
| ◎ | Rosettes – The AA's food award. Explanation on page 7 |
| ★★ | Stars – Accommodation rating. Explanation on pages 6–7 |
| ⊕ | Barrel – Name of Brewery, Company or Free House |
| ◧ | Tankard – Principal beers sold |
| Ŏ | Apple – Real cider available |
| ♆ | Wine glass – Indicates that at least eight wines are available by the glass. For the exact number of wines served this way, see notes at the bottom of each entry |
| NEW | Pubs appearing in the guide for the first time in 2011 |

## AA Classifications & Awards

Many of the pubs in this Guide offer accommodation. Where a Star rating appears next to an entry's name in the Guide, the establishment has been inspected by the AA under common Quality Standards agreed between the AA, VisitBritain, VisitScotland and VisitWales. These ratings are for the accommodation, and ensure that it meets the highest standards of cleanliness, with an emphasis on professionalism, proper booking procedures and prompt and efficient services. Some of the pubs in this Guide offer accommodation but do not belong to a rating scheme. In this case the accommodation is not included in their entry.

AA recognised establishments pay an annual fee that varies according to the classification and the number of bedrooms. The establishments receive an unannounced inspection from a qualified AA inspector who recommends the appropriate classification. Return visits confirm that standards are maintained; the classification is not transferable if an establishment changes hands.

The annual *AA Hotel Guide* and *AA Bed & Breakfast Guide* give further details of recognised establishments and the classification schemes. Details of AA recognised hotels, guest accommodation, restaurants and pubs are also available at **theAA.com,** along with a useful Route Planner.

## AA Hotel Classification

Hotels are classified on a 5-point scale, with one star ★ being the simplest, and five stars offering a luxurious service at the top of the range. The AA's top hotels in Britain and Ireland are identified by red stars. (★)

In addition to the main **Hotel** (HL) classification which applies to some pubs in this Guide, there are other categories of hotel which may be applicable to pubs, as follows:

**Town House Hotel** (TH) - A small, individual city or town centre property, which provides a high degree of personal service and privacy.

**Country House Hotel** (CHH) - Quietly located in a rural area.

**Small Hotel** (SHL) - Has fewer than 20 bedrooms and is owner managed.

**Metro Hotel** (MET) - A hotel in an urban location that does not offer an evening meal.

**Budget Hotel** (BUD) - These are usually purpose-built modern properties offering inexpensive accommodation. Often located near motorways and in town or city centres. **They are not awarded stars.**

## AA Guest Accommodation

Guest accommodation is also classified on a scale of one to five stars, with one ★ being the most simple, and five being more luxurious. Yellow stars (★) indicate the very best B&Bs, Guest Houses, Farmhouses, Inns and Guest Accommodation in the 3, 4 and 5 star ratings. Stars have replaced the Diamond Classification for this type of accommodation, in accordance with Common Standards agreed between the AA and the UK tourist authorities of VisitEngland, VisitScotland and VisitWales. To differentiate them from Hotel Stars, they have been given a series of designators appropriate to the type of accommodation they offer, as follows:

**Inn** (INN) – Accommodation provided in a fully licensed establishment. The bar will be open to non-residents and provide food in the evenings.

**Bed & Breakfast** (B&B) – Accommodation provided in a private house, run by the owner and with no more than six paying guests.

**Guest House** (GH) – Accommodation provided for more than six paying guests and run on a more commercial basis than a B&B. Usually more services, for example dinner, provided by staff as well as the owner.

**Farmhouse** (FH) – B&B or guest house rooms provided on a working farm or smallholding.

**Restaurant with Rooms** (RR) – Destination restaurant offering overnight accommodation. The restaurant is the main business and is open to non-residents. A high standard of food should be offered, at least five nights a week. A maximum of 12 bedrooms. Most Restaurants with Rooms have been awarded AA Rosettes for their food.

**Guest Accommodation** (GA) – Any establishment which meets the entry requirements for the Scheme can choose this designator.

**U** A small number of pubs have this symbol because their Star classification was not confirmed at the time of going to press.

**A** Refers to hotels rated by another organisation, eg VisitBritain.

## Rosette Awards

Out of the thousands of restaurants in the British Isles, the AA identifies, with its Rosette Awards, around 1900 as the best. What to expect from restaurants with AA Rosette Awards is outlined here; for a more detailed explanation of Rosette criteria please see **theAA.com**

⊛ Excellent local restaurants serving food prepared with care, understanding and skill and using good quality ingredients.

⊛⊛ The best local restaurants, which consistently aim for and achieve higher standards and where a greater precision is apparent in the cooking. Obvious attention is paid to the selection of quality ingredients.

⊛⊛⊛ Outstanding restaurants that demand recognition well beyond their local area.

⊛⊛⊛⊛ Amongst the very best restaurants in the British Isles, where the cooking demands national recognition.

⊛⊛⊛⊛⊛ The finest restaurants in the British Isles, where the cooking stands comparison with the best in the world.

# AA Pub of the Year

The AA Pub of the Year for England, Scotland and Wales have been selected with the help of our AA inspectors, we have chosen three very worthy winners for this prestigious annual award.

The winners stand out for being great all-round pubs or inns, combining a good pub atmosphere, a warm welcome from friendly, efficient hosts and staff, excellent food and well-kept beers.

## ENGLAND

### THE BLACK SWAN AT OLDSTEAD ★ ★ ★ ★ ★ ◎◎ RR
**OLDSTEAD, NORTH YORKSHIRE  Page 533**

Generations of the Banks family have farmed in the area, and now they own and run The Black Swan. It has a stunning rural location near Helmsley in The North York Moors National Park. Dating from the 16th century the bar features a stone-flagged floor, an open log fire, antique furniture window seats, soft cushions and fittings by Robert 'Mousey' Thompson, a prolific maker of traditional handcrafted English oak furniture in the 1930s. Choice here includes real ales, good wines by the glass, malt whiskies and vintage port, while food on offer changes with seasons and comes mainly from local farms. In the bar you can find excellent versions of pub classics, like the 'Fish and Chips' - or more specifically - east coast haddock, deep-fried in Black Sheep Ale batter, with hand-cut chips, pea purée and home-made tartare sauce, plus a selection of light lunches and sandwiches. The welcoming restaurant has two AA Rosettes, and, with its oak floor, Persian rugs, antique furniture and soft light from candles in old brass holders, might offer starters like Jerusalem artichoke soup with shiitake mushroom ravioli and chestnut foam. Follow with line-caught wild sea trout with Spillman's asparagus, crushed potatoes, roast salsify and crab bisque, ending with pear tart Tatin with pear purée, mascarpone and toasted almonds. Lovely bedrooms are situated in a quiet south-facing wing, each opening onto an individual terrace, and have solid oak floors, antiques, stylish soft fabrics and paintings. Luxurious bathrooms include iron roll-top baths and walk-in wet-room shower areas.

## SCOTLAND

### THE SUN INN ★★★★ ◉ INN

**DALKEITH, MIDLOTHIAN Page 575**

Recently refurbished, and with new owners, The Sun Inn offers all that's best in the world of the gastro-pub. Log fires, oak beams, exposed stone and wood panelling feature, alongside more modern comforts, while in the bar, local cask ales and Innis & Gunn's Edinburgh-brewed, oak-aged bottled beer have pride of place. The wine list is pretty special, too, the result of hard work by owner Bernie MacCarron, and chef and self-styled wine snob, Craig Minto. You can eat informally in the bar, or try the more formal restaurant, which holds an AA Rosette. Lunch might start with grilled Queenie scallops with garlic butter and gruyère, followed maybe with Eyemouth fish pie, or roast chicken supreme with fat chips and a roast tomato, tarragon and mushroom sauce. At dinner you could try the twice-baked Strathdon blue cheese soufflé; main courses might include milk fed calves' liver with dry cured bacon, caramelised shallots and creamy mash, or loin of venison on a garlic croute, with

Macsweens haggis, duck fat roasties and a port jus. The desserts are splendidly indulgent – perhaps you'll still have room for the sticky toffee and ginger pudding with hot butterscotch sauce and vanilla ice cream. There are afternoon teas every day except Sunday. Meanwhile, upstairs the bedrooms have been treated to monsoon showers and king-size beds with Egyptian cotton.

## WALES

### THE SWAN INN

**LITTLE HAVEN, PEMBROKESHIRE Page 600**

It's not that long ago that The Swan was boarded up; now, thanks to Paul and Tracey Morris, there's a buzz in the air, the place glows with attention and there are plenty of contented diners. In a spectacular setting perched above a rocky cove overlooking St Bride's Bay, this is a real gem, an unspoilt 200-year-old seaside inn with views across the water to Solva and Ramsay Island, particularly from the terrace, the sea wall outside or from the sought-after bay window in the beamed bar. Expect well-kept real ales at the spectacular pewter-topped bar, a more than adequate wine choice, rustic old settles, polished oak tables, leather armchairs fronting a blazing log fire and an intimate dining room. Upstairs is an elegant contemporary-style restaurant. Cooking is modern British with a commitment to seasonal and local produce, so look out for Welsh rib eye steaks, St Bride's Bay crab, local diver caught scallops and Welsh cheeses.

We aim to bring you the country's best pubs, selected for their atmosphere, great food and good beer. Ours is the only major pub guide to feature colour photographs, and to highlight the 'Pick of the Pubs', revealing Britain's finest hostelries. Updated every year, this edition includes lots of old favourites, as well as plenty of new destinations for eating and drinking, and great places to stay across Britain.

## Who's in the Guide?

We make our selection by seeking out pubs that are worth making a detour - 'destination' pubs - with publicans exhibiting real enthusiasm for their trade and offering a good selection of well-kept drinks and good food. We also choose neighbourhood pubs supported by locals and attractive to passing motorists or walkers. Our selected pubs make no payment for their inclusion in our guide. They are included entirely at our discretion.

## Tempting Food

We are looking for menus that show a commitment to home cooking, making good use of local produce wherever possible, and offering an appetising range of freshly-prepared dishes. Pubs presenting well-executed traditional dishes like ploughman's or pies, or those offering innovative bar or restaurant food, are all in the running. In keeping with recent trends in pub food, we are keen to include those where particular emphasis is placed on imaginative modern dishes and those specialising in fresh fish. Occasionally we include pubs that serve no food, or just snacks, but are very special in other ways.

## That Special Place

We look for pubs that offer something special: pubs where the time-honoured values of a convivial environment for conversation while supping or eating have not been forgotten. They may be

attractive, interesting, unusual or in a good location. Some may be very much a local pub or they may draw customers from further afield, while others may be included because they are in an exceptional place. Interesting towns and villages, eccentric or historic buildings, and rare settings can all be found within this guide.

## Pick of the Pubs and Full Page Entries

Some of the pubs included in the guide are particularly special, and we have highlighted these as Pick of the Pubs. For 2011 over 600 pubs have been selected by the personal knowledge of our editorial team, our AA inspectors, and suggestions from our readers.

These pubs have a coloured panel and a more detailed description. From these, over 200 have chosen to enhance their entry in the 2011 Guide by purchasing two photographs as part of a full-page entry.

## Smoking Regulations

A law banning smoking in public places came into force in July 2007. This covers all establishments in this guide. Some pubs provide a private area in, for example an outbuilding, for smokers. If the freedom to smoke is important to you, we recommend that you check with the pub when you book.

## Tell us what you think

We welcome your feedback about the pubs included and about the guide itself. We are also delighted to receive suggestions about good pubs you have visited and loved. A Reader Report form appears at the back of the book, so please write in or e-mail us at lifestyleguides@theAA.com to help us improve future editions. The pubs also feature on the AA website, **theAA.com**, along with our inspected restaurants, hotels and bed & breakfast accommodation.

Have dining pubs had their

# CHIPS?

*By Mark Taylor*

As is often the case, the Daily Mail headline of February 10, 2010, cut to the chase and told it as it was: "Staff storm out after owner says food is 'too poncey'". The story went on to explain how an acclaimed chef of a famous Oxfordshire dining inn walked out a few days after winning a Michelin star because the owner wanted to change the direction of the operation as it was losing money. He wanted the inn to go back to basic pub grub – burgers and chips – rather than the chef's signature dishes such as scallops with veal sweetbreads. The chef and four members of staff walked out, leaving the owner to deal with the huge media interest.

Even Raymond Blanc went public and lent his support to the chef, saying "a chef has their own individuality and creativity and will create a certain type of food – they shouldn't be expected to change".

It may have all seemed like a storm in a Villeroy & Boch teacup, but this one incident triggered huge debate about whether fine dining was ruining pub food. Those of us who ate at the inn will know that it hadn't really been a pub for years. It was a restaurant masquerading as one, and one imagines that anybody turning up for a pint with muddy boots and a wet dog may have been discreetly shown the door before they could say 'amuse bouche'.

And yet, pub or not, the story of the chef whose food was hailed as 'too poncey' did trigger the question of 'What do people really want in a pub setting?'

## How pub food has changed

British pubs have come a long way since the days when the only food available was a packet of crisps or a pickled egg, but does it matter that you can't get ham, egg or chips but you can have 'a symphony

Previous page: The One Elm, Stratford-upon-Avon

Left: The Walnut Tree, near Abergavenny

Opposite: Rose and Crown, Warwick

> *The clue is in the title – it's a public house and that means you have to cook what your public wants to eat*

of pork' or 'boneless quail, three ways'? A quick look through this guide and it soon becomes obvious that the line between pub and fine dining restaurant is as blurred as ever. For every inn serving cheese and pickle sandwiches or roast beef with all the trimmings on Sunday, there will be several more offering twice-cooked guinea fowl breast with Spanish ham, caramelised endive, game chips and sherry vinegar jus.

## Striking a balance

One pub that has struck the perfect balance is the King William in Bath. Owners Charlie and Amanda Digney took over this 19th-century tavern five years ago and turned it into a stylish and sophisticated gastro-pub – albeit one where the emphasis is as much on the 'gastro' as it is the 'pub' thanks to a bar that serves four local real ales and a selection of organic ciders. The bar menu offers upmarket burgers and sandwiches,

but also beer-battered hake and chips with tartare sauce. Charlie Digney says that if there is a problem with the 'gastro-pub' sector, it isn't necessarily about the pubs themselves, but more about the lack of skilled chefs.

"Good food is good food," he says. "Dishes such as jugged hare, steak and chips, or braised shin of beef are all fantastic and not 'fussy' but these are dishes that need to be cooked by a skilled chef. I think that the real problem is that there are not enough skilled chefs around and pubs are not generating enough profit to do anything about it. It's tough out there at the moment, the cost of everything keeps going up, yet we have a ceiling on what we can charge for our products. I know that the food at my pub is as good as any in the area, yet I can't charge £60 for three courses as they do at restaurants nearby even though we share most of the same suppliers."

## Cook what the customers want

Lee Cash runs the fast-expanding Peach Pub Company which includes the Rose and Crown at Warwick, The Swan in Salford, Bedfordshire, and The One Elm in Stratford-upon-Avon.

He says: "The clue is in the title – it's a public house and that means you have to cook what your public wants to eat on a menu that your guests like the look of. If your pub's in a beautiful village and does destination dining that attracts people from 50 miles around, that's obviously a very different ball game from one that's in the middle of a small market town. The principles are the same, though. You need to cook what your public wants to eat or the building dies on its feet. If the chef destroys the business by going too far, or the management is too weak, then you're only going to have yourself to blame if it all falls apart."

### The rise of gastro-pubs

At the other end of the gastronomic spectrum, Shaun Hill's esteemed restaurant The Walnut Tree near Abergavenny still has the understated charm of the former inn it once was. His ingredient-driven seasonal cooking has gained him three AA Rosettes and features deceptively simple dishes that wouldn't look out of place in any so-called gastro-pub: crab cakes with anchovy mayonnaise; calf's liver and bacon with cassis sauce; Bakewell tart with vanilla ice cream.

He welcomes the rise of gastro-pubs where the food is good and the cooking shows a good-skills set, but has his concerns about the ones that are masquerading as restaurants.

He says: "I don't know why some pubs try to emulate posh restaurants rather than anything more populist. Even more confusing is why they have taken on some of the dafter snobberies of restaurants, such as dress codes, that were best consigned to history. There is something incongruous about a pub offering pre-desserts or lifting domes, just as there is something uncomfortable about sommelier-endowed restaurants posturing about their rustic cuisine."

But as more and more pub chefs try to give posh restaurants a run for their money, they need to remember the simple fact they are cooking for the customers and not the guidebook inspectors. Ultimately, it's the customers who pay the bills.

Hill says: "There's a market for a good shepherd's pie, good smart grub and good almost anything else. I have turned out elaborate stuff at fine dining hotels like Gidleigh Park just as I have served less intricate food here at The Walnut Tree. I put the same work into each and am happy to be judged on that basis."

### A final thought

Back at the King William in Bath, Charlie Digney remains upbeat about gastro-pubs despite the challenges they face.

"The problem is there is now a gastro-pub formula – ham hock terrine, duck confit, scallops with black pudding etc. – all great dishes when done well but when cooked with cheap ingredients by undertrained, inexperienced cooks, they can be awful." But what if all people want is chicken in the basket or other pub classics? Is there still room for them amongst the 'trio of beef with horseradish foam'? Digney thinks so.

"I am sure if you were to put a local, organic chicken on a bed of fresh garlic, rub it with olive oil, season with sea salt and pepper, roast it until crispy and golden, quarter and pop it in a basket with some triple cooked chips and home-made garlic mayo it would rock your world. In fact I think I'm going to put this on the menu tomorrow!"

GIN
volution

*Gin has been going through a bit of a revolution lately as Fiona Griffiths discovers...*

There was a time when ordering a G&T in a pub was a straightforward request with a fairly predictable outcome. The bartender would half-fill a glass with ice, offer it up to the optic for a shot of gin (any gin would do), top up with tonic water, and then add a slice of lemon as a finishing touch.

But the G&T isn't quite what it used to be. Gin has gone all upmarket, with several premium brands having launched in the last few years, each traditionally distilled with an unusual mix of botanicals. Rose, chamomile, honeysuckle, lotus leaves, poppy, coul blush apple and rowanberries are amongst the extraordinary flavours being blended with the staple ingredient of juniper in the new wave of premium British gins.

Geraldine Coates, gin connoisseur and author of the website gintime.com, says: "Ten years ago people weren't that interested in gin - it was very much overtaken by vodka - but now it's a very vibrant and exciting category. Whereas pubs used to be incredibly limited with their range - really it would only be Gordon's or sometimes they might have Bombay Sapphire - now the slightly higher end pubs are being much more adventurous with gin, and I think that can only grow."

## New London gins

One of the pioneers of the gin 'renaissance' is *Sipsmith*, a small warehouse distillery tucked away in a residential street in Hammersmith, West London, which launched its London dry gin – infused with 10 natural botanicals including liquorice root, orris root, ground almond, cassia bark and cinnamon – in July 2009. Childhood friends Sam Galsworthy and Fairfax Hall were inspired to set up Sipsmith after witnessing the growth in artisanal spirits producers in America.

"We really felt we wanted to bring some of that energy back to London, because you don't have to go far back in history to realise that the roots of gin stem from the capital," says Galsworthy. "Gin is now enjoying a wonderful renaissance and Sipsmith is part of that renaissance, as it's the first copper distillery in London for nearly 200 years."

Four years ago Johnny Neill, who has a family history in the gin trade (his great-grandfather was one of the founders of G & J Greenall), gave up his job in the City to indulge his passion for gin, and

> *Rose, chamomile, honeysuckle, lotus leaves, poppy, coul blush apple and rowanberries are amongst the extraordinary flavours being blended with juniper in the new wave of premium British gins*

the result was *Whitley Neill* - a London dry gin with a South African twist.

"I've always had a fascination for gin and it was my dream to produce something a little bit different to your traditional London dry gin," explains Neill. "My wife is South African, so we have two South African botanicals which give the citrus side a little bit of a different flavour profile." Those botanicals are baobab fruit ("which has a very citrusy pulp and gives a soft grapefruit flavour when distilled") and "bittersweet and aromatic" cape gooseberries. Often Whitley Neill is served in a gin and tonic with a cape gooseberry - also known as physalis - as a garnish.

## New Scottish gins

If you order a gin and tonic with Hendrick's, don't be surprised if it comes complete with slices of cucumber.

*Hendrick's* - credited by many as responsible for kick-starting the gin revolution in the UK back in 2003 - is a small batch gin, produced in Scotland, which derives its unique flavour from the infusion of cucumber and rose petals. Nick Williamson, marketing controller for Hendrick's, says: "Like any gin, by law the main flavour has got to be juniper, but the rose and cucumber just gives it a much lighter, more floral and genuinely different taste."

Also from Scotland comes *Caorunn* (pronounced 'ka-roon'), which was launched in August 2009 and is a small batch gin infused with five Celtic botanicals - rowan berries, coul blush apple, heather, bog myrtle and dandelion. Iby Bakos, brand manager for Caorunn, says: "We're primarily a single malt whisky producer but we wanted to move into a different segment. The vodka market is pretty saturated, but the premium gin market is growing and it's exciting because of all the different flavours you can use in gin."

At the Ubiquitous Chip in Glasgow, Scottish gins Hendrick's and Caorunn take pride of place behind the bar. "Hendrick's is our most popular gin and I think that's because it's the most widely recognised as being different because of the cucumber," says bar manager Richard Burniston. "People tend to want to buy premium spirits these days, so they'll ask for a Hendrick's and tonic, not just a gin and tonic."

### Gin takes over from vodka

In fact, boredom with vodka has been largely blamed for the boom in premium gins, as Luke Tegner, brands director for Berry Bros & Rudd Spirits, explains. "What's going hand in hand with the rise in gin is the falling off of the excitement

in vodka. For bartenders, gin is a much more interesting drink to work with for creating cocktails than vodka, which is essentially a bland-tasting spirit."

## Other new London gins

Berry Bros & Rudd has launched its own premium gin, simply named *No. 3* after the address in St James's Street, London, which has been home to the wine and spirit merchant since 1698. The figure three has relevance to the recipe too, as - with the intention of keeping things simple - No. 3 is infused with just three fruits (juniper, sweet Spanish orange and grapefruit peel) and three spices (angelica root, Moroccan coriander seed and cardamom pods).

Joanne Moore, the world's only female master distiller, took the flowers in her garden and her love of chamomile tea as the inspiration for the premium London dry gin *Bloom*. Launched in 2009, its main elements are chamomile, honeysuckle, and the South East Asian citrus fruit pomelo. "No one was particularly concentrating on flowers in gin, and I wanted to encourage predominantly women into the category by creating a very light, delicate, floral gin, unlike the very earthy, overpowering juniper note gins," explains Moore.

Like Johnny Neill, investment banker Anshuman Vohra gave up his job in the City to launch his own gin brand, *Bulldog*.

He spent hours researching different potential botanicals on the internet, eventually sending his preferred list to a distillery in Essex, where it was worked up into a recipe featuring 12 exotic natural flavours, including lotus leaves, lavender, poppy and dragon eye. "They sent me some samples and I was the most popular person on the floor in the bank that day when all this gin turned

> *More and more people are coming in, seeing what's on offer and going, 'ooh, I'd like to try that'*

up," recalls Vohra. "The liquid they sent me that first day is pretty much what we have now." In common with all the new gins, Bulldog has a very distinctive, eye-catching bottle (smokey grey, with broad shoulders and a spiked collar), which certainly helps to sell it to customers in bars and pubs.

## What about the tonic?

With 95 per cent of gin drunk as a gin and tonic, the good news for G&T fans is that tonic water has been through a bit of a renaissance of its own. Tim Warrillow and Charles Rolls spotted a gap in the market for a high quality, natural tonic water that would complement all the new premium gins, and thus *Fever-Tree* was born in late 2005.

Warrillow explains: "We'd seen that consumers were becoming more interested in premium spirits and were paying more for them, and yet, incredibly, the mixer category was entirely dominated by one brand. It became apparent that people were actually being driven away from gin and tonic because of the quality of the tonic water. So often they thought it was the gin, but in many cases it was actually the saccharin, a cheap artificial sweetener used in tonic which has a very off-putting flavour." So Warrillow and Rolls set out to develop

a tonic water without any artificial ingredients, and sweetened only with cane sugar. "Quinine, from the fever tree, is the essence of tonic water, so we went to the source of the highest quality, most natural quinine, which is in Rwanda," explains Warrillow. "Rather like in a gin, we also use eight different botanical flavours, such as bitter orange oil from Tanzania, marigold, coriander and lime. "Three-quarters of a gin and tonic is usually the tonic, so our whole principle was to build up a subtle but complex tonic which really complements and enhances the gin."

Fever-Tree is now served in around 500 pubs and restaurants around the UK, including the Queens Arms in Corton Denham, Dorset, where the premium gin range includes Hendrick's, Sipsmith and Martin Miller.

"There's such a wide variety of gins around nowadays and, along with Fever-Tree tonic, they're gradually becoming more recognised," says Queens Arms manager James Scrancher. "More and more people are coming in, seeing what's on offer and going, 'ooh, I'd like to try that'. It's good for us to be able to offer a selection because people go away feeling they've had a better experience, having pushed onto something they've never tried before."

---

### DID YOU KNOW?

■ There are two basic legal categories of gin: distilled gin, which is crafted traditionally by re-distilling neutral spirit (made from wheat or rye) with juniper berries and other botanicals (herbs, spices and fruits); and compound gin, which is made by simply flavouring neutral spirit with essences or other natural flavourings without re-distillation.

■ The minimum bottled alcoholic strength for gin is 37.5% ABV in Europe or 40% in America.

■ A gin is generally considered premium if it's been handcrafted, distilled 3-5 times to remove impurities, and has a minimum alcohol content of 40%. It is also flavoured in a unique way, whereby during the final distillation the alcohol vapour wafts through a chamber in which dried juniper berries and other botanicals are suspended. The vapour gently extracts aromatic and flavouring oils and compounds from the fruits and spices as it travels through the chamber on its way to the condenser, producing a far more complex spirit.

■ London dry gin doesn't have to be produced in the capital, it's simply a style of gin. It cannot contain added sugar or colorants, with water being the only permitted additive.

■ By contrast, Plymouth gin can only legally be made in Plymouth.

# Beer Festivals

Beer festivals, or their equivalent, are as old as the hills. The brewing of hops goes back to the beginning of human civilisation, and the combination of common crop and a fermenting process that results in alcoholic liquid has long been a cause of celebration. Beer festivals officially began in Germany with the first Munich Oktoberfest in 1810. Wherever in the world beer is brewed, today and for the last few millennia, admirers, enthusiasts, aficionados – call them what you will – have gathered together to sample and praise its unique properties. It happens throughout Europe, in Australia and New Zealand, and in America and Canada, and annual events are held in pubs all over Britain.

Beer festivals are often occasions for the whole family, when entertainment is laid on for children as well as adults. Summer is naturally a popular season for festivals, when the action can be taken outdoors. Other festivals are held in October, traditionally harvest time, but they can be at any time of the year. They can be large and well-advertised gatherings that attract a wide following for sometimes several days of unselfconscious consumption of unusual or award-winning ales; or they might be local but none the less enthusiastic get-togethers of neighbourhood or pub micro-breweries.

We list here a selection of pubs that appear in this guide, who usually hold annual beer festivals. *For up-to-date information, please check directly with the pub.* We would love to hear from our readers about their favourite beer festivals.

E-mail us at lifestyleguides@theAA.com

**The Stag & Huntsman, Hambleden, Buckinghamshire 01753 643225**
A weekend beer festival is held in early September.

**The White Horse, Hedgerley, Buckinghamshire 01753 643225**
An annual beer festival is held at the end of May Bank Holiday.

**The Derehams Inn, Loudwater, Buckinghamshire 01494 530965**
5th annual beer festival the 1st weekend of July with 20 real ales and 3 ciders plus entertainment and barbecue each night, ending with ferret racing on the Sunday.

**Cambridge Blue, Cambridge, Cambridgeshire 01223 471680**
The summer festival in June with 140 real ales, the winter festival in February with 60 real ales and the October Festival specialises in a large selection of German beers.

**The Crown Inn, Elton, Cambridgeshire 01832 280232**
Annual treats include a May Day hog roast and a summer beer festival.

**Bhurtpore Inn, Aston, Cheshire 01270 780917**
An annual beer festival in November and early July, reputedly Cheshire's largest, is in its sixteenth year, with around 130 real ales to be sampled.

**The Smugglers Den Inn, Cubert, nr Newquay, Cornwall & Isles of Scilly 01637 830209**
The impressive selection of real ales is at its best during the real ale and pie festival over the May Day weekend.

**The Boot Inn, Boot, Cumbria 019467 23224**
The Boot's annual June beer festival is a great event for all the family with over 50 real ales.

**Queens Head Inn, Tirril, Cumbria 01768 863219**
In August every year the Cumbrian beer and sausage festival is held here.

**Greyhound Inn, Corfe Castle, Dorset 01929 480205**
A full diary of events features two annual beer festivals in May and August, and a West Country sausage and cider festival in October half term.

**Bankes Arms, Studland, Dorset 01929 450225**
The annual beer festival held in August in its large garden showcases 60 real ales and live music, Morris dancing and stone carving.

**The Hoop, Stock, Essex 01277 841137**
The annual 9-day beer festival starts last Bank Holiday in May with 200 real ales and 90 ciders with food also a major draw.

**The Hurdle Makers Arms, Woodham Mortimer, Essex 01245 225169**
With over 20 real ales the beer festival is held the last weekend in June with live music.

**Boat Inn, Ashleworth, Gloucestershire 01452 700272**
Renowned for its real ales, the Boat Inn hosts a popular annual beer festival with a great selection of ciders.

**The Yew Tree, Clifford's Mesne, Gloucestershire 01531 820719**
In October there's a beer and cider festival.

**Old Spot Inn, Dursley, Gloucestershire 01453 542870**
The inn holds four real ale festivals a year; landlord Steve Herbert organises a host of events, including brewery visits.

**New Forest Inn, Lyndhurst, Hampshire 023 80284690**
There is an annual 3-day beer festival the second week of July with 25 real ales, back to back entertainment, including live bands, acoustic singers and children's entertainment.

**The White Horse, Petersfield, Hampshire 01420 588387**
Longest Day beer festival in June with bouncy castle, live music, barbecue plus

# Looking for a better deal?

## Zoom in on a rewarding Credit Card from the AA

- Earn AA Reward Points on your everyday card purchases, and earn double points on motoring, fuel and AA products[1] – plus AA Members earn twice as fast.

- AA Members can earn 4% cash back on the AA Credit Card reward scheme when they redeem points earned on motoring or fuel spend against other AA products

- Points can also be redeemed against other offers too, including motoring and travel essentials or treats including wine, days out or high street shopping vouchers

- 0% for 12 months on motoring, fuel and AA card purchases[2]

- 0% for 12 months on balance and money transfers made in the first 90 days (3% fee)[3]

## 16.9% APR Typical rate (variable)

Call now on **0800 171 2038**
and quote GUIDE
or visit **theaa.com/cardxs**

[1]Motoring purchases includes: purchases from any car garage (eg for parts, repairs, servicing, MOT testing); fuel purchases (diesel, petrol or LPG Autogas) from any fuel stations including supermarkets; AA products and services purchased directly from the AA. [2]From the date of account opening, if you do not pay your balance in full we will use your payments to reduce lower rate balances before higher rate balances. If promotional rate balances are the same we will repay them in the following order: first, the one with the earliest expiry date, if the expiry dates are the same then the one which started first; if expiry dates, and start dates are the same then one with the lowest standard rate. [3]Applies to all balances transferred in the first 90 days from the date of account opening. The AA Credit Card is issued by MBNA Europe Bank Limited. Registered Office: Stansfield House, Chester Business Park, Chester CH4 9QQ. Registered in England number 2783251. Credit is available, subject to status, only to UK residents aged 18 or over. You cannot transfer balances from another MBNA account. We will monitor or record some phone calls. MBNA's consumer credit activities are licensed by the Office of Fair Trading (OFT) and our general insurance activities are authorised and regulated by the Financial Services Authority (FSA). Offers subject to change. Rates correct at time of going to press 04/10.

# Quality-assured accommodation at over 6,000 establishments throughout the UK & Ireland

- ☑ Quality-assured accommodation
- 🔒 Secure online booking process
- 🏠 Extensive range and choice of accommodation
- ⓘ Detailed, authoritative descriptions
- 💷 Exclusive discounts for AA Members

lots more entertainment. The Longest Night beer festival is in December.

**Tichborne Arms, Tichborne, Hampshire 01962 733760**
A beer festival is held on the third weekend in August.

**The Bowl Inn, Charing, Kent 01233 712256**
An annual beer festival takes place in mid July.

**Chequers Inn, Smarden, Kent 01233 770217**
Much involved with the local community throughout the year, the Chequers hosts an annual beer festival in August plus other events.

**The Stag's Head, Goosnargh, Lancashire 01772 864071**
Sixth annual beer festival with over 20 guest cask ales held over May Bank Holiday weekend.

**The Eagle and Child, Parbold, Lancashire 01257 462297**
The annual May Bank Holiday beer festival attracts up to 2,000 people to the huge marquee in the pub grounds.

**Swan in the Rushes, Loughborough, Leicestershire 01509 217014**
Two annual beer festivals second weekend November and last weekend May with live music and around 20 beers.

**Cow and Plough, Oadby, Leicestershire 0116 272 0852**
St George's beer festival - 30 beers and 10 ciders and live music.

**Junction Tavern, London NW5 020 7485 9400**
Two large beer festivals held in May and October with over 40 real ales. Also many mini festivals held throughout the year specialising in ales from various regions.

**White Horse, London, SW6 020 7736 2115**
The 2-day beer festival held annually in November with over 300 beers waiting to be sampled is a magnet for lovers of real

ale and European beers; Belgian beer festival August Bank Holiday; American beer festival Independence weekend; London Beer Festival in May.

**The Stuart House Hotel, Kings Lynn, Norfolk 01553 772169**
A programme of events includes an annual beer festival last weekend of July with live music.

**Angel Inn, Larling, Norfolk 01953 717963**
Each August the Angel hosts Norfolk's largest outdoor beer festival.

**White Hart, Fyfield, Oxfordshire 01865 390585**
An annual beer festival is held during the May Day Bank Holiday, with hog roasts and at least 13 real ales.

**The Grainstore Brewery, Oakham, Rutland 01572 770065**
Attend the annual beer festival during the August Bank Holiday.

**The Bat & Ball Freehouse, Farnham, Surrey 01252 792108**
Beer, cider and music festival in June with up to 30 cask ales and cider, barbecue and entertainment.

**The Surrey Oaks, Newdigate, Surrey 01306 631200**
Late May Bank Holiday and August Bank Holiday beer festivals, live music - rock and roll, blues and jazz bands.

**The Dog & Duck, Kingsfold, West Sussex 011306 627295**
A big beer festival and fundraising activities for St George's Hospital.

**The Smoking Dog, Malmesbury, Wiltshire 01666 825 823**
A renowned beer and sausage festival over Whitsun weekend with over 30 brews and 15 banger varieties.

**The Bridge Inn, West Lavington, Wiltshire 01380 813213**
Charity beer festival is held over August Bank Holiday weekend.

# England

River Wye, Monsal Head, Peak District National Park

## BEDFORDSHIRE

### BEDFORD     Map 12 TL04

## PICK OF THE PUBS

### The Knife & Cleaver Inn ♥

**The Grove, Houghton Conquest MK45 3LA**
☎ 01234 740387   📠 01234 740900
e-mail: info@theknifeandcleaver.com
**dir:** *11m from M1 junct 12/13. 5m S of Bedford. Off A6. In village opp church*

Originally called the Butchers Arms, the pub was owned as part of the manor house properties by the Conquest family, who had the manor from the 13th century. Records date from 1796, but the building is thought to be older. It stands opposite the medieval church of All Saints, Bedfordshire's largest parish church. Historical features include the Jacobean oak panelling in the lounge bar, which came from Houghton House. Light meals and hand-drawn ales are served in the bar, where leather sofas and winter log fires bring welcome comfort. The seasonal menu in the conservatory restaurant is strong on fresh seafood, and also offers a varied choice of meat and vegetarian dishes, such as pan-fried lamb rump with apricots, couscous and Moroccan-style tagine sauce, or chargrilled aubergine tower with pesto dressing.

**Open** all wk 12-3 6-11 (Sun noon-10.30pm) ◀ Village Bike, Potton Brewery, Adnams Broadside. ♥ 20 **Facilities** Family room Dogs allowed Garden Parking

---

### The Three Tuns

**57 Main Rd, Biddenham MK40 4BD** ☎ 01234 354847
e-mail: enquiries@threetunsbiddenham.com
**dir:** *On A428 from Bedford towards Northampton 1st left signed Biddenham. Into village, pub on left*

A stone-built, thatch roofed pub, The Three Tuns stands in the heart of the beautiful village of Biddenham. It has a large garden with a patio and decking, and a separate children's play area with swings and a climbing frame. The old morgue, situated between the two garden areas, is the oldest building in the village and is said to be haunted. Home-cooked dishes on the regularly-changing menus include pies, steaks, curries, fish, local sausages, burgers and vegetarian specialities; all washed down with award-winning Greene King beers. Recent change of hands.

**Open** all wk 12-3 6-11 (Sun 12-4 7-10.30; 12-11 in summer) **Bar Meals** L served all wk 12-2 D served Mon-Sat 6-9 **Restaurant** L served all wk 12-2 booking required D served Mon-Sat 6-9 booking required ⊕ GREENE KING ◀ Greene King IPA, Abbot Ale, guest ale, Guinness. **Facilities** Play area Family room Dogs allowed Garden Parking

---

### BLETSOE     Map 11 TL05

## PICK OF THE PUBS

### The Falcon ♥

**Rushden Rd MK44 1QN**
☎ 01234 781222   📠 01234 781222
e-mail: thefalcona6@aol.com
**dir:** *9m from M1 junct 13, 3m from Bedford*

The 17th-century Falcon stands in rolling downland, beside the River Great Ouse. Before becoming a coaching inn in 1727 it was a mill, and in 1859 Edward FitzGerald translated *The Rubaiyat of Omar Khayyam* here, describing The Falcon as 'The cleanest, the sweetest, the civilest, the quietest, the liveliest and the cheapest that was ever built'. Not one to prevaricate, then. Inside are an inglenook fireplace, beams galore, a splendidly oak-panelled restaurant and a secret tunnel to Bletsoe Castle. In winter, you can enjoy the crackling log fires and in summer there is a large riverside garden and marquee. Small and big appetites are catered for - 'Little Plates' choices include home-made soup of the day; moules marinière; and chicken liver pâté with confit de figues, cornichons and melba toast. The 'Large plates' could include creamy winter vegetable gnocchi with leeks, squash, carrots and sweet potato; oven baked monkfish on crushed new potatoes with caperberry and caviar sauce; slow roasted pork belly, colcannon, oven-baked brandied apples and Calvados cream. A change of hands has taken place.

**Open** all day all wk **Bar Meals** L served 12-2.45 D served 6-9.15 **Restaurant** L served 12-2.45 D served 6-9.15 ⊕ CHARLES WELLS ◀ Wells Bombardier, Wells Eagle, Red Stripe. ♥ 15 **Facilities** Children's menu Play area Garden Parking

---

### BOLNHURST     Map 12 TL05

## PICK OF THE PUBS

### The Plough at Bolnhurst ⊛ ♥

**Kimbolton Rd MK44 2EX** ☎ 01234 376274
e-mail: theplough@bolnhurst.com
**dir:** *On B660 N of Bedford*

This homely inn stoops in the landscape as only a late-medieval inn can; with tiny windows, thick walls and mellow pitched roof, matched inside by great open fires, wizened beams and characterful decor. Great real ales and a truly inspiring wine list partner a mouth-watering menu prepared in the open kitchen by Raymond Blanc-trained Martin Lee and his team of chefs, willing to create and experiment both with the freshest local and regional produce and specialist foods gathered from all corners. The result is an ever-changing menu of dishes unique to The Plough and which have gained an AA Rosette. Start with blood orange, chicory, Stitchelton cheese and walnut salad with a walnut and orange dressing before sampling slow cooked pork cheeks with bubble and squeak, home-made black pudding and caramelised apple; roast fillet of gurnard with sprouting broccoli, caper and parsley butter and new potatoes, or an old favourite like Aberdeenshire rib eye steak sandwich. But do leave room for the cheese board, with an astonishing choice of British, Italian and French varieties on offer.

**Open** Tue-Sun 12-3 6.30-11 Closed: 1 Jan, 2wks Jan, Mon **Bar Meals** L served Tue-Sun 12-2 booking required D served Tue-Sat 6.30-9.30 booking required **Restaurant** L served Tue-Sun 12-2 booking required D served Tue-Sat 6.30-9.30 booking required Fixed menu price fr £14 Av 3 course à la carte fr £32.50 ⊕ FREE HOUSE ◀ Adnams Broadside, Nethergate Azzanewt, Batemans XB, Village Bike Potton, Fuller's London Pride. ♥ 13 **Facilities** Children's portions Dogs allowed Garden Parking

---

### BROOM     Map 12 TL14

### The Cock

**23 High St SG18 9NA**
☎ 01767 314411   📠 01767 314284
**dir:** *Off B658 SW of Biggleswade. 1m from A1*

Unspoilt to this day with its intimate quarry-tiled rooms with latched doors and panelled walls, this 17th-century establishment is known as 'The Pub with no Bar'. Real ales are served straight from casks racked by the cellar steps. A straightforward pub grub menu includes ham off the bone, eggs and chips; breaded plaice filled with prawns and mushrooms; 3-egg omelettes; beef lasagne; battered fish medley (haddock, plaice, salmon and cod). There is a skittle room for hire and a camping and caravanning site at the rear of the pub.

**Open** 12-4 6-11 Closed: Sun eve **Bar Meals** L served all wk 12-2.15 D served all wk 7-9 Av main course £9 **Restaurant** L served all wk 12-2.15 D served all wk 7-9 Av 3 course à la carte fr £16 ⊕ GREENE KING ◀ Greene King Abbot Ale, IPA, Ruddles County. **Facilities** Children's menu Children's portions Play area Family room Dogs allowed Garden Parking

## EATON BRAY    Map 11 SP92

### The White Horse ☻

Market Square LU6 2DG
☎ 01525 220231  📄 01525 222485
e-mail: davidsparrow@onetel.net
web: www.the-whitehorse.co.uk
dir: *A5 N of Dunstable onto A505, left in 1m, follow signs*

For almost 20 years, David and Janet Sparrow have built their reputation on a warm and cosy atmosphere, great home cooked food and well kept real ales at this traditional 300-year-old village inn with its oak beams and horse brasses. There's a wide ranging menu including comfort food like beef in ale pie and curry of the day, steaks with a choice of sauces to accompany and a specials board that always includes a fresh fish dish. It's worth booking for the restaurant, but the same menu is also available in the bar.

**Open** all wk Closed: Sun eve Jan-Mar **Bar Meals** L served all wk 12-2.15 D served all wk 7-9.30 booking required Av main course £9.25 **Restaurant** L served all wk 12-2.15 D served all wk 7-9.30 booking required Av 3 course à la carte fr £18.75 ⊕ PUNCH TAVERNS ◀ Greene King IPA, Shepherd Neame Spitfire ♂ Aspall. ☻ 10
**Facilities** Children's menu Children's portions Play area Family room Garden Parking

## HARROLD    Map 11 SP95

### PICK OF THE PUBS

### The Muntjac

71 High St MK43 7BJ ☎ 01234 721500
e-mail: muntjacharrold@hotmail.co.uk
dir: *Telephone for directions*

This 17th-century former coaching inn stands in the picturesque village of Harrold, within easy reach of Bedford, Northampton and Milton Keynes. Its rural location close to the Harrold-Odell country park is also perfect for lovers of the English countryside. Alan and Collette Cooper have built up a reputation for excellent real ales, lagers, ciders, wines, spirits and soft drinks and, in the winter months, a real fire reflects the warmth of their welcome. The owners support local micro-breweries including Frog Island and White Park, giving plenty of scope for unusual guest ales and ciders. The independently-run Indian restaurant at the rear of the pub offers excellent dishes cooked to order to eat in or take away. The extensive menu includes fish, chicken and lamb, as well as vegetarian dishes, and the restaurant also offers a local home delivery service.

**Open** all wk Mon-Thu 5.30-11 (Fri 3-mdnt Sat noon-mdnt Sun 1-10.30) **Restaurant** D served Mon-Thu 5.30-11, Fri-Sat 5.30-11.30, Sun 5.30-10.30 ⊕ FREE HOUSE ◀ Frog Island, London Pride, guest ales ♂ Stowford Press, Harrold Calvados Society. **Facilities** Children's portions Dogs allowed Garden Parking **Notes** ☻

## IRELAND    Map 12 TL14

### The Black Horse ☻

SG17 5QL ☎ 01462 811398  📄 01462 817238
e-mail: countrytaverns@aol.com
dir: *From S: M1 junct 12, A5120 to Flitwick. Onto A507 by Redbourne School. Follow signs for A1, Shefford (cross A6). Left onto A600 towards Bedford*

Homely, village-inn looks combine with a bright, airy, chic interior where a comfy mix of light and dark wood old beams, inglenook fire and low ceilings invites closer inspection; a great flower-rich garden and courtyard dining area prove popular in clement weather. Grab a pint of Black Sheep (a good wine list too) and settle to appreciate the tempting range of dishes, from confit of duck hash starter to smoked haddock with Cornish yarg cheese or roast Bedfordshire lamb mains, topped off by a raspberry and Drambuie soufflé.

**Open** all wk 12-3 6-12 (Sun noon-6pm) Closed: 25-26 Dec, 1 Jan **Bar Meals** L served Mon-Sat 12-2.30, Sun 12-5 booking required D served Mon-Sat 6.30-10 booking required Av main course £10.95 **Restaurant** L served Mon-Sat 12-2.30, Sun 12-5 booking required D served Mon-Sat 6.30-10 booking required Fixed menu price fr £28.95 Av 3 course à la carte fr £28.95 ⊕ FREE HOUSE ◀ Black Sheep, London Pride, Adnams ♂ Westons Stowford Press. ☻ 17 **Facilities** Children's portions Garden Parking

## KEYSOE    Map 12 TL06

### The Chequers

Pertenhall Rd, Brook End MK44 2HR ☎ 01234 708678
e-mail: chequers.keysoe@tesco.net
dir: *On B660, 7m N of Bedford. 3m S of Kimbolton*

This peaceful 15th-century country pub has been in the same safe hands for over 25 years. No games machines, pool tables or jukeboxes disturb the simple pleasures of well-kept ales and great home-made food. The menu offers pub stalwarts like Ploughman's; home-made steak and ale pie; fried scampi and a variety of grilled steaks, and a blackboard displays further choice plus the vegetarian options. For a lighter option try the home-made chicken liver pâté or soup, fried brie with cranberries or plain or toasted sandwiches.

**Open** Wed-Mon L Closed: Mon eve & Tue **Bar Meals** Av main course £8.50 ⊕ FREE HOUSE ◀ Hook Norton Best, Fuller's London Pride. **Facilities** Children's menu Children's portions Play area Family room Garden Parking **Notes** ☻

## LINSLADE    Map 11 SP92

### The Globe Inn ☻

Globe Ln, Old Linslade LU7 2TA
☎ 01525 373338  📄 01525 850551
e-mail: 6458@greeneking.co.uk
dir: *N of Leighton Buzzard*

Originally a farmhouse and stables, this friendly waterside inn was converted to serve passing boat crews on the Grand Union Canal. Open fires and candles set the scene for winter evenings, whilst for warmer days there's a large garden and children's play area. Expect an appetising range of light bites and mixed smoked deli board for sharing, as well as hot dishes like pan-seared Barbary duck with dauphinoise potatoes; sweet potato, chick pea and spinach curry; and daily fresh fish specials.

**Open** all day all wk 11-11 (Sun 11-10.30) **Bar Meals** L served all wk 12-10 D served all wk 12-10 Av main course £8.95 food served all day **Restaurant** Av 3 course à la carte fr £20 food served all day ⊕ GREENE KING ◀ Greene King Abbot Ale, Old Speckled Hen ♂ Aspall, Suffolk. ☻ 16 **Facilities** Play area Dogs allowed Garden Parking

## MILTON BRYAN    Map 11 SP93

### The Red Lion

Toddington Rd, South End MK17 9HS ☎ 01525 210044
e-mail: paul@redlion-miltonbryan.co.uk
dir: *Telephone for directions*

Set in a pretty village near Woburn Abbey, this attractive brick-built pub is festooned with dazzling hanging baskets in the summer months. Comfortable, neatly maintained interior, with beams, rugs on wooden floors, and well-kept ales. Wide-ranging menu offering the likes of roast rump of lamb with potato purée, wilted spinach and ratatouille sauce; supreme of chicken stuffed with ricotta cheese, basil and Parma ham on wild rocket and roasted cherry tomato; and baked Cornish cod.

**Open** 12-3 6-11 (Sun 12-4) Closed: 25-26 Dec, 1 Jan, Sun eve & Mon eve in winter ◀ Greene King IPA, Old Speckled Hen, Abbot Ale, plus guest ales. **Facilities** Garden Parking

# PICK OF THE PUBS

## Hare and Hounds ♀

**OLD WARDEN**      Map 12 TL14

**SG18 9HQ**
☎ 01767 627225   📄 01767 627209
web:
www.thehareandhoundsoldwarden.co.uk
**dir:** *From Bedford turn right off A603 (or left
from A600) to Old Warden. Also accessed
from Biggleswade rdbt on A1*

Now the only pub in Old Warden, this
attractive 200 year-old building was
known as The Crown until 1822. It lies
at the heart of a prosperous, leafy
village on the Shuttleworth estate,
which is home to the famous collection
of classic cars and vintage aeroplanes.
In winter months you'll be greeted by the
warmth of two log fires as you head
either for the bar, or for one of the three
chic country dining rooms. The interiors
feature timbered walls, warm red and
cream colours, fresh flowers and
contemporary furnishings. Wines from
around the world include some from the
local Warden Abbey vineyard, whilst
cracking beers come courtesy of Youngs
and Charles Wells.

Food is taken very seriously here; the
printed menu lists a well-balanced
choice of rustic traditional dishes and
more modern offerings, with every effort
made to use local and organic produce.
Ingredients might include pork reared
on the estate, as well as herbs and
vegetables from the kitchen garden; fish
is delivered daily from Billingsgate, and
bread and ice creams are made on the
premises.

Typical starters include garlic foccacia
bread; roasted pepper and goat's
cheese ravioli with rocket, toasted pine
nuts and parmigiano reggiano; and crab
spring rolls with a soy, lime and chilli
dip. For main course, try the pan-fried
Norfolk pigeon with dauphinoise
potatoes and braised red cabbage;
spiced chickpea, potato and tomato
curry served with naan bread, steamed
rice and cucumber raita; or roasted
whole sea bass marinated in lemon,
garlic and rosemary. On warmer days,
enjoy the super views from the garden
and patio area.

**Open** Tue-Sat 12-3 6-11 (Sun 12-10.30)
Closed: 25 & 26 Dec, 1 Jan, Mon (ex BH)
**Bar Meals** L served all wk 12-2 D served
all wk 6.30-9 Av main course £16
**Restaurant** L served all wk 12-2
D served Mon-Sat 6.30-9, Sun 12-3.30
Av 3 course à la carte fr £22 ⊕ CHARLES
WELLS ◢ Wells, Youngs, Eagle IPA. ♀ 13
**Facilities** Garden Parking

## NORTHILL      Map 12 TL14

### The Crown ♟

**2 Ickwell Rd SG18 9AA**
☎ **01767 627337** 📠 **01767 627279**
**e-mail:** info@thecrown-northill.com
**dir:** *Telephone for directions*

A delightful 16th-century pub with chocolate box setting between Northill church and the village duck pond. Its acre of garden includes a children's play area, and plenty of tables for alfresco eating. Inside, the unique copper-covered bar leads to an informal dining area, where the bar menu of pub favourites applies. The candlelit split-level restaurant boasts much locally sourced produce served in home-cooked dishes such as roasted lamb chump with port and rosemary jus; smoked hake fillets on tomato sauce; and pork tenderloin medallions wrapped in bacon.

**Open** all wk Mon-Thu 11.30-3 6-11 (Fri-Sun & BHs 11.30-11) Closed: 25 Dec eve **Bar Meals** L served Mon-Fri 12-2.30, Sat-Sun 12-10.30 **Restaurant** L served Mon-Fri 12-2.30, Sat-Sun 12-10.30 booking required ⊕ GREENE KING ◀ Greene King IPA, Abbot Ale, Old Speckled Hen, Olde Trip plus, Guest ales. ♟ 9 **Facilities** Children's menu Children's portions Play area Dogs allowed Garden Parking

## ODELL      Map 11 SP95

### The Bell ♟

**Horsefair Ln MK43 7AU** ☎ **01234 720254**
**dir:** *Telephone for directions*

A Grade II listed 16th-century thatched pub with a patio and aviary outside, situated next to a spacious garden leading down to the River Ouse. The lunch menu offers a wide choice of baguettes and jacket potatoes as well as classics like fried whitebait; home cooked ham and free range eggs; and steak, mushroom and ale pie. Many of these dishes are also available at dinner, along with pan fried lamb's liver with smoked bacon and red wine gravy and leek and mushroom stroganoff with basmati rice. Portions are generous - the website warns 'if you are brave enough to attempt three courses you may need a snooze!'

**Open** all wk Mon-Fri 11.30-3 6-11.30 (Sat 11.30-4 6-11.30 Sun 12-4 7-10.30) **Bar Meals** L served all wk 12-2 booking required D served Tue-Sat 7-9 booking required Av main course £8 ⊕ GREENE KING ◀ Greene King IPA, Abbot Ale, Ruddles County, Seasonal ales Ò Stowford Press. ♟ 8 **Facilities** Children's menu Children's portions Family room Dogs allowed Garden Parking

## OLD WARDEN      Map 12 TL14

### PICK OF THE PUBS

### Hare and Hounds ♟

*See Pick of the Pubs on opposite page*

## SALFORD      Map 11 SP93

### PICK OF THE PUBS

### *The Swan* ♟

**2 Warendon Rd MK17 8BD** ☎ **01908 281008**
**e-mail:** swan@peachpubs.com
**dir:** *M1 junct 13, follow signs to Salford*

Not far from central Milton Keynes is this attractive village and the tile-hung Edwardian Swan, which has earned a great local reputation in recent years. In the kitchen Neil Simons and his team take pride in using top ingredients from ethical British producers, not least to cut down on air freight, to produce starters of pheasant, apricot and smoked bacon terrine with Cumberland sauce; and Thai crab beignet with pickled ginger and chilli dressing. From the plentiful main courses come free-range coq au vin; sea bass with crunchy winter vegetable slaw; and leek, red onion, broccoli and blue cheese strudel with Meaux mustard sauce. Deli boards - mixed, charcuterie, cheese, antipasti, fish and Indian - are a house speciality. The kitchen will happily prepare children's versions of anything the grown-ups eat. A short, sensibly priced wine list changes frequently. On sunny days, check for a barbecue on the terrace.

**Open** all day all wk 11am-mdnt (Sun 12-10.30) Closed: 25 Dec ◀ IPA, Black Sheep, Guinness. ♟ 8 **Facilities** Dogs allowed Garden Parking

## SOUTHILL      Map 12 TL14

### The White Horse ♟

**High St SG18 9LD** ☎ **01462 813364**
**e-mail:** paul.e.cluett@virgin.net
**dir:** *Telephone for directions*

A village pub with traditional values, happily accommodating the needs of children in the large mature garden and those who like to sit outside on cool days enjoying a well-kept pint (the patio has heaters). Grilled steaks are a big draw here but other main courses from the extensive menu include Cumberland sausages, home-made steak, Stilton and stout pie and Whitby seafood platter. Vegetarians and children have a tempting choice too, and the chef's daily-changing specials board is worth a look at.

**Open** all wk **Bar Meals** L served Mon-Fri 12-2.30, Sat-Sun 12-10 booking required D served Mon-Fri 6-10, Sat-Sun 12-10 booking required Av main course £7.50 **Restaurant** L served Mon-Fri 12-2.30, Sat-Sun 12-10 booking required D served Mon-Fri 6-10, Sat-Sun 12-10 booking required Fixed menu price fr £5.50 Av 3 course à la carte fr £15 ⊕ ENTERPRISE INNS ◀ Greene King IPA, Golden Fox, John Smith's, Sharp's Doom Bar. ♟ 8 **Facilities** Children's menu Play area Dogs allowed Garden Parking

## STANBRIDGE      Map 11 SP92

### PICK OF THE PUBS

### The Five Bells ♟

**Station Rd, Stanbridge LU7 9JF** ☎ **01525 210224**
**e-mail:** fivebells@fullers.co.uk
**dir:** *Off A505 E of Leighton Buzzard*

A stylish and relaxing setting for a drink or a meal is offered by this white-painted 400-year-old village inn, which has been delightfully renovated and revived. The bar features lots of bare wood as well as comfortable armchairs and polished, rug-strewn floors. The modern decor extends to the bright, airy 75-cover dining room. There's also a spacious garden with patio and lawns. The inn offers bar meals, set menus and a carte choice for diners. The bar menu typically includes dishes such as beer battered fish, chips and mushy peas; rib-eye steak with hand-cut chips; home-made beef and venison burger; red onion charlotte and roasted vegetable tart; and pan roasted duck breast with sour cherry sauce.

**Open** all day all wk 11-11 (Sun 12-10.30) **Bar Meals** L served all wk 12-10, Sun 12-10.30 D served all wk 12-10, Sun 12-10.30 food served all day **Restaurant** food served all day ⊕ FREE HOUSE ◀ Fullers London Pride, Fullers Chiswick Bitter, Gales Seafairers Ò Aspall. ♟ 8 **Facilities** Children's menu Children's portions Dogs allowed Garden Parking

## SUTTON      Map 12 TL24

### John O'Gaunt Inn ♟

**30 High St SG19 2NE** ☎ **01767 260377**
**dir:** *Off B1040 between Biggleswade & Potton*

Situated in one of Bedfordshire's most picturesque villages, the John O'Gaunt is a pretty village inn at the centre of the community and many rural walks. A guest ale features alongside the regular beers supplied in rotation from various breweries. Piped music is notable by its absence, though you may be encouraged to join in the regular folk music sessions; thirty different clubs and societies are hosted here. Good traditional fayre is on offer such as steak and kidney pudding; lamb shank with mint and onion gravy; fisherman's pie; and a variety of balti dishes. The pub has a large garden, and welcoming winter fires.

**Open** all wk 12-3 7-11 (Fri 12-3 6-11, Sun 12-5 7-11) **Bar Meals** L served all wk 12.30-1.45 D served all wk 7-9 Av main course £8 ⊕ ADMIRAL TAVERNS ◀ Rotating - Woodforde's Wherry, Black Sheep, London Pride, Timothy Taylor Landlord Ò Westons Old Rosie. ♟ 8 **Facilities** Dogs allowed Garden Parking **Notes** ⊛

## TILSWORTH      Map 11 SP92

### The Anchor Inn ♥

**1 Dunstable Rd LU7 9PU**
☎ 01525 210289   📄 01525 211578
**e-mail:** tonyanchorinn@aol.com
**dir:** *Exit A5 at Tilsworth. In 1m pub on right at 3rd bend*

The only pub in a Saxon village, The Anchor dates from 1878. The restaurant is a recent addition to the side of the pub, and the whole building has been refurbished. The licensees pride themselves on their fresh food and well-kept beers and guest ales. An acre of garden includes patio seating for alfresco dining, an adventure playground and a barbecue.

**Open** all day all wk noon-11.30pm **Bar Meals** L served all day 12-9 D served all day 12-9 food served all day **Restaurant** food served all day ⊕ GREENE KING ◀ Greene King IPA, Abbot Ale, Wadworth 6X, guest ales. ♥ 12 **Facilities** Children's menu Children's portions Play area Family room Dogs allowed Garden Parking

## WOBURN      Map 11 SP93

### The Birch at Woburn ♥

**20 Newport Rd MK17 9HX**
☎ 01525 861414   📄 01525 861323
**e-mail:** ctaverns@aol.com
**dir:** *Telephone for directions*

A beautifully presented family-run establishment, The Birch is located opposite Woburn Championship Golf Course, close to Woburn Abbey and the Safari Park. It has built its reputation on the friendly service of freshly cooked food. A comprehensive menu offers a range of English and Continental dishes, and there is a griddle area where customers can make their selection from the array of fresh steaks and fish, which are then cooked to their preference by the chefs.

**Open** 12-3 6-12 Closed: 25-26 Dec, 1 Jan, Sun eve **Bar Meals** L served 12-2.30 booking required D served 6-10 **Restaurant** L served 12-2.30 booking required D served 6-10 Av 3 course à la carte fr £29.95 ⊕ FREE HOUSE ◀ London Pride, Adnams, Guinness. ♥ 12 **Facilities** Children's portions Parking

## BERKSHIRE

### ALDERMASTON      Map 5 SU56

### Hinds Head ♥

**Wasing Ln RG7 4LX**
☎ 0118 971 2194   📄 0118 971 4511
**e-mail:** hindshead@fullers.co.uk
**dir:** *M4 junct 12, A4 towards Newbury, left on A340 towards Basingstoke, 2m to village*

This 17th-century inn with its distinctive clock and bell tower still incorporates the village lock-up, which was last used in 1865. The former brew house behind the pub has been refurbished to create an additional dining area. Menu choices range from jacket potatoes and filled baguettes to whole baked sea bass; carbonara pasta; and cauliflower cheese. Recent change of hands.

**Open** all wk Mon-Sat 12-3 6-9 (Sun 12-8) ⊕ FULLERS BREWERY ◀ Fullers HSB. ♥ 12 **Facilities** Children's menu Children's portions Family room Dogs allowed Garden Parking

### ALDWORTH      Map 5 SU57

### PICK OF THE PUBS

### The Bell Inn

**RG8 9SE** ☎ 01635 578272
**dir:** *Just off B4009 (Newbury to Streatley road)*

One might be surprised to discover that an establishment without a restaurant can hold its own in a world of smart dining pubs and modish gastro-pubs. Well, be surprised. The Bell not only survives, it positively prospers and, to be fair, it does serve some food, if only hot, crusty, generously filled rolls. And since it is one of the few truly unspoiled country pubs left, and serves cracking pints of Arkell's, West Berkshire and guest real ales, this limitation has been no disadvantage. The Bell is old, very old, beginning life in 1340 as a five-bay cruck-built manor hall. It has reputedly been in the same family for 200 years: ask Mr Macaulay, the landlord - he's been here for more than thirty of them, and he has no plans to change it from the time warp it is. A 300-year-old, one-handed clock still stands in the taproom 'keeping imperfect time', and the rack for the spit-irons and clockwork roasting jack are still over the fireplace. Taller customers may bump their heads at the glass-panelled bar hatch.

**Open** Mon-Sat 11-3 6-11 (Sun 12-3, 7-10.30) Closed: 25 Dec, Mon (BH Mon lunch only) ⊕ FREE HOUSE ◀ Arkell's Kingsdown, 3B, West Berkshire Old Tyler & Maggs Magnificent Mild, guest ales ♂ Uptons Farmhouse, Tutts Clump. **Facilities** Dogs allowed Garden Parking **Notes** ⊜

### ASCOT      Map 6 SU96

### The Thatched Tavern ♥

**Cheapside Rd SL5 7QG**
☎ 01344 620874   📄 01344 623043
**e-mail:** thethatchedtavern@4cinns.co.uk
**dir:** *Follow Ascot Racecourse signs. Through Ascot 1st left (Cheapside). 1.5m, pub on left*

Just a mile from the famous racecourse, a 17th-century building of original beams, flagstone floors and very low ceilings. In summer the sheltered garden makes a fine spot to enjoy real ales and varied choice of food; in the cooler months there is the cosy bar and warming fires. The kitchen brigade produces dishes like venison and mushroom pudding, seared calves' liver on bubble and squeak, and beef stew and dumplings.

**Open** all wk Mon-Thu 12-3.30 5.30-11 (all day Fri-Sun) **Bar Meals** L served Mon-Sat 12-2.30 Av main course £8 **Restaurant** L served Mon-Sat 12-2.30, Sun 12-3 booking required D served Mon-Sat 7-9.45, Sun 7-9 booking required Fixed menu price fr £11.95 Av 3 course à la carte fr £25 ⊕ FREE HOUSE ◀ Fuller's London Pride, IPA, Guinness ♂ Stowford Press. ♥ 11 **Facilities** Children's portions Dogs allowed Garden Parking

### ASHMORE GREEN      Map 5 SU56

### The Sun in the Wood ♥

**Stoney Ln RG18 9HF** ☎ 01635 42377   📄 01635 528392
**e-mail:** info@suninthewood.co.uk
**dir:** *From A34 at Robin Hood Rdbt left to Shaw, at mini-rdbt right then 7th left into Stoney Ln 1.5m, pub on left*

The name promises woodland beauty and the setting delivers it, yet the centre of Newbury is surprisingly close by. Expect stone floors and plenty of wood panelling within, and a country garden, decking terrace for alfresco dining and crazy golf outside. Sample a pint of Wadworth's or one of 15 wines by the glass, and enjoy food made on the premises using local ingredients. There is a classic British pub menu and an à la carte: perhaps a salmon and haddock fishcake, then roast breast of duck on a bourguignon cassoulet with mini fondant potatoes, followed by one of the wonderful home-made puddings.

**Open** 12-3 6-11 Closed: 25-26 Dec, Mon **Bar Meals** L served Tue-Sat 12-2, Sun 12-4 booking required D served Tue-Sat 6-9.30 booking required Av main course £9.50 **Restaurant** L served Tue-Sat 12-2, Sun 12-4 booking required D served Tue-Sat 6-9.30 booking required Fixed menu price fr £8.95 Av 3 course à la carte fr £20 ⊕ WADWORTH ◀ Wadworth 6X, Henrys Original IPA, Badger Tanglefoot ♂ Westons Stowford Press. ♥ 15 **Facilities** Children's menu Children's portions Play area Garden Parking

## BOXFORD   Map 5 SU47

### The Bell at Boxford ⬛ ★★★ INN 🍷

**Lambourn Rd RG20 8DD**
☎ **01488 608721** 📠 **01488 658502**
e-mail: paul@bellatboxford.com
dir: *M4 junct 14 onto A338 towards Wantage. Turn right onto B4000 to x-rds, signed Boxford*

This mock Tudor country pub is at the heart of the glorious Lambourn Valley, noted for its pretty villages and sweeping Downland scenery. Cosy log fires add to the appeal in winter, and the patio is popular throughout the year with its array of flowers and outdoor heating, hog roasts, barbecues and parties. Menus might include pan-fried Wantage duck breast with leeks and baby spinach, new potatoes, cranberry and orange sauce; confit of duck with a casserole of beans and chorizo; or beef bourguignon, Yorkshire pudding and grain mustard mash.

**Open** all wk 11-3 6-11 (Sun noon-10.30) **Bar Meals** L served Mon-Sat 12-2, Sun 12-9 D served Mon-Sat 7-9.30, Sun 7-9 Av main course £8.95 **Restaurant** L served Mon-Sat 12-2.30, Sun 12-7 D served Mon-Sat 7-9.30, Sun 7-9 Fixed menu price fr £13.95 Av 3 course à la carte fr £26 ⊕ FREE HOUSE ◀ Bishop's Tipple, Henry's IPA, 1664, Guinness, 6X. 🍷 60 **Facilities** Children's portions Dogs allowed Garden Parking **Rooms** 11

*See advertisement under NEWBURY*

## BRAY   Map 6 SU97

### PICK OF THE PUBS

**The Hinds Head** ◉◉ 🍷

*See Pick of the Pubs on page 34*

## CHADDLEWORTH   Map 5 SU47

### The Ibex

**Main St RG20 7ER** ☎ **01488 638311**
e-mail: inn@the-ibex.co.uk
dir: *A338 towards Wantage, through Great Shefford then right, then 2nd left, pub on right in village*

An award-winning hard-working community pub in a Grade II listed building with low beams. The only pub in the UK called The Ibex, it's the headquarters for local cricket teams; it has strong connections with horse-racing (it used to be run by ex-jockey Colin Brown of Desert Orchid fame); it has its own golf society; it runs film, quiz and curry nights; it sells home-made bread, free range eggs and local honey; it will even take your dry cleaning and deliver a bouquet. All this, and it serves with a smile Greene King ales and real ciders, and comprehensive menus of traditional pub grub.

**Open** all wk 11-3 6-mdnt (all day Sat-Sun & BHs) **Bar Meals** L served all wk 12-3 D served all wk 6-9 **Restaurant** L served all wk 12-3 D served all wk 6-9 ⊕ GREENE KING ◀ IPA, Morland Original, Guinness Ò Tutts Clump, Stowford Press, Ciderworks. **Facilities** Children's menu Children's portions Dogs allowed Garden Parking

## CHIEVELEY   Map 5 SU47

### The Crab at Chieveley ★★★★ GA ◉◉ 🍷

**North Heath, Wantage Rd RG20 8UE**
☎ **01635 247550** 📠 **01635 247440**
e-mail: info@crabatchieveley.com
dir: *M4 junct 13. 1.5m W of Chieveley on B4494*

A great seafood restaurant, this lovely old thatched dining pub is a perfect place to break a tedious M4 journey. Specialising in mouth-watering fish dishes, with fresh deliveries daily, the Fish Bar offers, for example, fresh Irish oysters followed by fish and chips. In the elegant, maritime-themed restaurant, try corn fed chicken ballotine with quail and raisin mousse or fruits de mer. Beers are from West Berkshire breweries and 13 boutique bedrooms complete the package.

**Open** all day all wk 11-11 **Bar Meals** L served all wk 12-2.30 D served all wk 7-9.30 Av main course £23 **Restaurant** Fixed menu price fr £15.95 Av 3 course à la carte fr £40 ⊕ FREE HOUSE ◀ West Berkshire Breweries. 🍷 20 **Facilities** Children's menu Children's portions Garden Parking **Rooms** 13

## COOKHAM DEAN   Map 5 SU88

### PICK OF THE PUBS

**The Chequers Brasserie** 🍷

**Dean Ln SL6 9BQ** ☎ **01628 481232** 📠 **01628 481237**
e-mail: info@chequersbrasserie.co.uk
dir: *From A4094 in Cookham High St towards Marlow, over rail line. 1m on right*

Kenneth Grahame, who wrote *The Wind in the Willows*, spent his childhood in these parts. He would surely have enjoyed this historic pub, tucked away between Marlow and Maidenhead in one of the prettiest villages in the Thames Valley. Striking Victorian and Edwardian villas around the green set the tone, whilst the surrounding wooded hills and dales have earned Cookham Dean a reputation as a centre for wonderful walks. The bar presents a good selection of ales from Adnams and Brakspear, amongst others, backed by top-flight real ciders from the likes of Thatchers, Aspall and Westons. The Anglo-French menu is dedicated to the use of fresh and high quality produce. Expect the likes of seared calves' liver with smoked bacon; and slow-cooked belly of Norfolk pork with crackling, Savoy cabbage and gratin potato. Accompanying children can be served smaller portions from the menu, and dogs are welcome in the garden.

**Open** all day all wk 11-11 **Bar Meals** L served Mon-Sat 12-2.30, Sun 12-9.30 D served Mon-Thu 6.30-9.30, Fri-Sat 6.30-10, Sun 12-9.30 **Restaurant** L served Mon-Sat 12-2.30, Sun 12-9.30 D served Mon-Thu 6.30-9.30, Fri-Sat 6.30-10, Sun 12-9.30 Fixed menu price fr £13.95 Av 3 course à la carte fr £25.95 ⊕ FREE HOUSE ◀ Guinness, Greene King IPA, Rebellion Marlow Brewery, Adnams Bitter, Brakspears Ò Stowford Press, Thatchers Cox, Aspall, Thatchers Katy. 🍷 14 **Facilities** Children's portions Garden Parking

# PICK OF THE PUBS

## The Hinds Head

**BRAY**  Map 6 SU97

**High St SL6 2AB**
☎ **01628 626151**  📠 **01628 623394**
e-mail: info@hindsheadbray.com
web: www.hindsheadbray.com
dir: *M4 junct 8/9 take exit to Maidenhead Central. Next rdbt take exit for Bray & Windsor. After 0.5m take B3028 to Bray*

The Hinds Head is owned by internationally acclaimed chef (some say culinary alchemist) Heston Blumenthal, and business partner Jamie Lee. Not surprisingly, it has become a gastronomic destination, yet remains very much a village local. With origins in Tudor times, celebrated past patrons include Prince Philip, who held his stag night here in 1947, and Princess Margaret and Lord Snowdon, who celebrated their engagement here in 1963.

Sturdy oak panelling and beams, leather chairs and real fires characterise the interior. On the ground floor is the two-AA Rosette main restaurant and a cosy bar area with comfortable seating and small alcoves. Upstairs are two further dining areas, the Vicars Room, and the larger Royal Room.

Blumenthal worked alongside the Tudor Kitchens at Hampton Court Palace, rediscovering the origins of British cuisine, and has reintroduced dishes from a bygone era. Starters include pea and ham soup; Hinds Head tea-smoked salmon with soda bread; spiced fig tart with goat's cheese and hazelnuts; or potted shrimps with watercress salad. Among typical main dishes are oxtail and kidney pudding; fish pie; and a variety of steaks with bone marrow sauce and triple cooked chips. Finish with Sussex pond pudding; banana Eton Mess, the traditional pudding from Eton College tuck shop; or treacle tart with milk ice cream; and British cheese with oatcakes and quince paste. In addition, a wide selection of specials is available Monday to Friday, while a separate lunchtime bar menu includes home-made Scotch quail egg; devils on

horseback; and smoked salmon with cucumber and cream cheese. Guest ales and well selected, widely sourced wines complete the picture.

**Open** all wk Closed: 25-26 Dec
**Bar Meals** L served Mon-Sat 12-2.30, Sun 12-4 D served Mon-Sat 6.30-9.30
**Restaurant** L served Mon-Sat 12-2.30, Sun 12-4 booking required D served Mon-Sat 6.30-9.30 booking required
⊕ FREE HOUSE ◀ Greene King IPA, Greene King Abbot Ale, Marlow Rebellion, Timothy Taylor Landlord, London Pride, Guest Ales ♂ Stowford Press. ♟15 **Facilities** Children's menu Parking

## CRAZIES HILL     Map 5 SU78

### PICK OF THE PUBS

### The Horns ♥

**RG10 8LY ☎ 0118 940 6222**
**dir:** *Off A321 NE of Wargrave*

Steve Wiltshire and his wife Dawn took over The Horns in mid-2009, and immediately started turning the garden into a paradise for children, with two Shetland ponies to pet and a large guinea pig and rabbit run. For grown-up diners there's a free minibus service, a large purpose-built BBQ, a hog-roast machine, and a free marquee for parties and weddings. Inside the restored Tudor hunting lodge are three interconnecting terracotta-coloured oak beamed rooms full of old pine tables, stripped wooden floors, and open fires; a barn added 200 years ago forms the dining area. The peaceful atmosphere makes it a great place to enjoy a pint of Brakspear ale. The menu of pub favourites ranges from starters like home-made soup of the day to mains such as home-cooked gammon steak with egg; home-made lasagne; and curry of the day.

**Open** all wk 12-3 6-11 **Bar Meals** L served 12-3 D served 6-9 Av main course £8.95 **Restaurant** L served 12-3 D served 6-9 ⊕ BRAKSPEAR ◀ Brakspear Bitter. ♥ 8 **Facilities** Children's menu Children's portions Play area Family room Dogs allowed Garden Parking

## CURRIDGE     Map 5 SU47

### The Bunk Inn ♥

**RG18 9DS ☎ 01635 200400**
**e-mail:** thebunkinn@btconnect.com
**dir:** *M4 junct 13, A34 N towards Oxford. Take 1st slip road then right for 1m. Right at T-junct, 1st right signed Curridge*

Owned by the Liquorish family since 1991, this village free house is renowned for its cuisine and friendly atmosphere. Stay in the log fire-warmed bar in winter or, in summer, head for the attractive garden and patio. The only question is, where to dine - stylish restaurant or lovely conservatory? All food is fresh, and wherever possible, seasonal and local. An impressive carte menu, plus specials that usually include fresh Brixham fish.

**Open** all day all wk 11am-11.30pm **Bar Meals** L served Mon-Fri 12-2.30, Sat 12-9.30, Sun 12-9 D served Mon-Fri 6-9.30, Sat 12-9.30, Sun 12-9 **Restaurant** L served Mon-Fri 12-2.30, Sat 12-9.30, Sun 12-9 D served Mon-Fri 6-9.30, Sat 12-9.30, Sun 12-9 ⊕ FREE HOUSE ◀ Fuller's London Pride, Good Old Boy ♂ Stowford Press. ♥ 10 **Facilities** Children's menu Children's portions Play area Dogs allowed Garden Parking

## EAST GARSTON     Map 5 SU37

### PICK OF THE PUBS

### *The Queen's Arms Country Inn*

**RG17 7ET ☎ 01488 648757   📄 01488 648642**
**e-mail:** info@queensarmshotel.co.uk
**dir:** *M4 junct 14, 4m onto A338 to Great Shefford, then East Garston*

This 18th-century inn is pleasantly located in a small village in the Lambourn Valley, with its many racehorse training yards. It is also an excellent area for walking, being quite close to the Ridgeway. Now part of the small and select Miller's Collection of pubs, the Queen's Arms offers a warm welcome in stylishly traditional setting. The menu offers a good selection of traditional country food made from fresh local ingredients. On the main menu are dishes such as goats' cheese and black pudding salad; wild boar and leek sausages; lamb cutlets; and roast peppers stuffed with brie, mushrooms and red onion served with tagliatelle. The terrace and large garden are popular in the summer, when barbecues and hog roasts take place.

**Open** all wk ◀ Guinness, 1664 Ringwood Best, Ringwood Fortyniner, guest ale. **Facilities** Dogs allowed Garden Parking

## HERMITAGE     Map 5 SU57

### The White Horse of Hermitage ♥

**Newbury Rd RG18 9TB ☎ 01635 200325**
**e-mail:** thewh@btconnect.com
**dir:** *5m from Newbury on B4009. Follow signs to Chieveley, right into Priors Court Rd, turn left at mini-rdbt, pub approx 1m*

The White Horse has achieved a solid reputation for its pub food, using the freshest and finest local produce to create a daily menu, including signature dishes such as BBQ babyback ribs. The interior bar and restaurant is contemporary in decor, and outside you choose between the Mediterranean-style patio or the large garden which is equipped with swings and a football area.

**Open** all wk noon-3 5-11 Closed: Mon (ex BH) **Bar Meals** L served Mon-Sat 12-3 D served Mon-Sat 5-10, Sun 5-8 ⊕ GREENE KING ◀ Abbot Ale, Greene King IPA, Guinness ♂ Stowford Press. ♥ 9 **Facilities** Children's menu Play area Dogs allowed Garden Parking

## HUNGERFORD     Map 5 SU36

### PICK OF THE PUBS

### The Crown & Garter ★★★★ INN ♥

**Inkpen Common RG17 9QR ☎ 01488 668325**
**e-mail:** gill.hern@btopenworld.com
**dir:** *From A4 to Kintbury & Inkpen. At village store left into Inkpen Rd, follow signs for Inkpen Common 2m*

Standing on a former coach road to Salisbury, this traditional 17th-century free house is said to have been used by James II on his way to visit one of his

mistresses. Today, the ancient charm of this family-run inn is best seen in the bar, where there's a huge inglenook fireplace and criss-crossing beams. You can eat here, in the wood-panelled restaurant, or outside under an oak tree in the enclosed beer garden. The daily-changing menu might feature roast fillet of salmon hollandaise with new potatoes; venison, pheasant and plum sausages with creamed potatoes; or spinach and Stilton tart with tomato and basil salsa. Typical desserts include bread and butter pudding with custard, and fresh raspberry and almond tart with vanilla ice cream. Nine spacious en suite bedrooms have been built around a pretty cottage garden, making a good base for walking, cycling or fishing in the surrounding countryside.

**Open** all wk 12-3 5.30-11 (Sun 12-5 7-10.30, closed Mon & Tue lunch) **Bar Meals** L served Wed-Sat 12-2, Sun 12-2.30 booking required D served Mon-Sat 6.30-9.30 booking required **Restaurant** L served Wed-Sat 12-2, Sun 12-2.30 booking required D served Mon-Sat 6.30-9.30 booking required ⊕ FREE HOUSE ◀ Mr Chubbs, Good Old Boy, Guinness, Moonlight, Ramsbury Gold. ♥ 9 **Facilities** Garden Parking **Rooms** 9

---

### The Pheasant Inn ★★★★ INN ♥ NEW

**Ermin St, Shefford Woodlands RG17 7AA**
**☎ 01488 648284   📄 01488 648971**
**e-mail:** enquiries@thepheasant-inn.co.uk
**dir:** *From M4 junct 14 take A338 towards Wantage. Left onto B4000 towards Lambourn*

Once called The Paraffin House, this old drovers' stopover has now been much enlarged by the addition of eleven new bedrooms, but the beamed, wood-panelled and stone-floored old pub remains unchanged, ready to cater for, among others, the refreshment needs of the local horse-racing communities. So when the favourite romps home at nearby Newbury, liberate your winnings with honey and thyme-marinated baby spring chicken; seared calves' liver; or grilled lemon sole from the daily changing menu.

**Open** all day all wk **Bar Meals** L served all wk 12-2.30 D served all wk 7-9 Av main course £14 **Restaurant** L served all wk 12-2.30 D served all wk 7-9 Av 3 course à la carte fr £25 ⊕ FREE HOUSE ◀ Wadworth, Loddon. ♥ 12 **Facilities** Children's portions Dogs allowed Garden Parking **Rooms** 11

**HUNGERFORD** *continued*

## PICK OF THE PUBS

### The Swan Inn ★★★★ INN

**Craven Rd, Lower Green, Inkpen RG17 9DX**
☎ 01488 668326  📠 01488 668306
e-mail: enquiries@theswaninn-organics.co.uk
web: www.theswaninn-organics.co.uk
dir: *S down Hungerford High St (A338), under rail bridge, left to Hungerford Common. Right signed Inkpen (3m)*

Organic beef farmers Mary and Bernard Harris preside over this rambling 17th-century free house, which stands in fine walking country just below Combe Gibbet and Walbury Hill. An attractive terraced garden sets the scene for alfresco summer dining, in contrast to the heavily beamed interior with its old photographic prints and open winter fires. Almost everything on the menu is prepared using their own fresh produce; meats — 100% organic and butchered on the premises — can be bought from the farm shop attached to the pub. The bar menu offers traditional English favourites, while the Cygnet restaurant may serve a gravadlax starter, followed by a tournedos Rossini; a pan-fried fillet of turbot; or a half shoulder of lamb with rosemary, garlic and red wine jus. Even the wine is organic, with over twenty choices from seven countries. There is an organic farm shop to visit, and 10 en suite bedrooms available.

**Open** all wk 11-11 (Sat noon-11pm Sun noon-4) Closed: 25-26 Dec **Bar Meals** L served all wk 12-2 booking required D served all wk 7-9.30 booking required Av main course £9.50 **Restaurant** L served Wed-Sun 12-2.30 booking required D served Wed-Sat 7-9.30 booking required Av 3 course à la carte fr £19.50 ⊕ FREE HOUSE ◄ Butts Traditional & Jester Bitter, Butts Blackguard, Adnams, guest ales. **Facilities** Children's menu Children's portions Play area Garden Parking **Rooms** 10

### HURST                                    Map 5 SU77

### The Green Man 🍷

**Hinton Rd RG10 0BP**
☎ 0118 934 2599  📠 0118 934 2939
e-mail: simon@thegreenman.uk.com
dir: *Off A321, adjacent to Hurst Cricket Club*

The pub gained its first licence in 1602, and Brakspear purchased a 1,000 year lease on the building in 1646. The old black beams, low in places, are still to be seen and the building has been developed to include all the

old features, while newer areas reflect a similar theme. Inside you'll find open fires, hand drawn beer and good food, from sandwiches to Sunday roasts. The garden, open to fields and woodland, includes a children's play area. As we went to press we learnt that the pub was due to change hands.

**Open** all wk 11-3 5.30-11 (Sun noon-10.30) **Bar Meals** L served 12-2.30 D served 6-9.30 **Restaurant** L served 12-2.30 D served 6-9.30 booking required ⊕ BRAKSPEAR ◄ Brakspear Bitter, Hobgoblin, seasonal ales. 🍷 8 **Facilities** Children's menu Children's portions Play area Garden Parking

### KINTBURY                                 Map 5 SU36

## PICK OF THE PUBS

### The Dundas Arms

**53 Station Rd RG17 9UT**
☎ 01488 658263  📠 01488 658568
e-mail: info@dundasarms.co.uk
dir: *M4 junct 13 take A34 to Newbury, then A4 to Hungerford, left to Kintbury. Pub 1m by canal & rail station*

Set in an Area of Outstanding Natural Beauty on the banks of the Kennet and Avon Canal, this free house has been welcoming travellers since the end of the 18th century. The pub has been in the same family for nearly 45 years, and proprietor David Dalzell-Piper has worked and cooked here throughout that time. Traditional beers like West Berkshire's Good Old Boy are served in the bar, whilst the simply styled restaurant is redolent of a French auberge. Here a typical meal might start with bubbly tempura king prawns with chilli mayonnaise, or grilled goat's cheese on Italian bread with sweet tomato purée. The modern British style of cooking continues in main course dishes such as Creedy Carver duck with cider and apple sauce, and grilled sea bass with Asian coleslaw. Puddings such as treacle sponge with custard are reassuringly traditional. On warm days, outdoor tables offer views of the narrow boats and wildlife on the canal.

**Open** all wk 11-2.30 6-11 Closed: 25 & 31 Dec, Sun eve **Bar Meals** L served Mon-Sat 12-2 D served Tue-Sat 7-9 Av main course £13 **Restaurant** L served Mon-Sat 12-2 D served Tue-Sat 7-9 booking required Av 3 course à la carte fr £30 ⊕ FREE HOUSE ◄ West Berkshire, Mr Chubbs Lunchtime Bitter, Adnams, West Berkshire Good Old Boy, Ramsbury Gold. **Facilities** Children's menu Family room Parking

### KNOWL HILL                               Map 5 SU87

## PICK OF THE PUBS

### Bird In Hand Country Inn ★★★ HL 🍷

**Bath Rd RG10 9UP**
☎ 01628 826622 & 822781  📠 01628 826748
e-mail: sthebirdinhand@aol.com
web: www.birdinhand.co.uk
dir: *On A4, 5m W of Maidenhead, 7m E of Reading*

In the same family for three generations, the inn's owners pride themselves on personal service, a friendly atmosphere, and keeping the warm and cosy inglenook fire burning in winter. Parts of the building date from the 14th century, and legend has it that in the late 1700s George III wet his regal whistle here while his horse was being re-shod at the forge next door. A range of constantly changing hand-pumped guest ales and a multitude of wines by the glass are served in the wood-panelled Oak Lounge bar, while an attractive restaurant overlooks a courtyard and fountain. The same menu is served throughout, offering both exotic and traditional dishes as well as light meals such as salad bowls, mezze, jacket potatoes, omelettes and pizzas. A typical three-course selection could begin with baked button mushrooms in garlic butter and breadcrumbs; grilled halibut supreme with Mediterranean vegetables and couscous; and a dessert from the board.

**Open** all day all wk **Bar Meals** Av main course £10 food served all day **Restaurant** L served all wk 12-2.30 booking required D served all wk 7-10 booking required Fixed menu price fr £10.50 Av 3 course à la carte fr £25 ⊕ FREE HOUSE ◄ Guest ales ♂ Thatchers. 🍷 20 **Facilities** Children's menu Children's portions Dogs allowed Garden Parking **Rooms** 15

### LECKHAMPSTEAD                            Map 5 SU47

## PICK OF THE PUBS

### The Stag 🍷

*See Pick of the Pubs on opposite page*

# PICK OF THE PUBS

## The Stag 🍷

**Shop Ln RG20 8QG ☎ 01488 638436**
e-mail:
enquiries@stagleckhampstead.co.uk
dir: *6m from Newbury on B4494*

To look at, the white-painted Stag could only be a pub. It lies just off the village green in a sleepy downland village and close by are the Ridgeway long-distance path and Snelsmore Common, home to nightjar, woodlark and grazing Exmoor ponies. Needless to say, with such beautiful countryside all around, muddy wellies and wet dogs are expected – in fact, the latter are as genuinely welcome as their owners. During the winter months the wood-burning stove is always ready with its dancing flames. The bar and restaurant walls are painted in warm red, or left as bare brick, while old black and white photographs tell of village life many years ago.

Surrounding farms and growers supply all produce, including venison, pheasant and fresh river trout. These fish often appear on the specials board, courtesy of a regular customer who barters them for a few glasses of Rioja, depending on their size. Aberdeen Angus beef from cattle raised next door may also feature as a special, and those lucky enough to find it there agree that its taste and texture are sublime.

Other possibilities, depending on the prevailing menu, are chicken liver pâté with onion marmalade; salmon and dill fishcake with sweet chilli sauce, followed by venison and redcurrant sausages with butternut squash mash, onion gravy and seasonal vegetables; pork loin with creamy mushroom sauce with sautéed cabbage and smoked bacon, and creamy mash; or traditional beer battered fish and chips with mushy peas. Home-made desserts include warm pecan pie and custard, or raspberry and white chocolate cheesecake with fruit compote. There are around 20 red and white wines, among them varieties from Australia, California and France. The Stag changed hands in February 2010.

Compulsive workers can take advantage of a wireless internet connection, although in a pub like this it would have to be pretty urgent work.

**Open** 12-3 6-11 Closed: Sun eve, Mon L **Bar Meals** L served Tue-Sat 12-2, Sun 12-3.30 booking required D served Mon-Sat 6-9 booking required **Restaurant** L served Tue-Sat 12-2, Sun 12-3.30 booking required D served Mon-Sat 6-9 ⊕ FREE HOUSE ◧ Morlands Original, Greene King IPA, Guest ales ♂ Aspall. ♟ 8 **Facilities** Children's menu Dogs allowed Garden Parking

## MAIDENHEAD — Map 6 SU88

### The Belgian Arms ♀

**Holyport SL6 2JR ☎ 01628 634468 📠 01628 777952**
e-mail: enquiries@thamessideevents.com
dir: *In Holyport, 2m from Maidenhead, off Ascot road*

Originally known as The Eagle, the Prussian eagle inn sign attracted unwelcome attention during the First World War. As a result, the name was changed to reflect an area where the fiercest fighting was taking place. Things are more peaceful now, and details of local walks are listed outside the pub. The attractive menu includes snacks and light lunches, as well as hot dishes like sausages, mash and onion gravy, and spicy beanburger and chips.

**Open** all wk 12-3 5.30-11.30 (Fri-Sat 11-11.30 Sun noon-10.30) **Bar Meals** L served Mon-Sat 12-3 D served Mon-Sat 6-10 ⊕ BRAKSPEAR ◀ Brakspear Best, Brakspear Organic Gold. ♀ 8 **Facilities** Dogs allowed Garden Parking

### The White Hart

**Moneyrow Green, Holyport SL6 2ND**
**☎ 01628 621460 📠 01628 621460**
e-mail: admin@thewhitehartholyport.co.uk
dir: *2m S from Maidenhead. M4 junct 8/9, follow Holyport signs then Moneyrow Green. Pub by petrol station*

A busy 19th-century coaching inn offering quality home-made food, with most vegetables and herbs used freshly picked from its own organic allotment. Typical mains are caramelised breast of duck; calves' liver and bacon; venison sausages; grilled fillet of plaice; and slow-roasted tomato tart with Somerset brie. The wood-panelled lounge bar is furnished with leather chesterfields and warmed by an open fire. There are large gardens to enjoy in summer with a children's playground and a petanque pitch.

**Open** all day all wk 12-11.30 (Fri-Sat 12-1am, Sun 12-11) **Bar Meals** L served Tue-Sat 12.30-3, Sun 12-4 D served Tue-Sat 6-9 Av main course £7.50 ⊕ GREENE KING ◀ Guinness, IPA, Morland Original Ŏ Stowford Press, Aspall. **Facilities** Children's portions Play area Dogs allowed Garden Parking

## NEWBURY — Map 5 SU46

### PICK OF THE PUBS

### Marco Pierre White's Yew Tree Inn ◎◎ ♀

**Hollington Cross, Andover Rd, Highclere RG20 9SE**
**☎ 01635 253360 📠 01635 255035**
e-mail: info@theyewtree.net
dir: *M4 junct 13, A34 S, 4th junct on left signed Highclere/Wash Common, turn right towards Andover A343, inn on right*

Immaculate styling at this 16th-century free house blends original features like old beams, tiled floors, and inglenook fireplaces with the contemporary refinements of crisp linen and sparkling glassware. The former coaching inn stands just south of the village on the A343, and is well placed for refreshments after a visit to nearby Highclere Castle. Unusual real ales and ciders and fifteen wines by the glass are served in the bar. Celebrated chef turned restaurateur Marco Pierre White offers both traditional British food and time-honoured classics from the French culinary canon. The Anglo-French cooking takes a brasserie approach, with the menu split into sections like hors d'oeuvres, fish and seafood, pies and puddings and roasts and grills, and delivers accomplished, well-presented dishes that are driven by quality ingredients. A memorable meal might kick off with boiled ham en gelée, before moving on to smoked haddock with colcannon and beurre blanc. The dessert menu — tellingly described as 'puddings' — could include Box Tree Eton mess.

**Open** all day all wk **Bar Meals** L served Mon-Sat 12-2.30, Sun 12-3 D served Mon-Sat 6-9.30, Sun 6-9 Av main course £15 **Restaurant** L served Mon-Sat 12-2.30, Sun 12-3 D served Mon-Sat 6-9.30, Sun 6-9 Fixed menu price fr £18.50 Av 3 course à la carte fr £33 ⊕ FREE HOUSE ◀ Timothy Taylor, Adnams, Butt's Barbus Barbus, Mr Chubbs Ŏ Westons Old Rosie, Mr Whitehead's Cirrus Minor. ♀ 15 **Facilities** Children's portions Dogs allowed Garden Parking

## PALEY STREET — Map 5 SU87

### PICK OF THE PUBS

### The Royal Oak ◎◎ ♀

**SL6 3JN ☎ 01628 620541**
e-mail: royaloakmail@aol.com
dir: *From Maidenhead take A330 towards Ascot for 2m, turn right onto B3024 signed Twyford, 2nd pub on left*

Owned by Nick Parkinson, son of Sir Michael Parkinson, this traditional English inn achieves the right balance between gastro and pub. The well-kept ales are supplied by Fullers but it is the wine list that really catches the eye with 15 served by the glass. In the kitchen, head chef Dominic Chapman uses the best seasonal produce to create excellent British food. Choose from a small selection of bar snacks — rabbit on toast, Scotch eggs or roll mops - or sample the lunch and dinner menus. In the restaurant you might begin with pickled South Devon mackerel with beetroot and horseradish cream or warm salad of Somerset smoked eel with frisee and bacon. Typical mains include roast Scottish halibut with samphire, cockles and mussels; oxtail and kidney pie; or fillet of Black Angus beef and veal sweetbread with chips, marrowbone and red wine sauce. In warmer weather, grab a table in the large beer garden.

**Open** 12-3 6-11 (Sun 12-4) Closed: 1st wk Jan, Sun eve **Restaurant** L served Mon-Sat 12-3, Sun 12-4 booking required D served Mon-Thu 6.30-9.30, Fri-Sat 6.30-10 Fixed menu price fr £17.50 Av 3 course à la carte fr £40 ⊕ FULLERS ◀ Fuller's London Pride. ♀ 15 **Facilities** Children's portions Garden Parking

## READING
Map 5 SU77

### The Crown ♥

**Playhatch RG4 9QN**
☎ 0118 947 2872    📠 0118 946 4586
e-mail: info@thecrown.co.uk
dir: *From Reading take A4155 towards Henley-on-Thames. At 1st rdbt take 1st exit, pub 400mtrs on left*

This charming 16th-century country inn with its lovely garden and excellent restaurant nestles between the Thames and the Chilterns, an Area of Outstanding Natural Beauty. Head Chef Nana Akuffo is behind the move to buy fresh local produce wherever possible. Dinner starters may include grilled Brixham sardine fillets, or Thai beef salad; main course examples are confit of duck en croûte, and slow-roasted Cornish lamb; typical desserts are hot sticky toffee pudding, and carpaccio of fresh pineapple.

**Open** all day all wk 10am-11.20pm (Fri-Sat 10am-12.20am) ◀ Brakspear Bitter, Brakspear Special, Brakspear Seasonal, Oxford Gold, Guinness. ♥ 12
**Facilities** Garden Parking

---

### The Flowing Spring

**Henley Rd, Playhatch RG4 9RB** ☎ 0118 969 9878
e-mail: flowingspring@aol.com
dir: *3m N of Reading*

A lovely country pub on the Henley road, much favoured by walkers and cyclists. It's family friendly too, with a menu for under-12s and a small play area in the large well-kept garden. Representative dishes on the combined bar/restaurant menu include chicken goujons with chips and salad; battered cod and chips; spotted dick; and sticky toffee pudding. Being a Fullers pub, Chiswick, London Pride and ESB are all well kept on tap.

**Open** all wk 11-11 **Bar Meals** L served all wk D served all wk food served all day **Restaurant** L served all wk D served all wk food served all day ⊕ FULLERS ◀ London Pride, ESB, Chiswick, Discovery Ò Aspall.
**Facilities** Children's menu Children's portions Play area Family room Dogs allowed Garden Parking

---

### The Shoulder of Mutton

**Playhatch RG4 9QU** ☎ 0118 947 3908
e-mail: shoulderofmutton@hotmail.co.uk
dir: *From Reading follow signs to Caversham, then onto A4155 to Henley-on-Thames. At rdbt left to Binfield Heath, pub on left*

An inviting combination of rustic, cosy village inn and chic, contemporary dining in the airy conservatory restaurant draws in a dedicated crowd of regulars and appreciative diners keen to share head chef Alan Oxlade's passion for the finest local foodstuffs. A nearby farm provides the meat for both the eponymous signature dish and the mutton pie as featured on the BBC's *The One Show*; or try a 'Seafood between the Sheets' (salmon, haddock and prawn lasagne). The walled garden is a popular retreat, or you can relax by the open fire over a glass of Loddon ale.

---

**Open** Mon-Sun L Closed: 26-30 Dec, 1 Jan, Sun pm ⊕ GREENE KING ◀ Greene King IPA, Hullabaloo Loddon.
**Facilities** Garden Parking

## SINDLESHAM
Map 5 SU76

### The Walter Arms ♥ NEW

**Bearwood Rd RG41 5BP** ☎ 0118 977 4903
e-mail: mail@thewalterarms.com
dir: *From Wokingham take A329 towards Reading. In 1.5m left onto B3030. 5m left into Bearwood Rd. Pub 200yds on left*

Built in the 1850s for a member of the Walter family, founders of The Times newspaper, the pub was once a meeting place for the villagers; in fact the family built the village of Sindlesham. Today's dining pub is a pleasing mix of chic modern with Edwardian overtones. Warm summer days see the wrap-around beer garden busy with families and diners keen to sample the diverse menu of English grills, smorgasbords, stone-baked pizzas and pasta choices: seafood Strozzapreti or Greek mezze may tempt, followed by Eton Mess and accompanied by a choice of reliable real ales and a good bin of wines.

**Open** all day all wk **Bar Meals** L served Mon-Fri 12-3, Sat 12-10, Sun 12-9 D served Mon-Fri 6-10, Sat-Sun all day Av main course £11.50 **Restaurant** L served Mon-Fri 12-3, Sat 12-10, Sun 12-9 booking required D served Mon-Fri 6-10, Sat-Sun all day booking required Av 3 course à la carte fr £17 ⊕ FREE HOUSE ◀ London Pride, Black Sheep Best, Timothy Taylor Landlord Ò Stowford Press. ♥ 10 **Facilities** Children's menu Children's portions Garden Parking

## STANFORD DINGLEY
Map 5 SU57

### The Old Boot Inn ♥

**RG7 6LT** ☎ 0118 974 4292    📠 0118 974 4292
dir: *M4 junct 12, A4/A340 to Pangbourne. 1st left to Bradfield. Through Bradfield, follow Stanford Dingley signs*

Set in the glorious Pang Valley in a charming village, with the River Pang running through it, the 18th-century Old Boot has been extended to include a popular dining conservatory. Fresh seafood choices are announced daily, and include the likes of grilled sardines with warm potato salad served with anchovy vinaigrette. Other tempting dishes might be ostrich fillet with caramelised shallots, or lamb shank with mash and a light lamb jus. There is an excellent choice of real ales always available.

**Open** all wk 11-3 6-11 **Bar Meals** L served all wk 12-2 D served all wk 7-9 **Restaurant** L served all wk 12-2 D served all wk 7-9 ⊕ FREE HOUSE ◀ Brakspear Bitter, Interbrew Bass, West Berkshire Dr Hexters, Archers Best, Thomas Hardy Royal Oak Ò Stowford Press. ♥ 10
**Facilities** Children's menu Children's portions Play area Dogs allowed Garden Parking

---

## SWALLOWFIELD
Map 5 SU76

### PICK OF THE PUBS

### The George & Dragon

**Church Rd RG7 1TJ**
☎ 0118 988 4432    📠 0118 988 6474
e-mail: nikita.staen@yahoo.co.uk
dir: *M4, junct 11, A33 towards Basingstoke. Left at Barge Ln to B3349 into The Street, right into Church Rd*

Don't judge a pub by its façade, at least not this one. It may look unassuming, but it has a smart, cosy interior with stripped low beams, terracotta-painted walls, log fires and rug-strewn floors, and it has earned quite a reputation for its real ales, excellent wines and great food. Dining takes precedence over drinking, and booking for lunch or dinner would be prudent. The chef sources as much local produce as he can for his internationally inspired dishes. A typical starter could be duck and spring onion parcel with pickled vegetables; New England clam chowder; or grilled tiger prawns with garlic ciabatta and aïoli. Main courses include scallop and smoked bacon salad with sauté potatoes; risotto alla Milanese; beef and venison casserole with herb dumplings; and local French partridge with seasonal vegetables. The garden overlooks beautiful countryside, and the pub makes a great place to halt a while after a walk in the area, perhaps along the long distance Blackwater Valley Footpath.

**Open** all day all wk **Bar Meals** L served Mon-Sat 12-2.30, Sun 12-3 D served Mon-Sat 7-9.30, Sun 7-9 **Restaurant** L served Mon-Sat 12-2.30, Sun 12-3 D served Mon-Sat 7-9.30, Sun 7-9 ⊕ FREE HOUSE ◀ Fuller's London Pride, Brakspears Ò Thatchers Gold.
**Facilities** Children's menu Children's portions Dogs allowed Garden Parking

## THATCHAM
Map 5 SU56

### The Bladebone Inn

**Chapel Row, Bucklebury RG7 6PD** ☎ 0118 971 2326
e-mail: simon.kelly2@btconnect.com
dir: *2m NE of Thatcham, 5m from Newbury*

Above the entrance to this historic inn hangs a bladebone, which, according to legend, originally came from a mammoth that once stalked the Kennet valley. A more probable explanation is that it was used to indicate that whale oil was sold here for use in oil-burning lamps and probably of 17th-century origin. These days the Bladebone is a stylish dining venue with a mixture of English and Mediterranean influences.

**Open** all day all wk noon-11 (Sun noon-6) ◀ Good Old Boy. **Facilities** Dogs allowed Garden Parking

## WALTHAM ST LAWRENCE — Map 5 SU87

### The Bell ♀

**The Street RG10 0JJ ☎ 0118 934 1788**
**e-mail:** scott@thebellinn.biz
**dir:** *On B3024 E of Twyford. From A4 turn at Hare Hatch*

In 1608 this 14th-century building was given to the village; it now runs as a free house with the rent going towards village charities. The Bell is renowned for its ever-changing range of real ales selected from smaller micro-breweries all over the country, and ciders too. It also has a growing reputation for its food - perhaps ham and confit pork belly terrine with apple chutney; pot roast partridge with braised red cabbage; home-made faggots with mash and onion gravy; or goujons of sole with fat chips and home-made ketchup.

**Open** all wk 12-3 5-11 (Sat noon-11 Sun noon-10.30)
**Bar Meals** L served Mon-Fri 12-2, Sat-Sun 12-3 D served all wk 7-9.30 ⊕ FREE HOUSE ◀ Waltham St Lawrence No.1 Ale, 4 Guest ales ♂ 3 Guest ciders. ♀ 19
**Facilities** Play area Dogs allowed Garden Parking

## WARGRAVE — Map 5 SU77

### St George and Dragon ♀

**High St RG10 8HY ☎ 0118 9404474**
**dir:** *3.5m from Henley on A321*

A friendly Thames-side pub, in one of the river's most scenic locations. Heaters on the outdoor decking make it possible to enjoy the view all year round, while inside are open kitchens, stone-fired ovens and log-burning fires. The menu offers the familiar - pizza, pasta and steaks - and the not so familiar, such as duck confit with pak choi, egg noodles, black bean and chilli sauce; and swordfish with Tuscan bean cassoulet and chorizo.

**Open** all day all wk noon-11 (Fri-Sat noon-mdnt Sun noon-10.30) ◀ Loddon Hulabaloo, Timothy Taylor Landlord ♂ Aspalls. ♀ 14 **Facilities** Dogs allowed Garden Parking

## WINKFIELD — Map 6 SU97

### Rose & Crown ♀

**Woodside, Windsor Forest SL4 2DP**
**☎ 01344 882051 ▤ 01344 885346**
**e-mail:** info@roseandcrownascot.com
**dir:** *M3 junct 3 from Ascot Racecourse on A332 take 2nd exit from Heatherwood Hosp rdbt, then 2nd left*

A 200-year-old traditional pub complete with old beams and low ceilings. Hidden down a country lane, it has a peaceful garden overlooking open fields where you can see horses and llamas at pasture. A typical menu may include pan-fried fillet steak with blue cheese gratin potatoes, with seasonal vegetables and a bourguignon sauce; pavé of halibut with rosemary sauté potatoes, chargrilled asparagus and baby leeks, with horseradish cream sauce; or asparagus tortellini with basil and parmesan cheese.

**Open** all day all wk **Bar Meals** L served Mon-Sat 12-2.15, Sun 12-3.15 D served Tue-Sat 7-9.15 booking required Av main course £10 **Restaurant** L served Mon-Sat 12-2.15, Sun 12-3.15 booking required D served Tue-Sat 7-9.15 booking required Av 3 course à la carte fr £25 ⊕ GREENE KING ◀ Morland Original, Greene King IPA, guest ale. ♀ 12 **Facilities** Children's menu Children's portions Play area Garden Parking

## WINTERBOURNE — Map 5 SU47

### The Winterbourne Arms ♀

**RG20 8BB ☎ 01635 248200 ▤ 01635 248824**
**e-mail:** winterbournearms@tiscali.co.uk
**dir:** *M4 junct 13 into Chieveley Services, follow Donnington signs to Winterbourne sign. Turn right into Arlington Ln, right at T-junct, left into Winterbourne*

This pretty black and white village pub is over 300 years old and once housed the village shop and bakery - the remains of the bread oven survive in the restaurant. Enjoy candlelit dinners and a log fire in winter, while the extensive landscaped gardens offer alfresco dining in summer. Local game and daily fresh fish from Brixham provide the basic ingredients for modern British dishes such as chicken liver and brandy pâté with onion marmalade followed by chargrilled fillet steak with brandy and mushroom sauce or home-made pie of the day.

**Open** all wk noon-3 6-11 (Sun noon-10.30) **Bar Meals** L served all wk 12-2.30 D served all wk 6-10 Av main course £6.95 **Restaurant** L served all wk 12-2.30 D served all wk 6-10 Av 3 course à la carte fr £20 ⊕ FREE HOUSE ◀ Ramsbury Gold, Guinness, Whistle Wetter. ♀ 20 **Facilities** Children's portions Dogs allowed Garden Parking

## WOKINGHAM — Map 5 SU86

### The Broad Street Tavern ♀ NEW

**29 Broad St RG40 1AU ☎ 0118 9773706**
**e-mail:** broadstreettavern@wadworth.co.uk
**dir:** *In town centre, adjacent to Pizza Express*

In a handsome detached period building fronted by elegant railings, the Wadworth-owned "Tav" offers leather armchairs and sofas in the bar, and an extensive decked garden area with a summer bar and barbecues. Meals include sausages sizzler board to share; gammon and eggs; salmon and spinach in tarragon sauce; rib-eye steaks; and hand-made pies. Then there are deli plates,

ciabattas and nibbles, such as spicy fries, lamb samosas and duck spring rolls; and quite a reputation for well-kept beers, Champagnes and cocktails too. The pub hosts four beer festivals a year.

**Open** all day all wk **Bar Meals** L served all wk 12-2.30 D served all wk 6-9.30 Av main course £7.95 ⊕ WADWORTH & CO ◀ Wadworth 6X, Henrys IPA, Bishops Tipple ♂ Old Rosie. ♀ 17 **Facilities** Dogs allowed Garden

WORLD'S END　　　　Map 5 SU47

## The Langley Hall Inn ♀

RG20 8SA ☎ 01635 248332 ◻ 01635 248571
**dir:** *Exit M4 junct 13 north, take 1st slip road signed Beedon & Chieveley. Left & immediately right, inn 1.5m on left*

Friendly, family-run bar/restaurant with a reputation for freshly prepared food, real ales and a good selection of wines. Fresh fish dishes vary according to the daily catch - maybe pan-fried crevettes, grilled Dover sole, salmon fishcakes with spinach and parsley sauce, or roast cod fillet with cheese and herb crust. Other favourites are braised lamb, beef stir-fry, and Thai chicken curry. Outside there is a large patio and garden, plus a petanque court for fine weather use.

**Open** all wk 12-3.30 5.30-11 (Sun 12-6) Closed: 26 Dec-2 Jan ◀ West Berkshire Brewery - Good Old Boy, Mr Chubbs, Lunchtime Bitter, Deuchars IPA, London Pride, Brakspears ♂ Stowford Press. ♀ 12 **Facilities** Dogs allowed Garden Parking

YATTENDON　　　　Map 5 SU57

### PICK OF THE PUBS

## The Royal Oak Hotel ♀

The Square RG18 0UG
☎ 01635 201325 ◻ 01635 201926
**e-mail:** info@royaloakyattendon.com
**web:** www.royaloakyattendon.co.uk
**dir:** *M4 junct 12, A4 to Newbury, right at 2nd rdbt to Pangbourne then 1st left. From junct 13, A34 N 1st left, right at T-junct. Left then 2nd right to Yattendon*

Once known simply as 'The Oak', this 16th-century free house reputedly played host to Oliver Cromwell before the battle of Newbury. Nowadays the pub is rarely interrupted by anything more menacing than the clip-clop of passing horse-riders. New owner Rob McGill offers beautifully kept real ales from the nearby West Berkshire Brewery, and delicious home-cooked food to

satisfy many different tastes and budgets. Lunchtime brings sandwiches and potted shrimps, as well as hot options like devilled kidneys on toast, or rich venison pie. A more formal dinner might begin with roast parsnip soup, before moving on to main course options like saffron noodles with roast butternut squash, or seared pavé of Cornish salmon with seafood risotto and crispy leeks. Desserts include golden bread and butter pudding, and vanilla and peach parfait. There are four roaring log fires in winter, as well as beautiful gardens and a boules pitch for the warmer months.

**Open** all day all wk **Bar Meals** L served Mon-Fri 12-2.30, Sat 12-3, Sun 12-4 D served Sun-Thu 7-9.30, Fri- Sat 7-10 Av main course £14 **Restaurant** L served Mon-Fri 12-2.30, Sat 12-3, Sun 12-4 D served Mon-Thu 7-9.30, Fri- Sat 7-10 Fixed menu price fr £11.50 Av 3 course à la carte fr £25 ⊕ FREE HOUSE ◀ West Berkshire, Good Old Boy, Mr Chubbs, 1 guest ale. ♀ 10 **Facilities** Children's menu Children's portions Dogs allowed Garden Parking

*See advert on opposite page*

## BRISTOL

BRISTOL　　　　Map 4 ST57

## Cornubia

142 Temple St BS1 6EN
☎ 0117 925 4415 ◻ 0117 929 1523
**e-mail:** philjackithecornubia@hotmail.co.uk
**dir:** *Opposite Bristol Fire Station*

This characterful Georgian city-centre pub was originally built as two houses, and now owned by the Hidden Brewery company. Office workers love it, not just because of its convenience, but also for its choice of seven changing real ales, two draught ciders and a serious collection of malts and bottled beers. And then there's the food — pork and apple sausages and mash or home-made soups for example - chalked up on a blackboard. Cornubia, by the way, is the Latinised name for Cornwall.

**Open** Mon-Wed 12-3 5-11 (Thu-Fri noon-11.30 Sat 6-11.30) Closed: 25-26 Dec, 1 Jan, Sun **Bar Meals** L served Mon-Sat 12-2.30 Av main course £6 ⊕ FREE HOUSE ◀ All Hidden Brewery ales, Erdinger, guest ales ♂ Cheddar Valley, Thatchers Gold, Sheepdip, Glastonbury. **Facilities** Children's portions Dogs allowed Parking

## The Hare on the Hill

Dove St, Kingsdown BS2 8LX ☎ 0117 908 1982
**e-mail:** harehill@bathales.co.uk
**dir:** *Telephone for directions*

If you can find it in the maze of streets that is Kingsdown, this is a gem – a small, street-corner local from the good old days, remaining close to the heart of the community. If all you want is a pint of one of Bath Ales award-winning brews, a real cider or a European-style beer, come here. All food (except fresh fish) is sourced from within a 40-mile radius. Typical are steak baguette; home-made quiche; five-bean chilli and rice; plus a roast on Sundays with live music in the evening.

**Open** all wk 12-2.30 5-11 (Sat 12-11.30 Sun 12-11)

**Bar Meals** L served Mon-Sat 12-2 (Sun 12-4) D served Mon-Sat 6-9 Av main course £7 ⊕ BATH ALES ◀ Gem, Spa, Barnstormer, Golden Hare, Dark Hare.

## Highbury Vaults

164 St Michaels Hill, Cotham BS2 8DE
☎ 0117 973 3203
**e-mail:** highburyvaults@youngs.co.uk
**dir:** *Take A38 to Cotham from inner ring dual carriageway*

Once a turnpike station, this 1840s pub has retained much of its Victorian atmosphere. In days when hangings took place on nearby St Michael's Hill, many victims partook of their last meal in the vaults. Today, it's a business crowd by day and students at night feasting on chilli, meat and vegetable curries, casseroles, pasta dishes, and jacket potatoes. No fried foods, no music or fruit machines here, but a popular heated garden terrace.

**Open** all day all wk noon-mdnt (Sun 12-11) **Bar Meals** L served Mon-Fri 12-2, Sat 12-2.30, Sun 12-3 D served Mon-Fri 5.30-8.30 Av main course £5.50 ⊕ YOUNG & CO BREWERY PLC ◀ Bath Ales Gem, St Austells Tribute, Brains SA, Young's Special & Bitter, Guest ales rotating ♂ Addlestones, Thatchers Gold. **Facilities** Garden Notes ⊜

## Robin Hood's Retreat ♀

197 Gloucester Rd BS7 8BG ☎ 0117 924 8639
**e-mail:** info@robinhoodsretreat.gmail.com
**web:** www.robinhoodsretreat.co.uk
**dir:** *At main rdbt at Broad Mead take Gloucester Rd exit, St Pauls. Road leads into Gloucester Rd (A38)*

In the heart of Bristol, this Victorian red-brick pub is popular with real ale lovers, who usually have eight to choose from. The interior has been superbly appointed, with original features retained and with the addition of richly coloured wood panelling and furniture. There's plenty of attention to detail in the food too, which is all prepared on the premises. Favourites are slow-cooked British dishes with a French accent, and several seafood options.

**Open** all wk Sun-Wed noon-11pm (Thu-Sat noon-mdnt) Closed: 25 Dec **Bar Meals** Av main course £15 **Restaurant** L served all wk D served all wk booking required Av 3 course à la carte fr £26 ⊕ ENTERPRISE INNS ◀ Doom Bar, Butcombe, Tribute, Tanglefoot ♂ Stowford Press. ♀ 15 **Facilities** Children's portions Garden

## BUCKINGHAMSHIRE

### AMERSHAM
Map 6 SU99

## Hit or Miss Inn ⚲

**Penn Street Village HP7 0PX**
☎ 01494 713109 📠 01494 718010
e-mail: hit@ourpubs.co.uk
**dir:** *M25 junct 18, A404 (Amersham to High Wycombe road) to Amersham. Past crematorium on right, 2nd left into Whielden Ln (signed Winchmore Hill). 1.25m, pub on right*

Michael and Mary Macken welcome you to their 18th-century cottage-style dining pub with its fires and old world beams. The Hit or Miss overlooks the cricket ground from which the pub takes its name, and there's a beautiful country garden with lawn, patio and picnic tables for warmer days. Home-cooked dishes range from tempting well-filled sandwiches and light meals like tempura battered prawns to grilled sea bass fillets on chorizo and basil risotto, and seared calves' liver, crispy bacon with mash and onion gravy. There are daily specials and Sunday roasts, too.

**Open** all day all wk 11-11 (Sun 12-10.30) **Bar Meals** L served Mon-Sat 12-2.30, Sun 12-8 D served Mon-Sat 6.30-9.30, Sun 12-8 Av main course £13 **Restaurant** L served Mon-Sat 12-2.30, Sun 12-8 D served Mon-Sat 6.30-9.30, Sun 12-8 Av 3 course à la carte fr £18 ⊕ HALL & WOODHOUSE ◀ Badger Best, Tanglefoot, Sussex, Hopping Hare ♻ Stowford Press. ⚲ 10 **Facilities** Children's menu Children's portions Dogs allowed Garden Parking

### BEACONSFIELD
Map 6 SU99

## PICK OF THE PUBS

## The Royal Standard of England ⚲

**Brindle Ln, Forty Green HP9 1XT** ☎ 01494 673382
e-mail: theoldestpub@btinternet.com
**dir:** *A40 to Beaconsfield, right at church rdbt onto B474 towards Penn, left onto Forty Green Rd, 1m*

Ramblers can use the large car park here before setting out on one of the circular walks around the pub. Situated in the beautiful Chilterns village of Forty Green, this award-winning country inn traces its roots to Saxon times. During the Civil War the pub was a mustering place for Royalists. Today, good hearty food is served amid the striking stained glass windows, beams and flagstone floors, whilst in winter a large inglenook fireplace warms the old walls. Seasonal wild game is a regular feature on the specials board, supported by an extensive bill of fare. Start, perhaps, with garlic prawns pan-fried in olive oil; continue with braised Elwy Valley Welsh lamb shoulder; and finish with a hot pudding such as spotted Dick, or chilled Eton mess. The bar boasts extensive lists of interesting beers, ciders and whiskies, with many popular wines served by the glass.

**Open** all day all wk 11-11 **Bar Meals** Av main course £11 food served all day **Restaurant** food served all day

⊕ FREE HOUSE ◀ Marston's Pedigree, Brakspear Bitter, Rebellion IPA, Theakston Old Peculier, Guest Ales ♻ Westons Stowford Press, Old Rosie Scrumpy, Orchard Pig Cider, Westons Perry. ⚲ 11 **Facilities** Children's portions Family room Dogs allowed Garden Parking

### BLEDLOW
Map 5 SP70

## The Lions of Bledlow ⚲

**Church End HP27 9PE**
☎ 01844 343345 📠 01844 343345
**dir:** *M40 junct 6, B4009 to Princes Risborough, through Chinnor into Bledlow*

This unspoilt 16th-century free house is a popular location for television series, including *Midsomer Murders* and *Miss Marple*. It overlooks the village green in a conservation area close to the Chiltern Hills, making it ideal for walkers, bird watchers and other outdoor enthusiasts. Pop in just for a drink, or choose dishes such as sea bass tagliatelle or pork fillet in cream and mushroom sauce from the daily specials and vegetarian selection boards.

**Open** all wk 11.30-3 6-11 (Sat 11.30-11 Sun noon-11) **Bar Meals** L served Mon-Sat 12-2.30, Sun 12-4 D served Mon-Sat 6.30-9.30, Sun 7-9 Av main course £8 **Restaurant** L served Mon-Sat 12-2.30, Sun 12-4 D served Mon-Sat 6.30-9.30, Sun 7-9 ⊕ FREE HOUSE ◀ Wadworth 6X, Guest ales ♻ Stowford Press. ⚲ 12 **Facilities** Children's menu Children's portions Family room Dogs allowed Garden Parking

### BLETCHLEY
Map 11 SP83

## PICK OF THE PUBS

## The Crooked Billet ◉ ⚲

**2 Westbrook End, Newton Longville MK17 0DF**
☎ 01908 373936
e-mail: john@thebillet.co.uk
**dir:** *M1 junct 13, follow signs to Buckingham. 6m, signed at Bottledump rdbt to Newton Longville*

Top sommelier John Gilchrist and wife/chef Emma took on the run-down Billet a decade ago and realised their dream of running a classy gastro-pub together. Although firmly placed on Buckinghamshire's culinary map, with a serious restaurant, the pretty 18th-century thatched pub is still very much a traditional village pub with oak beams, open log fires, real ale at the bar and a grand, bench-filled lawn for fine-weather

drinking. Local foodies flock to the two intimate wine-themed dining rooms for Emma's regularly-changing dinner menus, which are based on the finest, freshest ingredients from a multitude of small, local specialist food producers and suppliers. The emphasis is on taste, combined with modern presentation and a typical meal may take in scallops with bubble and squeak, pan-fried black pudding and bacon, followed by chargrilled beef fillet with Madeira reduction, and espresso coffee mousse served with home-made doughnuts. Lunchtime in the relaxed bar area brings sandwiches, salads and pastas, together with traditional pub dishes and a great value set menu. Expect an impeccable list of wines – all are available by the glass.

**Open** noon-2.30 5-11 (Sun noon-4) **Closed:** Mon L **Bar Meals** L served Tue-Sat 12-2, Sun 12-4 D served Mon-Sat 7-9.30 Av main course £12 **Restaurant** L served Tue-Sat 12-2, Sun 12-4 D served Mon-Sat 7-9.30 booking required Fixed menu price fr £22 Av 3 course à la carte fr £25 ⊕ GREENE KING ◀ Old Speckled Hen, Badger Tanglefoot, Hobgoblin, Ruddles County. ⚲ 200 **Facilities** Children's portions Garden Parking

### BOVINGDON GREEN
Map 5 SU88

## PICK OF THE PUBS

## The Royal Oak ⚲

*See Pick of the Pubs on opposite page*

### BRILL
Map 11 SP61

## The Pheasant Inn

**Windmill St HP18 9TG** ☎ 01844 239370
e-mail: info@thepheasant.co.uk
**dir:** *In village centre, by windmill*

High on the edge of Brill Common, this recently refurbished 17th-century beamed inn benefits from a large garden, and a veranda from which you can see the village windmill and across seven counties. A simple menu offers British, Mediterranean and Asian cooking, including pan-fried halibut with sweet potato mash and citrus sauce; roast rump of lamb hotpot; chicken curry and rice; and pear, red onion and Stilton tart. With locally brewed ales on offer, there are many wines available from smaller vineyards.

**Open** all day all wk Mon-Thu noon-11pm (Fri-Sat noon-mdnt Sun noon-10.30 ) **Bar Meals** L served all wk 12-2 D served all wk 6.30-9, Sun 12-7 Av main course £10 **Restaurant** L served all wk 12-2 D served all wk 6.30-9 ⊕ FREE HOUSE ◀ London Pride, Local Vale Ale ♻ Thatchers. **Facilities** Children's portions Garden Parking

# PICK OF THE PUBS

## The Royal Oak 🍷

**BOVINGDON GREEN** **Map 5 SU88**

**Frieth Rd SL7 2JF**
**☎ 01628 488611 📠 01628 478680**
**e-mail:** info@royaloakmarlow.co.uk
**web:** www.royaloakmarlow.co.uk
**dir:** *From Marlow, take A4155. In 300yds right signed Bovingdon Green. In 0.75m pub on left*

Less than a mile up the hill from Marlow you'll find this little old whitewashed pub, set in sprawling gardens with a pétanque piste, fragrant herbs and a sunny terrace. Don't be surprised to see red kites soaring above the building before you go in, as these magnificent birds are now thriving after their re-introduction to the Chilterns. Inside, the pub is at once both spacious yet cosy. Dark floorboards, rich fabrics and a woodburning stove set the tone, and the early evening regulars gather around the crossword.

Meanwhile the kitchen brigade can offer something for everyone, and will be just as happy rustling up a snack as they are when preparing some serious gastronomy. The imaginative British menu makes good use of fresh local produce, and an exclusively European wine list includes some twenty varieties available by the glass. The menu's 'small plates' selection begins with rustic breads, roast garlic and olive oil, and also includes horseradish cured gravadlax with buckwheat blinis and roast beetroot rémoulade. Main course options range from Oxfordshire beef shin bourguignon with dauphinoise potatoes and buttered Savoy cabbage; through roast butternut squash, macaroni and three cheese gratin with herb salad and vegetable crisps; to crispy-skinned sea bass fillet with sweet potato purée, caramelised fennel and béarnaise sauce. Among the decent selection of puddings is warm treacle tart with stem ginger ice cream; dark chocolate sludge cake with chilli; and apple tarte Tatin with cinnamon ice cream.

The beers come from Brakspears in Henley and the Rebellion Brewery in Marlow Bottom, whilst free Wi-fi is available if you're planning a working lunch or dinner.

**Open** all day all wk 11-11 (Sun 12-10.30) Closed: 26 Dec **Bar Meals** L served Mon-Fri 12-2.30, Sat 12-3, Sun 12-4 D served Sun-Thu 6.30-9.30, Fri-Sat 6.30-10 Av main course £13.75 **Restaurant** L served Mon-Fri 12-2.30, Sat 12-3, Sun 12-4 booking required D served Sun-Thu 6.30-9.30, Fri-Sat 6.30-10 Av 3 course à la carte fr £25.75 ⊕ SALISBURY PUBS LTD 🍺 Brakspears, Marlow Rebellion IPA, Marlow Rebellion Smuggler 🍏 Thatchers. 🍷 20 **Facilities** Dogs allowed Garden Parking

**BRILL** *continued*

## The Red Lion

27 Church St HP18 9RT ☎ 01844 238339
e-mail: lyngarh@aol.com
dir: *Off B4011 (Thame to Bicester road)*

The Red Lion dates back to the early 17th century and was originally five separate buildings. Plenty of walking and cycling routes converge upon the village, which is overlooked by a famous windmill. Simple, traditional menus change regularly and may feature pork medallions; beer-battered cod, or lamb shank braised in red wine. In summer the secluded garden is home to fierce competitions of Aunt Sally - a local form of skittles.

**Open** all day all wk noon-11.30 ◀ Greene King IPA, Olde Trip, Fireside, Old Speckled Hen. **Facilities** Dogs allowed Garden

| BUCKINGHAM | Map 11 SP63 |
|---|---|

## The Old Thatched Inn ⬤

Main St, Adstock MK18 2JN
☎ 01296 712584  ⬛ 01296 715375
e-mail: manager@theoldthatchedinn.co.uk
web: www.theoldthatchedinn.co.uk
dir: *Telephone for directions*

Dating back to 1702, this lovely old thatched and beamed inn still boasts the traditional beams and inglenook fireplace. The spacious interior consists of a formal conservatory and a bar with comfy furniture and a welcoming, relaxed atmosphere. Using the freshest, seasonal ingredients from local and regional suppliers, meat options might include roast Suffolk pheasant breast and ballotine, bubble and squeak, with wild mushrooms. Fresh fish is a speciality - fish soup, rouille, gruyère and crouton for example, and there are always two additional fish specials on a Friday.

**Open** all wk noon-11 (Mon-Tue 12-2.30 6-11 Sun noon-10.30) **Bar Meals** L served Mon-Fri 12-2.30, Sat 12-3, Sun 12-8 D served Mon-Sat 6-9.30 Av main course £11.95 **Restaurant** Av 3 course à la carte fr £25 ⊕ FREE HOUSE ◀ Hook Norton Best, Timothy Taylor, Old Speckled Hen, London Pride ♂ Aspall. ⬤ 14 **Facilities** Children's menu Children's portions Dogs allowed Parking

*See advert on opposite page*

## The Wheatsheaf ⬤

Main St, Maids Moreton MK18 1QR
☎ 01280 815433  ⬛ 01280 814631
dir: *M1 junct 13, (or M40 junct 9, A34 to Bicester) A421 to Buckingham, then A413 to Maids Moreton*

This traditional, thatched village inn has been a pub since 1750, and offers an appetising à la carte menu in the spacious conservatory overlooking the secluded beer garden. Eating options include baked cod and prawns in cream; roast aubergine stuffed with ratatouille; and home-made Thai chicken curry. Real ales and snacks can also be enjoyed in the bar, with its cosy inglenook fireplaces. Children will be delighted with the outdoor play equipment.

**Open** all wk 12-3 6-11 (Sun 12-8) **Bar Meals** L served Mon-Sat 12-2.15, Sun 12-3 D served all wk 7-9.15 **Restaurant** L served Mon-Sat 12-2.15, Sun 12-3 D served all wk 7-9.15 ⊕ FREE HOUSE ◀ John Smith's, Side Pocket For A Toad, Reverend James, Pitstop, Batemans GHA, John Smith's Smooth ♂ Thatchers. ⬤ 10 **Facilities** Children's menu Children's portions Play area Family room Dogs allowed Garden Parking

| CHALFONT ST GILES | Map 6 SU99 |
|---|---|

### PICK OF THE PUBS

## The Ivy House ⬤

*See Pick of the Pubs on page 46*

## The White Hart ⬤

Three Households HP8 4LP
☎ 01494 872441  ⬛ 01494 876375
e-mail: enquiries@thewhitehartstgiles.co.uk
dir: *Off A413 (Denham to Amersham road)*

Oak and brown leather furniture and a refurbished bar characterise the quiet, relaxed atmosphere of this prettily-located 100-year-old inn, giving it a welcoming, contemporary feel. The menu offers the likes of loin of pork en croute, carpet bag fillet steak, supreme of chicken, lamb shank, and calves' liver. Fish dishes include baked sea bass with vegetables and Thai fish sauce, and seared blue-fin tuna.

**Open** all wk 11-3.30 5-11.15 (Sun noon-3.30 5-10.30) ◀ Greene King Morland Original, Abbot Ale, Rev. James. ⬤ 12 **Facilities** Garden Parking

| CHALFONT ST PETER | Map 6 TQ09 |
|---|---|

### PICK OF THE PUBS

## The Greyhound Inn ⬤

SL9 9RA ☎ 01753 883404  ⬛ 01753 891627
e-mail: reception@thegreyhoundinn.net
dir: *M40 junct 1/M25 junct 16, follow signs for Gerrards Cross, then Chalfont St Peter*

For more than 600 years travellers, Oliver Cromwell among them, generation after generation of locals have sought hospitality and refreshment here. It was one of many places that the notorious Judge Jeffreys held his assize court, despatching the guilty to the gallows that once stood by the River Misbourne nearby. Now under new ownership it has been refurbished, although retains its flagstoned bar and original timbered ceiling. The restaurant offers British and European cooking, including starters of poached free-range eggs with basil hollandaise and crispy ham; and Bury black pudding on rösti with smoked bacon and caramelised apple. Among the well-balanced list of main courses find roast Scottish salmon herb crust with pan-seared scallops, potato scones and chive butter sauce; confit duck leg marinated in rosemary and thyme on a potato cake with port sauce; and wild mushroom risotto with rocket salad and parmesan shavings.

**Open** all day all wk Mon-Wed 6.30am-10.30pm (Thu 6.30am-11.30pm, Fri-Sat 6.30am-1am, Sun 8.30am-10.30pm) **Bar Meals** L served Mon-Sat 12-2.30, Sun 12-3 D served Mon-Sat 6-9.30 Av main course £12 **Restaurant** L served Mon-Sat 12-2.30, Sun 12-3 booking required D served Mon-Sat 6-9.30 booking required Av 3 course à la carte fr £20 ⊕ ENTERPRISE INNS ◀ London Pride, Greene King, IPA, Speckled Hen. ⬤ 10 **Facilities** Children's menu Children's portions Dogs allowed Garden Parking

| CHEDDINGTON | Map 11 SP91 |
|---|---|

## The Old Swan ⬤

58 High St LU7 0RQ ☎ 01296 668226  ⬛ 01296 663811
e-mail: oldswancheddington@btconnect.com
dir: *From Tring towards Marsworth take B489, 0.5m. Left towards Cooks Wharf onto Cheddington, pub on left*

Formed out of three cottages in the 15th century, this delightful thatched pub is known not only for its real ales and traditional charm but also for its food. Using fresh, locally-sourced ingredients dishes range from lunchtime ham, cheese and tomato panini and ham, egg and chips, to more imaginative evening meals, perhaps lamb shank with port and redcurrant sauce, 21-day aged sirloin steak with all the trimmings, and game pie. Children are made very welcome and there's a good play area in the attractive garden

**Open** all wk Mon-Wed 12-3, 5-11 (Thu all day Fri-Sun noon-11) **Bar Meals** L served Mon-Sat 12-2.30, Sun 12-4 D served Mon-Thu 6-9, Fri-Sat 6-9.30 Av main course £10 **Restaurant** L served Mon-Sat 12-2.30, Sun 12-4 D served Mon-Thu 6-9, Fri-Sat 6-9.30 ⊕ PUNCH TAVERNS ◀ Courage Best, St Austell Tribute, Everard's Tiger, Shepherd Neame Spitfire, Adnams Broadside ♂ Stowford Press. ⬤ 20 **Facilities** Children's portions Play area Dogs allowed Garden Parking

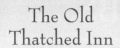

**www.theoldthatchedinn.co.uk**

# The Old Thatched Inn

Gastro Pub, Adstock

# Fine Food & Warm Welcome...

## 01296 712584

A great atmosphere awaits you at Buckinghamshire's favourite owner-managed gastropub, the Old Thatched Inn, in the picturesque village of Adstock.

Our passion is freshly made, delicious food that is, where possible sourced locally and doesn't break the bank. Our delightful stylish listed Inn dates back to 1702 and oozes character and atmosphere – a perfect backdrop for our great food and friendly service.

So come and discover this hidden rural gem in Adstock, between Buckingham, Milton Keynes and Winslow. Nearby attractions: Stowe Gardens and Silverstone Race Track... Come enjoy...

- 5 Real Ales
- Home-made food
- Extensive menus
- Daily specials

The Old Thatched Inn, Main Street, Adstock, (bet. Buckingham & Winslow), Buckinghamshire, MK18 2JN

# PICK OF THE PUBS

## The Ivy House 🍷

**CHALFONT ST GILES**   Map 6 SU99

**London Rd HP8 4RS**
☎ **01494 872184**   📠 **01494 872870**
e-mail: ivyhouse@fullers.co.uk
dir: *On A413 2m S of Amersham & 1.5m N of Chalfont St Giles*

A beautiful 250-year-old brick and flint coaching inn, enjoying amazing views of the Chiltern Hills and set close to John Milton's cottage. In a great location for country walks as well as several nearby golf courses, the pub is well known for its friendly welcome, great food and extensive wine list. Old beams, open fires, comfy armchairs and brasses all give the place a welcoming, cosy atmosphere. Naturally there's the odd ghost story to be told, and whisky lovers will appreciate the range of over 30 malts, including some of the landlord's favourite rarities.

Meals are served in the bar and the former coach house restaurant, and in fine weather you can dine alfresco in the courtyard and garden, with fantastic views over the Chiltern Hills. The fresh rustic menu changes every season, and also features daily specials, with the emphasis on quality local produce and fresh fish. The lunchtime bar menu brings a selection of sandwiches, salads, and good value hot dishes such as hand-carved ale and honey roasted ham with free range eggs and handcut chips or beer-battered fish and chips.

More formal dining might begin with starters like chargrilled halloumi and chorizo with sweet peppers, pan-fried curried mackerel, or duck liver, smoked duck and Cointreau pâté. Moving on, choose from squash, Parmesan and red onion marmalade tart; Buckinghamshire country pork sausages with bubble and squeak; confit tuna Niçoise; or poached chicken and spring vegetable broth. Desserts include apricot bread and butter pudding, pecan pie, or rich chocolate and Amaretto truffle torte.

**Open** all day all wk **Bar Meals** L served Mon-Fri 12-2.45, Sat-Sun all day D served Mon-Fri 6-9.15, Sat-Sun all day **Restaurant** L served Mon-Fri 12-2.45, Sat-Sun all day booking required D served Mon-Fri 6-9.15, Sat-Sun all day booking required ⊕ FULLERS ◀ Fuller's London Pride, Guest Ale ♨ Symons Founders Reserve. 🍷 10 **Facilities** Children's menu Dogs allowed Garden Parking

# PICK OF THE PUBS

## The Red Lion

**CHENIES**     Map 6 TQ09

**WD3 6ED**
☎ 01923 282722   📄 01923 283797
**e-mail:**
theredlionchenies@hotmail.co.uk
**dir:** *Between Rickmansworth & Amersham on A404, follow signs for Chenies & Latimer*

Set in the Chess Valley, in a picture-book village, complete with a pretty green and an ancient parish church, and just up the lane from Chenies Manor. The unassuming, white-painted Red Lion's owners Mike and Heather Norris have over 20 years' experience behind them, and they firmly believe the 17th-century inn's popularity stems from being a pub that serves good food, not a restaurant that serves beer. Expect a plain, simply furnished main bar, a charming, snug dining area housed in the original cottage to the rear with a tiled floor, old inglenook and rustic furniture, a new restaurant, and

Mike talking passionately about his real ales. Lion's Pride, brewed by Rebellion in Marlow, is available here and here alone; other local beers come from Vale Brewery in Haddenham.

Heather cooks everything, including fresh daily pastas; bangers with bubble-and-squeak; big chunks of oven-baked leg of lamb (much like Greek kleftiko); roast pork belly on leek and potato mash; game pie; fishcakes with horseradish and beetroot dip; Orkneys rump steak; curries; poached haddock with peppered red wine sauce; and sausage, apple and cheddar pie. Speaking of pies, brace yourself for the famous lamb version, which a visiting American serviceman once declared beat a rival pub's pies hands down. Ever since, its entry on the menu has acquired an additional adjective every time it is rewritten. Today, therefore, it reads (take a deep breath) 'The awesome, internationally acclaimed, world-renowned, aesthetically and palatably pleasing, not knowingly genetically modified, hand-crafted, well-balanced, famous, original Chenies lamb pie'. Outside, on the pub's sunny side, is a small seating area.

**Open** all wk Mon-Sat 11-2.30 5.30-11 (Sun 12-3 6.30-10.30) Closed: 25 Dec
**Bar Meals** L served Mon-Sat 12-2, Sun 12-2.15 D served Mon-Sat 7-10, Sun 7-9.30 **Restaurant** L served Mon-Sat 12-2, Sun 12-2.15 D served Mon-Sat 7-10, Sun 7-9.30 booking required
⊕ FREE HOUSE ◀ Wadworth 6X, Rebellion's, Lion's Pride, Vale Best, plus guest ales ♂ Thatchers Gold. ♟ 10
**Facilities** Dogs allowed Garden Parking

## CHENIES — Map 6 TQ09

### PICK OF THE PUBS

## The Red Lion ♥

*See Pick of the Pubs on page 47*

## CHESHAM — Map 6 SP90

## The Black Horse Inn ♥

**Chesham Vale HP5 3NS** ☎ **01494 784656**
**e-mail:** mgoodchild@btconnect.com
**dir:** *A41 from Berkhamsted, A416 through Ashley Green, 0.75m before Chesham right to Vale Rd, at bottom of Mashleigh Hill, 1m, inn on left*

Set in some beautiful valley countryside, this 500-year-old pub is ideal for enjoying a cosy, traditional environment without electronic games or music. During the winter there are roaring log fires to take the chill off those who may spot one of the resident ghosts. An ever-changing menu includes an extensive range of snacks, while the main menu may feature steak and Stallion Ale pie, trout and almonds, various home-made pies, steaks and gammon, stuffed plaice, or salmon supreme.

**Open** all wk 11-3 5.30-11 (Sat-Sun all day) **Bar Meals** L served all wk 12-2.30 D served Mon-Sat 6-9 ⊕ PUNCH TAVERNS ◄ Adnams Bitter, Speckled Hen, Wadworth 6X, Guest ale ♂ Stowford Press. ♥ 10 **Facilities** Dogs allowed Garden Parking

## The Swan

**Ley Hill HP5 1UT** ☎ **01494 783075**
**e-mail:** swanleyhill@btconnect.com
**dir:** *1.5m E of Chesham by golf course*

Once three cottages, the first built around 1520, qualifying it as one of Buckinghamshire's oldest pubs; now a free house. Condemned prisoners, heading for nearby gallows, would drink 'a last and final ale' here. During the Second World War, Clark Gable, James Stewart and Glenn Miller frequently drank here after cycling from Bovingdon airbase. Menus change several times monthly, and a blackboard features daily specials. Corn-fed chicken and home honey-roasted ham pie, and venison wrapped in smoked pancetta with confit new potatoes are typical dinner choices.

**Open** all wk 12-3 5.30-11 (Sun 12-10.30) **Bar Meals** L served all wk 12-2.30 D served Tue-Sat 6.30-9.30 **Restaurant** L served Tue-Sun 12-2.30 D served Tue-Sat 6.30-9.30 booking required ⊕ FREE HOUSE ◄ Adnams Bitter, Fuller's London Pride, Timothy Taylor Landlord, Brakspears, guest ales. **Facilities** Children's menu Garden Parking

## CHOLESBURY — Map 6 SP90

### PICK OF THE PUBS

## The Full Moon ♥

**Hawridge Common HP5 2UH**
☎ **01494 758959** 📱 **07092 875764**
**e-mail:** annie@alberto1142.freeserve.co.uk
**dir:** *At Tring on A41 follow signs for Wiggington & Cholesbury. On Cholesbury Common pub by windmill*

When this 17th-century former coaching inn was first built, the local Chiltern Hills were overrun with alehouses. These days, only three remain. Fortunately, the Full Moon, which graduated from The Half Moon in 1812, is something of an ideal country pub, complete with beams, flagstones, winter fires and a windmill-backed setting. Comprehensive menus cover a range of possibilities, from baguettes and jacket potatoes to more adventurous fare. Smoked fish platter, Barnsley lamb chops and Szechuan sirloin stir-fry give an indication of the choice. If you like your desserts there is a good variety, from cold mixed berry soufflé to hot sticky toffee pudding with sticky toffee sauce and custard. In 1907, the landlord was fined for permitting drunkenness on the premises: these days the clientele is much better behaved when it comes to the eclectic selection of real ales.

**Open** all day all wk 12-11 (Sun 12-10.30) Closed: 25 Dec **Bar Meals** L served Mon-Fri 12-2, Sat 12-9, Sun 12-8 D served Mon-Fri 6.30-9, Sat 12-9, Sun 12-8 Av main course £9.95 **Restaurant** L served Mon-Fri 12-2, Sat 12-9, Sun 12-8 D served Mon-Fri 6.30-9, Sat 12-9, Sun 12-8 Av 3 course à la carte fr £20 ⊕ ADMIRAL TAVERNS ◄ Greene King IPA, Adnams, Fuller's London Pride, Timothy Taylor Landlord, guest ales. ♥ 9 **Facilities** Children's menu Children's portions Dogs allowed Garden Parking

## CUDDINGTON — Map 5 SP71

### PICK OF THE PUBS

## The Crown ♥

*See Pick of the Pubs on page 49*

## DENHAM — Map 6 TQ08

## The Falcon Inn ★★★★ INN

**Village Rd UB9 5BE** ☎ **01895 832125**
**e-mail:** mail@falcondenham.com
**dir:** *M40 junct 1, follow A40/Gerrards Cross signs. Approx 200yds turn right onto Old Mill Rd. Pass church on right, enter village. Pub opposite village green*

Traditional historic 16th-century inn, located opposite the green in beautiful Denham village – an ideal refreshment stop when exploring the Colne Valley Country Park. Very little altered, it retains its old world charm. Expect excellent real ales and brasserie-style food: deep-fried calamari or whitebait to start; and main courses such as a Falcon burger with smoked bacon, mature Cheddar and home-made chips; wild boar sausages and mash; and

chicken and mushroom pie. Desserts may include roasted figs or sherry trifle. Beamed en suite bedrooms with original features are also available.

*The Falcon Inn*

**Open** all wk 11-3 5-11 (Fri-Sun all day) **Bar Meals** L served all wk 12-2.30 D served all wk 5-9.30 Av main course £9 **Restaurant** L served all wk 12-2.30 D served all wk 5-9.30 Av 3 course à la carte fr £19 ⊕ ENTERPRISE INNS ◄ Timothy Taylor Landlord, Bombardier, Archers, Brakspear & Guest Ale ♂ Stowford Press. **Facilities** Children's menu Dogs allowed Garden **Rooms** 4

### PICK OF THE PUBS

## The Swan Inn ♥

*See Pick of the Pubs on page 50*

## DORNEY — Map 6 SU97

## The Palmer Arms ♥

**Village Rd SL4 6QW** ☎ **01628 666612**
**e-mail:** chrys@thepalmerarms.com
**dir:** *From A4 take B3026, over M4 to Dorney*

The Palmer Arms, dating from the 15th century, is well-located in the beautiful conservation village of Dorney. Its owners are passionate about providing high standards of food and service, and like to think of their cooking as 'English with a twist'. Seasonal game dishes and fish is well represented on the menus, and the daily specials might include sea bass with fennel and artichoke; oven roasted salmon on watercress mash; game pie, or roasted butternut squash with feta, pine nuts and beetroot.

**Open** all day all wk 11am-11.30pm (Sun 11-9) **Bar Meals** L served all wk 11-9 D served all wk 11-9 Av main course £6 food served all day **Restaurant** Fixed menu price fr £10 Av 3 course à la carte fr £20 food served all day ⊕ GREENE KING ◄ Greene King Abbot Ale, IPA, Guinness ♂ Aspall. ♥ 18 **Facilities** Children's menu Children's portions Play area Dogs allowed Garden Parking

# PICK OF THE PUBS

## The Crown ♀

**CUDDINGTON**  Map 5 SP71

**Spurt St HP18 0BB ☎ 01844 292222**
**e-mail:** david@anniebaileys.com
**web:** www.thecrowncuddington.co.uk
**dir:** *Off A418 between Aylesbury & Thame*

The Crown is a Grade II listed building with bags of character that plays a dual role as a popular local and a serious dining pub. Customers are just as welcome to drop in for a friendly pint as they are when booking a table for a great meal. Fans of the television series *Midsomer Murders* may recognise the thatched and whitewashed exterior, which has been used several times as a location. Whilst the real life inhabitants of Cuddington may have a longer life expectancy than their fictional counterparts, one thing's for certain - they know a good pub when they see one. The Crown's atmospheric interior includes a locals' bar and several low-beamed dining areas filled with charming prints and the glow of evening candlelight.

Fullers London Pride, Adnams and Guinness are on tap in the bar, and there's also an extensive wine list that suggests a perfect match for every dish on the regularly-changing menus. Sandwiches, pasta and salads are a constant feature, supported by appetising light bites and starters such as goat's cheese and Mediterranean vegetable tartlet with a herb crust; seafood platter; and smoked chicken risotto cake with mango sauce.

Typical main courses include ribeye steak with spinach and gorgonzola; smoked haddock with Welsh rarebit topping on tomato and basil salad; glazed breast of duck served with stir-fry vegetables and sticky rice; and fillet of sea bass with celeriac purée, tomato and saffron fondue. Consult the blackboard for an ever-changing selection of desserts.

A small patio area provides outside seating, as well as an opportunity for alfresco summer dining.

**Open** all wk 12-3 6-11 (Sun all day) **Bar Meals** L served all wk 12-2.15 D served Mon-Sat 6.30-9.15 Av main course £11 **Restaurant** L served all wk 12-2.15 D served Mon-Sat 6.30-9.15 Fixed menu price fr £12.50 Av 3 course à la carte fr £22 ⊕ FULLERS ◀ Fullers London Pride, Adnams, Guinness. ♀ 12 **Facilities** Garden Parking

# PICK OF THE PUBS

## The Swan Inn ♟

**DENHAM**                    Map 6 TQ08

**Village Rd UB9 5BH**
☎ **01895 832085**    📠 **01895 835516**
**e-mail:** info@swaninndenham.co.uk
**web:** www.swaninndenham.co.uk
**dir:** *From A40 take A412. In 200yds follow Denham Village sign on right. Through village, over bridge, last pub on left*

The Swan is the embodiment of a traditional country inn – a double fronted Georgian property swathed in wisteria and set in the beautiful village of Denham. Though the location is wonderfully secluded, it is not too far from the bright lights, being handy for a choice of nearby motorways.

The interior is cosily welcoming with a large log fire and a collection of pictures picked up at auction, while outside is a peaceful sunny terrace and gardens large enough to lose your children in. A private dining room is also available for family occasions or business meetings.

Though The Swan is still very much a pub, with a thriving bar trade in the likes of Marlow Rebellion IPA, the quality of the food is also a great attraction here. Fresh seasonal produce underpins a menu that re-invigorates some old favourites, and makes the most of market availability with a daily-changing specials board. For a starter or light meal look to the 'small plates' section of the menu, which may feature seared 'Little Marlow' pigeon breast on black pudding rösti, with roast beetroot and watercress salad. Among the main courses you'll find plenty of variety, from breaded English veal escalope on hand-made linguini carbonara; to braised Oxfordshire shin of beef with horseradish dumpling and sticky red cabbage. Puddings follow traditional lines, usually with a twist. Classic lemon tart with mascarpone, for example, is served with a local elderberry drizzle; blackberry crème brûlée comes with a pistachio crisp. A goodly range of 'stickies' (dessert wines) has its own list, or you could round off with a hot chocolate with marshmallows. The whole experience is expertly managed by smiling and attentive staff who are clearly well trained and enjoying their job.

**Open** all day all wk 11-11 (Sun 12-10.30) Closed: 26 Dec **Bar Meals** L served Mon-Fri 12-2.30, Sat 12-3, Sun 12-4 D served Sun-Thu 6.30-9.30, Fri-Sat 6.30-10 Av main course £13.75 **Restaurant** L served Mon-Fri 12-2.30, Sat 12-3, Sun 12-4 booking required D served Sun-Thu 6.30-9.30, Fri-Sat 6.30-10 booking required Av 3 course à la carte fr £25.75 ⊕ SALISBURY PUBS LTD ◼ Wadworth 6X, Courage Best, Marlow Rebellion IPA ♂ Thatchers. ♟ 20 **Facilities** Dogs allowed Garden Parking

Save on Hotels. Book at **theAA.com/hotel**

**BUCKINGHAMSHIRE** 51 **ENGLAND**

## FARNHAM COMMON — Map 6 SU98

### The Foresters ♥

**The Broadway SL2 3QQ**
☎ 01753 643340 📠 01753 647524
**e-mail:** info@theforesterspub.com
**dir:** *Telephone for directions*

Dating from the 1930s but newly refurbished, The Foresters' bright gastro-pub decor lends a great atmosphere to the interior; brand new gardens to front and rear complete this well presented hostelry. The bar stocks reliable ales from Fullers and Young's, usually with a guest alongside, while the regularly changing gastro element offers fresh seasonal menu choices with a bias to exciting and modern British flavours. After lunch, head off for a walk in Burnham Beeches, the world's largest ancient beech woodlands.

**Open** all day all wk **Bar Meals** L served all wk 12-3 D served all wk 6.30-10 Av main course £10 **Restaurant** L served all wk 12-3 D served all wk 6.30-10 Fixed menu price fr £13.50 Av 3 course à la carte fr £25 ⊕ PUNCH TAVERNS ◀ Fuller's London Pride, Youngs, guest ale. **Facilities** Children's menu Children's portions Dogs allowed Garden Parking

## FARNHAM ROYAL — Map 6 SU98

### The Emperor ♥

**Blackpond Ln SL2 3EG** ☎ 01753 643006
**e-mail:** manager@theemperorfarnhamroyal.com
**dir:** *Telephone for directions*

This old inn has a wealth of polished wood floors and original beams running through its bar, conservatory and refurbished barn. A log fire burns in winter, and tables outside beckon on summer days. British food based on fresh seasonal fare is the overriding emphasis on the menus. You may find potted Aylesbury duck with baby leaf salad to start, followed by canon of Welsh lamb with dauphinoise potatoes, and fresh fruit meringue to finish.

**Open** all day all wk **Bar Meals** L served Mon-Thu 12-3, Fri-Sat 12-10, Sun 12-8 D served Mon-Thu 6-10, Fri-Sat 12-10, Sun 12-8 ⊕ OPENING COUNTY LEISURE ◀ London Pride, Timothy Taylor Landlord. ♥ 8 **Facilities** Children's menu Children's portions Dogs allowed Garden Parking

## FORD — Map 5 SP70

### PICK OF THE PUBS

### The Dinton Hermit     INN ♥

**Water Ln HP17 8XH**
☎ 01296 747473 📠 01296 748819
**e-mail:** relax@dintonhermit.co.uk
**dir:** *Off A418 between Aylesbury & Thame*

Deep in the Vale of Aylesbury, this traditional stone-built inn is a comfortable and friendly place to pop in for a quick drink in front of the open fire in winter. You'll find guest beers and locally brewed ales at the bar, as well as a wide selection of wines. In summer, the large garden is just the place to enjoy the sunshine

in the peace and quiet of the Buckinghamshire countryside. Both the restaurant and the bar menus offer a range of quality dishes, with locally sourced ingredients wherever possible. Menus change with the seasons, but might include chargrilled lamb chops, colcannon, roasted baby carrots and rosemary gravy; baked vine tomato, olive and goat's cheese tart with purple broccoli and new potatoes; grilled whole lemon sole with purple potatoes and garlic caper butter. And, if you can't bear to leave, just book into one of the contemporary bedrooms.

**Open** all day all wk 10am-11pm (Sun noon-10.30pm) **Bar Meals** Av main course £11.95 food served all day **Restaurant** L served Mon-Fri 12-2, Sat-Sun 12-3 D served Mon-Sun 6.30-9 ⊕ FREE HOUSE ◀ Vale Best Bitter, Beechwood, Copper Beech Wytchert VPA ♻ Stowford Press. ♥ 10 **Facilities** Children's menu Children's portions Dogs allowed Garden Parking **Rooms** 13

## FRIETH — Map 5 SU79

### The Prince Albert ♥

**RG9 6PY** ☎ 01494 881683
**dir:** *4m N of Marlow. Follow Frieth road from Marlow. Straight across at x-rds on Fingest road. Pub 200yds on left*

Set in the Chilterns, close to Hambledon and Marlow, this traditional country pub prides itself on old world values. There are no televisions, juke boxes or games - just good conversation, great beers and a welcoming atmosphere. With copper pots and pans and jugs hanging in the bar, warming open fires enhance the mood in winter and there is a garden with seating to admire the views. Expect traditional pub food with jacket potatoes and ploughman's lunches among the light bites, while the evening menu typically offers jumbo battered cod, chilli con carne, lamb shank, and home-made steak and kidney pie.

**Open** all day all wk 11-11 (Sun noon-10.30pm) **Bar Meals** L served Mon-Sat 12.15-2.30, Sun 12.30-3 D served Fri-Sat 7.30-9.30 ⊕ BRAKSPEAR ◀ Brakspear Bitter, Brakspear seasonal ales. ♥ 9 **Facilities** Children's portions Dogs allowed Garden Parking

### The Yew Tree

**RG9 6PJ** ☎ 01494 882330 📠 01494 883497
**e-mail:** infos@theyewtreerestaurant.com
**dir:** *From M40 towards Stokenchurch, through Cadmore End, Lane End right to Frieth*

Deep in the Chiltern Hills, the 16th-century, red-brick Yew Tree manages to be both traditional rustic country pub and contemporary restaurant, its unexpected pale beams contributing to the effect. Bar meals are available, although you may prefer the dining room where main courses include crispy-skinned sea bass with stir-fried vegetables and honey and soy glaze; and lamb shank, dauphinoise potatoes and garlic and thyme jus. A paddock with three llamas adjoins the substantial rear garden.

**Open** 11-3 6-11, Sun 11-5 Closed: Sun eve, Mon ◀ Fuller's Honeydew, Rebellion, IPA, Smuggler, Guinness, guest ale. **Facilities** Play area Dogs allowed Garden Parking

## FULMER — Map 6 SU98

### The Black Horse ♥ NEW

**Windmill Ln SL3 6HD** ☎ 01753 663183
**e-mail:** info@blackhorsefulmer.co.uk
**dir:** *A40 east of Gerrards Cross. Take turning to Fulmer/Wexham. Pub in centre of village after 1.5m*

Newly opened in Spring 2010, The Black Horse is the fifth and latest addition to the Salisbury group. Its owners have placed the emphasis firmly on recreating a home-from-home atmosphere suitable for the relaxed consumption of spanking real ales, an eclectic selection of European wines (20 sold by the glass), and award-winning British colonial food. A range of 'small plates' may embrace sautéed lamb's kidneys, while roast 'label anglais' chicken with lemon thyme bread pudding would follow on nicely.

**Open** all day all wk 11-11 (Sun noon-10.30) Closed: 26 Dec **Bar Meals** L served Mon-Fri 12-2.30, Sat 12-3, Sun 12-4 D served Sun-Thu 6.30-9.30, Fri-Sat 6.30-10 Av main course £13.75 **Restaurant** L served Mon-Fri 12-.2.30, Sat 12-3, Sun 12-4 booking required D served Sun-Thu 6.30-9.30, Fri-Sat 6.30-10 booking required Av 3 course à la carte fr £25.75 ⊕ SALISBURY PUBS LTD ◀ Greene King IPA, Ruddles County, Abbot Ale. ♥ 20 **Facilities** Children's portions Dogs allowed Garden Parking

## GREAT HAMPDEN    Map 5 SP80

### The Hampden Arms

**HP16 9RQ** ☎ **01494 488255** 📠 **01494 488094**
dir: *From M40 junct 4 take A4010, turn right before Princes Risborough. Great Hampden signed*

Constantine and Louise Lucas have run this mock-Tudor pub restaurant in the wooded Hampden Estate in the Chilterns since 2003. It's a free house, so expect beers from breweries such as Vale in Brill, and plenty of guests. The menu may well feature salmon and king prawn risotto; roast pheasant and cranberry sauce; and home-made steak and kidney pie, while kleftiko could show up as one of the Greek signature dishes usually available.

**Open** all wk noon-3 6-mdnt **Bar Meals** L served Mon-Sat 12-2, Sun 12-3 D served Mon-Sat 6-9.30 Sun 7-9.30 Av main course £7.95 **Restaurant** Fixed menu price fr £10 Av 3 course à la carte fr £20 ⊕ FREE HOUSE ◀ Adnams Bitter, Guest ales, Vale Brewery, London Pride.
**Facilities** Children's portions Family room Dogs allowed Garden Parking

## GREAT MISSENDEN    Map 6 SP80

### PICK OF THE PUBS

### The Nags Head ★★★★ INN ◉ ♥

*See Pick of the Pubs on page 53*

### PICK OF THE PUBS

### The Polecat Inn ♥

**170 Wycombe Rd, Prestwood HP16 0HJ**
☎ **01494 862253** 📠 **01494 868393**
e-mail: polecatinn@btinternet.com
dir: *On A4128 between Great Missenden & High Wycombe*

John Gamble bought the closed and dilapidated Polecat over 20 years ago, renovating and extending it to create an attractive free house, while retaining many original features. The inn dates back to the 17th century, and its beautiful three-acre garden, set amidst rolling Chilterns countryside, is part of its great attraction. The small low-beamed rooms radiating from the central bar give many options when it comes to choosing where to sit and relax with a pint or a plate of freshly cooked food. Dishes are prepared from local ingredients, including herbs from the garden. Lunchtime snacks (sandwiches, warm baguettes, jackets and ploughman's) are backed by a main menu ranging from crab cakes rolled in lemon crumbs; to main courses such as roast magret of duck; and puddings like sherry trifle. Daily blackboard specials add to the choice – venison and rabbit pie; or lamb's liver and bacon casserole with cheese bubble and squeak may be on offer.

**Open** 11-2.30 6-11 (Sun noon-3) Closed: 25-26 Dec, 1 Jan, Sun eve **Bar Meals** L served all wk 12-2 booking required D served Mon-Sat 6.30-9 booking required Av

main course £11.90 ⊕ FREE HOUSE ◀ Marston's Pedigree, Morland, Old Speckled Hen, Interbrew Flowers IPA, Brakspears Bitter Ŏ Scrumpy Jack. ♥ 16
**Facilities** Children's portions Play area Family room Garden Parking

## HAMBLEDEN    Map 5 SU78

### The Stag & Huntsman Inn

**RG9 6RP** ☎ **01491 571227** 📠 **01491 413810**
e-mail: andy@stagandhuntsman.com
dir: *5m from Henley-on-Thames on A4155 towards Marlow, left at Mill End towards Hambleden*

Close to the glorious beech-clad Chilterns, this 400-year-old brick and flint village pub has featured in countless films and television series. Ever-changing guest ales are served in the public bar, larger lounge bar and cosy snug. Food is available in the bars as well as the dining room, from an extensive menu of home-made dishes prepared with local seasonal produce. Hambleden estate game features in season. A weekend beer festival is held in early September.

**Open** all wk 11-2.30 (Sat-Sun 11-3), 6-11 (Sun 7-10.30), 25 Dec 12-1 Closed: 25-26 Dec & 1 Jan evenings **Bar Meals** L served all wk 12-2 D served Mon-Sat 7-9.30 ⊕ FREE HOUSE ◀ Rebellion IPA, Wadworth 6X, guest ales. **Facilities** Garden Parking

## HEDGERLEY    Map 6 SU98

### The White Horse ♥

**SL2 3UY** ☎ **01753 643225**
dir: *Telephone for directions*

The original part of the pub is 500 years old, and over 1000 beers take their turn at the pumps during each year. At least seven real ales are always available, served by gravity, and an annual beer festival is held during the end of May bank holiday. Home-made food ranges from a salad bar with pies, quiches, sandwiches and ploughman's through to curries, chilli, pasta dishes, pies and steaks.

**Open** all wk 11-2.30 5-11 (Sat 11-11, Sun 11-10.30) **Bar Meals** L served Mon-Fri 12-2, Sat-Sun 12-2.30 ⊕ FREE HOUSE ◀ Regularly changing Ŏ Regularly changing. ♥ 10 **Facilities** Children's portions Family room Dogs allowed Garden Parking

## KINGSWOOD    Map 11 SP61

### *Crooked Billet* ♥

**Ham Green HP18 0QJ**
☎ **01296 770239** 📠 **01296 770094**
dir: *On A41 between Aylesbury & Bicester*

Located in peaceful Buckinghamshire countryside, this 200-year-old pub offers an extensive and tempting choice of food. Starters may include port and Stilton rarebit with date and walnut bread, and tomato Cumberland sauce, or salad of queenie scallops with smoked salmon. Among the main courses can be found pasta alla Fiorentina smothered in cream cheese and spinach; roasted sea bass fillet with shrimp velouté and parsley mash; or gratin of fine herb gnocchi with chard, turnips and carrots.

**Open** all day all wk ◀ Hook Norton, Guinness, Tetley's. ♥ 15 **Facilities** Play area Garden Parking

## LACEY GREEN    Map 5 SP80

### The Whip Inn ♥ NEW

**Pink Rd HP27 0PG** ☎ **01844 344060** 📠 **01844 346044**
dir: *1m of A4010 (Princes Risborough to High Wycombe road). Adjacent to windmill*

A picturesque old smock windmill catches the breeze on the ridgetop where also stands this 150 year old pub, high above the Vale of Aylesbury; five counties are visible on clear days. Ramblers on The Chiltern Way join locals in appreciating some of 700 real ales offered each year, as well as real Millwhites cider. A robust menu of home-made classic favourites and seasonally based specials seals the deal at this rustic, music- and fruit-machine free country inn.

**Open** all day all wk **Bar Meals** L served all wk 12-2.30 booking required D served all wk 6.30-9 booking required Av main course £8 **Restaurant** L served all wk 12-2.30 booking required D served all wk 6.30-9 booking required Av 3 course à la carte fr £17 ⊕ FREE HOUSE ◀ Over 700 different guest ales every year Ŏ Thatchers, Millwhites. ♥ 22 **Facilities** Children's portions Dogs allowed Garden

# PICK OF THE PUBS

## The Nags Head ★★★★ INN

**GREAT MISSENDEN**          Map 6 SP80

**London Rd HP16 0DG**
☎ **01494 862200** 📄 **01494 862685**
e-mail: goodfood@nagsheadbucks.com
web: www.nagsheadbucks.com
dir: *1m from Great Missenden on London Rd. From A413 (Amersham to Aylesbury) turn left signed Chiltern Hospital. After 500 mtrs pub on corner of Nags Head Lane & London Rd.*

Originally built in the late 15th century as three small cottages, this free house is situated along the valley of the River Missbourne in the glorious Chiltern Hills. The cottages were originally known as 'bodger cottages' for the craftsmen who produced chair spindles and other half finished parts of furniture. These were collected from the many similar 'bodger cottages' in the area, and were assembled as finished pieces of furniture in London. Because of its location on the London Road, the pub was later converted into a coaching inn, offering rest and refreshment to weary travellers and their horses.

More recently The Nags Head has welcomed numerous Prime Ministers and heads of state on their journey to Chequers, and it was a favourite of the late Harold Wilson. Now in the hands of the Michaels family, The Nags Head underwent an extensive restoration in 2008 and it continues to gain a formidable reputation for hospitality.

Original features including the low oak beams and inglenook fireplace have been carefully retained as a backdrop for the stylish new bar and beautifully refurbished en suite bedrooms. The dining room is decorated with limited edition prints by the late Roald Dahl, the children's author who lived locally and who was a regular.

Food is a passion here, and executive head chef Claude Paillet sources the finest ingredients from local suppliers wherever possible for the Anglo-French menu. The varied menus offer starters like crab with home smoked salmon served with a chive cream and blinis. Main courses range from ox cheek pie with whole grain mustard mash served with leaf salad or chicken fillets wrapped in chorizo with a sweet chilli and tarragon yoghurt sauce. Leave room for a tempting pudding; typical choices include hot apple and cinnamon tart or hot chocolate sponge pudding. In summer, relax over a drink or a meal whilst gazing out over the Chiltern Hills from the pub's lovely informal garden.

**Open** all day all wk **Bar Meals** L served Mon-Sat 12-2.30, Sun 12-3.30 booking required D served all wk 6.30-9.30 booking required **Restaurant** L served Mon-Sat 12-2.30, Sun 12-3.30 booking required D served all wk 6.30-9.30 booking required Fixed menu price fr £14.95 Av 3 course à la carte fr £25.30 ⊕ FREE HOUSE ◀ London Pride, Rebellion, Tring, Vale ♂ Aspall. 🍷 19 **Facilities** Dogs allowed Garden Parking **Rooms** 5

## LONG CRENDON
Map 5 SP60

### PICK OF THE PUBS

## The Angel Inn ☺ ♥

**47 Bicester Rd HP18 9EE**
☎ **01844 208268** 📠 **01844 202497**
e-mail: angelrestaurant@aol.com
dir: *M40 junct 7, A418 to Thame, B4011 to Long Crendon. Inn on B4011*

Set in a picturesque village on the Bucks and Oxfordshire borders, this 15th century coaching inn has retained its original fireplaces and wattle and daub walls which are complemented by a modern, airy conservatory at the rear and tasteful natural materials and fabrics throughout. Cask real ales are served, along with cocktails, champagne, wine by the glass and an impressive selection of single malt whiskies, but food is the main focus here. At lunch, choose between tempting sandwiches and the more substantial fare on offer, typically roast fillet of pork wrapped in Parma ham on braised red cabbage and apple mash with apple mustard butter and cider jus, or breast of Gressingham duck glazed with honey on apple and potato rösti with steamed baby bok choi and blueberry sauce. Vegetarian options, like caramelised leek tart glazed with goat's cheese on a wild mushroom ragout, can be taken as a starter or main course. In warmer weather, head for the heated alfresco terrace.

**Open** all day Closed: Sun eve **Bar Meals** L served all wk 12-3 D served all wk 7-10 Av main course £9.95 **Restaurant** L served all wk 12-3 D served all wk 7-10 Fixed menu price fr £15.95 Av 3 course à la carte fr £28.70 ⊕ FREE HOUSE ◀ Oxford Blue, IPA, Brakspear. ♥ 18 **Facilities** Children's portions Garden Parking

## LOUDWATER
Map 6 SU99

## The Derehams Inn NEW

**5 Derehams Ln HP10 9RH ☎ 01494 530965**
e-mail: derehams@hotmail.co.uk
dir: *From A40 (London Rd) from High Wycombe towards Beaconsfield turn left onto Derehams Ln*

All low beams and brasses, panelling and pewter, The Derehams, which originated as 18th century farm cottages, shouts timeless English village pub loud and clear. A bevy of beer-wickets dispense a great range of local ales: Maggie's kitchen rustles up anything from light bites and sandwiches to goat curry and solid Sunday roasts. They also host an annual beer festival here and a classic car and bike meet every month.

**Open** all wk Mon-Thu 11.30-3.30 5.30-11 (Fri-Sun all day) **Bar Meals** L served Mon-Sat 12-2.30, Sun 2-5 Av main course £6 food served all day ⊕ FREE HOUSE ◀ London Pride, Loddon, Brakspears, Rebellion, Vale. **Facilities** Children's menu Children's portions Dogs allowed Garden Parking

## MARLOW
Map 5 SU88

### PICK OF THE PUBS

## The Hand and Flowers ☺☺☺ ♥

*See Pick of the Pubs on page 56*

## The Kings Head ♥

**Church Rd, Little Marlow SL7 3RZ**
☎ **01628 484407** 📠 **01628 484407**
e-mail: clive.harvison@sky.com
dir: *M40 junct 4 take A4040 S, then A4155 towards Bourne End. Pub 0.5m on right*

Together with the Old Forge, this flower-adorned, 17th-century pub forms part of an attractive group of buildings a few minutes' walk from a church dating back to 1400 and the Thames Footpath. It has an open-plan but cosy interior with original beams and warming fires. In addition to hot-filled French bread and jacket potatoes, the menu offers a range of more substantial meals, including breaded deep-fried Cornish sardine fillets; pan fried lambs' liver and bacon with onion gravy; and smoked haddock and spring onion fishcakes.

**Open** all day all wk **Bar Meals** L served Mon-Sat 12-2.15, Sun 12-7 booking required D served all wk 6.30-9.30 booking required Av main course £9.75 **Restaurant** L served Mon-Sat 12-2.15, Sun 12-7 booking required D served all wk 6.30-9.30 booking required Fixed menu price fr £9.75 ⊕ ENTERPRISE INNS ◀ Fuller's London Pride, Timothy Taylor Landlord, Adnam Broadside, Rebellion IPA, Rebellion Smuggler Ö Aspall. ♥ 13 **Facilities** Children's menu Children's portions Garden Parking

## MEDMENHAM
Map 5 SU88

## Ye Olde Dog and Badger NEW

**Henley Rd SL7 2HE ☎ 01491 571362**
e-mail: dogandbadger@googlemail.com
dir: *On A4155, midway between Marlow & Henley-on-Thames*

You'll sit in the shadows of robust company here, where past patrons have included Nell Gwynne and the notorious Hell Fire Club. Cocooned in its memorable 650 year old frame, beers from Rebellion Brewery entice walkers and boaters from the nearby Thames towpath to share in a great menu, from firm favourites to modern cuisine taken in the bar or restaurant. Indulge in asparagus, pea and artichoke risotto or slow roast belly of pork. Look our for the regular music evenings.

**Open** all day all wk **Bar Meals** Av main course £12 food served all day **Restaurant** Av 3 course à la carte fr £23 food served all day ⊕ ENTERPRISE INNS ◀ Rebellion IPA, London Pride, John Smith's, Guinness. **Facilities** Children's portions Dogs allowed Garden Parking

## MENTMORE
Map 11 SP91

### PICK OF THE PUBS

## The Stag Inn ♥

**The Green LU7 0QF**
☎ **01296 668423** 📠 **01296 660264**
e-mail: info@thestagmentmore.com
dir: *Telephone for directions*

High quality service is the keynote at the imposing Stag Inn, which offers a distinctive fusion of British and Mediterranean cuisine. The pub stands in a picture-postcard village overlooking the huge Elizabethan-style stately home of Mentmore Towers, which was built in 1855 for Baron Amschel de Rothschild. This idyllic area supplies head chef Mani Rebelo with fresh, seasonal produce to create his diverse range of popular dishes. An authentic selection of fresh pasta dishes complements the choice of home-made rustic pizzas (the pizza dough is made daily from a closely guarded secret recipe), with toppings that include The Stag's own combination of mozzarella, tomato, salami, onions, capers and fresh basil. For something a little more traditional, you could try a grilled Woburn venison steak with seasonal vegetables, or grilled sea bass with herbs and garlic. The full menu is available in the bar and restaurant, as well as in the pub's lovely summer garden.

**Open** all wk ⊕ CHARLES WELLS ◀ Youngs Bitter, Guinness, Bombardier. ♥ 8 **Facilities** Dogs allowed Garden Parking

## MILTON KEYNES
Map 11 SP83

## The Swan Inn ♥

**Broughton Rd, Milton Keynes Village MK10 9AH**
☎ **01908 665240** 📠 **01908 395091**
e-mail: info@theswan-mkvillage.co.uk
dir: *M1 junct 14 towards Milton Keynes. Pub off V11 or H7*

Everything you could wish for from an ancient thatched pub in the heart of the original Milton Keynes village. Sympathetically renovated, the interior is an eclectic mix of traditional charm and contemporary chic. Flagstone floors, an open fire in the inglenook in winter keep things cosy, and an orchard garden for those warmer days. Real ales and over 30 wines served by the glass are backed by a range of organic fruit juices and lemonades. The open-plan kitchen creates simple yet creative dishes that change monthly according to availability of produce, which includes herbs from the pub's own garden.

**Open** all day all wk **Bar Meals** L served all wk 12-3
D served all wk 6-9.30 Av main course £10.50
**Restaurant** L served all wk 12-3 booking required
D served all wk 6-9.30 booking required Av 3 course à la
carte fr £25 ⊕ FRONT LINE INNS ◀ Bombardier, Youngs,
guest ales. ♟ 34 **Facilities** Children's portions Dogs
allowed Garden Parking

---

### MOULSOE    Map 11 SP94

## The Carrington Arms ★★★ INN ♟

**Cranfield Rd MK16 0HB**
☎ **01908 218050**    ▤ **01908 217850**
e-mail: carringtonarms@aol.com
dir: *M1 junct 14, A509 to Newport Pagnell 100yds, turn
right signed Moulsoe & Cranfield. Pub on right*

This Grade II listed building is surrounded by farm land in
a conservation area. Customers can 'create' their own
menu from the meat and seafood counter, which the chef
then cooks in full view of his expectant diners. Aberdeen
beef, monkfish, tiger prawns, Colchester oysters are all on
offer, along with unusual meats like ostrich, crocodile
and kangaroo, plus vegetarian dishes and chef's
specials. Friday night is fish night and lobster is
available for pre-order. Recent change of hands.

**Open** all day all wk **Bar Meals** L served Mon-Fri 12-3, Sun
all day D served Mon-Fri 6-10, Sun all day ⊕ FREE HOUSE
◀ Morland Old Speckled Hen, Greene King IPA, London
Pride, Guest ales Ö Aspall. ♟ 10 **Facilities** Children's
menu Garden Parking **Rooms** 8

---

### OVING    Map 11 SP72

## The Black Boy ♟

**Church Ln HP22 4HN**
☎ **01296 641258**    ▤ **01296 641271**
e-mail: theblackboyoving@aol.com
dir: *4.6m N of Aylesbury*

Oliver Cromwell and his soldiers camped in the Black
Boy's huge garden after sacking nearby Bolebec Castle
during the Civil War. Today, the 16th-century pub is a
rural oasis, with spectacular views over the Vale of
Aylesbury to Stowe School and beyond. Choices in the
dining room include Scottish salmon with new potatoes
and seasonal greens; local lamb shank with minted gravy
and root vegetables; and a vegetarian cheese and onion
filo parcel. Recent change of hands.

**Open** noon-3 6-11 (Sun noon-5) Closed: 25 Dec
**Bar Meals** L served Mon-Sat 12-2, Sun 12-3 D served
Mon-Thu 6.30-9, Fri-Sat 6-9.30 ⊕ FREE HOUSE ◀ Hale
Best, Guest ales Ö Aspalls. ♟ 10 **Facilities** Children's
portions Dogs allowed Garden Parking

---

### PENN    Map 6 SU99

### PICK OF THE PUBS

## The Old Queens Head ♟

*See Pick of the Pubs on page 57*

---

### PRESTON BISSETT    Map 11 SP62

## The White Hart

**Pound Ln MK18 4LX** ☎ **01280 847969**
dir: *2.5m from A421*

Seek out this pretty thatched free house in the winter
months for traditional game dishes from the local shoots.
The Grade II listed building dates from 1545 and lies
amid the rolling hills of rural Buckinghamshire. There's a
good selection of wines and local real ales, and a small
select menu that changes with the seasons; expect
classic dishes like steak and ale pie, and slow-cooked
belly of pork. There's a nice, secluded garden, too.

**Open** 12-2.30 6-11 (Sat-Sun noon-11pm) Closed: Mon
**Bar Meals** L served Tue-Sun 12-2.30 D served Tue-Sun
6-11 Av main course £10 **Restaurant** L served Tue-Sun
12-2.30 booking required D served Tue-Sun 6-10 booking
required Av 3 course à la carte fr £22 ⊕ FREE HOUSE
◀ Hooky Best Bitter, Old Hooky, Timothy Taylor Landlord,
Rev James, Tribute. **Facilities** Children's menu Children's
portions Dogs allowed Garden Parking

---

### RADNAGE    Map 5 SU79

## The Three Horseshoes Inn ♟

**Horseshoe Rd, Bennett End HP14 4EB** ☎ **01494 483273**
e-mail: threehorseshoe@btconnect.com
dir: *From M40 junct 5, A40 towards High Wycombe, after
unrestricted mileage sign turn left signed Radnage
(Mudds Bank). 1.8m, 1st left into Bennett End Rd, inn
on right*

Dating from 1748, this delightful little inn is tucked away
down a leafy lane. Stone floors, original beams, a bread
oven and an open fire are among the features. The
modern English and European menu changes daily, and
award-winning chef/owner Simon Cranshaw uses as
much local produce as possible. Enjoy a Rebellion ale at
the bar, or wander outside in the lovely gardens. Themed
evenings (such as lobster night; Italian night; tapas and
jazz night) on the last Thursday of every month prove so
popular that booking is essential.

**Open** 12-3 6-11 (Sun 12-4) Closed: Sun eve Mon L
**Bar Meals** L served Wed-Sat 12-2.30, Sun 12-4 D served
Tue-Sat 6-9.30 Av main course £11 **Restaurant** L served
Tue-Sat 12-2.30, Sun 12-4 D served Mon-Sat 6-9.30 Fixed
menu price fr £16.50 Av 3 course à la carte fr £30
⊕ FREE HOUSE ◀ Rebellion beers. ♟ 12
**Facilities** Children's portions Dogs allowed Garden
Parking

---

### SKIRMETT    Map 5 SU79

### PICK OF THE PUBS

## The Frog ♟

**RG9 6TG** ☎ **01491 638996**    ▤ **01491 638045**
e-mail: info@thefrogatskirmett.co.uk
web: www.thefrogatskirmett.co.uk
dir: *Turn off A4155 at Mill End, pub in 3m*

This privately owned pub and restaurant is tucked
away in the beautiful Hambleden valley. Dating back
300 years in parts, the building has been designed to
make the most of its history while still having a fresh,
contemporary feel. The bar dates to the 18th century
and is the heart of the operation, with a cosy, friendly
atmosphere – there's comfortable leather and oak
seating and a fire burns in the winter. Head chef and
co-owner Jim Crowe has developed excellent
relationships with his suppliers, resulting in fantastic
local produce. The simple set menu offers great value
for money with options like warm potato rösti, black
pudding and smoked salmon with poached egg; grilled
mackerel with marinated cucumber and mustard crème
fraîche; or potted shrimp and watercress salad to start
with, followed by poached pork fillet in a butter bean
broth, with smoked bacon and garden peas; chargrilled Hambleden venison cheeseburger, pickled red
cabbage and chips; or buttered gnocchi with
asparagus, sun-blushed tomatoes, chargrilled peppers
and basil pesto with parmesan shavings. There are
also daily specials and on Sunday a roast of the day is
also available. If you still have room for dessert, the
sticky toffee pudding is recommended.

**Open** 11.30-3 6-11 Closed: Sun eve (Oct-Apr)
**Bar Meals** L served all wk 12-2.30 D served all wk
6.30-9.30 Av main course £11.95 **Restaurant** Av 3
course à la carte fr £25 ⊕ FREE HOUSE ◀ Adnams
Best, Hook Norton, Rebellion, Fuller's London Pride, IPA,
Guest ale Ö Thatchers Dry. ♟ 15 **Facilities** Children's
menu Children's portions Family room Dogs allowed
Garden Parking

# PICK OF THE PUBS

## The Hand and Flowers

**126 West St SL7 2BP**
☎ **01628 482277**   📄 **01628 401913**
e-mail:
theoffice@thehandandflowers.co.uk
web: www.thehandandflowers.co.uk
dir: *M4 junct 9, A404 N into Marlow, A4155 towards Henley-on-Thames. Pub on outskirts on right*

Upmarket Marlow beside the Thames is being trumpeted as being England's latest gastronomic hotspot and dedicated chef Tom Kerridge is leading the way at his unassuming pub on the outskirts of the town. He took pub cooking to a new level when he bought the lease to this whitewashed 18th-century Greene King pub in 2005 and it remains a class act and an inspiration for all to follow. Despite gaining three AA rosettes in the first year, the pub remains a relaxed and unpretentious place, with flagstone floors, old beams and timbers, roaring winter log fires,

walls lined with striking modern art, leather banquettes and cloth-less, smartly-set tables. A small bar area serves decent Abbot Ale, and a cracking £10 set lunch that features dishes like pork pie with piccalilli, chicken and mushroom pie, and slow roasted leg of pork with chorizo, butter beans and crackling. The informed and enthusiastic service also helps to set the tone of the place.

Tom's cooking is intelligently straightforward and elegant, with simplicity, flavour and skill top of his agenda, and the style is broadly modern British, with classical French cooking at the root of much of it, and the seasonally-changing menu is built around top-notch produce.

Considerable technical skill and confidence can be seen in his signature dishes, such as his fried duck egg with duck boudin, girolles and butter sauce; slow braised shin of Hambleden Estate beef with broad beans, marjoram and beef marrow; and warm pistachio sponge cake with melon sorbet and marzipan vanilla crème brûlée. Be wowed, also, by pea soup with poached egg, crispy bacon and mint oil; Weymouth plaice with sea purslane, mousseron mushrooms, brown shrimps and burnt butter dressing; and passion

fruit and white chocolate trifle with coffee sorbet and mango. Great patio for summer alfresco dining.

**Open** 12-2.30 6.30-9.30 (Sun 12-3.30) Closed: 24-26 Dec, 1 Jan D, Sun eve **Bar Meals** L served Mon-Sat 12-2.30 booking required D served Mon-Sat 6.30-9.30 booking required Av main course £13 **Restaurant** L served all wk 12-2.30 booking required D served all wk 6.30-9.30 booking required Av 3 course à la carte fr £35 ⊞ GREENE KING ◾ Abbot Ale, IPA. ☙ 11 **Facilities** Garden Parking

# PICK OF THE PUBS

## The Old Queens Head ♀

**PENN**      Map 6 SU99

**Hammersley Ln HP10 8EY**
☎ **01494 813371** 📄 **01494 816145**
e-mail: info@oldqueensheadpenn.co.uk
web: www.oldqueensheadpenn.co.uk
dir: *B474 (Penn road) through Beaconsfield
New Town towards Penn, approx 3m left into
School Rd, left in 500yds into Hammersley
Ln. Pub on corner opp church*

As the Great Fire of London swept
through the City's countless wooden
houses in 1666, a new wooden building
was rising just thirty miles away in rural
Buckinghamshire. The builders of Tylers
Green made good use of the plentiful
local timber to build the barn that, with
several additions, today houses the
dining room of this charming old pub.
But the fact that, with its cosy corners,
real fires and frequent changes in floor
level, the restaurant is still standing
perhaps serves to vindicate their choice
of material.

The owners have clearly spent many
hours at local auctions finding lovely old
furniture and pictures in keeping with
the age of the pub, whose warm
heritage colours harmonise well with the
dark floorboards, flagstones, rugs and
classic fabrics. A sunny terrace
overlooks the village church, and there's
a large garden in which to eat and
drink.

The highly versatile kitchen team has
created a modern British menu offering
good choice, with starters such as
steamed mussels with chilli, lemon
grass and coconut; local game terrine
with elderberry and apple jam and
toasted beer bread; and warm goat's
cheese and red onion marmalade
strudel with pickled beetroot and beet
leaves. Main course options are
similarly appetising; Little Marlow
venison and pearl barley stew with
rosemary dumplings and purple
sprouting; creamy wild mushroom and
baby spinach vol au vent with sautéed
spring greens and Parmesan crisp; and
roast hake fillet with tomato and
cannellini bean cassoulet and crispy
chilli squid are typical choices. Leave
room for puddings like dark chocolate
truffle cake with pistachio ice cream;

and Bramley apple and blackberry
crumble tart. Free Wi-fi is useful for
those business lunches where
yesterday's sales figures are suddenly
needed.

**Open** all day all wk 11-11 (Sun
12-10.30) Closed: 26 Dec **Bar Meals**
L served Mon-Fri 12-2.30, Sat 12-3, Sun
12-4 D served Sun-Thu 6.30-9.30, Fri &
Sat 6.30-10 Av main course £13.75
**Restaurant** L served Mon-Fri 12-2.30,
Sat 12-3, Sun 12-4 booking required
D served Sun-Thu 6.30-9.30, Fri & Sat
6.30-10 booking required Av 3 course à
la carte fr £25.75 ⊞ SALISBURY PUBS
LTD ◀ Ruddles County, Greene King IPA,
Guinness. ♀ 20 **Facilities** Dogs allowed
Garden Parking

## TURVILLE　Map 5 SU79

### PICK OF THE PUBS

## The Bull & Butcher ♥

**RG9 6QU ☎ 01491 638283**
e-mail: info@thebullandbutcher.com
dir: *M40 junct 5 follow Ibstone signs. Right at T-junct. Pub 0.25m on left*

You'll probably recognise The Bull & Butcher, even if you've never been there before. For Turville, with its delightful 16th-century pub and 10th-century church, has won celebrity status in numerous film and television productions: *Midsomer Murders, The Vicar of Dibley, Goodnight Mr Tom*, and *Chitty Chitty Bang Bang*. After an exhilarating walk amid the glorious Chilterns scenery, drop down from the windmill on Turville Hill and unwind with a pint from a fantastic choice of real ales in the Well Bar or Windmill Lounge with their natural oak beams and open fires. There's also a function room ideal for leisure and corporate occasions, and a large garden and patio area. Menu choices begin with starters that include a platter of cured meats with olives and bread, whilst main course dishes range from cod, chips and mushy peas or pan-fried duck with rice and stir-fried vegetables to roasted vegetable cannelloni with spinach.

**Open** all day all wk 11-11 (Sun noon-10.30pm) **Bar Meals** L served Mon-Fri 12-2.30, Sat 12-3.30 Sun 12-4 booking required D served Mon-Sat 6.30-9.30, Sun 7-9 booking required **Restaurant** L served Mon-Fri 12-2.30, Sat 12-3.30, Sun 12-4 booking required D served Mon-Sat 6.30-9.30, Sun 7-9 booking required ⊕ BRAKSPEAR ◀ Brakspear Bitter, Hooky Dark, Oxford Gold, Brewers selections. ♥ 36 **Facilities** Children's menu Dogs allowed Garden Parking

## WEST WYCOMBE　Map 5 SU89

### PICK OF THE PUBS

## The George and Dragon Hotel ♥

**High St HP14 3AB**
**☎ 01494 535340 📄 01494 400121**
dir: *On A40*

Visitors to the area will enjoy exploring West Wycombe Caves, and the stately houses at Cliveden and Hughenden Manor. After a day's hard touring, a visit to this traditional coaching inn with 14th-century origins in a National Trust village will be nicely relaxing. It wasn't always the case – it was once a hideout for highwaymen stalking travellers between London and Oxford; indeed, one unfortunate guest robbed and murdered here is rumoured still to haunt its corridors. The hotel is reached through a cobbled archway and comprises a delightful jumble of whitewashed, timber-framed buildings. A change of hands at the end of 2009 has restocked the bar with different albeit reliable real ales, including Doom Bar, Tribute and Rebellion IPA. Also reliable is the varied menu which offers freshly-prepared dishes cooked to order such as

beef and ale pie; beer battered haddock; a button mushroom, brie and cranberry filo parcel; and succulent rib-eye steaks.

**Open** all wk 11-3 5.30-11 **Bar Meals** L served 12-2.30 D served 6-9.30 Av main course £10 **Restaurant** L served 12-2.30 D served 6-9.30 ⊕ ENTERPRISE INNS ◀ Sharp's Doom Bar, Tribute, Rebellion IPA. ♥ 9 **Facilities** Play area Family room Dogs allowed Garden Parking

## WHEELER END　Map 5 SU89

## The Chequers Inn ♥

**Bullocks Farm Ln HP14 3NH ☎ 01494 883070**
e-mail: chequersinn2@btconnect.com
dir: *4m N of Marlow*

Styling itself 'a traditional village pub with old style values in an adult environment', this picturesque 17th-century inn, with its roaring winter fires and two attractive beer gardens, is ideally located for walkers on the edge of Wheeler End Common. A solid choice of mouth-watering sandwiches and bar meals supplements the main menu, which features plenty of fresh fish and local estate game. Grilled witch sole; pork fillet with Stilton sauce; stuffed pheasant breast followed by a selection of home-made puddings all might tempt.

**Open** 12-3 6-11 (Sun 12-3 7-10.30) Closed: Mon L **Bar Meals** L served Tue-Sat 12-2, Sun 12-3.30 D served Tue-Sat 6.30-9 **Restaurant** L served Tue-Sat 12-2, Sun 12-3.30 D served Tue-Sat 6.30-9 ⊕ FULLER SMITH TURNER PLC ◀ Fuller's ESB, London Pride, Guest ale. ♥ 12 **Facilities** Children's portions Dogs allowed Garden Parking

## WHITELEAF　Map 5 SP80

## Red Lion

**Upper Icknield Way HP27 0LL**
**☎ 01844 344476 📄 01844 344476**
e-mail: tim_hibbert@hotmail.co.uk
dir: *A4010 through Princes Risborough, turn right into The Holloway, at T-junct turn right, pub on left*

Family-owned 17th-century traditional country inn in the heart of the Chilterns, surrounded by National Trust land and situated close to the Ridgeway national trail. There are plenty of good local walks with wonderful views. A cosy fire in winter and a secluded summer beer garden add to the appeal. Hearty pub fare is served in the bar area and includes rib-eye steak, sausage and mash, vegetarian lasagne, haddock and chips, warm baguettes and jacket potatoes. You can also dine in the recently built restaurant.

**Open** all wk 12-3 5-11 (Fri Sat Sun all day) **Bar Meals** L served all wk 12-2 D served Mon-Sat 7-9 booking required **Restaurant** L served all wk 12-2 booking required D served Mon-Sat 7-9 booking required ⊕ FREE HOUSE ◀ Brakspear Bitter, Hook Norton, Tribute, Guinness Ö Aspall. **Facilities** Children's portions Family room Dogs allowed Garden Parking

## WOOBURN COMMON　Map 6 SU98

### PICK OF THE PUBS

## Chequers Inn ★★★ HL ◉ ♥

**Kiln Ln HP10 0JQ ☎ 01628 529575 📄 01628 850124**
e-mail: info@chequers-inn.com
dir: *M40 junct 2, A40 through Beaconsfield Old Town towards High Wycombe. 2m from town left into Broad Ln. Inn 2.5m*

Oak posts and beams, flagstone floors and a wonderful open fireplace blackened by a million blazing logs: this 17th-century inn is an absolute charmer. It has been owned and run by the same family for over 35 years, ensuring a friendly, relaxed and welcoming atmosphere. Overlooking open Chiltern Hills countryside, its interior includes an attractively decorated restaurant, but an alternative dining option is the extensive lunch and dinner bar menu backed by a large selection of beers, guest ales and wines; the same menu is served in the contemporary lounge. The restaurant is as ideal for a quick business lunch as for a long romantic dinner. Fresh, predominantly local ingredients are used in dishes such as traditional duck rillettes with red onion chutney; corn fed lemon chicken with black pudding fritters; lemongrass steamed salmon and confit red cabbage. Pineapple parfait with chocolate sauce; and bread and butter pudding might be on offer too. Outside is a large garden area where barbecues are held in summer. There are 17 beautifully appointed bedrooms available.

**Open** all day all wk noon-mdnt **Bar Meals** L served Mon-Fri 12-2.30, Sat 12-10, Sun 12-9.30 D served Mon-Thu 6-9.30, Fri 6-10, Sat 12-10, Sun 12-9.30 Av main course £9.95 **Restaurant** L served all wk 12-2.30 booking required D served all wk 7-9.30 booking required Fixed menu price fr £13.95 Av 3 course à la carte fr £27.95 ⊕ FREE HOUSE ◀ IPA, Rebellion Smuggler, Old Speckled Hen. ♥ 14 **Facilities** Children's menu Children's portions Garden Parking **Rooms 17**

## WOOBURN GREEN　Map 6 SU98

## Old Bell ♥ NEW

**Town Ln HP10 0PL ☎ 01628 520406**
e-mail: peterlim@oldbell.co.uk
dir: *On A4094. Pub adjacent to church in village*

This almost 300-year-old village inn stands at the edge of the Chilterns, just a short distance from Burnham Beeches woods. In a former guise it was an oriental restaurant and bar; nowadays traditional English pub food is the mainstay, with a nod to contemporary European influences. In the part-timber framed inn, visitors can tuck into home-made houmous with feta cheese, mixed olives and pitta bread before launching into pork chop with mustard, cider and cream sauce or seafood crêpes with lobster sauce and mixed salad.

Open all wk noon-3 5-11 **Bar Meals** L served Tue-Sat 12-2.30 D served Tue-Sat 6.30-9.30 Av main course £6 **Restaurant** L served Tue-Sun 12-2.30 booking required D served Tue-Sat 6.30-9.30 booking required Av 3 course à la carte fr £19 ⊕ ENTERPRISE INNS ◀ London Pride, Woodforde's Wherry. ♚ 10 **Facilities** Children's portions Garden Parking

## CAMBRIDGESHIRE

### BABRAHAM   Map 12 TL55

## PICK OF THE PUBS

### The George Inn at Babraham ♚

**High St CB2 4AG ☎ 01223 833800**
e-mail: info@thegeorgebabraham.co.uk
dir: *In High St, just off A11/A505 & A1307*

An 18th-century coaching inn once renowned for the Whitsun and May Day revels hosted here. Set in the heart of rural Cambridgeshire, it was devastated by fire in 2004 but new kitchens and three restaurant areas have restored the village dining pub to its former glory. It came under the new management of Stuart and Karen Laurie in March 2010, with daughter Joanna taking the reins on a day-to-day basis. At the bar, you'll find Old Speckled Hen and IPA, with Aspall's cider in support and eight wines served by the glass. As this guide goes to press the food operation is focussing on traditional British favourites such as steak and ale pie and fresh fish dishes, with menus that change every two months.

Open all wk Mon-Fri 12-3 5-11 (Sat-Sun all day) **Bar Meals** L served all wk 12-2 D served all wk 5.30-9 Av main course £8.65 **Restaurant** L served Mon-Fri 12-2, Sat-Sun 12-3 D served all wk 5.30-9 ⊕ GREENE KING ◀ Old Speckled Hen, Greene King IPA, Guest ale Ö Aspall. ♚ 8 **Facilities** Children's menu Children's portions Dogs allowed Garden Parking

### BARRINGTON   Map 12 TL34

### The Royal Oak ♚

**31 West Green CB22 7RZ**
**☎ 01223 870791 ▤ 01223 870791**
e-mail: info@royaloak.uk.net
dir: *From Barton off M11, S of Cambridge*

One of the oldest thatched pubs in England, this rambling, timbered 13th-century building overlooks one of the largest village greens in England. It's only six miles from Cambridge, three miles from the M11 and a mile from Shepreth Station. A wide range of fish dishes includes scallops, trout, scampi, tuna, swordfish, tiger prawns, squid and other seasonal offerings. There is also a carvery on Sunday which could be accompanied by a pint of IPA Potton Brewery or Young's Bitter.

Open all wk noon-2.30 6-11 (Sun noon-3 6.30-10.30) **Restaurant** L served 12-2, Sun 12-2.30 booking required D served 6.30-9.30, Sun 7-9 booking required ⊕ FREE HOUSE ◀ IPA Potton Brewery, Adnams, Young's Bitter, Morland Original. ♚ 8 **Facilities** Children's menu Children's portions Dogs allowed Garden Parking

### BROUGHTON   Map 12 TL27

## PICK OF THE PUBS

### The Crown ♚

*See Pick of the Pubs on page 60*

### CAMBRIDGE   Map 12 TL45

## PICK OF THE PUBS

### The Anchor ♚

**Silver St CB3 9EL ☎ 01223 353554**
e-mail: 7614@greeneking.co.uk
dir: *Telephone for directions*

Situated at the end of the medieval lane that borders Queens' College in the heart of the University city, this attractive waterside pub appeals to students and visitors alike. Hard by the bridge over the River Cam, in fine weather the riverside patio is an ideal spot for enjoying one of a range of good ales including guest beers while watching the activities on the water. The more adventurous can hire a punt for a leisurely trip to Grantchester (of Rupert Brooke and Jeffrey Archer fame), and on return sample a choice of hearty meals from a range that includes lasagne, home-made pie, and roast beer.

Open all wk Mon-Fri 11am-11pm (Fri-Sat 11am-12.30am, Sun 11am-10.30pm) Closed: 25 Dec **Bar Meals** food served all day ⊕ GREENE KING ◀ Greene King, IPA, Abbot Ale, Old Speckled Hen Ö Aspall. ♚ 12 **Facilities** Children's menu Dogs allowed

## PICK OF THE PUBS

### Cambridge Blue ♚

**85 Gwydir St CB1 2LG ☎ 01223 471680**
dir: *In city centre*

A friendly 1860s backstreet pub, built to serve the terrace that housed railway workers, with an unexpected garden and an amazing range of beers, from unusual bottled beers from around the world to a mind-boggling choice of 12 real ales from micro-breweries on handpump in the tap room – try a pint of Oakham Bishops Farewell or Woodforde's Wherry. Inside are two real fires, lots of memorabilia and a lively, buzzy vibe. Good value pub grub made on the premises comes in the form of steak and kidney pie, fish pie, sausages and mash, a daily curry and a range of filled ciabatta sandwiches and jacket potatoes. Don't miss the summer (June) and winter (Feb) beer festivals.

Open all day Tue-Sat noon-11 (Sun noon-10.30, Mon noon-2.30 5-11) Closed: Mon 3-5 **Bar Meals** L served Mon 12-2, Tue-Sun 12-4 D served all wk 6-10 Av main course £7 ⊕ FREE HOUSE ◀ Woodforde's Wherry, Oakham Bishops Farewell, guest ales Ö Pickled Pig, Thatchers. ♚ 8 **Facilities** Children's portions Family room Dogs allowed Garden

### Free Press ♚

**Prospect Row CB1 1DU ☎ 01223 368337**
e-mail: craig.bickley@ntlworld.com
dir: *Telephone for directions*

Students, academics, locals and visitors rub shoulders in this atmospheric and picturesque back-street pub near the city centre. It has open fires and a beautiful walled garden - but no music, mobile phones or gaming machines. Punters are attracted by first-rate real ales and great home-made food such as chilli with garlic bread; goat's cheese salad; filled toasted ciabattas; venison sausages; and salmon filled with couscous and vegetables. There is now a 3-course evening meal for £10 Mon-Wed.

Open all wk noon-2.30 6-11 (Fri noon-2.30 4.30-11, Sat noon-11, Sun noon-3 7-10.30) Closed: 25-26 Dec, 1 Jan **Bar Meals** L served Mon-Fri 12-2, Sat-Sun 12-2.30 D served Mon-Sat 6-9, Sat 7-9 Av main course £7.50 **Restaurant** Fixed menu price fr £10 ⊕ GREENE KING ◀ Greene King IPA, Abbot Ale, Dark Mild, guest ales. ♚ 10 **Facilities** Children's portions Dogs allowed Garden

### The Old Spring ♚ NEW

**1 Ferry Path CB4 1HB**
**☎ 01223 357228 ▤ 01223 357235**
e-mail: theoldspring@hotmail.co.uk
dir: *Just off Chesterton Rd, (A1303) in city centre, near Midsummer Common*

A popular local serving Cambridge's leafy suburb of Defreville, a few hundred yards back from boathouses on the river Cam. The lovely decked patio is a magnet for rowers in summer, while the bright and airy interior offers rug-covered wood floors, comfy sofas and large family tables. Sip a guest ale or one of 19 wines sold by the glass while choosing from the array of freshly prepared food ranging from jerk chicken wraps to specials such as roast loin of Grasmere Farm pork.

Open all day all wk 11.30-11 (Sun 12-10.30) **Bar Meals** L served Mon-Fri 12-2.30 Sat-Sun 12-3 D served Mon-Fri 6-9 Av main course £9.50 ⊕ GREENE KING ◀ IPA, Abbot Ale, Olde Trip, Old Speckled Hen, Guest ales Ö Stowford Press. ♚ 19 **Facilities** Children's menu Children's portions Garden Parking

# PICK OF THE PUBS

## The Crown ♙

**BROUGHTON** Map 12 TL27

**Bridge Rd PE28 3AY ☎ 01487 824428**
**e-mail:**
info@thecrowninnrestaurant.co.uk
**dir:** *Just off A141 between Huntingdon &*
*Warboys, by church in village centre*

This picturesque 18th-century free
house, a near neighbour of the village
church, is at the heart of a thriving local
community. In the mid-19th century,
however, it was serving the population
rather differently, since it also
incorporated a saddler's shop, thatched
stables and piggeries. The livestock has
long gone, and today it focuses on being
a popular village pub and highly
regarded restaurant, so it's hard to
believe that in 2000 it closed. But the
villagers rallied round, bought and
renovated it, and for several years ran it
as a village-owned tenancy.

The bar offers real ales from Elgoods
and Nethergate local breweries, and
you'll also find Aspall cyders (the
makers insist on the correct spelling).
The restaurant combines a traditional
pub look with contemporary design and
it's here you'll be able to eat Modern
European dishes cooked using the best
sustainable fish caught by day boats,
the highest quality meats, and excellent
seasonal vegetables.

Menus change regularly, so when you
visit you may find one offering starters
of salad of Atlantic prawns, creamy
avocado and smoked salmon; grilled
goat's cheese with rocket, pine-nuts,
sun-blushed tomatoes and pesto; or
potted chicken liver pâté with drawn
butter, warm toast and fruit compote.
Typical main courses are chargrilled
rib-eye steak with chips, button
mushrooms and mixed salad; twice-
cooked leg of duck, bubble and squeak,
braised red cabbage and red wine
sauce; pan-fried fillets of mackerel,
Italian ratatouille, parmesan and
tomato and lime dressing; and three-
cheese, spinach and tomato lasagne.
Round off with crème brûlée; sticky
toffee pudding with hazelnut and toffee

ice cream; or hot chocolate fondant with
poached rhubarb and rhubarb syrup.
You should also check the specials.
Wines begin at £13.50, with ten by the
glass. The garden is huge.

**Open** 11.30-3 6.30-11 (Sun 11.30-3)
Closed: Mon-Tue **Light Bites** L served
Wed-Sun 12-2.30 Av main course £11
**A la carte** L served Wed-Sun 12-2.30
D served Wed-Sun 7-10 Av 3 course fr
£24 ⊞ FREE HOUSE ◖ Elgoods, Greene
King IPA, Nethergates Suffolk County
and other guest ales Ö Aspalls. ♙ 10
**Facilities** Garden Parking

Save on Hotels. Book at **theAA.com/hotel**

**CAMBRIDGESHIRE** 61 **ENGLAND**

**CAMBRIDGE** continued

## The Punter **NEW**

**3 Pound Hill CB3 0AE** ☎ **01223 363322**
dir: *Telephone for directions*

Just two minutes' walk from the city centre and popular with visitors, locals and students alike, this beautifully renovated old coaching house is furnished with an eclectic mix of pine furniture that creates a comfortable, relaxed ambience where drinkers can sit alongside diners and enjoy well-priced rustic food. The daily-changing seasonal menu includes a £5 set lunch, whilst other choices might include beetroot, spinach and goat's cheese risotto; wild boar Barnsley chop with stuffing, greens and mash; and smoked haddock with rarebit topping. In the delightful courtyard garden pots of home-grown produce are sold.

**Open** all day all wk Closed: 25 Dec **Bar Meals** L served Mon-Fri 12-3, Sat-Sun all day D served Mon-Fri 6-10, Sat-Sun all day Av main course £12 **Restaurant** L served Mon-Fri 12-3, Sat-Sun all day D served Mon-Fri 6-10, Sat-Sun all day Av 3 course à la carte fr £20 ◂ Adnams Explorer, Adnams Broadside ♻ Aspall.
**Facilities** Children's portions Dogs allowed Garden

---

**DUXFORD** Map 12 TL44

### PICK OF THE PUBS

## The John Barleycorn

**3 Moorfield Rd CB2 4PP**
☎ **01223 832699** 🖷 **01223 832699**
e-mail: info@johnbarleycorn.co.uk
dir: *Exit A505 into Duxford*

Tucked at the far end of the village, a mile from the A1301 and close to Cambridge, this newly spruced-up 17th-century thatched and beamed pub is resplendent with hanging baskets, tubs and borders in high summer. Step through the latch door to find a delightful, single low-beamed and softly-lit bar with a rustic mix of country furniture, a large brick fireplace,

an old tiled floor, cushioned painted pews and hop-adorned beams. It's a cosy, comfortable and relaxing place in which to enjoy a hearty home-cooked meal, washed down with a cracking pint of Greene King Abbot or Old Speckled Hen. Typically, tuck into smoked haddock fishcakes and asparagus and broad bean risotto, follow with traditional bangers mash or deep-fried haddock and chips, or choose the pan-fried sea bass served on roasted Mediterranean vegetable couscous, or the beef fillet with sweet potato chips and béarnaise sauce, and finish with blueberry frangipane tart. Summer alfresco eating can be enjoyed on the flower-festooned rear patio.

**Open** all wk **Bar Meals** L served all wk D served all wk Av main course £7.50 **Restaurant** Fixed menu price fr £7.50 Av 3 course à la carte fr £12 ⊕ GREENE KING ◂ Greene King IPA, Abbot Ale, Old Speckled Hen, Ruddles Best & County. **Facilities** Dogs allowed Garden Parking

---

**ELSWORTH** Map 12 TL36

## The George & Dragon ₽

**41 Boxworth Rd CB3 8JQ**
☎ **01954 267236** 🖷 **01954 267080**
e-mail: www.georgeanddragon-elsworth.co.uk
dir: *SE of A14 between Cambridge & Huntingdon*

Set in a pretty village just outside Cambridge, this pub offers a friendly, relaxed environment, great beers and a wide range of satisfying food for locals and visitors alike. Aberdeen Angus steaks and fish fresh from Lowestoft are a draw here. Look out for grilled sea bass fillets with prawns and lemon butter or surf 'n' turf – succulent rib-eye steak with king prawns. Every Monday, British favourites are on the menu such as steak and kidney pudding and braised pheasant in port sauce. There are special menus for occasions such as Valentine candlelit dinner and Mother's Day.

**Open** all wk 11-2.30 6-11 **Bar Meals** L served all wk 11-2.30 D served all wk 6-11 Av main course £13 **Restaurant** L served all wk 11-2.30 D served all wk 6-11 ⊕ FREE HOUSE ◂ Greene King IPA, Ruddles County, Greene King Old Speckled Hen ♻ Aspall. ₽ 13 **Facilities** Children's menu Children's portions Garden Parking

---

**ELTON** Map 12 TL09

### PICK OF THE PUBS

## The Black Horse ₽

**14 Overend PE8 6RU**
☎ **01832 280240 & 280875** 🖷 **01832 280875**
e-mail: blackhorseelton@btconnect.com
dir: *Off A605 (Peterborough to Northampton road)*

Antique furnishings and open log fires crank up the old world charm in this 17th-century inn, while the delightful one-acre rear garden overlooks Elton's famous church and rolling open countryside. The real ales include Everards Tiger, seasonal Nethergate brews, and Barnwell Bitter, which is brewed locally. The superb selection of food ranges from bar snacks to a full à la carte. Among the 'snacks' are sandwiches, filled baguettes jacket potatoes, a home-made pie of the day, and seasonal salads. Or you might start with Portobello mushrooms topped with bacon and cheese gratin; or freshly dressed crab with brown bread and salad. Typical main courses include guinea fowl stuffed with black pudding and chorizo sausage, wrapped in Parma ham and served with a rich red wine jus; fillet of sea bass with braised pak choi, pesto and sun-blushed tomatoes; and bangers and mash.

**Open** all day noon-11.30pm Closed: Sun eve **Bar Meals** L served Mon-Fri 12-2.30, Sat all day, Sun 12-3 D served Mon-Fri 6-9, Sat all day **Restaurant** L served Mon-Fri 12-2.30, Sat all day, Sun 12-3 D served Mon-Fri 6-9, Sat all day ⊕ FREE HOUSE ◂ Everards Tiger, Barnwell Bitter, Oakham J H B ♻ Thatchers. ₽ 14 **Facilities** Children's menu Play area Family room Dogs allowed Garden Parking

---

# PICK OF THE PUBS

## The Anchor Inn ★★★★RR

**ELY**  Map 12 TL58

**Sutton Gault CB6 2BD**
☎ **01353 778537**  📠 **01353 776180**
e-mail: anchorinn@popmail.bta.com
web: www.anchorsuttongault.co.uk
dir: *From A14, B1050 to Earith, take B1381 to Sutton. Sutton Gault on left*

Built in 1650, The Anchor Inn has evolved to combine modern comforts with timeless charm and character. Scrubbed pine tables on gently undulating tiled floors, antique prints and winter log fires all enhance the cosy, intimate atmosphere of this family-run free house. Sutton Gault lies on the western edge of the Isle of Ely, which until the 17th century stood with its ancient cathedral high above the surrounding waterlogged swamps. Then, in 1630, the Earl of Bedford engaged the Dutch engineer Cornelius Vermuyden to drain the lawless and disease-ridden fens for agricultural use. The Anchor was originally constructed on the bank of the New Bedford River to accommodate Vermuyden's workforce, largely Scottish prisoners of war conscripted by Oliver Cromwell. Despite this rather grim provenance the Anchor has been a pub ever since, whilst the fens themselves have blossomed into a fine agricultural landscape.

The pub has won wide recognition for its stylish en suite accommodation and modern British cuisine. There's an emphasis on seasonal and traditional ingredients and, in summer, meals can be enjoyed on the terrace overlooking the New Bedford River.

Weekday lunch might begin with ham hock and chicken terrine with apple and sultana chutney; poached pear and Stilton bruschetta with rocket pesto; or smoked mackerel, roasted beetroot and horseradish salad. Main course options include sea bass fillet on a warm pumpkin, pine nut and watercress salad; bacon-wrapped stuffed whole quail with baby fondant potatoes, roasted vegetables and a port reduction; and oven-baked butternut squash stuffed with pearl barley, goat's cheese, red onion and Parmesan risotto. Typical dessert choices range from bread and butter pudding with custard, to spiced mulled wine jelly with ginger and cinnamon cream.

**Open** all wk 12-2.30 7-10.30 (Sat 12-3 6.30-11 Sun 12-4 6.30-10) Closed: 25-26 Dec eve **Restaurant** L served Mon-Sat 12-2, Sun 12-2.30 booking required D served Mon-Fri 7-9, Sat 6.30-9.30, Sun 6.30-8.30 booking required ⊕ FREE HOUSE ◀ Pegasus, guest ales. ♈ 12 **Facilities** Garden Parking **Rooms** 4

Save on Hotels. Book at **theAA.com/hotel**

**CAMBRIDGESHIRE** 63 **ENGLAND**

**ELTON** continued

## The Crown Inn ★★★★★ INN ◉

**8 Duck St PE8 6RQ ☎ 01832 280232**
e-mail: inncrown@googlemail.com
dir: *A1(M) junct 17, W on A605 signed Oundle/
Northampton. In 3.5m right to Elton, 0.9m left signed
Nassington. Inn 0.3m on right*

Almost hidden by a towering chestnut tree, The Crown is
a beautiful, 17th-century thatched building opposite the
village green. Chef/owner Marcus Lamb places great
emphasis on the food, using local supplies for everything
from sandwiches to salmon and prawn ravioli in a Thai
broth followed by pork loin layered with mushroom, leek
and Stilton, and served with mashed potato and a
mustard sauce. Annual treats include a May Day hog
roast and a summer beer festival. There are five en suite
bedrooms, each with its own individual appeal.

**Open** all wk noon-11 (Mon 5-11 (BH noon-11)) Closed:
1-7 Jan (Restaurant ) **Bar Meals** L served Tue-Sun 12-2
D served Mon-Sat 6.30-8.45 Av main course £10
**Restaurant** L served Tue-Sun 12-2 booking required
D served Tue-Sat 6.30-8.45 booking required Fixed menu
price fr £12 Av 3 course à la carte fr £30 ⊕ FREE HOUSE
◀ Golden Crown Bitter, Greene King IPA, Adnams, Jeffrey
Hudson Bitter, Black Sheep. **Facilities** Children's portions
Dogs allowed Garden Parking **Rooms** 5

*See advert on page 61*

| **ELY** | **Map 12 TL58** |
|---|---|

### PICK OF THE PUBS

## The Anchor Inn ★★★★ RR ◉ ☐

*See Pick of the Pubs on opposite page*

| **FEN DITTON** | **Map 12 TL46** |
|---|---|

### PICK OF THE PUBS

## Ancient Shepherds ☐

**High St CB5 8ST ☎ 01223 293280 📠 01223 293280**
e-mail: ancientshepherds@hotmail.co.uk
dir: *From A14 take B1047 signed Cambridge/Airport*

Located three miles from Cambridge in the riverside
village of Fen Ditton, this heavily-beamed pub and
restaurant provides a welcome escape for those who
like to enjoy their refreshments without the addition of
music, darts or pool. Named after the ancient order of
Shepherders who used to meet here, it was built

originally as three cottages in 1540. The two bars, a
lounge and a dining room all boast inglenook
fireplaces.

**Open** noon-2.30 6-11 Closed: 25-26 Dec, 1 Jan, Sun
eve, Mon eve **Bar Meals** L served all wk 12-2 Av main
course £7.95 **Restaurant** L served all wk 12-2 D served
Tue-Sat 6.30-9 booking required Av 3 course à la carte
fr £22 ⊕ PUNCH TAVERNS ◀ Adnams Bitter, Greene
King IPA ⚬ Aspall. ☐ 8 **Facilities** Dogs allowed Garden
Parking

| **FENSTANTON** | **Map 12 TL36** |
|---|---|

## King William IV ☐

**High St PE28 9JF ☎ 01480 462467**
e-mail: kingwilliamfenstanton@btconnect.com
dir: *Off A14 junct 27 between Cambridge & Huntingdon*

Three 17th-century cottages make up this rambling old
inn, set beside the clock tower in the heart of the village.
Inside are low beams, a lively bar and the appropriately
named Garden Room. Food ranges from bar food such as
hot baguettes, ciabatta, wraps or sandwiches through to
an evening meal of home-made soup or potted mackerel
with horseradish cream, followed by pan-fried pheasant
breast with confit leg meat, braised pearl barley, red
cabbage and game sauce; and sticky toffee pudding with
pecan and toffee sauce. Now under new ownership.

**Open** all wk Mon-Thu 12-3 5-11 (Fri-Sun all day)
**Bar Meals** L served all wk 12-3 D served all wk 6-9
**Restaurant** L served all wk 12-3 D served all wk 6-9
⊕ GREENE KING ◀ Greene King Abbot Ale & IPA, guest
ales ⚬ Aspall. ☐ 11 **Facilities** Children's portions Dogs
allowed Garden Parking

| **FORDHAM** | **Map 12 TL67** |
|---|---|

### PICK OF THE PUBS

## White Pheasant ☐

**CB7 5LQ ☎ 01638 720414**
e-mail: chef@whitepheasant.com
web: www.whitepheasant.com
dir: *From Newmarket A142 to Ely, approx 5m to
Fordham. Pub on left in village*

This 18th-century building stands in a fenland village
between Ely and Newmarket. In recent years its
considerable appeal has been subtly enhanced by
improvements that preserve its period charm. You can
enjoy locally brewed ale, a glass of wine, home-made

lemonade or strawberryade while perusing the menus.
Food is taken seriously here, with quality, presentation
and flavour taking top priority, using produce sourced
as locally as possible. A tasting menu features up to
ten combinations of ingredients that the kitchen
matches faultlessly. These dishes can often be found
in starters such as goat's cheese and beetroot salad;
or chicken liver parfait. European touches appear in
main courses such as Blythburgh pork belly, Bramley
apple and balsamic baby onion; and fricassée of
mushrooms with tarragon and parmesan. Cox's apple
and rhubarb crumble with vanilla ice cream is among
the more traditional desserts.

**Open** noon-3 6-11 (Sun 12-4) Closed: 26-29 Dec, 1
Jan, Sun eve, Mon **Bar Meals** L served Tue-Sat 12-2.30
booking required Av main course £12 **Restaurant**
L served Tue-Sun 12-2.30 booking required D served
Tue-Sat 6-9.30 booking required Fixed menu price fr
£10 Av 3 course à la carte fr £28 ⊕ FREE HOUSE
◀ Rusty Bucket, Woodforde's Wherry, Nethergate
⚬ Aspall. ☐ 12 **Facilities** Children's portions Garden
Parking

*See advert on page 64*

| **FOWLMERE** | **Map 12 TL44** |
|---|---|

## The Chequers ☐

**High St SG8 7SR ☎ 01763 208369 📠 01763 208944**
e-mail: info@thechequersfowlmere.co.uk
dir: *From M11, A505, 2nd right to Fowlmere. 8m S of
Cambridge, 4m E of Royston*

The pub dates from the 16th century, and was visited by
Samuel Pepys in 1660, but the pub's sign - blue and red
chequers - honours the British and American squadrons
based nearby during World War II. These days The
Chequers is known for its imaginative cooking served in
the galleried restaurant, bar or attractive garden. Their
wide-ranging menu could include a starter of warm
smoked chicken, pancetta and pear mixed leaf salad;
mains of Malaysian chicken or prawn curry with
cardamom rice, or perhaps sautéed breast of guinea fowl
stuffed with confit with sweet potato mash.

**Open** all wk 12-3 6-11 Closed: 25-26 Dec eve & 1 Jan eve
**Bar Meals** L served Mon-Fri 12-2, Sat 12-2.30, Sun 12-3
D served Mon-Sat 7-9.30, Sun 7-9 Av main course £15
**Restaurant** L served Mon-Fri 12-2, Sat 12-2.30, Sun 12-3
D served Mon-Sat 7-9.30, Sun 7-9 Av 3 course à la carte
fr £28 ⊕ FREE HOUSE ◀ Adnams, Buntingford, Sharps,
Fullers ⚬ Aspall. ☐ 19 **Facilities** Garden Parking

---

**GRANTCHESTER**     Map 12 TL45

## The Rupert Brooke ☕

**2 Broadway CB3 9NQ**
☎ 01223 840295   📠 01223 841251
**e-mail:** info@therupertbrooke.com
**dir:** *M11 junct 12, follow Grantchester signs*

Only five minutes from the centre of Cambridge and the M11, yet set in an idyllic location overlooking the meadows close to the River Cam, sits The Rupert Brooke, named after the WWI poet. Inside, you'll find timber beams and winter log fires, with relaxing sofas and tub chairs. Using local, seasonal produce and with regularly changing menus, watch the chefs at work in the theatre-style kitchen, creating their range of modern British dishes - winter squash and sage risotto; Grasmere Farm sausages with creamy mash are typical choices. The pub provides newspapers and Wi-fi.

**Open** all wk 11.30-11 (Fri-Sun 11.30-mdnt) **Bar Meals** L served Mon-Sat 12-3, Sun 12-4 D served Mon-Fri 6-9.30 **Restaurant** L served Mon-Sat 12-3, Sun 12-4 booking required D served Mon-Sat 6-9.30 booking required ⊕ ENTERPRISE INNS ◀ Harveys Sussex Best, Woodforde's Wherry, London Pride, Timothy Taylor Landlord, Sharp's Doom Bar, Flowers IPA ◔ Westons Stowford Press. ☕ 12 **Facilities** Children's menu Children's portions Family room Garden Parking

---

**GREAT CHISHILL**     Map 12 TL43

## The Pheasant ☕

**24 Heydon Rd SG8 8SR** ☎ 01763 838535
**dir:** *Off B1039 between Royston & Saffron Walden*

Stunning views and roaring log fires characterise this traditional, beamed village free house, where Nethergates, Woodforde's Wherry and Greene King ales are some of the choices. There are no gaming machines or piped music to disturb the friendly, sociable bar, and children under 14 are not allowed in. In summer, bird song holds sway in the idyllic pub garden. Freshly-made sandwiches come complete with chips and salad garnish or there is a deal to include home-made soup as well, whilst home-made dishes like four-rib rack of lamb; calves' liver and bacon; and wild mushroom and tarragon linguini cater for larger appetites.

**Open** all wk noon-3 6-11 (all day Sat-Sun) **Bar Meals** L served all wk 12-2 D served all wk 6-9.30 Av main course £14 **Restaurant** L served all wk 12-2 D served all wk 6-9.30 Av 3 course à la carte fr £25 ⊕ FREE HOUSE ◀ Nethergates, Greene King IPA, London Pride, Woodforde's Wherry, Oakham JHB ◔ Stowford Press. ☕ 10 **Facilities** Dogs allowed Garden Parking

---

**HEMINGFORD GREY**     Map 12 TL27

### PICK OF THE PUBS

## The Cock Pub and Restaurant ☕

**47 High St PE28 9BJ**
☎ 01480 463609   📠 01480 461747
**e-mail:** cock@cambscuisine.com
**dir:** *2m S of Huntingdon and 1m E of A14*

Oliver Thain and Richard Bradley's pretty 17th-century pub stands in an idyllic village of thatched, timbered and brick cottages, where you can enjoy peaceful views across the willow-bordered Great Ouse river. It's a world away from the busy A14, just a mile away, and famished travellers should look for the turning for Hemingford Grey as the food on offer at this thriving dining pub is worth the detour – the set lunch menu is a steal. No longer an ordinary village local, the stylishly revamped interior comprises a contemporary bar and restaurant with bare boards, dark or white-painted beams, a pale green and cream decor, wood-burning stoves, and church candles on an eclectic mix of old dining tables. In keeping with the surroundings, cooking is modern British and fresh local produce is used in preparing the short, imaginative carte, while daily deliveries of fresh fish dictate the chalkboard menu choice. A typical meal might kick off with Stilton and walnut terrine with sultana purée and rocket, followed by mustard glazed pork belly with sweet potato, creamed Savoy cabbage and apple and celeriac slaw, and pear and rosemary tarte Tatin with

---

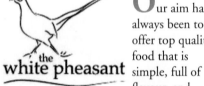

mascarpone and honey. Excellent ales from East Anglian breweries, 14 wines by the glass, and a glorious summer garden complete the attractive picture.

**Open** all wk 11.30-3 6-11 **Restaurant** L served all wk 12-2.30 D served all wk 6.15-9.30 Fixed menu price fr £13 Av 3 course à la carte fr £24 ⊕ FREE HOUSE ◀ Golden Jackal, Wolf Brewery, IPA, Great Oakley, Potbelly Brewery ♻ Cromwell. ♟ 14 **Facilities** Children's portions Dogs allowed Garden Parking

### HILDERSHAM　　　　　Map 12 TL54

## The Pear Tree ♟

**High St CB21 6BU** ☎ 01223 891680
**e-mail:** peartreeinn@btconnect.com
**dir:** *5m E of Cambridge, take A1307 to Haverhill, turn left to Hildersham*

Standing opposite the village green and close to a Roman road, The Pear Tree is ideally situated for walkers. Paul and Sonya Fisher offer home-cooked food from locally-sourced ingredients; vegetarian options are always available, and their expanding range of freshly prepared pies is gaining an enviable local reputation. The present building took over the Pear Tree name in the 19th century, and there's a picture of the former thatched pub in the bar. Look out for the monthly themed menus.

**Open** 12-2.30 6.30-11 (Fri 6-11, Sun 11.30-2.30 6.30-10.30) Closed: Tue & Mon L **Bar Meals** L served Wed-Sun 12-2.30 D served all wk 6.30-9.30 Av main course £8.50 ⊕ FREE HOUSE ◀ Greene King IPA , Abbot Ale. ♟ 12 **Facilities** Children's menu Children's portions Dogs allowed Garden Parking

### HILTON　　　　　Map 12 TL26

## The Prince of Wales ★★★ INN ♟

**Potton Rd PE28 9NG** ☎ 01480 830257
**e-mail:** simon@hiltonpow.co.uk
**dir:** *On B1040 between A14 & A428 S of St Ives*

The Prince of Wales is a traditional, 1830s-built, two-bar village inn with four comfortable bedrooms. Food options range from bar snacks to full meals, among which are grills, fish, curries brought in from a local Indian restaurant, and daily specials, such as lamb hotpot. Home-made puddings include crème brûlée and sherry trifle. The village's 400-year-old grass maze was where locals used to escape the devil.

**Open** 12-2.30 6-11 Closed: Mon L **Bar Meals** L served all wk 12-2 D served all wk 7-9 ⊕ FREE HOUSE ◀ Adnams, Timothy Taylor Landlord, Smoothflow, Worthingtons, guest ales. ♟ 9 **Facilities** Children's menu Children's portions Garden Parking **Rooms** 4

### HINXTON　　　　　Map 12 TL44

## PICK OF THE PUBS

## The Red Lion ★★★★ INN ◉ ♟

**32 High St CB10 1QY**
☎ 01799 530601　📄 01799 531201
**e-mail:** info@redlionhinxton.co.uk
**dir:** *N'bound only: M11 junct 9, towards A11, left onto A1301. Turn left to Hinxton. Or M11 junct 10, take A505 towards A11/Newmarket. At rdbt take 3rd exit onto A1301, right to Hinxton*

With its low ceilings, chesterfield sofas and wooden floor, the bar at this 16th-century pink-washed free house simply oozes charm. Many customers choose to eat informally on settles in the bar, whilst others opt for the spacious, airy restaurant with its lofty ceilings and pegged oak rafters. Guests are encouraged to eat or drink wherever they feel most comfortable – which, in summer, might include the lovely walled garden. Lighter options include freshly made soup, sandwiches and baguettes, supplemented by more substantial pub favourites like steak and Woodforde's Wherry ale pie. A typical à la carte dinner might begin with saffron grilled red mullet, followed by wild mushroom and garden pea ballantine with steamed vegetables; rounded off with poached pear and brandy snap baskets, or the chef's pudding taster plate. Enjoy your meal with a pint of Rusty Bucket or Aspall cider. Eight purpose-built flint and brick guest rooms are set apart from the rest of the pub within a private garden area.

**Open** all wk Sun-Fri 11-3 6-11 (Sat all day) **Bar Meals** L served Mon-Thu 12-2, Fri-Sun 12-2.30 D served Sun-Thu 7-9, Fri-Sat 7-9.30 Av main course £8 **Restaurant** L served Mon-Thu 12-2, Fri-Sun 12-2.30 D served Sun-Thu 7-9, Fri-Sat 7-9.30 Av 3 course à la carte fr £23 ⊕ FREE HOUSE ◀ Adnams, Greene King IPA, Woodforde's Wherry, Rusty Bucket, guest ales ♻ Aspall. ♟ 20 **Facilities** Children's portions Dogs allowed Garden Parking **Rooms** 8

### HOLYWELL　　　　　Map 12 TL37

## The Old Ferryboat Inn ★★★ INN ♟

**Back Ln PE27 4TG** ☎ 01480 463227　📄 01480 463245
**e-mail:** 8638@greeneking.co.uk
**dir:** *From Cambridge on A14 right onto A1096, then right onto A1123, right to Holywell*

Renowned as England's oldest inn, built some time in the 11th century, but with a hostelry history that goes back to the 6th. In a tranquil setting beside the Great Ouse river, The Old Ferryboat has immaculately maintained thatch, white stone walls, cosy interior and bags of charm and character. A pleasant atmosphere - despite the resident ghost of a lovelorn teenager - in which to enjoy grilled bacon and warm poached egg salad; British beef and Ruddles ale pie, mash, seasonal vegetables and onion gravy; or sweet potato, chick pea and spinach curry. There are seven en suite bedrooms available.

**Open** all wk 11-11 (Sun noon-10.30) ◀ Greene King Abbot Ale/IPA, guest ales. ♟ 18 **Facilities** Garden Parking **Rooms** 7

### HORNINGSEA　　　　　Map 12 TL46

## The Crown & Punchbowl

**CB5 9JG** ☎ 01223 860643　📄 01223 441814
**e-mail:** info@thecrownandpunchbowl.co.uk
**dir:** *Telephone for directions*

Soft colours and wooden floors create a warm and cosy atmosphere beneath the tiled roof of this whitewashed free house, just ten minutes from Cambridge city centre. The large restaurant caters equally for business lunches and those with more time to relax; expect roast guinea fowl with braised lentils; stuffed field mushroom with goat's cheese, spinach and beans; and home-made pie with seasonal vegetables. Fresh fish and home-made sausages also feature on the chalkboard menus.

**Open** noon-2.30 6.30-9 Closed: Sun eve & BH eve **Bar Meals** Av main course £11.95 **Restaurant** L served all wk 12-2.30 booking required D served Mon-Sat 6.30-9 booking required Fixed menu price fr £18 Av 3 course à la carte fr £25 ⊕ FREE HOUSE ◀ Hobson's Choice. **Facilities** Garden Parking

### KEYSTON　　　　　Map 11 TL07

## PICK OF THE PUBS

## Pheasant Inn ◉

*See Pick of the Pubs on page 66*

### KIMBOLTON　　　　　Map 12 TL16

## The New Sun Inn ♟

**20-22 High St PE28 0HA**
☎ 01480 860052　📄 01480 869353
**e-mail:** newsuninn@btinternet.com
**dir:** *From A1 N take B645 for 7m. From A1 S take B661 for 7m. From A14 take B660 for 5m*

An impressive array of flowers greets visitors to this 16th-century inn near Kimbolton Castle. As well as being a real ale pub, it offers a good choice of wines by the glass. Dishes from the restaurant menu include king prawns in hot garlic and ginger oil, or whole baked camembert to start, then venison sausages with grain mustard mash or home-made steak and kidney pudding as mains. Lighter meals, such as jacket potatoes or sandwiches are also available.

**Open** all wk 11.30-2.30 6-11 (Sun all day) ◀ Wells Bombardier & Eagle IPA, Greene King Old Speckled Hen, Guest Ale. ♟ 12 **Facilities** Dogs allowed Garden

# PICK OF THE PUBS

## Pheasant Inn

**Village Loop Rd PE28 0RE**
☎ **01832 710241**
**e-mail:**
info@thepheasant-keyston.co.uk
**dir:** *0.5m off A14, clearly signed, 10m W of Huntingdon, 14m E of Kettering*

An unspoilt bar full of oak beams, simple wooden furniture, and warmed by large open fires greets visitors to this 15th-century, thatched English inn. The quiet village setting is in total contrast to the former central London haunts of licensees Jay and Taffeta Scrimshaw: Jay was formerly in charge of the White Swan in Fetter Lane, whilst Taffeta ran Chelsea's busy Japanese restaurant, Itsu. Nevertheless, the metropolitan efficiency shines through. Three distinct dining areas are all comfortable, intimate and relaxed, whilst in fine weather you can enjoy the garden at the rear of the pub or sit on one of the benches out front.

Expect good things of the restaurant, which has an AA Rosette. The cooking style owes much to the South of France, as well as to the fresh seasonal produce delivered by the chef's preferred suppliers, who are listed on the back of the menu. The selection changes daily, but typical starters might include bubble and squeak with fried duck's egg and home-made salad cream; salted calves' tongue with sauce gribiche and watercress; or dressed Dorset crab with blood orange salad. Main course choices range from boiled ham with carrot and swede purée and parsley sauce; through wild mushroom risotto with a poached egg and green salad; to Cornish fish stew with red mullet, cuttlefish, mussels, clams, tomato and saffron. Desserts such as caramel and amaretto parfait with peanut brittle, and lemon tart with thyme yoghurt are typical choices.

There's also a children's menu, featuring favourites such as spaghetti Bolognese or cheese omelette; followed by apple cobbler with Chantilly cream or home-made ice cream.

**Open** all day all week
**Bar Meals** L served Mon-Sat 12-2.30, Sun 12-12.30 booking required D served Mon-Sat 6.30-9.30 booking required Av main course £17.50
**Restaurant** L served all wk 12-2.30 booking required D served all wk 6.30-9.30 booking required Fixed menu price fr £19.95 Av 3 course à la carte fr £30 ◼ Adnams, Village Bike Potton Brewery, Augustinian Nethergate Brewery. **Facilities** Children's menu Dogs allowed Garden Parking

| LITTLE WILBRAHAM | Map 12 TL55 |
|---|---|

## PICK OF THE PUBS

## Hole in the Wall ◉ ♥

**2 High St CB21 5JY ☎ 01223 812282**
e-mail: jenniferleeton@btconnect.com
dir: *Telephone for directions*

As its name implies, there was once a hole in the wall of the main bar – so the local farm workers could collect their beer when only the gentry were allowed in the pub. Nowadays, this heavily timbered 15th-century village pub welcome all-comers for pints of Cambridge Bitter and some first-class modern British cooking prepared from fresh local produce by chef-patron Chris Leeton. In a relaxing and comfortable setting of hop-adorned exposed beams, gleaming brass, roaring log fires and rustic country furnishings, you can choose from imaginative and sensibly-short daily menus. Take chicken liver parfait with forced rhubarb chutney and toasted soda bread or twice-baked broccoli and goat's cheese soufflé with toasted walnut sauce for starters, with main course options ranging from a classic fish pie and seared calves' liver with bubble-and-squeak, pancetta, peppercorn and bandy cream, to baked organic salmon with clam chowder. The one-AA Rosette menu also features puddings like hot banana fritters in cinnamon butter with caramel sauce and rum and raisin ice cream.

**Open** 11.30-3 6.30-11 Closed: 2wks Jan, 25 Dec, Mon (ex BH L), Sun eve **Bar Meals** L served Tue-Sun 12-2 booking required D served Tue-Sat 7-9 booking required Av main course £12 **Restaurant** L served Tue-Sun 12-2 booking required D served Tue-Sat 7-9 booking required Av 3 course à la carte fr £24 ⊕ FREE HOUSE ◀ Woodforde's Wherry, Cambridge Bitter, Sparta, Nelsons Revenge Ŏ Stowford Press. ♥ 10 **Facilities** Children's portions Dogs allowed Garden Parking

| MADINGLEY | Map 12 TL36 |
|---|---|

## PICK OF THE PUBS

## The Three Horseshoes ♥

**High St CB3 8AB ☎ 01954 210221  📄 01954 212043**
e-mail: 3hs@btconnect.com
dir: *M11 junct 13, 1.5m from A14*

This picturesque thatched inn enjoys a charming location; its large garden extends towards meadowland and the local cricket pitch. Inside is a small, bustling bar serving a great selection of beers and a pretty conservatory restaurant. Chef-Patron Richard Stokes is a local from the fens who has eaten his way around the world, and his success can be gauged by the long queues for tables. Richard's own style is a modern take on Italian cuisine, characterised by seasonal and imaginative dishes with intense flavours. After antipasti, you could try gnudi bianco (sheeps' milk ricotta dumplings); or tagliatelle con coniglio (pasta with slow cooked rabbit sauce and sage gremolata), followed by spatchcock poussin marinated with chilli,

black pepper, garlic and lemon; or roast leg of Cornish lamb stuffed with pecorino, mint, anchovy and garlic. Desserts might include pressed chocolate cake with caramel ice cream. Prior booking is advisable.

**Open** all wk 11.30-3 6-11 (Sun 6-9.30) **Bar Meals** L served Mon-Fri 12-2, Sat-Sun 12-2.30 D served all wk 6.30-9.30 Av main course £14 **Restaurant** L served all wk 12-2.30 D served Mon-Sat 6.30-9.30 Av 3 course à la carte fr £30 ⊕ FREE HOUSE ◀ Adnams Bitter, Hook Norton Old Hooky, Smile's Best, Cambridge Hobsons Choice, guest ales Ŏ Stowford Press. ♥ 22 **Facilities** Children's portions Garden Parking

| MILTON | Map 12 TL46 |
|---|---|

## Waggon & Horses

**39 High St CB24 6DF ☎ 01223 860313**
e-mail: winningtons.waggon@ntlworld.com
dir: *A14/A10 junct. Past Tesco, through village, approx 1m set back on left*

Elgood Brewery's most southerly house, the pub is an imposing mock-Tudor building famed for its large collection of hats. As well as a great selection of ales, real cider is also served, from local producer Cassells. A challenging quiz is set on Wednesday nights and baltis are the speciality on Thursdays. All meals are good value and the chilli is particularly recommended. Bar billiards is popular inside, and outside there is a large child-safe garden with a slide and swings, and a pétanque terrain.

**Open** all wk noon-2.30 5-11 (Fri 5-mdnt, Sat noon-3 6-11.30, Sun noon-3 7.30-10.30) **Bar Meals** L served all wk 12-2 D served all wk 7-9 Av main course £5 ⊕ ELGOOD & SONS LTD ◀ Elgoods Cambridge Bitter, Black Dog Mild, Golden Newt, seasonal and guest ales Ŏ Cassells. **Facilities** Children's portions Dogs allowed Garden Parking

| NEWTON | Map 12 TL44 |
|---|---|

## The Queen's Head

**Fowlmere Rd CB22 7PG ☎ 01223 870436**
dir: *6m S of Cambridge on B1368, 1.5m off A10 at Harston, 4m from A505*

Best described as 'quintessentially English', this 17th-century village pub has been run by the same family for nearly 50 years. They continue to steadfastly ban fruit machines and piped music from the two small bars. Keeping things simple, lunches are limited to home-made soup, Aga-baked potatoes, and sandwiches. In the evening it's just soup and cold platters. There's no specials board since, as the landlord says, 'We have no specialist'! There is a green opposite where customers can eat and drink.

**Open** all wk 11.30-2.30 6-11 (Sun noon-2.30 7-10.30) Closed: 25-26 Dec **Bar Meals** L served all wk 12-2.15 D served all wk 7-9.30 Av main course £5 ⊕ FREE HOUSE ◀ Adnams Southwold, Broadside, Fisherman, Bitter, Regatta Ŏ Crones. **Facilities** Children's portions Family room Dogs allowed Parking **Notes** ⊛

| PETERBOROUGH | Map 12 TL19 |
|---|---|

## The Brewery Tap

**80 Westgate PE1 2AA**
**☎ 01733 358500  📄 01733 310022**
e-mail: brewerytap@hotmail.com
dir: *Opposite bus station*

This is the home of multi-award-winning Oakham Ales, moved here from their home in Rutland when Peterborough's spacious old labour exchange opened its doors as the Brewery Tap in 1998. Visitors to this striking pub can see the day-to-day running of the brewery through a glass wall spanning half the length of the bar. As if the appeal of the beer range were not enough, Thai chefs beaver away producing delicious snacks, soups, salads, stir-fries and curries. Look out for live music nights.

**Open** all day all wk noon-11pm (Fri-Sat noon-mdnt) Closed: 25-26 Dec, 1 Jan **Bar Meals** L served Sun-Thu 12-2.30, Fri-Sat 12-10.30 D served Sun-Thu 6-9.30, Fri-Sat 12-10.30 **Restaurant** L served Sun-Thu 12-2.30, Fri-Sat 12-10.30 D served Sun-Thu 6-9.30, Fri-Sat 12-10.30 ⊕ FREE HOUSE ◀ Oakham Inferno, Jeffery Hudson Bitter, Bishops Farewell, White Dwarf, Elgoods Black Dog, 7 guest ales Ŏ Westons 1st Quality. **Facilities** Children's portions Dogs allowed

## Charters Bar & East Restaurant

**Upper Deck, Town Bridge PE1 1FP**
**☎ 01733 315700 & 315702 (bkgs)  📄 01733 315700**
e-mail: charters.manager@oakagroup.com
dir: *A1/A47 towards Wisbech, 2m for city centre & town bridge (River Nene). Barge moored at Town Bridge (west side)*

Moored in the heart of Peterborough on the River Nene, this 176-foot converted barge promises 'brews, blues and fine views'. It motored from Holland across the North Sea in 1991, and is now a haven for real ale and cider lovers. Twelve hand pumps dispense a continually changing repertoire of brews, while Friday and Saturday nights bring live blues music. The East part of the name applies to the oriental restaurant on the upper deck which offers a comprehensive selection of Asian dishes.

**Open** all day all wk noon-11pm (Fri-Sat noon-2am) Closed: 25-26 Dec, 1 Jan **Bar Meals** L served all wk 12-2.30 Av main course £5.95 **Restaurant** L served Mon-Sat 12-2.30, Sun 12-3.30 booking required D served Sun-Thu 5.30-10.30, Fri-Sat 5.30-11 booking required Fixed menu price fr £10 Av 3 course à la carte fr £17.95 ⊕ FREE HOUSE ◀ Oakham JHB, Oakham Bishops Farewell, Abbeydale Absolution, Elgoods Black Dog Ŏ Westons Old Rosie, Westons Traditional Draught Scrumpy. **Facilities** Dogs allowed Garden Parking

## REACH
Map 12 TL56

### Dyke's End ☆

CB25 0JD ☎ 01638 743816
dir: *Telephone for directions*

In 1996/7 villagers saved this pub from closure and ran it as a co-operative until 2003, when it was bought by Frank Feehan, who has further refurbished and extended it. Frank's additions include the Devil's Dyke micro-brewery, which produces four real ales, including a strong mild. The pub's local reputation for the quality of its food means restaurant booking is strongly advised, particularly at weekends. A fenced front garden overlooks the village green.

**Open** Mon-Fri 12-2.30 6-11 (Sat-Sun noon-11) Closed: Mon L **Bar Meals** L served all wk 12-2 D served all wk 7-9 ⊕ FREE HOUSE ◀ Devil's Dyke micro-brewery beer, Woodforde's Wherry, Adnams Bitter ♂ Aspall, Old Rosie. ☆ 8 **Facilities** Play area Family room Dogs allowed Garden Parking

## STAPLEFORD
Map 12 TL45

### The Rose at Stapleford ☆

81 London Rd CB22 5DE ☎ 01223 843349
e-mail: paulnbeer@aol.com
dir: *Telephone for directions*

Having made a success of The George and Dragon at Elsworth, Paul and Karen Beer weave their magic at The Rose, a traditional village pub close to Cambridge and Duxford Imperial War Museum. Expect a stylish interior, replete with low beams and inglenook fireplaces, and extensive menus that draw on local Suffolk produce, particularly meat, with fish from Lowestoft. Typical dishes take in steak and kidney pudding, ale battered haddock or cod fillet, and braised lamb shank.

**Open** 12-2.30 6-11 Closed: Sun eve **Bar Meals** L served all wk 12-2.30 D served all wk 6-9.30 Av main course £12 food served all day **Restaurant** L served all wk 12-2.30 D served all wk 6-9.30 Fixed menu price fr £11 Av 3 course à la carte fr £20 food served all day ◀ IPA, Tribute, Guest Ale ♂ Aspall. ☆ 13 **Facilities** Dogs allowed Garden Parking

## STILTON
Map 12 TL18

### PICK OF THE PUBS

### The Bell Inn Hotel ★★★ HL ☺ ☆

Great North Rd PE7 3RA
☎ 01733 241066 ▤ 01733 245173
e-mail: reception@thebellstilton.co.uk
dir: *From A1(M) junct 16 follow signs for Stilton. Hotel on main road in village centre*

Steeped in history and reputedly the oldest coaching inn on the Great North Road, the Bell's impressive 16th-century stone façade hides a fine interior that boasts original features, including a grand stone fireplace in the Village Bar. In its time the inn has hosted highwayman Dick Turpin, Lord Byron and, more recently, Clark Gable and Joe Louis, who were stationed nearby in World War II. The Bell is also famous as the birthplace of Stilton cheese, which was first served here in the early 1700s. Imaginative modern British dishes are served in the atmospheric, galleried restaurant, the set menu offering pumpkin, Stilton and rosemary soup, chargrilled lamb with pea and mint purée and redcurrant jus, and prune and Armagnac tart. Tuck into pasta with crab and chorizo or steak and kidney suet pudding in the more informal bistro. Note the magnificent inn sign, it's a replica of the original weighing two and three quarter tonnes. There are 22 comfortable en suite rooms available.

**Open** all wk noon-2.30 6-11 (Sat-Sun noon-11) Closed: 25 Dec **Bar Meals** L served Mon-Sat 12-2.30, Sun all day D served all wk 6-9.30 Av main course £10 **Restaurant** L served Sun-Fri 12-2 booking required D served Mon-Sat 7-9.30 booking required Fixed menu price fr £19.50 Av 3 course à la carte fr £29.50 ⊕ FREE HOUSE ◀ Greene King Abbot Ale, Oakham JHB, Fuller's London Pride, Greene King IPA, Brewers Gold. ☆ 8 **Facilities** Children's menu Children's portions Garden Parking **Rooms** 22

## STRETHAM
Map 12 TL57

### The Lazy Otter ☆

Cambridge Rd CB6 3LU ☎ 01353 649780
e-mail: thelazyotter@btconnect.com
dir: *Telephone for directions*

Just off the A10 between Ely and Cambridge, the Lazy Otter stands overlooking the marina beside the River Great Ouse. There's been a pub on this site since the 18th century, and this one now has new owners. Today, the large beer garden and riverside restaurant are popular summer attractions. Menus might feature steak and kidney pudding, seafood tagliatelle, or Thai green curry (both chicken a vegetarian varieties) plus grills, burgers, baguettes and Sunday roasts. Perhaps enjoy your meal with a glass of locally produced, award-winning Pickled Pig cider.

**Open** all day all wk 11-11 (Sun noon-10.30pm) **Bar Meals** L served Mon-Sat 12-3, Sun 12-6 booking required D served Mon-Sat 6-9 booking required Av main course £9 **Restaurant** L served Mon-Sat 12-3, Sun 12-6 booking required D served Mon-Sat 6-9 booking required Av 3 course à la carte fr £20 ⊕ FREE HOUSE ◀ Greene King, IPA, Guest ales ♂ Pickled Pig. ☆ 10 **Facilities** Children's menu Children's portions Play area Garden Parking

## CHESHIRE

## ALDFORD
Map 15 SJ45

### PICK OF THE PUBS

### The Grosvenor Arms ☆

Chester Rd CH3 6HJ
☎ 01244 620228 ▤ 01244 620247
e-mail: grosvenor.arms@brunningandprice.co.uk
dir: *On B5130, S of Chester*

Described by its owners as a 'large, rather austere Victorian governess of a building which looks a little ungainly from the road side', the Grosvenor was the work of a locally infamous mid-Victorian architect who, in the name of progress, destroyed many fine medieval buildings in and around Chester. It is endearing nonetheless, and viewed from the garden it's 'a delight of higgledy-piggledy rooflines and soft, warm Cheshire brick'. The spacious, open-plan interior includes an airy conservatory and a panelled, book-filled library. On the bistro-style menu are a range of sandwiches and unusual starters such as crispy chilli beef, bok choi and sesame salad; and open lasagne of seared scallops and king prawns with a saffron and spinach sauce. Main courses range from pan-fried sea bream fillets with shallot risotto, tomato, pancetta and clam sauce, to ham (served cold) with free range eggs and hand-cut chips. Sandwiches and light bites are also available, with a great selection of beers to wash it all down. Desserts include warm apple pie with custard or cinnamon ice cream; and Belgian waffle with butterscotch ice cream and butterscotch sauce. An outside terrace leads into a small but pleasing garden which, in turn, takes you out to the village green.

**Open** all day all wk **Bar Meals** Av main course £10.95 food served all day ⊕ FREE HOUSE ◀ Weetwood-Eastgate, Phoenix, Brunning & Price Original, Thwaites Original, guest ales. ☆ 20 **Facilities** Children's portions Dogs allowed Garden Parking

# PICK OF THE PUBS

## The Bhurtpore Inn 🍷

**ASTON**      Map 15 SJ64

**Wrenbury Rd CW5 8DQ**
☎ **01270 780917**
**e-mail:** simonbhurtpore@yahoo.co.uk
**dir:** *Just off A530 between Nantwich & Whitchurch. Turn towards Wrenbury at x-rds in village*

A pub since at least 1778, when it was called the Queen's Head. It subsequently became the Red Lion, but it was Lord Combermere's success at the Siege of Bhurtpore in India in 1826 that inspired the name that has stuck. Simon and Nicky George came across it in 1991, boarded-up and stripped-out. Simon is a direct descendant of Joyce George, who leased the pub from the Combermere estate in 1849, so was motivated by his family history to take on the hard work of restoring the interior; the pub reopened in early 1992. Since then, 'award winning' hardly does justice to the accolades heaped upon this hostelry.

In the bar, eleven ever-changing real ales are always available, mostly from local micro-breweries, as are real ciders, continental draught lagers and around 150 of the world's bottled beers. An annual beer festival, reputedly Cheshire's largest, is in its sixteenth year, with around 130 real ales to be sampled. Beers are only part of the story; the pub has been short-listed five times for the 'National Whisky Pub of the Year' award, and the soft drinks menu is as long as your arm.

Recognition extends to the kitchen too, where unfussy dishes of classic pub fare are acceptable to both the palate and the wallet. Among the hearty British ingredients you'll find seasonal game, such as venison haunch on cabbage with smoked bacon and cream; and rabbit loin with a pork and black pudding stuffing. As you might expect, curries and balti dishes are always to be found on the blackboard; these usually comprise at least six options, based on beef, mutton and goat, as well as vegetables and quorn.

Vintage vehicles bring their owners here on the first Thursday of the month, and folk musicians play on the third Tuesday.

**Open** all wk 12-2.30 6.30-11.30 (Fri-Sat 12-12, Sun 12-11) Closed: 25-26 Dec, 1 Jan **Bar Meals** L served Mon-Fri 12-2 D served Mon-Fri 6.30-9.30 (Sat 12-9.30, Sun 12-9) Av main course £10.50 **Restaurant** L served Mon-Fri 12-2 D served Mon-Fri 6.30-9.30 (Sat 12-9.30, Sun 12-9) Av 3 course à la carte fr £19 ⊕ FREE HOUSE ◼ Salopian Golden Thread, Abbeydale Absolution, Weetwood Oasthouse Gold, Copper Dragon Golden Pippin, Townhouse Audley Gold ♂ Cheddar Valley, Moonshine, Cheshire. ♟ 11 **Facilities** Children's menu Dogs allowed Garden Parking

## ASTON — Map 15 SJ64

### PICK OF THE PUBS

**The Bhurtpore Inn** ☑

*See Pick of the Pubs on page 69*

## BOLLINGTON — Map 16 SJ97

### The Church House Inn ★★★ INN

Church St SK10 5PY
☎ 01625 574014 📠 01625 562026
e-mail: info@thechurchhouseinn-bollington.co.uk
dir: *From A34 take A538 towards Macclesfield. Through Prestbury, then follow Bollington signs*

Exposed beams, log fires and agricultural decorations lend a homely feel to this stone-built village free house, which hit the headlines when it was bought by a group of local residents. The varied menu includes home-made soup, the inn's own sausages and pies, and other traditional British favourites. Vegetarian options feature on the daily specials board. The pub also has a small enclosed beer garden. Comfortable, well-equipped accommodation is available.

**Open** all wk 12-3 5.30-11 (Sun 12-10.30) **Bar Meals** L served Mon-Sat 12-2, Sun 12-8 D served Mon-Sat 6-9.30, Sun 12-8 Av main course £10.50 ⊕ FREE HOUSE ◀ Adnams, Timothy Taylor Golden Best, Beartown. **Facilities** Children's menu Children's portions Parking **Rooms** 5

## BUNBURY — Map 15 SJ55

### PICK OF THE PUBS

**The Dysart Arms** ☑

Bowes Gate Rd CW6 9PH
☎ 01829 260183 📠 01829 261286
e-mail: dysart.arms@brunningandprice.co.uk
dir: *Between A49 & A51, by Shropshire Union Canals*

Built as a farmhouse in the mid-18th century, and licensed since the late 1800s, this is a quintessentially English village pub, right down to its pretty garden with views of two castles and the parish church next door. Around its central bar are several airy rooms for eating or just drinking with solid wood furnishings, bare floors, open fires and a couple of large bookcases. Home-grown herbs are used in a please-all menu, which opens with starters such as smoked salmon on a potato cake with a poached egg; crayfish cocktail; and farmhouse terrine with home-made chutney. Among the main courses are beef, ale and tarragon pie with red cabbage and roasted new potatoes; and pan-fried sea bass fillet, smoked paprika and hazelnut risotto and roasted fennel. Decadent desserts might include bread and butter pudding with orange sauce and clotted cream, and golden syrup sponge and custard; or select from the British farmhouse cheese board.

**Open** all day all wk 11.30-11 (Sun noon-10.30)
**Bar Meals** L served all wk D served all wk food served

all day **Restaurant** L served all wk D served all wk food served all day ⊕ FREE HOUSE ◀ Weetwood Eastgate ☼ Stowford Press. ☑ 17 **Facilities** Children's portions Dogs allowed Garden Parking

## BURLEYDAM — Map 15 SJ64

### The Combermere Arms ☑

SY13 4AT ☎ 01948 871223 📠 01948 661371
e-mail: combermere.arms@brunningandprice.co.uk
dir: *From Whitchurch take A525 towards Nantwich, at Newcastle/Audlem/Woore sign, turn right at junct. Pub 100yds on right*

Popular with local shoots, walkers and town folk alike, this busy 17th-century inn retains great character and warmth. Three roaring fires complement the wealth of oak, nooks and crannies, pictures and old furniture. Dishes range from light bites like Welsh rarebit with leeks, bacon and tomatoes to venison sausages with mash, cabbage and cranberry gravy; roast guinea fowl with Puy lentils; and raspberry Bakewell tart and custard. There is a great choice of real ales and ciders, an informative wine list and very impressive cheese list.

**Open** all wk 11.30-11 **Bar Meals** Av main course £9.45 food served all day **Restaurant** food served all day ⊕ FREE HOUSE ◀ Woodlands Oak Beauty, Weetwood Cheshire Cat, Thornbridge Jaipur Monsoon, St Austells Tribute, Storm Hurricane Hubert ☼ Weston Stowford Press, Thatchers Gold, Inch's Stonehouse. ☑ 28 **Facilities** Children's portions Dogs allowed Garden Parking

## BURWARDSLEY — Map 15 SJ55

### PICK OF THE PUBS

**The Pheasant Inn** ★★★★★ INN

*See Pick of the Pubs on page 71*

## CHESTER — Map 15 SJ46

### PICK OF THE PUBS

**Albion Inn**

*See Pick of the Pubs on page 72*

### Old Harkers Arms ☑

1 Russell St CH1 5AL
☎ 01244 344525 📠 01244 344812
e-mail: harkers.arms@brunningandprice.co.uk
dir: *Follow steps down from City Road onto canal path*

A buzzy meeting place with the feel of a gentlemen's club, this former Victorian chandler's warehouse on the Shropshire Union Canal is one of Chester's more unusual pubs. The bar offers over 100 malt whiskies (there's a helpful booklet to aid decision making), over 15 wines by the glass, and hand pumps dispensing regular and guest ales mostly from local micro-breweries. The daily-changing menu runs from light dishes such as breaded

tiger prawns with pineapple salsa, through to main courses of braised lamb shoulder or Gloucester Old Spot sausages.

**Open** all day all wk 11.30-11 (Sun noon-10.30) Closed: 25 Dec **Bar Meals** Av main course £11.25, à la carte fr £21.45 food served all day ⊕ FREE HOUSE ◀ Weetwood Cheshire Cat, Flowers Original, Titanic Stout, Spitting Feathers, Brunning and Price Original ☼ Westons Organic, Scrumpy, Old Rosie. ☑ 15 **Facilities** Dogs allowed

## CHOLMONDELEY — Map 15 SJ55

### PICK OF THE PUBS

**The Cholmondeley Arms** INN ☑

SY14 8HN ☎ 01829 720300 📠 01829 720123
e-mail: info@cholmondeleyarms.co.uk
dir: *On A49, between Whitchurch & Tarporley*

Formerly the village school built in 1862, this elegant gastro-pub is located in quiet Cheshire countryside adjoining the parks and gardens of historic Cholmondeley Castle, home to Lord and Lady Cholmondeley, and is also close to the Sandstone Trail, the Shropshire Union Canal, Beeston Castle and historic Chester. All food is freshly prepared, using local produce wherever possible, and is offered from a daily-changing menu. You might start with home-cured salt beef fritter, poached egg and brown sauce; hot crab pâté with brown toast; or foie gras stuffed mushrooms with Guinness rarebit. Main courses range from lamb rump, harissa with sultana and herb couscous; Cornish Black bream fillet, olive mash and Chantenay carrots; steak, kidney and oyster pudding, dauphinoise potatoes and onion gravy. Perhaps try the Headmaster's Lunch – sliced rare ribeye steak in a baguette with lettuce, mustard and mayonnaise. Puddings are old favourites such as syrup tart, Bakewell tart and sticky toffee pudding. Accommodation is available if you would like to stay over.

**Open** all day all wk Closed: 25 Dec **Bar Meals** L served Mon-Fri 12-2.30, Sat-Sun 12-9.30 D served Mon-Fri 6-10, Sat-Sun 12-9.30 Av main course £10 ⊕ FREE HOUSE ◀ Weetwood Eastgate Ale, Salopian Gold, Black Sheep, Brakspear. ☑ 10 **Facilities** Children's menu Children's portions Dogs allowed Garden Parking **Rooms** 6

# PICK OF THE PUBS

## The Pheasant Inn ★★★★★INN

**BURWARDSLEY**   Map 15 SJ55

**CH3 9PF**
☎ **01829 770434**   📠 **01829 771097**
**e-mail:** info@thepheasantinn.co.uk
**web:** www.thepheasantinn.co.uk
**dir:** *A41 (Chester to Whitchurch), after 4m left to Burwardsley. Follow 'Cheshire Workshops' signs*

Tucked away in a peaceful corner of rural Cheshire, this 300-year-old half-timbered former farmhouse is just quarter of an hour's drive from historic Chester. Standing way up in the Peckforton Hills, the views from the terrace are magnificent. Since it became an alehouse in the mid-17th century, only five families have been licensees.

Four real ales are always on tap in the wooden-floored bar as well as a list of well-chosen wines, where hefty beams support the storey above; drinks are also to be enjoyed in the stone-flagged conservatory and flower-filled courtyard. The wholesome food is good using the best of local and free range produce, the service friendly and relaxed, and children are welcome during the day.

The menu breaks down into nibbles, deli-boards and sandwiches for those who want to make a quick pit-stop; a selection for those who fancy eating gastro-pub style; and principally British and European main courses for those who want something more substantial. Among these are beer-battered North Sea haddock, mushy peas and hand-cut chips; pan fried lambs' liver with Lyonnaise potatoes, crispy bacon and oatmeal cabbage; slow roasted belly pork with choucroute, champ mash and apple jus; and vine tomato tart and red onion tart with baked goat's cheese, balsamic and red pepper dressing.

Puddings follow traditional lines with sticky toffee pudding, toffee sauce and ice cream; and warm cherry and Kirsch tart with crème anglaise. There's also a selection of ice creams made by Gog's Cheshire Farm just down the road. If the thought of driving home threatens to spoil your evening, why not stay in one of the en suite country-style bedrooms.

**Open** all day all wk **Bar Meals** L served all wk (no food Mon 3-6) D served all wk (no food Mon 3-6) Av main course £11.95 food served all day
**Restaurant** L served all wk (no food Mon 3-6) D served all wk (no food Mon 3-6) food served all day ⊕ FREE HOUSE
◗ Weetwood Old Dog, Eastgate, Best, guest Bitter ♂ Stowford Press.
**Facilities** Children's menu Dogs allowed Garden Parking **Rooms** 12

# PICK OF THE PUBS

## Albion Inn

**CHESTER**        Map 15 SJ46

**Park St CH1 1RN** ☎ **01244 340345**
**e-mail:** christina.mercer@tesco.net
**web:** www.albioninnchester.co.uk
**dir:** *In city centre adjacent to Citywalls &
Newgate*

The home fires still burn on winter
nights at this living memorial to the
Great War of 1914-18. With its splendid
cast-iron fireplaces and original three-
room layout, the pub is filled with sepia
photographs and prints, whilst leather
sofas, enamelled advertisements and
artefacts from the First World War
complete the period look. The lounge
wallpaper was designed on the first day
of the Great War, and other objects of
interest include a 1928 Steck Duo Art
player piano, which still performs on
occasions. The Albion is the creation of
Michael Mercer, who has run Chester's
last Victorian corner pub in the shadow
of the city's Roman wall for over 37
years.

'Trench rations' are locally and
regionally sourced wherever possible.
Expect lunchtime choices like Great
British butties filled with cold ham and
tomato; or Stilton, walnut and celery; as
well as a selection of wholemeal club
sandwiches. Hot dishes range from
savoury minced beef steak and tatties;
to roast Cheshire turkey and savoury
stuffing with cranberry and apple sauce,
creamed potatoes and fresh vegetables.

The house speciality is Tunstall
Staffordshire oatcakes with a range of
fillings that includes bangers, beans
and bacon; and McSween's haggis with
melted cheese. Meanwhile, the specials
board might feature cold poached
salmon with potato salad; organic
chicken Madras curry and basmati rice
with mango and ginger chutney; or
naturally smoked haddock kedgeree
with a mild curry sauce.

There are four cask ales on tap, a good
range of malts and a decent list of New
World wines. Please note that – in true
wartime spirit - this is a grown-ups only
pub.

**Open** all wk 12-3, Tue-Fri 5-11, Sat
6-11, Sun 7-10.30, Mon 5.30-11 Closed:
25-26 Dec, 1-2 Jan **Bar Meals** L served
all wk 12-2 D served Mon-Sat 5-8
Av main course £10.50
**Restaurant** L served all wk 12-2 D
served Mon-Sat 5-8 Fixed menu price fr
£10.50 ⊕ PUNCH TAVERNS ◀ Black
Sheep, Batemans, Deuchars, Adnams,
Guest ales ♻ Westons Organic bottled
cider. **Facilities** Dogs allowed **Notes** ⌘

Save on Hotels. Book at **theAA.com/hotel**

**CHESHIRE** 73 **ENGLAND**

## CONGLETON Map 16 SJ86

### The Plough At Eaton ★★★★ INN ♥

**Macclesfield Rd, Eaton CW12 2NH**
☎ 01260 280207 📠 01260 298458
**e-mail:** theploughinn@hotmail.co.uk
**web:** www.theploughinnateaton.co.uk
**dir:** On A536 (Congleton to Macclesfield road)

Like a giant jigsaw puzzle, an ancient Welsh barn was transported here in hundreds of pieces to become a marvellously atmospheric restaurant adjoining this Elizabethan inn. From the specials menu come poached fresh salmon and prawn salad; chicken Madras with rice; and lamb Henry with mash. The carte offers lightly grilled turbot with lemon butter, and fillet steak cooked at the table. Apple crumble and custard and chocolate fudge cake are typical desserts. There are 17 modern annexe en suite bedrooms available, and gardens with sitting areas.

**Open** all day all wk 11am-mdnt **Bar Meals** L served Mon-Thu 12-2.30, Fri-Sun 12-9.30 D served Mon-Sat 6-9.30, Fri-Sun 12-9.30 **Restaurant** L served Mon-Thu 12-2.30, Fri-Sun 12-9.30 D served Mon-Sat 6-9.30, Fri-Sun 12-9.30 ⊕ FREE HOUSE ◀ Boddingtons, Hydes, Moore Houses, Storm Brew, Guest ales. ♥ 10 **Facilities** Dogs allowed Garden Parking **Rooms** 17

## GAWSWORTH Map 16 SJ86

### Harrington Arms ♥ NEW

**Church Ln SK11 9RJ** ☎ 01260 223325
**dir:** From Macclesfield take A536 towards Congleton. Turn left for Gawsworth

A truly memorable old pub, part of a three-storey Cheshire brick farmhouse, with a warren of quirky little rooms, open fires, rustic furnishings; the hum of locals' conversations diverting from its bucolic location near to Gawsworth's wonderful old church, village ponds and magnificent half-timbered hall. Good, simple, filling pub food, from sandwiches, sausage and mash to home-made pies using the wealth of Cheshire produce available locally. Autumn sees the annual conker championship here.

**Open** all wk Mon-Sat noon-3 5-11 Sun noon-4 7-11 **Bar Meals** L served Mon-Sat 12-2.30 Sun 12-3.30 D served Mon-Sat 5-8.30 Av main course £6.50 ⊕ ROBINSONS ◀ Unicorn, Hatters, Robinsons Seasonal Ale, Guinness ♻ Stowford Press. ♥ 8 **Facilities** Children's portions Dogs allowed Garden Parking

## HANDLEY Map 15 SJ45

### The Calveley Arms

**Whitchurch Rd CH3 9DT**
☎ 01829 770619 📠 01829 770901
**e-mail:** calveleyarms@btconnect.com
**dir:** 5m S of Chester, signed from A41. Follow signs for Handley & Aldersey Green Golf Course

Built as a coaching in the early 17th century, the smart black-and-white pub stands opposite the church with views of the distant Welsh hills. Chock full of old timbers, jugs, pots, pictures, prints and ornaments, the rambling bars provide an atmospheric setting in which to sample some good beers and pub food. Perhaps salmon teriyaki; home-made steak and kidney pie; moules marinière; or Gressingham duck breast with pink rhubarb and ginger sauce.

**Open** all wk noon-3 6-11 (Sun 7-11) **Bar Meals** food served all day **Restaurant** food served all day ⊕ ENTERPRISE INNS ◀ Castle Eden Ale, Marston's Pedigree, Black Bull, Bombardier, Greene King IPA. **Facilities** Children's portions Play area Dogs allowed Garden Parking

## HAUGHTON MOSS Map 15 SJ55

### The Nags Head ♥

**Long Ln CW6 9RN** ☎ 01829 260265 📠 01829 261364
**e-mail:** roryk1@btinternet.com
**dir:** Exit A49 S of Tarporley at Beeston/Haughton sign into Long Ln. 1.75m to pub

Dating back to 1629, this timbered black and white free house was once the village smithy. Inside you'll find low ceilings, crooked beams, exposed brickwork and real fires. Outside, there's a bowling green and spacious gardens. Rory and Debbie are committed to providing quality food and service in a warm and friendly atmosphere. The extensive menu offers wholesome, traditional dishes such as poached salmon supreme; steak, ale and mushroom pie; and vegetable cannelloni. More imaginative dishes are featured on the 'Chef's Creative Journey', and there's a specials board, too.

**Open** all day all wk 11am-mdnt **Bar Meals** L served all wk 12-10 D served all wk 12-10 Av main course £10 food served all day **Restaurant** L served all wk 12-10 D served all wk 12-10 Fixed menu price fr £8.85 Av 3 course à la carte fr £20 food served all day ⊕ FREE HOUSE ◀ Flowers IPA, Sharp's Doom Bar, guest ales. **Facilities** Children's menu Children's portions Play area Dogs allowed Garden Parking

## HUXLEY Map 15 SJ56

### Stuart's Table at the Farmer's Arms ♥

**Huxley Ln CH3 9BG** ☎ 01829 781342 📠 01829 781794
**e-mail:** stuart@stuartstable.com
**dir:** Telephone for directions

A pub since 1802, the Farmer's Arms stands in beautiful Cheshire countryside and prides itself on its menu reflecting the seasons and using the best produce available. It specialises in quality British steaks, served with an appealing range of sauces and accompaniments. Other choices might include cod with cassoulet of white beans, roast lamb rump or wild mushroom risotto. Lighter lunchtime bites include tapas or open sandwiches served with hand-cut chips. There are monthly fine dining evenings and thirty wines by the glass.

**Open** all wk noon-3 5-11 (Fri-Sat noon-mdnt, Sun noon-10.30, Mon 5-11) **Bar Meals** L served Tue-Sat 12-2 Av main course £11 **Restaurant** L served Tue-Sat 12-2, Sun 12-4 D served Tue-Thu 6.30-9, Fri-Sat 6.30-9.30 booking required Fixed menu price fr £10 Av 3 course à la carte fr £25 ⊕ ADMIRAL TAVERNS ◀ Black Sheep, Adnams, guest ale. ♥ 30 **Facilities** Children's menu Children's portions Dogs allowed Garden Parking

## KETTLESHULME Map 16 SJ97

### Swan Inn NEW

**SK23 7QU** ☎ 01663 732943
**e-mail:** the.swan.kettleshulme@googlemail.co.uk
**dir:** On B5470 between Whaley Bridge (2m) and Macclesfield (5m)

A glorious, tiny 15th-century village inn huddled in the shadow of the impressive Windgather Rocks crags in the Cheshire Peak District. A consortium of locals bought the place in 2004 to save it from closure; now safe and thriving in private hands, an eclectic, robust menu is strong on seafood, including monkfish Thai curry and Dorset char, as well as local farm beef and pork dishes. From the cosy little bar in this cottagey pub, a generous array of local craft brewery beers keeps ramblers and locals very contented.

**Open** all wk Mon 5-11 Tue 12-3 5-11 Wed-Sun all day Closed: 25-26 Dec, 1 Jan, Mon L **Bar Meals** L served Tue 12-2, Wed 12-9, Thu-Fri 12-7, Sat 12-9, Sun 12-4 booking required D served Mon-Tue 6.30-8.30, Wed 12-9, Thu-Fri 12-7, Sat 12-9 Av main course £12.50 **Restaurant** Fixed menu price fr £11.50 Av 3 course à la carte fr £20 ⊕ FREE HOUSE ◀ Marstons, Marble, Thornbridge, Phoenix. **Facilities** Children's portions Dogs allowed Garden

## KNUTSFORD
Map 15 SJ77

### PICK OF THE PUBS

## The Dog Inn ★★★★ INN ♚

**Well Bank Ln, Over Peover WA16 8UP**
☎ 01625 861421 📠 01625 864800
**e-mail:** thedoginnpeover@btconnect.com
**web:** www.doginn-overpeover.co.uk
**dir:** S from Knutsford take A50. Turn into Stocks Ln at
The Whipping Stocks pub. 2m

Colourful flowerbeds, tubs and hanging baskets in
summer create quite a setting for the timbered Dog
Inn, which has served ale to locals and travellers since
the turn of the 19th century. In its time it has been a
row of cottages, a grocer's, a shoemaker's and a farm,
but now faithful regulars and visitors come for its
range of cask ales from small regional breweries, for
its large array of malt whiskies, and for a classic
English menu prepared from ingredients sourced
largely within a six-mile radius. Starters include
breaded crab and salmon fishcakes, and Manx kippers
served with brown bread and butter. Typical main
courses are macaroni cheese; stir-fried chicken; and
deep-fried cod in home-made beer batter. Ever popular
desserts include chocolate fudge cake and bread and
butter pudding. If a 'lite bite' is all you need to soak up
your pint of Weetwood Best, choose from the excellent
range of sandwiches and hot baguettes.

**Open** all wk 11.30-3 4.30-11 (Sat-Sun all day)
**Bar Meals** L served all wk 12-2.30 D served all wk 6-9
Av main course £12 **Restaurant** L served all wk
12-2.30 D served all wk 6-9 Av 3 course à la carte fr
£18 ⊕ FREE HOUSE ◀ Hydes Traditional Bitter,
Weetwood Best, Skipton Brewery, Moorhouses. ♟ 10
**Facilities** Children's menu Children's portions Dogs
allowed Garden Parking **Rooms** 6

## LACH DENNIS
Map 15 SJ77

## The Duke of Portland

**Penny's Ln CW9 7SY** ☎ 01606 46264
**e-mail:** info@dukeofportland.com
**web:** www.dukeofportland.com
**dir:** M6 junct 19, A556 towards Northwich. Left onto
B5082 to Lach Dennis

Expect to eat well at this family-run pub set in the heart
of the glorious Cheshire plain. The sunny, landscaped
garden complements the attractive building, and there is
a genuine commitment to local producers, artisans and
farmers, many of whom have never supplied other
commercial customers. Menus might include 'Belle
Epoque's' black pudding or goat's cheese and tomato tart
for a light bite; The Duke's legendary fish and chips; or
secret recipe black pepper and pork sausages will satisfy
larger appetites.

**Open** all day all wk **Bar Meals** L served all wk 12-3
booking required D served all wk 5.30-9.30 booking
required **Restaurant** L served all wk 12-3 booking
required D served all wk 5.30-9.30 booking required Fixed
menu price fr £13 Av 3 course à la carte fr £26.50 food
served all day ⊕ MARSTONS ◀ Banks Cocker Hoop
Original, Oxford Gold, Cumberland Ale ♂ Thatchers Gold.
**Facilities** Garden Parking

## LITTLE NESTON
Map 15 SJ27

## The Harp Inn

**19 Quay Side CH64 0TB**
☎ 0151 336 6980 📠 0151 336 6980
**e-mail:** jonesalbert@sky.com
**dir:** From Neston town centre, at 2nd mini-rdbt, turn right
onto Marshlands Rd. At bottom turn left, 200yds ahead

Overlooking the River Dee and across to Wales, this
isolated pub enjoys beautiful scenery and sunsets. The
building was formerly miners' cottages before becoming
a pub 150 years ago; on the walls mining artefacts and
pictures testify to its history. Although renovated over the
years, it remains a simple two-roomed pub, with quarry-
tiled floors and low beams. A good range of real ales is
kept, and simple plates of food include home-made soup,
and steak and onion pie with chips and peas. There is a
boules pitch in the beer garden

**Open** all day all wk noon-mdnt **Bar Meals** L served Mon-
Fri 12-2 Av main course £5 ⊕ ADMIRAL TAVERNS
◀ Joseph Holts, Timothy Taylor Landlord, Wadworth 6x,
Guest ales. **Facilities** Children's portions Family room
Dogs allowed Garden Parking **Notes** ⊛

## MACCLESFIELD
Map 16 SJ97

## The Windmill Inn ♚

**Holehouse Ln, Whitely Green, Adlington SK10 5SJ**
☎ 01625 574222
**e-mail:** mail@thewindmill.info
**web:** www.thewindmill.info
**dir:** Between Macclesfield & Poynton. Follow brown tourist
signs on main road. Pub in 1.5m

Just two minutes walk from the Macclesfield Canal and
close to the Middlewood Way, this former farmhouse is an
ideal place to start or end a country stroll. It has an
extensive landscaped garden, complete with children's
maze, while the interior is made cosy with a real fire and
sofas. The aim here is to create 'simple, fresh and tasty
food' from produce sourced from trusted local suppliers
and from neighbouring counties. In addition to tempting
sandwiches and light lunches, the menu might offer pan-
fried pigeon breast on garlic rosemary crumpet, baby
spinach and shallot vinaigrette; the Windmill's own fish
pie; Barrows' 28-day aged locally reared rib-eye steak
with hand-cut chips; and mulled plums topped with
hazelnut crumble and ginger ice cream.

**Open** all wk noon-3 5-11 (Fri-Sat noon-11, Sun noon-
10.30) **Bar Meals** L served Mon-Fri 12-2.30, Sat-Sun 12-4
D served Mon-Fri 5.30-9.30, Sat 12-9.30, Sun 12-8 Av
main course £10 **Restaurant** L served Mon-Fri 12-2.30,
Sat 12-9, Sun 12-8 D served Mon-Fri 5.30-9.30, Sat
12-9.30, Sun 12-8 ⊕ MOYO LTD ◀ Black Sheep, Old
Speckled Hen, Bombardier, changing Storm Ales. ♟ 16
**Facilities** Children's menu Dogs allowed Garden Parking

## MARTON
Map 16 SJ86

### PICK OF THE PUBS

## The Davenport Arms ♚

*See Pick of the Pubs on opposite page*

# PICK OF THE PUBS

## The Davenport Arms ♉

**MARTON**  Map 16 SJ86

**Congleton Rd SK11 9HF**
☎ **01260 224269**  📠 **01260 224565**
**e-mail:**
enquiries@thedavenportarms.co.uk
**web:**www.thedavenportarms.co.uk
**dir:** *3m from Congleton off A34*

Cushioned settles and leather armchairs by the log fire characterise the traditional bar of this 18th-century free house. Meanwhile, an authentic well adds its own appeal to the restaurant, though nowadays this is purely for decoration. As hereditary royal foresters, the Davenports once wielded considerable power, including the right to try, convict and hang highwaymen. Trials took place in the living room above the pub – which was then a farmhouse – and it is thought that miscreants were hanged from a gibbet attached to a nearby farm building. The Ancient Tree Forum reckons that the

somewhat battered Marton Oak is at least 1200 years old, and probably the oldest tree in England. This remarkable survivor still stands in the village and, amazingly, it still produces acorns.

All food, including chutneys, sauces and desserts, is freshly made on the premises using ingredients from local suppliers. The specials board is changed daily, and the menu is updated to reflect the changing seasons. Lunchtime brings a range of speciality baguettes, wraps and soft tortillas, supplemented by hot dishes like pan-fried liver, bacon and mash, and vegetarian crêpe paysanne. The dinner menu might begin with black pudding fritters with apple and cider chutney, or hot smoked salmon and prawn tian with farmhouse bread. Main course offerings include Davenport chicken in red wine, bacon, mushroom and shallot gravy; haddock in real ale batter with mushy peas, chips and tartare sauce; and stuffed field mushrooms with fruit chutney, apple and Welsh brie.

Outside, there's a lovely beer garden and a discreet children's play area. The pub hosts Marton's annual gooseberry show on the first Saturday in August each year. In 1978 the show was entered in the Guinness Book of Records for displaying the world's largest gooseberry.

**Open** noon-3 6-mdnt (Fri-Sun noon-mdnt) Closed: Mon L (ex BH)
**Bar Meals** L served Tue-Sat 12-2.30, Sun 12-3 D served Tue-Fri 6-9, Sun 6-8.30 Av main course £7 **Restaurant** L served Tue-Fri 12-2.30, Sat 12-9, Sun 12-8 booking required D served Tue-Fri 6-9, Sat 12-9, Sun 12-8 booking required Av 3 course à la carte fr £20.25 ⊕ FREE HOUSE ◖ Copper Dragon, Storm Brewing, Directors, Weetwood, Theakstons. ♉ 9
**Facilities** Children's menu Play area Garden Parking

## MOBBERLEY                     Map 15 SJ77

### The Roebuck 🍷 NEW

**Mill Ln WA16 7HX** ☎ **01565 873322**
**e-mail:** mail@theroebuck.com
**dir:** Just off B5085 NE of Knutsford

Grade II-listed and long one of Cheshire's most attractive country inns, where Timothy Taylor Landlord is accompanied by up to four cask ales and a cosmopolitan wine list. Food is freshly and locally sourced for the traditional/contemporary menu, which includes beer-battered haddock with home-made mushy peas; braised steak and onions with horseradish mash; and goat's cheese and shallot tarte Tatin with red pepper dressing. When the sun shines sit under one of the trees in the three-tiered rear garden.

**Open** all wk 12-3 5-11 (Sat-Sun all day) **Bar Meals** Av main course £13 **Restaurant** L served Mon-Fri 12-2.30, Sat 12-9.30, Sun 12-8 booking required D served Mon-Fri 5.30-9.30, Sat 12-9.30, Sun 12-8 booking required ⊕ FREE HOUSE ◖ Timothy Taylor Landlord, Black Sheep, Guest ales. 🍷 12 **Facilities** Children's menu Children's portions Garden Parking

## MOULDSWORTH                     Map 15 SJ57

### PICK OF THE PUBS

### The Goshawk 🍷

**Station Rd CH3 8AJ**
☎ **01928 740900** 📠 **01928 740965**
**dir:** A51 from Chester onto A54. Left onto B5393 towards Frodsham. Enter Mouldsworth, pub on left opposite rail station

A welcoming pub with log fires and stripped pine floors, The Goshawk is conveniently located opposite the railway station in Mouldsworth, one stop from Chester on the Manchester to Stockport line. Close by are the Delamere Forest and Country Park, and the Mouldsworth Motor Museum. The menu has something for everyone, with light snacks of Bury black pudding with chicken and beetroot, or eggs Benedict, and shellfish starters like potted shrimps or seared scallops. There is a good choice of salads, and more substantial fare, with up to 12 fish dishes, steaks from the chargrill, and vegetarian options such as stuffed roasted red peppers. House favourites are lobster thermidor and steak and kidney pudding made with Timothy Taylor's Ale, while alternatives include braised lamb shank with dauphinoise potatoes and honey roast Chantenay carrots, or halibut topped with pesto and crab crust served with couscous, chickpeas and Thai asparagus.

---

**Open** all wk noon-11 (Sun noon-10.30) Closed: 25 Dec & 1 Jan **Bar Meals** food served all day **Restaurant** food served all day ⊕ WOODWARD & FALCONER PUBS ◖ Weetwoods Eastgate, Old Speckled Hen. 🍷 14 **Facilities** Play area Family room Garden Parking

## NANTWICH                     Map 15 SJ65

### The Thatch Inn 🍷

**Wrexham Rd, Faddiley CW5 8JE** ☎ **01270 524223**
**dir:** Follow signs for Wrexham from Nantwich, inn 4m from Nantwich on A534

Believed to be the oldest (and one of the prettiest) pubs in south Cheshire, the black-and-white Thatch Inn has a three quarter acre garden, while inside there are plentiful oak beams, and open fires in winter. Starters might be salmon and spring onion fishcakes with dill crème fraîche or black pudding on wilted spinach and caramelised pear, topped with streaky bacon and creamy mustard sauce. For mains, perhaps slow roasted belly pork on red cabbage with a creamy cider sauce or posh sausages and chips. Children have their own menu.

**Open** Mon-Tue 6-11, Wed-Thu 12-3 6-11, Fri-Sat 12-11, Sun 12-10.30 Closed: Mon L & Tue L **Bar Meals** L served Wed-Thu 12-3, Fri-Sat 12-9, Sun 12-8.30 D served Mon-Thu 6-9, Fri-Sat 12-9, Sun 12-8.30 ⊕ ENTERPRISE INNS ◖ Timothy Taylor Landlord, Weetwoods. 🍷 24 **Facilities** Play area Family room Garden Parking

## PARKGATE                     Map 15 SJ27

### The Boat House 🍷

**1 The Parade CH64 6RN**
☎ **0151 336 4187** 📠 **01928 740965**
**dir:** On B5135, 3m from Heswall

Situated beside the RSPB's Parkgate Reserve, with magnificent views across the Dee estuary to Wales, this striking black-and-white timbered building is a haven for bird-watchers and food lovers. Eat in the airy dining room looking out across salt marshes, or in the cosy, modernised bars. The extensive menu favours fresh fish and seafood, perhaps halibut with crab and a pesto crust or a bowls of mussels with chips. Alternatives include steak and kidney pie and braised lamb shank. Look out for the flooding, about four times a year, where the water laps right up to the walls of the pub!

**Open** all wk noon-11 (Sun noon-10.30) Closed: 25 Dec, 1 Jan **Bar Meals** L served Mon-Sat 12-9.30, Sun 12-9 D served Mon-Sat 12-9.30, Sun 12-9 **Restaurant** L served all wk 12-5 D served Mon-Sat 5-9.30, Sun 5-9 ⊕ FREE HOUSE ◖ Theakstons, John Smith's, Greene King IPA, Timothy Taylor Landlord, Old Speckled Hen. 🍷 17 **Facilities** Children's portions Family room Garden Parking

---

### The Ship Hotel ★★ HL NEW

**The Parade CH64 6SA**
☎ **0151 336 3931** 📠 **0151 203 1636**
**e-mail:** info@the-shiphotel.co.uk
**dir:** A540 (Chester towards Neston) left then immediately right onto B5136 (Liverpool Rd). In Neston town centre, left onto B5135. Follow to The Parade in Parkgate, hotel 50yds on right

Sits in a delightful parade on the River Dee estuary with fabulous views to the coastline and mountains of North Wales. During the 18th century this was a thriving port, especially for trade with Ireland, before silt rendered access impossible for sea-going vessels. Locals and visiting bird-watchers are made welcome as they enjoy award-winning cask ales and traditional home-made pub food such as roast topside of beef; and poached fillet of salmon. Why not stay over and explore the area.

**Open** all day all wk **Bar Meals** L served all wk 12-2.30 D served all wk 6-8 Av main course £6 **Restaurant** L served all wk 12-2.30 D served all wk 6-8 ⊕ FREE HOUSE ◖ Trapper's Hat, Storr, Oak Beauty, Peerless, Oast House Gold. **Facilities** Dogs allowed Parking **Rooms** 24

## PLUMLEY                     Map 15 SJ77

### The Golden Pheasant Hotel 🍷

**Plumley Moor Rd WA16 9RX**
☎ **01565 722261** 📠 **01565 723804**
**dir:** M6 junct 19, A556 signed Chester. 2m, left at Plumley/Peover signs. Through Plumley, pub 1m opp rail station

Set in the beautiful Cheshire countryside, The Golden Pheasant is convenient for Chester and Manchester, with trains from the station opposite hourly. This 200-year-old, traditional wayside inn has a wealth of beams, low ceilings and a magnificent carved oak bar servery. Privately owned, the pub is proud of its real ales, extensive wine list and home-cooked, locally sourced food served in the more formal dining rooms and lounge bar area. There is wonderful fresh fish and Tabley Estate game to enjoy. Expect roaring log fires, comfy sitting areas, alfresco dining, a children's play area and a locals' bar with a darts board.

**Open** all day all wk 11-11 (Sun noon-10.30) **Bar Meals** Av main course £10 food served all day **Restaurant** Fixed menu price fr £16.95 Av 3 course à la carte fr £19.95 food served all day ⊕ J W LEES ◖ J W Lees Bitter, John Willies Bitter, Guinness. 🍷 14 **Facilities** Children's menu Children's portions Play area Garden Parking

### The Smoker 🍷

**WA16 0TY** ☎ **01565 722338**
**e-mail:** smoker@plumley.fsword.co.uk
**dir:** From M6 junct 19 take A556 W. Pub 1.75m on left

This 400-year-old thatched coaching inn is actually named after a white racehorse bred by the Prince Regent. The pub's striking wood-panelled interior of three connecting rooms provides a traditional welcoming atmosphere, with log fires, beams and copper kettles.

The menu has an appealing and lengthy array of starters such as Bury black pudding fritter and crisp streaky bacon, while main courses include red Thai chicken curry; pork fillet in a sage, apple and brandy sauce; and Welsh sea bass with ginger and spring onions.

**Open** all wk 10-3 6-11 (Sun 10am-10.30pm) **Bar Meals** L served Mon-Fri 10-2.30, Sun 10-9 D served Mon-Fri 6-9.30, Sun 10-9 Av main course £10 **Restaurant** L served Mon-Fri 10-2.30, Sun 10-9 booking required D served Mon-Fri 6-9.30, Sun 10-9 booking required Av 3 course à la carte fr £18.50 ⊕ FREDERIC ROBINSON ◀ Robinson's Best, Double Hop, Robinsons Smooth. ♟ 10 **Facilities** Children's menu Children's portions Play area Garden Parking

### SHOCKLACH                        Map 15 SJ44

## The Bull ♟

**SY14 7BL** ☎ 01829 250239
**e-mail:** info@thebullshocklach.com
**dir:** 12m S of Chester, 3m W of Malpas

A traditional village pub, set in a picturesque village a stones throw from the River Dee, with lots of old beams, a funky new bar with an open fire and what the owners call 'unusual' furniture, in which hand pumps dispense five local and national real ales. High quality, locally sourced ingredients are the basis for roast treacle-cured bacon chop; pan-fried sea bass; braised blade of beef; and sweet and sour aubergine chargrilled in vermouth. A growing single malt collection sits alongside an extensive wine list. The pub organises brewery tours, farmers' markets, and two real ale and food festivals (Easter and August).

**Open** all wk Mon-Thu 12-3 5-11 (Fri-Sat noon-11 Sun noon-10.30) **Bar Meals** L served Mon-Fri 12-2.30, Sat 12-10, Sun 12-8 booking required D served Mon-Thu 6-9.30, Fri 6-10, Sat 12-10, Sun 12-8 booking required Av main course £11 **Restaurant** L served Mon-Fri 12-2.30, Sat 12-10, Sun 12-8 booking required D served Mon-Thu 6-9.30, Fri 6-10, Sat 12-10, Sun 12-8 booking required Av 3 course à la carte fr £20 ⊕ ADMIRAL TAVERNS ◀ Stonehouse Station Bitter, guest ales. ♟ 9 **Facilities** Children's menu Children's portions Dogs allowed Garden Parking

### SUTTON LANE ENDS                 Map 16 SJ97

## Sutton Hall ♟ NEW

**Bullocks Ln SK11 0HE**
☎ 01260 253211   ▤ 01260 252538
**e-mail:** sutton.hall@brunningandprice.co.uk

A converted 480-year-old manor house, formerly the family home of the Earls of Lucan; the 6th Earl famously disappeared in 1974, leaving behind the unresolved murder of his nanny. With a warren of seven dining areas, nooks and crannies everywhere, a snug, a library, and plenty of sun-filled terraces and gardens, Sutton Hall has plenty of space. Real ales and ciders are numerous, as are the 100-plus malt whiskies and bourbons. The brasserie-style menu of robust dishes may include beef fillet carpaccio, and braised shoulder of lamb.

**Open** all day all wk Mon-Sat 11.30-11 Sun noon-10.30 **Bar Meals** Av main course £10.25 food served all day **Restaurant** food served all day ⊕ BRUNNING AND PRICE ◀ Brunning & Price Original, Flowers Original, Weetwood Cheshire Cat, Wincle Mr Mullins, Roosters Silver Lining ⭕ Westons Traditional Scrumpy, Westons Organic, Thatchers Old Rascal. ♟ 30 **Facilities** Children's portions Dogs allowed Garden Parking

### SWETTENHAM                       Map 15 SJ86
### PICK OF THE PUBS

## The Swettenham Arms ♟

**Swettenham Ln CW12 2LF**
☎ 01477 571284   ▤ 01477 571284
**e-mail:** info@swettenhamarms.co.uk
**dir:** M6 junct 18 to Holmes Chapel, then A535 towards Jodrell Bank. 3m right (Forty Acre Lane) to Swettenham

Hard by the ancient parish church, this delightful 16th-century inn lies deep in the Dane Valley. It was once a nunnery, but before that probably provided funeral parties with bed and board; corpses were 'rested' too, in the underground passage linking the pub to the church. An excellent selection of changing real ales and ciders attracts plenty of awards. Recent mysterious sightings keep alive the legend that a nun was murdered here. Eyes peeled then as you enjoy high standards of locally sourced, home-prepared food, chosen from a short menu listing steak, oyster, mushroom and ale pie; Lancashire hotpot; seared braised oxtail; local breast of pheasant; salmon fillet; and home-made cannelloni. If it's too warm for a log fire inside, sit outside on the flower-festooned patio, to one side of which is a nature reserve created by astronomer Sir Bernard Lovell, and to the rear a lavender and sunflower meadow.

**Open** all wk noon-3.30 6-11 (Sat-Sun noon-11) **Bar Meals** L served Mon-Fri 12-2.30, Sat-Sun 12-9.30 booking required D served Mon-Fri 6.30-9.30, Sat-Sun 12-9.30 booking required Av main course £12 **Restaurant** L served Mon-Fri 12-2.30, Sat-Sun 12-9.30 booking required D served Mon-Fri 6.30-9.30, Sat-Sun 12-9.30 booking required Fixed menu price fr £12.50 Av 3 course à la carte fr £25 ⊕ FREE HOUSE ◀ Landlord, Hydes, Beartown, Sharp's Doom Bar, Bollington Best, Black Sheep ⭕ Addlestones, Westons Cider Ice. ♟ 12 **Facilities** Children's menu Children's portions Dogs allowed Garden Parking

### TARPORLEY                        Map 15 SJ56

## Alvanley Arms Inn ★★★★ INN ♟

**Forest Rd, Cotebrook CW6 9DS** ☎ 01829 760200
**e-mail:** info@alvanleyarms.co.uk
**dir:** On A49, 1.5m N of Tarporley

A charming 16th-century, family-run coaching inn with shire horse-themed decor: rosettes, harnesses and horseshoes decorate the walls, linking the inn to the landlords' Cotebrook Shire Horse Centre next door. Hand-pulled ales in the oak-beamed bar complement a range of freshly prepared dishes, based on ingredients from local family businesses. Dishes range from traditional steak and ale pie or gammon steak with egg and chips to oriental duck pancakes or Thai fish goujons. Seven individually designed bedrooms are available.

**Open** all wk noon-3 5.30-11.30 (Sat-Sun noon-11) **Bar Meals** L served Mon-Sat 12-2, Sun 12-9 D served Mon-Sat 6-9, Sun 12-9 **Restaurant** L served Mon-Sat 12-2, Sun 12-9 D served Mon-Sat 6-9, Sun 12-9 booking required ⊕ FREDERIC ROBINSON ◀ Robinsons Best & guest ales. ♟ 12 **Facilities** Dogs allowed Garden Parking **Rooms** 7

### TUSHINGHAM CUM GRINDLEY           Map 15 SJ54
### PICK OF THE PUBS

## Blue Bell Inn

**SY13 4QS** ☎ 01948 662172   ▤ 01948 662172
**dir:** A41, 4m N of Whitchurch, signed Bell O' the Hill

In what must be a unique tale from the annals of pub-haunting, this inn reputedly has a ghost duck, whose spirit is sealed in a bottle buried in the bottom step of the cellar. Believe that or not, the Blue Bell remains a charming pub. A lovely black-and-white building that oozes character with its abundance of beams, open fires and horse brasses, its oldest part dates to approximately 1550, and the main building was completed in 1667. It has all the features you'd expect of a timber-framed building of this date, including one of the largest working chimneys in Cheshire and a priest hole. Curios that have been discovered from within the wall structure are on show in the pub. A menu of hearty, home-cooked pub food includes curries, steak and chips, and chilli with garlic bread. Drink options include well kept ales, Skinners cider and a selection of wines.

**Open** noon-3 6-11.30 Closed: Mon (ex BH) **Bar Meals** L served Tue-Sun 12-2 D served Tue-Sun 6-9 Av main course £8.75 **Restaurant** L served Tue-Sun 12-2 D served Tue-Sun 6-9 booking required Av 3 course à la carte fr £18 ⊕ FREE HOUSE ◀ Shropshire Gold, Oakham JHB, guest ales ⭕ Skinners. **Facilities** Children's portions Family room Dogs allowed Garden Parking

---

**WARMINGHAM**     Map 15 SJ76

## PICK OF THE PUBS

### The Bear's Paw ★★★★★ INN ♥

**School Ln CW11 3QN ☎ 01270 526317**
e-mail: info@thebearspaw.co.uk
web: www.thebearspaw.co.uk
dir: *M6 junct 18, A54, A533 towards Sandbach. Follow signs for village*

Reopened after a complete rebuild in 2009, this 19th-century inn is now a strikingly appointed gastro-pub with rooms. Gastro-pub maybe, but with two open fires, reclaimed antique oak flooring and more than 200 pictures on the oak-panelled walls, it still feels for all the world like a traditional village pub. The bar (home to a carved wooden bear with a salmon in its mouth) features six real ales from local micro-breweries, including the appropriately named Beartown in Congleton, and Weetwood in Tarporley. Wide-ranging menus offer starters of sizzling king prawns 'pil pil' style, and chicken liver parfait with red onion marmalade, and mains that include fresh roast rump of Bowland lamb; sesame-coated hake with egg noodles; tagliatelle frutti di mare; braised crisp belly pork; and filo parcel of feta cheese. Dessert options are chocolate bread and butter pudding with custard, and baked Alaska with raspberry sauce.

**Open** all day all wk noon–11 **Bar Meals** L served Mon-Thu 12-9.30, Fri-Sat 12-10, Sun 12-8 D served Mon-Thu 12-9.30, Fri-Sat 12-10, Sun 12-8 **Restaurant** L served Mon-Thu 12-9.30, Fri-Sat 12-10, Sun 12-8 D served Mon-Thu 12-9.30, Fri-Sat 12-10, Sun 12-8 ⊕ FREE HOUSE ◄ Weetwood, Beartown, Storm Brewery, Wincle, Titanic Ö Westons Stowford Press. ♥ 10 **Facilities** Children's menu Children's portions Dogs allowed Garden Parking **Rooms** 14

---

**WRENBURY**     Map 15 SJ54

### *The Dusty Miller* ♥

**CW5 8HG ☎ 01270 780537**
dir: *Telephone for directions*

A beautifully converted 16th-century mill building beside the Shropshire Union Canal. A black and white lift bridge, designed by Thomas Telford, completes the picture postcard setting. The menu, which mainly relies on ingredients from the region, offers light bites including filled rolls and a cheese platter alongside the more substantial baked hake with buttery mash and a white wine and parsley sauce, and home-made Aberdeen Angus burger with pear and apple chutney.

---

**Open** 12-3 6.30-11 Closed: Mon in winter ◄ Robinson's Unicorn, Double Hop, Old Tom, Hatters Mild, Hartleys XB Ö Stowford Press, Westons Traditional Scrumpy. ♥ 12 **Facilities** Dogs allowed Garden Parking

---

**WYBUNBURY**     Map 15 SJ64

### The Swan ♥

**Main Rd CW5 7NA ☎ 01270 841280 🖺 01270 841200**
e-mail: jacqueline.harris7@btinternet.com
web: www.swaninnwybunbury.co.uk
dir: *M6 junct 16 towards Chester & Nantwich. Turn left at lights in Wybunbury*

The Swan, a pub since 1580, is situated in the village centre next to the church. All the food is freshly prepared on the premises and includes pork and liver pâté with apple and cider brandy chutney; root vegetable casserole with Cheddar cheese mash; Thai green curry; and beer battered haddock and handcut chips. Light bites feature spicy chicken tortilla wrap and penne pasta with roasted Tuscan vegetables. Sit in the garden overlooking the famous leaning church tower.

**Open** all wk noon-mdnt, (Mon 5-mdnt) **Bar Meals** L served Tue-Sat 12-2, Sun 12-3.30 D served Mon-Sat 6.30-9.30, Sun 5-8 **Restaurant** L served Tue-Sat 12-2, Sun 12-3.30 booking required D served Mon-Sat 6.30-9.30, Sun 5-8 booking required Fixed menu price fr £7.25 ⊕ ROBINSON ◄ Unicorn, Cumbria Way, guest ales Ö Stowford Press. ♥ 9 **Facilities** Children's menu Dogs allowed Garden Parking

---

## CORNWALL & ISLES OF SCILLY

**BLISLAND**     Map 2 SX17

### The Blisland Inn

**PL30 4JF ☎ 01208 850739**
dir: *5m from Bodmin towards Launceston. 2.5m off A30 signed Blisland. On village green*

An award-winning inn in a very picturesque village on the edge of Bodmin Moor. The superb parish church was a favourite of John Betjeman who wrote about it extensively. Most of the traditional pub fare is home cooked, including a variety of puddings. Leek and mushroom bake is a perennial favourite, while lasagne, sausage and mash, and traditional farmhouse ham, egg and chips are also popular.

---

**Open** all day all wk **Bar Meals** L served all wk 12-2 D served all wk 6.30-9 booking required ⊕ FREE HOUSE ◄ Sharps, Skinners, Guest ales Ö Cornish Orchard, Winkleigh, Haye Farm. **Facilities** Children's portions Family room Dogs allowed Garden

---

**BODINNICK**     Map 2 SX15

### Old Ferry Inn ♥

**PL23 1LX ☎ 01726 870237 🖺 01726 870116**
e-mail: royce972@aol.com
dir: *A38 towards Dobwalls, left onto A390. After 3m left onto B3359 then right to Bodinnick/Polruan for 5m*

This friendly family-run free house stands just 50 yards from the scenic River Fowey, where the car ferry still makes regular crossings to Fowey itself. Inside the 400-year-old building, old photographs and nautical bric-a-brac set the scene. Sample an ale, stout or continental lager while perusing the extensive lunchtime bar menu which embraces hot and spicy chicken wings, creamy garlic mushrooms, burgers, home-made chilli, and fresh pasta of the day. Daily specials and an evening carte serving local fish, meat and produce complete the dining options.

**Open** all day all wk 11-11 (summer), noon-10 (winter) Closed: 25 Dec **Bar Meals** L served all wk 12-3 (summer), 12-2.30 (winter) D served all wk 6-9 (summer), 6.30-8.30 (winter) Av main course £9 **Restaurant** D served all wk 7-8.30 booking required Av 3 course à la carte fr £22.50 ⊕ FREE HOUSE ◄ Sharp's Bitter, Guinness Ö Cornish Orchard. ♥ 12 **Facilities** Children's menu Children's portions Family room Dogs allowed Garden Parking

# PICK OF THE PUBS

## Cadgwith Cove Inn

**CADGWITH**                    Map 2 SW71

**TR12 7JX**
☎ 01326 290513   📠 01326 291018
**e-mail:**
enquiries@cadgwithcoveinn.com
**web:** www.cadgwithcoveinn.com
**dir:** *10m from Helston on main Lizard road*

Formerly the haunt of smugglers and now popular with coast path walkers and local fishermen, this 300-year-old pub is set in an unspoilt fishing hamlet of thatched cottages on the rugged Lizard coastline. In summer, ramblers mingle with tourists and locals on the sunny front patio, which affords views across the old pilchard cellar to the peaceful cove. The atmospheric, simply furnished bars are adorned with relics that record a rich seafaring history, and it's easy to imagine that the ghosts of smugglers still gather within these cosy walls.

The pub offers a warm welcome and authentic local colour – come on a Friday night and relax with pint of Sharp's Doom Bar and listening to sea shanties sung by the Cadgwith Singers late into the night. On Tuesday nights the inn hosts a thriving folk club when guests are invited to join in or just sit back and enjoy the music. On any night of the week you might find yourself swapping tales with one of the fishermen whose catches feature on the popular menus – their colourful boats rest on the shingle a few steps down the lane from the pub.

As may be expected, these are positively laden with seafood - lobster and crab of course, but also grilled red mullet or bass, moules marinière, the special Cadgwith fish casserole, and traditional fish and chips. Meat eaters and vegetarians are also well provided for, with ingredients coming from local butchers and surrounding farms. Meals can be served in the garden in clement weather, and the large terrace is also an ideal spot during the summer gig races, or for one of the regular seafood barbecues prepared by local fishermen.

**Open** all wk **Bar Meals** L served all wk 12-2 D served all wk 7-9 **Restaurant** L served all wk 12-2 D served all wk 7-9 ⊕ PUNCH TAVERNS 🍺 Sharp's, guest ales. **Facilities** Children's menu Family room Dogs allowed Garden Parking

## BOLVENTOR
Map 2 SX17

### Jamaica Inn ♟

PL15 7TS ☎ 01566 86250 📄 01566 86177
e-mail: enquiry@jamaicainn.co.uk
dir: Follow A30 from Exeter. 10m after Launceston take Bolventor road, follow signs

The setting for Daphne du Maurier's famous novel, this 18th-century inn stands high on Bodmin Moor. Its Smugglers Museum houses fascinating artefacts, while the Daphne du Maurier room honours the great writer. The place is big on atmosphere, with a cobbled courtyard, beamed ceilings and roaring fires, plus a children's play area and beautiful gardens. Breakfasts, mid morning snacks and lunches provide an inviting choice, while the evening menu offers steaks, fish, chicken and vegetarian options.

**Open** all day all wk 9am-11pm **Bar Meals** L served all wk Av main course £12.50 food served all day ⊕ FREE HOUSE 🍺 Sharp's Doom Bar, Tribute, Jamaica Inn Ale. ♟ 8
**Facilities** Play area Dogs allowed Garden Parking

## BOSCASTLE
Map 2 SX09

### PICK OF THE PUBS

### The Wellington Hotel ★★ HL ◉◉ ♟

The Harbour PL35 0AQ ☎ 01840 250202
e-mail: info@boscastle-wellington.com
dir: A30/A395 at Davidstowe follow Boscastle signs. B3266 to village. Right into Old Rd

Known affectionately as 'The Welly' by both locals and loyal guests, this listed 16th-century coaching inn with its castellated tower nestles on one of England's most stunning coastlines at the end of a glorious wooded valley where the rivers Jordan and Valency meet. It was fully refurbished after the devastating floods in 2004, but retains much of its original charm, including beamed ceilings and real log fires. The traditional beamed bar complete with minstrels' gallery proffers a good selection of Cornish ales and ciders, malt whiskies and bar snacks. Nearly all the food uses Cornish ingredients, if available, "no matter what the cost". So expect the likes of Cornish crab and samphire cake with mixed leaf salad; Cornish ale-battered fish with home-made tartare sauce; roasted Cornish sardines with preserved lemon; and West Country cheeses in the traditional ploughman's. Alternatively, if you're not calorie counting, the Cornish cream tea is not to be missed. There is also a fine dining restaurant.

**Open** all day all wk 11am-11pm (Sun noon-10pm)
**Bar Meals** L served Mon-Fri 12-3, Sat-Sun 12-9 D

served Mon-Fri 6-10, Sat-Sun 12-9 Av main course £7
Restaurant D served Fri-Wed 6-9 Av 3 course à la carte
fr £25 ⊕ FREE HOUSE 🍺 St Austell HSD, St Austell Tribute, Skinners Ales Spriggan, Betty Stogs, Tintagel ○ Rattler Apple, Thatchers Dry. ♟ 15
**Facilities** Children's menu Children's portions Dogs allowed Garden Parking **Rooms** 15

## CADGWITH
Map 2 SW71

### PICK OF THE PUBS

### Cadgwith Cove Inn

See Pick of the Pubs on page 79

## CALLINGTON
Map 3 SX36

### The Coachmakers Arms

6 Newport Square PL17 7AS
☎ 01579 382567 📄 01579 384679
dir: Between Plymouth & Launceston on A388

There's plenty of choice on the menu at this traditional stone-built pub, from chargrilled steaks, steak and kidney pie or hot-pot, to oven-baked plaice, vegetable balti or salads. Clocks, plates, pictures of local scenes, old cars and antique trade advertisements contribute to the atmosphere, as do the fish tank and aviary. Regulars range from the local football team to the pensioners dining club. On Wednesday there's a charity quiz night, and Thursday is steak night.

**Open** all day all wk **Bar Meals** L served all wk 12-2 D served all wk 7-9.30 Av main course £7 **Restaurant** L served all wk 12-2 D served all wk 7-9.30 Fixed menu price fr £15 ⊕ ENTERPRISE INNS ◀ Sharp's Doom Bar, Worthing Best Bitter, Bass. **Facilities** Children's menu Children's portions Dogs allowed Parking

## Manor House Inn

**Rilla Mill PL17 7NT ☎ 01579 362354**
**dir:** *5m from Callington, just off B3257*

Set by the River Lynher on the edge of Bodmin Moor, once a granary for the mill next door, Manor House is a traditional pub that offers real ales and ciders, a bespoke wine list and a reasonably-priced selection of home-made food. Careful attention is paid to sourcing quality local ingredients, mainly within a 10-mile radius, including fresh fish. Typical choices include steak and ale pie, battered haddock and chips, chicken chasseur, and curry of the week. Lighter options include club sandwich, tuna melt, toasted sandwiches and salads. The inn makes an ideal resting spot for walkers and day trippers.

**Open** Mon-Fri 11-3 5.30-11 (all day Sat-Sun) Closed: Mon L **Bar Meals** L served Tue-Sun 11.30-2 D served Tue-Sun 6-9 Av main course £8 **Restaurant** L served Tue-Sun 11.30-2 D served Tue-Sun 6-9 Fixed menu price fr £10.95 Av 3 course à la carte fr £18 ⊕ FREE HOUSE ◀ Sharp's Own & Special, Doom Bar, Betty Stogs Ö Thatchers Gold, Westons Scrumpy, Cornish Rattler. **Facilities** Children's menu Children's portions Dogs allowed Garden Parking

| **CONSTANTINE** | **Map 2 SW72** |

### PICK OF THE PUBS

## Trengilly Wartha Inn ★★★ INN ⊛ ♟

*See Pick of the Pubs on page 82*

| **CUBERT** | **Map 2 SW75** |

## The Smugglers' Den Inn ♟

**Trebellan TR8 5PY ☎ 01637 830209   🖻 01637 830580**
**e-mail:** info@thesmugglersden.co.uk
**web:** www.thesmugglersden.co.uk
**dir:** *From Newquay take A3075 to Cubert x-rds, then right, then left signed Trebellan, 0.5m*

Set in a valley leading to the coast, this thatched 16th-century pub comprises a long bar, family room, children's play area, courtyards and huge beer garden. The no-nonsense, modern menu might offer houmous and

flatbread with rocket and sun-blushed tomatoes at lunch, or tempura king prawns followed by Falmouth Bay moules marinière in the evening. The impressive selection of real ales is at its best during the real ale and pie festival over the May Day weekend.

**Open** all day all wk 11.30-3 6-11 (Sat 11-3 6-mdnt, Sun & summer open all day) Closed: Jan-Mar closed Mon-Tue L **Bar Meals** L served all wk 12-2.30 (winter 12-2) D served all wk 6-9.30 (winter Sun-Thu 6-9, Fri-Sat 6-9.30) **Restaurant** L served all wk 12-2.30 (winter 12-2) D served all wk 6-9.30 (winter Sun-Thu 6-9, Fri-Sat 6-9.30) booking required ⊕ FREE HOUSE ◀ Skinner's Smugglers Ale, Sharp's Doom Bar, St Austell Tribute, Rotating Guest ales Ö Healey's Cornish Rattler. ♟ 10 **Facilities** Children's menu Play area Family room Dogs allowed Garden Parking
**See advert on opposite page**

| **DUNMERE** | **Map 2 SX06** |

## The Borough Arms

**PL31 2RD ☎ 01208 73118**
**dir:** *From A30 take A389 to Wadebridge, pub approx 1m from Bodmin*

Although it was built in the 1850s to refresh rail workers transporting china clay from the moors down to the port at Padstow, the Borough seems much older. These days walkers, cyclists, horseriders and summertime tourists drop in as they follow the now-disused railway line which has become the 17-mile Camel Trail. Food from both the menu of pub favourites and the specials board is served all day, with a carvery also operating at lunch and dinner and all day on Sundays. Children's portions are marked on the menu.

**Open** all day all wk **Bar Meals** L served all wk 12-9 D served all wk 12-9 Av main course £7 food served all day **Restaurant** L served all wk 12-9 D served all wk 12-9 Fixed menu price fr £8.50 Av 3 course à la carte fr £18 food served all day ⊕ ST AUSTELL ◀ Tribute, IPA. **Facilities** Children's menu Children's portions Play area Family room Dogs allowed Garden Parking

| **FEOCK** | **Map 2 SW83** |

## *The Punch Bowl & Ladle* ♟

**Penelewey TR3 6QY**
**☎ 01872 862237   🖻 01872 870401**
**dir:** *Off Truro to Falmouth road, after Shell garage at 'Playing Place' rdbt follow signs for King Harry Ferry to right. 0.5m, pub on right*

This ancient and fascinating thatched building comprises three cob-built 17th-century farm workers' cottages and a former custom house. There are delightful rural views from the inn's patio, and in warmer weather you can enjoy a drink in the walled garden. The menu uses 99 per cent Cornish goods, and choices include fish pie; local mussels in Cornish cider; Malaysian chicken; and venison steak in chocolate sauce. There is live music monthly, and regular food theme nights.

**Open** all day all wk 11.30am-11pm (Fri 11.30am-mdnt, Sun noon-10.30) ◀ Tribute, Tinners, Proper Job, Cornish Cream. ♟ 8 **Facilities** Dogs allowed Garden Parking

| **FOWEY** | **Map 2 SX15** |

## The Ship Inn

**Trafalgar Square PL23 1AZ ☎ 01726 832230**
**e-mail:** shipinnfowey@hotmail.com
**dir:** *From A30 take B3269 & A390*

One of Fowey's oldest buildings, The Ship was built in 1570 by John Rashleigh, who sailed to the Americas with Walter Raleigh. Given Fowey's riverside position, assume a good choice of fish, including River Fowey mussels, pan-fried scallops with mushrooms and bacon, and Ship Inn fish pie. Other options include beef and Guinness pie or local butcher's sausages and mash. St Austell ales, real fires and a long tradition of genial hospitality add the final touches. As we went to press, a change of hands was about to take place.

**Open** all day all wk 11am-mdnt (Thu-Sat 11am-1am) **Bar Meals** L served Mon-Sat 12-2.30, Sun 12-4 D served Mon-Sat 6-9 **Restaurant** L served Mon-Sat 12-2.30 (summer only), Sun 12-4 D served Mon-Sat 6-9, (Sun 6-9 summer only) ⊕ ST AUSTELL BREWERY ◀ St Austell Tinners Ale, Tribute, Proper Job Ö Cornish Rattler. **Facilities** Children's menu Children's portions Family room Dogs allowed

| **GOLDSITHNEY** | **Map 2 SW53** |

## The Trevelyan Arms ♟

**Fore St TR20 9JU ☎ 01736 710453**
**e-mail:** mikehitchens@hotmail.com
**dir:** *5m from Penzance. A394 signed to Goldsithney*

The former manor house for Lord Trevelyan, this 17th-century property stands at the centre of the picturesque village just a mile from the sea. It has also been a coaching inn and a bank/post office in its time, but these days is very much the traditional family-run Cornish pub. Food is fresh and locally sourced, offering good value for money. Typical dishes are T-bone steaks, home-made pies and curries, pasta dishes and local fish.

**Open** all wk 4-mdnt (Sat-Sun noon-mdnt) **Bar Meals** L served Sun D served all wk 6-9 **Restaurant** L served Sun D served all wk 6-9 ⊕ PUNCH TAVERNS ◀ Morland Speckled Hen, Guinness, St Austell Tribute Ö Green Goblin. ♟ 10 **Facilities** Children's menu Children's portions Dogs allowed Garden

# PICK OF THE PUBS

## Trengilly Wartha Inn ★★★INN

Nancenoy TR11 5RP
☎ 01326 340332 📠 01326 340332
e-mail: reception@trengilly.co.uk
dir: *Follow signs to Constantine, left towards Gweek until 1st sign for inn, left & left again at next sign, continue to inn*

William and Lisa Lea have been running this friendly Cornish inn for more than a decade, and in that time the couple have built it into one of the county's leading residential inns. The pub is situated in a small hamlet about a mile from the village of Constantine. Its unusual name means a settlement above the trees — in this case, the wooded valley of Polpenwith Creek, which is an offshoot of the lovely Helford River.

The bar offers a choice of unusual ales, several of which are served straight from the stillages. It features around fifteen wines by the glass, as well as over forty malt whiskies, which can be enjoyed by a blazing fire in the wintertime. The bar menu is available during both lunchtimes and evenings.

There's also a small bistro on one side of the inn, with hand-made furniture made by local cabinet-making students. The bistro menu includes a choice of regulars' favourites, as well as the burgeoning specials board that features the work of three excellent Cornish chefs. Choose from a range of locally produced meats and game; fish and shellfish from local waters; and modern vegetarian dishes, all cooked under the owners' supervision. Leave space for one of the rich, imaginative desserts and a Cornish cheeseboard with home-made biscuits.

The six acres of gardens and meadows surrounding the inn include a pretty beer garden and a vine-shaded pergola that's perfect for summer dining. The pub also offers six attractively furnished en suite bedrooms, and two superior garden rooms overlooking the lake.

**Open** all wk 11-3 6-12
**Bar Meals** L served all wk 12-2.15 D served all wk 6.30-9.30 Av main course £10 **Restaurant** L served all wk 12-2.15 booking required D served all wk 6.30-12 booking required Fixed menu price fr £10 Av 3 course à la carte fr £25 ⊕ FREE HOUSE ◖ Skinners Cornish Knocker, Betty Stogs, Sharp's Doom Bar, Sharp's Edenale, Guest Ales ♂ Cornish Rattler, Thatchers Gold. ♟ 15
**Facilities** Children's menu Play area Family room Dogs allowed Garden Parking **Rooms** 8

Save on Hotels. Book at **theAA.com/hotel**

**CORNWALL & ISLES OF SCILLY** 83 **ENGLAND**

---

## GUNNISLAKE
Map 3 SX47

### The Rising Sun Inn

**Calstock Rd PL18 9BX ☎ 01822 832201**
**dir:** *From Tavistock take A390 to Gunnislake. Left after lights into Calstock Rd. Inn approx 500mtrs on right*

With its wonderful display of hanging baskets, this traditional two-roomed picture-postcard pub is set in award-winning terraced gardens overlooking the beautiful Tamar Valley. Great walks start and finish at the Rising Sun, which is understandably popular with hikers and cyclists, locals and visitors. Enjoy a pint of real ales like Cornish Coaster or Betty Stogs and local real cider.

**Open** all wk 12-3 5-11 ⊕ FREE HOUSE ◀ Spitfire, Otter, Sharp's Cornish Coaster, Skinner's Betty Stogs Bitter, Bass Ö Stowford Press. **Facilities** Dogs allowed Garden Parking **Notes** ⊜

---

## GUNWALLOE
Map 2 SW62

### PICK OF THE PUBS

### The Halzephron Inn ♥

**TR12 7QB ☎ 01326 240406 ▤ 01326 241442**
**e-mail:** halzephroninn@tiscali.co.uk
**dir:** *3m S of Helston on A3083, right to Gunwalloe, through village. Inn on left*

The name of this ancient inn derives from Als Yfferin, old Cornish for 'cliffs of hell', an appropriate description of its situation on this hazardous stretch of coastline. Once a haunt of smugglers, the pub stands just 300 yards from the famous South Cornwall footpath and is the only pub on the stretch between Mullion and Porthleven. Originally called The Ship, it changed its name in the late 1950s when it regained its licence after 50 'dry' years. Today it offers a warm welcome, a wide selection of ales including Organic Halzephron Gold and whiskies, and meals prepared from fresh local produce. Lunch brings a choice of platters accompanied by home-made granary or white rolls, plus specials such as seafood chowder. The evening menu shifts comfortably from the classic (beef bourguignon) to the modern: perhaps whole roast partridge en croûte; or roast saddle of rabbit wrapped in prosciutto filled with mushroom and herb duxelle. There is an excellent Junior Menu available.

---

**Open** all wk Closed: 25 Dec **Bar Meals** L served all wk 12-2 D served all wk 7-9 **Restaurant** L served all wk 12-2 D served all wk 7-9 ⊕ FREE HOUSE ◀ Sharp's Own, Doom Bar & Special, St Austell Tribute, Skinners Betty Stogs Ö Cornish Rattler. ♥ 8 **Facilities** Family room Garden Parking

---

## GWEEK
Map 2 SW72

### The Gweek Inn

**TR12 6TU ☎ 01326 221502 ▤ 01326 221164**
**e-mail:** steve.gilks@btinternet.com
**dir:** *2m E of Helston near Seal Sanctuary*

The lovely location of this traditional family-run village pub at the mouth of the pretty Helford River makes booking a table a wise precaution. It is known for value-for-money food, typically steak, kidney and ale pie; tagliatelle con pollo; filled jacket potatoes; and a range of salads. The chalkboard lists locally caught seafood.

**Open** all day all wk 11.30-closing ◀ Sharp's Doom Bar, Sharp's Own, Sharp's Special, Skinners Betty Stogs, Guest ale. **Facilities** Play area Dogs allowed Garden Parking

---

## KINGSAND
Map 3 SX45

### The Halfway House Inn ♥

**Fore St PL10 1NA ☎ 01752 822279 ▤ 01752 823146**
**e-mail:** info@halfwayinn.biz
**dir:** *From Torpoint Ferry or Tamar Bridge follow signs to Mount Edgcumbe*

Set among the narrow lanes and colour-washed houses of a quaint fishing village, this picturesque inn has been licensed since 1850. Its name comes from the fact that the stream at the rear of the premises once marked the border between Devon and Cornwall. The pleasant stone-walled bar with low-beamed ceilings and large central fireplace is ideal for a relaxing pint of Cornish real ale. Locally caught seafood is a feature of the small restaurant, whose menu includes a platter of smoked fish to start, and main courses such as garlic monkfish; whole sea bass with orange butter sauce; and sautéed scallops.

**Open** all wk **Bar Meals** L served all wk 11-2 6-9 D served all wk 11-2 6-9 Av main course £8 **Restaurant** L served all wk 11-2 6-9 D served all wk 11-2 6-9 Fixed menu price fr £14 Av 3 course à la carte fr £14 ⊕ FREE HOUSE ◀ Sharp's Doom Bar & Own, Guinness, John Smith's Smooth, Skinners Ö Stowford Press, Old Rosie. ♥ 12 **Facilities** Dogs allowed

---

## LAMORNA
Map 2 SW42

### Lamorna Wink

**TR19 6XH ☎ 01736 731566**
**dir:** *4m on B3315 towards Land's End, then 0.5m to turn on left*

This oddly-named pub was one of the original Kiddleywinks, a product of the 1830 Beer Act that enabled any householder to buy a liquor licence. Popular with walkers and not far from the Merry Maidens standing stones, the Wink provides a selection of local beers and a simple menu that includes sandwiches, jacket potatoes and fresh local crab. The management have been at the Wink for over thirty years, and pride themselves on providing diners with as much local produce as possible.

**Open** all wk Mon-Sat 11-2.30 (Sun 12-2.30) **Bar Meals** L served Mon-Sat 11-2, Sun 12-2 ⊕ FREE HOUSE ◀ Sharp's Doom Bar, Betty Stogs Ö Scrumpy Jack. **Facilities** Family room Dogs allowed Garden Parking **Notes** ⊜

---

## LANLIVERY
Map 2 SX05

### PICK OF THE PUBS

### The Crown Inn
INN

*See Pick of the Pubs on page 84*

---

## LOSTWITHIEL
Map 2 SX15

### The Royal Oak ♥

**Duke St PL22 0AG**
**☎ 01208 872552 & 872922 ▤ 01208 872922**
**e-mail:** rawlings309@btinternet.com
**dir:** *A30 from Exeter to Bodmin then onto Lostwithiel. Or A38 from Plymouth towards Bodmin then left onto A390 to Lostwithiel*

A secret tunnel is believed to run between this 12th-century inn and Restormel Castle a short way up the River Fowey. The stone-flagged public bar is cosy and welcoming with a log fire; here and in the separate lounge bar real ales such as Sharp's Doom Bar are served. Quality local produce is used wherever possible in a menu of home-made dishes such as chilli and garlic stirfry prawns; and chicken stuffed with sun-dried tomatoes and mushrooms.

**Open** all day all wk noon-mdnt **Bar Meals** Av main course £8.95 food served all day **Restaurant** food served all day ⊕ PUNCH TAVERNS ◀ Fuller's London Pride, Sharp's Doom Bar, Tribute. ♥ 8 **Facilities** Children's portions Family room Dogs allowed Garden Parking

---

# PICK OF THE PUBS

## The Crown Inn ★★★ INN

**LANLIVERY** Map 2 SX05

**PL30 5BT** ☎ **01208 872707**
**e-mail:** thecrown@wagtailinns.com
**dir:** *Signed from A390. Follow brown sign about 1.5m W of Lostwithiel*

Built in the 12th century to house the stonemasons constructing the next-door church of St Brevita, past which runs Saints' Way, the old coast-to-coast path linking Padstow and Fowey, this ancient pub has been extensively, but sympathetically, restored. The work uncovered a huge, deep well under the porch, which is now covered by glass enabling you to peer down as you walk over it. Needless to say, with such a history, everything about this charming pub oozes tradition - its thick stone walls, granite and slate floors, low beams, open fireplaces, and large,

unusual bread oven. Fowey harbour is only a few miles away, so expect the menu to offer fresh crab, scallops, mackerel and much more. Other local produce also features strongly, including meats from a butcher's in Par, fruit and vegetables from Bodmin and dairy products from Lostwithiel.

A typical meal might begin with an appetiser of marinated olives and ciabatta bread, then a starter of locally smoked duck, Cornish charcuterie, or pan-seared scallops. Main courses could include slow roasted belly pork; fresh Cornish crab gratin; and wild mushroom risotto. Have a fresh Fowey crab sandwich at lunchtime, or a Cornish brie, bacon and watercress ciabatta; or just a proper Cornish pasty.

The beers come from Sharp's in Rock and Skinners of Truro, while a reasonably priced wine list offers seven wines by the glass. The pretty front garden is a lovely spot to enjoy a summer evening, perhaps with a glass of Pimms. Bed and breakfast rooms are available.

**Open** all day all wk **Bar Meals** booking required food served all day **Restaurant** booking required food served all day ⊕ FREE HOUSE ◀ Sharp's Doom Bar, Skinners Betty Stogs, guest ales. **Facilities** Children's menu Dogs allowed Garden Parking **Rooms** 9

## LUDGVAN
Map 2 SW53

### White Hart 🍷

**Churchtown TR20 8EY ☎ 01736 740574**
dir: From A30 take B3309 at Crowlas

Built somewhere between 1280 and 1320, the White Hart is one of the oldest pub's in Cornwall. It retains the peaceful atmosphere of a bygone era and offers splendid views across St Michael's Mount and Bay. A great selection of real ales is sold from the back of the bar, with different guest ales every month, and the food is as popular as ever. Mr and Mrs Gibbard, the owners, also run The Turk's Head Inn in Penzance.

**Open** all wk **Bar Meals** L served all wk 12-2.30 booking required D served all wk 6-9.30 booking required Av main course £7 **Restaurant** L served all wk 12-2.30 booking required D served all wk 6-9.30 ⊕ PUNCH TAVERNS ◀ Sharp's Doom Bar, Flowers IPA, Betty Stogs, Abbots Õ Thatchers. 🍷 10 **Facilities** Children's menu Children's portions Dogs allowed Garden Parking

## MALPAS
Map 2 SW84

### The Heron Inn 🍷

**Trenhaile Ter TR1 1SL**
**☎ 01872 272773 📠 01872 272773**
e-mail: theheron@hotmail.co.uk
dir: From Trafalgar rdbt in Truro exit towards BBC Radio Cornwall, & pub sign. Follow Malpas Rd for 2m into village. Pub on left

Set in the picturesque village of Malpas just two miles from Truro's city centre, this pub enjoys panoramic River Fal views from its large terrace. The building may be old but its interior is light and airy, echoing the colours of the river. Along with St Austell Brewery ales, local produce is sourced in traditional home-made dishes such as local roast ham, fried egg and chips; beef lasagne with garlic bread; and a pan-fried trio of Cornish fish. Open all day through the summer months and afternoon cream teas available. The pub can be reached by boat at Malpas Marina.

**Open** all wk 11.30-3 6-11 (Fri-Sat all day (Sun till 10.30) summer all day every day) **Bar Meals** Av main course £9 **Restaurant** L served Mon-Fri 12-2, Sat-Sun 12-2.30 booking required D served all wk 6.30-9 booking required ⊕ ST AUSTELL BREWERY ◀ Tribute, IPA, Black Prince Õ Cornish Rattler. 🍷 11 **Facilities** Children's menu Children's portions Garden Parking

## MANACCAN
Map 2 SW72

### The New Inn 🍷

**TR12 6HA ☎ 01326 231323**
e-mail: penny@stmartin.wanadoo.co.uk
dir: 7m from Helston

This thatched village pub, deep in Daphne du Maurier country, dates back to Cromwellian times, although obviously Cromwell forbade his men to drink here. Attractions include the homely bars and large, natural

garden full of flowers. At lunchtime you might try a locally made pasty or moules marinière, and in the evening perhaps sea bass and chive fishcakes with tomato coulis and sautéed vegetables, or slow-roasted lamb shank with red wine and redcurrant gravy.

**Open** all wk 12-3 6-11 (Sat-Sun all day in summer) **Bar Meals** L served Mon-Sun 12-2.30 D served Mon-Sun 6-9 **Restaurant** L served all wk D served all wk ⊕ PUNCH TAVERNS ◀ Sharp's Doom Bar Õ Stowford Press. 🍷 10 **Facilities** Children's menu Play area Dogs allowed Garden Parking

## MARAZION
Map 2 SW53

### PICK OF THE PUBS

### Godolphin Arms ★★★★ INN

**TR17 0EN ☎ 01736 710202 📠 01736 710171**
e-mail: enquiries@godolphinarms.co.uk
dir: From A30 just outside Penzance follow Marazion signs. Pub 1st large building on right in Marazion, opposite St Michael's Mount

Locations don't come much more spectacular than this: the Godolphin Arms stands atop a sea wall directly opposite St Michael's Mount, and has superb views across the bay. It's so close that the sea splashes at the windows in the winter, and you can watch the movement of seals, dolphins, ferries, and fishing boats returning to Newlyn with their daily catch. From the traditional bar and beer terrace to the more homely restaurant and most of the stylishly decorated bedrooms, the Mount is clearly visible. Seafood figures prominently in the restaurant: the specials blackboard lists daily choices such as lemon sole pan fried in butter and capers; moules; scallops; or seafood tagliatelle. Aside from the view, the highlight of any stay is breakfast, which includes everything from a full English breakfast to kippers on toast.

**Open** all day all wk 11am-mdnt (Sun noon-mdnt) **Bar Meals** L served all wk 8am-9pm D served all wk 8am-9pm food served all day **Restaurant** L served all wk 8am-9pm D served all wk 8am-9pm food served all day ⊕ FREE HOUSE ◀ Special, St Austell Tribute, St Austell Tinners Õ Cornish Rattler. **Facilities** Dogs allowed Garden Parking **Rooms** 10

## MEVAGISSEY
Map 2 SX04

### The Ship Inn ★★★ INN 🍷

**Fore St PL26 6UQ ☎ 01726 843324 📠 01726 844368**
e-mail: shipinnian@hotmail.co.uk
dir: 7m S of St Austell

This 400-year-old inn stands just a few yards from Mevagissey's picturesque fishing harbour, so the choice of fish and seafood dishes comes as no surprise: moules marinière, beer-battered cod, and oven-baked fillet of haddock topped with prawns and Cornish Tiskey cheese, and served with a lemon and dill sauce. The popular bar has low-beamed ceilings, flagstone floors and a strong nautical feel. The inn has attractively decorated bedrooms if you would like to extend your visit.

**Open** all day all wk **Bar Meals** L served all wk 12-6 D served all wk 6-9 food served all day ⊕ ST AUSTELL BREWERY ◀ St Austell Ales. 🍷 8 **Facilities** Children's menu Family room Dogs allowed **Rooms** 5

## MITCHELL
Map 2 SW85

### PICK OF THE PUBS

### The Plume of Feathers ★★★★ INN

**TR8 5AX ☎ 01872 510387 📠 01637 839401**
e-mail: enquiries@theplume.info
dir: Exit A30 to Mitchell/Newquay

Over the years, this 16th century building has welcomed various historical figures - John Wesley preached Methodism from the pillared entrance, and Sir Walter Raleigh used to live locally. The present owners have established it as a successful destination pub restaurant; the imaginative kitchen has an excellent reputation for its food, based on a fusion of modern European and classical British dishes, with an emphasis on fresh fish and the best Cornish ingredients. Lunch brings starters such as home-made fishcake with sweet chilli and mixed leaves followed by a home-made beef burger with home-made relish and fries or venison stew with creamed potato and Savoy cabbage. Dinner could start with smoked mackerel fillet with houmous and toasted crostini followed by confit of Cornish duck leg with Toulouse sausage, tomato and mixed bean cassoulet. Finish with baked cheesecake of the day with clotted cream.

**Open** all day all wk 9am-11/mdnt (25 Dec 11-4) **Bar Meals** Av main course £10 food served all day **Restaurant** Av 3 course à la carte fr £22 food served all day ⊕ FREE HOUSE ◀ Doom Bar, John Smith's Smooth, Various Skinners Ales. **Facilities** Play area Dogs allowed Garden Parking **Rooms** 7

## MORWENSTOW
Map 2 SS21

### PICK OF THE PUBS

### The Bush Inn 🍷

**EX23 9SR ☎ 01288 331242**
web: www.bushinn-morwenstow.co.uk
dir: Exit A39, 3m N of Kilkhampton, 2nd right into village of Shop. 1.5m to Crosstown. Inn on village green

The Bush is a 13th-century pub set in an isolated cliff-top hamlet, close to a dramatic stretch of the north Cornish coast, a natural haunt for smugglers and wreckers a couple of centuries ago. The historic interior features stone-flagged floors, old stone fireplaces and a 'leper's squint', a tiny window through which the needy grabbed food scraps. Today meals are prepared from fresh local produce, including beef from the inn's own farm, and lamb, pork, salad and vegetables from others near by; seafood comes from home waters. The menu is concise but packed with flavour: a bowl of mixed olives, sun-blushed tomatoes and crusty bread; or a mixed game terrine with Cumberland sauce and

*continued*

## MORWENSTOW *continued*

wholemeal toast to start. Follow with steak and ale casserole; or an organic chargrilled sirloin with peppercorn sauce and garlic mushrooms. Desserts are all home made using Cornish butter and organic free-range eggs. There is a large garden overlooking the beautiful Tidna Valley and Atlantic Ocean.

*The Bush Inn*

**Open** all day all wk 11am-12.30am **Bar Meals** L served all wk D served all wk Av main course £12 food served all day **Restaurant** L served all wk D served all wk Fixed menu price fr £8 Av 3 course à la carte fr £19 food served all day ◖ St Austell HSD, Sharp's Doom Bar, Skinners Betty Stogs, St Austell Tribute Ö Thatchers & Cornish Orchard. ♇ 9 **Facilities** Children's menu Children's portions Play area Dogs allowed Garden Parking

---

### MYLOR BRIDGE     Map 2 SW83

## PICK OF THE PUBS

### The Pandora Inn ♇

**Restronguet Creek TR11 5ST**
☎ 01326 372678   ▤ 01326 378958
**e-mail:** info@pandorainn.com
**dir:** *From Truro/Falmouth follow A39, left at Carclew, follow signs to pub*

You can reach this thatched white-painted inn on foot, by bicycle or boat, as well as by car. Its breathtakingly beautiful situation, right on the banks of the Restronguet Creek, affords panoramic views across the water. You can even dine on the pontoon, where up to twenty boats can moor at high tide; inside, the Upper Deck restaurant offers a more traditional experience. The inn itself dates back in part to the 13th century, and its flagstone floors, low-beamed ceilings and thatched roof suggest little has changed. The name stems from the good ship *Pandora*, sent to Tahiti in 1790 to capture the Bounty mutineers. Sadly it was

wrecked and the captain, court-martialled upon his return, reputedly bought the inn. Today you can ponder the story over a casual lunch of crispy olive oil jacket potato filled with hand-picked white Cornish crab. In the evening make a meal of quenelles of Cornish smoked mackerel, followed by Falmouth scallops baked in their shells.

**Open** all day all wk 10.30am-11pm Closed: 25 Dec **Bar Meals** L served Sun-Thu 10.30-9, Fri-Sat 10.30-9.30 Av main course £14 ⊕ ST AUSTELL BREWERY ◖ St Austell Tinners Ale, HSD, Bass, Tribute. ♇ 15 **Facilities** Children's menu Children's portions Dogs allowed Garden Parking

---

### NEWQUAY     Map 2 SW86

## The Lewinnick Lodge Bar & Restaurant

**Pentire Headland TR7 1NX**
☎ 01637 878117   ▤ 01637 870130
**e-mail:** ask@lewinnick-lodge.info
**dir:** *From Newquay take Pentire Rd 0.5m, pub on right*

Originally built as a small stone cottage in the late 18th century, the Lodge enjoys stunning views of Cornwall's Atlantic coast. One of only two properties on the rugged Pentire Headland, the pub has established a great reputation, built up by the current owners over the last 20 years, with locals and visitors alike. Menu choices include Cornish mussels and brown shrimp gratin; ham hock terrine with sourdough and piccalilli; pan-fried gurnard fillet with chorizo, red peppers and onion; roasted aubergine and pepper caponata; orchard pear and plum crumble; and glazed lemon tart with clotted cream.

**Open** all day all wk **Bar Meals** L served all wk 12-5 D served all wk 5-10 Av main course £10 food served all day **Restaurant** L served all wk 12-5 D served all wk 5-10 Av 3 course à la carte fr £20 food served all day ⊕ FREE HOUSE ◖ Sharp's Doom Bar, Skinner's Betty Stogs Ö Cornish Orchards. **Facilities** Children's menu Dogs allowed Garden Parking

---

### PENZANCE     Map 2 SW43

## Dolphin Tavern ★★★ INN ♇

**Quay St TR18 4BD** ☎ 01736 364106
**e-mail:** dolphin@tiscali.co.uk
**dir:** *Telephone for directions*

The infamous Judge Jeffries held court in this harbourside pub during the 18th century, sending many poor souls to the gallows. Back in 1585, John Hawkins used the tavern as his headquarters to recruit Cornishmen to fight in the Armada. Said to be the most haunted pub in Cornwall, the Dolphin now serves great home-made food, accompanied by a full range of St Austell beers, an extensive wine list and accommodation too. The food specials board changes daily, and features meat, fish and vegetarian dishes using produce from within a 10-mile radius of the pub.

**Open** all day all wk Closed: 25 Dec **Bar Meals** Av main course £6 food served all day **Restaurant** Av 3 course à la carte fr £20 food served all day ◖ St Austell HSD, Tinners Tribute Ö Cornish Rattler. **Facilities** Children's menu Children's portions Play area Family room Dogs allowed Garden **Rooms** 2

---

## The Turks Head Inn ♇

**Chapel St TR18 4AF**
☎ 01736 363093   ▤ 01736 360215
**e-mail:** turkshead@gibbards9476.fsworld.co.uk
**dir:** *Telephone for directions*

Dating from around 1233, making it Penzance's oldest pub, it was the first in the country to be given the Turks Head name. Sadly, a Spanish raiding party destroyed much of the original building in the 16th century, but an old smugglers' tunnel leading directly to the harbour and priest holes still exist. Typically available are fresh seafood choices like crab, ray wing, gurnard and tandoori monkfish, along with others such as pan-fried venison, chicken stir-fry, pork tenderloin, steaks, mixed grill and salads. A sunny flower-filled garden lies at the rear.

**Open** all day all wk **Bar Meals** L served all wk 12-2.30 booking required D served all wk 6-9.30 booking required Av main course £8.95 **Restaurant** L served all wk 12-2.30 booking required D served all wk 6-9.30 booking required Fixed menu price fr £10 ◖ Betty Stogs, 6X, Sharp's Doom Bar, Guest ale Ö Thatchers. ♇ 22 **Facilities** Children's menu Children's portions Family room Dogs allowed Garden

---

### PERRANUTHNOE     Map 2 SW52

## PICK OF THE PUBS

### The Victoria Inn ★★★ INN ◉

**TR20 9NP** ☎ 01736 710309
**e-mail:** enquiries@victoriainn-penzance.co.uk
**dir:** *Off A394 (Penzance to Helston road), signed Perranuthnoe*

Reputedly Cornwall's oldest inn, the striking, pink-washed Victoria, built to accommodate the masons who extended the parish church in the 12th century, stands within sight of the sea. On fine summer days arrive early as the restful, Mediterranean-style garden and the comfortable, typically Cornish stone-walled bar, adorned with various seafaring and fishing memorabilia, fill up with famished coast path walkers and families strolling up from the beach. Food is taken seriously here, with chef-patron Stewart Eddy, who trained with Raymond Blanc and Michael Caines, cooking the best fish, seafood and seasonal ingredients with care and simplicity. The result is earthy, flavoursome dishes that pack a punch. At dinner, follow duck liver and port pâté, with roast belly of St Buryan pork with onion marmalade, black pudding and apple sauce, or local crab with a oli and herb salad, and sticky toffee pudding with banana ice cream. Add traditional lunch dishes and Sunday roasts, tip-top Doom Bar Bitter on tap, and two individually-decorated, en suite bedrooms, and you have a cracking Cornish coastal gem.

**Open** 12-2 6.30-11 (all day Jun-Sep) **Closed:** 25-26 Dec, 1 Jan, Sun eve & Mon (off season) **Bar Meals** L served all wk 12-2 booking required D served all wk 6.30-11 booking required Av main course £15 **Restaurant** L served all wk 12-2 booking required D served all wk 6.30-11 booking required ⊕ FREE HOUSE ◀ Doom Bar, Tribute ♂ Cornish Orchards. **Facilities** Children's menu Children's portions Dogs allowed Garden Parking **Rooms** 2

---

### POLKERRIS                    Map 2 SX05

## The Rashleigh Inn

**PL24 2TL** ☎ **01726 813991**   📄 **01726 815619**
**e-mail:** jonspode@aol.com
**web:** www.rashleighinnpolkerris.co.uk
**dir:** Off A3082 outside Fowey

Once a boathouse and coastguard station, this 300-year-old, stone-built building became the village pub in 1915 when the previous one was swept away during a storm. There are panoramic views across St Austell Bay from the multi-level heated and panelled terrace. In the refitted bar there's an excellent real ale selection, with real cider and local organic soft drinks are also on offer. There's superb food too, using the best of locally sourced ingredients (suppliers listed on the menu): local mussels, lobster thermidor, West Country chicken with herb dumplings and parsnip and apple mash, Cornish steaks and tapas platters.

**Open** all day all wk **Bar Meals** L served all wk 12-2 D served all wk 6-9 Av main course £8.95 food served all day **Restaurant** L served all wk 12-2 booking required D served all wk 6-9 booking required Fixed menu price fr £8.95 ⊕ FREE HOUSE ◀ Sharp's Doom Bar, Timothy Taylor Landlord, Skinners Betty Stogs, St Austell HSD, Otter Bitter ♂ Stowford Press. **Facilities** Garden Parking

---

### POLPERRO                    Map 2 SX25

## Old Mill House Inn

**Mill Hill PL13 2RP** ☎ **01503 272362**
**e-mail:** enquiries@oldmillhouseinn.co.uk
**dir:** Telephone for directions

In the heart of historic Polperro, this 16th-century inn has been extensively refurbished. Here you can sample well-kept local ales and 'scrumpy' cider beside a log fire in the bar, or sit out over lunch in the riverside garden during fine weather. Local ingredients, with an emphasis on freshly caught fish, are the foundation of dishes on the restaurant menu. Traditional roasts are served on Sundays.

---

**Open** all day all wk 10am-12.30am (Sun 10am-11.30pm) **Bar Meals** L served all wk 10-2.30 D served all wk 5.30-9 ⊕ FREE HOUSE ◀ Skinners, Skinners Mill House Ale, Sharps, Guest ales ♂ Stowford Press, Old Rosie. **Facilities** Children's menu Dogs allowed Garden Parking

---

### PORT GAVERNE                    Map 2 SX08

### PICK OF THE PUBS

## Port Gaverne Hotel ★★ HL ♀

**PL29 3SQ** ☎ **01208 880244**   📄 **01208 880151**
**dir:** Signed from B3314, S of Delabole via B3267 on E of Port Isaac

Just up the lane from a secluded cove is this delightful 17th-century inn. In this once thriving port, women unloaded coal and general merchandise from ships then loaded them up again with slate from the great Delabole quarry until, in 1893, the coming of the railway put paid to the port's prosperity. A meandering building with plenty of period detail, the hotel has long association with fishing and smuggling. As you might expect, locally supplied produce includes plenty of fresh fish, and it appears on all the menus. For example, along with a selection of ploughman's, you might fancy a half pint of prawns at lunchtime, or a seafood pie. At dinner expect starters like tomato, red onion and Cornish goat's cheese salad; crab soup; or lobster and monkfish Thermidor; and mains of sautéed trio of Cornish fish on vegetable rösti; pan-fried John Dory with olive oil mash; or chargrilled sirloin steak au poivre. Walkers from the Heritage Coast Path can pause for a pint in the comfortable, picture-adorned bar or in the small beer garden.

**Open** all day all wk **Bar Meals** L served all wk 12-2.30 D served all wk 6-9 Av main course £8.95 **Restaurant** D served all wk 7-9 Av 3 course à la carte fr £27 ⊕ FREE HOUSE ◀ Sharp's Doom Bar, Bass, St Austell Tribute. ♀ 9 **Facilities** Children's menu Children's portions Dogs allowed Garden Parking **Rooms** 14

---

### PORTHLEVEN                    Map 2 SW62

## The Ship Inn ♀

**TR13 9JS** ☎ **01326 564204**   📄 **01326 564204**
**e-mail:** cjoakden@yahoo.co.uk
**dir:** From Helston follow signs to Porthleven, 2.5m. On entering village continue to harbour. Take W road by side of harbour to inn

Dating from the 17th century, this smugglers' inn is actually built into the cliffs, and is approached by a flight of stone steps. During the winter, two log fires warm the interior, while the flames of a third flicker in the separate Smithy children's room. Expect a good selection of locally caught fish and seafood, such as crab and prawn mornay, or the smoked fish platter, all smoked in Cornwall. The pub has declared itself a 'chip-free zone'.

---

**Open** all day all wk 11.30am-11.30pm (Sun noon-10.30) **Bar Meals** L served all wk 12-2 D served all wk 6.30-9 Av main course £10 ⊕ FREE HOUSE ◀ Courage Best, Sharp's Doom Bar & Special, guest ales ♂ Cornish Orchard. ♀ 8 **Facilities** Children's menu Family room Dogs allowed Garden

---

### PORTREATH                    Map 2 SW64

## Basset Arms

**Tregea Ter TR16 4NG** ☎ **01209 842077**
**e-mail:** bassettarms@btconnect.com
**dir:** From Redruth take B3300 to Portreath. Pub on left near seafront

Tin-mining and shipwreck paraphernalia adorn the low-beamed interior of this early 19th-century Cornish stone cottage, built as a pub to serve harbour workers. At one time it served as a mortuary for ill-fated seafarers, so there are plenty of ghost stories! The menu makes the most of local seafood, such as mussels and fries, and home-made fish pie, but also provides a wide selection of alternatives, including half chicken in barbecue sauce; 12oz gammon steak; curry of the day; and salads including crab, when available. Wash down your meal with a pint of John Smith's.

**Open** all day all wk 11am-11pm (Fri-Sat 11am-mdnt, Sun 11-10.30) **Bar Meals** L served all wk 12-2 D served all wk 6-9 Av main course £9 **Restaurant** L served all wk 12-2 D served all wk 6-9 Av 3 course à la carte fr £20 ⊕ FREE HOUSE ◀ Sharp's Doom Bar, John Smith's Smooth, Skinners Real Ales. **Facilities** Children's menu Children's portions Play area Dogs allowed Garden Parking

---

### RUAN LANIHORNE                    Map 2 SW84

## The Kings Head

**TR2 5NX** ☎ **01872 501263**
**e-mail:** contact@kings-head-roseland.co.uk
**dir:** 3m from Tregony Bridge on A3078

Expect a warm welcome at this traditional country pub set deep in the Roseland countryside. Roaring winter fires, beamed ceilings and mulled wine contrasts with summer days relaxing on the terrace with a jug of Pimms, a pint of Betty Stogs or Rattler Cornish cider. Whatever the time of year, the chef responds with seasonal dishes using the best of local produce, ranging from Cornish crab pâté with cognac with sweet and sour red onion marmalade to pork loin steak pan fried with sherry, garlic and bay leaf. Look out for the signature dish, too - slow-roasted Ruan duckling with a warm pepper sauce.

**Open** 12-2.30 6-11 **Closed:** Sun eve, Mon (Nov-Etr) **Restaurant** L served all wk 12.30-2 booking required D served all wk 6.30-9 booking required Av 3 course à la carte fr £25 ⊕ FREE HOUSE ◀ Skinners Kings Ruan, Cornish Knocker, Betty Stogs ♂ Cornish Rattler. **Facilities** Dogs allowed Garden Parking

## ST AGNES — Map 3 SW75

### PICK OF THE PUBS

#### Driftwood Spars ★★★★ GA ☻

Trevaunance Cove TR5 0RT
☎ 01872 552428   📠 01872 553701
e-mail: info@driftwoodspars.co.uk
dir: A30 onto B3285, through St Agnes, down steep hill, left at Peterville Inn, onto road signed Trevaunance Cove

Just off the South West Coastal Path, this family-run pub occupies a 300-year-old tin miners' store, chandlery and sail loft, complete with its own smugglers' tunnel. It takes its name from spars salvaged from nearby shipwrecks and used in the construction of this 17th-century building. Fifteen bedrooms; a dining room with sea view; two beer gardens; three bars sparkling with real fires, old brass and lanterns; a micro-brewery; and a shop complete this award-winning establishment. Two of the eight ales brewed here are on sale at any one time, alongside guests and a 40-bin wine list. On the menu seafood figures strongly, as do platters of Cornish meats and cheeses; and cream teas with cupcakes. Specials may range from pressed ox tongue terrine to main courses of oven-roasted hake with confit cherry tomatoes and black olive tapenade; and confit leg of Terras Farm duck with sweet potato and sage gratin. Dark chocolate tart with Cornish clotted cream is a typical dessert.

**Open** all day all wk 11-11 (Fri-Sat 11-1am, 25 Dec 11am-2pm) **Bar Meals** L served all wk 12-2.30 D served all wk 6.30-9.30 (winter 6.30-9) Av main course £9.95 **Restaurant** L served Sun 12-2.30 booking required D served all wk 7-9, (winter Thu-Sat 7-9) booking required Av 3 course à la carte fr £24 ⊕ FREE HOUSE ◀ Blue Hills Bitter, Tribute, Betty Stogs, Doom Bar, Dartmoor ♻ Cornish Rattler, Thatchers. ☻ 10 **Facilities** Children's menu Children's portions Dogs allowed Garden Parking **Rooms** 15

## ST AGNES (ISLES OF SCILLY) — Map 2 SV80

### Turks Head

TR22 0PL ☎ 01720 422434
dir: By boat or helicopter to St Mary's & boat on to St Agnes

Named after the 16th-century Turkish pirates who arrived from the Barbary Coast, the Turks Head is Britain's most southwesterly inn. Noted for its atmosphere and superb location overlooking the island quay, this former coastguard boathouse is packed with fascinating model ships and maritime photographs. Lunchtime brings soup, salads and open rolls, while evening dishes might include blackened swordfish steak in Cajun spices, or sirloin steak with all the trimmings.

**Open** all wk Closed: Nov-Feb ⊕ FREE HOUSE ◀ Skinners Betty Stogs, Sharp's Doom Bar, Ales of Scilly, Scuppered, Turks Ale. **Facilities** Dogs allowed Garden

## ST BREWARD — Map 2 SX07

### The Old Inn & Restaurant ☻

Churchtown, Bodmin Moor PL30 4PP
☎ 01208 850711   📠 01208 851671
e-mail: theoldinn@macace.net
dir: A30 to Bodmin. 16m, right just after Temple, follow signs to St Breward. B3266 (Bodmin to Camelford road) turn to St Breward, follow brown signs

Located high up on Bodmin Moor, one of Cornwall's oldest inns is owned and run by local man Darren Wills, the latest licensee in its 1,000-year history. The solid granite pub has slate flagstone floors (where dogs are welcome to sit!), sloping beamed ceilings and two huge granite fireplaces with real fires in winter. It is well-known throughout this glorious area for its wholesome home-cooked food served in the bars or restaurant, frequented by many regulars who are drawn by its Moorland mixed grills and Sunday carvery. Check out the local Cornish wines as well. There is also a large beer garden.

**Open** all day all wk **Bar Meals** L served Sun-Fri 11-2, Sat 11-9 D served Sun-Fri 6-9, Sat 11-9 Av main course £8.95 **Restaurant** L served Mon-Fri 11-2, Sat-Sun 12-9 booking required D served Mon-Fri 6-9, Sat-Sun 12-9 booking required Av 3 course à la carte fr £20 ⊕ FREE HOUSE ◀ Sharp's Doom Bar & Special, guest ales ♻ Sharp's Orchard Cider. ☻ 15 **Facilities** Children's menu Children's portions Family room Dogs allowed Garden Parking

## ST EWE — Map 2 SW94

### The Crown Inn

PL26 6EY ☎ 01726 843322   📠 01726 844720
e-mail: linda@thecrowninn737.fsnet.co.uk
dir: From St Austell take B3273. At Tregiskey x-rds turn right. St Ewe signed on right

The Crown's chef John Nelson co-founded and helped to restore the famous 'Lost Gardens of Heligan', just a mile from this delightful 16th-century inn. Hanging baskets add plenty of brightness and colour to the outside, while indoors you'll find well-kept St Austell ales complementing an extensive menu and daily specials. Expect cod in beer batter, local steaks, rack of lamb, and liver and bacon among other favourites. Try a glass of Polmassick wine from the vineyard only half a mile away.

**Open** all wk **Bar Meals** L served all wk 12-2 D served all wk 6-9.30 Av main course £7.50 **Restaurant** L served all wk 12-2 D served all wk 6-9.30 Fixed menu price fr £10.50 ⊕ ST AUSTELL BREWERY ◀ Tribute, Tinners, guest ale ♻ Cornish Rattler. **Facilities** Children's menu Children's portions Play area Family room Dogs allowed Garden Parking

## ST IVES — Map 2 SW54

### The Watermill

Lelant Downs TR27 6LQ ☎ 01736 757912
e-mail: watermill@btconnect.com
dir: Exit A30 at junct for St Ives/A3074, turn left at 2nd mini rdbt

Built in the 1700s to mill grain for the local estate, the watermill was converted into a pub/restaurant in the 1970s. Old mill machinery is still in place and the iron waterwheel still turns, gravity fed by the mill stream. It is a family friendly establishment, with extensive gardens and fantastic views up the valley towards Trencrom Hill. Bar meals are served, and there is a separate restaurant where steaks and fish (sea bass, sardines and mackerel perhaps) are specialities. Cornish Rattler cider is served along with a range of real ales including Betty Stogs.

**Open** all day all wk noon-11 **Bar Meals** L served all wk 12-2.30 D served all wk 6-9 Av main course £7.50 **Restaurant** D served all wk 6-9 booking required Av 3 course à la carte fr £15 ⊕ FREE HOUSE ◀ Sharp's Doom Bar, Skinner's Betty Stogs, Guest ales ♻ Cornish Rattler. **Facilities** Children's menu Play area Dogs allowed Garden Parking

## ST JUST (NEAR LAND'S END) — Map 2 SW33

### PICK OF THE PUBS

#### Star Inn

TR19 7LL ☎ 01736 788767
dir: Telephone for directions

Plenty of tin mining and fishing stories are told at this traditional Cornish pub, located in the town of St Just, near Land's End. It dates back a few centuries, and was reputedly built to house workmen constructing the 15th-century church. John Wesley is believed to have been among the Star's more illustrious guests over the years, but these days the pub is most likely to be recognised for having featured in several television and film productions. A choice of local beers is served, but there is no food. Monday night is folk night, and there's live music on Thursdays and Saturdays, too, in a whole range of styles.

**Open** all day all wk 11am-12.30am ◄ St Austell HSD, Tinners Ale, Tribute, Dartmoor ○ Cornish Rattler. **Facilities** Family room Dogs allowed Garden **Notes** ✇

## The Wellington ★★ INN

**Market Square TR19 7HD**
☎ 01736 787319    📠 01736 787906
e-mail: wellingtonhotel@msn.com
dir: *Take A30 to Penzance, then A3071 W of Penzance to St Just*

Standing in the market square of an historic mining town, this family-run, stunning granite inn makes an ideal base for exploring the spectacular beaches and countryside of West Penwith. Low ceilings, solid stonework and a secluded walled garden help evoke the atmosphere of Cornwall as it once was. St Austell beers and Cornish Rattler cider are served in the bar, while the kitchen specialises in fresh local produce – crab, Newlyn fish, beef, and Cornish cheeses. There are comfortable en suite rooms available if you would like to stay over.

**Open** all day all wk **Bar Meals** L served all wk 12-2 D served all wk 6-9 (winter 6-8.30) Av main course £8 **Restaurant** D served all wk 6-9 (summer) Av 3 course à la carte fr £17.50 ⊕ ST AUSTELL BREWERY ◄ St Austell Tinners, St Austell Tribute, HSD ○ Cornish Rattler. **Facilities** Play area Dogs allowed Garden **Rooms** 11

### ST MAWES    Map 2 SW83

## PICK OF THE PUBS

## The Victory Inn

**Victory Hill TR2 5DQ**
☎ 01326 270324    📠 01326 270238
e-mail: contact@victory-inn.co.uk
dir: *Take A3078 to St Mawes. Pub up Victory Steps adjacent to harbour*

Named after Nelson's flagship, this friendly fishermen's local near the harbour adopts a modern approach to its daily lunch and dinner menus. You may eat downstairs in the bar, or in the first-floor Seaview Restaurant, with a terrace that looks across the town's rooftops to the harbour and the River Fal. High on the

list of ingredients is fresh seafood - all from Cornish waters, of course - the choice changing virtually daily to include crab risotto; fisherman's pie; and beer-battered cod and hand-cut chips, for example, with chicken breast cordon bleu; lamb shank provençale; and curry or casserole of the day among the other favourites. Children are provided with paper, crayons and their own menu; dogs are given treats too. Wines are all carefully chosen and excellent in quality, as are the real ales from Cornwall's own Roseland, Sharp's and Skinners breweries.

**Open** all day all wk 11am-mdnt **Bar Meals** L served all wk 12-3 D served all wk 6-9.30 booking required Av main course £9.95 **Restaurant** L served all wk 12-3 D served all wk 6-9.15 booking required ⊕ PUNCH TAVERNS ◄ Sharp's, Bass, Wadworth 6X, Roseland Brewery Cornish Shag, Skinner's Betty Stogs. **Facilities** Children's menu Children's portions Dogs allowed Garden

### ST MAWGAN    Map 2 SW86

## PICK OF THE PUBS

## The Falcon Inn ★★★★ INN ⬤

**TR8 4EP** ☎ 01637 860225    📠 01637 860884
e-mail: info@thefalconinn-stmawgan.co.uk
dir: *From A30 (8m W of Bodmin) follow signs to Newquay/St Mawgan Airport. After 2m right into village, pub at bottom of hill*

You'll find this pub nestling in the sheltered Vale of Lanherne, in a village of outstanding tranquility and natural beauty. Nearby, traces of a 6th-century Celtic monastery can be found in what became the Arundel family manor house – today a convent housing nuns and friars. The wisteria-covered Falcon has a large attractive garden, magnificent magnolia tree and cobbled courtyard. The interior is cosy and relaxed, with flagstone floors and log fires in winter; plus comfortable accommodation is available. Beers from St Austell Brewery are augmented by Rattler cider, and a dozen wines are served by the glass. At lunchtime home-made soups, sandwiches, jacket potatoes, and main courses such as chicken and mushroom pie are the order of the day. An à la carte evening menu is served in the more formal restaurant. Dishes may feature starters of antipasto misto or roast vegetable bruschetta. Main courses always include fresh fish options, and vegetarians are well catered for.

**Open** all wk 11-3 6-11 (Jul-Aug open all day) Closed: 25 Dec (open 12-2) **Bar Meals** L served all wk 12-2 D served all wk 6-9 **Restaurant** L served all wk 12-2 D served all wk 6-9 ⊕ ST AUSTELL BREWERY ◄ St Austell HSD, Tinners Ale, Tribute, Proper Job IPA ○ Cornish Rattler. ⬤ 12 **Facilities** Children's menu Children's portions Dogs allowed Garden Parking **Rooms** 2

### ST MERRYN    Map 2 SW87

## PICK OF THE PUBS

## The Cornish Arms ⬤

**PL28 8ND** ☎ 01841 520288    📠 01841 521496
e-mail: cornisharms@rickstein.com
dir: *From Padstow follow signs for St Merryn then Churchtown*

Rick Stein and his ex-wife Jill liked their local pub so much that they bought it. Actually, they're tenants, but that spoils the story. Initially, the locals were concerned they were going to turn it into a gastro-pub, but that was never their intention. Head chef Julian Lloyd's no-nonsense British pub menu lists goujons of lemon sole with salad and tartare sauce; pan-fried polenta with field mushroom, rocket and aïoli; Tywardreath pork and garlic sausages, mash and onion gravy; and hot and spicy Goan chicken curry with steamed rice. As happy St Austell Brewery tenants, they serve Tribute, Tinners, HSD and Proper Job cask ales, while Rick has developed a couple of recipes to go with their bottled beer, Clouded Yellow, as an alternative to his own Chalky's Bark and Chalky's Bite, named after his much-missed rough-haired Jack Russell.

**Open** all wk (25 Dec open 2hrs only, winter 3-5pm) **Bar Meals** L served all wk 12-3 D served all wk 6-9 (summer & school hol open all day) Av main course £9.60 ◄ St Austell Tribute, Proper Job, Tinners, Sharp's Chalky's Bite ○ Cornish Rattler. ⬤ 11 **Facilities** Children's menu Dogs allowed Garden Parking

### ST NEOT    Map 2 SX16

## The London Inn ⬤

**PL14 6NG** ☎ 01579 320263    📠 01579 321642
e-mail: ho@ccinns.com
dir: *Telephone for directions*

Dating back to the 18th century, this pub was the first coaching inn on the route from Penzance to London. The bar and dining areas have old beamed ceilings and polished flagstone floors. Seafood platter, salmon, and halibut are among the fish dishes, while other main courses include lamb shank in a spiced port sauce. Lighter fare ranges from ciabatta bread with a variety of fillings, including roast beef, chicken, bacon and cheese, to a choice of ploughman's lunches.

**Open** all wk Mon-Fri 12-3 (Sat-Sun 12-11) ⊕ PIRAN INNS LTD ◄ Doom Bar, Tribute, Guest Ales ○ Stowford Press. ⬤ 16 **Facilities** Dogs allowed Parking

# PICK OF THE PUBS

# The Mill House Inn

**TREBARWITH**  Map 2 SX08

**PL34 0HD**
☎ 01840 770200  📠 01840 770647
e-mail:
management@themillhouseinn.co.uk
web: www.themillhouseinn.co.uk
dir: *From Tintagel take B3263 S, right after Trewarmett to Trebarwith Strand. Pub 0.5m on right*

Tintagel Castle, famously associated with the legend of King Arthur, stands on its 'island' at the bottom of the next valley to this charming 18th century corn mill. Dating from 1760, it was still working in the late 1930s, then became successively a private house, a guest house and finally, in 1960, a pub.

Set in seven acres of wooded gardens on the north Cornish coast, it's a beautifully atmospheric stone building, with log fires in the residents' lounge

and an informally furnished, slate-floored bar, where wooden tables and chapel chairs help to create a relaxed, family-friendly feel. Locally brewed real ales come from Sharp's, Skinner's and Tintagel, and ciders made by Cornish Orchards and Rattler.

Lunches, evening drinks and barbecues are particularly enjoyable outside on the attractive split-level terraces, while dinner in the restaurant over the millstream is also an appealing experience. Regularly changing dishes use the best fresh fish, meat, vegetables and other ingredients, all North Cornwall sourced. The bar menu lists crispy sweet chilli beef or pork with stir-fry noodles; scampi with lemon, chips and peas; and season-dependent winter stew of the day. A typical dinner might be tian of Port Isaac crab and smoked salmon; then Thai-style crispy pork belly with Asian noodles, sautéed bok choi and sesame; or wild mushroom and rocket pappardelle pasta in white wine cream sauce; followed by Kirsch-cured cherry and almond tartlet.

An unusual and creative wine list ensures a good choice of complementary

wines. Live music is often a possibility. The surfing beach at Trebarwith Strand, half a mile from the inn, is one of the finest in Cornwall.

**Open** all wk 11-11 (Fri-Sat 11am-mdnt, Sun noon-10.30) Closed: 25 Dec
**Bar Meals** L served Mon-Sat 12-2.30, Sun 12-3 D served all wk 6.30-8.30
**Restaurant** D served all wk 7-9
⊕ FREE HOUSE 🍺 Sharp's Doom Bar, Skinners Cornish Knocker, Tintagel Brewery Harbour Special Ò Cornish Orchards, Rattler.
**Facilities** Children's menu Play area Family room Dogs allowed Garden Parking

## SALTASH — Map 3 SX45

### The Crooked Inn ★★★ GA

Stoketon Cottage, Trematon PL12 4RZ
☎ 01752 848177 📄 01752 843203
e-mail: info@crooked-inn.co.uk
dir: *Telephone for directions*

A family-run inn that overlooks the lush Lyher Valley, and once housed staff from Stoketon Manor, whose ruins lie the other side of the courtyard. Traditional, home-made dishes include pie, pasta or curry of the day; battered fresh cod; breaded wholetail scampi; and 'generous, hefty, ample or copious' steaks. Boards list lunchtime, evening and vegetarian specials and there's also a 'Little Horrors' menu. The children's playground has friendly animals, swings, slides, a trampoline and a treehouse. Spacious bedrooms are well equipped.

**Open** all wk Closed: 25 Dec ⊕ FREE HOUSE ◀ Hicks Special Draught, Sharp's Own Ale, Skinner's Cornish Knocker Ale. **Facilities** Play area Dogs allowed Garden Parking **Rooms** 18

## SENNEN — Map 2 SW32

### The Old Success Inn

Sennen Cove TR19 7DG
☎ 01736 871232 📄 01736 871457
e-mail: oldsuccess@staustellbrewery.co.uk
dir: *Telephone for directions*

Once the haunt of smugglers and now a focal point for the Sennen Lifeboat crew, this 17th-century inn enjoys a glorious location overlooking Cape Cornwall. Its name comes from the days when fishermen gathered here to count their catch and share out their 'successes'. Fresh local seafood is to the fore, and favourites include cod in Doom Bar batter, steaks, chilli, and vegetable lasagne. Live music every Saturday night in the bar.

**Open** all wk Mon-Sat 10-11 ( Sun 12-10.30) **Bar Meals** L served all wk 12-2 D served all wk 6-9 **Restaurant** L served all wk 12-2 D served all wk 6-9 ⊕ St Austell Brewery ◀ Tribute, HSD, Proper Job ⚬ Rattler. **Facilities** Children's menu Dogs allowed Garden Parking

## TINTAGEL — Map 2 SX08

### The Port William ♟

Trebarwith Strand PL34 0HB
☎ 01840 770230 📄 01840 770936
e-mail: theportwilliam@btinternet.com
dir: *Off B3263 between Camelford & Tintagel, pub signed*

Occupying one of the best locations in Cornwall, this former harbourmaster's house lies directly on the coastal path, 50 yards from the sea. There is an entrance to a smugglers' tunnel at the rear of the ladies' toilet! Focus on the daily-changing specials board for such dishes as artichoke and roast pepper salad, warm smoked trout platter, and spinach ricotta tortelloni. There has been a change of hands.

**Open** all wk Mon-Sat 10-11 12-3, 3-6, 6-9 ⊕ ST AUSTELL BREWERY ◀ Tribute, Tinners, Guest ales ⚬ Cornish Rattler. ♟ 8 **Facilities** Family room Dogs allowed Garden Parking

## TORPOINT — Map 3 SX45

### PICK OF THE PUBS

### Edgcumbe Arms

Cremyll PL10 1HX
☎ 01752 822294 📄 01752 829086
dir: *Telephone for directions*

The inn dates from the 15th century and is located right on the Tamar estuary, next to the National Trust Park, close to the foot ferry from Plymouth. Views from the bow window seats and waterside terrace are glorious, taking in Drakes Island, the Royal William Yard and the marina. Real ales from St Austell like Cornish Cream, Proper Job, Tribute HS and Tinners, and quality home-cooked food are served in a series of rooms, which are full of character with American oak panelling and stone flagged floors. A good choice of bar snacks is also offered. The inn has a first floor function room with sea views, and a courtyard garden; it also holds a civil wedding licence.

**Open** all day all wk 11am-11pm **Bar Meals** L served Mon-Fri 12-6, Sat-Sun 12-8 D served Mon-Fri 6-9, Sat-Sun 12-9 **Restaurant** food served all day ⊕ ST AUSTELL BREWERY ◀ St Austell HSD, Tribute HS, IPA, guest ales ⚬ Cornish Rattler. **Facilities** Children's menu Children's portions Dogs allowed Garden Parking

## TREBARWITH — Map 2 SX08

### PICK OF THE PUBS

### The Mill House Inn

*See Pick of the Pubs on opposite page*

## TREBURLEY — Map 3 SX37

### PICK OF THE PUBS

### The Springer Spaniel

*See Pick of the Pubs on page 92*

## TREGADILLETT — Map 3 SX28

### Eliot Arms ♟

PL15 7EU ☎ 01566 772051
dir: *From Launceston take A30 towards Bodmin. Then follow brown signs to Tregadillett*

The extraordinary decor in this charming creeper-clad coaching inn, dating back to 1625, includes Masonic regalia, horse brasses and grandfather clocks. It was believed to have been a Masonic lodge for Napoleonic prisoners, and even has its own friendly ghost! Customers can enjoy real fires in winter and lovely hanging baskets in summer. Food, based on locally sourced meat and fresh fish and shellfish caught off the Cornish coast, is served in the bar or bright and airy restaurant. Expect home-made soups, pie and curry of the day; steak and chips; chargrills; and home-made vegetarian dishes.

**Open** all day all wk 11.30-11 (Fri-Sat 11.30am-mdnt, Sun noon-10.30) **Bar Meals** L served all wk 12-2 booking required D served all wk 6-9 booking required Av main course £8.95 **Restaurant** L served all wk 12-2 booking required D served all wk 6-9 booking required ⊕ FREE HOUSE ◀ Sharp's Doom Bar, Courage Best. ♟ 9 **Facilities** Family room Dogs allowed Parking

## TRESCO (ISLES OF SCILLY) — Map 2 SV81

### PICK OF THE PUBS

### The New Inn ★★★★ INN ◉ ♟

New Grimsby TR24 0QQ
☎ 01720 422844 📄 01720 423200
e-mail: newinn@tresco.co.uk
dir: *By New Grimsby Quay*

As the sole survivor of the once-thirteen island pubs this has to be, as landlord Robin Lawson says, the "Best Pub on Tresco". Everywhere you look is maritime history, much of it, such as the signboard, mahogany bar and wall-planking, salvaged from wrecks. An AA Rosette recognises the quality of food in the quiet restaurant, the livelier Driftwood Bar, the Pavillion, and outside, all singing from the same menu. Accompany a lunchtime grilled pollock and chips with a pint of Scillonian real ale or Cornish Rattler cider. For dinner, seek out salmon fishcakes with spinach and white wine cream; braised Cornish pork sausages with creamed mash and onion gravy; or roasted red pepper, pear, walnut and goat's cheese gnocchi. Traditional roasts are served on Sundays. Some of the rooms available have ocean views. A 10:10 signatory, the New Inn is aiming for a ten per cent carbon emissions cut this year.

**Open** all wk all day (Apr-Oct) phone for winter opening **Bar Meals** L served all wk 12-2.30 D served all wk 6-9 Av main course £12.50 **Restaurant** D served all wk 6-9 booking required Av 3 course à la carte fr £21 ⊕ TRESCO ESTATE ◀ Skinner's Betty Stogs Bitter, Tresco Tipple, Ales of Scilly Scuppered & Firebrand, St Austell IPA ⚬ Cornish Rattler. ♟ 13 **Facilities** Children's menu Children's portions Garden **Rooms** 16

# PICK OF THE PUBS

## The Springer Spaniel

**TREBURLEY** Map 3 SX37

PL15 9NS ☎ 01579 370424
e-mail:
enquiries@thespringerspaniel.org.uk
web: www.thespringerspaniel.org.uk
dir: *On A388 halfway between Launceston & Callington*

The creeper-clad walls of this 200 year-old free house shelter a cosy bar with high-backed wooden settles, farmhouse-style chairs and a wood-burning stove. You can bring your dog, join in with the chat, read the papers or cast an eye over the many books in the snug. Owner-managers Roger and Lavinia Halliday aim to provide the best that a traditional Cornish hostelry can offer - reliable ales, delicious food, fine wines and friendly service.

The restaurant is full of plants and flowers, with flickering candles in the evenings adding to the romantic atmosphere. In summer the landscaped, sheltered garden is a great place to relax and enjoy the sunshine with a pint of St Austell Tribute. The fully stocked bar also includes other local brews and guest ales, as well as a wine list designed to complement the food on offer.

Food is a big draw here, with beef from the owners' neighbouring organic farm supplementing ingredients from the best local suppliers. Bar lunches range from the ever-popular ploughman's, and a selection of hot filled foccacias; to pub favourites like organic beef sausages and mash. Meanwhile a three-course meal from the specials board might begin with smoked mackerel with gooseberry and elderflower chutney, before moving on to rack of lamb with a rosemary crust and red wine jus. Desserts include vanilla pannacotta with kiwi and orange, and mulled wine poached pears with a cinnamon shortbread biscuit. Children are always welcome, and will enjoy the 'Little Jack Russell' menu which serves up soft drinks, organic burgers and sausages, as well as a seasonal vegetable pasta bake.

**Open** all wk noon-2.30 6-10.30
**Bar Meals** L served all wk 12-1.45 D served all wk 6.15-8.45 **Restaurant** L served all wk 12-1.45 D served all wk 6.15-8.45 ⊕ FREE HOUSE ◄ Sharp's Doom Bar, Skinner's Betty Stogs, St Austell Tribute, guest ale ♂ Cornish Rattler, Cornish Orchard's Black & Gold.
**Facilities** Children's menu Family room Dogs allowed Garden Parking

## TRURO                                    Map 2 SW84

### Old Ale House ♀

**7 Quay St TR1 2HD** ☎ **01872 271122**   📠 **01872 271817**
**e-mail:** old.ale.house@btconnect.com
**dir:** *In town centre*

Olde-worlde establishment with a large selection of real
ales on display, as well as more than twenty flavours of
fruit wine. Lots of attractions, including live music and
various quiz and games nights. Food includes 'huge
hands of hot bread', oven-baked jacket potatoes,
ploughman's lunches and daily specials. Vegetable stir
fry, five spice chicken and sizzling beef feature among
the sizzling skillets.

**Open** all wk 11-11 (Fri-Sat 11-12 Sun 12-10.30) Closed:
25 Dec, 26 Dec, 1 Jan **Restaurant** L served Mon-Sun 12-2
⊕ ENTERPRISE INNS ◀ Skinners Kiddlywink, Shepherd
Neame Spitfire, Courage Bass, Greene King Abbot Ale,
Fuller's London Pride. ♀ 9

### The Wig & Pen Inn

**Frances St TR1 3DP**
☎ **01872 273028**   📠 **01872 277351**
**dir:** *In city centre near Law Courts. 10 mins from rail
station*

A listed city centre pub originally known as the Star, that
became the Wig & Pen when the county court moved to
Truro. There is a ghost called Claire who lives in the
cellar, but she is friendly! The choice of food includes
such home-made dishes as steak and ale pie, curry,
casseroles, steaks and vegetarian dishes, and a range of
fish options such as sea bass, John Dory, mullet or
monkfish.

**Open** all wk ◀ St Austell, Tribute, IPA, HSD, guest ales.
**Facilities** Dogs allowed Garden

## TYWARDREATH                             Map 2 SX05

### The Royal Inn ★★★★ INN ♀

**66 Eastcliffe Rd PL24 2AJ**
☎ **01726 815601**   📠 **01726 816415**
**e-mail:** info@royal-inn.co.uk
**dir:** *A3082 Par, follow brown tourist signs for 'Newquay
Branch line' or railway station. Pub opp rail station*

Travellers and employees of the Great Western Railway
once frequented this 19th-century inn, which was named
after a visit by King Edward VII to a local copper mine.
These days it's much extended and smartly refurbished,
with an open-plan bar serving a variety of real ales.
Leading off are the dining areas which comprise a cosy
beamed room and the Ladybird conservatory. Pub
classics include home-made steak and ale pie, or chef's
favourites like bacon and brie chicken. Fifteen
comfortable rooms are available. There has been a
change of hands.

**Open** all day all wk 11.30am-11pm (Sun 12-10.30)
**Bar Meals** L served all wk 12-2 D served Mon-Sat 6.30-9,
Sun 7-9 **Restaurant** L served all wk 12-2 D served Mon-
Sat 6.30-9, Sun 7-9 booking required ⊕ FREE HOUSE

◀ Sharp's Doom Bar & Special Ale, Wells Bombardier,
Shepherd Neame Spitfire, Cotleigh Barn Owl ♦ Cornish
Rattler. ♀ 13 **Facilities** Children's menu Dogs allowed
Garden Parking **Rooms** 15

## VERYAN                                   Map 2 SW93

### The New Inn ♀

**TR2 5QA** ☎ **01872 501362**
**dir:** *From St Austell take A390 towards Truro, in 2m left to
Tregony. Through Tregony, follow signs to Veryan*

Based in a pair of 16th-century cottages, this unspoilt
pub, now in new hands, is found in the centre of a pretty
village on the Roseland Peninsula. It has a single bar,
open fires and a beamed ceiling, and the emphasis is on
good ales and home cooking. Simple, satisfying dishes
abound, with seafood featuring heavily: expect deep-fried
whitebait; red mullet fillets with pink peppercorn
dressing; goat's cheese tart; and lamb shank roasted in
white wine and mint.

**Open** all day all wk **Bar Meals** L served all wk 12-2 D
served all wk 6.30-9 Av main course £10 **Restaurant** L
served all wk 12-2 booking required D served all wk
6.30-9 booking required ⊕ ST AUSTELL BREWERY ◀ St
Austell HSD, Dartmoor Ale & Tribute, IPA ♦ Cornish
Rattler. **Facilities** Children's menu Children's portions
Dogs allowed Garden

## WADEBRIDGE                               Map 2 SW97

### The Quarryman Inn

**Edmonton PL27 7JA** ☎ **01208 816444**
**dir:** *Off A39 opposite Royal Cornwall Showground*

Close to the famous Camel Trail, this friendly 18th-
century free house has evolved from a courtyard of
cottages once home to slate workers from the nearby
quarry. Several bow windows, one of which features a
stained-glass quarryman panel, add character to this
unusual inn. The pub's signature dishes are chargrilled
steaks served on sizzling platters and fresh local
seafood; puddings are on the blackboard. The first
Tuesday night of the month features curries made to
authentic recipes.

**Open** all day all wk noon-11pm **Bar Meals** L served all wk
12-2.30 booking required D served all wk 6-9 booking
required Av main course £12.90 ⊕ FREE HOUSE
◀ Sharp's, Skinners, Timothy Taylor Landlord, Alton's
Pride, guest ales. **Facilities** Children's menu Children's
portions Dogs allowed Garden Parking

### Swan ♀

**9 Molesworth St PL27 7DD**
☎ **01208 812526**   📠 **01208 812526**
**e-mail:** reservations@smallandfriendly.co.uk
**dir:** *In centre of Wadebridge on corner of Molesworth St
& The Platt*

A town centre hotel that is family friendly, it was
originally called the Commercial Hotel, and sits alongside
the Camel Trail. Typical pub food includes doorstep
sandwiches and baguettes, light snacks like cheesy
chips, salads, chargrill dishes, full Cornish breakfast and
main courses like Tribute beer-battered cod, or curry of
the day. Children's dishes include chicken nuggets made
of 100% chicken breast; pizza or pork sausage.

**Open** all day all wk Mon-Sun 9.30-mdnt **Bar Meals** L
served all wk 12-9 ⊕ ST AUSTELL BREWERY ◀ Tribute,
IPA, Guinness ♦ Rattler. ♀ 13 **Facilities** Children's menu
Family room Dogs allowed Garden

## WIDEMOUTH BAY                            Map 2 SS20

### Bay View Inn ♀

**EX23 0AW** ☎ **01288 361273 & 01288 361145**
**e-mail:** thebayviewinn@aol.com
**dir:** *On Marine Drive adjacent to beach in Widemouth Bay*

As its name implies, this pub has wonderful views of the
rolling Atlantic from its restaurant and the large raised
decking area outside. About a hundred years old, it was a
guest house for many years before becoming an inn in
the 1960s. The menu makes excellent use of Cornish
produce, including fresh fish (perhaps in Betty Stogs beer
batter) and signature dish of fillet steak with spinach,
porcini mushroom pâté, pancetta and a red wine
reduction. There are barbecues in the garden during July
and August. Dogs allowed in the bar area only.

**Open** all day all wk **Bar Meals** L served Mon-Sat 12-2.30,
Sun 12-9 D served Mon-Sat 6-9, Sun 12-9 food served all
day **Restaurant** L served Mon-Sat 12-2.30, Sun 12-9 D
served Mon-Sat 6-9, Sun 12-9 ◀ Sharp's Doom Bar,
Skinner's Betty Stogs, Bayview Sunset ♦ Stowford Press.
♀ 17 **Facilities** Children's menu Play area Dogs allowed
Garden Parking

## ZENNOR                                   Map 2 SW43

### PICK OF THE PUBS

### The Gurnard's Head ★★★ INN ⊕⊕ ♀

**Treen TR26 3DE** ☎ **01736 796928**
**e-mail:** enquiries@gurnardshead.co.uk
**dir:** *5m from Penzance. 5m from St Ives on B3306*

An imposing, colour-washed building dominating the
coast above Gurnard's Head, this refurbished
restaurant and pub with rooms is just the place to stay
on a windswept night, when Cornwall is at its most
brutal. When the weather's good (which it often is) the
coastal path and rugged Penwith Moors walks are
fantastic. The bar has old tables and chairs, rugs on a
stone floor, log fires, and loads of books; the snug

*continued*

## ZENNOR continued

leads to the simply furnished, candlelit restaurant. Here, food is taken seriously, hence the two AA Rosettes. Frequently appearing as main courses are stuffed pork loin with sage gnocchi, carrots and purple sprouting broccoli; mackerel with chorizo, Puy lentils and rocket; and butternut squash with spinach, sage and walnut risotto. There are many vegetarian options available. Skinner's Press Gang cider accompanies the same brewery's Betty Stogs real ale at the bar.

**Open** all day all wk Closed: 24-25 Dec,
**Bar Meals** L served all wk 12.30-2.30 booking required D served all wk 6.30-9.30 booking required Av main course £11.50 **Restaurant** L served all wk 12.30-2.30 booking required D served all wk 6.30-9.30 booking required ◀ Betty Stogs, Tribute Ö Skinner's Press Gang. ♀ 16 **Facilities** Children's menu Dogs allowed Garden Parking **Rooms** 7

## The Tinners Arms ♀

TR26 3BY ☎ 01736 796927
**e-mail:** tinners@tinnersarms.com
**dir:** Take B3306 from St Ives towards St Just. Zennor approx 5m

The only pub in the village, this 13th-century, granite-built free house is close to the South West coastal path and is particularly popular with walkers. Built to house the masons who built the church next door, it has changed very little over the years, with its stone floors and low ceilings. During WWI DH Lawrence stayed here for some months. The main bar has open fires at both ends and outside there is a large terrace with sea views. A dinner menu, based on ingredients from local suppliers, might include half a pint of shell-on prawns, Cornish sirloin and brisket stew, 21-day hung steak, or wild brill with thyme and mushroom butter.

**Open** all wk **Bar Meals** L served all wk 12-2.30 D served all wk 6.30-9 Av main course £12.50 ⊕ FREE HOUSE ◀ Zennor Mermaid, Tinners Ale, Sharps Own Ö Burrow Hill. ♀ 10 **Facilities** Children's menu Children's portions Family room Dogs allowed Garden Parking

---

### CUMBRIA

| AMBLESIDE | Map 18 NY30 |
|---|---|

### PICK OF THE PUBS

## Drunken Duck
Inn ★★★★★ INN ⊛⊛ ♀

*See Pick of the Pubs on opposite page*

---

## Wateredge Inn ★★★★ INN ♀

Waterhead Bay LA22 0EP
☎ 015394 32332    📠 015394 31878
**e-mail:** stay@wateredgeinn.co.uk
**dir:** M6 junct 36, A591 to Ambleside, 5m from Windermere station

The inn's name sums up its idyllic position on the banks of Lake Windermere, with Ambleside just a short stroll away. Run by the same family for over 25 years, the inn was originally developed from two 17th-century fishermen's cottages. Real ales and 13 wines by the glass can be sipped whilst appreciating the spectacular views from the heated lakeside patio. On the bar and bistro menu, choose from classic pub fare augmented by some gastro dishes. There are pretty, spacious bedrooms available.

**Open** all wk 10.30-11 **Bar Meals** L served Mon-Fri 12-2.30, Sat 12-4 D served Mon-Fri 6-9.30, Sat 5.30-8.30 ⊕ FREE HOUSE ◀ Theakstons, Barn Gates Brewery, Colly Wobbles, Tag Lag, Cat Nap, Ö Simmons. ♀ 13 **Facilities** Children's menu Dogs allowed Garden Parking **Rooms** 22

---

| APPLEBY-IN-WESTMORLAND | Map 18 NY62 |
|---|---|

## The Royal Oak ♀

Bongate CA16 6UN ☎ 017683 51463    📠 017683 52300
**e-mail:** jan@royaloakappleby.co.uk
**dir:** M6 junct 38 take B6260 to Appleby-in-Westmorland

Parts of this venerable former coaching inn date back to 1100, with 17th-century additions. The building has been sympathetically and painstakingly refurbished to provide a classic dog-friendly tap-room with blackened beams, an oak-panelled lounge with open fire, and a comfortable restaurant. The modern British menu uses the best of local ingredients and features dishes like rosemary and garlic studded lamb shank; stuffed chicken fillet with celery, onion and peppers; and sun-dried tomato, roasted red pepper and goat's cheese tart. Enjoy your visit with a pint of Hawkshead.

**Open** all day all wk **Bar Meals** L served Mon-Fri 8-3, Sat-Sun all day D served Mon-Fri 5-9, Sat-Sun all day Av main course £10 **Restaurant** L served Mon-Fri 8-3, Sat-Sun all day D served Mon-Fri 5-9, Sat-Sun all day Av 3 course à la carte fr £22.50 ⊕ FREE HOUSE ◀ Hawkshead, Black Sheep, Timothy Taylor. ♀ 9 **Facilities** Children's menu Children's portions Dogs allowed Garden Parking

---

### PICK OF THE PUBS

## Tufton Arms Hotel ♀

Market Square CA16 6XA
☎ 017683 51593    📠 017683 52761
**e-mail:** info@tuftonarmshotel.co.uk
**dir:** In town centre

Appleby-in-Westmorland is a medieval market town nestling in the heart of a valley so magically unspoilt that the only possible name for it is Eden. The Milsom family have lovingly restored the Tufton Arms to its

---

former Victorian splendour with rich drapes, period paintings and antique furniture. The elegant conservatory restaurant overlooks a cobbled mews courtyard; light and airy in the daytime, this room takes on an attractive glow in the evening when the curtains are closed and the lighting is low. Chef David Milsom and his kitchen team have won many accolades for their superb food, which comprises a selection of delicious dishes made from the finest and freshest local ingredients. Typical starters include creamy garlic mushrooms or a platter of oak-smoked salmon. Move on to roast rack of Eden Valley lamb; loin of pork chop; or baked cod steak. Round off with home-made lemon cheesecake or brandy snap basket filled with chocolate mousse.

**Open** all day all wk 7am-11pm Closed: 25-26 Dec **Bar Meals** L served all wk 12-2 D served all wk 6.30-9 **Restaurant** L served all wk 12-2 D served all wk 6.30-9 ⊕ FREE HOUSE ◀ Tufton Arms Ale, Flowers IPA, Tennants. ♀ 15 **Facilities** Dogs allowed Parking

---

| ARMATHWAITE | Map 18 NY54 |
|---|---|

## The Dukes Head Inn ★★★ INN ♀

Front St CA4 9PB ☎ 016974 72226
**e-mail:** info@dukeshead-hotel.co.uk
**dir:** 9m from Penrith, 10m from Carlisle between junct 41 & 42 of M6

First licensed when the Carlisle to Settle railway was being built, this homely, whitewashed inn stands in the heart of a tiny village in the beautiful Eden Valley. Follow a fabulous walk along the banks of the River Eden with a pint of Black Sheep and a hearty meal in the civilised lounge bar, with its stone walls, open fires and sturdy oak settles and tables. Follow hot potted Solway shrimps, with venison, pheasant and rabbit hotpot with pickled red cabbage, or steak, kidney and pie, leaving room for sticky toffee pudding with toffee sauce. There are five comfortable bedrooms available.

**Open** all wk 11.30-11.30 Closed: 25 Dec **Bar Meals** L served Mon-Sat 12-2, Sun 12-2.30 D served all wk 6.30-9 Av main course £11.75 **Restaurant** L served Mon-Sat 12-2, Sun 12-2.30 D served all wk 6.30-9 Av 3 course à la carte fr £17.50 ⊕ PUNCH TAVERNS ◀ Jennings Cumberland Ale, Black Sheep Bitter, Black Cat Mild, Lancaster Blonde Ö Aspall's Premier Cru, Westons, Thatchers. ♀ 9 **Facilities** Children's menu Children's portions Dogs allowed Garden Parking **Rooms** 5

---

| BAMPTON | Map 18 NY51 |
|---|---|

## Mardale Inn

CA10 2RQ ☎ 01931 713244
**e-mail:** info@mardaleinn.co.uk
**dir:** Telephone for directions

Situated in one of the most rural parts of the Lake District, this whitewashed, early 18th-century inn is perfect for walking, biking and fishing. The interior is a refreshing mix of rural beams and rustic furniture and

*continued on page 96*

# PICK OF THE PUBS

## Drunken Duck Inn ★★★★★INN   ♟

**AMBLESIDE**                    Map 18 NY30

**Barngates LA22 0NG**
☎ 015394 36347    📄 015394 36781
**e-mail:** info@drunkenduckinn.co.uk
**web:** www.drunkenduckinn.co.uk
**dir:** *From Kendal on A591 to Ambleside, then follow Hawkshead sign. In 2.5m inn sign on right, 1m up hill*

Located on a crossroads high above Lake Windermere, this traditional whitewashed free house is just a short drive from the local beauty spot of Tarn Hows. In the same ownership since the mid-1970s, the 17th-century inn continues to offer good service, with excellent food and drink in a friendly, relaxed atmosphere.

The amusing title dates back to Victorian times, when the landlady found her ducks motionless in the road. Thinking that they were dead, she began to pluck them for the pot, unaware that they were merely legless from drinking beer that had leaked into their feed. Legend has it that after the ducks recovered on their way to the oven, the good lady knitted them waistcoats to wear until their feathers grew back. No such risk today - the adjoining Barngates Brewery takes good care of its award-winning real ales, which are served in the oak-floored bar with its open fire, leather club chairs and beautiful slate bar top.

Excellent, locally-sourced food is served in three informal restaurant areas. Lunchtime brings a range of soups, cob sandwiches and ploughman's, as well as hot dishes like Cullen skink with poached egg; wild mushrooms on toast; and corn-fed chicken with fondant potato, wilted spinach and pan jus. A three course restaurant meal might begin with crab and shrimp tortellini with prawn bisque and rocket, followed by braised belly pork and black pudding with boulangère wilted lettuce, Calvados apples and sauce. Leave room for rhubarb and duck egg custard tart with clotted cream.

Each of the seventeen bedrooms comes complete with antique furniture, prints and designer fabrics. After an invigorating walk there's nothing better than relaxing on the front verandah with a pint of Barngates Cracker Ale, whilst soaking up the view to Lake Windermere.

**Open** all wk Closed: 25 Dec
**Bar Meals** L served all wk 12-4 Av main course £20 **Restaurant** D served all wk 6-9.30 booking required Av 3 course à la carte fr £40 🛢 FREE HOUSE ◼ Barngates Cracker Ale, Chesters Strong & Ugly, Tag Lag, Catnap, Mothbag, 1 guest ale. ♟ 17
**Facilities** Garden Parking **Rooms** 17

## BAMPTON *continued*

more modern colours and design. There is a great selection of real ales to enjoy while perusing the menu. A sample dinner menu may include Morecambe Bay potted shrimp followed by Withnail venison burgers topped with local blue cheese and served with home-made chips. Dogs are welcome in all public areas, and fans of cult movie, *Withnail and I*, will find plenty of the film's locations in the area.

**Open** all wk 11-11 **Bar Meals** L served all wk 12-6 D served all wk 6-9 food served all day ⊕ FREE HOUSE ◀ Coniston Bluebird, Timothy Taylor Landlord, Hesket Newmarket High Pike, Dent Aviator, Tirril.
**Facilities** Children's menu Children's portions Dogs allowed Parking

---

### BARBON — Map 18 SD68

## The Barbon Inn ♀

LA6 2LJ ☎ 015242 76233 📄 051242 76574
**e-mail:** info@barbon-inn.co.uk
**dir:** *3.5m N of Kirkby Lonsdale on A683*

A 17th-century coaching inn with oak beams and open fires, the Barbon is situated in a quiet village between the lakes and dales. Pockmarks in a settle tell of a 19th-century shooting, and there's also a tale of a hanged highwayman. A good choice of wines and real ales is offered alongside dishes like Morecambe Bay potted shrimps and roast fillet of pork with Marsala sauce and apricot compote. Special diets are happily catered for.

**Open** all wk 12-2 6-11 (Sun 6-10.30) Closed: 25 Dec
**Bar Meals** L served all wk 12-2 D served all wk 6-9 ⊕ FREE HOUSE ◀ York Brewery, Dent, Tirril, Kirby Lonsdale Ö Old English. ♀ 20 **Facilities** Children's portions Dogs allowed Garden Parking

---

### BASSENTHWAITE — Map 18 NY23

## PICK OF THE PUBS

## The Pheasant ★★★ HL ⊕ ♀

*See Pick of the Pubs on opposite page*

---

### BEETHAM — Map 18 SD47

## PICK OF THE PUBS

## The Wheatsheaf at Beetham ♀

LA7 7AL ☎ 015395 62123 📄 015395 64840
**e-mail:** info@wheatsheafbeetham.com
**dir:** *On A6 5m N of junct 35*

Records show that this 16th-century former coaching inn has been welcoming guests since 1609. Run by the Skelton family, it's sited in the village centre, close to the little River Bela in an Area of Outstanding Natural Beauty. A small bar services the dining areas, all decorated with fresh flowers and illuminated with candles in the evening. Jennings Cumberland heads up the choice of three real ales, while ten wines by the glass span classic European with New World offerings.

As far as possible, seasonal menus use the freshest and finest local produce. Lunchtime light meals include hot and cold sandwiches, and simple dishes such as naturally smoked haddock rarebit. An evening meal could start with the Wheatsheaf's own potted shrimps, and continue with pan-fried duck breast served pink with an orange liqueur jus. Desserts may proffer peach and brandy trifle, or chocolate brioche and butter pudding with creamy custard.

**Open** all day all wk noon-11pm Closed: 25 Dec
**Bar Meals** L served Mon-Sat 12-9, Sun 12-8.30 D served Mon-Sat 12-9, Sun 12-8.30 Av main course £7 food served all day **Restaurant** Fixed menu price fr £10 Av 3 course à la carte fr £12 ⊕ FREE HOUSE ◀ Jennings Cumberland Ale, Wainwright, Queen Jean Ö Kingston Press. ♀ 10 **Facilities** Garden Parking

---

### BLENCOGO — Map 18 NY14

## The New Inn ♀

CA7 0BZ ☎ 016973 61091 📄 016973 61091
**dir:** *From Carlisle take A596 towards Wigton, then B5302 towards Silloth. After 4m Blencogo signed on left*

This late Victorian sandstone pub has superb views of the north Cumbrian fells and Solway Plain. It is located in a farming hamlet, and the impressive menu makes good use of produce from the region - perhaps chargrilled tenderloin of pork topped with apricot and herb crust; fresh salmon served with hollandaise sauce and asparagus; or yellow-fin tuna with mild curried mango and Armagnac sauce. A selection of malt whiskies is kept.

**Open** 6.30-11 Closed: 1st 2wks Jan, Mon-Wed
**Bar Meals** Av main course £15 **Restaurant** L served Sun 12-2 booking required D served Thu-Sun 6-9 booking required Fixed menu price fr £18.50 Av 3 course à la carte fr £26 ⊕ FREE HOUSE ◀ Boddingtons, guest ales. ♀ 10
**Facilities** Garden Parking

---

### BLENCOWE — Map 18 NY43

## The Crown Inn NEW

CA11 0DG ☎ 017684 83369
**e-mail:** crowninn@talktalk.net
**dir:** *From Penrith take B5288. Approx 3m turn right, follow Blencowe signs. Pub in village centre*

Parts of this traditional village free house date from the 16th century, and the inn enjoys far reaching views to the Pennines and Northern fells being situated just outside the Lake District National Park. Very much part of the community, the inn offers a good selection of well kept cask ales and a comprehensive wine list. Choices from the modern British menu might include herb stuffed chicken with roasted vegetables and red pesto drizzle; salmon fillet with black pepper crust, rosemary and baby tomato; spinach and ricotta cannelloni; or game dishes when in season. There are also regular themed dining nights like Celebration of Cumbrian beef.

**Open** all wk Mon-Sat 5-close (Sun noon-3 5-close)
**Bar Meals** L served Sun 12-2 D served all wk 6-9 Av main course £10 **Restaurant** L served Sun 12-2 D served all wk 6-9 Fixed menu price fr £12.95 Av 3 course à la carte fr £16 ⊕ FREE HOUSE ◀ Doris's 90th Birthday Ale, Cumberland Ale, Corby Ale, Yates ales, Timothy Taylor Landlord. **Facilities** Children's menu Children's portions Dogs allowed Garden Parking

---

### BOOT — Map 18 NY10

## PICK OF THE PUBS

## The Boot Inn

*See Pick of the Pubs on page 98*

---

## PICK OF THE PUBS

## Brook House Inn ★★★★ INN ♀

CA19 1TG ☎ 019467 23288 📄 019467 23160
**e-mail:** stay@brookhouseinn.co.uk
**dir:** *M6 junct 36, A590 follow Barrow signs. A5092, then A595. Past Broughton-in-Furness then right at lights to Ulpha. Cross river, next left signed Eskdale, & on to Boot. (NB not all routes to Boot are suitable in bad weather conditions)*

The La'al Ratty steam railway terminates just 200 metres from Brook House, making it a popular spot for refreshment. The inn's position is superb, with glorious views and fabulous walking country all around, so the provision of a small drying room for wet walkers is greatly appreciated, as is dedicated bike accommodation. Between three and seven real ales are kept, including Hawkshead Bitter and Jennings Cumberland, and an amazing selection of 170 malt whiskies. Home-made food prepared from locally supplied fresh produce is available in the restaurant, bar and snug all day. These quality ingredients include ribeye steak, sea bream, venison, mussels and pigeon. Home-made chutney, biscuits, bread, sauces and stocks are also a feature. The dinner menu is the same throughout the inn, offering an evening of fine dining on fresh Islay scallops; brill with saffron sauce; pigeon and bacon salad: sea bass with roasted red pepper and vine tomato salsa; local organic steaks; trio of lamb chops with Madeira and mushroom sauce; and Moroccan vegetable and bean casserole. The inn is run by two generations of the Thornley family who also offer tastefully furnished rooms with views of the fells.

**Open** all wk Closed: 25 Dec **Bar Meals** food served all day **Restaurant** L served by arrangement booking required D served 6-8.30 ⊕ FREE HOUSE ◀ Timothy Taylor Landlord, Hawkshead Bitter, Jennings Cumberland, Yates, guest ales Ö Westons Old Rosie. ♀ 10 **Facilities** Children's menu Family room Garden Parking **Rooms** 7

# PICK OF THE PUBS

## The Pheasant ★★★HL 🌹 🍷

**BASSENTHWAITE** Map 18 NY23

**CA13 9YE**
☎ **017687 76234** 📠 **017687 76002**
**e-mail:** info@the-pheasant.co.uk
**web:** www.thepheasantinn.co.uk
**dir:** *A66 to Cockermouth, 8m N of Keswick on left*

First a farmhouse, then a coaching inn, this 500-year-old Lake District favourite is surrounded by lovely gardens and today combines the role of traditional Cumbrian hostelry with that of an internationally renowned modern hotel. Even so, you still sense the history the moment you walk through the door - the legendary foxhunter John Peel, who's "view halloo would awaken the dead", according to the song, was a regular. In the warmly inviting bar, with polished parquet flooring, panelled walls and oak settles, hang two of Cumbrian artist and former customer Edward H Thompson's paintings. Here, order a

pint of Cumberland Ale from Jennings, the Cockermouth brewery that resumed production within weeks of catastrophic flood damage in November 2009, or cast your eyes over the extensive selection of malt whiskies.

The high standard of food, recognised by an AA Rosette, is well known for miles around; meals are served in the attractive beamed dining room, bar and lounges overlooking the gardens. (A bistro was due to open in June 2010). Light lunches served in the lounge and bar include open sandwiches, ploughman's, home-made pork pie, and chicken Caesar, while a three-course dinner could feature crab and cucumber cannelloni with soy marshmallow and chilled cucumber velouté; fillet of smoked haddock with creamed leeks; slowly cooked loin of wild Cumbrian venison with creamy pearl barley, jellied balsamic, beetroot and peanut butter; or poached breast of wood pigeon with apricot chutney, watercress, cumin jus and natural yoghurt. Treat the family to afternoon tea with home-made scones and rum butter.

A private dining room is available for small parties, and there are individually decorated en suite bedrooms with beautiful fabrics, antique pieces and impressive bathrooms.

**Open** all wk Closed: 25 Dec
**Bar Meals** L served all wk 12-2 D served all wk 6-9 Av main course £12.95
**Restaurant** L served all wk 12-1.15 booking required D served all wk 7-8.30 booking required Fixed menu price fr £35 ⊕ FREE HOUSE ◀ Coniston Bluebird, Interbrew Bass, Jennings Cumberland Ale. 🍷 12 **Facilities** Dogs allowed Garden Parking **Rooms** 15

# PICK OF THE PUBS

# The Boot Inn

**BOOT** Map 18 NY10

**CA19 1TG** ☎ **019467 23224**
e-mail: enquiries@bootinn.co.uk
web: www.bootinn.co.uk
dir: *From A595 follow signs for Eskdale then Boot*

Pubs called The Boot often commemorate The Iron Duke's famous military footwear, but not this one. The charming Eskdale village of Boot lies at the bottom of Hardknott Pass, the steepest road in the Lake District. Surrounded by glorious peaks on every side, the area contains some of England's finest walking country, for which, of course, the right boots are essential, just as they were for Wellington. Scafell Pike, England's highest mountain, and Wastwater,

England's deepest lake, are within rambling distance and, naturally enough, the pub attracts many, sometimes cold, sometimes wet, but usually hungry and thirsty, hikers and climbers.

Whether you are in the bar with its log fire, in the conservatory, from which there are splendid views, outside, or in the 16th-century beamed Burnmoor Room restaurant, Caroline and Sean will provide you with a hearty, unfussy meal. At lunch start with, for example, potato wedges or Cumberland mushrooms in white wine and garlic sauce; and at dinner with prawn cocktail or deep-fried brie. Main courses, regardless of time of day, include wholetail Whitby scampi; fish pie; Boot pie, which is choice cuts of Cumbrian steak slow-cooked in real ale encased in shortcrust pastry; chilli con carne; and vegetable lasagne. Of course, lunch doesn't have to be any of these; if you prefer, it can be a chicken burger; lamb kebab; home-made chip butty; or tuna mayonnaise jacket potato.

Children have their own menu. The Boot's annual beer festival, in June, is a great event for all the family – you can arrive on the The Ravenglass and Eskdale Railway, known locally as the La'al Ratty.

**Open** all wk Closed: 25 Dec
**Bar Meals** L served all wk 12-4 D served all wk 6-9 **Restaurant** D served all wk 6-8.30 booking required ⊕ ROBINSONS ◀ Double Hop, Unicorn, Dizzy Blonde, Dark Hatters ♻ Westons Stowford Press Organic. **Facilities** Children's menu Children's portions Play area Family room Dogs allowed Garden Parking

**BORROWDALE** Map 18 NY21

## The Langstrath Country Inn

**CA12 5XG ☎ 017687 77239**
**e-mail:** info@thelangstrath.com
**dir:** *B5289 past Grange, through Rosthwaite, left to Stonethwaite. Inn on left after 1m*

This lovely 16th-century, family-run inn must surely enjoy one of the most spectacular locations in the country, with spectacular views up the Langstrath valley. Refurbishments over the years include the addition of a restaurant ideally placed to make the most of the views. A meal here could start with Alf Bennet's hand-potted local shrimps; followed by slow cooked Rosthwaite Herdwick with carrot and swede mash, hot pot potatoes and green beans, or vegetarian cottage pie – made with lentils and sun blush tomatoes and topped with cheesy mash. Finish with sticky toffee pudding with butterscotch sauce and ice cream. The bar offers decent ales and an extensive wine list. Set on the coast-to-coast and Cumbrian Way walks, this is an ideal spot for hikers.

**Open** noon-10.30 Closed: Jan, Mon **Bar Meals** L served Tue-Sun 12-2 D served Tue-Sun 6-9 Av main course £10 **Restaurant** L served Tue-Sun 12-2 D served Tue-Sun 6-9 FREE HOUSE Jennings Bitter, Black Sheep, Hawkshead Bitter, Cocker Hoop Thatchers Gold. 9 **Facilities** Children's menu Children's portions Dogs allowed Garden Parking

**BOUTH** Map 18 SD38

## The White Hart Inn

**LA12 8JB ☎ 01229 861229 01229 861836**
**e-mail:** nigelwhitehart@aol.com
**dir:** *1.5m from A590. 10m from M6 junct 36*

Bouth today reposes quietly in the Lake District National Park, although once it housed an occasionally noisy gunpowder factory. When this closed in 1928 villagers turned to woodland industries and farm labouring instead, and some of their tools now adorn this 17th-century coaching inn. Peruse the menu over a pint of Black Sheep Best. Ever-changing specials are served in the upstairs restaurant that looks out over woods, fields and fells, or in the horseshoe-shaped bar.

**Open** all day all wk noon-11 (Sun noon-10.30) **Bar Meals** L served Mon-Fri 12-2 booking required D served all wk 6-8.45 booking required Av main course £12.95 **Restaurant** L served Mon-Fri 12-2 booking required D served all wk 6-8.45 booking required FREE HOUSE Black Sheep Best, Jennings Cumberland Ale, Coniston Bluebird, Ulverston. **Facilities** Children's menu Dogs allowed Garden Parking

**BOWLAND BRIDGE** Map 18 SD48

**PICK OF THE PUBS**

## Hare & Hounds Country Inn

**LA11 6NN ☎ 015395 68333 015395 68777**
**dir:** *M6 onto A591, left after 3m onto A590, right after 3m onto A5074, after 4m sharp left & next left after 1m*

This 17th-century coaching inn is set in the pretty little hamlet of Bowland Bridge, not far from Bowness. A traditional country pub atmosphere is fostered by the flagstone floors, exposed oak beams, ancient pews warmed by open fires, and cosy niches. The bar menu offers local Cumberland sausage with egg and chips; toasted muffin with smoked haddock; confit of duck; and king prawns in filo pastry. The seasonal main menu could offer asparagus and saffron risotto; and smoked salmon and prawn roulade as starters, followed by butternut squash, spinach and mozzarella strudel; fresh cod in batter with home-made chips; or steak and ale pie. There is also a specials board with fresh fish and game always available. A safe garden with play area and swings for the children makes this pub particularly family friendly, and there are gorgeous views all round, especially of Cartmel Fell.

**Open** all day all wk 11am-11pm **Bar Meals** L served 12-9 D served 12-9 food served all day MARSTONS Jennings, Marstons Pedigree, Cumberland Ale, guest beers. 10 **Facilities** Play area Family room Dogs allowed Garden Parking

**BRAITHWAITE** Map 18 NY22

## Coledale Inn

**CA12 5TN ☎ 017687 78272**
**e-mail:** info@coledale-inn.co.uk
**dir:** *M6 junct 50, A66 towards Cockermouth for 18m. Turn to Braithwaite then towards Whinlatter Pass. Follow sign on left, over bridge to Inn*

Set in a peaceful spot above Braithwaite village, this inn is ideal for exploring the fells via footpaths that lead off from its gardens. The building started life as a woollen mill in the 1820s, and became a pencil factory before its transition to licensed premises. The interior is attractively decked out with Victorian prints, furnishings and antiques; two homely bars serve a selection of local ales. A short but traditional menu extends from Greek salad to herb and garlic chicken, and jam roly-poly served with custard.

**Open** all day all wk **Bar Meals** L served all wk 12-2 D served all wk 6-9 Av main course £9 FREE HOUSE Yates, Theakstons, Jennings, Keswick, Tirril. **Facilities** Children's menu Children's portions Play area Dogs allowed Garden Parking

## The Royal Oak ★★★ INN

**CA12 5SY ☎ 017687 78533 017687 78533**
**e-mail:** tpfranks@hotmail.com
**dir:** *Exit M6 junct 40, A66 to Keswick, 20m. Bypass Keswick & Portinscale juncts, take next left, pub in village centre*

The Royal Oak is set in the centre of the village in a walkers' paradise surrounded by high fells and beautiful scenery. The interior is all oak beams and log fires, and the menu offers hearty pub food, such as giant Yorkshire pudding with home-made Cumberland sausage casserole or pork chops with apple and cinnamon sauce, (including a section for smaller appetites) in the bar area or restaurant, served alongside local ales, such as Jennings Lakeland or Cocker Hoop. Visitors can extend the experience by staying over in the comfortable en suite bedrooms, some with four-poster beds.

**Open** all day all wk **Bar Meals** L served all wk 12-2 D served all wk 6-9 Av main course £8 **Restaurant** L served all wk 12-2 D served all wk 6-9 Av 3 course à la carte fr £20 MARSTONS Jennings Lakeland Ale, Cumberland Ale, Cocker Hoop, Sneck Lifter. 8 **Facilities** Children's menu Children's portions Dogs allowed Garden Parking **Rooms** 10

**BRAMPTON** Map 21 NY56

## Blacksmiths Arms ★★★★ INN

**Talkin Village CA8 1LE**
**☎ 016977 3452 016977 3396**
**e-mail:** blacksmithsarmstalkin@yahoo.co.uk
**dir:** *From M6 take A69 E, after 7m straight over rdbt, follow signs to Talkin Tarn then Talkin Village*

Enjoy warm hospitality and a pint of ale from Brampton Brewery at this attractive, 18th-century free house. The original smithy, dating from 1700, remains part of the inn along with the bar, restaurant and accommodation. Choose from menus that range from bar snacks and daily-changing specials board to full à la carte offerings like spinach and ricotta cannelloni; poached fillet of salmon; and beef medallions in red wine sauce. The inn stands in some of northern Cumbria's most scenic countryside, close to the Borders, Hadrian's Wall and the Lakes.

**Open** all wk noon-3 6-mdnt **Bar Meals** L served all wk 12-2 D served all wk 6-9 Av main course £8.50 **Restaurant** L served all wk 12-2 D served all wk 6-9 Fixed menu price fr £8.50 FREE HOUSE Yates, Brampton, Black Sheep, Getsdale Cold Fell. 16 **Facilities** Children's menu Children's portions Garden Parking **Rooms** 8

# PICK OF THE PUBS

## Blacksmiths Arms

**BROUGHTON-IN-FURNESS** Map 18 SD28

**Broughton Mills LA20 6AX**
☎ **01229 716824**
e-mail: blacksmithsarms@aol.com
web: www.theblacksmithsarms.com
dir: *A593 from Broughton-in-Furness towards Coniston, in 1.5m left signed Broughton Mills, pub 1m on left*

This quaint whitewashed free house was originally a farmhouse called Broadstones, serving beer from the kitchen to travellers and local farmers. By 1748 it was recorded as being an inn, as well as a blacksmiths and working farm with 34 acres. The original interior has been beautifully preserved and oozes charm and character. Each of the four rooms have glowing log fires in winter, including one in the old farmhouse range. There are low beams, oak-panelled corridors, and worn slate floors sourced from the local quarries. Gaslights in the dining room and bar are called into service when the electricity fails and, in time-honoured fashion, there are classic pub games like dominoes, cribbage and board games. Michael and Sophie Lane serve a cracking pint of local ale, with Jennings Cumberland, Dent Aviator and Hawkshead Bitter all tapped straight from the cask.

Interesting, freshly-cooked food makes good use of local produce from quality Cumbrian suppliers, and locally-reared Herdwick lamb is often on the menu. Lunchtime brings an appetising range of sandwiches and ploughman's, as well as mixed leaf salads with new potatoes. The main menu might begin with smoked haddock fishcakes and poached egg, or roasted pigeon breast with apple, black pudding and crispy pancetta salad. Main course options include slow-braised belly pork with roasted butternut squash, green beans and celeriac mash, and pan-roasted sea bass with thyme-crushed new potatoes. Round things off with Bramley apple and cinnamon brûlée, or warm chocolate brownie with hot fudge sauce.

There's a sheltered, flower-filled front patio garden for alfresco summer dining. The inn is set in a secluded South Lakeland valley, with miles of glorious walks radiating from the front door.

**Open** all wk Closed: 25 Dec
**Bar Meals** L served all wk 12-2 booking required D served all wk 6-9 booking required Av main course £10.95 ⊕ FREE HOUSE ◼ Jennings Cumberland Ale, Dent Aviator, Barngates Tag Lag, Moorhouses Pride of Pendle, Hawkshead Bitter. **Facilities** Children's menu Dogs allowed Garden Parking

Save on Hotels. Book at **theAA.com/hotel**

CUMBRIA 101 ENGLAND

## PICK OF THE PUBS

### Blacksmiths Arms

*See Pick of the Pubs on opposite page*

### The Old Kings Head

**Church St LA20 6HJ**
☎ 01229 716293 ▤ 01229 716401
e-mail: theoldkingsheadbroughton@btconnect.com
dir: *Telephone for directions*

With a history spanning 400 years, the spick-and-span former coaching inn is one of the oldest buildings in the town. Perfectly located for exploring the southern Lakes, the pub offers great beers and freshly prepared food using local ingredients. Look to the chalkboard for daily fish specials, perhaps hot potted prawns, and whole bass with lemon and lime cream, or tuck into winter lamb casserole, rack of lamb, or a classic steak and ale pie.

**Open** all wk noon-3 5-mdnt **Bar Meals** L served all wk 12-2 booking required D served all wk 5-9 booking required Av main course £9.95 **Restaurant** L served all wk 12-2 booking required D served all wk 5-9 booking required ⊕ ENTERPRISE INNS ◀ Golden Pippin, Black Sheep, Adnams. **Facilities** Children's menu Play area Garden Parking

### Bridge Hotel ★★★ CHH

**CA13 9UZ** ☎ 017687 70252 ▤ 017687 70215
e-mail: enquiries@bridge-hotel.com
web: www.bridge-hotel.com
dir: *M6 junct 40, A66 to Keswick. Continue on A66 to avoid Keswick centre, exit at Braithwaite. Over Newlands Pass, follow Buttermere signs. (if weather bad follow Whinlatter Pass via Lorton). Hotel in village*

An 18th-century former coaching inn set between Buttermere and Crummock Water in an outstandingly beautiful area, surrounded by the Buttermere Fells. There are wonderful walks right from the front door. Good food and real ales are served in the character bars (Cumberland sausage, rainbow trout or Scottish salmon), and a four-course dinner in the dining room - including, perhaps, roast Lakeland lamb with Cumberland sauce and crispy leeks, or venison braised with mushrooms and Old Peculier jus. The bedrooms are tastefully appointed and have stylish bathrooms.

**Open** all day all wk 10.30am-11.30pm **Bar Meals** L served all wk 12-9.30 D served all wk 12-9.30 Av main course £8.50 food served all day **Restaurant** D served all wk 6-8.30 booking required Fixed menu price fr £29.50 ⊕ FREE HOUSE ◀ Theakston's Old Peculier, Black Sheep Best, Buttermere Bitter, Boddingtons, Hawkshead Gold. **Facilities** Children's menu Children's portions Garden Parking **Rooms** 21

### Oddfellows Arms

**CA7 8EA** ☎ 016974 78227 ▤ 016974 78056
dir: *Telephone for directions*

This 17th-century former coaching inn is set in a scenic conservation village in the northern fells. Popular with coast-to-coast cyclists and walkers on the Cumbrian Way, the Oddfellows serves Jennings Bitter and Cumberland Ale. Lunchtime snacks include jacket potatoes, sandwiches, or hot beef in a roll, whilst specials and vegetarian blackboards supplement the regular menu. Expect Jennings Ale and beef pie; bacon chops with Stilton; sirloin steaks; daily-changing curry and local trout fillets. The beer garden is the place to enjoy the peace and quiet, and admire the views.

**Open** all day all wk **Bar Meals** L served all wk 12-2 D served all wk 6.15-8.30 Av main course £8.50 **Restaurant** L served all wk 12-1.30 booking required D served all wk 6.15-8.30 booking required Av 3 course à la carte fr £15 ⊕ MARSTONS ◀ Jennings Bitter, Cumberland Ale. **Facilities** Children's menu Children's portions Dogs allowed Garden Parking

## PICK OF THE PUBS

### The Cavendish Arms ▼

**LA11 6QA** ☎ 015395 36240
e-mail: food@thecavendisharms.co.uk
dir: *M6 junct 36, A590 signed Barrow-in-Furness. Cartmel signed. In village take 1st right*

Situated within the village walls, this 450-year-old coaching inn is Cartmel's longest-surviving hostelry. Many traces of its history remain, from the mounting block outside the main door to the bar itself, which used to be the stables. Oak beams, uneven floors and an open fire create a traditional, cosy atmosphere, and outside a stream flows past a tree-lined garden. The food, from the lunchtime sandwiches to the cheeses served at the end of dinner, owes much to its local origins (and, of course, to the skilled kitchen team). Perhaps begin your meal with seafood chowder or mushroom and feta cheese risotto. Then move on to supreme of chicken with cherry tomato, mushroom and air-dried ham sauce; steak and ale pie; or goat's cheese lasagne. Desserts include sticky toffee pudding with butterscotch sauce and tiramisu. The owners have teamed up with a local company that offers carriage tours of the village. This popular area is ideal for walking, horse riding, visiting Cartmel races, Lake Windermere and car museum.

**Open** all wk ⊕ FREE HOUSE ◀ Greene King IPA, Cumberland, Theakstons. ▼ 8 **Facilities** Dogs allowed Garden Parking

### The Trout Hotel ▼

**Crown St CA13 0EJ** ☎ 01900 823591 ▤ 01900 827514
e-mail: enquiries@trouthotel.co.uk
dir: *In town centre*

Overlooking the River Derwent, the Trout's well-appointed rooms make a good base for horse riding, cycling, fell walking, climbing and fishing trips. The patio of the Terrace Bar and Bistro, with its large heated parasols, offers alfresco dining any time of the year, while the Derwent Restaurant, dominated by a classic fireplace and ornate mirrored sideboard, offers daily changing menus featuring the best local produce, such as pheasant and pigeon breast, grilled sea bass, and mushroom risotto.

**Open** all day all wk **Bar Meals** food served all day **Restaurant** food served all day ⊕ FREE HOUSE ◀ Jennings Cumberland Ale, Theakston Bitter, John Smith's, Marston's Pedigree, Courage Directors. ▼ 24 **Facilities** Children's menu Garden Parking

## PICK OF THE PUBS

### The Black Bull Inn & Hotel ▼

**1 Yewdale Rd LA21 8DU**
☎ 015394 41335 & 41668 ▤ 015394 41168
e-mail: i.s.bradley@btinternet.com
dir: *M6 junct 36, A590. 23m from Kendal via Windermere & Ambleside*

A cosy refuge in the heart of the Lake District, this 400-year-old coaching inn has been run by the same family for nearly 30 years. Set at the foot of the Old Man of Coniston and adjacent to Coniston Water, it has welcomed some famous faces over the years, from Coleridge and Turner to Donald Campbell when attempting his water speed records, and Anthony Hopkins who starred in the film of Campbell's last 60 days. Back in the 1990s the owners' son started a micro-brewery behind the inn. It has gone from strength to strength, the award-winning ales being sold not only behind the bar, but also delivered to 30 neighbouring hostelries. For hungry ramblers calling in at lunchtime, there is an unfussy range of snacks. Alternatively the restaurant menu runs from hearty winter warmers such as a 10-ounce platter of famous Cumberland sausage, to a half shoulder of slow-roasted English lamb.

**Open** all day all wk Closed: 25 Dec **Bar Meals** Av main course £8.95 food served all day **Restaurant** D served all wk 6-9 booking required Av 3 course à la carte fr £20 ⊕ FREE HOUSE ◀ Coniston Bluebird, Old Man Ale, Opium, Blacksmith, XB, Oatmeal Stout. ▼ 10 **Facilities** Children's menu Children's portions Family room Dogs allowed Garden Parking

**CONISTON** *continued*

## PICK OF THE PUBS

### Sun Hotel & 16th Century Inn

**LA21 8HQ** ☎ 015394 41248 📄 015394 41219
**e-mail:** thesun@hotelconiston.com
**dir:** *From M6 junct 36, A591, beyond Kendal & Windermere, then A598 from Ambleside to Coniston. Pub signed from bridge in village*

A 16th-century inn with a 10-room hotel attached, this was Donald Campbell's base during his final water speed record attempt. Coniston Bluebird is one of the ales behind the bar, along with guest ales like Black Cat, Black Sheep Special and Speckled Hen. The menu offers seafood paella; pan-roasted pheasant with baby spinach ragout; and Hungarian goulash with dumplings. Outside is a large quiet garden with benches, and the conservatory offers exceptional views that can be enjoyed whatever the weather.

**Open** all day all wk 11am-mdnt **Bar Meals** L served all wk 12-3 D served all wk 6-9 ⊕ FREE HOUSE
◀ Coniston Bluebird, Hawkshead, Copper Dragon, 4 guest ales. **Facilities** Play area Family room Dogs allowed Garden Parking

## CROOK
Map 18 SD49

### The Sun Inn

**LA8 8LA** ☎ 01539 821351 📄 01539 821351
**dir:** *Off B5284*

A welcoming inn which has grown from a row of cottages built in 1711, when beer was served to travellers from a front room. The same pleasure is dispensed today by the winter fires or on the summer terrace. The bar and regular menus feature steak and mushroom pie, beer battered cod and chips, curries, steaks, salads and vegetarian dishes. Enjoy dining in the restaurant for that special occasion. The seasonal menus use locally sourced produce.

**Open** all wk Mon-Fri 12-2.30 6-11 (Sat 12-11 Sun 12-10.30) **Bar Meals** L served Mon-Fri 12-2.30, Sat 12-9, Sun 12-8 D served Mon-Fri 6-9, Sat 12-9, Sun 12-8 Av main course £9 **Restaurant** L served Mon-Fri 12-2.30, Sat 12-9, Sun 12-8 D served Mon-Fri 6-9, Sat 12-9. Sun 12-8 booking required Av 3 course à la carte fr £20
⊕ SCOTTISH & NEWCASTLE ◀ Theakston, John Smith's, Courage Directors, Coniston Bluebird, Hawkshead. **Facilities** Children's menu Children's portions Dogs allowed Garden Parking

## CROSTHWAITE
Map 18 SD49

## PICK OF THE PUBS

### The Punch Bowl Inn ★★★★★ INN ⊚⊚ ♥

**LA8 8HR** ☎ 015395 68237 📄 015395 68875
**e-mail:** info@the-punchbowl.co.uk
**web:** www.the-punchbowl.co.uk
**dir:** *M6 junct 36, A590 towards Barrow, A5074 & follow signs for Crosthwaite. Pub by church on left*

Located in the stunning Lyth Valley beside the ancient parish church, this classy inn operates as a bar serving locally brewed Barngates beers, an elegant restaurant noted for using local seasonal ingredients, as well as swish, boutique-style rooms, and the village post office. Although stylishly remodelled with a contemporary feel, it retains bags of character. Witness oak beams, roaring log fires and gleaming wooden floors here, and elegant dining rooms with white linen and colourful local artwork. The award-winning menus are served throughout the bar and restaurant and champion local suppliers, many of them organic. Start with Italian fish soup; twice baked mature Lancashire cheese soufflé; or home-smoked saddle of venison; followed by baked fillet of skate with wholegrain mustard, orange and parsley crust; or braised shoulder of lamb, garlic mousseline potatoes and rosemary jus. Beautiful rooms boast flat-screen TVs, Roberts Revival radios and a freestanding roll-top bath. Great walks from the front door.

**Open** all day all wk 11am-mdnt **Bar Meals** Av main course £16 food served all day **Restaurant** Av 3 course à la carte fr £32.50 food served all day ⊕ FREE HOUSE
◀ Erdinger, Westmorland Gold, Coniston Bluebird, Hawkshead Gold ♂ Thatchers Gold. ♥ 14
**Facilities** Children's portions Dogs allowed Garden Parking **Rooms** 9

## ELTERWATER
Map 18 NY30

## PICK OF THE PUBS

### The Britannia Inn

**LA22 9HP** ☎ 015394 37210 📄 015396 78075
**e-mail:** info@britinn.co.uk
**dir:** *In village centre*

Built around 500 years ago as a gentleman farmer's house, the Britannia stands amidst the imposing mountains of the Langdale valley. Within its thick stone walls, the bar seating areas are a cluster of small and cosy rooms with low-beamed oak ceilings and winter coal fires. There's generally a quiz night on Sundays, and the pub really comes to life in summer when colourful hanging baskets dazzle the eye and the garden fills up with customers and, occasionally, Morris dancers. Featured ales include Jennings Bitter and Coniston Bluebird, supplemented by guest beers from around the country. The inn offers a wide choice of fresh, home-cooked food, and a typical evening meal might start with Morecambe Bay shrimps with chervil and lemon butter, followed by chicken, ham and leek pie in suet pastry with fresh vegetables and a choice of potatoes. Round off with home-made profiteroles and dark chocolate sauce.

**Open** all day all wk 10am-11pm **Bar Meals** L served 12-9.30 D served 12-9.30 Av main course £11 food served all day **Restaurant** D served 6.30-9.30 booking required Av 3 course à la carte fr £19 ⊕ FREE HOUSE
◀ Jennings Bitter, Coniston Bluebird, Thwaites Wainwright, Dent Aviator, Hawkshead Bitter.
**Facilities** Children's menu Children's portions Dogs allowed Garden Parking

## ENNERDALE BRIDGE
Map 18 NY01

## PICK OF THE PUBS

### The Shepherd's Arms Hotel

**CA23 3AR** ☎ 01946 861249 📄 01946 861249
**e-mail:** shepherdsarms@btconnect.com
**dir:** *A66 to Cockermouth (25m), A5086 to Egremont (5m) then follow sign to Ennerdale*

Located on one of the most beautiful stretches of Wainwright's Coast to Coast footpath, this informal free house is a favourite with walkers. The bar has a long serving counter, a long case clock and wood-burning stove below a large beam hung with copper and brass. The main area has an open log fire and comfortable seating, and is a venue for local musicians; it opens into a small conservatory with tables and an additional outdoor sitting area. Shepherd's Arms own brew heads a list of beers that includes Jennings Bitter and a regular guest ale. A nicely varied menu is served throughout, with plenty of choice for vegetarians, as well as daily specials and carte options in the dining room. Using locally sourced produce where possible, dinner might begin with fresh home-made soup, or deep-fried brie with a hot redcurrant sauce, before moving on to nut and mushroom fettuccine; Herdwick lamb half shoulder slow cooked in a mint and garlic jus; grilled swordfish; or local sirloin steak with brandy and black pepper sauce.

**Open** all wk Mon-Fri 12-2 6-11 (Winter) noon-11 (Summer) ◀ Jennings Bitter, Cumberland, Guest ales.
**Facilities** Dogs allowed Garden Parking

# PICK OF THE PUBS

## Bower House Inn

### ESKDALE GREEN    Map 18 NY10

**CA19 1TD**
☎ **019467 23244**   📠 **019467 23308**
**e-mail:** info@bowerhouseinn.co.uk
**web:** www.bowerhouseinn.co.uk
**dir:** *4m off A595, 0.5m W of Eskdale Green*

In gloriously unspoilt Eskdale overlooking Muncaster Fell, the traditional appeal of this 17th-century inn finds favour with an eclectic clientele, from walkers and tourists to business folk and wedding parties. Less than four miles from the Cumbria coast road, it's ideally placed for visitors heading to the western lakes – and has been welcoming people through its doors for over 400 years.

Headquarters of the village cricket team (the pitch is next door), the bar has a distinctly clubby feel with oak beams, ticking clocks, crackling log fires and local Coniston, Hawkshead and

Jennings ales on tap; the bar opens out on to a delightful enclosed garden.

The rambling restaurant is a charming room with candlelit tables, exposed stone, log fires and equestrian pictures. Here typical starters may include steamed Scottish mussels in a white wine and cream sauce, and roasted duck breast salad with raspberry and balsamic dressing. For a main course you can choose between the likes of Woodalls belly pork with black pudding mash; or something a little more exotic, such as seared swordfish with sautéed potatoes. Vegetarians will enjoy the vegetable stroganoff with parsnip ribbons and white truffle oil.

Why not time your visit to coincide with one of the special events running throughout the year? The annual bonfire night weekend, for example, starts on the Friday with a family get-together in the bar with traditional fare and live entertainment. On Saturday you go orienteering in the safe hands of the Bower House's own guides, before returning for a memorable bonfire and firework display. Before departing on Sunday, join the inn's famous bracing walk after a legendary breakfast. Then

return to the crackling Cumberland fireplace for a final warm-up before departing fully refreshed.

**Open** all day all wk **Bar Meals** L served Mon-Fri 12-2, Sat-Sun 12-9 D served Mon-Fri 6-9, Sat- Sun 12-9 food served all day ⊕ FREE HOUSE 🍺 Theakston Bitter, Ennerdale, Yates.
**Facilities** Children's menu Dogs allowed Garden Parking

## ESKDALE GREEN
Map 18 NY10

### PICK OF THE PUBS

## Bower House Inn

See Pick of the Pubs on page 103

## FAUGH
Map 18 NY55

### The String of Horses Inn ★★★ INN ♟

**CA8 9EG ☎ 01228 670297**
e-mail: info@stringofhorses.com
dir: *M6 junct 43, A69 towards Hexham. In 5-6m right at 1st lights at Corby Hill/Warwick Bridge. 1m, through Heads Nook, in 1m bear sharp right. Left into Faugh. Pub on left down hill*

Tucked away in a sleepy village close to Talkin Tarn, this traditional Lakeland inn oozes old world charm. It dates from the 17th century, when it was a packhorse inn. The bar and restaurant have oak beams, roaring log fires, wood panelling and oak settles, and you'll find a good range of real ales and imaginative pub food on offer – maybe moules marinière followed by sizzling fajitas. A comfortable base for exploring the North Lakes.

**Open** Tue-Sun Closed: Mon **Bar Meals** D served Tue-Sun 6-8.45 Av main course £7.95 **Restaurant** D served Tue-Sun 6-8.45 ⊕ FREE HOUSE ◄ Brampton Bitter, Theakston Best, John Smith's, Guinness. ♟ 8 **Facilities** Parking **Rooms** 11

## GRASMERE
Map 18 NY30

### The Travellers Rest Inn ♟

**Keswick Rd LA22 9RR**
**☎ 015394 35604 📄 017687 72309**
e-mail: stay@lakedistrictinns.co.uk
dir: *From M6 take A591 to Grasmere, pub 0.5m N of Grasmere*

Located on the edge of picturesque Grasmere and handy for touring and exploring the ever-beautiful Lake District, the Travellers Rest has been a pub for more than 500 years. Inside, a roaring log fire complements the welcoming atmosphere of the beamed and inglenooked bar area. An extensive menu of traditional home-cooked fare is offered, ranging from Westmorland terrine and eggs Benedict, to wild mushroom gratin and rump of Lakeland lamb.

**Open** all day all wk Mon-Sat 11-11 (Sun noon-10.30) **Bar Meals** food served all day ⊕ FREE HOUSE ◄ Jennings Bitter & Cocker Hoop, Cumberland Ale, Sneck Lifter, guest ales. ♟ 10 **Facilities** Family room Dogs allowed Garden Parking

## GREAT LANGDALE
Map 18 NY20

### The New Dungeon Ghyll Hotel ★★ HL ♟

**LA22 9JY ☎ 015394 37213 📄 015394 37666**
e-mail: enquiries@dungeon-ghyll.com
dir: *From Ambleside follow A593 towards Coniston for 3m, at Skelwith Bridge right onto B5343 towards 'The Langdales'*

Traditional Cumberland stone hotel standing in its own lawned grounds in a spectacular position beneath the Langdale Pikes and Pavey Ark. The hotel dates back to medieval times, and is full of character and charm. Local specialities, expertly cooked, are served in the smart dining room. A sample dinner menu offers pan-fried venison steak on a parsnip rösti with blood orange sauce; griddled grey mullet with stir-fried vegetables and a sweet chilli sauce, venison casserole; or spinach and ricotta cannelloni.

**Open** all wk ⊕ FREE HOUSE ◄ Thwaites Bitter, Langdale Top Ö Kingston Press, Wainwrights. ♟ 8 **Facilities** Family room Dogs allowed Garden Parking **Rooms** 20

## GREAT SALKELD
Map 18 NY53

### PICK OF THE PUBS

## The Highland Drove Inn and Kyloes Restaurant ♟

See Pick of the Pubs on opposite page

## HAWKSHEAD
Map 18 SD39

### Kings Arms ★★★ INN

**The Square LA22 0NZ**
**☎ 015394 36372 📄 015394 36006**
e-mail: info@kingsarmshawkshead.co.uk
dir: *M6 junct 36, A590 to Newby Bridge, right at 1st junct past rdbt, over bridge, 8m to Hawkshead*

Overlooking the picturesque square at the heart of this virtually unchanged Elizabethan Lakeland village, made famous by Beatrix Potter who lived nearby, this 16th-century inn throngs in summer. In colder weather, bag a table by the fire in the traditional carpeted bar, quaff a pint of Hawkshead bitter and tuck into lunchtime rolls (bacon and brie with cranberry sauce), or for dinner try lamb Henry (slow braised shoulder with red wine and rosemary gravy), or chargrilled rib-eye steak with peppercorn sauce. Look out for the carved figure of a king in the bar. Cosy, thoughtfully equipped bedrooms are available.

**Open** all day all wk 11am-mdnt **Bar Meals** L served all wk 12-2.30 D served all wk 6-9.30 Av main course £7 **Restaurant** L served all wk 12-2.30 booking required D served all wk 6-9.30 booking required ⊕ FREE HOUSE ◄ Tetley Bitter, Black Sheep Best, Hawkshead Gold, Hawkshead Bitter, Coniston Bluebird, guest ales. **Facilities** Children's menu Dogs allowed Garden **Rooms** 8

### PICK OF THE PUBS

## The Queen's Head ★★★★ INN ◉ ♟

See Pick of the Pubs on page 106

### The Sun Inn ★★★★ INN

**Main St LA22 0NT ☎ 015394 36236**
e-mail: rooms@suninn.co.uk
dir: *N on M6 junct 36, A591 to Ambleside, B5286 to Hawkshead. S on M6 junct 40, A66 to Keswick, A591 to Ambleside, B5286 to Hawkshead*

The Sun is a listed 17th-century coaching inn at the heart of the charming village where Wordsworth went to school. Inside are two resident ghosts - a giggling girl and a drunken landlord - and outside is a paved terrace with seating. The wood-panelled bar has low, oak-beamed ceilings, and hill walkers and others will enjoy the log fires, real ales and locally-sourced food. There are 8 attractive bedrooms, some with four-posters.

**Open** all day all wk 11am-11pm (Sun noon-10.30pm) **Bar Meals** L served all wk 12-2.30 D served all wk 6-9 ⊕ FREE HOUSE ◄ Jennings, Timothy Taylor Landlord, Hawkshead Bitter, Cocker Hoop, plus two guest ales. **Facilities** Children's portions Dogs allowed Garden **Rooms** 8

## HESKET NEWMARKET
Map 18 NY33

### The Old Crown ♟

**CA7 8JG ☎ 016974 78288**
e-mail: theoldcrown@btinternet.com
dir: *From M6 junct 41, B5305, left after 6m towards Hesket Newmarket*

Regulars here can sleep soundly, in the knowledge that their favourite beers will always be waiting for them. That's because the pub and its associated micro-brewery, which stands at the rear, are owned by a dedicated co-operative of local people. Real ales aside, traditional home-cooked food includes steak in Hesket Newmarket ale; breaded haddock with chips and peas; lamb and vegetarian curries; and Normandy-style chicken with bacon and mushrooms in a cream and cider sauce.

**Open** 12-2.30 5.30-11 Closed: 25 Dec eve, Mon-Thu L ex Sch hols **Bar Meals** L served all wk 12-2 D served all wk 6.30-9 ⊕ FREE HOUSE ◄ Doris, Skiddaw, Blencathra, Catbells, Great Cockup, Old Carrock Ö Stowford Press. ♟ 11 **Facilities** Children's portions Family room Dogs allowed Garden

# PICK OF THE PUBS

## The Highland Drove Inn and Kyloes Restaurant 🍷

**GREAT SALKELD**  Map 18 NY53

**CA11 9NA**
☎ 01768 898349  📄 01768 898708
e-mail:
highlanddroveinn@btinternet.com
**dir:** *Exit M6 junct 40, take A66 E'bound then A686 to Alston. After 4m, left onto B6412 for Great Salkeld & Lazonby*

Kyloes were the original Highland cattle that were bred in the Western Isles and then driven over the short channels of water to the mainland. Donald and Paul Newton's 300-year-old country inn stands on an old drove road, nestling by the church in a picturesque village deep in the lovely Eden Valley. Looking more like an old farmhouse, the pub is a great all-round inn, the area's social hub with a well-deserved reputation for high quality food and conviviality.

Inside, there's an attractive brick and timber bar, old tables and settles in the main bar area, and a lounge with log fire, dark wood furniture and tartan fabrics. The restaurant is upstairs and has a unique hunting lodge feel, with a verandah and lovely country views.

Menus list traditional local dishes, alongside daily specials reflecting the availability of local game and fish, and meat from herds reared and matured in Cumbria. Expect to find sea bass, brill or wild salmon sharing the menu with innovative chicken dishes, succulent steaks, and even mallard. Typical meals might be braised belly pork and crispy bacon with beetroot salad and sage crème fraîche, or spicy devilled mushrooms with dressed leaves and crusty bread, followed by Cranston's Cumberland sausage with mashed potato, seasonal vegetables and onion gravy, or honey roasted ham hock with parsnip and Dijon mustard mash.

Despite the excellence of the food, the Highland Drove is still a pub where locals come to enjoy the wide range of cask-conditioned real ales, plenty of other beers and ciders, and a good selection of wines. The area's many attractions include Hadrian's Wall.

**Open** all wk noon-2 6-late (Closed Mon L) **Bar Meals** L served Tue-Sun 12-2 D served all wk 6-9 **Restaurant** L served Tue-Sun 12-2 D served all wk 6-9 🍺 Theakston Black Bull, John Smiths Cask, John Smiths Smooth, Theakstons Best, Theakstons Mild, guest ale. 🍷 25 **Facilities** Dogs allowed Garden Parking

# PICK OF THE PUBS

## Queen's Head ★★★★ INN ✿ 🍷

**Main St LA22 0NS**
☎ **015394 36271** 📠 **015394 36722**
**e-mail:**
enquiries@queensheadhotel.co.uk
**web:** www.queensheadhotel.co.uk
**dir:** *M6 junct 36, A590 to Newby Bridge, 1st right, 8m to Hawkshead*

Surrounded by fells and forests, a stone's throw from Esthwaite Water, close to Lake Windermere, the Queen's Head is the perfect base for exploring the Lakes. Part of picturesque Hawkshead since the 16th century, this inn is located in a village with impressive literary links. William Wordsworth attended the local grammar school here and the writer and illustrator Beatrix Potter lived just up the road. Her husband William Heelis was the local solicitor and his old offices, now the Beatrix Potter Gallery, are full of her wonderful illustrations.

Behind the pub's flower-bedecked exterior you'll find low oak-beamed ceilings, wood-panelled walls, an original slate floor and a welcoming open fire.

An extensive wine list and a selection of real ales is offered, plus a full menu and an ever-changing specials board. Dishes draw from the wealth of quality produce on the doorstep: organic trout from Esthwaite Water, wild pheasant from Graythwaite, traditionally cured hams and Cumberland sausage from Waberthwaite, and slow-maturing Herdwick lamb.

For lunch, try sandwiches, salads or light bites. An evening meal might open with warm goat's cheese served with sun-blushed tomatoes, rocket leaves, fresh fig, roasted pine nuts and balsamic vinaigrette, followed by Winster Valley pheasant with caramelised Bramley apples, prunes and baby onions, or pan-fried corn-fed chicken breast with haricot bean ragout, truffle and sage sauce. Vegetarians might like to choose leek and Lancashire blue cheese risotto or open ravioli of wild mushrooms fricassee. The surrounding area is a haven for walkers, and for those wishing to stay, there are 13 very attractive en suite rooms.

**Open** all day all wk 11am-11.45pm Sun 12-11.45 **Bar Meals** L served 12-2.30 Sun 12-5 D served all wk 6.15-9.30 Av main course £12.95 **Restaurant** L served 12-2.30 Sun 12-5 booking required D served all wk 6.15-9.30 booking required ⊕ FREDERIC ROBINSON ◀ Hartleys Cumbria Way, Double Hop, Guest Ale. 🍷 16 **Facilities** Children's menu Family room Garden **Rooms** 13

## KENDAL　　Map 18 SD59

### Gateway Inn ▼

**Crook Rd LA8 8LX ☎ 01539 724187 📠 01539 720581**
**dir:** *From M6 junct 36 take A590/A591, follow signs for Windermere, pub on left after 9m*

Located within the Lake District National Park, this Victorian country inn offers delightful views, attractive gardens, Thwaites beers and welcoming log fires. A good range of appetising dishes includes chicken casserole with red wine and herb dumplings, grilled fillets of sea bass with ratatouille and mussels, and roasted butternut squash filled with leeks and Stilton. Traditional English favourites of liver and onions or rabbit pie are also a feature.

**Open** all wk 🍺 Thwaites Bitter, Thwaites Smooth & Cask Ales. ▼ 11 **Facilities** Play area Dogs allowed Garden Parking

## KESWICK　　Map 18 NY22

### The Farmers

**Portinscale CA12 5RN ☎ 01768 773442**
**dir:** *M6 junct 40, A66, bypass Keswick. After B5289 junct turn left to Portinscale*

Set in a small village a mile from bustling Keswick, this historic village pub has traditional decor and long-standing ties with the local hunt. Expect good quality, well-kept ales, a friendly welcome and traditional home-cooked food. Typical offerings include home-made lasagne; fish and chips; home-made steak and ale pie; and sweet and sour chicken in batter. Leave room for dessert, perhaps a chocolate brownie or home-made strawberry pie.

**Open** all wk noon–11pm (winter Mon-Fri 3-11 Sat-Sun noon-11) **Bar Meals** L served Sat-Sun 12-3 D served all wk 5-9, Av main course £7.95 **Restaurant** Fixed menu price fr £12.95 ⊕ MARSTONS 🍺 Jennings Bitter, Jennings Cumberland Ale, guest ale. **Facilities** Dogs allowed Garden

### The George ★★★ INN ▼ NEW

**3 St John's St CA12 5AZ**
**☎ 017687 72076 📠 017687 75968**
**e-mail:** rooms@thegeorgekeswick.co.uk
**dir:** *M6 junct 40 onto A66, take left filter road signed Keswick, pass pub on left. At x-rds turn left onto Station St, 150 yds on left*

Keswick's oldest coaching inn is a handsome 17th-century building in the heart of this popular Lakeland town. Restored to its former glory, retaining its traditional black panelling, Elizabethan beams, ancient settles and log fires, it makes a comfortable base (13 comfortable en suite rooms) from which to explore the fells and lakes. Expect to find local Jennings ales on tap and classic pub food prepared from local ingredients. Typical dishes include Cumberland ale battered haddock and chips, Borrowdale rainbow trout with herb butter, venison casserole, cow (steak) pie, and sticky toffee pudding.

**Open** all day all wk **Bar Meals** L served Mon-Thu 12-2.30 (Fri-Sun 12-5) D served all wk 5.30-9 Av main course £11 **Restaurant** D served all wk 5.30-9 booking required Fixed menu price fr £8.95 Av 3 course à la carte fr £14.95 ⊕ Jennings 🍺 Jennings, Cumberland, Sneck Lifter, Cocker Hoop, Guest ales. ▼ 10 **Facilities** Children's menu Dogs allowed Garden Parking **Rooms** 13

### PICK OF THE PUBS

### The Horse & Farrier Inn ▼

*See Pick of the Pubs on page 108*

### PICK OF THE PUBS

### The Kings Head ▼

**Thirlspot CA12 4TN**
**☎ 017687 72393 📠 017687 72309**
**e-mail:** stay@lakedistrictinns.co.uk
**dir:** *From M6 take A66 to Keswick then A591, pub 4m S of Keswick*

Standing at the foot of Helvellyn near the shores of Lake Thirlmere, this 17th-century coaching inn offers spectacular views towards Blencathra and Skiddaw. On warmer days the garden is the best place to enjoy a meal or drink, whilst indoors the traditional bar features old beams and inglenook fireplaces. Popular real ales include beers from the Jennings Brewery in nearby Cockermouth, and there is a fine selection of wines and malt whiskies. The flexible and extensive menu begins with lunchtime soups and sandwiches, whilst in the elegant restaurant you can linger over a four-course seasonal menu of traditional English dishes and local specialities. Start, perhaps, with potted Morecambe Bay shrimps or black pudding, Stilton and apple tart. Braised lemon-rosemary lamb Henry with couscous and spring vegetables might form the main course, rounded off with blackcurrant and vanilla sundae with shortbread biscuits. A steak menu is offered during the week, and booking is advisable to enjoy the choice of roasts on Sunday lunchtimes.

**Open** all day all wk **Bar Meals** Av main course £10 food served all day **Restaurant** D served all wk 7-8.30 booking required Av 3 course à la carte fr £20 ⊕ FREE HOUSE 🍺 Jennings Bitter, Cumberland Ale, Sneck Lifter, Cocker Hoop, guest ales. ▼ 9 **Facilities** Children's menu Family room Dogs allowed Garden Parking

### Pheasant Inn NEW

**Crosthwaite Rd CA12 5PP ☎ 017687 72219**
**e-mail:** peter@peter909.wanadoo.co.uk

Famous local artist John William Wilkinson – 'Wilk' – would sit in the corner here near the open fire, sketching the locals; some of his work is still on display. The Pheasant is also widely known hereabouts for its range of Jennings ales on tap, Cocker Hoop and Cumberland being two of the most popular. It's always been associated with the local hunt, which continues to meet here on Boxing Day to enjoy a pint or a local whisky. The kitchen

produces seasonal and local food of excellent quality in dishes such as pan-roasted chicken breast stuffed with haggis; and pork, black pudding and smoked bacon sausages on sage and onion mash.

**Open** all wk noon-2 5.30-11 (all day in summer) Closed: 25 Dec **Bar Meals** L served all wk 12-2 D served all wk 6-9 Av main course £9.50 **Restaurant** L served all wk 12-2 D served all wk 6-9 ⊕ MARSTON PLC 🍺 Jennings Bitter, Cumberland, Cockerhoop, Sneck Lifter. **Facilities** Children's menu Children's portions Dogs allowed Garden Parking

### The Swinside Inn

**Newlands Valley CA12 5UE ☎ 017687 78253**
**e-mail:** swinsideinn@btconnect.com
**dir:** *1m from A66, signed for Newlands/Swinside*

Situated in the quiet Newlands Valley, the Swinside Inn is a listed building dating back to about 1642. From the pub there are superb views of Causey Pike and Cat Bells among other landmarks. The current tenants have been busy refurbishing the pub and a new lounge bar and landscaped beer garden were due to be ready as we went to press. Inside you'll find traditional open fires and oak-beamed ceilings, and from Easter to late October food is served all day. Extensive bar menu may offer lamb Henry, Cumberland sausage, Swinside chicken, and fresh, grilled Borrowdale trout. Friday fish night specials.

**Open** all wk 11-3 6-11 winter (all day summer) **Bar Meals** L served all wk 11-3 D served all wk 6-9 Av main course £8.95 ⊕ SCOTTISH & NEWCASTLE 🍺 Jennings Cumberland Ale, John Smith's Smooth, Deuchars, guest ales. **Facilities** Children's menu Children's portions Dogs allowed Garden Parking

## KIRKBY LONSDALE　　Map 18 SD67

### PICK OF THE PUBS

### The Pheasant Inn ▼

**Casterton LA6 2RX**
**☎ 01524 271230 📠 01524 274267**
**e-mail:** info@pheasantinn.co.uk
**dir:** *M6 junct 36, A65 for 7m, left onto A683 at Devils Bridge, 1m to Casterton centre*

A whitewashed 18th-century coaching inn, The Pheasant nestles beneath the fells in the quiet hamlet of Casterton, just a mile from the market town of Kirkby Lonsdale in the beautiful Lune Valley. The Dixon family and staff ensure a warm welcome and traditional food

*continued on page 109*

# PICK OF THE PUBS

## The Horse & Farrier Inn 🍷

**Threlkeld Village CA12 4SQ**
☎ **017687 79688** 📠 **017687 79823**
**e-mail:** info@horseandfarrier.com
**web:** www.horseandfarrier.com
**dir:** *M6 junct 40 follow Keswick (A66) signs,*
*after 12m turn right signed Threlkeld.*
*Pub in village centre*

For over 300 years this solid old Lakeland inn has seen poets, playwrights and lead miners wend along the Glenderamackin Valley, an ancient route between Keswick and Penrith tucked in beneath the challenging mountains of Blencathra, Skiddaw and Helvellyn in this northern outpost of the Lake District National Park. Little wonder that it's a hot-spot for serious walkers reflecting in the beer garden on a day well-spent - a case of up hill and down ale, perhaps. Less energetic visitors may be taken by an underground tour at the nearby mining museum.

Within the thick, whitewashed stone walls of this long, low old building you'll find slate-flagged floors, beamed ceilings and crackling log fires, with hunting prints decorating the traditional bars and a memorable panelled snug.

The inn has an excellent reputation for good food, from hearty Lakeland breakfasts to home-cooked lunches and dinners served in either the bar, or the charming period restaurant. The chefs make full use of local, seasonal produce when preparing their varied menus. The lunchtime bar menu has all the old favourites, from baguettes and filling platter sandwiches, pies and fish and chips to more individual dishes like hot oak fillet of smoked Scottish salmon or mushroom, tomato and garlic tagliatelle with fresh spinach pasta.

The dinner menu considerably extends the choice, including the pub signature dish of Farrier lamb shoulder with a speciality marinade, slowly braised in Jennings Cumberland ale and served with chive mash and a redcurrant and mint sauce. Local Cumberland beef and pork sausage also makes the grade, served with butterbean and chive mash, onion and thyme gravy. A specials board ups the ante with a great choice of Lakeland surf, turf and game.

**Open** all day all wk 7.30am-mdnt
**Bar Meals** food served all day
**Restaurant** food served all day
⊕ JENNINGS BROTHERS PLC 🛢 Jennings Bitter, Cocker Hoop, Sneck Lifter, Cumberland Ale, guest ale. 🍷 10
**Facilities** Children's menu Family room Dogs allowed Garden Parking

Save on Hotels. Book at **theAA.com/hotel**

**CUMBRIA** 109 **ENGLAND**

**KIRKBY LONSDALE** *continued*

is served daily in both the oak-panelled restaurant and the bar, where beams and open fireplaces add to the relaxing atmosphere. Local ales, malt whiskies and a broad choice of wines can be sampled while perusing the menu of quality produce sourced from the valley farms. The reasonably priced lunch selection may include grilled gammon steak, and Cumbrian chicken breast cooked in tomato sauce with peppers, red onions, garlic, white wine and rosemary. Dinner could start with poached fresh pears with Stilton dressing, and continue with roast crispy duckling off the bone with sage and onion stuffing. In fine weather you can sit outside and enjoy the lovely views of the fells.

Open all wk noon-3 6-11 Closed: 2wks mid Jan **Bar Meals** L served all wk 12-2 D served all wk 6-9 Av main course £13 **Restaurant** L served all wk 12-2 booking required D served all wk 6-9 booking required Av 3 course à la carte fr £19 ⊕ FREE HOUSE ◀ Theakston Best & Cool Cask, Black Sheep Best, Dent Aviator, Timothy Taylor Landlord, John Smith's. ▼ 8 **Facilities** Children's portions Garden Parking

### PICK OF THE PUBS

**The Sun Inn** ★★★★★ INN ◉ ▼

Market St LA6 2AU
☎ 015242 71965 📠 015242 72485
e-mail: email@sun-inn.info
*dir: From M6 junct 36 take A65 for Kirkby Lonsdale. In 5m left signed Kirkby Lonsdale. At next T-junct turn left. Right at bottom of hill*

You'll find this welcoming 17th-century free house in the heart of Kirkby Lonsdale, just a few minutes' walk from the famous Ruskin's View. Natural stone and oak floors, log fires and window seats create a relaxed atmosphere in the bar, just perfect for enjoying the selection of cask ales from Wainwright, Timothy Taylor and Hawkshead. Lunchtime choices feature soup-and-sandwich options, as well as hot dishes like steak and kidney pudding. The restaurant menu changes regularly, perhaps encompassing starters such as ham hock terrine with pineapple chutney as a prelude to the main course. Typical choices include belly of pork and black pudding with creamed cabbage and dry-cured bacon, and stuffed squash with wild mushroom, parsnip, swede and parmesan. Eleven deluxe bed and breakfast rooms blend modern comforts with character and charm, making The Sun an ideal base from which to explore the Lake District and Yorkshire Dales.

Open all day all wk 10am-11pm **Bar Meals** L served Tue-Sun 12-2.30 D served all wk 7-9 Av main course £16.95 **Restaurant** L served Tue-Sun 12-2.30 D served all wk 7-9 Av 3 course à la carte fr £25 ⊕ FREE HOUSE ◀ Timothy Taylor Landlord, Thwaites Wainwright, Hawkshead Best Bitter. ▼ 9 **Facilities** Children's menu Children's portions Dogs allowed **Rooms** 11

### The Whoop Hall ★★ HL ▼

Skipton Rd LA6 2HP
☎ 015242 71284 📠 015242 72154
e-mail: info@whoophall.co.uk
*dir: From M6 junct 36 take A65. Pub 1m SE of Kirkby Lonsdale*

This 16th-century converted coaching inn was once the kennels for local foxhounds. In an imaginatively converted barn you can relax and enjoy Yorkshire ales and a good range of dishes based on local produce. Oven baked fillet of sea bass with tagliatelle verde and tiger prawns, and stir-fried honey roast duck with vegetables and water chestnuts are among the popular favourites. The bar offers traditional hand-pulled ales and roaring log fires, while outside is a terrace and children's area.

Open all wk **Bar Meals** L served all wk 12-9 ⊕ FREE HOUSE ◀ Black Sheep, Greene King IPA, Tetley Smooth ᵔ Thatchers Gold. ▼ 14 **Facilities** Play area Family room Dogs allowed Garden Parking **Rooms** 24

| **LITTLE LANGDALE** | **Map 18 NY30** |
| --- | --- |

### PICK OF THE PUBS

**Three Shires Inn** ★★★★ INN

*See Pick of the Pubs on page 110*

| **LOWESWATER** | **Map 18 NY12** |
| --- | --- |

### PICK OF THE PUBS

**Kirkstile Inn** ★★★★ INN ▼

CA13 0RU ☎ 01900 85219 📠 01900 85239
e-mail: info@kirkstile.com
*dir: From A66 Keswick take Whinlatter Pass at Braithwaite. Take B5292, at T-junct left onto B5289. 3m to Loweswater. From Cockermouth B5289 to Lorton, past Low Lorton, 3m to Loweswater. At red phone box left, 200yds*

Kirkstile Inn has offered shelter and hospitality amidst the stunning Cumbrian fells for some 400 years, and makes an ideal base for walking, climbing, boating and fishing. If you're a fan of real ale, be sure to try something from the Loweswater Brewery, which is attached to the inn. Alternatively, Stowford Press is on offer for cider drinkers. The dining room dates back to 1549 and is the oldest part of the inn, facing south down to the Buttermere Valley. Here the food matches the quality of the views, with plenty of choice from both the regular menus and the daily changing blackboard

specials. Expect a choice of baguettes and jacket potatoes at lunchtime, as well as hot dishes like Lakeland steak and ale pie. The evening menu might begin with Crofton goat's cheese stumpy, or smoked chicken salad with olive dressing. Move on, perhaps, to home-made chicken, leek and mustard pudding, or slow-cooked Lakeland lamb shoulder with rosemary mash. The friendly atmosphere extends through to the accommodation – comfortable en suite rooms and a family suite.

Open all day all wk Closed: 25 Dec **Bar Meals** L served all wk 12-2 booking required D served all wk 6-9 booking required Av main course £9.50 **Restaurant** D served all wk 6-9 booking required Av 3 course à la carte fr £21 ⊕ FREE HOUSE ◀ Kirkstile Gold, Yates Bitter, Melbreak, Grasmoor Ale, LPA ᵔ Stowford Press. ▼ 9 **Facilities** Children's menu Children's portions Family room Dogs allowed Garden Parking **Rooms** 9

| **MILNTHORPE** | **Map 18 SD48** |
| --- | --- |

### The Cross Keys ★★★★ INN **NEW**

1 Park Rd LA7 7AB ☎ 015395 62115 📠 015395 62446
e-mail: stay@thecrosskeyshotel.co.uk
*dir: M6 junct 35, to junct 35A then A6 N ot Milnthorpe; or M6 junct 36, A65 towards Kendal. At Crooklands left onto B6385 to Milnthorpe. Pub at x-rds in village centre*

With Levens Hall, Leighton Moss Nature Reserve and Morecambe Bay on the doorstep, this refurbished former coaching inn in the heart of Milnthorpe village makes a good pit-stop for comfortable accommodation, cask conditioned ales, and hearty pub food. Served in the traditional bar and dining room, menus offers sandwiches, salads and pub classics like steak and ale pie, lamb Henry, home-made lasagne, and sirloin steak with peppercorn sauce.

Open all day all wk **Bar Meals** L served Mon-Fri 12-2 Sat-Sun all day D served Mon-Fri 5.30-8.30 Sat-Sun all day Av main course £8 **Restaurant** L served Mon-Fri 12-2 Sat-Sun all day D served Mon-Fri 5-8.30 Sat-Sun all day Fixed menu price fr £8 Av 3 course à la carte fr £16 ⊕ ROBINSONS ◀ Hartley XB, Dizzy Blond, Veltins, Guest ale ᵔ Stowford Press. **Facilities** Children's menu Children's portions Dogs allowed Garden Parking **Rooms** 8

# PICK OF THE PUBS

## Three Shires Inn ★★★★INN

**LITTLE LANGDALE**          Map 18 NY30

**LA22 9NZ**
☎ **015394 37215**  📄 **015394 37127**
**e-mail:** enquiry@threeshiresinn.co.uk
**web:** www.threeshiresinn.co.uk
**dir:** *Turn off A593, 2.3m from Ambleside at 2nd junct signed 'The Langdales'. 1st left 0.5m. Inn in 1m*

The traditional Cumbrian slate and stone inn was built in 1872 and enjoys a stunning location in the beautiful Little Langdale valley. Just as it did in the late 19th century, it provides a much-needed resting place and watering hole for travellers on the journey over the high passes of Hardknott and Wrynose, and is the perfect pit-stop for lunch on walks in the Langdale and Skelwith area. Named after its situation near the meeting point of three county shires - Westmorland, Cumberland and Lancashire — it has been personally run by the Stephenson family since 1983.

The bars boasting bare beams and slate walls are warmed in winter by cosy log fires, whilst on fine summer days, locals, walkers and tourists head for the picnic tables by a lakeland stream in the landscaped garden with its magnificent views of the fells.

Refreshments include tip-top Cumbrian ales from Jennings, Hawkshead and Coniston breweries. Food is locally sourced and very popular, with evening booking advisable. Light lunches range from home-made soup, sandwiches and baguettes, to hot dishes such as locally made Cumberland sausages with vegetables, onion rings and a choice of potatoes. A fixed price dinner menu might begin with courgette and mint soup, followed by pan-fried salmon fillet and steamed asparagus with lemon and herb butter; or sweet potato and butternut squash curry with a timbale of herb rice and naan bread. For dessert, choose strawberry shortcake with vanilla crème Anglaise, ice cream and strawberries; or a selection of English Lakes ice creams. All of the inn's ten prettily furnished bedrooms offer a high standard of accommodation, with lovely views of the valley.

**Open** all wk 11-3 6-10.30 Dec-Jan, 11-10.30 Feb-Nov (Fri-Sat 11-11 ) **Closed:** 25 Dec **Bar Meals** L served all wk 12-2 (ex 24 & 25 Dec) D served all wk 6-8.45 (ex mid wk Dec-Jan) booking required Av main course £12.95 **Restaurant** D served all wk 6-8.45 (ex mid wk Dec-Jan) booking required Fixed menu price fr £18.95 Av 3 course à la carte fr £18 ⊕ FREE HOUSE ◄ Jennings Best & Cumberland, Coniston Old Man, Hawkshead Bitter, Ennerdale Blonde. **Facilities** Children's menu Dogs allowed (in bar only) Garden Parking **Rooms** 10

Save on Hotels. Book at theAA.com/hotel

CUMBRIA 111 ENGLAND

MUNGRISDALE Map 18 NY33

## The Mill Inn

CA11 0XR ☎ 017687 79632 📠 017687 79981
e-mail: enquiries@the-millinn.co.uk
dir: From Penrith A66 to Keswick, after 10m right to
Mungrisdale, pub 2m on left

Set in a peaceful village, this 17th-century coaching inn,
now with new licensees, is handy for spectacular fell
walks. Charles Dickens and John Peel once stayed here.
In summer, visitors can sit in the beer garden beside the
river, and in winter warm themselves by a log fire. The
menus are based on traditional Cumbrian dishes and
steaks are a speciality. Other choices include
Cumberland sausages, home-made steak and kidney pie
and vegetarian options.

**Open** all day all wk **Closed:** 25 Dec **Bar Meals** L served all
wk 12-2 booking required D served all wk 6-9 booking
required **Restaurant** L served all wk 12-2 booking
required D served all wk 6-9 booking required
⊕ ROBINSONS ◀ Robinsons ale, Hartleys XB ⏧ Stowford
Press. **Facilities** Children's menu Children's portions
Dogs allowed Garden Parking

NEAR SAWREY Map 18 SD39

### PICK OF THE PUBS

## Tower Bank Arms

LA22 0LF ☎ 015394 36334
e-mail: enquiries@towerbankarms.com
dir: On B5285 SW of Windermere.1.5m from
Hawkshead. 2m from Windermere via ferry

Devotees of Beatrix Potter may find this 17th-century
Lakeland inn familiar: it stands next to the author's
home, Hill Top, now owned by the National Trust, and
featured in the *Tale of Jemima Puddleduck*. Follow a
visit to Hill Top with lunch at this traditional and
delightfully unspoilt little pub but time your arrival
carefully as it can get swamped during the summer
months. Its rustic charm is best enjoyed out of season,
when you can relax and soak up atmosphere in the
low-beamed main bar, with its slate floor, crackling log
fire, fresh flowers and ticking grandfather clock. Tip-
top local ales on handpump include Hawkshead Bitter,
Barngates Tag Lag and Cumbrian Legendary, and
hearty country food makes good use of local produce.
At lunch, tuck into home-baked ham and mustard
sandwiches or beef and ale stew, with evening
additions taking in pork tenderloin with black pudding
mousse and Calvados and apple sauce, and Cumbrian
lamb shoulder with mint and rosemary jus. Puddings
include traditional sticky toffee pudding and a slate of
local cheeses.

**Open** all wk all day Etr-Oct **Bar Meals** L served all wk
12-2 D served Mon-Sat 6-9, Sun & BH 6-8 (Mon-Thu in
winter) Av main course £11 **Restaurant** D served Mon-
Sat 6-9, Sun & BH 6-8 (Mon-Thu in winter) Av 3 course
à la carte fr £18.95 ⊕ FREE HOUSE ◀ Barngates Tag
Lag, Hawkshead Bitter, Brodies Prime, Ulverston,
Cumbrian Legendary ⏧ Westons Organic Vintage, Old
Rosie. **Facilities** Children's portions Dogs allowed
Garden Parking

NETHER WASDALE Map 18 NY10

### The Screes Inn

CA20 1ET ☎ 019467 26262 📠 019467 26262
e-mail: info@thescreesinnwasdale.com
dir: A595 to Gosforth, in 3m turn right signed Nether
Wasdale. In village on left

This friendly family-run pub is situated in the picturesque
village of Nether Wasdale and makes an excellent base
for walking, mountain biking or diving in this lovely area,
particularly Scawfell. It dates back 300 years and offers
a log fire, real ales and large selection of malt whiskies.
There is a good choice of sandwiches at lunchtime, and
other dishes include lasagne, roast leg of lamb off the
bone, vegetarian chilli, chick pea and sweet potato curry.
There has been a change of hands.

**Open** all day all wk 11-11 (Sun 11-10.30) **Closed:** 25 Dec,
1 Jan ◀ Yates Bitter, Derwent, Black Sheep.
**Facilities** Dogs allowed Garden Parking

OUTGATE Map 18 SD39

### Outgate Inn ▼

LA22 0NQ ☎ 015394 36413
e-mail: outgate@outgate.wanadoo.co.uk
dir: Exit M6 junct 36, by-passing Kendal, A591 towards
Ambleside. At Clappersgate take B5285 to Hawkshead
then Outgate 3m

A 17th-century Lakeland inn with oak beams, once a
mineral water manufacturer and now part of Robinson's
and Hartley's Brewery. During the winter there's a real
fire, while the secluded beer garden at the rear is a
tranquil place to enjoy the summer warmth. Pub lunches
range from sandwiches and jackets to hot plates such as
home-made beef and Guinness casserole, while dinner
choices continue the traditional route: pan-fried rump
steak medallions, perhaps, or poached chicken supreme
in a chasseur sauce.

**Open** all wk all day Mar-Nov **Bar Meals** L served all wk
12-2 D served all wk 6-9 **Restaurant** L served all wk 12-2
D served all wk 6-9 ⊕ FREDERIC ROBINSON ◀ Hartleys
XB, Old Stockport Bitter, Robinsons Smooth ⏧ Stowford
Press. ▼ 12 **Facilities** Children's menu Children's
portions Dogs allowed Garden Parking

RAVENSTONEDALE Map 18 NY70

### PICK OF THE PUBS

## The Black Swan    INN

CA17 4NG ☎ 015396 23204
e-mail: enquiries@blackswanhotel.com
dir: M6 junct 38 take A685 E towards Brough

A grand, family-run Victorian inn in a peaceful
conservation village in the upper Eden Valley. Its lovely
riverside garden is home to red squirrels, which will let
you share their space to relax after you've walked the
Howgill Fells, explored the Lakes or toured the Yorkshire
Dales. Local ales are served in the bar, while in the
beautifully decorated dining rooms main meals include
award-winning local sausages casseroled with red
wine, mushrooms and shallots; whole horseshoe of
local gammon served with grilled tomato, mushrooms,
chips and egg or pineapple; aromatic Mughlai chicken
or vegetable curry with almonds, sultanas, basmati
rice and coriander; fresh cod or haddock in Black
Sheep beer batter with mushy or garden peas and
chips; and vegetable and lentil shepherd's pie with
goats' cheese mash. In 2009 the Black Swan earned an
AA Breakfast and Dinner award for its food and use of
freshly prepared local ingredients (There is menu
sourcing information about all their suppliers.) There
are individually-styled bedrooms available.

**Open** all wk 8am-11.30pm **Bar Meals** L served all wk
12-2 D served all wk 6-9 **Restaurant** L served all wk
12-2 booking required D served all wk 6-9 ⊕ FREE
HOUSE ◀ Black Sheep, John Smith's, Dent, Tirril
Brewery, Hawkshead Brewery ⏧ Thatchers.
**Facilities** Dogs allowed Garden Parking **Rooms** 14

### PICK OF THE PUBS

## The Fat Lamb Country Inn ★★ HL

*See Pick of the Pubs on page 113*

## SEDBERGH — Map 18 SD69

### The Dalesman Country Inn ☕

**Main St** LA10 5BN ☎ 015396 21183 ▤ 015396 21311
**e-mail:** info@thedalesman.co.uk
**dir:** *M6 junct 37, A684 to Sedbergh, 1st pub in town on left*

Restored 16th-century coaching inn, noted for its dazzling floral displays and handy for a choice of glorious walks along the River Dee or up to the Howgill Fells. The menu changes every fortnight, and among the main courses are trio of chargrilled lamb chops, wild salmon fillet, home-made mushroom stroganoff, fresh swordfish Niçoise, and organic chicken breast. Popular patio and garden, and a good wine selection.

**Open** all wk ◀ Carlsberg-Tetley, Theakston Best Bitter, Black Sheep. ☕ 9 **Facilities** Family room Garden Parking

## TIRRIL — Map 18 NY52

### PICK OF THE PUBS

### Queen's Head Inn ☕

CA10 2JF ☎ 01768 863219
**e-mail:** bookings@queensheadinn.co.uk
**dir:** *A66 towards Penrith then A6 S towards Shap. In Eamont Bridge turn right just after Crown Hotel. Tirril in 1m on B5320*

Situated on the edge of the Lake District National Park, this traditional English country inn dates from 1719 and is chock-full of beams, flagstones and memorabilia as you would expect from an old inn. While enjoying a pint of Unicorn, Cumbrian Way and Dizzy Blonde in the bar, look for the Wordsworth Indenture, signed by the great poet himself, his brother, Christopher, and local wheelwright John Bewsher, to whom the Wordsworths sold the pub in 1836. You can eat in the bar or restaurant, and a meal might include bacon and black pudding salad; oven-baked chicken stuffed with Blengdale Blue and spinach; and chocolate and orange tart. In August every year the Cumbrian beer and sausage festival is held here. The village shop is located at the back of the inn.

**Open** all day all wk noon–11pm Sun–Thu, noon–mdnt Fri–Sat ◀ Unicorn, Cumbria Way, Dizzy Blonde. ☕ 10 **Facilities** Dogs allowed Parking

## TORVER — Map 18 SD29

### Church House Inn NEW

LA21 8AZ ☎ 01539 441282
**e-mail:** churchhouseinn@hotmail.co.uk
**dir:** *Take A539 from Coniston towards Broughton-in-Furness. Inn on left in Torver before junct with A5084 towards Ulverston*

Footpaths wind to the bank of Coniston Water whilst the ridges of the Coniston Horseshoe mountains rise steeply from sloping pastures opposite. Sitting plum in the middle, the 15th century Church House Inn revels in this idyllic location, offering a great range of Lakeland beers

and satisfying meals sourced from local farms and estates; Cumberland Tattie hot pot based on slow braised Herdwick lamb hits the spot, enjoyed in the olde-worlde rambling interior or sheltered beer garden.

**Open** all day all wk Dec-Mar noon-3 5-11 Closed: Dec-Mar Mon-Tue fr 5pm, Wed-Thu noon-3 5-mdnt
**Bar Meals** L served all wk 12-3 D served all wk 6-9 booking required Av main course £13.50 **Restaurant** L served all wk 12-3 booking required D served all wk 6-9 booking required ⊕ ENTERPRISE INNS ◀ Hawkshead Bitter, Hawkshead Gold, Ennerdale Bitter, Tag Lag, Loweswater Gold. **Facilities** Children's portions Family room Dogs allowed Garden Parking

## TROUTBECK — Map 18 NY40

### PICK OF THE PUBS

### Queen's Head ★★★★ INN ☕

**Townhead** LA23 1PW
☎ 015394 32174 ▤ 015394 31938
**e-mail:** reservations@queensheadtroutbeck.co.uk
**dir:** *M6 junct 36, A590/591, W towards Windermere, right at mini-rdbt onto A592 signed Penrith/Ullswater. Pub 2m on left*

The lovely undulating valley of Troutbeck, with its maze of footpaths and stunning felltop views, is a magnet for ramblers. True to its roots, this smart 17th-century coaching inn offers sustenance and comfortable accommodation to the weary and footsore. The bar is perhaps its most remarkable feature, carved from a four-poster bed that once resided in Appleby Castle. Nooks and crannies, low beams stuffed with old pennies by farmers on their way home from market, and a log fire throughout the year complete the heart-warming picture. Robinson's Brewery furnishes the likes of Cumbria Way, Old Tom and Dizzy Blonde at the pumps, while the chef's reputation for accomplished cooking is well established. The menu proffers hearty fare – from tempting baguettes filled with smoked local cheese and roasted vine tomatoes, to exotic main courses such as Bobotie (a South African dish of best minced lamb, nibbed almonds, apricots and topped with a brandied egg custard).

**Open** all day all wk **Bar Meals** Av main course £18.50 food served all day **Restaurant** booking required Av 3 course à la carte fr £22.95 food served all day ⊕ FREDERIC ROBINSON ◀ Hartleys XB, Cumbria Way, Double Hop, Old Tom, Dizzy Blonde. ☕ 8 **Facilities** Children's menu Dogs allowed Parking **Rooms** 15

*See advert on page 114*

## ULVERSTON — Map 18 SD27

### Farmers Arms ☕

**Market Place** LA12 7BA
☎ 01229 584469 ▤ 01229 582188
**dir:** *In town centre*

A warm welcome is extended at this lively 16th-century inn located at the centre of the attractive, historic market town. Visitors will find a comfortable and relaxing beamed front bar with an open fire in winter. Landlord Roger Chattaway takes pride in serving quality ales and food. His Sunday lunches are famous locally, and there's a varied and tempting specials menu, deli boards to share, pub classics, chargrilled steaks and seafood delights like roasted whole sea bass encased in salt. Pizzas have now made an appearance on the menu; perhaps Pizza de la Mer, American Hot, or the vegetarian option Vitabella.

**Open** all wk **Bar Meals** L served all wk 9-3 booking required D served all wk 6-9 booking required ⊕ FREE HOUSE ◀ Hawkshead Best Bitter, John Smith's, Directors, Yates ♂ Symons. ☕ 12 **Facilities** Garden

## WASDALE HEAD — Map 18 NY10

### Wasdale Head Inn ☕

CA20 1EX ☎ 019467 26229 & 26333 ▤ 019467 26334
**e-mail:** wasdaleheadinn@msn.com
**dir:** *From A595 follow Wasdale signs. Inn at head of valley*

Famous historic mountain inn dramatically situated at the foot of England's highest mountains and beside her deepest lake, with views to Great Gable, Kirk Fell and Yewbarrow. The oak-panelled walls are hung with photographs reflecting a passion for climbing. Exclusive real ales are brewed in the pub's own micro-brewery. Bar menu choices (lasagne, goulash, chilli, scampi from Whitby, lamb Henry) are served with mash, rice, chips or new potatoes; the restaurant menu steps up a notch with sautéed garlic tiger prawns, steaks, and grilled salmon fillet.

**Open** all day all wk **Bar Meals** L served all wk 12-9 D served all wk 12-9 Av main course £9 food served all day **Restaurant** D served all wk 7-8 booking required Av 3 course à la carte fr £23 ⊕ FREE HOUSE ◀ Yates Best Bitter, Rannerdale Robin, Coniston Bluebird, Loweswater Gold. **Facilities** Children's menu Children's portions Dogs allowed Garden Parking

# PICK OF THE PUBS

## The Fat Lamb Country Inn ★★HL

**RAVENSTONEDALE**      Map 18 NY70

**Crossbank CA17 4LL**
☎ **015396 23242**   📄 **015396 23285**
e-mail: enquiries@fatlamb.co.uk
*dir: On A683 between Sedbergh & Kirkby Stephen*

No matter which way you look from The Fat Lamb's gardens, your gaze will fall on some of England's most precious, under-visited and remote countryside. To the west rise the great, grassy whalebacks of The Howgill Fells whilst north are the limestone scars, vales and plateaux secreting the glorious Smardale National Nature Reserve. Throw in the top end of Swaledale in the Yorkshire Dales and the viridian Vale of Eden, and you'll realise why ramblers and country lovers compete to stay in the comfy AA-rated en suite bedrooms at this stone coaching inn high above the green meadows of Ravenstonedale in the furthest corner of old Westmorland.

Modern amenities blend with old fashioned hospitality at this 350 year-old free house. An open fire in the traditional Yorkshire range warms the bar in winter; this is the oldest part of the building and was converted from the former kitchen and living area. Here, visitors and locals can mingle and natter without the intrusion of electronic entertainments.

Snacks and meals are served here and in the most traditional and relaxed restaurant, which is decorated with old prints and plates. The carte menu might feature an opening salvo of spiced chicken roulade with a honey and mustard seed dressing, preparing the way for roast leg of local shearling lamb in a port wine and rosemary gravy or grilled Bessy Beck trout with a lime, dill and cream cheese stuffing; non-meat options include brie and broccoli filo pastry parcels in a spicy tomato sauce. Whatever you choose, it will have been prepared on site using the best available local ingredients.

A short, post-prandial constitutional could take you through the inn's own Crossbank Nature Reserve, where over 80 species of bird are recorded, sharing with badgers, otters, roe deer and bats.

**Open** all day all wk **Bar Meals** L served all wk 12-2 booking required D served all wk 6-9 booking required Av main course £9.60 **Restaurant** L served all wk 12-2 booking required D served all wk 6-9 booking required Fixed menu price fr £23 Av 3 course à la carte fr £13.50 ⊕ FREE HOUSE 🛢 Black Sheep Bitter. **Facilities** Play area Dogs allowed Garden Parking **Rooms** 12

## WATERMILLOCK — Map 18 NY42

### PICK OF THE PUBS

## Brackenrigg Inn ★★★ INN ♥

*See Pick of the Pubs on page 115*

## WINDERMERE — Map 18 SD49

### The Angel Inn ♥

Helm Rd LA23 3BU ☎ 015394 44080
e-mail: rooms@the-angelinn.com
dir: *From Rayrigg Rd (parallel to lake) into Crag Brow,
then right into Helm Rd*

City chic style is offered at this sophisticated gastro-pub in a great location five minutes' from Lake Windermere in the centre of Bowness-on-Windermere. Local ales vie with international beers at the bar, and good food based on local produce is available throughout the day from a choice of menus: breakfast/brunch; sandwiches and light lunches; starters, nibbles and salads; main courses - braised Cumbrian farmed pork belly with parmentier potatoes, carrot purée and black pudding - desserts and a children's menu. In warmer weather head for the garden terrace where there are great views.

**Open** all day all wk 9am-11pm **Closed:** 25 Dec
**Bar Meals** L served all wk 9.30-4 D served all wk 5-9
**Restaurant** L served all wk 9.30-4 D served all wk 5-9
⊕ FREE HOUSE ◀ Coniston Bluebird Bitter, Hawkshead Bitter. ♥ 12 **Facilities** Children's menu Garden Parking

### Eagle & Child Inn ★★★ INN ♥

Kendal Rd, Staveley LA8 9LP ☎ 01539 821320
e-mail: info@eaglechildinn.co.uk
web: www.eaglechildinn.co.uk
dir: *M6 junct 36, A590 towards Kendal then A591 towards
Windermere. Staveley approx 2m*

The rivers Kent and Gowan meet at the gardens of this friendly inn, and it's surrounded by miles of excellent walking, cycling and fishing country. Several pubs in Britain share the same name, which refers to a legend of a baby found in an eagle's nest. With a good range of beers to chose from, dishes include Fleetwood mussels in tomato, garlic and white wine sauce, local rump steak braised with onions; and roast cod loin in anchovy and parsley butter. Comfortable accommodation is available.

*Eagle & Child Inn*

**Open** all day all wk **Bar Meals** L served Mon-Fri 12-2.30, Sat-Sun 12-3 D served Mon-Fri 6-8.45, Av main course £9.95 **Restaurant** Fixed menu price fr £12.95 ⊕ FREE HOUSE ◀ Coniston, Hawkshead Bitter, Dent Ales, Yates Bitter, Tirril Brewery ⚬ Westons, Ancient Orchard, Cumbrian. ♥ 10 **Facilities** Children's menu Children's portions Dogs allowed Garden Parking **Rooms** 5

## WORKINGTON — Map 18 NY02

### The Old Ginn House

Great Clifton CA14 1TS
☎ 01900 64616 🖬 01900 873384
e-mail: enquiries@oldginnhouse.co.uk
dir: *Just off A66, 3m from Workington & 4m from
Cockermouth*

The inn was converted from a 17th-century farmstead. It contained a rounded room in which horses were harnessed to a grindstone to crush crops, called
*continued on page 116*

---

# Luxury in the Lakes – The Queen's Head Hotel

The UK has some of the most stunning landscape in the world, boasting superb scenery, rolling hills, and views to remember. No more so is this true than in the Lake District, so we've found the ideal base from which you can experience all this and more - The Queen's Head Hotel.

Tucked away in the Troutbeck Valley near Windermere (only three miles away), this warm and welcoming accommodation awaits your arrival, where you'll experience first hand the luxurious rooms on offer, as well as an array of tantalising dishes. Plus, you'll have no trouble discovering all the area has to offer, with a maze of footpaths linking ancient hamlets, as well as luring you into some beautiful gardens.

Take a break from the stresses and strains of everyday life and savour the moment within comfortable and attractive surroundings. You can expect a choice of double and fabulous four-poster beds, as well as being enticed by the textures and themes that complement each room. From the original coaching inn to the beautifully transformed ancient barn, your room will just be the tip of the iceberg when it comes to comfort.

During your stay you'll also no doubt want to sample the extensive menu on offer, with locally sourced produce, including poached local duck eggs, 100% homemade pure beef burgers, and even there own cumberland sausage, as well as the old favourite of real ale battered fish and chips! With so much choice, it seems that the most stressful part of your break will be what to choose from the menu and there's even a selection of local ales to wash everything down!

*So, take advantage of The Queen's Head Hotel NOW and book your next Lakeland adventure.*

The Queen's Head Hotel
Townhead, Troutbeck
Near Windermere,
Cumbria, LA23 1PW
**Tel 015394 32174**
**www.queensheadtroutbeck.co.uk**

# PICK OF THE PUBS

## Brackenrigg Inn ★★★INN 🍷

**WATERMILLOCK**      Map 18 NY42

**CA11 0LP**
☎ **017684 86206**   📄 **017684 86945**
e-mail: enquiries@brackenrigginn.co.uk
dir: *M6 junct 40 take A66 signed Keswick. Then A592 signed Ullswater. Right at lake. Inn 6m from M6 & Penrith*

This long, white-washed free house makes a superb base for exploring the delights of the north Lakes, which include walking, climbing, watersports, and golf, as well as simply touring by car. Originally an 18th-century coaching inn, guests can still enjoy the breathtaking landscape of Ullswater and the surrounding fells from the pub's elevated terrace and fine gardens. There's a good choice of real ales such as Coniston Bluebird, Jennings Cumberland and Copper Dragon 1816. Meanwhile, the wine list is well balanced and full of interest, with a choice of fifteen wines by the glass and helpful suggestions on tasting.

The award-winning menu caters for all tastes, and meals are freshly prepared from local produce by the inn's team of resident chefs. Expect a range of traditional or more modern dishes in the restaurant, or choose from the all-day bar menu. Typical options include starters like crispy breaded duck egg with piccalilli sauce; pan-seared scallops with a white chocolate and white truffle risotto; and grilled goat's cheese en croute with honey, treacle and seasonal fruits. Main course choices might feature pan-fried red mullet, chorizo, ratatouille of vegetables and new potatoes; Martindale venison and blue cheese lasagne topped with roquefort and rocket; or roast butternut squash and blue cheese risotto with rocket and balsamic. If time is short, the interesting range of sandwiches like three cheese and red onion mayonnaise; and tuna, red onion and salad cream might fit the bill.

Finally, if you can't tear yourselves away from the peace and beauty of this place, then make yourself at home in one of the smart bedrooms, some housed on the ground floor in Stable Cottages. A good night's sleep and a traditional Cumbrian breakfast are guaranteed.

**Open** all day all wk **Bar Meals** L served all wk 12-5 D served all wk 5-9 food served all day **Restaurant** L served all wk 12-2.30 D served all wk 6-9 Av 3 course à la carte fr £28 ⊕ FREE HOUSE 🛢 Jennings Cumberland, Coniston Bluebird, Copper Dragon, Tirril Brewery, Old Faithful, Guinness. 🍷 15 **Facilities** Children's menu Dogs allowed Garden Parking **Rooms** 17

**WORKINGTON** *continued*

'ginning'. Today this unique room houses the warmly hospitable main bar where a good selection of ales, lagers and wines are served. The butter yellows, bright check curtains and terracotta tiles of the dining areas exude a warm Mediterranean glow. Take your choice of traditional home-cooked fare such as chicken and ham pie; pasta carbonara; local Cumberland sausage; or mixed grill.

**Open** all day all wk Closed: 24-26 Dec, 1 Jan **Bar Meals** L served all wk 12-2 D served all wk 6-9.30 Av main course £8 **Restaurant** L served all wk 12-2 D served all wk 6-9.30 Av 3 course à la carte fr £16 ⊕ FREE HOUSE ◀ Jennings Bitter, John Smith's Bitter, Local Bluebird. **Facilities** Children's menu Children's portions Garden Parking

**YANWATH**     Map 18 NY52

### PICK OF THE PUBS

## The Yanwath Gate Inn ♀

**CA10 2LF ☎ 01768 862386**
**e-mail:** enquiries@yanwathgate.com
**dir:** *Telephone for directions*

Matt Edwards, mine host at the 'Yanworth Yat', is an enthusiastic supporter of Cumbria's burgeoning micro-breweries, with at least three represented at any one time; Tirril beers from just up the road are a favourite. He's no shrinking violet with local food either, and has received many awards for the quality of the inn's meals, the raw material for much of which is sourced from producers close to home in this enviable location between the Eden Valley and the mountains embracing Ullswater, possibly England's loveliest lake. There's an easy-going mix of traditional ambience (the pub is nearly 330 years old) with modern overtones here, and this is reflected in the choice of top notch staple fodder; the challenging Gate Inn Platter (mussels, smoked salmon, cheese, smoked duck breast and Penrith pepperpot sausage with all the trimmings) or wild venison steak in redcurrant and game sauce with sage mash – or something a little more modern, such as chestnut mushroom, chive and feta risotto. There's a marvellous local cheeseboard, too.

**Open** all day all wk **Bar Meals** L served all wk 12-2.30 booking required D served all wk 6-9 booking required Av main course £10 **Restaurant** L served all wk 12-2.30 booking required D served all wk 6-9 booking required Av 3 course à la carte fr £30 ⊕ FREE HOUSE ◀ Hesket Newmarket, Tirril, Loweswater, Keswick Ŏ Westons Old Rosie. ♀ 12 **Facilities** Children's menu Dogs allowed Garden Parking

## DERBYSHIRE

**ASHBOURNE**     Map 10 SK14

## Barley Mow Inn

**Kirk Ireton DE6 3JP ☎ 01335 370306**
**dir:** *Telephone for directions*

On the edge of the Peak District National Park, this imposing 17th-century inn has remained largely unchanged over the years. Close to Carsington Water, ideal for sailing, fishing and bird watching. There are also good walking opportunities on nearby marked paths. Ales from the cask and traditional cider; fresh granary rolls at lunchtime and evening meals for residents only.

**Open** all wk noon-2 7-11 (Sun noon-2 7-10.30) Closed: 25 Dec, 1 Jan ◀ Changing micro-breweries. **Facilities** Dogs allowed Garden Parking

**BAKEWELL**     Map 16 SK26

### PICK OF THE PUBS

## The Bull's Head

**Church St, Ashford-in-the-Water DE45 1QB**
**☎ 01629 812931**
**e-mail:** bullshead.ashford@virgin.net
**dir:** *Off A6, 2m N of Bakewell, 5m from Chatsworth Estate*

A family affair for several generations, the Bull's Head has seen the London and Manchester coaches come and go, though the village's famous well dressing is still a sight to enjoy. Everything about this cosy pub is smartly turned out, from the roses climbing round the door to the shiny brassware in the bar where you may choose between a pint of Robinson's Old Stockport, Unicorn or Double Hop. The interior is unpretentious, with dark wooden beams, open brick fires and comfy banquettes. There is no restaurant as such; dishes from a frequently changing menu are cooked to order and served in the small lounge bar. Lunchtime sees a range of sandwiches on offer, or delicious home-made soups such as tomato and lovage; or yellow split pea. Steak and Old Stockport ale pie served with braised red cabbage and dripping-roasted potatoes is a popular main course choice, with blueberry crumble pie and vanilla ice cream to finish.

**Open** all wk 11-3 (summer) noon-3 (winter) 6-11 (Sun noon-3 7-10.30) **Bar Meals** L served all wk 12-2 D served Mon-Sat (ex Thu in winter) 6.30-9, Sun 7-9 ⊕ ROBINSONS ◀ Old Stockport, Unicorn, Double Hop. **Facilities** Family room Dogs allowed Garden Parking

### PICK OF THE PUBS

**The Monsal Head Hotel ★★ HL ⊛ ♀**

*See Pick of the Pubs on opposite page*

**BAMFORD**     Map 16 SK28

### PICK OF THE PUBS

**Yorkshire Bridge Inn ★★★★ INN ♀**

*See Pick of the Pubs on page 118*

**BARLOW**     Map 16 SK37

## The Trout at Barlow ♀

**33 Valley Rd S18 7SL**
**☎ 0114 289 0893 ▤ 0114 289 0893**
**e-mail:** mikenorie@btconnect.com
**dir:** *From Chesterfield follow the Newbold Rd B619 for 4.5m*

This country pub is a few miles outside Chesterfield at the start of the Peak District. It is strong on food and jazz, with Jazz Club every Saturday night and Jazz Dining the first Monday of the month. There is also a quiz on a Wednesday night. A weekly-changing choice of two real ales along with regulars is offered and plenty of freshly prepared, home-cooked food. All special occasions are catered for, such as weddings and parties.

**Open** all wk 12-3 6-11 (Sun noon-9.30) **Bar Meals** booking required Av main course £7.95 **Restaurant** L served Mon-Sat 12-2, Sun 12-4 booking required D served Mon-Sat 6-9 booking required Av 3 course à la carte fr £10.95 ⊕ MARSTONS ◀ Marstons Pedigree, Mansfield Smooth, Marston's Finest Creamy, Guest. ♀ 9 **Facilities** Children's menu Children's portions Dogs allowed Garden Parking

**BARROW UPON TRENT**     Map 11 SK32

## Ragley Boat Stop ♀

**Deepdale Ln, Off Sinfin Ln DE73 1HH ☎ 01332 703919**
**e-mail:** ragley@king-henry-taverns.co.uk
**dir:** *Telephone for directions*

When King Henry's Taverns bought this canalside pub, its outbuildings were in a dangerous condition, there was no sewerage, and four acres of overgrown garden sloped down to the waterside. Today it offers pub grub at sensible prices to satisfy the appetites of boaters hungry after hours sitting motionless at the tiller. Traditional favourites include steak and ale pie; scampi; calves' liver and bacon; and garlic chicken goujons. Look out for a free wine offer if you 'dine after nine'. There is a huge balcony overlooking the gardens and canal.

**Open** all day all wk **Bar Meals** Av main course £3.50 food served all day **Restaurant** food served all day ⊕ KING HENRY TAVERNS ◀ Greene King IPA, Marstons Pedigree, Guinness. ♀ 16 **Facilities** Children's menu Children's portions Play area Family room Garden Parking

# PICK OF THE PUBS

## The Monsal Head Hotel ★★HL

**BAKEWELL** Map 16 SK26

**Monsal Head DE45 1NL**
☎ 01629 640250 🖷 01629 640815
**e-mail:** enquiries@monsalhead.com
**dir:** A6 from Bakewell towards Buxton. 1.5m
to Ashford. Follow Monsal Head signs, B6465
for 1m

Commanding superb views over Monsal
Dale, this distinctive balconied free
house is set in the heart of the Peak
District National Park just three miles
from Bakewell. The hotel's real ale pub,
the Stable Bar, reflects its earlier role as
the home of railway horses which
collected passengers from Monsal Dale
station.

Today, this delightful venue features
original flagstone floors and seating in
the former horse stalls, with horse tack

on the walls and a hay rack at the back
of the bar. You'll find welcoming winter
fires and a range of cask ales that
includes Theakstons and Lloyds Monsal.
Lagers, wheat beers and wines by the
bottle or glass are also on offer.

Food is served all day in the bar and
Longstone restaurant, or in fine weather
you may prefer to eat in the large
enclosed garden. Expect lunchtime
sandwiches and jacket potatoes,
supplemented by wraps, fajitas and a
children's menu. For something more
ambitious, head for the restaurant,
where the substantial portions of tried
and tested dishes are sure to please.
Starters like Thai-spiced duck spring
rolls with Asian vegetable salad and
sweet chilli dip, or goat's cheese and
spinach tartlet with pecan, pear, red
chard and rocket salad might set the
ball rolling, to be followed by vegetable
cottage pie; whole roasted flounder with
tomato and chilli jam and sour cream;
or venison and mushroom pie with red
wine and herbs. Raspberry Pavlova or
chocolate nemesis with honeycomb ice
cream are typical desserts, or you might
opt for a selection of farmhouse
cheeses.

There are seven en suite bedrooms, and
the complex is ideally located for touring
and walking. Chatsworth House and
Haddon Hall are a ten-minute drive
away.

**Open** all day all wk 8am-11pm
**Bar Meals** L served Mon-Sat 12-9.30,
Sun 12-9 D served Mon-Sat 12-9.30,
Sun 12-9 food served all day
**Restaurant** L served Mon-Sat 12-9.30,
Sun 12-9 D served Mon-Sat 12-9.30,
Sun 12-9 food served all day ⊕ FREE
HOUSE ◗ Bradfield ales, Lloyds Monsal,
Thornbridge ales, Abbeydale,
Peakstones Black Hole. ▼ 17
**Facilities** Children's menu Dogs allowed
Garden Parking **Rooms** 7

# PICK OF THE PUBS

## Yorkshire Bridge Inn ★★★★ INN ♀

**BAMFORD** Map 16 SK28

Ashopton Rd S33 0AZ
☎ 01433 651361   📄 01433 651361
e-mail: info@yorkshire-bridge.co.uk
web: www.yorkshire-bridge.co.uk
dir: *A57 from M1, left onto A6013, pub 1m on right*

Taking its name from the old packhorse bridge over the River Derwent near Derbyshire's border with Yorkshire, this early 19th-century inn is surrounded by wonderful Peak District walking country. A short stroll to the north is the Ladybower and other reservoirs, where the RAF's Dambuster training runs took place in 1943 before they headed for Germany. Although the reservoirs caused heated controversy when they were created in the first half of the 20th century, they are now as much part of the scenery as the moorland itself.

The inn's beamed and chintz-curtained bars are cosy and welcoming in winter, although when warm you might prefer your pint of Easy Rider or Scott's 1816 in the stone-built conservatory, the courtyard, or the spacious beer garden.

The kitchen prepares good quality, freshly made pub food using local produce; the standard menu lists submarines, toasted sandwiches and filled jacket potatoes (lunchtime only), plus grills and other hot dishes, and salads (available throughout the day). Starters include home-made soup; nachos; and garlic bread with mozzarella and tomato, while among the main courses are roast chicken breast with stuffing, sausage, Yorkshire pudding and chips; breaded fried scampi with new potatoes and vegetables; lasagne verde with garlic bread; and quiche of the day. There are also daily specials including giant prawn cocktail; rosemary and garlic lamb steaks with onions, mushrooms and Stilton; and buttered grilled fillet of tilapia. For dessert, you could try chocolate fudge and mousse cake; warm caramel apple pie; or ginger and clementine cheesecake.

The en suite bedrooms, including one with a four-poster, and self-catering apartments over the road make a good base for touring the nearby attractions of Chatsworth, Dovedale and Bakewell.

**Open** all day all wk **Bar Meals** L served Mon-Sat 12-2, Sun 12-8.30 D served Mon-Thu 6-9, Fri-Sat 6-9.30, Sun 12-8.30 Av main course £9.25 ⊕ FREE HOUSE 🛢 Bakewell Best, Pale Rider, Scotts 1816, Chatsworth Gold, Easy Rider. ♀ 11 **Facilities** Children's menu Garden Parking **Rooms** 14

| BASLOW | Map 16 SK27 |
| --- | --- |

## PICK OF THE PUBS

### Rowley's ⊛⊛ ⍷

**Church Ln DE45 1RY ☎ 01246 583880**
e-mail: info@rowleysrestaurant.co.uk
dir: *A619/A623 signed Chatsworth. Baslow on edge of Chatsworth Estate*

Set in peaceful village overlooking the church, the former Prince of Wales pub was spruced up and transformed into a modern bar and restaurant in 2006 by the team behind Fischer's Restaurant in nearby Baslow Hall. The sibling venue offers an informal mix of stone-flagged bar area, where you sup a pint of local Abbeydale ale, alongside the chic, more contemporary feel of its three dining areas upstairs. The food (awarded two AA Rosettes) is an appealing mix of modern and traditional British, with an emphasis on quality local produce. At lunch, simply presented dishes may take in saffron risotto with seared squid and chorizo; venison and smoked paprika burger with tomato chutney and parsnip crisps; and classic fish and chips with pea purée and fat chips. Dinner options may include roast cod with cockle and linguini broth, Moroccan spiced shoulder of lamb with apricot couscous, and coconut and lemongrass rice pudding. The alfresco terrace has lovely church views.

**Open** all day Closed: Sun eve **Bar Meals** L served Mon-Fri 12-2, Sat 12-2.30, Sun 12-3 D served Mon-Thu 5.30-7.30 Av main course £10 **Restaurant** L served Mon-Fri 12-2, Sat 12-2.30, Sun 12-3 D served Mon-Thu 5.30-9, Fri-Sat 6-10 Fixed menu price fr £23.50 Av 3 course à la carte fr £26 ⊕ FREE HOUSE ◀ Thornbridge, Abbeydale Brewery ♻ Aspall. ⍷ 10 **Facilities** Children's menu Children's portions Parking

| BIRCHOVER | Map 16 SK26 |
| --- | --- |

## PICK OF THE PUBS

### The Druid Inn

**Main St DE4 2BL ☎ 01629 650302**
e-mail: thedruidinn@hotmail.co.uk
dir: *From A6 between Matlock & Bakewell take B5056 signed Ashbourne. Approx 2m left to Birchover*

Built in 1607, this family-run gastro-pub offers freshly prepared traditional and contemporary food, largely sourced from within the Peak District. You can choose from four different dining areas: lunch (and maybe a pint of Druid Bitter) in the bar and snug; a more formal meal in the upper or lower restaurant; or outside on the terrace, from where you can survey the surrounding countryside. Each dining area has the same varied and ever-changing menu, ranging from light bites and sandwiches to two- and three-course meals. A starter such as Bakewell black pudding with streaky bacon, onions and poached free-range egg could precede classic coq au vin; curried smoked haddock and garden pea risotto; or penne pasta creamed with wild mushrooms and Stilton. End with chocolate marquise, or crumble of the day. If you want to walk up on the moors behind the inn, it's best to do that first.

**Open** 11-3 6-11 (Sat 11am-mdnt) Closed: 25 Dec, Sun eve **Bar Meals** L served Mon-Sat 12-2.30, Sun 12-3 booking required D served Mon-Thu 6-9, Fri-Sat 6-9.30 booking required Av main course £10 **Restaurant** L served Mon-Sat 12-2.30, Sun 12-3 booking required D served Mon-Thu 6-9, Fri-Sat 6-9.30 booking required Fixed menu price fr £13 Av 3 course à la carte fr £20 ⊕ FREE HOUSE ◀ Druid Bitter, Guest ale. **Facilities** Children's menu Children's portions Garden Parking

## PICK OF THE PUBS

### Red Lion Inn

**Main St DE4 2BN ☎ 01629 650363**
e-mail: red.lion@live.co.uk
dir: *5.5m from Matlock, off A6 onto B5056*

Originally a farmhouse, The Red Lion was built in 1680, and gained its first licence in 1722, and its old well, now glass-covered, still remains in the Tap Room. Follow a walk to nearby Rowter Rocks, a gritstone summit affording stunning valley and woodland views, cosy up in the character bar, with its old oak beams, exposed stone walls, scrubbed oak tables, worn quarry-tiled floor, and welcoming atmosphere. Quaff a pint of locally brewed Swift Nick or Old Rosie cider and refuel with a plate of home-cooked food prepared from local ingredients. Start with a Sardinian speciality from owner Matteo Frau's homeland, perhaps courgette, tomato and pecorino rösti with pickled onion chutney and pistoccu, or carpaccio of venison with cranberry glaze, then follow with pheasant supreme; lamb shank with braised red cabbage; sirloin steak and chips; or roast squash, sage Derby and mushroom crumble. Leave room for chocolate brownie with clotted cream, or a hearty sticky toffee pudding with vanilla ice cream. Don't miss the Sunday lunches and the Sardinian nights in winter.

**Open** 12-2.30 6-11.30 (Sat & BH Mons noon-mdnt Sun 12-11) Closed: Mon in winter **Bar Meals** L served Tue-Sat 12-2, Sun 12-7(winter) D served Tue-Sat 6-9 Av main course £7.95 **Restaurant** L served Tue-Sat 12-2, Sun 12-7(winter) D served Tue-Sat 6-9 Av 3 course à la carte fr £16 ⊕ FREE HOUSE ◀ Worthingtons, Nine Ladies, Swift Nick, Ichinusa (Sardinian), Peakstone's Rock Brewery Bitters ♻ Westons Scrumpy, Perry, Old Rosie. **Facilities** Children's portions Dogs allowed Garden Parking

| BIRCH VALE | Map 16 SK08 |
| --- | --- |

## PICK OF THE PUBS

### The Waltzing Weasel Inn ⍷

**New Mills Rd SK22 1BT**
**☎ 01663 743402　🖷 01663 743402**
e-mail: waltzingweasel@mailauth.co.uk
dir: *Village at junct of A6015 & A624, halfway between Glossop & Chapel-en-le-Firth*

Dramatic views of Kinder Scout set this 400-year-old quintessential English inn apart from the crowd. Situated beside the Sett Valley trail, it is an ideal spot for walkers. Early 2010 saw a change of management here, followed by a complete refurbishment. But the bar is still warmed by a real fire and furnished with country antiques, while the restaurant enjoys more of those wonderful views from its mullioned windows. No games machines or piped music sully the atmosphere, so sit back with a pint of Marston's and choose from a menu of robust and reasonably priced dishes. In addition to soups, filled jackets, sandwiches and light bites, the lunch menu embraces starters such as button mushroom and blue cheese bake; or corned beef hash with soft poached egg. Main courses include proper steak and ale pie in a puff pastry case; and chargrilled gammon steak with hand-cut chunky chips.

**Open** all day all wk **Bar Meals** L served all wk 12-3 D served all wk 6-9.30 Av main course £8 **Restaurant** L served all wk 12-3 D served all wk 6-9.30 Fixed menu price fr £10 Av 3 course à la carte fr £12 ⊕ FREE HOUSE ◀ Marston's Best & Pedigree, Jennings Sneck Lifter, Greene King IPA, Old Speckled Hen. ⍷ 10 **Facilities** Children's menu Children's portions Dogs allowed Garden Parking

| BRADWELL | Map 16 SK18 |
| --- | --- |

### Ye Old Bowling Green Inn

**Smalldale S33 9JQ ☎ 01433 620450**
e-mail: dalesinns@aol.com
dir: *Off A623 onto B6049 to Bradwell. Onto Gore Ln by playing field to Smalldale & inn*

An early 16th-century coaching inn with impressive views over glorious Hope Valley and Win Hill, and reports of a resident ghost or ghosts. With its old world atmosphere and warming winter fires, the pub is popular with the locals who discuss all kinds of matters especially those ghosts. Traditional country cooking features pub classics such as BBQ chicken breast with bacon and cheese; home-made pie of the day (look out for Desperate Dan Pie); a range of steaks from the griddle plus sandwiches, baguettes, salads and light bites. This is a great place for setting out for a walk or hike.

**Open** all day all wk **Bar Meals** L served Mon-Sat 12-2.30, Sun 12.30-4 D served Mon-Sat 6-9 (booking required) Av main course £9 **Restaurant** L served Mon-Sat 12-2.30, Sun 12.30-4 D served Mon-Sat 6-9 (booking required) ⊕ ENTERPRISE INNS ◀ Tetleys, Copper Dragon, Black Sheep, John Smith's, Hobgoblin **Facilities** Children's menu Children's portions Play area Garden Parking

## BRASSINGTON — Map 16 SK25

### PICK OF THE PUBS

### Ye Olde Gate Inne

**Well St DE4 4HJ** ☎ 01629 540448 📠 01629 540448
e-mail: theoldgateinn@supanet.com
dir: *2m from Carsington Water off A5023 between Wirksworth & Ashbourne*

Built in 1616 out of local stone and timbers allegedly salvaged from the wrecked Armada fleet, this venerable inn stands beside an old London to Manchester turnpike in the heart of Brassington, a hill village on the southern edge of the Peak District. Oak beams, black cast iron log burner, an antique clock, charmingly worn quarry-tiled floors and a delightful mishmash of polished furniture give the inn plenty of character. Hand-pumped Marston's Pedigree Bitter takes pride of place behind the bar, alongside guest ales such as Jennings Cumberland. The menu offers firm lunchtime favourites, such as home-roasted ham, egg and home-made chips; and Cumberland sausages with creamed mash and onion gravy. In the evening, start with crevettes cooked in garlic butter and choose from the likes of roast pheasant breast wrapped in bacon with a port sauce, or pan-fried fillet of beef served with an oxtail broth.

**Open** Tue eve-Sun Closed: Mon (ex BH), Tue L
🍺 Marston's Pedigree, Jennings Cumberland, guest ales. **Facilities** Family room Dogs allowed Garden Parking

## CASTLETON — Map 16 SK18

### The Peaks Inn ☕

**How Ln S33 8WJ** ☎ 01433 620247 📠 01433 623590
e-mail: info@peaks-inn.co.uk
dir: *On A625 in town centre*

An attractive, stone-built village pub standing below the ruins of Peveril Castle, after which Castleton is named. The bar is warm and welcoming, with leather armchairs for weary walkers, and open log fires. The menu offers old favourites of steak and ale pie; bangers and mash; ham, egg and chips; beer battered cod; and a range of steaks.

**Open** all wk 🍺 Black Sheep, Deuchars IPA, Tetley Smooth, 1 guest on rotation. ☕ 9 **Facilities** Dogs allowed Garden Parking

### Ye Olde Nag's Head

**Cross St S33 8WH** ☎ 01433 620248 & 620443
e-mail: info@yeoldenagshead.co.uk
dir: *A625 from Sheffield, W through Hope Valley, through Hathersage & Hope. Pub on main road*

A traditional 17th-century inn in grey stone situated in the heart of the Peak District National Park, close to Chatsworth House, Haddon Hall and miles of wonderful walks. Walkers are welcome to seek refreshment in the cosy bars, warmed by open fires and kitted out with antiques. Here you'll find three ales and a good choice of pub food: starters such as whitebait or Thai fishcake can be followed by roast beef with all the trimmings; or spaghetti carbonara.

**Open** all day all wk **Bar Meals** food served all day **Restaurant** food served all day ⊕ FREE HOUSE 🍺 Black Sheep, Guinness. **Facilities** Children's menu Children's portions Dogs allowed Parking

## CHELMORTON — Map 16 SK16

### The Church Inn NEW

**SK17 9SL** ☎ 01298 85319
e-mail: justinsatur@tiscali.co.uk
dir: *From A515 or A6 take A5270 between Bakewell & Buxton. Chelmorton signed*

There has been an inn here since 1742, when a certain George Holme opened it as an alehouse called the Blacksmith's Arms. It was renamed the Church Inn in 1884, about the time it was bought by Gresley's Brewery of Burton-on-Trent, later taken over by Marston's. These ales are still sold at the warm and welcoming, newly decorated bar, with its tiled floor and carefully preserved old features. Home-cooked ingredients are freshly prepared daily, appearing in dishes such as rabbit pie, fresh battered haddock, and chicken balti.

**Open** all wk 12-3 6.30-11.30 (Sat-Sun noon-11.30) **Bar Meals** L served Mon-Fri 12-2.30 Sat-Sun 12-5 D served Mon-Fri 6.30-9, Sat-Sun 12-9 Av main course £7.50 ⊕ FREE HOUSE **Facilities** Children's menu Dogs allowed Garden

## CHESTERFIELD — Map 16 SK37

### PICK OF THE PUBS

### Red Lion Pub & Bistro ☕

**Darley Rd, Stone Edge S45 0LW**
☎ 01246 566142 📠 01246 591040
e-mail: redlionpubandbistro@yahoo.com
dir: *Telephone for directions*

Built in 1788, the Red Lion has seen many changes, including a recent refurbishment and the addition of two function rooms. Despite its wooden beams and stone walls, the building is an effortless blend of old and new, with discreet lighting and comfy leather armchairs that place the spacious interiors firmly in the 21st century. Ian Daisley's striking black and white photographs decorate the walls, whilst local jazz bands liven up the bar on Thursdays evenings. Meals are served in the bar and bistro, or beneath white umbrellas in the large garden. Home-grown salads and fresh, seasonal produce, especially game and fish, feature on the menus, and the chefs make everything from chutneys to black pudding. Typical choices might start with crayfish and mango salad, or chorizo and herb risotto, followed by slow-cooked pork belly with pan-seared scallops, or hazelnut and parmesan crusted shallot tart. Leave space for desserts like vanilla bean pannacotta and pomegranate ice.

**Open** all day all wk **Bar Meals** Av main course £11 food served all day **Restaurant** food served all day ⊕ FREE HOUSE 🍺 Black Sheep. **Facilities** Children's menu Children's portions Garden Parking

## CHINLEY — Map 16 SK08

### Old Hall Inn ★★★★ INN ☕ NEW

**Whitehough SK23 6EJ** ☎ 01663 750529
e-mail: info@old-hall-inn.co.uk
dir: *From Chapel-en-le-Frith take B5470 W. Right into Whitehough Head Ln. 0.8m to inn*

Smack in the heart of prime walking country, with Kinder Scout, Mam Tor and Stanage Edge all within easy reach, this family-run, 16th-century traditional pub adjoins Whitehough Hall and offers an impressive choice of ciders and local cask ales (Thornbridge, Abbeydale, Storm), alongside daily menus that make good use of local produce, and comfortable en suite bedrooms. Typical dishes range from steak and kidney pudding and ham, egg and chips to Chatsworth venison with redcurrant and port sauce, and roast leg of lamb. Classic puddings include sticky toffee pudding.

**Open** all day all wk **Bar Meals** L served Mon-Sat 12-2, Sun 12-7.30 booking required D served Mon-Thu 5-9 Fri-Sat 5-9.30 Sun 12-7.30 booking required Av main course £9 **Restaurant** L served Mon-Sat 12-2, Sun 12-7.30 booking required D served Mon-Thu 5-9 Fri-Sat 5-9.30 Sun 12-7.30 booking required Av 3 course à la carte fr £18 ⊕ FREE HOUSE 🍺 Marstons, Thornbridge, Phoenix, Abbeydale, Storm Ö Thatchers, Sheppy's, Westons. ☕ 12 **Facilities** Children's menu Children's portions Dogs allowed Garden Parking **Rooms** 4

*See advert on opposite page*

## DERBY — Map 11 SK33

### The Alexandra Hotel

**203 Siddals Rd DE1 2QE** ☎ 01332 293993
dir: *150yds from rail station*

This two-roomed hotel is filled with railway memorabilia. It is noted for its real ale (11 hand pumps and 450 different brews on tap each year), range of malt whiskies, real ciders, and friendly atmosphere. A typical menu offers chilli con carne; liver and bacon; home-baked ham with free range egg and chips; filled Yorkshire puddings; ploughman's lunches; and freshly-made filled hot and cold cobs.

Save on Hotels. Book at **theAA.com/hotel**

DERBYSHIRE **121** ENGLAND

Open all day all wk 11-11 (Sun 12-3 7-10) Closed: 25 Dec ◄ Castle Rock, Elsie Mo, Harvest Pale Ö Old Rosie, Stowford Press. **Facilities** Dogs allowed Garden Parking **Notes** ⊜

## The Brunswick Inn NEW

**1 Railway Ter DE1 2RU**
☎ **01332 290677** 📠 **01332 370226**
**e-mail:** thebrunswickinn@yahoo.co.uk
**dir:** *From rail station turn right. Pub 100yds*

Built in 1841 by the railway, this Grade II listed building is the oldest brewery in Derby producing its own range of traditional Everards ales. There are sixteen handpumps –six Brunswick ales and ten guest beers. Food is served Monday to Saturday with cobs and snacks on Sundays. So choose your ale and sit back with a pint and relax by the cosy coal fire.

Open all day all wk **Bar Meals** L served Mon-Wed 11.30-2.30, Fri 11.30-7, Thu & Sat 11.30-5, Sun (cold food) D served Fri 11.30-7, Sun (cold food) Av main course £4 ⊕ EVERARDS BREWERY ◄ Various Ö Westons Old Rosie, Westons 1st Quality. **Facilities** Children's portions Family room Dogs allowed Garden **Notes** ⊜

---

## Hardwick Inn ▼

**Hardwick Park S44 5QJ**
☎ **01246 850245** 📠 **01246 856365**
**e-mail:** batty@hardwickinn.co.uk
**web:** www.hardwickinn.co.uk
**dir:** *M1 junct 29 take A6175. 0.5m left (signed Stainsby/ Hardwick Hall). After Stainsby, 2m, left at staggered junct. Follow brown tourist signs*

The historic atmosphere of this 15th-century inn has been retained, particularly when the coal fires are lit in winter. Built from locally quarried sandstone, the pub stands by the south gate of the National Trust's Hardwick Hall, and has been run by three generations of the same family. Expect an extensive salad bar, as well as home-cooked dishes like grilled sea bass with cracked black pepper and fresh lemon, and steak and Stilton pie from the specials board.

---

Open all day all wk **Bar Meals** food served all day **Restaurant** L served Tue-Sat 12-2, Sun 12-1 & 4-5.30 booking required D served Tue-Sat 7-8.30 booking required ⊕ FREE HOUSE ◄ Theakston Old Peculier & XB, Black Sheep, Bombardier, Bess of Hardwick Ö Westons. **Facilities** Play area Family room Garden Parking

## Miners Arms

**Water Ln S32 5RG** ☎ **01433 630853**
**dir:** *Off B6521, 5m N of Bakewell*

This welcoming 17th-century inn and restaurant in the famous plague village of Eyam gets its name from the local lead mines of Roman times. The menu features the likes of pork loin steak topped with black pudding and wholegrain mustard sauce; sausage ring and onion gravy; chicken jalfrezi with rice and naan bread. A specials board adds more choices. Wash it all down with a pint of Theakston's Best, or Greene King IPA.

Open all day all wk Closed: 26 Dec eve **Bar Meals** L served Mon-Sat 12-2, Sun 12-3 D served Mon 6-8, Tue-Fri 6-9, Sat 7-9 Av main course £8.95 **Restaurant** L served Mon-Sat 12-2, Sun 12-3 D served Mon 6-8, Tue-Fri 6-9, Sat 7-9 Av 3 course à la carte fr £20 ⊕ FREE HOUSE ◄ Theakstons Best, Greene King IPA, Pedigree, Old Speckled Hen. **Facilities** Children's menu Children's portions Dogs allowed Garden Parking

---

## FENNY BENTLEY — Map 16 SK14

### PICK OF THE PUBS

**Bentley Brook Inn** INN ♥

*See Pick of the Pubs on page 123*

### The Coach and Horses Inn

DE6 1LB ☎ 01335 350246
e-mail: coachandhorses2@btconnect.com
dir: *On A515 (Ashbourne to Buxton road), 2.5m from Ashbourne*

A cosy refuge in any weather, this family-run, 17th-century coaching inn stands on the edge of the Peak District National Park. Besides the beautiful location, its charms include stripped wood furniture and low beams. Expect a selection of real ales and good home cooking along the lines of a ramekin of home-made smoked salmon mousse; slow cooked beef in red wine puff pastry pie; and feta, red onion and spinach turnover with a tomato and basil sauce. Hot and cold sandwiches and baguettes provide lighter options from 12 to 5.

**Open** all day all wk 11-11 (Sun 12-10.30) **Bar Meals** Av main course £9.95 food served all day **Restaurant** food served all day ⊕ FREE HOUSE ⬦ Marston's Pedigree, Timothy Taylor Landlord, Black Sheep Best, Oakham JHB, Peak Ales Swift Nick. **Facilities** Family room Garden Parking

## FOOLOW — Map 16 SK17

### The Bulls Head Inn ★★★★ INN

S32 5QR ☎ 01433 630873 📄 01433 631738
e-mail: wilbnd@aol.com
dir: *Just off A623, N of Stoney Middleton*

Open fires, oak beams, flagstone floors, great views and good food are among the attractions at this 19th-century former coaching inn, tucked away in a conservation village high up in the Peak District. A welcome pit-stop for walkers and visitors for lunchtime sandwiches, minted lamb casserole, beef Wellington with red wine gravy, and roast sea bass with fennel, washed down with a pint of Black Sheep. Bedrooms are comfortable and well equipped.

**Open** 12-3 6.30-11 (all day Sun) Closed: Mon (ex BH) **Bar Meals** L served Tue-Sun 12-2 D served Tue-Sun 6.30-9 **Restaurant** L served Tue-Sun 12-2 D served Tue-Sun 6.30-9 ⊕ FREE HOUSE ⬦ Black Sheep, Peak Ales, Adnams, Tetley. **Facilities** Dogs allowed Parking **Rooms** 3

## FROGGATT — Map 16 SK27

### PICK OF THE PUBS

**The Chequers Inn ★★★★ INN** ⊛ ♥

Froggatt Edge S32 3ZJ
☎ 01433 630231 📄 01433 631072
e-mail: info@chequers-froggatt.com
dir: *On A625, 0.5m N of Calver*

The Chequers is an excellent base for exploring the Peak District, with Chatsworth House in close proximity. Originally four stone-built 18th-century cottages, this traditional country inn nestles in the valley below beautiful Froggatt Edge. A haven for walkers, its westward panorama is reached by a steep, wild woodland footpath from the elevated secret garden. The comfortable interior of wooden floors, antiques and blazing log fires is perfect for a relaxing pint of Bakewell Best Bitter or your choice from an innovative modern European menu. The food is prepared from locally sourced produce, ranging from sandwiches and salads through to starters as varied as game terrine with pear jelly, and smoked haddock and blue cheese soufflé with pea purée. Mains take in pot-roasted lamb shank with braised winter vegetables, and slow-cooked pork shoulder with parsley mash and apple and vanilla compote. Finish with blackcurrant and elderflower mousse. There are five en suite bedrooms available.

**Open** all wk 12-2 6-9.30 (Sat 12-9.30, Sun 12-9) Closed: 25 Dec **Bar Meals** L served Mon-Fri 12-2, Sat-Sun 12-6 D served Mon-Sat 6-9.30, Sun 6-9 Av main course £13 **Restaurant** Av 3 course à la carte fr £22 ⊕ FREE HOUSE ⬦ Greene King IPA, Black Sheep, Kelham Island Easy Rider, Bakewell Best Bitter, Bombardier. ♥ 10 **Facilities** Children's menu Children's portions Garden Parking **Rooms** 5

## GREAT HUCKLOW — Map 16 SK17

### The Queen Anne Inn ★★★ INN ♥

SK17 8RF ☎ 01298 871246 📄 01298 873504
e-mail: angelaryan100@aol.com
dir: *A623 onto B6049, turn off at Anchor pub towards Bradwell, 2nd right to Great Hucklow*

Enjoy stunning open views from the sheltered south-facing garden of this traditional country free house. The inn dates from 1621; a licence has been held for over 300 years, and the names of all the landlords are known. Inside you'll find log fires, good food, and an ever-changing range of cask ales.

Specialities include chicken breast stuffed with Stilton cheese; rack of lamb on herby mash; and Thai red king prawn curry.

**Open** noon-2.30 5-11 (Fri-Sun noon-11) Closed: Mon **Bar Meals** L served Tue-Sun 12-2 D served Tue-Thu 6-8.30 (Fri-Sat 6-9, Sun 6-8) Av main course £8.95 **Restaurant** L served Tue-Sun 12-2 D served Tue-Thu 6-8.30 (Fri-Sat 6-9, Sun 6-8) ⊕ FREE HOUSE ⬦ Tetleys Cask Ales, Copper Dragon, Peak Ales, Brampton, Theakstons ♂ Stowford Press. ♥ 9 **Facilities** Children's menu Children's portions Family room Garden Parking **Rooms** 2

## GRINDLEFORD — Map 16 SK27

### PICK OF THE PUBS

**The Maynard ★★★ HL** ⊛⊛

Main Rd S32 2HE ☎ 01433 630321 📄 01433 630445
e-mail: info@themaynard.co.uk
dir: *From M1 junct 30 take A619 into Chesterfield, then onto Baslow. A623 to Calver, right into Grindleford*

This fine stone-built inn stands grandly in immaculately kept grounds overlooking the Derwent Valley, in the heart of the Peak District National Park. You may eat in either the Longshore Bar or in the Padley Restaurant, with its large windows facing the gardens. Choose the bar, and the menu may well offer seared breast of chicken with mushroom risotto and balsamic oil; Moroccan-spiced braised lamb with couscous; or grilled sea bass on champ with tomato and olive salsa. Opt for the restaurant and discover other possibilities, such as eggs Benedict with chive oil, or smoked haddock fishcake as starters; main courses of fillet of beef with fondant potato, wild mushrooms and caramelised red wine onion; pan-fried calf's liver with olive oil mash, onion fritters and grilled pancetta; and pan-seared red mullet with shellfish paella and lobster oil. For dessert, try sticky toffee parkin pudding with stem ginger ice cream.

**Open** all day all wk noon-9 **Bar Meals** L served Sun-Fri 12-2 D served Sat 7-9 ⊕ FREE HOUSE ⬦ Abbey Dale Moonshine, Bakewell Bitter. **Facilities** Dogs allowed Garden Parking **Rooms** 10

## HARTSHORNE — Map 10 SK32

### The Mill Wheel ★★★★ INN

Ticknall Rd DE11 7AS
☎ 01283 550335 📄 01283 552833
e-mail: info@themillwheel.co.uk
dir: *M42 junct 2 follow signs for A511 to Woodville, left onto A514 towards Derby to Hartshorne*

This old building's huge mill wheel has survived for some 250 years. In 1945 a dispute over water rights cut off the supply and the site became derelict. Since being restored in 1987, the wheel has been slowly turning once again, and is very much the focus of attention in the bar and restaurant. Mill Wheel Bitter is available along with dishes

*continued on page 124*

# PICK OF THE PUBS

## Bentley Brook Inn ★★★ INN ♉

**FENNY BENTLEY**          Map 16 S14

**DE6 1LF**
☎ 01335 350278   📠 01335 350422
e-mail: all@bentleybrookinn.co.uk
web: www.bentleybrookinn.co.uk

The Bentley Brook flows through a field behind this lovely building, originally a medieval farmhouse. From its car park you can see a square tower, the only one of five remaining of the farm's one-time neighbour, a fortified manor house. Between the World Wars, two elderly ladies lived here in considerable style, attended to by five servants, a gardener, an under-gardener and a coachman. It became a restaurant in 1954, a full drinks licence was granted in the early 1970s, and in 2006/7 it was completely restored and refurbished.

You can all too easily settle by the central open log fire in the bar and play dominoes, cards or chess, while

sampling one of the several real ales from Leatherbritches brewery, the inn's own craft brewery housed in the old washhouse and coal store.

In the restaurant, which overlooks the terrace and garden, locally sourced, seasonal menus provide lunches and dinners that might begin with deep-fried Dovedale Blue cheese with home-made Cumberland sauce; salmon fishcake on tomato salsa; or locally made black pudding and home-cured bacon tartlet with mustard sauce. One of these could be followed by rump or gammon steak; free-range chicken breast in pesto with tagliatelle; or haddock in crisp beer batter, chips and peas. Other possibilities are home-made steak and ale pie with suet pastry crust; chicken curry with basmati rice and naan bread; and roasted vegetable tartlet with goat's cheese and home-made red onion marmalade. Desserts include sticky toffee pudding with butterscotch sauce and ice cream; and fresh fruit Pavlova with fruit coulis.

The Sunday carvery offers a choice of traditional roast meats, fish and vegetarian options; during the summer

the barbecue in the garden is fired up. There are eleven well appointed and thoughtfully equipped en suite bedrooms.

**Open** all day all wk **Bar Meals** L served all wk 12-9 (Oct-Mar 12-3) booking required D served all wk 12-9 (Oct-Mar 6-9) booking required
 **Restaurant** L served all wk 12-9 (Oct-Mar 12-3) booking required D served all wk 12-9 (Oct-Mar 6-9) booking required ⊕ FREE HOUSE
◖ Leatherbritches Bespoke, Leatherbritches Hairy Helmet, Goldings, Marstons Pedigree. ♉ 10
**Facilities** Play area Dogs allowed Garden Parking **Rooms** 11

**HARTSHORNE** *continued*

such as pan-fried Cornish mackerel, followed perhaps by roast loin of lamb with dauphinoise potatoes. If you want to stay over, there are modern bedrooms available.

**Open** all wk all day Sat-Sun **Bar Meals** L served Mon-Sat 12-2.30, Sun 12-7 D served Mon-Thu 6-9.15, Fri-Sat 6-9.30, Sun 12-7 food served all day **Restaurant** L served Mon-Sat 12-2.30, Sun 12-7 D served Mon-Thu 6-9.15, Fri-Sat 6-9.30, Sun 12-7 food served all day ⊕ FREE HOUSE ◀ Abbot Ale, Summer Lightning, Bass, Pedigree, Mill Wheel Bitter. **Facilities** Children's portions Garden Parking **Rooms** 4

### HASSOP                                    Map 16 SK27

## Eyre Arms ♈

DE45 1NS ☎ 01629 640390
e-mail: nick@eyrearms.com
dir: *On B6001 N of Bakewell*

Formerly a farmstead and 17th-century coaching inn, this traditional ivy-clad free house stands in one of the most beautiful parts of rural Derbyshire. Oak settles, low ceilings and cheery log fires create a cosy atmosphere, while the views of rolling Peak District countryside from the secluded garden can only be improved with a pint of Bakewell Best in hand. Typical dishes include sliced breast of duck interleaved with mango; Derbyshire oatcake filled with Cheddar and asparagus; and chicken Hartington, stuffed with leeks and Stilton.

**Open** all wk 11-3 6.30-11 Closed: 25 Dec **Bar Meals** L served all wk 12-2 D served all wk 6.30-9 Av main course £8 **Restaurant** Av 3 course à la carte fr £20 ⊕ FREE HOUSE ◀ Marston's Pedigree, Black Sheep Special, Bakewell Best Bitter ⌀ Westons Stowford Press. ♈ 9 **Facilities** Garden Parking

### HATHERSAGE                                Map 16 SK28

## *Millstone Inn* ★★★★ INN ♈

Sheffield Rd S32 1DA
☎ 01433 650258 ⌷ 01433 650276
e-mail: jerry@millstone.co.uk
dir: *Telephone for directions*

Striking views over the picturesque Hope Valley are afforded from this former coaching inn, set amid the beauty of the Peak District yet convenient for the city of Sheffield. The atmospheric bar serves six traditional cask ales all year round and the menu offers a good choice of dishes prepared from local produce, including a popular

Sunday carvery of freshly roasted joints. A range of accommodation is available from single to family rooms.

**Open** all day all wk 11.30am-11pm ◀ Timothy Taylor Landlord, Black Sheep, guest ales. ♈ 16 **Facilities** Dogs allowed Garden Parking **Rooms** 8

### PICK OF THE PUBS

## The Plough Inn ★★★★ INN ◉ ♈

Leadmill Bridge S32 1BA
☎ 01433 650319 & 650180 ⌷ 01433 651049
e-mail: sales@theploughinn-hathersage.co.uk
dir: *M1 junct 29, take A617W, A619, A623, then B6001 N to Hathersage*

Its hard to believe now, but The Plough started life as a grimy smelting mill processing lead ore from the Peak District's mines. Records as an ale house stretch back 300 years, but today's comfy dining inn is a far cry from such humble beginnings. Set in a nine-acre estate beside the River Derwent, it's the ideal base for exploring the eastern valleys and moors of the National Park; Chatsworth House and the Castleton caverns are a short drive away from the inn's AA-rated accommodation, moulded into the main building or across a private cobbled courtyard. The impressive menu offers modern European and traditional dishes, taken in the fire-warmed bar or intimate restaurant; perhaps a warm salad of partridge, Jerusalem artichoke and pancetta to precede pumpkin and goat's cheese risotto or pot roast guinea fowl with creamed Savoy cabbage, coquette potatoes and port. With 15 wines by the glass and beers from Black Sheep, allow plenty of time to relax in the flower-bedecked beer garden afterwards.

**Open** all day all wk 11-11 (Sun noon-10.30pm) Closed: 25 Dec **Bar Meals** L served all wk 12-9 D served all wk 6.30-9.30 booking required Av main course £12 food served all day **Restaurant** L served all wk 12-2.30 booking required D served all wk 6.30-9.30 booking required Fixed menu price fr £20.50 Av 3 course à la carte fr £25 ⊕ FREE HOUSE ◀ London Pride, Old Speckled Hen, Black Sheep, Youngs Bitter, Bombardier. ♈ 15 **Facilities** Children's portions Garden Parking **Rooms** 5

## The Scotsmans Pack Country Inn ★★★★ INN ♈

School Ln S32 1BZ ☎ 01433 650253 ⌷ 01433 650712
e-mail: scotsmans.pack@btinternet.com
web: www.scotsmanspack.com
dir: *Hathersage is on A625 8m from Sheffield. Pub near church and Little John's Grave*

This historic inn in the beautiful Hope Valley is located on one of the old packhorse trails used by Scottish 'packmen' or travelling drapers. Just a short walk away from Hathersage church and Little John's Grave, the inn is ideally placed for walking and touring the Peak District, with five individually designed en suite bedrooms. Hearty pub dishes include sautéed queen scallops with roast pumpkin risotto; noisettes of Derbyshire lamb and dauphinoise potatoes; and large pork loin cutlets with apple and sage stuffing. Wash your meal down with a great choice of real ales.

**Open** all day all wk 11-3 6-mdnt (all day Fri-Sun) **Bar Meals** L served Mon-Fri 12-2 booking required D served Mon-Fri 6-9, Sat-Sun 12-9 booking required ⊕ MARSTONS PLC ◀ Jennings Cumberland, Pedigree, Mansfield Bitter. ♈ 10 **Facilities** Children's menu Children's portions Family room Garden Parking **Rooms** 5

### HAYFIELD                                  Map 16 SK08

## The Royal Hotel ♈

Market St SK22 2EP ☎ 01663 742721
e-mail: enquiries@theroyalhayfield.co.uk
web: www.theroyalhayfield.co.uk
dir: *Off A624*

Dating from 1755, The Royal Hotel is situated in the heart of the picturesque village of Hayfield in the High Peak. A fine-looking, mid-18th-century former vicarage, the Grade II listed building has an oak-panelled bar with log fire and a wide selection of traditional ales, and a dining room with a self-contained function room. Food is served

Save on Hotels. Book at **theAA.com/hotel**

DERBYSHIRE 125 ENGLAND

daily from the bar snack menu or the full à la carte menu with its wide range of specials. Kinder Scout looks impressive from the patio.

**Open** all day all wk 9am-mdnt **Bar Meals** L served Mon-Fri 12-2.30, Sat 12-9, Sun 12-6 D served Mon-Fri 6-9, Sat 12-9, Sun 12-6 **Restaurant** L served Mon-Fri 12-2.30, Sat 12-9, Sun 12-6 D served Mon-Fri 6-9, Sat 12-9, Sun 12-6 ⊕ FREE HOUSE ◀ Hydes, Guest Ales ○ Stowford Press. **Facilities** Children's menu Children's portions Family room Dogs allowed Garden Parking

### HOGNASTON — Map 16 SK25

## The Red Lion Inn ♥

**Main St DE6 1PR** ☎ 01335 370396 ▤ 01335 370396
**e-mail:** redlion@w3z.co.uk
**web:** www.redlionhognaston.co.uk
**dir:** *From Ashbourne take B5035 towards Wirksworth. Approx 5m follow Carsington Water signs. Turn right to Hognaston*

One of the original destination gastro-pubs, the Red Lion still does the business with a great rack of specials that change frequently and major on Derbyshire produce. Work up an appetite with a walk at the nearby Carsington Water, bag a fireside seat in the antique-rich, rustic bar, chinwag with the locals and look forward to the game pie with rabbit, venison and hare, or draw on a Derbyshire beer in the tranquil garden and snack on quail eggs and Avruga caviar.

**Open** all wk 12-3 6-11 **Bar Meals** L served all wk 12-2.30 D served all wk 6.30-9 Av main course £9.95 **Restaurant** L served all wk 12-2.30 D served all wk 6.30-9 Av 3 course à la carte fr £24.50 ⊕ FREE HOUSE ◀ Marston's Pedigree, Guinness, Ruddles County, Derbyshire Brewing Co, Black Sheep ○ Old Rosie. ♥ 9 **Facilities** Children's portions Garden Parking

### HOPE — Map 16 SK18

## Cheshire Cheese Inn

**Edale Rd S33 6ZF** ☎ 01433 620381
**e-mail:** carol.o@btconnect.com
**dir:** *On A6187 between Sheffield & Chapel-en-le-Frith, turn off at Hope Church down Edale Rd*

Originally a farm, this 16th-century inn stands on the old trans-Pennine salt route in the heart of the Peak District, and owes its name to the tradition of accepting cheese as payment for lodgings. It has a reputation for good home-made food and a great selection hand-pulled beer served in a relaxed atmosphere with open fires. There is a

choice of light bites and main meals, ranging from toasted sandwiches or jacket potatoes to Aberdeen Angus lasagne or steak and ale pie.

**Open** all day Sat-Sun Closed: Mon **Bar Meals** L served Tue-Sun booking required D served Tue-Sun booking required ⊕ ENTERPRISE INNS ◀ Golden Pippin, Copper Dragon, Swift Nick, Deuchars IPA, Farmers Blonde, Youngs Best. **Facilities** Children's portions Dogs allowed Garden Parking

### LITTLE HAYFIELD — Map 16 SK08

## Lantern Pike NEW

**45 Glossop Rd SK22 2NG** ☎ 01663 747590
**e-mail:** sales@lanternpikeinn.co.uk
**dir:** *On A624, between Glossop and Chapel-en-le-Frith*

A local's pub and country dining inn with tremendous views from the rambling patio-garden to the eponymous beacon-hill nearby and walks to the challenging heights of Kinder Scout from the door. Coronation Street was perhaps first mooted here in 1960 (the original doors from the 'Rovers Return' are here), where beers from local micro-breweries can accompany a reliable menu of pub favourites and freshly cooked home-made specials taken at the bar or in a cosy restaurant.

**Open** Mon 5-mdnt, Tue-Fri noon-3 5-mdnt (Sat-Sun all day) Closed: 25 Dec, Mon L **Bar Meals** L served Tue-Fri 12-2.30, Sat-Sun 12-8.30 D served Tue-Fri 5-8.30, Sat-Sun 12-8.30 Av main course £9 **Restaurant** L served Tue-Fri 12-2.30, Sat-Sun 12-8.30 D served Tue-Fri 5-8.30, Sat-Sun 12-8.30 Av 3 course à la carte fr £17 ⊕ ENTERPRISE INNS ◀ Timothy Taylor Landlord, Black Sheep, Longendale Lights. **Facilities** Children's menu Children's portions Garden Parking

### LITTON — Map 16 SK17

## Red Lion Inn ♥

**SK17 8QU** ☎ 01298 871458 ▤ 01298 871458
**e-mail:** theredlionlitton@yahoo.co.uk
**dir:** *Just off A623 (Chesterfield to Stockport road), 1m E of Tideswell*

The Red Lion is a beautiful, traditional pub on the village green, very much at the heart of the local community. It became a pub in 1787 when it was converted from three farm cottages. With its wood fires, selection of well kept real ales and friendly atmosphere, it's a favourite with walkers and holiday-makers too. The menu offers hearty pub food at reasonable prices, such as Thai fishcakes with sweet chilli dip to start; Derbyshire lamb hotpot; steak and kidney pie; or South African bobotie to follow; and apple and berry crumble with custard to finish. A gluten-free menu is available.

**Open** all day all wk **Bar Meals** Av main course £8.95 food served all day **Restaurant** food served all day ⊕ ENTERPRISE INNS ◀ Barnsley Bitter, Abbeydale, Absolution, guest ales. ♥ 10 **Facilities** Children's portions Dogs allowed

### LONGSHAW — Map 16 SK27

## Fox House ♥

**Hathersage Rd S11 7TY** ☎ 01433 630374
**dir:** *From Sheffield follow A625 towards Castleton*

A delightfully original 17th-century coaching inn and, at 1,132 feet above sea level, one of the highest pubs in Britain. The Longshaw dog trials originated here, after an argument between farmers and shepherds as to who owned the best dog. A simple menu lists sandwiches, starters, Sunday roasts, and mains like chicken and ham pie, ground Scottish beefsteak burger, spicy prawn pasta, and lamb cutlets.

**Open** all wk ◀ Guest ales ○ Aspall. ♥ 20 **Facilities** Garden Parking

### MATLOCK — Map 16 SK35

## The Red Lion ★★★★ INN

**65 Matlock Green DE4 3BT** ☎ 01629 584888
**dir:** *From Chesterfield, A632 into Matlock, on right just before junct with A615*

This friendly, family-run free house makes a good base for exploring local attractions like Chatsworth House, Carsington Water and Dovedale. Spectacular walks in the local countryside help to work up an appetite for bar lunches, steaks and a wide selection of home-cooked meals. In the winter months, open fires burn in the lounge and games room, and there's a boules area in the garden for warmer days. There are 6 comfortable bedrooms.

**Open** all wk ◀ Courage Directors, John Smith's, Theakstons Bitter, Peak Ales, guest ales. **Facilities** Garden Parking **Rooms** 6

### MELBOURNE — Map 11 SK32

## The Melbourne Arms ★★★ INN ♥

**92 Ashby Rd DE73 8ES**
☎ 01332 864949 & 863990 ▤ 01332 865525
**e-mail:** info@melbournearms.co.uk
**dir:** *Telephone for directions*

This restaurant on the village outskirts was tastefully converted from an 18th-century pub about 13 years ago. There are two bars, a coffee lounge and the restaurant itself, traditionally decorated, - no, not red flock wallpaper - where an extensive menu of authentic Indian dishes is offered. With a range of English dishes and a children's menu too, there's no reason why the whole family can't find plenty to enjoy. You can stay over in one of the modern bedrooms.

**Open** all day all wk 11.30am-11.30pm ◀ Pedigree, Tetley's Smooth, Guinness. ♥ 12 **Facilities** Play area Family room Garden Parking **Rooms** 9

## MILLTOWN                           Map 16 SK36

### The Nettle Inn ♀

**S45 0ES ☎ 01246 590462**
**dir:** *Telephone for directions*

A 16th-century hostelry on the edge of the Peak District, this inn has all the traditional charm you could wish for, from flower-filled hanging baskets to log fires and a stone-flagged taproom floor. Expect well-kept Bradfield ales and impressive home-made food (including breads, pickles and sauces), using the best of seasonal produce. Typical dishes are grilled Cornish mackerel; organic goat's cheese and green olive tapenade crostini; and braised wild rabbit with Bramley apple and cider sauce.

**Open** all wk Sat-Sun all day **Bar Meals** Av main course £6.75 food served all day **Restaurant** Av 3 course à la carte fr £25 food served all day ⊕ FREE HOUSE ◀ Bradfield Farmers Best Bitter, Bradfield Farmers Blonde, Hardy & Hansons, Olde Trip, Bradfield Belgian Blue, Bradfield Farmers Brown Cow. ♀ 9
**Facilities** Children's menu Children's portions Dogs allowed Garden Parking

## RIPLEY                            Map 16 SK35

### *The Moss Cottage Hotel*

**Nottingham Rd DE5 3JT ☎ 01773 742555**
**e-mail:** doug-ashley@hotmail.co.uk
**dir:** *Telephone for directions*

This red-brick free house specialises in carvery dishes, with four roast joints each day. Expect popular menu choices like prawn cocktail or mushroom dippers; ham, egg and chips; liver and onions; or battered haddock. Hot puddings include rhubarb crumble and chocolate fudge cake. Wash down your meal with a pint of Olde Trip.

**Open** 12-3 5-11 (Sun 5-8) Closed: Sun eve Mon L ◀ Olde Trip, Guinness, Guest ale ♂ Old Rosie Scrumpy.
**Facilities** Parking

## ROWSLEY                           Map 16 SK26

### The Grouse & Claret ★★★★ INN ♀

**Station Rd DE4 2EB ☎ 01629 733233 ▤ 01629 735194**
**dir:** *On A6 between Matlock & Bakewell*

A popular venue for local anglers, this 18th-century pub takes its name from a fishing fly. Situated at the gateway to the Peak District National Park, it is handy for touring the Peak District or visiting the stately homes of Haddon Hall and Chatsworth House. A meal from the cosmopolitan menu might include beef goulash with herb dumplings, or pork and black pudding stack. For the more traditionally minded, pâté in a pot for a starter; and either a lamb steak or beer battered fish and chips might fit the bill. Comfortable accommodation is available.

**Open** all day all wk **Bar Meals** L served Mon-Sat 12-9, Sun 12-8 D served Mon-Sat 12-9, Sun 12-8 Av main course £7.50 food served all day **Restaurant** L served Mon-Sat 12-9, Sun 12-8 D served Mon-Sat 12-9, Sun 12-8 food served all day ⊕ WOLVERHAMPTON & DUDLEY BREWERIES PLC ◀ Marston's Pedigree, Mansfield, Bank's Bitter. ♀ 16 **Facilities** Children's menu Children's portions Play area Garden Parking **Rooms** 8

## SHARDLOW                          Map 11 SK43

### The Old Crown Inn

**Cavendish Bridge DE72 2HL ☎ 01332 792392**
**e-mail:** the.oldcrowninn@btconnect.com
**dir:** *M1 junct 24 take A6 towards Derby. Left before river, bridge into Shardlow*

A family-friendly pub on the south side of the River Trent, where up to seven guest ales are served. It was built as a coaching inn during the 17th century, and retains its warm and atmospheric interior. Several hundred water jugs hang from the ceilings, while the walls display an abundance of brewery and railway memorabilia. Traditional food is lovingly prepared by the landlady, including sandwiches; jackets; thick-cut ham and eggs; smoked haddock fishcakes; and chilli con carne. Home-made specials are available daily.

**Open** all day all wk 11am-11.30pm (Fri-Sat 11am-12.30am, Sun 11am-11pm) **Bar Meals** L served Mon-Fri 12-2, Sat 12-8, Sun 12-3 D served Mon-Fri 5-8, Sat 12-8 Av main course £6.95 **Restaurant** L served Mon-Fri 12-2, Sat 12-8, Sun 12-3 D served Mon-Fri 5-8, Sat 12-8 ⊕ MARSTONS ◀ Marston's Pedigree, Jennings Cocker Hoop, Guest ales. **Facilities** Children's menu Children's portions Play area Dogs allowed Garden Parking

## TIDESWELL                         Map 16 SK17

### The George Hotel ♀

**Commercial Rd SK17 8NU**
**☎ 01298 871382 ▤ 01298 871382**
**e-mail:** georgehoteltideswell@yahoo.co.uk
**dir:** *A619 to Baslow, A623 towards Chapel-en-le-Frith, 0.25m*

A 17th-century coaching inn in a quiet village conveniently placed for exploring the National Park and visiting Buxton, Chatsworth and the historic plague village of Eyam. Quality home-cooked food includes venison cooked in red wine sauce, roast pheasant with bacon, potatoes and mushrooms, seafood crumble, and whole rainbow trout with almonds.

**Open** all wk ◀ Kimberley Cool, Olde Trip Bitter, Best Bitter. ♀ 12 **Facilities** Dogs allowed Garden Parking

### Three Stags' Heads

**Wardlow Mires SK17 8RW ☎ 01298 872268**
**dir:** *At junct of A623 (Baslow to Stockport road) & B6465*

Grade II listed 17th-century former farmhouse, designated by English Heritage as one of over 200 heritage pubs throughout the UK. It is located in the limestone uplands of the northern Peak District, and is now combined with a pottery workshop. Well-kept real ales and hearty home-cooked food for ramblers, cyclists and locals includes chicken and spinach curry; pork, leek and Stilton pie, and game in season. No children under eight.

**Open** noon-mdnt (Fri 7-mdnt) Closed: Mon-Thu (ex BH) ◀ Abbeydale Matins, Absolution, Black Lurcher, Brimstone Bitter. **Facilities** Dogs allowed Parking **Notes** ⊜

## WESSINGTON                        Map 16 SK35

### The Three Horseshoes

**The Green DE55 6DQ ☎ 01773 834854**
**dir:** *A615 towards Matlock, 3m after Alfreton, 5m before Matlock*

A century ago horses were still being traded over the bar at this late 17th-century former coaching inn and associated blacksmith's forge, to both of which activities it no doubt owes its name. For a true taste of the Peak District, try Derbyshire chicken with black pudding and apple, or braised lamb shank with celeriac purée. Several local walks start or end at the pub.

**Open** all day all wk **Bar Meals** L served all wk 12-2.30 served all wk 5-8 Av main course £7 ⊕ GREENE KING ◀ Guinness, Hardys & Hansons Olde Trip, guest ale. **Facilities** Children's menu Play area Dogs allowed Garden Parking

# DEVON

## ASHBURTON                         Map 3 SX77

### The Rising Sun ★★★★ INN ♀

**Woodland TQ13 7JT ☎ 01364 652544**
**e-mail:** admin@therisingsunwoodland.co.uk
**dir:** *From A38 E of Ashburton take lane signed Woodland/Denbury. Pub on left, approx 1.5m*

A former drovers' inn, largely rebuilt following a fire in 1989, the Rising Sun is set in beautiful Devon countryside. Owner Paul is the chef and is dedicated to using local and seasonal produce on his menus. There's a good choice of fish from Brixham – baked sea bass - and excellent West Country cheeses; children's menu too. The pub is well known for its home-made pies (available to take home) and regularly changing ales. There are five en suite bedrooms available.

**Open** all wk noon-3 6-11 (Sun noon-3 6.30-11, all day mid Jul-mid Sep) Closed: 25 Dec **Bar Meals** L served Mon-Sat 12-2.15, Sun 12-2.30 D served Mon-Sat 6-9.15, Sun 6.30-9.15 Av main course £8.95 **Restaurant** L served Mon-Sat 12-2.15, Sun 12-2.30 D served Mon-Sat 6-9.15, Sun 6.30-9.15 Av 3 course à la carte fr £22 ⊕ FREE HOUSE ◀ Princetown Jail Ale, Guest Ales ♂ Thatchers. ♀ 16 **Facilities** Children's menu Children's portions Play area Family room Dogs allowed Garden Parking **Rooms** 5

## AVONWICK    Map 3 SX75

### The Avon Inn

**TQ10 9NB ☎ 01364 73475**
**dir:** *Telephone for directions*

There's been a change of ownership at this handsome whitewashed free house, just off the busy Exeter to Plymouth trunk road. The Needs family, with many years of experience between them, make it a welcoming stop. Father Gary and son Brad both have cellar management certificates, so expect to find Otter ales and real ciders in excellent condition. Karen presides over the kitchen's menu of traditional pub grub, such as the home-made 'Giant Avon Inn Pasty', also available in vegetarian form.

**Open** all day all wk 11am-12.30am (Sun noon-11.30pm)
**Bar Meals** Av main course £7.95 food served all day
**Restaurant** food served all day ⊕ FREE HOUSE ◖ Otter, Doom Bar, Hunters Gold ♂ Thatchers Gold.
**Facilities** Children's menu Children's portions Play area Dogs allowed Garden Parking

### PICK OF THE PUBS

### The Turtley Corn Mill ☆ ☆ ☆ INN ▾

**TQ10 9ES ☎ 01364 646100  🖹 01364 646101**
**e-mail:** mill@avonwick.net
**dir:** *From A38 at South Brent/Avonwick junction, take B3372, then follow signs for Avonwick, 0.5m*

In its idyllic South Hams location, this sprawling old building began life as a corn mill, then spent many years as a chicken hatchery before being converted to a pub in the 1970s. The six-acre site is bordered by a river and includes a lake with its own small island, whilst the interior is light and fresh with old furniture and oak and slate floors. There are plenty of newspapers and books to browse through while supping a pint of Tribute or Doom Bar. Daily-changing menus, based extensively on local produce, feature starters like black pudding hash cake with apple purée and air-dried ham. Main course options include vegetable and goat's cheese spring rolls with mixed salad, and Cullen Skink pie. Desserts such as warm pear and almond frangipane can also be served to take away if you're already full. Four comfortable bedrooms make this an attractive stopover.

**Open** all day all wk Closed: 25 Dec **Bar Meals** L served all wk 12-11pm booking required D served all wk 12-11pm booking required Av main course £13.45 food served all day **Restaurant** L served all wk 12-11pm booking required D served all wk 12-11pm booking required Av 3 course à la carte fr £17.50 food served all day ⊕ FREE HOUSE ◖ Tamar Ale, Jail Ale, Tribute, Sharp's Doom Bar, IPA, guest ales ♂ Thatchers. ▾ 8 **Facilities** Children's portions Dogs allowed Garden Parking **Rooms** 4

## AXMOUTH    Map 4 SY29

### PICK OF THE PUBS

### The Harbour Inn

**Church St EX12 4AF ☎ 01297 20371**
**e-mail:** theharbourinn@live.co.uk
**dir:** *Main street opposite church, 1m from Seaton*

The River Axe meanders through its valley into Lyme Bay, but just before they meet is Axmouth harbour, which accounted for one sixth of Devon's trade during the 16th century. This cosy, oak-beamed, harbourside inn was built four centuries earlier, however. Gary and Graciela Tubb have maintained three principles - local ingredients bought from small family businesses, nothing frozen, and everything home made. A bar and bistro menu offers scampi and chips, lasagne, sausages or faggots with mash and gravy, jacket potatoes, baguettes and sandwiches. From a daily updated blackboard menu, you might want to consider pork tenderloin with prunes and bacon; swordfish steak with Niçoise salad; or tagliatelle, wild mushrooms and spicy tomato sauce. The Harbour makes a great stop if you are walking the South West Coast Path between Lyme Regis and Seaton.

**Open** all wk ◖ Badger 1st Gold, Tanglefoot, Sussex ♂ Stowford Press, Applewood. **Facilities** Play area Dogs allowed Garden Parking

### The Ship Inn

**EX12 4AF ☎ 01297 21838**
**dir:** *1m S of A3052 between Lyme & Sidmouth. Signed to Seaton at Boshill Cross*

There are long views over the Axe estuary from the beer garden of this creeper-clad family-run inn. It was built soon after the original Ship burnt down on Christmas Day 1879, and is able to trace its landlords back to 1769. Well kept real ales complement an extensive menu including daily blackboard specials where local fish and game feature, cooked with home-grown herbs. The pub has a skittles alley.

**Open** all day all wk **Bar Meals** L served all wk 12-2.30 booking required D served all wk 6-9 booking required Av main course £6.95 **Restaurant** L served all wk 12-2.30 booking required D served all wk 6-9 booking required Fixed menu price fr £6.95 ⊕ PUNCH TAVERNS ◖ Otter Bitter, Guinness, Sharp's Doom Bar ♂ Stowford Press. **Facilities** Children's menu Children's portions Play area Family room Dogs allowed Garden Parking

## BARBROOK    Map 3 SS74

### The Beggars Roost

**EX35 6LD ☎ 01598 752404**
**e-mail:** info@beggarsroost.co.uk
**dir:** *A39, 1m from Lynton*

Originally a manor farmhouse with attached cow barn, the buildings were converted into a hotel in the 1970s with the barn becoming the Beggars Roost. The long, low bar has tables around a warm log-burner; the restaurant on the floor above extends up into the beamed apex and is popular for parties. The pub menu offers a great range of reasonably priced favourites such as casseroles, terrines and ploughman's, while the restaurant focuses on more sophisticated fare.

**Open** noon-2.30 6-close Closed: Mon (Nov-Feb) ◖ Exmoor Ale, Cotleigh Barn Owl, Exmoor Silver Stallion, Cotleigh Tawny ♂ Thatchers. **Facilities** Dogs allowed Garden Parking

## BEER    Map 4 SY28

### Anchor Inn ★★★★ INN ▾

**Fore St EX12 3ET ☎ 01297 20386  🖹 01297 24474**
**e-mail:** 6403@greeneking.co.uk
**dir:** *A3052 towards Lyme Regis. At Hangmans Stone take B3174 into Beer. Pub on seafront*

Fish caught by local boats feature strongly on the menu at this pretty colour-washed inn, which overlooks the sea in the picture-perfect Devon village of Beer. Starters to tempt might be grilled Cornish sardines; home-made crab chowder; or duck liver parfait and plum and apple chutney, followed by warm salad of salmon and broccoli fishcakes; slow cooked lamb shank with grain mustard mash; moules marinière; or chargrilled pork rib steak. There are six comfortable guest rooms available.

**Open** all day all wk 8am-11pm **Bar Meals** L served Mon-Fri 11-2.30, Sat-Sun 11-4 D served Sun-Thu 6-9, Fri-Sat 6-9.30 Av main course £7.95 **Restaurant** L served Mon-Fri 12-2.30, Sat-Sun 12-3 D served Sun-Thu 6-9, Fri-Sat 6-9.30 Fixed menu price fr £15 Av 3 course à la carte fr £21 ⊕ GREENE KING ◖ Otter Ale, Greene King IPA, Abbot Ale ♂ Aspall. ▾ 14 **Facilities** Children's menu Garden **Rooms** 6

## BERE FERRERS    Map 3 SX46

### Olde Plough Inn

**PL20 7JL ☎ 01822 840358**
**e-mail:** info@oldeploughinn.co.uk
**dir:** *A390 from Tavistock*

Originally three cottages, dating from the 16th century, this inn has bags of character, with its old timbers and flagstones, which on closer inspection are revealed to be headstones. To the rear is a fine patio overlooking the River Tavey, and there are lovely walks in the Bere Valley on the doorstep. The area is ideal for birdwatchers. Dishes on offer range through fresh fish, crab, local pies, curries and stir-fries.

**Open** all wk 11-3 6-11 (Sat end May-end Aug 11-11 Sun noon-11) Closed: 1st wk Jan ◖ Sharp's Doom Bar & Own, guest ale ♂ Winkleigh. **Facilities** Family room Dogs allowed Garden

## BICKLEIGH — Map 3 SS90

### Fisherman's Cot ♀

EX16 8RW ☎ 01884 855237 📠 01884 855241
e-mail: fishermanscot.bickleigh@marstons.co.uk
dir: *Telephone for directions*

Well-appointed thatched inn by Bickleigh Bridge over the River Exe with food all day and large beer garden, just a short drive from Tiverton and Exmoor. The Waterside Bar is the place for snacks and afternoon tea, while the restaurant incorporates a carvery and à la carte menus. Sunday lunch is served, and champagne and smoked salmon breakfast is optional.

**Open** all day all wk 11am-11pm (Sun noon-10.30pm) ♀ 8 **Facilities** Garden Parking

## BIGBURY-ON-SEA — Map 3 SX64

### Pilchard Inn ♀

Burgh Island TQ7 4BG
☎ 01548 810514 📠 01548 810243
e-mail: reception@burghisland.com
dir: *From A38 turn off to Modbury then follow signs to Bigbury & Burgh Island*

Accessible at low tide by foot or by the unique hydraulic sea tractor at high tide, this small 14th-century smugglers' inn is located on a tiny island off the Devon coast. Soup, baguettes and bar snacks are on offer at lunchtime and organic produce is used where possible.

Evening meals served on Thursdays, Fridays (set curry night menu) and Saturdays must be booked in advance. South Hams and St Austell ales sit alongside Heron Valley cider in the bars.

**Open** all day all wk **Bar Meals** food served all day **Restaurant** D served Fri 7-9 (curry buffet) booking required Fixed menu price fr £18.75 ⊕ FREE HOUSE ◀ St Austell, South Hams, Exeter Brewery ♂ Thatchers Gold, Heron Valley. ♀ 16 **Facilities** Family room Dogs allowed Garden

*See advert below*

## BRAMPFORD SPEKE — Map 3 SX99

### The Lazy Toad Inn ♀

EX5 5DP ☎ 01392 841591 📠 01392 841591
e-mail: thelazytoadinn@btinternet.com
web: www.thelazytoadinn.co.uk
dir: *From Exeter take A377 towards Crediton 1.5m, right signed Brampford Speke*

Beamed ceilings and slate floors characterise this Grade II listed 19th-century free house, with its cobbled courtyard and winter log fires. There are many glorious walks along the banks of the River Exe. Home grown fruit, vegetables, herbs and even lamb complement the dishes, and meat and fish are cured in the pub's own smokery. Menu choices might include deep-fried local rabbit; or sweet potato and leek roulade, washed down with a great selection of real ales and ciders.

**Open** 11.30-2.30 6-11 (Sun 12-3) Closed: 3wks Jan, Sun eve & Mon **Bar Meals** L served Tue-Sun 12-2 booking required D served Tue-Sat 6-9 booking required Av main course £11.50 **Restaurant** Av 3 course à la carte fr £24 ⊕ FREE HOUSE ◀ Exmoor Fox, Otter Ale & Bitter, Exe Valley Exeter Old, Sharp's Doom Bar ♂ Sandford Devon Red, Traditional Farmhouse, Shaily Bridge. ♀ 12 **Facilities** Children's menu Children's portions Family room Dogs allowed Garden Parking

*See advert on opposite page*

## BRANSCOMBE — Map 4 SY18

### PICK OF THE PUBS

### The Masons Arms ★★ HL ◉ ♀

*See Pick of the Pubs on page 130*

## BRAUNTON — Map 3 SS43

### The Williams Arms

Wrafton EX33 2DE ☎ 01271 812360 📠 01271 816595
e-mail: info@williamsarms.co.uk
dir: *On A361 between Barnstaple & Braunton*

Spacious thatched pub dating back to the 16th century, and adjacent to the popular Tarka Trail, named after the much-loved otter created by author Henry Williamson. The restaurant has a carvery serving fresh locally-sourced meat and various vegetable dishes. Breakfast all day.

**Open** all day all wk 8.45am-11pm ◀ Guinness, Creamflow, Doom Bar ♂ Thatchers. **Facilities** Play area Garden Parking

# The
# Lazy Toad Inn

Brampford Speke, Exeter EX5 5DP
**Tel:** 01392 841591
**Email:** thelazytoadinn@btinternet.com
**Website:** www.thelazytoadinn.co.uk

The Lazy Toad is a Grade II listed Inn dating back to the late 19th century with light oak beamed ceilings and slate floors, log fire in winter, a cobbled courtyard and a lovely intimate walled beer garden.

The Inn is situated just off the Exe Valley Way and the Devonshire Heartland Way just a few hundred yards from many glorious walks along the River Exe.

Brampford Speke is an unspoilt, picturesque, atmospheric village with thatched cottates, listed buildings and high garden walls in its conservation area.

We attach great importance to our food, ambience and service. Our team of chefs produce an imaginative, daily changing menu featuring local seasonal produce. Many of our herbs, vegetables and fruit are produced in our garden in season. We cater for all tastes especially vegetarians and those with allergies.

Dogs on leads and well behaved children are welcome.

# PICK OF THE PUBS

## The Masons Arms ★★ HL 🌸 🍷

**BRANSCOMBE**   Map SY18

**EX12 3DJ**
☎ **01297 680300** 📠 **01297 680500**
**e-mail:** reception@masonsarms.co.uk
**dir:** *Turn off A3052 towards Branscombe,
down hill, hotel at bottom of hill*

This fine creeper-clad inn was at one time a well-documented haunt of smugglers. It stands in the picturesque village of Branscombe, just a ten-minute stroll from the beach, with wonderful local walks including the South West Coast Path. The building dates from 1360, when it was just a simple cider house squeezed into the middle of a row of cottages. Today, that row of cottages is an independent, family-run pub and hotel offering accommodation that includes cottage bedrooms and suites set in their own peaceful gardens with views across the valley and out to sea.

The Masons Arms has a bar that can hardly have changed in 200 years, with stone walls, ancient ships' beams, slate floors, and a splendid open fireplace used for spit-roasts, including Sunday lunchtimes. Five real ales are always available, including several that are locally brewed.

Food is a serious business here; where possible, all ingredients are grown, reared or caught locally, and the restaurant maintains a standard of cooking worthy of its AA Rosette. Expect starters such as seared West Country scallops with roasted butternut squash purée; and fresh herb risotto with a deep-fried poached egg. Main course choices might include roast rack of West Country lamb with aubergine caviar and light lamb jus; or grilled sea bass with West Country mussel and chervil cream velouté; followed, perhaps, by Devon clotted cream crème brûlée; or iced chocolate and roasted hazelnut parfait with crème Anglaise.

Meanwhile, the simpler bar menu also offers a range of more substantial dishes like crispy fried haddock in Branscombe Ale batter and cumin-grilled lamb cutlets. Outside there is a walled terrace with seating for around 100 people.

**Open** all wk Mon-Fri 11-3 6-11 (Sat 11-11 Sun 12-10.30) **Bar Meals** L served Mon-Fri 12-2, Sat-Sun 12-2.15 booking required D served all wk 7-9 booking required Av main course £13 **Restaurant** D served all wk 7-9 booking required Fixed menu price fr £29.95 🛢 FREE HOUSE 🍺 Otter Ale, Masons Ale, Tribute, Branoc, guest ales 🍏 Addlestones. 🍷 14 **Facilities** Children's menu Dogs allowed Garden Parking **Rooms** 21

## BRENDON — Map 3 SS74

### Rockford Inn ♟

**EX35 6PT** ☎ 01598 741214
e-mail: enquiries@therockfordinn.com
dir: *A39 through Minehead follow signs to Lynmouth. Turn left off A39 to Brendon approx 5m before Lynmouth*

This traditional 17th-century free house stands on the banks of the East Lynn River, and is handy for several Exmoor walking routes. Thatchers ciders complement local ales served from the cask, and there's a choice of good home-made pub meals. Game pie, salmon with shrimps, capers and parsley, and wild mushroom crumble are typical menu choices; the specials board changes daily. Eat in the garden in fine weather, or come indoors to the open fire as the nights draw in.

**Open** all day Closed: Mon L **Bar Meals** L served Tue-Sun 12-3 D served Tue-Sun 6-8.30 booking required Av main course £5 **Restaurant** Fixed menu price fr £7.95 Av 3 course à la carte fr £21.95 ⊕ FREE HOUSE ◀ Barn Owl, Tribute, Cotleigh 25, Exmoor, Cavalier ♂ Thatchers. **Facilities** Children's menu Dogs allowed Garden Parking

## BROADHEMPSTON — Map 3 SX86

### The Monks Retreat Inn

**The Square TQ9 6BN** ☎ 01803 812203
dir: *Exit A381 (Newton Abbot to Totnes road) at Ipplepen, follow for Broadhempston signs for 3.5m*

Apparently a friendly ghost of a monk inhabits this 1456 inn, formerly called Church House Inn. Certainly it's the sort of place you'd want to linger in: the building (listed as of outstanding architectural interest) is full of fascinating features, including a panelled oak screen typical of ancient Devon houses. Sit by one of the cosy log fires and enjoy a pint of Otter Bitter or Jail Ale.

**Open** Tue-Sun Closed: Mon **Bar Meals** L served Tue-Sun 12-1.45 D served Tue-Sun 6.30-9 **Restaurant** L served Tue-Sun 12-1.45 booking required D served Tue-Sun 6.30-9 booking required ⊕ ENTERPRISE INNS ◀ Jail Ale, Otter Bitter ♂ Thatchers Gold. **Facilities** Dogs allowed

## BUCKFASTLEIGH — Map 3 SX76

### *Dartbridge Inn* ▲ ★★★ INN ♟

**Totnes Rd TQ11 0JR** ☎ 01364 642214 ▤ 01364 643839
e-mail: dartbridge.buckfastleigh@oldenglishinns.co.uk
dir: *From Exeter A38, take 1st Buckfastleigh turn, then right to Totnes. Inn on left*

Standing close to the River Dart, this 19th-century building was originally a simple dwelling, then a teashop before becoming a pub. Well known for its eye-catching floral displays, inside are open fires and oak beams. The lunch/bar menu includes slow-cooked Welsh lamb, and spinach and ricotta girasole, while dinner mains are typically baked rainbow trout with pan-fried tiger prawns, gammon and other steaks, sausages and mash, and chicken Caesar salad.

**Open** all wk ◀ Scottish Courage, Abbot Ale, IPA, Otter Ale. ♟ 12 **Facilities** Parking **Rooms** 10

## BUCKLAND MONACHORUM — Map 3 SX46

### Drake Manor Inn ♟

**The Village PL20 7NA** ☎ 01822 853892 ▤ 01822 853892
e-mail: drakemanor@drakemanorinn.co.uk
dir: *Off A386 near Yelverton*

The 12th-century Drake Manor Inn was originally built to accommodate masons constructing the nearby St Andrew's church. Today, licensee Mandy Robinson prides herself on running a proper pub with a locals' bar, where friends gather to chat and drink fine ales and whisky. The locally-sourced menu includes steaks, fish dishes and pub favourites, as well as vegetarian choices and bar snacks. Main dishes might include venison sirloin with forest fruits and port wine sauce or fillet of natural smoked haddock on pea risotto. The sunny cottage garden is popular in fine weather.

**Open** all wk 11.30-2.30 (Sat 11.30-3) 6.30-11 (Fri-Sat 6.30-11.30) (Sun noon-11) **Bar Meals** L served all wk 12-2 D served Mon-Sat 7-10, Sun 7-9.30 Av main course £6 **Restaurant** L served all wk 12-2 D served Mon-Sat 7-10, Sun 7-9.30 Av 3 course à la carte fr £15 ⊕ PUNCH TAVERNS ◀ John Smith's & Courage Best, Sharp's Doom Bar, Jail Ale, Otter Ale. ♟ 9 **Facilities** Children's portions Family room Dogs allowed Garden Parking

## BUTTERLEIGH — Map 3 SS90

### The Butterleigh Inn

**EX15 1PN** ☎ 01884 855407 ▤ 01884 855600
dir: *3m from M5 junct 28 turn right by Manor Hotel in Cullompton. Follow Butterleigh signs*

This 400-year-old traditional free house has a mass of local memorabilia throughout. At this friendly local, customers can choose from a selection of real ales including O'Hanlon's Yellow Hammer, and ciders including Sam's Medium from Winkleigh Cider. On fine days, the garden with its huge flowering cherry tree is very popular. Booking is recommended for the restaurant, where home-made dishes and daily specials are always available.

**Open** 12-2.30 6-11 (Fri-Sat 6-12 Sun 12-3) Closed: Sun eve Nov-Apr **Bar Meals** L served Mon-Sat 12-2 D served Mon-Sat 7-9 Av main course £9 **Restaurant** L served Mon-Sat 12-2 D served Mon-Sat 7-9 ⊕ FREE HOUSE ◀ Cotleigh Tawny Ale, Yellow Hammer, guest ale ♂ Sams Medium, Thatchers Gold. **Facilities** Children's menu Children's portions Dogs allowed Garden Parking

## CHAGFORD — Map 3 SX78

### PICK OF THE PUBS

### The Sandy Park Inn ♟

**TQ13 8JW** ☎ 01647 433267
e-mail: sandyparkinn@btconnect.com
dir: *From A30 exit at Whiddon Down, turn left towards Moretonhampstead. Inn 5m from Whiddon Down*

Everything about the thatched Sandy Park is just as it should be. Dogs are frequently to be found slumped in front of the fire, horse-brasses and sporting prints adorn the walls, and the beamed bar attracts locals and tourists alike, all happily setting the world to rights with the help of an eclectic wine list and good range of traditional local ales like Otter and Dartmoor Legend. The candlelit restaurant is equally appealing, offering a brasserie-style menu which changes daily to make the most of local produce. Starters might include artichoke, sun-blushed tomato, spinach and feta cheese tartlet; or parsnip and apple soup, to be followed by beer-battered cod with home-cut chips or pheasant casserole - the perfect fare after a day spent stomping on the moors.

**Open** all day all wk noon-11pm **Bar Meals** L served all wk 12-2.30 booking required D served all wk 6-9 booking required Av main course £9 **Restaurant** L served all wk 12-2.30 booking required D served all wk 6-9 booking required ⊕ FREE HOUSE ◀ Otter Ale, O'Hanlons, Dartmoor Legend ♂ Pound House. ♟ 8 **Facilities** Children's portions Family room Dogs allowed Garden Parking

### Three Crowns Hotel ♟

**High St TQ13 8AJ** ☎ 01647 433444 & 433441 ▤ 01647 433117
dir: *Telephone for directions*

This impressive, 13th-century town centre inn is now run as a joint venture by St Austell Brewery and well-established publicans, John Milan and Steve Bellman. Period features include its famous leaning granite façade, mullioned windows, sturdy oak beams and massive open fireplace, while a refurbishment programme is revealing even more historic features. Dine in the lounge bar with its inglenook fireplace or in the cosy softly-lit restaurant. Menu specialities are caramelised breast of Gressingham duck; Dartmoor steak or lamb; beer-battered haddock fillet; and wild mushroom tagliatelle.

**Open** all day all wk 8am-11pm **Bar Meals** L served all wk 12-2.30 booking required D served all wk 6-9 booking required Av main course £14 **Restaurant** L served all wk 12-2.30 booking required D served all wk 6-9 booking required ⊕ ST AUSTELL BREWERY ◀ Tribute, IPA, Proper Job, HSD, Dartmoor ♂ Cornish Rattler, Pear Rattler. ♟ 11 **Facilities** Children's menu Children's portions Dogs allowed Parking

## CHARDSTOCK     Map 4 ST30

### The George Inn

**EX13 7BX ☎ 01460 220241**
**e-mail:** info@george-inn.co.uk
**dir:** *A358 from Taunton through Chard towards Axminster, left at Tytherleigh. Signed from A358*

A glorious, thatched 15th century village inn with superb oak panelling removed from a ship, a ghostly parson named Copeland and robust, long-standing locals who preside in 'Compost Corner', perhaps ruminating over local ales or awaiting a feast from the kitchen, anything from filled baguettes to home-made pies and slow-roast belly of pork with cider sauce, before tackling a game of skittles against visiting foes.

**Open** all wk 11.30-3 6-12 (all day Sat-Sun) **Bar Meals** L served all wk 12-2 D served all wk 6.30-9.30 Av main course £7.95 **Restaurant** L served all wk 12-2 D served all wk 6.30-9.30 ⊕ FREE HOUSE ◀ Otter Bitter, Sharp's Doom Bar, guest ales ♂ Stowford Press.
**Facilities** Children's menu Children's portions Dogs allowed Garden Parking

## CHERITON BISHOP     Map 3 SX79

### PICK OF THE PUBS

### The Old Thatch Inn ♀

*See Pick of the Pubs on opposite page*

## CLAYHIDON     Map 4 ST11

### PICK OF THE PUBS

### The Merry Harriers ♀

**Forches Corner EX15 3TR**
**☎ 01823 421270   🖷 01823 421270**
**e-mail:** peter.gatling@btinternet.com
**dir:** *Wellington A38, turn onto Ford Street (marked by brown tourist sign). At top of hill turn left, 1.5m on right*

Set high on the Blackdown Hills, the Merry Harriers stands on the once notorious Forches Corner, which was the scene of ambushes during the 17th-century Monmouth Rebellion. The black and white free house features beamed ceilings, a cosy inglenook and attractive dining areas, whilst the large mature garden is popular during the summer months. Peter and Angela Gatling have worked tirelessly to build the local drinks trade and expand the food operation. More than 90 per cent of kitchen ingredients come from the surrounding hills or further afield in the West Country. A light bar lunch might feature a smoked bacon and West Country brie baguette, or a more substantial dish of roasted salmon fillet on sautéed new potatoes with dill sauce. Evening main courses include local steak and kidney pie with rich Otter ale gravy; and wild mushroom and spinach risotto with seasonal salad.

**Open** noon-3 6.30-11 Closed: Sun eve & Mon **Bar Meals** L served Tue-Sat 12-2, Sun 12-2.15 booking required D served Tue-Sat 6.30-9 booking required Av main course £9 food served all day **Restaurant** L served Tue-Sat 12-2, Sun 12-2.15 booking required D served Tue-Sat 6.30-9 booking required Av 3 course à la carte fr £18 food served all day ⊕ FREE HOUSE ◀ Otter Head, Cotleigh Harrier, Exmoor Gold, St Austell Tinners, Otter Amber ♂ Thatchers Gold, Bollhayes. ♀ 14 **Facilities** Children's menu Children's portions Play area Family room Dogs allowed Garden Parking

## CLEARBROOK     Map 3 SX56

### The Skylark Inn

**PL20 6JD ☎ 01822 853258**
**e-mail:** skylvic@btinternet.com
**dir:** *5m N of Plymouth on A386 towards Tavistock. Take 2nd right signed Clearbrook*

The Skylark is set in the Dartmoor National Park just ten minutes from Plymouth and the area is ideal for cyclists and walkers. The beamed bar with its large fireplace and wood-burning stove characterises this attractive village inn, where good wholesome food is served from an extensive menu. Dishes include classics like ham and eggs; gammon steak; or a mixed grill.

**Open** all wk 11.30-3 6-11.30 **Bar Meals** L served all wk 12-2 booking required D served all wk 6.30-9 booking required Av main course £9.70 **Restaurant** L served all wk 12-2 booking required D served all wk 6.30-9 booking required ⊕ UNIQUE PUB CO LTD ◀ Otter Ale, St Austell Tribute, Dartmoor Best Bitter. **Facilities** Play area Family room Dogs allowed Garden Parking

## CLOVELLY     Map 3 SS32

### PICK OF THE PUBS

### Red Lion Hotel ★★ HL

**The Quay EX39 5TF**
**☎ 01237 431237   🖷 01237 431044**
**e-mail:** redlion@clovelly.co.uk
**dir:** *From Bideford rdbt, follow A39 to Bude for 10m. At Clovelly Cross rdbt turn right, follow past Clovelly Visitor Centre entrance, bear to left. Hotel at bottom of hill*

Clovelly, the famously unspoilt 'village like a waterfall', descends down broad steps to a 14th-century harbour and this charming hostelry is located right on the quay. Guests staying in the whimsically decorated bedrooms can fall asleep to the sound of waves lapping the shingle and wake to the cries of gulls squabbling for scraps. Seafood, unsurprisingly, is a priority on the modern menu, which could offer home-made wild rabbit terrine with red onion marmalade to start, followed by chargrilled turbot steak. Daytime visitors can tuck into a locally-made Cornish pasty, or a plate of cod and chips.

**Open** all day all wk **Bar Meals** L served all wk 12-2.30 D served all week 6-8.30 Av main course £6.95 **Restaurant** D served all wk 7-9 booking required Fixed menu price fr £29.50 Av 3 course à la carte fr £29.50 ⊕ FREE HOUSE ◀ Doom Bar, Old Appledore, Guinness, Clovelly Cobbler ♂ Thatchers. **Facilities** Children's menu Children's portions Family room Parking **Rooms** 11

## CLYST HYDON     Map 3 ST00

### PICK OF THE PUBS

### The Five Bells Inn ♀

**EX15 2NT ☎ 01884 277288**
**e-mail:** info@fivebellsclysthydon.co.uk
**dir:** *B3181 towards Cullompton, right at Hele Cross towards Clyst Hydon. 2m turn right, then sharp right at left bend at village sign*

Originally a 16th-century thatched farmhouse, this attractive country pub in rolling east Devon countryside started serving ale about a hundred years ago, and takes its name from the five bells hanging in the village church tower. It's gone from strength to strength in recent years, thanks to its family-friendly owners and a focus on real ales, good food and cheerful hospitality. The well-maintained garden is a delight in summer, with twenty tables enjoying lovely views, and a children's play area. The interior boasts two wood fires, numerous prints and watercolours, and brass and copper artefacts. Excellent real ales are augmented by draught lagers, cider and bottled beers. When it comes to food, why not start with bacon and garlic mushroom tart, or crab cakes with sweet chilli dip. Then indulge in a West Country steak served with mushrooms, peas and chips; or a slowly cooked duck leg on a bed of colcannon with orange and spring onion.

**Open** 11.30am-3 6.30-11pm Closed: 25 Dec, Mon L **Bar Meals** L served Tue-Sun 11.30-2 D served all wk 6.30-9 ◀ Cotleigh Tawny Ale, Otter Bitter, O'Hanlon's. ♀ 8 **Facilities** Play area Family room Garden Parking

## COCKWOOD     Map 3 SX98

### PICK OF THE PUBS

### The Anchor Inn ♀

**EX6 8RA ☎ 01626 890203   🖷 01626 890355**
**dir:** *Off A379 between Dawlish & Starcross*

Overlooking a small landlocked harbour on the River Exe, this former Seamen's Mission has been a haven to sailors and smugglers for centuries. In summer customers spill out onto the veranda and harbour wall, while real fires and low beams make the interior cosy in winter. Nautical bric-a-brac abounds, with lights inside divers' helmets, ropes and pulleys, binnacles, and a wall displaying over 200 cast ship badges. For fish dish lovers, this comprehensive menu might prove a challenge in just what to choose - 30 different ways to eat mussels for one thing! But if that doesn't

*continued on page 134*

# PICK OF THE PUBS

# The Old Thatch Inn ♟

**CHERITON BISHOP**  Map 3 SX79

**EX6 6HJ** ☎ **01647 24204**
e-mail: mail@theoldthatchinn.f9.co.uk
dir: *0.5m off A30, 7m SW of Exeter*

This charming 16th-century free house is just outside the eastern border of Dartmoor National Park. Stagecoaches would stop here when the old road to Cornwall went through the village, but today the pub stands half a mile away from its successor, the A30 dual-carriageway that takes holiday traffic to and from all points west. For a time during its long history the inn was in private hands, then became a tea room, before its licence was renewed in the early 1970s. Following a fire, major refurbishment was necessary in 2007, but it was carried out thoughtfully and sympathetically so as not to compromise its period appeal. Four real ales are served in the bar and there's an extensive wine list.

Owners David and Serena London are proud of their high standards, and prepare all their food from fresh, regionally sourced ingredients, with seafood featuring strongly. Light snacks at lunchtime include filled pumpkin and sunflower seed mini-loaves, and soup of the day with ciabattas. Main menu starters include warm pigeon breast rocket salad with strawberry and balsamic dressing; terrine of wild boar, red onion confit, toasted bread; Bantry Bay mussels with white wine and garlic cream sauce; Cornish crab gateau, cucumber and lemon mayonnaise; and buffalo mozzarella and beef tomato, black olive and pesto dressing. Appearing as main courses may be fillet of beef medallions layered with fresh spinach with sautéed potatoes and wild mushroom and port sauce; sirloin steak with pan-fried cherry tomatoes, mushrooms and chips; pan-fried calves' liver with celeriac mash, caramelised red onion and balsamic jus; fresh sea bass fillets on a bed of pak choi, new potatoes and crab bisque; and goat's cheese and asparagus filo parcel with tomato coulis.

**Open** all wk 11.30-3 6-11 Closed: 25-26 Dec, Sun eve **Bar Meals** L served Mon-Thu 12-2.30 (Fri-Sun 12-3) D served Mon-Thu 6.30-9 (Fri-Sat 6.30-9.30) Av main course £9.50 **Restaurant** L served Mon-Thu 12-2.30 (Fri-Sun 12-3) D served Mon-Thu 6.30-9 (Fri-Sat 6.30-9.30) Av 3 course à la carte fr £24.00 ◀ Otter Ale, Port Stout, O'Hanlon's Stormstay, Sharp's Doom Bar, Dartmoor Legend, Yellowhammer ♂ Thatchers. ♟ 9 **Facilities** Children's menu Family room Dogs allowed Garden Parking

## COCKWOOD *continued*

appeal, there are scallops, oysters, crab, lobster, whole grilled plaice, lemon sole and marlin. There are set meals for two, and for four; and meat eaters and vegetarians are not forgotten. Try and save a little room for at least one of the twelve varieties of treacle tart. There is live music Wednesday and Thursday nights and Sunday lunchtime.

**Open** all day all wk 11-11 (Sun noon-10.30, 25 Dec 12-2) **Bar Meals** Av main course £8.95 food served all day **Restaurant** L served all wk 12-2.15 D served Mon-Sat 6.30-10, Sun 6.30-9.30 booking required Av 3 course à la carte fr £25 ⊕ HEAVITREE ◀ Interbrew Bass, Timothy Taylor Landlord, Fuller's London Pride, Otter Ale, Abbot, Adnams Broadside. ♚ 20 **Facilities** Children's menu Dogs allowed Garden Parking

---

### COLEFORD      Map 3 SS70

## PICK OF THE PUBS

### The New Inn ★★★★ INN ♚

EX17 5BZ ☎ 01363 84242 ▤ 01363 85044
e-mail: enquiries@thenewinncoleford.co.uk
dir: *From Exeter take A377, 1.5m after Crediton turn left for Coleford, 1.5m to inn*

The ancient, slate floored bar with its old chests and polished brass blends effortlessly with the fresh white walls, original oak beams and simple wooden furniture in the dining room of this pretty, 13th-century inn. Set beside the babbling River Cole, the pub was once used by travelling Cistercian monks, and Charles I reviewed his troops from a nearby house during the English Civil War. With a menu changing every eight weeks, reliable, home-made bar food includes a range of ploughman's and filled baguettes, supported by pub classics like beer-battered cod, chips and peas, and Clannaborough red ruby beefburgers with melting Stilton, chips and salad. Main menu choices include herb-crusted baked haddock fillet with smoked cheese and crème fraîche; seasonal venison and mushroom pie with port and pickled walnut flakes; and mushroom, mascarpone and hazelnut tartlet. Comfortable overnight accommodation is available in six well-appointed en suite bedrooms, whilst the riverside garden is perfect for alfresco summer dining.

**Open** all wk 12-3 6-11 (Sun 7-10.30 winter) Closed: 25-26 Dec **Bar Meals** L served all wk 12-2 D served all wk 6.30-9.30 Av main course £8 **Restaurant** L served all wk 12-2 D served all wk 6.30-9.30 Av 3 course à la carte fr £19.95 ⊕ FREE HOUSE ◀ Doom Bar, Otter Ale, Exmoor Ale, Spitfire, Rev James Ö Thatchers, Winkleigh Sam's. ♚ 20 **Facilities** Children's menu Children's portions Dogs allowed Garden Parking **Rooms** 6

---

### COLYFORD      Map 4 SY29

## The Wheelwright Inn ♚

Swanhill Rd EX24 6QQ
☎ 01297 552585 ▤ 01297 553841
e-mail: gary@wheelwright-inn.co.uk
dir: *Telephone for directions*

This pretty thatched inn has earned a reputation for outstanding food and service since the current landlords took over. The exterior of the 17th-century building belies the contemporary interior, but the low beams, wooden floors and log fire ensure that it retains its authentic country feel. Well kept beers include Badger First Gold and Hopping Hare. Expect a varied modern menu, including well-filled sandwiches on locally baked bread; local pork cutlet with creamy potato and swede mash; and moules marinière with crusty bread.

**Open** all day all wk Closed: 26 Dec **Bar Meals** food served all day **Restaurant** food served all day ⊕ HALL & WOODHOUSE ◀ Badger First Gold, Hopping Hare, Guinness, Sussex Ö Stowford Press. **Facilities** Children's menu Children's portions Family room Dogs allowed Garden Parking

---

### DALWOOD      Map 4 ST20

## PICK OF THE PUBS

### The Tuckers Arms ♚

*See Pick of the Pubs on page 135*

---

### DARTMOUTH      Map 3 SX85

## PICK OF THE PUBS

### Royal Castle Hotel ★★★ HL ♚

11 The Quay TQ6 9PS
☎ 01803 833033 ▤ 01803 835445
e-mail: becca@royalcastle.co.uk
dir: *In town centre, overlooking inner harbour*

Overlooking Dartmouth's inner harbour, this old building dates from the 1630s when two merchants built adjacent quayside houses. A century later, one had become The New Inn and by the 1780s had been joined by its neighbour to become The Castle Inn. Further rebuilds resulted in the battlemented cornice and front entrance supported by Doric columns. Tudor fireplaces, spiral staircases and priest holes are other intriguing features, along with many fine antique pieces, including four-poster and brass beds. The Nu

---

first floor restaurant looks out over the river and is decorated in a classic contemporary style; non-residents may come in for breakfast, lunch or dinner. A supporter of Taste of the West's 'buy local' campaign, the hotel offers an extensive seasonal menu of local crab, oysters, sautéed monkfish loin, braised ox cheek in Guinness, and in the Galleon and Harbour Bars a good range of bar meals.

*Royal Castle Hotel*

**Open** all day all wk 8am-11.30pm **Bar Meals** Av main course £10 food served all day **Restaurant** L served all wk 12-2 D served all wk 6-9 Fixed menu price fr £12.50 Av 3 course à la carte fr £25 ⊕ FREE HOUSE ◀ Jail Ale, Bays Gold, Doom Bar Ö Thatchers Gold, Orchards Cider. ♚ 29 **Facilities** Children's menu Children's portions Family room Dogs allowed Parking **Rooms** 25

---

### DENBURY      Map 3 SX86

## The Union Inn ♚

Denbury Green TQ12 6DQ
☎ 01803 812595 ▤ 01803 814206
e-mail: unioninn@aol.com
dir: *2m form Newton Abbot, signed Denbury*

The Union Inn is at least 400 years old and counting. Inside are the original stone walls that once rang to the hammers of the blacksmiths and cartwrights who worked here many moons ago. Choose freshly prepared, mouth-watering starters such pea and ham soup, crayfish cocktail and spiced smoked duck breast with pink ginger, and follow with beer battered cod and hand-cut chips; venison sausage toad-in-the-hole; or wild mushroom risotto. There is a menu gastronomique served five evenings a week. The guest ale is changed on a keg-by-keg basis.

**Open** all wk noon-3 6-11.30 (Fri-Sat noon-mdnt) **Bar Meals** L served all wk 12-2 D served all wk 6-9 Av main course £17 **Restaurant** L served all wk 12-2 D served all wk 6-9 Fixed menu price fr £14 Av 3 course à la carte fr £20 ⊕ ENTERPRISE INNS ◀ Otter bitter, Denbury Dreamer, Jail ale Ö Sams cider. ♚ 10 **Facilities** Children's menu Children's portions Dogs allowed Garden Parking

# PICK OF THE PUBS

## The Tuckers Arms

**DALWOOD**      Map 4 ST20

**EX13 7EG**
☎ 01404 881342   🖷 01404 881138
**e-mail:**
tuckersarms@tuckersarms.com
**web:** www.tuckersarms.com
**dir:** *Off A35 between Honiton & Axminster*

An 800-year-old, family-run Devon longhouse in a pretty setting between two ridges of the Blackdown Hills, a tranquil landscape of high plateaux, valleys and springs, dotted with farms and villages. Some sources suggest that the pub was built as living accommodation for the labourers constructing St Peters church across the way, although at least one other source credits the Duke of Beaulieu for building it as a hunting lodge.

The present management arrived from Yorkshire about three years ago and are delighted with how welcome they've been made to feel. The interior is everything you would expect of a traditional, thatched inn – inglenook fireplaces, low beams and flagstone floors.

Local ales on tap come from the Otter and Branscombe breweries, and other regularly changing brews from around the region are also served.

As the pub is only fifteen minutes from the coast at Lyme Regis, fish and seafood have only a short distance to travel, so its freshness is assured. At lunchtime, begin with goat's cheese and wild mushroom terrine; then perhaps beer-battered catch of the day with hand-cut chips and pea purée; or maybe prime beefburger, topped with cheese, celeriac, coleslaw, onion ring, salad and mayonnaise.

The fine dining evening menu offers freshly netted local mussels, cooked marinière style; followed by venison haunch with beetroot gratin, parsnip purée in Malbec sauce and wilted greens: or hazelnut and mushroom parcel. Traditionalists might settle for West Country ham, two free-range eggs and chips, or a 10oz gammon steak. Finish with a home-made sweet or a malt whisky from the wide selection.

**Open** all wk 11.30-3 6.30-11 **Bar Meals** L served all wk 12-2 D served all wk 7-9 **Restaurant** L served all wk 12-2 D served all wk 7-9 ⊕ FREE HOUSE ◀ Otter Bitter, Branoc Ale, Guest ales. ☐ 8 **Facilities** Children's menu Dogs allowed Garden Parking

# PICK OF THE PUBS

## The Nobody Inn ★★★★INN ♟

**DODDISCOMBSLEIGH** — Map 3 SX88

**EX6 7PS**
☎ **01647 252394** 📄 **01647 252978**
**e-mail:** info@nobodyinn.co.uk
**dir:** *3m SW of Exeter Racecourse (A38)*

For many years this late 16th-century free house served as the village's unofficial church house and meeting place, becoming a de facto inn along the way. It was officially licensed as the New Inn in 1838, and acquired its unusual name after an unfortunate incident following the innkeeper's death in 1952. His corpse was accidentally left in the mortuary while the funeral took place around an empty coffin with 'no body'.

The present owners — only the fifth since 1838 - have recently undertaken a major investment programme, but have wisely bypassed the bar, which retains its traditional ambience. Here, the low ceilings, blackened beams, inglenook fireplace and antique furniture all contribute to the timeless atmosphere, and you can sample some 260 wines and 230 whiskies in addition to an ever-changing range of real ales.

The pub is also famous for its selection of local cheeses - there are usually about fifteen varieties — and fresh fish is delivered daily from Brixham. Imaginative bar meals are served every lunchtime and evening from a regularly changing menu. Dinner might begin with scallops baked in Devon Oke cheese sauce, continuing with pheasant and apricot pie, mashed potatoes and seasonal vegetables; or roasted vegetable and Sharpham brie pie in herb pastry, with salad and garlic olive bread; and finish with warm chocolate brownie, clotted cream and chocolate sauce. The inn is set in a pretty cottage garden in rolling countryside between the Haldon Hills and the Teign Valley. A small bar shop sells some of the items you are likely to have enjoyed in the pub. Five attractive bedrooms are available.

**Open** all day all wk 11-11 (Sun 12-10.30) Closed: 25-26 Dec, 1 Jan
**Bar Meals** L served Mon-Sat 12-2, Sun 12-3 D served Mon-Thu 6.30-9, Fri-Sat 6.30-9.30, Sun 7-9 Av main course £8
**Restaurant** D served Mon-Thu 6.30-9, Fri-Sat 6.30-9.30, Sun 7-9 booking required Av 3 course à la carte fr £23
🍺 FREE HOUSE 🛢 Branscombe Nobody's Bitter, 2 guest ales
🍏 Brimblecombes Local cider, Westons Stowford Press. ♟ 28 **Facilities** Dogs allowed Garden Parking **Rooms** 5

## DITTISHAM — Map 3 SX85

### PICK OF THE PUBS

## The Ferry Boat 🍷

**Manor St TQ6 0EX ☎ 01803 722368**
**dir:** *Telephone for directions*

Set right at the water's edge with a pontoon outside its front door, this riverside inn (the only one on the River Dart) dates back 300 years. Tables at the front enjoy views across the river to Greenway House and Gardens, the National Trust property that used to be Agatha Christie's home. The pub has plenty of marine connections, being just a few miles upriver from the Royal Naval College in Dartmouth. The pontoon guarantees popularity with the boating fraternity, but the pub is also a favourite with walkers and families. Menus of home-cooked food vary seasonally, based on fresh fish, crab and mussels, and local meats and cheeses. A beach barbecue in summer produces a wonderful paella, sometimes accompanied by live music from local musicians. With its year-round selection of four or five real ales, and open log fires crackling in the grates in winter, this really is a pub for all seasons.

**Open** all day all wk **Bar Meals** L served all wk 12-2 booking required D served all wk 7-9 booking required Av main course £10 ⊕ PUNCH TAVERNS ◗ Youngs, Adnams, St Austell Tribute, IPA, Sharp's Doom Bar, Otter Ale. 🍷 10 **Facilities** Children's menu Children's portions Family room Dogs allowed

## DODDISCOMBSLEIGH — Map 3 SX88

### PICK OF THE PUBS

## The Nobody Inn ★★★★ INN 🍷

*See Pick of the Pubs on opposite page*

## DOLTON — Map 3 SS51

## Rams Head Inn 🍷

**South St EX19 8QS ☎ 01805 804255 📠 01805 804509**
**e-mail:** ramsheadinn@btopenworld.com
**dir:** *8m from Torrington on A3124*

Huge old fireplaces and bread ovens are amongst the original features that give this 15th-century free house its traditional character. The inn's central location places it on many inland tourist routes, whilst the Tarka Trail and Rosemoor Gardens are both nearby. Expect cask ales on tap, accompanied by popular bar meals like liver and bacon, or sausage and mash. Salmon supreme, chicken Imperial and double lamb chops all feature on the restaurant menu.

**Open** all wk 10-3 5-11 (Fri-Sat noon-mdnt Sun noon-4 6-11) **Bar Meals** Av main course £9 food served all day **Restaurant** food served all day ⊕ FREE HOUSE ◗ Flowers IPA Cask, Trophy, Sharps Own Ö Winkleigh. 🍷 14 **Facilities** Dogs allowed Garden Parking

## DREWSTEIGNTON — Map 3 SX79

### PICK OF THE PUBS

## The Drewe Arms 🍷

**The Square EX6 6QN**
**☎ 01647 281224 📠 01647 281179**
**e-mail:** mail@thedrewearms.co.uk
**dir:** *W of Exeter on A30 for 12m. Left at Woodleigh junct follow signs for 3m to Drewsteignton*

In a sleepy village square, this traditional thatched pub lies just within Dartmoor National Park. Built in 1646, it used to be the Druid Arms, but in the 1920s the Drewe family, who had commissioned Sir Edwin Lutyens to design nearby Castle Drogo, persuaded the brewery to change the pub's name. The Drewe's contribution? They paid for a pub sign showing the family coat of arms. Real ales are served from the cask in the tap room and served through a hatchway into the bar. Dine in The Dartmoor or Card Rooms, or in Aunt Mabel's Kitchen, named after Mabel Mudge, landlady for 75 years from 1919 to 1994. Enjoy grilled steaks; pizzas; fillet of cod; steak and kidney pudding; fresh mussels cooked several ways; and Teign Valley venison pie, as well as sandwiches and ploughman's lunches. In summer relax in the attractive gardens or enjoy a game of boules.

**Open** all day all wk 11am-mdnt (winter 11-3 6-mdnt) **Bar Meals** L served all wk 12-10 (winter 12-2.30) D served all wk 12-10 (winter 6-9.30) Av main course £9.50 food served all day **Restaurant** L served all wk 12-10 (winter 12-2.30) D served all wk 12-10 (winter 6-9.30) Av 3 course à la carte fr £20 food served all day ⊕ ENTERPRISE INNS ◗ Otter Ale, Tribute, Tanglefoot, Druid's, Sharp's Doom Bar Ö Winkleigh Autumn Scrumpy. 🍷 10 **Facilities** Children's menu Children's portions Dogs allowed Garden Parking

## EAST ALLINGTON — Map 3 SX74

## Fortescue Arms

**TQ9 7RA ☎ 01548 521215**
**e-mail:** info@fortescue-arms.co.uk
**dir:** *Telephone for directions*

This charming old country inn is run by Werner Rott, the Austrian chef/proprietor and spare-time sculptor. Being the only pub in the village, it is very much the centre of the community. In the flagstone-floored bar he offers Butcombe Bitter, guest real ales and a short menu. In the restaurant, expect fine sirloin steak with green peppercorn and brandy sauce; chicken schnitzel; pheasant wrapped in Black Forest ham with lentils and tangy berry sauce; roasted monkfish tail with spinach and red pepper sauce; and three-bean chilli with rice and corn cake.

**Open** 12-2.30 6-11 Closed: Mon lunch **Bar Meals** L served all wk 12-2.30 booking required D served all wk 6.30-10 booking required Av main course £8.50 **Restaurant** L served all wk 12-2.30 booking required D served all wk 6.30-10 booking required Av 3 course à la carte fr £22.50 ⊕ FREE HOUSE ◗ Butcombe Bitter, Dartmoor IPA, Guinness, Guest ales. **Facilities** Children's menu Family room Dogs allowed Garden Parking

## EXETER — Map 3 SX99

## Red Lion Inn 🍷

**Broadclyst EX5 3EL ☎ 01392 461271**
**dir:** *On B3181 (Exeter to Cullompton)*

A 16th-century, listed building set at the heart of a delightful village which is part of the National Trust's Killerton Estate. Inside the inn there is a wealth of beams and warming open fires on cooler days. The restaurant menus offer dishes based on locally sourced produce including seasonal game. In the bar expect traditional fare – beer battered cod and chips; curries, steaks and salads.

**Open** all wk 11-3.30 5.30-11.30 (Sat-Sun 11am-11.30pm) **Bar Meals** L served all wk 12-2.30 D served all wk 6-9.30 Av main course £7.50 **Restaurant** L served all wk 12-2.30 D served all wk 6-9.30 Fixed menu price fr £8.95 Av 3 course à la carte fr £25 ⊕ FREE HOUSE ◗ Bass, Fuller's London Pride, O'Hanlons Local Blakelys Red, Old Speckled Hen. 🍷 8 **Facilities** Children's menu Children's portions Dogs allowed Garden Parking

## *The Twisted Oak*

**Little John's Cross Hill EX2 9RG ☎ 01392 273666**
**e-mail:** info@twistedoakpub.com
**dir:** *A30 to Okehampton, follow signs for pub*

Set in a beautiful part of Ide just outside Exeter, this large pub has been turned into a quality, food-driven venue in the last few years. There is a choice of dining areas - an informal place where you can relax on the leather sofas and eat; a separate lounge bar restaurant; and a more formal conservatory area, which is adult only in the evenings. During the summer months the huge garden provides seating and a children's play area.

**Open** all wk 11am-3 5-11pm (Fri-Sun 11am-mdnt) ◗ Sharp's Doom Bar, Exmoor Ale. **Facilities** Play area Family room Dogs allowed Garden Parking

## EXMINSTER — Map 3 SX98

## *Swans Nest* 🍷

**Station Rd EX6 8DZ ☎ 01392 832371**
**dir:** *From M5 junct 30 follow A379 (Dawlish road)*

A much extended pub in a pleasant rural location whose facilities, unusually, extend to a ballroom, dance floor and stage. The carvery is a popular option for diners, with a choice of meats served with freshly prepared vegetables, though the salad bar is a tempting alternative, with over 39 items, including quiches, pies and home-smoked chicken. A carte of home-cooked fare includes grilled lamb steak, Devon pork chop, and five-bean vegetable curry.

**Open** all wk 11-2.30 6-11 (Sun 12-3 6-11) ◗ Otter Ale, Guest Ales Ö Stowford Press. 🍷 8 **Facilities** Play area Family room Garden Parking

## EXTON
Map 3 SX98

### PICK OF THE PUBS

### The Puffing Billy ☙

**Station Rd EX3 0PR ☎ 01392 877888**
**e-mail:** enquiries@thepuffingbilly.co.uk
**dir:** *A376 signed Exmouth, through Ebford. Follow signs for Puffing Billy, turn right into Exton*

Acquired in September 2009 by an expanding Devon-based hotel and restaurant group, the 16th-century Puffing Billy overlooks the Exe estuary near its confluence with the River Clyst. Local breweries Otter, Exmoor and Teignworthy supply their real ales to the smartly designed bar, while the restaurant serves food from a modern British seasonal menu. Examples from a spring version were starters of Cornish sardines with aubergine caviar, cherry tomato compote and basil vinaigrette; and salad of local asparagus with watercress, radish, herb croutons and warm poached duck egg. Main courses included fresh, locally caught fish in light beer batter with chips, garden peas and home-made tartare sauce; roasted chicken, baby leek and smoked pancetta pie in tarragon cream sauce with puff pastry top and creamed mash; and stuffed roasted bell pepper with yellow and green tomatoes, home-made pesto and new potatoes. Watch the river traffic go by from the secluded garden.

**Open** all wk noon-3 6-11 (all day Apr-Sep) Closed: selected days over Xmas **Bar Meals** L served Mon-Sat 12-2 **Restaurant** L served Mon-Sat 12-2 (Sun 12-2.30) booking required D served Mon-Sat 6.30-9.30 (Sun 6-9) booking required ⊕ FREE HOUSE ◖ Otter Ale, Otter Bitter. ☙ 15 **Facilities** Children's menu Garden Parking

## HARBERTON
Map 3 SX75

### The Church House Inn ☙

**TQ9 7SF ☎ 01803 863707**
**dir:** *From Totnes take A381 S. Turn right for Harberton, pub by church in village centre*

Built to house masons working on the church next door around 1100, the inn's fascinating historic features include a Tudor window frame and latticed window with 13th-century glass. It passed from church to private ownership in the 1950s, and is one of 18 church houses that have become pubs in the county. In addition to a menu of popular favourites, the blackboard displays daily specials such as traditional steak and kidney pie; chicken piri-piri; and crêpe florentine au gratin.

**Open** all wk noon-3 6-11 Closed: 25 Dec eve, 1 Jan eve **Bar Meals** L served all wk 12-2 D served all wk 6.30-9 Av main course £9.50 **Restaurant** L served all wk 12-2 booking required D served all wk 6.30-9 booking required Av 3 course à la carte fr £19 ⊕ FREE HOUSE ◖ Skinners, Dartmoor IPA, Dartmoor Jail Ale, Guest ales. ☙ 10 **Facilities** Children's menu Children's portions Family room Dogs allowed

## HAYTOR VALE
Map 3 SX77

### PICK OF THE PUBS

### The Rock Inn ★★ HL ◉

*See Pick of the Pubs on opposite page*

## HOLSWORTHY
Map 3 SS30

### The Bickford Arms ⋃

**Brandis Corner EX22 7XY**
**☎ 01409 221318 📠 01409 220085**
**e-mail:** info@bickfordarms.com
**dir:** *On A3072, 4m from Holsworthy towards Hatherleigh*

This pub stood on the Holsworthy to Hatherleigh road for 300 years before it was gutted by fire in 2003. Although totally rebuilt by the current owners, it retains much period charm, with beams, a welcoming bar and two fireplaces. The bar, which serves both real ales and ciders, and restaurant menu offers food prepared with locally-sourced ingredients - perhaps free-range Devon duck breast with redcurrant and red wine sauce or home-made steak and ale pie.

**Open** all wk 11-11 (11-3 5.30-11 winter) Closed: 25-26 Dec **Bar Meals** L served all wk 12-2 D served all wk 6-9 Av main course £9 ⊕ FREE HOUSE ◖ Skinners Betty Stogs, Lazy Daze, Tribute ♂ Sams, Thatchers. **Facilities** Children's menu Children's portions Garden Parking **Rooms** 5

## HONITON
Map 4 ST10

### PICK OF THE PUBS

### The Holt ◉

*See Pick of the Pubs on page 141*

### The Otter Inn

**Weston EX14 3NZ ☎ 01404 42594**
**dir:** *Just off A30 W of Honiton*

On the banks of the idyllic River Otter, this ancient 14th-century inn is set in over two acres of grounds and was once a cider house. Enjoy one of the traditional real ales, try your hand at Scrabble, dominoes or cards, or peruse the inn's extensive book collection. A wide-ranging menu caters for all tastes and includes fresh fish, game, steak, vegetarian dishes, bar meals and Sunday lunch.

**Open** all wk ◖ Otter Ale, London Pride, guest ales. **Facilities** Family room Dogs allowed Garden Parking

## HORNDON
Map 3 SX58

### *The Elephant's Nest Inn*

**PL19 9NQ ☎ 01822 810273 📠 01822 810273**
**e-mail:** info@theelephantsnest.co.uk
**dir:** *Off A386 N of Tavistock*

The pub got its unique name in the 1950s when a regular made a humorous remark about the then rather portly landlord. An isolated inn on the flanks of Dartmoor National Park reached via narrow lanes from Mary Tavy, the 16th-century building retains its real fires, slate floors and low beamed ceilings decorated with elephant memorabilia. Meals include lunchtime baguettes, interesting vegetarian options and a good seafood selection - smoked haddock chowder, for example.

**Open** all wk ◖ Palmers IPA, Copper, Otter Bright, Sail Ale, guest ales. **Facilities** Family room Dogs allowed Garden Parking

## HORSEBRIDGE
Map 3 SX47

### The Royal Inn

**PL19 8PJ ☎ 01822 870214**
**e-mail:** paul@royalinn.co.uk
**dir:** *S of B3362 (Launceston-Tavistock road)*

The pub, with a façade enlivened by superb pointed arched windows, was once a nunnery until Henry VIII dissolved the monastery. Standing near a bridge built over the Tamar in 1437 by Benedictine monks, it became the Packhorse Inn until Charles I pitched up one day - his seal is in the doorstep. Beef for the steaks, casseroles and stews, and the pheasant and venison on the specials board are all locally supplied. Chilli cheese tortillas are much appreciated; so is the absence of noisy machines.

**Open** all wk noon-3 6.30-11pm **Bar Meals** L served all wk 12-2 booking required D served all wk 6.30-9 booking required Av main course £8.50 **Restaurant** L served all wk 12-2 booking required D served all wk 6.30-9 booking required Av 3 course à la carte fr £17 ⊕ FREE HOUSE ◖ Dartmoor Jail Ale, Dartmoor Legend, Bass, Skinners, St Austell Proper Job ♂ Cornish Rattler, Thatchers Gold. **Facilities** Dogs allowed Garden Parking

## ILFRACOMBE
Map 3 SS54

### The George & Dragon

**5 Fore St EX34 9ED ☎ 01271 863851**
**e-mail:** linda.quinn5@btinternet.com
**dir:** *Telephone for directions*

The oldest pub in town, The George & Dragon dates from 1360 and is reputedly haunted. The food is of the simple, no-nonsense variety - typical examples include home-cooked boozy beef; chicken curry; mixed grills; and home-cooked crab from the harbour when available. No fruit machines or pool table, but if you are lucky there will be a little home-produced background music, along with a good choice of real ales and ciders.

*continued on page 140*

# PICK OF THE PUBS

## The Rock Inn ★★HL 🏵

**HAYTOR VALE**                    Map 3 SX77

**TQ13 9XP**
☎ **01364 661305** 🖷 **01364 661242**
**e-mail:** inn@rock-inn.co.uk
**web:** www.rock-inn.co.uk
**dir:** *A38 from Exeter, at Drum Bridges rdbt take A382 for Bovey Tracey, 1st exit at 2nd rdbt (B3387), 3m left to Haytor Vale*

Dating back over 200 years, this old coaching inn stands in a tiny Dartmoor village below Haytor, the best known of the Dartmoor tors. It's a stunning location, with wonderful surrounding walks, and the nine, upgraded and comfortable en suite bedrooms, all named after Grand National winners, make this well-established, family-run inn a peaceful base for exploring Dartmoor and South Devon's superb coastline.

The old stables recall the pub's strategic position on the road between Widecombe-in-the-Moor and Newton Abbot. The characterful, traditional beamed interior has sturdy old furnishings, plenty of antique tables, settles, prints and paintings, a grandfather clock, and various pieces of china over the two fireplaces, where logs crackle constantly on wild winter days.

Both the classic main bar and the attractive adjoining rooms are popular settings in which to appreciate some good modern British cooking, using top-notch local produce in nicely presented dishes. After a day on the moor, healthy appetites can be satisfied with crab and leek risotto or a bowl of River Teign mussels cooked in garlic and white wine, followed by rump of Devon lamb with dauphinoise potatoes and red wine sauce, or pan-fried halibut on roasted Mediterranean vegetables with tomato pesto. Leave room for a rich chocolate tart, vanilla pannacotta with plum compote, or a platter of West Country cheeses.

Simpler, more traditional lunch dishes include steak and Jail Ale pie, pork and leek sausages with mash and red wine gravy, and cheese ploughman's with chutneys, pickles and crusty bread – best enjoyed alfresco in the sheltered courtyard or in the peaceful garden across the lane. Devon cheese is a particular feature, alongside wine from the Sharpham Vineyard in Totnes and local ales, including Dartmoor Best.

**Open** all day all wk 11-11 (Sun noon-10.30) Closed: 25-26 Dec
**Bar Meals** L served all wk 12-2 booking required Av main course £11
**Restaurant** D served all wk 7-9 booking required Fixed menu price fr £23 Av 3 course à la carte fr £35 ⊕ FREE HOUSE ◼ Otter Bright, Dartmoor Brewery Jail Ale. **Facilities** Children's menu Family room Garden Parking
**Rooms** 9

## ILFRACOMBE *continued*

**Open** all day all wk 10am–mdnt (Sun noon–mdnt) **Bar Meals** L served all wk 12-3 D served all wk 6.30-9 Av main course £7 **Restaurant** L served all wk 12-3 D served all wk 6.30-9 Av 3 course à la carte fr £14 ⊕ PUNCH TAVERNS ◖ Spitfire, Betty Stogs, Courage Best, ♂ Aspall. **Facilities** Children's menu Children's portions Dogs allowed **Notes** ⊗

### KINGSBRIDGE — Map 3 SX74

## The Crabshell Inn

**Embankment Rd TQ7 1JZ**
☎ 01548 852345  📠 01548 852262
**dir:** *A38 towards Plymouth, follow signs for Kingsbridge*

A traditional sailors' watering hole on the Kingsbridge estuary quayside (arrive by boat and you may moor free). As you would expect, the views from the outside tables and from the first-floor Waters Edge Restaurant are wonderful. The extensive menu and specials board range through grills, pies, pasta, jacket potatoes, salads and sandwiches, but the house speciality is fresh fish, with dishes such as monkfish provençale, and scallop and smoked bacon gratin.

**Open** all wk ◖ Bass Bitter, Crabshell Bitter, Old Speckled Hen, Worthington Cream Flow. **Facilities** Play area Family room Dogs allowed Garden Parking

### KINGSKERSWELL — Map 3 SX86

## Barn Owl Inn ♥

**Aller Mills TQ12 5AN** ☎ 01803 872130
**e-mail:** barnowl.allermills@hall-woodhouse.co.uk
**dir:** *Telephone for directions*

Flagged floors, a black-leaded range and oak beams are amongst the many charming original features at this 16th-century former farmhouse. The renovated building, which is handy for Dartmoor and the English Riviera towns, also boasts a high-vaulted converted barn with a minstrels' gallery. Lunchtime snacks include toasties, wraps and baguettes, while the main menu features plenty of traditional pub favourites all washed down with a pint of Tanglefoot or Badgers First Gold.

**Open** all day all wk noon–11 (Sun noon-10.30) Closed: 26 Dec **Bar Meals** food served all day **Restaurant** Fixed menu price fr £4.99 Av 3 course à la carte fr £12 food served all day ⊕ WOODHOUSE INNS ◖ Tanglefoot, Badger First Gold. ♥ 16 **Facilities** Children's menu Children's portions Dogs allowed Garden Parking

### PICK OF THE PUBS

## Bickley Mill Inn ♥

**TQ12 5LN** ☎ 01803 873201
**e-mail:** info@bickleymill.co.uk
**dir:** *From Newton Abbot on A380 towards Torquay. Right at Barn Owl Inn, follow brown tourist signs*

The inn is a family-owned free house occupying a former flour mill, which dates from the 13th century. The beautiful property blends old and new in a fresh contemporary style and comprises an attractive bar, restaurant and rooms. It is located in the wooded Stoneycombe Valley, within convenient reach of Torquay, Newton Abbot and Totnes. An 18th-century former barn, the Millers Room, has been transformed into a function room catering for groups of 25 to 125 guests. Dishes are freshly prepared using quality produce from the southwest. Fish from Brixham is a feature of the daily specials, along with regulars like tomato, roast pepper and basil risotto; baked field mushrooms, Devon Blue cheese and thyme; Moroccan lamb shoulder, couscous, with lemon and mint yoghurt; grilled sea bass fillets, roast fennel, white wine and dill sauce; mango and passionfruit crème brûlée; chocolate and Grand Marnier cheesecake. While perusing the menu enjoy a pint of Otter or Teignworthy ale.

**Open** all wk Mon-Sat 11.30-3 6.30-11 (Sun 6-10.30) Closed: 27-28 Dec & 1 Jan **Bar Meals** L served Mon-Sat 12-2 (Sun 12-2.30) D served Mon-Sat 6.30-9.15 (Sun 6-8.30) **Restaurant** L served Mon-Sat 12-2 (Sun 12-2.30) D served all wk 6.30-9.15 booking required ⊕ FREE HOUSE ◖ Otter Ale, Boddingtons, Teignworthy, Bays. ♥ 9 **Facilities** Children's menu Children's portions Dogs allowed Garden Parking

### KING'S NYMPTON — Map 3 SS61

### PICK OF THE PUBS

## The Grove Inn ♥

**EX37 9ST** ☎ 01769 580406
**e-mail:** enquiry@thegroveinn.co.uk
**dir:** *2.5m from A377 (Exeter to Barnstaple road)*

A true taste of Devon is offered at this 17th-century thatched inn, set in a beautiful conservation village deep in rolling, unspoilt Devon countryside. Real Devon ales (Teignworthy Springtide), real Devon ciders (Sam's Dry) and Devon wines (Sharpham) are on offer to accompany imaginative dishes on changing menus that evolve with the seasons and champion top-notch ingredients from local farmers and artisan producers.

A typical menu may take in Head Mill trout with horseradish cream sauce, village-grown beetroot risotto, or grilled Capricorn goat's cheese salad for starters, with minted Twitchen Farm lamb burger with melted Sharpham brie and chunky chips; Lakeland Farm beef Wellington with dauphinoise potatoes; and North Devon fish and Exmouth mussel stew for main course. For pudding, try the local damson cobbler with clotted cream, or a trio of Parsonage Farm ice creams. The setting is suitable cosy and welcoming – beamed and stone-walled bar and dining areas with rustic furnishings, flagstoned floor, and blazing winter log fires.

**Open** noon-3 6-11 (BH noon-3) Closed: Mon L ex BH **Bar Meals** L served Tue-Sat 12-2 Av main course £12 **Restaurant** L served Tue-Sun 12-2 booking required D served Tue-Sat 7-9 booking required ⊕ FREE HOUSE ◖ Exmoor Ale, Otter Ale, Bath Gem Ale, Teignworthy Springtide, O'Hanlons Firefly ♂ Winkleigh, Sams dry. **Facilities** Children's menu Children's portions Dogs allowed Garden

### KINGSTON — Map 3 SX64

## The Dolphin Inn

**TQ7 4QE** ☎ 01548 810314  📄 01548 810314
**e-mail:** info@dolphininn.eclipse.co.uk
**dir:** *From A379 (Plymouth to Kingsbridge road) take B3233 for Bigbury-on-Sea. Follow brown inn signs*

The Dolphin is just a mile from the beaches of the South Hams and the beautiful Erme Estuary, ideal for walkers, golfers and surfers. This 16th-century inn was originally built as cottages for stone masons working on the village church; now expanded to buildings across the road the owners put up a sign saying 'Drive carefully through the pub'! All the food is home made and the menu includes pies, crab bake, lobster bisque, lamb stew, and stuffed chicken breast. Specials provide daily fish and game dishes.

**Open** all wk noon-3 6-11 (Sun 7-10.30) Closed: Sun eve Winter **Bar Meals** L served Mon-Fri 12-2 (Sat-Sun 12-2.30) D served all wk 6-9 (closed Sun & Mon eve winter) **Restaurant** L served Mon-Fri 12-2 (Sat-Sun 12-2.30) D served all wk 6-9 (closed Sun & Mon eve winter) ⊕ PUNCH TAVERNS ◖ Teignworthy Springtide, Courage Best, Sharp's Doom Bar, Otter. **Facilities** Children's menu Play area Family room Dogs allowed Garden Parking

# PICK OF THE PUBS

## The Holt ❀

**178 High St EX14 1LA ☎ 01404 47707**
**e-mail:** enquiries@theholt-honiton.com
**web:** www.theholt-honiton.com

The Holt is situated in the historic market town of Honiton, and is part of a jigsaw of a local food-and-drink business that puts environmental responsibility at the top of its agenda and traceability at the forefront of its business ethos. Thus the beers come from the McCaig family's Otter Brewery based at nearby Luppit, using barley malted nearby and pure water from the head-springs of the River Otter to produce five quaffable ales. In a similar vein, the pub has its own smokery, where locally sourced poultry, meats, game, fish, shellfish and cheese are prepared.

In this appealing pub-restaurant, the bar is downstairs, busy with time-worn pub tables and chairs and a spread of sofas, amidst which is sewn the open-plan kitchen, providing plenty of activity and buzz; in the candlelit dining area upstairs tables look down on the bar below, so you can still feel totally involved.

The frequently changing menu is supplemented by daily specials and tapas, both at lunchtimes and in the evenings; such inventive cooking has gained The Holt an AA Rosette. Wing in with a starter of smoked pigeon, caramelised chicory tart, pickled beetroot and watercress before settling in to a guinea fowl supreme with bacon, sweetcorn, parsley and mustard sauce or perhaps glazed pork cheek, nose to tail terrine, smoked mash and sherry vinegar sauce, completing the treat with passionfruit shortcake with Greek yoghurt sorbet.

Brewing has been in the family for three generations, and in addition to the beers, the McCraigs have developed a

range of flavoured UK grain spirit vodkas in a bid to provide a natural alternative to the artifically flavoured vodkas often found behind the bar; their 'Traffic Light' three-shooter cocktail is much more than an aperitif!

**Open** 11-3 5.30-mdnt Closed: 25, 26 Dec & 1 Jan, Sun & Mon
**Bar Meals** L served all wk 12-2 D served all wk 7-9.30 Av main course £8
**Restaurant** L served all wk 12-2 booking required D served all wk 7-9.30 booking required Av 3 course à la carte fr £23 ⊕ FREE HOUSE ◀ Otter Bitter, Otter Ale, Otter Bright, Otter Amber ♻ Aspall. **Facilities** Dogs allowed

## KINGSWEAR — Map 3 SX85

### The Ship Inn ♀

**Higher St TQ6 0AG ☎ 01803 752348**
*dir:* Telephone for directions

Historic village pub overlooking the scenic River Dart towards Dartmouth and Dittisham. Located in one of South Devon's most picturesque corners, this tall, character inn is very much a village local with a friendly, welcoming atmosphere inside. Well-prepared fresh food is the hallmark of the menu. Sandwiches, baguettes and pies are available in the bar, while the restaurant menu offers crispy duck with stir-fried vegetables on egg noodles, or oven-baked cod with lemon and lime crust.

**Open** all day all wk noon-mdnt (winter noon-3 6-mdnt) ◀ Greene King IPA, Otter, Adnams, Timothy Taylor, Otter Bright ♂ Aspall. ♀ 12 **Facilities** Family room Dogs allowed Garden

## LIFTON — Map 3 SX38

### PICK OF THE PUBS

### The Arundell Arms ★★★ HL ◉◉ ♀

**PL16 0AA ☎ 01566 784666 📠 01566 784494**
**e-mail:** reservations@arundellarms.com
**web:** www.arundellarms.com
*dir:* 1m off A30 dual carriageway, 3m E of Launceston

An 18th-century creeper-clad inn named after William Arundell, who took over the 'best and most respectable inn in the village' in 1815. Now it's been in Anne Voss-Bark's family for over 40 years, and is renowned among the hunting, shooting and fishing fraternity for some of the best beats in the country; the River Tamar flows along the bottom of the garden, and guests enjoy 20 miles of fishing rights along its banks. The inn exudes warmth and a truly civilised air pervades the interior — not only in the 'locals' bar, with its babble of conversation and simple food at lunchtime, but also in the smarter dining bar which has won two AA Rosettes for its food. Here you'll find an appetiser of chicken, artichoke and rosemary soup; dishes such as an escalope of organic salmon, or a fillet of Aylesbury duck with wild garlic crust; and desserts like caramelised crème brûlée with a mango sorbet and berry syrup.

**Open** all wk 12-3 6-11 ◀ Tribute, Guest Ales ♂ Thatchers, Cornish Rattler. ♀ 9 **Facilities** Dogs allowed Garden Parking **Rooms** 21

## LITTLEHEMPSTON — Map 3 SX86

### Tally Ho Inn

**TQ9 6NF ☎ 01803 862316 📠 01803 862316**
**e-mail:** tally.ho.inn@btconnect.com
*dir:* Off A38 at Buckfastleigh. A381 between Newton Abbot & Totnes

A traditional, family-owned 14th-century thatched inn in a pretty village, with inglenook fireplaces and a flower-filled patio. Local suppliers are the mainstay of seasonal menus offering tiger prawns in ginger tempura butter with chilli jam; slow roasted brisket beef with asparagus, pomme allumette, tarragon and Dijon mustard sauce; butternut squash, roasted red onion and smoked garlic risotto; or home-made steak and kidney pie. Real ales come from Devon breweries.

**Open** noon-3 6.30-11 Closed: 25 Dec, Sun Eve (win) **Bar Meals** L served all wk 12-2 booking required D served all wk 6.30-9 booking required Av main course £10 **Restaurant** Av 3 course à la carte fr £20 ⊕ FREE HOUSE ◀ Exmoor Ale, Teignworthy Brewery Ales, Guinness, guest ales ♂ Thatchers Gold. **Facilities** Children's menu Children's portions Dogs allowed Garden Parking

## LUTON (NEAR CHUDLEIGH) — Map 3 SX97

### The Elizabethan Inn ♀

**Fore St TQ13 0BL ☎ 01626 775425 📠 01626 775151**
**e-mail:** elizabethaninn@btconnect.com
*dir:* Between Chudleigh & Teignmouth

With log fires in winter and a pretty beer garden for warmer days, this welcoming 16th-century free house is a great destination for diners and drinkers alike. Known locally as the Lizzie, the pub offers a good selection of Devon ales, as well as Thatcher's Gold and local Reddaways cider. The pub prides itself in producing good, honest Devon food using the best of local ingredients. The specials board might include home-made lamb and mint sausages; locally farmed steaks; fisherman's pie; or linguine with roasted Mediterranean vegetables.

**Open** all wk 12-3 6-11.30 (Sun all day) Closed: 25-26 Dec, 1 Jan **Bar Meals** L served Mon-Sat 12-2 (Sun 12-2.30) booking required D served all wk 6-9.30 booking required Av main course £8.95 **Restaurant** L served Mon-Sat 12-2 (Sun 12-2.30) booking required D served all wk 6-9.30 booking required Fixed menu price fr £14.50 ⊕ FREE HOUSE ◀ London Pride, Teignworthy Reel Ale, Otter Ale, O'Hanlon's Yellowhammer, Dartmoor IPA ♂ Thatchers Gold, Local Reddaways. ♀ 11 **Facilities** Children's menu Children's portions Dogs allowed Garden Parking

## LYDFORD — Map 3 SX58

### PICK OF THE PUBS

### Dartmoor Inn ◉◉

**EX20 4AY ☎ 01822 820221 📠 01822 820494**
**e-mail:** info@dartmoorinn.co.uk
*dir:* On A386 S of Okehampton

Owners Karen and Philip Burgess have made their mark at this distinctive free house, which Charles Kingsley almost certainly described in his novel *Westward Ho!* The stylish, restrained decor extends through the cosy dining rooms and small bar, where real ales and high class pub classics are on offer. Food is based on seasonal ingredients, sourced locally, and turned into top-notch dishes. In the New England-style restaurant you might start with corned beef terrine with mustard dressing, followed by pan fried lamb's kidneys, bacon, black pudding and red wine sauce. After your meal, you can even browse for beautiful accessories and home ware in the inn's own boutique.

**Open** all day noon-2.30 6.30-11pm Closed: Mon L ex BHs **Bar Meals** L served Tue-Sun 12-2.15 D served all wk 6.30-9.15 ⊕ FREE HOUSE ◀ Otter Ale, Tribute. **Facilities** Dogs allowed Garden Parking

## LYMPSTONE — Map 3 SX98

### The Globe Inn ♀

**The Strand EX8 5EY ☎ 01395 263166**
*dir:* Telephone for directions

Set in the estuary village of Lympstone, this traditional beamed inn has a good local reputation for seafood. The separate restaurant area serves as a coffee bar during the day. Look out for bass fillets with plum sauce; monkfish kebabs; seafood platter; and seafood grill. Weekend music and quiz nights are a feature.

**Open** all wk 10am-3 5.30-mdnt (Sun all day) ◀ London Pride, Otter, Bass ♂ Aspall. ♀ 10 **Facilities** Dogs allowed

## LYNMOUTH — Map 3 SS74

### PICK OF THE PUBS

### Rising Sun Hotel ★★ HL ◉

**Harbourside EX35 6EG**
**☎ 01598 753223 📠 01598 753480**
**e-mail:** reception@risingsunlynmouth.co.uk
*dir:* From M5 junct 25 follow Minehead signs. A39 to Lynmouth

Overlooking Lynmouth's tiny harbour and bay is this 14th-century thatched smugglers' inn. In turn, overlooking them all, are Countisbury Cliffs, the highest in England. The building's long history is evident from the uneven oak floors, crooked ceilings and thick walls. Literary associations are plentiful: R D Blackmore wrote some of his wild Exmoor romance, *Lorna Doone*, here; the poet Shelley is believed to have honeymooned in the garden cottage, and Coleridge stayed too. Immediately behind rises Exmoor Forest and

National Park, home to red deer, wild ponies and birds of prey. With moor and sea so close, game and seafood are in plentiful supply; appearing in dishes such as braised pheasant with pancetta and quince and Braunton greens; and roast shellfish – crab, mussels, clams and scallops in garlic, ginger and coriander. At night the oak-panelled, candlelit dining room is an example of romantic British inn-keeping at its best.

*Rising Sun Hotel*

**Open** all day all wk 11am-mdnt Closed: 25 Dec **Bar Meals** L served all wk 12-2.30 D served all wk 6-9 Av main course £12.95 **Restaurant** D served all wk 7-9 booking required Av 3 course à la carte fr £30 ⊕ FREE HOUSE ◄ Exmoor Gold, Fox, Exmoor Antler ○ Thatchers Gold. **Facilities** Dogs allowed **Rooms** 14

### LYNTON                                   Map 3 SS74

## The Bridge Inn

**Lynbridge Hill EX35 6NR**
☎ 01598 753425     📠 01598 753225
**dir:** *Exit A39 at Barbrook onto B3234. In 1m pub on right just beyond Sunny Lyn camp site*

Attractive 17th-century riverside inn overlooked by National Trust woodlands. In the cellars the remains of 12th-century salmon fishermen's cottages are still visible, and the unusually shaped windows at the front originally belonged to Charles I's hunting lodge at Coombe House, salvaged following flood damage in the 1680s. The 1952 Lynmouth Flood destroyed the Lyn Bridge and car park, but most of the pub survived intact.

**Open** Tue-Sun Closed: Mon & Tue-Thu L Jan-Feb ◄ St. Austell Tribute, Sharp's Doom Bar, Exmoor Fox. **Facilities** Dogs allowed Garden Parking

### MARLDON                                  Map 3 SX86

## The Church House Inn

**Village Rd TQ3 1SL** ☎ 01803 558279   📠 01803 664865
**dir:** *Take Torquay ring road, follow signs to Marldon & Totnes, follow brown signs to pub*

This ancient country inn dates from 1362, when it was a hostel for the builders of the adjoining village church. It was rebuilt in 1740 and many features from that period

still remain including beautiful Georgian windows. These days it has an uncluttered, contemporary feel. Typical lunch offerings include cullen skink, and sausages with red wine gravy and mash. Evening menus include chicken liver pâté with spiced tomato chutney followed by fillet of salmon with a spring onion, mussel and white wine sauce.

**Open** all wk 11.30-2.30 5-11 (Fri-Sat 5-11.30 Sun 12-3 5.30-10.30) **Bar Meals** L served all wk 12-2 D served all wk 6.30-9.30 Av main course £11 **Restaurant** L served all wk 12-2 D served all wk 6.30-9.30 Av 3 course à la carte fr £26 ⊕ FREE HOUSE ◄ Dartmoor Best, Bass, Old Speckled Hen, Greene King IPA, London Pride. **Facilities** Dogs allowed Garden Parking

### MEAVY                                    Map 3 SX56

## The Royal Oak Inn ☺

**PL20 6PJ** ☎ 01822 852944
**e-mail:** sjearp@aol.com
**dir:** *B3212 from Yelverton to Princetown. Right at Dousland to Meavy, past school. Pub opposite village green*

Flagstone floors, oak beams and a welcoming open fire set the scene at this traditional 15th-century free house – the perfect Dartmoor hideaway for drinking and dining. Standing by the village green and close to the shores of Burrator reservoir on the edge of Dartmoor, the inn is popular with cyclists and walkers – 'muddy boots and muddy paws are always welcome'. Local cask ales, ciders and fine wines accompany the carefully sourced ingredients in a menu ranging from lunchtime baguettes, ploughman's and jackets to blackened Cajun chicken, a Dartmoor steak or mushroom and goat's cheese tartlets.

**Open** all wk Mon-Fri 11-3 6-11 (Sat-Sun & May-Sep all day) **Bar Meals** L served Mon-Fri 12-2.30, Sat-Sun 12-3 D served all wk 6-9 Av main course £7 **Restaurant** L served Mon-Fri 12-2.30, Sat-Sun 12-3 D served all wk 6-9 Fixed menu price fr £10 ⊕ FREE HOUSE ◄ Dartmoor Jail Ale, Dartmoor IPA, St Austell Tribute, Royal Oak, Guest ales ○ Westons Scrumpy, Old Rosie, Thatchers Gold. ☺ 12 **Facilities** Children's menu Children's portions Dogs allowed Garden

### MODBURY                                  Map 3 SX65

### PICK OF THE PUBS

## California Country Inn

*See Pick of the Pubs on page 144*

### MOLLAND                                  Map 3 SS82

## The London Inn

**EX36 3NG** ☎ 01769 550269
**dir:** *Telephone for directions*

A 15th-century former coaching inn crammed with inglenooks and bare beams, this inn harks back to an era that has almost disappeared. Its owners passionately believe that Exmoor needs to retain at least one of its

traditional pubs, and this inn, with its parlour and servery bar with an open fireplace and beer and cider straight from the cask, really does them proud. Popular with the shooting and hunting crowd, The London offers traditional home-cooked food made with the best local produce; maybe wood pigeon salad, venison sausages with bubble and squeak and gravy, and jam roly poly. There are two beer gardens so you can take in the beautiful surroundings.

**Open** all wk 12-3 6-11 **Bar Meals** L served all wk 12-3 D served Mon-Sat 6-9 **Restaurant** L served all wk 12-3 booking required D served Mon-Sat 6-9 booking required ⊕ FREE HOUSE ◄ Exmoor Ale, Cotleigh Tawny Bitter ○ Winkleigh Cider. **Facilities** Children's portions Family room Dogs allowed Garden Parking

### MORETONHAMPSTEAD                         Map 3 SX78

## The White Hart Hotel ★★★ HL ◉ ☺

**The Square TQ13 8NF**
☎ 01647 441340     📠 01647 441341
**e-mail:** enquiries@Whitehartdartmoor.co.uk
**dir:** *From A30 at Whiddon Down take A382 for Chagford & Moretonhampstead. Pub in village centre. Parking in 20yds*

Set in the heart of Dartmoor, this Grade II listed building dates from 1639 and has a recently refurbished bar, lounge and brasserie restaurant area for informal dining and drinking. Locally brewed ales are served alongside locally sourced food and dishes include an assiette of fish; asparagus, pea and mint risotto; succulent Devon steaks; and pork and apple sausages, mash and onion gravy. Customers can also call in for morning coffee or afternoon tea.

**Open** all day all wk 11-11 **Bar Meals** L served all wk 12-2.30 D served all wk 6-9.30 Av main course £7.95 **Restaurant** L served all wk 12-2.30 booking required D served all wk 6-9.30 booking required Fixed menu price fr £15.95 Av 3 course à la carte fr £25 ⊕ HART INNS LTD ◄ St Austell Tribute, Otter Ale, Sharp's Doom Bar ○ Thatchers. ☺ 12 **Facilities** Dogs allowed Garden **Rooms** 28

### NEWTON ABBOT                             Map 3 SX87

## The Wild Goose Inn ☺

**Combeinteignhead TQ12 4RA** ☎ 01626 872241
**dir:** *From A380 at Newton Abbot rdbt take B3195 (Shaldon road), signed Milber, 2.5m into village, right at sign*

Set in the heart of the village at the head of a long valley, this charming free house boasts a sunny garden sheltered by the adjacent 14th-century church tower. Originally licensed as the Country House Inn in 1840, it was renamed in the 1960s when nearby geese began intimidating the pub's customers. A good range of real ales and ciders accompanies home-made pub food prepared from local ingredients. Expect dishes such as Torbay mussels, local trout fillet in saffron and vermouth sauce, succulent steaks and beef in red wine.

*continued on page 145*

# PICK OF THE PUBS

# California Country Inn

**MODBURY** Map 3 SX65

California Cross PL21 0SG
☎ 01548 821449 📄 01548 821566
e-mail:
enquiries@californiacountryinn.co.uk
dir: *Telephone for details*

This centuries old inn stands in some of the most tranquil countryside in southern England, just a few miles from Dartmoor to the north and the cliffs and estuaries of the coast to the south, part of the South Devon Area of Outstanding Natural Beauty. In fact, this stretches inland to include the hills and vales seen from the pub's gardens.

Dating from the 14th-century; its unusual name is thought to derive from local adventurers in the mid 19th century who heeded the call to 'go west' and waited at the nearby crossroads for the stage to take them on the first part of their journey to America's west coast.

They must have suffered wistful thoughts of home when recalling their local pub, which retains character, with wizened old beams, exposed dressed-stone walls and a fabulous, huge stone fireplace. Old rural prints and photos, copper kettles, jugs, brasses and many other artefacts add to the rustic charm of the whitewashed pub's atmospheric interior.

The food part of the package is largely sourced from the bounty of the local countryside and waters, with meats from a supplier in nearby Loddiswell and fish from the renowned 'Catch of the Day' in Kingsbridge. Meals can be taken from the bar menu, or indulge in the à la carte menu from the inn's restaurant. Appetizing starters from the latter include pheasant wrapped in Parma ham with wild mushroom and shallot fricassee and crispy leeks or crispy Woolston belly pork with black pudding, apple purée and beetroot salad. Mains range across the board from four cheeses and wild mushroom pasta; roasted loin of lamb with lemon and mint stuffing, ratatouille, garlic creamed potatoes and jus to a medley of local seafood (salmon, lemon sole, scallop and king prawn) or old stalwarts

such as home-made chilli con carne or local mixed sausages, mash, onion gravy and peas.

Carefully selected wines include some from the nearby Sharpham Vineyard, whilst real ales to savour come from the likes of Sharp's brewery.

**Open** all day all wk **Bar Meals** L served Mon-Sat 12-2, Sun 12-2.30 D served Mon-Sat 6-9, Sun 6-8.30 Av main course £10 **Restaurant** L served Sun 12-2 D served Wed-Sun 6-9 booking required Av 3 course à la carte fr £25 ⊕ FREE HOUSE ◢ Guinness, Abbot Ale, London Pride, Sharp's Doom Bar **Facilities** Children's menu Family room Dogs allowed Garden Parking

### NEWTON ABBOT *continued*

**Open** all wk 11-3 5.30-11 (Sun 12-3 7-11) **Bar Meals** L served all wk 12-2 D served all wk 7-9.30 booking required Av main course £8.50 **Restaurant** L served all wk 12-2 D served all wk 7-9.30 booking required ⊕ FREE HOUSE ◀ Otter Ale, Cotleigh, Sharp's Bitter, Skinner's Bitter, Teignworthy, Branscombe, Exe Valley ☼ Skinners Press Gang, Wiscombe Suicider, Milltop Gold. ♀ 10 **Facilities** Children's menu Children's portions Family room Dogs allowed Garden Parking

---

### NEWTON ST CYRES          Map 3 SX89

## The Beer Engine

**EX5 5AX ☎ 01392 851282** 🖷 **01392 851876**
**e-mail:** info@thebeerengine.co.uk
**dir:** *From Exeter take A377 towards Crediton. Signed from A377 towards Sweetham. Pub opp rail station in village*

Originally opened as a railway hotel in 1852, this pretty, whitewashed free house is now acknowledged as one of Devon's leading micro-breweries. Engine ales with names like Piston bitter, Rail ale and Sleeper Heavy evoke the pub's antecedents. With local suppliers listed, expect a wide choice of vegetarian and fresh fish dishes, as well as braised lamb shank, breaded veal escalope, and pan-fried venison sausages on bubble and squeak.

**Open** all day all wk 11am-11pm (Sun noon-10.30) **Bar Meals** L served Mon-Wed 12-2.15, Thu-Sat 3-6 D served all wk 6.30-8.30 Av main course £9 **Restaurant** L served all wk 12-2.15 booking required D served all wk 6.30-8.30 booking required ⊕ FREE HOUSE ◀ Engine Ales: Piston Bitter, Rail Ale, Sleeper Heavy ☼ Stowford Press. **Facilities** Children's menu Dogs allowed Garden Parking

---

### NORTH BOVEY          Map 3 SX78

### PICK OF THE PUBS

## The Ring of Bells Inn ♀

**TQ13 8RB ☎ 01647 440375** 🖷 **01647 440746**
**e-mail:** info@ringofbells.net
**dir:** *1.5m from Moretonhampstead off B3212. 7m S of Whiddon Down junct on A30*

Built in the 13th century to house the stonemasons building the parish church, the thatched Ring of Bells overlooks the green in this idyllic edge of Dartmoor village. Refurbished and back on song since the arrival of new owners in December 2008, the ancient, spruced-up pub is the hub of the community and

draws Dartmoor visitors and walkers in for good food and locally-brewed ales. Served in cosy low-beamed bars, with heavy oak doors, rustic furnishings, crackling winter log fires and evening candlelight, the short daily menu may list roast garlic and sweet potato soup and warm pigeon and black pudding salad for starters. Hearty main dishes might include beer battered cod and chips and a big bowl of mussels with chips, to roast rack of lamb with lemon polenta and tahini dressing, and pork belly with pumpkin risotto. Round off with bread-and-butter pudding. Chef Andy Burkin uses fresh, locally-sourced produce and menus reflect the changing seasons.

**Open** all day all wk Closed: 25 Dec **Bar Meals** L served all wk 12-2.30 (closed Mon in win) booking required D served all wk 6-9 (closed Sun & Mon in win) booking required Av main course £14 **Restaurant** L served all wk 12-2.30 (closed Mon in win) booking required D served all wk 6-9 (closed Sun & Mon in win) booking required ⊕ FREE HOUSE ◀ Otter Ale, St Austell Tribute, Sharps Doom Bar. ♀ 15 **Facilities** Children's portions Family room Dogs allowed Garden

---

### NOSS MAYO          Map 3 SX54

### PICK OF THE PUBS

## The Ship Inn ♀

*See Pick of the Pubs on page 146*

---

### OTTERY ST MARY          Map 3 SY19

## The Talaton Inn

**Talaton EX5 2RQ ☎ 01404 822214** 🖷 **01404 822214**
**dir:** *Take A30 to Fairmile, then follow signs to Talaton*

Run by a brother and sister partnership, this well-maintained, timber-framed 16th-century inn offers a good selection of real ales and malts, and a fine collection of bar games. Specials set menus are available at lunch and dinner. Dishes might include crispy bacon, chicken and brie Caesar salad, braised lamb steak with rosemary, red wine and chive sauce, with Eton mess to finish. At Sunday lunchtimes, as well as the popular roast, there is also a pie and vegetarian choice. There is a patio for summer dining and themed food nights.

**Open** all wk 12-3 7-11 **Bar Meals** L served all wk 12-2 D served Tue-Sat 7-9 **Restaurant** L served all wk 12-2 D served Tue-Sat 7-9 booking required Fixed menu price fr £7.95 Av 3 course à la carte fr £9.25 ⊕ FREE HOUSE ◀ Otter, Fuller's London Pride, O'Hanlon's, Badger Tanglefoot, Seasonal Brew. **Facilities** Children's menu Children's portions Dogs allowed Garden Parking

---

### PARRACOMBE          Map 3 SS64

### PICK OF THE PUBS

## The Fox & Goose ♀

*See Pick of the Pubs on page 147*

---

### PLYMOUTH          Map 3 SX45

## The Fishermans Arms ♀ NEW

**31 Lambhay St, The Barbican PL1 2NN**
**☎ 01752 661457**
**e-mail:** thefishermansarms@ymail.com
**dir:** *At top of Lambhay Hill turn right, pass large car park, 2nd right into Lambhay St*

Plymouth's second oldest pub stands in the Barbican, the city's historic Elizabethan quarter, and one wall is the only surviving part of Plymouth Castle, which was demolished in the 15th century. There is also a 3ft wide tunnel underneath the bar which runs to the shoreline – smugglers perhaps? Devoid of modern-day intrusions, it's a bustling local with log fires, regular quiz nights, tip-top St Austell ales, and good pub food cooked by a finalist in the Great British Pie Competition. Dishes range from ham, egg and chips to crispy belly pork with apple and celeriac purée, and lemon and sage dressing.

**Open** all wk Mon 6pm-11pm Tue-Thu noon-3 6-11 Fri-Sun all day from noon **Bar Meals** L served Tue-Sat 12-2 Sun 12-3 D served all wk 6.30-9.30 Av main course £8 **Restaurant** L served Tue-Sat 12-2 Sun 12-3 D served all wk 6.30-9.30 Av 3 course à la carte fr £23 ⊕ ST AUSTELL ◀ Tribute, HSD, Proper Job ☼ Rattler Apple, Rattler Pear. ♀ 12 **Facilities** Children's portions Dogs allowed

---

### PLYMTREE          Map 3 ST00

## The Blacksmiths Arms ♀ NEW

**EX15 2JU ☎ 01884 277474**
**e-mail:** blacksmithsplymtree@yahoo.co.uk
**dir:** *From A373 (Cullompton to Honiton road) follow Plymtree signs. Pub in village centre*

Visitors often do a double-take here, half-recognising the bar that is modelled on the *EastEnders'* 'Queen Vic'. That's where the similarities end; this heavily beamed cheery, community village inn dispenses a selection of local beers and an appealing, tight menu drawing on Devon's best – rabbit and venison sausage cassoulet is a favourite. Chow down near the log fire in the lively bar where you might here the locals discussing the only pub in the village's past, relax in the superb beer garden or maybe get a touch of exercise on the skittles alley.

**Open** all wk Mon-Fri 6-11 Sat noon-11 Sun noon-10 (Sun noon-4 Oct-Mar) Closed: Mon (Apr-Sep) **Bar Meals** L served Sat-Sun 12-2 D served Tue-Sun 6-9 Av main course £5 **Restaurant** L served Sun 12-2 D served Tue-Sun 6-9 Av 3 course à la carte fr £18 ⊕ FREE HOUSE ◀ O'Hanlons, Otter, Exe Valley, Bays, Exmoor Ales ☼ Stowford Press, Cornish. ♀ 8 **Facilities** Children's menu Children's portions Play area Family room Dogs allowed Garden Parking

# PICK OF THE PUBS

## The Ship Inn ♇

**NOSS MAYO**       Map 3 SX54

**PL8 1EW**
☎ **01752 872387** 📄 **01752 873294**
**e-mail:** ship@nossmayo.com
**web:** www.nossmayo.com
**dir:** *5m S of Yealmpton on River Yealm estuary*

Huddled on Noss Mayo's tidal waterfront on the south bank of the stunning Yealm estuary, this beautifully renovated 16th-century free house is especially popular with sailing enthusiasts. The estuary is surrounded by rolling wooded hills, with the lower trees dipping their branches into its tidal waters. It is very well protected from the storms of the Channel and the Atlantic, making it ideal for both novices and experienced sailors, who can tie up their boats right outside. Walkers, too, throng the bar, and dogs are allowed downstairs.

The deceptively spacious building, refurbished using reclaimed materials such as local stone and English oak, remains cosy thanks to its wooden floors, old bookcases, log fires and dozens of local pictures. Beers from nearby Summerskill's are supported by Butcombe Blonde, as well as a selection from Princetown Breweries.

The ever-changing menu of home-made dishes majors on local produce, especially fish. Stilton and Devon brie are amongst the choices with your ploughman's lunch, whilst alternatives include baguettes and main courses such as warm marinated chicken, bacon and avocado salad. For the hearty three-course appetite, classic starters like duck liver pâté with red onion marmalade, or broccoli and Stilton soup with crusty bread might precede fillet of cod with sun-dried tomato tapenade, creamed potato and roasted cherry tomatoes; fillet steak with pâté crouton, wild mushroom sauce, fries and green vegetables, or leek, blue cheese and walnut pie. Round off with treacle tart and Chantilly cream, or chocolate brownie with vanilla ice cream.

As well as an interesting and reasonably priced global wine choice, a decent list of malts, liqueurs and hot drinks completes the menu, which you can study at leisure while enjoying the great views from the waterside garden.

**Open** all day all wk **Bar Meals** L served Mon-Sat 12-9.30, Sun 12-9 D served Mon-Sat 12-9.30, Sun 12-9 Av main course £14 **Restaurant** L served Mon-Sat 12-9.30, Sun 12-9 D served Mon-Sat 12-9.30, Sun 12-9 Av 3 course à la carte fr £25 ⊕ FREE HOUSE ◀ Tamar, Jail Ale & Butcombe Blonde, Dartmoor IPA. ♇ 13 **Facilities** Dogs allowed Garden Parking

# PICK OF THE PUBS

## The Fox & Goose ♍

**PARRACOMBE**      Map 3 SS64

**EX31 4PE**
☎ 01598 763239   📄 01598 763621
**web:**
www.foxandgoose-parracombe.co.uk
**dir:** *1m from A39 between Blackmoor Gate (2m) & Lynton (6m). Signed to Parracombe. Fox & Goose sign on approach*

Once just a couple of tiny thatched cottages serving the local farming community, this imposing Victorian building was changed beyond recognition when it was rebuilt at the end of the 19th century. The trigger was the arrival of the legendary narrow gauge Lynton and Barnstaple Railway, which linked Parracombe with the outside world in 1898. Later, in 1925, the village's narrow street was sidelined by an early bypass, which may have contributed to the closure of the railway just ten years later.

Through all this, the village has remained unspoilt and the pub continues to thrive. Locals and visitors alike enjoy local Cotleigh and Exmoor ales, as well as good home-made food listed on the blackboard menus. Food is served in the homely bar and restaurant, adorned with farm memorabilia and old village photographs, or in the paved courtyard garden overlooking the river.

Menus may champion meat and seasonal game from surrounding farms and estates, as well as fish landed locally along the North Devon coast. Lobster, for example, is caught off Lundy Island, or there could be grilled lemon sole fillets with broccoli, lemon and parsley; and halibut steak, served on a bed of creamed leeks. Meat-lovers will not be disappointed, however. Main course choices feature prime lamb chops with seasonal vegetables, tomatoes and mint gravy, and venison steak served on a bed of spiced red cabbage with cherry vine tomatoes, rich redcurrant gravy and parsnip crisps. Vegetarians aren't forgotten either, with a choice of interesting dishes that includes fresh egg tagliatelle topped with home-made tomato, mozzarella and basil sauce, served with garlic bread. But leave room for indulgent desserts like hot lemon sponge pudding with lemon sauce and clotted cream, and chocolate peppermint pot.

**Open** all day all wk **Bar Meals** L served all wk 12-2 D served 6-9 (Sun 7-9) **Restaurant** L served 12-2 D served 6-9 (Sun 7-9) 🛢 FREE HOUSE ◀ Cotleigh Barn Owl, Dartmoor Best, Exmoor Fox, Guinness ♂ Winkleigh. ♍ 10 **Facilities** Children's menu Dogs allowed Garden Parking

## PORTGATE — Map 3 SX48

### PICK OF THE PUBS

### The Harris Arms ♀

EX20 4PZ ☎ 01566 783331 📠 01566 783359
e-mail: info@theharrisarms.co.uk
dir: From A30 at Broadwoodwidger/Roadford Lake exit follow signs to Lifton then for Portgate

This 16th-century inn, with wonderful views to Brent Tor, certainly lives up to its promotional strapline: 'Eat real food and drink real wine'. Located on the old A30 close to the boundary between Devon and Cornwall, it's an accessible spot for honest food with substance and style, plus real ales and excellent wines. Owners Rowena and Andy Whiteman have previously run vineyards in France and New Zealand, so their wine list, with over 150 wines, is both eclectic and extensive; twenty are served by the glass. The pub's reputation for excellent food, which reaches far beyond the local area, is built on exact cooking and locally-sourced ingredients. Examples from the specials board may include starters such as a bowl of Fowey River mussels; grilled marinated Cornish sardines; or griddled fresh Cornish squid. Main dishes continue the emphasis on good ingredients in plates of roasted halibut fillet, and vegetarian options such as spinach and ricotta cheese torte.

Open Tue-Sun L Closed: Mon & Sun eve Bar Meals L served Tue-Sun 12-2 booking required D served Tue-Sat 6.30-9 booking required Restaurant L served Tue-Sun 12-2 booking required D served Tue-Sat 6.30-9 booking required Av 3 course à la carte fr £25 ⊕ FREE HOUSE ◀ Sharp's Doom Bar, Otter Ale, Bays Best. ♀ 20 Facilities Children's menu Children's portions Dogs allowed Garden Parking

## RATTERY — Map 3 SX76

### Church House Inn ♀

TQ10 9LD ☎ 01364 642220 📠 01364 642220
e-mail: ray.hardy@btconnect.com
dir: 1m from A38 Exeter to Plymouth Rd & 0.75m from A385 Totnes to South Brent Rd

This venerable inn dates from 1028 and its interior burgeons with brasses, bare beams, large fireplaces and other historic features. Some customers encounter the wandering spirit of a monk; fortunately he seems to be friendly. In the character dining room, the menu includes fresh fish (devilled whitebait, crab mornay), as well as

Stilton and vegetable crumble; the Church House Inn fry-up; and rump steak and scampi combo. There is a lawn beer garden and patio to enjoy in warmer months.

Open all wk 11-2.30 6-11 (Sun noon-3 6-10.30) Bar Meals L served Mon-Sat 11.30-2, Sun 12-2 booking required D served all wk 6.30-9 booking required Av main course £9 Restaurant L served Mon-Sat 11.30-2, Sun 12-2 booking required D served all wk 6.30-9 booking required ⊕ FREE HOUSE ◀ Princetown Jail Ale, Butcombe Gold, Otter Ale, Dartmoor Best Bitter ♂ Thatchers Gold, Thatchers Katy. ♀ 10 Facilities Children's menu Children's portions Dogs allowed Garden Parking

## ROCKBEARE — Map 3 SY09

### PICK OF THE PUBS

### Jack in the Green Inn ◉◉ ♀

See Pick of the Pubs on opposite page

## SALCOMBE — Map 3 SX73

### PICK OF THE PUBS

### The Victoria Inn ♀

Fore St TQ8 8BU ☎ 01548 842604 📠 01548 844201
e-mail: info@victoriainn-salcombe.co.uk
dir: In town centre, overlooking estuary

Tim and Liz Hore run this friendly and inviting pub in the centre of town, keeping the log fire roaring in winter, and in milder weather welcoming mums, dads, children and pets to the huge family garden with its shady terrace and enclosed children's play area. The bar presents a veritable smörgåsbord of St Austell ales, in addition to a diverse selection of wines and spirits; if you have something to celebrate, champagne is served by the glass as well as the bottle. The first-floor restaurant gives stunning views of the pretty harbour and fishing boats bringing in the catch of the day. So expect to find an open sandwich of Salcombe white crabmeat; starters such as smoked haddock kedgeree or pan-fried West Country scallops; and a heart-warming selection of main dishes: sautéed pork fillet; chef's own steak and kidney pudding; and the inn's own 'scrummy' fish pie.

Open all day all wk 11.30am-11pm (Fri-Sat 11.30am-11.30pm) Closed: 25 Dec pm Bar Meals L served all wk 12-2.30 D served all wk 6-9 Av main course £9.95 ⊕ ST AUSTELL BREWERY ◀ St Austell Tribute, Black Prince, Proper Job IPA ♂ Rattler. ♀ 20 Facilities Children's portions Play area Dogs allowed Garden

## SHEEPWASH — Map 3 SS40

### Half Moon Inn

EX21 5NE ☎ 01409 231376 📠 01409 231673
e-mail: info@halfmoonsheepwash.co.uk
dir: From M5 take A30 to Okehampton then A386, at Hatherleigh, left onto A3072, after 4m right for Sheepwash

A very popular venue for anglers, this white-painted inn overlooking the village square in a remote Devon village is a Grade II listed building with fishing rights for ten miles of the River Torridge. Inside you'll find slate floors and a huge inglenook fireplace where a log fire burns in cooler weather. Bar snacks are available at lunchtime and a set menu of traditional English fare at dinner.

Open all wk 11-3 6-11.30 ◀ Greene King Ruddles Best Bitter, St Austell Tribute, Bombardier ♂ Thatchers Gold. Facilities Dogs allowed Parking

## SIDMOUTH — Map 3 SY18

### PICK OF THE PUBS

### The Blue Ball ★★★★★ INN ♀

See Pick of the Pubs on page 151

### PICK OF THE PUBS

### Dukes ★★★★ INN ♀

See Pick of the Pubs on page 152

## SLAPTON — Map 3 SX84

### PICK OF THE PUBS

### The Tower Inn

Church Rd TQ7 2PN ☎ 01548 580216
e-mail: towerinn@slapton.org
dir: Off A379 S of Dartmouth, turn left at Slapton Sands

Tucked away in the heart of Slapton village, this 14th-century free house owes its name to the ruined tower of the Collegiate Chantry of St Mary, which overlooks the award-winning walled garden. Approached down a narrow lane, the pub is a fascinating series of low-ceilinged, interconnecting rooms with stone walls and fireplaces, beams, pillars and pews. There are open fires and candlelit dinners in winter, and the inn is a haven for lovers of real ales, local ciders and fine wines. The menus are based on locally produced ingredients including Devon beef and smoked fish from Dartmouth. Lunchtime brings a sandwich selection on locally baked bread, as well as hot dishes like slow-roast belly of pork with confit apples and crackling. The dinner menu might feature local seafood bouillabaisse; local rump steak with tomato and mushroom Provençale; and grilled courgette, tomato and bean salad with marinated halloumi.

*continued on page 150*

# PICK OF THE PUBS

## Jack in the Green Inn

**London Rd EX5 2EE**
☎ **01404 822240** 🖨 **01404 823445**
**e-mail:** info@jackinthegreen.uk.com
**web:** www.jackinthegreen.uk.com
**dir:** *From M5 take old A30 towards Honiton, signed Rockbeare*

Eighteen years on and Paul Parnell, the 'well travelled, rosy-cheeked rugby aficionado' owner of this unassuming, white-painted roadside inn, continues to improve its well-deserved reputation for upmarket modern pub food, recently adding a new state-of-the-art kitchen and further developing his links with local artisan producers. He's a passionate foodie and top-drawer, locally-sourced raw ingredients underpin chef Matthew Mason's innovative menus, be it Carolyn Bellinger's free range chickens, game from local shoots, or salad leaves and seasonal vegetables grown within six miles of the pub. So, it's a cracking award winning dining destination with

two AA Rosettes and a simple philosophy to serve the best of Devon's produce in stylish surroundings — neat open-plan bar with wood-burning stoves and leather armchairs, and a warren of cosy dining rooms adorned with fresh flowers and Simon Drew prints.

Simple pub classics are deliciously updated, even the humble ploughman's is given the VIP treatment, and a prawn cocktail, for example, is poshed-up with slow-roasted tomatoes and 'Bloody Mary' sauce. For a 'Totally Devon' experience, kick off with braised Kenniford Farm pork belly with black pudding and apple, then follow with rack of Whimple lamb with honey-roast garlic purée and basil mash, and finish with a plate of Quicke's cheddar cheeses with home-made pickle.

Alternatives may include Lyme Bay crab salad with herb mayonnaise and shellfish vinaigrette or Jerusalem artichoke soup for starters, with main course options like duck breast with fondant potato, poached rhubarb and juniper, line-caught pollack with watercress cream sauce, and marinated chicken with pea and mint risotto. Scott's twist on the 'Jaffa Cake' makes for an intriguing finale. Why not push the boat out and experience the new tasting menu, which showcases the

superb local ingredients. The wine list offers over 100 bins, each selected for character and excellent value. There is a spacious courtyard for alfresco dining.

**Open** all wk 11-3 5.30-11 (Sun noon-11) Closed: 25 Dec-5 Jan
**Bar Meals** L served Mon-Sat 12-2, Sun 12-9 D served Mon-Sat 6-9.30, Sun 12-9 Av main course £15
**Restaurant** L served Mon-Sat 12-2, Sun12-9 D served Mon-Sat 6-9.30, Sun 12-9 Fixed menu price fr £25 Av 3 course à la carte fr £39.50 🍺 FREE HOUSE 🛢 Otter Ale, Sharp's Doom Bar, Butcombe Bitter ♂ Dragon Tears, Luscombe, St Georges. ♀ 12
**Facilities** Children's menu Family room Garden Parking

## SLAPTON *continued*

**Open** 12-3 6-11 Closed: 1st 2wks Jan, Mon winter **Bar Meals** L served all wk 12-2 D served all wk 7-9 Av main course £14.95 **Restaurant** L served all wk 12-2 D served all wk 7-9 Av 3 course à la carte fr £25 ⊕ FREE HOUSE ◀ Butcombe Bitter, St Austell Tribute, Otter Bitter, Otter Ale, guest ales ♂ Sharps Orchard. **Facilities** Children's menu Children's portions Family room Dogs allowed Garden Parking

### SOURTON  Map 3 SX59

## The Highwayman Inn

EX20 4HN ☎ 01837 861243  📄 01837 861196
**e-mail:** info@thehighwaymaninn.net
**dir:** *On A386 (Okehampton to Tavistock road). Exit A30 towards Tavistock. Pub 4m from Okehampton, 12m from Tavistock*

A strong contender for the title 'Britain's most unusual inn'. The Highwayman is indeed a fascinating old place full of legend, strange architecture, eccentric furniture and obscure bric-a-brac. Since 1959 the vision of Welshman John 'Buster' Jones, and now run by his daughter Sally, it is made from part of a galleon, wood hauled from Dartmoor's bogs, and Gothic church arches. Popular with holidaymakers and international tourists, the drinks include real farmhouse cider and organic wines, while the menu offers pasties, platters and nibbles. Outside the kids will enjoy Mother Hubbard's Shoe, and the Pumpkin House.

**Open** 11.30-2 6-10.30 (Sun 12-2 7-10.30) Closed: 25-28 Dec **Bar Meals** L served all wk 12-1.45 D served all wk 6-9 Av main course £4 ⊕ FREE HOUSE ◀ St Austell Duchy ♂ Grays. **Facilities** Play area Family room Dogs allowed Garden Parking **Notes** ☺

### SOUTH POOL  Map 3 SX74

## The Millbrook Inn ♥

TQ7 2RW ☎ 01548 531581
**e-mail:** info@millbrookinnsouthpool.co.uk
**dir:** *Take A379 from Kingsbridge to Frogmore then E for 2m to South Pool*

This quaint 16th-century village pub is cosy and unspoilt inside, with open fires, fresh flowers, cushioned wheelback chairs, and beams adorned with old banknotes and clay pipes. Set at the head of the creek, its summer barbecues attract small boats from Salcombe and Kingsbridge. Fish is a speciality, and there's a peaceful sunny rear terrace overlooking a stream with ducks. At least two real ales always kept.

**Open** all wk 12-11 (Sun 12-10.30) **Bar Meals** L served all wk 12-2 D served Mon-Sat 7-9 ⊕ FREE HOUSE ◀ Otter Ale, Redrock ♂ Thatchers Heritage. ♥ 10
**Facilities** Children's portions Dogs allowed Garden

### SOUTH ZEAL  Map 3 SX69

## Oxenham Arms ★★★★ INN ♥

EX20 2JT ☎ 01837 840244  📄 01837 840791
**e-mail:** relax@theoxenhamarms.co.uk
**dir:** *Just off A30 4m E of Okehampton, in village centre*

Probably built by monks in the 12th century, this inn on the edge of Dartmoor is one of the oldest in England. First licensed in 1477, the pub retains a historical feel with beams, flagstone floors, blazing fires and a prehistoric monolith – archaeologists believe the monks just built around it. Burgoynes restaurant serves an eclectic seasonal menu based on fine local produce. Expect the likes of a choice of home-made pâtés, followed by coq au vin, Cornish crab salad, and The Oxenham chicken curry.

**Open** all wk 10.30-3.30 5-11 ◀ Sharp's Doom Bar, Otter, guest. ♥ 8 **Facilities** Dogs allowed Garden Parking **Rooms** 7

### SOWTON  Map 3 SX99

## The Black Horse Inn ♥ NEW

Old Honiton Rd EX5 2AN ☎ 01392 366649
**e-mail:** enquiries@blackhorseinnexeter.co.uk
**dir:** *On old A30 from Exeter towards Honiton, 0.5m from M5 junct 29; 1m from Exeter International Airport. Inn between Sowton & Clyst Honiton*

Recent refurbishment has seen this village roadside pub emerge as a fresh, contemporary dining inn, with crisp decor and a relaxed atmosphere. Using produce from local suppliers, the menu offers great specials adding to a base of wholesome favourites. Pan-fried Lyme Bay scallops are the lead-in to supreme of guinea fowl on a confit of leek and bacon with cider and wholegrain mustard sauce; or perhaps a panini or a lamb balti will hit the spot. Try the local Otter ale or from the decent hand of wines by the glass while sitting on the terrace on warmer days.

**Open** all wk 11.45-2.30 5-11 **Bar Meals** L served all wk 11.45-2 D served all wk 6-9 Av main course £9.95 **Restaurant** L served all wk 11.45-2 D served all wk 6-9 Av 3 course à la carte fr £20 ⊕ FREE HOUSE ◀ Otter, 6X, Guinness ♂ Thatchers. ♥ 11 **Facilities** Children's menu Garden Parking

### SPREYTON  Map 3 SX69

### PICK OF THE PUBS

## The Tom Cobley Tavern

EX17 5AL ☎ 01647 231314
**dir:** *From A30 at Whiddon Down take A3124 N. Take 1st right after services then 1st right over bridge.*

This peaceful, whitewashed pub stands in a sleepy Dartmoor village and draws the crowds in summer due to its name and associations with Widecombe Fair. It was from this pub, one day in 1802, a certain Thomas Cobley and his companions set forth for Widecombe Fair, an event immortalised in song, and his cottage still stands in the village. The pub remains a traditional village local and the unspoilt main bar has a roaring log fire, cushioned settles and dispenses a mind-boggling range of 20 tip-top real ales straight from the cask, for which it has won many awards. Typically, order a pint of Cotleigh Tawny Ale or Sharp's Doom Bar to accompany some hearty pub food, which ranges from simple bar snacks to decent pies, salads, duck and fish dishes, as well as a good vegetarian selection. Finish off with one of the great ice creams or sorbets. Summer alfresco drinking can be enjoyed on the pretty flower-decked gravel terrace or in the rear garden with its far-reaching views.

**Open** 12-3 6-11 (Sun 12-4 7-11 Mon 6.30-11 Fri-Sat 6-1am) Closed: Mon L **Bar Meals** L served Tue-Sat 12-3 D served Sun-Thu 7-10 Av main course £6 **Restaurant** L served all wk 12-3 booking required D served all wk 7-10 Fixed menu price fr £10 ⊕ FREE HOUSE ◀ Cotleigh Tawny Ale, Doom Bar, Tribute, Otter Ale, Proper Job, ♂ Winkleigh Cider, Stowford Press. **Facilities** Dogs allowed Garden Parking

### STOCKLAND  Map 4 ST20

### PICK OF THE PUBS

## The Kings Arms Inn

EX14 9BS ☎ 01404 881361  📄 01404 881387
**e-mail:** info@thekingsarmsinn.org.uk
**dir:** *Off A30 to Chard, 6m NE of Honiton*

Set in the village of Stockland within the Blackdown Hills, this traditional 16th-century thatched, whitewashed former coaching inn is a haven for walkers and a good base for exploring Lyme Regis and the Jurassic coast. Pass through the impressive flagstone entrance and you'll encounter two interesting features - a medieval oak screen and an original bread oven. Locals and visitors in the bar can enjoy Otter and Exmoor real ales, as well as pub food using local suppliers. The bar menu might include sandwiches, ploughman's and specials such as pan-fried lamb's liver and crispy bacon with mashed potato and onion gravy, or steak, mushroom and Guinness pie.

*continued on page 153*

# PICK OF THE PUBS

## The Blue Ball ★★★★ INN

SIDMOUTH Map 3 SY18

**Stevens Cross, Sidford EX10 9QL**
☎ **01395 514062** 📠 **01395 519584**
**e-mail:** rogernewton@blueballinn.net
**web:** www.blueballinn.net
**dir:** *M5 junct 30 exit to A3052. Through Sidford towards Lyme Regis, on left after village, approx 13m*

Painstakingly rebuilt after a disastrous fire destroyed the building in 2006, this marvellous 14th-century thatched, cob-and-flint pub has been run by the Newton family since 1912. Roger and Linda Newton sourced old furniture, pictures and memorabilia to re-capture the unique atmosphere of the original inn. They also added contemporary-styled en suite bedrooms, including a ground floor disabled room, as well as a function room with full conference facilities.

The new-look inn is a hugely attractive and lovingly maintained building, festooned with colourful hanging baskets in summer, when the patio and landscaped gardens come into their own. Arrive early in winter to bag a seat by one of the three log fires within the rambling carpeted bars, which specialise in hand-pumped cask conditioned ales.

The food bar and large family dining area offer extensive menus, beginning at 8am with a tempting breakfast choice – fruit juice, fresh fruit and cereal; followed, perhaps, by poached smoked haddock; eggs Benedict; or the full cooked English.

Later in the day, the main menu offers starters like sweet potato and parsnip soup with walnut bread, and Tregida smoked salmon and prawn mousse purse with dressed rocket. Main course options are just as appetising, and typical choices include lemon sole fillets with lime and chilli-scented vegetables in Parma ham; grilled fillet steak; and roasted vegetables in tomato and basil sauce with penne pasta and Parmesan.

Within easy reach of the M5, A303 and Exeter, and just minutes from stunning walks along the Devon coastline, the Blue Ball is an ideal base for exploring Devon, or for stopping over en route to the west.

**Open** all day all wk Closed: 25 Dec eve **Bar Meals** L served all wk 12-3 D served all wk 6-9 Av main course £10 **Restaurant** L served all wk 12-3 D served all wk 6-9 ⊕ PUNCH TAVERNS ◗ Otter Bitter, Tribute, John Smiths, Guest Ale Ŏ Stowford Press. ♟ 13 **Facilities** Children's menu Play area Family room Dogs allowed Garden Parking **Rooms** 9

# PICK OF THE PUBS

## Dukes ★★★★ INN 🍷

**SIDMOUTH** Map 3 SY18

**The Esplanade EX10 8AR**
**☎ 01395 513320 📠 01395 519318**
**e-mail:** dukes@hotels-sidmouth.co.uk
**dir:** *M5 junct 30 onto A3052, take 1st exit to Sidmouth on right then left onto Esplanade*

Situated at the heart of Sidmouth town centre on the beautiful Regency Esplanade, Dukes might be a contemporary inn but its values are traditional. The interior is stylish and lively, with a relaxed continental feel in the bar and public areas. In fine weather the patio garden overlooking the sea is perfect for soaking up the sun while tasting a mid-morning Italian freshly ground coffee and home-baked pastry; a little later on, sit out with your pint of Branscombe's or Burrow Hill cider, or one of the 20 wines served by the glass. Varied menu choices include traditional English-style favourites, fresh fish from Brixham and Lyme Bay, and prime meats from West Country farms.

Lunch options include smoked mackerel kedgeree; chicken and tarragon tagliatelli; roasted onion and cheese quiche; and a lamb and sweet mint burger. If you just want a snack, possibilities range from stone-baked pizzas to sandwiches made from hand-cut locally baked white or granary bread: crab and mayonnaise; brie and cranberry; and roasted pork with cider chutney are three options. Loaded nachos, home-made jacket wedges and garlic bread are always popular, but it may be wise to hold back for a Devon cream tea later.

After a day breathing sea air, the dinner choices can be as robust as your appetite. You could start with chicken and apricot rillette, or locally smoked salmon; and continue with pan-fried marinated venison; or Creedy carver duck confit. Desserts, such as sticky toffee pudding or caramelised apple and cider trifle, are all made on the premises. Sundays mean traditional roasts – topside of West Country beef, leg of lamb, loin of pork.

Refurbished bed and breakfast accommodation is available, with most rooms overlooking the bay; all are en suite and come with free Wi-fi.

**Open** all day all wk **Bar Meals** L served Sun-Thu 12-9, Fri-Sat 12-9.30 D served Sun-Thu 12-9, Fri-Sat 12-9.30 Av main course £11.50 **Restaurant** L served Sun-Thu 12-9, Fri-Sat 12-9.30 booking required D served Sun-Thu 12-9, Fri-Sat 12-9.30 booking required Av 3 course à la carte fr £20 FREE HOUSE Branscombe Vale Branoc & Summa That, O'Hanlon's Firefly, Otter Ale, Yeovil Ale Stowford Press, Burrow Hill. 🍷 20 **Facilities** Children's menu Play area Dogs allowed Garden Parking **Rooms** 13

**STOCKLAND** *continued*

The restaurant offers other choices: pan-fried scallops with black pudding and beetroot purée, slow-roasted belly pork served on champ with an apple and elderflower sauce, and vegetarian options such as roasted butternut squash, spinach and ricotta pie. Look out for the lively annual Stockland Fair.

**Open** all wk 11-3 6-11 (Sun 12-3 6.30-10.30) **Bar Meals** L served Mon-Sat 12-2 Av main course £8.95 **Restaurant** L served all wk 12-2 booking required D served all wk 6.30-9 booking required Fixed menu price fr £9.95 ⊕ FREE HOUSE ◀ Otter Ale, Exmoor Ale, Otter Amber ♂ Thatchers. **Facilities** Children's portions Dogs allowed Garden Parking

### STOKE FLEMING     Map 3 SX84

## The Green Dragon Inn ♥

Church Rd TQ6 0PX
☎ 01803 770238 ▤ 01803 770238
**e-mail:** pcrowther@btconnect.com
**dir:** *Off A379 (Dartmouth to Kingsbridge coast road) opposite church*

An ancient pub built by masons labouring on the nearby church, first recorded as purveying ales in 1607. The current landlord, a keen solo sailor, has turned the interior into a haven of boating memorabilia, including charts, flags, sextants and sailing pictures. Aspall ciders back up the real ales in the bar, while the reasonably priced menu includes unusual options such as manuka smoked duck; Molly Parkin (sliced parsnips layered with tomatoes, cheese and cream); and chorizo and bean stew.

**Open** all wk **Bar Meals** L served all wk 12-2 D served all wk 6.30-8.30 Av main course £10 ⊕ HEAVITREE ◀ Otter, Tribute, guest ale ♂ Aspall. ♥ 10 **Facilities** Children's menu Children's portions Play area Dogs allowed Garden Parking

### STRETE     Map 3 SX84

### PICK OF THE PUBS

## Kings Arms ⊚ ♥

Dartmouth Rd TQ6 0RW
☎ 01803 770377 ▤ 01803 771008
**e-mail:** kingsarms_devon_fish@hotmail.com
**dir:** *On A379 (Dartmouth-Kingsbridge road), 5m from Dartmouth*

You can't miss this striking, 18th-century pub, with its unique cast-iron balcony, as it stands smack beside the coast road and the South West coast path passes the front door. Pop in for a pint of Otter Ale, bag a seat by the fire in the traditional, terracotta-walled bar, or head up the few steps into the light and airy contemporary-styled restaurant, replete with modern artwork and stunning views across Start Bay. Chef Rob Dawson's motto is 'keep it fresh, keep it simple' and on his daily lunch and dinner menus you'll find

wonderfully fresh seafood, simply prepared with some modern twists, including crab, lobster and fish from a local boat (the boat trawls exclusively for the pub once a week). At lunch, tuck into delicious fish soup with saffron and rouille, a plate of smoked sprats, or smoked haddock and rocket fishcake with wholegrain mustard sauce. Evening choices extend to cod with local clams, peas and asparagus, red gurnard with scallion mash and roasted red pepper cream, and sirloin steak with Café de Paris butter. In summer, head for the flower-filled garden and dine alfresco overlooking the bay.

**Open** 11.30-3 6-11 (Sat-Sun 11.30-11) Closed: Mon winter **Bar Meals** L served Mon-Fri 12-2, Sat-Sun 11.30-11 booking required D served Mon-Fri 6.30-9, Sat-Sun 11.30-11 booking required Av main course £12 **Restaurant** L served Tue-Fri 12-2, Sat-Sun 11.30-11 booking required D served Tue-Fri 6.30-9, Sat Sun 11.30-11 booking required Av 3 course à la carte fr £24 ⊕ HEAVITREE ◀ Otter Bitter, Adnams Bitter, Guinness ♂ Aspall. ♥ 15 **Facilities** Dogs allowed Garden Parking

### THURLESTONE     Map 3 SX64

## The Village Inn ♥

TQ7 3NN ☎ 01548 563525
**e-mail:** enquiries@thurlestone.co.uk
**dir:** *Take A379 from Plymouth towards Kingsbridge, at Bantham rdbt straight over onto B3197, then right into a lane signed Thurlestone, 2.5m*

Built in the 16th century as a farmhouse, this old pub prides itself on good service, well-kept ales and decent food. Like the nearby Thurlestone Hotel, it has been owned by the Grose family for over a century. Seafood is a speciality, with Salcombe crabmeat, River Exe mussels and other local fish and shellfish to choose from on the seasonal menus. Other possibilities are Cajun roasted chicken breast, sirloin and rump steaks, and beef burgers.

**Open** all wk 11.30-3 6-11.30 (Sun & summer all day) **Bar Meals** L served Mon-Sat 12-2.30, Sun 12-4 D served Mon-Sat 6.30-9.30, Sun 7-9 ⊕ FREE HOUSE ◀ Palmers IPA, Interbrew Bass, Sharp's Doom Bar, guest ale ♂ Heron Valley. ♥ 10 **Facilities** Children's menu Family room Dogs allowed Garden Parking

### TIPTON ST JOHN     Map 3 SY09

### PICK OF THE PUBS

## The Golden Lion Inn ♥

*See Pick of the Pubs on page 154*

### TOPSHAM     Map 3 SX98

### PICK OF THE PUBS

## Bridge Inn

Bridge Hill EX3 0QQ ☎ 01392 873862
**e-mail:** su3264@eclipse.co.uk
**dir:** *M5 junct 30 follow Sidmouth signs, in approx 400yds right at rdbt onto A376 towards Exmouth. In 1.8m cross mini-rdbt. Right at next mini rdbt to Topsham. 1.2m, cross River Clyst. Inn on right*

This 'museum with beer' is substantially 16th century, although its constituent parts vary considerably in age. Most of the fabric is local stone, while the old brewhouse at the rear is traditional Devon cob. Four generations of the same family have run it since great-grandfather William Gibbings arrived in 1897, and it remains eccentrically and gloriously old fashioned – mobile phones are definitely out. Usually around ten real ales from local and further flung breweries are served straight from their casks, the actual line-up varying by the week. There are no lagers and only a few wines, two from a local organic vineyard. Traditional bar food includes ploughman's, pasties, sandwiches and soup, all made with local ingredients, while in the evenings there's chunky pork pie with home-made coleslaw. Queen Elizabeth II visited in 1998, believed to be the only time she has officially stepped inside an English pub.

**Open** all wk 12-2 6-10.30 (Sun 7-10.30) **Bar Meals** L served all wk 12-2 Av main course £6.90 ⊕ FREE HOUSE ◀ Branscombe Vale-Branoc, Adnams Broadside, Exe Valley, O`Hanlons, Blackawton, Teignworthy. **Facilities** Dogs allowed Garden Parking Notes ⊚

## The Lighter Inn ♥

The Quay EX3 0HZ ☎ 01392 875439 ▤ 01392 876013
**e-mail:** lighterinn.topsham@hall-woodhouse.co.uk
**dir:** *Telephone for directions*

The imposing 17th-century customs house on Topsham Quay has been transformed into a popular waterside inn. A strong nautical atmosphere is reinforced with pictures, ship's instruments and oars beneath the pub's wooden ceilings, and the attractive quayside sitting area is popular in summer. Dishes may include whole sea bass or plaice, steaks, curries and salads, or steak, ale and mushroom pie.

**Open** all wk 11-11 (Sun noon-10.30) ◀ Badger Best, Badger Tanglefoot, Sussex, Hopping Hare. ♥ 12 **Facilities** Family room Dogs allowed Parking

# PICK OF THE PUBS

# The Golden Lion Inn ♉

**TIPTON ST JOHN**          Map 3 SY09

**EX10 0AA ☎ 01404 812881**
**e-mail:** info@goldenliontipton.co.uk
**web:** www.goldenliontipton.co.uk

Locally brewed Otter ales are the order of the day at Franky and Michelle Teissier's inviting pub situated in a picturesque village, where Art Deco prints vie for attention with Tiffany lamps and paintings by Devonian and Cornish artists. The pub retains that traditional pub feel with low wooden beams, stone interior walls and a blazing log fire in winter.

The Teissiers' penchant for British, Mediterranean and rustic French cooking translates on the lunchtime menu into chunky fish soup; crevettes in garlic butter; goat's cheese salad with Italian ham; smoked duck salad with onion marmalade; breaded plaice and chips; and steak and kidney pudding with a suet crust. The French influence comes through particularly strongly on the dinner version, as illustrated by starters of escargots de Bourgogne; and scallops Marseillaise, alongside the less Gallic prawns in filo with chilli jam, and smoked duck salad. Breast of chicken with light sherry and cream sauce might follow, or there could be pork Normande, namely pork tenderloin with creamy cider and apple sauce; marinated lamb kebab; griddled breast of duck with balsamic plum sauce; and prime local fillet steak with port and Stilton sauce.

With the seaside town of Sidmouth just down the road, you can virtually bank on daily specials of fresh fish and seafood, such as sea bass stuffed with cream cheese and sage; monkfish kebabs; and lobster in garlic butter. If you're a vegetarian, you have plenty of choice, from vegetable lasagne to butter bean cassoulet. White and granary bread sandwiches are filled with roast beef, chicken and mayonnaise, home-made gravadlax with honey and mustard dressing, or fresh Lyme Bay crab. The Sunday lunch menu offers roast West Country beef with Yorkshire pudding; roast lamb with mint sauce; salmon fishcake with tartare sauce; Breton chicken with smoky bacon and leeks in cream; and winter vegetable crêpe. The half-price Sunday roast for children is good value. Outside there is a grassy beer garden plus a terracotta-walled terrace area with tumbling grapevines.

**Open** all wk 12-2.30 (Sat-Sun 12-3.30) 6-11 (Sun 7-10.30) **Bar Meals** L served all wk 12-2 D served Mon-Sat 6.30-8.30, Sun 7-8.30 booking required **Restaurant** L served all wk 12-2 D served Mon-Sat 6.30-8.30, Sun 7-8.30 ◖ Otter Ale, Bass, Otter Bitter. ♉ 12 **Facilities** Children's menu Garden Parking

# PICK OF THE PUBS

## The Durant Arms ★★★★INN

**TOTNES** | Map 3 SX86

**Ashprington TQ9 7UP ☎ 01803 732240**
**dir:** *Exit A38 at Totnes junct, to Dartington & Totnes, at 1st lights right for Kingsbridge on A381, in 1m left for Ashprington*

With stunning views of the River Dart, the award-winning 18th-century Durant Arms has a local reputation as a dining pub. Set in the picturesque village of Ashprington, just outside the Elizabethan town of Totnes in the heart of the South Hams, the building was originally the counting house for the neighbouring 500-acre Sharpham Estate.

Formerly known as The Ashprington Inn, a smaller establishment than the Durant, proprietors Graham and Eileen Ellis have expanded the business into an adjoining property. The small bar is fitted out in a traditional style, with work by local artists on display alongside the horse brasses, ferns and cheerful red velvet curtains.

All dishes at the Durant are cooked to order, using locally sourced ingredients wherever possible. Typical dishes from the daily-changing blackboard menu include pub favourites such as fisherman's pie; chicken curry; and traditional steak and kidney pie. A more formal meal might begin with chargrilled fresh asparagus with lemon and chive oil, or pan-seared scallops with pea purée. Follow on, perhaps, with pork tenderloin with Stilton and mushroom sauce; braised lamb shank on herb mash with red wine and rosemary; or a fish selection of monkfish, scallops and tiger prawns in a white wine and cream sauce.

Leave space for desserts such as Eton mess; date chocolate brownie with clotted cream; and Grand Marnier crème brûlée; or opt for the hand-made English cheeses from nearby Sharpham's organic dairy.

The little courtyard to the rear provides a cosy spot to linger over a summer meal, and eight comfortably furnished and attractively decorated en suite bedrooms complete the package.

**Open** all wk Sat-Sun all day **Bar Meals** L served all wk 12-2 D served all wk 7-9.15 **Restaurant** L served all wk 12-2 D served all wk 7-9.15 ⊕ FREE HOUSE ◀ Dartmoor Bitter, Tetley, Tribute ♂ Luscombe. ♟ 10 **Facilities** Children's menu Family room Dogs allowed Garden Parking **Rooms** 8

## TORCROSS
Map 3 SX84

## Start Bay Inn ☞

**TQ7 2TQ ☎ 01548 580553** 📠 **01548 581285**
**e-mail:** clair@startbayinn.co.uk
**dir:** *Between Dartmouth & Kingsbridge on A379*

The fishermen who work from the beach right in front of this 14th-century pub deliver their catch direct to the kitchen; so does a local crabber, while the former landlord (father of landladies Clair and Gail) dives for scallops. Be in no doubt therefore about the freshness of all the fish appearing on the specials board. Look also for locally-sourced steaks, ham, home-made burgers, vegetable curry, sandwiches and jacket potatoes. Try the local Sharpham white wine – while sitting on the seafront patio in summer.

**Open** all day all wk 11.30am-11.30pm **Bar Meals** L served all wk 11.30-2.15 D served all wk 6-9.30 winter, 6-10 summer ⊕ HEAVITREE ◀ Interbrew Flowers Original & Bass, Otter Ale. ☙ 8 **Facilities** Children's menu Children's portions Family room Garden Parking

## TORQUAY
Map 3 SX96

## The Cary Arms ★★★★★ INN ☞ NEW

**Beach Rd TQ1 3LX ☎ 01803 327110** 📠 **01803 323221**
**e-mail:** enquiries@caryarms.co.uk
**dir:** *From Exeter A380 towards Torquay. Left onto B3192. On entering Teignmouth, at bottom of hill at lights, right signed Torquay/A379. Cross R. Teign. At mini rdbt follow Babbacombe/Seafront signs. Pass Babbacombe Model Village & Bygones, through lights, left into Babbacombe Downs Rd, left into Beach Rd*

Not just an inn on the beach, more a classic English pub with boutique-style luxury accommodation. In the stone-walled bar, perhaps with a pint of Otter in hand, you'll stand on planked floors beneath beamed ceilings contemplating the views across the bay and the seasonal menu - Devon beef or Lyme Bay lobster, perhaps, or maybe line-caught seafood; roasted supreme of guinea fowl; or wild mushroom strudel. There are jazz, gastro, quiz and steak nights dotted throughout the year. En suite rooms are sea facing with a balcony.

**Open** all wk noon-11pm **Bar Meals** L served all wk 12-3 booking required D served all wk 6.30-9 booking required Av main course £14.95 **Restaurant** Av 3 course à la carte fr £26.50 ⊕ FREE HOUSE ◀ Otter Ale, Otter Bitter, Bays Gold ⊘ Cornish Rattler, Thatchers Gold, Healeys Oak Matured. ☙ 14 **Facilities** Children's menu Children's portions Family room Dogs allowed Garden **Rooms** 8

## TOTNES
Map 3 SX86

## PICK OF THE PUBS

## The Durant Arms
INN ☞

*See Pick of the Pubs on page 155*

## Royal Seven Stars Hotel ☞

**The Plains TQ9 5DD ☎ 01803 862125** 📠 **01803 867925**
**e-mail:** enquiry@royalsevenstars.co.uk
**dir:** *From A382 signed Totnes, left at 'Dartington' rdbt. Through lights towards town centre, through next rdbt, pass Morrisons car park on left. 200yds on right*

A Grade II listed pub in the heart of Totnes, dating from 1640. The traditional saloon bar with open fire serves Jail Ale and Doom Bar among others, with home-cooked bar meals available all day. Bar 7's more contemporary atmosphere, with slate floors and black leather sofas, is the setting for Mediterranean-inspired snacks, fruit smoothies, speciality coffees and a selection of cakes. The restaurant, called TQ9 after its town centre location, serves good local produce– including a Sunday carvery – in a relaxed, stylish environment.

**Open** all day all wk **Bar Meals** Av main course £8 food served all day **Restaurant** L served Sun 12-2.30 booking required D served all wk 6.30-9.30 booking required Av 3 course à la carte fr £20 ⊕ FREE HOUSE ◀ Jail Ale, Doom Bar, Bays Gold, Courage Best. ☙ 20 **Facilities** Children's menu Children's portions Family room Dogs allowed Parking

## Rumour ☞

**30 High St TQ9 5RY ☎ 01803 864682**
**dir:** *Follow signs for Totnes castle/town centre. On main street up hill above arch on left. 5 min walk from rail station*

Named after Fleetwood Mac's landmark 1977 album, this 17th-century building had a chequered history as a milk bar, restaurant and wine bar. Now comprehensively refurbished, including innovative heating and plumbing systems which reduces the pub's environmental footprint. Rumour's hospitable staff deliver an extensive hand-made pizza menu alongside more formal à la carte offerings like slow-roast pork belly with puréed garlic, fennel potatoes and rosemary, and grilled salmon with spiced lentils, avocado and rocket. Desserts include prune and pistachio tart with clotted cream.

**Open** all wk **Bar Meals** L served Mon-Sat 12-3 D served all wk 6-10 booking required Av main course £12 **Restaurant** L served Mon-Sat 12-3 D served all wk 6-10 booking required Av 3 course à la carte fr £30 ⊕ FREE HOUSE ◀ Erdinger, Abbots Ale, Leffe, Half Bore ⊘ Thatchers. ☙ 12 **Facilities** Children's portions

## Steam Packet Inn ★★★★ INN ☞

**St Peter's Quay TQ9 5EW**
**☎ 01803 863880** 📠 **01803 862754**
**e-mail:** steampacket@buccaneer.co.uk
**dir:** *Exit A38 towards Plymouth, 18m. A384 to Totnes 6m. Left at mini-rdbt, pass Morrisons on left, over mini-rdbt, 400yds on left*

Named after the passenger, cargo and mail steamers that once plied the Dart, this riverside pub, with four en suite rooms, makes full use of its riverside position. Great views, particularly from the conservatory restaurant, and

plenty of waterside seating contribute to its popularity. Typical dishes are fresh Dartmoor Ale-battered cod; salmon and smoked haddock Wellington; slow-cooked belly pork; steak and kidney suet pudding; and butternut squash, spinach and tomato lasagne.

*Steam Packet Inn*

**Open** all day all wk **Bar Meals** L served Mon-Fri 12-2.30, Sat-Sun 12-3 D served Mon-Sat 6-9.30, Sun 6-9 Av main course £9.95 **Restaurant** L served Mon-Fri 12-2.30, Sat-Sun 12-3 D served Mon-Sat 6-9.30, Sun 6-9 Av 3 course à la carte fr £16.50 ⊕ BUCCANEER HOLDINGS LTD ◀ Sharp's Doom Bar, Otter Ale, Jail Ale, Guest ale ⊘ Stowford Press. ☙ 11 **Facilities** Children's menu Dogs allowed Garden Parking **Rooms** 4

## PICK OF THE PUBS

## The White Hart ☞

**Dartington Hall TQ9 6EL**
**☎ 01803 847111** 📠 **01803 847107**
**e-mail:** bookings@dartingtonhall.com
**dir:** *From A38 take Totnes turn onto A384. Turn by Dartington church into Dartington Hall Estate*

Surrounded by landscaped gardens and an ancient deer park, the White Hart stands within the courtyard of the magnificent 14th-century Dartington Hall. Ancient tapestries hang above the original kitchen fire in the main restaurant, recently fully refurbished, which is floored with flagstones and oak, lit by gothic chandeliers, and furnished with limed oak settles. Otter real ales and Yarde cider are available in the bar, again with a fire, and there's a patio for the warmer weather. The daily changing bar and restaurant menu uses fresh, seasonal ingredients from South Devon and the estate itself – single-suckled beef, grass-reared lamb, additive-free and free-range chickens and eggs, and fish. Typical dishes might be grilled field mushroom burger with caramelised onions, beefsteak tomato and goat's cheese; confit of free-range Crediton duck leg with apple and celeriac purée, and cranberry and balsamic compote; and grilled salmon fillet with sautéed spinach and garlic, and herb butter sauce.

**Open** all day all wk Closed: 24-29 Dec **Bar Meals** L served all wk 12-2.30 booking required D served all wk 6-9 booking required Av main course £13 **Restaurant** L served all wk 12-2.30 booking required D served all wk 6-9 booking required Av 3 course à la carte fr £25 ⊕ FREE HOUSE ◀ Otter Brewery Ale & Bitter ⊘ Yarde Real Cider. ☙ 14 **Facilities** Children's portions Garden Parking

Save on Hotels. Book at **theAA.com/hotel**

DEVON 157 **ENGLAND**

| TRUSHAM | Map 3 SX88 |
|---|---|

## PICK OF THE PUBS

### Cridford Inn ▾

*See Pick of the Pubs on page 158*

| TUCKENHAY | Map 3 SX85 |
|---|---|

## The Maltsters Arms ▾

TQ9 7EQ ☎ 01803 732350 🖹 01803 732823
e-mail: pub@tuckenhay.demon.co.uk
dir: *A381 from Totnes towards Kingsbridge. 1m, at hill top turn left, follow signs to Tuckenhay, 3m*

Accessible only along high-banked lanes, or by boat either side of high tide, this old stone country inn on Bow Creek off the River Dart was once owned by TV chef, the late Keith Floyd. The daily-changing menu may feature local mussels with garlic, white wine and herbs; grilled gurnard and hake fillets with a prawn and herb sauce; Goan-style chicken breast with lemon and coriander butter; or celeriac, fennel and pepper gratin. Famous for summer barbecues and music events.

**Open** all day all wk 11-11 (25 Dec 12-2) **Bar Meals** L served all wk 12-3 D served all wk 7-9.30 Av main course £11 food served all day **Restaurant** L served all wk 12-3 booking required D served all wk 7-9.30 booking required Av 3 course à la carte fr £20 ⊕ FREE HOUSE ◀ Princetown Dartmoor IPA, Teignworthy Maltsters Ale, Sharps Doom Bar ♂ Westons Perry, Heron Valley 'Shag', Bays Breaker Yarde Dry. ▾ 18 **Facilities** Children's menu Children's portions Family room Dogs allowed Garden Parking

| TYTHERLEIGH | Map 4 ST30 |
|---|---|

## Tytherleigh Arms Hotel

EX13 7BE
☎ 01460 220400 & 220214 🖹 01460 220814
e-mail: tytherleigharms@aol.com
dir: *Equidistant from Chard & Axminster on A358*

Beamed ceilings and huge roaring fires are notable features of this family-run, 16th-century former coaching inn. It is a food-led establishment, situated on the Devon, Somerset and Dorset borders. Great pride is taken in sourcing local ingredients, and fish dishes are a speciality with fish caught locally – perhaps trout fillet with bacon and mushroom. Other fresh home-cooked dishes might include chicken liver and smoked bacon pâté; red pepper and lentil lasagne; lamb cutlets with minted gravy. Save some room for the delicious home-made puds.

**Open** all wk 11-2.30 6.30-11 (Sun eve in winter) **Bar Meals** L served all wk 11-2.30 D served all wk 6.30-9 (booking required) Av main course £11 **Restaurant** L served all wk 11-2.30 D served all wk 6.30-9 (booking required) ⊕ FREE HOUSE ◀ Butcombe Bitter, Otter, Murphy's, Boddingtons ♂ Ashton Press **Facilities** Children's menu Children's portions Garden Parking

| UMBERLEIGH | Map 3 SS62 |
|---|---|

## PICK OF THE PUBS

### The Rising Sun Inn

EX37 9DU ☎ 01769 560447 🖹 01769 560835
e-mail: digby.rees@btconnect.com
dir: *On A377 (Exeter-Barnstaple road) at junct with B3227*

Idyllically set beside the River Taw and with a very strong fly fishing tradition, The Rising Sun dates back in part to the 13th century. The traditional flagstoned bar is strewn with comfortable chairs and adorned with fishing memorabilia; daily papers and magazines put the finishing touches to a relaxing atmosphere. Outside is a sunny raised terrace with beautiful views over the valley, and the riverside walk is enjoyable before or after a meal. A choice of à la carte restaurant or regularly revised bar menus feature the best of West Country produce, with seasonal delights like seafood from the North Devon coast, salmon and sea trout from the Taw, game from Exmoor, and local cheeses. The daily changing specials board could be the best place to start looking. There's also a carvery every Sunday.

**Open** all wk 11.30am-3 6-11pm (Sat 11.30am-11pm Sun noon-11pm) **Bar Meals** L served Mon-Sun 12-2.30 D served all wk 6-9 Av main course £10 ⊕ FREE HOUSE ◀ Cotleigh Barn Owl, Guinness, St Austell Tribute, Exmoor Fox ♂ Thatchers Gold. **Facilities** Children's menu Children's portions Dogs allowed Garden Parking

| WIDECOMBE IN THE MOOR | Map 3 SX77 |
|---|---|

## The Old Inn ▾

TQ13 7TA ☎ 01364 621207 🖹 01364 621407
e-mail: oldinn.widecombe@hall-woodhouse.co.uk
dir: *Telephone for directions*

Set in the heart of Dartmoor, this 600-year-old inn is a pub for all seasons and the ideal place for walkers. Sit outside in summer and admire the views, or enjoy the five log fires when the weather turns cold. Award-winning cask ales include seasonal guests, with over 20 wines by the glass. Lunchtime brings baked jackets and baguettes with a range of fillings, while those with larger appetites can tuck into plates of bangers and mash, chicken tikka Marsala, or grilled tuna steak.

**Open** all day all wk **Bar Meals** Av main course £8 food served all day **Restaurant** food served all day ⊕ HALL & WOODHOUSE ◀ Badger, Guest ales ♂ Applewood. ▾ 23 **Facilities** Children's menu Children's portions Dogs allowed Garden Parking

## PICK OF THE PUBS

### The Rugglestone Inn ▾ NEW

TQ13 7TF ☎ 01364 621327
e-mail: enquiries@rugglestoneinn.co.uk
dir: *From village centre take road by church towards Venton. Inn down hill on left*

Unspoilt gem of a rural pub set beside moorland within walking distance of the picturesque village. Named after the Ruggle Stone, a huge mass of granite nearby,

and converted from a farm cottage in 1832, this rustic stone inn comprises three cosy rooms, one a delightful, old-fashioned parlour with beams, stone floors, crackling winter log fires and simple furnishings, all are devoid of modern-day intrusions. Tip-top Butcombe, Dartmoor Best and Otter Bitter are among the ales tapped straight from cask, while cider drinkers have a good choice of heady local farm ciders. Hearty, home-cooked traditional pub food ranges from simple bar snacks like hot pork baps with apple sauce and ham ploughman's to chicken and leek pie, Stilton and mushroom quiche, fish pie, fresh beer battered haddock and chips, and oven-baked trout. Across the babbling brook to the front of the pub lies a lawn with benches and peaceful moorland views.

**Open** all wk Sat-Sun all day **Bar Meals** L served 12-2 D served all wk 6.30-9 Av main course £5 **Restaurant** L served all wk 12-2 D served all wk 6.30-9 ⊕ FREE HOUSE ◀ Dartmoor Bitter, Butcombe, O'Hanlons Yellowhammer, Blackawton Original, Otter Bitter ♂ Ashton Press, Lower Widdon Farm, Riches. ▾ 10 **Facilities** Children's menu Children's portions Dogs allowed Garden Parking

| WINKLEIGH | Map 3 SS60 |
|---|---|

## PICK OF THE PUBS

### The Duke of York ▾

Iddesleigh EX19 8BG
☎ 01837 810253 🖹 01837 810253
dir: *Telephone for directions*

The atmosphere of this venerable thatched inn is blissfully unsullied by juke box, fruit machine or karaoke. Set deep in rural mid-Devon, it was originally three cottages housing craftsmen who were rebuilding the parish church; local records accurately date this work to 1387. All the timeless features of a classic country pub remain - heavy old beams, scrubbed tables, farmhouse chairs and a huge inglenook fireplace with winter fires. Popular with all, it offers decent real ales (Cotleigh Tawny, for example) and hearty home cooking, with everything freshly prepared using local produce such as meat reared on nearby farms. Examples of bar meals taken from the large blackboard menu include rainbow trout, liver and bacon, and casseroles. From the dining room menu could come Dartmouth smokehouse salmon followed by pork loin with port and tarragon sauce, then a choice of more than a dozen classic home-made desserts.

**Open** all day all wk 11am-11pm **Bar Meals** L served all wk 11-10 D served all wk 11-10 food served all day ⊕ FREE HOUSE ◀ Adnams Broadside, Cotleigh Tawny, guest ales ♂ Winkleigh. ▾ 10 **Facilities** Dogs allowed Garden

# PICK OF THE PUBS

## Cridford Inn ♟

**TRUSHAM**       Map 3 SX88

**TQ13 0NR ☎ 01626 853694**

**e-mail:** reservations@vanillapod-cridfordinn.com

**dir:** *A38 take junct for Teign Valley, turn right follow signs Trusham for 4m*

Heritage enthusiasts will be in seventh-heaven here, where researchers have pieced together a remarkable history dating back over a thousand years, putting a 9th century longhouse on the site before a modern rebuild took place in the 13th century. A mosaic floor in the Vanilla Pod restaurant and what is probably the oldest surviving stained glass window in a secular building add immense warmth and character, as do the rough stone walls, old fireplaces and the general atmosphere of this architectural treasure, which has medieval masons' marks still visible

above the bar. The only chill in the air may be from the ghost of a nun (the place also served as a nunnery), whilst the shade of a cavalier is also occasionally spotted abroad.

This picturesque thatched inn crouches like an owl below towering trees near a brook in the Teign Valley just a brace of miles from Dartmoor National Park; a pretty terrace is an ideal summertime spot to mull over the extensive menu with a pint of local Teignworthy bitter.

Quite apart from the fine destination dining of the chic Vanilla Pod restaurant, the bar menu boasts dishes prepared from the finest Devonshire ingredients and changes regularly to reflect seasonal largesse. The moules in the marinière are sourced from the Teign or Exe estuaries, whilst estate game goes into the Gamekeeper's cobbler — slowly braised venison, rabbit and pheasant in a rich red wine and thyme gravy baked with herb scones, coming with seasonal vegetables. The chargrilled rib eye steak is topped with red onion marmalade and Exmoor blue cheese with a port wine jus. Specials and vegetarian choices are on the blackboard near the bar.

**Open** all wk 11-3 6-11 (Sat 11-11 Sun noon-10.30) **Bar Meals** L served all wk 12-2.30 D served all wk 7-9.30 Av main course £8.95 **Restaurant** L served Sun 12-1 booking required D served Mon-Sat 7-9.30 booking required Fixed menu price fr £25 ◀ Doom Bar, Otter Ale, Teighworthy Ales, Bays ♂ Thatchers. ♟ 10 **Facilities** Children's menu Family room Garden Parking

# PICK OF THE PUBS

## The Digger's Rest 🍷

**WOODBURY SALTERTON** Map 3 SY08

**EX5 1PQ**
**☎ 01395 232375 📠 01395 232711**
**e-mail:** bar@diggersrest.co.uk
**dir:** *2.5m from A3052. Signed from Westpoint*

Standing in the delightful East Devon village of Woodbury Salterton, this charming whitewashed inn is just a few minutes drive from Exeter and the M5. The 500 year-old building with its thatched roof, thick walls and heavy beams was originally a cider house, but the choice in today's bar is much wider. Draught Stowford Press maintains the cider tradition, but you'll also find a changing guest ale list that might include Tribute and Doom Bar from Cornwall and Wild Cat from Exmoor, as well as offerings from the Otter Brewery up the road.

The interior features West Country art and antique furniture, and is just the place to sit by the fire with a pint or catch up with e-mails using the free Wi-fi. There's also a skittle alley, whilst the patio garden provides alfresco drinking and dining for up to forty people.

Simple, freshly cooked food is prepared from English produce, including fish from Brixham and Looe, West Country beef, and East Devon pork. The kitchen is committed to supporting good animal husbandry and buys organic where possible. Starters include chicken liver parfait with red onion jam and toasted brioche, and twice-baked smoked cheese soufflé with pickled peppers and toasted pine nut salad. Amongst the main course choices are Kenniford Farm tendersweet pork belly with thyme and garlic fondant potato, crackling and buttered spinach; linguine Provençale with roasted vegetables, pesto, rocket and Parmesan shavings; and Devon steak and Otter ale pie with thick cut chips and fresh vegetables. The dessert menu features baked passionfruit cream with shortbread, and pistachio tart with macerated fruit. Alternatively, you could opt for a selection of West Country cheeses served with quince paste and wheat wafers.

**Open** all wk 11-3 5.30-11 (Sun 12-3.30 5.30-10.30) **Bar Meals** L served Mon-Sat 11-2.15, Sun 12-2.15 D served Mon-Sat 6.30-9.30, Sun 6.30-9 **Restaurant** L served Mon-Sat 11-2.15, Sun 12-2.15 D served Mon-Sat 6.30-9.30, Sun 6.30-9 ⊕ FREE HOUSE ◀ Otter Bitter, Otter Ale, Exmoor Ales, Tribute St Austell Brewery, Wildcat, Sharps Doom Bar 🍎 Stowford Press. 🍷 13 **Facilities** Children's menu Dogs allowed Garden Parking

**WINKLEIGH *continued***

## The Kings Arms

**Fore St EX19 8HQ ☎ 01837 83384 📠 01834 83055**
**e-mail:** kingsarmswinkleigh@googlemail.com
**dir:** *Village signed from B3220 (Crediton to Torrington road)*

Scrubbed pine tables and traditional wooden settles set the scene at this ancient thatched country inn in Winkleigh's central square. Wood-burning stoves keep the beamed bar and dining rooms warm in chilly weather, and traditional pub games are encouraged. Generous servings of freshly made, and locally sourced, food include sandwiches and hot snacks, as well as steak and kidney parcel, loin of lamb with rosemary and redcurrant sauce, and Lucy's fish pie. Booking is recommended at weekends. The village's own cider is available and Devon cream teas are served every day.

**Open** all day all wk 11-11 (Sun noon-10.30) **Bar Meals** L served Mon-Sat 11-9.30, Sun 12-9 D served Mon-Sat 11-9.30, Sun 12-9 food served all day **Restaurant** L served Mon-Sat 11-9.30, Sun 12-9 D served Mon-Sat 11-9.30, Sun 12-9 food served all day ENTERPRISE INNS Butcombe Bitter, Sharp's Doom Bar, Otter Bitter Winkleigh Cider. **Facilities** Children's portions Dogs allowed Garden

**WOODBURY SALTERTON** **Map 3 SY08**

**PICK OF THE PUBS**

## The Digger's Rest

*See Pick of the Pubs on page 159*

**YEALMPTON** **Map 3 SX55**

**PICK OF THE PUBS**

## Rose & Crown

**Market St PL8 2EB**
**☎ 01752 880223 📠 01752 881058**
**e-mail:** info@theroseandcrown.co.uk
**web:** www.theroseandcrown.co.uk
**dir:** *Telephone for directions*

From the classic brown and cream decor to the comfy leather sofas and open fire, the interior of this stylish bar restaurant reflects a perfect balance between contemporary and traditional. New owner Simon Warner took over in December 2009, adding Thatcher's Gold cider to the grand selection of real ales at the bar, which includes Sharp's Doom Bar. The short menu, around seven choices at each stage, proffers traditional classics with an extra touch of class, allowing the kitchen's focus on quality, freshness and local supply to be maintained. Another of the menu's attractions is the no-nonsense pricing – everything is listed in round pounds, there's no messing here with the ubiquitous 95p. A typical three-course choice could start with mackerel salad with toasted brioche; continue with shellfish marinière with skinny chips; and finish with mango and pineapple crumble with passionfruit sorbet. The newly landscaped terraced garden is the perfect place to enjoy your meal if the weather permits.

*Rose & Crown*

**Open** all wk **Bar Meals** L served all wk 12-2.30 D served all wk 6.30-9.30 **Restaurant** L served all wk 12-2.30 booking required D served all wk 6.30-9.30 booking required FREE HOUSE Doom Bar, London Pride, Courage Best, IPA Greene King, Otter, Tribute Thatchers Gold. **Facilities** Children's menu Children's portions Dogs allowed Garden Parking

# DORSET

**ABBOTSBURY** **Map 4 SY58**

## *Ilchester Arms*

**9 Market St DT3 4JR**
**☎ 01305 871243 📠 01305 871225**
**dir:** *Telephone for directions*

Rambling 16th-century coaching inn set in the heart of one of Dorset's most picturesque villages, the Ilchester Arms is warm and welcoming, with heavy oak beamed ceilings, quarry tiles and bare boards. Abbotsbury is home to many crafts including woodwork and pottery. A good area for walkers, and handy for the Tropical Gardens and Swannery.

**Open** all wk Fuller's HSB, Courage Best, Tribute, Speckled Hen, Abbot. 12 **Facilities** Dogs allowed Garden Parking

**BISHOP'S CAUNDLE** **Map 4 ST61**

## The White Hart NEW

**☎ 01963 23519**
**e-mail:** info@whitehartbishopscaundle.co.uk
**dir:** *From Salisbury take A3030 towards Sturminster Newton*

At the heart of the village, deep in Blackmore Vale with views across rolling countryside from its garden, this 17th-century pub has seen its fortunes restored following the arrival of new tenants in 2009. In a setting of thick stone walls, original old beams and a roaring log fire, you can quaff Hall & Woodhouse beers and tuck into some good pub food that utilises the best local seasonal produce, notably fresh fish. Typical dishes include rabbit curry, roast hake with spicy chorizo and potato salad, home-made pies, and apple and rhubarb crumble. There are special dining events.

*The White Hart*

**Open** 12-2.30 5.30-11 Closed: Mon (seasonal closures) **Bar Meals** L served all wk 12-2.30 D served all wk 5.30-9.30 Av main course £9.95 **Restaurant** L served all wk 12-2.30 booking required D served all wk 6-9.30 booking required Fixed menu price fr £9.95 Av 3 course à la carte fr £15.95 HALL & WOODHOUSE Badger 1st Gold, Tanglefoot, Seasonal ales, Fursty Ferret Stowford Press. 20 **Facilities** Children's menu Children's portions Play area Dogs allowed Garden Parking

**BLANDFORD FORUM** **Map 4 ST80**

## The Anvil Inn ★★★★ INN

**Salisbury Rd, Pimperne DT11 8UQ**
**☎ 01258 453431 📠 01258 480182**
**e-mail:** theanvil.inn@btconnect.com
**dir:** *Telephone for directions*

A thatched roof, crooked beams and a cavernous fireplace are just a few of the rustic charms of this family-run 16th-century inn located in the pretty village of Pimperne, two miles from Blandford Forum. The two bars offer a range of real ales and light bites, while the charming beamed restaurant with log fire offers a full menu and in warmer months meals can be enjoyed outside. There are 12 en suite bedrooms available.

**Open** all wk **Bar Meals** food served all day **Restaurant** food served all day FREE HOUSE Guinness, London Pride, IPA, Copper Ale. **Facilities** Dogs allowed Garden Parking **Rooms** 12

## Crown Hotel

**West St DT11 7AJ ☎ 01258 456626 📠 01258 451084**
**e-mail:** crownhotel.blandford@hall-woodhouse.co.uk
**web:** www.innforanight.co.uk/crownthink.html
**dir:** *M27 junct 1 W onto A31 to A350 junct, right to Blandford Forum. 100mtrs from town bridge*

An 18th-century coaching inn which replaces an original inn destroyed by fire in 1731. Standing on the banks of the River Stour, the Crown has plenty of period atmosphere, and a separate restaurant. Begin a meal, perhaps, with roast squash and feta salad or roast chicken tart; followed by lamb shank shepherd's pie or honey glazed pork belly. An extensive bar menu includes sandwiches and light bites.

Save on Hotels. Book at **theAA.com/hotel**

**DORSET** 161  ENGLAND

*Crown Hotel*

**Open** all wk 10am-11.30pm (Sun 12-10.30) **Bar Meals** L served all wk 12-3 D served all wk 6-9 Av main course £13 **Restaurant** Av 3 course à la carte fr £25 ⊕ HALL & WOODHOUSE ◀ Badger Tanglefoot, Badger 1st Gold. ♀ 12 **Facilities** Children's menu Dogs allowed Garden Parking

---

### BOURTON                            Map 4 ST73

## The White Lion Inn

**High St SP8 5AT ☎ 01747 840866**
e-mail: office@whitelionbourton.co.uk
dir: *Off A303, opposite B3092 to Gillingham*

Dating from 1723, the White Lion is a beautiful, stone-built, creeper clad Dorset inn. The bar is cosy, with beams, flagstones and an open fire, and serves a range of real beers and ciders. Imaginative menus draw on the wealth of quality local produce, and dishes range from twice-baked Cheddar soufflé or duck rillette to Moroccan tagine or roast venison.

**Open** all wk Mon-Thu noon-3 5-11 (Fri, Sat Sun all day) **Bar Meals** L served Mon-Sat 12-2.30, Sun 12-3.30 D served all wk 6-9 Av main course £11 **Restaurant** L served Mon-Sat 12-2.30, Sun 12-3.30 D served all wk 6-9 Av 3 course à la carte fr £20 ⊕ ADMIRAL TAVERNS ◀ Otter Amber, Sharp's Doom Bar, St Austell Tribute Ō Thatchers. **Facilities** Children's menu Children's portions Dogs allowed Garden Parking

---

### BRIDPORT                            Map 4 SY49

## The George Hotel

**4 South St DT6 3NQ ☎ 01308 423187**
dir: *In town centre, 1.5m from West Bay*

Handsome Georgian town house, with a Victorian-style bar and a mellow atmosphere, which bustles all day, and offers a traditional English breakfast, decent morning coffee and a good menu featuring fresh local plaice, natural smoked haddock, avocado and bacon salad, and the famous rabbit and bacon pie. Everything is home cooked using local produce and can be enjoyed with a selection of real ales.

---

**Open** all wk 10am-11.30pm (Fri-Sat 10am-12.30am Sun noon-10.30) **Bar Meals** L served all wk 12-2.30 D served Tue-Sat 6-9.30 Av main course £9 ⊕ PALMERS ◀ Palmers - IPA, Copper & 200, Tally Ho.
**Facilities** Children's portions Family room Dogs allowed Notes ⊛

---

### PICK OF THE PUBS

## The Shave Cross Inn ✩✩✩✩✩ INN ♀

**Shave Cross, Marshwood Vale DT6 6HW**
**☎ 01308 868358   📠 01308 867064**
e-mail: roy.warburton@virgin.net
dir: *From Bridport take B3162. In 2m left signed 'Broadoak/Shave Cross', then Marshwood*

Remote down winding Dorset country lanes in the verdant Marshwood Vale, the gleaming old thatch draws the wanderer to this 700-year-old inn where pilgrims rested in Edward III's reign on their way to the church of St Candida and St Cross in nearby Whitchurch Canonicorum, as well as monastic visitors, who frequently had their tonsures trimmed while staying, hence the pub's name. Today's travellers enjoy a curious mix of olde England – great local beers, beams, inglenook, flagstone floors, rustic furnishings, log fire – and Caribbean-influenced award-winning food; hot spicy Cuban seafood bouillabaisse or Guyanese lamb cutlet crown with a balsamic vinegar sauce may hit the spot. More hesitant British palates also have ample award winning dishes to choose from. The flower-filled sun-trap garden is a delight in summer, and through the oldest thatched skittle alley in the country, kids will find their play area. On Twelfth Night traditions are lovingly retained with morris dancing and ashen-faggot burning. There are individually designed rooms available, all furnished with luxurious fittings.

**Open** 11-3 6-11.30 Closed: Mon (ex BH) **Bar Meals** L served Tue-Sun 12-2.30 D served Tue-Sun 6-7 Av main course £10 **Restaurant** L served Tue-Sun 12-2.30 booking required D served Tue-Sun 6-9 (closed Sun eve winter) booking required Fixed menu price fr £28 Av 3 course à la carte fr £32.50 ⊕ FREE HOUSE ◀ Local guest ales, Branoc (Branscombe Valley), Quay Brewery Weymouth Ō Old Rosie, Thatchers, Stowford Press, Pitford. ♀ 8 **Facilities** Children's menu Children's portions Play area Dogs allowed Garden Parking **Rooms** 7

---

## The West Bay

**Station Rd, West Bay DT6 4EW**
**☎ 01308 422157   📠 01308 459717**
dir: *From A35 (Bridport by-pass) take B3157 (2nd exit) towards West Bay. After mini-rdbt 1st left (Station Road). Pub on left*

Built in 1739, this traditional bar/restaurant lies at the foot of East Cliff, part of the impressive World Heritage Jurassic Coast. Now under new ownership, the pub continues to specialise in fish and seafood with the latest catch shown as blackboard specials. Perhaps choose Portland mussels steamed in white wine and cream as a

---

starter; then grilled Lyme Bay lemon sole stuffed with shrimp tails, lemon and herbs. For meat eaters there's a good choice of steaks or maybe Dorset rack or lamb with garlic and herb potatoes. Palmers Brewery in Bridport furnishes the real ales, or you can ring the changes with a pint of Thatcher's Gold cider.

**Open** all wk Mon-Thu noon-3 6-11 (Fri-Sun all day) **Bar Meals** L served all wk 12-2.30 D served all wk 6-9 Av main course £10 **Restaurant** L served all wk 12-2.30 booking required D served all wk 6-9 booking required Fixed menu price fr £10 Av 3 course à la carte fr £20 ⊕ PALMERS ◀ Palmers IPA, Palmers Copper, Palmers 200, Guinness, Tally Ho! Ō Thatchers Gold. **Facilities** Children's portions Dogs allowed Garden Parking

---

### BUCKHORN WESTON              Map 4 ST72

### PICK OF THE PUBS

## Stapleton Arms ♀

**Church Hill SP8 5HS ☎ 01963 370396**
e-mail: relax@thestapletonarms.com
dir: *3.5m from Wincanton in village centre*

Tucked away in a pretty village, the Stapleton Arms is a modern country pub on the Somerset, Wiltshire and Dorset border. Stylish but unstuffy, with a spacious bar, elegant dining room and secluded garden, it offers real ales such as Moor's Revival and Butcombe, and draught ciders including Cheddar Valley and Orchard Pig. There are also organic fruit juices and wines from new, old and emerging wine regions. With a philosophy – quality food cooked simply with the freshest local ingredients - produce is sourced from small producers for the daily changing menu. For starters try Cornish mussels in a white wine, shallot, garlic and thyme cream sauce. Main courses include braised oxtail with swede mash, and fish caught off Dorset's south coast is delivered daily. Typical desserts are sticky date pudding with butterscotch sauce and vanilla ice cream. Alternatively the cheeseboard offers local cheeses including Somerset brie, Exmoor Blue and Montgomery Cheddar.

**Open** all wk 11-3 6-11 (Sun noon-10.30) **Bar Meals** L served all wk 12-3 D served all wk 6-10 Av main course £12 **Restaurant** L served all wk 12-3 booking required D served all wk 6-10 booking required Av 3 course à la carte fr £24 ⊕ FREE HOUSE ◀ Butcombe, Moor's Revival Ō Thatchers Cheddar Valley, Butcombe's Ashton Press, Orchard Pig. ♀ 12 **Facilities** Children's menu Children's portions Play area Dogs allowed Garden Parking

## BUCKLAND NEWTON     Map 4 ST60

### PICK OF THE PUBS

### Gaggle of Geese ☻

**DT2 7BS ☎ 01300 345249**
e-mail: goose@thegaggle.co.uk
dir: On B3143 N of Dorchester

In its own secluded five acres of land, with an orchard, its own cricket club, croquet lawn and skittles alley, this is a proper village pub which ticks all the right boxes – a lived-in, loved feeling to the beamed bar with its comfy sofas, copper-topped fireplace and well used bookshelves; first rate West Country beers and tempting farm ciders add to this and the owners and locals offer huge support for local charities and community events, including goose and poultry auctions. On top of this is a great, totally home-made menu, most of it bartered or bought very locally, including a home-butchery using meat from licensee Mark Hammick's family farm: think game terrine starter; mains like pan-fried pheasant breast and confit leg with Puy lentils, swede and carrot purée or mussels in a creamy cider sauce. And how can anyone resist finishing with Dorset Blue Vinny, Dorset Red, Coastal Cheddar and Goldilocks with Dorset Thick and Thins and Piddle Honey?

**Open** all wk 11.30-3 6-11.30 (Sun 11.30-11.30, Sat 11.30-11.30 in summer) Closed: 1wk Jan, 25 Dec **Bar Meals** L served Mon-Sat 12-2, Sun 12-3 booking required D served Sun-Thu 7-9, Fri-Sat 7-9.30 booking required Av main course £11 **Restaurant** L served Mon-Sat 12-2, Sun 12-3 booking required D served Sun-Thu 7-9, Fri-Sat 7-9.30 booking required Av 3 course à la carte fr £21 ⊕ FREE HOUSE ◀ Ringwood, Proper Job, Tribute, Hop Back Summer Lightning, Otter Amber Ö Thatchers Gold, Lulworth Skipper, Bridge Farm Traditional. ☻ 10 **Facilities** Children's portions Play area Dogs allowed Garden Parking

## BURTON BRADSTOCK     Map 4 SY48

### PICK OF THE PUBS

### The Anchor Inn ☻

**High St DT6 4QF ☎ 01308 897228**
e-mail: info@dorset-seafood-restaurant.co.uk
dir: 2m SE of Bridport on B3157 in centre of Burton Bradstock

Located near Chesil Beach, just inland from the Jurassic Coast World Heritage Site, this 300-year-old coaching inn is full of marine memorabilia. Fishing nets hang from ceilings, whilst old fishing tools and seafood shells adorn the walls. The well-stocked bar offers a wide range of draught beers including Otter, Tribute and Courage Best, as well as Thatcher's cider. Lunchtime brings hot baked baguettes, open crab sandwich, and baked ham, egg and chips; other dishes such as salmon, scallop and prawn chowder, and shellfish combo reflect The Anchor's reputation for superb seafood dishes. This theme continues in the main menu, with starters like Cornish mussels with garlic bread, and lobster and prawn bisque. Main courses also offer plenty of seafood, including swordfish steak, and smoked haddock with poached egg. Meanwhile, roast Gressingham duck with wild mushroom sauce; beef stroganoff; and Olde English sirloin will satisfy the meat-eaters, and there are vegetarian options, too.

**Open** all wk 11.30-3 5.30-12 (Sat-Sun 11.30am-mdnt) **Bar Meals** L served all wk 12-2 booking required D served all wk 6-9.30 booking required Av main course £8.95 **Restaurant** L served all wk 12-2 booking required D served all wk 6-9.30 booking required Av 3 course à la carte fr £30 ⊕ PUNCH TAVERNS ◀ Otter Bitter, Tribute, Theakston Best Bitter, John Smith's Ö Thatchers Traditional. ☻ 10 **Facilities** Children's menu Dogs allowed Parking

## CATTISTOCK     Map 4 SY59

### Fox & Hounds Inn

**Duck St DT2 0JH ☎ 01300 320444 📄 01300 320444**
e-mail: lizflight@yahoo.co.uk
dir: On A37, between Dorchester & Yeovil, follow signs to Cattistock

An attractive 16th-century inn in a picturesque village, winner of the title 'Dorset's Best Local'. At the rear, spare ground is being turned into allotments for the villagers, who donate their excess produce to the pub's kitchen.

Features include beams, open fires in winter and huge inglenooks, one with an original bread oven. Palmers real ales are on tap, along with Thatchers ciders, while traditional home-made meals include locally made faggots and mash, fresh fish, oxtails, and steaks from nearby farms. There are monthly folk music nights.

**Open** noon-2.30 7-11 (Thu-Sat 12-2.30 6-11) Closed: Mon L **Bar Meals** L served Tue-Sun 12-2 D served Tue-Sat 7-11 booking required Av main course £8.95 **Restaurant** L served Tue-Sun 12-2 D served Tue-Sat 7-11 booking required ⊕ PALMERS ◀ Palmers IPA, Copper Ale, Palmers 200, Dorset Gold Ö Thatchers Traditional, Thatchers Gold. **Facilities** Children's portions Play area Dogs allowed Garden Parking

## CHEDINGTON     Map 4 ST40

### Winyards Gap Inn ☻

**Chedington Ln DT8 3HY ☎ 01935 891244**
e-mail: enquiries@winyardsgap.com
web: www.winyardsgap.com
dir: 5m S of Crewkerne on A356

Tucked beneath an ancient earthwork, and surrounded by National Trust property, this pub has a view from the beamed bar and the terraced garden that's truly worth savouring. With a pint of Piddle (named after a Dorset river, since you ask) in one hand, menu in the other, choose a 12oz rump steak with plum tomatoes, garlic mushrooms and chunky chips; smoked haddock fishcake on avocado salsa; or maybe Somerset brie with thyme and courgette tagliatelle. There are regular quiz and jazz nights held.

**Open** all wk 11.30-3 6-11 (Sat-Sun 11.30am-11) Closed: 25 Dec **Bar Meals** L served Mon-Sat 12-2 D served all wk 6-9 Av main course £8 **Restaurant** L served all wk 12-2 booking required D served all wk 6-9 booking required Av 3 course à la carte fr £20 ⊕ FREE HOUSE ◀ Doom Bar, Exmoor Ale, Otter Ale, Dorset Piddle Ö Thatchers Gold, Old Rosie, 1st Quality Cider. ☻ 8 **Facilities** Children's menu Children's portions Dogs allowed Garden Parking

## CHIDEOCK     Map 4 SY49

### The Anchor Inn

**Seatown DT6 6JU ☎ 01297 489215**
dir: On A35 turn S in Chideock opp church & follow single track rd for 0.75m to beach

Originally a smugglers' haunt, The Anchor has an incredible setting in a little cove surrounded by National Trust land, beneath Golden Cap. The large sun terrace and cliff-side beer garden overlooking the beach make it a premier destination for throngs of holidaymakers in the summer, while on winter weekdays it is blissfully quiet. The wide-ranging menu starts with snacks and light lunches - three types of ploughman's and a range of sandwiches might take your fancy. For something more substantial choose a freshly caught fish dish accompanied with one of the real ales or ciders.

**Open** all wk 11.30am-10.30pm **Bar Meals** L served all wk 12-9 D served all wk 12-9 ⊕ PALMERS ◀ Palmers 200 Premium Ale, IPA, Copper Ale ♂ Thatchers Tradition, Thatchers Pear. **Facilities** Children's menu Children's portions Family room Dogs allowed Garden Parking

---

### CHRISTCHURCH                    Map 5 SZ19

## Fishermans Haunt

**Salisbury Rd, Winkton BH23 7AS**
☎ 01202 477283   ≣ 01202 478883
**e-mail:** fishermanshaunt@fullers.co.uk
**dir:** *2.5m N on B3347 (Christchurch to Ringwood road)*

Dating from 1673, this inn overlooks the River Avon and is a popular place for walkers, and anglers visiting some of the local fisheries. The area is also well endowed with golf courses. The menu offers a daily fish selection, usually including trout and whole plaice, and staples such as steak and kidney pie, battered cod, and mixed grill along with sandwiches and baked potatoes. There's a more extensive carte menu in the restaurant.

**Open** all wk 11-11 (Fri 11am-mdnt, Sun 11.30-10.30) ◀ Seafairers ale, HSB, London Pride, Fullers ESB. **Facilities** Family room Dogs allowed Garden Parking

---

## The Ship In Distress

**66 Stanpit BH23 3NA**
☎ 01202 485123   ≣ 01202 483997
**e-mail:** enquiries@theshipindistress.com
**dir:** *Telephone for directions*

This 300-year-old family-run pub close to Mudeford Quay was once the haunt of smugglers and the two bars are awash with nautical memorabilia to keep its smuggling history alive. The pub's award-winning modern seafood restaurant showcases local fish – lemon and Dover sole, sea bass, crabs and lobster. Typical dishes are diver-caught scallops with garlic and herb butter, followed by fillets of locally caught sea bass with dauphinoise potatoes, green beans and pesto. Home-made daily desserts include lemon posset and sticky toffee pudding. On warmer days head for the sun trap terrace.

**Open** all day all wk 11am-mdnt (Sun 11-11) **Bar Meals** L served Mon-Fri 12-2, Sat- Sun 12-2.30 D served Sun-Thu 6.30-9, Fri-Sun 6.30-9.30 Av main course £5.95 **Restaurant** L served Mon-Fri 12-2, Sat- Sun 12-2.30 D served Sun-Thu 6.30-9, Fri-Sun 6.30-9.30 Fixed menu price fr £9.95 Av 3 course à la carte fr £24.50 ⊕ PUNCH TAVERNS ◀ Ringwood Best, Fortyniner, Adnams Broadside, Guest Ales. **Facilities** Children's menu Children's portions Dogs allowed Garden Parking

---

### CHURCH KNOWLE                    Map 4 SY98

## The New Inn ⚑

**BH20 5NQ** ☎ 01929 480357   ≣ 01929 480357
**e-mail:** maurice@newinn-churchknowle.co.uk
**dir:** *From Wareham take A351 towards Swanage. At Corfe Castle turn right for Church Knowle. Pub in village centre*

Set in a picturesque village overlooking the Purbeck Hills, this quaint 16th-century stone and thatched country inn has been run by the Estop family for 25 years. Real ales include Jurassic, while ciders include a guest from Weston. Freshly pressed apple juice is purchased direct from the farm, and an elderflower bubbly, ginger beer and Sicilian lemonade are also popular. Fresh seafood is the house speciality, with whole crabs to crack, Cornish hake, Torbay sole, local mussels and Brixham plaice all found on the menu, along with traditional favourites. There is a large garden with wonderful views.

**Open** 11-3 6-11 Closed: Mon eve Jan & Feb **Bar Meals** L served all wk 12-2.15 booking required D served all wk 6-9.15 booking required Av main course £8.50 **Restaurant** L served all wk 12-2.15 booking required D served all wk 6-9.15 booking required ⊕ PUNCH TAVERNS ◀ Old Speckled Hen, Original, DBC Jurassic, St Austell Tribute ♂ Old Rosie, Stowford Press. ⚑ 10 **Facilities** Children's menu Children's portions Family room Garden Parking

---

## CORFE CASTLE — Map 4 SY98

### The Greyhound Inn ♀

**The Square BH20 5EZ**
☎ 01929 480205 🖹 01929 480205
e-mail: eat@greyhoundcorfe.co.uk
web: www.greyhoundcorfe.co.uk
dir: *W from Bournemouth, take A35 to Dorchester, after 5m left onto A351, 10m to Corfe Castle*

A classic pub set beneath the ruins of Corfe Castle, the Greyhound warmly welcomes locals and visitors, children and pets. Its large sun-drenched beer garden with views of Swanage Steam Railway is ideal for sampling a summer ale or cider. Food for all the family make it a popular choice for walkers, cyclists and nearby campsites, but emphasis is nonetheless put on sourcing and cooking fresh seasonal produce in dishes such as Dorset crab salad; prime Dorset beef steaks; and home-cooked Wiltshire ham. The pub hosts food, beer and cider festivals throughout the year.

**Open** all day all wk **Bar Meals** L served all wk 12-3 booking required D served all wk 6-9.30 booking required Av main course £11 food served all day **Restaurant** food served all day ⊕ ENTERPRISE INNS ◀ Ringwood Best, Sharps Doom Bar, London Pride ♂ Westons Organic, Stowford Press, Thatchers Gold. ♀ 9 **Facilities** Children's menu Children's portions Play area Family room Dogs allowed Garden

***See advert on page 163***

## CORFE MULLEN — Map 4 SY99

### The Coventry Arms ◉ ♀

**Mill St BH21 3RH** ☎ 01258 857284
e-mail: info@coventryarms.co.uk
dir: *On A31 (Wimborne-Dorchester road)*

Built in the 13th-century, this friendly pub was once a watermill with its own island. Beer is served direct from the cask, while an annual spring seafood festival attracts many visitors. The inn specialises in fish and game from local estates, and most of the produce is sourced from within the area. Expect such creative dishes as open ravioli of monkfish medallions and mussels; or pan-seared Sika deer's liver with smoked bacon. There's a lovely garden to enjoy in warmer weather.

**Open** all wk 8am-3 5.30-11 (Sat-Sun 8-3 7-11) ◀ Timothy Taylor Landlord, Guest Ales ♂ Stowford Press. ♀ 17 **Facilities** Dogs allowed Garden Parking

## EAST MORDEN — Map 4 SY99

### PICK OF THE PUBS

### The Cock & Bottle

**BH20 7DL** ☎ 01929 459238
dir: *From A35 W of Poole turn right B3075, pub 0.5m on left*

A cob-walled Dorset longhouse built some 400 years ago, the pub acquired a brick skin around 1800 and remained thatched until 1966. The original interiors are comfortably rustic with quaint, low-beamed ceilings, attractive paintings and lots of nooks and crannies around the log fires. Additional to the lively locals' bar are a lounge bar and modern rear restaurant extension. Lovely pastoral views over farmland include the pub's paddock, where vintage car and motorcycle meetings are occasionally hosted during the summer. A new management team was introduced in early 2010 as this guide prepares for press, with Hall and Woodhouse brews as reliable as ever. Bar and light lunch menus are supported by a daily carte, and a children's choice is also available.

**Open** all wk 11.30-2.30 6-11 (Sun noon-3 7-10.30) **Bar Meals** L served all wk 12-2 D served Mon-Sat 6-9 (Sun 7-9) **Restaurant** L served all wk 12-2 booking required D served Mon-Sat 6-9 (Sun 7-9) booking required ⊕ HALL & WOODHOUSE ◀ Badger Dorset Best, Tanglefoot & Sussex. **Facilities** Children's menu Dogs allowed Garden Parking

## EVERSHOT — Map 4 ST50

### PICK OF THE PUBS

### The Acorn Inn ★★★★ INN ◉

**DT2 0JW** ☎ 01935 83228 🖹 01935 83707
e-mail: stay@acorn-inn.co.uk
web: www.acorn-inn.co.uk
dir: *A303 to Yeovil, Dorchester Rd, on A37 right to Evershot*

Attractively set at the heart of a quaint, historic village and surrounded by unspoiled countryside, this traditional 16th-century inn was the model for Thomas Hardy's Sow and Acorn in *Tess of the D'Urbervilles*. With cosy and comfortable bedrooms, several with four-posters, it makes an excellent rural base from which to explore Hardy Country. Throughout the oak-panelled bars and elegantly decorated dining areas, both warmed by blazing winter log fires, there's some imaginative food to choose from. Using local, seasonal

produce from local farms and estates, the modern British repertoire takes in chicken liver parfait with red onion marmalade, wild rabbit stuffed with ceps and wrapped in Parma ham, with toasted barley sauce, red gurnard with butternut squash terrine and lemon, thyme and caper dressing, and dark chocolate pannacotta. More rustic and traditional bar meals include seafood pie, sausages, mash and red onion gravy, and rare roast beef and horseradish sandwiches. Wonderful walks from the front door.

**Open** all day all wk 11-11.30pm **Bar Meals** L served all wk 12-2 D served all wk 7-9 Av main course £6.50 **Restaurant** L served all wk 12-2 booking required D served all wk 7-9 booking required Fixed menu price fr £19.50 Av 3 course à la carte fr £23.50 ⊕ FREE HOUSE ◀ Sharp's Doom Bar, Otter ♂ Thatchers Gold, Thatchers Scrumpy. **Facilities** Children's portions Family room Dogs allowed Garden Parking **Rooms** 10

## FARNHAM — Map 4 ST91

### PICK OF THE PUBS

### The Museum Inn ◉ ♀

**DT11 8DE** ☎ 01825 516261 🖹 01825 516988
e-mail: enquiries@museuminn.co.uk
dir: *From Salisbury take A354 to Blandford Forum, 12m. Farnham signed on right. Pub in village centre*

Now an award-winning free house and restaurant, this part-thatched country inn dates back to the 17th century when it was built by the father of modern archaeology, General Pitt-Rivers, who took over the Gypsy School nearby to house one of his museums. Sympathetically refurbished, the inn retains many original features throughout its convivial beamed rooms, from the stone flagged floors and inglenook fireplace to a traditional bread oven. The same attention to detail is evident in the kitchen, where head chef Patrick Davy sources seasonal produce from local suppliers for the modern British dishes. Try Portland crab risotto with tempura of soft shell crab, dressed pea shoots and langoustine oil, followed by roasted Brixham monkfish tail, Bombay potatoes, spinach, shallot bhaji and curried mussel sauce. The cooking is backed up by an excellent list of wines (12 by the glass) and hand-pulled ales include local Ringwood Old Thumper.

**Open** all wk noon-3 6-11 **Bar Meals** L served 12-2 D served 7-9 Av main course £13 **Restaurant** L served Sun 12-2.30 booking required D served Fri-Sat 7-9 booking required Av 3 course à la carte fr £34 ⊕ FREE HOUSE ◀ Ringwood Old Thumper, Timothy Taylor, Jimmy Riddle, Sunchaser ♂ Stowford Press, Westons Organic. ♀ 12 **Facilities** Children's menu Children's portions Dogs allowed Garden Parking

Save on Hotels. Book at **theAA.com/hotel**

DORSET 165 ENGLAND

## GILLINGHAM
Map 4 ST82

### The Kings Arms Inn ☻

**East Stour Common SP8 5NB ☎ 01747 838325**
e-mail: nrosscampbell@aol.com
dir: *4m W of Shaftesbury on A30*

This family-run village inn makes a great base for
exploring Dorset's countryside and coast. A 200-year-old
free house, it has a public bar with a log fire, several
dining rooms and an enclosed acre of attractive beer
garden. The menus offer an extensive choice of
restaurant fare and traditional pub grub. Popular choices
include Geo Cockburn's famous haggis and black
pudding with streaky bacon, mini sausage, tattie scone
and fried egg (which you can have as a starter or a main
course); slow roast belly pork on bubble and squeak
mash with fried black pudding, Granny Smith apples and
crackling; or breast of chicken cooked with chorizo,
shallots, chestnut mushrooms and spinach, finished with
double cream and pasta. A separate menu is available
for children.

**Open** all wk **Bar Meals** L served Mon-Sat 12-2.30, Sun
12-9.15 booking required D served Mon-Sat 5.30-9.15,
Sun 12-9.15 booking required **Restaurant** L served Mon-
Sat 12-2.30, Sun 12-9.15 booking required D served
Mon-Sat 5.30-9.15, Sun 12-9.15 booking required
⊕ FREE HOUSE ◄ London Pride, Copper Ale, Tribute,
Wadworth 6X. **Facilities** Children's menu Children's
portions Family room Dogs allowed Garden Parking

## GUSSAGE ALL SAINTS
Map 4 SU01

### *The Drovers Inn* ☻

**BH21 5ET ☎ 01258 840084**
e-mail: info@thedroversinn.biz
dir: *A31 Ashley Heath rdbt, right onto B3081*

Rural 16th-century pub with a fine terrace and wonderful
views from the garden. Popular with walkers, its
refurbished interior retains plenty of traditional appeal
with flagstone floors and oak furniture. Ales include
Ringwood's seasonal ales and guest beers. The menu
features home-cooked pub favourites: fresh cod in home-
made beer batter, curry, steak and kidney pie, and steak
and chips.

**Open** all wk 12-3 6-12 (Sat-Sun 11am-mdnt) Closed: 26
Dec ◄ Ringwood Best, Old Thumper, Ringwood seasonal
ales, Fortyniner, guest ales ♂ Thatchers Gold. ☻ 10
**Facilities** Dogs allowed Garden Parking

## KING'S STAG
Map 4 ST71

### The Greenman ☻

**DT10 2AY ☎ 01258 817338 📄 01258 818358**
dir: *E of Sherborne on A3030*

Legend has it that King's Stag in the Blackmore Vale
owes its name to Henry III's favourite white hart, hunted
down and killed by a local nobleman. Built around 1775
and full of oak beams, the pub has five separate dining
areas where you can order anything from a snack to a

banquet. The Sunday carvery offers a choice of five meats
and eight vegetables - booking is essential. Children will
enjoy the play area while parents can relax and enjoy a
drink.

**Open** all wk 11-3 5.30-11 **Bar Meals** L served all wk 12-2
D served all wk 6-9 Av main course £8 **Restaurant** L
served all wk 12-2 D served all wk 6-9 Fixed menu price
fr £8 Av 3 course à la carte fr £19.95 ⊕ ENTERPRISE
INNS ◄ Exmoor, Spitfire, HBC, London Pride, Old
Speckled Hen. ☻ 9 **Facilities** Play area Family room Dogs
allowed Garden Parking

## LODERS
Map 4 SY49

### Loders Arms

**DT6 3SA ☎ 01308 422431**
e-mail: mike.webb@orange.net
dir: *Off A3066, 2m NE of Bridport*

Long-serving Palmers Brewery tenants Mike and Julie
Webb have returned to the Bridport area to run this
unassuming stone-built local, tucked away in a pretty
thatched village near the Dorset coast. Bag a seat in the
long cosy bar or in the homely dining room for gammon
steak with pineapple and egg; pan-fried scallops; home-
made fishcakes; and brie, mushroom and nut Wellington.
Or check for a barbecue in the lovely garden, with views
of Boarsbarrow Hill.

**Open** all wk **Bar Meals** L served all wk 12-2 booking
required D served all wk 6.30-9 Av main course £10.95
**Restaurant** L served all wk 12-2 D served all wk 6.30-9
⊕ PALMERS ◄ Palmers Copper, Palmers IPA, Palmers
200, Tally Ho. **Facilities** Children's menu Children's
portions Dogs allowed Garden Parking

## LOWER ANSTY
Map 4 ST70

### The Fox Inn ★★★★ INN ☻

**DT2 7PN ☎ 01258 880328 📄 01258 881440**
e-mail: fox@anstyfoxinn.co.uk
dir: *A35 from Dorchester towards Poole for 4m, exit
signed Piddlehinton/Athelhampton House, left to
Cheselbourne, then right. Pub in village opposite post
office*

The 250-year-old house was built for Charles Hall, later
to co-found Blandford's Hall & Woodhouse Brewery. When
Ansty's original Fox burnt down in 1915, the Woodhouse
family decided to move it to the family home. Badger
beers are, naturally enough, served in the bar. The oak-
panelled main restaurant is now augmented by a light
and airy garden eatery. Bar food proffers doorstep toastie

melts, or curry of the day; the carte has the likes of
Portland mussels marinière, and chicken breast wrapped
in smoked bacon. Comfortable accommodation is
available.

**Open** all day all wk **Bar Meals** L served all wk 12-2.30 D
served all wk 6.30-9 Av main course £7.50 **Restaurant** L
served all wk 12-2.30 D served all wk 6.30-9 Av 3 course
à la carte fr £18 ⊕ HALL & WOODHOUSE ◄ Badger
Tanglefoot, Badger Best, Badger Smooth, seasonal guest
ale. ☻ 12 **Facilities** Children's menu Children's portions
Dogs allowed Garden Parking **Rooms** 11

## LYME REGIS
Map 4 SY39

### Pilot Boat Inn ☻

**Bridge St DT7 3QA ☎ 01297 443157**
dir: *Telephone for directions*

Old smuggling and sea rescue tales are associated with
this busy town centre pub, close to the sea front. However
its biggest claim to fame is as the birthplace of the
original Lassie, Hollywood's favourite collie. Along with
Palmers ales, there is a good range of food on regularly
changing menus. Sandwiches, salads and cold platters
are offered, plus local crab, real scampi and chips, and
other fresh fish as available. There's also a good
vegetarian choice.

**Open** all day all wk Closed: 25 Dec **Bar Meals** food
served all day **Restaurant** food served all day
⊕ PALMERS ◄ Palmers, IPA, 200, Bridport Bitter. ☻ 9
**Facilities** Children's menu Children's portions Dogs
allowed Garden

## MARSHWOOD
Map 4 SY39

### PICK OF THE PUBS

### The Bottle Inn

**DT6 5QJ ☎ 01297 678254**
e-mail: thebottleinn@googlemail.com
dir: *On B3165 (Crewkerne to Lyme Regis road) 5m from
the Hunters Lodge*

The thatched Bottle Inn was first mentioned as an ale
house back in the 17th century, and was the first pub
in the area during the 18th century to serve bottled
beer rather than beer from the jug - hence the name.
Standing beside the B3165 on the edge of the glorious
Marshwood Vale, its rustic interior has simple wooden
settles, scrubbed tables and a blazing fire. Now under
new management the pub's lunch menu keeps it
simple with jacket potatoes, grilled paninis, burgers
like wild boar and apple, ploughman's, baguettes, lite
bites (perhaps crab cakes; pâté; or deep fried brie)
plus haddock and chips, chilli; and gammon steak. At
dinner the choices could be smoked duck with
raspberry coulis or king prawns in garlic and cream,
followed by traditional suet steak and kidney pudding
or supreme of chicken stuffed with smoked salmon
with whisky and mustard cream sauce. The pub is
home to the annual World Stinging-Nettle Eating
Championships. Look out for live music evenings, and
remember Tuesday night is steak night and Thursday
night is curry night.

*continued on page 166*

**MARSHWOOD** *continued*

Open all wk Mon-Fri noon-3 6-11, Sat-Sun all day noon-11 **Bar Meals** L served all wk 12-2.30 booking required D served Mon-Sat 6.30-9, Sun 6.30-8.30 **Restaurant** L served all wk 12-2.30 booking required D served Mon-Sat 6.30-9, Sun 6.30-8.30 booking required ⊕ FREE HOUSE ◀ Otter Ale, Otter Bitter, guest ale Ŏ Stowford Press, Thatchers Dry. **Facilities** Play area Family room Garden Parking

---

### MILTON ABBAS          Map 4 ST80

## The Hambro Arms ⬤

DT11 0BP ☎ 01258 880233
e-mail: info@hambroarms.co.uk
dir: *A354 (Dorchester to Blandford road), turn off at Royal Oak*

This 18th-century thatched pub, now owned by a partnership of villagers, is set in the midst of a picturesque village of thatched, whitewashed cottages, believed to be the first planned settlement in England. The owners' aim is to provide a traditional country pub atmosphere with exceptional food, most of it locally sourced, whether you're looking for a lunchtime snack or fine dining experience. Regular gourmet and oriental evenings are featured.

Open all wk 11-3 6-11 (Sat-Sun 11-11) ◀ Ringwood, Piddle Ales, Durdle Door Ŏ Stowford Press. ⬤ 8 **Facilities** Garden Parking

---

### MOTCOMBE          Map 4 ST82

## The Coppleridge Inn ★★★ INN ⬤

SP7 9HW ☎ 01747 851980   📠 01747 851858
e-mail: thecoppleridgeinn@btinternet.com
web: www.coppleridge.com
dir: *Take A350 towards Warminster for 1.5m, turn left at brown tourist sign. Follow signs to inn*

A working farm until the late 1980s, this 18th-century building retains plenty of traditional features, including flagstone floors and log fires. Run by the Goodinge family for nearly 20 years, it offers an excellent range of real ales and a daily-changing menu of sophisticated pub dishes such as seafood linguine with mixed fish, mussels and prawns. Outside is a large garden and terrace with Blackmore Vale views, and a secure children's playground. There are ten spacious bedrooms available situated around a tastefully converted courtyard.

---

Open all wk 11-3 5-11 (Sat 11am-mdnt Sun noon-11)
**Bar Meals** L served all wk 12-2.30 D served all wk 6-9 Av main course £9.50 **Restaurant** L served all wk 12-2.30 D served all wk 6-9 Av 3 course à la carte fr £18 ⊕ FREE HOUSE ◀ Butcombe Bitter, Greene King IPA, Wadworth 6X, Fuller's London Pride, Sharp's Doom Bar Ŏ Ashton Press. ⬤ 10 **Facilities** Children's menu Children's portions Play area Family room Dogs allowed Garden Parking **Rooms** 10

---

### NETTLECOMBE          Map 4 SY59

## Marquis of Lorne

DT6 3SY ☎ 01308 485236
e-mail: enquiries@marquisoflorne.com
dir: *From A3066 (Bridport-Beaminster road) approx 1.5m N of Bridport follow Loders & Mangerton Mill signs. At junct left past Mangerton Mill, through West Milton. 1m to T-junct, straight over. Pub up hill, approx 300yds on left*

A 16th-century farmhouse converted into a pub in 1871, when the Marquis himself named it to prove land ownership. Membership of the Campaign for Real Food means that much local produce is used. Daily menus offer such dishes as pigeon breast with juniper and red wine sauce, home-made curry, and mushroom and pepper stroganoff. This family-friendly pub also offers a children's menu and play area. Eat, drink and enjoy superb views from the beautiful gardens.

Open all wk 12-2.30 6-11 Closed: 25 Dec **Bar Meals** L served all wk 12-2 D served all wk 6-9 Av main course £11 **Restaurant** L served all wk 12-2 D served all wk 6-9 Av 3 course à la carte fr £20 ⊕ PALMERS ◀ Palmers Copper, IPA, 200 Premium Ale. **Facilities** Children's menu Children's portions Play area Dogs allowed Garden Parking

---

### NORTH WOOTTON          Map 4 ST61

## The Three Elms

DT9 5JW ☎ 01935 812881
e-mail: mark@threeelms.co.uk
dir: *From Sherborne take A352 towards Dorchester then A3030. Pub 1m on right*

On the edge of the beautiful Blackmore Vale, with views of Bulbarrow Hill, this family-friendly pub and restaurant is a clever mix of original and contemporary features. The bar is well stocked with real ales, ciders and local beers. Freshly cooked British classics are served at candlelit tables, including Sunday roasts and weekly changing blackboard specials. A typical meal might be West Country sardines, followed by liver, bacon and onions, and a home-made dessert to finish. The large beer garden hosts summer BBQs and beer festivals.

---

Open all wk 11-2.30 6.30-11 (Sun noon-3 7-10.30)
Closed: 25-26 Dec **Bar Meals** L served Mon-Sat 12-2, 12-2.30 booking required D served Mon-Sat 6.30-9.30, Sun 7-9 booking required Av main course £8.50 **Restaurant** L served Mon-Sat 12-2, Sun 12-2.30 booking required D served Mon-Sat 6.30-9.30, Sun 7-9 booking required Fixed menu price fr £9.50 Av 3 course à la carte fr £19.95 ⊕ FREE HOUSE ◀ Butcombe Bitter, Otter Bitter, Tribute Ŏ Thatchers Burrow Hill, Thatchers Dry, Ashton Press. **Facilities** Children's menu Children's portions Dogs allowed Garden Parking

---

### OSMINGTON MILLS          Map 4 SY78

## The Smugglers Inn ⬤

DT3 6HF ☎ 01305 833125
e-mail: smugglers.weymouth@hall-woodhouse.co.uk
dir: *7m E of Weymouth towards Wareham, pub signed*

Set on the cliffs at Osmington Mills with the South Coast Footpath running through the garden, the inn has beautiful views across Weymouth Bay. In the late 18th century (the inn dates back to the 13th century) it was the base of infamous smuggler Pierre La Tour who fell in love with the publican's daughter, Arabella Carless, who was shot dead while helping him to escape during a raid. Things are quieter now and you can enjoy a pint of Tanglefoot or one of the guest ales like Pickled Partridge. On the menu typical dishes are smoked haddock Benedict; venison sausages and mash; and steak and Tanglefoot pie.

Open all wk 11-11 (Sun noon-10.30) **Bar Meals** L served all wk 12-9.30 D served all wk 12-9.30 Av main course £9 food served all day **Restaurant** L served all wk 12-9.30 D served all wk 12-9.30 food served all day ⊕ HALL & WOODHOUSE ◀ Badger, Tanglefoot, guest ale. ⬤ 12 **Facilities** Children's menu Children's portions Play area Dogs allowed Garden Parking

---

### PIDDLEHINTON          Map 4 SY79

## The Thimble Inn

DT2 7TD ☎ 01300 348270
e-mail: thimbleinn@googlemail.com
dir: *A35 W'bound, right onto B3143, Piddlehinton in 4m*

Friendly village local with open fires, traditional pub games and good food cooked to order. The pub stands in a pretty valley on the banks of the River Piddle, and the riverside patio is popular in summer. Along with an excellent range of beers, the extensive menu ranges from sandwiches, ploughman's and jacket potatoes to special's such as pigeon, beef and mushroom pudding; fish crumble topped with cheesy mash; pheasant breast casserole; and a vegetarian option of three bean smoky chilli with basmati rice.

Open all wk 11.30-2.30 6-11 Closed: 25 Dec **Bar Meals** L served all wk 11.30-2 booking required D served all wk 6.30-9 booking required Av main course £7.50 **Restaurant** L served all wk 11.30-2 booking required D served all wk 6.30-9 booking required ⊕ FREE HOUSE ◀ Ringwood Best, Palmer Copper Ale & Palmer IPA, Ringwood Old Thumper, Summer Lightning Ŏ Thatchers Gold, Thatchers Dry. **Facilities** Children's menu Children's portions Dogs allowed Garden Parking

## PIDDLETRENTHIDE    Map 4 SY79

### The European Inn ♀

**DT2 7QT** ☎ **01300 348308**
**e-mail:** info@european-inn.co.uk
**web:** www.european-inn.co.uk
**dir:** 5m N of Dorchester on B3143

The name dates from as long ago as 1860, when the landlord, a soldier, returned from fighting in the Crimean War. New owners Julie and Angus Troup have refurbished the inside to provide a welcoming place to enjoy a pint of Palmers Copper or one of the twelve wines by the glass. The regularly-changing menu uses produce as fresh, seasonal and local as possible. Expect starters like leek, potato and Piddle Valley nettle soup or toasted Woolsery goat's cheese with red pepper chutney. Mains might include fillet of West Country cod with pink grapefruit and ginger dressing, sprouting broccoli and Cornish new potatoes, or succulent Black Angus Simon Harvell steaks. Head outside in warmer weather to the garden or decked area.

**Open** Tue-Sat 11.30-11 (Sun 12-7) Closed: Sun eve & Mon **Bar Meals** L served Tue-Sun 12-2 D served Tue-Sat 7-9 ⊕ FREE HOUSE ◄ Palmers Copper, Sharp's Doom Bar, Otter Bright ♂ Thatchers Gold. ♀ 12
**Facilities** Children's portions Dogs allowed Garden Parking

### The Piddle Inn ★★★★ INN

**DT2 7QF** ☎ **01300 348468** 🖹 **01300 348102**
**e-mail:** piddleinn@aol.com
**dir:** 7m N of Dorchester on B3143, in village centre

In the heart of rolling Dorset downland, tucked away in the unspoilt Piddle Valley north of Dorchester, the pub takes its name from the river flowing through the beer garden. It's a welcoming place, 18th-century, and popular for food, drink and accommodation. In the bar real ales are served straight from the barrel, and the pool table, dart board and large screen TV entertain. Traditional chargrilled meats are locally sourced and cooked fresh to order, augmented by a speciality fish board, daily specials and home-made puddings.

**Open** all day all wk **Bar Meals** L served all wk 12-2 D served all wk 6.30-9 Av main course £7.95 **Restaurant** L served all wk 12-2 D served Mon-Sat 6.30-9, Sun 7-9 booking required Av 3 course à la carte fr £23 ⊕ FREE HOUSE ◄ St Austell Tribute, Dorset Piddle ♂ Thatchers Gold, Cornish Rattler. **Facilities** Children's menu Children's portions Dogs allowed Garden Parking **Rooms** 3

### The Poachers Inn ♀

**DT2 7QX** ☎ **01300 348358** 🖹 **01300 348153**
**e-mail:** info@ thepoachersinn.co.uk
**dir:** 6m N from Dorchester on B3143. At church end of village

Saxon King Ethelred's wife Emma founded the village; Thomas Hardy loved it and today's licensees at The Poachers continue this deeply ingrained sense of heritage with a comfortably welcoming, traditional inn beside the River Piddle. Classic pub meals (steak and ale pie) vie with contemporary alternatives (yellow fin sole with brown butter) in the fashionably furnished bar and restaurant, or relax in the pool-side beer garden with a glass of local Palmer's bitter.

**Open** all day all wk 8am-mdnt **Bar Meals** L served all wk 12-2.30 D served all wk 6-9.30 Av main course £8 **Restaurant** L served all wk 12-2.30 D served all wk 6-9.30 Av 3 course à la carte fr £15 ⊕ FREE HOUSE ◄ Wadworth 6X, Palmers Copper Ale, Guinness, John Smith's, Tinners, Doom Bar ♂ Thatchers Gold. ♀ 9
**Facilities** Children's menu Children's portions Dogs allowed Garden Parking

## PLUSH    Map 4 ST70

### The Brace of Pheasants ♀

**DT2 7RQ** ☎ **01300 348357** 🖹 **01300 348959**
**e-mail:** info@braceofpheasants.co.uk
**dir:** A35 onto B3143, 5m to Piddletrenthide, then right to Mappowder & Plush

Tucked away in a fold of the hills in the heart of Hardy's beloved county is this small 16th-century thatched village inn. With a welcoming open fire, oak beams and fresh flowers, it's an ideal place to start or end a walk. Along with a good selection of real ales and 18 wines by the glass, a menu might offer beer battered pigeon breast strips with Scandinavian style cabbage and beetroot salad; caramelised leek, garden pea and basil risotto; garlic and herb marinated local venison steak. Home-made desserts could be mocha crème brûlée; or treacle tart and double cream.

**Open** noon-3 7-11 Closed: 25 Dec, Mon (ex BH) Sun eve **Bar Meals** L served Tue-Sun 12-2.30 D served Tue-Sat 7-9.30 **Restaurant** L served Tue-Sun 12-2.30 D served Tue-Sat 7-9.30 ⊕ FREE HOUSE ◄ Dorset Brewing Co, Palmers, Dorset Piddle, Sharp's Doom Bar ♂ Stowford Press. ♀ 18 **Facilities** Children's portions Dogs allowed Garden Parking

## POOLE    Map 4 SZ09

### The Guildhall Tavern

**15 Market St BH15 1NB**
☎ **01202 671717** 🖹 **01202 242346**
**e-mail:** sewerynsevfred@aol.com
**dir:** 2 mins from Quay

Originally a cider house, this pub stands in the heart of Poole's old town, just two minutes from the historic quay. Beautifully fresh fish and seafood dominate the bilingual menus, which reflect the owners' Gallic roots. So you could find mini bouillabaisse de Marseille (a home-made fish soup), with pan-fried fresh skate wing to follow. But meat eaters will be more than satisfied with Charolais beef and a sauce of your choice, or duck breast served with raspberry and shallot gravy. French themed evenings are held every month.

**Open** Tue-Sat Closed: 1st 2wks Nov, Mon, Sun **Bar Meals** L served Tue-Sat 11.30-3 Av main course £17 **Restaurant** L served Tue-Sun 11.30-3 D served Tue-Sun 6-10 Fixed menu price fr £14.25 Av 3 course à la carte fr £30 ⊕ PUNCH TAVERNS ◄ Ringwood Best.
**Facilities** Children's menu Children's portions Dogs allowed Parking

## PICK OF THE PUBS

### The Rising Sun ◉◉ ♀

**3 Dear Hay Ln BH15 1NZ** ☎ **01202 771246**
**e-mail:** paul@risingsunpoole.co.uk
**dir:** 7m from Wimborne B3073, A349 take A350 signed Poole/Channel Ferries

Spruced-up and reinvented as a stylish gastro-pub, this 18th-century pub just off the High Street in Poole offers a warm and relaxing atmosphere, whether you are popping for a pint of Ringwood Best in the elegant lounge bar, or heading for the charming restaurant to explore Greg Etheridge's innovative menus (two AA Rosettes). Both lunch and dinner menus successfully combine traditional pub classics with more adventurous dishes and make sound use of fresh local ingredients. Lunch offers salads, inventive sandwiches, starters like potted shin of beef with home-made piccalilli and toasted soda bread, and a tapas board of cured meat, cheese and olives, and main courses like salmon fishcakes with chive butter sauce, and beer battered cod with pea purée and chunky chips. Evening extras may include roast rack of Honeybrook Farm lamb with curly kale and cannellini and butter bean stew, and whole baked anchovy stuffed bream with caper and shallot butter. Round off, perhaps, with lemon posset and poached figs.

**Open** all day Closed: 25 Dec, Sun eve **Bar Meals** L served Mon-Sat 12-2.30, Sun 12-4 D served Mon-Sat 6-9.30 booking required Av main course £12 **Restaurant** L served Mon-Sat 12-2.30, Sun 12-5 booking required D served Mon-Sat 6-10 booking required ⊕ ENTERPRISE INNS ◄ Amstel, Ringwood Best Bitter, ♂ Stowford Press. ♀ 12
**Facilities** Children's portions Garden Parking

## POWERSTOCK  Map 4 SY59

### PICK OF THE PUBS

## Three Horseshoes Inn

**DT6 3TF** ☎ **01308 485328** 🖹 **01308 485229**
dir: *3m from Bridport off A3066 (Beaminster road)*

Now in new hands, the "Shoes" is a pretty Victorian inn belonging to Bridport's Palmers Brewery. The patio, terraced garden and guest rooms look out over the village, which lies at the foot of Eggardon hill fort, from which you can see Start Point in South Devon on a clear day. A reputation for excellent cooking owes much to the kitchen's devotion to local produce, especially game in winter and fresh fish in the summer. Typical starters of watercress soup with goat's curd, toast and pesto; or hot smoked eel could be followed by partridge with creamed sprout tops, bacon and chestnuts; macaroni cheese with wild mushrooms, spinach and Dorset Blue Vinny cheese; or Lyme Bay whiting in beer batter with hand-cut chips, crushed peas and chunky tartare sauce. Desserts - all home made - include treacle tart and whisky cream; and plum, apple and walnut crumble with custard.

**Open** 12-3 6.30-11.30 (Sun noon-3 6.30-10.30pm) Closed: Mon L **Bar Meals** L served Tue-Sat 12-2.30, Sun 12-3 D served Tue-Sat 7-9, Sun 7-8.30 Av main course £12 **Restaurant** L served Tue-Sat 12-2.30, Sun 12-3 D served Tue-Sat 6.30-9.30 Av 3 course à la carte fr £25 ⌗ PALMERS ⬛ Palmer's IPA, Copper Ale ♨ Thatchers Gold. **Facilities** Children's menu Children's portions Play area Family room Dogs allowed Garden Parking

## PUNCKNOWLE  Map 4 SY58

## The Crown Inn ♀

**Church St DT2 9BN** ☎ **01308 897711**
e-mail: crownpuncknowle@btinternet.com
dir: *From A35, into Bridevally, through Litton Cheney. From B3157, inland at Swyre*

There's a traditional atmosphere within the rambling, low-beamed bars at this picturesque 16th-century thatched inn, which was once the haunt of smugglers on their way from nearby Chesil Beach to visit prosperous customers in Bath. Food ranges from light snacks and sandwiches to home-made dishes like lamb chops with mint sauce and tuna steak with basil and tomato sauce. Accompany your meal with a glass of real ale or one of the eight wines by the glass.

**Open** 12-3 6-11 Closed: Sun eve in Winter **Bar Meals** L served all wk 12-2 D served Mon-Sat 6-9 Av main course £8 **Restaurant** L served all wk 12-2 D served Mon-Sat 6-9 Av 3 course à la carte fr £18 ⌗ PALMERS ⬛ Palmers IPA, 200 Premium Ale, Copper, Tally Ho! ♨ Thatchers Gold. ♀ 8 **Facilities** Children's menu Children's portions Family room Dogs allowed Garden Parking

## SHAPWICK  Map 4 ST90

## The Anchor Inn ♀ NEW

**West St DT11 9LB** ☎ **01258 857269**
e-mail: anchorshapwick@btconnect.com
dir: *From Wimborne or Blandford Forum take B3082. Pub signed. From A31, A350 towards Blandford Forum, turn right to Sturminster Marshall then follow Shapwick signs*

The discreet changes Mark Thornton has made to this village centre pub have made it more comfortable, without compromising its rural feel. So you can still sit by an open fire, or head outside, where a waitress will bring your pan-fried halibut with samphire and citrus butter sauce; marinated goat chops with Moroccan almond and apricot sauce; or fennel and lemon risotto with pine-nuts. As well as the enticing menu, the bar offers four real ales and a keenly priced wine list.

**Open** noon-3 6-11 Closed: Sun eve **Bar Meals** L served 12.15-2.30 booking required D served 6.15-9.30 booking required Av main course £12.50 ⌗ FREE HOUSE ⬛ Ringwood Best, Keystone, Jennings ♨ Thatchers, Rosie. ♀ 16 **Facilities** Children's portions Play area Dogs allowed Garden Parking

## SHERBORNE  Map 4 ST61

## *The Digby Tap*

**Cooks Ln DT9 3NS** ☎ **01935 813148** 🖹 **01935 816768**
dir: *Telephone for directions*

Old-fashioned town pub with stone-flagged floors, old beams and a wide-ranging choice of real ale. A hearty menu of pub grub includes lasagne, steak and kidney pie, rump steak, gammon steak, and plaice or cod. The pub was used as a location for the 1990 TV drama *A Murder of Quality*, that starred Denholm Elliot and Glenda Jackson. Scenes from the film can be seen on the pub walls.

**Open** all day all wk 11-11 (Sun noon-11) ⬛ Otter Bitter, Sharp's Cornish Coaster, St Austell Tinners ♨ Thatchers Gold. **Facilities** Family room Dogs allowed **Notes** ◉

### PICK OF THE PUBS

## The Kings Arms ★★★★★ INN ♀ NEW

**North Rd, Charlton Horethorne DT9 4NL**
☎ **01963 220281** 🖹 **01963 220496**
e-mail: admin@thekingsarms.co.uk
dir: *On A3145, N of Sherborne. Pub in village centre*

Tony and Sarah Lethbridge's 17-month restoration of this striking village inn ended in March 2009, when they flung open the doors of their now chic country inn.

Business has been brisk ever since, with both locals and visitors finding favour with the 10 swish new bedrooms, named and decorated after gemstones and replete with marble en suite bathrooms, and Sarah's innovative menu, which offers a successful blend of modern British and classic pub dishes. Either bag a table in the stone-flagged front bar, kitted out with Farrow and Ball hues, old dining tables and bold artwork, or head for the contemporary-styled rear restaurant, or the super rear terrace and garden, with its posh teak tables and croquet lawn, and order from the daily lunch and dinner menus. Typical choices from the latter include duck liver parfait with red onion marmalade, lamb rump with parsnip purée and ricotta and mint gnocchi, and rhubarb and custard pannacotta. Lighter lunchtime additions take in warm crab bruschetta, ham, egg and chips, and steak and Guinness pie. A cracking addition to the Dorset pub scene.

**Open** all day all wk **Bar Meals** L served all wk 12-2.30 booking required D served Mon-Thu 7-9.30, Sat 7-10, Sun 7-9 booking required **Restaurant** L served all wk 12-2.30 booking required D served Mon-Tu 7-9.30, Sat 7-10, Sun 7-9 booking required ⌗ FREE HOUSE ⬛ Butcombe, Kings Arms Tipple, Bishops Tipple, 6X, Keystone Gold ♨ Lawrences. ♀ 19 **Facilities** Children's menu Children's portions Dogs allowed Garden Parking **Rooms** 10

## Queen's Head

**High St, Milborne Port DT9 5DQ** ☎ **01963 250314**
e-mail: info@queenshead.co.uk
dir: *On A30, 2.5m W of Sherborne towards Sailsbury*

Milborne Port has no facilities for shipping, the suffix being Old English for 'borough', a status it acquired in 1249. The building came much later, in Elizabethan times, although no mention is made of it as a hostelry until 1738. This popular old inn offers great real ales and dishes along the lines of grilled pork loin steaks with gin and coriander sauce; red snapper supreme with vegetable risotto; crispy battered cod; curry of the day; and vegetable paella.

**Open** all wk 11-2.30 5.30-11.30 (Fri-Sat 11am-mdnt) **Bar Meals** L served all wk 12-2.30 booking required D served all wk 5.30-9.30 booking required Av main course £7.50 **Restaurant** L served all wk 12-2.30 booking required D served all wk 5.30-9.30 booking required ⌗ ENTERPRISE INNS ⬛ Butcombe Bitters, Fuller's London Pride, Hopback Summer Lightning. **Facilities** Dogs allowed Garden Parking

## *Skippers Inn* ♀

**Horsecastles DT9 3HE** ☎ **01935 812753**
e-mail: chrisfrowde@tiscali.co.uk
dir: *From Yeovil A30 to Sherborne*

'You don't need a newspaper in Skippers, read the walls'. So says the proprietor about his end-of-terrace converted cider house, and Sherborne's self-styled premier fish restaurant. The crammed blackboard menu has everything from game, duck, chicken and venison to steaks, sandwiches, soup, and around 12 fresh fish dishes. On Sunday there are three roasts to choose from.

**Open** all wk 11-2.30 6-11 (Sun 12-2 7-10.30) Closed: 25 Dec ◀ Wadworth 6X, Henrys IPA, Guest ales ♻ Stowford Press. ♟ 8 **Facilities** Garden Parking

---

### SHROTON OR IWERNE COURTNEY    Map 4 ST81

## PICK OF THE PUBS

# The Cricketers

DT11 8QD ☎ 01258 860421 📄 01258 861800
e-mail: cricketers@heartstoneinns.co.uk
dir: *7m S of Shaftesbury on A350, turn right after Iwerne Minster. 5m N of Blandford Forum on A360, past Stourpaine, in 2m left into Shroton. Pub in village centre*

The Cricketers nestles under Hambledon Hill, known for its Iron Age hill forts. A classic English hostelry built at the turn of the 20th century, themed nights and regular events put The Cricketers firmly at the heart of the community; you may very well meet the village cricket team here in the summer months. The pub is also popular with hikers, lured from the Wessex Way which runs conveniently through the garden. The open plan interior comprises a main bar decorated with a collection of sporting memorabilia, comfy seating and pleasant eating areas – all light and airy rooms leading to the restaurant at the rear. This in turn overlooks a lovely garden, well stocked with trees and flowers. Butcombe and Otter are among the real ales on offer. Home-made chilli con carne, luxury fish pie and the Cricketers' ultimate burger give a flavour of the menu; the specials board includes the catch of the day.

**Open** all wk 11-3 6-11 (Sat-Sun 11-11 summer only) **Bar Meals** L served all wk 12-2.30 booking required D served Mon-Sat 6-9.30 booking required Av main course £10 **Restaurant** L served all wk 12-2.30 booking required D served Mon-Sat 6-9.30 booking required Av 3 course à la carte fr £10 ⊕ FREE HOUSE ◀ Tribute Cornish Ale, Butcombe, Otter Ale ♻ Stowford Press. **Facilities** Children's menu Children's portions Garden Parking

---

### STOKE ABBOTT    Map 4 ST40

## The New Inn

DT8 3JW ☎ 01308 868333
dir: *1.5m from Beaminster*

A welcoming 17th-century farmhouse turned village inn, with thatched roof, log fires and a beautiful garden. It offers three real ales, and an extensive menu of light meals such as grilled black pudding with caramelised apples, and cold smoked duck breast with plum chutney, plus a good choice of baguettes, sandwiches and vegetarian dishes. Specials might include pork schnitzel with sweet chili dip, scallops wrapped in bacon, and beef and mushroom pie.

**Open** Tue-Sun Closed: Mon ◀ Palmers IPA & 200 Premium Ale, Tally Ho, Copper IPA. **Facilities** Dogs allowed Garden Parking

---

### STRATTON    Map 4 SY69

## Saxon Arms ♟

DT2 9WG ☎ 01305 260020
e-mail: rodsaxonlamont1@yahoo.co.uk
dir: *3m NW of Dorchester on A37. Pub between church & village hall*

With its solid oak beams, log-burning stove and flagstone floors, this pretty thatched free house makes a great first impression. Popular with fishermen and cycling clubs, the pub is also handy for riverside walks. Stowford Press cider offers a fresh alternative to the good selection of beers, whilst menu choices include Dorset ham, egg and chips; smoked haddock and spring onion fishcake; and warm spinach and feta cheese pie.

**Open** all wk 11-3 5.30-late (Sat-Sun 11am-late) **Bar Meals** L served Mon-Sat 11-2.15, Sun 12-9 booking required D served Mon-Sat 6-9.15, Sun 12-9 booking required Av main course £6.95 **Restaurant** L served Mon-Sat 11-2.15, Sun 12-9 booking required D served Mon-Sat 6-9.15, Sun 12-9 booking required Fixed menu price fr £8.95 ⊕ FREE HOUSE ◀ Fuller's London Pride, Palmers IPA, Ringwood, Timothy Taylor, Butcombe, Abbot, Ruddles ♻ Stowford Press. ♟ 15 **Facilities** Children's menu Children's portions Dogs allowed Garden Parking

---

### STUDLAND    Map 5 SZ08

## The Bankes Arms Hotel

Watery Ln BH19 3AU
☎ 01929 450225 📄 01929 450307
web: www.bankesarms.com
dir: *B3369 from Poole, across on Sandbanks chain ferry, or A35 from Poole, A351 then B3351*

Close to sweeping Studland Bay, across which can be seen the prime real estate enclave of Sandbanks, is this part 15th-century, creeper-clad inn, once a smugglers' dive. It specialises in fresh fish and seafood, but also offers game casserole, lamb noisettes in mint, honey and orange sauce, and spicy pork in chilli, coriander and

caper sauce. The annual beer festival held in its large garden showcases 60 real ales, music, Morris dancing and stone carving.

*The Bankes Arms Hotel*

**Open** all day all wk 11-11 (Sun 11-10.30) Closed: 25 Dec **Bar Meals** L served all wk 12-3 (Summer & BH 12-9) D served all wk 6-9 (Summer & BH 12-9) ⊕ FREE HOUSE ◀ Isle of Purbeck Fossil Fuel, Studland Bay Wrecked, Solar Power, IPA ♻ Westons Old Rosie, Thatchers Cheddar Valley. **Facilities** Children's menu Dogs allowed Garden Parking

---

### SYDLING ST NICHOLAS    Map 4 SY69

## PICK OF THE PUBS

# The Greyhound Inn ★★★★ INN ⑧ ♟

DT2 9PD ☎ 01300 341303
e-mail: info@thegreyhounddorset.net
dir: *Off A37 (Yeovil to Dorchester road), turn off at Cerne Abbas/Sydling St Nicholas*

Tucked away in a tranquil village in a glorious valley north of Dorchester, the 17th-century Greyhound Inn is the perfect pub from which to explore Hardy Country. Bedrooms in the converted skittle alley are individually decorated and well appointed, some have four-poster beds and all have smart en suite bathrooms. Visit postcard-pretty Cerne Abbas or head to the coast for an invigorating cliff path walk, before returning to relax in the neat open-plan bar, replete with traditional pine and darkwood furnishings and country prints, with a pint of local Palmer's IPA. The food will not disappoint either, the modern British menu and interesting daily specials make sound use of local produce. Best enjoyed in the warmly decorated dining room, the choice may include scallops with pea shoot and pancetta salad, or pigeon breast and oxtail faggot with port and shallot marmalade for starters, with rack of lamb with pea and mint purée or monkfish with chorizo, fresh basil, cherry tomatoes and sherry for main course. Round off with vanilla and passionfruit brûlée. Super, sun-trap front terrace for summer alfresco dining.

**Open** all wk 11-2.30 6-11 Closed: Sun eve **Bar Meals** L served all wk 12-2 booking required D served Mon-Sat 6-9 booking required **Restaurant** L served all wk 12-2 booking required D served Mon-Sat 6-9 booking required Av 3 course à la carte fr £20 ⊕ FREE HOUSE ◀ Palmer IPA, Wadworth 6X, St Austell Tinners, Old Speckled Hen, Spitfire ♻ Thatchers Gold. ♟ 12 **Facilities** Children's menu Children's portions Play area Dogs allowed Garden Parking **Rooms** 6

## TARRANT MONKTON — Map 4 ST90

### PICK OF THE PUBS

## The Langton Arms ★★★★ INN

DT11 8RX ☎ 01258 830225 📄 01258 830053
e-mail: info@thelangtonarms.co.uk
dir: *A31 from Ringwood, or A357 from Shaftesbury, or A35 from Bournemouth*

Occupying a peaceful spot close to the village church, this attractive 17th-century thatched inn serves real ales from four pumps; the house beer, Hidden Pint, comes from the Hidden Brewery at Dinton near Salisbury. Two bars, the Farmers and the Carpenters, are relaxing places for both drinkers and diners; the carte and traditional pub dishes are served in each, as well as in the Stables restaurant and conservatory. Here, a fulfilling meal on a weekday might comprise local game terrine, followed by duo of free-range duck, and then apple, pear and cinnamon crumble with custard. If traditional fayre is more your style, you will have to choose between the likes of ham, egg and chips; locally-made faggot with a mild horseradish mash; a trio of venison and wild boar sausages; and the Langton Arms game pie. Sharing platters are popular too. Vegetarians will be delighted with baked aubergine and roasted tomato coulis, stuffed with sweet peppers, courgettes and glazed with mozzarella. All the comfortable and well equipped bedrooms are on the ground floor.

**Open** all day all wk **Bar Meals** L served Mon-Fri 12-2.30, Sat-Sun all day D served Mon-Thu 6-9.30, Fri 6-10, Sat-Sun all day **Restaurant** L served Mon-Fri 12-2.30, Sat-Sun all day D served Mon-Thu 6-9.30, Fri 6-10, Sat-Sun all day ⊕ FREE HOUSE ◀ Guest ales (all local). **Facilities** Children's menu Children's portions Play area Family room Dogs allowed Garden Parking **Rooms** 6

## TRENT — Map 4 ST51

### PICK OF THE PUBS

## Rose & Crown Trent ♥

DT9 4SL ☎ 01935 850776 📄 01935 850776
e-mail: hkirkie@hotmail.com
dir: *Just off A30 between Sherborne & Yeovil*

This ivy-clad, thatched inn is situated in the conservation village of Trent. The original building dates from the 14th century, when workers erecting the spire of the church opposite lived in it, although the structure as it is now is 18th century, and was first a farmhouse before becoming an inn. Recently refurbished, the interior still speaks eloquently of its past, especially in the Trent Barrow Room, which has a massive open fire, plenty of seating, old bottles, books and walls that must resonate with whatever a former landlord called Buff Biggins got up to that made him 'infamous'. Generations of farmers have beaten a path here for a pint, these days brewed by Wadworth in Devizes. Apart from the restaurant, which has wonderful views, you can eat in the beer garden, or at the front of the pub. Look out for the popular sausage menu.

**Open** 12-3 6-11 (Sat-Sun 12-11) Closed: Mon **Bar Meals** L served Tue-Sun 12-3 booking required D served Tue-Sat 6-9 booking required Av main course £8.95 **Restaurant** L served Tue-Sun 12-3 D served Tue-Sat 6-9 booking required Fixed menu price fr £12.95 Av 3 course à la carte fr £26.95 ⊕ WADWORTH ◀ 6X, Henry's IPA, Horizon, Bishops Tipple, guest ale ♂ Stowford Press, Thatchers Gold. ♥ 8 **Facilities** Family room Dogs allowed Garden Parking

## WEST BEXINGTON — Map 4 SY58

## The Manor Hotel ★★ HL

DT2 9DF ☎ 01308 897616 📄 01308 897704
e-mail: themanorhotel@btconnect.com
dir: *On B3157, 5m E of Bridport*

Overlooking the Jurassic Coast's most famous feature, Chesil Beach, parts of this ancient manor house date from the 11th century. It offers an inviting mix of flagstones, Jacobean oak panelling, roaring fires, comfortable en suite rooms, and a cosy cellar bar serving Dorset beer and organic cider. Locally sourced dishes include grilled John Dory; Peggy's Gloucester Old Spot sausages; butternut squash risotto; and, in season, jugged hare. Muddy boots, dogs or children won't raise any eyebrows. There has been a recent change of hands.

**Open** all day all wk 11.30am-11pm **Bar Meals** L served all wk 12-2 D served all wk 6.30-9 ⊕ FREE HOUSE ◀ Good Choice, guest ales. **Facilities** Children's menu Play area Family room Dogs allowed Garden Parking **Rooms** 13

## WEST LULWORTH — Map 4 SY88

## The Castle Inn ♥

Main Rd BH20 5RN ☎ 01929 400311 📄 01929 400415
e-mail: office@lulworthinn.com
dir: *Follow village signs from A352 (Dorchester to Wareham road). Inn on right on B3070 through West Lulworth. Car park opposite*

In a delightful setting near Lulworth Cove, this family-run thatched village inn lies close to plenty of good walks. The friendly bars offer a traditional atmosphere in which to enjoy a pint of well-kept Isle of Purbeck. Outside, you'll find large tiered gardens packed with plants, and in summer there's a giant outdoor chess set. The wide-ranging menu includes chicken stroganoff, seafood stew, sirloin steak grill, and tuna steak. There's also a good vegetarian choice.

**Open** all wk Closed: 25 Dec ◀ John Smith's, Sharps, Isle of Purbeck, Piddle Ales, Palmers. ♥ 8 **Facilities** Dogs allowed Garden Parking

## Lulworth Cove Inn ★★★ INN ♥ NEW

Main Rd BH20 5RQ ☎ 01929 400333 📄 01929 400453
e-mail: inn@lulworth-cove.com
dir: *From A352 (Dorchester to Wareham road) follow Lulworth Cove signs. Innat end of B3070, opposite car park*

Lulworth Cove's fabulous horseshoe bay, one of England's greatest natural wonders, is just steps away from this striking old inn; many of the letting rooms of which have memorable views of Dorset's Jurassic Coast World Heritage Site. Ramblers can sate their appetites with locally-sourced wild boar and apple faggots or hand-made Dorset pork and herb sausages; more simple fare includes coastal Cheddar baguettes and crab hot pot, taken in the bar, restaurant or alfresco. A Sunday carvery is now available.

**Open** all day all wk **Bar Meals** L served all day Etr-Oct (Winter Mon-Fri 1-3) D served all day Etr-Oct (Winter Mon-Fri 6-9) Av main course £8.95 **Restaurant** L served all day Etr-Oct (Winter Mon-Fri 1-3) D served all day Etr-Oct (Winter Mon-Fri 6-9) Fixed menu price fr £15.95 Av 3 course à la carte fr £25 ⊕ HALL & WOODHOUSE ◀ Badger Ales, HB Extra Cold, HB Export, HB Premium ♂ Applewood. ♥ 10 **Facilities** Children's menu Children's portions Dogs allowed Garden **Rooms** 13

*See advert on opposite page*

## WEYMOUTH — Map 4 SY67

## The Old Ship Inn

7 The Ridgeway DT3 5QQ ☎ 01305 812522
e-mail: theoldshippinn@googlemail.com
dir: *3m from Weymouth town centre, at bottom of The Ridgeway*

Thomas Hardy refers to this pub in his novels *Under the Greenwood Tree* and *The Trumpet Major*. It is the oldest pub in the village and has been welcoming travellers for 400 years. Copper pans, old clocks and a beamed open fire create just the right atmosphere inside, while outside the garden offers views over Weymouth. With a frequently changing menu, you will find good home cooked pub food here along with great real ales and traditional ciders.

**Open** all day all wk **Bar Meals** L served Mon-Sat 12-2.30, Sun 12-6 D served Mon-Sat 6-9 ⊕ PUNCH TAVERNS ◀ Otter, Jurassic, Sharp's Doom Bar, guest ales ♂ Westons Old Rosie, Scrumpy. **Facilities** Children's menu Children's portions Dogs allowed Garden Parking

## WINTERBORNE ZELSTON    Map 4 SY89

### Botany Bay Inne ♟

**DT11 9ET ☎ 01929 459227**
**dir:** *A31 between Bere Regis & Wimborne Minster*

Built in the 1920s as The General Allenby, the pub's name was changed during the 1990s in belated recognition of prisoners from Dorchester jail who spent their last nights in the area before transportation to Australia. Modern travellers are spared this fate, so drop by to enjoy varied menus that range from traditional pub favourites like battered cod with chips and peas; to leek and Stilton tart; and herby roasted rack of lamb.

**Open** all wk 10-3 6-11.30 **Bar Meals** L served all wk (breakfast)10-12, (lunch)12-2.15 D served all wk 6.30-9.30 Av main course £8 **Restaurant** L served all wk (breakfast)10-12, (lunch) 12-2.15 booking required D served all wk 6.30-9.30 booking required Av 3 course à la carte fr £16 ⊕ HALL & WOODHOUSE ◀ Badger First Gold, Tanglefoot, Guest ales. ♟ 10 **Facilities** Children's menu Children's portions Dogs allowed Garden Parking

## WORTH MATRAVERS    Map 4 SY97

### PICK OF THE PUBS

### The Square and Compass

**BH19 3LF ☎ 01929 439229**
**dir:** *Between Corfe Castle & Swanage. From B3069 follow signs for Worth Matravers*

Overlooking the English Channel, an unspoilt stone-built pub which has been run by the Newman family since 1907. A book on sale in the bar captures its fascinating history, and is crammed with stories, anecdotes and pictures collected during the 'Newman century'; its simple interior – there is no bar, just a serving hatch – can have seen few radical changes in that time. Stone flags on the floor come from local quarries, there's a wood-burner in the tap-room, an open fire in the oak-panelled larger room, and a museum of local artefacts (some dating from Roman times) together with a collection of fossils from the nearby Jurassic Coast. Award-winning Wessex and West Country beers come straight from the barrel; real ciders include an award-winning seasonal traditional cider home-pressed by landlord Charlie Newman. Any of these will perfectly accompany a traditional hot pasty or pie with various fillings, these being the only food options. Live music is played in the evenings throughout the year.

Open all wk 12-3 6-11 (12-11 in summer) **Bar Meals** L served all wk D served all wk food served all day ⊕ FREE HOUSE ◀ Palmer's Copper Ale & Dorset Gold, RCH Pitchfork, Hop Back Summer Lightning Ŏ Hecks Farmhouse, Single Variety, Seasonal home-produced. **Facilities** Dogs allowed Garden Notes ⊛

## DURHAM, CO

### AYCLIFFE    Map 19 NZ22

### The County ★★★★ RR ♟

**13 The Green, Aycliffe Village DL5 6LX**
**☎ 01325 312273  🖹 01325 317131**
**e-mail:** info@thecountyaycliffevillage.com
**dir:** *Off A167 into Aycliffe Village. Off Junct 59 A1(M)*

This award-winning, self-styled restaurant with rooms overlooks the village green. Within doorstep distance are top quality suppliers of fish, meat, game and many of the other ingredients that make up the seasonal menus and daily specials, such as chargrilled steaks; fillet of lemon sole; home-made steak and kidney pie; and wild mushroom and spinach risotto. Locally sourced food deserves locally produced real ales – the County's very own brew is one that clamours for attention.

*continued on page 172*

# *Lulworth Cove Inn*

Main Road, West Lulworth, Wareham, Dorset BH20 5RQ
Tel: 01929 400333    Fax: 01929 400534
Email: inn@lulworth-cove.co.uk    Web: www.lulworth-cove.co.uk

Situated 500 metres from Lulworth Cove on the Jurassic Coast. The inn has gained an enviable reputation for locally caught seafood and award winning real ales.

Owned by Blandford Brewers, Hall & Woodhouse this traditional coastal inn is set firmly amongst its 17th century colourful past.

The inn boasts 13 en-suite 3 star rated letting rooms, many with lovely sea views. The large bar opens to a sea view garden.

Crab, lobster and seafood are provided by Joe Miller of Cove Fish whose family has fished the coastal Jurassic waters for many generations.

Chefs specials include seasonal hand dived scallops. Year round crab, lobster, bass, skate and many more species as well as a full bar menu including char-grilled steaks, fish, handmade burgers and our own crispy beer battered cod. Open all year round. Free Wifi internet throughout.

**AYCLIFFE** *continued*

Open all wk 12-3 6-11 Closed: 25 Dec, 1 Jan **Bar Meals** L served Mon-Sat 12-2, Sun 12-2.30 **D** served all wk 6-9 Av main course £8.95 **Restaurant** L served Mon-Sat 12-2, Sun 12-2.30 D served all wk 6-9 Fixed menu price fr £9.95 Av 3 course à la carte fr £25 ⊕ FREE HOUSE ◀ Yorkshire Dales, Hawkshead, Jennings County Best Bitter, Black Sheep, Cooper Hoop. ♚ 10 **Facilities** Children's portions Parking **Rooms** 7

### BARNARD CASTLE　　　　　Map 19 NZ01

## PICK OF THE PUBS

## The Bridge Inn

**Whorlton Village DL12 8XD** ☎ **01833 627341**
e-mail: info@thebridgeinnrestaurant.co.uk
dir: *Telephone for directions*

Chef/patron Paul O'Hara's idea at his 'eating and drinking house' is to fuse together the creativity and excitement of the city, with great local produce, so now the good people of Teesdale enjoy good real ales, an extensive wine list and a wide choice of fine food. The menus are concise and food treated in a simple and honest way. In either the bar, the restaurant (open in the evening) or outside, start with pigeon breast, crispy bacon, black pudding and nettle risotto; sweet cured herrings with horseradish and beetroot; potted Craster kipper, melba toast; and then try to decide between caramelised onion and cherry tomato tart; roast rump of lamb and mushy peas; Hanger steak au poivre; saffron risotto with salsa verde; or Bridge Inn fishcake with buttered spinach. To finish, leave room for rhubarb fool; chocolate truffle cake; or iced cinder toffee parfait.

Open Tue-Fri noon-2 6.30-11 (Mon-Sat 6.30-11) Closed: 24 Dec eve, 25-26 Dec, 1-10 Jan, Sun, Sat L, Mon L **Bar Meals** L served Tue-Fri 12-2 booking required D served Mon-Sat 6.30-11 booking required Av main course £6 **Restaurant** L served Tue-Fri 12-2 booking required D served Mon-Sat 6.30-11 booking required Fixed menu price fr £7.50 Av 3 course à la carte fr £19 ◀ Timothy Taylor Landlord, Theakstons Black Bull, Adnams Best Bitter, Greene King IPA. **Facilities** Children's portions Dogs allowed Garden Parking

## PICK OF THE PUBS

## The Morritt Arms Hotel ★★★ HL ♚

**Greta Bridge DL12 9SE**
☎ 01833 627232　📠 01833 627392
e-mail: relax@themorritt.co.uk
dir: *At Scotch Corner take A66 towards Penrith, after 9m turn at Greta Bridge. Hotel over bridge on left*

Situated in rural Teesdale, The Morritt Arms has been an inn for two centuries. Full of character, the Dickens bar, with its interesting mural, is the place to go for a lunchtime pint of Black Sheep and a snack or bar meal. Very much focused on food, The Morritt can meet most demands, from morning coffee or a traditional afternoon tea, to a contemporary à la carte menu in the evening.

The establishment's approach to fine dining has been totally revamped, as has the decor and the pricing – all aimed at encouraging more people to treat themselves more often without incurring a huge bill. Expect continental flavours to appear in a typical dinner choice of Mediterranean vegetable frittata, home-made houmous, and black olives; a main course of butter-fried rainbow trout with pea and prawn risotto; and a dessert of strawberry tiramisu, strawberry wonton and chocolate scroll. En suite bedrooms, 27 in total, make this a popular function and wedding venue.

Open all day all wk 7am-11pm (Sun 7-10.30pm) **Bar Meals** Av main course £14 food served all day **Restaurant** L served all wk 12-3 D served all wk 7-9.30 Av 3 course à la carte fr £25 ⊕ FREE HOUSE ◀ John Smith's, Timothy Taylor Landlord, Black Sheep Best. ♚ 16 **Facilities** Children's menu Children's portions Play area Family room Dogs allowed Garden Parking **Rooms** 27

### COTHERSTONE　　　　　Map 19 NZ01

## The Fox and Hounds

**DL12 9PF** ☎ **01833 650241**
e-mail: ianswinburn999@btinternet.com
dir: *4m W of Barnard Castle. From A66 onto B6277, signed*

Huddled above one of the village greens in pretty Cotherstone, at the heart of beautiful Teesdale and just a stone's throw from the river's wooded gorge. Beams, open fires and cosy corners tempt you to linger at this 360 year old inn, sip Yorkshire Terrier bitter and contemplate the well-balanced menu drawing on the bountiful largesse of the Tees Valley's farms and estates. Both starters and mains include choices using the tasty local Cotherstone cheese, or sample slow braised venison shank or Teesdale spring lamb chops on rosemary mash.

Open all wk 12-2.30 6.30-11 (Sun 6.30-10.30) Closed: 25-26 Dec **Bar Meals** L served all wk 12-2 D served all wk 6.30-9 Av main course £8.90 **Restaurant** D served all wk 6.30-9 Fixed menu price fr £13.50 Av 3 course à la carte fr £18.90 ⊕ FREE HOUSE ◀ Black Sheep Best, Village Brewer Bull Bitter, Black Sheep Ale, Daleside Special, Yorkshire Terrier. **Facilities** Garden Parking

### DURHAM　　　　　Map 19 NZ24

## Victoria Inn

**86 Hallgarth St DH1 3AS** ☎ **0191 386 5269**
dir: *In city centre*

This unique listed inn has scarcely changed since it was built in 1899. Just five minutes walk from the cathedral, it has been carefully nurtured by the Webster family for over 35 years. Small rooms warmed by coal fires and a congenial atmosphere include the unusual off-sales booth and tiny snug, where a portrait of Queen Victoria still hangs above the upright piano. You'll find a few simple snacks to tickle the taste buds, but it's the cracking well-kept local ales, single malts, and over 40 Irish whiskeys that are the main attraction.

Open all wk 11.45-3 6-11 ⊕ FREE HOUSE ◀ Wylam Gold Tankard, Durham Magus, Big Lamp Bitter, Hambleton ☋ Stud Hill Island Juniper. **Facilities** Family room Dogs allowed Parking

### FIR TREE　　　　　Map 19 NZ13

## Duke of York Inn

**DL15 8DG** ☎ **01388 767429**　📠 **01388 767429**
e-mail: julie.donaghue3@yahoo.co.uk
dir: *On A68, 12m W of Durham. From Durham take A690 W. Left onto A68 to Fir Tree*

A former drovers' and coaching inn dating from 1749, the Duke of York stands on the tourist route (A68) to Scotland. Refurbished inside and out to a high standard, keeping the traditional country feel with contemporary touches. Typical dishes include steak and ale pie, and chicken with pepper sauce, plus choices from the carvery and grill.

Open all day all wk **Bar Meals** food served all day **Restaurant** food served all day ⊕ CAMERONS BREWERY ◀ Camerons Smooth, John Smith's, Guinness. **Facilities** Children's menu Children's portions Dogs allowed Garden Parking

### HUTTON MAGNA　　　　　Map 19 NZ11

## PICK OF THE PUBS

## The Oak Tree Inn

**DL11 7HH** ☎ **01833 627371**
dir: *From A1 at Scotch Corner take A66. 6.5m, right for Hutton Magna*

Expect a warm welcome at this whitewashed, part 18th-century free house run by Alastair and Claire Ross. Alastair previously spent 14 years in London working at the Savoy, Leith's and, more recently, a private members' club on The Strand. Meals in the simply furnished dining room are based around the finest local ingredients, and dishes change daily depending on produce available. The fish choices, in particular, rely on what comes in on the boats. The refined cooking style combines classic techniques and occasional modern flavours: you could start with watercress and potato soup; garlic and saffron salt cod fish cake; or warm salad of pork belly and black pudding. A fish main event could feature halibut, John Dory or wild sea bass; alternatively a roast breast of guinea fowl is served with crispy leg confit, olive oil mashed potato and rosemary vegetables. As well as fine real ales, there's a menu of bottled beers from around the globe, and a list of 20 malt whiskies.

Open 6-11 (Sun 5.30-10.30) Closed: Xmas & New Year, Mon **Restaurant** D served Tue-Sun 6-9 booking required Av 3 course à la carte fr £32 ⊕ FREE HOUSE ◀ Wells Bombardier, Timothy Taylor Landlord, Black Sheep Best. **Facilities** Dogs allowed Parking

# PICK OF THE PUBS

## Rose & Crown ★★HL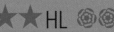

**ROMALDKIRK** Map 19 NY92

**DL12 9EB**
☎ 01833 650213 📠 01833 650828
e-mail: hotel@rose-and-crown.co.uk
dir: *6m NW from Barnard Castle on B6277*

This splendid, ivy-clad, 18th-century inn stands on the village green next to the Saxon church, known locally as the 'Cathedral of the Dale', and opposite the ancient stocks and water pump. It's a great all-rounder pub - cosy bar, smart two-Rosette restaurant and classy bedrooms. Step inside and you'll see fresh flowers, varnished oak panelling, old beams, gleaming copper and brass artefacts, and maybe encounter the odd creaking stair.

From your oak settle, as a fire crackles in the grate, and armed with the daily newspaper and pint of Allendale Best Bitter, you can savour the buzziness of the bar. You may prefer to retreat to a comfortable wingchair in the quiet of the grandfather-clock-ticking lounge, and order a pot of tea, or to the Brasserie, decorated with big pictures of crusty old waiters, and where the tables are lit by candles in wax-run bottles. Here you can order seared pink trout with juniper, sea salt, cucumber relish and sherry dressing as a starter; and chicken liver crostini with chestnuts, smoked bacon, oloroso sherry and salad as a main. There are sandwiches, ploughman's, and cheese - or steak-filled stotty cakes, a type of bread popular in the north-east. Children might prefer spaghetti, scrambled eggs on toast, or maybe smoked Scottish salmon.

In the restaurant, there's more of that oak panelling, crisp white tablecloths, sparkling silver and soft lights - the perfect setting for a fixed-price, four-course dinner of, say, matured Cumberland farmhouse ham with honey-roast figs; courgette and sweet pear soup; baked slice of baby halibut with local Cotherstone cheese, cream and red onion marmalade; and hot sticky walnut tart with vanilla ice cream.

Bose music systems help to make an overnight stay in one of the twelve beautifully furnished en suite bedrooms even more enjoyable.

**Open** all wk 11-11 Closed: 23-27 Dec **Bar Meals** L served all wk 12-1.30 D served all wk 6.30-9.30 Av main course £13.50 **Restaurant** L served Sun 12-1.30 booking required D served all wk 7.30-8.45 booking required Fixed menu price fr £32.50 ⊕ FREE HOUSE ◀ Theakston Best, Black Sheep Best, Allendale ale. ♀ 14 **Facilities** Children's menu Dogs allowed Parking **Rooms** 12

## MIDDLESTONE — Map 19 NZ23

### Ship Inn ♀

**Low Rd DL14 8AB ☎ 01388 810904**
**e-mail:** tony.theshipinn@googlemail.com
**dir:** On B6287 (Kirk Merrington to Coundon road)

Beer drinkers will appreciate the string of real ale-related accolades received by this family-run pub on the village green. In the last five years regulars could have sampled well over 800 different beers. Home-cooked food is served in the bar and restaurant, using beef, pork and lamb reared locally. The Ship is 550 feet above sea level and unusually the cellar is 9 feet above the bar! The rooftop patio has spectacular views over the Tees Valley and Cleveland Hills.

**Open** all wk 4-11 (Fri-Sun noon-11) **Bar Meals** L served Fri-Sun 12-2 D served all wk 6-9 Av main course £4.90 ⊕ FREE HOUSE ◀ 6 guest ales ♂ Westons. ♀ 9 **Facilities** Children's menu Children's portions Play area Family room Dogs allowed Parking

## MIDDLETON-IN-TEESDALE — Map 18 NY92

### The Teesdale Hotel ★★ HL

**Market Square DL12 0QG**
**☎ 01833 640264** ▤ 01833 640651
**e-mail:** enquiries@teesdalehotel.com
**dir:** A1 to Scotch Corner, A66 to Barnard Castle, follow signs for Middleton-in-Teesdale

Just off the Pennine Way, this tastefully modernised, family-run former coaching inn enjoys some of Britain's loveliest scenery. It has a striking 18th-century stone exterior and archway, while the interior is warm and friendly, with an open fire in the bar and well-kept real ales hand-pumped from the ancient cellar. All food is home-made using local produce. A typical meal might include garlic and chilli butter prawns, followed by Teesdale lamb chops on mashed potato with rosemary and red wine gravy. There is a decked area for the warmer months.

**Open** all day all wk **Bar Meals** L served all wk 12.30-2.30 D served all wk 7-9 Av main course £7.50 **Restaurant** D served all wk 7-9 Fixed menu price fr £8.75 Av 3 course à la carte fr £16.70 ⊕ FREE HOUSE ◀ Guinness, Jennings Smooth, Black Sheep Best Bitter, Bitburger ♂ Aspall. **Facilities** Children's menu Children's portions Dogs allowed Parking **Rooms** 14

## NEWTON AYCLIFFE — Map 19 NZ22

### Blacksmiths Arms ♀

**Preston le Skerne, (off Ricknall Lane) DL5 6JH**
**☎ 01325 314873**
**dir:** Turn off A167 next to Gretna pub, into Ricknall Ln. Blacksmiths Arms 0.5m

Enjoying an excellent reputation locally as a good dining pub, this former smithy dates from the 1700s, and is still relatively isolated in its farmland setting. The menu offers starters of hot smoked mackerel and potato salad; cod and prawn brandade; chicken fillet goujons; and potted mushrooms. Requiring their own page on the menu are fish dishes such as grilled halibut steak with risotto, and gingered salmon. Chef's specialities include Gressingham duck breast, and pork au poivre.

**Open** 11.30-2.30 6-11 Closed: 1 Jan, Mon **Bar Meals** L served 11.30-2.30 D served 6-11 **Restaurant** L served 11.30-2.30 D served 6-11 ⊕ FREE HOUSE ◀ Ever changing selection of real ales. ♀ 10 **Facilities** Children's menu Play area Dogs allowed Garden Parking

## ROMALDKIRK — Map 19 NY92

### PICK OF THE PUBS

### Rose & Crown ★★ HL ◉◉ ♀

**See Pick of the Pubs on page 173**

## SEDGEFIELD — Map 19 NZ32

### Dun Cow Inn ♀

**43 Front St TS21 3AT**
**☎ 01740 620894** ▤ 01740 622163
**e-mail:** dunn_cow@btconnect.com
**dir:** At junct of A177 & A689. Inn in village centre

An interesting array of bric-a-brac can be viewed inside this splendid old village inn, which has many flower baskets bedecking its exterior in summer. Typical offerings include Angus sirloin steaks, locally-made sausages, spring lamb cutlets, fresh Shetland mussels, and mushroom stroganoff. Pudding choices often include gooseberry crumble and chocolate fudge cake with butterscotch sauce.

**Open** all wk 11am-3pm, 6pm-mdnt ◀ Theakston Best Bitter, John Smith's Smooth, Black Sheeps Bitter, Guest ales. ♀ 8 **Facilities** Parking

## TRIMDON — Map 19 NZ33

### The Bird in Hand

**Salters Ln TS29 6JQ ☎ 01429 880391**
**dir:** Telephone for directions

Village pub nine miles west of Hartlepool with fine views over surrounding countryside from an elevated position. There's a cosy bar and games room, stocking a good choice of cask ales and guest beers, a spacious lounge and large conservatory restaurant. Traditional Sunday lunch goes down well, as does breaded plaice and other favourites. In summer you can sit outside in the garden, which has a roofed over area for climbing plants.

**Open** all wk **Facilities** Family room Dogs allowed Garden Parking

## ESSEX

## ARKESDEN — Map 12 TL43

### PICK OF THE PUBS

### Axe & Compasses ♀

**See Pick of the Pubs on opposite page**

## AYTHORPE RODING — Map 6 TL51

### Axe & Compasses ♀

**Dunmow Rd CM6 1PP ☎ 01279 876648**
**e-mail:** axeandcompasses@msn.com
**dir:** From A120 take junct for Dunmow

A weather-boarded, 17th-century pub where the owners like to create a 'nostalgic pub experience'. In the bar, ales from small regional brewers such as Nethergate Old Growler and Saffron Walden Gold are backed by Weston's ciders. David, a skilled self-taught chef, uses the best of seasonal produce and loves to offer dishes such as pan-fried pigeon breast, bacon salad and parsnip crisp or Mersea oysters to start; then calves' liver, crispy bacon, sage mash and caper butter; and ginger parkin, toffee sauce and home-made brandy ice cream to finish.

**Open** all day all wk 11am-11.30pm (Sun noon-11) **Bar Meals** L served all wk 12-10 Av main course £10 food served all day **Restaurant** L served all wk 12-2.30 booking required D served Mon-Sat 6-10, Sun 12-8 booking required Av 3 course à la carte fr £22.50 ⊕ FREE HOUSE ◀ Brentwood Best, Nethergate Old Growler, Crouch Vale Brewers Gold, Woodforde's Wherry, Saffron Walden Gold ♂ Westons Old Rosie, Weston's Scrumpy, Herefordshire Perry. ♀ 15 **Facilities** Children's portions Dogs allowed Garden Parking

## BLACKMORE — Map 6 TL60

### PICK OF THE PUBS

### The Leather Bottle

**The Green CM4 0RL ☎ 01277 823538**
**e-mail:** leatherbottle@tiscali.co.uk
**dir:** M25 junct 8 onto A1023, left onto A128, 5m. Left onto Blackmore Rd, 2m. Left towards Blackmore, 2m. Right then 1st left

According to local legend, Henry VIII used to stable his horses here when he came to visit his mistress. There has been a pub on the site for over 400 years, but the original building burned down in 1954 and was rebuilt

*continued on page 176*

# PICK OF THE PUBS

## Axe & Compasses 🍷

**ARKESDEN** Map 12 TL43

**High St CB11 4EX**
☎ **01799 550272** 📄 **01799 550906**
**dir:** *From Buntingford take B1038 towards Newport. Then left for Arkesden*

Known as 'the Axe' in the local vernacular, this old pub stands in the centre of a pretty village through which runs Wicken Water, a gentle stream spanned by footbridges leading to picture-postcard white, cream and pink-washed thatched cottages. The main section of the building, itself also thatched and dating from 1650, is now the comfortable lounge. Easy chairs and settees, antique furniture, clocks and horse brasses bask in the warming glow of an open fire in the winter months. The part to the right is the public bar, built in the early 19th century as stabling, a function it performed until the 1920s.

Locals sip pints of Greene King IPA or Abbot ale, perhaps with a sandwich or a plate of fresh plaice fillets rolled and lightly cooked with mushrooms, white wine and cream. In the cosy, softly lit restaurant area, which seats 50 on various levels, agricultural implements adorn the old beams. Here, the menu offers a good selection of starters, including seafood platter of smoked salmon, prawns, mussels and smoked mackerel with remoulade sauce; king prawns and green lipped mussels grilled with garlic butter; and Parma ham with nectarines in a mint vinaigrette.

There's a good choice of main courses too, examples being pan-fried duck breast with black cherries and finished with cherry brandy; medallions of beef fillet, with rösti potatoes and finished with soft green peppercorns, brandy and cream; and lightly grilled sea bass fillets with a leek and potato cake served on a lemon parsley butter sauce.

Vegetarians may choose spinach and potato cakes, breadcrumbed and fried on a tomato and basil sauce. Round off with popular desserts from the trolley such as trifle of the day, or summer pudding. House wines are modestly priced. On a fine day many drinkers and diners head for the patio.

**Open** all wk noon-2.30 6-11 (Sun noon-3 7-10.30) **Bar Meals** L served all wk 12-2 D served all wk 6.45-9.30 booking required Av main course £16 **Restaurant** L served all wk 12-2 D served all wk 6.45-9.30 booking required Av 3 course à la carte fr £27 🍺 GREENE KING ◀ Greene King IPA, Abbot Ale, Old Speckled Hen. 🍷 14 **Facilities** Garden Parking

**BLACKMORE** *continued*

two years later. The bar is a cosy, inviting place to savour real ales, while the restaurant is smart, with modern furnishings. There's also an airy conservatory which opens onto the spacious enclosed garden. There is always a good selection of real ales and ciders, and all food is prepared with the finest freshest ingredients mainly from local suppliers. Options include a very reasonably priced lunchtime menu, which might include smoked trout tart with beetroot relish followed by roast chicken breast stuffed with Stilton and walnuts with pancetta cream sauce. Typical dishes at other times are creamy seafood chowder topped with tiger prawns; pan-fried lambs' kidneys, spicy tomato sauce and toasted ciabatta; wild mushroom and spinach risotto; and slow braised lamb shank with garlic and rosemary mash and redcurrant jus.

**Open** all day all wk **Bar Meals** L served all wk 12-2 D served all wk 7-9 Av main course £10 **Restaurant** L served all wk 12-2 booking required D served all wk 7-9 booking required Fixed menu price fr £10.95 Av 3 course à la carte fr £20 ● Adnams Best, Adnams Broadside, Sharp's Doom Bar, Woodforde's Wherry, Cottage Cactus Jack ♻ Aspall, Westons Old Rosie. **Facilities** Children's portions Dogs allowed Garden Parking

---

## PICK OF THE PUBS

## The Green Dragon at Young's End ♥

**Upper London Rd, Young's End CM77 8QN**
☎ **01245 361030**   📠 **01245 362575**
**e-mail:** info@thegreendragonyoungsend.co.uk
**dir:** *At Braintree bypass take A131 S towards Chelmsford, exit at Young's End on Great Leighs bypass*

The Green Dragon provides a comfortable venue for good drinking and dining, with winter fires creating a cosy atmosphere in the friendly bars, which are smartly decked in contemporary designs and lots of original exposed beams and stylish furnishings. The spacious restaurant maintains the rustic theme with bare brick walls and wonderful old beams. Outside there's a large garden and heated patio area. The bar menu offers the likes of beer-battered cod and chips, Essex bangers and mash, omelettes, jackets and sandwiches, while the restaurant goes in for dishes like chicken breast stuffed with brie and bacon, steak and ale pie, or halibut with mussels and tagliatelle of leek. There is also the option of private dining in the Hayloft Restaurant.

**Open** all wk Mon-Sat 12-3 6-11 (Sun 12-6) **Bar Meals** L served Mon-Sat 12-2.30, Sun 12-5 D served Mon-Thu 6-9, Fri-Sat 6-9.30, **Restaurant** L served Mon-Sat 12-2.30, Sun 12-5 booking required D served Mon-Thu 6-9, Fri-Sat 6-9.30 booking required ● GREENE KING ● Greene King IPA , Abbot Ale ♻ Aspall. ♥ 10 **Facilities** Children's menu Garden Parking

---

## The Rosebud ♥ NEW

**66-67 Hurst Green CO7 0EH** ☎ **01206 304571**
**e-mail:** mark@rosebudpub.co.uk
**dir:** *From Colchester take A120 towards Harwich. Right to Brightlingsea. Follow High St (away from war memorial). 0.5m to Hurst Green*

Apparently, only the locals know about this quaint little pub propping up a row of fishermen's cottages, named after a wrecked ship – at least until this entry appears! Opened in 1849 for the oyster fishermen, the pub has been in the same family for two generations. Expect fresh fish and seafood like seafood platter and moules marinière, plus meat from the local butcher; lamb's liver and bacon, gammon and steaks. Look for the recently found tail in a bottle behind the bar – some say it belonged to a cat on the doomed Rosebud. An on-site micro-brewery is planned.

**Open** all wk Mon-Thu 4.30-11 Fri-Sat noon-11 Sun noon-7 (open all day in Spring/Summer) **Bar Meals** L served Fri-Sun 1-4 booking required D served Wed-Sat 6-9 booking required Av main course £8 **Restaurant** L served Fri-Sun 1-4 booking required D served Wed-Sat 6-9 booking required Av 3 course à la carte fr £14 ● FREE HOUSE ● Woodforde's Wherry, Nelson's Revenge, Adnams Best. ♥ 13 **Facilities** Children's portions Garden

---

## Ye Olde White Harte Hotel

**The Quay CM0 8AS** ☎ **01621 782106**   📠 **01621 782106**
**dir:** *Along high street, right before clocktower, right into car park*

Directly overlooking the River Crouch, the hotel dates from the 17th century and retains many original features, including exposed beams. It also has its own private jetty. The food is mainly English-style with such dishes as roast leg of English lamb, local roast Dengie chicken, and grilled fillet of plaice and lemon. There is also a range of bar snacks including toasted and plain sandwiches, jacket potatoes and soup.

**Open** all day all wk **Bar Meals** L served all wk 12-2.15 D served all wk 6.30-9 Av main course £9 **Restaurant** L served all wk 12-2.15 D served all wk 7-9 Av 3 course à la carte fr £21 ● FREE HOUSE ● Adnams Bitter, Crouch Vale Best. **Facilities** Dogs allowed Parking

---

## PICK OF THE PUBS

## The Bell Inn

**Saint James St CO9 3EJ** ☎ **01787 460150**
**e-mail:** bell-castle@hotmail.co.uk
**dir:** *On A1124 N of Halstead, right to Castle Hedingham*

Scratch the imposing Georgian façade of The Bell and a much older inn is revealed. In one of the rooms a stretch of medieval wattle and daub walling was exposed, dating back to its origins as a pub in the 15th

---

century. Lots of exposed beams and brickwork retain that rustic charm, enhanced by the magpie collection of tables and chairs; winter log fires draw in the locals and in summer the orchard garden and vine-covered patio are popular retreats at this village inn which has been in the same family for over 40 years. Good, solid English food has a strong hand here, with home-made pies, lamb chops and rump steaks all hitting the mark. More unusual are the daily Turkish specials such as fish stew made with grouper, tomatoes and peppers or Mediterranean grilled fish options. Beer aficionados will delight in the selection of real ales stillaged behind the bar and gravity-served; ales from Maldon and Mighty Oak Breweries are a favourite as is local Delvin End cider.

*The Bell Inn*

**Open** all wk 11.45-3 6-11 (Fri-Sat noon-mdnt Sun noon-11) Closed: 25 Dec eve **Bar Meals** L served Mon-Fri 12-2, Sat-Sun 12-2.30 D served Sun-Mon 7-9, Tue-Sat 7-9.30 Av main course £9 ● GRAYS ● Maldon Gold, Mighty Oak, Adnams Bitter, IPA, guest ale ♻ Stowford Press, Delvin Ends Orchard Express. **Facilities** Children's menu Children's portions Play area Family room Dogs allowed Garden Parking

---

## The Swan Inn ♥

**CO6 2DD** ☎ **01787 222353**   📠 **01787 220012**
**e-mail:** theswan@cipubs.com
**web:** www.theswaninnchappel.co.uk
**dir:** *Pub visible just off A1124 (Colchester to Halstead road), from Colchester 1st left after viaduct*

This rambling low-beamed free house stands in the shadow of a magnificent Victorian railway viaduct, and boasts a charming riverside garden with overflowing flower tubs. Fresh meat arrives daily from Smithfield, and fish from Billingsgate. Typically the seafood may include crispy sole fillets or poached skate, while the grill comes into its own with prime steaks and platters of surf 'n' turf. There are daily vegetarian specials, and home-made

Save on Hotels. Book at **theAA.com/hotel**

ESSEX 177 ENGLAND

desserts. The bar serves up a well-kept pint and offers 15 wines by the glass.

**Open** all wk 11-3 6-11 (Sat 11-11 Sun noon-10.30) **Bar Meals** L served Mon-Sat 12-2.30, Sun 12-8 D served Mon-Sat 6-9.30, Sun 12-8 Av main course £8.95 **Restaurant** Av 3 course à la carte fr £20 ⊕ FREE HOUSE ◀ Adnam Bitter, Broadside, Guest Ale ⊙ Aspalls. ⚑ 15 **Facilities** Children's menu Children's portions Play area Dogs allowed Garden Parking

### CHELMSFORD                           Map 6 TL70

# The Alma ⚑

**37 Arbour Ln CM1 7RG** ☎ **01245 256783**
**e-mail:** alma@cipubs.com
**dir:** *Telephone for directions*

Named after the bloodiest battle of the Crimean war, The Alma was built in the late 19th century as an alehouse for soldiers recovering in the neighbouring hospital. The present owners have created a contemporary edge for the pub, and the menu follows suit with a stylish mix of traditional and modern dishes - perhaps pan seared pigeon breast as a starter; smoked haddock with mash, mange tout and cheese sauce, or breast of duck with creamed parsnip tart for a main.

**Open** all day all wk 11-11 (Fri-Sat 11-mdnt, Sun noon-10.30) **Bar Meals** L served Mon-Sat 12-2.30, Sun 12-8 D served Mon-Sat 6-9.30, Sun 12-8 Av main course £7.50 **Restaurant** L served Mon-Sat 12-2.30, Sun 12-8 D served Mon-Sat 6-9.30, Sun 12-8 Fixed menu price fr £10.95 Av 3 course à la carte fr £15 ⊕ FREE HOUSE ◀ Adnams ⊙ Aspall. ⚑ 12 **Facilities** Children's menu Children's portions Garden Parking

### CLAVERING                            Map 12 TL43

## PICK OF THE PUBS

# The Cricketers ⚑

*See Pick of the Pubs on page 178*

### COLCHESTER                           Map 13 TL92

# The Rose & Crown Hotel ★★★ HL

**East St CO1 2TZ** ☎ **01206 866677**   📠 **01206 866616**
**e-mail:** info@rose-and-crown.com
**dir:** *From M25 junct 28 take A12 N. Follow Colchester signs*

The Rose & Crown is a beautiful timber-framed building dating from the 14th century, believed to be the oldest hotel in the oldest town in England, just a few minutes' from Colchester Castle. The Tudor bar with its central roaring fire is a great place to relax with a drink. Food is served in the Oak Room, or the Tudor Room brasserie, an informal alternative serving classic bar food.

**Open** all wk **Bar Meals** L served all wk 12-2.30 D served all wk 6.30-9.30 Av main course £8.95 ⊕ FREE HOUSE ◀ Tetley's Bitter, Rose & Crown Bitter, Adnams Broadside. **Facilities** Family room Parking **Rooms** 39

### DEDHAM                               Map 13 TM03

# Marlborough Head Inn ★★★ INN ⚑

**Mill Ln CO7 6DH** ☎ **01206 323250**
**e-mail:** jen.pearmain@tiscali.co.uk
**dir:** *E of A12, N of Colchester*

Tucked away in glorious Constable Country, a 16th-century building that was once a clearing-house for local wool merchants. In 1660, after a slump in trade, it became an inn. Today it is as perfect for a pint, sofa and newspaper as it is for a good home-cooked family meal. Traditional favourites such as steak, Guinness and mushroom pie; and lamb shank with red wine and rosemary appear on the menu, plus fish is given centre stage on Fridays. There is a terrace and walled garden to enjoy in the warmer weather. Three en suite bedrooms are available.

**Open** all day all wk 11.30-11 **Bar Meals** Av main course £8.95 food served all day **Restaurant** food served all day ⊕ PUNCH TAVERNS ◀ Adnams Southwold, Greene King IPA, Woodforde's Wherry ⊙ Aspall. ⚑ 12 **Facilities** Children's menu Children's portions Family room Dogs allowed Garden Parking **Rooms** 3

## PICK OF THE PUBS

# The Sun Inn ☆☆☆☆☆ INN ◉ ⚑

**High St CO7 6DF** ☎ **01206 323351**
**e-mail:** office@thesuninndedham.com
**dir:** *From A12 follow signs to Dedham for 1.5m, pub on High Street*

Owner Piers Baker has transformed the Sun from a run-down village boozer to an inn of fine repute. With open fires, oak beams, a sun-trap terrace and walled garden, you'll find character everywhere you look. Here, a quiet pint goes hand in hand with robust food; there's a decent selection of real ales, and a respectable wine list with over twenty served by the glass. Locally sourced seasonal ingredients drive the daily-changing menu of Mediterranean-style dishes, many with a pronounced Italian flavour. On a lovely summer's day you could choose a plate of antipasti to share; or fresh pasta with summer girolles. Follow with leg of salt marsh lamb with aubergines, pine nuts, sultanas, tomatoes and basil. And round off with peaches in Pinot Nero with star anise and vanilla ice cream. If you can't quite tear yourself away, five en suite guest rooms with large comfy beds, crisp linen, character furniture and great showers are available. Look out for produce for sale at Victoria's Plums.

**Open** all day all wk 11am-11pm Closed: 25-27 Dec **Bar Meals** L served Mon-Thu 12-2.30, Fri-Sun 12-3 D served Sun-Thu 6.30-9.30, Fri-Sat 6.30-10 Av main course £6.75 **Restaurant** L served Mon-Thu 12-2.30, Fri-Sun 12-3 D served Sun-Thu 6.30-9.30, Fri-Sat 6.30-10 Fixed menu price fr £13.50 Av 3 course à la carte fr £21 ⊕ FREE HOUSE ◀ Brewer's Gold Crouch Vale, Adnams Broadside, 2 guest ales ⊙ Aspall. ⚑ 25 **Facilities** Children's menu Children's portions Dogs allowed Garden Parking **Rooms** 5

### ELSENHAM                             Map 12 TL52

# The Crown

**The Cross, High St CM22 6DG** ☎ **01279 812827**
**e-mail:** enquiries@thecrownelsenham.co.uk
**dir:** *M11 junct 8 towards Takeley. Left at lights*

A pub for 200 years, with oak beams, open fireplaces and Essex pargetting at the front. The menu, which has a large selection of fresh fish, might offer baked trout with toasted almonds, steak and kidney pie, Crown mixed grill with onion rings, a choice of steaks cooked to order, or breast of duck with peppercorn sauce. There's a good choice of vegetarian choices as well, plus lighter bites and jacket potatoes.

**Open** all day all wk noon-mdnt ◀ IPA, Guinness, Guest Ale. **Facilities** Dogs allowed Garden Parking

### FAIRSTEAD                            Map 7 TL71

# The Square and Compasses ⚑

**Fuller St CM3 2BB** ☎ **01245 361477**   📠 **01245 362633**
**e-mail:** info@thesquareandcompasses.co.uk
**web:** www.thesquareandcompasses.co.uk
**dir:** *From A131 (Chelmsford to Braintree) take Great Leighs exit, enter village, turn right into Boreham Rd. Turn left signed Fuller St & Terling. Pub on left on entering hamlet*

Known locally as The Stokehole, this lovingly restored free house dates from about 1652. Originally two farm cottages, the building still retains its original exposed beams and inglenook fireplaces. Food is simple and straightforward, served alongside a good selection of cider and East Anglian ales. As well as pub classics, the daily-changing chalkboard specials might include Essex coast cod loin fillet with spiced coconut cream sauce; pan-fried local ox liver; or caramelised red onion, brie and flat mushroom tart.

**Open** all wk 11.30-3 6-11 (Sat-Sun noon-11) **Bar Meals** L served Mon-Fri 12-2, Sat 12-2.30, Sun 12-6 D served Mon-Sat 6.30-9.30 booking required **Restaurant** L served Mon-Fri 12-2, Sat 12-2.30, Sun 12-4 D served Mon-Sat 6.30-9.30 booking required ⊕ FREE HOUSE ◀ Square and Compasses Stokers Ale, Essex Maldon Gold, Might Oak, Essex Nelson Blood, Farmers, Essex Hophead, Dark Starr, Sussex ⊙ Stowford Press, Westons. ⚑ 14 **Facilities** Children's portions Dogs allowed Garden Parking

# PICK OF THE PUBS

## The Cricketers

**CLAVERING** Map 12 TL43

**CB11 4QT**
☎ **01799 550442** 📠 **01799 550882**
e-mail: info@thecricketers.co.uk
web: www.thecricketers.co.uk
dir: *From M11 junct 10, A505 E. Then
A1301, B1383. At Newport take B1038*

Well over 30 years in the hands of the
Oliver family, this celebrated 16th-
century inn stands at the heart of a
beautiful unspoilt Essex village, along
the road from the local cricket pitch.

The Cricketers is the family home of
Jamie Oliver and it was here that the
young Jamie first discovered his passion
for cooking — he remains involved by
supplying the pub with wonderful
seasonal vegetables, herbs and salads
from his certified organic garden
nearby.

The front has a pretty terrace with
tables, benches and brollies. Within the
refurbished beamed and cosy bar and
intimate dining room, expect polished
tables, gleaming brassware and
glasses, crackling winter log fires and a
warm, friendly atmosphere.

Head chef, Justin Greig, is passionate
about quality local produce and
developing his Italian-inspired
seasonally changing menus and daily
chalkboard specials. From the main
menu, kick off an excellent meal with
squid linguini, served with garlic, chilli,
tomato and parsley, or home-made
tagliatelle with braised wild rabbit,
follow with rump of Braxted Hall Farm
lamb with sage-infused swede and
balsamic jus, 28-day aged Dedham Vale
sirloin steak with polenta chips and
harissa sauce, or pan-fried gurnard
with a warm salad of roasted peppers,
asparagus and wild rocket. Finish with
oozy chocolate pot with marmalade ice
cream or vanilla rice pudding with
rhubarb compôte.

In the bar, tuck into salad niçoise, a
rustic platter of Italian meats or a
classy sandwich, perhaps filled with

Priors Hall Farm ham, mature cheddar
and pickle. The children's menu steers
clear of the 'dreaded nuggets', offering
instead home-made fusilla pasta with
sausage bolognaise sauce, or lightly
battered fish of the day. A chalkboard
lists a great selection of 17 wines by the
glass.

**Open** all day all wk Closed: 25-26 Dec
**Bar Meals** L served all wk 12-2 D served
all wk 6.30-9.30 Av main course £15
**Restaurant** L served all wk 12-2
D served all wk 6.30-9.30 Fixed menu
price fr £29.95 Av 3 course à la carte fr
£29.95 ⊕ FREE HOUSE ◀ Adnams
Bitter, Tetley Bitter, Greene King IPA,
Adnams Broadside, Woodforde's Wherry,
Nog ♉ Aspall. ☿ 17 **Facilities** Children's
menu Garden Parking

| FEERING | Map 7 TL82 |

## The Sun Inn ☆

**Feering Hill CO5 9NH**
☎ 01376 570442 📠 01376 570442
e-mail: andy.howard@virgin.net
dir: *On A12 between Colchester & Witham. Village 1m*

Real ale and real food are at the heart of this pretty, timbered pub that dates from 1525. There's a large garden for the summer months, while winter warmth comes from two inglenook fireplaces. There are no TVs or games machines; instead the customers create the atmosphere. Food-wise, expect simple, seasonal dishes; perhaps tempura-battered prawns followed by fresh fish in a Spitfire ale batter with chips, peas and home-made tartare sauce, with plum crumble for pudding.

**Open** all wk Sat-Sun all day **Bar Meals** L served Mon-Sat 12-2.30, Sun 12-8 D served Mon-Sat 6-9.30, Sun 12-8 Av main course £5 **Restaurant** L served Mon-Sat 12-2.30, Sun 12-8 D served Mon-Sat 6-9.30, Sun 12-9 Fixed menu price fr £13.50 ⊕ SHEPHERD NEAME ◀ Master Brew, Spitfire, Bishops Finger, seasonal ale, guest ales. ☆ 8 **Facilities** Children's menu Children's portions Dogs allowed Garden Parking

| FELSTED | Map 6 TL62 |

## PICK OF THE PUBS

### The Swan at Felsted ☆

*See Pick of the Pubs on page 180*

| FINGRINGHOE | Map 7 TM02 |

## The Whalebone ☆

**Chapel Rd CO5 7BG ☎ 01206 729307**
e-mail: vicki@thewhaleboneinn.co.uk
dir: *Telephone for directions*

This Grade II listed 18th-century free house has panoramic views of the Roman river valley. The Whalebone has wooden floors, aubergine walls, unique artwork and sculptures, and roman blinds. The unusual name comes from bones, once fastened above the door of the pub, which came from a locally beached whale. Another unusual feature is the oak tree nearby, thought to be the largest in Essex. Legend has it that the tree grew from an acorn in the mouth of a pirate executed and buried there some centuries ago. No acorns on the menu though, just hearty home-made dishes like Gerald's Suffolk Farm sausages, mash, spring greens and gravy; dressed fresh Cromer crab, mixed leaves, potato salad, and granary bread; or roast leg of local lamb with minted mash, seasonal vegetables and gravy.

**Open** all wk noon-3 5.30-11 (Sat noon-11 Sun noon-10.30) **Bar Meals** L served Mon-Sat 12-2.30, Sun 12-6.45 booking required D served Mon-Thu 6.30-9, Fri-Sat 6.30-9.30, Sun 12-6.45 booking required Av main course £10.95 **Restaurant** L served Mon-Sat 12-2.30, Sun 12-6.45 booking required D served Mon-Thu 6.30-9, Fri-Sat 6.30-9.30, Sun 12-6.45 booking required ⊕ FREE HOUSE ◀ 4 Guest Ales ☼ Aspall. ☆ 13 **Facilities** Children's menu Children's portions Play area Family room Dogs allowed Garden Parking

| GOSFIELD | Map 13 TL72 |

## The Green Man ☆

**The Street CO9 1TP ☎ 01787 273608**
e-mail: info@thegreenmangosfield.co.uk
dir: *Take A131 N from Braintree then A1017 to village*

Situated close to Gosfield Lake, this pink-washed medley of buildings houses a recently refurbished village dining pub. At lunchtime, enjoy a pint of Abbot ale with a choice of thick cut sandwiches and crusty filled baguettes, plus dishes such as breaded scampi and chips; and mussels in white wine, shallots and cream. The dinner menu is based around classic British and international fare and offers the likes of slow roast pork belly, champ, apple chutney and bay infused gravy; or roast sea bass fillet, Singapore noodles and shell fish broth; and wild meat night every Wednesday. This pub is now under new ownership and has been refurbished.

**Open** all wk **Bar Meals** L served Mon-Sat 12-2.30, Sun 12-5 D served Mon-Sat 6-9 Av main course £7.95 **Restaurant** L served Mon-Sat 12-2.30, Sun 12-5 D served Mon-Sat 6-9 Av 3 course à la carte fr £20 ⊕ GREENE KING ◀ Greene King IPA, Abbot Ale, Guest Ales ☼ Aspall. ☆ 16 **Facilities** Children's menu Children's portions Dogs allowed Garden Parking

| GREAT BRAXTED | Map 7 TL81 |

## The Ducane ☆

**The Village CM8 3EJ**
☎ 01621 891697 📠 01621 890009
e-mail: eat@theducane.co.uk
dir: *Great Braxted signed between Witham & Kelvedon on A12*

A friendly, mid-Thirties pub in delightful gardens, fronted by a mighty oak tree. Tastefully renovated and hung with local artworks, it's clear that chef/patron Jonathan Brown and his partner, Louise Partis, care hugely about the place. They offer locally brewed real ales and an extensive wine list in the central bar, while the kitchen makes full use of local Braxted lamb and beef, vegetables and fruits from nearby farms, and East Coast fish and shellfish. There is an exchange scheme at The Ducane where budding gardeners can exchange pints of real ale for produce.

**Open** Tue-Fri 12-3 6-11.30 (Sat 12-3 6-12 Sun 12-4) Closed: Sun eve & Mon **Bar Meals** L served Tue-Sun 12-2.30 booking required D served Tue-Sat 7-9.30 booking required Av main course £9.50 **Restaurant** L served Tue-Sun 12-2.30 booking required D served Tue-Sat 7-9.30 booking required Fixed menu price fr £13.50 Av 3 course à la carte fr £27.50 ⊕ FREE HOUSE ◀ Adnams Bitter, Bass Bitter, Maldon Gold, Farmers Ales. ☆ 10 **Facilities** Children's menu Children's portions Dogs allowed Garden Parking

| GREAT YELDHAM | Map 13 TL73 |

## PICK OF THE PUBS

### The White Hart ★★★★★ RR ◉◉

**Poole St CO9 4HJ**
☎ 01787 237250 📠 01787 238044
e-mail: mjwmason@yahoo.co.uk
dir: *On A1017 between Haverhill & Halstead*

Highwaymen were once locked up in a small prison beneath the stairs of this impressive 500-year-old timber-framed inn. Situated on the border of Essex and Suffolk, the White Hart enjoys a setting within four and a half acres of gardens, close to Heddingham Castle, the Colne Valley and Newmarket. With its blend of traditional and contemporary, it's a popular wedding venue on the one hand, and a great place to sample Brandon's Rusty Bucket on the other. The hard work put in by the establishment's owner, Matthew Mason, has resulted in many awards, including two AA Rosettes for its food. The express bar menu lists favourites such as Cumberland sausage ring with Cheddar mash and onion gravy, while the à la carte choice includes ballotine of Yeldham wood pigeon among its starters, and Auberies Estate roast loin of venison as a main course. For dessert there's baked Alaska or warm pear frangipane. Eleven en suite and fully equipped rooms complete the picture.

**Open** all day wk **Bar Meals** Av main course £8.95 food served all day **Restaurant** Fixed menu price fr £11.95 Av 3 course à la carte fr £25 food served all day ⊕ FREE HOUSE ◀ Adnams Bitter, Black Sheep, Rusty Bucket. **Facilities** Children's menu Children's portions Play area Garden Parking **Rooms** 11

| HORNDON ON THE HILL | Map 6 TQ68 |

## PICK OF THE PUBS

### Bell Inn & Hill House ☆

*See Pick of the Pubs on page 181*

# PICK OF THE PUBS

## The Swan at Felsted ♉

**FELSTED**                    Map 6 TL62

**Station Rd CM6 3DG**
☎ **01371 820245**  📠 **01371 821393**
**e-mail:** info@theswanatfelsted.co.uk
**dir:** *Exit M11 junct 8 onto A120 signed Felsted. Pub in village centre*

Venture through the door of this red brick-and-timber building and a pleasant surprise awaits. Rebuilt after a disastrous fire in the early 1900s, the building was formerly the village bank, then a run-down boozer. In 2002 it was rescued and stylishly refurbished by Jono and Jane Clark. Today it's very much a gastro-pub, with polished wood floors, leather sofas, chunky furnishings and colourful modern art, yet it successfully balances traditional pub attributes with a quality dining experience. There are roaring log fires in winter and a courtyard garden to enjoy in the warmer months. The atmosphere is friendly and informal and locals beat a path to the door for cracking Greene King ales and over a dozen world wines served by the glass; if sharing a bottle, allow time to peruse the 80-plus choices on the list.

Seasonally changing food menus champion locally sourced produce. The à la carte menu offers an imaginative selection of modern European dishes whilst the lunch menu keeps them in touch with their pub roots. Tasters begin with olives or garlic bread, before brasserie starters such as confit duck leg and wild mushroom terrine; and classic crayfish and prawn cocktail with Marie Rose sauce. Main courses cater to all tastes: slow-braised pork cheeks with cider fondant and braised red cabbage; or pan-roasted halibut with Cromer crab, crushed new potatoes and basil dressing. Old favourites include pork sausages with creamy mash potato; and classic shepherd's pie to name just two examples. Home-made treacle tart or Bramley apple and sultana crumble with crème anglaise may feature on the dessert list.

Special offers, such as ladies' night on Tuesdays and steak night on Wednesdays succeed in keeping the clientele coming. And with Stansted airport just 15 minutes away, the Swan makes a great last port of call before the holiday begins.

**Open** all wk noon-3 5-11 (Sun noon-6) **Bar Meals** L served Mon-Sat 12-2.30, Sun 12-4 D served Mon-Sat 6-9.30 **Restaurant** L served Mon-Sat 12-2.30, Sun 12-4 booking required D served Mon-Sat 6-9.30 booking required ⊕ GREENE KING ▄ IPA, Prospect, Guinness, guest ale ♻ Stowford Press. ♉ 14 **Facilities** Children's menu Dogs allowed Garden Parking

# PICK OF THE PUBS

## Bell Inn & Hill House ♟

**HORNDON ON THE HILL**          Map 6 TQ68

**High Rd SS17 8LD**
☎ **01375 642463**   📄 **01375 361611**
**e-mail:** info@bell-inn.co.uk
**dir:** *M25 junct 30/31 signed Thurrock*

The Bell has been run by generations of the same family for over 70 years. Much of the structure of this historic building was complete when the first Tudor king, Henry VII, came to the throne in 1445. From its earliest days it served as a coaching inn, as the archway through to the courtyard testifies. From the first-floor gallery that runs above the courtyard, luggage would have been transferred to and from the top of the London stagecoaches. Once inside, look for the original king post that supports the inn's ancient roof timbers. You cannot help but notice hot cross buns hanging from the beams in the saloon bar. Every year the oldest willing villager hangs another, an unusual tradition that dates back about 100 years when the pub happened to change hands on a Good Friday; during the food shortages of World War II the tradition was maintained with a bun made of concrete.

The bars serve a selection of regularly changing guest ales, usually two or three per week, which are backed by regulars such as Ruddles and Spitfire; from the extensive wine list, many bottles are served by the glass. The lunchtime bar menu offers open sandwiches such as hot roast beef with horseradish; and light meals – moules marinière with fat chips; game suet pudding with caramelised onions; and Cumberland sausages with creamed potato and onion rings are all very popular. From the daily-changing restaurant menu, built around the freshest produce, you might start with crab dim sum with sauté bok choy and white onion purée; and continue with roast Priors Hall suckling pig with sage stuffing and cinnamon apple compôte. Stylish puddings include blackberry baked Alaska with toasted apple and vanilla sauce; and a white chocolate mousse in a dark chocolate cup with raspberries.

**Open** all wk Mon-Fri 11-3 5.30-11 (Sat 11-3 6-11 Sun 12-4 7.10.30) Closed: 25-26 Dec **Bar Meals** L served all wk 12-1.45 D served all wk 6.30-9.45 Av main course £8.95 **Restaurant** L served Mon-Sat 12-1.45, Sun 12-2.30 booking required D served Mon-Fri 6.30-9.45, Sat 6-9.45 booking required Av 3 course à la carte fr £23.95 ⊕ FREE HOUSE ◀ Greene King IPA, Interbrew Bass, Crouchvale Brewers Gold, Ruddles County, Spitfire. ♟ 16 **Facilities** Dogs allowed Garden Parking

# Lion & Lamb | The White House

*Restaurant and Bar now offering Accommodation in conjunction with*
*The White House Luxury Country House*

A traditional country restaurant and bar complete with oak beams and a large secluded garden overlooking farmland. Side the B1256 (the old A120) 5 mins from M11–J8 and Stansted Airport is the Lion & Lamb, a traditional country pub combined with a restaurant serving very modern food all day long – kangaroo, grilled dover sole, pork belly and roasted loin with a pumpkin puree, parsnips and a tarragon jus and wild mushroom risotto are just some of the temptations that could be offered. With its oak beams and cosy fireplace, the Lion & Lamb dates back to the 16th century and is very inviting. Bar snacks are available and diners are welcome to eat in the bar, dining area or conservatory. Children are welcome, making the Lion & Lamb a popular choice for family groups.

This carefully refurbished family home displays many original 16th-century features alongside modern comforts. The Grade II listed building is close to Stansted Airport and is enclosed by extensive gardens. Accommodation is stylish with large beds and ensuite and there is a luxurious Victorian bathroom.

Served around one table in the farmhouse-style kitchen, the full cooked breakfast is a wholesome start to the day. For other meals a range of interesting dishes, using quality local ingredients, is available in the Lion and Lamb pub a mile up the road, which is owned by the same proprietors who offer free transport to and fro.

**Stortford Road (B1256), Little Canfield, Dunmow, Near Takeley CM6 1SR**
**Tel: 01279 870257   Fax: 01279 870423**
**Email: info@lionandlamb.co.uk or enquiries@whitehousestansted.co.uk**
**www.lionandlamb.co.uk or www.whitehousestansted.co.uk**

Johansen
Conde
Nast

INGATESTONE Map 6 TQ69

## The Red Lion 🍷

**Main Rd, Margaretting CM4 0EQ** ☎ **01277 352184**
**e-mail:** the_redlion@msn.com
**dir:** *From Chelmsford take A12 towards Brentwood. Margaretting in 4m*

The phrase 'quintessential English pub' is something of a cliché, but how else to describe the 17th-century Red Lion? The bar is decorated in burgundy and aubergine, the restaurant in coffee and cream. Seasonal highlights include spring onion, feta and courgette fritters; sausage and mustard mash; lamb hotpot; a daily roast; deep-fried Lowestoft cod and chips (or to take away); and aubergine, tomato and mozzarella pie. Watch the chefs gathering produce from the large gardens.

**Open** all wk 12-3 5.30-11.30 (Sat-Sun 11am-11pm)
**Bar Meals** L served all wk 12-2.30 D served all wk 6-9.30 Av main course £7.95 **Restaurant** L served all wk 12-2.30 D served all wk 6-9.30 Fixed menu price fr £10 ⊕ GREENE KING ◀ Greene King IPA, Tribute, Abbot, Speckled Hen ☼ Aspall. 🍷 14 **Facilities** Children's menu Children's portions Play area Garden Parking

### LANGHAM Map 13 TM03

## The Shepherd and Dog

**Moor Rd CO4 5NR** ☎ **01206 272711** 🖳 **01206 273136**
**dir:** *A12 from Colchester towards Ipswich, take 1st left signed Langham*

Situated on the Suffolk/Essex border, in Constable country, this 1928 freehouse has the classic styling of an English country pub. Widely renowned for its food, the Shepherd and Dog serves an extensive variety of meat, fish and poultry dishes, plus a vegetarian selection and a children's menu.

**Open** all wk **Bar Meals** L served Mon-Fri 12-3, Sat-Sun 12-9.30 D served Mon-Fri 6-9.30, Sat-Sun 12-9.30 Av main course £8.95 **Restaurant** L served Mon-Fri 12-3, Sat-Sun 12-9.30 D served Mon-Fri 6-9.30, Sat-Sun 12-9.30 Av 3 course à la carte fr £13.95 ⊕ FREE HOUSE ◀ Greene King IPA, Abbot Ale, guest ales. **Facilities** Children's menu Children's portions Dogs allowed Garden Parking

### LITTLEBURY Map 12 TL53

## The Queens Head Inn 🍷 NEW

**High St CB11 4TD** ☎ **01799 522251**
**e-mail:** thequeenshead@fsmail.net
**dir:** *M11 junct 9A take B184 towards Saffron Walden. Right onto B1383, S towards Wendens Ambo*

A beautiful 16th-century family-run inn with open fires, exposed beams and one of only two remaining full-length settles in England. Very much at the centre of the local community, the pub runs darts and football teams and pétanque competitions; a large beer garden with bouncy castle confirms its family-friendly credentials. The kitchen aims to produce good home-made pub grub at realistic prices, with a menu of popular favourites from pizzas to pies, ciabattas to curries.

**Open** all wk Mon-Thu 12-3 5.30-11 Fri 12-3 5.30-mdnt Sat noon-mdnt Sun noon-10.30 **Bar Meals** L served all wk 12-2.30 D served all wk 6.30-9 Av main course £7.50 **Restaurant** L served all wk 12-2.30 booking required D served all wk 6.30-9 booking required Av 3 course à la carte fr £13 ⊕ GREENE KING ◀ Greene King IPA, Morland Old Speckled Hen, Guest ale ☼ Stowford Press, Aspall. 🍷 9 **Facilities** Children's menu Children's portions Play area Dogs allowed Garden Parking

### LITTLE CANFIELD Map 6 TL52

## The Lion & Lamb 🍷

**CM6 1SR** ☎ **01279 870257** 🖳 **01279 870423**
**e-mail:** info@lionandlamb.co.uk
**dir:** *M11 junct 8, B1256 towards Takeley & Little Canfield*

Ideal for business or leisure, this traditional country pub and restaurant is handy for Stansted airport and the M11. Inside you'll find oak beams, winter log fires, an extensive food selection, real ales and up to 11 wines available by the glass. From the bar menu choose sandwiches, steak and ale pie, Lion & Lamb beef burger, lasagne or sausage and mash. In the restaurant sample vegetable moussaka of red lentils and aubergine or Thai red beef curry. Children's menu and portions available.

**Open** all day all wk **Bar Meals** food served all day **Restaurant** food served all day ⊕ GREENE KING ◀ Old Speckled Hen, Greene King IPA, Old Bob, guest ales. 🍷 11 **Facilities** Children's menu Children's portions Play area Garden Parking

*See advert on opposite page*

### LITTLE DUNMOW Map 6 TL62

## Flitch of Bacon

**The Street CM6 3HT**
☎ **01371 820323** 🖳 **01371 820338**
**dir:** *B1256 to Braintree for 10m, turn off at Little Dunmow, 0.5m pub on right*

A charming 15th-century country inn whose name refers to the ancient gift of half a salted pig, or 'flitch', to couples who have been married for a year and a day, and 'who have not had a cross word'.

**Open** Mon eve-Sun. Closed: Mon lunch ◀ Fuller's London Pride, Greene King IPA. **Facilities** Family room Dogs allowed Garden Parking

### MANNINGTREE Map 13 TM13

### PICK OF THE PUBS

## The Mistley Thorn ☺☺ 🍷

**High St, Mistley CO11 1HE**
☎ **01206 392821** 🖳 **01206 390122**
**e-mail:** info@mistleythorn.com
**dir:** *From Ipswich A12 junct 31 onto B1070, follow signs to East Bergholt, Manningtree & Mistley. From Colchester A120 towards Harwich. Left at Horsley Cross. Mistley in 3m*

In the 17th century, Witchfinder General Matthew Hopkins held court in a building here. Today's comfy Georgian coaching inn is far less stressful on guests lucky enough to be enjoying the views across the serene Stour estuary. Relaxing in the clean-cut, modish interior that has a whiff of New England about it, patrons can look forward to an eclectic menu that has gained executive chef Sherri Singleton two AA Rosettes. Unsurprisingly, local seafood is to the fore, with rock oysters and Colchester oysters popular in season. The fare changes daily to reflect the availability of the locally-sourced produce; an entrée may be duck terrine with home-made rhubarb chutney and toast or a smoked haddock chowder before indulging in a Cioppino, a 'Cal Ital' seafood stew with local fresh fish, shellfish, tomato and herbs served with garlic crostini, or pork belly hotpot with chilli, baby beetroot, ginger and miso will hit the spot. Sherri also runs the Mistley Kitchen cookery school here.

continued on page 184

**MANNINGTREE** *continued*

**Open** all wk 12-2.30 6.30-9 (Sat-Sun all day) **Bar Meals** L served Mon-Fri 12-2.30, Sat-Sun all day D served Mon-Fri 6.30-9, Sat 6.30-9.30 Av main course £11 **Restaurant** L served Mon-Fri 12-2.30, Sat-Sun all day D served Mon-Fri 6.30-9, Sat 6.30-9.30 Fixed menu price fr £11.95 Av 3 course à la carte fr £14.95 ⊕ FREE HOUSE ◀ Mersea Bitter, Adnams Bitter. ♟17 **Facilities** Children's menu Children's portions Dogs allowed Parking

### NORTH FAMBRIDGE     Map 7 TQ89

## The Ferry Boat Inn

**Ferry Ln CM3 6LR ☎ 01621 740208**
e-mail: sylviaferryboat@aol.com
dir: *From Chelmsford take A130 S, then A132 to South Woodham Ferrers, then B1012. Turn right to village*

A 500-year-old traditional weatherboard inn tucked away in a lovely village beside the River Crouch and marina. Popular with the sailing fraternity, walkers and birdwatchers (Essex Wildlife Trust's 600-acre sanctuary is close by), it boasts low beams and roaring log fires in character bars, and offers tip-top Greene King ales on tap and an extensive menu listing traditional pub food. Typical choices include ham, egg and chips and steaks with all the trimmings.

**Open** all wk 11.30-3 6.30-11 (Sun 12-4 6.30-10.30 & all day in summer) **Bar Meals** L served all wk 12-2 D served all wk 7-9.30 Av main course £8 **Restaurant** L served all wk 12-2 booking required D served all wk 7-9.30 booking required Av 3 course à la carte fr £15 ⊕ FREE HOUSE ◀ Greene King IPA, Abbot Ale, Morland. **Facilities** Children's menu Children's portions Family room Dogs allowed Garden Parking

### PATTISWICK     Map 13 TL82

## PICK OF THE PUBS

### The Compasses at Pattiswick ♟

*See Pick of the Pubs on opposite page*

### PELDON     Map 7 TL91

## The Peldon Rose

**Colchester Rd CO5 7QJ**
**☎ 01206 735248 📠 01206 736303**
e-mail: enquiries@thepeldonrose.co.uk
dir: *On B1025 Mersea Rd, just before causeway*

The Peldon Rose simply exudes character - locally famous as an old smugglers' inn, it boasts log fires in the bar in winter, original beams and leaded windows. An airy conservatory leads out to the garden, which is ideal for summer dining. Fresh local ingredients including Mersea island fish and oysters feature on the menu; other dishes include lamb and vegetable casserole with herb dumplings; and field mushrooms with spinach, pine nut and Stilton stuffing.

**Open** all day all wk Closed: 25 Dec **Restaurant** L served all wk 12-2.15 D served all wk 6.30-9 ⊕ FREE HOUSE ◀ Adnams Broadside, Adnams Bitter, IPA, local guest bitter. **Facilities** Children's menu Garden Parking

### SHALFORD     Map 12 TL72

## The George Inn

**The Street CM7 5HH**
**☎ 01371 850207 📠 01371 851355**
e-mail: info@thegeorgeshalford.com
dir: *5m Braintree*

A hundred years ago there were five pubs in Shalford, but the George Inn, which dates back some 500 years, is the only one now. It's a traditional village pub, with oak beams and open fires, surrounded by lovely countryside. Shalford Brewery ales are available in the bar, and menu is written up on the blackboard daily, including steaks, chicken breast specialities and popular Oriental and Indian dishes. Fish goes down well too, particularly battered plaice, cod mornay, and salmon en croute.

**Open** all wk ◀ Woodforde's Wherry, Adnams Bitter, Shalford. **Facilities** Garden Parking

### STANSTED AIRPORT

**See also Little Canfield**

### STOCK     Map 6 TQ69

## The Hoop

**21 High St CM4 9BD ☎ 01277 841137**
e-mail: thehoopstock@yahoo.co.uk
dir: *On B1007 between Chelmsford & Billericay*

This 15th-century free house on Stock's village green is every inch the country pub. Expect a warm welcome, real ales and a pleasing lack of music or fruit machines. The annual beer festival enjoys growing popularity, but the food is also a major draw. In keeping with the traditional interior, a meal might include toad in the hoop with mash and onion gravy; roast saddle of venison; pan-seared Cornish scallops with vanilla and artichoke purée and crispy pancetta; or wild mushroom risotto. Hot chocolate fondant with pistachio ice cream and vanilla crème brûlée might be a temptation for dessert.

**Open** all day all wk 11-11 (Sun 12-10.30) **Bar Meals** L served Mon-Sat 12-2.30, Sun 12-5 D served Mon-Sat 6-9 Av main course £9 **Restaurant** L served Tue-Fri 12-2.30, Sun 12-5 booking required D served Tue-Sat 6-9 booking required Av 3 course à la carte fr £30 ⊕ FREE HOUSE ◀ Adnams Bitter, 4 guest ales ♂ Westons, Thatchers, Aspalls. **Facilities** Children's portions Dogs allowed Garden

### WICKHAM BISHOPS     Map 7 TL81

## The Mitre

**2 The Street CM8 3NN**
**☎ 01621 891378 📠 01621 894932**
dir: *Off B1018 at Witham exit A12. Right at Jack & Jenny pub. Right at end of road. 1st left & follow road over bridge. 2nd pub on left*

Originally the Carpenter's Arms, this friendly pub changed its name in the mid-1890s, presumably to reflect the one-time possession of the village by the Bishops of London. The pub's regular range of meat choices includes mixed grills, pies and curries, steaks, and dishes featuring duck, pork, lamb and chicken. Fish is strongly represented by dishes based on haddock, cod, trout, sea bass, swordfish, plaice, Dover sole, red mullet and sea halibut to name a few.

**Open** all wk ◀ Greene King IPA, Greene King Abbot, Fireside, Ruddles, Old Bob. **Facilities** Play area Dogs allowed Garden Parking

### WOODHAM MORTIMER     Map 7 TL80

## Hurdle Makers Arms ♟

**Post Office Rd CM9 6ST**
**☎ 01245 225169 📠 01245 225169**
e-mail: info@hurdlemakersarms.co.uk
dir: *From Chelmsford A414 to Maldon/Danbury. 4.5m, through Danbury into Woodham Mortimer. Over 1st rdbt, 1st left, pub on left. Behind golf driving range*

This Grade II listed building was formerly two cottages, but has been a pub since 1837. The beamed interior still retains its open log fire, and real ale lovers will be delighted by the wide range of micro-brewery products and ciders on offer. Home-made specials might include local rabbit casserole; fresh mackerel; pigeon breasts in red wine; or Stilton chicken. In summer there are weekend barbecues in the large beer garden and a beer festival in June.

**Open** all wk Mon-Sat all day (Sun 12-9) **Bar Meals** L served Mon-Fri 12-3, Sat 12-9.30, Sun 12-8 D served Mon-Fri 6-9.30, Sat 12-9.30, Sun 12-8 **Restaurant** L served Mon-Fri 12-3, Sat 12-9.30, Sun 12-8 D served Mon-Fri 6-9.30, Sat 12-9.30, Sun 12-8 ⊕ GRAY & SONS ◀ Abbot, Mighty Oak, Crouch Vale, Farmers ales, Guest ales ♂ Old Rosie, Westons Scrumpy, Westons Organic. ♟8 **Facilities** Children's menu Children's portions Play area Garden Parking

# PICK OF THE PUBS

## The Compasses at Pattiswick

PATTISWICK       Map 13 TL82

**Compasses Rd CM77 8BG**
☎ **01376 561322** 🖷 **01376 564343**
**e-mail:** info@
thecompassesatpattiswick.co.uk
**dir:** *From Braintree take A120 E towards
Colchester. After Bradwell 1st left to
Pattiswick*

Years ago, two farm-workers cottages were amalgamated to form this friendly pub, still surrounded by the meadows and pocket woodlands of the Holifield Estate, tucked away deep in the north Essex countryside. Connections with the estate run deeper than mere location, however: the pub's owners source some of the raw materials for the extensive menu direct from the estate, so you'll be confident in knowing just where your pheasant, venison, rabbit or partridge grew to maturity. Support for local producers is at the centre of the pub's ethos, with minimising food miles a guiding principle; hence meats are traceable to local farms and seafood comes from inshore fishermen on the Essex coast.

Hearty rural recipes and uncomplicated cooking allow the dishes to do the talking; the monthly changing menu is supplemented by a daily specials board allowing the chefs to take full advantage of seasonal produce and the freshest ingredients. Starters range from deep-fried goat's cheese with a cranberry compote to smoked duck Waldorf salad with beetroot dressing or a classic moules marinière, paving the way for reliable mains such as braised lamb shank with crushed root vegetables and creamy mashed potatoes or grilled sea bass with chervil-crushed potatoes, watercress and a red pepper coulis. Specials will vary with the seasons, so you may be tempted by pan seared swordfish with sun blushed tomato and fine bean salad, salsa verde and olive tapenade. The desserts list favours the classics — steamed strawberry jam sponge with home-made custard or sticky toffee pudding with vanilla ice cream and sorbets. The wine list is very comprehensive, with 13 available by the glass, a generous range of old and new world bins and a fine wine list featuring some exclusive Bordeaux and Burgundies.

A roaring log fire makes a welcoming sight in winter after a local walk, while in summer the large garden is inviting. Families are very well catered for here, with a play area, child menus and even a toy box to keep little diners entertained.

**Open** all wk 11-3 5.30-11 (Sat 5.30-mdnt, Sun noon-4.30, Sun eve in summer) **Bar Meals** L served all wk 12-3 D served Mon-Thu 6-9.30, Fri-Sat 6-9.45 **Restaurant** L served Mon-Sat 12-3, Sun 12-4.30 booking required D served Mon-Thu 6-9.30, Fri-Sat 6-9.45 booking required ⊕ FREE HOUSE ◀ Woodforde's Wherry, Adnams, Adnams Broadside, St Austell Tribute ♂ Aspall. ☿ 13 **Facilities** Children's menu Play area Dogs allowed Garden Parking

## GLOUCESTERSHIRE

### ALDERTON — Map 10 SP03

## The Gardeners Arms

Beckford Rd GL20 8NL ☎ 01242 620257
e-mail: gardeners1@btconnect.com
web: www.gardenersarms.biz
dir: Telephone for directions

This charming family-run, 16th-century thatched free house is in a quiet Cotswolds village. Play boules in the large beer garden, and shove ha'penny or other traditional bar games in the stone-walled bar. Seasonal local produce and daily fresh fish underpin simple dishes such as home-made beef lasagne and tiger prawn Thai green curry. Monthly-changing specials include slow-braised Cotswold lamb shoulder and pan-fried halibut steak. Two annual beer festivals are held; one in May and the other at Christmas. The bar serves a good range of ales all year round.

Open all wk 10-2 5.30-10.30 (Sun all day, Fri til mdnt) Bar Meals L served all wk 12-2 D served all wk 5.30-9 Av main course £8.95 Restaurant L served Mon-Sat 12-2, Sun all day booking required D served all wk 5.30-9.30 booking required ⊕ FREE HOUSE ◀ Doom Bar, Butcombe Best, Courage Best, Local Guest Ales ♂ Westons Stowford. Facilities Children's menu Children's portions Dogs allowed Garden Parking

### ALMONDSBURY — Map 4 ST68

## The Bowl

16 Church Rd BS32 4DT
☎ 01454 612757 ▤ 01454 619910
e-mail: bowlinn@sabrain.com
dir: M5 junct 16 towards Thornbury. 3rd left onto Over Ln, 1st right onto Sundays Hill, next right onto Church Rd

The Bowl nestles on the southeastern edge of the Severn Vale, hence its name. Part of the inn dates from 1146, when monks were building the village church, so it was getting on when it became an inn in 1550. Up to six real ales and great wines are on offer, and freshly prepared food includes chicken quesadilla with tomato salsa and guacamole; slow-roasted leg of lamb with roasted vegetables and thyme jus; mussels in white wine, garlic and parsley sauce; and fabulous Celtic Pride Farm steaks.

Open all day all wk Bar Meals Av main course £9 food served all day Restaurant booking required Av 3 course à la carte fr £28 food served all day ⊕ BRAINS BREWERY ◀ Butcombe, Tribute, Brains ♂ Stowford Press. Facilities Children's menu Children's portions Parking

### ANDOVERSFORD — Map 10 SP01

## PICK OF THE PUBS

### The Kilkeney Inn ♥

Kilkeney GL54 4LN ☎ 01242 820341
e-mail: info@kilkeneyinn.co.uk
dir: On A436 1m W of Andoversford

A charming country dining pub with rolling landscapes stretching away on all sides, where the aim is to mix traditional values with a certain sophistication and style, so beer drinkers are more than welcome and will find real ales served in good condition. Inside, fresh flowers, polished quarry floor tiles and twinkling lights illuminating the impressive wine display create a relaxing ambience. A wood-burner warms the bar whenever there's a nip in the air. The Conservatory restaurant has an airy feel and striking prints adorn the walls; on suitable summer days the doors open on to garden patio, ideal for a romantic alfresco meal. Lunches include lite bites and main courses like Cajun spiced chicken breast with chips. The dinner menu kicks off with home-made soup such as celeriac and apple or Thai salmon, crab and polenta cakes, followed by the inn's special of slow roast shoulder of lamb. Desserts, all crafted in the kitchen, could include a Cointreau spiked warm dark chocolate and orange brownie.

Open all wk Mon-Sat 11.30-3 5.30-11 Sun 11.30-11 Bar Meals L served 12-2 Sun 12-3 D served 6.30-9 ⊕ CHARLES WELLS ◀ Youngs Best Bitter, St Austells Tribute. ♥ 9 Facilities Garden Parking

## The Royal Oak Inn ♥

Old Gloucester Rd GL54 4HR ☎ 01242 820335
e-mail: royal.oak1@unicombox.co.uk
dir: 200mtrs from A40, 4m E of Cheltenham

The 17th-century Royal Oak stands on the banks of the River Coln, in the heart of Andoversford. Originally a coaching inn, it has been sympathetically refurbished in recent times; its main dining room, galleried on two levels, occupies the converted former stables. Two log fires, three or more real ales and a draught cider are part of the allure, coupled with a restaurant menu of seasonal produce sourced locally; the specials board changes twice a week. Ask about meal deals, often on offer.

Open all wk Mon-Sat 12-2.30 5-11 (all day Sun) Bar Meals L served all wk 12-2 D served all wk 6.30-9 Av main course £6.95 Restaurant L served all wk 12-2 D served all wk 6.30-9 Fixed menu price fr £9.75 ⊕ ENTERPRISE INNS ◀ Stanway Ales, Doom Bar, Otter Ale, Broadside ♂ Westons Vintage Organic. ♥ 13 Facilities Children's menu Children's portions Dogs allowed Garden Parking

### ARLINGHAM — Map 4 SO71

## PICK OF THE PUBS

### The Old Passage Inn ★★★★ RR ⑧⑧ ♥

Passage Rd GL2 7JR
☎ 01452 740547 ▤ 01452 741871
e-mail: oldpassage@ukonline.co.uk
dir: 5m from A38 adjacent M5 junct 13

For centuries this ancient inn, surrounded by fields, provided refreshment to ferry passengers across the tidal River Severn. Today it is more seafood-restaurant-with-rooms than drinking establishment, although you'll still find real ales like Wickwar and Westons Organic cider on tap. Eating in the open and airy dining room is a delight, as it's on the popular riverside terrace. Years ago the Severn would have supplied much of the fish, but its elvers and salmon are now in short supply and rarely feature on the menu; freshwater crayfish may turn up, though, and the inn's own saltwater tanks virtually guarantee Pembrokeshire or Cornish lobsters. Simply prepared dishes include roast hake with warm fennel and tomato salad; grilled kippers with sauté potatoes; roast gurnard with brown shrimp, fennel and pine-nut risotto; and whole lemon sole with nut-brown butter. Non-fish alternatives, such as roast sirloin of beef, are there if you want them. There are three modern en suite bedrooms here.

Open 11-3 6-finish (all day Etr-Sep) Closed: 25 Dec, Sun eve & Mon Restaurant L served Tue-Sat 12-2.30, Sun 12-3 booking required D served Tue-Sat 6-9 booking required Fixed menu price fr £17.50 Av 3 course à la carte fr £45 ⊕ FREE HOUSE ◀ Wickwar ♂ Westons Organic. ♥ 12 Facilities Children's portions Dogs allowed Garden Parking Rooms 3

### ASHLEWORTH — Map 10 SO82

## Boat Inn

The Quay GL19 4HZ ☎ 01452 700272 ▤ 01452 700272
e-mail: elisabeth_nicholls@yahoo.co.uk
dir: From Gloucester take A417 towards Ledbury. At Hartpury follow signs for Ashleworth Quay

This picturesque pub on the banks of the Severn has been in the same family for over 400 years, and has changed very little in that time. Renowned for its real ales, it hosts a popular annual beer festival but is also has a great selection of ciders supplied by the local cider house, Westons. Traditionally filled rolls, perhaps with home-made tomato chutney, form the hub of the simple but delicious food offering, available only at lunchtimes.

Open Tue & Wed (eve)-Sun Closed: Mon & Wed L Bar Meals L served Tue, Thu-Sun 12-2 ⊕ FREE HOUSE ◀ Wye Valley, Church End, Arkells, RCH Pitchfork ♂ Westons Stowford Press, Westons Old Rosie Scrumpy, Westons Stowford Export. Facilities Garden Parking Notes ⑧

Save on Hotels. Book at **theAA.com/hotel**

**GLOUCESTERSHIRE** 187 **ENGLAND**

## PICK OF THE PUBS

### The Queens Arms ♟

**The Village GL19 4HT ☎ 01452 700395**
**dir:** *From Gloucester N on A417 for 5m. At Hartpury, opp Royal Exchange turn right at Broad St to Ashleworth. Pub 100yds past village green*

Just a short step from the village green in this pretty Severn-side village stands this engaging 16th-century inn. Sitting in the peaceful garden behind its 200-year-old clipped yews, treat yourself to a leisurely pint of Donnington's Best Bitter, watch the antics of pub dog Bonnie threading between the garden furniture or simply appreciate the great tubs and hanging baskets and enjoy views to the hills of Dean and the Cotswolds. The interior was given a makeover by the Victorians; thankfully the original beams and iron fireplaces were untouched, now complemented by comfy armchairs and antiques. It's a reliable village pub, with friendly locals keen to share their watering hole with visitors drawn to the tempting cuisine that offers an inventive and wide-ranging choice. Good Gloucestershire produce is made-over into rabbit casserole in white wine with bacon, mustard, tarragon and baby onions or a large rack of pork spare ribs marinated in home-made honey and BBQ sauce. Fish lovers may score with fresh monkfish or salmon fillet or for a change try the exotic South African Bobotie, spicy mince topped with savoury egg custard, almonds and raisins.

**Open** noon-3 7-11 Closed: 25-26 Dec & 1 Jan, Sun eve (ex BH wknds) **Bar Meals** L served all wk 12-2 booking required D served Mon-Sat 7-9 booking required Av main course £12 **Restaurant** L served all wk 12-2 booking required D served Mon-Sat 7-9 booking required Av 3 course à la carte fr £21 ⊕ FREE HOUSE ◄ Timothy Taylor Landlord, Donnington BB, S A Brain & Company Rev James, Shepherd Neame Spitfire Ö Stowford Press. ♟ 14 **Facilities** Garden Parking

### AWRE                                    Map 4 SO70

## PICK OF THE PUBS

### The Red Hart Inn at Awre ♟

**GL14 1EW ☎ 01594 510220**
**dir:** *E of A48 between Gloucester & Chepstow, access is from Blakeney or Newnham villages*

The history of this cosy traditional free house goes back to 1483, when it was built to house the workmen who were renovating the nearby 10th-century church. The charming interior includes all the hoped-for historic features such as flagstone floors, stone fireplaces, lots of exposed beams, and an original working well, which is now attractively illuminated. It's the kind of atmospheric place where one quick post-walk pint of Wye Valley Butty Bach could turn into a lengthy sojourn, probably involving a meal. Close to the beautiful River Severn, the setting is ideal for serious hikers, or for those simply seeking a relaxing, attractive place to walk off dinner – there's even a map by the front door for inspiration. Now under new ownership.

**Open** 12-3 6.30-12 (Sun 6.30-10) Closed: Mon ex BHs **Bar Meals** L served Tue-Sun 12-3 D served Tue-Sat 6.30-9 Av main course £7.95 **Restaurant** L served Tue-Sun 12-3 D served Tue-Sat 6.30-9 Fixed menu price fr £10 Av 3 course fr £17.25 ⊕ FREE HOUSE ◄ Wye Valley Butty Bach, guest ales, Sharp's, London Pride, Butcombe Ö Westons, Thatchers, Searn Cider. ♟ 10 **Facilities** Children's menu Children's portions Dogs allowed Garden Parking

### BARNSLEY                              Map 5 SP00

## PICK OF THE PUBS

### The Village Pub ⊛⊛ ♟

**GL7 5EF ☎ 01285 740421     📠 01285 740925**
**e-mail:** reservations@thevillagepub.co.uk
**dir:** *On B4425 4m NE of Cirencester*

Unique in preserving its unusual name, this 'Village Pub' is not your average local. Set in a charming Cotswold village, this enduringly popular pub-restaurant has been beautifully refurbished, yet retains its polished flagstones, oak floorboards, exposed timbers and open fireplaces. Expect a civilised atmosphere in the five rambling dining rooms, which sport an eclectic mix of furniture, rug-strewn floors, warm terracotta walls and crackling log fires. Innovative modern British pub food draws a discerning dining crowd, the daily menus featuring quality local ingredients, including traceable or organic meats, and fresh seasonal fish. Starters may take in potted rabbit with celeriac and mustard, and fresh asparagus with parmesan hollandaise, with main dishes ranging from John Dory with braised octopus, and roast cod with Niçoise salad, to lambs' sweetbreads with wild mushroom risotto cake. A recent change of hands has taken place.

**Open** all wk 11-11 (Sun 11-10) **Bar Meals** L served Mon-Fri 12-2.30, Sat-Sun 12-3 D served Mon-Thu 6-9.30, Fri-Sat 6-10, Sun 6-9 ⊕ FREE HOUSE ◄ Hook Norton Bitter, Butcombe Traditional, guest ales Ö Ashton Press. ♟ 12 **Facilities** Children's portions Dogs allowed Garden Parking

### BERKELEY                              Map 4 ST69

### The Malt House ★★★ INN

**Marybrook St GL13 9BA**
**☎ 01453 511177     📠 01453 810257**
**e-mail:** the-malthouse@btconnect.com
**web:** www.themalthouse.uk.com
**dir:** *M5 junct 13/14, A38 towards Bristol. Pub on main road towards Sharpness*

Within walking distance of Berkeley Castle and its deer park, this family-run free house is also handy for the Edward Jenner museum, dedicated to the life of the founding father of immunology. Inside the heavily beamed pub you'll find a varied selection of lunchtime bar food with a choice of real ales and ciders, as well as weekly home-made specials in the restaurant. Pub favourites like steak and ale pie rub shoulders with vegetarian stuffed peppers, and grilled halibut, butter and lime. Accommodation is available.

**Open** all wk Mon-Thu 4-11 (Fri 3-mdnt Sat noon-mdnt Sun noon-4) **Bar Meals** L served Sat-Sun 12-2 D served Mon-Sat 6.30-9 Av main course £8.50 **Restaurant** L served Sat-Sun 12-2 D served Mon-Sat 6.30-9 ⊕ FREE HOUSE ◄ Old Speckled Hen, Theakstons Best Ö Stowford Press, Thatchers Gold. **Facilities** Children's menu Garden Parking **Rooms** 10

### BIBURY                                 Map 5 SP10

### Catherine Wheel

**Arlington GL7 5ND ☎ 01285 740250**
**e-mail:** info@catherinewheel-bibury.co.uk
**dir:** *On B4425, W of Bibury*

This beautiful Cotswold stone inn, stable courtyard and orchard date back to the 15th century. The Catherine Wheel has changed hands many times since J Hathaway opened it as an inn in 1856 – but a warm welcome, good local ales and quality food remain the hallmarks. The short but appetising menu includes a duo of local venison with Savoy cabbage and parsnip purée; and vegetarian hotpot with butternut squash, spinach and spiced tomato sauce.

**Open** all day all wk 10am-11pm **Bar Meals** Av main course £9 food served all day **Restaurant** booking required food served all day ⊕ WHITE JAYS LTD ◄ Hook Norton, Sharp's Doom Bar Ö Westons Stowford Press. **Facilities** Children's menu Children's portions Dogs allowed Garden Parking

## BIRDLIP — Map 10 SO91

### The Golden Heart ♛

**Nettleton Bottom GL4 8LA**
☎ 01242 870261 ▤ 01242 870599
e-mail: cathstevensgh@aol.com
dir: *On A417 (Gloucester to Cirencester road). 8m from Cheltenham. Pub at base of dip in Nettleton Bottom*

Expect glorious views from the terraced gardens of this centuries-old Cotswold stone inn. It probably started life as a drovers' inn, and retains plenty of original features. Excellent local ales and traditional ciders are the focus of the bar, while the extensive menus show an equal commitment to local produce, particularly prize-winning meat from livestock markets and shows. Choices range from ribeye steak with wild mushrooms to whole rainbow trout with lemon and parsley butter.

**Open** all wk 11-3 5.30-11 (Fri-Sun open all day) Closed: 25 Dec **Bar Meals** L served Mon-Sat 12-3, Sun all day D served Mon-Sat 6-10, Sun all day Av main course £11.25 **Restaurant** L served Mon-Sat 12-3, Sun all day D served Mon-Sat 12-3, Sun all day ⊕ FREE HOUSE ◀ Otter Bitter, Wickwar, Cotswolds Way, Wye Valley, Otter, Gold Festival ♻ Westons, Henney, Thatchers. ♛ 10 **Facilities** Family room Dogs allowed Garden Parking

## BLEDINGTON — Map 10 SP22

### PICK OF THE PUBS

### The Kings Head Inn ★★★★ INN ◉ ♛

*See Pick of the Pubs on opposite page*

## BOURTON-ON-THE-HILL — Map 10 SP13

### PICK OF THE PUBS

### Horse and Groom ♛

**GL56 9AQ** ☎ 01386 700413 ▤ 01386 700413
e-mail: greenstocks@horseandgroom.info
dir: *2m W of Moreton-in-Marsh on A44*

Owned and run by the Greenstock brothers, this is a honey-coloured Grade II listed Georgian building with a contemporary feel combined with original period features. This is a serious dining pub, as well as a friendly place for the locals to drink. The bar offers a selection of local favourites and guest ales, whilst the blackboard menu of regularly changing dishes provides plenty of appeal for even the most regular diners. With committed local suppliers backed up by the pub's own vegetable patch, the Horse and Groom's kitchen has plenty of good produce to work with. A typical menu might feature creamed fennel and white bean soup; linguine of roasted wild mushrooms, thyme, parmesan, pine nuts and cream; griddled Dexter sirloin steak, garlic and parsley butter; roast rack of 'old farm' lamb, parsnip and Dijon purée with thyme jus. Leave room for puddings like chocolate tart, salted caramel and Jersey cream. In summer, the mature garden offers panoramic hilltop views.

---

**Open** 11-3 6-11 Closed: 25 Dec, Sun eve **Bar Meals** L served all wk 12-2 booking required D served Mon-Sat 7-9 booking required Av main course £12.50 **Restaurant** L served all wk 12-2 booking required D served Mon-Sat 7-9 booking required Av 3 course à la carte fr £25 ⊕ FREE HOUSE ◀ Wye Valley Bitter, Pure UBU, Goffs Jouster, Cotswold Wheat, Prescott Brewery's Track Record ♻ Westons Stowford Press. ♛ 13 **Facilities** Children's portions Garden Parking

## CHARLTON KINGS — Map 10 SO92

### PICK OF THE PUBS

### The Reservoir ♛

**London Rd GL54 4HG** ☎ 01242 529671
e-mail: alexwynn007@hotmail.co.uk
dir: *On A40, 5m E of Cheltenham*

Mark Streeter and his talented team have recently arrived at the Reservoir Inn, bringing with them a fresh approach and plenty of experience – Mark has worked at The Savoy and The Vineyard at Stockcross amongst other places. Real food, prepared fresh every day and at affordable prices is the ethos – Mark wants everyone to be able to enjoy the food he works so hard to produce. The surroundings here are beautiful - opposite is the reason for the pub's name, Dowdeswell Reservoir – and the pub is undergoing refurbishment to make it even more welcoming to all. Expect Abbot Ale, Morland Original and Old Speckled Hen in the spacious bar, while menus use fresh, seasonal and locally sourced ingredients in a range broad enough to satisfy everyone – there's an excellent Sunday lunch, new vegetarian menu, various good value offers are available and Wednesday night is steak night – two sirloin steaks cooked as you like with all the trimmings and a bottle of house wine for £25.

**Open** 11-3 5-11 (Fri-Sun open all day) Closed: Mon winter **Bar Meals** Av main course £8 food served all day **Restaurant** L served Tue-Sat 12-2.30, Sun 12-8 D served Tue-Sat 5.30-9.30 Fixed menu price fr £10 Av 3 course à la carte fr £22 ⊕ THE TROUBLED PUB COMPANY ◀ IPA, Abbot, Old Speckled Hen ♻ Stowford Press. ♛ 9 **Facilities** Dogs allowed Garden Parking

## CHEDWORTH — Map 5 SP01

### PICK OF THE PUBS

### Hare & Hounds ★★★★ INN ◉ ♛

**Foss Cross GL54 4NN** ☎ 01285 720288
e-mail: stay@hareandhoundsinn.com
dir: *On A429 (Fosse Way), 6m from Cirencester*

Situated on the Fosse Way, close to Cirencester, this 14th-century inn is an ideal base for exploring the Cotswolds or attending Cheltenham race meetings. With its interconnecting dining areas, open fires, beams and stone and polished wood floors, it retains a great deal of old world charm. There's a daily changing blackboard with at least two extra fish dishes, along with a menu typically listing marinated lambs' kidneys

---

cooked in red wine, grilled red snapper with oriental tamarind, lemon grass and ginger sake, and trio of lamb – confit shoulder, cutlet and stuffed belly. At lunch enjoy a glass of Arkells ale with bacon and eggs with bubble and squeak, or Old Spot sausage and mash with onion gravy. In warmer weather, sit outside in the garden or at anytime in the orangery. There are ten comfortable en suite rooms set around a tranquil courtyard.

*Hare & Hounds*

**Open** all wk 11-3 (Sat 6-close Sun 7- close) **Bar Meals** L served all wk 12-2.30 booking required D served Mon-Sat 6.30-9.30, Sun 7-9 booking required Av main course £6.95 **Restaurant** L served all wk 12-2.30 booking required D served Mon-Sat 6.30-9.30, Sun 7-9 booking required Av 3 course à la carte fr £22.50 ⊕ ARKELLS ◀ Arkells 2B, 3B, Moonlight ♻ Stowford Press. ♛ 8 **Facilities** Children's menu Children's portions Family room Dogs allowed Garden Parking Rooms 10

### PICK OF THE PUBS

### Seven Tuns ♛

**Queen St GL54 4AE**
☎ 01285 720242 ▤ 01285 720933
e-mail: theseventuns@clara.co.uk
dir: *Exit A429, turn off at junct to Chedworth. Approx halfway between Northleach & Cirencester, follow signs to pub*

Directly opposite this creeper-covered, unmistakably Cotswold inn, are a waterwheel, a spring and a raised terrace for summer dining. The pub dates back to the 17th century, and the name derives from the seven chimney pots that deck the roof. The lunch menu offers nothing too heavy - baguettes, ploughman's, soup of the day and appealing Mediterranean dishes like melted brie and ham croque-madame with a fried egg; goat's cheese bruschetta with black cherry compote, or courgette, garden pea and basil risotto. Typical of a

*continued on page 190*

# PICK OF THE PUBS

## The Kings Head Inn ★★★★INN

**BLEDINGTON** Map 10 SP22

**The Green OX7 6XQ**
**☎ 01608 658365 01608 658902**
**e-mail:** info@kingsheadinn.net
**dir:** *On B4450 4m from Stow-on-the-Wold*

A more delightful spot would surely be hard to find: facing the village green with its brook and border-patrolling ducks, this is certainly a quintessential Cotswold inn. Stone-built and dating back to the 15th century, this perfect country retreat on the Gloucester border is a former cider house. Much of the original structure has survived, leaving sturdy beams, low ceilings, flagstone floors, exposed stone walls, and inglenook fireplace – all of which have been preserved and enhanced by more recent additions.

Archie and Nicola Orr-Ewing have worked hard to earn an excellent reputation for their Cotswold treasure – one built on well-kept real ales, an extensive wine list and wonderful fresh produce in the kitchen. Ingredients are locally sourced and organic as far as possible, with beef (hung for 21 days) from Archie's uncle's farm and fish delivered fresh from Cornwall. In the bar, Hook Norton Bitter is a mainstay, alongside guest ales from local microbreweries, organic cider, local lagers, over 25 malt whiskies, and eight wines served by the glass.

The menu is concise but some of the starters can be served as main courses, so choice is more than ample: lamb kofta kebabs with Bombay potato and cucumber salad, or baked Cornish scallops with garlic and chorizo, cheddar and herb crust. Although the cuisine offers main courses like whole baked Cornish lemon sole with brown shrimp dressing and Charlotte potatoes, the kitchen nevertheless may offer a heart-warming favourite such as a Fifield farm Angus steak and ale pie with puff pastry and fries. Desserts too are all home made and familiar, with the likes of apple, plum and pear crumble with crème anglaise, and sticky toffee pudding with Dorset clotted cream.

The thoughtfully and tastefully decorated bedrooms are split between the pub and a converted barn.

**Open** all wk 11.30-3 6-11 Closed: 25-26 Dec **Bar Meals** L served Mon-Fri 12-2, Sat-Sun 12-2.30 D served Mon-Thu 7-9, Fri-Sat 7-9.30, Sun 7-9 Av main course £12 **Restaurant** L served Mon-Fri 12-2, Sat-Sun 12-2.30 D served Mon-Thu 7-9, Fri-Sat 7-.9.30, Sun 7-9 Av 3 course à la carte fr £24 FREE HOUSE Hook Norton Bitter, Doom Bar, Vale Pale Ale, Wye Valley & Brakspear Stowford Press. 8 **Facilities** Children's menu Dogs allowed Garden Parking **Rooms** 12

**CHEDWORTH** *continued*

winter evening might be wild boar pâté with spiced apple chutney; braised oxtail and cranberry casserole with mustard mash; and rope mussels in creamy cider and white wine sauce. In the beer garden there's a revolving South African barbecue and a renovated skittle alley. Live music evenings held.

**Open** all wk noon-3 6-11 (Sat noon-mdnt Sun noon-10.30pm) Jul-Aug all day **Bar Meals** L served Mon-Fri 12-2.30, Sat-Sun 12-3 D served Mon-Sat 6.30-9.30, Sun 6.30-9 Av main course £9.95 **Restaurant** L served Mon-Fri 12-2.30, Sat-Sun 12-3 D served Mon-Sat 6.30-9.30, Sun 6.30-9 Av 3 course à la carte fr £20 ◀ Young's Bitter, Winter Warmer, Waggledance, Bombardier, Tribute. ♟ 12 **Facilities** Children's menu Children's portions Family room Dogs allowed Garden Parking

---

## CHIPPING CAMPDEN    Map 10 SP13

### The Bakers Arms

**Broad Campden GL55 6UR ☎ 01386 840515**
dir: *1m from Chipping Campden*

There is a friendly family atmosphere at this country Cotswold inn, where you can expect to find exposed stone walls, beams and an inglenook fireplace. A choice of four to five real ales is offered alongside reasonably priced meals. Choose from ploughman's, warm baguettes and filled giant Yorkshire puddings, or specials such as lamb shank with mint gravy; smoked haddock bake; or pork steaks in cider cream sauce.

**Open** all wk 11.30-2.30 5.30-11 (Fri-Sun 11.30-11 Apr-Oct all wk 11.30-11) Closed: 25-26 Dec & 31 Dec eve **Bar Meals** L served Mon-Fri 12-2, Sat 12-2.30, Sun 12-6 D served Mon-Sat 6-9 **Restaurant** L served Mon-Fri 12-2, Sat 12-2.30, Sun 12-6 D served Mon-Sat 6-9 ⊕ FREE HOUSE ◀ Stanway Bitter, Bombardier, Donnington BB. **Facilities** Children's menu Children's portions Play area Garden Parking **Notes** ⊜

---

### PICK OF THE PUBS

### Eight Bells ♟

*See Pick of the Pubs on opposite page*

---

### PICK OF THE PUBS

### The Kings ☆☆☆☆☆ RR ◉ ♟

**The Square GL55 6AW**
**☎ 01386 840256 ▤ 01386 841598**
e-mail: info@kingscampden.co.uk
dir: *Telephone for directions*

A lovely old townhouse facing the square of one of England's prettiest towns. Sympathetically restored, yet packed with character, the oldest parts include the 16th-century stone mullioned windows on the first floor. The bar offers at least two real ales, including local Hook Norton, as well as daily papers and traditional pub games, but no noisy gaming machines. Bar snacks include a good range of sandwiches and baguettes,

---

while main meals are served in the informal bar brasserie or more formal AA Rosette restaurant overlooking the square. The packed menu offers some imaginative delights: tian of Salcombe crab with cherry tomatoes and herb crème fraîche; braised shank of Lighthorne lamb with dauphinoise potatoes, roast root vegetables and rosemary sauce; risotto of the day. The large grassed garden and dining terrace is good to find in a town centre pub. Individually decorated bedrooms offer period features with plenty of modern comforts.

**Open** all day all wk **Bar Meals** L served all wk 12-2.30 booking required D served all wk 6.30-9.30 booking required **Restaurant** L served all wk 12-2.30 booking required D served all wk 6.30-9.30 booking required ⊕ FREE HOUSE ◀ Hook Norton Best. ♟ 10 **Facilities** Children's menu Children's portions Garden Parking **Rooms** 19

---

### PICK OF THE PUBS

### Noel Arms Hotel ★★★ HL

**High St GL55 6AT ☎ 01386 840317 ▤ 01386 841136**
e-mail: reception@noelarmshotel.com
dir: *On High St, opposite Town Hall*

Charles II stayed in this 16th-century coaching inn, built of golden Cotswold stone like so many places around here. It was through the carriage arch that packhorse trains used to carry bales of wool, the source of the town's prosperity, to Bristol and Southampton. Absorb the hotel's atmosphere with a real ale in front of the log fire in Dover's Bar; read the papers over a coffee and pastry in the Austrian coffee shop; and enjoy brasserie style food in the restaurant, with ingredients sourced from the lush Cotswolds. Classic starters include potted shrimps on toast; Welsh rarebit; and devilled whitebait. Longhorn steaks matured for 28 days are served with triple-cooked chips and all the trimmings. Alternatively old favourites include Barnsley lamb chop and kidney; Gloucester Old Spot sausages with mash and onion gravy; and Madgett's Farm chicken, mushroom and leek pie. Replete, you can retire to bed in a four-poster made in 1657.

**Open** all day all wk **Bar Meals** L served all wk 12-7 D served all wk 12-7 Av main course £12.50 food served all day **Restaurant** food served all day ⊕ FREE HOUSE ◀ Hook Norton Best Bitter, Guinness ♖ Westons Stowford Press. **Facilities** Children's menu Children's portions Dogs allowed Garden Parking **Rooms** 28

---

### The Volunteer Inn

**Lower High St GL55 6DY ☎ 01386 840688**
e-mail: mark_gibbo@yahoo.co.uk
dir: *From Shipston on Stour take B4035 to Chipping Campden*

A 300-year-old inn where, in the mid-19th-century, the able-bodied used to sign up for the militia. Ramblers can set off from here to walk the Cotswold Way. Food options are provided by the Pan-Asian Maharaja Restaurant found at the inn which serves a wide choice of options in the evenings. Volunteer Ale is among the regulars on offer.

**Open** all wk **Bar Meals** Av main course £7.90 **Restaurant** D served all wk 5-10.30 booking required ⊕ FREE HOUSE ◀ Hook Norton, Hobgoblin, Volunteer Ale. **Facilities** Children's portions Play area Family room Dogs allowed Garden

---

## CIRENCESTER    Map 5 SP00

### PICK OF THE PUBS

### The Crown of Crucis ★★★ HL

**Ampney Crucis GL7 5RS**
**☎ 01285 851806 ▤ 01285 851735**
e-mail: reception@thecrownofcrucis.co.uk
dir: *On A417 to Lechlade, 2m E of Cirencester*

Overlooking the village cricket green, this 16th-century former coaching inn retains its historical charm while feeling comfortably up-to-date. The building stands beside the Ampney brook at the gateway to the Cotswolds, and the quiet stream meandering past the lawns creates a perfect picture of quintessential rural England. The name 'Crucis' refers to the Latin cross in the nearby churchyard. With its traditional beams, log fires and warm, friendly atmosphere, the bar has been recently restored. Bar food is served all day, along with a range of daily specials. The busy bar offers a large selection of draught and real ales and a choice of wines by the glass. The restaurant menu offers starters of pan-fried pigeon breast, and prawn and avocado cocktail; followed perhaps by peppered venison steak on garlic cream potatoes with rich red wine sauce, or ginger and spring onion risotto with infused lemon oil and parmesan crisp. Round things off with Cotswold crème brûlée and home-made shortbread biscuits.

**Open** all day all wk Closed: 25 Dec **Bar Meals** food served all day **Restaurant** L served all wk 12-2.30 booking required D served all wk 7-9.30 booking required ⊕ FREE HOUSE ◀ Sharp's Doom Bar, Archers Village, John Smith's. **Facilities** Dogs allowed Garden Parking **Rooms** 25

# PICK OF THE PUBS

## Eight Bells 🍷

**Church St GL55 6JG**
☎ 01386 840371  📄 01386 841669
**e-mail:**
neilhargreaves@bellinn.fsnet.co.uk
**dir:** *8m from Stratford-upon-Avon, M40 junct 15*

A lovely, flower basket-hung inn, just off the High Street of this showpiece Cotswold town, the Eight Bells was built in the 14th century to house stonemasons working on the nearby church; later it was used to store its bells, thus its name. During the 17th century the inn was rebuilt, using the rough-hewn stones and timbers you see around you today.

The way in is through a cobbled entranceway leading into two atmospheric beamed bars with open fireplaces and, in the floor of one, a surviving priest's hole; outside is an enclosed courtyard and terraced garden overlooking the almshouses and church. Interpret as you wish the website comment that the owners have resisted transforming the inn into a "so-called gastro-pub"; just enjoy the Hook Norton and Purity (from Stratford-upon-Avon) real ales and freshly prepared, locally sourced dishes offered, such as lunchtime sandwiches on freshly baked ciabatta bread; home-made soup; cod and smoked haddock pie; and autumn vegetable and melting Stilton risotto.

From a main menu come starters of warm salad of pan-fried calamari, chorizo and sesame seeds with chilli and lime dressing; and chicken ballottine stuffed with sage and black pudding, wrapped in bacon. Appearing as a main course might be prime 10oz gammon steak with 'rumbledy thump' potatoes; grilled fillet of sea bass on mildly spiced Catalan bean cassoulet; Mr Lashford's Gloucestershire sausage toad-in-the-hole with Old Rosie cider and grain mustard sauce; and wild mushroom and walnut tagliatelle with white wine and herb cream sauce. Hot ginger sponge and poached pear in a brandy-snap basket are typical home-made desserts. Children will be tempted by their own menu.

**Open** all day all wk noon-11 (Sun noon-10.30) Closed: 25 Dec
**Bar Meals** L served Mon-Thu 12-2, Fri-Sun 12-2.30 D served Mon-Thu 6.30-9, Fri-Sat 6.30-9.30, Sun 6.30-8.45
**Restaurant** L served Mon-Thu 12-2, Fri-Sun 12-2.30 D served Mon-Thu 6.30-9, Fri-Sat 6.30-9.30, Sun 6.30-8.45 🍺 Hook Norton Best & guest ales, Goff's Jouster, Marston Pedigree, Purity UBU 🍏 Old Rosie. 🍷 8
**Facilities** Family room Dogs allowed Garden

# PICK OF THE PUBS

## The Yew Tree 🍷

**CLIFFORD'S MESNE**    Map 10 SO72

Clifford's Mesne GL18 1JS
☎ 01531 820719
e-mail: cass@yewtreeinn.com
dir: *From Newent High Street follow signs to Clifford's Mesne. Pub at far end of village on road to Glasshouse*

With satnav or an OS map, you should find this welcoming pub with little trouble; without one, it might prove a bit trickier, as it's up a little lane on the slopes of the National Trust's May Hill, Gloucestershire's highest point. Up here, horses and sheep graze wild and, weather permitting, from its 296m summit you can see the Welsh Mountains, the Malvern Hills and the River Severn - a seven-county panorama in fact.

Many centuries ago the building was a cider press, but it looks very different now, pleasingly floored with quarry tiles, warmed by winter log fires, and a bar with an excellent choice of locally brewed real ales and ciders. All the wines are imported by the inn and sold in its own wine shop; twelve wines by the glass are available in the pub.

Study the seasonal menu while you snack on bowls of nuts, olives and peppers, or nibble home-made breadsticks with a selection of dips. All dishes on the menu are freshly prepared; only the cheeses and some of the breads and ice creams are bought in. Starters could include potted Stilton and toast; kidneys in creamy Dijon sauce on a garlic croûte; and chargrilled courgette and sun-dried tomato risotto. For a main course, consider Moroccan baked lamb shank with savoury couscous; Gloucester Old Spot loin steak with roast vine tomatoes, apricot butter and hand-cut chips; pheasant and fig pudding with mash; sea bass fillets on creamed potato with sautéed spinach and vermouth sauce; or wild mushroom and chestnut strudel. A blackboard lists

the daily specials. As an alternative to one of the home-made desserts, try a plate of regional and artisan cheeses.

Regular events include monthly quiz and supper nights throughout the winter, and occasional performances during dinner by guest artistes; while in October there's a beer, cider and local produce festival.

**Open** 12-2.30 6-11 (Sun 12-5) Closed: Mon, Tue L, Sun eve **Bar Meals** L served Wed-Sat 12-2 booking required D served Tue-Sat 6-9 booking required Av main course £11 **Restaurant** L served Sun 12-4 booking required Av 3 course à la carte fr £20 ⊕ FREE HOUSE ◀ Wye Valley HPA, Cotswold Spring Brewery Glory, Goffs, Spinning Dog, Local Ales ⚙ Stowford Press, Lyne Downe, Black Dragon, Gwatkins. ♙ 12
**Facilities** Children's menu Play area Dogs allowed Garden Parking

| CLIFFORD'S MESNE | Map 10 SO72 |

## PICK OF THE PUBS

## The Yew Tree ☻

*See Pick of the Pubs on opposite page*

| COATES | Map 4 SO90 |

## PICK OF THE PUBS

## The Tunnel House Inn

*See Pick of the Pubs on page 194*

| COLESBOURNE | Map 10 SP01 |

## PICK OF THE PUBS

## The Colesbourne Inn ☻

GL53 9NP ☎ 01242 870376
e-mail: colesbourneinn@wadworth.co.uk
dir: *Midway between Cirencester & Cheltenham on A435*

A handsome 17th-century stone pub on the Colesbourne estate at the heart of the Cotswolds. Set between the historic towns of Cheltenham and Cirencester, it is ideal for exploring the villages and gentle, very English countryside of Gloucestershire. Nearby is the source of the River Thames, which can be reached on foot along delightful field and meadow paths. Dating back to 1827 and set in two acres of grounds, the Colesbourne Inn has been sympathetically restored over the years. Among the distinguishing features are a host of beams, roaring log fires, four separate dining areas, and a superb terrace and garden with stunning rural views. There is even a side entrance from the bar originally used as a chamber for smoking ham. Food is all important at the Colesbourne Inn, and fresh local produce is used wherever possible; there is an appetising range of light bites.

**Open** all wk 11-11 (Sun 11-10.30) ⊕ WADWORTH ◄ Wadworth 6X, Henrys IPA, Horizon, Summersault ♂ Stowford Press. ☻ 20 **Facilities** Play area Dogs allowed Garden Parking

| COLN ST ALDWYNS | Map 5 SP10 |

## PICK OF THE PUBS

## The New Inn At Coln ★★ HL ◉◉

GL7 5AN ☎ 01285 750651 📄 01285 750657
e-mail: info@thenewinnatcoln.co.uk
dir: *Between Bibury (B4425) & Fairford (A417), 8m E of Cirencester*

The setting for this handsome Elizabethan coaching inn is perfect: a sleepy Cotswold village close to the River Coln and historic Bibury, with a postcard-pretty frontage of flower baskets and ivy. Tastefully furnished rooms within include the Courtyard Bar, with its old beams, tiled floor, stone walls and open fires, and the more intimate, red-walled dining room. Modern menus

are built around fresh, high quality ingredients. In the bar, share a deli board of cold meats, pâté and pickles, enjoy a light goat's cheese and shallot tart, a roast beef and horseradish sandwich, or the traditional pork sausages, mash and onion gravy, or choose for great value set lunch menu. At dinner, order seared scallops with beetroot and smoked salmon salad, follow with braised pork belly with confit Savoy cabbage and red wine jus, and round off with iced banana and Bailey's parfait with caramel sauce. You can also eat outside on the terrace. Individually designed bedrooms ooze comfort and style – each has a view, over the village, terrace or watermeadows.

**Open** all wk **Bar Meals** L served all wk 12.30-3 D served all wk 7-9 Av main course £10 **Restaurant** L served all wk 12.30-3 D served all wk 7-9 Av 3 course à la carte fr £30 ⊕ FREE HOUSE ◄ Hook Norton Best Bitter, Wadworth 6X, Donningtons BB. **Facilities** Play area Dogs allowed Garden Parking **Rooms** 13

| COWLEY | Map 10 SO91 |

## PICK OF THE PUBS

## The Green Dragon Inn ★★★★ INN ☻

*See Pick of the Pubs on page 195*

| CRANHAM | Map 10 SO81 |

## The Black Horse Inn ☻

GL4 8HP ☎ 01452 812217
dir: *A46 towards Stroud, follow signs for Cranham*

Set in a small village surrounded by woodland and commons, a mile from the Cotswold Way and Prinknash Abbey. The owner neatly sums up the pub: 'Very popular with walkers. Open fires, Morris dancers, pub cricket team, pub dogs Baxter and Percy. Home-cooked traditional pub food – ham, faggots, toad-in-the-hole, pies (steak and kidney, beef and Guinness); melted brie, bacon and walnut salad; very popular Sunday roasts; home-made puds – meringues, sticky toffee, lemon shortcake'. All this, real ales and ciders too, and a sloping garden with lovely views across the valley.

**Open** 12-2.30 6.30-11 (Sun 12-3.30 6.30-11) Closed: 25 Dec, Mon **Bar Meals** L served Tue-Sat 12-2, Sun 12-2.30 D served Tue-Sun 6.45-9 Av main course £9 **Restaurant** L served Sat 12-2, Sun 12-2.30 booking required D served Sat-Sun 6.45-9 booking required ⊕ FREE HOUSE ◄ Wickwar Brand Oak, Archers, Golden Train & Village, Hancocks HB & guest ales, Cats Whiskers, Gem, Bath Ales, Butcombe, Stroud Brewery Buddings ♂ Thatchers Gold, Stowford Press, Westons Country Perry & Scrumpy. ☻ 9 **Facilities** Children's portions Dogs allowed Garden Parking

| DURSLEY | Map 4 ST79 |

## PICK OF THE PUBS

## The Old Spot Inn ☻ NEW

Hill Rd GL11 4JQ ☎ 01453 542870
e-mail: steveoldspot@hotmail.co.uk
dir: *From Tetbury on A4135 (or Uley on B4066) into Dursley, round Town Hall. Straight on at lights towards bus station, pub behind bus station. From Cam to lights in Dursley immediately prior to pedestrianised street. Right towards bus station*

Smack on the Cotswold Way and named after the Gloucestershire Old Spot Pig, this classic 18th-century free house is a former real ale pub of the year, so it's worth visiting to sample the eight tip-top real ales on handpump, and to savour the cheerful buzzing atmosphere as The Old Spot is a cracking community local. As well as organising four real ale festivals a year, landlord Steve Herbert organises a host of events, including brewery visits, cricket matches and celebrity chef nights. Devoid of modern-day intrusions, the rustic and traditional low-beamed bars are havens of peace, with just the comforting sound of crackling log fires and the hubbub of chatting locals filling the rambling little rooms. Food is wholesome and home made, ranging from ploughman's lunches and doorstep sandwiches to pork and apple burgers, sausages and mash with rich gravy, cottage pie with home-made bread and salad, and steak and ale pie with proper shortcrust pastry. Puddings include treacle tart and bread-and-butter pudding. There's also a pretty garden for summer alfresco sipping.

**Open** all day all wk **Bar Meals** L served all wk 12-3 booking required Av main course £8 ⊕ FREE HOUSE ◄ Otter, Butty Bach, Golden Hare ♂ Ashton Press, Happy Days, Stowford Press. ☻ 8 **Facilities** Children's portions Family room Dogs allowed Garden Parking

| EBRINGTON | Map 10 SP14 |

## PICK OF THE PUBS

## The Ebrington Arms ★★★★ INN ◉

*See Pick of the Pubs on page 196*

# PICK OF THE PUBS

## The Tunnel House Inn

**COATES** Map 4 SO90

**GL7 6PW**
☎ 01285 770280 📄 01285 700040
**e-mail:** bookings@tunnelhouse.com
**web:** www.tunnelhouse.com
**dir:** *From Cirencester on A433 towards Tetbury, in 2m turn right towards Coates, follow brown signs to Canal Tunnel & Inn*

Lying between the Cotswold villages of Coates and Tarlton, the Tunnel House enjoys a glorious rural location down a bumpy track leading to the mouth of the two-mile long Sapperton Tunnel on the Thames and Severn Canal; it provided accommodation for navvies building the canal, and is not far from the source of the Thames. In appropriate weather the garden is an ideal place for relaxing with a pint of Wye Valley or Hook Norton and enjoying the views across the fields.

In the winter months three log fires warm the welcoming bar, where oddities include an upside-down table on the ceiling.

Now under new management, the pub is open and serves food all day, every day. You may dine on simple, home-made cooking in the restaurant area or relax in the comfortable seating in the bar. Eat lightly at lunchtime with a beef and horseradish sandwich on granary bread, or a warm white baguette of honey-roast ham and mustard.

In the evening, indulge in Mediterranean flavours with the likes of an asparagus, parmesan, Parma ham and soft boiled egg salad; or ravioli filled with sun-dried tomato, roasted pepper, ricotta and basil. Main courses reflect classic English flavours in dishes such as a rump or rib-eye steak served with chips and mixed leaves; Gloucester Old Spot sausages with creamed mashed potatoes and red onion marmalade; or a braised pork chop with mustard mash, glazed apples and green vegetables.

Children will probably opt for the usual favourites of sausage and mash with gravy; mini beefburger with cheese; and chicken goujons with chips and peas. Desserts will be hard to resist if they include Belgian waffles with home-made chocolate ripple ice cream; or Kahlua crème brûlée with chocolate truffles. A kiddie's play area and spectacular walks in the surrounding countryside add to the pub's popularity.

**Open** all wk **Bar Meals** Av main course £9.95 food served all day
**Restaurant** food served all day ⊕ FREE HOUSE ◀ Uley Old Spot, Uley Bitter, Wye Valley Bitter, Hook Norton, Budding, Butcombe ♂ Cornish Rattler, Black Rat, Westons Organic. **Facilities** Children's menu Play area Family room Dogs allowed Garden Parking

# PICK OF THE PUBS

## The Green Dragon Inn ★★★★INN ♈

COWLEY      Map 10 SO91

**Cockleford GL53 9NW**
☎ 01242 870271   📄 01242 870171
**e-mail:** green-dragon@buccaneer.co.uk
**web:** www.green-dragon-inn.co.uk
**dir:** *Telephone for directions*

This beautiful Cotswold-stone inn has surveyed the heart of the pretty little village of Cockleford for well over 300 years. Behind the striking, rose and creeper covered façade lies a stunning interior crafted at the workshops of Robert Thompson, the 'Mouse Man of Kilburn' (that's Kilburn, North Yorkshire, not London), so-called for his trademark mouse, after whom the popular Mouse Bar, with its stone-flagged floors, beamed ceilings and crackling log fires, is named. See if you can find the craftily hidden, playful little rodents carved into the Yorkshire oak. Once your eye is in, they're surprisingly easy to spot, aided by a glass of Butcombe bitter.

With comfy AA-listed accommodation on site, it's an ideal base for exploring the Cotswolds; Miserden Gardens and Chedworth Roman villa are a short way away and there are easy strolls in the Churn Valley. In summer the secluded patio garden overlooking a lake is a great space; colder times see the Mouse Bar and Lower Bar both busy with diners who make a bee-line for The Green Dragon from many miles around to experience the superb meals that cater for both snackers and indulgents keen to try the happy mix of traditional and modern cuisines.

A light lunch could be a smoked trout and horseradish roulade with garlic and anchovy focaccia or a trio of Gloucester Old Spot sausages with mash and rich gravy. Mains are very wide ranging and change weekly; look for crabmeat, haddock, cod and prawn bread and butter pudding with a mature Cheddar cheese sauce, or slow-braised lamb shank on minted mashed potato with a shallot, redcurrant and rosemary sauce; vegetarian options include Mediterranean vegetable risotto quesadillas with a provençale sauce.

**Open** all day all wk **Bar Meals** L served Mon-Fri 12-2.30, Sat 12-3, Sun 12-3.30 D served all wk 6-10 Av main course £15 **Restaurant** L served Mon-Fri 12-2.30, Sat 12-3, Sun 12-3.30 D served all wk 6-10 Av 3 course à la carte fr £25 ⊕ BUCCANEER ◀ Hook Norton, Directors, Butcombe, guest ale ♻ Stowford Press. ♈ 9
**Facilities** Children's menu Dogs allowed Garden Parking **Rooms** 9

# PICK OF THE PUBS

## The Ebrington Arms ★★★★INN

**EBRINGTON**  Map 10 SP14

**GL55 6NH** ☎ **01386 593223**
**e-mail:** info@theebringtonarms.co.uk
**dir:** *Chipping Campden on B4035 towards Shipston on Stour. Left to Ebrington signed after 0.5m, by village green*

Every inch the real McCoy of a village pub, this award-winning, hidden gem is in the Cotswolds — the hills look lovely from the walled beer garden. Built in 1640, its abundance of character owes much to the heavy beams and original flagstones in both the bar and Old Bakehouse dining room, and the large inglenook fireplaces, which recall the building's days as the village bakery.

Very much the hub of community life, it's where lucky locals (and visitors too, of course) are spoilt for choice with several real ales, some from nearby breweries like Stroud and Uley, while cider drinkers can enjoy traditional Robinson's Flagon, and even Cotswold-brewed lagers. Wine-wise, owners Jim and Claire Alexander researched the market thoroughly before plumping for a selection of local merchants, including Savage Wines, of whose proprietor wine critic Oz Clarke has said: "I don't think Mark Savage could buy a dull wine if he tried".

As for the food, chef James Nixon knows how to get his hands on the best freshly harvested, organic produce, as most of it is grown or reared in fields around the pub. That his culinary talents are recognised with an AA Rosette should therefore come as no surprise. One of his typical evening meals could feature tuna carpaccio with radish, parmesan shavings and lemon olive oil; noisettes of Cotswold lamb topped with wild mushroom gratin, celeriac dauphinoise, roasted squash and thyme jus; and passionfruit and orange glaze. A vegetarian's first two courses on the other hand might be bruschetta of marinated wild mushrooms with feta, spinach and basil mousse; and roasted root vegetable cassoulet with rocket salad.

Music, games and quiz nights, and monthly themed food evenings are held. If you would like to stay, there are luxurious en suite bedrooms available.

**Open** all wk all day **Food** Mon-Thu 12-2.30 6.30-9, Fri-Sat 12-2.30 6.30-9.30, Sun 12-3.30 (full menu inc Sunday roast) 6.30-8.30 (summer only, limited menu) ⊕ FREE HOUSE ◀ Butty Bach, Uley Bitter, Stroud Organic, Hooky Bitter ♂ Robinsons Flagon. ♑ 7 **Facilities** Dogs allowed Garden Parking **Rooms** 3

Save on Hotels. Book at **theAA.com/hotel**

**GLOUCESTERSHIRE** 197 **ENGLAND**

---

**EWEN** | Map 4 SU09

## The Wild Duck ★★ HL ▾ NEW

**GL7 6BY** ☎ **01285 770310** 📠 **01285 770924**
**e-mail:** wduckinn@aol.com
**dir:** *From Cirencester take A429 towards Malmesbury. At kemble left to Ewen. Inn in village centre*

Built of honeyed Cotswold stone in 1563 and situated near to the source of the Thames, this former farm has been family-owned for more than 20 years. Deep red walls lined with old portraits give the Post Horn bar a warm feel; the rambling restaurant offers prime beef fillet Wellington with red wine glaze and wild mushroom sauce; bouillabaisse with parmesan croutons and truffle oil; and home-made burger with bacon and chips. The unusual clock on the façade was a gift from Longines. There is a delightful garden and comfortable rooms if you would like to stay over.

**Open** all day all wk **Bar Meals** L served Mon-Fri 12-2, Sat-Sun 12-10 booking required Av main course £10 **Restaurant** L served Mon-Fri 12-2, Sat-Sun 12-10 booking required D served all wk 6.30-10 booking required Av 3 course à la carte fr £25 ⊕ FREE HOUSE ◀ Duckpond Bitter, Butcombe Bitter, Dorothy Goodbody, Abbot Ale, Old Speckled Hen ♂ Ashton Press, Stowford Press, Aspall. ▾ 32 **Facilities** Children's menu Children's portions Dogs allowed Garden Parking **Rooms** 12

---

**FORD** | Map 10 SP02

### PICK OF THE PUBS

## The Plough Inn ★★★★ INN

**GL54 5RU** ☎ **01386 584215** 📠 **01386 584042**
**e-mail:** info@theploughinnatford.co.uk
**dir:** *4m from Stow-on-the-Wold on B4077 towards Tewkesbury*

Cheltenham racecourse is but a short drive from this 16th-century inn, and the famous Jackdaws Castle racing stables are just across the street. Trainers, jockeys and stable hands are always in the bar, which features an award that recognises the pub's love of all things racing. So committed is landlord Craig Brown

that he rode as a novice at Aintree on Grand National day in April 2009. If you want to stay over after a day at the races, there are bedrooms situated in a restored stable block, adjacent to the beer garden. It's a traditional English pub, with flagstone floors and log fires, sturdy pine furnishings, and remnants of the stocks that once held convicted sheep-stealers. Excellent Donnington Ales served in the bar are made from water drawn from a spring next to the brewery, and hops which travel only from neighbouring Worcestershire. Meals are cooked to order from local produce and usually include Asian duck salad with spring onion, sesame and soy sauce; chef's own pâté of the day with Melba toast; home-made cottage pie topped with cheesy mash; and chargrilled steaks.

*The Plough Inn*

**Open** all wk Closed: 25 Dec **Bar Meals** L served Mon-Fri 10-2, Sat-Sun all day D served Mon-Fri 6-9, Sat-Sun all day food served all day **Restaurant** L served Mon-Fri 10-2, Sat-Sun all day D served Mon-Fri 6-9, Sat-Sun all day food served all day ⊕ DONNINGTON ◀ Donnington BB, SBA & XXX (summer only) ♂ Stowford Press. **Facilities** Play area Garden Parking **Rooms** 3

---

**FOSSEBRIDGE** | Map 5 SP01

### PICK OF THE PUBS

## The Inn at Fossebridge ★★★★ INN

*See Pick of the Pubs on page 198*

---

**FRAMPTON MANSELL** | Map 4 SO90

### PICK OF THE PUBS

## The Crown Inn ★★★★ INN ▾

**GL6 8JG** ☎ **01285 760601**
**e-mail:** enquiries@thecrowninn-cotswolds.co.uk
**dir:** *A419 halfway between Cirencester & Stroud*

A handsome 17th-century inn right in the heart of the village, surrounded by the peace and quiet of the Golden Valley. Once a simple cider house, this classic Cotswold stone inn is full of old world charm, with honey-coloured stone walls, beams and open fireplaces where log fires are lit in winter. There is also plenty of seating in the large garden for the warmer months. Gloucestershire beers, such as Stroud Organic and Laurie Lee's Bitter, are usually showcased alongside others from the region, and a good choice of wines by the glass is served in the restaurant and three inviting bars. Fresh local food with lots of seasonal specials

may include king prawn skewers with sweet chilli sauce, Old Spot sausages with creamy mash and onion gravy, braised lamb shank with roasted root vegetables, and rump steak with thick-cut chips and peppercorn sauce. Comfortable annexe rooms are well appointed and ideal for both business and leisure guests.

**Open** all day all wk noon-11 **Bar Meals** L served Mon-Sat 12-2.30, Sun 12-8.30 booking required D served Mon-Sat 6-9.30, Sun 12-8.30 booking required Av main course £9.50 ⊕ FREE HOUSE ◀ Butcombe Bitter, Laurie Lee's Bitter, Stroud Organic. ▾ 16 **Facilities** Children's portions Dogs allowed Garden Parking **Rooms** 12

---

**GLOUCESTER** | Map 10 SO81

## Queens Head ▾

**Tewkesbury Rd, Longford GL2 9EJ**
☎ **01452 301882** 📠 **01452 524368**
**e-mail:** queenshead@aol.com
**dir:** *On A38 (Tewkesbury to Gloucester road) in Longford*

Under the same ownership since 1995, this 250 year-old pub/restaurant is just out of town but there's no missing it in summer when it is festooned with hanging baskets. Inside, there's a lovely old flagstone-floored locals' bar which proffers a great range of real ales, while two dining areas tempt with comprehensive menus. These may include pan-fried Isle of Man scallops with bacon lardons, apple salad and port dressing; followed by fillet of pork with apricot and thyme sausage meat with red wine sauce, or the pub's famous Longford lamb — slow-roasted in mint gravy.

**Open** all wk 11-3 5.30-11 **Bar Meals** L served all wk 12-2 D served all wk 6.30-9.30 Av main course £4.95 **Restaurant** D served all wk 6.30-9.30 booking required Fixed menu price fr £12.50 Av 3 course à la carte fr £18.95 ⊕ FREE HOUSE ◀ Butty Bach, Dursley Steam, Otter, Butcombe, Hobgoblin ♂ Ashton Press, Stowford Press. **Facilities** Parking

---

**GREAT BARRINGTON** | Map 10 SP21

### PICK OF THE PUBS

## The Fox

**OX18 4TB** ☎ **01451 844385**
**e-mail:** info@foxinnbarrington.com
**dir:** *3m W on A40 from Burford, turn N signed The Barringtons, pub approx 0.5m on right*

This picturesque 17th-century former coaching house is set in the heart of the Cotswolds. It has a delightful patio and large beer garden overlooking the River Windrush - on warm days a perfect summer watering hole and very popular with those attending Cheltenham racecourse. Built of mellow Cotswold stone and characterised by low ceilings, beams and log fires, the inn offers a range of well-kept Donnington beers and a select wine list. Enjoy a meal in the main bar or the riverside dining room.

*continued on page 199*

# PICK OF THE PUBS

## The Inn at Fossebridge ★★★★INN

**FOSSEBRIDGE**          Map 5 SP01

**GL54 3JS**
☎ 01285 720721  📄 01285 720793
e-mail: info@fossebridgeinn.co.uk
dir: *From M4 junct 15, A419 towards
Cirencester, then A429 towards Stow. Pub
approx 6m on left in dip*

This 18th-century, family run free house
is immersed in more than 300 years of
history. Set in extensive grounds with a
lake, it was once a coaching inn on the
ancient Fosseway when it was known as
Lord Chedworth's Arms. Wealthy
landowner Lord Chedworth still lends
his name to the characterful old bar
even though the pub changed its name
to The Fossebridge Inn in the early 19th
century.

The two bars and restaurant are divided
by stone archways and each area boasts
exposed beams, stone walls, flagstone
floors and open fires. They provide the
setting for the varied bar food and
restaurant menus, ranging from
sandwiches and baguettes to light
meals such as the inn's own chargrilled
burger with tomato relish and skinny
chips, Cumberland sausages, Cheddar
mash and caramelised onion gravy, and
scampi, chips and tartare sauce.

French head chef Damien Dupuis and
his team create well presented dishes
with well defined flavours, using as
much local produce as possible. Main
courses could include oven-baked
halibut; Cornish potted crab; game
terrine with red onion marmalade;
grilled lemon sole with parsley and
lemon butter; or slow-braised lamb
shanks in a rich tomato jus. Puddings
may include dishes such as sticky toffee
pudding with butterscotch ice cream or
cherry sauce, or raspberry crème brûlée.
There are also changing daily specials.

All eight bedrooms have been
refurbished to a high standard with
excellent shower and bathroom
facilities. All rooms are named after
local towns and villages.

**Open** all day all wk noon-mdnt (Sun
noon-11.30) **Bar Meals** L served all wk
12-2.30, Sun 12-3.30 D served Mon-Sat
6-10, Sun 6.30-9.30 Av main course
£15 **Restaurant** L served all wk 12-3,
Sun 12-3.30 booking required D served
Mon-Sat 6.30-10, Sun 6.30-9.30
booking required Av 3 course à la carte
fr £30 ⊕ FREE HOUSE 🍺 St Austell
Tribute, St Austell Proper Job, Prescott
Hill Climb, Brains Rev James
🍎 Stowford Press, Kingston Press.
**Facilities** Children's menu Dogs allowed
Garden Parking **Rooms** 8

**GREAT BARRINGTON** *continued*

Wholesome food is prepared using produce from local suppliers. Expect dishes like beef in ale pie; local pigeon breasts casseroled with button mushrooms; chicken peri-piri; and Thai tuna steak.

**Open** all day all wk **Bar Meals** L served Mon-Fri 12-2.30, Sat-Sun 12-9.30 D served Mon-Fri 6.30-9.30, Sat-Sun 12-9.30 Av main course £12 **Restaurant** L served Mon-Fri 12-2.30, Sat-Sun 12-9.30 D served Mon-Fri 6.30-9.30, Sat-Sun 12-9.30 ⊕ DONNINGTON ◀ Donnington BB, SBA ♂ Stowford, Perry. **Facilities** Children's portions Dogs allowed Garden Parking

### GREET　　Map 10 SP03

## The Harvest Home ♀

Evesham Rd GL54 5BH
☎ 01242 602430　▤ 01242 602094
**e-mail:** harvesthome07@btinternet.com
**dir:** *M5 junct 9 take A435 towards Evesham, then B4077 & B4078 towards Winchcombe, 200yds from station*

Set in the beautiful Cotswold countryside, this traditional country inn draws steam train enthusiasts aplenty, as a restored stretch of the Great Western Railway runs past the end of the garden. Built around 1903 for railway workers, the pub is handy for Cheltenham Racecourse and Sudeley Castle. Expect a good range of snacks and mains, including locally-reared beef and tempting seafood dishes, along with beers like Goffs Jouster.

**Open** all wk 12-3 6-11 (Sun 12-10.30) **Bar Meals** L served all wk 12-3 D served all wk 6.30-9 **Restaurant** L served all wk 12-3 D served all wk 6.30-9 ⊕ ENTERPRISE INNS ◀ Goffs Jouster, Timothy Taylor Landlord, Courage Directors ♂ Stowford Press. ♀ 11 **Facilities** Children's menu Children's portions Dogs allowed Garden Parking

### GUITING POWER　　Map 10 SP02

## *The Hollow Bottom*

GL54 5UX ☎ 01451 850392　▤ 01451 850945
**e-mail:** hello@hollowbottom.com
**dir:** *Telephone for directions*

There's a horse-racing theme at this 18th-century Cotswold free house, often frequented by the Cheltenham racing fraternity. Its nooks and crannies lend themselves to an intimate drink or meal, and there's also a separate dining room, plus outside tables for fine weather. Specials include prawn cocktail on seasonal leaves with a spicy tomato sauce; grilled salmon; breast of pan-fried chicken with Stilton, olive oil, tomato and spring onion; and home-made raspberry cheesecake to finish.

**Open** all wk ◀ Hollow Bottom Best Bitter, Goffs Jouster, Timothy Taylor Landlord, Fuller's London Pride, Caledonian IPA. **Facilities** Dogs allowed Garden Parking

### HINTON　　Map 4 ST77

## The Bull Inn ♀

SN14 8HG ☎ 0117 937 2332
**e-mail:** diserwhite@aol.com
**web:** www.thebullathinton.co.uk
**dir:** *From M4 junct 18, A46 to Bath 1m, turn right 1m, down hill. Pub on right*

The interior of this 17th-century inn retains two inglenook fireplaces and original flagstone flooring; outside, there's a front-facing terrace and a large rear garden with a children's play area. In former times the building was a farm and dairy, and the owners now rear their own pigs for the restaurant table. Food served draws in locally supplied produce and home-grown fruit and vegetables. Look out for pan-roasted breast of guinea fowl; beer-battered haddock and hand-cut chips; marinated roasted pork loin; and button mushroom and parmesan risotto.

**Open** noon-3 6-11.30 (Sat-Sun & BH open all day) Closed: Mon L (ex BH) **Bar Meals** L served Tue-Sat 12-2, Sun 12-8.30 D served Mon-Thu 6-9, Fri-Sat 6-9.30 Av main course £11 **Restaurant** L served Tue-Sat 12-2, Sun 12-8.30 booking required D served Mon-Thu 6-9, Fri-Sat 6-9.30 booking required Av 3 course à la carte fr £22 ⊕ WADWORTH ◀ Wadworth 6X & Henrys IPA, Wadworth Bishops Tipple, Wadworth Summersault, guest ale ♂ Thatchers Gold, Stowford Press. ♀ 11 **Facilities** Children's menu Play area Dogs allowed Garden Parking

### LECHLADE ON THAMES　　Map 5 SU29

## The Trout Inn ♀

St Johns Bridge GL7 3HA
☎ 01367 252313　▤ 01367 252313
**e-mail:** chefpjw@aol.com
**dir:** *A40 onto A361 then A417. From M4 junct 15, A419, then A361 & A417 to Lechlade*

In 1220, when workmen constructed a new bridge over the Thames, they built an almshouse to live in. In 1472 it became an inn, which it has been ever since. The bar, all flagstone floors and beams, overflows into the old boathouse, and serves a range of ales and 15 wines by the glass. Top of the menu are favourites like rich lamb and vegetable hotpot; locally made faggots; and tempura-battered hake fillets. This family-friendly pub has a large garden which often pulsates with tractor and steam events, and jazz and folk festivals.

**Open** all wk 10-3 6-11 (summer all wk 10am-11pm) Closed: 25 Dec **Bar Meals** L served all wk 12-2 D served all wk 7-10 **Restaurant** L served all wk 12-2 D served all wk 7-10 ⊕ ENTERPRISE INNS ◀ Courage Best, Doom Bar, Cornish Coaster, guest ales. ♀ 15 **Facilities** Children's menu Children's portions Play area Family room Dogs allowed Garden Parking

### LITTLETON-ON-SEVERN　　Map 4 ST58

## White Hart ♀

BS35 1NR ☎ 01454 412275
**e-mail:** whitehart@youngs.co.uk
**web:** www.whitehartbristol.com
**dir:** *M48 junct 1 towards Chepstow left on rdbt, follow for 3m, 1st left to Littleton-on-Severn*

A traditional English country pub dating back to the 1680s. It was originally a farmhouse, from which flagstone floors and other features of the old building, including two large inglenook fireplaces, survive. Food ranges from home-cooked pub classics, such as beef and ale winter stew with herb dumpling and vegetables, to modern Anglo-French dishes that usually feature among the specials. After all-day sun in the front garden, watch it set over the Severn estuary.

**Open** all day all wk noon-11 **Bar Meals** L served Mon-Sat 12-9.30, Sun 12-8 ⊕ YOUNGS ◀ Youngs Bitter, Youngs Special, St Austell Tribute, Bath Ales Gem ♂ Thatchers Heritage, Thatchers Gold. ♀ 18 **Facilities** Children's menu Children's portions Family room Dogs allowed Garden Parking

### LITTLE WASHBOURNE　　Map 10 SO93

## *The Hobnails Inn*

GL20 8NQ ☎ 01242 620237　▤ 01242 620458
**dir:** *M5 junct 9, A46 towards Evesham then B4077 to Stow-on-the-Wold. Inn 1.5m on left*

Established in 1473, the Hobnails is one of the oldest inns in the county. Inside you'll find winter log fires, and you can tuck yourself into a private corner, or relax with a pint of ale on one of the leather sofas. A good range of bar snacks is supplemented by a lunchtime carvery and a fresh fish range. Outside is a lovely large garden for warmer days with views over surrounding countryside.

**Open** all wk ◀ London Pride, Flowers IPA, Hook Norton Best, Deuchars IPA. **Facilities** Dogs allowed Garden Parking

## The Glasshouse Inn ♥

**May Hill GL17 0NN ☎ 01452 830529**
e-mail: glasshouseinn@btconnect.com
dir: Village off A40 between Gloucester & Ross-on-Wye

The Glasshouse is unique and its popularity confirms the need for traditional pubs with no gimmicks. The inn dates back to 1450 and gets its name from Dutch glassmakers who settled locally in the 16th century. It is located in a wonderful rural setting with a country garden outside and a tranquil and dignified interior. The inn serves a range of real ales and home-cooked dishes. Remember to book for Sunday lunch.

**Open** Mon-Sat 11.30-3 7-11 (Sun 11.30-3) Closed: Sun eve **Bar Meals** L served all wk 12-2 booking required D served Mon-Sat 6.30-9 ⊕ FREE HOUSE ◀ Butcombe, Spitfire, Black Sheep, London Pride, Greene King Ö Stowford Press. ♥ 12 **Facilities** Garden Parking

## The Farmers Arms ♥

**Ledbury Rd GL19 4DR ☎ 01452 780307**
e-mail: danieljrpardoe@googlemail.com
dir: From Tewkesbury take A38 towards Gloucester/ Ledbury. 2m, right at lights onto B4213 (signed Ledbury). 1.5m, pub on left

A popular, 16th-century, timber-framed pub on the village fringe and close to the River Severn. Low beams, an open fire, regular guest ales and an extensive menu are to be found within. Home-made dishes using locally sourced produce include steak and kidney pie; honey roast ham with free range eggs and chips; and luxury fish pie. Look lout for special themed nights - Italian, French, Irish.

**Open** all wk 11-3 6-12 (Sat-Sun & summer 11-mdnt) ◀ Wadworth 6X, Henry's Original IPA, guest ales Ö Stowford Press, Thatchers Gold. ♥ 12 **Facilities** Play area Dogs allowed Garden Parking

### PICK OF THE PUBS

## The Fox ♥

**GL56 0UR**
☎ 01451 870555 & 870666 ▤ 01451 870666
e-mail: info@foxinn.net
dir: A436 from Stow-on-the-Wold then right to Lower Oddington

Set in a quintessential Cotswold village, this stone-built and creeper-clad free house dates back to the 17th century. Fresh flowers and antique furniture complete the period feel in the bar, with its polished flagstone floors, beams and log fires. The Fox's reputation for well kept beers, good food and wine at reasonable prices draws people in to enjoy the atmosphere of a traditional English pub. The regularly changing menus and the daily specials take full

advantage of seasonal local produce and freshly-caught Cornish fish. Starters like baked crab gratin; and spinach and parmesan risotto herald main course options that include guinea fowl with wild mushrooms and Madeira; sea bass with lemon and herb butter; and individually baked steak and kidney pie. Desserts such as home-made tiramisu and chocolate bread and butter pudding and cream provide a satisfying conclusion. In summer, there's a heated terrace for alfresco dining, as well as a pretty, traditional cottage garden.

**Open** all wk Closed: 25 Dec **Bar Meals** L served Mon-Sat 12-2, Sun 12-4 booking required D served Mon-Sat 6.30-10, Sun 7-9.30 booking required Av main course £12.25 **Restaurant** L served Mon-Sat 12-2, Sun 12-4 booking required D served Mon-Sat 6.30-10, Sun 7-9.30 booking required Av 3 course à la carte fr £25 ⊕ FREE HOUSE ◀ Hook Norton Best, Abbot Ale, Ruddles County, Wickwar's Old Bob, Purity UBU Ö Stowford Press. ♥ 13 **Facilities** Children's portions Dogs allowed Garden Parking

## The George Inn ♥

**St Briavels GL15 6TA ☎ 01594 530228**
dir: Telephone for directions

In a quiet village high above the Wye Valley and close to the Forest of Dean, this pretty white-washed pub overlooks a moody 12th-century castle ruin. The interior includes an 8th-century Celtic coffin lid set into one of the walls. The pub is famous for braised shoulder of lamb and Moroccan lamb, along with popular dishes such as traditional steak and kidney, and beef and Guinness pies.

**Open** all wk 12-3 6.30-11 ◀ 6X, IPA, JCB Ö Stowford Press. ♥ 10 **Facilities** Dogs allowed Garden Parking

## The Catherine Wheel

**39 High St SN14 8LR ☎ 01225 892220**
e-mail: bookings@thecatherinewheel.co.uk
dir: Between Bath, Bristol & Chippenham on A420. 5m from M4 junct 18

Simple, stylish decor complements the clean lines of this impressive, mainly 17th-century inn on the edge of the Cotswolds, with its exposed brickwork and large open fireplaces. Menus are also simple and well presented, with favourites at lunchtime including jacket potatoes and ploughman's. In the evening look forward to smoked mackerel and crab fishcakes, followed by one of the specials such as venison and pheasant stew. A small but sunny patio is a lovely spot for a summertime pint brewed by nearby Cotswold and Bath-based breweries.

**Open** all wk noon-3 6-11 (Sun noon-11) ◀ Courage Best, guest ales Ö Stowford Press. **Facilities** Dogs allowed Garden Parking

## The Lord Nelson Inn ★★★ INN ♥

**1 & 2 High St SN14 8LP ☎ 01225 891820**
e-mail: thelordnelsoninn.@btinternet.com
dir: M4 junct 18 onto A46 towards Bath. Left at Cold Ashton rdbt towards Marshfield

Located in a village at the edge of the Cotswolds, this 17th-century coaching inn is family run and has a reputation for good home-made food and quality cask ales. The spacious bar, candlelit restaurant, log fires in winter and a patio for summer use complete its attractions, along with comfortable accommodation in peaceful surroundings. With the food emphasis on simplicity and quality, dishes include terrine of pressed ham hock; Nailey Farm sausages with mash and mushy peas; Artingstall's faggots; and home-made warm treacle tart.

**Open** all day all wk **Bar Meals** L served Mon-Sat 12-2, Sun 12-3 booking required D served Mon-Sat 6.30-9, Sun 6-8 booking required Av main course £10.50 **Restaurant** L served Mon-Sat 12-2, Sun 12-3 booking required D served Mon-Sat 6.30-9, Sun 6-8 booking required Fixed menu price fr £13.95 Av 3 course à la carte fr £20.95 ⊕ ENTERPRISE INNS ◀ Courage Best, Bath Gem, Sharp's Doom Bar Ö Stowford Press. ♥ 9 **Facilities** Children's menu Children's portions Play area Dogs allowed Garden **Rooms** 3

## The Masons Arms ♥

**28 High St GL7 5JT ☎ 01285 850164 ▤ 01285 850164**
dir: 6m E of Cirencester off A417, beside village green

Nestling alongside the green in the heart of the village, this is a quintessential 17th-century stone-built Cotswold inn. The hub of the community and welcoming to visitors, it offers something for everyone, from a warming log fire in the large inglenook to the range of well-kept Arkell's ales and Weston's cider served in the convivial beamed bar. Good value home-made food. Worth noting if visiting the Cotswold Water Park near by.

**Open** all wk 12-2 5.30-11 (Sat 12-11 Sun 12-10) **Bar Meals** L served all wk 12-2 D served all wk 6-9 booking required Av main course £7 **Restaurant** L served all wk 12-2 D served all wk 6-9 booking required Fixed menu price fr £18 ⊕ ARKELLS ◀ 3B's, 2B's Kingsdown SBA Moonlight Ö Westons Vintage, Perry. **Facilities** Children's portions Dogs allowed Parking

## The Old Lodge ♥

**Minchinhampton Common GL6 9AQ**
☎ 01453 832047 ▤ 01453 834033
e-mail: old-lodge@food-club.com
dir: Telephone for details

A 400-year-old Cotswold inn, high on Minchinhampton Common, where cattle range free and from where you can see Wales. The stylish restaurant, adorned with paintings and sculptures, has floor-to-ceiling windows that look directly onto the common. Typically on the menu are roast monkfish tail with curried parsnip purée and mussel broth; braised shank of lamb with dauphinoise potato, french beans and paprika sauce; and porcini mushroom risotto with shaved parmesan.

**Open** all day all wk 11-11 (Sun 11-10.30) Closed: 25 Dec ⬛ Stroud Budding, Tom Long, Otter Bitter ○ Stowford Press. ⬗ 10 **Facilities** Dogs allowed Garden

## PICK OF THE PUBS

### The Weighbridge Inn ⬗

*See Pick of the Pubs on page 202*

---

**MORETON-IN-MARSH** Map 10 SP23

## The Red Lion Inn ★★★ INN ⬗ NEW

GL56 0RT ☎ 01608 674397
**e-mail:** info@theredlionlittlecompton.co.uk
**dir:** *Between Chipping Norton & Moreton-in-Marsh on A44*

One of 15 Donnington Brewery pubs, the Red Lion is Warwickshire's most southerly pub. You can walk to all of them but not in one day! The traditional Cotswold stone building quietly located on the edge of the village has been under new management since late 2009. Set in a large mature garden, the building features exposed stone walls and beams, inglenook fireplaces and real fires; there is accommodation, too. Public bar games include darts, dominoes, a juke box and pool table. The restaurant offers a seasonal menu and sensibly priced daily-changing specials.

**Open** all wk 12-3 6-12 **Bar Meals** L served all wk 12-2 D served all wk 6-9 booking required Av main course £10 **Restaurant** L served all wk 12-2 booking required D served all wk 6-9 booking required Fixed menu price fr £10 ⬛ DONNINGTON BREWERY ⬛ Donnington BB, Donnington Double D. ⬗ 10 **Facilities** Children's portions Dogs allowed Garden Parking **Rooms** 2

---

**NAILSWORTH** Map 4 ST89

## PICK OF THE PUBS

### The Britannia ⬗

Cossack Square GL6 0DG ☎ 01453 832501
**e-mail:** pheasantpluckers2003@yahoo.co.uk
**dir:** *From A46 S'bound right at town centre rdbt. 1st left. Pub directly ahead*

This stone-built 17th-century former manor house occupies a delightful position on the south side of Nailsworth's Cossack Square. The interior is bright and uncluttered with low ceilings, cosy fires and a blue slate floor. Outside you'll find a pretty garden with plenty of tables, chairs and parasols for sunny days. Whether inside or out, a pint of well-kept ale is sure to go down well. The brasserie-style menu offers an interesting blend of modern British and continental food, with ingredients bought from local suppliers and from Smithfield Market. You can go lightly with just a starter from a tapas-style list that includes houmous,

deep-fried brie and moules marinière; or plunge into hearty classics such as steak and ale pie or ham, egg and chips. Other options include stone-baked pizzas and impressive meat-free options such as butternut squash and chilli risotto. Great wines, too.

**Open** all wk Mon-Thu 11-11 (Fri-Sat 11-mdnt Sun 11-10.30) Closed: 25 Dec **Bar Meals** L served Mon-Fri 11-2.45, Sat-Sun 11-10 D served Mon-Fri 5.30-10, Sat-Sun 11-10 ⬛ FREE HOUSE ⬛ Tom Longstroud, Greene King IPA, Buckham ○ Ashton Press. ⬗ 10 **Facilities** Dogs allowed Garden Parking

## PICK OF THE PUBS

### Egypt Mill ★★★ HL ⬗

GL6 0AE ☎ 01453 833449 📄 01453 839919
**e-mail:** reception@egyptmill.com
**dir:** *M4 junct 18, A46 N to Stroud. M5 junct 13, A46 to Nailsworth*

Situated in the charming Cotswold town of Nailsworth, this converted corn mill contains many features of great character, including the original millstones and lifting equipment. The ground floor bar and bistro enjoy a picturesque setting, and its views over the pretty water gardens complete the scene. There is a choice of eating in the bistro or restaurant, and in both there is a good selection of wines by the glass. For those who like to savour an aperitif before dining, try the large Egypt Mill Lounge. Tempting starters might offer ham hock and pea risotto; smoked salmon and avocado parcels; and salmon and lobster sausages. Main courses include the likes of saddle of lamb Greek style; calves' liver and bacon; breast of duck with apple and blackberry risotto; and Brixham fish and potato pie.

**Open** all day all wk 11am-11pm **Bar Meals** L served Mon-Fri 12-2, Sat 12-2.30, Sun 12-6 D served Mon-Thu 6-9.30, Fri-Sat 6-9.45, Sun 6.30-9 ⬛ FREE HOUSE ⬛ Stroud Brewery, Nailsworth, ○ Stowford Press. ⬗ 10 **Facilities** Garden Parking **Rooms** 28

## PICK OF THE PUBS

### Tipputs Inn ⬗

Bath Rd GL6 0QE ☎ 01453 832466
**e-mail:** pheasantpluckers2003@yahoo.co.uk
**dir:** *A46, 0.5m S of Nailsworth*

Mellow Cotswold stone and stripped floorboards blend nicely with modern, clean-lined furniture in this impeccably decorated 17th-century pub-restaurant. A giant candelabra adds a touch of grandeur. Located in the heart of the Cotswolds, the Tipputs Inn is owned by Nick Beardsley and Christophe Coquoin. They started out as chefs together more than 12 years ago, but admit to spending less time in the kitchen these days now that they have to create menus for this and their other Gloucestershire food pubs, plus they select and import some wines and wines direct from France.

There are dishes for every eventuality, starting with tapas-style appetisers and extending through starters such as pan-fried halloumi or spicy prawn cocktail to pub classics (fish and chips; home-made burger and chips) and classy options such as confit duck leg with black pudding, mashed potato and seasonal vegetables or cherry tomato, basil and ricotta risotto. Classic desserts include Eton mess and vanilla crème brûlée.

**Open** all wk ⬛ FREE HOUSE ⬛ Abbot Ale, Stroud Brewery, Otter Ale ○ Stowford Press. ⬗ 12 **Facilities** Dogs allowed Garden Parking

---

**NAUNTON** Map 10 SP12

## The Black Horse

GL54 3AD ☎ 01451 850565
**dir:** *Telephone for directions*

Renowned for its home-cooked food and Donnington real ales, this friendly inn enjoys a typical Cotswold village setting beloved of ramblers and locals alike. The Black Horse provides a traditional English menu featuring liver and bacon, cottage pie, and broccoli and cheese bake.

**Open** all wk 11-3 6-11 (Fri-Sat 11-11, Sun 12-11) ⬛ Donnington BB, SBA ○ Stowford Press. **Facilities** Dogs allowed Garden Parking

---

**NEWLAND** Map 4 SO50

## PICK OF THE PUBS

### The Ostrich Inn

GL16 8NP ☎ 01594 833260
**e-mail:** kathryn@theostrichinn.com
**dir:** *Follow Monmouth signs from Chepstow (A466), Newland signed from Redbrook*

A 13th-century inn situated in a pretty village on the western edge of the Forest of Dean and adjoining the Wye Valley, both Areas of Outstanding Natural Beauty. To this day it still retains many of its ancient features, including a priest hole. With wooden beams and a welcoming log fire in the large lounge bar throughout the winter, visitors can enjoy a relaxed and friendly setting for a wide selection of cask-conditioned beers and good food. Diners are served in the small, intimate restaurant, the larger lounge bar, the garden and the patio. In the bar expect simpler dishes, such as salmon spinach fishcakes; steak and ale pie; and penne pasta. The monthly changing menu in the restaurant offers more sophistication in the form of slow-roasted spiced belly pork with pak choi; and supreme of Nile perch from Lake Victoria with black tiger prawns and chive cream sauce. No one will frown at your muddy boots.

**Open** all wk 12-3 (Mon-Sat 6-11.30 Sun 6-10.30) ⬛ FREE HOUSE ⬛ Timothy Taylor Landlord, Butty Bach, Pigs Ear, Old Hooky, Adnams ○ Stowford Press, Old Rosie. **Facilities** Dogs allowed Garden

# PICK OF THE PUBS

## The Weighbridge Inn

**MINCHINHAMPTON** Map 4 SO80

**GL6 9AL**
**01453 832520** **01453 835903**
**e-mail:** enquiries@2in1pub.co.uk
**dir:** *Between Nailsworth & Avening on B4014*

This 17th-century freehouse stands beside the old packhorse trail between London and Bristol, now a footpath and bridleway. In the 1820s, the road in front (now the B4014) became a turnpike and a weighbridge was installed to serve the local woollen mills. As well as looking after his customers, the innkeeper had to ensure the tolls were paid - a penny for a horse, threepence for a score of pigs and tenpence for herd of cattle. Associated memorabilia and other rural artefacts are displayed around the inn, which has been carefully renovated to retain original features. Up in the restaurant, which used to be the hayloft, for example, the old roof timbers reach almost to the floor.

The drinking areas are, as you would expect, tailor-made for a decent pint - Uley Old Spot, maybe, but if beer is not to your taste, a heady Westons Bounds Brand scrumpy. On the short wine list, the seven reds and seven whites come from just seven countries, with all available by the glass. From the patios and sheltered landscaped garden the Cotswolds are in full view.

The inn prides itself on the quality of its food, all cooked from scratch to appear on the regular menu as simple starter dishes of garlic mushrooms; Thai-style mussels; and whitebait, for example. Don't expect nouvelle cuisine here (and we mean this as a compliment), as hearty dishes include beef bourguignon; grilled salmon steak; chicken Kiev; and mixed bean lasagne. The Weighbridge is the home of '2 in 1' pies, half containing one of seven fillings of your choice, the rest with home-made cauliflower cheese. Typical desserts include chocolate fondant; Eton mess; tiramisu; and crème brûlée. Lighter meals are available as salads, omelettes, jacket potatoes and filled baguettes. The future for the inn is really more of the same – great food, a warm welcoming atmosphere and great beers.

**Open** all day all wk noon-11 (Sun noon-10.30) Closed: 25 Dec
**Bar Meals** L served all wk 12-9.30 booking required D served all wk 12-9.30 booking required Av main course £12.50 food served all day
**Restaurant** L served all wk 12-9.30 booking required D served all wk 12-9.30 booking required food served all day FREE HOUSE Wadworth 6X, Uley Old Spot, Palmers IPA Wicked Witch, Westons Bounds Brand, Thatchers Gold. 15
**Facilities** Children's menu Family room Dogs allowed Garden Parking

## NORTH CERNEY    Map 5 SP00

### PICK OF THE PUBS

### Bathurst Arms ♀

**GL7 7BZ ☎ 01285 831281**
**e-mail:** james@bathurstarms.com
**dir:** 5m N of Cirencester on A435

Set in the picturesque village of North Cerney, the 17th-century Bathurst Arms offers the intimacy of a traditional inn combined with high standards of food and wine. The rambling, creeper-covered building stands on the Earl of Bathurst's estate, with a pretty flower-filled garden running down to the River Churn. The stone-flagged bar exudes character with its beams and log fires, and draws walkers and locals for pints of Cotswold Way or Festival Gold and decent pub food prepared from locally sourced ingredients. The fixed-price lunchtime menu includes a glass of wine, or you can choose from the main menu. A typical three course meal might begin with Cerney goat's cheese pannacotta, roasted walnuts, pea salad and garlic bread crisps, followed by fillet of Gloucestershire pork Wellington with confit root vegetables, spring cabbage and red wine gravy. The scrummy dessert menu might feature lemon pannacotta with berry compote.

**Open** all wk 12-3 6-12 (all day Sat-Sun all wk summer) **Bar Meals** L served all wk 12-2 D served all wk 6-9 **Restaurant** L served all wk 12-2 D served all wk 6-9 Fixed menu price fr £9.95 Av 3 course à la carte fr £25 ⊕ FREE HOUSE ◀ Cotswold Way, Tournament, Festival Gold ♂ Stowford Press. ♀ 25 **Facilities** Children's menu Children's portions Dogs allowed Garden Parking

## NORTHLEACH    Map 10 SP11

### PICK OF THE PUBS

### The Puesdown Inn ★★★★ INN ◉◉ ♀

**Compton Abdale GL54 4DN**
**☎ 01451 860262 ▤ 01451 861262**
**e-mail:** inn4food@btopenworld.com
**dir:** On A40 between Oxford & Cheltenham, 3m W of Northleach

The unique name of this comfortable coaching inn comes from an old English expression meaning 'windy ridge'. It's also an anagram for 'snowed up' — and guests were indeed marooned here in 1947, during the worst blizzard of the century. Dating from 1236, the inn is set high on the old Salt Way between Burford and Cheltenham. Inside, you'll find cosy sofas, log fires and warm, rich colours on the walls, providing a welcome refuge from the winter weather. Lunchtime brings a range of paninis, omelettes and hot meals, whilst the restaurant has earned two AA Rosettes for dishes such as rump of lamb with dauphinoise potatoes; red onion and tomato tarte Tatin; and tournedos of roast hake with parsley mash, Pernod and rosemary jus. The inn offers three individually styled en suite bedrooms, as well as a delightful hidden garden with views over the surrounding Cotswold countryside.

**Open** 10-3 6-11 Closed: Sun eve, Mon eve **Bar Meals** L served Mon-Sat 12-3 D served Tue-Sat 6-10.30 Av main course £7.50 **Restaurant** L served all wk 12-3 (booking required Sun L) booking required D served Tue-Sat 6-10.30 booking required Fixed menu price fr £1 Av 3 course à la carte fr £24.50 ⊕ FREE HOUSE ◀ Hook Norton Best Bitter, Hooky Dark, Old Hooky, Haymaker, Twelve Days ♂ Stowford Press. ♀ 11 **Facilities** Children's portions Dogs allowed Garden Parking Rooms 3

## OAKRIDGE    Map 4 SO90

### The Butcher's Arms

**GL6 7NZ ☎ 01285 760371**
**e-mail:** jemorgan@vwclub.net
**dir:** From Stroud A419, left for Eastcombe & Bisley signs. Just before Bisley right to Oakridge, follow brown signs for pub

Traditional Cotswold country pub with stone walls, beams and log fires in the renowned Golden Valley. Once a slaughterhouse and butchers shop. A full and varied restaurant menu offers steak, fish and chicken dishes, while the bar menu ranges from ploughman's lunches to home-cooked daily specials.

**Open** all wk 12-3 6-11 (Summer Fri-Sun noon-11) Closed: 1 Jan ◀ Henrys IPA, 6X, JCB, ♂ Stowford Press. **Facilities** Family room Dogs allowed Garden Parking

## OLDBURY-ON-SEVERN    Map 4 ST69

### The Anchor Inn ♀

**Church Rd BS35 1QA ☎ 01454 413331**
**e-mail:** info@anchorinnoldbury.co.uk
**dir:** From N A38 towards Bristol, 1.5m then right, village signed. From S A38 through Thornbury

Located on the original river bank in the village of Oldbury-on-Severn, parts of this Cotswold stone pub date from 1540. The village has a long history dating back to the Iron Age, whilst the pub itself was formerly a mill. There is a large garden to enjoy, flower-filled in summer, and a boules area. Fresh river Exe mussels and home-baked ham, eggs and bubble and squeak are available in the traditional bar, supported by dishes like home-made cassoulet; grilled venison steak with green peppercorn and brandy sauce; or mushroom and leek pudding in the dining room.

**Open** all wk all day Sat-Sun **Bar Meals** L served Mon-Fri 12-2, Sat 12-2.30, Sun 12-3 D served Sat-Sun 6-9 Av main course £9.75 food served all day **Restaurant** L served Mon-Fri 12-2, Sat 12-2.30, Sun 12-3 booking required D served Sat-Sun 6-9 booking required Av 3 course à la carte fr £18.95 food served all day ⊕ FREE HOUSE ◀ Interbrew Bass, Butcombe Best, Otter Bitter, Guest ales ♂ Ashton Press, Stowford Press. ♀ 16 **Facilities** Children's menu Dogs allowed Garden Parking

## PAINSWICK    Map 4 SO80

### PICK OF THE PUBS

### The Falcon Inn

**New St GL6 6UN ☎ 01452 814222 ▤ 01452 813377**
**e-mail:** enquiries@falconinn-cotswolds.co.uk
**dir:** On A46 in centre of Painswick

Built in 1554, this former coaching inn has been licensed since the 17th century. It was a courthouse for over two hundred years, but today its friendly service extends to a drying room for walkers' gear. The chef is passionate about local and seasonal produce, and lists his suppliers on a blackboard for all to see. Expect an appetising lunchtime menu of traditional English fare such as pan-fried lamb's liver with Old Spot bacon and mash, and home-made cottage pie with seasonal vegetables, while the monthly-changing seasonal dinner menu might include grilled sea bream with crayfish tails, lime and coriander butter. The Falcon stands at the heart of the village opposite St Mary's church, famous for the 99 yew trees growing within its grounds. It makes an ideal base for exploring Painswick and the surrounding area.

**Open** all day all wk 10am-11pm **Bar Meals** L served all wk 12-3 D served all wk 7-9.30 Av main course £7 **Restaurant** D served all wk 6-9.30 (food served all day Fri-Sun) Av 3 course à la carte fr £22 ⊕ ENTERPRISE ◀ Otters Ale, Butcombe Blend, Butcombe Bitter ♂ Stowford Press, Ashton Press. **Facilities** Children's portions Dogs allowed Garden Parking

## PAXFORD    Map 10 SP13

### PICK OF THE PUBS

### The Churchill Arms ★★★★ INN ◉◉

See Pick of the Pubs on page 204

## SAPPERTON    Map 4 SO90

### PICK OF THE PUBS

### The Bell at Sapperton ♀

See Pick of the Pubs on page 205

# PICK OF THE PUBS

## The Churchill Arms ★★★★ INN

**PAXFORD**      Map 10 SP13

**GL55 6XH**
☎ 01386 594000 📄 01386 594005
**e-mail:** info@thechurchillarms.com
**web:** www.thechurchillarms.com
**dir:** *2m E of Chipping Campden, 4m N of Moreton-in-Marsh*

An unpretentious 17th-century pub in mellow stone which enjoys an enchanting location near the historical town of Chipping Campden. With glorious views over a stone chapel and rolling hills, the Churchill is no different in appearance to any other Cotswold village local.

Owners Sheridan Mather and Richard Shore took over the pub in January 2009, intent on maintaining a relaxed and informal atmosphere and serving food of good quality. It draws an eclectic mix of customers, including drinkers, well-informed foodies and muddy walkers — the starting point of the Cotswold Way is a short stroll away. Hook Norton and Wye Valley ales are on tap, among others, and an impressive list of wines ensures there's a tipple to suit every taste and pocket.

Classic bar snacks include pickled quails' eggs with celery salt; Welsh rarebit with rocket salad; and scampi in a basket with tartare sauce. The setting for savouring the imaginative food and tip-top ales is suitably cosy with a rustic interior — expect flagstones, a beamed ceiling and large inglenook fireplace with wood-burning stove.

Head chef William Guthrie makes sound use of quality local supplies, and prepares innovative modern British dishes that evolve with the seasons, with clever twists on pub classics. For starters try, perhaps, carrot and cumin soup with onion fritter; cured trout and crab beignet with lemon and caviar dressing; or pressing of confit duck and foie gras with Cumberland sauce. Then follow with roast monkfish, braised chicory and fennel risotto with an orange butter sauce; stuffed breast of guinea fowl with beetroot and carrot ribbons; or braised shoulder of Lighthorne lamb, aubergine caviar and white bean jus. Leave room for a delicious sticky toffee pudding; honey and walnut parfait, apple purée and coffee ice; or dark chocolate tart, orange curd and chocolate crisp. Four en suite rooms complete the picture.

**Open** all wk 11-3 6-11 Closed: 25 Dec
**Bar Meals** L served all wk 12-2 booking required D served all wk 7-9 booking required Av main course £8.50
**Restaurant** L served all wk 12-2 booking required D served all wk 7-9 booking required Fixed menu price fr £12 Av 3 course à la carte fr £32
🛢 ENTERPRISE INNS 🍺 Hook Norton Bitter, Butty Bach, Wye Valley, Mad Goose, Purity, 🍎 Stowford Press.
**Facilities** Children's menu Dogs allowed Garden

# PICK OF THE PUBS

## The Bell at Sapperton ♉

**SAPPERTON**     Map 4 SO90

**GL7 6LE**
☎ 01285 760298   🖹 01285 760761
**e-mail:**
thebell@sapperton66.freeserve.co.uk
**web:** www.foodatthebell.co.uk
**dir:** *From A419 halfway between Cirencester & Stroud follow signs for Sapperton. Pub in village centre near church*

Restored and refurbished with style by Paul Davidson and Pat LeJeune in 1999, the 300-year-old Bell continues to wow Cotswold walkers, drinkers and diners. Built of mellow Cotswold stone and set in an idyllic hillside village close to Cirencester Park, The Bell is civilised in every way, attracting discerning folk from miles around for innovative pub food served throughout three cosy dining areas, where exposed stone walls, polished flagstones, bare boards, open log fires and individual tables and chairs set the style. Added touches

include tasteful wine prints, daily newspapers to peruse, and fresh flowers. There's a secluded rear courtyard and a landscaped front garden for summer drinking and dining, the latter replete with horse-tethering rail.

Use of top-notch seasonal produce is key to the popularity of the daily menus and includes home-made bread, fish from Cornwall and organic and rare breed meats, notably Ryland lamb from Huntsham Farm at Goodrich on Wye, and free-range duck and chicken from Madgett's Farm near Chepstow. Follow pork liver and bacon terrine with house chutney, or pan-fried squid and pickled endive with soy, balsamic and ginger dressing, with hand-raised veal and ham pie, duck with red cabbage and spices, chump of Lighthorne lamb with sweetbreads and tarragon, and wild sea bass with Portland crab and parmesan risotto. Walkers calling in for a snack can tuck into a three-cheese ploughman's lunch, best washed down by a pint of local ale, perhaps Uley Old Spot or Wickwar Cotswold Way. The wine list has 20 by the glass and is strong on single-supplier wines.

**Open** all wk 11-2.30 6.30-11 (Sun 12-10.30) Closed: 25 Dec
**Bar Meals** L served all wk 12-2.15 booking required D served all wk 7-9.15 booking required Av main course £15
**Restaurant** Av 3 course à la carte fr £30 ⊞ FREE HOUSE ◀ Uley Old Spot, Bath Ales, Otter Bitter, Cotswold Way ⚹ Stowford Press. ☐ 20
**Facilities** Dogs allowed Garden Parking

## SHEEPSCOMBE
Map 4 SO81

### PICK OF THE PUBS

### The Butchers Arms

**GL6 7RH** ☎ **01452 812113** 🖶 **01452 814358**
**e-mail:** mark@butchers-arms.co.uk
**dir:** *1.5m S of A46 (Cheltenham to Stroud road), N of Painswick*

Set in the heart of Cider with Rosie country, with glorious views over the rolling Sheepscombe Valley, this mellow-stone pub dates from 1620 and was originally a butchery for deer hunted in Henry VIII's deer park – hence the pub's name. Note the famous pub sign showing a butcher supping a pint of ale with a pig tied to his leg. The pub draws walkers, riders and tourists exploring this unspoiled rural backwater. On sunny days take in the view from the front terrace or bag a bench in the glorious steep garden behind the pub. In the winter, the homely, rustic bar and adjoining beamed dining room, both featuring crackling log fires, are the setting for cooking that relies on locally-sourced raw materials. Tuck into ham and mustard mayonnaise sandwiches (lunch only), a warm chorizo, bacon and potato salad, share an oozy baked camembert, or order something more substantial, perhaps chicken, leek and ham pie, sirloin steak with cracked pepper sauce, or stuffed saddle of lamb with cranberry and mint jus. Wash down with a pint of Otter Ale or Westons Scumpy cider.

**Open** all wk 11.30-2.30 6.30-11 (Sat 11.30-11.30 Sun noon-10.30) **Bar Meals** L served Mon-Fri 12-2.30, Sat-Sun all day booking required D served Mon-Sat 6.30-9.30, Sun 6.30-9 (ex Sun Jan & Feb) booking required Av main course £9.50 **Restaurant** L served Mon-Fri 12-2.30, Sat-Sun all day booking required D served Mon-Sat 6.30-9.30, Sun 6.30-9 (ex Sun Jan & Feb) booking required Av 3 course à la carte fr £19 🍺 Otter Bitter, Goffs Camelot, Butcombe Bitter, St Austell Proper Job, Wye Valley Dorothy Goodbody Ö Westons Stowford Press, Westons Traditional Scrumpy. **Facilities** Children's menu Children's portions Dogs allowed Garden Parking

## SOMERFORD KEYNES
Map 4 SU09

### The Bakers Arms

**GL7 6DN** ☎ **01285 861298**
**dir:** *Exit A419 signed Cotswold Water Park. Cross B4696, 1m, follow signs for Keynes Park & Somerford Keynes*

A beautiful chocolate box pub built from Cotswold stone, with low-beamed ceilings and inglenook fireplaces, and now with a new licensee. Dating from the 15th century, the building was formerly the village bakery and stands in mature gardens ideal for alfresco dining. Discreet children's play areas and heated terraces add to its broad appeal. Somerford Keynes is in the Cotswold Water Park, and the man-made beach of Keynes Park is within easy walking distance, while the nearby Thames Path and Cotswold Way make the pub popular with walkers.

**Open** all day all wk 11-11 (Sun 12-10.30) **Bar Meals** L served Mon-Fri 12-2.30, Sat-Sun 12-9 D served Mon-Fri 6-9, Sat-Sun 12-9 **Restaurant** L served Mon-Fri 12-2.30, Sat-Sun 12-9 D served Mon-Fri 6-9, Sat-Sun 12-9 ⊕ ENTERPRISE INNS 🍺 Courage Best, Butcombe Bitter, Stroud Budding Ö Stowford Press. **Facilities** Children's menu Children's portions Play area Dogs allowed Garden Parking

## SOUTHROP
Map 5 SP10

### PICK OF THE PUBS

### The Swan at Southrop ◉◉

**GL7 3NU** ☎ **01367 850205** 🖶 **01367 850517**
**e-mail:** info@theswanatsouthrop.co.uk
**dir:** *Off A361 between Lechlade & Burford*

This early 17th-century, creeper-clad establishment is a classic Cotswold inn on the village green, and is run by Sebastian and Lana Snow, both protegés of Antony Worrall-Thompson. The interior - bar, snug and award-winning restaurant - is surprisingly light and airy for such an historic building, but homely too, especially when the log fire is ablaze. In the kitchen, impeccable local produce is used in the modern British cooking with Mediterranean touches. Typical of the extensive menus are Puy lentil soup with lardons and croutons; butternut, pine nuts and sage risotto; carpaccio of line caught tuna with avocado, lime ginger and coriander dressing; and escargot Bourgogne. Mains might include roast fillet of cod in herb crust with Lyonnaise potatoes; roast haunch of local wild venison with caramelised apples, bubble and squeak, pickled beetroot and horseradish; minute steak of salmon with a warm salad of samphire, crab, avocado and cherry tomatoes; and osso buco with Milanese risotto. The bar menu offers the likes of the Swan burger, and the Swan club sandwich with fries; moules marinière; whitebait; and home-made pork scratching. There's a children's menu too.

**Open** all wk **Bar Meals** L served all wk 12-3 D served all wk 6-10.30 Av main course £7 **Restaurant** L served all wk 12-3 booking required D served all wk 6-10.30 booking required Fixed menu price fr £14.50 Av 3 course à la carte fr £28 ⊕ FREE HOUSE 🍺 Hook Norton, Wadworth 6X, Cotswold Way, guest ale. **Facilities** Children's menu Children's portions Dogs allowed

## STONEHOUSE
Map 4 SO80

### The George Inn ⬤

**Peter St, Frocester GL10 3TQ**
☎ **01453 822302** 🖶 **01453 791612**
**e-mail:** paul@georgeinn.co.uk
**dir:** *M5 junct 13, onto A419 at 1st rdbt 3rd exit signed Eastington, left at next rdbt signed Frocester. Approx 2m on right in village*

A family-run 18th-century inn at the centre of this rural community, unsullied by juke box or fruit machine. Instead crackling log fires and a sunny courtyard garden overlooked by the original coaching stables give the place all-year-round appeal. The Cotswold Way and a network of leafy paths are on the doorstep. Expect a warm welcome, a selection of real ales including three local brews, and good home-cooked food from nearby suppliers; 'surf and turf' and the mixed grill are both very popular. Diary dates include regular gigs for charity.

**Open** all day all wk 7.30am-mdnt **Bar Meals** L served all wk 12-9.30 D served all wk 12-9.30 food served all day **Restaurant** L served all wk 12-9.30 D served all wk 12-9.30 food served all day ⊕ ENTERPRISE INNS 🍺 Deuchars IPA, Black Sheep, 3 guest ales Ö Old Rosie, Stowford Press. ⬤ 10 **Facilities** Children's menu Children's portions Play area Family room Dogs allowed Garden Parking

## STOW-ON-THE-WOLD
Map 10 SP12

### The Eagle and Child ⬤

**GL54 1HY** ☎ **01451 830670** 🖶 **01451 870048**
**e-mail:** stay@theroyalisthotel.com
**dir:** *From Moreton-in-Marsh rail station take A429 to Stow-on-the-Wold. At 2nd lights left into Sheep St, A436. Establishment 100yds on left*

Reputed the oldest inn in England, dating back to 947 AD and once a hospice to shelter lepers, The Eagle and Child is part of the Royalist Hotel. The social hub of the hotel and village, serving local ales on handpump, it also delivers pub food that manages to be both rustic and accomplished. Informality and flexibility go hand-in-hand with flagstone floors, oak beams and rustic tables; the light-flooded conservatory offering a striking contrast to the character, low-ceilinged dining room. Expect range of pub classics, from Old Spot sausages with leek mash to steak and Guinness pie, and more innovative food like seafood and charcuterie deli plates, and braised duck leg with redcurrant and butterbean stew.

Save on Hotels. Book at **theAA.com/hotel**

**GLOUCESTERSHIRE** 207 **ENGLAND**

**Open** all wk Mon-Sat 11-11 (Sun 11-10.30) ⊕ FREE HOUSE ◀ Hook Norton, Goffs, Donnington, Jouster, Hooky ♂ Stowford Press. ♛ 8 **Facilities** Dogs allowed Garden Parking

## The Unicorn

**Sheep St GL54 1HQ** ☎ **01451 830257** ▤ **01451 831090**
**e-mail:** reception@birchhotels.co.uk
**dir:** *Telephone for directions*

Attractive hotel of honey-coloured limestone, hand-cut roof tiles and abundantly flowering window boxes, set in the heart of Stow-on-the-Wold. The interior is stylishly presented with Jacobean pieces, antique artefacts and open log fires. The pub menu offers a good choice of dishes which can be served in the oak-beamed bar, the stylish contemporary restaurant or in the secluded garden if the weather is fine.

**Open** all wk **Bar Meals** Av main course £9.95 **Restaurant** L served all wk 12-2 D served all wk 7-9 ⊕ FREE HOUSE ◀ Hook Norton, Dorothy Goodbody ♂ Westons. **Facilities** Children's menu Children's portions Dogs allowed Garden Parking

| STROUD | Map 4 SO80 |
|---|---|

### PICK OF THE PUBS

## Bear of Rodborough Hotel ★★★ HL ♛

*See Pick of the Pubs on page 208*

## The Ram Inn

**South Woodchester GL5 5EL**
☎ **01453 873329** ▤ **01453 873329**
**e-mail:** raminnwoodchester@hotmail.co.uk
**dir:** *A46 from Stroud to Nailsworth, right after 2m into South Woodchester, follow brown tourist signs*

From the plentiful seating on terrace of the 17th-century Cotswold stone Ram Inn, there are splendid views over five valleys, although proximity to the huge fireplace may prove more appealing in winter. Rib-eye steak, at least two fish dishes, home-made lasagne and Sunday roasts can be expected, washed down with a glass of Uley Old Spot or Stroud Budding and regularly changing guests. Enjoy a display by the Stroud Morris Men who regularly perform here.

**Open** all day all wk **Bar Meals** L served all wk 12-2 D served all wk 6-9 **Restaurant** L served all wk 12-2 D served all wk 6-9 ⊕ FREE HOUSE ◀ Uley Old Spot, Stroud Budding, Butcombe Bitter, Guests. **Facilities** Children's menu Children's portions Family room Dogs allowed Garden Parking

### PICK OF THE PUBS

## Rose & Crown Inn

**The Cross, Nympsfield GL10 3TU** ☎ **01453 860240**
**dir:** *M5 junct 13 off B4066, SW of Stroud*

An imposing, 400-year-old coaching inn of honey-coloured local stone that could well be the highest pub in the Cotswolds, a fact that hardly matters since the views over the Severn are stunning anyway. Occupying a central position in the village, the closeness of the Cotswold Way makes it a popular stop for hikers and bikers. Inside, the inn's character is preserved with natural stone, wood panelling, a lovely open fire and some local real ales, like Pig's Ear from the Uley brewery, and proper ciders, like Black Rat. In the galleried restaurant, the new owners' menu offers main courses at lunch and dinner of chicken and bacon Caesar salad; fresh Devonshire mussels; and home-cooked honey-roast ham and free-range egg. At lunchtime there are sandwiches, home-made burgers and toasted filled baguettes. In the large garden children will enjoy the playground area, which has a swing, slides and a climbing bridge.

**Open** all day all wk noon-mdnt **Bar Meals** L served all wk 12-3 D served all wk 6-9 Av main course £8 ⊕ FREE HOUSE ◀ Uley, Pigs Ear, Butcombe Bitter, Hooky Bitter ♂ Thatchers, Stowford Press, Black Rat. **Facilities** Children's menu Children's portions Play area Dogs allowed Garden Parking

## The Woolpack Inn

**Slad Rd, Slad GL6 7QA** ☎ **01452 813429**
**e-mail:** info@thewoolpackinn-slad.com
**dir:** *2m from Stroud, 8m from Gloucester*

The Woolpack is a friendly local in the beautiful Slad Valley close to the Cotswold Way, an area immortalised by Laurie Lee; indeed, the author was a regular here. Now under new management, the place is popular with walkers, so muddy boots are not frowned upon, and children and dogs are welcome. The menu of honest and freshly prepared food from local suppliers may include Gressingham duck breast with braised red cabbage; butternut squash and broccoli pie; and chocolate and beetroot brownie.

**Open** all day all wk **Bar Meals** L served Mon-Sat 12-2, Sun 12-3.30 booking required D served Tue-Sat 6.30-9 booking required Av main course £10 **Restaurant** L served Mon-Sat 12-2, Sun 12-3.30 booking required D served Tue-Sat 6.30-9 booking required Av 3 course à la carte fr £18 ⊕ FREE HOUSE ◀ Uley Pig's Ear, Old Spot, Uley Bitter, Budding, Butcombe Bitter ♂ Old Rosie, Stowford Press. **Facilities** Children's menu Children's portions Dogs allowed Garden Parking

| TETBURY | Map 4 ST89 |
|---|---|

### PICK OF THE PUBS

## Gumstool Inn ♛

**Calcot Manor GL8 8YJ**
☎ **01666 890391** ▤ **01666 890394**
**e-mail:** reception@calcotmanor.co.uk
**dir:** *3m W of Tetbury*

A traditional country inn, the Gumstool is part of Calcot Manor Hotel, which is set in 220 acres of Cotswold countryside. The hotel is a successful conversion of a 14th-century stone farmhouse built by Cistercian monks, set around a flower-filled courtyard. As a free house, the Gumstool stocks a good selection of some unusual real ales, mostly from the West Country, and an excellent choice of wines. Food is top notch gastro-pub quality – starters of devilled lamb's kidneys with crisp puff pastry; and twice-baked Arbroath smokies and Cheddar cheese soufflé indicate the calibre. A section of the menu proffers light main courses such as warm Cornish crab and leek tart, or seared scallop salad with avocado and crispy pancetta. Among the main courses may be found slow braised lamb hotpot; venison steak au poivre; spiced halibut fillet; and grilled calves' liver. There is a pretty sun terrace, while winter evenings are warmed with cosy log fires.

**Open** all wk 11.30-2.30 5.30-11 **Bar Meals** L served all wk 11.30-2 booking required D served Mon-Sat 7-9.30, Sun 7-9 booking required Av main course £9.50 **Restaurant** L served all wk 12-2 booking required D served Mon-Sat 7-9.30, Sun 7-9 booking required Av 3 course à la carte fr £22 ⊕ FREE HOUSE ◀ Atlantics Sharp's IPA, Matthews Bob Wool, Wickwar Cotswold Way, Butcombe Blonde. ♛ 21 **Facilities** Children's menu Children's portions Play area Family room Garden Parking

### PICK OF THE PUBS

## The Priory Inn ★★★ SHL ♛

**London Rd GL8 8JJ**
☎ **01666 502251** ▤ **01666 503534**
**e-mail:** info@theprioryinn.co.uk
**dir:** *M4 junct 17, A429 towards Cirencester. Left onto B4014 to Tetbury. Over mini-rdbt onto Long St, pub 100yds after corner on right*

Thriving gastro-pub, hotel and coffee bar at the centre of Tetbury life. The excellent selection of real ales from local breweries includes a premium lager from the

*continued on page 209*

# PICK OF THE PUBS

## Bear of Rodborough Hotel ★★★ HL ♀

**STROUD**  Map 4 SO80

**Rodborough Common GL5 5DE**
☎ 01453 878522  📠 01453 872523
**e-mail:** info@bearofrodborough.co.uk
**web:**
www.cotswold-inns-hotels.co.uk/bear
**dir:** *From M5 junct 13 follow signs for
Stonehouse then Rodborough*

Standing 600 feet above sea level and
surrounded by 300 acres of National
Trust land, this 17th-century former
Cotswolds alehouse takes its name from
the bear-baiting that used to take place
nearby. The hotel is worth seeking out
for all sorts of reasons. There's the
comfortable accommodation, open log
fires, stone walls and solid wooden
floors, as well as an interesting
inscription over the front doors that
reads 'Through this wide opening gate
none come too early, none return too
late'. The motto was reputedly carved by
the renowned sculptor and typographer,

Eric Gill. A running bear design is
incorporated into the ceiling beams in
the elegant Box Tree restaurant and
Tower Room, while the identity of a
resident ghost is often discussed in the
Grizzly Bar over pints of Gloucestershire
brews from Uley and Wickwar. Outside,
there's a delightful York stone terrace,
as well as a walled croquet lawn
created in the 1920s by a former
resident called Edmunds, a partner in a
well-known firm of Stroud nurserymen.

The bar menu begins with an attractive
range of hot and cold sandwiches, the
former served with mixed leaf salad and
spicy potato wedges. Then there are
starters, salads and main course dishes
like warm aubergine tart with Greek
salad and tzatziki, and steak and
Guinness pie with herb mash and
vegetables.

A full afternoon tea menu with cakes,
scones and clotted cream fills in the
time before dinner in the restaurant.
Start, perhaps, with smoked salmon
salad with purple rocket, Thai grass and
Parmesan; followed by a duet of guinea
fowl, smoked bacon and Savoy cabbage,
served with pear purée and roasted
cocotte potato. Warm chocolate tart with

English raspberries brings the meal to
an appealing conclusion.

**Open** all day all wk **Bar Meals** L served
all wk 12-2.30 D served all wk 6.30-10
Av main course £10.95
**Restaurant** D served all wk 7-10 Fixed
menu price fr £28.95 Av 3 course à la
carte fr £28.95 ⊕ FREE HOUSE
🛢 Butcombe, Stroud Life, London Pride,
Uley Bitter, Bob from Wickwar
Brewery. ♀ 10 **Facilities** Play area Dogs
allowed Garden Parking **Rooms** 46

## TETBURY *continued*

Cotswold Brewing Company; real cider from Thatchers is also on tap; and a local bubbly from Bow in the Cloud vineyard near Malmesbury is sold by the glass. Since 2008 a '30-mile food zone' has demonstrated the pub's commitment to serving food and drink from farms and suppliers within a 30-mile radius. Children are particularly welcome, with a specialised menu of home-made dishes and junior cocktails, plus the opportunity to decorate a personalised wood-fired pizza. An evening meal could begin with smoked pigeon breast salad with bacon, beetroot and black pudding; and continue with a seven-ounce Willesley Farm beef burger with smoked tomato and cucumber salsa. Try an upside down apple tart with Ceri's vanilla ice cream for dessert; or a vanilla pannacotta with poached pear and hazelnut biscotti. There is live music every Sunday evening, and local ale and cider days twice a year.

**Open** all day all wk **Restaurant** L served Mon-Thu 12-3, Fri-Sun & BHs all day booking required D served Mon-Thu 5-10, Fri-Sun & BHs all day booking required Av 3 course à la carte fr £21 ⊕ FREEHOUSE ◀ Uley Bitter, Archers Ale ♻ Thatchers. ☂ 13 **Facilities** Children's menu Children's portions Play area Family room Dogs allowed Garden Parking **Rooms** 14

### PICK OF THE PUBS

## The Trouble House ◉◉ ☂

**Cirencester Rd GL8 8SG** ☎ **01666 502206**
dir: *On A433 between Tetbury & Cirencester*

The aptly named Trouble House has something of a chequered past. It was the scene of agricultural riots and civil war conflicts and original features like ancient beams, fireplaces and a charmingly crooked ceiling all add to the pub's very English allure. Now under new management of Liam Parr, previously front of house at Calcot Manor, and Shane who was a chef there, the pub continues to be a draw for its food. On the menu could be confit chicken, ham and foie gras terrine, pear and saffron chutney; Salcombe crab gratin; slow cooked Old Spot pork shoulder; steamed bream fillet, lemon tabouleh, roast peppers and fennel roast and braised local lamb with grilled leeks and celeriac. Desserts run along the lines of cherry and almond crumble, and caramelised lemon tart. There's a roast on Sundays.

**Open** 11.30-3 7-11 Closed: 25-26 Dec, Sun eve, Mon **Bar Meals** L served Tue-Fri 12-2 booking required Av main course £10.50 **Restaurant** L served Tue-Sun 12-2 booking required D served Tue-Sat 7-9.30 booking required Av 3 course à la carte fr £25.50 ⊕ WADWORTH ◀ Wadworth 6X, Henrys IPA ♻ Stowford Press. ☂ 12 **Facilities** Dogs allowed Garden Parking

### TODENHAM                    **Map 10 SP23**

### PICK OF THE PUBS

## The Farriers Arms ☂

**Main St GL56 9PF** ☎ **01608 650901**
e-mail: info@farriersarms.com
dir: *Right to Todenham at N end of Moreton-in-Marsh. 2.5m from Shipston on Stour*

Dating back to 1650, when it was a church house, this traditional Cotswold pub was also an ironworks before becoming a pub in 1830. The pub ticks all the country pub boxes with its polished flagstone floors, exposed stone walls, wooden beams and large inglenook fireplace, whilst the suntrap patio garden offers views of the church. The bar and recently refurbished restaurant offers a daily-changing menu packed with local produce. Starters range from black pudding topped with rarebit and served with tomato chutney, or smoked salmon and prawn cornets, while typical main courses include local steak with mushrooms, tomatoes and black pepper sauce, and whole grilled lemon sole with lemon and dill butter. In the Aunt Sally season maybe have a game yourself, or just watch 'the professionals' as they compete against other local league players in this traditional pub game.

**Open** all wk noon-3 6-11 (6.30 winter) **Bar Meals** L served Mon-Sat 12-2, Sun 12-2.30 D served Mon-Sun 6-9, Sun 6.30-9 in winter Av main course £11.95 **Restaurant** L served Mon-Sat 12-2, Sun 12-2.30 D served Mon-Sun 6-9, Sun 6.30-9 in winter Fixed menu price fr £11.95 Av 3 course à la carte fr £20 ⊕ FREE HOUSE ◀ Hook Norton Best, Wye Valley Butty Bach, Black Sheep, Goffs Brewery Ales ♻ Stowford Press. ☂ 10 **Facilities** Children's menu Children's portions Dogs allowed Garden Parking

### TORMARTON                    **Map 4 ST77**

## Best Western Compass Inn ☂

**GL9 1JB** ☎ **01454 218242**  🖹 **01454 218741**
e-mail: info@compass-inn.co.uk
web: www.compass-inn.co.uk
dir: *M4 junct 18, A46 N towards Stroud. After 200mtrs 1st right towards Tormarton. Inn in 300mtrs*

A charming 18th-century creeper-clad inn, set in six acres of grounds in the heart of the Gloucestershire countryside, right on the Cotswold Way. Light bites and more filling meals can be taken in the bar, while the restaurant offers the likes of oven roasted Scottish

salmon fillet; traditional beef or vegetable lasagne; three Cumberland sausages and mash; and parmesan, sage and tomato risotto cakes.

*Best Western Compass Inn*

**Open** all day all wk 7am-11pm (Sat-Sun 8am-11pm) Closed: 25-26 Dec **Bar Meals** Av main course £8.45 food served all day **Restaurant** Av 3 course à la carte fr £20 food served all day ⊕ FREE HOUSE ◀ Interbrew Bass, London Pride, Butcombe ♻ Ashton Press. ☂ 11 **Facilities** Children's menu Children's portions Dogs allowed Garden Parking

### UPPER ODDINGTON                    **Map 10 SP22**

### PICK OF THE PUBS

## The Horse and Groom Inn ☂

**GL56 0XH** ☎ **01451 830584**
e-mail: info@horseandgroom.uk.com
dir: *1.5m S of Stow-on-the-Wold, just off A436*

A 16th-century stone-built inn, The Horse and Groom is located in a Cotswold conservation village just a mile and a half from Stow-on-the-Wold. It is immaculately kept, with pale polished flagstone floors, beams, stripped stone walls and log fires in the inglenook. In fine weather you can enjoy the terrace and gardens, with grape vines bounded by dry stone walls. A great selection of cask ales is offered from local breweries and the wine list, including 25 available by the glass, is ever growing. Menus comprise regional food sourced from as close to the kitchen door as possible. Bread, for example, is made daily from Cotswold Flour Millers flour. Dishes might include deep fried beer battered king prawns with tomato crème fraîche; baked haddock topped with Welsh rarebit and poached egg; slow braised crispy Old Spot pork belly with cider, honey caramelised shallot mash and juniper scented greens; lemon glazed tart and raspberry sorbet. Fish is featured on the daily blackboard menu.

**Open** all wk noon-3 5.30-11 (Sun 6.30-10.30) **Bar Meals** L served all wk 12-2 D served Mon-Sat 6.30-9, Sun 7-9 **Restaurant** L served all wk 12-2 D served Mon-Sat 6.30-9, Sun 7-9 ⊕ FREE HOUSE ◀ Wye Valley Butty Bach, Wye Valley Best, Hereford Pale Ale, Wickwar Bob ♻ Kingston Press. ☂ 25 **Facilities** Children's menu Children's portions Dogs allowed Garden Parking

## WINCHCOMBE — Map 10 SP02

### The White Hart Inn and Restaurant ♈

High St GL54 5LJ ☎ 01242 602359 📠 01242 602703
e-mail: info@wineandsausage.com
dir: In centre of Winchcombe on B4632

In a pretty small town on the Cotswold Way, close to
Sudeley Castle and glorious rolling countryside, this
smart 16th-century inn provides welcome refreshment to
walkers and tourists. Quaff a pint of Uley Bitter in
traditional pubby front bar, with its wood floor, scrubbed
old tables and cricketing memorabilia, and tuck into
simple and unpretentious British food sourced from local
farmers and suppliers. Typical dishes include ham hock
terrine with piccalilli, beef Wellington, dressed crab, and
rhubarb fool. Don't miss the wine shop next to the bar!

**Open** all day all wk 10am-11pm (Fri-Sat 10am-mdnt Sun
10am-10.30pm) ⬤ Uley Old Spot, Whittingtons Cats
Whiskers, Greene King IPA, Wadworth 6X, Old Speckled
Hen, Butcombe, Otter, Jouster ♺ Stowford Press. ♈ 8
**Facilities** Dogs allowed Garden Parking

## WITHINGTON — Map 10 SP01

### The Mill Inn

GL54 4BE ☎ 01242 890204 📠 01242 890195
dir: 3m from A40 between Cheltenham & Oxford

Until 1914 the innkeeper also had to find time to grind
corn in this 450-year-old inn on the banks of the River
Coln. Inside are stone-flagged floors, oak panelling and
log fires, while outside is a peaceful lawned garden with
40 tables. Lunch or dinner is selected from a wide
selection of light meals and more substantial main
courses, including blackened Cajun chicken, steak and
ale pie and Barnsley chop.

**Open** all wk ⬤ Samuel Smith Old Brewery Bitter, Samuel
Smith Sovereign, Alpine Lager, Pure Brew Lager, Extra
Stout. **Facilities** Family room Dogs allowed Garden
Parking

## WOODCHESTER — Map 4 SO80

### PICK OF THE PUBS

### The Old Fleece ♈

Bath Rd, Rooksmoor GL5 5NB ☎ 01453 872582
e-mail: pheasantpluckers2003@yahoo.co.uk
dir: 2m S of Stroud on A46

Set amid beautiful countryside with miles of footpaths
to explore, this delightful coaching inn was built in the
18th century from Cotswold stone and has a traditional
stone roof. From the Old Fleece, you can walk to
Rodborough, Minchinhampton and Selsley Commons, or
go one step further and connect eventually with the
scenic Cotswold Way long distance trail. The beautifully
refurbished interior includes wooden floors, wood
panelling and exposed stone, and the bar serves well
kept Greene King Abbot Ale and Otter Bitter.

Predominantly French chefs offer a comprehensive
menu of British and continental dishes, ranging from
classics such as Old Spot sausage and mash with
onion gravy to the likes of confit duck leg with hoi sin
noodles, whole sea bream with braised fennel, or pork
loin steak with apple and Calvados purée.

**Open** all day all wk 11-11 (Sun 11-10.30) Closed: 25
Dec **Bar Meals** L served all wk 11-2.45 D served all wk
5.30-10 **Restaurant** L served all wk 11-2.45 D served
all wk 5.30-10 ⊕ PHEASANT PLUCKERS LTD ⬤ Otter
Bitter, Buckham Bitter, Tom Long ♺ Ashton Press. ♈ 12
**Facilities** Dogs allowed Garden Parking

# GREATER MANCHESTER

## ALTRINCHAM — Map 15 SJ78

### PICK OF THE PUBS

### The Victoria ♈

*See Pick of the Pubs on opposite page*

## BIRTLE — Map 15 SD81

### Pack Horse Inn ♈ NEW

Elbut Ln BL9 7TU ☎ 0161 764 3620
e-mail: pack@jwlees.co.uk
dir: From Bury towards Rochdale take B6222 (Bury &
Rochdale Old Rd). Left at Fairfield General Hospital

Just beyond the Pack Horse the lane gives way to marked
moorland paths and tracks into the spectacular wooded
chasm of the Cheesden Gorge. Ramblers in this heritage
hotspot rest awhile at this converted farmhouse, which
offers classic English pub meals and some interesting
specials served in a comfy inn busy with artefacts and
boasting a great patio with fine views over farmland high
above Bury. It is a great community pub with events all
year through, also popular with families, and horse-riders
hitch up here en route to the moorland bridlepaths.

**Open** all day all wk **Bar Meals** food served all day
**Restaurant** food served all day ⊕ JW LEES ⬤ JW Lees
Bitter, Coronation Street. ♈ 20 **Facilities** Children's
menu Children's portions Garden Parking

## DENSHAW — Map 16 SD91

### The Rams Head Inn ♈

OL3 5UN ☎ 01457 874802 📠 01457 820978
e-mail: ramsheaddenshaw@aol.com
dir: M62 junct 22, A672 towards Oldham, 2m to inn

From its position 1212 feet above sea level, this
400-year-old country inn offers panoramic views over
Saddleworth. Log fires and collections of memorabilia are
features of the interior, where blackboard menus list
everything available and food is cooked to order. Game
and seafood figure strongly, with dishes such as crayfish
tails with ginger crème fraîche, and monkfish wrapped in
Parma ham. Another attraction is The Pantry (open 9am-
4.30pm Tue-Sat, 11am-4.30pm Sun), a farm shop, deli,
bakery, and coffee shop.

**Open** noon-2.30 6-11 Closed: 25 Dec, Mon (ex BH)
**Bar Meals** L served Tue-Sat 9-4.30, Sun 11-4.30
**Restaurant** food served all day ⊕ FREE HOUSE
⬤ Timothy Taylor Landlord, Black Sheep Bitter
♺ Thatchers Gold. ♈ 16 **Facilities** Children's portions
Parking

## DIDSBURY — Map 16 SJ89

### PICK OF THE PUBS

### The Metropolitan ♈

2 Lapwing Ln M20 2WS
☎ 0161 438 2332 📠 0161 282 6544
e-mail: info@the-metropolitan.co.uk
dir: M60 junct 5, A5103, right onto Barlow Moor Rd,
left onto Burton Rd. Pub at x-rds. Right onto Lapwing
Ln for car park

Originally a hotel for passengers riding the old Midland
Railway into Manchester, the 'Met' still punches above
its weight architecturally, but then that's how Victorian
railway companies liked to gain a competitive edge
over their rivals. Look in particular at the decorative
floor tiling, the ornate windows the impressive roof
timbers and the delicate plasterwork. During the latter
part of the 20th century the building became very run
down, until in 1997 it was given a sympathetic
renovation, reopening as a gastro-pub. Its huge, airy
interior is filled with antique tables and chairs, and
deep sofas, which suit the mainly young, cosmopolitan
clientele. Food ranges from starters and light bites
(pea and ham risotto; Thai-style mussels) to main
courses such as pork loin with sweet potato and
rosemary mash and steamed pak choi, fish and chips,
and sirloin steak with pepper sauce. Outside terraces
buzz with drinkers and diners in the summer.

**Open** all day all wk 11.30-mdnt (Sun noon-11) Closed:
25 Dec **Bar Meals** L served Mon-Sat 12-7, Sun 12-6
food served all day **Restaurant** L served Mon-Thu
12-9.30, Fri-Sat 12-10, Sun 12-9 food served all day
⬤ Timothy Taylor Landlord, Deuchars IPA, Guinness
♺ Westons, Rekorderlig. ♈ 28 **Facilities** Children's
portions Garden Parking

# PICK OF THE PUBS

## The Victoria ♥

**Stamford St WA14 1EX**
☎ **0161 613 1855**
**e-mail:** the.victoria@yahoo.co.uk
**dir:** *From rail station, cross main road, turn right. 2nd left onto Stamford St*

Tucked away behind the main shopping street, the beautifully restored Victoria re-opened in 2006 following a period of closure. Rachel Wetherill and Kevin Choudhary have breathed new life into the place, establishing it as a stylish, food-led tavern. On one side is a wood-panelled dining area, set with linens and tableware, on the other a more casual bar area, with lots of wood, slate and exposed brickwork.

The food is imaginative and freshly prepared using locally-sourced ingredients, and appears on seasonal menus as classic British dishes with a modern twist. This approach leads to starters such as seared pigeon pasty with creamy lentil sauce; warm cockle and dill tart with watercress and herb dressing; and sweet onion and cider soup topped with Stilton crumble. Any of these could be followed by a main course such as jugged wild rabbit (slow-braised with prunes and sherry); cottage pie (beef cheek, oxtail and winter vegetables); rib-eye steak with hand-cut fat chips and a red wine and shallot butter; or pan-fried sea bass served with a beetroot and Jerusalem artichoke salad. On Sundays a traditional roast rib of beef (hung for four weeks) is available. And are the puddings given a modern makeover too? Judge for yourself – there could be forced rhubarb and sweet ginger roly poly; and home-made rum baba with sweet vanilla cream. There are also lunchtime sandwiches, ploughman's, omelettes, battered butties, and light meals, such as chorizo Scotch egg, and smoked duck crumpet.

The wine list features more than 30 carefully chosen bins, and there are several hand-pulled real ales. For drivers, The Victoria has a temperance bar offering locally produced old favourites like dandelion and burdock and sarsaparilla.

**Open** all day all wk noon-11 (Sun noon-6) Closed: 26 Dec & 1 Jan
**Bar Meals** L served Mon-Sat 12-3 D served Mon-Sat 5.30-9 Av main course £15 **Restaurant** L served Mon-Sat 12-3, Sun 12-4 D served Mon-Sat 5.30-9 Fixed menu price fr £15.95 Av 3 course à la carte fr £23.95 ⊕ FREE HOUSE ◄ Old Speckled Hen, Jennings Cumberland, Flowers IPA ♻ Westons Organic. ♥ 10

## DOBCROSS
Map 15 SD90

### Swan Inn NEW

**The Square OL3 5AA** ☎ **01457 873451**
**e-mail:** swandobcross@hotmail.com
**dir:** *A62 outside Oldham. Follow brown tourist signs towards Saddleworth*

A picture-perfect South-Pennine weaving village in magnificent walking country, Dobcross was a main location for the 1979 film 'YANKS'. Fronting the steeply sloping little cobbled square, the Swan is a commanding gritstone inn with a warren of characterful rooms off the passageway bar; think open fires, slabbed floors and centuries of service to discerning locals. Offering reliable real ales and robust, traditional pub grub (try the home-made pies), the inn is on the route of the remarkable Longwood Thump rushcart festival each August.

**Open** all wk Mon-Thu 12-3 5-11, Fri 12-3 5-11.30, Sat noon-11.30, Sun noon-10.30 Closed: 25 Dec **Bar Meals** L served all wk 12-2 D served Mon-Sat 5.30-8 Av main course £8 ⊕ MARSTONS/JENNINGS ◀ Cumberland, Pedigree, Cockerhoop, Oxford Gold. **Facilities** Children's menu Children's portions Family room Dogs allowed Garden

## LITTLEBOROUGH
Map 16 SD91

### The White House ♀

**Blackstone Edge, Halifax Rd OL15 0LG**
☎ **01706 378456**
**dir:** *On A58, 8m from Rochdale, 9m from Halifax*

A coaching house built in 1671, standing 1,300 feet above sea level on the Pennine Way, with panoramic views of the moors and Hollingworth Lake far below. Not surprising, then, that it attracts walkers and cyclists who rest up and sup on Theakstons and regular guest ales. It's been known as The White House for over 100 years and has been in the same hands for just over 26 of them. A simple menu of pub grub ranges from sandwiches and starters like garlic and herb mushrooms, to grills, curries, chillies and traditional plates of home-made steak and kidney pie.

**Open** all wk Closed: 25 Dec **Bar Meals** L served all wk 12-2 D served all wk 6-9 **Restaurant** L served all wk 12-2 D served all wk 6.30-9.30 ⊕ FREE HOUSE ◀ Timothy Taylor Landlord, Theakstons Bitter, Exmoor Gold, Black Sheep, Phoenix. **Facilities** Parking

## MANCHESTER
Map 16 SJ89

### Dukes 92 ♀

**14 Castle St, Castlefield M3 4LZ**
☎ **0161 839 8646** 🖹 **0161 832 3595**
**e-mail:** info@dukes92.com
**dir:** *In Castleford town centre, off Deansgate*

Beautifully-restored 19th-century stable building with a vast patio beside the 92nd lock of the Duke of Bridgewater canal, opened in 1762. The interior is full of surprises, with minimalist decor downstairs and an upper

gallery displaying local artistic talent. A grill restaurant supplements a lunchtime bar menu and evening pizza choices, as well as the renowned cheese and pâté counter with its huge range of British and continental cheeses which can be enjoyed with one of the 15 wines served by the glass or a pint of Interbrew.

**Open** all day all wk Closed: 25-26 Dec, 1 Jan **Bar Meals** Av main course £8 food served all day **Restaurant** Fixed menu price fr £10 Av 3 course à la carte fr £25 food served all day ⊕ FREE HOUSE ◀ Interbrew Boddingtons Bitter, Boddingtons Ò Koppaberg. ♀ 15 **Facilities** Children's menu Children's portions Garden Parking

### Marble Arch

**73 Rochdale Rd M4 4HY**
☎ **0161 832 5914** 🖹 **0161 819 2694**
**dir:** *In city centre (Northern Quarter)*

A listed building with a strikingly original interior, the Marble Arch is a fine example of Manchester's Victorian heritage. It's also home to the award-winning organic Marble Brewery, with six regular and eight seasonal house beers. Snacks and more substantial meals are served in the bar - the pies are deservedly popular. Sample the likes of steak and Marble ale pie; black pudding and potato salad; and pot-roast chicken in Marble ginger beer.

**Open** all wk Closed: 25-26 Dec ◀ GSB, Marble Best, Ginger Marble, Lagonda.

### The Queen's Arms

**6 Honey St, Cheetham M8 8RG** ☎ **0161 834 4239**
**e-mail:** shirleygreenwood@tiscali.co.uk
**dir:** *Telephone for directions*

The Queen's is part of a loose grouping of real ale pubs in Manchester's Northern Quarter. The original tiled frontage shows that it was once allied to the long-vanished Empress Brewery. Its clientele spans the socio-economic spectrum from 'suits' to bikers to pensioners, all seemingly happy with the heavy rock on the jukebox. Food is available, but it's the brewed, distilled and fermented products that attract, including an impressive 'menu' of bottled lagers, fruit beers, vodkas and wines. Now under new ownership.

**Open** all day all wk Closed: 25 Dec **Bar Meals** L served all wk 12-5 Av main course £3.50 ⊕ FREE HOUSE ◀ Hopsack, guest ales. **Facilities** Children's menu Play area Dogs allowed Garden **Notes** ⊛

## MARPLE BRIDGE
Map 16 SJ98

### Hare & Hounds NEW

**19 Mill Brow SK6 5LW** ☎ **0161 4274042**
**e-mail:** gmarsh@bwanorth.co.uk
**dir:** *From Marple Bridge travelling towards Mellor, turn left up Hollins Lane. Follow road to T junct with Ley Lane. Turn right, pub is 0.25m on left.*

Dating from 1805 the Hare & Hounds is a hidden gem in the beautiful hamlet of Mill Brow, a genuine village community in a great rural setting. Recently sympathetically refurbished, this is now a comfortable country pub with great atmosphere, roaring fires in winter and a get away from loud music and big TV screens. You can enjoy a pint of real ale or cider here or peruse the menu if you like. Freshly prepared food is offered using local ingredients where possible. Expect exciting dishes like starters of chorizo frittata, mussels buzarra or pork and black pudding meatballs. Follow with roasted rump of lamb on mint crusted fondant potato and redcurrant gravy, or ribeye steak with triple-cooked chips.

**Open** all wk Mon-Thu 5-mdnt, Fri noon-3 5-mdnt, Sat-Sun noon-mdnt **Bar Meals** L served Fri-Sat 12-2, Sun 1-7 D served Wed-Sat 6-9.30 booking required **Restaurant** Fixed menu price fr £16.95 Av 3 course à la carte fr £19 ⊕ FREDERIC ROBINSON ◀ Unicorn Bitter, Hatters Mild, Dizzy Blonde Ò Stowford Press, Westons Original Scrumpy. **Facilities** Children's portions Dogs allowed Garden Parking

## MELLOR
Map 16 SJ98

### The Moorfield Arms ★★★★ INN ♀

**Shiloh Rd SK6 5NE**
☎ **0161 427 1580** 🖹 **0161 427 1582**
**e-mail:** info@moorfieldarms.co.uk
**dir:** *From Marple station down Brabyns Brow to lights. Right into Town St. 3m, left into Shiloh Rd. 0.5m, pub on left*

Magnificent views of Kinder Scout and Lantern Pike make this traditional old moorland pub an ideal Peak District base. The building dates from 1640 and retains plenty of old world charm and atmosphere. A bit of fell-walking should generate an appetite for a hot tandoori chicken sandwich; grilled gammon steak; savoury tortilla wrap; steak and ale pie; cod mornay; slow-roasted lamb Henry (the house signature dish); or one of the many specials. Situated in a barn conversion, en suite rooms are comfortable and stylish.

**Open** Mon-Sat 12-2.30 6-9.30 (Sun 12-9) Closed: Mon in Winter **Bar Meals** L served Mon-Sat 12-2, Sun 12-9 D served all wk 6-9.30 Av main course £10 **Restaurant** L served all wk 12-2 D served all wk 6-9.30 Fixed menu price fr £5.95 Av 3 course à la carte fr £25 ⊕ FREE HOUSE ♀ 12 **Facilities** Children's menu Garden Parking **Rooms** 4

## The Oddfellows Arms ⚑

**73 Moor End Rd SK6 5PT** ☎ **0161 449 7826**
dir: *Telephone for directions*

A friendly welcome can be expected in this c1650 building, which has had a liquor licence since 1805. It changed its name from 'The Angel Inn' in 1860 to accommodate the Oddfellows Society, a forerunner of the Trades Unions. There are always plenty of real ales to choose from.

**Open** all wk 4-late (Thu-Fri 12-late Sat 11-late Sun 11-6) Closed: 25-26 Dec, 31 Dec-1 Jan ◀ Adnams Southwold, Marston's Pedigree, Bitter, Fennicks Arizona, Guest. ⚑ 8 **Facilities** Dogs allowed Garden Parking

---

### OLDHAM                            Map 16 SD90

## The Roebuck Inn ⚑

**Strinesdale OL4 3RB**
☎ **0161 624 7819**  📄 **0161 633 6210**
e-mail: sehowarth1@hotmail.com
dir: *From Oldham Humps Bridge take Huddersfield Rd, right at 2nd lights onto Ripponden Rd, after 1m right at lights onto Turfpit Ln, follow for 1m*

Historic inn located on the edge of Saddleworth Moor in the rugged Pennines, 1,000 feet above sea level. This may explain the presence of the ghost of a girl who drowned in the local reservoir. The menu offers an extensive choice from vegetarian dishes and steaks to fish dishes; from the fish board perhaps smoked haddock with poached egg and hollandaise sauce. Food and drink can be enjoyed in the garden in the summer months.

**Open** all wk 12-3 5-11 **Bar Meals** L served all wk 12-2.15 D served all wk 5-9.15 Av main course £11 food served all day **Restaurant** L served all wk 12-2.15 D served all wk 5-9.15 booking required Fixed menu price fr £6.95 Av 3 course à la carte fr £16 food served all day ⊕ FREE HOUSE ◀ Tetleys, Guest ale. ⚑ 9 **Facilities** Children's menu Children's portions Play area Dogs allowed Garden Parking

---

### PICK OF THE PUBS

## The White Hart Inn ◉◉ ⚑

**Stockport Rd, Lydgate OL4 4JJ**
☎ **01457 872566**  📄 **01457 875190**
e-mail: bookings@thewhitehart.co.uk
dir: *From Manchester A62 to Oldham. Right onto bypass, A669 through Lees. In 500yds past Grotton, at brow of hill turn right onto A6050*

There's been a pub on this site – high on the hillside overlooking Oldham and Manchester – since 1788, when the place had vast cellars for brewing its own beer using water from the well. A barn was subsequently added to house the local foxhounds and this later served as a police station, school and weaver's cottage, before the ground floor became a smart bar and brasserie when current owner Charles Brierley took over in 1994. The inn also has a contemporary restaurant, an intimate library dining

area and the Oak Room, which is a luxury function and conference venue. The cosmopolitan menu makes good use of local ingredients, offering some classic dishes, perhaps potted shrimps and beer battered haddock with pea purée and chunky chips, alongside lamb rump with parsley and mint risotto, and wild sea bass and scallop with chorizo butter sauce, with chocolate tart and sticky toffee pudding among the pudding choice. There are also open sandwiches, local ales on tap and an extensive wine list.

**Open** all day all wk Closed: 26 Dec **Bar Meals** L served Mon-Sat 12-2.30, Sun 1-7 booking required D served all wk 6-9.30 booking required Av main course £17 **Restaurant** L served Sun 1-3 booking required D served Mon-Sat 6-9.30 booking required Av 3 course à la carte fr £30 ⊕ FREE HOUSE ◀ Timothy Taylor Landlord, J W Lees Bitter, Copper Dragon, Golden Best. ⚑ 12 **Facilities** Children's menu Dogs allowed Garden Parking

---

### STALYBRIDGE                        Map 16 SJ99

## The Royal Oak

**364 Huddersfield Rd, Millbrook SK15 3EP**
☎ **0161 338 7118**
dir: *From Stalybridge turn onto Huddersfield road, pub on right adjacent to Country Park*

This family-run pub, once a coroner's evidence room, was later owned by the late Jackie Blanchflower of Manchester United, who took it on in the 1960s, and rumour has it that the players used to drink here. It stands next to a country park, which is great for walks before or after eating. The food is Italian influenced, and everything is freshly prepared and cooked to order. The wine list is short but well chosen.

**Open** Wed-Fri 5.30-11 (Tue 6-9 only by prior reservation, Sat 4.30-11, Sun noon-10.30) Closed: 1 Jan, Mon **Bar Meals** D served Tue 6-9, Wed-Fri 5.30-9, Sat 4.30-9, Sun 12-7 Av main course £8.25 **Restaurant** D served Tue 6-9, Wed-Fri 5.30-9, Sat 4.30-9, Sun 12-7 Fixed menu price fr £13.50 Av 3 course à la carte fr £20 ⊕ ENTERPRISE INN ◀ Boddingtons, John Smith's. **Facilities** Children's menu Children's portions Garden Parking

---

## Stalybridge Station Buffet Bar

**The Railway Station, Rassbottom St SK15 1RF**
☎ **0161 303 0007**
dir: *Telephone for directions*

Unique Victorian railway station refreshment rooms dating from 1885, including original fittings such as the marble-topped bar and open fire. The first-class ladies' waiting room, with ornate ceiling, and a conservatory provide additional space. Decorated throughout with railway memorabilia and photographs, the place is famous locally for its range of real ales and draught cider, as well as simple home-cooked and inexpensive food: black pudding and black peas, pasta bake, pies, liver and onions, and sausages and mash.

**Open** all wk 11-11 (Sun noon-10.30) **Bar Meals** food served all day ◀ Boddingtons, Flowers IPA, Millstone, Phoenix. **Facilities** Dogs allowed Garden Parking **Notes** ◉

---

### STOCKPORT                          Map 16 SJ89

## The Arden Arms ⚑

**23 Millgate SK1 2LX** ☎ **0161 480 2185**
e-mail: steve@ardenarms.com
dir: *M60 junct 27 to town centre. Across mini-rdbt, at lights turn left. Pub on right of next rdbt behind Asda*

The classic unspoilt layout and original tiled floors of this Grade II listed late Georgian coaching inn rank high among the country's timeless gems. The building was last modernised in 1908, giving drinkers the opportunity to order from the traditional curved bar before settling down by the coal fire in the tiny snug. Lunchtime brings interesting sandwiches and home-made soup, with a selection of hot dishes that might include grilled lamb cutlet; or pan-fried sea bass. There is a jazz night on Mondays and charity quiz on Tuesday evenings.

**Open** all wk noon-11.45 Closed: 25-26 Dec, 1 Jan **Bar Meals** L served Mon-Fri 12-2.30, Sat-Sun 12-4 Av main course £6 ⊕ ROBINSONS ◀ Unicorn Bitter, Hatters Mild, Double Hop, Old Town, seasonal ales. ⚑ 8 **Facilities** Dogs allowed Garden **Notes** ◉

---

## The Nursery Inn

**Green Ln, Heaton Norris SK4 2NA**
☎ **0161 432 2044**  📄 **0161 442 1857**
e-mail: nurseryinn@hydesbrewery.com
dir: *Green Ln off Heaton Moor Rd. Pass rugby club on Green Ln, at end on right. Narrow cobbled road, pub 100yds on right*

Down a narrow cobbled lane in a pleasant Manchester suburb, The Nursery is a classic unspoilt 1930s pub with a unique and immaculately kept bowling green to the rear. In the rambling interior, which includes a vast panelled lounge with big banquettes, you can quaff cracking beers brewed by Hydes and enjoy some good value, home-cooked lunchtime food. A former real ale national pub of the year winner so it's well worth seeking out.

**Open** all wk **Bar Meals** L served Tue-Fri 12-2.30, Sat-Sun 12-4 D served Tue-Fri 5.30-7.30 **Restaurant** L served Tue-Sun 12-2.30 ⊕ HYDES BREWERY ◀ Hydes Bitter, Hydes Jekylls Gold, Hydes Seasonal Ales, Guest ales. **Facilities** Children's portions Dogs allowed Garden Parking **Notes** ◉

## HAMPSHIRE

### ALTON
Map 5 SU73

#### PICK OF THE PUBS

**The Anchor Inn** ✕✕✕ INN ⊛⊛ ℗

**Lower Froyle GU34 4NA**
☎ 01420 23261 ▤ 01420 520467
e-mail: info@anchorinnatlowerfroyle.co.uk
**dir:** A31 signed Bentley, follow brown tourist signs to
Anchor Inn

Tucked away in the centre of the quaint Hampshire
village of Lower Froyle, slap bang in the middle of horse
racing territory, this boarded and tile-hung gastro-pub
with rooms has bags of atmosphere and appeal. The
intimate snug and saloon bar are decked out with low
beams, open fires, wooden floors and lots of original
features, whilst antiques and old prints hint at a
bygone era. In the dining room, candlesticks and
polished wooden tables combine with the painted wall
panelling to create a romantic interior. The seasonal
menu is driven by fresh local produce, blending modern
presentation with simplicity and clear flavours in the
classic English cooking. Typical menu choices might
start with soused mackerel, horseradish cream and
watercress, before moving on to fillet of bass with
fennel gratin, or fillet of beef with pan haggerty,
spinach and meat juices. The dessert selection
includes jam roly poly and Cambridge burnt cream with
poached Yorkshire rhubarb.

**Open** all day all wk **Bar Meals** L served all wk 12-2.30
D served all wk 6.30-9.30 **Restaurant** L served Mon-Sat
12.30-2.30, Sun 12-4 booking required D served Mon-
Fri 6.30-9.30, Sat 6.30-10, Sun 7-9 booking required
⊕ THE MILLERS COLLECTION ◖ Ringwood Best,
Ringwood Fortyniner, guest ales ♂ Thatchers. ℗ 9
**Facilities** Children's portions Dogs allowed Garden
Parking **Rooms** 5

### ANDOVER
Map 5 SU34

### Wyke Down Country Pub & Restaurant

**Wyke Down, Picket Piece SP11 6LX**
☎ 01264 352048 ▤ 01264 324661
e-mail: info@wykedown.co.uk
**dir:** 3m from Andover town centre/A303. Follow signs for
Wyke Down Caravan Park

Combining a pub/restaurant with a caravan park and
golf driving range, this establishment is a diversified
farm on the outskirts of Andover. It still raises beef cattle,
but the pub started in a barn 25 years ago and the
restaurant was built 12 years ago. Dishes range from
lasagne, curry and Cajun chicken supreme on the bar
menu to restaurant fare such as roast tenderloin of pork,
nut loaf, or steaks from the griddle.

**Open** all wk noon-3 6-11 Closed: 25 Dec-2 Jan
**Bar Meals** L served all wk 12-2 booking required D served
all wk 6-9 booking required Av main course £7
**Restaurant** L served all wk 12-2 booking required D
served all wk 6-9 booking required Fixed menu price fr
£15 Av 3 course à la carte fr £20 ⊕ FREE HOUSE
◖ Guinness, London Pride, Butcombe Bitter.
**Facilities** Children's menu Children's portions Play area
Garden Parking

### AXFORD
Map 5 SU64

#### PICK OF THE PUBS

### The Crown at Axford

**RG25 2DZ** ☎ 01256 389492
e-mail: info@crownataxford.co.uk
**dir:** From Basingstoke take A339 towards Alton. Under
M3 bridge, turn next right onto B3046 towards New
Alresford. Axford in approx 5m

The Crown is a small country inn set at the northern
edge of the pretty Candover Valley. Here you can enjoy
your choice from a selection of real ales and wines,
with some bread and olives to keep you going, and
order dishes like pork, beer and watercress sausages.
The food is all home cooked from local produce
wherever possible, including fish, game, and
vegetarian dishes from the board. Organic specials are
a feature. There has been a change of hands.

**Open** all wk Mon-Fri noon-2.30 6-11 (Sat noon-11pm
Sun noon-10.30pm) **Bar Meals** L served Mon-Fri 12-2,
Sun 12-4 D served Mon-Fri 6-9 ⊕ FREE HOUSE
◖ Triple fff, Hogsback ales ♂ Stowford Press, Hex
Ciders. **Facilities** Dogs allowed Garden Parking

### BALL HILL
Map 5 SU46

### The Furze Bush Inn

**Hatt Common, East Woodhay RG20 0NQ**
☎ 01635 253228 ▤ 01635 254883
e-mail: info@furzebushinn.co.uk
**dir:** Telephone for directions

Tucked away in a glorious rural location, this
whitewashed free house is handy for Highclere Castle,
Newbury Races and walking on the Berkshire Downs. The
bar menu features a good range of pub favourites, with
more adventurous dishes like wild mushroom risotto with
parmesan and nutmeg, and pan-fried fillet of grouper
with crushed garlic new potatoes available in the
restaurant. There's a large front beer garden.

**Open** all day all wk **Bar Meals** L served Mon-Fri 12-2.30,
Sat-Sun & BH all day D served all wk 6-9.30 Av main
course £9 **Restaurant** L served Mon-Fri 12-2.30, Sat-Sun
& BH 12-6 booking required D served all wk 6-9.30
booking required Av 3 course à la carte fr £20 ⊕ FREE
HOUSE ◖ London Pride, Greene King, Abbot Ale.
**Facilities** Children's menu Play area Dogs allowed Garden
Parking

### BAUGHURST
Map 5 SU56

#### PICK OF THE PUBS

### The Wellington Arms ⊛⊛ ℗

**Baughurst Rd RG26 5LP** ☎ 0118 982 0110
e-mail: hello@thewellingtonarms.com
web: www.thewellingtonarms.com
**dir:** M4 junct 12 follow Newbury signs on A4. At rdbt
left signed Aldermaston. Through Aldermaston. Up hill,
at next rdbt 2nd exit, left at T-junct, pub 1m on left

Fields and woodland surround the large lawned garden
of this tiny whitewashed free house. It's the ideal
setting for the free-range chickens whose eggs are
used in the kitchen, a practical expression of the
owners' concern for slow food and food miles. There are
beehives too; herbs and vegetables are grown in the
pub's own polytunnel and raised beds, whilst bread
comes from a local craft baker. Indoors, Edwardian
furniture and blackboard menus set the scene for
meals that are prepared daily in small quantities,
allowing regular changes to the bill of fare. Start,
perhaps, with home-grown salad leaves, nasturtium
flowers and Cornish crab, before moving on to main
course options like roast guinea fowl with Puy lentils,
roast shallots and morel mushrooms; and Cornish
skate with capers, flat leaf parsley and sautéed greens.
Leave space for dessert; flourless dark chocolate cake
with espresso ice cream is a typical choice.

**Open** 12-3.30 6-11 Closed: Sun eve **Bar Meals** Av main
course £14 **Restaurant** L served all wk 12-2.30 booking
required D served Mon-Sat 6-9.30 booking required
Fixed menu price fr £15 Av 3 course à la carte fr £22
⊕ FREE HOUSE ◖ Wadworth 6X, West Berks Brewery,
Good Old Boy. ℗ 11 **Facilities** Children's portions Dogs
allowed Garden Parking

### BEAUWORTH
Map 5 SU52

### The Milburys

**SO24 0PB** ☎ 01962 771248 ▤ 01962 7771910
e-mail: info@themilburys.co.uk
**dir:** A272 towards Petersfield, after 6m turn right for
Beauworth

A rustic hill-top pub dating from the 17th century and
named after the Bronze Age barrow nearby. It is noted for
its massive, 250-year-old treadmill that used to draw
water from the 300ft well in the bar, and for the far-
reaching views across Hampshire that can be savoured
from the lofty garden. Inside you will find great real ales

Save on Hotels. Book at **theAA.com/hotel**

HAMPSHIRE 215 ENGLAND

with a guest one changing weekly and traditional pub food. There's a skittle alley and rallies and club meetings are held here.

**Open** all wk **Bar Meals** L served all wk 12-2.30 D served all wk 6-9.30 Av main course £8 **Restaurant** L served all wk 12-2.30 D served all wk 6-9.30 Fixed menu price fr £8.95 ⊕ FREE HOUSE ◀ Theakstons Old Peculier, Triple fff Altons Pride, Deuchars, Ale of Wight, Summer Lightning, Guest ale. **Facilities** Dogs allowed Garden Parking

## BENTLEY
Map 5 SU74

# The Bull Inn

**GU10 5JH ☎ 01420 22156**
**dir:** *2m from Farnham on A31 towards Winchester*

A 15th-century beamed coaching inn, under new ownership since early 2010, with open log fires, two separate bars and a restaurant. Regular pub food is complemented by beef bourguignon with creamy mash; braised, curried shank of lamb with rice; saltimbocca cod fillet with chargrilled vegetables; and wild mushroom risotto with truffle oil. Specials boards change daily and all desserts are home made, apart from the locally sourced ice cream. Beers include Alton's Pride and Moondance.

**Open** all day all wk 11-11 (Sun 12-10.30) **Bar Meals** L served Mon-Sat 12-2.30, Sun 12-8.30 D served Mon-Sat 6.30-9.30, Sun 12-8.30 Av main course £9.95 ⊕ ENTERPRISE INNS ◀ Courage Best, Westcott Bitter, Moondance, Alton's Pride ♂ Thatchers Pear. **Facilities** Children's portions Dogs allowed Garden Parking

## BENTWORTH
Map 5 SU64

### PICK OF THE PUBS

# The Sun Inn ♥

*See Pick of the Pubs on page 217*

## BOLDRE
Map 5 SZ39

# The Hobler Inn ♥

**Southampton Rd, Battramsley SO41 8PT**
**☎ 01590 623944**
**e-mail:** hedi@alcatraz.co.uk
**dir:** *2m from Brockenhurst, towards Lymington on main road*

On the main road between Brockenhurst and Lymington, with a large grassed area and trestle tables ideal for

families visiting the New Forest. It's more London wine bar than local, but still serves a well-kept pint of Ringwood. Hot lunchtime snacks like Welsh rarebit or Boston baked beans on toast are good value. Mains include a variation on the classic shepherd's pie but with added Nepalese spices.

**Open** all wk ◀ Ringwood, Ringwood Best, Timothy Taylor. ♥ 10 **Facilities** Garden Parking

### PICK OF THE PUBS

# The Red Lion ♥

**Rope Hill SO41 8NE**
**☎ 01590 673177** 🖷 **01590 674036**
**dir:** *1m from Lymington off A337. From M27 junct 1 through Lyndhurst & Brockenhurst towards Lymington, follow signs for Boldre*

A quintessential New Forest pub on the crossroads in the centre of the village. Consistent with 15th-century origins, its rambling interior contains beamed rooms, log fires and authentic rural memorabilia; outdoors are gardens and heated patios. Traditional, home-made meals incorporate the best local, seasonal produce. For instance, with the sea being so close, the daily specials feature fresh fish and shellfish, all Marine Security Council approved, while the New Forest's sustainable deer management policy ensures a supply of venison in season. More specifically, the menu lists steak and Ringwood Ale pie; free range chicken breast with bacon, barbecue sauce and Cheddar cheese; half a roasted duck in bitter cherry sauce; and filo pastry parcel of spinach and feta. Home-made puddings are all displayed on a board (monthly Pie and Pudding evenings are good value). In the summer, cook your own meat, fish, seafood or game on a patio 'hot table'.

**Open** all wk 11-3 5.30-11 (Winter Sun noon-6 10.30, Summer Sat 11-11 Sun noon-10.30) **Bar Meals** L served Mon-Sat 12-2.30, Sun 12-3.30 (Summer Sat 12-9.30, Sun 12-9) D served Mon-Sat 6-9.30, Sun 6-9 (Summer Sat 12-9.30, Sun 12-9) Av main course £10 **Restaurant** L served Mon-Sat 12-2.30, Sun 12-3.30 (Summer Sat 12-9.30, Sun 12-9) D served Mon-Sat 6-9.30, Sun 6-9 (Summer Sat 12-9.30, Sun 12-9) ⊕ FREE HOUSE ◀ Ringwood Best, Ringwood Fortyniner, Marstons Pedigree, Guinness, guest ales ♂ Thatchers Gold. ♥ 17 **Facilities** Children's portions Dogs allowed Garden Parking

*See advert under Lymington*

## BRAMDEAN
Map 5 SU62

# The Fox Inn

**SO24 0LP ☎ 01962 771363**
**e-mail:** thefoxinn@bramdean.net
**dir:** *A272 between Winchester & Petersfield*

The crest fixed to the exterior of this 400-year-old pub commemorates the day when the Prince of Wales (later King George IV) stopped by for refreshments. Situated in the beautiful Meon Valley surrounded by copper beech trees, The Fox serves locally sourced food including a good blackboard selection of fresh fish dishes - perhaps supreme of halibut with lime and chilli butter. Other typical choices include pork fillet with Stilton and brandy sauce.

**Open** 11-3 6.30-11 Closed: Sun eve ◀ IPA Smooth, Morlands Original. **Facilities** Dogs allowed Garden Parking

## BRANSGORE
Map 5 SZ19

### PICK OF THE PUBS

# The Three Tuns Country Inn ⊛⊛ ♥

*See Pick of the Pubs on page 218*

## BUCKLERS HARD
Map 5 SU40

### PICK OF THE PUBS

# The Master Builders House Hotel ★★★ HL ⊛ ♥

**SO42 7XB ☎ 01590 616253** 🖷 **01590 616297**
**e-mail:** enquiries@themasterbuilders.co.uk
**dir:** *From M27 junct 2 follow signs to Beaulieu. Left onto B3056. Left to Bucklers Hard. Hotel 2m on left*

Previously home to master shipwright Henry Adams, this idyllic 18th-century inn is situated on the banks of the River Beaulieu, in the historic village of Bucklers Hard. The New Forest National Park, Lord Montagu's Beaulieu Palace and the National Motor Museum are all on the doorstep, with plentiful ducks and boats to see on picturesque riverside walks. Sit next to the roaring winter fires while supping a pint of Ringwood, or enjoy a glass of Stowford Press cider with one of the summer barbecues which take place every weekend after Easter. A simple wholesome menu has fish choices such as rock oysters; Lymington dressed crab; or a bucket of Atlantic prawns. Meats include chipolatas and steaks; and vegetarian options may embrace New Forest wild mushrooms on toast. Finish with a plate of local cheeses with water biscuits and grapes, or famous New Forest ice creams sold by the scoop.

*continued on page 216*

**BUCKLERS HARD** *continued*

**Open** all day all wk 11-11 (Sun 11-10.30) **Bar Meals** L served Mon-Fri 12-2.30, Sat-Sun 12-3 D served all wk 6-9.30 Av main course £9 food served all day **Restaurant** L served Mon-Fri 12-2.30, Sat-Sun 12-3 booking required D served all wk 7-9.30 booking required ⊕ HILLBROOKE HOTELS ◄ Ringwood Best, Ringwood Fortyniner, Marston's Pedigree ⬧ Stowford Press. ♀ 11 **Facilities** Children's menu Dogs allowed Garden Parking **Rooms** 25

| BURGHCLERE | Map 5 SU46 |

## PICK OF THE PUBS

**Carnarvon Arms** ♀

*See Pick of the Pubs on page 219*

| BURLEY | Map 5 SU20 |

## The Burley Inn ♀

**BH24 4AB ☎ 01425 403448**
e-mail: info@theburleyinn.co.uk
dir: *4m SE of of Ringwood*

No more is "The doctor will see you now" heard in the bar and dining areas of this fine Edwardian pub, once the GP's surgery. Food is served all day, with a menu offering freshly cut sandwiches, hot snacks, freshly baked pies, grills and vegetarian dishes. Take a glass of Ringwood Best Bitter or locally produced fruit wine out to the new patio and decking area and watch the ponies, donkeys and cattle wandering freely through the village.

**Open** all day all wk **Bar Meals** L served all wk 12-10 D served all wk 12-10 Av main course £7 food served all day **Restaurant** L served all wk 12-10 D served all wk 12-10 food served all day ⊕ FREE HOUSE ◄ Ringwood Best, Ringwood Old Thumper, Gales HSB, Youngs Special ⬧ Thatchers Old Rascal. ♀ 10 **Facilities** Children's menu Dogs allowed Garden Parking

| CADNAM | Map 5 SU31 |

## Sir John Barleycorn ♀

**Old Romsey Rd SO40 2NP ☎ 023 8081 2236**
e-mail: hedi@alcatraz.co.uk
dir: *From Southampton M27 junct 1 into Cadnam*

Reputedly the oldest inn in the New Forest, this friendly establishment is formed from three 12th-century cottages, one of which was once home to the charcoal burner who discovered the body of King William Rufus. A thorough menu covers all the options from quick snacks and sandwiches to toad-in-the-hole; chicken, leek and bacon pie; and Thai chicken curry. The name derives from a folksong celebrating the transformation of barley to beer.

**Open** all day all wk 9am-11pm (Sat-Sun 11-11) ◄ Ringwood, Ringwood Fortyniner ⬧ Stowford Press. ♀ 10 **Facilities** Garden Parking

| CHALTON | Map 5 SU71 |

## PICK OF THE PUBS

## The Red Lion ♀

**PO8 0BG ☎ 023 9259 2246** 🖷 **023 9259 6915**
e-mail: redlionchalton@fullers.co.uk
dir: *Just off A3 between Horndean & Petersfield. Follow signs for Chalton*

Believed to be Hampshire's oldest pub, The Red Lion was built in 1147 as a workshop and residence for the craftsmen working on St Michael's church across the road. By 1460 it had become a hostel for church dignitaries, and was later extended to accommodate coachmen on their regular journey from London to Portsmouth. Constructed from wood, white daub and thatch, the ancient building blends effortlessly into the hills and trees of the South Downs, and original features inside include an inglenook fireplace. There are spectacular views from the large garden and modern dining room. The pub has a good reputation locally for the quality of its food. You can choose from the daily changing menu of freshly cooked dishes, which relies heavily on locally sourced produce, or the popular snack menu of traditional pub fare, all washed down with a pint of real ale or cider.

**Open** all day all wk 11.30-11 (Sun 12-10.30) **Bar Meals** food served all day **Restaurant** food served all day ⊕ FULLER, SMITH & TURNER PLC ◄ Fuller's, HSB, London Pride, Discovery, ESB, seasonal ales ⬧ Kopparberg. ♀ 20 **Facilities** Family room Dogs allowed Garden Parking

| CHARTER ALLEY | Map 5 SU55 |

## The White Hart Inn

**White Hart Ln RG26 5QA**
**☎ 01256 850048** 🖷 **01256 850524**
e-mail: enquiries@whitehartcharteralley.com
dir: *From M3 junct 6 take A339 towards Newbury. Turn right to Ramsdell. Right at church, then 1st left into White Hart Lane*

On the outskirts of the village overlooking open farmland and woods, this pub draws everyone from cyclists and walkers to real ale enthusiasts. Dating from 1818, it originally refreshed local woodsmen and coach drivers visiting the farrier next door. Today's more modern menu is likely to include pheasant and ham hock terrine; winter lamb cassoulet; Mediterranean sea bass fillet; and three fruit marmalade sponge. Look to the blackboard for specials and fish dishes.

**Open** all wk noon-2.30 7-11 (Sun noon-10.30) Closed: 25-26 Dec, 1 Jan **Bar Meals** L served all wk 12-2 D served Tue-Sat 7-9 Av main course £12.50 **Restaurant** L served Tue-Sun 12-2 booking required D served Tue-Sat 7-9 booking required Av 3 course à la carte fr £24 ⊕ FREE HOUSE ◄ Palmers IPA, Triple fff Alton Pride, Stonehenge Great Bustard, Loddon Ferryman's Gold, Bowmans Swift One. **Facilities** Children's menu Children's portions Family room Dogs allowed Garden Parking

| CHAWTON | Map 5 SU73 |

## The Greyfriar

**Winchester Rd GU34 1SB**
**☎ 01420 83841** 🖷 **01420 83841**
e-mail: peter@thegreyfriar.co.uk
dir: *Just off A31 near Alton. Access to Chawton via A31/A32 junct. Follow Jane Austen's House signs*

A terrace of 16th-century cottages opposite Jane Austen's house, which was divided into a beer shop and grocery in the 1860s. Proper pub status followed with a licence granted to the Chawton Arms; for reasons unknown it became The Greyfriar in 1894. Today it's a family-run and friendly place to enjoy Fuller's beers and quality food from a varied and imaginative menu. Steaks are sourced from Ballindalloch Castle, home of the oldest Aberdeen Angus herd in the world. Handouts of local walks are available from the pub.

**Open** all day all wk noon-11 (Sun noon-10.30) **Bar Meals** L served Mon-Sat 12-2.30, Sun 12-3 D served Mon-Sat 7-9.30, Sun 6.30-8 Av main course £12 ⊕ FULLERS ◄ Fuller's London Pride, ESB, Seasonal ales. **Facilities** Children's menu Children's portions Play area Dogs allowed Garden Parking

| CHERITON | Map 5 SU52 |

## PICK OF THE PUBS

## The Flower Pots Inn

**SO24 0QQ ☎ 01962 771318**
dir: *A272 towards Petersfield, left onto B3046, pub 0.75m on right*

In the 1840s the head gardener of nearby Avington Park built himself a farmhouse; today it's this popular village pub, known almost universally as the Pots. There are two bars: one rustic and pine-furnished, with a glass-covered well, the other with a sofa; both have open fires when it's cold. Local beer drinkers know the pub well for its award-winning Pots Ale and Goodens Gold, brewed across the car park. Simple home-made food includes toasted sandwiches, jacket potatoes and different hotpots - chilli con carne, spicy mixed bean, and lamb and apricot - served with garlic bread, basmati rice or jacket potato. Ploughman's feature various cheeses, ham or beef, and baps come filled with rib-eye steak and onions; prawns; bacon and mushroom; or coronation chicken. A large, safe garden, with a covered patio, allows children to let off steam (under 12s are not allowed in the bar).

**Open** all wk noon-2.30 6-11 (Sun noon-3 7-10.30) **Bar Meals** L served all wk 12-2 D served Mon-Sat 7-9 Av main course £6.50 ⊕ FREE HOUSE ◄ Flower Pots Bitter, Goodens Gold ⬧ Westons Old Rosie. **Facilities** Children's portions Dogs allowed Garden Parking **Notes** ⊜

# PICK OF THE PUBS

## The Sun Inn ♀

**BENTWORTH**       Map 5 SU64

**Sun Hill GU34 5JT ☎ 01420 562338**
dir: *Telephone for directions*

Hidden down a tiny lane on the village edge, this pretty flower-decked and unspoilt rural pub dates from the 17th century when it was a pair of traditional cottages. Little has changed inside over the years, where brick and board floors are laid with a rustic mix of scrubbed pine tables, benches and settles, original beams are hung with sparkling horse brasses, walls are adorned with prints and plates, and tasteful cosmetic touches – magazines to peruse, fresh flowers, flickering candlelight – enhance the overall unblemished atmosphere. Crackling log fires warm the three inter-linked rooms and you can expect a friendly, relaxed atmosphere throughout.

As well as The Sun's charm, real ale and an extensive selection of hearty home-cooked dishes (listed on the changing chalkboard menu) are prime reasons for visiting. Dishes range from ploughman's lunches, home-made soup and sandwiches (chicken and avocado), to beef stew and dumplings, beer-battered cod, calves' liver and bacon, pork and Stilton pie, and half-shoulder of lamb with redcurrant and mint gravy. Game in season includes venison, cooked in Guinness with pickled walnuts, and pheasant. For pudding, tuck into apple and raspberry crumble, white chocolate and strawberry cheesecake, or a warm chocolate brownie.

A thriving free house, the bar groans with hand-pumps, dispensing Ringwood Best and Old Thumper, both from Hampshire breweries, plus Fuller's London Pride and regular guest beers.

There is much to see and do in the area: Gilbert White's House and the Oates Museum in Selborne are not far away, and neither are Jane Austen's House at Chawton, nor the Watercress Line at Alresford, where you can enjoy a 10-mile steam train ride through glorious Hampshire countryside to Alton.

**Open** all wk 12-3 6-11 (Sun 12-10.30) **Bar Meals** L served 12-2 D served 7-9.30 Av main course £10.95 ⊕ FREE HOUSE ◀ AMD Wells Resolute, Timothy Taylor Landlord, Ringwood Best & Old Thumper, Brakspear Bitter, Fuller's London Pride, Hogs Back TEA. ♀ 12 **Facilities** Children's menu Family room Dogs allowed Garden Parking

# PICK OF THE PUBS

## The Three Tuns Country Inn

**BRANSGORE**  Map 5 SZ19

**Ringwood Rd BH23 8JH**
☎ **01425 672232**
**e-mail:** threetunsinn@btconnect.com
**dir:** *1.5m from A35 Walkford junct. 3m from Christchurch & 1m from Hinton Admiral railway station*

Festooned with a riot of flowers and with a glorious south-facing garden, this picture-perfect 17th-century thatched pub is located in the heart of the New Forest National Park. One of the few pubs in the Forest remaining under thatch, it is worth noting following a walk or cycle ride for its relaxing buzzy vibe and award-winning food.

The inn offers five distinct public areas: a comfortable Lounge Bar, with no music, TV screens or games, and in winter a log fire; an oak-beamed Snug Bar, again with a log fire, and biscuits and water for dogs; a large terrace with

its water feature; a vast garden, surrounded by fields, trees and ponies, and not a bouncy castle in sight, but space galore (on sunny days, out comes the barbecue); and finally, the restaurant. Here you'll find how fresh local produce and seasonings from around the world are fused into classic dishes and seasonal specials, recognised for their quality by two AA Rosettes.

The eclectic menus offers something for everyone, whether you are popping in for a pint of Exmoor Gold or Ringwood Best and a light bar snack, or you plan to linger over three courses, and both menus are served throughout the pub. Expect to find Wiltshire ham and mustard sandwiches, bangers and mash, calves' liver and bacon and deep-fried cod, alongside venison suet pudding, braised Dorset lamb with Puy lentils and New Forest wild mushrooms, and sea bass with fricassée of squid, olives, tomatoes and artichokes. For pudding, try the vanilla, chocolate and almond Pavlova, the tonka bean crème brûlée with cinnamon fig, or a plate of British and French artisan and farmhouse cheeses with home-made pickles.

**Open** all day all wk 11.30-11 (Sun 12-10.30) **Bar Meals** L served Mon-Fri 12-2.15, Sat-Sun 12-9.15 booking required D served Mon-Fri 6.30-9.15, Sat-Sun 12-9.15 booking required Av main course £12 **Restaurant** L served Mon-Fri 12-2.15, Sat-Sun 12-9.15 booking required D served Mon-Fri 6.30-9.15, Sat-Sun 12-9.15 booking required Av 3 course à la carte fr £20 ⊕ ENTERPRISE INNS ◀ St Austell Tribute, Ringwood Best Bitter, Fortyniner, Exmoor Gold, Timothy Taylor ♂ Thatchers Gold, New Forest Traditional Farmhouse. ♀ 9
**Facilities** Children's menu Dogs allowed Garden Parking

# PICK OF THE PUBS

## Carnarvon Arms ♀

**BURGHCLERE**      Map 5 SU46

**Winchester Rd RG20 9LE**
☎ **01635 278222** 📄 **01635 278444**
**e-mail:** info@carnarvonarms.com
**web:** www.carnarvonarms.com
**dir:** *M4 junct 13, A34 S to Winchester.*
*Exit A34 at Tothill Services, follow*
*Highclere Castle signs. Pub on right*

Outside it's a Grade II listed coaching inn; inside a great contemporary look ticks all the boxes, and there's a quiet, grassy beer garden in which to relax. The Carnarvon Arms was a stop-off for visitors to nearby Highclere Castle, still the family seat of the Earls of Carnarvon. It was the 5th Earl who famously opened Tutankhamun's tomb in 1922, dying the following year and triggering suggestions of a Mummy's Curse. He is buried on nearby Beacon Hill, an ancient hill fort – quite appropriate for an archaeologist.

Today's traveller will find the large bar is all open-plan, airy and fresh, tastefully appointed with leather sofas and chairs blending seamlessly with more traditional seating, modern match-boarding and screens dividing up the space. Here, a bar menu of inviting sandwiches and traditional bites like beer battered fish and chips or home-made sausages with creamed potato in a broccoli and shallot sauce will take the edge off an appetite.

In the stunning dining room, with its high vaulted ceiling, the Egyptian-inspired wall carvings pay homage to those remarkable excavations in the Valley of the Kings. Modern British food, with a strong emphasis on seasonal ingredients at sensible prices, is head chef Justin Brown's objective; his lunch and carte menus are fulsome and wholesome. Kick in with a celeriac and thyme soup with white truffle oil or pan-roasted Cornish scallops with butternut squash. Clean the palate with a draught from the extensive wine list before progressing to the main event, perhaps favouring double-cooked shoulder of lamb with a roast garlic mash, baby carrots and red wine jus; or a red onion marmalade and Cerney goat's cheese filo tart with a mixed leaf salad or fish broth with cod, mullet, sole and mackerel.

The freshest local produce will offer tempting alternatives; venison pie is an award-winning special. And should there be a crevice still unsated, then some great puddings include caramel vanilla choux bun or apple and ginger tart Tatin with vanilla bean ice-cream. Vegetarian and set-price lunch menus are also available. There is an excellent menu for children called 'Proper food for small people'.

**Open** all day all wk **Bar Meals** L served all wk 12-2.30 D served all wk 6.30-9 **Restaurant** L served all wk 12-2.30 D served all wk 6.30-9.30 🍺 Guinness, guest ales. ♀ 15 **Facilities** Children's menu Dogs allowed Garden Parking

## CHILWORTH — Map 5 SU41

### Chilworth Arms ♀

**Chilworth Rd SO16 7JZ ☎ 023 8076 6247**
**dir:** *3m N of Southampton on A27 (Romsey road)*

Formerly known as the Clump Inn, this gastro-pub is warmed by log fires and furnished with leather sofas. There's a great mix of freshly prepared dishes, from simple pizzas to well-aged steaks, fresh fish and traditional pub classics, many with a hint of Italian about them. Regularly changing real ales vie for popularity with continental beers, fine wines and fresh juices. Eat in the spacious dining area, or out on the covered patio.

**Open** all day all wk 11-10.30 (Sun noon-8.30) ◀ Timothy Taylor Landlord. ♀ 15 **Facilities** Garden Parking

## CRAWLEY — Map 5 SU43

### The Fox and Hounds ♀

**SO21 2PR ☎ 01962 776006 ▤ 01962 776006**
**e-mail:** liamlewisairey@aol.com
**dir:** *A34 onto A272 then 1st right into Crawley*

Just north west of Winchester, at the heart of a peaceful Hampshire village, this mock Tudor traditional inn enjoys a burgeoning reputation for simple well-cooked food. Typical dishes are roast beetroot salad with goat's cheese; smokey chicken with bacon, leek and cream sauce; home-made beef lasagne; and sticky toffee pudding. Restored to former glories, the interior features beamed rooms warmed by log fires that create a welcoming, lived-in atmosphere; perfect for dining or just supping a pint of Bombardier.

**Open** all wk 11-3 6-mdnt **Bar Meals** L served all wk 12-2 booking required **Restaurant** L served all wk 12-2 booking required D served all wk 6.30-9.30 booking required ⊕ ENTERPRISE INNS ◀ Wadworth 6X, Ringwood Best, Ringwood Fortyniner, Bombardier. ♀ 36 **Facilities** Play area Garden Parking

## CRONDALL — Map 5 SU74

### PICK OF THE PUBS

### The Hampshire Arms ♀

**Pankridge St GU10 5QU ☎ 01252 850418**
**e-mail:** gary@thehampshirearms.co.uk
**dir:** *From M3 junct 5 take A287 S towards Farnham. Follow signs to Crondall on right*

The Hampshire Arms bar is light and elegant, as are the two main dining areas and intimate alcoves. Throughout the public rooms open fires, exposed beams and candlelight combine to create a delightfully welcoming atmosphere. The building dates from the 18th century and began as two cottages, but over the years it has also been a courthouse, a post office and a bakery. Outside there is a large landscaped garden with a patio area. New licensee, award winning chef Gary Webster, offers country pub classics along with fine dining options. For a leisurely lunch you could try chef's special pie of the day, home-made beefburger,

beer-battered cod, or one of the vegetarian options. For something more imaginative, there is pan-fried breast of duck with lime and chillies; Chinese-spiced slow-roasted belly of pork with sausage and sauerkraut; or chargrilled sea bass with pea and crayfish risotto.

**Open** all day all wk Mon-Thu 11am-11pm (Fri-Sat 11am-mdnt Sun 11am-10.30pm) **Meals** L served Mon-Fri 12-2.30, Sat 12-9.30, Sun 12-7.30 D served Mon-Fri 6-9.30 ⊕ GREENE KING ◀ Greene King IPA, Olde Trip, guest ales. ♀ 10 **Facilities** Dogs allowed Garden Parking

## CROOKHAM VILLAGE — Map 5 SU75

### The Exchequer ♀ NEW

**Crondall Rd GU51 5SU ☎ 01252 615336**
**e-mail:** inbox@theexchequer.co.uk
**dir:** *M3 junct 5, A287 towards Farnham for 5m. Left to Crookham Village*

Re-launched under new owners at the end of 2009, this whitewashed free house is just a stone's throw from the A287 in the beautiful setting of Crookham Village. Capitalising on the wealth of local small breweries, the Exchequer aims to become one of southern England's top real ale houses. And there's something for everyone on the richly varied menu – butternut squash curry; slow-cooked belly pork with sage mash, sautéed apple and maple syrup; and smoked haddock with mustard mash are typical choices.

**Open** all wk Mon-Fri 12-3 6-11 (Sat-Sun noon-11) **Bar Meals** L served Mon-Fri 12-2, Sat-Sun all day D served Mon-Fri 6.30-9, Sat-Sun all day Av main course £9.50 **Restaurant** L served Mon-Fri 12-2, Sat-Sun all day D served Mon-Fri 6.30-9, Sat-Sun all day booking required Fixed menu price fr £13.50 Av 3 course à la carte fr £25 ⊕ FREE HOUSE ◀ Exchequer Ale, Hogs Back TEA, Otter Ale Ŏ Aspalls. ♀ 15 **Facilities** Children's menu Children's portions Dogs allowed Garden Parking

## DOWNTON — Map 5 SZ29

### The Royal Oak ♀

**Christchurch Rd SO41 0LA ☎ 01590 642297**
**e-mail:** royal.oak.downtown@gmail.com
**dir:** *On A337 between Lymington & Christchurch*

Two miles south of the New Forest and just one mile from the beach at Lymington, this renovated pub is now under new ownership. Enjoy a glass of Ringwood Best Bitter and snack on a traditional ploughman's platter or daytime sandwiches such as chicken and avocado, classic BLT or creamed cheese, cucumber and smoked salmon. A comprehensive list of main meals includes steak and ale pie; pork, cider and apple casserole; butternut squash risotto; and beer battered haddock and chips.

**Open** all day all wk 11-11.30 **Bar Meals** L served Mon-Fri 12-2.30, Sat-Sun all day D served Mon-Fri 6-9.30, Sat-Sun all day Av main course £9.95 **Restaurant** L served Mon-Fri 12-2.30, Sat-Sun all day booking required D served Mon-Fri 6-9.30, Sat-Sun all day booking required Fixed menu price fr £8.95 Av 3 course à la carte fr £23 ⊕ ENTERPRISE INNS ◀ Ringwood Best Bitter, Ringwood Fortyniner Ŏ Thatchers Gold. ♀ 9 **Facilities** Children's menu Children's portions Dogs allowed Garden Parking

## DROXFORD — Map 5 SU61

### PICK OF THE PUBS

### The Bakers Arms ◉

**High St SO32 3PA ☎ 01489 877533**
**e-mail:** enquiries@thebakersarmsdroxford.com
**dir:** *10m E of Winchester on A32 between Fareham & Alton. 7m SW of Petersfield. 10m inland from Portsmouth*

This unpretentious, white-painted pub and restaurant could teach many pubs that never feature in this guide a thing or two. It has been opened up inside but still oozes country charm and character, the staff are smiley, and the locals clearly love it. Over the big log fire a blackboard menu lists the simple, well cooked and locally sourced food, while in the bar customers make short work of its barrels of Swift One from the village's own Bowman Brewery. They can snack too, on home-made Cornish pasties, pickled eggs and onions, and hot filled baguettes. But the kitchen cooks to AA Rosette standard, so make the most of your visit if you're just passing through: lamb's kidneys fried with mustard and onions on toast; fillet of gurnard with brown shrimps, preserved lemon and crushed potatoes; and treacle tart with custard will make you wish every village had a pub like this.

**Open** 11.45-3 6-11 (Sun 12-3) Closed: Sun eve & Mon **Bar Meals** L served Tue-Sun 12-2 booking required D served Tue-Sun 7-9 booking required Av main course £10 **Restaurant** L served Tue-Sun 12-2 booking required D served Tue-Sun 7-9 booking required Fixed menu price fr £13 Av 3 course à la carte fr £23.50 ⊕ FREE HOUSE ◀ Bowman Swift One, Bowman Wallops Wood Ŏ Stowford Press. **Facilities** Children's portions Dogs allowed Garden Parking

## DUMMER — Map 5 SU54

### The Queen Inn

**Down St RG25 2AD ☎ 01256 397367 ▤ 01256 397601**
**e-mail:** richardmoore49@btinternet.com
**dir:** *M3 junct 7, follow Dummer signs*

You can dine by candlelight from the restaurant menu at this 16th-century village pub with its low beams and huge open log fire. Alternatively you'll find lunchtime savouries like Welsh or Scottish rarebits alongside sandwiches and jackets. The bar menu offers everything from starters and healthy options to flame grills, house favourites, and specials like chargrilled half chicken piri

piri and beef bourguignon. Food can be washed down with one of the guest ales.

**Open** all wk 11-3 6-11 (Sun 12-3 7-10.30) **Bar Meals** L served all wk 12-2.30 D served all wk 6.30-9.30 Av main course £12.50 **Restaurant** L served all wk 12-2.30 booking required D served all wk 6.30-9.30 booking required Fixed menu price fr £12.50 ⊕ ENTERPRISE INNS ◀ Courage Best, Fuller's London Pride, Old Speckled Hen, guest ales. **Facilities** Children's menu Children's portions Garden Parking

### EAST END                                    Map 5 SZ39

## PICK OF THE PUBS

### The East End Arms

**Main Rd SO41 5SY**
☎ **01590 626223** 🖷 **01590 626223**
**e-mail:** manager@eastendarms.co.uk
**dir:** *From Lymington towards Beaulieu (past Isle of Wight ferry), 3m to East End*

Close to Beaulieu and historic Bucklers Hard, this New Forest inn, owned by John Illsley, the bass player of Dire Straits, combines the authenticity of a proper local with a good reputation as a gastro-pub. Ringwood ales are drawn straight from the wood in the Foresters Bar, where stone floors and open fires create a homely, traditional feel. The atmospheric lounge bar, with its sofas and winter fires, is a comfortable setting for a meal from the daily-changing brasserie-style menu. Locally sourced fish/seafood make a strong showing in dishes such as lightly spiced Cajun mullet fillet with hazelnut coleslaw, straw potatoes, fried aubergine parcels in breadcrumbs filled with feta and sun-blushed tomatoes. For a lighter lunch you may find a freshly baked ciabatta filled with beef and horseradish, or mozzarella and tomato, and served with hand-cooked crisps. The pub is well worth the drive down country lanes, or a short diversion from the nearby Solent Way long distance footpath.

**Open** all wk **Restaurant** L served all wk 12-2.30 booking required D served Mon-Sat 7-9.30 booking required ⊕ FREE HOUSE ◀ Ringwood Best, Ringwood Fortyniner, Andwell Brewery, Jennings, Cottage Brewing ♂ Thatchers, Katy Cider. **Facilities** Children's portions Dogs allowed Garden Parking

### EAST MEON                                   Map 5 SU62

## Ye Olde George Inn 🍷

**Church St GU32 1NH** ☎ **01730 823481**
**e-mail:** yeoldegeorge@live.co.uk
**dir:** *S of A272 (Winchester/Petersfield). 1.5m from Petersfield turn left opposite church*

This delightful 15th-century coaching inn, with the River Meon running alongside, is located close to a magnificent Norman church. If you want heavy beams, inglenook fireplaces and wooden floors, look no further – they're all here, the ideal setting for a choice of real ales, freshly prepared bar snacks and monthly changing menus. Tuck into fig and shallot tarte Tatin; local pork sausages in

Parma ham; braised crispy Gressingham duck; or smoked haddock, salmon and king prawn fish pie, all made using local seasonal produce. Children and dogs always welcome.

**Open** all wk Mon-Sat 11-3 6-11 (Sun 11-10) Closed: 25 Dec **Bar Meals** L served Mon-Sat 12-2.30, Sun 12-3 D served Mon-Sat 6.30-9.30, Sun 6.30-9 food served all day **Restaurant** L served Mon-Sat 12-2.30, Sun 12-3 D served Mon-Sat 6.30-9.30, Sun 6.30-9 food served all day ⊕ HALL & WOODHOUSE ◀ Badger Best, Hopping Hare, King & Barnes Sussex. 🍷 9 **Facilities** Children's menu Children's portions Dogs allowed Garden Parking

### EASTON                                      Map 5 SU53

## PICK OF THE PUBS

### The Chestnut Horse 🍷

**SO21 1EG** ☎ **01962 779257** 🖷 **01962 779037**
**e-mail:** info@thechestnuthorse.com
**dir:** *From M3 junct 9 take A33 towards Basingstoke, then B3047. Take 2nd right, then 1st left*

It's worth packing your walking boots when you visit this 16th-century pub in the pretty village of Easton in the Itchen Valley. There are a number of enjoyable walks directly from the door of this charming inn which is packed with character. Old tankards hang from the low-beamed ceilings in the two bar areas, where a large open fire is the central focus through the winter months. Award-winning English beers can be enjoyed in the bar or the garden. A good-value set price menu is offered Monday to Saturday lunchtime (12-2pm) or Monday to Friday early evening (6-7.30pm). This might include rib-eye steak and salad, pork and leek sausage with mash and onion gravy, or roasted vegetable penne pasta. Typical main menu dishes are slow roasted duck with Bramley apple mash and vegetable filo parcel, or lamb medallions with boulangère potatoes, French beans, bacon and red wine jus. A vegetarian alternative could be smoked cheese glazed ratatouille crêpes with dressed leaves.

**Open** all wk noon-3.30 5.30-11 (Sun eve closed winter) **Bar Meals** L served all wk 12-2.30 booking required D served Mon-Sat 6-9.30 booking required Av main course £12 **Restaurant** L served all wk 12-2 booking required D served Mon-Sat 6-9.30 booking required Fixed menu price fr £12 Av 3 course à la carte fr £27 ⊕ HALL & WOODHOUSE ◀ Chestnut Horse Special, Badger First Gold, Tanglefoot ♂ Stowford Press. **Facilities** Children's portions Dogs allowed Garden Parking

### The Cricketers Inn 🍷

**SO21 1EJ** ☎ **01962 779353** 🖷 **01962 779010**
**e-mail:** cricketersinn@btconnect.com
**dir:** *M3 junct 9, A33 towards Basingstoke, right at Kingsworthy onto B3047. In 0.75m turn right. Pub signed*

Standing on a corner in the heart of a popular village, this 1904 pub is a real local, with a single L-shaped bar and cricketing memorabilia on the walls. Look out for crusty doorstep sandwiches and open toasties, in

addition to filled Yorkshires and specials of ribs, sweet and sour chicken and cottage pie.

**Open** all wk ◀ Ringwood, guest ales. 🍷 8 **Facilities** Dogs allowed Garden Parking

### EAST TYTHERLEY                              Map 5 SU22

## PICK OF THE PUBS

### The Star Inn
### Tytherley ★★★★ INN ⑱ 🍷

**SO51 0LW** ☎ **01794 340225**
**e-mail:** info@starinn.co.uk
**dir:** *5m N of Romsey off A3057, left for Dunbridge on B3084. Left for Awbridge & Kents Oak. Through Lockerley then 1m*

The 16th-century Star Inn stands overlooking the village cricket green in the smallest village in the Test Valley. You'll find Hidden Brewery beers and other guest ales behind the bar, plus an extensive international wine list. Dine where you like, in the bar, at dark-wood tables in the main dining room, or outside on the patio in summer, where you can also play king-sized chess. Lunchtime brings a variety of platters (fish, Barkham Blue, or Winchester farmhouse cheese), sandwiches (perhaps smoked salmon, crème fraîche and dill, or Cumberland sausage with caramelised onion), and a good value two-course menu (stir-fried tiger prawns with chorizo and gremolata, and roast chicken supreme). The evening menu might offer crab soufflé with watercress and saffron cream, and braised belly pork with sage polenta and celeriac purée. There's a good choice at Sunday lunch, too, including traditional roasts. Children of well behaved parents are welcome.

**Open** 11-2.30 6-10 Closed: Sun eve & Mon (ex BH) **Bar Meals** L served Tue-Sun 12-2 booking required D served Tue-Fri 7-9 booking required **Restaurant** L served Tue-Sun 12-2 booking required D served Tue-Sat 7-9 booking required ⊕ FREE HOUSE ◀ Cottage Brewery, Andwell Brewery, guest ales ♂ Thatchers Gold. 🍷 8 **Facilities** Dogs allowed Garden Parking **Rooms** 3

### EMSWORTH                                    Map 5 SU70

## The Sussex Brewery 🍷

**36 Main Rd PO10 8AU**
☎ **01243 371533** 🖷 **01243 379684**
**e-mail:** info@sussexbrewery.com
**dir:** *On A259 (coast road), between Havant & Chichester*

The Sussex Brewery is set in the picturesque village of Emsworth, renowned for its annual food festival in September. This 17th-century pub upholds traditional values with its sawdust covered floors, real ales and open fires. The menu includes a large variety of sausages, from Cumberland and Lincolnshire to Cajun and Mexican (there's a good choice for vegetarians too). Other dishes include slow roasted belly of pork on pea mash with caramelised apple and cider sauce, or fillet steak stuffed with Stilton on a bed of truffle mash.

*continued on page 222*

**EMSWORTH** *continued*

**Open** all day all wk 7am-mdnt **Bar Meals** L served all wk 12-2.30 D served all wk 6.30-9.30 Av main course £9 **Restaurant** L served all wk 12-2.30 booking required D served all wk 6.30-9.30 booking required Fixed menu price fr £9 ⊕ YOUNG & CO BREWERY PLC ◀ Youngs Special, Youngs Ordinary, Waggle Dance, Bombardier Tribute Ŏ Stowford Press. ♀ 12 **Facilities** Children's portions Dogs allowed Garden Parking

---

### EVERSLEY
Map 5 SU76

## The Golden Pot ♀

**Reading Rd RG27 0NB ☎ 0118 973 2104**
**e-mail:** jcalder@golden-pot.co.uk
**web:** www.golden-pot.co.uk
**dir:** *Between Reading & Camberley on B3272 approx 0.25m from Eversley cricket ground*

Dating back to the 1700s, this well-established hostelry has recently converted to a free house. Expect three pumps rotating ales by Andwell Brewing Company, Loddon Brewery and Hogs Back among others. A warming fire connects the bar and restaurant, while the Snug and Vineyard are comfortable outside areas surrounded by colourful tubs and hanging baskets for summer relaxation. All food is home made, such as Welsh rarebit with smoked bacon; slow cooked duck breast with Chinese five spice; and pan-fried cod fillet with chorizo butter sauce; children are not only welcome but also specially catered for.

**Open** all wk 11.30-3 5.30-10.30 Closed: 25-26 & 31 Dec, 1 Jan, (Sun eve) **Bar Meals** L served all wk 12-2.45 booking required D served Mon-Sat 6-9 booking required **Restaurant** L served all wk 12-2.45 booking required D served Mon-Sat 6-9 booking required ⊕ FREE HOUSE ◀ Andwell Brewery, Loddon Brewery, West Berkshire, Hogs Back Brewery, Itchen Valley. ♀ 9 **Facilities** Children's menu Dogs allowed Garden Parking

---

### EXTON
Map 5 SU62

## The Shoe Inn ♀

**Shoe Ln SO32 3NT ☎ 01489 877526**
**e-mail:** theshoeexton@googlemail.com
**dir:** *Exton on A32 between Fareham & Alton*

In the heart of the Meon Valley, a popular village pub maintaining its appeal since Annabel Terry took it over. Food is key – local ingredients include those from its ever-expanding herb and organic vegetable garden, nourished by compost from the local stud farm. A typical

selection of dishes could include tempura soft-shell crab with fennel salad; and roast loin of pork with sage and onion stuffing. The bar offers well-kept Wadworth ales, ciders and over a dozen wines served by the glass. Enjoy the views of Old Winchester Hill from the garden on warmer days.

**Open** all wk 11-3 6-11 Closed: 25 Dec **Bar Meals** L served all wk 12-2.15 **Restaurant** L served all wk 12-2.15 D served all wk 6-9 ⊕ WADWORTH ◀ Wadworth 6X, IPA, Bishops Tipple Ŏ Stowford Press. ♀ 13 **Facilities** Children's menu Children's portions Dogs allowed Garden Parking

---

### FORDINGBRIDGE
Map 5 SU11

## The Augustus John

**116 Station Rd SP6 1DG ☎ 01425 652098**
**e-mail:** enquiries@augustusjohnfordingbridge.co.uk
**dir:** *12m S of Salisbury on A338 towards Ringwood*

A moving force in British art, Augustus John used to drink in this former station pub, where Lorraine Smallwood has been in command since 2009, having worked here for the previous thirteen years. Sheila, the chef, has been here just as long, cooking seared duck breast with zingy plum sauce; baked haddock with Mornay sauce; and fusilli Napolitano. With Ringwood real ales too, it's easy to see why locals and visitors enjoy coming here.

**Open** all wk Mon-Sat 11.30-3 6.30-11.30 (Sun noon-3 7-11.30) **Bar Meals** L served all wk 12-2.30 D served all wk 6.30-9 (booking advised Fri-Sun) Av main course £9.95 **Restaurant** L served all wk 12-2.30 D served Mon-Sat 6.30-9 (Sun 7-9) (booking advised Fri-Sun) ⊕ MARSTONS ◀ Ringwood Best, Fortyniner Ŏ Thatchers Gold. **Facilities** Children's portions Dogs allowed Garden Parking

---

### FRITHAM
Map 5 SU21

## The Royal Oak ♀

**SO43 7HJ ☎ 023 8081 2606 ▤ 023 8081 4066**
**e-mail:** royaloak-fritham@btopenworld.com
**dir:** *M27 junct 1, B3078 signed Fordingbridge. 2m, then left at x-rds signed Ocknell & Fritham. Then follow signs to Fritham*

An award-winning small traditional thatched pub and working farm dating from the 15th century, deep in the New Forest. Walkers, cyclists and horse-riders delight in the large garden overlooking woodland. Unaltered for 100 years and with no jukebox or fruit machine, the three small bars focus on serving a great selection of good real ales and draught ciders. Simple plates of food include quiches, sausages, pork pies and sausage rolls, all home made using the farm's pigs.

**Open** all wk all day wknds & Jul-Sep **Bar Meals** L served Mon-Fri 12-2.30, Sat-Sun 12-3 Av main course £7 ⊕ FREE HOUSE ◀ Ringwood Best & Fortyniner, Hop Back Summer Lightning, Palmers Dorset Gold, Bowman Ales Swift One Ŏ Aspall, Thatchers. ♀ 12 **Facilities** Dogs allowed Garden **Notes** ☺

---

### GOSPORT
Map 5 SZ69

## The Seahorse ♀

**Broadsands Dr PO12 2TJ ☎ 023 9251 2910**
**e-mail:** simonl29@aol.com
**dir:** *A32 onto Military Rd, 2nd exit rdbt onto Gomer Ln, 0.5m on left*

Much more than just a local pub, the refurbished Seahorse includes Leonard's restaurant, as well as a large bar with terrace. This is a family-run business, where head chef Simon Leonard uses locally sourced ingredients to create a wide range of traditional and speciality dishes. Typical choices include boiled ham, duck egg and hand-cut chips; mutton suet pudding; and chargrilled steak with wild mushrooms.

**Open** all day all wk 11-11 Closed: 25 Dec ◀ London Pride, Worthington. ♀ 8 **Facilities** Dogs allowed Garden Parking

---

### HAMBLEDON
Map 5 SU61

## The Vine Inn ♀

**West St PO7 4RW ☎ 023 9263 2419**
**e-mail:** ag.vine@yahoo.co.uk
**dir:** *Just off B2150 between Droxford (A32) & Waterlooville (A3)*

An old country inn with a welcoming atmosphere, tucked away in the main street of the pretty village of Hambledon. New owners Alan Gill and Sonia Tidmarsh have made an impression with their menus built around traditional British cooking. There are plenty of real ales to enjoy in the bar or outside in the garden.

**Open** all wk ⊕ MARSTONS ◀ Ringwood Best, Jennings Cockerhoop, Marstons Best Bitter, Brakspears Oxford Gold Ŏ Thatchers. ♀ 11 **Facilities** Dogs allowed Garden

---

### HAMBLE-LE-RICE
Map 5 SU40

## PICK OF THE PUBS

### The Bugle ◉ ♀
*See Pick of the Pubs on opposite page*

---

### HANNINGTON
Map 5 SU55

## PICK OF THE PUBS

### The Vine at Hannington ♀
*See Pick of the Pubs on page 224*

# PICK OF THE PUBS

## The Bugle ❀ ♀

### HAMBLE-LE-RICE
Map 5 SU40

**High St SO31 4HA**
☎ 023 8045 3000 📄 023 8045 3051
**e-mail:** manager@buglehamble.co.uk
**dir:** *M27 junct 8, follow signs to Hamble. In village centre turn right at mini-rdbt into one-way cobbled street, pub at end*

A proposal to demolish this Grade II listed waterside pub and build houses was kicked into touch a little while back, thanks to a successful campaign by villagers. To great relief all round, a local business bought the pub and lovingly refurbished it, using traditional methods and materials, in close consultation with English Heritage. Old features include exposed beams and brickwork, natural flagstone floors and an oak bar, while among the new is a large heated terrace with lovely views over the River Hamble - perfect for outdoor dining. A pint of one of the regionally brewed real ales on a rotating roster makes an ideal partner for a doorstep sandwich, honey-roast ham and grain mustard, maybe, or smoked Lyburn cheese and home-made chutney. Alternatively, try home-made merguez sausages with minted yogurt, or chargrilled polenta with New Forest wild mushrooms and sage butter.

The seasonal menu is based on top quality local ingredients, with dishes ranging from deep-fried balls of Laverstoke Park mozzarella; and local ale-battered fish and hand-cut chips in the bar, to grilled South Coast sole with caper flower butter; Hampshire free range rib-eye steak; and pan-fried local bream with chorizo-crushed potatoes in the dining room. Factor in the daily specials and the choice becomes even wider. Finish with chocolate torte and Dorset clotted cream, or sticky toffee pudding. The concise wine list offers plenty of scope, with prices starting at below £15 and ten served by the carafe or glass.

For private dining, there is the Captain's Table upstairs. Regular events at The Bugle include the wine club, and quiz and live music nights.

**Open** all day all wk **Bar Meals** L served Mon-Thu 12-2.30, Fri 12-3, Sat 12-10, Sun 12-9 D served Mon-Thu 6-9.30, Fri 6-10, Sat 12-10, Sun 12-9 Av main course £10 **Restaurant** L served Mon-Thu 12-2.30, Fri 12-3, Sat 12-10, Sun 12-9 D served Mon-Thu 6-9.30, Fri 6-10, Sat 12-10, Sun 12-9 Av 3 course à la carte fr £22.50 ⊕ FREE HOUSE
◀ Rotating locally brewed ales, Courage Best. ♀ 10
**Facilities** Children's portions

# PICK OF THE PUBS

## The Vine at Hannington ♀

**HANNINGTON**       Map 5 SU55

**RG26 5TX**
☎ 01635 298525   🖷 01635 298027
**e-mail:**
info@thevineathannington.co.uk
**web:** www.thevineathannington.co.uk
**dir:** *Hannington signed from A339 between
Basingstoke & Newbury*

A traditional village pub high up on the
beautiful Hampshire Downs, with views
across the countryside from its
sheltered garden and attractive
conservatory. It was originally the
Wellington Arms, since the land once
belonged to the Iron Duke, then it
became the Shepherd's Crook and
Shears until 1960, when it was renamed
after the local Vine and Craven Hunt.
Visitors can be assured of friendly

service, well kept beers, a compact wine
list that will satisfy most tastes, and
great home-made pub food. Indeed,
many of the herbs, salad leaves and
vegetables used come from the pub
garden.

Seasonal menus of home-cooked,
affordable dishes, including daily
specials, might suggest starting with
goat's cheese and red onion tart with a
honey and balsamic dressed salad;
Scottish smoked salmon on a
chargrilled potato cake; or warm
chicken salad with bacon, feta and pine
nuts; or maybe a share of a generous
plate of antipasti. Then follows a
selection of mains, among which you'll
find honey, ginger and balsamic glazed
salmon fillet; Manydown Farm's locally
reared Aberdeen Angus rump steak; and
steak and Ringwood Best ale pie. Turn
your attention to the specials board for
skate wing in black caper butter,
crushed potato and vegetables; roasted
pheasant wrapped in bacon with port
and redcurrant gravy; and seared tuna
Niçoise salad perhaps. Should you just
want a bar snack, there are jackets,
ploughman's and home-made soup.

The garden behind The Vine is large, but
a cosy wood-burner might make staying
inside preferable when the sun isn't
shining. There are plenty of excellent
countryside walks and cycle routes
nearby, including the Wayfarers Walk,
which runs from Emsworth to Inkpen
Beacon.

**Open** 12-3 6-11 (Sat-Sun all day)
Closed: 25 Dec, Sun eve & Mon in winter
**Bar Meals** L served Mon-Fri 12-2, Sat-
Sun 12-2.30 D served all wk 6-9
**Restaurant** L served Mon-Fri 12-2, Sat-
Sun 12-2.30 D served all wk 6-9
⊞ FREE HOUSE ◗ Black Sheep,
Bombardier. ♀ 11 **Facilities** Children's
menu Play area Family room Dogs
allowed Garden Parking

### HAVANT Map 5 SU70

## The Royal Oak ⚑

19 Langstone High St, Langstone PO9 1RY
☎ 023 9248 3125
e-mail: 7955@greeneking.co.uk
dir: *Telephone for directions*

Occupying an outstanding position overlooking Langstone Harbour, this historic 16th-century pub is noted for its rustic, unspoilt interior. Flagstone floors, exposed beams and winter fires contrast with the waterfront benches and secluded rear garden for alfresco summer drinking. Light lunches such as rich tomato soup or chicken Caesar salad support a dinner menu that includes slow-cooked Welsh lamb; baked salmon fillet; and British ham hock glazed with honey mustard.

Open all day all wk 11-11 ◀ Greene King IPA, Ruddles County, Ruddles Best, Abbot Ale, Speckled Hen. ⚑ 16 Facilities Family room Dogs allowed Garden

### HOLYBOURNE Map 5 SU74

## The White Hart Hotel ⚑ NEW

◀ 39 London Rd GU34 4EY ☎ 01420 87654
e-mail: whitehart-holybourne@btconnect.com
dir: *From M3 junct 5 follow Alton signs (A339). In Alton take A31 towards Farnham. Follow Holybourne signs*

Located on the old London Road between Alton and Farnham, the village of Holybourne is steeped in history. An old Roman fort lies under the cricket field, and the village also stands on the Pilgrims' Way. Here, The White Hart offers a well-kept glass of real ale along with a daily-changing menu of freshly cooked old English fare that includes home-made soups, pies and daily specials. Regular main course options also include Brock's Farm beef, vegetarian dishes, mid-week and Sundays roasts and plenty of fresh fish, such as Test Valley trout with watercress sauce, and grilled whole gilt head bream or sea bass.

Open all day all wk Bar Meals L served all wk 12-3 D served all wk 6.30-9.30 Av main course £8.50 food served all day Restaurant L served all wk 12-3 D served all wk 6.30-9.30 ⊕ GREENE KING/MERLIN INNS ◀ Courage Best, Greene King IPA, 2 Guest ales. ⚑ 10 Facilities Children's menu Children's portions Play area Dogs allowed Garden Parking

### HOOK Map 5 SU75

## Crooked Billet

▲London Rd RG27 9EH
☎ 01256 762118 ◻ 01256 761011
e-mail: richardbarwise@aol.com
web: www.thecrookedbillethook.co.uk
dir: *From M3 take Hook ring road. At 3rd rdbt turn right onto A30 towards London, pub on left 0.5m by river*

The present pub dates back to 1935, though there has been a hostelry on this site since the 1600s. Food to suit all appetites includes half shoulder of lamb in mint

gravy; Billet toad in the hole with mash and onion gravy; home-made steak and kidney pie; fresh cod fillets in beer batter; and a range of ploughman's with hot French bread. The pub is family-friendly, offering a children's menu and play area. Guest ales are a speciality here, along with beers from Andwells brewery.

*Crooked Billet*

Open all wk Bar Meals L served Mon-Sat 12-2.30, Sun 12-3 booking required D served Mon-Fri 6.30-9.30, Sat-Sun 6.30-10 booking required Av main course £10 ⊕ FREE HOUSE ◀ Courage Best, Andwells Brewery, guest ♂ Thatchers. Facilities Children's menu Children's portions Play area Dogs allowed Garden Parking

## The Hogget ⚑

London Rd, Hook Common RG27 9JJ ☎ 01256 763009
e-mail: home@hogget.co.uk
dir: *M3 junct 5, A30, 0.5m, between Hook & Basingstoke*

The Hogget has established a reputation, locally and further afield, for its good food and relaxed setting; indeed the pub's popularity means that food times have now been extended. Beers from Ringwood, Jennings and Marston's support a sensible wine list, with plenty of choice by the glass. Local ingredients from named suppliers are the foundation of freshly-cooked dishes like duck and port parfait; venison and celeriac stew with herb and Stilton dumplings; and orange and apricot brioche and butter pudding with crème anglaise.

Open all day all wk Closed: 25 Dec Bar Meals L served all wk 10-6.30 booking required D served all wk 6.30-9 booking required Av main course £11.50 food served all day Restaurant L served all wk 10-6.30 booking required D served all wk 6.30-9 booking required Fixed menu price fr £9.50 food served all day ⊕ MARSTONS PUB COMPANY ◀ Ringwood Best, Jennings Sneck Lifter, Marston's Pedigree, Guest ales ♂ Thatchers Gold. ⚑ 16 Facilities Children's menu Children's portions Dogs allowed Garden Parking

### HORSEBRIDGE Map 5 SU33

## John O'Gaunt Inn ⚑

SO20 6PU ☎ 01794 388394
e-mail: keithnigeldavid@hotmail.com
dir: *A3057 (Stockbridge to Romsey road). Horsebridge 4m from Stockbridge, turn right at brown information board*

Walkers from the nearby Test Way, fishermen from the River Test and the winter shooting fraternity all frequent this small country inn, six miles north of Romsey. It provides a great atmosphere for well-kept ales and

generously priced food. The menu showcases fresh local produce, with dishes such as home-made steak and kidney pudding, liver and bacon, followed by a good selection of puddings. A traditional roast at Sunday lunchtime too.

Open 11-3 6-11 (Sat 11-11 Sun noon-10) Closed: Mon L ◀ Ringwood Best Bitter, Ringwood Fortyniner, Palmers IPA ♂ Thatchers. ⚑ 8 Facilities Dogs allowed Garden Parking

### HURSLEY Map 5 SU42

## The Dolphin Inn ⚑

SO21 2JY ☎ 01962 775209
e-mail: mandy@dolphininn.demon.co.uk
web: www.dolphinhursley.co.uk
dir: *Telephone for directions*

Reputedly built from the timbers of an early HMS Dolphin, hence the pub name, the roadside village inn dates from the 16th century and was once a thriving coaching inn. Follow a stroll through nearby Farley Mount Country Park with a traditional pub lunch in the mature garden or in the beamed bars. Quench your thirst with a cold glass of Summer Lightning, while the children enjoy the play area. Look out for the local butcher's meat draw on Fridays nights.

Open all wk Mon-Sat 11-11 (Sun 12-10.30) Bar Meals L served Mon-Thu 12-2, Fri-Sat 12-2.30, Sun 12-8.30 booking required D served Mon-Thu 6-9, Fri-Sat 6.30-9.30, Sun 12-8.30 booking required Av main course £8 ⊕ ENTERPRISE INNS ◀ Ringwood, Summer Lightning, HSB ♂ Thatchers Dry, Thatchers Premium. ⚑ 12 Facilities Children's menu Children's portions Play area Family room Dogs allowed Garden Parking

### IBSLEY Map 5 SU10

## Old Beams Inn ⚑

Salisbury Rd BH24 3PP
☎ 01425 473387 ◻ 01202 743080
e-mail: oldbeams@alcatraz.co.uk
dir: *On A338 between Ringwood & Salisbury*

Old Beams is a beautiful 14th-century thatched and timber-framed village inn located at the heart of the New Forest, with views of lovely countryside and the famous native ponies. It has a beer garden with a decked area and patio, and a cosy old world interior. Pub food favourites, based on local and New Forest produce, dominate the menu, and on Friday night (fish night) there's a large selection.

*continued on page 226*

**IBSLEY** *continued*

**Open** all wk 11am-11.30pm **Bar Meals** food served all day **Restaurant** food served all day ⊕ ALCATRAZ ◀ IPA, Old Speckled Hen. ▼ 10 **Facilities** Children's menu Garden Parking

## ITCHEN ABBAS
Map 5 SU53

### The Trout

**Main Rd SO21 1BQ** ☎ **01962 779537** 📄 **01962 791046**
**dir:** *M3 junct 9, A34, right onto A33, follow signs to Itchen Abbas, pub 2m on left*

A 19th-century coaching inn in the Itchen Valley close to the river itself. Originally called the Plough, it is said to have been the location that inspired Charles Kingsley to write *The Water Babies*. Freshly cooked, locally sourced produce is served in the bar and restaurant: watercress soup, of course, smoked trout from the Avington fishery, steak and ale pie, and Scottish haddock and chips - ideal for hungry walkers. A lunchtime selection of light meals includes baguettes, wraps, focaccias and salads.

**Open** all wk 12-3 6-11 Closed: 26 Dec & 1 Jan **Bar Meals** booking required food served all day **Restaurant** booking required food served all day ⊕ GREENE KING ◀ Greene King IPA, Abbots Ale, Olde Trip. **Facilities** Children's menu Children's portions Play area Dogs allowed Garden Parking

## LINWOOD
Map 5 SU10

### PICK OF THE PUBS

### The High Corner Inn ▼

*See Pick of the Pubs on page 228*

## LITTLETON
Map 5 SU43

### PICK OF THE PUBS

### The Running Horse ★★★★ INN ⊛ ▼

*See Pick of the Pubs on page 229*

## LONGPARISH
Map 5 SU44

### PICK OF THE PUBS

### The Plough Inn

**SP11 6PB** ☎ **01264 720358**
**e-mail:** eat@theploughinn.info
**dir:** *M3 junct 8, A303 towards Andover. In approx 6m take B3048 towards Longparish*

This charming old 18th-century inn stands close to the centre of Longparish, just a few minutes' drive from Andover. The nearby River Test is one of southern England's finest chalk streams and the Test Way footpath runs through the inn's car park. This delightful location makes The Plough a popular stop for walkers, as well as for the fishermen and cyclists who are also drawn to this lovely valley. Expect Hampshire ales from the Ringwood and Itchen Valley breweries, and a food offering that encompasses fish specials and pub classics as well as the à la carte menu. Typical dishes include duo of duck on rösti potato with sautéed Savoy cabbage and five spice jus; award-winning local sausages with mash and onion gravy; grilled goat's cheese and pimento polenta with balsamic glazed rocket; and locally-smoked trout on toasted brioche with creamed leeks and dill dressing.

**Open** 12-2.30 6-9.30 Closed: Sun eve **Bar Meals** L served 12-2.30 booking required D served 6-9.30 booking required Av main course £10 **Restaurant** L served 12-2.30 booking required D served 6-9.30 booking required Av 3 course à la carte fr £20 ⊕ ENTERPRISE INNS ◀ Itchen Valley, Black Sheep, Ringwood Best. **Facilities** Children's portions Dogs allowed Garden Parking

## LOWER SWANWICK
Map 5 SU40

### Old Ship NEW

**261 Bridge Rd SO31 7FN** ☎ **01489 575646**

A 17th-century inn of great character, a stone's throw from the marina on the Hamble River. It's popular with both locals and sailors, with an open fire in winter, serving well-kept Fuller's ales and a home-cooked menu of typical pub food. Light bites, sandwiches and baguettes, ploughman's and jackets all feature, backed by good ranges of starters (breaded mushrooms), meats (sweet chilli pork), fish (smoked haddock fishcakes), grills (gammon steak) and vegetarian options (macaroni cheese). A kiddies' menu and chef's specials on the blackboard complete the comprehensive choices.

**Open** all day all wk **Bar Meals** L served Mon-Sat 12-2.15, Sun 12-9 booking required D served Mon-Sat 6.30-9.15, Sun 12-9 booking required **Restaurant** L served Mon-Sat 12-2.15, Sun 12-9 booking required D served Mon-Sat 6.30-9.15, Sun 12-9 booking required ⊕ MERLIN INNS / FULLERS ◀ HSB, Seafarers, London Pride. **Facilities** Children's menu Children's portions Family room Dogs allowed Garden Parking

## LOWER WIELD
Map 5 SU64

### PICK OF THE PUBS

### The Yew Tree ▼

**SO24 9RX** ☎ **01256 389224** 📄 **01256 389224**
**dir:** *Take A339 from Basingstoke towards Alton. Turn right for Lower Wield*

In glorious countryside, opposite a picturesque cricket pitch, this free house first served ale in 1845, when the eponymous, now 650-year-old yew tree was just getting into its stride. The popular landlord's simple mission statement promises "Good honest food; great local beers; fine wines (lots of choice); and, most importantly, good fun for one and all". Triple fff is the house beer, with 20 guest ale brewers on rotation. Most

of the food is sourced from Hampshire or neighbouring counties, with dishes reflecting the season, while keeping the regular favourites "to avoid uproar". Sample dishes include salmon fillet marinated in Chinese spices with oriental noodles; half shoulder of lamb with parsley mash and olive, rosemary and tomato jus; and roasted onion stuffed with leek and courgette provençale topped with cheese. The wines, mainly New World, but with some classic Burgundies, are sourced from ten suppliers, with plenty available by the glass. There is an annual cricket match and sports day in summer and quiz nights in winter.

**Open** Tue-Sat 12-3 6-11 (Sun all day) Closed: 1st 2wks Jan, Mon **Bar Meals** L served Tue-Sun 12-2 D served Tue-Sat 6.30-9, Sun 6.30-8.30 Av main course £11.50 **Restaurant** L served Tue-Sun 12-2 D served Tue-Sat 6.30-9, Sun 6.30-8.30 Av 3 course à la carte fr £22.50 ⊕ FREE HOUSE ◀ Cheriton Pots, Hidden Pint, Triple fff Moondance, Hogs Back TEA, Itchen Valley Hampshire Rose. ♥ 14 **Facilities** Children's menu Dogs allowed Garden Parking

---

### LYMINGTON                    Map 5 SZ39

## The Kings Arms

**Saint Thomas St SO41 9NB** ☎ 01590 672594
**dir:** *Approach Lymington from N on A337, left onto Saint Thomas St. Pub 50yds on right*

King Charles I is reputed to have patronised this historic coaching inn, which these days enjoys an enviable reputation for its cask ales, housed on 150-year-old stillages. Local Ringwood ales as well as national brews are served. It is a real community pub, with a dartboard and Sky TV, and the open brick fireplaces are used in winter.

**Open** all wk ◀ Weekly rotating guest ales.
**Facilities** Garden **Notes** ⊕

## Mayflower Inn ♥

**Kings Saltern Rd SO41 3QD**
☎ 01590 672160   📠 01590 679180
**e-mail:** info@themayflower.uk.com
**dir:** *A337 towards New Milton, left at rdbt by White Hart, left to Rookes Ln, right at mini-rdbt, pub 0.75m*

A favourite with yachtsmen and dog walkers, this solidly built mock-Tudor inn overlooks the Lymington River, with glorious views to the Isle of Wight. There's a magnificent garden with splendid sun terraces, a purpose-built play area for children and an on-going summer barbecue in fine weather. Menu prices are reasonable, with dishes that range from light bites like mezze plate or home-made smoked haddock fish cakes to main courses such as chargrilled tuna steak with warm Niçoise salad, or Thai chicken noodles.

**Open** all day all wk **Bar Meals** Av main course £6.50 food served all day **Restaurant** Fixed menu price fr £10 Av 3 course à la carte fr £12 food served all day ⊕ ENTERPRISE INN/COASTAL INNS & TAVERNS LTD ◀ Ringwood Best, Fuller's London Pride, 6X, Goddards Fuggle Dee Dum ♂ Thatchers. ♥ 9 **Facilities** Children's menu Play area Dogs allowed Garden Parking

---

### LYNDHURST                    Map 5 SU30

## New Forest Inn

**Emery Down SO43 7DY** ☎ 023 8028 4690
**e-mail:** info@thenewforestinn.co.uk
**dir:** *M27 junct 1 follow signs for A35/Lyndhurst. In Lyndhurst follow signs for Christchurch, turn right at Swan Inn towards Emery Down*

The inn, which prides itself on its friendliness and great local atmosphere, is located in the heart of the New Forest, with ponies constantly trying to get in the front door. The pub has its own local walk and dogs are made welcome. Inside you'll find oak beams and floors, two open fires in feature fireplaces and three seating areas. There are guest cask ales throughout the year and a 3-day beer festival. Home-cooked food includes local game, locally sourced meat and vegetarian options. Outside there's a lovely garden for summer use.

**Open** all day all wk **Bar Meals** food served all day **Restaurant** food served all day ⊕ ENTERPRISE INNS ◀ Ringwood Best, Ringwood Fortyniner, guest ales ♂ Stowford Press. **Facilities** Children's menu Children's portions Dogs allowed Garden Parking

## The Oak Inn ♥

**Pinkney Ln, Bank SO43 7FE**
☎ 023 8028 2350   📠 023 8028 4601
**e-mail:** oakinn@fullers.co.uk
**dir:** *From Lyndhurst signed A35 to Christchurch, follow A35 1m, turn left at Bank sign*

New Forest ponies, pigs and deer graze outside this small, but perfectly formed former cider house, behind whose bay windows lie a traditional woodburner, antique pine and bric-a-brac galore. With well-kept Fuller's ales changing regularly, your can enjoy your pint with lunchtime doorstep sandwiches filled with crayfish and rocket; beef, horseradish, mayo and salad; ham, cheese and green tomato chutney, and more. Typical menus feature pan-fried calves' liver and bacon; cod, dill and potato casserole; and chargrilled rib-eye steak. Dogs love the large beer garden.

**Open** all wk Mon-Fri 11.30-3.30 6-11 (Sat 11.30-11 Sun 12-10.30) **Bar Meals** L served Mon-Sat 12-2.30, Sun 12-9 booking required D served Mon-Sat 6-9.30, Sun 12-9 booking required Av main course £9.95 **Restaurant** L served Mon-Sat 12-2.30, Sun 12-9 booking required D served Mon-Sat 6-9.30, Sun 12-9 booking required ⊕ FULLERS BREWERY ◀ London Pride, Fuller's HSB, Gale's Seafarer Ale ♂ Aspall. ♥ 9
**Facilities** Children's menu Dogs allowed Garden Parking

---

## The Trusty Servant

**Minstead SO43 7FY** ☎ 023 8081 2137
**dir:** *Telephone for directions*

Popular New Forest pub overlooking the village green and retaining many Victorian features. The famous sign is taken from a 16th-century Winchester scholar's painting portraying the qualities of an ideal college servant. The menu prides itself on its real food, good value and generous portions. You might sample snacks, home-made pies, steaks from the grill, venison or tenderloin of pork. There's also a good choice of vegetarian dishes, such as sizzling Thai vegetable stir-fry.

**Open** all wk ◀ Ringwood Best, Fuller's London Pride, Wadworth 6X, Timothy Taylor Landlord. **Facilities** Family room Dogs allowed Garden Parking

---

### MAPLEDURWELL                    Map 5 SU65

## The Gamekeepers ♥

**Tunworth Rd RG25 2LU**
☎ 01256 322038   📠 01256 322038
**e-mail:** costellophil@hotmail.co.uk
**dir:** *M3 junct 6, take A30 towards Hook. Turn right after The Hatch pub. The Gamekeepers signed*

A 19th-century pub/restaurant with an indoor well, The Gamekeepers has a very rural location with a large secluded garden. Relax on a leather settee with a pint of Fursty Ferret or Hopping Hare and enjoy the cosy atmosphere of low beams and flagstone floors. An impressive range of game in season and seafood (Dover sole, John Dory, monkfish) is offered, with dishes like oven-baked salmon topped with fontina cheese and wrapped in Parma ham, or chargrilled beef fillet on dauphinoise potatoes with blue cheese and pink peppercorn butter. Children's portions are also available.

**Open** all wk Mon-Fri 11-3 5.30-mdnt (Sat 11-mdnt Sun 11-11) **Bar Meals** L served Mon-Fri 11-2.30, Sat-Sun 11-9 booking required D served Mon-Fri 5.30-9, Sat-Sun 11-9 booking required Av main course £9.95 **Restaurant** L served Mon-Fri 11-2.30, Sat-Sun 11-9 booking required D served Mon-Fri 5.30-9, Sat-Sun 11-9 booking required Fixed menu price fr £25.95 Av 3 course à la carte fr £28.95 ⊕ HALL & WOODHOUSE ◀ Badgers First Gold, Tanglefoot, Sussex Best, Fursty Ferret, Hopping Hare ♂ Stowford Press. ♥ 10 **Facilities** Children's portions Dogs allowed Garden Parking

# PICK OF THE PUBS

## The High Corner Inn ♀

**LINWOOD**  Map 5 SU10

**BH24 3QY**
☎ **01425 473973**  📄 **01425 480015**
**e-mail:** highcorner@wadworth.co.uk
**dir:** *From A338 (Ringwood to Salisbury road) follow brown tourist signs into forest. Pass Red Shoot Inn, after 1m turn down gravel track at Green High Corner Inn*

Lost down a quarter-mile gravel track a mile from the village of Linwood, off the narrow lane linking Lyndhurst and the A338 near Ringwood, this much extended and modernised, early 18th-century inn is set in seven beautiful acres of woodland deep in the heart of the New Forest. The cluster of rambling buildings began life as a farm in the early 1700s and the old stables have over time been connected to the main inn to create family and function rooms, the latter proving very popular for weddings in this gloriously peaceful forest location. A quiet hideaway in winter, mobbed in summer, it is a popular retreat for families with its numerous bar-free rooms, an outdoor adventure playground and miles of wildlife-rich forest and heathland walks and cycle trails.

The beamed bars, replete with roaring winter log fires and the full range of Wadworth ales on tap, and the lovely forest garden are very agreeable settings for sampling an extensive range of home-cooked meals and bar snacks; daily specials are shown on chalkboards and a carvery is available on Sunday.

Rest and refuel during or following a forest ramble with a refreshing pint of 6X and a bowl of home-made soup and a plate of sandwiches or a ploughman's lunch, best enjoyed on the flower-filled terrace or in the garden with its forest views, or tuck into something more substantial from the traditional pub menu, perhaps home-made game terrine; hunter's chicken; beer battered cod; steak and kidney pie; gammon, egg and chips; decent steak with all the trimmings; or the High Corner hot pot. Leave room for a nursery-style pudding, perhaps a traditional crumble. Dogs and horses are welcome.

**Open** all wk 11-3 6-11 (3-6 winter)
**Bar Meals** L served Mon-Fri 12-2.30, Sat 12-2, Sun 12-8 D served Mon-Sat 6-9, Sun 12-8 **Restaurant** L served Mon-Fri 12-2.30, Sat 12-2, Sun 12-8 D served Mon-Sat 6-9, Sun 12-8
⊕ WADWORTH ◀ Wadworth 6X, Horizon, IPA, Red Shoot New Forest Gold, Toms Tipple ♻ Westons, Thatchers Gold. ♀ 14
**Facilities** Children's menu Play area Dogs allowed Garden Parking

# PICK OF THE PUBS

## The Running Horse ★★★★ INN

LITTLETON Map 5 SU43

**88 Main Rd SO22 6QS**
☎ **01962 880218**  📄 **01962 886596**
**e-mail:**
runninghorseinn@btconnect.com
**web:** www.runninghorseinn.co.uk
**dir:** *3m from Winchester, signed from Stockbridge Rd*

Good food and luxurious accommodation is what makes this attractive rural gastro-pub on the western outskirts of Winchester such a popular place.

The bar with its limestone counter is a successful blend of the traditional and the modern, with stripped wooden floor, leather tub chairs around an original fireplace, and white walls. The rear garden and the patio to the front are large and peaceful and are overlooked by elegant en suite rooms.

The focus here is undoubtedly on good eating, and the chefs' sourcing of seasonal produce of impeccable freshness helped The Running Horse to gain its AA Rosette for the quality of its contemporary international cuisine.

Choose between dining outside, casually in the bar, or more formally in the stylish restaurant. Dinner might begin with roasted butternut squash and sage risotto with feta cheese and rocket parcel, or pan-seared pigeon breast with beetroot purée, spiced red wine jelly and pickled walnuts. Main courses include duo of Salisbury spring lamb with ratatouille terrine, basil scented mash, carrot ribbons and a red wine reduction, or venison fillet with butter garlic and thyme, parsnip purée, confit potato, wilted spinach and a chocolate scented red wine sauce. Vegetarians are well served too, a typical choice being potato and herb gnocchi with asparagus spears, peas, poached hen's egg, mixed shoots and Parmesan foam. Locally brewed beers include Flower Pots from nearby Cheriton, and a comprehensive wine list completes the package. Look out for Wednesday fish and chip supper nights.

**Open** all wk **Bar Meals** L served all wk 12-2 D served all wk 6-9.30 **Restaurant** L served all wk 12-2 D served all wk 6-9.30 🍺 Ringwood Best, Flower Pots. ♟ 10 **Facilities** Dogs allowed Garden Parking **Rooms** 9

## MICHELDEVER — Map 5 SU53

### Half Moon & Spread Eagle ?

**Winchester Rd SO21 3DG ☎ 01962 774339**
*dir: From Winchester take A33 towards Basingstoke. In 5m turn left after small car garage. Pub 0.5m on right*

Old drovers' inn located in the heart of a pretty thatched and timbered Hampshire village, overlooking the cricket green. The pub, comprising three neatly furnished interconnecting rooms, has a real local feel, and a few years back reverted to its old name having been the Dever Arms for eight years. An extensive menu ranges through Sunday roasts, fresh battered cod, and half shoulder of minted lamb. Recent change of hands.

**Open** all wk 13-3 6-11 (Sun 12-3) **Bar Meals** L served all wk 12-2 D served all wk 6-9 ⊕ GREENE KING ◀ Greene King IPA, Abbot Ale, guest ales. ♀ 9 **Facilities** Children's menu Children's portions Play area Dogs allowed Garden Parking

## MORTIMER WEST END — Map 5 SU66

### The Red Lion

**Church Rd RG7 2HU ☎ 0118 970 0169**
*dir: Telephone for directions*

Original oak beams and an inglenook fireplace are the mark of this traditional pub, which dates back to 1650. Quality food and a range of real ales are served, with dishes to suit all tastes under the headings of 'smaller or more', 'considerable' and 'puddings'. Where possible produce is locally sourced, including free-range chicken and eggs, and English beef hung for 21 days. Perhaps start with ham hock terrine, onion marmalade and pepper toast, followed by baked supreme of salmon, fondant potatoes, chorizo and broad bean sauce; then finishing with pear, apple and raisin strudel.

**Open** all day all wk **Bar Meals** Av main course £8.95 food served all day **Restaurant** Fixed menu price fr £9.95 Av 3 course à la carte fr £18.95 food served all day ⊕ HALL & WOODHOUSE ◀ Tanglefoot, Badger First Gold, Guinness, Sussex ♂ Stowford Press. **Facilities** Children's menu Children's portions Play area Family room Dogs allowed Garden Parking

## NEW ALRESFORD — Map 5 SU53

### The Bell ♀ NEW

**12 West St SO24 9AT ☎ 01962 732429**
**e-mail:** info@bellalresford.com
*dir: In village centre*

A restored 17th-century former coaching inn situated in the heart of a picturesque Georgian town in the peaceful Itchen Valley. Take a steam train ride on the Watercress Line, browse the boutiques and galleries, or enjoy a riverside stroll, then rest and refuel in the homely bar and restaurant at The Bell. Follow local trout and watercress terrine or watercress and spinach soufflé, with monkfish wrapped in Parma ham with clam and Pernod risotto, or confit duck leg with cherry jus, and round off with sticky

toffee sundae or a plate of Hampshire cheeses. Wash down with tip-top pint of Itchen Valley Winchester Bitter.

**Open** all day all wk **Bar Meals** L served all wk 12-3 D served Mon-Sat 6-9 Av main course £13 **Restaurant** L served Mon-Sat 12-3, Sun 12-4 D served Mon-Sat 6-9 Fixed menu price fr £10 ⊕ FREE HOUSE ◀ Sharp's Doom Bar, Winchester, Otter, Resolute, Upham Ale ♂ Mr Whiteheads, Heart of Hampshire, Scrumpy. ♀ 18 **Facilities** Children's portions Dogs allowed Garden Parking

## NORTHINGTON — Map 5 SU53

### The Woolpack Inn ★★★★ INN ◉ ♀

**Totford SO24 9TJ ☎ 0845 293 8066  ▤ 0845 293 8055**
**e-mail:** info@thewoolpackinn.co.uk
*dir: From Basingstoke take A339 towards Alton. Under motorway & turn right (across dual carriageway) onto B3036 signed Candovers & Alresford. Pub between Brown Candover & Northington*

Approach this old drovers' inn at night and just as you prepare to descend a steep hill you'll see its welcoming lights twinkling below. Since taking over in 2008, the current owners have really smartened it up, creating a sense of calm modernity while still retaining a traditional feel. The menu, awarded one AA Rosette, offers bacon butty on farmhouse bread and beer-battered fish and chips in the traditional bar area; and in the dining room, warm smoked trout and crispy bacon salad; pot-roast Candover Park partridge; and pan-roasted salmon with bacon, pea and potato broth. There are seven stylish rooms available.

**Open** all wk 11.30am-3 6-close (Sat-Sun open all day) Closed: 25 Dec eve **Bar Meals** L served all wk 11.30-3 D served Mon-Sat 6-close Av main course £8 **Restaurant** L served all wk 11.30-3 D served Mon-Sat 6-close Av 3 course à la carte fr £20 ⊕ FREE HOUSE ◀ Palmers IPA, Palmers Copper, Moondance Triple fff ♂ Thatchers Gold. ♀ 10 **Facilities** Children's menu Children's portions Play area Dogs allowed Garden Parking **Rooms** 7

## NORTH WALTHAM — Map 5 SU54

### PICK OF THE PUBS

### The Fox ♀

**See Pick of the Pubs on opposite page**

## OLD BASING — Map 5 SU65

### The Millstone ♀

**Bartons Ln RG24 8AE ☎ 01256 331153**
**e-mail:** millstone@wadworth.co.uk
*dir: From M3 junct 6 follow brown signs to Basing House*

Basingstoke is just a stone's throw away, which makes this attractive old building's rural location, beside the River Loddon, all the more delightfully surprising. Nearby are the extensive ruins of Old Basing House, one of Britain's most famous Civil War sites. Typical main dishes might include battered or grilled cod; creamy

vegetable korma; and spinach, mushroom and brie filo parcel. Snacks include baguettes, ciabattas, jacket potatoes and ploughman's.

**Open** all day all wk 11.30-11 ◀ Wadworth 6X, Wadworth JCB, Henrys Smooth, Henrys IPA. ♀ 9 **Facilities** Dogs allowed Garden Parking

## OVINGTON — Map 5 SU53

### PICK OF THE PUBS

### The Bush

**See Pick of the Pubs on page 232**

## PETERSFIELD — Map 5 SU72

### The Good Intent ♀

**40-46 College St GU31 4AF ☎ 01730 263838**
**e-mail:** info@goodintentpetersfield.co.uk
*dir: Telephone for directions*

Candlelit tables, open fires and well-kept ales characterise this 16th-century pub, and in summer, flower tubs and hanging baskets festoon the front patio. Curry nights are held on the last Thursday in the month, for which booking is advisable. Menus feature starters such as potted trout and salmon with chive and sour cream dip; spicy chicken goujons with sweet chilli mayonnaise; followed by vegetable goulash with chive dumplings; pork stroganoff and rice; lambs' liver and bacon, mash and onion gravy; and game casserole. Sandwiches and baguettes are also available at lunchtime. Gluten free and lactose free diets can be catered for.

**Open** all wk 11-3 5.30-11 (Sun 12-3 7-11) **Bar Meals** L served all wk 12-2.30 D served Sun-Mon 7-9, Tue-Sat 6.30-9.30 food served all day ⊕ FULLERS BREWERY ◀ Fuller's HSB, London Pride, Guest ales. ♀ 9 **Facilities** Children's menu Children's portions Dogs allowed Garden Parking

# PICK OF THE PUBS

## The Fox 🍷

**NORTH WALTHAM**      Map 5 SU54

**RG25 2BE ☎ 01256 397288**
**e-mail:** info@thefox.org
**dir:** *From M3 junct 7 take A30 towards Winchester. Village signed on right. Take 2nd signed road*

A strong local following should prove that this peaceful village pub down a quiet country lane just off the M3 is also an ideal lunch or dinner stop for those from further afield. Built as three farm cottages in 1624, the Fox welcomes families - witness the children's adventure play area in an extensive beer garden that becomes a tapestry of colour in summer when the pretty flower borders and hanging baskets are blooming.

In the bar, in addition to the good choice of real ales with monthly guest ale, which Rob Mackenzie looks after passionately, is an ever-growing collection of 1,100 miniatures. Needless to say, these aren't for sampling, but there's an interesting selection of malt whiskies, which are available on conventional pub terms.

Rob's wife Izzy is responsible for dishes on the seasonally rolling monthly menus and the daily specials, which, from the mayonnaise upwards, are prepared in her kitchen. A simple bar menu leads you towards plates of Whitby scampi; sausage and mash; and chicken and leek pie, while in the tartan-carpeted restaurant there's a wider choice. Begin with smoked mackerel mousse; goat's cheese with honey, sesame and mint chilli; or fresh soup of the day; continue with a main course of baked sea bass fillets with ginger and coriander; pork tenderloin medallions with sauté potatoes, green beans and wholegrain mustard and cream sauce; chicken breast cordon bleu with dauphinoise potatoes and redcurrant and wine sauce; or Stilton and wild mushroom Wellington.

The Fox is known for its events calendar — 2010, for instance, saw a pig-racing evening, a wine-tasting dinner, and an oyster festival with a pipe band, Morris dancers and a beer tent.

**Open** all day all wk 11-11 **Bar Meals** L served all wk 12-2.30 D served all wk 6-9.30 Av main course £7.30 **Restaurant** L served all wk 12-2.30 booking required D served all wk 6-9.30 booking required Av 3 course à la carte fr £20.20 ⊞ FREE HOUSE ◀ Ringwood Best Bitter, Brakspear, West Berkshire Good Old Boy, guest ale ♂ Aspall, Thatchers Gold. ♟ 14 **Facilities** Children's menu Play area Dogs allowed Garden Parking

# PICK OF THE PUBS

## The Bush

| OVINGTON | Map 5 SU53 |
| --- | --- |

**SO24 ORE**
☎ **01962 732764** 📠 **01962 735130**
**e-mail:** thebushinn@wadworth.co.uk
**web:** www.wadworth.co.uk
**dir:** *A31 from Winchester, E to Alton & Farnham, approx 6m turn left off dual carriageway to Ovington. 0.5m to pub*

Located just off the A31 on a peaceful lane, this unspoilt 17th-century rose-covered cottage enjoys an enviable picturesque setting, close to one of Hampshire's famous chalk trout streams – the River Itchen. Gentle riverside strolls are very popular, as are the rustic bars and bench-filled garden of this one-time refreshment stop on the Pilgrim's Way between Winchester and Canterbury, both of which are often crammed with people replenishing their energy after a walk, especially on fine summer weekends.

Don't expect to find a juke box or fruit machine, the intimate, softly-lit and atmospheric rooms boast dark-painted walls, an assortment of sturdy tables, chairs and high-backed settles and a wealth of old artefacts, prints and stuffed fish. On cold winter nights the place to sit with a pint of traditional ale is in front of the roaring log fire.

The regularly-changing menu is based on the freshest food the owners, Nick and Cathy Young, can source, including local farm cheeses, meats from Wiltshire, Hampshire and Scotland, and fish from the Dorset and Cornish coasts. Choices range from sandwiches, ploughman's lunches and other bar snacks, through to satisfying meals such as chicken liver pâté with grape chutney, or local smoked trout mousse; followed by steak, red wine and mushroom pie, chargrilled rib-eye steak with chips and a garlic and anchovy butter; and a daily seasonal special like roast partridge with turnip gratin and bread sauce. Finish with sticky toffee pudding with caramel sauce, or Valhrona dark chocolate and raspberry crème brûlée.

You will certainly find a wine to suit your palate, including from among the dozen or so served by the glass. Real ales keep their end up too, with Wadworth 6X and guest ales. Traditional afternoon tea is available on Fridays and every weekend throughout the year.

**Open** all day all wk **Bar Meals** L served 12-2.30 D served 7-9 ⊕ WADWORTH ▥ Wadworth 6X, IPA, Farmers Glory, JCB, Summersault, Old Timer, guest ales. **Facilities** Children's menu Family room Dogs allowed Garden Parking

## PICK OF THE PUBS

### The Trooper Inn ⌁

**Alton Rd, Froxfield GU32 1BD ☎ 01730 827293**
📄 01730 827103
e-mail: info@trooperinn.com
dir: *From A3 take A272 Winchester exit towards Petersfield (NB do not take A272 to Petersfield). 1st exit at mini-rdbt for Steep. 3m, pub on right*

Rescued from closure by the present owners in the mid-1990s, this 17th-century free house stands in an isolated location at one of Hampshire's highest points. Said to have been a recruiting centre at the outset of the Great War, The Trooper now boasts a pine furnished interior, winter log fires, spacious bar and a charming restaurant with a vaulted ceiling and wooden settles. Expect country cooking with fresh fish and game, much of it from local suppliers and producers. Lunchtime sandwiches and baguettes are served with chips and salad, whilst squash, butterbean and leek stew, and roasted duck breast with red cabbage and red wine sauce are typical main course choices. The inn backs onto Ashford Hangers nature reserve, and is well positioned for the South Downs, Jane Austen's Chawton and Gilbert White's Selborne.

**Open** noon-3 6-11 Closed: 25-26 Dec & 1 Jan, Sun eve & Mon L **Bar Meals** L served Tue-Sat 12-2, Sun 12-2.30 booking required D served Mon-Thu 6.30-9, Sat 7-9.30 booking required **Restaurant** L served Tue-Sat 12-2, Sun 12-2.30 booking required D served Mon-Fri 6.30-9, Sat 7-9.30 booking required ⊕ FREE HOUSE
◀ Ringwood Best, Ballards, local guest ales.
**Facilities** Children's menu Children's portions Dogs allowed Garden Parking

### The White Horse Inn

**Priors Dean GU32 1DA ☎ 01420 588387**
📄 01420 588387
e-mail: details@pubwithnoname.co.uk
dir: *A3/A272 to Winchester/Petersfield. In Petersfield left to Steep, 5m then right at small x-rds to East Tisted, take 2nd drive on right*

Also known as the 'Pub With No Name' as it has no sign, this splendid 17th-century farmhouse was originally used as a forge for passing coaches. The blacksmith sold beer to the travellers while their horses were attended to. Today there is an excellent range of beers and daily specials such as coarse pork and herb terrine; pea and broad bean risotto; oriental style crispy pork with egg noodles, watercress and cucumber salad; and grilled halibut fillet with lemon butter.

**Open** all wk Mon-Wed 12-3 6-12 (Thu-Sun all day) **Bar Meals** L served all wk 12-2.30 D served all wk 6-9.30 Av main course £11 **Restaurant** L served all wk 12-2.30 booking required D served all wk 6-9.30 booking required Av 3 course à la carte fr £22 ⊕ FULLERS BREWERY ◀ No Name Best, No Name Strong, Ringwood Fortyniner, Sharp's Doom Bar, Seafarers, London Pride.
**Facilities** Children's menu Children's portions Family room Dogs allowed Garden Parking

### PILLEY　　　　　　　　　　Map 5 SZ39

### The Fleur de Lys ⌁

**Pilley St SO41 5QG ☎ 01590 672158**
e-mail: hrh7@btinternet.com
dir: *From Lymington A337 to Brockenhurst. Cross Ampress Park rdbt, right to Boldre. At end of Boldre Ln turn right. Pub 0.5m*

Dating from 1014, parts of the building pre-date the forest which surrounds it; as the Fleur de Lys, it has been serving ales since 1498. Today this traditional thatched inn exudes centuries of character, warmed by an open fire and two wood burning stoves; outside is a large landscaped garden with wooden tables and chairs. The emphasis here is on fine dining, with a concise menu which may feature pan-fried rabbit loin; marinated saddle of New Forest venison; and chocolate and marshmallow soufflé.

**Open** 11-3 6-11 (Sun noon-4) Closed: Sun eve, Mon all day ◀ Ringwood Best, Guest ales ♨ Stowford Press. ⌁ 10 **Facilities** Family room Dogs allowed Garden Parking

### PORTSMOUTH & SOUTHSEA　　Map 5 SZ69

### The Wine Vaults ⌁

**43-47 Albert Rd, Southsea PO5 2SF ☎ 023 9286 4712**
e-mail: wine.vaults@fullers.co.uk
dir: *Telephone for directions*

Originally several Victorian shops, now converted into a Victorian-style alehouse with wooden floors, panelled walls, and seating from old churches and schools. Partly due to the absence of a jukebox or fruit machine, the atmosphere is relaxed, and there is a good range of real ales and good-value food. A typical menu includes beef stroganoff, Tuscan vegetable bean stew, grilled gammon steak, salads, sandwiches, and Mexican specialities.

**Open** all day all wk noon-11 (Fri-Sat noon-mdnt Sun noon-10.30) ◀ Fuller's London Pride, Discovery, Fuller's ESB, Fuller's HSB, Guest ales. ⌁ 20 **Facilities** Family room Dogs allowed Garden

### ROCKBOURNE　　　　　　Map 5 SU11

## PICK OF THE PUBS

### The Rose & Thistle ⌁

**See Pick of the Pubs on page 234**

### ROCKFORD　　　　　　　Map 5 SU10

### The Alice Lisle ⌁

**Rockford Green BH24 3NA ☎ 01425 474700**
e-mail: alicelisle@fullers.co.uk
dir: *Telephone for directions*

Well-known New Forest pub with landscaped gardens overlooking a lake, popular with walkers and visitors to the region. It was named after the widow of one of Cromwell's supporters who gave shelter to two fugitives from the Battle of Sedgemoor. Fullers beers are on offer

here with a choice of 11 wines by the glass. Choose from a varied menu which might include salmon and crab cakes, honey minted lamb shoulder, liver and bacon, and Mexican enchilada. There's a good variety of children's dishes too.

**Open** all day all wk 10am-11pm **Bar Meals** Av main course £8.95 food served all day ⊕ FULLERS BREWERY ◀ HSB, London Pride, Discovery. ⌁ 11
**Facilities** Children's menu Children's portions Play area Family room Dogs allowed Garden Parking

### ROMSEY　　　　　　　　Map 5 SU32

## PICK OF THE PUBS

### The Dukes Head ⌁

**Greatbridge Rd SO51 0HB ☎ 01794 514450**
dir: *Telephone for directions*

The main part of this long, whitewashed pub dates back to 1468. It is situated a little way out of Romsey, and little more than a hefty cast from the Test, England's foremost trout river. There are large gardens at the front and rear, while inside are the main bar, the snug and four other rooms. In 2008 the pub closed for a year, reopening in 2009 under the new management of Karen Slowen. She is building a strong customer base around her range of real ales – at least four change on a weekly basis. Fresh fish, another priority, appears on the daily specials board, supplied by an excellent fish wholesaler and local fishermen who bring in their catch. On the supper menu you'll find 'Things you expect on a pub menu' such as the Dukes' burger; other main courses like herb-crumbed chicken escalope with mozzarella and pancetta; and desserts such as banoffee pie with caramel sauce.

**Open** all day all wk Closed: 25 Dec **Bar Meals** L served all wk 12-2.30 booking required D served all wk 6-9.30 booking required Av main course £10.95 **Restaurant** L served all wk 12-2.30 booking required D served all wk 6-9.30 booking required ⊕ ENTERPRISE INNS
◀ Fuller's London Pride, Ringwood Best Bitter, 49ers, Summer Lightning, Guinness, 4 guest ales. ⌁ 10
**Facilities** Children's menu Children's portions Dogs allowed Garden Parking

### The Three Tuns ⌁

**58 Middlebridge St SO51 8HL ☎ 01794 512639**
e-mail: guru.palmer@yahoo.co.uk
dir: *Romsey bypass, 0.5m from main entrance of Broadlands Estate*

Centrally located in the abbey town, the 400-year-old Three Tuns is just a short walk from the front gates of Broadlands, country seat of Earl Mountbatten. In the last couple of years new owners Hannah and David have sought out local suppliers, aiming at a gastro-pub style operation. Typical dishes are braised shoulder of Romsey lamb, and Swish and Chips (plaice, haddock, king prawn and scallop in beer batter with real tartare and pea purée).

*continued on page 235*

# PICK OF THE PUBS

## The Rose & Thistle ♗

**ROCKBOURNE**  Map 5 SU11

**SP6 3NL** ☎ **01725 518236**
**e-mail:** enquiries@roseandthistle.co.uk
**dir:** *Follow Rockbourne signs from A354 (Salisbury to Blandford Forum road), or from A338 at Fordingbridge follow signs to Rockbourne*

Originally two 17th-century thatched cottages, this delightful, long and low whitewashed pub enjoys a most tranquil location within one of Hampshire's most picturesque downland villages. It stands at the top of the fine main street lined with idyllic thatched cottages and period houses, and is a true picture postcard pub if ever there was one, with a stunning rose arch, flowers around the door and a quaint dovecot in the glorious front garden. Country-style fabrics, impressive floral arrangements and magazines to peruse and tasteful touches in the charming beamed bars, which boast a collection of polished oak tables and chairs, carved settles and benches, and two huge fireplaces with blazing winter log fires – perfect to hunker down beside following a breezy downland walk.

Expect a relaxing atmosphere, Timothy Taylor Landlord on tap and interesting pub food from well-balanced lunch and dinner menus and daily dishes that favour fresh fish and local game in season. Bar snacks take in beef and horseradish sandwiches, Welsh rarebit with bacon and tomato, scrambled eggs on toast with crispy proscuitto, and locally made pork sausages with wholegrain mustard mash and onion gravy. From the main menu, order roasted squash, feta and pine nut salad, creamy garlic mushrooms, or a fish platter (smoked salmon and prawns, salmon and trout pâté) for starters. Follow with steak and kidney pudding, New Forest sirloin steak with slow-roasted tomatoes and shallots and a wholegrain mustard and tarragon sauce, free range belly pork on parsnip and rosemary mash with crab apple gravy, or one of the fish specials. Round off with a traditional sticky toffee and date pudding, a seasonal fruit crumble, served with lashings of custard, or tuck into a bowl of home-made ice creams.

The pub is conveniently placed for visiting Rockbourne's Roman Villa, the New Forest, Salisbury and Breamore House.

**Open** all wk Mon-Sat 11-3 6-11 (Sun 12-8) **Bar Meals** L served all wk 12-2.30 booking required D served Mon-Sat 7-9.30 booking required Av main course £7 **Restaurant** L served all wk 12-2.30 booking required D served Mon-Sat 7-9.30 booking required Av 3 course à la carte fr £14 ⊕ FREE HOUSE ◄ Fuller's London Pride, Palmers Copper Ale, Timothy Taylor Landlord, Six D Bitter Ⴠ Westons Scrumpy, Black Rat. ♗ 12 **Facilities** Children's menu Dogs allowed Garden Parking

Save on Hotels. Book at **theAA.com/hotel**

HAMPSHIRE 235 **ENGLAND**

**ROMSEY** *continued*

**Open** all day Closed: Mon L ◀ Ringwood Best, Ringwood Fortyniner, Sharp's Doom Bar, Hobgoblin ♻ Old Rosie. 🍷 8 **Facilities** Dogs allowed Garden Parking

### ROWLAND'S CASTLE     Map 5 SU71

## *The Castle Inn* 🍷

**1 Finchdean Rd PO9 6DA**
☎ 023 9241 2494   📠 023 9241 2494
**e-mail:** rogerburrell@btconnect.com
**dir:** *N of Havant take B2149 to Rowland's Castle. Pass green, under rail bridge, pub 1st on left opposite Stansted Park*

A Victorian building directly opposite Stansted Park, part of the Forest of Bere. Richard the Lionheart supposedly hunted here, and the house and grounds are open to the public for part of the year. Traditional atmosphere is boosted by wooden floors and fires in both bars. Menu options include pies, lasagne, curry, steaks, local sausages, and chilli.

**Open** all day all wk ◀ Fuller's Butser, HSB, London Pride, guest ales. 🍷 8 **Facilities** Dogs allowed Garden Parking

## *The Fountain Inn*

**34 The Green PO9 6AB**
☎ 023 9241 2291   📠 023 9241 2291
**e-mail:** fountaininn@amserve.com
**dir:** *Telephone for directions*

Set by the village green in pretty Rowlands Castle, The Fountain is a lovingly refurbished Georgian inn complete with resident ghost. Food is served in Sienna's bistro, where dishes include hand rolled, stone baked pizzas, pasta dishes, and specials like flame-grilled chicken and Serrano ham salad, and crusted fillet steak with a roasted vegetable chutney.

**Open** all wk ◀ Ruddles IPA, Abbot, Ruddles Cask. **Facilities** Play area Dogs allowed Garden Parking

### ST MARY BOURNE     Map 5 SU45

## *The Bourne Valley Inn* 🍷

**SP11 6BT** ☎ 01264 738361   📠 01264 738126
**e-mail:** enquiries@bournevalleyinn.com
**dir:** *Telephone for directions*

Surrounded by fields on the outskirts of St Mary Bourne, this popular traditional inn is an oasis of tranquility. There is a large character bar with plenty of guest ales and a more intimate dining area, as well as a riverside garden abounding with wildlife where children can let off steam in the special play area. Old favourites on the menu include pork and leek sausages with creamy mash and red wine gravy; hand-carved ham with free range eggs and fries; and home-made lasagne with salad.

**Open** all day all wk **Bar Meals** L served all wk 12-2.30 D served all wk 6-9 Av main course £8.95 **Restaurant** L served all wk 12-2.30 D served all wk 6-9 Fixed menu price fr £8.95 Av 3 course à la carte fr £17 ⊕ FREE HOUSE ◀ Guest ales ♻ Jacques. 🍷 12 **Facilities** Children's menu Children's portions Play area Dogs allowed Garden Parking

### SELBORNE     Map 5 SU73

## *The Selborne Arms* 🍷

**High St GU34 3JR** ☎ 01420 511247   📠 01420 511754
**e-mail:** info@selbornearms.co.uk
**web:** www.selbornearms.co.uk
**dir:** *From A3 follow B3006, pub on left in village centre*

A traditional village pub with real fires and a friendly atmosphere. On entering, you must turn either left or right for the bars as a massive brick chimney blocks the way. There's a surprising amount to do in Selborne, so either before or after you've looked around or walked up the zig-zag path, enjoy a pint of Suthwyk's Old Dick, then eat here, perhaps Devonshire dressed crab salad; locally hand-made Toulouse-style sausages and mash with onion gravy; or home-made curry with rice.

**Open** all wk 11-3 6-11 (Sat-Sun 11-11) **Bar Meals** L served all wk 12-2 D served Mon-Sat 7-9, Sun 7-8.30 **Restaurant** L served all wk 12-2 D served Mon-Sat 7-9, Sun 7-8.30 ⊕ FREE HOUSE ◀ Courage Best, Ringwood Fortyniner, Suthwyk Old Dick,local guest ales ♻ Mr Whiteheads. 🍷 10 **Facilities** Children's menu Play area Garden Parking

### SILCHESTER     Map 5 SU66

## *Calleva Arms* 🍷

**Little London Rd, The Common RG7 2PH**
☎ 0118 970 0305
**dir:** *A340 from Basingstoke, signed Silchester. M4 junct 11, 20 mins signed Mortimer then Silchester*

Standing opposite the village green, the pub is popular with walkers, cyclists, and visitors to the nearby Roman town of Calleva Atrebatum with the remains of its town walls and amphitheatre. A pleasant, airy conservatory added to the 19th-century building overlooks a large enclosed garden. Lunchtime favourites include steaks, bangers and mash and special salads. A typical dinner selection could start with Thai spiced crab cakes with mango salsa or Indian, nacho or antipasti sharing platters; followed by aromatic half duck with hoi sin sauce; and chef's fruit crumble served with custard.

**Open** all wk 11-3 5.30-11.30 (Sat 11am-11.30pm Sun noon-11) ◀ London Pride, HSB, Guinness, Butser Bitter. 🍷 8 **Facilities** Dogs allowed Garden Parking

### SOUTHAMPTON     Map 5 SU41

## *The White Star Tavern, Dining & Rooms* ★★★★★ INN ⚙ ⚙ 🍷

**28 Oxford St SO14 3DJ**
☎ 023 8082 1990   📠 023 8090 4982
**e-mail:** reservations@whitestartavern.co.uk
**dir:** *M3 junct 13, take A33 to Southampton, towards Ocean Village & Marina*

Named after the famous shipping line, this ex-seafarers' hotel has become a vibrant gastro-pub and boutique inn, with thirteen smart bedrooms. Awarded two AA Rosettes, the restaurant provides modern British cooking, typified by parsnip gnocchi, New Forest mushrooms and shaved Old Winchester cheese; pan-fried bream with Scottish mussels, chorizo mash and fish gravy; honey-roast ham, frazzled duck egg and hand-cut skinny chips; and shallot tarte Tatin with truffled mash. Live musicians perform every Friday night and there are pavement tables in the summer.

**Open** all day all wk 7am-11pm (Fri 7am-mdnt, Sat 9am-mdnt, Sun 9am-10.30pm) Closed: 25 Dec **Bar Meals** L served Mon-Thu 7-2.30, Fri 7-3, Sat 9-3, Sun 9-4 D served Mon-Thu 6-9, Fri 6-10, Sat 6-9, Sun 6-9.30 Av main course £9 **Restaurant** L served Mon-Thu 12-2.30, Fri-Sat 11-3, Sun 12-8 D served Mon-Thu 6-9.30, Fri-Sat 6-10 Av 3 course à la carte fr £22 ⊕ ENTERPRISE INNS ◀ London Pride, Ringwood, Swift One. 🍷 11 **Facilities** Children's portions **Rooms** 13
*See advert on page 237*

### SOUTHSEA

## See Portsmouth & Southsea

### SPARSHOLT     Map 5 SU43

### PICK OF THE PUBS

## *The Plough Inn* 🍷

*See Pick of the Pubs on page 236*

# PICK OF THE PUBS

## The Plough Inn ♟

**SPARSHOLT**      Map 5 SU43

**Main Rd SO21 2NW**
☎ **01962 776353**   📄 **01962 776400**
**dir:** *From Winchester take B3049 (A272) W,*
*left to Sparsholt, Inn 1m*

In beautiful countryside, just a few miles out of Winchester, this popular village pub has been a local winner for years. It was built about 200 years ago as a coach house to serve Sparsholt Manor opposite, but within 50 years it had become an alehouse.

Inside, the main bar and dining areas blend harmoniously together, with judiciously placed farmhouse-style pine tables, wooden and upholstered seats, and miscellaneous agricultural implements, stone jars, wooden wine box end-panels and dried hops. Wadworth of Devizes supplies all the real ales, and there's a good wine selection.

The dining tables to the left of the entrance look over open fields to wooded downland, and it's at this end of the pub you'll find a blackboard offering lighter dishes such as salmon and crab fishcakes with saffron sauce; lamb's liver and bacon with mash and onion gravy; beef, ale and mushroom pie; and whole baked camembert with garlic and rosemary. The menu board at the right-hand end of the bar offers the more substantial venison steak with celeriac mash and roasted beetroot; roast pork belly with bubble-and-squeak, five spice and sultana gravy; chicken breast with black pudding, apple and bacon and bean jus; and moules marinière with crusty bread. Lunchtime regulars know that 'doorstep' is a most apt description for the great crab and mayonnaise, beef and horseradish and other sandwiches. Puddings include rich chocolate tart with clotted cream, and banana pannacotta with chocolate sauce.

The Plough is very popular, so it's best to book for any meal. The delightful flower- and shrub-filled garden has plenty of room for children to run around and play in.

**Open** all wk Mon-Sat 11-3 6-11 (Sun 12-3 6-10.30) Closed: 25 Dec
**Bar Meals** L served all wk 12-2 booking required D served Sun-Thu 6-9, Fri-Sat 6-9.30 booking required Av main course £8.95 **Restaurant** L served Mon-Sun 12-2 booking required D served Sun-Thu 6-9, Fri-Sat 6-9.30 booking required Fixed menu price fr £11.95
⊕ WADWORTH ◀ Wadworth Henry's IPA, 6X, Old Timer, JCB. ♟ 15
**Facilities** Children's menu Play area Family room Dogs allowed Garden Parking

## STEEP  Map 5 SU72

### PICK OF THE PUBS

## Harrow Inn

**GU32 2DA ☎ 01730 262685**
dir: *A3 to A272, left through Sheet, take road opposite church (School Ln) then over A3 by-pass bridge*

This 16th-century, tile-hung gem has changed little over the years. The McCutcheon family has run it since 1929; sisters Claire and Nisa, both born and brought up here, are now the third generation with their names over the door. Tucked away off the road, it comprises two tiny bars - the 'public' is Tudor, with beams, tiled floor, inglenook fireplace, scrubbed tables, wooden benches, tree-trunk stools and a 'library'; the saloon (or Smoking Room, as it is still called) is Victorian. Beers are dispensed from barrels, there is no till and the toilets are across the road. Food is in keeping: ham and pea soup; hot scotch eggs (some days); Cheddar ploughman's; and various quiches. The garden has a dozen tables surrounded by country-cottage flowers and fruit trees. Quiz nights raise huge sums for charity, for which Claire's partner Tony grows and sells flowers outside.

**Open** all wk 12-2.30 6-11 (Sat 11-3 6-11 Sun 12-3 7-10.30) Closed: Sun eve in winter **Bar Meals** L served all wk 12-2 D served all wk 7-9 Av main course £8 ⊕ FREE HOUSE ◀ Ringwood Best, Palmers Best, Hop Back GFB, Bowman Ales, Otter Ale Ŏ Thatchers Heritage. **Facilities** Dogs allowed Garden Parking **Notes** ⊕

## STOCKBRIDGE  Map 5 SU33

### PICK OF THE PUBS

## The Greyhound Inn ⊕⊕ ♥ NEW

**31 High St SO20 6EY ☎ 01264 810833**
e-mail: enquiries@thegreyhound.info
dir: *In village centre*

Refurbished and remodelled in recent years, this classy 15th-century village inn stands in the heart of fishing country midway between Winchester and Salisbury. It backs on to the River Test and the beautiful riverside garden is one of only a handful to be found along its length, and the inn has fishing rights on this stretch of the magnificent chalk stream. The history-steeped bar and more contemporary lounge sport polished wood floors, old beams and timbers, subtle spot-lighting, open log fires, and scatter cushions on deep comfy sofas. The draw is the first-class modern British cooking, with the occasional influences from France and Italy, and simplicity is key to the kitchen's approach, delivering cracking modern dishes with care, finesse and thoughtful composition. Take potted duck confit with red onion jam, followed by sea bass with brown shrimp risotto and tomato and broad bean velouté, and plum tarte Tatin with cinnamon ice cream. At lunchtime you can pop in for a pint of Butcombe and a bar meal, perhaps fish pie or a smoked ham and Cheddar sandwich. There's a carefully selected list of wines, with eight served by the glass.

**Open** all day Closed: 24-26 & 31 Dec, 1 Jan, Sun eve **Bar Meals** L served Mon-Thu 12-2, Fri-Sat 12-2.30 booking required Av main course £12 **Restaurant** L served Mon-Thu 12-2, Fri-Sun 12-2.30 booking required D served Mon-Thu 7-9, Fri-Sat 7-9.30 booking required Av 3 course à la carte fr £30 ⊕ FREE HOUSE ◀ Butcombe Bitter Ŏ Aspalls Draught. ♥ 8 **Facilities** Children's portions Dogs allowed Garden Parking

## Mayfly ♥

**Testcombe SO20 6AZ ☎ 01264 860283**
dir: *Between A303 & A30, on A3057*

Situated right on the banks of the swiftly flowing River Test, this beamed old farmhouse has a traditional bar, a bright conservatory and a splendid riverside terrace. This idyllic, tranquil setting makes the Mayfly a popular drinking spot so arrive early on warm summer days to sup a pint of Adnams Broadside on a waterside bench. All-day bar food includes fisherman's pie, rib-eye steak, herb-crusted pork fillet with mustard jus, and lasagne with garlic bread. Look out for the impressive wine list.

**Open** all day all wk 10am-11pm Closed: 25 Dec **Bar Meals** L served all wk 11.30-9 D served al wk 11.30-9 food served all day ⊕ FREE HOUSE ◀ Wadworth 6X, Adnams Broadside, Adnams Best, guest ales Ŏ Aspall. ♥ 21 **Facilities** Children's portions Family room Dogs allowed Garden Parking

### PICK OF THE PUBS

## The Peat Spade ⊕ ♥

**Longstock SO20 6DR ☎ 01264 810612**
e-mail: info@peatspadeinn.co.uk
dir: *Telephone for directions*

Unusual paned windows overlook the peaceful village lane and idyllic heavily thatched cottages at this striking, redbrick and gabled Victorian pub, which

*continued on page 239*

---

## STOCKBRIDGE *continued*

stands tucked away in the heart of the Test Valley, only 100 yards from the famous trout stream. Former Hotel du Vin chefs Lucy Townsend and Andrew Clark have created a classy country inn, one where you will find a relaxed atmosphere in the cosy fishing and shooting themed bar and dining room, and a simple, daily-changing menu listing classic English food. Using locally-sourced produce, including allotment fruit and vegetables and game from the Leckford Estate, the choice may take in devilled whitebait with tartare sauce for starters, with main dishes ranging from rump steak with garlic butter to roast halibut with squid ink risotto and sweet fennel. For pudding, try the Cambridge burnt cream or the lemon meringue pie. To drink, there's Ringwood Fortyniner on tap and a choice of 10 wines by the glass – quaff them on the super summer terrace.

**Open** all day all wk Mon-Sat 11am-11pm (Sun 11am-10.30pm) Closed: 25-26 Dec **Bar Meals** L served all wk 12-2 booking required D served all wk 7-9 booking required **Restaurant** L served all wk 12-2 booking required D served all wk 7-9 booking required ⊕ FREE HOUSE ◀ Ringwood Best, Ringwood Fortyniner, guest ales. ⬤ 10 **Facilities** Dogs allowed Garden Parking

*See advert opposite*

---

### PICK OF THE PUBS

## The Three Cups Inn ⭐ ⭐ ⭐ INN ⬤

*See Pick of the Pubs on page 240*

---

### STRATFIELD TURGIS          Map 5 SU65

## The Wellington Arms ⬤

RG27 0AS ☎ 01256 882214 📠 01256 882934
e-mail: wellington.arms@hall-woodhouse.co.uk
dir: *On A33 between Basingstoke & Reading*

Looking at this Grade II listed hotel today, it is hard to believe it was originally a farmhouse. The Wellington Arms is an ideal base for visiting the nearby Stratfield Saye estate, formerly the home of the Duke of Wellington. Well-kept real ales complement a good selection of eating options, including liver and bacon served with bubble and squeak; steak and kidney pudding; fanned avocado, cherry, tomato and bacon salad; and smoked salmon and prawn platter.

**Open** all day all wk noon-11 (Sun noon-10.30) ◀ Badger 1st Gold, Seasonal Ales. ⬤ 12 **Facilities** Dogs allowed Garden Parking

---

### TANGLEY          Map 5 SU35

## The Fox Inn ⬤

SP11 0RU ☎ 01264 730276 📠 01264 730478
e-mail: info@foxinntangley.co.uk
dir: *A343, 4m from Andover*

The 300-year-old brick and flint cottage that has been The Fox since 1830 stands on a small crossroads, miles,

---

it seems, from anywhere. Enjoy a pint of London Pride or Ramsbury in the tiny, friendly bar or try some fresh, authentic Thai cuisine available to eat in or take away from the restaurant. There is a menu for children, while adults can enjoy one of the changing, weekly specials.

**Open** all day all wk noon-11 (Sun noon-10.30) Closed: 25 Dec, 1 Jan **Bar Meals** L served Mon-Sat 12-2.30, Sun 12-3 booking required D served Mon-Sat 6-10, Sun 6-8 booking required **Restaurant** L served Mon-Sat 12-2.30, Sun 12-3 booking required D served Mon-Sat 6-10, Sun 6-8 booking required ⊕ FREE HOUSE ◀ London Pride, Ramsbury, Ö Stonehenge. ⬤ 12 **Facilities** Children's menu Children's portions Dogs allowed Garden Parking

---

### TICHBORNE          Map 5 SU53

### PICK OF THE PUBS

## The Tichborne Arms ⬤

SO24 0NA ☎ 01962 733760 📠 01962 733760
e-mail: tichbornearms@xln.co.uk
dir: *Off A31 towards Alresford, after 200yds right at Tichborne sign*

A picturesque thatched free house in the heart of the Itchen valley. Three pubs have been built on this site, the first in 1429, but each has been destroyed by fire; the present red-brick building was erected in 1939. An interesting history is attached to this idyllic rural hamlet, which was dramatised in feature film *The Tichborne Claimant*; it told the story of a butcher's boy from Australia who impersonated the son of Lady Tichborne to claim the family title and estates. The pub interior displays an eclectic mix of artefacts, from stuffed animals and antiques to a chiming grandfather clock. A glowing wood-burning stove matches the warmth of the welcome from owners Patrick and Nicky Roper, who cook to order daily changing menus of fresh local and seasonal produce. So expect a wide range of game dishes in winter; the fish menu is also extensive. A beer festival is held on the third weekend in August.

**Open** 11.30-3 6-11.30 Closed: Sun eve **Bar Meals** L served all wk 11.30-2 D served all wk 6.30-9 Av main course £10.95 ⊕ FREE HOUSE ◀ Hopback Brewery, Palmers, Bowman, Sharp's Downton Ö Mr Whitehead's Cirrus, Mr Whitehead's Strawberry. ⬤ 10 **Facilities** Children's portions Dogs allowed Garden Parking

---

### UPPER FROYLE          Map 5 SU74

## The Hen & Chicken Inn ⬤

GU34 4JH ☎ 01420 22115
e-mail: info@henandchicken.co.uk
dir: *2m from Alton, on A31 next to petrol station*

Bishops travelling between Winchester and Canterbury once rested at this 18th-century coaching inn, and highwayman Dick Turpin may well have laid low here. Today its still traditional atmosphere owes much to its large inglenook fireplace complete with empty post boxes above, wood panelling and beams. Twenty-first century travellers, both ecclesiastical and lay, can enjoy saddle

---

of venison Wellington with parsnip purée; 8oz sirloin steak with grilled field mushrooms; steamed Scottish mussels; and Moroccan-style chickpea stew. There's a children's play area in the garden.

**Open** all wk 11.45-3 5.30-close (Sat-Sun all day) **Bar Meals** L served Mon-Sat 12-2.30, Sun 12-8 booking required D served Mon-Thu 6-9, Fri-Sat 6-9.30, Sun 12-8 booking required Av main course £10 **Restaurant** L served Mon-Sat 12-2.30, Sun 12-8 booking required D served Mon-Thu 6-9, Fri-Sat 6-9.30, Sun 12-8 booking required Av 3 course à la carte fr £20 ⊕ HALL & WOODHOUSE ◀ Badger Best, Tanglefoot, King, Barnes Sussex Ale Ö Stowford Press. **Facilities** Children's menu Children's portions Play area Dogs allowed Garden Parking

---

### WARSASH          Map 5 SU40

## The Jolly Farmer Country Inn ⬤

29 Fleet End Rd SO31 9JH
☎ 01489 572500 📠 01489 885847
e-mail: mail@thejollyfarmeruk.com
dir: *Exit M27 junct 9 towards A27 Fareham, right onto Warsash Rd. Follow for 2m, left onto Fleet End Rd*

This friendly pub close to the Hamble River is unmissable thanks to the multi-coloured classic cars lined up outside. The bars are furnished in a rustic style with farming equipment on the walls and ceilings. There's also a patio, large beer garden and a purpose-built children's play area. Catch of the day seafood specials appear on the chalkboard, backed up with prime grills, light bites and house specialities such as chicken and seafood paella, confit of duck or chicken stroganoff.

**Open** all day all wk 11am-11pm **Bar Meals** L served Mon-Sat 12-2.30 (Sun all day) D served Mon-Sat 6-10 (Sun all day) Av main course £9.95 **Restaurant** L served all wk 12-2.30 D served all wk 6-10 Fixed menu price fr £9.95 ⊕ WHITBREAD ◀ Fuller's London Pride & HSB, Interbrew Flowers IPA. ⬤ 14 **Facilities** Play area Family room Dogs allowed Garden Parking

---

### WELL          Map 5 SU74

## The Chequers Inn ⬤

RG29 1TL ☎ 01256 862605 📠 01256 861116
e-mail: roybwells@aol.com
dir: *From Odiham High St turn right into Long Ln, follow for 3m, left at T-junct, pub 0.25m on top of hill*

Set deep in the heart of the Hampshire countryside, in the village of Well near Odiham, this 15th-century pub is full of charm and old world character, with a rustic, low-beamed bar, log fires, scrubbed tables and vine-covered front terrace. The menu offers good pub food such as steak and Tanglefoot pie, fishcakes, slow whole roast pheasant; and the chef's ultimate beefburger, served with home-made chips, new potatoes or creamy mash.

**Open** all wk noon-3 6-11pm (Sat noon-11pm Sun noon-10.30pm) ◀ Badger First Gold, Tanglefoot, Seasonal Ales, Guinness Ö Stowford Press. ⬤ 8 **Facilities** Family room Dogs allowed Garden Parking

# PICK OF THE PUBS

## The Three Cups Inn ★★★INN ♒

**STOCKBRIDGE** Map 5 SU33

**High St SO20 6HB** ☎ **01264 810527**
**e-mail:** manager@the3cups.co.uk
**web:** www.the3cups.co.uk
**dir:** *M3 junct 8, A303 towards Andover. Left onto A3057 to Stockbridge*

Almost at the far western end of Stockbridge's unusually wide main street, stands this 15th-century, timber-framed building. The pub's name apparently comes from an Old English phrase for a meeting of three rivers, although there's only one river here. The river happens to be the Test, generally regarded as the birthplace of modern fly fishing, but it splits into several channels through the town, so maybe that's how the name came about. One of these channels flows through the delightful rear garden.

Lucia Foster, the owner, has run the place for nearly 35 years and in most respects it must look much as it did more than three decades ago. The low-beamed bar to the right of the front door can be warmed by the centrally placed log fire; Ringwood, Itchen Valley and Flower Pots, all Hampshire real ales, and a guest, are served here. You can eat in the bar, but the main, candlelit dining area is at the other end of the building.

Modern European and traditional selections on the seasonal lunch, early evening and cartes, including a daily changing blackboard, blend fresh regional ingredients to create starters such as confit duck en croûte; tian of Selsey cock crab; and baked goat's cheese summer salad; and main courses of line-caught Solent sea bass; mature English sirloin; saddle of Southdown lamb; braised rabbit leg; and a vegetarian dish of the day. Desserts include orange and lemon caramelised tart with orange sorbet; peach Melba; and white and dark chocolate bavarois with Malibu and vanilla ice cream.

A covered patio extends into a rose-filled garden, where you can dine while trying to spot wild brown trout in the aforementioned stream. Accommodation suites provide Egyptian cotton sheets and real ground coffee.

**Open** all day all wk 10am-10.30pm
**Bar Meals** L served all wk 12-2.30 D served all wk 6-9.30 Av main course £10.95 **Restaurant** L served all wk 12-2.30 D served all wk 6-9.30 Fixed menu price fr £14.95 Av 3 course à la carte fr £20 ⊕ FREE HOUSE ◼ Fagin's Itchen Valley, Ringwood, Flower Pots, guest ales Ŏ Stowford Press. ♉ 10
**Facilities** Dogs allowed Garden Parking
**Rooms** 8

# PICK OF THE PUBS

## The Wykeham Arms ♀

**WINCHESTER** Map 5 SU42

**75 Kingsgate St SO23 9PE**
☎ **01962 853834** 🖶 **01962 854411**
e-mail: wykehamarms@fullers.co.uk
web: www.fullershotels.com/rte.
asp?id=129
**dir:** *Near Winchester College & Winchester Cathedral*

The 271-year-old Wyk, owned by London brewery Fuller's, is now in the capable hands of manager and landlord, Jon Howard. A thoroughly delightful place, it stands on the corner of two of Winchester's most charismatic thoroughfares: Kingsgate Street, lined with old buildings associated with Winchester College, and Canon Street, whose 19th-century terraced houses climb pleasingly uphill. Through the Wyk's unusual curved front doors, you may take one of two routes – straight on into the main bar, or left into another; both immediately convey what Germans call gemütlichkeit, the notion of belonging and warm friendliness, which for here is the perfect definition.

Photographs, paintings and Nelson-related ephemera fill most walls, and pewter tankards, walking canes and heaven knows what else hang from ceilings. Beyond each bar are warren-like, tucked-away dining areas, although you may also eat in the bars themselves at one of the old Winchester College desks. The wine cellar is particularly well stocked, with twenty or so by the glass chalked on a blackboard.

For a lunchtime snack, the sandwiches – smoked salmon and cream cheese, for example - are good. The frequently changing lunchtime and evening menus typically offer starters of grilled brie and onion marmalade tartlets with dressed rocket; grilled sardines with beef tomato and olive salad; and pan-fried mixed wild mushrooms with red onion and Isle of White soft cheese, and mains of chargrilled beef fillet with wilted spinach, blue Vitelotte potato chips and pepper sauce; beer-battered (Fuller's Organic Honey Dew) cod fillet with mint pea purée, hand-cut chips and tartare sauce; and asparagus and ricotta ravioli with chilli and garlic. Or try the famous Wyk (cottage) pie. There's a patio outside to enjoy in the warmer months.

**Open** all day all wk 11-11 (Sun 11-10.30) **Bar Meals** L served Mon-Sat 12-3 Av main course £9 **Restaurant** L served all wk 12-3 booking required D served all wk 6.30-9.30 booking required Fixed menu price fr £18.95 Av 3 course à la carte fr £25 🛢 FULLERS ◀ HSB, London Pride, Chiswick, Seafarer, guest ales. ♀ 20 **Facilities** Dogs allowed Garden Parking

## WHERWELL                              Map 5 SU34

### The White Lion ♀

**Fullerton Rd SP11 7JF ☎ 01264 860317**
*dir: M3 junct 8, A303, then B3048 to Wherwell; or A3057 (S of Andover), B3420 to Wherwell*

The White Lion is a well-known historic pub in the heart of the Test Valley. Parts of the building date back to before the Civil War, during which one of Cromwell's cannon balls supposedly fell down the chimney and is on display today. Enjoy a pint of Ringwood Best while reflecting upon other historical features, such as the bricked-up windows which resulted from the Window Tax introduced in 1696. Food consists of traditional favourites and a seasonal specials board. Recent change of hands.

**Open** all wk 11-2.30 6-10.30 (Thu-Sat 6-11 Sun noon-3) Closed: 25 Dec ◀ Ringwood Best Bitter, John Smith's Smooth. ♀ 12 **Facilities** Dogs allowed Garden Parking

## WHITCHURCH                            Map 5 SU44

### Watership Down Inn ♀

**Freefolk Priors RG28 7NJ ☎ 01256 892254**
e-mail: watershipdowninn@live.co.uk
*dir: On B3400 between Basingstoke & Andover*

Enjoy an exhilarating walk on Watership Down before relaxing with a pint of well-kept local ale at this homely 19th-century inn named after Richard Adams' classic tale of rabbit life. Now under new ownership, the pub offers a menu that includes scampi, chips and peas; steak and ale pie; Caribbean chicken; plus baguettes, sandwiches and jacket potatoes. All dishes are available in smaller portions for children, and as takeaways.

**Open** all day all wk **Bar Meals** Av main course £8 food served all day **Restaurant** food served all day ⊕ PUNCH TAVERNS ◀ Ringwood Best, Youngs Special, Sharp's Doom Bar, Bombardier. ♀ 11 **Facilities** Children's portions Play area Dogs allowed Garden Parking

## WICKHAM                                Map 5 SU51

### Greens Restaurant & Pub ♀

**The Square PO17 5JQ ☎ 01329 833197**
e-mail: DuckworthGreens@aol.com
*dir: 2m from M27, on corner of historic Wickham Square. 3m from Fareham*

Set on a corner of Wickham's picturesque square, Frank and Carol Duckworth have been welcoming customers to Greens for over 25 years. Drinkers will find award-winning local ales and high standards of customer service that ensure a warm and welcoming reception. The modern British menu includes starters like twice-baked Winchester cheese soufflé, whilst main course options might include loin of free-range Hampshire pork; or Caesar salad with a choice of chicken or salmon. Finish your meal with home-made ice cream. To celebrate their successful 25 years at Greens, Frank and Carol Duckworth are running a series of promotions during the year.

**Open** 10-3 6-11 (Sun & BH noon-4) Closed: Sun eve & Mon **Bar Meals** L served Tue-Sat 12-2.30, Sun 12-3 booking required D served Tue-Sat 6.30-9.30 booking required **Restaurant** L served Tue-Sat 12-2.30, Sun 12-3 booking required D served Tue-Sat 6.30-9.30 booking required ⊕ FREE HOUSE ◀ Hopback Summer Lightning, Youngs Special, Guinness, Timothy Taylor, Local ales. ♀ 10 **Facilities** Children's portions Garden Parking

## WINCHESTER                            Map 5 SU42

### The Bell Inn ♀

**83 St Cross Rd SO23 9RE ☎ 01962 865284**
e-mail: the_bellinn@btconnect.com
*dir: M3 junct 11, B3355 towards city centre. Approx 1m pub on right*

Edge of town local that's worth noting as it stands close to the 12th-century St Cross Hospital, with its fine Norman church, and glorious walks through the River Itchen water meadows to Winchester College and the city centre. Very much a community local, with Greene King ales and good value food served in the main bar and the pine-furnished lounge, plus a warm welcome to families and dogs. Head for the sunny walled garden on warm summer days.

**Open** all day all wk 11-11 (Fri-Sat 11am-mdnt Sun noon-10.30) **Bar Meals** L served Mon-Sat 12-2.30, Sun 12-4 D served Mon-Sat 6-9, Sun 12-4 ⊕ GREENE KING ◀ IPA, 2 guest ales Ò Stowford Press. ♀ 10 **Facilities** Children's portions Play area Dogs allowed Garden Parking

### The Westgate Inn ★★★ INN

**2 Romsey Rd SO23 8TP**
**☎ 01962 820222 ▤ 01962 820222**
e-mail: wghguy@yahoo.co.uk
*dir: On corner of Romsey Rd & Upper High St, opposite Great Hall & Medieval West Gate*

When the railway developed its routes to the west, brewer Eldridge Pope saw the potential to transport its ales to London and provide accommodation and refreshment to travellers since the 1850s. This quirky building in Winchester's main shopping street was created from three buildings opposite the medieval West Gate. Home-cooked meals are served along with real ales and ciders, including succulent steaks, fish and chips and share platters. Attractive and good-sized accommodation is available.

**Open** all day all wk noon-11.30 **Bar Meals** L served all wk 12-2.30 D served all wk 6-9.30 Av main course £7.50 **Restaurant** L served all wk 12-2.30 D served all wk 6-9.30 ⊕ MARSTONS ◀ Jennings Cumberland, Banks Original, Marstons Burton Bitter, guest ales Ò Thatchers Gold, Wychwood Green Goblin. **Facilities** Dogs allowed **Rooms** 8

See Pick of the Pubs on page 241

## PICK OF THE PUBS

### The Wykeham Arms ♀

*See Pick of the Pubs on page 241*

# HEREFORDSHIRE

## ASTON CREWS                           Map 10 SO62

## PICK OF THE PUBS

### The Penny Farthing Inn

**HR9 7LW ☎ 01989 750366 ▤ 01989 750366**
e-mail: thepennyfarthinginn@hotmail.co.uk
*dir: 5m E of Ross-on-Wye*

New owners have taken over this whitewashed 17th-century blacksmith's shop and coaching inn, located high above the Wye Valley, with stunning views of the Malvern Hills, the Black Mountains and the Forest of Dean from the restaurant and charming garden. Inside are lots of nooks and crannies with oak beams, antiques, saddlery and warming log fires. The menu capitalises on the wealth of local vegetable and fruit growers' produce, and some of the best meat in the country. Begin with chicken liver pâté with red onion marmalade or creamy garlic mushrooms, then follow with braised lamb shank with creamy mash and rosemary sauce, duck breast with port and raspberry sauce, or one of the daily chalkboard specials, perhaps whole lemon sole with garlic butter, or lambs' liver on bubble-and-squeak with onion gravy. Footpaths radiate from the front door.

**Open** Mon-Thu 12-3 6-11 (Sun 12-3) Closed: Mon in winter **Bar Meals** L served Tue-Sun 12-3 D served Tue-Sat 6.30-9 Av main course £8.95 **Restaurant** L served Tue-Sun 12-3 D served Tue-Sat 6.30-9 ⊕ PUBFOLIO ◀ John Smith's, Black Sheep, 6x Ò Westons Stowford Press. **Facilities** Children's menu Children's portions Dogs allowed Garden Parking

## AYMESTREY                             Map 9 SO46

## PICK OF THE PUBS

### The Riverside Inn

*See Pick of the Pubs on opposite page*

## BODENHAM                              Map 10 SO55

### England's Gate Inn

**HR1 3HU ☎ 01568 797286 ▤ 01568 797768**
*dir: Hereford A49, turn onto A417 at Bosey Dinmore hill, 2.5m on right*

A pretty black and white coaching inn dating from around 1540, with atmospheric beamed bars and blazing log fires in winter. A picturesque garden attracts a good summer following, and so does the food. The menu features such dishes as Moroccan-style lamb tagine with apricot and almond couscous; slow roast pork belly with black pudding and home-made faggot; and classic steak

*continued on page 244*

# PICK OF THE PUBS

## The Riverside Inn

**AYMESTREY**　　　　Map 9 SO46

**HR6 9ST ☎ 01568 708440**
e-mail: theriverside@btconnect.com
dir: *On A4110, 18m N of Hereford*

This eye-catching old inn snuggles down beside a bridge over the river Lugg deep in the north Herefordshire countryside, an area dappled by old orchards and threaded by sinuous, wooded ridges above age-old watermeadows. Over 300 years old, it's a popular pit-stop for walkers hiking the Mortimer Trail from Ludlow to Kington as the pub stands at the halfway point, and numerous circular walks start from the front door. Anglers are also drawn to inn and it offers a mile of private fishing for brown trout and grayling.

The interior, with its wood panelling, low beams and log fires, engenders a relaxed atmosphere reflecting its long history. Real ales and ciders, drawing on the Marches' long tradition of brewing and cider making, include beers from Hereford's Spinning Dog brewery and Brook Farm cider made in nearby Wigmore.

Owner Richard Gresko has a very focused approach to food, and locally grown and reared produce is used as much as possible in his kitchen. Visitors are welcome to take a stroll round the pub's extensive vegetable, herb and fruit gardens, strung above the secluded riverside beer garden, one of the nicest you'll find anywhere.

Diners are promised a synergy of finest ingredients and imaginative cooking from the award winning team of chefs, producing local country style dishes. Judge for yourself as the impressive starters choice includes baked flat field mushroom topped with Ragstone cheese with roasted pinenuts and balsamic dressing or pan-fried breast of local wood pigeon with black pudding, pickled apple purée and a damson vinaigrette. Mains major on the extraordinary range of turf and woodland meats available literally just down the lane from local estates and shoots.

On the day you may find seared tenderloin of organic rare breed pork stuffed with apricots, prunes and pistachios, Herefordshire apple and gooseberry compote with an aromatically spiced sauce, or pan-fried haunch of local wild venison, spiced apple and pear purée, braised garden red cabbage with a red wine sauce. Of course, the famous Herefordshire beef gets a look in, with pan-fried rare-breed Herefordshire fillet steak, Provençal tomatoes, Wye Valley beer battered onion rings with red wine and shallot jus doing the business.

**Open** 11-3 6-11 (Sun 12-3 6-10.30)
Closed: 26 Dec & 1 Jan, Sun eve, Mon L, Mon eve in winter **Bar Meals** L served Tue-Sun 12-2 booking required D served Mon-Sat 7-9 booking required Av main course £9.95 **Restaurant** L served Tue-Sun 12-2 booking required D served Mon-Sat 7-9 booking required Av 3 course à la carte fr £21.50 ⊕ FREE HOUSE ◼ Wye Valley Bitter & Butty Bach, Hobsons Best Bitter, Spinning Dog, Owd Bull ♂ Brooke Farm Medium Dry, Westons Stowford Press.
**Facilities** Children's menu Dogs allowed Garden Parking

**BODENHAM** *continued*

and ale pie — melt-in-the-mouth beef slowly cooked in Butty Bach real ale.

**Open** all day all wk **Bar Meals** L served all wk 12-2.30 D served all wk 6-9.30 Av main course £9.95 **Restaurant** L served all wk 12-2.30 D served all wk 6-9.30 booking required ⊕ FREE HOUSE ◀ Wye Valley Bitter, Butty Bach, Shropshire Lad, guest ales. **Facilities** Children's menu Children's portions Dogs allowed Garden Parking

### BRINGSTY COMMON            Map 10 SO75

## Live and Let Live NEW

**WR6 5UW ☎ 01886 821462**
**e-mail:** theliveandletlive@tiscali.co.uk
**dir:** *From A44 (Bromyard to Worcester road) turn at sign with cat onto track leading to the common. At 1st fork bear right. Pub 200yds on right*

Secluded amidst bracken-covered common and old orchards, this lovely old thatched cider house reopened in 2007 after several years closure and truly inspirational work by owner Sue Dovey. Local Oliver's cider is joined by beers from south Marches micro-breweries. Bar meals and the intimate Thatch restaurant major on seasonal food from the home area, including Hereford Hop Cheese, Bringsty Black Welsh Mountain lamb and Whitbourne organic pork sausages. The common has superb, easy walks to raise an appetite.

**Open** Tue-Fri 12-2.30 5.30-11 Sat-Sun all day Closed: Mon (ex BHs) **Bar Meals** L served all wk 12-2 D served all wk 6-9 Av main course £10 **Restaurant** D served all wk 6-9 Fixed menu price fr £10 ⊕ FREE HOUSE ◀ MHB, Ludlow, Wye Valley, Hobsons ♂ Olivers, Robinsons. **Facilities** Children's portions Dogs allowed Garden Parking Notes ⊛

### CRASWALL            Map 9 SO23

## The Bulls Head

**HR2 0PN ☎ 01981 510616**
**e-mail:** info@thebullsheadcraswall.co.uk
**dir:** *From A465 turn at Pandy. Village in 11m*

Set in a remote spot at the foot of the Black Mountains, this old drovers' inn is not easy to find but well worth the effort. Just six miles from Hay on Wye, it is popular with walkers and riders, who tie their horses at the rail outside. Real ales and farmhouse ciders are served through the hole in the wall servery in the character bar with flagstone floors, and there are log fires in winter. Typical dishes include the house speciality rib of Herefordshire beef cooked on the bone (for two), Italian style sausages, beef pie and local black pudding with apples. Wimberry tart is a popular summer dessert.

**Open** 12-3 6.30-11 Closed: Winter months ex school hols, Mon & Tue **Bar Meals** L served all wk 12-2 D served all wk 6.30-9 Av main course £11 **Restaurant** L served all wk 12-2 D served all wk 6.30-9 Av 3 course à la carte fr £20 ⊕ FREE HOUSE ◀ Butty Bach, Wye Valley Organic Bitter ♂ Gwatkin's Farmhouse & Norman, Westons Old Rosie Scrumpy. **Facilities** Dogs allowed Garden

### DORSTONE            Map 9 SO34

## PICK OF THE PUBS

### *The Pandy Inn*

**HR3 6AN ☎ 01981 550273 ▤ 01981 550277**
**e-mail:** magdalena@pandyinn.wanadoo.co.uk
**dir:** *Off B4348 W of Hereford*

The Pandy is one of the oldest inns in the country and has a fascinating history. One of the four Norman knights who killed Thomas à Becket in Canterbury Cathedral in 1170, Richard de Brito, built a chapel at Dorstone as an act of atonement after 15 years in the Holy Land. He also built the Pandy to house the workers, subsequently adapting it to become an inn. Later, during the Civil War in the 17th century, Oliver Cromwell is known to have taken refuge here. The ancient hostelry is located opposite the village green and part of it retains its original flagstone floors and beams. The large garden, which offers 19 tables and a children's playground, has views of Dorstone Hill. Food is freshly prepared daily and the seasonal menu includes Pandy pies and home-made puddings. Farmhouse ciders are served alongside local cask ales.

**Open** all wk Closed: Mon Oct-Jun ◀ Wye Valley Bitter & Butty Bach. **Facilities** Play area Dogs allowed Garden Parking

### FOWNHOPE            Map 10 SO53

### The Green Man Inn ⬤

**HR1 4PE ☎ 01432 860243 ▤ 01432 860920**
**e-mail:** greenman.hereford@thespiritgroup.com
**dir:** *From M50 junct 4 take A449 then B4224 towards Hereford to Fownhope*

This white-painted 15th-century coaching inn has a host of beams inside and out. Set in an attractive garden close to the River Wye, it's an ideal base for walking, touring and salmon fishing. The extensive menu has something for everyone, with a range of chunky sandwiches, jacket potatoes, burgers and ciabatta melts. Then there are hand-made pies, gourmet grills, and main course favourites like sausages and mash. Recent change of hands.

**Open** all day all wk 11am-11pm (Sun noon-10.30pm) ◀ John Smith's Smooth, Bombardier, Adnams ♂ Stowford Press. ⬤ 8 **Facilities** Garden Parking

### HAMPTON BISHOP            Map 10 SO53

### The Bunch of Carrots ⬤

**HR1 4JR ☎ 01432 870237 ▤ 01432 870237**
**e-mail:** bunchofcarrots@buccaneer.co.uk
**dir:** *From Hereford take A4103, A438, then B4224*

The name has nothing to do with crunchy orange vegetables - it comes from a rock formation in the River Wye, which runs alongside this friendly pub. Inside, expect real fires, old beams and flagstones.

There is an extensive menu plus a daily specials board, a carvery, salad buffet, and simple bar snacks. Real ale aficionados should certainly sample the local organic beer, or enjoy a pint of Wye Valley Bitter or Black Bull.

**Open** all wk ◀ Directors, Wye Valley Bitter, Black Bull Bitter, Organic Bitter ♂ Westons Stowford Press. ⬤ 11 **Facilities** Play area Dogs allowed Garden Parking

### HEREFORD            Map 10 SO53

### The Crown & Anchor ⬤

**Cotts Ln, Lugwardine HR1 4AB**
**☎ 01432 851303 ▤ 01432 851637**
**dir:** *2m from Hereford on A438. Left into Lugwardine down Cotts Lane*

Old Herefordshire-style black-and-white pub with quarry tile floors and a large log fire, just up from the bridge over the River Lugg. Among the many interesting specials you might find fillets of Torbay sole with mussels and white wine; mushrooms in filo pastry with wild mushroom and marsala sauce; seafood tagliolini; supreme of chicken stuffed with wild mushrooms and chestnuts with cranberry and white wine sauce; or Brother Geoffrey's pork sausages with juniper and red wine sauce and mash. A long lunchtime sandwich list is available.

**Open** all wk Closed: 25 Dec ◀ Worthington Bitter, Timothy Taylor Landlord, Marstons Pedigree, Butcombe Ale, Ruddles. ⬤ 8 **Facilities** Dogs allowed Garden Parking

### HOARWITHY            Map 10 SO52

## The New Harp Inn NEW

**HR2 6QH ☎ 01432 840900**
**dir:** *From Ross-on-Wye take A49 towards Hereford. Turn right for Hoarwithy*

A real country pub, with the slogan: 'Kids, dogs and muddy boots all welcome'. Situated on the river Wye, the pub is popular with locals, fishermen, campers and visitors to the countryside. Begin with a local real ale, an unusual foreign bottled beer or a home-produced cider. The menu spoils for choice with 28-day, chargrilled Herefordshire sirloin steak; rack of Holme Lacey lamb; pork fillet and boudin noir with apple and pork faggot; beer-battered Cornish fish and home-made chips; and leek and feta cakes. Outside are a real babbling brook and extensive gardens.

**Open** all wk Mon-Thu noon-3 6-11 Fri-Sun all day **Bar Meals** L served all wk 12-3 D served all wk 6-9 Av main course £11 **Restaurant** L served all wk 12-3 D served all wk 6-9 Fixed menu price fr £19 Av 3 course à la carte fr £23.50 ◀ Timothy Taylor Landlord, Wye Valley, Malvern Pear ♂ Stowford Press, New Harp Reserve. **Facilities** Children's menu Children's portions Play area Dogs allowed Garden Parking

Save on Hotels. Book at **theAA.com/hotel**

**HEREFORDSHIRE** 245 **ENGLAND**

## KIMBOLTON
Map 10 SO56

### PICK OF THE PUBS

## Stockton Cross Inn ♀

HR6 0HD ☎ 01568 612509 📄 01568 620238
e-mail: mb@ecolots.co.uk
dir: On A4112, 0.5m off A49, between Leominster & Ludlow

A drovers' inn dating from the 16th century, the Stockton Cross Inn stands beside a crossroads where witches, rounded up from the surrounding villages such as Ludlow, were allegedly hanged. This grisly past is at odds with the peace and beauty of the setting, which includes a pretty country garden with umbrellas and trees for shade. The building itself is regularly photographed by tourists and featured on calendars and chocolate boxes. Landlord Mike Bentley tends a range of ales which include Wye Valley Butty Bach and HPA, Hobson's Town Crier and Tetleys Smooth Flow. Children are welcome and enjoy their own menu. In addition to the specials board dishes on the menu might include smoked haddock and risotto cake; glazed goat's cheese, black olive and sundried tomato salad and basil pesto; beer battered fish and home made chips; cottage pie and vegetables; locally made sausages with mash and onion gravy. If you've room left maybe tuck into a dessert of rhubarb and apple crumble with. All meals are prepared on the premises using organic produce wherever possible.

**Open** 12-3 7-11 Closed: Sun eve & Mon **Bar Meals** L served Tue-Sun 12-2 D served Tue-Sat 7-9 Av main course £10 **Restaurant** L served Tue-Sun 12-2 D served Tue-Sat 7-9 ⊕ FREE HOUSE ◀ Wye Valley Butty Bach & HPA, Hobson's Town Crier, Flowers Best Bitter, Murphys, Tetley's Smooth Flow, guest ales ♂ Robinsons Flagon. ♀ 8 **Facilities** Children's menu Children's portions Garden Parking

## KINGTON
Map 9 SO25

### PICK OF THE PUBS

## The Stagg Inn and Restaurant ◉◉ ♀

Titley HR5 3RL ☎ 01544 230221 📄 01544 231390
e-mail: reservations@thestagg.co.uk
dir: Between Kington & Presteigne on B4355

Titley stands amid unspoilt Welsh border country at the junction of two drovers' roads, and wool would have been weighed here. The inn was known as The Balance until 1833, when Eliza Greenley of Titley Court gave the

building its brick frontage and re-named the inn after her family crest. Farmhouse tables and crackling log fires make for a relaxed atmosphere in the rambling dining rooms and homely bar, where local farmers gather for pints of Hobson's and Ralph's Radnorshire cider, accompanied by bar snacks like home-made sausages from the inn's own pigs, steak sandwich or scallops on parsnip purée. Local boy and Roux-trained chef Steve Reynolds has a passion for local produce, and his assured modern approach to cooking allows key flavours to shine through in such robust, earthy starters as local goat's cheese and fennel tart. Main course options might feature herbed chicken breast with potato fondant, or monkfish on mussel risotto with green salad. Home-made puddings complete the picture along with a cheese board menu.

**Open** Tue-Sun 12-3 (Tue-Sat 6.30-10.30) Closed: 2wks Nov, 2wks Jan & Feb, Sun eve & Mon **Bar Meals** L served Tue-Sat 12-2 D served Tue-Thu 6.30-9 Av main course £9.90 **Restaurant** L served Tue-Sun 12-2 booking required D served Tue-Sat 6.30-9 booking required Av 3 course à la carte fr £25 ⊕ FREE HOUSE ◀ Hobsons-Town Crier, Old Henry & Best Bitter, Brains Rev James, Timothy Taylor Landlord, Ludlow Best ♂ Dunkertons Black Fox, Ralph's Cider. ♀ 12 **Facilities** Children's portions Dogs allowed Garden Parking

## LEDBURY
Map 10 SO73

## The Farmers Arms ♀

Horse Rd, Wellington Heath HR8 1LS ☎ 01531 632010
dir: Through Ledbury, pass rail station, right into Wellington Heath, 1st right for pub

Standing at the bottom of a country lane, this charming country inn has an elevated position over the village green. Wood's Shropshire Lad and Wye Valley's Butty Bach beers are among those in the bar. The comprehensive menu makes good use of local produce, such as Pontypool loin of lamb; grilled 10oz Hereford rib-eye steak; escalope of Severn and Wye salmon; and Maynard Farm caramelised ham. Heated, covered seating on the patio is tailor-made for outdoor eating; there's a children's play area too.

**Open** all wk ⊕ BERMILL LTD ◀ London Pride, Wye Valley, Doom Bar, Guest ales. ♀ 8 **Facilities** Children's menu Play area Dogs allowed Garden Parking

## The Talbot ♀

14 New St HR8 2DX ☎ 01531 632963 📄 01531 636107
e-mail: talbot.ledbury@wadworth.co.uk
dir: Follow Ledbury signs, turn into Bye St, 2nd left into Woodley Rd, over bridge to junct, left into New St. Pub on right

Step back in time with a visit to this late 16th-century black-and-white coaching inn. Dating from 1596, the oak-panelled dining room, with fine carved overmantle, still displays musket-shot damage after a skirmish here between Roundheads and Cavaliers in 1645. Choose from a good selection of Wadworth ales, and menus listing

starters like smoked mackerel pâté, and traditional favourites such as home-cooked ham with a brace of free range eggs. Puddings, also home-made, include apple and berry crumble with damson and sloe gin ice cream.

**Open** all day all wk **Bar Meals** L served all wk 12-2.30 D served all wk 6-9.15 Av main course £10.95 **Restaurant** L served all wk 12-2.30 D served all wk 6-9.15 ⊕ WADWORTH ◀ Wadworth 6X & Henrys Original IPA, Wye Valley Butty Bach, Wadworth guest ales, Henry's Smooth ♂ Stowford Press, Westons Organic, Westons Perry. ♀ 15 **Facilities** Children's portions Garden Parking

## The Trumpet Inn

Trumpet HR8 2RA ☎ 01531 670277
dir: 4m from Ledbury, at junct of A438 & A417

This traditional black and white free house dates back to the late 14th century. The former coaching inn and post house takes its name from the days when mail coaches blew their horns on approaching the crossroads. The cosy bars feature a wealth of exposed beams, with open fireplaces and a separate dining area. Light sandwich lunches and salad platters complement main dishes like salmon fishcakes; kleftiko; or vegetable stroganoff.

**Open** all wk ◀ Wadworth 6X, Henrys IPA, Old Father Time. **Facilities** Dogs allowed Garden Parking

## LEOMINSTER
Map 10 SO45

## The Grape Vaults

Broad St HR4 8BS ☎ 01568 611404
e-mail: jusaxon@tiscali.co.uk
dir: Telephone for directions

An unspoilt pub with a small, homely bar complete with real fire - in fact it's so authentic that it's Grade II listed, even down to the fixed seating. Real ale is a popular feature, and includes micro-brewery products. The good food includes turkey and ham pie, bubble and squeak with bacon and egg, steak and ale pie, and various fresh fish dishes using cod, plaice, salmon and whitebait. No music, gaming machines, or alcopops!

**Open** all day all wk 11-11 **Bar Meals** L served all wk 12-2 D served Mon-Sat 5.30-9 ⊕ PUNCH TAVERNS ◀ guest ales. **Facilities** Children's portions Dogs allowed **Notes** ◉

## The Royal Oak Hotel

South St HR6 8JA ☎ 01568 612610 📄 01568 612710
e-mail: reservations@theroyaloakhotel.net
dir: Town centre, near A44/A49 junct

Coaching inn dating from around 1733, with log fires, antiques and a minstrels' gallery in the original ballroom. The pub was once part of a now blocked-off tunnel system that linked the Leominster Priory with other buildings in the town. Good choice of ales, and a hearty menu offering traditional British food with a modern twist.

**Open** all wk ◀ Shepherd Neame Spitfire, Wye Valley Butty Bach. **Facilities** Dogs allowed Garden Parking

## LITTLE COWARNE — Map 10 SO65

### The Three Horseshoes Inn ♥

**HR7 4RQ ☎ 01885 400276 🖹 01885 400276**
**e-mail:** janetwhittall@threehorseshoes.co.uk
**dir:** *Off A456 (Hereford/Bromyard). At Stokes Cross follow Little Cowarne/Pencombe signs*

They no longer shoe horses at the blacksmith next door, but this old ale house's long drinking pedigree - 200 years and counting - looks secure. Norman and Janet Whittall have seen 20 years here and have newly redecorated throughout; their son Philip, the head chef, creates dishes sourced mainly from fresh, local ingredients; some are grown in the inn's garden. There's a good range of bar snacks but the restaurant menu could feature pork and pheasant pâté with pickled damsons; pan-fried Herefordshire venison with sloe gin sauce; or pheasant breast stuffed with spiced pear with elderberry sauce. Well travelled Philip turns his talents to more exotic dishes for an 'all you can eat' curry night each Wednesday.

**Open** 11-3 6.30-mdnt (Sun noon-4 7-mdnt) Closed: 25-26 Dec, 1 Jan & Sun eve in Winter **Bar Meals** L served all wk 12-2.30 D served all wk 6.30-9 Av main course £10 **Restaurant** L served all wk 12-2.30 D served Mon-Sat 6.30-9, Sun summer 7-9 ⊕ FREE HOUSE ◀ Greene King Old Speckled Hen, Wye Valley Bitter, Ruddles Best ♂ Stowford Press, Olivers Cider, Perry. ♥ 12
**Facilities** Children's menu Children's portions Family room Garden Parking

## MADLEY — Map 9 SO43

### The Comet Inn

**Stoney St HR2 9NJ ☎ 01981 250600**
**e-mail:** thecometinn-madley@hotmail.co.uk
**dir:** *6m from Hereford on B4352*

Originally three cottages, this black and white 19th-century inn occupies a prominent corner position and is set in two and a half acres — no surprise, then, that there's a large beer garden where food can be served on fine days. Inside it retains many original features and a roaring open fire. Vicky Willison, the enthusiastic and welcoming owner, serves simple and hearty pub food in the conservatory off the main bar, with smaller portions for smaller appetites if required.

**Open** all wk 12-3 6-11 (Fri-Sun all day) **Bar Meals** food served all day **Restaurant** food served all day ⊕ FREE HOUSE ◀ Wye Valley Bitter ♂ Stowford Press.
**Facilities** Children's menu Children's portions Play area Garden Parking

## MUCH MARCLE — Map 10 SO63

### The Slip Tavern ♥

**Watery Ln HR8 2NG ☎ 01531 660246 🖹 01531 660700**
**e-mail:** thesliptavern@aol.com
**dir:** *Follow signs off A449 at Much Marcle junction*

Curiously named after a 1575 landslip which buried the local church, this country pub is delightfully surrounded by cider apple orchards. An attractive conservatory overlooks the award-winning garden, where summer dining is popular, and there's also a cosy bar with roaring fires in winter. Being situated next to Weston's Cider Mill, cider is a favourite in the bar along with real ales from the cask. There are regular jazz and folk evenings.

**Open** all wk Tue-Sun 12-3 6-11.30 Closed: Mon
**Bar Meals** L served Tue-Sun 12-2 D served Tue-Sun 6.30-9 Av main course £6.95 **Restaurant** L served Tue-Sun 12-2 booking required D served Tue-Sun 6.30-9 booking required Fixed menu price fr £9.95 Av 3 course à la carte fr £20 ⊕ FREE HOUSE ◀ John Smith's, Butcombe, Guest ales ♂ Stowford Press. Vintage Organic. ♥ 9 **Facilities** Children's portions Play area Dogs allowed Garden Parking

## ORLETON — Map 9 SO46

### The Boot Inn

**SY8 4HN ☎ 01568 780228**
**e-mail:** thebootinn@villagegreeninns.com
**dir:** *Follow A49 S from Ludlow (approx 7m) to B4362 (Woofferton), 1.5m off B4362 turn left. Inn in village centre*

A black and white half timbered village inn, The Boot dates from the 16th century, and in winter a blazing fire in the inglenook warms the bar. You will be welcomed with excellent service, a good quality English menu with locally sourced produce and a fine range of cask ales. The wine list has been chosen to compliment the menu and to suit all pockets. Recent change of ownership.

**Open** all wk 12-3 5.30-11 (Sat-Sun noon-11) **Bar Meals** L served Mon-Sat 12-2, Sun 12-3.30 D served all wk 6.45-9 Av main course £10 **Restaurant** L served all wk 12-3 D served all wk 6-9 ⊕ VILLAGE GREEN INNS ◀ Hobsons Best, Local Real Ales, Woods, Wye Valley ♂ Robinsons.
**Facilities** Children's menu Play area Dogs allowed Garden Parking

## PEMBRIDGE — Map 9 SO35

### New Inn

**Market Square HR6 9DZ**
**☎ 01544 388427 🖹 01544 388427**
**dir:** *From M5 junct 7 take A44 W through Leominster towards Llandrindod Wells*

Worn flagstone floors and open fires in winter characterise this unspoilt black and white timbered free house. Formerly a courthouse and jail, the building dates from the early 14th century. In summer, customers spill out into the pub's outdoor seating area in the Old Market Square. It attracts locals and summer tourists alike for the great selection of real ales, malts and ciders, and the home-cooked English food.

**Open** all wk 11-2.30 6-11 (summer 11-3) Closed: 1st wk Feb **Bar Meals** L served all wk 12-2 D served all wk 6.30-9 booking required Av main course £11.50 **Restaurant** L served all wk 12-2 D served all wk 6.30-9 booking required ⊕ FREE HOUSE ◀ Three Tuns from Bishops Castle, Ludlow Brewery, Hobsons, Doom Bar, Hook Norton ♂ Stowford Press, Westons Organic, Dunkertons.
**Facilities** Children's portions Family room Garden Parking

## ROSS-ON-WYE — Map 10 SO52

### The Moody Cow ♥

**Upton Bishop HR9 7TT ☎ 01989 780470**
**e-mail:** info@themoodycow.biz
**dir:** *From A449 take turn signed Newent , 1m into Upton Bishop. Or M50 junct 3 take Newent exit, left. Pub in 1.5m*

According to chef/proprietor Jonathan Rix, the pub — once the Wellington — is named after (but presumably not by) a former landlord's wife. He serves local ales such as Wye Valley as well as Weston's organic cider and a good selection of wines, and sources produce, or at least most of it, from within 20 miles. His tempting menus offer glazed lamb's liver with red cabbage and garlic mash; Caesar salad with grilled wood-pigeon, artichokes and bacon; Brixham hake fried in Wye Valley beer batter with triple-cooked chips and mushy peas; and Japanese-style seafood broth with rice noodles.

**Open** 11-3.30 6-11 (Sun 11-6.30) Closed: Mon
**Bar Meals** L served Tue-Sun 11.30-2.30 D served Tue-Sat 6.30-10 Av main course £11.95 **Restaurant** L served Tue-Sun 11.30-2.30 D served Tue-Sat 6.30-10 booking required Fixed menu price fr £19.95 Av 3 course à la carte fr £30 ⊕ ENTERPRISE ◀ Wye Valley Bitter, Butty Bach, Spitfire ♂ Stowford Press, Westons Organic. ♥ 9
**Facilities** Children's portions Dogs allowed Garden Parking

## ST OWENS CROSS — Map 10 SO52

### PICK OF THE PUBS

### The New Inn ♥

*See Pick of the Pubs on opposite page*

# PICK OF THE PUBS

# The New Inn ♟

### ST OWENS CROSS    Map 10 SO52

**HR2 8LQ**
☎ **01989 730274**  📠 **01989 730557**
**e-mail:** info@newinn.biz
**web:** www.newinn.biz
**dir:** *Off A4137 W of Ross-on-Wye*

A delightful, multi-award-winning 16th-century inn, under the caring eye of new owners who took over in late 2009. The spacious beer garden overlooks rolling Herefordshire countryside, with views stretching to the Black Mountains in the distance and is ideal for alfresco dining, weather permitting. Thankfully recent interior refurbishments have preserved the character of features like the exposed beams and woodwork, creating a cosy and traditional backdrop for a drink, a quick snack or a leisurely meal. Among the changing selection of ales you might find Wychwood's Hobgoblin and Marstons Burton Bitter. The ever-changing menus reveal a keen sense of the seasons and a real commitment to sourcing excellent local ingredients. Ross-on-Wye is just four miles away, and the surrounding area includes countless other attractions such as Symonds Yat rock, Goodrich Castle and Hereford Cathedral, all of which are within easy reach.

**Open** all day all wk 11-11
**Bar Meals** L served Mon-Sat 12-9, Sun 12-7.30 D served Mon-Sat 12-9, Sun 12-7.30 food served all day
**Restaurant** L served Mon-Sat 12-9, Sun 12-7.30 D served Mon-Sat 12-9, Sun 12-7.30 food served all day 🛢
MARSTONS ◀ Marstons Bitter, Hobgoblin. ♟ 8 **Facilities** Children's menu Play area Dogs allowed Garden Parking

## SHOBDON — Map 9 SO46

### The Bateman Arms ★★★★ INN

**HR6 9LX** ☎ **01568 708374**
e-mail: diana@batemanarms.co.uk
dir: *On B4362 off A4110 NW of Leominster*

An 18th-century three-storey coaching inn of striking appearance, with old cobbled paving lining its street frontage. The only pub in the village of Shobdon, there's character inside too; in the bar you can sit beneath ancient oak beams on 300-year-old wooden settles and enjoy a light meal, or head for the restaurant and its menu based on locally-sourced produce. Enjoy flat field mushroom rarebit, followed by Shobdon sausages with mash, peas and onion gravy; meat or vegetable lasagne; or a Herefordshire steak. Desserts are all home made. There is also a games room, large beer garden, and comfortable en suite bedrooms.

**Open** all day all wk **Bar Meals** L served all wk 12-2 D served Tue-Sat 7-9 Av main course £5.99 **Restaurant** L served all wk 12-2 D served Tue-Sat 7-9 ⊕ FREE HOUSE ◀ John Smith's, Hobgoblin, Guinness, Guest ale.
**Facilities** Children's portions Garden Parking **Rooms** 9

## STAPLOW — Map 10 SO64

### PICK OF THE PUBS

### The Oak Inn ★★★★ INN ⚑ NEW

**HR5 1NP** ☎ **01531 640954**
e-mail: oakinn@wyenet.co.uk
dir: *M50 junct 2, A417 to Ledbury. At rdbt take 2nd exit onto A449, then A438 (High St). Then take B4214 to Staplow*

Owners Hylton Haylett and Julie Woollard have sympathetically refurbished this lovely old 17th-century black and white free house in the heart of rural Herefordshire. The three cosy bar areas have log burning stoves, flagstone floors and old wooden beams. Four cask ales are on offer, including Wye Valley Bitter and Reverend James. The open plan kitchen serves home-cooked, locally sourced food in the rustic restaurant. The traditional lunchtime menu offers sandwiches; grilled ciabatta melts with chips and mixed salad; and a range of pub favourites that includes the ever-popular local ham, eggs and chips. Go à la carte in the evenings with roasted Mediterranean gateau; tenderloin free-range pork with garlic and chive mash; or poached organic salmon with 'risi bisi' rice. Don't miss The Oak's locally renowned bread and butter pudding. There is a large garden

adjacent to orchards with lovely views. Four luxury en suite bedrooms make The Oak Inn an ideal base for exploring the Malvern Hills and the nearby market town of Ledbury.

**Open** all wk Mon-Sat noon-3 5.30-11 (Sun noon-3.30 7-11) **Bar Meals** L served all wk 12-2.30 D served all wk 6.30-9.30 **Restaurant** L served Mon-Sat 12-2.30, Sun 12-3 booking required D served Mon-Sat 6.30-9.30, Sun 7-9 booking required Fixed menu price fr £25 ⊕ FREE HOUSE ◀ Marstons Pedigree, Reverend James, Wye Valley Bitter, Sharp's Doom Bar ♂ Westons Stowford Press. ⚑ 8 **Facilities** Children's portions Dogs allowed Garden Parking **Rooms** 4

## SYMONDS YAT (EAST) — Map 10 SO51

### PICK OF THE PUBS

### The Saracens Head Inn ★★★★ INN ⚑

*See Pick of the Pubs on opposite page*

## TILLINGTON — Map 9 SO44

### *The Bell*

**HR4 8LE** ☎ **01432 760395** 🖹 **01432 760580**
e-mail: beltill@aol.com
dir: *NE Hereford, on road to Weobley via Burghill*

Run by the same family since 1988, The Bell offers something for everybody, with quiet gardens, a formal dining area and a traditional public bar complete with oak parquet flooring, an open fire and a dart board. The varied menus cover all dining requirements, from bar snacks to more elaborate meals: smoked salmon terrine, followed by roast Madgett's Farm duck breast, or venison, wild boar and pheasant casserole, perhaps.

**Open** all wk ◀ London Pride, Hereford Bitter, other local ales. **Facilities** Play area Dogs allowed Garden Parking

## ULLINGSWICK — Map 10 SO54

### PICK OF THE PUBS

### *Three Crowns Inn* ⊚ ⚑

**HR1 3JQ** ☎ **01432 820279** 🖹 **08700 515338**
e-mail: info@threecrownsinn.com
dir: *From Burley Gate rdbt take A465 toward Bromyard, after 2m left to Ullingswick, left after 0.5m, pub 0.5m on right*

An unspoilt country pub in deepest rural Herefordshire, where food sources are so local that their distance away is measured in fields rather than miles. A hand-written sign offering to buy surplus fruit and veg gives locals a gentle reminder, as they sup their favourite real ale at the bar. Parterres in the garden grow varieties of produce that are not easy, or even possible, to buy commercially. Among them is a pea whose provenance can be traced back to a phial found by Lord Carnarvon in Tutankhamun's tomb. The daily-changing menus are refreshingly brief and uncomplicated; half a dozen options within each course are all priced the same - so eating to a budget is easily accomplished. A typical selection could be fish soup with rouille and croutons, followed by poached knuckle of Shropshire veal, or fish such as grilled Cornish gurnard. Puddings include chocolate truffle torte.

**Open** Tue-Sun Closed: 25-26 Dec, 1 Jan, Mon ◀ Hobsons Best, Wye Valley Butty Bach & Dorothy Goodbody's, guest ales. ⚑ 9 **Facilities** Dogs allowed Garden Parking

## WALFORD — Map 10 SO52

### PICK OF THE PUBS

### The Mill Race ⚑

*See Pick of the Pubs on page 251*

# PICK OF THE PUBS

# The Saracens Head Inn ★★★★ INN ♗

**SYMONDS YAT (EAST)**     Map 10 SO51

**HR9 6JL**
☎ **01600 890435**   ▤ **01600 890034**
**e-mail:**
contact@saracensheadinn.co.uk
**web:** www.saracensheadinn.co.uk
**dir:** *From Ross-on-Wye take A40 to Monmouth. In 4m take Symonds Yat East turn. 1st right before bridge. Right in 0.5m. Right in 1m*

For centuries this former cider mill has stood in its spectacular position on the east bank of the River Wye, where the river flows into a steep wooded gorge. This is the yat, the local name for a gate or pass, named after Robert Symonds who was a Sheriff of Herefordshire in the 17th century. The inn's own ferry across the river is still hand operated, just as it has been for the past 200 years. There's a relaxed atmosphere throughout the inn, from the flagstone bar to the cosy lounge and stylish dining room, and you can also eat on one of the two sunny riverside terraces.

Regularly changing menus and daily specials boards offer both the traditional – roast rib of Herefordshire beef with Yorkshire pudding and horseradish, for example – and modern, such as courgette and sweet potato gateau with chive mash, poached baby leeks and pesto. A typical three course meal might start with potted smoked mackerel with warm onion chutney and tossed leaves, followed by pan-roasted salmon fillet with saffron new potatoes and sautéed Mediterranean vegetables. A blackboard lists the selection of desserts, or you might opt for a slate of five local cheeses served with bread, wheat wafers, grapes and quince jelly.

The inn is situated in an Area of Outstanding Natural Beauty on the edge of the Royal Forest of Dean, so a stay in one of the ten en suite bedrooms is a must for exploring the unspoiled local countryside. Walking, cycling, mountain biking, canoeing, kayaking, climbing, abseiling and potholing are all available nearby, whilst fishing is free to residents.

**Open** all day all wk Closed: 25 Dec **Bar Meals** L served all wk 12-2.30 D served all wk 6.30-9 Av main course £9 **Restaurant** L served all wk 12-2.30 D served all wk 6.30-9 Av 3 course à la carte fr £27.50 ⊕ FREE HOUSE ◀ Theakstons Old Peculier, Old Speckled Hen, Wye Valley Hereford Pale Ale, Wye Valley Butty Bach, Butcombe Bitter Ŏ Westons Organic, Stowford Press, Lyne Down's Roaring Meg. ♗ 10 **Facilities** Children's menu Dogs allowed Garden Parking **Rooms** 10

## WALTERSTONE — Map 9 SO32

### Carpenters Arms

**HR2 0DX** ☎ 01873 890353
**dir:** Off A465 between Hereford & Abergavenny at Pandy

There's plenty of character in this 300-year-old free house located on the edge of the Black Mountains where the owner, Mrs Watkins, was born. Here you'll find beams, antique settles and a leaded range with open fires that burn all winter; a perfect cosy setting for enjoying a pint of Rambler's Ruin. Popular food options include beef and Guinness pie; beef lasagne; and thick lamb cutlets. Ask about the vegetarian selection, and large choice of home-made desserts.

**Open** all day all wk noon-11pm Closed: 25 Dec
**Bar Meals** food served all day ⊕ FREE HOUSE
◀ Wadworth 6X, Breconshire Golden Valley & Rambler's Ruin ♂ Weston's. **Facilities** Children's portions Play area Family room Garden Parking **Notes** ⊚

## WELLINGTON — Map 10 SO44

### The Wellington

**HR4 8AT** ☎ 01432 830367
**e-mail:** thewellington@hotmail.com
**dir:** Off A49 into village centre. Pub 0.25m on left

Owners Ross and Philippa Williams came from London to create one of Herefordshire's finest gastro-pubs. They've certainly done well, with Ross quickly becoming an award-winning champion of food prepared from local, seasonal produce. Start with Jerusalem artichoke and carrot soup; or Lay & Robson oak smoked salmon with celeriac remoulade, followed by pan-roasted saddle of local venison with beetroot and goat's cheese dauphinoise and redcurrant sauce; or wild mushroom and ricotta tortellini with creamy pesto dressing, and then rhubarb crème brûlée; or baked lemon and vanilla cheesecake.

**Open** 12-3 6-11 Closed: 25-26 Dec, Sun eve, Mon L
**Bar Meals** L served Tue-Sun 12-2 D served Mon-Sat 7-9 Av main course £7.50 **Restaurant** L served Tue-Sun 12-2 D served Mon-Sat 7-9 Av 3 course à la carte fr £25
⊕ FREE HOUSE ◀ Hobsons, Wye Valley Butty Bach, Wye Valley HPA, Guest ales ♂ Westons Scrumpy.
**Facilities** Children's portions Play area Dogs allowed Garden Parking

## WEOBLEY — Map 9 SO45

### PICK OF THE PUBS

### *The Salutation Inn*

**Market Pitch HR4 8SJ**
☎ 01544 318443  ▤ 01544 318405
**dir:** A44, then A4112, 8m from Leominster

A black and white timber-framed pub dating back more than 500 years and situated in a corner of the country renowned for its hops, cattle and apple orchards. The inn, sympathetically converted from an old ale house and adjoining cottage, is the perfect base for exploring the lovely Welsh Marches and enjoying a host of leisure activities, including fishing, horse riding, golf, walking, and clay shooting. The book capital of Hay-on-Wye and the cathedral city of Hereford are close by. The inn's restaurant offers a range of award-winning dishes created with the use of locally sourced ingredients. Chef's specials are also served in the traditional lounge bar with its welcoming atmosphere and cosy inglenook fireplace. A change of hands has taken place.

**Open** all day all wk noon-11 (Sun noon-10.30) ◀ Betty Stogs, Courage Directors Best ♂ Stowford Press.
**Facilities** Dogs allowed Garden Parking

## WHITNEY-ON-WYE — Map 9 SO24

### PICK OF THE PUBS

### *Rhydspence Inn* ★★★★ INN

**HR3 6EU** ☎ 01497 831262  ▤ 01497 831751
**e-mail:** info@rhydspence-inn.co.uk
**dir:** N side of A438, 1m W of Whitney-on-Wye

This charming inn dates from 1380 and was extended in the 17th and 20th centuries. It was most likely built to provide comfort for travellers and pilgrims from Abbey Cwmhir to Hereford Cathedral, but it later became a watering hole for drovers taking cattle, sheep and geese to market in London. These days the pub is rather more elegant, with a cosy bar and spacious dining room giving way to stunning views over the Wye Valley. Food options range from deep-fried cod in lemon batter and French fries or braised shank of lamb from the bar bites and brasserie selection, to main menu dishes such as peppered venison with fricassee of mushrooms and port and redcurrant reduction or pan-fried sea bass with tempura courgettes and lemon aïoli. There is also a good choice of steaks from the grill. Seven comfortable bedrooms are available.

**Open** all wk 11-2.30 7-11 ◀ Robinsons Best, Interbrew Bass. **Facilities** Family room Garden Parking **Rooms** 7

## WOOLHOPE — Map 10 SO63

### The Butchers Arms ⊛⊛ ♥ NEW

**HR1 4RF** ☎ 01432 860281  ▤ 01531 660461
**e-mail:** food@butchersarmswoolhope.co.uk
**dir:** From Hereford take B4224 towards Ross-on-Wye. Follow signs for Woolhope on left

This picturesque, half-timbered inn stands at the foot of the sublime Marcle Ridge at the heart of cider country. Dating from the 16th century, it was a butcher's shop that also brewed beer and baked the village's bread. The accessible gastro-pub menu is strong on Herefordshire fare: Goodrich longhorn beef and Kentchurch venison follow starters like artichoke and smoked Applewood cheese tart, created under the tutelage of the renowned Stephen Bull. Local beers, ciders and a classic list of bins complete the picture.

**Open** 12-2.30 6.30-11 Closed: Sun eve, Mon (ex BHs)
**Bar Meals** L served Mon-Sat 12-2, Sun 12-2.15 D served all wk 7-9 Av main course £11 **Restaurant** L served all wk 12-2 D served all wk 7-9 Av 3 course à la carte fr £22
⊕ FREE HOUSE ◀ Local cask ales ♂ Stowford Press, Olivers, Dragon, Orchard. ♥ 10 **Facilities** Children's portions Dogs allowed Garden Parking

### The Crown Inn ♥

**HR1 4QP** ☎ 01432 860468  ▤ 01432 860770
**e-mail:** menu@crowninnwoolhope.co.uk
**dir:** B4224 to Mordiford, left after Moon Inn. Pub in village centre

Featuring more than 150 guest ales every year as well as a list of over 18 ciders and perrys, this old-fashioned free house is well supported by locals and visitors alike. The pub is host to many clubs and societies. Food includes lunchtime baguettes and light snacks available at the bar, with main course options including slow-braised belly pork with caramelised apple; and stuffed vegetarian pasta with spicy tomato sauce and parmesan. There are stunning views from the large garden, and an outside summertime bar on Saturday nights.

**Open** all wk noon-2.30 6.30-11 (Sat-Sun all day)
**Bar Meals** L served all wk 12-2 D served all wk 6.30-9 Av main course £8.50 **Restaurant** L served all wk 12-2 D served all wk 6.30-9 Fixed menu price fr £11 ⊕ FREE HOUSE ◀ Wye Valley Best, Guest ales ♂ Westons Stowford Press, Country Perry, Bounds Brand Scrumpy, Local ciders. ♥ 8 **Facilities** Children's portions Garden Parking

# PICK OF THE PUBS

## The Mill Race

**WALFORD** Map 10 SO52

**HR9 5QS** ☎ **01989 562891**
**e-mail:** enquiries@millrace.info
**dir:** *From Ross-on-Wye take B4234 to Walford. Pub 3m on right after village hall*

Pick up a route map from the pub to see some beautiful countryside - the local Walford Loop walk takes forty-five minutes, the longer River Walk, about two hours. Afterwards, head for this free house and a pint of Wye Valley Bitter or Roaring Meg, a real cider named after a cannon used during the Civil War by the Parliamentarians to regain nearby Goodrich Castle. There is a great mix of old and new in this comfortable, contemporary village pub. In the winter are log fires, and in summer the sun shines on the large sun terrace.

Food sourcing is environmentally responsible, whether it comes from reliable local suppliers or the pub's own 1000-acre farm, where cattle, rare breed pigs, turkeys, geese and pheasant are reared, and fruit and vegetables grown. Regularly changing menus focus on simple food cooked well, lunch typically featuring chicken or vegetable curry; steamed mussels in white wine; sun-blushed tomato and pesto risotto; and tarragon chicken baguette. In the evening there might be calves' liver and bacon; fillets of bream with olives; Herefordshire pork loin with parsnip purée; and wild mushroom and sage tagliatelle. Afterwards, perhaps hot chocolate pudding with pistachio ice cream; prune parfait with Earl Grey syrup; or a good farmhouse cheese selection. Maybe you fancy dipping your biscotti in a glass of pudding wine.

Saturday brunch is a good idea: either a Full English; Welsh rarebit with tomato and herb salad; or maybe toasted crumpets with baked ham, spinach and hollandaise sauce. Sunday's lunch choice changes weekly depending on what's available and what's best. On the wine list is Monnow Valley, a white made from Huxelrebe/Seyval Blanc vines grown just north of Monmouth. Shooting parties are well catered for with a selection of breakfasts, lunches (including packed) and dinners.

The owners have been doing 'green things' since 2005 and their efforts were recognised in 2009 with a Green Initiative Pub award.

**Open** all wk 11-3 5-11 (Sat-Sun all day) **Bar Meals** L served Mon-Fri 12-2, Sat-Sun 12-2.30 booking required D served Mon-Sat 6-9.30, Sun 6-9 booking required Av main course £9 **Restaurant** L served Mon-Fri 12-2, Sat-Sun 12-2.30 booking required D served Mon-Sat 6-9.30, Sun 6-9 booking required Av 3 course à la carte fr £20 FREE HOUSE Wye Valley Bitter, Guest Ales, Guinness Westons, Stowford Press, Roaring Meg. 14 **Facilities** Children's menu Garden Parking

## HERTFORDSHIRE

### ALDBURY
Map 6 SP91

## The Greyhound Inn ♥

**19 Stocks Rd HP23 5RT**
☎ 01442 851228  📠 01442 851495
e-mail: greyhound@aldbury.wanadoo.co.uk
dir: *Telephone for directions*

Aldbury's ancient stocks and duckpond guarantee the village's frequent use as a film location, and customers here can find themselves in pole position to witness every clap of the clapperboard. In the oak-beamed restaurant, the long menu includes steak, ale and mushroom pie; Lancashire hot-pot; mixed grill; prawn and crayfish pie; monkfish and chorizo cassoulet; spaghetti bolognaise; and butternut squash risotto. Bar snacks are a local legend, especially when accompanied by Badger Best or Tanglefoot.

**Open** all day all wk 11.30-11 (Sun noon-10.30) Closed: 25 Dec **Bar Meals** L served all wk 12-2.30 D served all wk 6.30-9.30 Av main course £11 food served all day **Restaurant** L served all wk 12-2.30 D served all wk 6.30-9.30 Av 3 course à la carte fr £22 food served all day ⊕ HALL & WOODHOUSE ◀ Badger Best, Tanglefoot, King & Barnes Sussex. ♥ 13 **Facilities** Family room Dogs allowed Garden Parking

### PICK OF THE PUBS

## The Valiant Trooper

**Trooper Rd HP23 5RW** ☎ 01442 851203
e-mail: info@thevalianttrooper.co.uk
dir: *A41 at Tring junct, follow rail station signs 0.5m, at village green turn right, 200yds on left*

Lucky locals have been enjoying this old pub in this quintessential Chiltern-foot village beneath the beech-woods of Ashridge Park for several centuries. Originally The Royal Oak, its current name recalls times when the Duke of Wellington discussed strategy with his troops

here; when the famous warrior died it was renamed in his honour. Modern day strategists who may meet here include a dedicated and colourful team of Morris Men. Diners today also now have the chance to plan a strategy – do we play safe or go native? Good, solid standards of lamb rump or the inviting pheasant and boar sausages on mash with cranberry and onion jam need to be balanced against the bracing new specials offerings here. Chef Steve Mason is rediscovering very old and rustic meals, including squirrel braised with leeks and thyme gravy, braised pigs' trotters with a sage gravy, or jugged local hare with crushed new potatoes. Finish with a lemon posset and a glass of Tring Trooper ale before a stroll around the village green.

**Open** all day all wk noon-11pm (Sun noon-10.30) **Bar Meals** L served Mon-Fri 12-3, Sat 12-9, Sun 12-4.30 D served Mon-Fri 6.30-9, Sat 12-9 Av main course £9.50 **Restaurant** L served Mon-Fri 12-3, Sat 12-9, Sun 12-4.30 D served Mon-Fri 6.30-9, Sat 12-9 Fixed menu price fr £9 ⊕ FREE HOUSE ◀ Fuller's London Pride, Tring Trooper Ale, Brakspear Bitter. **Facilities** Children's menu Children's portions Play area Family room Dogs allowed Garden Parking

### ARDELEY
Map 12 TL32

## Jolly Waggoners

**SG2 7AH** ☎ 01438 861350  📠 01438 861350
dir: *From Stevenage take B1037, through Walkern, in 2m right to Ardeley*

This 500-year-old village pub has a large garden to enjoy in summer and open fires creating a cosy atmosphere in winter. Real ales are served along with guest beers, and fresh local ingredients are used in the seasonal menus – venison stew with caramelised shallots. Families are welcome and the pub is also dog friendly, so you can enjoy a meal in the bar with your best friend! This pub has reverted back to its original name.

**Open** all wk 12-3 6-11 ◀ Greene King IPA, 2 Guest ales. **Facilities** Dogs allowed Garden Parking

### ASHWELL
Map 12 TL23

## Three Tuns ★★★ INN ♥

**6 High St SG7 5NL** ☎ 01462 742107  📠 01462 743662
e-mail: info@threetunshotel.co.uk
dir: *Telephone for directions*

The building, dating from 1806, replaced an earlier one first recorded as a public house in 1700. Original features survive in the two traditional bars and the large dining room, which were refurbished in 2009 by the new landlord. The extensive menu offers classic burgers and steak dishes alongside home-made steak and kidney pie, sausages and mash and honey-glazed pork chops. Lighter meals include filled baguettes, salads and ploughman's lunches which can be enjoyed in the large garden.

**Open** all day all wk 11am-11.30pm (Fri-Sat 11am-12.30am) **Bar Meals** L served Mon-Fri 12-2.30, Sat-Sun all day booking required D served Mon-Fri 6.30-9.30, Sat-Sun all day booking required Av main course £10 **Restaurant** L served Mon-Fri 12-2.30, Sat-Sun all day booking required D served Mon-Fri 6.30-9.30, Sat-Sun all day booking required ⊕ GREENE KING ◀ Greene King IPA, Abbot, Guest ale ♂ Aspall. ♥ 9 **Facilities** Children's menu Children's portions Play area Family room Dogs allowed Garden Parking **Rooms** 6

Save on Hotels. Book at **theAA.com/hotel**

HERTFORDSHIRE 253 **ENGLAND**

## AYOT GREEN — Map 6 TL21

### The Waggoners ♀ NEW

Brickwall Close AL6 9AA
☎ 01707 324241   ▤ 01707 329882
e-mail: laurent@thewaggoners.co.uk
dir: *Ayot Green on unclassified road off B197, S of Welwyn*

Built in the 17th century to house the workers at nearby Brocket Hall before becoming a thriving coaching inn, this refurbished dining pub overlooks the beautiful village green. In the cosy beamed bar and smart restaurant extension, experienced French owners offer an upmarket, French inspired menu alongside classic English ales. Accompany a pint of Adnams Broadside with beef fillet au poivre, served with dauphinoise potatoes and braised shallots, and follow with vanilla crème brûlée. There is a sun-trap garden and sheltered terrace for summer alfresco dining.

**Open** all day **Closed**: Sun eve **Bar Meals** Av main course £8.95 food served all day **Restaurant** L served all wk 12-2.45 booking required D served all wk 6.30-9.30 Fixed menu fr £12.95 Av 3 course à la carte fr £30 ⌗ PUNCH TAVERNS ◖ Fuller's London Pride, IPA, Tribute, Adnams Broadside. ♀ 25 **Facilities** Children's portions Dogs allowed Garden Parking
**See advert on opposite page**

## BARLEY — Map 12 TL43

### The Fox & Hounds ♀

High St SG8 8HU ☎ 01763 848459   ▤ 01763 849080
e-mail: info@foxandhoundsbarley.co.uk
dir: *A505 onto B1368 at Flint Cross, pub 4m*

Set in a pretty village, this former 17th-century hunting lodge is notable for its pub sign which extends across the lane. It has real fires, a warm welcome and an attractive garden. A typical menu includes wild mushroom risotto, beef burger with chunky-cut chips, Irish stew, and beer-battered fish and chips. Recent change of hands.

**Open** 10-3 6-late (Sat 10am-late, Sun 10-6) **Closed**: Mon ◖ Adnams Best, Flowers IPA, Woodforde's Wherry. ♀ 12 **Facilities** Play area Garden Parking

## BUNTINGFORD — Map 12 TL32

### The Sword Inn Hand ★★★★ INN

Westmill SG9 9LQ ☎ 01763 271356
e-mail: welcome@theswordinnhand.co.uk
dir: *Off A10 1.5m S of Buntingford*

Midway between London and Cambridge in the lovely award-winning village of Westmill, this inn has been welcoming travellers since the 14th century. Inside there are oak beams, flag floor and an open fireplace. It styles itself a 'real English', family-run pub offering a large selection of snacks, specials and a range of real ales. Fresh produce is delivered daily to create herb-crushed rack of lamb, sea bass fillet with stir-fry vegetables, escalope of veal with melted brie, or Chef's cod and chips. There are four ground floor bedrooms available.

**Open** all wk 12-3 5-11 (Sun Sep-Apr 12-7, May-Aug 12-10) **Bar Meals** L served Mon-Sat 12-2.30, Sun 12-4 D served Mon-Sat 6.30-9.30 **Restaurant** L served Mon-Sat 12-2.30, Sun 12-4 D served Mon-Sat 6.30-9.30 ⌗ FREE HOUSE ◖ Greene King IPA, Young's Bitter, Timothy Taylor Landlord, Guest ales ◔ Aspall. **Facilities** Play area Dogs allowed Garden Parking **Rooms** 4

## COTTERED — Map 12 TL32

### The Bull at Cottered

SG9 9QP ☎ 01763 281243
e-mail: cordell39@btinternet.com
dir: *On A507 in Cottered between Buntingford & Baldock*

Low-beamed ceilings, antique furniture, cosy fires and pub games typify this charming traditional village local. The setting is picturesque, and a well-tended garden offers an alternative dining venue in summer. The menu presents a classy and comprehensive carte of all home-made brasserie-style food, ranging from smoked salmon and prawn parcel as a starter to calves' liver with sage and butter, or duck breast with honey and wholegrain mustard glaze for a main course. There are live music and dinner nights, plus quality beers and great Sunday lunches.

**Open** all wk 11.30-3 6.30-11 (Sun 12-10.30) **Bar Meals** L served Mon-Sat 12-2, Sun 12-4 D served Mon-Sat 6.30-9.30, Sun 6-9 Av main course £12 **Restaurant** L served Mon-Sat 12-2, Sun 12-4 D served Mon-Sat 6.30-9.30, Sun 6-9 booking required Fixed menu price fr £20 Av 3 course à la carte fr £25 ⌗ GREENE KING ◖ Greene King IPA, Abbot Ale. **Facilities** Garden Parking

## FLAUNDEN — Map 6 TL00

### PICK OF THE PUBS

### The Bricklayers Arms ♀

*See Pick of the Pubs on page 254*

## HEMEL HEMPSTEAD — Map 6 TL00

### PICK OF THE PUBS

### Alford Arms ♀

*See Pick of the Pubs on page 255*

## HEXTON — Map 12 TL13

### The Raven ♀

SG5 3JB ☎ 01582 881209   ▤ 01582 881610
e-mail: jack@ravenathexton.f9.co.uk
dir: *5m W of Hitchin. 5m N of Luton, just outside Barton-le-Clay*

This neat 1920s pub is named after Ravensburgh Castle in the neighbouring hills. It has comfortable bars and a large garden with a terrace and play area. Snacks include ploughman's and salad platters, plus tortilla wraps, filled baguettes and jacket potatoes. The main menu offers lots of steak options, and dishes like smoky American chicken, whole rack of barbecue ribs, Thai red vegetable curry and an all-day breakfast.

**Open** all wk ◖ Greene King, Old Speckled Hen, Fuller's London Pride, Greene King IPA. ♀ 24 **Facilities** Play area Garden Parking

## HINXWORTH — Map 12 TL24

### Three Horseshoes

High St SG7 5HQ ☎ 01462 742280
e-mail: margaretplatten@btinternet.com
dir: *E of A1 between Biggleswade & Baldock*

Thatched 18th-century country pub with a dining extension into the garden. Parts of the building date back 500 years, and the walls are adorned with pictures and photos of the village's history. Samples from a typical menu include lamb cutlets with champ, rainbow trout with almonds, sea bass provençale, steak and Guinness pie, bacon and cheese pasta bake, and roasted Tuscan red peppers.

**Open** all wk (all day Sat-Sun) **Bar Meals** L served all wk 12-3 D served all wk 6.30-9.30 Av main course £7.50 **Restaurant** L served all wk 12-3 D served all wk 6.30-9.30 ⌗ GREENE KING ◖ Greene King IPA, Abbot Ale, guest ales. **Facilities** Children's menu Children's portions Dogs allowed Garden Parking

# PICK OF THE PUBS

## The Bricklayers Arms

**FLAUNDEN**  Map 6 TL00

**Hogpits Bottom HP3 0PH**
☎ **01442 833322**  📄 **01442 834841**
e-mail: goodfood@bricklayersarms.com
web: www.bricklayersarms.com
dir: *M25 junct 18 onto A404 (Amersham road). Right at Chenies for Flaunden*

Coated in creeper, Flaunden's low, cottagey-tiled pub, formerly a pair of brick and flint 18th-century cottages, is a peaceful and inviting spot, especially in summer when its country-style garden becomes the perfect place to savour an alfresco pint or meal. It was in 1832 when Benskin's brewery converted one of them into an alehouse, which it remained until the 1960s, when the neighbouring cottage became part of the pub. Sympathetic conversion of an outbuilding and barn resulted in today's award-winning restaurant.

Tucked away in deepest Hertfordshire, it has featured in many fictional film and TV programmes, and is a favourite with locals, walkers, horse-riders and, well, just about everyone.

One reason for its success is an ivy-covered façade that gives way to an immaculate interior, complete with low beams, exposed brickwork, candlelight and open fires. Another is a happy marriage between traditional English and French fusion cooking.

The Gallic influence comes from Michelin-trained head chef, Claude Paillet, and his team who use fresh organic produce from local suppliers to create seasonal lunch and dinner menus, plus daily specials. Among many choices of starter are local game terrine with chunky piccalilli and foccacia bread; or a selection of home-smoked fish with lemon coriander butter and tomato chutney. To follow, might come saddle of venison with cranberry and game jus; cod with wholegrain mustard sauce and crispy root vegetables; or a lunchtime dish of steak, kidney and ale pie with chive mash. But don't stop there, as The

Bricklayers is also held in high esteem for its pudding menu, on which you're likely to find apple and cinnamon tart; hot chocolate sponge pudding; and vanilla crème brûlée. Choose one of the 120 wines from all corners of the world and, in the summer, enjoy it with your lunch in the terraced garden.

**Open** all wk 12-11.30 (25 Dec 12-3) **Bar Meals** L served Mon-Sat 12-2.30, Sun 12-3.30 booking required D served Mon-Sat 6.30-9.30, Sun 6.30-8.30 Av main course £13 **Restaurant** L served Mon-Sat 12-2.30, Sun 12-3.30 booking required D served Mon-Sat 6.30-9.30, Sun 6.30-8.30 Av 3 course à la carte fr £28 ⊕ FREE HOUSE ◀ Old Speckled Hen, Greene King IPA, London Pride, Jack O'Legs (Tring Brewery), Rebellion Ö Aspall. ♥ 16 **Facilities** Dogs allowed Garden Parking

# PICK OF THE PUBS

## Alford Arms ♟

HEMEL HEMPSTEAD          Map 6 TL00

**Frithsden HP1 3DD**
☎ 01442 864480   📠 01422 876893
e-mail: info@alfordarmsfrithsden.co.uk
web: www.alfordarmsfrithsden.co.uk
dir: *From Hemel Hempstead on A4146 take 2nd left at Water End. In 1m left at T-junct, right after 0.75m. Pub 100yds on right*

Set in the unruffled hamlet of Frithsden and surrounded by National Trust woodland, this pretty Victorian pub is full of surprises. Cross the threshold and you'll immediately pick up on the warm and lively atmosphere, derived partly from the buzz of conversation and the background jazz music, and partly from the rich colours and eclectic mixture of furniture and pictures in the dining room and bar. The staff are renowned for their good humour, and they take the trouble to ensure that customers have an enjoyable experience; and, if you can't make it back to the office, free Wi-fi is available.

The seasonal menus and daily specials balance innovative dishes with more traditional fare, and everything is prepared from fresh local produce whenever possible. There's a great choice of light dishes or 'small plates', from the daily soup with crusty bread; to herb-crusted Ashridge rabbit croquettes with spiced cauliflower dip. Main meals with a similarly imaginative approach include poached pollock with saffron infused cherry tomatoes; spinach and feta hot water pie with warm aubergine caviar; and label anglais chicken and black pudding suet pudding with caramelised shallots, spinach and Jerusalem artichoke. Puddings have an interesting tweak too, such as warm English rhubarb and ginger crumble, and Bramley apple steamed pudding with maple syrup and marsala ice cream. The British cheese plate is a tempting alternative to finish, with Alford oatcakes, sticky malt loaf and tomato chutney.

The pretty garden overlooks the village green, and historic Ashridge Forest is close by - the perfect place to tie in a walk with the dog, a stroll to admire the bluebells, or even a foraging trip for wild mushrooms.

**Open** all day all wk 11-11 (Sun 12-10.30) Closed: 26 Dec
**Bar Meals** L served Mon-Fri 12-2.30, Sat 12-3, Sun 12-4 D served Mon-Thu 6.30-9.30, Fri-Sat 6.30-10, Sun 7-9.30 Av main course £13.75
**Restaurant** L served Mon-Fri 12-2.30, Sat 12-3, Sun 12-4 booking required D served Mon-Thu 6.30-9.30, Fri-Sat 6.30-10, Sun 7-9.30 booking required Av 3 course à la carte fr £25.75
⊕ SALISBURY PUBS LTD ◖ Brakspear, Flowers Original, Marlow Rebellion IPA, Sharp's Doom Bar ♂ Thatchers. ♟ 20
**Facilities** Dogs allowed Garden Parking

## HITCHIN
Map 12 TL12

### The Greyhound ★★★ INN

London Rd, St Ippolyts SG4 7NL ☎ 01462 440989
e-mail: greyhound@freenet.co.uk
dir: 1.5m S of Hitchin on B656

There has been a pub on the site for 300 years although
the current building dates from 1900. The Greyhound was
rescued from dereliction by the present owner who
previously worked for the London Fire Brigade. The pub
prides itself on being a friendly, family-run hostelry;
located in pleasant countryside and open farmland, yet
handy for the M1 and Luton Airport. The shotguns over
the bars are said to have been owned by notorious
poacher twins who used each other as an alibi. The food
is unpretentious, generous and competitively priced.
There are five en suite bedrooms available.

Open all wk 7am-2.30 5-11 (Sun 7am-8pm) Bar Meals L
served Mon-Sat 7-2, Sun 7am-8pm D served Mon-Sat
5-9, Sun 7am-8pm Restaurant L served Mon-Sat 7-2,
Sun 7am-8pm D served Mon-Sat 5-9, Sun 7am-8pm
⊕ FREE HOUSE ◀ Adnams, guest. Facilities Dogs
allowed Parking Rooms 5

## HUNSDON
Map 6 TL41

### PICK OF THE PUBS

### The Fox and Hounds ♀

2 High St SG12 8NH
☎ 01279 843999 📄 01279 841092
e-mail: info@foxandhounds-hunsdon.co.uk
web: www.foxandhounds-hunsdon.co.uk
dir: From A414 between Ware & Harlow take B180 in
Stanstead Abbotts N to Hunsdon

There's an easy-going atmosphere at this renowned
gastro-pub, set in a sleepy village in the heart of the
Hertfordshire countryside, with a cosy winter fire
warming the old bar, liberally supplied with Victorian-
style furnishing and no pressure to do anything other
than enjoy a glass of Adnams brewery beer, the
welcome for local drinkers is genuine. The tree-shaded
garden too, together with the heated, covered terrace is
popular with both drinkers and alfresco diners. There's
no doubting that the food side of the pub equation is
the main attraction here, created with the flair that
saw owner James Rix in demand at top London
eateries. Taken in the bar or elegant, chandeliered
dining room, kick off with wood pigeon, snails and
spinach on toast before progressing to loin of wild
locally shot venison, gratin dauphinoise and braised

red cabbage, or rack of black-faced lamb, potato
gnocchi, butternut squash and garlic. Some great
calorific puddings top off the event, accompanied by an
impressive wine list.

Open noon-4 6-11 Closed: 26 Dec, Sun eve, Mon & BHs
eve (Tue after BHs) Bar Meals L served Tue-Sun 12-3 D
served Tue-Sat 6.30-9.30 Av main course £12
Restaurant L served Sun 12-3.30 booking required D
served Fri-Sat 7-9.30 booking required Av 3 course à la
carte fr £25 ⊕ FREE HOUSE ◀ Adnams Bitter, Adnams
Broadside, Guinness ♂ Aspall. ♀ 9 Facilities Children's
menu Children's portions Play area Dogs allowed
Garden Parking

## LITTLE HADHAM
Map 6 TL42

### The Nags Head

The Ford SG11 2AX ☎ 01279 771555 📄 01279 771555
e-mail: paul.arkell@virgin.net
dir: M11 junct 8 take A120 towards Puckeridge & A10.
Left at lights in Little Hadham. Pub 1m on right

Formerly a coaching inn, this welcoming 16th-century
pub has also been a brewery, a bakery and Home Guard
arsenal in its time. The 1960s folk-rock group Fairport
Convention once performed in concert opposite and the
pub ran dry! Open brickwork and an old bakery oven are
among the features at this village inn, as well as the
range of real ales behind the bar. The extensive menu
specialises in fish dishes and the Sunday roasts are
popular. Sit out the front on a good day and enjoy the
countryside.

Open all wk Bar Meals L served Mon-Sat 12-2, Sun 12-3
D served Mon-Sat 6-9, Sun 7-9 Restaurant L served Mon-
Sat 12-2, Sun 12-3 booking required D served Mon-Sat
6-9, Sun 7-9 booking required ⊕ GREENE KING ◀ Greene
King Abbot Ale, IPA, Old Speckled Hen & Ruddles County
Ale, Marstons Pedigree. Facilities Children's
menu Children's portions Garden

## OLD KNEBWORTH
Map 6 TL22

### The Lytton Arms ♀

Park Ln SG3 6QB ☎ 01438 812312 📄 01438 817298
e-mail: thelyttonarms@btinternet.com
dir: From A1(M) take A602. At Knebworth turn right at rail
station. Follow Codicote signs. Pub 1.5m on right

The pub was designed around 1877 by Lord Lytton's
brother-in-law, who happened to be the architect Sir
Edwin Lutyens. It replaced the previous inn, now a
residence next door. Also next door, but in a much grander
way, is the Lytton estate, the family home for centuries.
On the simple but wide-ranging menu are Mrs O'Keefe's
flavoured sausages; chicken or vegetable balti; honey-
roast ham; chargrilled lamb's liver and bacon; and
fisherman's pie.

Open all wk ◀ Fuller's London Pride, Adnams Best Bitter,
Broadside, Woodforde's Wherry, Deuchars IPA. ♀ 30
Facilities Dogs allowed Garden Parking

## POTTERS CROUCH
Map 6 TL10

### The Hollybush

AL2 3NN ☎ 01727 851792 📄 01727 851792
e-mail: info@thehollybushpub.co.uk
dir: Ragged Hall Ln off A405 or Bedmond Ln off A4147

Run by the same family for over 30 years, The Hollybush
is a picturesque country pub with a quaint, white-painted
exterior, attractively furnished interior and a large
enclosed garden. An antique dresser, a large fireplace
and various prints and paintings help to create a
delightfully welcoming atmosphere. Traditional pub fare
is offered: ploughman's, jacket potatoes, salads, platters
and share plates, plus toasted sandwiches, along with an
evening menu including Barnsley lamb chop with home-
made onion and rosemary sauce; salmon, sweet potato
and coriander fishcakes; and brie, pesto and cherry
tomato filo tart. The pub is close to St Albans with its
Roman ruins and good local walks.

Open all wk noon-2.30 6-11 (Sun 7-10) Bar Meals L
served all wk 12-2 D served Wed-Sat 6-9 ⊕ FULLER
SMITH TURNER PLC ◀ Fuller's Chiswick Bitter, Fuller's
London Pride, ESB, seasonal ales. Facilities Garden
Parking

## RICKMANSWORTH
Map 6 TQ09

### The Rose and Crown ♀

Harefield Rd WD3 1PP ☎ 01923 897680
e-mail: roseandcrown@morethanjustapub.com
dir: M25 junct 17/18, follow Northwood signs. Past Tesco,
pub 1.5m on right

This 16th-century former farmhouse first became licensed
in the mid-1700s. Around the wisteria-clad building,
you'll find a large garden looking out across the lovely
Colne Valley; the local stables, Field Ways, is popular with
the film industry and Russell Crowe has enjoyed a pint
here. The bar still retains its historic charm with low-
beamed ceilings and real fires, while the kitchen prepares
local produce such as meat from Daltons of Ickenham
and Flexmore Farm. Lunchtime sandwiches and sharing
platters are backed by favourite pies such as game or
fish, while the dinner range broadens to include
chargrilled steaks.

Open all day all wk 11am-11.30pm Bar Meals L served
Mon-Sat 12-6 D served Mon-Sun 6-9 Av main course £5
food served all day Restaurant L served Mon-Sun 12-6 D
served Mon-Sun 6-10 Fixed menu price fr £10 Av 3 course
à la carte fr £17.50 food served all day ⊕ MORE THAN
JUST A PUB CO LTD ◀ London Pride, Deuchars IPA,
Timothy Taylor Landlord. ♀ 12 Facilities Children's
menu Children's portions Play area Dogs allowed Garden
Parking

# PICK OF THE PUBS

## The Cabinet Free House and Restaurant

**High St, Reed SG8 8AH**
☎ 01763 848366
e-mail: thecabinet@btconnect.com
dir: *2m S of Royston, just off A10*

This famous 16th-century, white-painted clapboard inn is run as a joint venture by Tracey Hale and Angus Martin. The village is situated on a chalk ridge at almost the highest point in Hertfordshire, with the Roman Ermine Street passing just to the west. There has been a settlement here for centuries – the community is mentioned in the Domesday Book. The lovely surroundings lend themselves to special occasions, particularly weddings, and the premises are licensed for civil ceremonies.

A cabinet used to be a small room used as a study or retreat, although little studying and even less retreating gets done these days. A cabinet could also be a meeting place, which is more like it, because people come here to drink and eat with their friends, enjoying a wide range of real ales beneath low-beamed ceilings, and the 'eclectic menu based on personal taste and sound cooking techniques rather than a particular cuisine'.

Food is prepared from the best local produce, but draws inspiration from around the world to offer a possible three-course set lunch of leek and Cheddar omelette; mussels cooked in butter with leeks and cider; and croissant and marmalade butter pudding. Starters in the evening are equally appealing: Milano salami with artichoke, Moroccan olives and grilled baby gem salad; smoked haddock and Emmental frittata; and carpaccio of beef with rocket, shaved parmesan, truffle oil and balsamic.

Among the main courses are baked sea bass; pan-roasted duck; pies filled with steak or rabbit, chicken and morel, or salmon and crayfish, all with red cabbage and mash; red mullet in pastis and butter; and feta and roasted pumpkin risotto. Finally, desserts such as crème brûlée with coffee and Amaretto. Don't forget to check the specials board for, perhaps, scallops with sweet chilli sauce; steak and onion suet pudding; or 21-day sirloin with potato tartiflette and sautéed wild mushrooms. The compact wine list is keenly priced. Oh, and if you see an old gentleman in a dark coat, he could be the resident ghost.

**Open** 12-3 6-11 (Sat-Sun 12-11)
Closed: 26 Dec, 1 jan, Mon
**Bar Meals** L served Tue-Sun 12-3 D served Tue-Sat 6-9 **Restaurant** L served Tue-Sun 12-3 booking required D served Tue-Sat 6-9 booking required Fixed menu price fr £17 Av 3 course à la carte fr £25 ⊕ FREE HOUSE ◀ Woodforde's Wherry, Adnams, Old Speckled Hen, Nelson's Revenge, Timothy Taylor, Augustinian Ō Aspall. ♀ 12
**Facilities** Family room Dogs allowed Garden Parking

## ROYSTON — Map 12 TL34

### PICK OF THE PUBS

## The Cabinet Free House and Restaurant ♥

See Pick of the Pubs on page 257

## ST ALBANS — Map 6 TL10

### Rose & Crown ♥

10 Saint Michael St AL3 4SG
☎ 01727 851903 📠 01727 761775
e-mail: ruth.courtney@ntlworld.com
dir: Telephone for details

Traditional 16th-century pub situated in a beautiful part of St Michael's 'village', opposite the entrance to Verulanium Park and the Roman Museum. It has a classic beamed bar with a huge inglenook, open fire in winter and a lovely walled garden. The pub offers a distinctive range of American deli-style sandwiches, which are served with potato salad, kettle crisps and pickled cucumber. There is traditional folk music on Thursday nights, live music on Monday nights.

Open all day all wk 11.30-3 5.30-11 (Sat 11.30-11.30) ◀ Adnams Bitter, Tetley Bitter, Fuller's London Pride, Courage Directors, guest ales. ♥ 20 Facilities Dogs allowed Garden Parking

## STAPLEFORD — Map 6 TL31

### Papillon Woodhall Arms ★★★ INN ♥

17 High Rd SG14 3NW
☎ 01992 535123 📠 01992 587030
e-mail: info@papillon-woodhallarms.com
dir: On A119, between A602 & Hertford

A pink-washed twin-gabled building behind a neat white picket fence, just a five-minute drive from the centre of Hertford. The bar serves well-kept ales in a welcoming atmosphere, plus a huge selection of snacks and pub lunches — from toasted baguettes to sautéed lamb's liver and crispy bacon. Restaurant food includes plentiful fish dishes, such as fresh skate wing served with the traditional beurre noir and capers. Accommodation is available in ten en suite bedrooms.

Open all wk Bar Meals L served all wk 12-2 D served Sun-Fri 6.30-10 Restaurant L served all wk 12-2 booking required D served all wk 6.30-10 booking required ⊕ FREE HOUSE ◀ Greene King IPA, Archers, Cottage, Nethergate, Youngs Special. ♥ 10 Facilities Children's menu Children's portions Family room Garden Parking Rooms 10

## TEWIN — Map 6 TL21

### The Plume of Feathers ♥

Upper Green Rd AL6 0LX ☎ 01438 717265
dir: E from A1(M) junct 6 towards WGC, follow B1000 towards Hertford. Tewin signed on left

Built in 1596, this historic inn, firstly an Elizabethan hunting lodge and later the haunt of highwaymen, has bee refurbished. It boasts several ghosts including a 'lady in grey'. Interesting menus change daily, and include a tapas bar from noon till close. Other options available are Moroccan spiced baby shark with king prawns and couscous, honey-roast duck with sweet potato wontons, or slow-roasted belly pork with bacon and cabbage. Be sure to book in advance.

Open all day all wk 9am-11pm (Fri-Sat 9am-mdnt) ◀ IPA, Abbot Ales, Guest. ♥ 30 Facilities Dogs allowed Garden Parking

## WALKERN — Map 12 TL22

### The White Lion ♥

31 The High St SG2 7PA ☎ 01438 861251
e-mail: info@whitelionwalkern.co.uk
dir: B1037 from Stevenage

In rolling chalk downland, Walkern is on the outskirts of Stevenage. The bar in this 16th-century pub has oak beams, an inglenook, leather sofas, newspapers and a computer for those who still need to surf the net over a pint of Greene King or cup of hot chocolate. The informal restaurant offers a traditional pub menu, with ham, egg and chips, fillet of beef stroganoff, and succulent steaks.

Open noon-3 4.30-11 (Mon 4.30-11 Sat-Sun noon-mdnt) Closed: Mon L ◀ Greene King IPA, Abbot Ale, Guinness. ♥ 8 Facilities Play area Dogs allowed Garden Parking

## WELWYN — Map 6 TL21

### The White Hart ♥

2 Prospect Place AL6 9EN
☎ 01438 715353 📠 01438 714448
e-mail: bookings@thewhitehearthotel.net
dir: Just off A1(M) junct 6. On corner of Prospect Place (just past fire station)

Olde worlde beams and inglenook fireplace blend easily with contemporary wood floors, leather chairs and bold artwork in this elegant, refurbished 17th-century coaching inn on the old Great North Road at the hub of old Welwyn. In keeping, menus are modern and innovative, generally utilising local market and farm produce. Start with duck hash with mixed leaves and fried egg; continue with chicken and spinach mousseline wrapped in streaky bacon and top-up with a chocolate and Baileys pot. Classic beers are from Charles Wells and Young's.

Open all day all wk 7am-mdnt (Sun 9am-10.30pm) Bar Meals L served Mon-Sat 12-2.30 D served Mon-Sat 6.30-9.30 Av main course £6.50 Restaurant L served all wk 12-2.30 booking required D served Mon-Sat 6.30-9.30, Sun 6-8.30 booking required Fixed menu price fr £9.99 Av 3 course à la carte fr £25 ⊕ CHARLES WELLS ◀ Eagle IPA, Bombardier, Youngs Ö Stowford Press. ♥ 14 Facilities Children's menu Children's portions Parking

## WELWYN GARDEN CITY — Map 6 TL21

### The Brocket Arms ★★★ INN ♥ NEW

Ayot St Lawrence AL6 9BT
☎ 01438 820250 & 07984 282800
e-mail: booking@brocketarms.com
dir: A1(M) junct 4 follow signs to Wheathampstead, then Shaw's Corner. Pub past Shaw's Corner on right

Originally built as a monks' hostel, parts of The Brocket Arms date back to 1378 but it didn't become a tavern until the 1630s. Encircled by a picturesque village that was once home to George Bernard Shaw, the pub was refurbished and reopened in May 2009 by Howard and Suzy Sharp. Huge oak beams and hefty hearths greet you along with a great range of real ales and wines. Chef Andrew Knight uses the best seasonal ingredients for his simple menu which specialises in game. There are also six comfortable bedrooms, each full of character and charm.

Open all day all wk Bar Meals L served all wk 12-2.30 D served all wk 5-7 Av main course £7 Restaurant L served all wk 12-2.30 booking required D served all wk 7-9 booking required Fixed menu price fr £18.50 ⊕ FREE HOUSE ◀ Nethergate Brewery Brocket Bitter, Greene King IPA, Abbot Ale, Sharp's Doom Bar, Olde Trip Ö Westons, Aspalls. ♥ 12 Facilities Children's portions Dogs allowed Garden Parking Rooms 6

## WILLIAN — Map 12 TL23

### PICK OF THE PUBS

## The Fox ◉ ♥

See Pick of the Pubs on opposite page

# PICK OF THE PUBS

## The Fox

**WILLIAN** Map 12 TL23

**Baldock Ln SG6 2AE**
☎ 01462 480233 📄 01462 676966
e-mail: restaurant@foxatwillian.co.uk
dir: *A1(M) junct 9 towards Letchworth, 1st left to Willian, 0.5m on left*

A clean, crisp modern look defines the interior of this popular, award-winning dining pub; settees and cane chairs, themed paintings by local artists on the walls, chunky wooden furniture detain expectant diners, or look for space in the glazed restaurant atrium or enclosed courtyard. All of this in an imposing Georgian building opposite the village pond and right next door to the church, ideal company for the two beer gardens here.

It has answered to several names over the years, being the Orange Tree from c1750, then until 1870 the Dinsdale Arms (after the family who owned the village), when it became for a while the Willian Arms. In 1907, after its first incarnation as The Fox, the People's Refreshment House Association, whose aim was to bring respectability to public houses, took it over. It's now part of a select chain overseen by Cliff Nye, renowned for his Norfolk coast pubs – the choice of beer reflects this, with East Anglian brews from Woodforde's and Adnams to the fore.

Young and friendly staff serve food from the daily-changing, one-AA Rosette menu, which includes fish and shellfish brought in from north Norfolk - Brancaster mussels served marinière or in a korma cream sauce, for example. Hazelnut breaded chicken strips with soy and sweet chilli sauce or honey roasted swede and turnip soup with avocado oil may tickle the starter buds before progressing to seared grey mullet with caramelised turnip, truffle creamed butter beans and beurre noisette, or slow confit local farm pork belly with orange and chilli glaze, wasabi creamed potato, wilted red chard, crispy egg noodle lattice and plum compote. Helpfully, wines are suggested to accompany these mains, and the attractive desserts include lychee and apricot mille-feuille, roasted chestnut and chocolate torte and some very select British cheeses.

**Open** all day all wk Mon-Thu noon-11 (Fri-Sat noon-mdnt, Sun noon-10.30) **Bar Meals** L served Mon-Sat 12-2 Av main course £12.50 **Restaurant** L served Mon-Sat 12-2, Sun 12-2.45 booking required D served Mon-Fri 6.45-9, Sat 6.30-9.15 booking required Av 3 course à la carte fr £25.50 ⊕ FREE HOUSE ◀ Adnams Bitter, Woodforde's Wherry, Fuller's London Pride, weekly changing guest ales ⚬ Aspall. ♀ 14 **Facilities** Dogs allowed Garden Parking

## KENT

### BEARSTED      Map 7 TQ85

## The Oak on the Green NEW

**Bearsted Green ME14 4EJ**
☎ **01622 737976** 📄 **01233 820074**
**e-mail:** headoffice@villagegreenrestaurants.com
**dir:** *In village centre*

As its name suggests, this refurbished 17th-century pub overlooks Bearsted's pretty green and the front terrace, canopied under huge blue brollies, makes the most of its pleasant location. Once the village courthouse and prison, it is now a thriving gastro-pub. An eclectic modern menu offers an extensive choice including grills and pies (steak, port and Stilton), alongside classic dishes like local sausages and mash, and imaginative specials, perhaps seared squid with garlic, chilli and coriander and roast pork belly with rosemary and garlic gravy.

**Open** all day all wk **Bar Meals** Av main course £5 food served all day **Restaurant** Av 3 course à la carte fr £20 food served all day ⊕ FREE HOUSE ◖ Fuller's London Pride, ESB, Old Thumper, Beehead ♂ Biddenden. **Facilities** Children's menu Children's portions Dogs allowed Garden Parking

### BIDDENDEN      Map 7 TQ83

## PICK OF THE PUBS

## The Three Chimneys

**Biddenden Rd TN27 8LW** ☎ **01580 291472**
**dir:** *From A262 midway between Biddenden & Sissinghurst, follow Frittenden signs. (Pub seen from main road). Pub immediately on left in hamlet of Three Chimneys*

Worth remembering if visiting nearby Sissinghurst Castle, this 15th-century timbered treasure that has every natural advantage of being a classic country pub, its original, small-roomed layout and old-fashioned furnishings remain delightfully intact. There are old settles, low beams, wood-panelled walls, worn brick floors, crackling log fires, soft evening candlelight, absence of music and electronic games – glorious. Modern-day demand for dining space has seen the addition of the rear Garden Room and a tasteful conservatory, and drinkers and diners spill out onto the secluded heated side patio and vast shrub-filled garden, which are perfect for summer eating. Food is bang up-to-date and listed on daily-changing chalkboards. Tuck into a hearty ploughman's lunch or salmon and smoked haddock fishcakes with tartare sauce, or something more substantial, perhaps roast duck with bubble-and-squeak and port jus, pan-fried rib-eye steak with garlic butter, or scallops on roasted sweet potato with coconut and coriander velouté. If you have room for a pudding, try the delicious sticky toffee pudding. Adnams ales and the heady Biddenden cider are tapped direct from cask.

**Open** all wk 11.30-3 5.30-11 (Sat-Sun 11.30-4, 5.30-11) Closed: 25 Dec **Bar Meals** L served all wk 12-2.30 booking required D served all wk 6.30-9.30 booking required **Restaurant** L served all wk 12-2.30 booking required D served all wk 6.30-9.30 booking required ⊕ FREE HOUSE ◖ Adnams, Harveys Old, Special ♂ Biddenden. **Facilities** Dogs allowed Garden Parking

### BODSHAM GREEN      Map 7 TR14

## PICK OF THE PUBS

## Froggies At The Timber Batts

**School Ln TN25 5JQ**
☎ **01233 750237** 📄 **01233 750176**
**e-mail:** joel@thetimberbatts.co.uk
**dir:** *4m E of Wye*

French chef/proprietor Joel Gross built up a great reputation for his former restaurant in Wye; now he's built a similar one at this delightful 15th-century pub. Named after a nearby wood yard, Joel added the Froggies bit. The beamed bar, serving three real ales, has an inglenook fireplace the size of a small room, while the restaurant has a huge fireplace of its own, old pine tables and candles. Three different menus – bar snacks, carte and daily specials – offer locally sourced dishes, some classically French, naturally. An economy with words on the bar menu results in croque monsieur, stuffed mussels and beef bourguignon, for example. Restaurant favourites include stuffed mussels; duck breast in bigarade sauce; roasted rack of Romney Marsh lamb; and grilled local wild sea bass. As for wines, remember that Monsieur Gross is French, and his huge wine list fairly bristles with his mother country's products.

**Open** all wk 12-3 6.30-close Closed: 24 Dec-2 Jan **Bar Meals** L served all wk 12-2.30 D served all wk 7-9.30 **Restaurant** L served all wk 12-2.30 booking required D served all wk 7-9.30 booking required Fixed menu price fr £18 Av 3 course à la carte fr £33 ⊕ FREE HOUSE ◖ Adnams, London Pride, Woodforde's Wherry. **Facilities** Children's portions Dogs allowed Garden Parking

### BOSSINGHAM      Map 7 TR14

## The Hop Pocket

**The Street CT4 6DY** ☎ **01227 709866** 📄 **01227 709866**
**dir:** *Telephone for directions*

Birds of prey and an animal corner for children are among the more unusual attractions at this family pub in the heart of Kent. Canterbury is only five miles away and the county's delightfully scenic coast and countryside are within easy reach. Menu may include fish pie, supreme of chicken, spicy salmon, Cajun beef, chilli nachos and fish platter. There is also an extensive range of sandwiches and omelettes.

**Open** all wk 11-3 6-mdnt (Sat & Sun all day) **Bar Meals** L served all wk 12-2.30 D served Mon-Sat 7-9.30 **Restaurant** L served all wk 12-2.30 D served Mon-Sat 7-9.30 ⊕ FREE HOUSE ◖ London Pride, Adnams, Wadworth 6X, Purity Ales. **Facilities** Children's portions Play area Dogs allowed Garden Parking

### BRABOURNE      Map 7 TR14

## The Five Bells ♀

**The Street TN25 5LP**
☎ **01303 813334** 📄 **01303 814667**
**dir:** *5m E of Ashford*

A 16th-century free house pub surrounded by rolling hills and orchards and the perfect pit stop for walkers and cyclists. Originally a poor house, the old stocks are located across the road, while inside are whitewashed walls and a huge inglenook fireplace. An extensive menu and a range of popular daily specials include traditional steak and kidney pie; liver and bacon with sage and onion gravy; and fillet of salmon with creamed leeks and smoked salmon mash.

**Open** all wk ◖ Shepherd Neame Master Brew, London Pride, Greene King IPA, Adnams. ♀ 12 **Facilities** Play area Dogs allowed Garden Parking

### BROOKLAND      Map 7 TQ92

## PICK OF THE PUBS

## The Royal Oak ♀

**High St TN29 9QR** ☎ **01797 344215**
**e-mail:** info@royaloakbrookland.co.uk
**dir:** *A259, 5m E of Rye. In village by church*

This smart marshland pub began life as a house in 1570. A succession of parish clerks and sextons lived here until 1736 when it started to function as a pub – a role it has amply fulfilled ever since. These days its uncluttered interior is a pleasing combination of original features and modern furnishings. The menus cater for everything from speedy lunchtime snacks to leisurely three-course dining. Regularly changing dishes draw on local, seasonal produce. Simple options are freshly made sandwiches; beer-battered south coast cod with hand-cut chips and garden peas; and the ploughman's platter with home-cooked smoked ham, Cheddar cheese, chutney and crusty bread. For dinner, choose from the likes of pan-fried local pigeon breasts marinated in juniper and thyme; chargrilled chump of Romney Marsh lamb with rosemary and garlic oil; and warm chocolate brownie with chocolate sauce. A well-kept and tranquil garden borders the churchyard of St Augustine, one of only four churches in England with a separate bell tower.

**Open** 12-3 6-11 Closed: Sun eve & Mon eve **Bar Meals** L served all wk 12-2 D served all wk 6.30-9 **Restaurant** L served all wk 12-2 D served all wk 6.30-9 ⊕ ENTERPRISE INNS ◖ Harvey's Best Bitter, Adnams Best Bitter, guest ale ♂ Westons Stowford Press. ♀ 8 **Facilities** Dogs allowed Garden Parking

Save on Hotels. Book at **theAA.com/hotel**

KENT  261  ENGLAND

## PICK OF THE PUBS

### Woolpack Inn

*See Pick of the Pubs page 262*

---

### BURHAM                    Map 6 TQ76

## The Golden Eagle

80 Church St ME1 3SD ☎ 01634 668975
e-mail: kathymay@btconnect.com
web: www.thegoldeneagle.org
dir: *S from M2 junct 3 or N from M20 junct 6 on A229, follow signs to Burham*

Commanding striking views across the Medway Valley, this traditional Kentish village pub, which dates from 1850, has been famous locally for 30 years for its authentic Malaysian food. Expect to find an extensive menu, enhanced by chef specialities on the chalkboard, and featuring pork in satay sauce, pad Thai chicken, beef and mushrooms, duck royale, and traditional puddings like raspberry Pavlova and chocolate fudge cake.

**Open** all wk Closed: 25-26 Dec **Bar Meals** L served all wk 12-2 D served all wk 7-9.30 **Restaurant** L served all wk 12-2 D served all wk 7-9.30 ⊕ FREE HOUSE ◀ Wadworth 6X, Boddingtons ♂ Stowford Press. **Facilities** Parking

---

### CANTERBURY                Map 7 TR15

## The Chapter Arms ♀

New Town St, Chartham Hatch CT4 7LT
☎ 01227 738340
e-mail: david.durell@unicombox.co.uk
dir: *3m from Canterbury. Off A28 in Chartham Hatch or A2 at Upper Harbledown*

Situated on the North Downs Way, this charming and picturesque free house is set in over an acre of gardens overlooking apple orchards and oast houses. It was once three cottages owned by Canterbury Cathedral's Dean and Chapter – hence the name. A comely choice of ales is offered in the bar, and food ranges from lunchtime traditional (baguettes, steak and kidney pie) to a special fish menu (moules marinières, grilled whole lemon sole). Desserts such as chocolate covered profiteroles are made on the premises.

---

**Open** all wk 11-3 6-11 (all day Fri-Sun Jun-Sep) **Bar Meals** L served all wk 12-2.30 D served Mon-Sat 6.30-9 **Restaurant** L served all wk 12-2.30 D served Mon-Sat 6.30-9 ⊕ FREE HOUSE ◀ Shepherd Neame Master Brew, Adnams, Harveys, Youngs, Wells Bombardier, Guest ales. ♀ 10 **Facilities** Children's menu Children's portions Play area Dogs allowed Garden Parking

---

## PICK OF THE PUBS

### The Dove Inn ◉

Plum Pudding Ln, Dargate ME13 9HB
☎ 01227 751360  📠 01227 751360
e-mail: pipmacgrew@hotmail.com
dir: *5m NW of Canterbury. A299 Thanet Way, exit at Lychgate service station*

The Dove is a splendid vine-covered Victorian country gastro-pub, tucked away in a sleepy hamlet between Faversham and Whitstable, surrounded by orchards and farmland. It has established a reputation for well-kept Shepherd Neame ales and good food based on locally sourced ingredients. The interior is simple and relaxed with stripped wooden floors and scrubbed tables. Outside is a large formal garden where, appropriately, a dovecote and doves present an agreeably scenic backdrop for an alfresco meal or quiet pint. The Dove's menu is short but nonetheless offers something for most palates and appetites. You could lunch lightly with sardines on toast or Welsh rarebit; alternatively tuck into potted shrimps and toast before a bavette of beef with horseradish and potato gratin, or Kentish pork and ale sausages and mash. Half a dozen well executed desserts include sorbets, cheesecake, and crème brûlée. Children are offered smaller portions from the main menu.

**Open** noon-3 6-mdnt (Fri noon-mdnt Sun noon-9 (Apr-Oct) noon-4 (Nov-Mar)) Closed: Mon **Bar Meals** L served Tue-Sat 12-2.30 D served Tue-Thu 6.30-9 Av main course £10 **Restaurant** L served Tue-Sun 12-2.30 booking required D served Tue-Sat 7-9 booking required Av 3 course à la carte fr £25 ⊕ SHEPHERD NEAME ◀ Shepherd Neame Master Brew, Spitfire, seasonal ale. **Facilities** Children's portions Dogs allowed Garden Parking

---

## PICK OF THE PUBS

### The Granville ◉

Street End, Lower Hardres CT4 7AL
☎ 01227 700402  📠 01227 700925
dir: *On B2068, 2m from Canterbury towards Hythe*

Sister pub to the Sportsman in Whitstable (run by the brothers of the Granville's landlady, Gabrielle Harris), the interior here is fresh and spacious, with a double-height ceiling in the main restaurant (celebrating its first AA Rosette), whitewashed walls, and regularly changing local artworks. With ample parking, a patio and large beer garden where summer barbecues take place, this Shepherd Neame pub is good for families and dogs. Don't, however, expect typical pub grub from the short, lively menu, although it is good honest

---

British cooking. Starters include rock oysters with shallot vinegar; smoked local widgeon with mustard fruits; and antipasti. Main courses always feature three meat and three fish dishes: slow-roast Waterham Farm chicken with truffle cream sauce, and Dungeness brill fillet with grain mustard sauce are two examples. Finish with poached spiced pear with ginger ice cream and chocolate sauce. There is no children's menu as such, but items from the main menu can be served.

**Open** noon-3 5.30-11 Closed: 25-26 Dec, Mon eve **Bar Meals** L served Tue-Sat 12-2 D served Tue-Sat 7-9 Av main course £14.95 **Restaurant** L served Tue-Sun 12-2 booking required D served Tue-Sat 7-9 booking required Av 3 course à la carte fr £25 ◀ Master Brew, seasonal ale. **Facilities** Children's portions Dogs allowed Garden Parking

---

## PICK OF THE PUBS

### The Red Lion

High St, Stodmarsh CT3 4BA
☎ 01227 721339  📠 01227 721339
e-mail: tiptop-redlion@hotmail.com
dir: *From Canterbury take A257 towards Sandwich, left into Stodmarsh Rd to Stodmarsh*

Built in 1475 and burnt to the ground in 1720, the Red Lion was rebuilt and has remained much the same as you'll find it today. Set in a tiny hamlet, it is surrounded by reed beds which are home to marsh harriers, bearded tits and bitterns. The pub's interior, warmed by two large log fires, is adorned with traditional hop garlands, curios, antiques and a collection of international menus. Outside is an extensive garden where an antique forge doubles as a barbecue during the summer months; here you'll find an abundance of flowers, wandering ducks, chickens and the odd cat. The menu majors on produce from surrounding allotments and small holdings, mushrooms picked in the nearby woods, and unusual cuts of meat purchased as close to the village as possible. Seasonal game such as rabbits and pheasant are in plentiful supply thanks to local shoots; the famous Whigham family recipe for oxtail stew is another favourite.

**Open** all day all wk 10.30am-11pm (Sun 10.30-4.30) Closed: Sun eve **Bar Meals** L served all wk 12-2.30 booking required D served Mon-Sat 7-9.30 booking required Av main course £12.50 **Restaurant** L served all wk 12-2.30 booking required D served Mon-Sat 7-9.30 booking required Fixed menu price fr £22 Av 3 course à la carte fr £36 ⊕ FREE HOUSE ◀ Greene King IPA, Ruddles County, Old Speckled Hen. **Facilities** Play area Family room Dogs allowed Garden Parking

# PICK OF THE PUBS

## Woolpack Inn

**BROOKLAND**     Map 7 TQ92

Beacon Ln TN29 9TJ ☎ 01797 344321
web: www.thewoolpackbrookland.co.uk
dir: *1.5m past Brookland towards Rye on A259*

Partly built of old timbers salvaged from local shipwrecks and isolated down a lane deep in Kentish marshland, surrounded by dykes and reed beds, this low, white-painted 15th-century cottage oozes authentic character and charm. Built when smuggling was rife on Romney Marsh, it's rumoured that at one time the Woolpack had a secret tunnel used by smugglers to escape from the Excise men. The old spinning wheel mounted on the bar ceiling was used to divide up their contraband; but, nowadays, the pub is ideally situated for those who wish to explore this unique and beautiful area of Kent. There are many walks in the area to study nature at close quarters, go fishing, or just to stop and let the world go by. Open beams and a vast inglenook fireplace (you can sit in it!) add to the atmosphere, and landlord Barry Morgan and his staff extend a warm welcome to all.

The chef makes extensive use of fresh produce including fish from the local fishermen. The menu offers a wide variety of home-made meals, whilst dishes on the specials board make the most of seasonal produce. Lunchtime brings ploughman's, sandwiches and filled jacket potatoes (vegetable curry), and there are hog roasts and barbecues in the pub garden on summer evenings.

On the main menu, expect pub favourites like chicken kiev, lamb shank and battered cod. There are also game and vegetarian dishes like whole partridge with red wine and cream sauce, and Stilton and vegetable bake. Finish with the likes of honey and cinnamon pudding, steamed spotted Dick, or bitter chocolate and orange sponge. Wash down with a cracking pint of Shepherd Neame Spitfire.

**Open** all wk Mon-Fri 11-3 6-11 Sat 11-11 Sun noon-10.30 (open all day during school holidays)
**Bar Meals** L served Mon-Fri 12-2.30, Sat-Sun 12-9 D served Mon-Fri 6-9, Sat-Sun 12-9 Av main course £9.95
🍺 Shepherd Neame Spitfire Premium Ale, Master Brew Bitter.
**Facilities** Children's menu Play area Family room Dogs allowed Garden Parking

Save on Hotels. Book at **theAA.com/hotel**

KENT 263 **ENGLAND**

## CANTERBURY *continued*

### The White Horse Inn ♟

**53 High St, Bridge CT4 5LA**
☎ 01227 832814 ▤ 01227 832814
**dir:** *3m S of Canterbury, just off A2*

This medieval and Tudor building was originally a staging post close to a ford on the main Dover to Canterbury road, and still provides a stirling service to modern travellers. An enormous log fire burning in the beamed bar during the winter months provides a guaranteed warm welcome, whilst the extensive garden is popular for alfresco dining on warmer days. Fullers and Shepherd Neame are amongst the real ales served in the bar, with up to ten wines available by the glass. You'll find a strong emphasis on food, with seasonal dishes created from the best local ingredients. Choose between the relaxed blackboard bar menu, and more formal dining in the restaurant.

**Open** Mon-Sun L Closed: 25 Dec, 1 Jan, Sun eve
◼ Shepherd Neame Masterbrew, Greene King Abbot Ale, Fuller's London Pride, Greene King IPA, Gadds No. 5. ♟ 10
**Facilities** Garden Parking

---

### CHARING
Map 7 TQ94

### The Bowl Inn

**Egg Hill Rd TN27 0HG**
☎ 01233 712256 ▤ 01233 714705
**e-mail:** info@bowl-inn.co.uk
**dir:** *M20 junct 8/9, A20 to Charing, then A252 towards Canterbury. Left at top of Charing Hill down Bowl Rd, 1.25m*

Standing on top of the North Downs, The Bowl was built as a farmhouse in 1512 and converted to a brewhouse in 1606. Alan and Sue Paine have been here since 1992, and run a relaxed and welcoming hostelry. Excellent ales include local Kentish brews among handles for Adnams, Harvey's, and Sharp's. The small but varied menu proffers Kent-cured ham, English Cheddar ploughman's, and hot bacon and sausage sandwiches. Pool can be played on an unusual rotating hexagonal table. In summer enjoy the patio and garden, also an annual beer festival takes place in mid-July.

**Open** all wk Mon-Sat noon-mdnt Sun noon-11 (Mon-Thu 4-11 Fri-Sun noon-mdnt winter) **Bar Meals** Av main course £6 food served all day ⊕ FREE HOUSE ◼ Fuller's London Pride, Adnams Southwold, Harveys Sussex Best, Whitstable IPA, Youngs Best. **Facilities** Dogs allowed Garden Parking.

### The Oak ★★★★ INN ⑧ NEW

**5 High St TN27 0HU** ☎ 01233 712612
**e-mail:** info@theoakcharing.co.uk
**dir:** *M20 junct 9, A20 towards Maidstone. 5m to Charing. Right into High St*

Plumb in the middle of Charing's medieval centre at the foot of the North Downs, The Oak continues to mature as a classic English village inn, supporting local brewers

and a farming cooperative which supplies the meats for Simon Desmond's AA Rosette award-winning feasts. Unusual dishes like crispy stuffed pig's trotter sit easily alongside top-notch fish, lamb and game stalwarts; the choice evolves with the seasons, in summer alfresco dining on the colourful garden terrace is appealing. There are eight contemporary but cosy en suite rooms available at this newly refurbished free house.

*The Oak*

**Open** all wk 11-3 6-11 Closed: 25 Dec **Bar Meals** L served all wk 12-2.45 D served all wk 7-9.15 Av main course £12 **Restaurant** L served all wk 12-2.30 D served all wk 7-9.15 booking required Av 3 course à la carte fr £20 ⊕ FREE HOUSE ◼ Goachers, Golden Braid, Masterbrew. **Facilities** Children's menu Children's portions Dogs allowed Garden Parking **Rooms** 8

---

### CHIDDINGSTONE
Map 6 TQ54

#### PICK OF THE PUBS

### Castle Inn ♟

**TN8 7AH** ☎ 01892 870247 ▤ 01892 871420
**e-mail:** info@castleinn-kent.co.uk
**dir:** *1.5m S of B2027 between Tonbridge & Edenbridge*

Like the rest of the village street, this historic, tile-hung free house is owned by the National Trust. The building dates from 1420 and boasts leaded casement windows and projecting upper gables. The charming interior has also remained delightfully unchanged; its two traditional bars have quarry-tiled floors and an old brick fireplace, as well as rustic wall benches in the classic public bar. Expect Larkins real ales and carefully chosen wines. The lunchtime menu offers some interesting sandwiches, supported by light meals such as smoked salmon scrambled eggs on toasted muffin and fresh linguine carbonara. An evening dinner might begin with pressed ham collar, mustard potatoes and Castle salad cream, continuing with poached halibut served with sweet and sour tomato, tian Provençale and pesto. Round things off with treacle tart, almond and vanilla ice cream. For an alfresco drink, head for the vine-hung courtyard, or cross the bridge to the lawn and its beautifully tended flowerbeds.

**Open** all day all wk 11-11 (Sun 12-10.30) **Bar Meals** L served all wk 12-4 D served all wk 7-9.30 **Restaurant** L served Mon-Fri 12-2, Sat-Sun 12-4 D served all wk 7-9.30 ◼ Larkins Traditional, Harveys Sussex, Larkins Porter, Larkins Blonde ⌀ Stowford Press. ♟ 9 **Facilities** Children's menu Children's portions Dogs allowed Garden

---

### CHILHAM
Map 7 TR05

#### PICK OF THE PUBS

### The White Horse

**The Square CT4 8BY** ☎ 01227 730355
**dir:** *Take A28 from Canterbury then A252, in 1m turn left*

One of the most photographed pubs in Britain, The White Horse stands next to St Mary's church facing onto the 15th-century village square, where the May Fair is an annual event. The pub offers a traditional atmosphere and modern cooking from a monthly-changing menu based on fresh local produce. Dishes include fillet steak poached in red wine, and cod and smoked haddock fishcakes served with a sweet chilli sauce.

**Open** all day all wk noon-close ◼ Masterbrew, Guest. **Facilities** Dogs allowed Garden

---

### CHILLENDEN
Map 7 TR25

#### PICK OF THE PUBS

### Griffins Head ♟

*See Pick of the Pubs on page 264*

---

### DARTFORD
Map 6 TQ57

### The Rising Sun Inn ★★★ INN ♟

**Fawkham Green, Fawkham DA3 8NL**
☎ 01474 872291 ▤ 01474 872779
**dir:** *0.5m from Brands Hatch Racing Circuit & 5m from Dartford*

Standing on the green in a picturesque village not far from Brands Hatch, The Rising Sun has been a pub since 1702. Inside you will find a bar full of character, complete with inglenook log fire and a cosy restaurant. Starters include crispy soy duck; Stilton and bacon field mushrooms; and tempura tiger prawns. Follow with pork loin with honey and herb crust, or sea bass fillets with mango and garlic beurre. There is also a patio for alfresco dining in warmer weather, plus comfortable en suite bedrooms.

**Open** all day all wk **Bar Meals** food served all day **Restaurant** L served all wk 12-3 D served all wk 6.30-9.30 ⊕ FREE HOUSE ◼ Courage Best, Courage Directors, London Pride, Timothy Taylor Landlord, Harveys. ♟ 9 **Facilities** Children's portions Garden Parking **Rooms** 5

# PICK OF THE PUBS

## Griffins Head ♀

**CHILLENDEN**     Map 7 TR25

**CT3 1PS**
☎ **01304 840325**   📠 **01304 841290**
**dir:** *A2 from Canterbury towards Dover, then B2046. Village on right*

Dating from 1286, the Griffins Head is an architectural gem of a building, a fine black-and-white half-timbered Wealden hall house, nestling in a tiny farming hamlet amid rolling open countryside south-east of Canterbury. Originally built as a farmhouse to serve the local estate, ale and cider were always brewed on the premises for the workers but it was only granted an ale licence in 1743. The present Tudor structure is built around the original wattle and daub walls, remains of which can be viewed in one of the three delightfully unspoilt rooms, which also feature flagstone floors, exposed brick walls and beams and a tasteful mix of furnishings, from old scrubbed pine tables and chairs to church pews.

Fine Shepherd Neame ales and home-made food have helped this old inn to make its mark with visitors as well as locals, among them Kent's cricketing fraternity. The constantly changing seasonal menu is typically English, and specialises in game from local estates, and locally caught fish where possible. Typical dishes might include lamb stew; braised steak, onions and mash; warm salads with steak and roasted vegetables; or sautéed prawns and squid; and traditional pub dishes like cottage pie and ham, egg and chips. Desserts include apple crumble, or home-made ice creams like passionfruit, ginger, or raspberry and strawberry. The pretty garden, full of rambling roses and clematis, is the setting for popular summer weekend barbecues.

**Open** all wk Closed: Sun pm
**Bar Meals** L served all wk 12-2 D served Mon-Sat 7-9.30 booking required
**Restaurant** L served all wk 12-2 D served Mon-Sat 7-9.30 booking required 🍺 SHEPHERD NEAME
🍺Shepherd Neame. ♀ 10
**Facilities** Garden Parking

## DEAL                                  Map 7 TR35

### The King's Head

**9 Beach St CT14 7AH**
☎ 01304 368194  📠 01304 364182
**e-mail:** booking@kingsheaddeal.co.uk
**dir:** A249 from Dover to Deal, on seafront

A 250-year-old public house, The King's Head stands overlooking the sea only a minute's walk from the town centre. It has been established for over 28 years under the same ownership and is particularly well known for the annual display of flowers that adorns the building. Hand-pulled bitter and bar meals are served, including steaks, sandwiches and seafood, plus a daily-changing specials board.

**Open** all day all wk ◾ Shepherd Neame Master Brew, Spitfire, Fuller's London Pride. **Facilities** Dogs allowed Garden

## DOVER                                 Map 7 TR34

### The White Cliffs Hotel ★★★ HL ◉ ♥

**High St, St Margaret's at Cliffe CT15 6AT**
☎ 01304 852400 & 852229  📠 01304 851880
**e-mail:** mail@thewhitecliffs.com
**dir:** 3m NE of Dover

A contemporary atmosphere and a refreshingly independent way of thinking characterise this traditional Kentish weather-boarded establishment. The hotel has a stylish, contemporary feel without compromising the charm of this delightful historic building, with its winter log fires and bar leading out onto the rose-filled summer garden. Gavin Oakley brings imagination and flair to menus at The Bay Restaurant, where main course offerings might include roast pumpkin and squash with baby onions and talegio; slow-braised belly of free-range pork; or bouillabaisse of locally landed fish.

**Open** all wk **Bar Meals** Av main course £8 food served all day **Restaurant** L served all wk 12-2 D served all wk 7-9 Fixed menu price fr £15 Av 3 course à la carte fr £25 ⊕ FREE HOUSE ◾ Adnams, Bitburger, Erdinger, Fuller's London Pride ⭕ Westons Organic, Biddenden. ♥ 11 **Facilities** Children's menu Children's portions Play area Dogs allowed Garden Parking **Rooms** 15

## FAVERSHAM                             Map 7 TR06

### PICK OF THE PUBS

### Shipwright's Arms ♥

**Hollowshore ME13 7TU** ☎ 01795 590088
**dir:** A2 through Ospringe then right at rdbt. Right at T-junct then left opposite Davington School, follow signs

Built of homely brick and clad in weatherboard, this extraordinary creekside pub dates from the 17th century and stands in a remote location on the Swale marshes. Once the haunt of pirates and smugglers, it is best reached on foot or by boat and the effort in getting here is well rewarded as this unspoilt tavern

oozes historic character and charm. Step back in time in the classic bars, which boast nooks and crannies, original standing timbers, built-in settles, well-worn sofas, wood-burning stoves, a wealth of maritime artefacts, and relaxed, no-frills but comfortable atmosphere. In time-honoured fashioned, quaff locally-brewed Goachers and Whitstable ales tapped straight from the cask, and tuck into simple, traditional bar food, perhaps liver and bacon, fish pie, sausages and mash, ploughman's and locally caught fish.

**Open** 11-3 6-10 (Sat-Sun 11-4 6-11 in winter), 11-11 (Sun noon-10.30 in summer) Closed: Mon (Oct-Mar) **Bar Meals** L served Tue-Sat 11-2.30, Sun 12-2.30 D served Tue-Sat 7-9 (no food Tue-Thu eve in winter) **Restaurant** L served Tue-Sat 11-2.30, Sun 12-2.30 D served Tue-Sat 7-9 ⊕ FREE HOUSE ◾ Local ales, Goachers, Hop Daemon, Whitstable Brewery. ♥ 12 **Facilities** Children's menu Children's portions Family room Dogs allowed Garden Parking

## FOLKESTONE                            Map 7 TR23

### The Lighthouse Inn ★★★ INN ♥

**Old Dover Rd, Capel le Ferne CT18 7HT**
☎ 01303 223300  📠 01303 842270
**e-mail:** james@thelighthouseinn.net
**dir:** M20 junct 13 follow signs for Capel le Ferne

The Lighthouse began as an ale house in 1840, later becoming, successively, a billiard hall, convalescent home, psychiatric hospital and country club while, more recently still, Channel Tunnel builders headquartered here. There are sweeping Channel views from the pub, which is splendidly situated on the edge of Dover's famous White Cliffs. Expect decent home-made food; pan fried sea bass; local sausages with rustic mash; or liver and bacon. Check the blackboard for the chef's specials.

**Open** all day all wk 11-11 **Bar Meals** Av main course £12.50 food served all day **Restaurant** Fixed menu price fr £14 Av 3 course à la carte fr £25 food served all day ⊕ FREE HOUSE ◾ IPA, 6X, Adnams, Directors. ♥ 14 **Facilities** Play area Family room Dogs allowed Garden Parking **Rooms** 10

## FORDCOMBE                             Map 6 TQ54

### Chafford Arms ♥

**TN3 0SA** ☎ 01892 740267
**e-mail:** chaffordarms@btconnect.com
**web:** www.chaffordarms.com
**dir:** On B2188 (off A264) between Tunbridge Wells, East Grinstead & Penshurst

A lovely mid-19th-century tile-hung village pub, with a working red telephone kiosk in the car park and a large garden with great views across the weald. Larkins and Harveys ales are stocked at the bar, and the menu offers a great range of traditional pub food.

While mum and dad choose between chicken, ham and leek pie or a crock of chilli con carne, the children can pick their favourites.

*Chafford Arms*

**Open** all day all wk 11am-mdnt **Bar Meals** L served Mon-Sat 12-9, Sun 12-8 D served Mon-Sat 12-9, Sun 12-8 food served all day **Restaurant** food served all day ⊕ ENTERPRISE INNS ◾ Larkins Bitter, Harvey's Best. ♥ 9 **Facilities** Children's menu Dogs allowed Garden Parking

## GOODNESTONE                           Map 7 TR25

### The Fitzwalter Arms

**The Street CT3 1PJ** ☎ 01304 840303
**e-mail:** thefitzwalter arms@gmail.com
**dir:** Signed from B2046 & A2

The 'Fitz', hostelry to the Fitzwalter Estate, has been a pub since 1702. Quintessentially English, it is a place of conviviality and conversation. Jane Austen was a frequent visitor to nearby Goodnestone Park after her brother, Edward, married into the family. On the menu, brawn with a radish, celery, parsley and caper salad; or mackerel tartar with an oyster fritter and bloody Mary sauce; followed by poached halibut fillet, asparagus and hollandaise sauce; or confit pork belly, crackling and rhubarb. Dessert might be rhubarb and ginger crumble with custard.

**Open** all wk Mon-Fri noon-3 6-11 (Sat-Sun noon-11) Closed: 25 Dec, 1 Jan **Restaurant** L served Mon & Wed-Sun 12-2 booking required D served Mon & Wed-Sat 7-9 booking required Fixed menu price fr £15.50 Av 3 course à la carte fr £24 ⊕ SHEPHERD NEAME ◾ Master Brew, Spitfire. **Facilities** Dogs allowed Garden

## GOUDHURST                             Map 6 TQ73

### Green Cross Inn

**TN17 1HA** ☎ 01580 211200  📠 01580 212905
**dir:** A21 from Tonbridge towards Hastings turn left onto A262 towards Ashford. 2m, Goudhurst on right

In an unspoiled corner of Kent, close to Finchcocks Manor, and originally built to serve the Paddock Wood-Goudhurst railway line, which closed in 1968, this thriving dining pub specialises in fresh seafood. Arrive early to bag a table in the dining room, prettily decorated with fresh flowers, and tuck into oysters, crab, mussels, smoked eel, whole Dover sole, or Rye Bay skate, or order the duck cassoulet, followed by hot chocolate soufflé with chocolate sauce; all prepared and supervised by chef/owner who is Italian classically trained.

*continued on page 266*

**GOUDHURST** *continued*

**Open** all wk noon-3 6-11 Closed: Sun eve **Bar Meals** L served all wk 12-2.30 booking required D served Mon-Sat 7-9.45 booking required Av main course £12 **Restaurant** L served all wk 12-2.30 booking required D served Mon-Sat 7-9.45 booking required Av 3 course à la carte fr £30 ⊕ FREE HOUSE ◀ Harvey's Sussex Best Bitter, Guinness Ỏ Biddenden. **Facilities** Children's portions Garden Parking

### PICK OF THE PUBS

## The Star & Eagle ★★★★ INN ♀

**High St TN17 1AL** ☎ **01580 211512** 📄 **01580 212444**
**e-mail:** starandeagle@btconnect.com
**dir:** *Just off A21 towards Hastings. Take A262 into Goudhurst. Pub at top of hill next to church*

A commanding position at 400 feet above sea level gives the 14th-century Star & Eagle outstanding views of the orchards and hop fields that helped earn Kent the accolade 'The Garden of England'. The vaulted stonework suggests that this rambling, big-beamed building may once have been a monastery, and the tunnel from the cellars probably surfaces underneath the neighbouring parish church. The bedrooms and public rooms boast original features and much character. Adnams and Harvey's are the mainstays in the bar, and there's plenty of choice in wines served by the glass. While supping, unwind and enjoy choosing between the fine traditional and continental dishes prepared under the guidance of Spanish chef/proprietor Enrique Martinez. A typical bar meal might be fresh deep-fried calamari, which can be served either as an entrée or a main course. From the restaurant carte you may choose king scallops and crispy bacon on wilted spinach leaves, or escalope of veal with Parma ham. Puddings such as strawberry and kiwi Pavlova are fresh and hand made.

**Open** all wk 11-11 (Sun 12-3 6.30-10.30) **Bar Meals** L served all wk 12-2.30 D served all wk 7-9.30 Av main course £11.50 **Restaurant** L served all wk 12-2.30 D served all wk 7-9.30 Fixed menu price fr £25 Av 3 course à la carte fr £26.50 ⊕ FREE HOUSE ◀ Adnams Bitter, Harvey's, Grasshopper. ♀ 14 **Facilities** Children's portions Family room Garden Parking **Rooms** 10

### GRAVESEND Map 6 TQ67

## The Cock Inn

**Henley St, Luddesdowne DA13 0XB**
☎ **01474 814208** 📄 **01474 812850**
**e-mail:** andrew.r.turner@btinternet.com
**dir:** *Telephone for directions*

Seven hand pumps deliver a wonderful array of well-kept real beers at this traditional English alehouse in the beautiful Luddesdowne Valley. Wood burning stoves in the two bars with exposed beams set the warm ambience, with not a fruit machine, jukebox or television in sight. Orders for excellent home-made food (steak and ale pie, scampi, pork in apple and cider sauce) are taken at the

bar; there is no dedicated restaurant, so table reservations cannot be made. No children under 18.

**Open** all day all wk noon-11 (Sun noon-10.30) ◀ Adnams Southwold, Adnams Broadside, Shepherd Neame Master Brew, Goacher's Real Mild Ale, Woodforde's Wherry. **Facilities** Dogs allowed Garden Parking

### HARRIETSHAM Map 7 TQ85

## The Pepper Box Inn ♀

**ME17 1LP** ☎ **01622 842558**
**e-mail:** enquiries@thepepperboxinn.co.uk
**dir:** *From A20 in Harrietsham take Fairbourne Heath turn. 2m to x-rds, straight over, 200yds, pub on left*

A delightful 15th-century country pub enjoys far-reaching views over the Weald of Kent from its terrace, high up on the Greensand Ridge. The pub takes its name from an early type of pistol, a replica of which hangs behind the bar. Using the best of local seasonal produce, typical dishes might include rack of pork with apples and cider, chargrilled lamb fillet with beetroot and crème fraîche, and fillet of sea trout.

**Open** all wk 11-3 6.30-11 **Bar Meals** L served all wk 12-2.15 D served Tue-Sat 7-9.45, Sun 12-3 Av main course £8.50 **Restaurant** L served Tue-Sat 12-2 D served Tue-Sat 7-9.45 Av 3 course à la carte fr £23 ⊕ SHEPHERD NEAME ◀ Shepherd Neame Master Brew, Spitfire, seasonal ales. ♀ 10 **Facilities** Dogs allowed Garden Parking

### HAWKHURST Map 7 TQ73

### PICK OF THE PUBS

## The Great House ♀

**Gills Green TN18 5EJ**
☎ **01580 753119** 📄 **01622 880120**
**e-mail:** enquiries@thegreathouse.net
**dir:** *Just off A229 between Cranbrook & Hawkhurst*

The Great House is a wonderfully atmospheric 16th-century free house with a warm and comfortable ambience. There are three dining areas to choose from, and the Orangery which opens onto a Mediterranean-style terrace overlooking a pretty garden. The food is fresh and seasonal, and all meat is sourced from a local organic farm. Dishes range from favourites from the bar menu and might include Park Farm Cumberland sausages and mash, liver and bacon, or one of various ploughman's. Alongside the deli board selection (cheese, fish, antipasti, charcuterie), there

are starters of grilled goats' cheese with sesame crust and sweet chilli dressing, or Niçoise-style fish soup with potato aïoli, which may be followed by slow-cooked lamb shank with olive mash; sweet and sour pumpkin risotto; or roast breast of Norfolk chicken with haricot beans and bacon ragout. Imaginative desserts might take in Bailey's chocolate parfait with cherry sauce, or Kentish apple and cinnamon crumble. Part of the pub has been transformed into a deli/farmers' market.

**Open** all day all wk noon-11 **Bar Meals** L served Mon-Fri 12-3, Sat 12-10, Sun 12-9 D served Mon-Fri 6.30-9.30, Sat 12-10, Sun 12-9 Av main course £12 **Restaurant** L served Mon-Fri 12-3, Sat 12-10, Sun 12-9 D served Mon-Fri 6.30-9.30, Sat 12-10, Sun 12-9 Av 3 course à la carte fr £20 ⊕ FREE HOUSE ◀ Harvey's, Guinness, Youngs Ỏ Biddenden Cider. ♀ 20 **Facilities** Children's portions Garden Parking

### HEVER Map 6 TQ44

## The Wheatsheaf

**Hever Rd, Bough Beech TN8 7NU** ☎ **01732 700254**
**dir:** *M25 & A21 take exit for Hever Castle & follow signs. 1m past Castle on right*

Originally built as a hunting lodge for Henry V, this splendid creeper-clad inn has some stunning original features, including a crown post revealed during renovation in 1997. Timbered ceilings and massive Tudor fireplaces set off various curios, such as the mounted jaw of a man-eating shark, and a collection of musical instruments. Food served all day encompasses light lunches from Monday to Saturday; the daily board menu may include houmous with olives and pitta bread followed by lightly spiced pork casserole. Real ales include Harvey's Sussex best and interesting ciders like Kentish Biddenden cider served by handpump.

**Open** all day all wk 11am-11.30pm **Bar Meals** food served all day ⊕ FREE HOUSE ◀ Harveys Sussex Bitter, Grasshopper Ỏ Biddenden, Westons Stowford Press. **Facilities** Children's menu Dogs allowed Garden Parking

---

## HODSOLL STREET | Map 6 TQ66

# The Green Man

**TN15 7LE** ☎ **01732 823575**
e-mail: the.greenman@btinternet.com
dir: *On North Downs between Brands Hatch & Gravesend off the A227*

This 300-year-old, family-run pub is loved for its decent food and real ales. It stands in the picturesque village of Hodsoll Street on the North Downs, surrounded by beautiful Kent countryside. Food is prepared to order using fresh local produce, and includes a wide variety of fish such as roast cod with king prawns or smoked haddock with hollandaise sauce, poached eggs and bacon. As well as a range of steaks and grills find chicken breast stuffed with pork and leek sausage, or for a vegetarian option cherry tomato and Stilton risotto.

**Open** all wk 11-2.30 6-11 (all day Fri-Sun) **Bar Meals** L served Mon-Fri 12-2, Sat 12-3, Sun all day D served Mon-Sat 6.30-9.30, Sun all day **Restaurant** L served Mon-Fri 12-2, Sat 12-3, Sun all day D served Mon-Sat 6.30-9.30, Sun all day ⊕ HAYWOOD PUB COMPANY LTD ◼ Timothy Taylor Landlord, Harvey's, Old Speckled Hen, guest ale. **Facilities** Children's menu Children's portions Play area Dogs allowed Garden Parking

---

## HORTON KIRBY | Map 6 TQ56

# The Bull@Horton Kirby NEW

**Lombard St DA4 9DF** ☎ **01322 862274**
e-mail: landlord@thebullpub.co.uk
dir: *From A225 between Dartford & Eynsford follow signs for Horton Kirby. Pub 10 mins walk from Farningham Road Station in South Darenth*

You can savour lovely views over the Darenth Valley from the large garden at this small Victorian pub in a sleepy village just outside Dartford. Beer-lovers flock to the single bar for the tip-top ales from up and coming micro-breweries, perhaps Dark Star Hophead, Oakham Bishops Farewell or Thornbridge Jaipur. Food is simple and traditional and uses home-grown and local allotment produce as well as locally shot game. Dishes may include beer-battered haddock; lamb stew with mash; mutton curry; cheese and onion pie; beef and horseradish baguette; and Sunday roast lunches.

**Open** all day all wk **Bar Meals** L served all wk 12-2.30 booking required D served all wk 6-9 booking required Av main course £7.50 ⊕ FREE HOUSE ◼ Dark Star Hophead, Marble Pint, Oakham Bishops Farewell, Newby Wyke Kingston Topaz, Thornbridge Jaipur ♂ Millwhites Kingston Black, Westcroft Janet's Jungle Juice, Hecks Port Wine of Glastonbury. **Facilities** Children's portions Dogs allowed Garden Parking

---

## ICKHAM | Map 7 TR25

# The Duke William ★★★ INN ♥ NEW

**The Street CT3 1QP** ☎ **01227 721308**
e-mail: goodfood@dukewilliam.biz
dir: *A257 Canterbury to Sandwich. In Littlebourne turn left opposite The Anchor, into Nargate St. 0.5m turn right into Drill Ln, then right into The Street*

Traditional, locally sourced and home-cooked food is the keynote at this whitewashed free house in the heart of Ickham village. Menu choices include lamb steak with a mint and honey jus; baked sea bass with lemon and herb butter; and oven-roasted Mediterranean vegetables with goat's cheese. The lovely garden features a covered patio, as well as a children's play area with a swing and slide. Four comfortable en suite bedrooms complete the picture.

**Open** all day all wk **Bar Meals** L served all wk 12-3 booking required D served all wk 6.30-10 booking required Av main course £11.95 food served all day **Restaurant** L served all wk 12-2.30 booking required D served all wk 6.30-10 booking required ⊕ FREE HOUSE ◼ Masterbrew, Harveys. ♥ 9 **Facilities** Children's menu Children's portions Play area Dogs allowed Garden Parking **Rooms** 4

---

## IDEN GREEN | Map 6 TQ73

# The Peacock

**Goudhurst Rd TN17 2PB** ☎ **01580 211233**
dir: *A21 from Tunbridge Wells to Hastings, onto A262, pub 1.5m past Goudhurst*

A Grade II listed building dating from the 17th century with low beams, an inglenook fireplace, and ancient oak doors. Seasonal ales can be found amongst the Shepherd Neame handles in the convivial bar. Popular with families, the Peacock offers a wide range of traditional pub food; children may be served smaller portions from the main carte or choose from their own menu, and in summer they can use the large enclosed garden with fruit trees and picnic tables on one side of the building.

**Open** all day all wk 12-11 (Sun 12-6) **Bar Meals** L served Mon-Fri & Sun 12-2.30, Sat all day D served Mon-Fri 6-8.45, Sat all day Av main course £8.95 **Restaurant** L served Mon-Fri & Sun 12-2.30, Sat all day D served Mon-Fri 6-8.45, Sat all day ⊕ SHEPHERD NEAME ◼ Shepherd Neame Master Brew, Spitfire, seasonal ales. **Facilities** Children's menu Children's portions Family room Dogs allowed Garden Parking

---

## IGHTHAM | Map 6 TQ55

### PICK OF THE PUBS

# The Harrow Inn ♥

**Common Rd TN15 9EB** ☎ **01732 885912**
dir: *1.5m from Borough Green on A25 to Sevenoaks, signed Ightham Common, turn left into Common Rd. Inn 0.25m on left*

Tucked away down country lanes, yet easily accessible from both the M20 and M26, this creeper-hung, stone-

---

built free house dates back to at least the 17th century. The two-room bar area has a great brick fireplace, open to both sides and piled high with logs, while the restaurant's vine-clad conservatory opens on to a terrace that's ideal for a pint of Loddon Hoppit or Gravesend Shrimpers and warm weather dining. Menus vary with the seasons, and seafood is a particular speciality: fish lovers can enjoy dishes such as crab and ginger spring roll; swordfish with Cajun spice and salsa; or pan-fried fillets of sea bass with lobster cream and spinach. Other main courses may include baked sausage with gammon, fennel, red onions and garlic; and tagliatelle with wild mushroom, fresh herb, lemongrass and chilli ragout. The car park is fairly small, although there's adequate street parking.

**Open** noon-3 6-11 Closed: 26 Dec, 1 Jan, Sun eve & Mon **Bar Meals** L served Tue-Sun 12-2 D served Tue-Sat 6-9 Av main course £10.50 **Restaurant** L served Tue-Sun 12-2 booking required D served Tue-Sat 6-9 booking required ⊕ FREE HOUSE ◼ Loddon Hoppit, Gravesend Shrimpers. ♥ 9 **Facilities** Children's portions Family room Garden Parking

---

## IVY HATCH | Map 6 TQ55

### PICK OF THE PUBS

# The Plough at Ivy Hatch ♥

*See Pick of the Pubs on page 268*

---

## LAMBERHURST | Map 6 TQ63

# The Swan at the Vineyard ♥

**The Down TN3 8EU** ☎ **01892 890170**
dir: *Telephone for directions*

Outside the Swan, which dates from the 1700s, is a beautiful floral display; inside there are open fireplaces and leather couches, and as many as three ghosts. There are two dining areas, one traditional, the other a 'cellar restaurant', with high-back leather chairs and an art gallery. A comprehensive menu features coq au vin; coconut and galangal Thai risotto with tiger prawns; and spinach and chanterelle lasagne. Try one of the award-winning English wines.

**Open** all wk ◼ Harveys Best, Adnams Broadside, Bombardier, Adnams Regatta, guest ales. ♥ 11 **Facilities** Play area Dogs allowed Garden Parking

---

## LEIGH | Map 6 TQ54

# The Greyhound Charcott ♥

**Charcott TN11 8LG** ☎ **01892 870275**
e-mail: ghatcharcott@aol.com
dir: *From Tonbridge take B245 N towards Hildenborough. Left onto Leigh road, right onto Stocks Green road. Through Leigh, right then left at T-junct, right into Charcott (Camp Hill)*

This cosy pub has been welcoming locals and visitors for around 120 years. Tony French, who took over five years ago, has maintained the traditional atmosphere in which
*continued on page 269*

# PICK OF THE PUBS

## The Plough at Ivy Hatch 🍷

**IVY HATCH**      Map 6 TQ55

**High Cross Rd TN15 ONL**
☎ **01732 810100**
**e-mail:** info@theploughivyhatch.co.uk
**dir:** *Off A25 between Borough Green &*
*Sevenoaks, follow signs to Ightham Mote*

This tile-hung 17th-century free house stands in the picturesque village of Ivy Hatch, just a short walk from the National Trust's Ightham Mote, Britain's best preserved medieval house. Owners Miles and Anna have renovated the bar area, conservatory and dining room to restore the pub to the centre of its small community. The Plough offers everything from drinks for weary walkers to full meals for hungry families – and the smart oak flooring and seating area around the fireplace make this the perfect spot for a lingering lunch or

supper. Beers are from Harveys and Westerham breweries and the wine list covers new and old world.

The modern British menu with its European highlights aims to please all tastes and budgets. Menus are updated daily, driven by locally produced seasonal ingredients including south coast seafood and seasonal game from local shoots, and the food is freshly cooked with no frozen or bought-in dishes. The 'small lunch' menu begins with well-filled sandwiches served with chips or a cup of soup, and also features cheese ploughman's, home-made steak burgers and chicken Caesar salad. Starters from the main menu might include grilled Cornish sardines on toast with oven-dried tomatoes and sage and anchovy butter, or purple sprouting broccoli with poached free-range egg and hollandaise sauce. Moving on to the main course, expect dishes like roasted herb-stuffed chicken breast with rustic salad of sauté potatoes, curly endive, croutons and bacon; and pan-fried grey mullet with confit garlic aioli, shaved fennel and herb new potatoes. Desserts include

pear and almond tart with mascarpone and vanilla sauce, and bread and butter pudding with home-made vanilla custard.

There are lots of good walks in the area, with no need to worry about squelching back to the pub in muddy boots, as the terrace and garden are ideal for alfresco dining.

**Open** all wk noon-3 6-11 (Sat noon-11 Sun 10-6) Closed: 1 Jan
**Bar Meals** L served Mon-Sat 12-2.45, Sun 12-6 D served Mon-Sat 6-9.30
**Restaurant** L served Mon-Sat 12-2.45, Sun 12-6 D served Mon-Sat 6-9.30 ⊞ FREE HOUSE ◀ Harveys Best, Seasonal ales, Westerham Finchcocks ♨ Stowford Press. 🍷 10
**Facilities** Garden Parking

**LEIGH** *continued*

music, pool table and fruit machine have no place. Winter brings log fires, while in summer you can enjoy the garden. Meals could include local wild pigeon salad and crispy smoked bacon salad; salmon and lemon fishcakes; and home-made steak burgers, alongside ploughman's, sandwiches and ciabattas. Enjoy your meal with a good selection of well-kept ales.

*The Greyhound Charcott*

**Open** all wk noon-3 5.30-11 (Sat-Sun all day) **Bar Meals** L served Mon-Sat 12-2, Sun 12-3 D served Mon-Sat 6.30-9.30 Av main course £8.95 **Restaurant** L served Mon-Sat 12-2, Sun 12-3 D served Mon-Sat 6.30-9.30 Av 3 course à la carte fr £22 ⊕ ENTERPRISE INNS ◀ Harvey's, Woodforde's Wherry, Westerham British Bulldog Ö Stowford Press. ♀ 12 **Facilities** Children's portions Dogs allowed Garden Parking

### LINTON　　　Map 7 TQ75

## The Bull Inn

**Linton Hill ME17 4AW** ☎ **01622 743612**
**dir:** *S of Maidstone on A229 (Hastings road)*

A traditional 17th-century coaching inn in the heart of the Weald with stunning views from the glorious garden, and a large inglenook fireplace and wealth of beams inside. An inviting bar menu includes lasagne, spinach and ricotta tortellini, cod and chips, and bubble and squeak, as well as sandwiches, baguettes, and ploughman's. From the restaurant menu comes pan-fried venison steak wrapped in pancetta, served on sautéed oyster mushrooms.

**Open** all day all wk 11am-11.30pm (Sun noon-10.30pm) ◀ Shepherd Neame Master Brew, Kent's Best. **Facilities** Dogs allowed Garden Parking

### LITTLEBOURNE　　　Map 7 TR25

## Duke William Inn

**4 High St CT3 1UN** ☎ **01227 721244**　📠 **01227 721244**
**e-mail:** sam@bowwindow.co.uk
**dir:** *From A2 follow signs to Howletts Zoo. After zoo & at end of road, pub straight ahead*

Located just outside the city of Canterbury, the renamed Duke William Inn overlooks the village green and is well placed for Sandwich and Herne Bay. With open log fires and exposed oak beams, this friendly inn is a good place for visitors and locals.

**Open** all wk ◀ John Smith's, Sussex Harveys. **Facilities** Parking

### MAIDSTONE　　　Map 7 TQ75

## The Black Horse Inn ★★★★ INN ♀

**Pilgrims Way, Thurnham ME14 3LD**
☎ **01622 737185**　📠 **01622 739170**
**e-mail:** info@wellieboot.net
**dir:** *M20 junct 7, A249, right into Detling. Opposite Cock Horse Pub turn onto Pilgrims Way*

Smack beside the Pilgrim's Way and tucked just below the North Downs ridge, this popular free house was converted from a forge in the 18th century. Much extended, more recently with stylish annexe bedrooms to the rear, you'll find a charming beamed bar for quaffing pints of Harvey's Sussex Bitter and local Biddenden cider, and a candlelit restaurant serving a good range of imaginative food. Typical choices include rump of Romney Marsh lamb with redcurrant and rosemary jus, steak and kidney suet pudding, and apple pie and custard.

**Open** all day all wk **Bar Meals** Av main course £9.95 food served all day **Restaurant** Fixed menu price fr £13.95 Av 3 course à la carte fr £28.95 food served all day ⊕ FREE HOUSE ◀ Greene King IPA, Black Sheep, Hobgoblin, Grasshopper, Harveys Sussex Ö Biddenden. ♀ 21 **Facilities** Children's menu Dogs allowed Garden Parking **Rooms** 30

### MARKBEECH　　　Map 6 TQ44

## The Kentish Horse

**Cow Ln TN8 5NT** ☎ **01342 850493**
**dir:** *3m from Edenbridge & 7m from Tunbridge Wells*

Surrounded by Kent countryside, this pub is popular with ramblers, cyclists and families. The inn dates from 1340 and is said to have a smuggling history; it also boasts a curious street-bridging Kentish sign. The menu is cooked simply from fresh ingredients, and can be served anywhere in the pub or garden. Harvey's Larkins and regular guest ales available.

**Open** all day all wk ◀ Harvey's Larkins, guest ales. **Facilities** Play area Dogs allowed Garden Parking

### NEWNHAM　　　Map 7 TQ95

## The George Inn ♀

**44 The Street ME9 0LL**
☎ **01795 890237**　📠 **01795 890726**
**e-mail:** marieannand@btconnect.com
**dir:** *4m from Faversham*

The George is an attractive country inn with a large beer garden. Despite the passing of the centuries, the inn retains much of its historic character with beams, polished wooden floors, inglenook fireplaces and candlelit tables. Food is served in the bar and 50-seater restaurant. Bar snacks range from sandwiches to sausage and mash, while main meals could include pan-fried fillet of red snapper with crushed potatoes, baby fennel, fresh scampi and rosemary butter; or peppered duck breast with celeriac mash and cherry and port

sauce. Regular events include live jazz, quizzes and murder mystery evenings.

*The George Inn*

**Open** all wk 11-3 6.30-11 (Sun noon-10) **Bar Meals** L served Mon-Sat 12-2.30, Sun 12-9.30 booking required D served all wk 7-9.30 booking required Av main course £10 **Restaurant** L served Mon-Sat 12-2.30, Sun 12-9.30 booking required D served all wk 7-9.30 booking required Av 3 course à la carte fr £20 ⊕ SHEPHERD NEAME ◀ Shepherd Neame Master Brew, Spitfire, Bishops Finger, Kent Best, seasonal ale. ♀ 8 **Facilities** Children's menu Garden Parking

### PENSHURST　　　Map 6 TQ54

### PICK OF THE PUBS

## The Bottle House Inn ♀

*See Pick of the Pubs on page 270*

## The Leicester Arms

**High St TN11 8BT** ☎ **01892 870551**
**dir:** *From Tunbridge Wells take A26 towards Tonbridge. Left onto B21765 towards Penshurst*

A large and picturesque country inn at the centre of a picturesque village, the Leicester Arms stands in its own pretty gardens looking out over the River Medway. It was once part of the Penshurst Place estate. The wood-panelled dining room is worth a visit for the views over the weald and river alone. Dishes range from traditional pub food in the bar to the likes of pressed pork belly with crackling, chicken curry, or Moroccan vegetable tagine from the carte menu.

**Open** all wk 11am-mdnt **Bar Meals** L served all wk 12-9.30 Av main course £10 food served all day **Restaurant** Av 3 course à la carte fr £19 ⊕ ENTERPRISE INNS ◀ Harvey's Sussex Bitter, Shepherd Neame Master Brew, Sharp's Doom Bar Ö Stowford Press. **Facilities** Children's menu Dogs allowed Garden Parking

# PICK OF THE PUBS

## The Bottle House Inn ♇

**PENSHURST**     Map 6 TQ54

**Coldharbour Rd TN11 8ET**
☎ **01892 870306** 📠 **01892 871094**
e-mail:
info@thebottlehouseinnpenshurst.co.uk
web:
www.thebottlehouseinnpenshurst.co.uk
dir: *From Tunbridge Wells take A264 W, then*
*B2188 N. After Fordcombe left towards*
*Edenbridge & Hever. Pub 500yds after*
*staggered x-rds*

Remotely situated on a country lane two
miles south west of Penshurst, The
Bottle House was built as a farmhouse
in 1492, and later divided into two
properties. Thomas Scraggs, 'a common
beer seller of Speldhurst', leased one of
them in 1806 and obtained a licence to
sell ales and ciders. It was registered as
an alehouse at each subsequent change
of hands, at a time when hop-growing
was the major local industry.

During the 19th century it also housed a
shop, a farrier and a cobbler, and there
was a skittle alley at the back. The pub
was said to be the originator of the
ploughman's lunch, made with bread
from the old bakery next door and
cheese donated by Canadian soldiers
billeted nearby. The building was
completely refurbished in 1938 and
granted a full licence; it was reputedly
named after all the old bottles
discovered during these works.

These days the inn has had another
refurbishment, even the ancient beams.
The copper-topped counter gives the bar
a warm, welcoming atmosphere. Choose
from the range of Harveys and local
Larkins hand-pumped beers and eleven
wines by the glass before settling at a
bench seat on the patio or in the
garden.

The menu has something for everyone,
starting with rabbit and smoked bacon
terrine, seared scallops with pea purée
and pancetta, or potted shrimps with
mixed leaves. Lighter meals and shares
are also available, perhaps lasagne
with garlic ciabatta, or baked
camembert with fig and mustard

chutney. For main course, tuck into a
hearty game casserole with dumplings;
sea bass with brown shrimp and caper
butter; confit duck leg with thyme potato
cake and port sauce; or wild mushroom
and artichoke risotto with parmesan
crisps. Naturally, a ploughman's lunch
with rustic bread, pickles and home-
baked ham is also served.

**Open** all day all wk 11-11 (Sun
11-10.30) Closed: 25 Dec
**Bar Meals** Av main course £12 food
served all day **Restaurant** Fixed menu
price fr £20 Av 3 course à la carte fr
£22.50 food served all day ⊕ FREE
HOUSE ◖ Larkins Ale, Harveys Sussex
Best Bitter. ♇ 11 **Facilities** Children's
menu Dogs allowed Garden Parking

## PICK OF THE PUBS

### The Spotted Dog 🍷

Smarts Hill TN11 8EE
☎ 01892 870253  🖷 01892 870107
e-mail: info@spotteddogpub.co.uk
dir: Off B2188 between Penshurst & Fordcombe

Deep in the Kent countryside, this 16th-century white weather-boarded free house enjoys fine views over the Weald from the rear terrace. Inside, you'll encounter a rambling series of small rooms with tiled and oak floors, low beams and open fireplaces. Since Easter 2010 the pub has been under new ownership, with a new head chef, Matthew, who makes the most of fresh food and changes his menus regularly. Starters like duck and orange pâté; torpedo prawns with sweet chilli dip; and fresh asparagus with hollandaise and poached egg set the scene for main courses such as slow-cooked rolled shoulder of lamb; liver and bacon; a half rack of spare ribs; fruits de mer (including a whole lobster); mushroom stroganoff with basmati rice; and caramelised red onion and goat's cheese tartlet.

Open all wk noon-3 6-11 (Sun noon-10.30)
Bar Meals L served Mon-Sat 12-2.30 D served Mon-Sat 6-9 Av main course £9 Restaurant L served Mon-Sat 12-2.30, Sun 12-5 D served Mon-Fri 6-9, Sat 6-9.30
⊕ FREE HOUSE ◀ Sharp's Doom Bar, Larkins Traditional, Harveys, Guest ale ♻ Chiddingstone. 🍷 10
Facilities Children's menu Children's portions Dogs allowed Garden Parking

### PLUCKLEY                              Map 7 TQ94

## PICK OF THE PUBS

### *The Dering Arms*

Station Rd TN27 0RR
☎ 01233 840371  🖷 01233 840498
e-mail: jim@deringarms.com
dir: M20 junct 8, A20 to Ashford. Right onto B2077 at Charing to Pluckley

Pluckley's residents cherish its claim to fame as the most haunted village in England; they're also proud of its starring role in the 1990s TV series, *The Darling Buds of May*. The village was for centuries the home of the Dering family, hence the name. The inn has two simply furnished traditional bars with mounted stags' heads and fishing rods, roaring fires in winter, an intimate restaurant, and a family room with a baby grand piano (there to be played). The extensive daily menus reflect the chef's love of fresh fish and seafood, as in provençal fish soup and grilled sardines with rosemary butter. Appearing as main course options might be skate wing grilled with capers and lemon butter, and confit of duck, bubble and squeak and wild mushroom sauce. Blackboard specials add to the choice. Events such 7-course black tie evenings are scheduled for the winter months, and classic car meetings are held every second Sunday of the month.

Open 11.30-3.30 6-11 Closed: 26-29 Dec, Sun eve & Mon ◀ Goacher's Dering Ale, Maidstone Dark, Gold Star, Old Ale. Facilities Family room Dogs allowed Garden Parking

### The Mundy Bois

Mundy Bois TN27 0ST ☎ 01233 840048
e-mail: helen@mundybois.com
dir: From A20 at Charing exit towards Pluckley. Right into Pinnock at bottom of Pluckley Hill. Next right into Mundy Bois Rd. 1m left

An ale house since 1780 and formerly named the Rose and Crown, this creeper-clad pub is on the outskirts of Pluckley, considered to be the most haunted place in England. The pub is reported to have its own ghost. A blackboard menu features frequently changing dishes created from local produce where possible, and a nearby farm specializing in rare breeds – rare breed Welsh pork chops on mustard mash with caramelised apples and cider sauce. A patio dining area allows alfresco eating, and the garden has an adventure playground. The pub is located in a splendid walking area.

Open all wk 12-3 6-11 (Sun 12-5) Bar Meals L served all wk 12-2 D served all wk 6.30-9 Restaurant L served all wk 12-2 D served all wk 6.30-9 ◀ Master Brew, Guest beer. Facilities Children's menu Children's portions Play area Dogs allowed Garden Parking

### ST MARGARET'S AT CLIFFE          Map 7 TR34

## PICK OF THE PUBS

### The Coastguard

*See Pick of the Pubs on page 272*

### SANDWICH                              Map 7 TR35

### George & Dragon Inn 🍷

Fisher St CT13 9EJ ☎ 01304 613106
e-mail: enquiries@georgeanddragon-sandwich.co.uk
web: www.georgeanddragon-sandwich.co.uk
dir: Between Dover & Canterbury

Built in 1446 and first licensed in 1615, this town centre pub oozes charm and character, with its wood floors and open fires, and makes a welcome pit-stop when exploring historic Sandwich on foot. Run by two brothers and back on song, you can refuel with a pint of Shepherd Neame Master Brew or Wantsum and a decent plate of food prepared from local seasonal ingredients; perhaps

braised beef with horseradish mash, fish pie, and skate wing with caper and parsley hollandaise.

Open all wk 11-3 6-11 (Sat 11-11 Sun 11-10.30 summer, 11-6 winter) Bar Meals L served all wk 12-2 booking required D served all wk 6-9 booking required Av main course £10.50 Restaurant L served all wk 12-2 booking required D served all wk 6-9 booking required Av 3 course à la carte fr £25 ⊕ ENTERPRISE INNS ◀ Shepherd Neame Master Brew, Harvey's Sussex Best, Sharp's Doom Bar, Ringwood Best, Wantsum, Turbulent Priest. 🍷 9
Facilities Children's portions Dogs allowed Garden

### SELLING                                Map 7 TR05

### The Rose and Crown

Perry Wood ME13 9RY ☎ 01227 752214
e-mail: perrywoodrose@btinternet.co.uk
dir: From A28 right at Badgers Hill, left at end. 1st left signed Perry Wood. Pub at top

Set amidst 150 acres of woodland in the middle of an Area of Outstanding Natural Beauty, this 16th-century pub has won awards for its green credentials. The perfumed summer garden includes a children's play area, and strolling in the woods beyond is encouraged – ask at the bar for a map. Perhaps indulge in a pint of Harveys before you go, and enjoy the pub's beamed interior decorated with hop garlands, corn dollies, horse brasses and brass cask taps. Upon your return, order your favourite comfort food, such as Kent fish pie or liver and bacon.

Open all wk noon-3 6.30-11 Closed: 25-26 Dec eve, 1 Jan eve, Mon eve Bar Meals L served all wk 12-2 D served Tue-Sun 6.30-9 Av main course £8.95 Restaurant L served all wk 12-2 D served Tue-Sun 6.30-9 ⊕ FREE HOUSE ◀ Adnams Southwold, Harvey's Sussex Best Bitter, guest ale ♻ Stowford Press, Biddenden. Facilities Children's menu Children's portions Play area Dogs allowed Garden Parking

### SMARDEN                                Map 7 TQ84

### *The Bell* 🍷

Bell Ln TN27 8PW ☎ 01233 770283
e-mail: thesmardenbell@btconnect.com
dir: Telephone for directions

Built in the year 1536, The Bell was originally a farm building on a large estate. It was used as a blacksmiths forge right up until 1907, but it had also been an alehouse since 1630. A typical menu includes seared king scallops with spinach and a crab sauce, chargrilled chicken breast with mozzarella, basil and wild mushroom sauce, gammon steak with beetroot mash and parsley sauce, and tournedos of monkfish Rossini.

Open all day all wk noon-11 ◀ Shepherd Neame Master Brew, Spitfire, seasonal ales. 🍷 15 Facilities Dogs allowed Garden Parking

# PICK OF THE PUBS

# The Coastguard

**ST MARGARET'S AT CLIFFE**  Map 7 TR34

**St Margaret's Bay CT15 6DY**
☎ **01304 853176**
**e-mail:** thecoastguard@talk21.com
**dir:** *2m off A258 between Dover & Deal,
follow St Margaret's at Cliffe signs. Through
village towards sea*

The location, surely one of the best on
the south coast, gives this family-run
establishment the distinction of being
the closest British pub to France; in
fact, when you arrive your mobile phone
is likely to retune to a French network.
On a clear day, drink in hand, watch the
cross-channel ferries, container ships
and tankers from the terrace. Real ales,
with Kent and Scotland (co-owner Nigel
Wydymus is a Scot) change frequently,
and if you like real ciders you may also
find Biddenden Strong Kent or Westons
Old Rosie. Look at the website for those
currently on tap, as well as a long list of
those stocked in the past. A worldwide
wine list includes a couple of bottles
from, relatively speaking, just up the
road.

The food from Nigel's wife Sam and her
team is renown, and all freshly made on
the premises from local produce as far
as possible. Many dishes have a story
behind them: they might be based on an
old Roman recipe, a reworked classic
dish, or perhaps an original creation in
response to something particularly
outstanding that becomes available.
The menus change twice daily,
depending on the weather and what's
available.

Starters include Kentish pork and game
terrine with pickled beets; fresh king
scallops seared in garlic butter; and
roast aubergine soup with coriander,
cumin and home-made walnut bread.
Among the mains are Hoegaarden-
battered fresh day-boat cod with
braised peas and double-fried chips;
fillet of plaice with creamed spinach,
garden herbs and roast tomatoes; wild
boar braised with juniper, cider, honey,
mustard and celeriac mash; and curry
of Kentish autumn vegetables and
coconut with fresh spinach. For dessert
look for sea salt caramel and chocolate
tart with fresh berries; steamed stem
ginger pudding with cinnamon custard;
and an award-winning cheeseboard.

**Open** all day all wk 11-11 (Sun
11-10.30) **Bar Meals** L served all wk
12.30-2.45 D served all wk 6.30-8.45 Av
main course £12 food served all day
**Restaurant** L served all wk 12.30-2.45
D served all wk 6.30-8.45 Av 3 course à
la carte fr £22 ⊕ FREE HOUSE ◀ Gadds
of Ramsgate, Hop Daemon, Adnams,
Caledonian, Westerham ♂ Westons Old
Rosy, Biddenden Strong Kent Cider,
Rough Old Wife. **Facilities** Play area
Dogs allowed Garden Parking

## The Chequers Inn

**The Street TN27 8QA**
☎ 01233 770217 📄 01233 770623
e-mail: spaldings@thechequerssmarden.com
**dir:** *Through Leeds village, left to Sutton Valence/Headcorn then left for Smarden. Pub in village centre*

The former weavers' village of Smarden has around 200 buildings of architectural and historical interest; one of them is the clapboard façaded, 14th-century Chequers. In its beautiful landscaped garden are a large carp pond and an attractive south-facing courtyard. Real ales brewed by Harvey's and Adnams are served in the low-beamed bars, and seasonal menus and specials offer traditional and modern food. Beginning with the bar, there are sandwiches; ham, egg and chips; chicken and bacon salad; and curry, while restaurant starters include green-lipped mussels in white wine and garlic sauce; and haggis, tatties, neeps with whisky cream. Among the mains are pan-fried calf's liver and onions; sea bass with spinach, crispy bacon, lemon grass and chilli jus; chicken fajitas with sour cream and salsa; beef stew and dumplings; rabbit and pork casserole; and slow-roasted sweet bell pepper with creamy tikka-spiced vegetables. Pie nights are on Wednesdays, steak nights on Thursdays.

**Open** all wk **Bar Meals** L served all wk 12-3 D served all wk 6-9 **Restaurant** L served all wk 12-3 D served all wk 6-9 ⊕ FREE HOUSE ◀ Harvey's, IPA, Adnams, Hancock. **Facilities** Children's menu Children's portions Dogs allowed Garden Parking

---

SPELDHURST     Map 6 TQ54

## George & Dragon ☻

**Speldhurst Hill TN3 0NN**
☎ 01892 863125 📄 01892 863216
e-mail: julian@speldhurst.com
**dir:** *Telephone for directions*

Built around 1500, the award-winning George and Dragon is a venerable timber-clad village hostelry. Some say its origins are earlier, when Speldhurst would have seen archers departing for the Battle of Agincourt. At the beginning of the 17th century the curative powers of the village's iron-rich waters were discovered, which put nearby Tunbridge Wells on the map. Today's customers enjoy a modern gastro-pub, where refreshments include Larkin's bitter, made about three miles away, and a range of local organic fruit juices; in fact, just about every ingredient comes from within a 30-mile radius. The seasonal menu offers half a dozen eclectic choices at each stage: you could start with seared scallops with crisp sea purselane; or Weald Way goat's cheese, thyme and pine nut parfait. Follow this with slow-roast belly of pork with caramelised apple; or Turner's Hill pheasant breast and confit leg. Food can be served in either of the two gardens.

**Open** all day all wk **Bar Meals** L served all wk 12-2.30 D served Mon-Sat 7-9.45 Av main course £12.50 **Restaurant** L served Sat 12-3, Sun 12-4 booking required D served Fri 7-10, Sat 6.30-10 booking required Av 3 course à la carte fr £26 ⊕ FREE HOUSE ◀ Harvey's Best, Sussex Pale, Larkins, Porter ♻ Stowford Press. ♥ 11 **Facilities** Children's portions Family room Dogs allowed Garden Parking

---

TENTERDEN     Map 7 TQ83

## White Lion Inn

**57 High St TN30 6BD**
☎ 01580 765077 📄 01580 764157
e-mail: whitelion.tenterden@marstons.co.uk
**dir:** *On A28 (Ashford to Hastings road)*

A 16th-century coaching inn on a broad tree-lined street in 'the jewel of the Weald'. Renovated and rejuvenated, the pub combines its many original features with a contemporary look and feel. Reasonably priced fresh food ranges from starters of roasted Portobello mushrooms or shredded duck in crisp filo pastry; to mains such as harissa lamb kebabs or chicken Caesar salad. Look out for special offers on pub classics served all day. Reliable Marston ales are the mainstay in the bar.

**Open** all wk 10am-11pm (wknds 10am-mdnt) **Bar Meals** food served all day **Restaurant** food served all day ⊕ MARSTONS ◀ Marstons Pedigree, Cumberland. **Facilities** Children's menu Garden Parking

---

TONBRIDGE

## See Penshurst

---

TUNBRIDGE WELLS (ROYAL)     Map 6 TQ53

## The Beacon ★★★★★ INN ☻

*See Pick of the Pubs on page 274*

---

## The Crown Inn

**The Green, Groombridge TN3 9QH** ☎ 01892 864742
e-mail: crowngroombridge@aol.com
**dir:** *Take A264 W of Tunbridge Wells, then B2110 S*

Dating back to 1585, this charming free house was a favourite haunt for the cast of *Pride and Prejudice* during filming nearby a few years ago. Sir Arthur Conan Doyle was a frequent visitor while staying at Groombridge Place situated opposite. Also a haunt for smugglers once, low

beams and an inglenook fireplace are the setting for some great food and drink. Expect favourites such as pan fried black pudding, crispy bacon and wholegrain mustard sauce; deep fried whitebait; home-made pies; beef stroganoff; chicken Madras; and home-made lasagne.

**Open** all wk 11-3 6-11 (Sat 11-11 Sun noon-10.30 Sun noon-5 winter) **Bar Meals** L served Mon-Fri 12-2.30, Sat-Sun 12-3 D served Mon-Thu 6.30-9, Fri-Sat 6.30-9.30 Av main course £9.50 **Restaurant** L served Mon-Fri 12-2.30, Sat-Sun 12-3 booking required D served Mon-Thu 6.30-9, Fri-Sat 6.30-9.30 booking required Av 3 course à la carte fr £19.50 ⊕ FREE HOUSE ◀ Harvey's Best, Larkins, IPA ♻ Stowford Press. **Facilities** Children's menu Children's portions Play area Dogs allowed Garden Parking

## The Hare on Langton Green ☻

**Langton Rd, Langton Green TN3 0JA**
☎ 01892 862419 📄 01892 861275
e-mail: hare@brunningandprice.co.uk
**dir:** *From Tunbridge Wells follow A264 towards East Grinstead. Village on A264*

There has been an inn on this site, in what is now a well-to-do suburb of genteel Tunbridge Wells, since the 18th century. The current Hare's predecessor was extensively damaged in a fire in 1900, the present Victorian-Tudor edifice rising from the ashes a year later. The menu changes every day and it can take a pleasantly long time to study all the options, from Malaysian fish stew; and braised shoulder of lamb, to steak and venison pudding; and Kentish sausage with buttered mash. For vegetarians, sweet potato, chickpea and spinach curry is a possibility, while sandwiches are also available. In addition to Greene King's real ales and Westons ciders, there's an impressive range of malt whiskies and wines by the glass. A woman holding a child is said to haunt the main staircase and cellar, though nobody has been able to identify the period she comes from.

**Open** all day all wk 11.30-11 (Fri-Sat 11.30-mdnt, Sun noon-10.30) **Bar Meals** Av main course £11.95 food served all day **Restaurant** Av 3 course à la carte fr £19.95 food served all day ⊕ BRUNNING & PRICE ◀ Greene King IPA, Abbot Ale, Morland Orignal, Ruddles Best, Olde Trip ♻ Westons Old Rosie, Stowford Press, Westons Organic. ♥ 20 **Facilities** Children's portions Dogs allowed Garden Parking

---

WESTERHAM     Map 6 TQ45

## The Fox & Hounds ☻

**Toys Hill TN16 1QG** ☎ 01732 750328
e-mail: hickmott1@hotmail.com
**dir:** *Telephone for directions*

Set in an Area of Outstanding Natural Beauty high on Kent's Greensand Ridge, this late 18th century ale house adjoins a large National Trust estate incorporating an old water tower now protected as a home for hibernating bats. The pub has a traditionally styled restaurant, where

*continued on page 275*

# PICK OF THE PUBS

## The Beacon ★★★★ INN

**TUNBRIDGE WELLS (ROYAL)** Map 6 TQ53

**Tea Garden Ln, Rusthall TN3 9JH**
**☎ 01892 524252** **01892 534288**
**e-mail:** beaconhotel@btopenworld.com
**dir:** *From Tunbridge Wells take A264 towards East Grinstead. Pub 1m on left*

Standing in seventeen acres, the Beacon was built in 1895 for Sir Walter Harris, a former lieutenant of the City of London, as his country home, commissioning the finest craftsmen to create a host of impressive architectural features. After Harris's death the house passed through various hands until, during the Second World War, it became a hostel for Jewish refugees.

Today, the building still pulsates with country house charm; the bar, for example, with its moulded plaster ceiling, bookshelves and stained glass windows decidedly stands out from the crowd and is the perfect place to enjoy a pint of Harveys Best or Larkins Traditional real ale, or organic draught cider. Take it out to the terrace, from which there are truly glorious views.

Food is served in both the bar and the restaurant, with its large fireplace, or in one of three private dining rooms. Menus take full advantage of seasonal local produce, to which, as a member of Kentish Fare, the kitchen is strongly committed, although fruit, vegetables and herbs are increasingly grown in the Beacon's own kitchen garden.

Start perhaps with loin of rabbit wrapped in pancetta on chestnut and pearl barley broth; or pressed English goat's cheese and eggplant with piquant tomato relish. Select a main dish of Loch Duart salmon; stuffed leg of free-range chicken; maple-glazed Barbary duck breast; or beetroot hash cake.

A separate list of classic dishes includes local sausages with creamy mash; pie of the day; and tuna, red onion and lemon mayonnaise in a tortilla wrap. A good wine list offers plenty of choice by the glass. Why not stay over in one of the spacious, comfortable furnished bedrooms.

**Open** all day all wk Mon-Sat 11-11 (Sun 12-10.30) **Bar Meals** L served Mon-Thu 12-2.30, Fri-Sun 12-9.30 D served Mon-Thu 6.30-9.30, Fri-Sun 12-9.30 Av main course £9.50 **Restaurant** L served Mon-Thu 12-2.30, Fri-Sun 12-9.30 D served Mon-Thu 6.30-9.30, Fri-Sun 12-9.30 Av 3 course à la carte fr £22 FREE HOUSE Harveys Best, Timothy Taylor Landlord, Larkins Traditional Stowford Press Draught Cider, Westons Organic Bottled Pear Cider. 12 **Facilities** Play area Garden Parking **Rooms** 3

## WESTERHAM *continued*

starters might include moules marinière or deep fried brie with cranberry dressing. Follow with venison casserole with herb dumplings, Fox and Hounds fish pot or herb crusted lamb with boulangère potatoes.

**Open** 10-3 6-11 (Sat-Sun 10am-11pm) (all day in Summer) Closed: 25 Dec, Mon eve **Bar Meals** L served Mon-Sat 12-2, Sun 12-3 D served Tue-Sat 6-9 **Restaurant** L served Mon-Sat 12-2, Sun 12-3 D served Tue-Sat 6-9 ⊕ GREENE KING ◀ Greene King IPA, Abbot Ale, Ruddles County, Morlands. ♀ 10 **Facilities** Children's menu Dogs allowed Garden Parking

## Grasshopper on the Green ♀ NEW

**The Green TN16 1AS ☎ 01959 562926**
e-mail: info@grasshopperonthegreen.com
dir: *M25 junct 5, A21 towards Sevenoaks, then A25 to Westerham. Or M25 junct 6, A22 towards East Grinstead, A25 to Westerham*

This 700 year-old free house takes its name from the heraldic crest of the local 16th-century merchant and financier Thomas Gresham, founder of the Royal Exchange. With its log fires, mulled wine and peaceful summer garden, this is an inn for all seasons. Enjoy Grasshopper Kentish Bitter alongside home-cooked dishes like fishcakes with chilli dip, and whole chicken breast in Parma ham and smoked bacon sauce. There are special menus for children and the over-60s.

**Open** all day all wk **Bar Meals** L served (breakfast 10-12) Av main course £12.25 food served all day **Restaurant** food served all day ⊕ FREE HOUSE ◀ Grasshopper Ale, Adnams Broadside, Harveys Sussex, Courage Best, Brains SA Gold. ♀ 12 **Facilities** Children's menu Children's portions Play area Dogs allowed Garden Parking

### WEST MALLING    Map 6 TQ65

## PICK OF THE PUBS

## The Farmhouse ♀

**97 The High St ME19 6NA**
**☎ 01732 843257 ☐ 01622 851881**
e-mail: enquiries@thefarmhouse.biz
dir: *M20 junct 4, S on A228. Right to West Malling. Pub in village centre*

A modern gastro-pub, The Farmhouse occupies a handsome Elizabethan property at the heart of the village of West Malling. It has a relaxing atmosphere with a stylish bar and two dining areas, while outside is a spacious walled garden with an area of decking. There are stone-baked pizzas and toasted paninis alongside the blackboard menu which changes regularly. Starters range from asparagus, pea and mint soup with crusty bread to seared North Atlantic scallops, tomato compôte, sweet chilli and bacon. Main courses might include pan-fried monkfish tail, jasmine rice, crayfish, leek and mushroom ragout; and pan-fried duck magret, dauphinoise potatoes in puff pastry with French beans and red wine sauce. Bar food is available all day.

**Open** all day all wk 11am-11pm **Bar Meals** L served Mon-Thu 12-3, Fri-Sun 12-10 D served Mon-Thu 6-9.30, Fri-Sun 12-10 food served all day **Restaurant** L served Mon-Thu 12-3, Fri-Sun 12-10 D served Mon-Thu 6-9.30, Fri-Sun12-10 food served all day ⊕ ENTERPRISE INNS ◀ Harvey's, Guinness, Youngs ♂ Biddenden. ♀ 20 **Facilities** Children's portions Garden Parking

### WHITSTABLE    Map 7 TR16

## PICK OF THE PUBS

## The Sportsman ◉◉ ♀

**Faversham Rd CT5 4BP ☎ 01227 273370**
e-mail: contact@thesportsmanseasalter.co.uk
dir: *3.5m W of Whitstable, on coast road between Whitstable & Faversham*

The first evidence of an inn on this site dates back to 1642 but the surrounding area of Seasalter was entered in the Domesday book as belonging to the kitchens of Canterbury cathedral. Reached via a winding lane across open marshland from Whitstable, and tucked beneath the sea wall, The Sportsman has a rustic yet comfortable and welcoming interior, with wooden floors and stripped pine furniture. A range of Shepherd Neame ales is served, including seasonal brews, and there is an excellent wine list. The daily menu is based on local produce from farms, boats and game dealers. Fish dishes might include braised turbot fillet with a mussel tartare. Starters also feature lots of seafood, typically slip sole grilled in seaweed butter, follow this with mains such as roast Waterham Farm chicken with bread sauce, chestnuts and bacon, and jasmine tea junket with rosehip syrup and breakfast crunch to finish. There is also a tasting menu available for a maximum of 6 people. Remember that food is not served on Sunday evenings or Mondays, or you could be disappointed.

**Open** all wk noon-3 6-11 Closed: 25 Dec, 26 Dec, 1 Jan **Restaurant** L served Tue-Sun 12-2 booking required D served Tue-Sat 7-9 booking required Av 3 course à la carte fr £32 ⊕ SHEPHERD NEAME ◀ Shepherd Neame Late Red, Master Brew, Porter, Early Bird, Goldings, Whitstable Bay ♂ Thatchers Gold. ♀ 9 **Facilities** Children's portions Family room Dogs allowed Garden Parking

### WYE    Map 7 TR04

## The New Flying Horse ♀

**Upper Bridge St TN25 5AN**
**☎ 01233 812297 ☐ 01233 813487**
e-mail: newflyhorse@shepherd-neame.co.uk
dir: *Telephone for directions*

A feisty combination of village local (with a rare bat and trap game), contemporary 'restropub' and an amazing WW2 'Soldier's View of Blighty' garden which won an award at the 2005 Chelsea Flower Show. Dine alfresco at this 17th century posting inn with a great bag of pub classics, or snuggle up with award-winning beers in the

timeless, cosy interior and choose from a range of tempting specials based on Kentish produce.

**Open** all day all wk **Bar Meals** L served all wk 12-2 booking required D served all wk 6-9 booking required Av main course £8.95 **Restaurant** L served all wk 12-2 booking required D served all wk 6-9 booking required Av 3 course à la carte fr £20 ⊕ SHEPHERD NEAME ◀ Masterbrew Spitfire, Late Red, Canterbury Stack, Guest ales. ♀ 12 **Facilities** Children's menu Children's portions Play area Dogs allowed Garden Parking

# LANCASHIRE

### BASHALL EAVES    Map 18 SD64

## PICK OF THE PUBS

## The Red Pump Inn ♀

**Clitheroe Rd BB7 3DA ☎ 01254 826227**
e-mail: info@theredpumpinn.co.uk
dir: *3m from Clitheroe, NW, follow 'Whitewell, Trough of Bowland & Bashall Eaves' signs*

Enjoying panoramic views of Pendle Hill and Longridge Fell, this is one of the oldest inns in the Ribble Valley, its name coming from the old red pump that used to provide horses with water. Public areas divide into a snug with real fire, large and small dining rooms and a bar where you will find great real ales and plenty of wines by the glass. If you hear music in the bar it'll probably be an eclectic mix of 60s blues, jazz and whatever else matches the relaxed, slightly quirky atmosphere. The menu changes to reflect the seasons and the whims of the owners and chefs, while the supporting daily specials boards – where you'll find the fish - may change during the day. Local produce includes meat, game, cheeses and vegetables, with extra-matured local Pendle beef available every day. Typical dishes include pan-seared pigeon breast with local black pudding and caramelised apple; Pendle beef and pork sausages and champ; rich chocolate and rum mousse.

**Open** noon-3 6-11 ( Sun noon-9) Closed: 2wks end Feb, Mon (ex BH) **Bar Meals** L served Mon-Fri 12-2, Sat 12-2.30, Sun 12-7 D served Mon-Sat 6-9, Sun 12-7 **Restaurant** L served Mon-Fri 12-2, Sat 12-2.30, Sun 12-7 D served Mon-Sat 6-9, Sun 12-7 ⊕ FREE HOUSE ◀ Black Sheep, Moorhouses, Tirril Brewery. ♀ 10 **Facilities** Children's menu Garden Parking

### BILSBORROW    Map 18 SD53

## Owd Nell's Tavern ♀

**Guy's Thatched Hamlet, Canal Side PR3 0RS**
**☎ 01995 640010 ☐ 01995 640141**
e-mail: info@guysthatchedhamlet.com
dir: *M6 junct 32 N on A6. In approx 5m follow brown tourist signs to Guy's Thatched Hamlet*

This country-style tavern forms a part of Guy's Thatched Hamlet, a cluster of eating and drinking venues beside the Lancaster Canal that has been run by the Wilkinson

*continued on page 276*

**BILSBORROW** *continued*

family for nearly 30 years. Expect excellent ales, such as Owd Nell's Canalside Bitter or Pendle Witch, and an authentic country pub ambience enhanced by flagged floors, fireplaces and low ceilings. All-day fare is typified by fish and chips, and filled Yorkshire puddings. Children's menus are available. There is a cider festival at the end of July.

**Open** all day all wk 7am-2am Closed: 25 Dec **Bar Meals** Av main course £7 food served all day **Restaurant** L served Mon-Sat 12-2.30, Sun 12-10.30 D served Mon-Sat 5.30-10.30, Sun 12-10.30 Fixed menu price fr £12 Av 3 course à la carte fr £12.50 ⊕ FREE HOUSE ◀ Boddingtons Bitter, Jennings Bitter, Copper Dragon, Black Sheep, Owd Nells Canalside Bitter, Moorhouses Bitter, Pendle Witch, Thwaites ⚲ Thatchers Heritage, Cheddar Valley. ♀ 20 **Facilities** Children's menu Children's portions Play area Family room Dogs allowed Garden Parking

---

### BLACKBURN · Map 18 SD62

## PICK OF THE PUBS

## Clog and Billycock

Billinge End Rd, Pleasington BB2 6QB
☎ 01254 201163
e-mail: enquiries@theclogandbillycock.com
web: www.theclogandbillycock.com
**dir:** *M6 junct 29 onto M65 junct 3, follow signs for Pleasington*

A part of Pleasington's history for over 150 years, this stylish free house displays an engaging mix of contemporary and traditional styles following a £1.3 million refurbishment. Located on the quiet edges of Blackburn's western suburbs where the River Darwen flows out of town, this warm and relaxing building is just the place to appreciate Thwaites ales, draught ciders and fine wines, as well as tempting, contemporary twists on favourite traditional dishes created by Nigel Haworth, all prepared from quality Lancashire produce. Expect substantial snacks, grills and salads, alongside popular choices from the regular menu that might include Clog and Billy fish pie; Ribble Valley steak and kidney pudding with mashed potato and creamed Hesketh savoy cabbage; or forest mushroom, celeriac and spinach potato pancakes with Sandham's creamy Lancashire cheese. A comprehensive young person's menu delivers real food at sensible prices, with a refreshing choice of non-alcoholic drinks.

---

**Open** all wk noon-11 (Sun noon-10.30) Closed: 25 Dec **Bar Meals** L served Mon-Sat 12-2, Sun 12-8.30 (afternoon bites Mon-Sat 2-5.30) D served Mon-Fri 6-9, Sat 5.30-9, Sun 12-8.30 Av main course £12.50 **Restaurant** L served Mon-Sat 12-2, Sun 12-8.30 D served Mon-Fri 6-9, Sat 5.30-9, Sun 12-8.30 Fixed menu price fr £15 ⊕ FREE HOUSE ◀ Thwaites Bomber, Wainwright, Original. **Facilities** Children's menu Dogs allowed Garden Parking

## PICK OF THE PUBS

## The Millstone at Mellor ★★ HL ⓐⓐ ♀

*See Pick of the Pubs on opposite page*

---

### BLACKO · Map 18 SD84

## *Moorcock Inn*

Gisburn Rd BB9 6NG
☎ 01282 614186 · ▤ 01282 614186
e-mail: boo@patterson1047.freeserve.co.uk
**dir:** *M65 junct 13, take A682 to Blacko*

Family-run country inn with traditional log fires and good views towards the Pendle Way, ideally placed for non-motorway travel to the Lakes and the Yorkshire Dales. Home-cooked meals are a speciality, with a wide choice including salads and sandwiches, and vegetarian and children's meals. Starters like cheesy mushrooms, and garlic prawns are followed by lasagne, various steak choices, pork in orange and cider, and trout grilled with lemon and herb butter.

**Open** all day Tue-Sun & Mon L Closed: Mon eve ◀ Thwaites Best Bitter, Smooth. **Facilities** Garden Parking

---

### BURROW · Map 18 SD67

## PICK OF THE PUBS

## The Highwayman ♀

LA6 2RJ ☎ 01524 273338
e-mail: enquiries@highwaymaninn.co.uk
web: www.highwaymaninn.co.uk
**dir:** *M6 junct 36, A65 to Kirkby Lonsdale. Then A683 S. Burrow approx 2m*

The Highwayman is the sister pub to the Three Fishes at Mitton in Nigel Haworth's thriving Ribble Valley Inns empire of dining pubs. Following a £1.2 million renovation in partnership with local brewer Daniel

---

Thwaites, the 18th-century former coaching inn re-opened in 2007 and business has been brisk since. In a smart, civilised setting of stone floors, handsome wooden furniture, crackling log fires and wonderful terraced gardens you can sample cracking real ales and delicious food. Food is very much at the heart of the operation, and the philosophy of head chef Michael Ward focuses on an attractive contemporary interpretation of traditional specialities using regional produce – the menu celebrates local food heroes on every line. The ingredients they supply appear in dishes such as warm Flookburgh shrimps with blade mace butter; braised ox cheek pudding; Sillfield Farm dry-cured gammon steak; and Leagram's organic creamy curd cheese and onion pie. There are seasonal alternative menus too, for example one focussing on parsnip dishes, plus a very good childrens' menu.

**Open** all wk noon-11 (Sun noon-10.30) Closed: 25 Dec **Bar Meals** L served Mon-Sat 12-2, Sun 12-8.30 D served Mon-Fri 6-9, Sat 5.30-9, Sun 12-8.30 Av main course £12 food served all day ⊕ RIBBLE VALLEY INNS ◀ Lancaster Bomber, Wainwright, Thwaites Original ⚲ Kingston. ♀ 13 **Facilities** Children's menu Children's portions Dogs allowed Garden Parking

---

### CARNFORTH · Map 18 SD47

## The Longlands Inn and Restaurant

Tewitfield LA6 1JH ☎ 01524 781256 · ▤ 01524 781004
e-mail: info@longlandshotel.co.uk
web: www.longlandshotel.co.uk
**dir:** *Telephone for directions*

With its nooks and crannies, old beams and uneven floors, this family-run inn stands next to Tewitfield locks on the Lancaster canal. The bar comes to life for band night on Mondays, with a more relaxed feel during the rest of the week. The appetising menu includes slate platters with deli-style bread; and main course choices ranging from braised Silverdale lamb shank, and tamarind confit duck leg on Chinese noodles to the Longlands fish pie with melted cheese topping.

**Open** all day all wk 11am-1am (Sun 11-mdnt) **Bar Meals** L served Mon-Sat 12-2.30, Sun 12-9.30 D served Mon-Sat 5.30-9.30, Sun 12-9.30 **Restaurant** L served Mon-Sat 12-2.30, Sun 12-9.30 D served Mon-Sat 5.30-9.30, Sun 12-9.30 booking required ⊕ FREE HOUSE **Facilities** Children's menu Dogs allowed Garden Parking

# PICK OF THE PUBS

## The Millstone at Mellor ★★HL

**BLACKBURN**      Map 18 SD62

**Church Ln, Mellor BB2 7JR**
☎ **01254 813333**   📄 **01254 812628**
**e-mail:** info@millstonehotel.com
**web:** www.millstonehotel.co.uk
**dir:** *M6 junct 31, A59 towards Clitheroe, past British Aerospace. Right at rdbt signed Blackburn/Mellor. Next rdbt 2nd left. Hotel at top of hill on right*

The river Ribble meanders lazily in it's trough-like valley just to the north of the village of Mellor, beyond which rise the commanding heights of Longridge Fell. Nearby are the impressive half-timbered mansion of Samlesbury Hall, Whalley's ancient abbey and the legend-wreathed

slopes of Pendle Hill. All damn good reasons to spend a couple of days staying at the AA-listed accommodation at this lovely village inn and restaurant. Here the wealth of Lancashire's generous larder is gathered to your table via the classic and inventive dishes created by chef/patron Anson Bolton, who has gained two AA rosettes for each of the past eight years. The very English, oak-panelled Millers Restaurant is the place for a leisurely lunch or carte choice, or chose to dine in The Millers Bar, where signature dishes include braised and glazed Pendle lamb shank served with spring onion champ. Vegetarians may indulge in Ribblesdale goat's cheese and spinach risotto with soft poached egg and shaved parmesan, whilst surf fans can look forward to the renowned Millstone fish curry, featuring king prawns, scallops, haddock and salmon.

Daily specials make full use of the embarrassment of local suppliers hereabouts, or if you fancy just a nibble, then a Bowland roast beef sandwich or a crumbly Lancashire with Balderstone plum chutney should satisfy. The carte

restaurant menu tempts with starters such as tea smoked venison loin with horseradish crème fraîche prior to Goosnargh duck breast and confit duck leg, braised red cabbage and plum syrup. The menu has helpful suggestions as to appropriate wines and also bottled beers from Daniel Thwaites' varied range.

**Open** all day all wk **Bar Meals** L served Mon-Sat 12-9.30, Sun 12-9 Av main course £11 food served all day **Restaurant** L served all wk 12-2.30 booking required D served all wk 6.30-9.30 booking required Fixed menu price fr £27 🌐 SHIRE HOTELS LTD 🍺 Thwaites, Warsteiner, Lancaster Bomber, Thwaites Original Cash Bitter, Wainwrights ♻ Kingstone Press. 🍷 10 **Facilities** Children's menu Parking **Rooms** 23

## CHIPPING — Map 18 SD64

### Dog & Partridge ☻

**Hesketh Ln PR3 2TH** ☎ 01995 61201 📄 01995 61446
*dir: M6 junct 31A, follow Longridge signs. At Longridge left at 1st rdbt, straight on at next 3 rdbts. At Alston Arms turn right. 3m, pub on right*

Dating back to 1515, this pleasantly modernised rural pub in the Ribble Valley enjoys delightful views of the surrounding fells. The barn has been transformed into a welcoming dining area, where home-made food on the comprehensive bar snack menu is backed by a specials board featuring fresh fish and game dishes. A typical menu shows a starter of deep fried garlic mushrooms; then mains of braised pork chops with home-made apple sauce and stuffing; and home-made steak and kidney pie.

**Open** 11.45-3 6.45-11 (Sat 11.45-3 6-11 Sun 11.45-10.30) Closed: Mon **Bar Meals** L served Tue-Sat 12-1.45 **Restaurant** L served Tue-Sat 12-1.30, Sun 12-3 booking required D served Tue-Sat 7-9 Sun 3.30-8.30 booking required Fixed menu price fr £17.25 ⊕ FREE HOUSE ◀ Carlsberg-Tetley, Black Sheep. ☻ 8 **Facilities** Children's menu Children's portions Parking

## CLITHEROE — Map 18 SD74

### PICK OF THE PUBS

### The Assheton Arms ☻
*See Pick of the Pubs on opposite page*

---

### The Shireburn Arms ★★★ HL ☻

**Whalley Rd, Hurst Green BB7 9QJ**
☎ 01254 826518 📄 01254 826208
e-mail: sales@shireburnarmshotel.com
*dir: Telephone for directions*

A privately run, 17th-century inn with super views, in the heart of the Ribble Valley. *Lord of the Rings* author J R R Tolkien used to drink here when visiting his son at Stonyhurst College nearby, and the pub has become and home of the 'Tolkien Trail'. Using the finest local produce from around Lancashire, the menu ranges from sandwiches and salads to roasted Goosnargh duck with black cherry jus; wild sea trout on crushed peas; and mushroom, cranberry and brie Wellington. A conservatory links the restaurant with the patio and gardens.

**Open** all day all wk ◀ Theakstons Best Bitter, guest ales. ☻ 10 **Facilities** Play area Family room Dogs allowed Garden Parking **Rooms** 22

## DALTON — Map 15 SD40

### The Beacon at Dalton ☻ NEW

**Beacon Ln WN8 7RR** ☎ 01695 622771
e-mail: enquiries@thebeaconatdalton.co.uk
*dir: M6 junct 26 onto M58 towards Skelmersdale. At junct 5 follow signs for Up Holland & Beacon Country Park. In Up Holland 1st left by Victoria pub into Mill Ln which becomes Beacon Ln in approx 2m. Pub on right on brow of hill*

Nestling at the edge of a country park close to the renowned viewpoint of Ashurst's Beacon (look for Snowdonia and the Lakes on very clear days), this welcoming 300 year old pub is a true local serving the scattered Lancashire community and discerning diners who seek out dishes such as pork fillet on a bed of Lancashire cheese and black pudding. The period 19th century dining room is most refreshing, reflecting the care taken in a comprehensive 2008 refurbishment here.

**Open** all day all wk **Bar Meals** L served all wk 12-9.30 D served all wk 12-9.30 Av main course £7 **Restaurant** L served all wk 12-9.30 D served all wk 12-9.30 booking required Fixed menu price fr £11.95 Av 3 course à la carte fr £20 food served all day ⊕ MARSTONS ◀ Pedigree, Cumberland, Hobgoblin, Sneck Lifter. ☻ 10 **Facilities** Children's menu Children's portions Play area Dogs allowed Garden Parking

## FENCE — Map 18 SD83

### Fence Gate Inn ☻

**Wheatley Lane Rd BB12 9EE**
☎ 01282 618101 📄 01282 615432
e-mail: info@fencegate.co.uk
*dir: From M65 junct 13 towards Fence, 1.5m, pub set back on right opposite T-junct for Burnley*

An extensive property, the Fence Gate Inn was originally a collection point for cotton delivered by barge and distributed to surrounding cottages to be spun into cloth. Food is served both in the bar and the Topiary Brasserie. Highlights are a selection of sausages starring Lancashire's champion leek and black pudding with a hint of sage. Alongside the food, a good choice of wines and ales are also available and can be enjoyed outside under the parasols in good weather.

**Open** all day all wk **Bar Meals** L served Mon-Sat 12-2.30, Sun 12-8 D served Mon-Sat 6-9, Sun 12-8 Av main course £8.95 **Restaurant** L served Mon-Sat 12-2.30, Sun 12-8 D served Mon-Sat 6-9, Sun 12-8 Av 3 course à la carte fr £25 ⊕ FREE HOUSE ◀ Theakston, Directors, Deuchars, Moorhouse, Bowland ♂ Stowford Press. ☻ 10 **Facilities** Children's menu Children's portions Garden Parking

### Ye Old Sparrowhawk Inn ☻

**Wheatley Lane Rd BB12 9QG**
☎ 01282 603034 📄 01282 603035
e-mail: mail@thesparrowhawk.co.uk
web: www.thesparrowhawk.co.uk
*dir: M65 junct 13, A6068, at rdbt take 1st exit 0.25m. Turn right onto Carr Hall Rd, at top turn left 0.25m, pub on right*

Sipping a pint outside the half-timbered Sparrowhawk on a summer's evening is one of life's great pleasures. The pub stands at the gateway to Pendle Forest, famous for its witches, but here you'll find friendly service and stylish surroundings. The classically-trained chefs work with locally sourced fresh ingredients to create menus that include seared calves' liver, buttery mash, mustard onions and bacon jus; chicken and ham hock pie; and Lancashire hotpot with braised red cabbage. There are fabulous lunchtime sandwiches on offer.

**Open** all day all wk **Bar Meals** L served Mon-Sat 12-2.30, Sun 12-8 booking required D served Mon-Sat 5.30-9.30, Sun 12-8 booking required Av main course £9.95 **Restaurant** L served Mon-Sat 12-2.30, Sun 12-8 booking required D served Mon-Sat 5.30-9.30, Sun 12-8 booking required ⊕ MOYO LTD ◀ Thwaites Cask, Draught Bass, Greene King IPA, Banktop. ☻ 10 **Facilities** Children's menu Children's portions Dogs allowed Garden Parking

## FORTON — Map 18 SD45

### PICK OF THE PUBS

### The Bay Horse Inn ☻

**LA2 0HR** ☎ 01524 791204 📄 01524 791204
e-mail: yvonne@bayhorseinn.com
*dir: M6 junct 33 take A6 towards Garstang, turn left for pub, approx 1m from M6*

Mismatched furniture and a handsome stone fireplace with roaring winter log fires characterise this charming, 18th-century pub in the Trough of Bowland. Expect a warm welcome and real cask beers, as well as an extensive wine list and a good selection of malt whiskies. Award-winning chef Craig Wilkinson specialises in simple, fresh and imaginative dishes, exercising his culinary skills on the very best of local ingredients to produce pub fare of unashamedly gastro standards. Lunchtime brings sandwiches with fillings such as poached salmon with lemon and dill mayonnaise, and boiled Lancashire ham with English mustard; there are also hot dishes like roast sea bass with smoked bacon mash and shrimp butter. Duck

*continued on page 280*

# PICK OF THE PUBS

## The Assheton Arms

CLITHEROE      Map 18 SD74

**Downham BB7 4BJ**
☎ **01200 441227**   📄 **01200 440581**
**e-mail:** asshetonarms@aol.com
**web:** www.assheton-arms.co.uk
**dir:** *A59 to Chatburn, then follow Downham signs*

In the shadow of Pendle Hill, this stone-built country pub was originally a farmhouse, brewing beer just for the workers. It became a real pub, the George and Dragon, in 1872, then in 1950 was renamed in honour of the contribution Ralph Assheton, Lord Clitheroe, made to the Second World War effort. The Assheton family owns the whole, TV aerial-free village and their coat-of-arms on the sign above the door includes a man holding a scythe incorrectly. For an explanation, which involves the English Civil War, it's probably best to ask a local.

Visitors to the pub that Wendy and David Busby have run since 1983 will find the single bar and little rooms, with window seats and an original 1765 stone fireplace, attractively furnished with solid oak tables and wing-back settees. Real ales from Thwaites of Blackburn include Lancaster Bomber and Wainwright, named after the famous fell-walker.

A large blackboard lists the range of daily specials, particularly fish and shellfish, such as sea bream, monkfish, oysters, mussels, scallops and lobster. Local and traditional favourites on the main menu include Lancashire hot-pot; steak and kidney pudding; venison casserole; roast suckling pork; grilled Dover sole; and chicken and mushroom pie. The vegetarian section offers cauliflower and mushroom provençale; and vegetable chilli with rice.

An interesting selection of nibbles for while you wait includes Mrs Whelan's horseshoe-shaped Burnley black pudding with piccalilli and mustard; and Morecambe Bay potted shrimps served cold, or creamed and hot with toast. A fair few red, white and rosé wines are available by the standard or large glass. Children (who have their own menu) and dogs (who don't, although there's water) are welcome.

**Open** all wk Mon-Fri 12-3 6-11 (Sat-Sun noon-11pm) **Bar Meals** L served Mon-Sat 12-2, Sun 12-9 D served all wk 6-9 Av main course £10.95 **Restaurant** Fixed menu price fr £10 Av 3 course à la carte fr £18 ⊕ FREE HOUSE ◀ Thwaites Lancaster Bomber, Wainwright. ♀ 20 **Facilities** Children's menu Dogs allowed Parking

## FORTON *continued*

salad with walnut, beetroot and orange dressing kicks off the main menu, which also offers main course choices like roast Cumbrian lamb with carrot purée, peas, rosemary and anchovy butter. There are regular live music evenings, including jazz.

**Open** noon-3 6.30-mdnt Closed: Mon (ex BH L)
**Bar Meals** L served Tue-Sat 12-1.45, Sun 12-3 D served Tue-Sat 6.30-9.15 booking required Av main course £14.95 **Restaurant** L served Tue-Sat 12-1.45, Sun 12-3 D served Tue-Sat 6.30-9.15 booking required Av 3 course à la carte fr £18.95 ⊕ FREE HOUSE ◀ Thwaites Lancaster Bomber, Moorhouses Pendle Witch, Masham Brewery, Black Sheep. ☕ 11 **Facilities** Children's portions Garden Parking

### GOOSNARGH     Map 18 SD53

## The Stag's Head ☕ NEW

**990 Whittingham Ln, Whittingham PR3 2AU**
☎ 01772 864071
**e-mail:** clare@thestagshead.co.uk
**dir:** *From A6 at Broughton take B5260 signed Longridge. 3m to pub*

The search continues here for a tunnel rumoured to link this part-18th-century village pub to haunted Chingle Hall. In the bar five guest ales are always on tap (there's a beer festival each May). Dishes relying on quality local suppliers include slow-cooked Goosnargh duck on toast; Curwen Hill beef and ale pie; Pendle lamb Lancashire hot pot; and battered deep-fried Fleetwood cod. The cheeseboard reflects the fact that this area is known as the Cheese Triangle. The surrounding countryside is a rambler's dream, with the pub a welcome stopping point.

**Open** all day Closed: Tue **Bar Meals** L served Mon-Sat (ex Tue) 12-3 D served Mon-Sat (ex Tue) 6-9 Av main course £10 **Restaurant** L served Mon-Sat (ex Tue) 12-3 (Sun 12-8) D served Mon-Sat (ex Tue) 6-9 (Sun 12-8) booking required Av 3 course à la carte fr £14.95 ⊕ SCOTTISH & NEWCASTLE ◀ Theakstons, John Smith's, Guest ales. ☕ 11 **Facilities** Children's menu Children's portions Dogs allowed Garden Parking

### HESKIN GREEN     Map 15 SD51

## Farmers Arms

**85 Wood Ln PR7 5NP**
☎ 01257 451276   📠 01257 453958
**e-mail:** andy@farmersarms.co.uk
**dir:** *On B5250 between M6 & Eccleston*

Once known as the Pleasant Retreat, this country inn lives up to that name and offers a warm welcome and a traditional theme. The long, creeper-covered building houses two cosy bars decorated with old pictures and farming memorabilia. Very much a Rothwell family concern, traditional hand-pulled real ales are offered and hearty food cooked by son Andrew. Typical dishes include chicken curry; lasagne; pizzas; and a selection from the grill.

**Open** all wk ⊕ ENTERPRISE INNS ◀ Timothy Taylor Landlord, Pedigree, Black Sheep, Tetley, Tetley Bitter. **Facilities** Children's menu Children's portions Play area Dogs allowed Garden Parking

### HEST BANK     Map 18 SD46

## Hest Bank Hotel

**2 Hest Bank Ln LA2 6DN**
☎ 01524 824339   📠 01524 824948
**e-mail:** chef.glenn@btinternet.com
**dir:** *From Lancaster take A6 N, after 2m left to Hest Bank*

Comedian Eric Morecambe used to drink at this canalside former coaching inn, first licensed in 1554. Awash with history and 'many happy ghosts', it now offers cask ales and a wide selection of meals all day, with local suppliers playing an important role in maintaining food quality. The good-value menu may range from a large pot of Bantry Bay mussels to the pub's own lamb hotpot made to a traditional recipe. The pub is family-friendly and offers a children's menu and play area.

**Open** all day all wk 11.30-11.30 (Sun 11.30-10.30) **Bar Meals** L served Mon-Sat 12-9, Sun 12-8 D served Mon-Sat 12-9, Sun 12-8 Av main course £10 food served all day ⊕ PUNCH TAVERNS ◀ Timothy Taylor Landlord, Black Sheep Bitter, Guest ales. **Facilities** Children's menu Children's portions Play area Garden Parking

### LANCASTER     Map 18 SD46

## The Stork Inn ☕

**Conder Green LA2 0AN**
☎ 01524 751234   📠 01524 752660
**e-mail:** tracy@thestorkinn.co.uk
**dir:** *M6 junct 33 take A6 north. Left at Galgate & next left to Conder Green*

White-painted coaching inn spread along the banks of the Conder Estuary, with a colourful 300-year-history that includes several name changes. The quaint sea port of Glasson Dock is a short walk along the Lancashire Coastal Way, and the Lake District is easily accessible. In the bar you will find local ales such as Lancaster Amber and Black. Seasonal specialities join home-cooked English and South African food like pan-fried chicken breast topped with Lancashire cheese and bacon; Boerewors - lightly spiced pure beef farmer's sausage, served with sweet potato mash and a balsamic, red onion and tomato relish; and minted pea risotto.

**Open** all day all wk 10am-11pm (Sat-Sun 8.30am-11pm) **Bar Meals** L served all wk 12-9 (Sat-Sun breakfast 8.30am-10.30am) D served all wk 12-9 (Sat-Sun breakfast 8.30am-10.30am) food served all day **Restaurant** food served all day ⊕ ENTERPRISE INN ◀ Black Sheep, Timothy Taylor Landlord, Lancaster Amber, Lancaster Black, Marstons Pedigree. ☕ 10 **Facilities** Children's menu Children's portions Play area Dogs allowed Garden Parking

## The Sun Hotel and Bar ☕

**LA1 1ET** ☎ 01524 66006   📠 01524 66397
**e-mail:** info@thesunhotelandbar.co.uk
**dir:** *6m from M6 junct 33*

There's a full and fascinating history of this popular city centre pub on its website, including the fact that Turner, the painter, Charles Dickens and possibly even Bonnie Prince Charlie all drank here. Famous for its hospitality and wide selection of cask ales and wines, its lovely old bar is frequented throughout the day; first arrivals are the hotel guests and business breakfasters, then shoppers and people checking their emails over coffee. At lunchtime it's busy with customers keen to tuck into the locally sourced good food on the main and daily changing specials menus. And in the evening there are the real ale enthusiasts, draught and bottled lager connoisseurs and wine lovers. At the time of writing (when menus were being revamped) typical lunch and supper main courses include beef chilli; smoked chicken Caesar salad; Lancashire hotpot; Lancaster Brewery beer-battered fish and chips; vegetable moussaka; and Mexican three-bean chilli.

**Open** all day all wk from 7.30am until late **Bar Meals** food served all day ⊕ FREE HOUSE ◀ Thwaites Lancaster Bomber, Lancaster Amber, Timmermans Strawberry, Lancaster Blonde, Warsteiner. ☕ 23 **Facilities** Children's portions Garden

## The Waterwitch ☕

**The Tow Path, Aldcliffe Rd LA1 1SU**
☎ 01524 63828   📠 01524 34535
**e-mail:** thewaterwitch@mitchellsinns.co.uk
**dir:** *6m from M6 junct 33*

The Waterwitch takes its name from three longboats that worked the adjacent Lancaster canal in the late 18th century. It occupies an old stables, tastefully converted to retain original features such as stone walls and interior slab floors. In just a few years the pub has acquired celebrity status and a clutch of awards, yet it still remains a genuine pub with the broad appeal of a wine bar and restaurant. It is noted for its ever-changing selection of fine cask-conditioned real ales, impressive wine list and guest cheeses.

The talented team of chefs work with locally-sourced produce including fish that arrives daily from Fleetwood harbour. There has been a recent change of hands.

**Open** all wk ◄ Thwaites Lancaster Bomber, Warsteiner, Moorhouse Ales, Lancaster Brewery Bitters, Beacon Ales. ♥ 27 **Facilities** Garden

## NEWTON  Map 18 SD65

## Parkers Arms NEW

BB7 3DY ☎ 01200 446236

e-mail: enquiries@parkersarms.co.uk

dir: From Clitheroe take B6478 through Waddington to Newton-in-Bowland

Bowland's imposing fells swoop across the horizon above this refurbished dining inn just yards from the pretty river Hodder. It's the pub nearest to the geographical centre of the UK, and celebrates its rural location by gathering in the best Lancashire produce, with beers from Bowland Brewery, cheeses from local craft producers and meats raised on the grassy hills around. Edisford pork sausages or Anderton's cured Bowland gammon could be your introduction to the area's bounty, taken in the peaceful garden overlooking the valley. A cookery school is planned here in 2010.

**Open** all wk Mon-Fri noon-3 6-mdnt (Sat-Sun noon-mdnt) (open all day in summer) **Bar Meals** L served Mon-Fri 12-3 (Sat-Sun all day) D served Mon-Fri 6-9 (Sat-Sun all day) Av main course £9.50 **Restaurant** L served Mon-Fri 12-3 (Sat-Sun all day) D served Mon-Fri 6-9 (Sat-Sun all day) Fixed menu price fr £15 Av 3 course à la carte fr £20 ⊕ ENTERPRISE INNS ◄ Bowland Hen Harrier, Sawley Tempted, Lancaster Amber, Skipton Brewery Copper Dragon ♂ Stowford Press. **Facilities** Children's menu Children's portions Dogs allowed Garden Parking

## PARBOLD  Map 15 SD41

### PICK OF THE PUBS

## The Eagle & Child

Maltkiln Ln, Bispham Green L40 3SG
☎ 01257 462297  📠 01257 464718

dir: 3m from M6 junct 27. Over Parbold Hill, follow signs for Bispham Green on right

This traditional free house stands in a pretty and peaceful location, with seating to enjoy the action on the bowling green during the summer months. The pub's unusual name – which derives from a local legend about Lord Derby's illegitimate son being discovered in an eagle's nest – has also prompted the more prosaic local nickname of the Bird and Bastard. The pub maintains its traditional atmosphere with an offering of real ciders and five regularly-changing guest ales, whilst the annual May Bank Holiday beer festival attracts up to 2,000 people to the huge marquee in the pub grounds. Choices from the extensive menu might include roast Croston Hall pheasant; sautéed pork fillet with a brandy, mushroom, garlic and cream sauce; or braised ox tail with red wine sauce and mashed potato. The newly-opened farm shop next door offers butchery, wine sales, cheeses and much more!

**Open** all wk **Bar Meals** L served all wk 12-2 booking required D served Sun-Thu 5.30-8.30, Fri-Sat 5.30-9 booking required Av main course £9.50 **Restaurant** L served all wk 12-2 booking required D served Sun-Thu 5.30-8.30, Fri-Sat 5.30-9 booking required Fixed menu price fr £13.50 Av 3 course à la carte fr £20 ⊕ FREE HOUSE ◄ Moorhouse Black Cat Mild, Thwaites Bitter, Southport Golden Sands, guest ales ♂ Kingstone Press Traditional Cider. **Facilities** Children's menu Children's portions Family room Dogs allowed Garden Parking

## PRESTON  Map 18 SD52

### PICK OF THE PUBS

## Cartford Country Inn & Hotel

Little Eccleston PR3 0YP ☎ 01995 670166

e-mail: info@thecartfordinn.co.uk

dir: Off A586

This pleasantly rambling, three-storey inn former coaching inn stands sentinel by the toll bridge over the tidal River Wyre, a few miles from its meeting with the Irish Sea and close to Blackpool. There's a nice beer garden with views over the river to the shapely Lancashire fells, ideal to relax in with a beer from Moorhouses, Bowland or Lakeland Breweries. Comprehensively upgraded by owners Julie and Patrick Beaumé, the inn offers a pleasant mix of traditional and gastro elements; a timeless log fire still burns in the winter grate, while polished wood floors and chunky dining furniture are decidedly up-to-date. Imaginative food starts with a choice of nibbles, continues with wood platters of antipasti or seafood, and culminates in the full menu experience: Bury black pudding melt, followed by Pilling Marsh lamb hotpot, finishing with the renowned Cartmel sticky toffee pudding.

**Open** all day Closed: 25 Dec, Mon L **Restaurant** L served Tue-Sat 12-2, Sun 12-8 D served Mon-Thu 5-9, Fri-Sat 5-10 Av 3 course à la carte fr £20 ⊕ FREE HOUSE ◄ Pride of Pendle Moorhouse, Lakeland Gold Hawkshead, New Harrier Bowland Brewery, Old Peculier Theakston. **Facilities** Children's menu Children's portions Garden Parking

## RIBCHESTER  Map 18 SD63

### The White Bull ♥

Church St PR3 3XP ☎ 01254 878303

e-mail: enquiries@whitebullrib.co.uk

dir: M6 junct 31, A59 towards Clitheroe. B6245 towards Longridge. Pub 100mtrs from Roman Museum in town centre

Ancient Roman columns welcome patrons to this Grade II listed pub in the centre of Ribchester, with its beer garden overlooking the former Roman bathhouse. Despite its 18th-century origins as a courthouse, you'll find a warm and friendly atmosphere in which to sample the local hand-pumped beers. Lunchtime sandwiches and a variety of specials support the main menu. Recent change of hands.

**Open** all wk Mon open 6pm ◄ John Smith's, Copper Dragon Bitter, Bowland Brewery Bitter, Moorhouses. ♥ 8 **Facilities** Garden Parking

## SAWLEY  Map 18 SD74

### The Spread Eagle ♥

BB7 4NH ☎ 01200 441202  📠 01200 441973

e-mail: spreadeagle@zen.co.uk

dir: Just off A159 between Clitheroe & Skipton, 4m N of Clitheroe

This pub stands on the banks of the River Ribble, affording lovely views from every table. There is a 17th-century bar with oak beams and a log fire, where a great choice of real ale, malt whiskies and wines by the glass is offered. Dishes served in the modern dining room might include steamed steak and kidney pudding; pan-roasted Barnsley chop; or baked fish pie with cheesy mash. Mediterranean platters and light bites are also available like brushetta or grilled scallops.

**Open** all day all wk 11-11 (Sun noon-10.30) **Bar Meals** L served Mon-Sat 12-2, Sun 12-7.30 D served Mon-Sat 6-9.30, Sun 12-7.30 food served all day **Restaurant** L served Mon-Sat 12-2, Sun 12-7.30 D served Mon-Sat 6-9.30, Sun 12-7.30 food served all day ⊕ INDIVIDUAL INNS ◄ Timothy Taylor, Wainwrights. ♥ 16 **Facilities** Garden Parking

# PICK OF THE PUBS

## Freemasons Country Inn 🍷

**WISWELL**      Map 18 SD73

**8 Vicarage Fold BB7 9DF**
☎ **01254 822218**   🖨 **01254 824375**
**e-mail:**
enquiries@freemasonswiswell.co.uk
**web:** www.freemasonswiswell.co.uk
**dir:** *M6 junct 31, A59 towards Clitheroe.*
*A671 towards Whalley for 0.1m, turn left for*
*Wiswell. Pub opposite red phone box*

This beautiful country inn stands in the picture-perfect Wiswell in the heart of the Ribble Valley. The inn was formally three small cottages, one of which was a freemasons lodge. This is how the inn acquired its name. When the new owner along with head chef/patron Steven Smith took over in 2009, an exceptional renovation saw this rural village pub evolve into a stylish and inviting country inn where great food is served in elegant and relaxed surroundings.

Downstairs flag floors, roaring log fires, walls in muted heritage colours, antique rugs and furniture, period paintings and prints all unite to create a superbly relaxed and comfortable atmosphere. A period style oak staircase leads guests upstairs to the Derby room with its impressive collection of antique prints with a horse-racing theme and cast iron fireplace. To the left is the Tudor room with its oak tables and chairs, settles and Tudor artwork. The Portrait room has elegant Georgian furniture and period portraits. The magnificent Gun room is the place to relax with a coffee or liqueur in sumptuous surroundings.

Head chef/patron and local lad Steven Smith, ex-Gilpin Lodge and Box Tree Restaurant, has quickly established the Freemasons on the Ribble Valley food map, through his confident, modern British approach to cooking and his passion for the top-notch local produce available to him, or the best ingredients sourced throughout Great Britain if necessary. His diverse menus offer something for every taste. Starters such as a classic but modern chicken liver parfait with Melba toast, or sea scallops with tandoori roast pork belly, sweet potato apple and cumin, and mains of poached and roasted Goosnargh duck with beetroot and orange, and

traditional slow-cooked aged sirloin with hand-cut chips and pepper sauce. For those with a sweet tooth, classics such as lemon meringue pie, custard tart and rice pudding are created with Steve's light, modern touch.

At the bar you will find several fine cask ales from independent breweries such as Tirrils, Moorhouses, Bank Top and Bowland. The extensive wine list, with 240 wines, offers a fine selection from around the world.

**Open** all wk Mon-Fri 11.30-3 5.30-11 (Sat 11.30-mdnt, Sun 11.30-10.30)
**Bar Meals** L served Mon-Sat 12-2.30, Sun 12-3 D served Mon-Sat 5.30-9.30, Sun 5-8.30 Av main course £15
**Restaurant** L served Mon-Sat 12-2.30 D served Mon-Sat 5.30-9.30 Fixed menu price fr £15 Av 3 course à la carte fr £26 ⊕ FREE HOUSE ◀ Tirrils, Moorhouses, Bowland, Bank Top, Skipton Brewery ♂ Aspall. ♥ 15 **Facilities** Children's menu Children's portions Dogs allowed Garden

## SLAIDBURN                     Map 18 SD75

### Hark to Bounty Inn ☂

Townend BB7 3EP ☎ 01200 446246  📠 01200 446361
e-mail: manager@harktobounty.co.uk
dir: From M6 junct 31 take A59 to Clitheroe then B6478,
through Waddington & Newton, onto Slaidburn

A family-run 13th-century inn known as The Dog until
1875 when Bounty, the local squire's favourite hound,
disturbed a post-hunt drinking session with its loud
baying. The squire's vocal response obviously made a
lasting impact. View the ancient courtroom, last used in
1937. The current family of landlords have been here
some 25 years, and the kitchen offers the likes of black
pudding with brandy and Stilton; local organic pork with
mustard and brown sugar; Bowland lamb shoulder with
root vegetable and redcurrant gravy; or smoked mackerel
kedgeree.

Open all day all wk 11-mdnt ◾ Theakston Old Peculier,
Theakstons Bitter, Moorhouses, Guest ale. ☂ 8
Facilities Dogs allowed Garden Parking

## TUNSTALL                      Map 18 SD67

### PICK OF THE PUBS

### The Lunesdale Arms

LA6 2QN ☎ 015242 74203  📠 015242 74229
e-mail: info@thelunesdale.co.uk
dir: M6 junct 36. A65 Kirkby Lonsdale. A638 Lancaster.
Pub 2m on right

Emma Gillibrand's bright, cheery and welcoming pub
is set in a small rural village in the beautiful Lune
Valley. Well established, with quite a reputation for its
food, wines and fine regional beers (Black Sheep &
Dent), it draws diners from far and wide for changing
chalkboard menus that showcase locally sourced
produce, including bread baked on the premises, meat
from local farms and organically grown vegetables and
salads. Both lunch and evening menus change on a
daily basis according to the seasonality of ingredients
and new ideas. Country terrine with medlar jelly; slow-
roasted shoulder of lamb; butternut squash, sage and
Lancashire blue cheese risotto; steak, Guinness and
mushroom pie; and Yorkshire rhubarb pannacotta with
poached rhubarb show the style. In winter, cosy up by
the wood-burning stove in the light and airy bar, with
its bare boards, stripped dining tables, comfortable
sofas, and local artwork.

Open 11-3 6-11 (Sat Sun & BHs 11-4 6-1am) Closed:
25-26 Dec, Mon (ex BH) Bar Meals L served Tue-Fri
12-2, Sat-Sun 12-2.30 booking required D served Tue-
Sun 6-9 booking required Av main course £11
Restaurant L served Tue-Fri 12-2, Sat-Sun 12-2.30
booking required D served Tue-Sun 6-9 booking
required Av 3 course à la carte fr £18.50 ⊕ FREE
HOUSE ◾ Black Sheep, Dent Aviator, Guinness, Peroni,
Brysons Bitter ♻ Stowford Press. Facilities Children's
portions Family room Dogs allowed Garden Parking

## WHALLEY                       Map 18 SD73

### PICK OF THE PUBS

### The Three Fishes ◎ ☂

Mitton Rd, Mitton BB7 9PQ
☎ 01254 826888  📠 01254 826026
e-mail: enquiries@thethreefishes.com
web: www.thethreefishes.com
dir: M6 junct 31, A59 to Clitheroe. Follow signs for
Whalley, take B6246 for 2m

The original and now flagship pub in Nigel Haworth's
thriving mini-empire of dining pubs (Ribble Valley
Inns) opened in 2004 and business has boomed ever
since, thanks, in no small part to Haworth's inspired
menu, which features classic regional dishes and
champions Lancashire's 'local food heroes'. Dating
back some 400 years, the beautifully refurbished pub
is supposedly named after the 'three fishes pendant' in
the coat of arms of the last abbot of Whalley Abbey, a
carved stone from which is now incorporated over the
pub entrance. The spruced-up interior very much
respects the past and retains its most attractive
features, including the big open fires. The strength of
the menu of regional and British classics comes from
using top-notch local ingredients and the extensive
menu may take in Chadwick's black pudding with
caramelised onions and mustard; warm Morecambe
Bay shrimps; heather-reared Bowland lamb Lancashire
hotpot with pickled red cabbage; and 28-day aged
steaks from Ribble Valley farms. Salads, lunchtime
sandwiches and light meals are also available, while
children have their own, quite grown-up, menu. Enjoy
the sprawling sun terraces in summer and arrive early
to bag a seat.

Open all day all wk Closed: 25 Dec Bar Meals L served
Mon-Sat 12-2, Sun 12-8.30 D served Mon-Fri 6-9, Sat
5.30-9, Sun 12-8.30 Av main course £13.75 food
served all day Restaurant Av 3 course à la carte fr
£19.50 ⊕ FREE HOUSE ◾ Thwaites Traditional,
Thwaites Bomber, Bowland Brewery Hen Harrier. ☂ 13
Facilities Children's menu Children's portions Dogs
allowed Garden Parking

## WHITEWELL                     Map 18 SD64

### PICK OF THE PUBS

### The Inn at
### Whitewell ★★★★★ INN ◎ ☂

Forest of Bowland BB7 3AT
☎ 01200 448222  📠 01200 448298
e-mail: reception@innatwhitewell.com
dir: From B6243 follow Whitewell signs

An ancient stone inn set amid the wild beauty of the
Forest of Bowland, overlooking the River Hodder and
standing next to the parish church. In fact, the inn is
Whitewell, yet despite its splendid isolation there is
much to enjoy here: the inn has seven miles of fishing
rights, and the whole complex embraces a wine
merchant, an art gallery, a shop selling home-made
goodies, and 23 individually decorated bedrooms. The
somewhat eccentric interior is packed with a random
collection of bric-a-brac and furnishings, including a
vast collection of old prints and paintings. Bar lunch
dishes could include hot smoked trout with horseradish
cream or pan-fried chicken livers with black pudding
and red wine jus; more hearty plates may encompass
fish pie and Lancashire hotpot. Bar suppers follow
similar lines, or you can choose à la carte starters such
as chicken liver pâté, and follow with Goosnargh
chicken with roast garlic sauce, and a plate of British
and Irish cheese. There are stunning walks from the
front door.

Open all wk 10am-1am Bar Meals L served all wk 12-2
D served all wk 7.30-9.30 Av main course £23
Restaurant D served all wk 7.30-9.30 booking required
Av 3 course à la carte fr £29 ⊕ FREE HOUSE
◾ Marston's Pedigree, Bowland Bitter, Copper Dragon,
Timothy Taylor Landlord ♻ Dunkerton's Organic
Premium. ☂ 16 Facilities Children's portions Dogs
allowed Garden Parking Rooms 23

## WISWELL                       Map 18 SD73

### PICK OF THE PUBS

### Freemasons Country Inn ☂

*See Pick of the Pubs on opposite page*

## LEICESTERSHIRE

### BELTON — Map 11 SK42

## PICK OF THE PUBS

### *The Queen's Head* ★★★★ RR ◉◉ ♥

**2 Long St LE12 9TP**
☎ 01530 222359 📠 01530 224860
e-mail: enquiries@thequeenshead.org
web: www.thequeenshead.org
dir: *On B5324 between Coalville & Loughborough*

The clean, uncluttered exterior of this white-fronted, village centre pub suggests that its new owners might also have a fair idea of what constitutes good interior design. And so they have. The place has all-round appeal, whether you want to settle into a leather sofa in the contemporary bar, enjoy the food in the restaurant, garden or terrace, or stay overnight in a smartly designed bedroom. A Lite Bites/Classics menu incorporates club sandwiches; burger and fries; risotto of the day; and sausage and mash. The modern British set menu offers starters of grilled red mullet with houmous and cucumber spaghetti; and carpaccio of beef, tarragon cream and rocket, with mains including fillet or rump of beef with smoked mash and cauliflower cheese; sweet potato curry with jasmine rice and home-made naan bread; and assiette of rabbit with beetroot purée. The two AA Rosettes the Queen's Head has earned speak volumes.

**Open** all day all wk Closed: 25-26 Dec ◀ Worthington, Pedigree, Queens Special. ♥ 14 **Facilities** Play area Dogs allowed Garden Parking Rooms 6

### BIRSTALL — Map 11 SK50

## PICK OF THE PUBS

### The White Horse

**White Horse Ln LE4 4EF** ☎ 0116 267 1038
e-mail: info@thewhitehorsebirstall.co.uk
dir: *M1 junct 21A, A46 towards Newark 5.5m. Exit A46 at Loughborough*

Little did the builders of the Grand Union Canal realise, but their local coal wharf serving the village of Birstall would one day become the tranquil garden of this old canal-workers beerhouse, which has matured over the years since it was rebuilt in the 1920's into today's restful retreat. Overlooking Watermead Country Park, The White Horse (formerly The Mulberry Tree) delivers the very best expected of a village inn; reliable beers, good company, garden with views and a sought-after range of dishes. Boaters and ramblers alike can look forward to venison pâté, ciabatta crisps and onion jam or goat's cheese and red onion tart to whet the appetite prior to wild mushroom and spinach pancakes with white wine and parmesan sauce, a specialist stone-baked pizza or braised lamb shank, finishing with white chocolate bread and butter pudding or locally made ice cream. Or just follow the locals' lead and tuck in to the renowned pie of the week with all the trimmings.

**Open** all wk winter 12-3 5.30-11, summer all day, everyday **Bar Meals** L served Mon-Sat 12-2.30, Sun 12-4 D served Mon-Sat 6-9 **Restaurant** L served Mon-Sat 12-2.30, Sun 12-4 D served Mon-Sat 6-9 ⊕ TRUST INNS ◀ Timothy Taylor Landlord, Jennings Cumberland, Guest. **Facilities** Children's menu Children's portions Play area Dogs allowed Garden Parking

### BREEDON ON THE HILL — Map 11 SK42

### The Three Horseshoes

**Main St DE73 8AN** ☎ 01332 695129
e-mail: ian@thehorseshoes.com
dir: *5m from M1 junct 23a. Pub in village centre*

Originally a farrier's – the stables can still be seen in the courtyard – the Three Horseshoes is around 250 years old. Opposite the pub is the village's original round house lockup. Numerous original features and old beams are supplemented by antique furniture, and sea-grass matting completes the warm and welcoming atmosphere. Typical dishes are rabbit terrine with Cumberland sauce; lamb shank with parsnip mash and rosemary gravy; salmon with sweet potato curry; and mussels in white wine, garlic and cream with sea salt chips. There is also a brunch menu and gourmet food and gift shop.

**Open** Mon-Sun L Closed: 25-26, 31 Dec-1 Jan, Sun eve **Bar Meals** L served Mon-Sat 12-2 D served Mon-Sat 5.30-9.15 **Restaurant** L served Mon-Sat 12-2, Sun 12-3 booking required D served Mon-Sat 6.30-9.15 booking required ⊕ FREE HOUSE ◀ Marstons Pedigree, Old Speckled Hen, Theakstons. **Facilities** Dogs allowed Garden Parking

### BRUNTINGTHORPE — Map 11 SP68

### Joiners Arms ♥

**Church Walk LE17 5QH** ☎ 0116 247 8258
e-mail: stephen@thejoinersarms.co.uk
dir: *4m from Lutterworth*

More restaurant than village pub, with restored natural oak beams, tiled floor, pleasant decor, and lots of brassware and candles. Menus change constantly, and quality ingredients are sourced – beef from Scotland, Cornish lamb, Portland crab. Dishes might include mushrooms on duck fat toast with poached egg; salmon with shellfish risotto; sea bass, Chinese greens and ginger butter sauce; pear tart Tatin; or blueberry soufflé. Every Tuesday there's a 3-course fixed menu 'Auberge Supper'.

**Open** 12-2 6.30-11 Closed: Mon **Bar Meals** L served Tue-Sun 12-2 booking required Av main course £13.50 **Restaurant** L served Tue-Sun 12-2 booking required D served 6.30-9.30 booking required Fixed menu price fr £10.50 Av 3 course à la carte fr £26 ⊕ FREE HOUSE ◀ Greene King IPA, John Smith's, Guinness. ♥ 16 **Facilities** Parking

### BUCKMINSTER — Map 11 SK82

### Tollemache Arms ♥ NEW

**48 Main St NG33 5SA** ☎ 01476 860477
e-mail: info@tollemache-arms.co.uk
dir: *On the B676 4m off the A1 towards Melton Mowbray*

Recently reopened after a year long closure, enthusiastic new owners have refurbished the pub and returned it to part of the community but with a passion for food. The bar offers local ales, home-made nibbles and a place for people to relax. There is a dining area with a library where local meetings and toddler groups attend. The menu might include cream of watercress and Jerusalem artichoke soup or rabbit cakes with sauce gribiche, followed by 14-hour slow roast pork with cider sauce, or butternut squash risotto with sage and pine nuts.

**Open** all wk Mon noon-3, Tue-Sat noon-3 5-11, Sun noon-5 Closed: 26 Dec, 1 Jan, Sun eve, Mon eve **Bar Meals** L served Mon-Sat 12-2, Sun 12-3 booking required D served Tue-Sat 6.30-9.30 booking required Av main course £12 **Restaurant** L served Mon-Sat 12-2, Sun 12-3 booking required D served Tue-Sat 6.30-9.30 booking required Av 3 course à la carte fr £20 ⊕ FREE HOUSE ◀ Guinness, John Smith's, Ten Fifty, Red Star Ales, changing Guest ales. ♥ 10 **Facilities** Children's menu Children's portions Dogs allowed Garden Parking

### EVINGTON — Map 11 SK60

### The Cedars

**Main St LE5 6DN** ☎ 0116 273 0482
e-mail: cedars@king-henrys-taverns.co.uk
dir: *From Leicester take A6 towards Market Harborough. Left at lights, onto B667 to Evington. Pub in village centre*

King Henry's Taverns, the owners, like to say that you get two for the price of one here – and you can. The Bar

Save on Hotels. Book at theAA.com/hotel

LEICESTERSHIRE 285 ENGLAND

Restaurant serves the group's range of competitively priced, freshly prepared steaks, fish and seafood, rumpburgers, traditional favourites, and international and vegetarian dishes. Take the Titanic Challenge – a 48oz (uncooked) rump steak, too big to be cooked 'well done'. Panoramic windows in the main eating area overlook a fountain and pond, and the gardens are a great place for alfresco dining. Friday nights here are devoted to karaoke – you have been warned!

**Open** all day all wk **Bar Meals** L served all wk 12-10 D served all wk 12-10 food served all day **Restaurant** L served all wk 12-10 D served all wk 12-10 food served all day ⊕ KING HENRY'S TAVERNS ◀ Guinness, IPA, Marstons Pedigree. **Facilities** Children's menu Children's portions Play area Family room Garden Parking

## FLECKNEY                Map 11 SP69

### The Old Crown

**High St LE8 8AJ ☎ 0116 240 2223**
**e-mail:** old-crown-inn@fleckney7.freeserve.co.uk
**dir:** Telephone for directions

Close to the Grand Union Canal and Saddington Tunnel, a traditional village pub that is especially welcoming to hiking groups and families. Noted for good real ales and generous opening times (evening meals from 5pm) offering a wide choice of popular food. The garden has lovely views of fields and the canal, as well as a pétanque court.

**Open** all wk ◀ Everards Tiger & Beacon, Courage Directors, Adnams Bitter, Greene King Abbot Ale, Marston's Pedigree. **Facilities** Play area Family room Dogs allowed Garden Parking **Notes** ⊛

## GRIMSTON                Map 11 SK62

### The Black Horse

**3 Main St LE14 3BZ ☎ 01664 812358**
**e-mail:** wymeswold@supanet.com
**dir:** Telephone for directions

A traditional 16th-century coaching inn displaying much cricketing memorabilia in a quiet village with views over the Vale of Belvoir. Overlooking the village green, there are plenty of opportunities for country walks, or perhaps a game of pétanque on the pub's floodlit pitch. Good home-cooked meals with daily specials, including lots of game. Fish choices and specials include monkfish, lemon sole, whole grilled plaice, and Arctic char. There is an alfresco eating area for warmer weather.

**Open** all wk 12-3 6-11 (Sun 12-6) ◀ Adnams, Marston's Pedigree, St Austell Tribute, Belvoir Mild, guest ales ♂ Thatchers Gold. **Facilities** Dogs allowed Garden

## HATHERN                 Map 11 SK52

### The Anchor Inn ♥

**Loughborough Rd LE12 5JB ☎ 01509 842309**
**dir:** M1 junct 24, A6 towards Leicester. Pub 4.5m on left

The Anchor was once a coaching inn, with stables accessed through an archway off what is now the A6.

Alongside a good range of real ales are snacks galore, a lengthy restaurant menu and plenty of vegetarian options. Rosemary and garlic coated brie wedges could be followed with Cajun chicken; fillet steak sizzler; or beef Madras. Unquestionably family-friendly, there's a fenced-off children's play area in the garden.

◀ Everards Tiger, Original, Pitch Black, Abbot Ale. ♥ 20 **Facilities** Play area Garden Parking

## KNOSSINGTON             Map 11 SK80

### The Fox & Hounds ♥

**6 Somerby Rd LE15 8LY ☎ 01664 454676**
**dir:** 4m from Oakham in Knossington

High quality food and helpful, friendly service are the hallmarks of this 500-year-old pub. Set in the village of Knossington close to Rutland Water, the building retains lots of traditional features, and the large rear garden and sitting area are ideal for alfresco summer dining. A typical lunch menu might include grilled lamb rump with ratatouille and tapenade; vegetable tart with Stilton; or salmon with roasted aubergine, red pepper and coriander salsa.

**Open** noon-3 6-11 (Fri noon-3 5-11 Sat-Sun noon-11) Closed: Mon ◀ Bombardier, London Pride, IPA. ♥ 8 **Facilities** Play area Dogs allowed Garden Parking

## LONG CLAWSON            Map 11 SK72

### The Crown & Plough

**East End LE14 4NG ☎ 01664 822322 📠 01664 822322**
**e-mail:** crownandplough@btconnect.com
**dir:** In village centre, 3m from A606 (Melton Mowbray to Nottingham road)

Following an extensive programme of refurbishment, the pub retains the atmosphere of a village local but with a contemporary flavour. It has a good reputation for the quality of its food served from one menu throughout the bar, snug, restaurant and landscaped garden. There's a good choice of fish (pan-fried sea bass with home-made tagliatelle, mussels and clams), and the likes of whole roast partridge with gratin potatoes and Savoy cabbage.

**Open** all wk ◀ Shepherd Neame, Spitfire, Lancaster Bomber, Marstons Pedigree, Adnams Explorer. **Facilities** Garden Parking

## LOUGHBOROUGH            Map 11 SK51

### The Falcon Inn ★★★ INN

**64 Main St, Long Whatton LE12 5DG**
**☎ 01509 842416 📠 01509 646802**
**e-mail:** enquiries@thefalconinnlongwhatton.com
**dir:** Telephone for directions

Decked out with award-winning flower displays in summer, this traditional country inn is just ten minutes' drive from East Midlands airport and the M1. It offers great food, plus stylish en suite accommodation in a converted stable and school house at the rear of the pub. Food choices range from classic pub favourites like filled

jacket potatoes, spare ribs of pork in chilli barbecue sauce or gammon and chips to more exotic dishes including a full Lebanese mezze that reflects the traditions of Lebanese-born proprietor Jad Otaki. There is a beautiful terrace and outside bar. Look out for special events throughout the year.

**Open** all day all wk **Bar Meals** L served Mon-Sat 12-2, Sun 12-4 D served Mon-Sat 6.30-9 **Restaurant** L served Mon-Sat 12-2, Sun 12-4 D served Mon-Sat 6.30-9 booking required ⊕ EVERARDS ◀ Tiger Best Bitter, Everards Original, guest ale. **Facilities** Family room Garden Parking **Rooms** 11

### The Swan in the Rushes ♥

**21 The Rushes LE11 5BE**
**☎ 01509 217014 📠 01509 217014**
**e-mail:** swanintherushes@castlerockbrewery.co.uk
**dir:** On A6 (Derby road). Pub in front of Sainsbury's, 1m from railway station.

A 1930s tile-fronted real ale pub, it was acquired by the Castle Rock chain in 1986, making it the oldest in the group. There's a first-floor drinking terrace, a function room and bar that seats 80, and a family/dining area. This real ale pub with a friendly atmosphere always offers ten ales, including seven guests, a selection of real ciders and fruit wines, and two annual beer festivals. Expect traditional pub grub. Music nights, folk club and a skittle alley complete the picture.

**Open** all day all wk 11-11 (Fri-Sat 11-mdnt Sun noon-11) **Bar Meals** L served all wk 12-3 D served Mon-Fri 5-9.30, Sat 12-9.30 Av main course £6.50 ⊕ CASTLE ROCK ◀ Castle Rock Harvest Pale, Castle Rock Sheriff's Tipple, Adnams Bitter, Castle Rock Elsie Mo, 7 guests ♂ Westons Old Rosie Scrumpy, Broadoak Moonshine. ♥ 12 **Facilities** Children's portions Family room Dogs allowed Parking

## LUTTERWORTH             Map 11 SP58

### Man at Arms ♥

**The Green, Bitteswell LE17 4SB ☎ 01455 552540**
**e-mail:** man@king-henrys-taverns.co.uk
**dir:** From Lutterworth take Lutterworth Rd towards Ullesthorpe. Turn left at small white cottage. Pub on left after college on village green

Named after a bequest left by the Dowse Charity to the nearby village of Bitteswell to provide a 'man at arms' in time of war, this was the first pub bought by the King Henry's Taverns group. Now, after 25 years, the pub shares a common menu with others in the group. Expect some sizeable options, including a pound of lamb chops; Superman's mixed grill; and Cajun chicken and ribs combo.

**Open** all day all wk **Bar Meals** food served all day **Restaurant** Fixed menu price fr £3.50 food served all day ⊕ KING HENRY'S TAVERNS ◀ Greene King IPA, Marstons Pedigree, Guinness. ♥ 16 **Facilities** Children's menu Children's portions Play area Family room Garden Parking

# PICK OF THE PUBS

## The Staff of Life ♉

**MOWSLEY**  Map 11 SP68

**Main St LE17 6NT ☎ 0116 240 2359**
**dir:** *M1 junct 20, A4304 to Market Harborough. Left in Husbands Bosworth onto A5199. In 3m turn right to pub*

Converted from a well-proportioned private Edwardian home, the pub welcomes customers with a small patio area to the front and additional outside seating in the rear garden. The interior has traditional features that include high-backed settles, flagstone floors and a fine wood-panelled ceiling in the bar. Many wines are served by the glass, and there are usually four real ales to choose from.

Carefully prepared and presented dishes mix British and international influences in the dining area, which overlooks the patio garden. The classic pub lunch menu is served from Wednesday to Saturday, and shares choices from the early evening carte that appears from Tuesday to Friday: expect dishes like classic cottage pie with leek and Cheddar topping, gravy and vegetables; beer battered fish, hand cut chips and mushy peas; and penne pasta with red pesto, sun blushed tomatoes, spinach and wild mushrooms.

The more extensive à la carte menu uses seasonal produce, with meats supplied by local butcher Joseph Morris. Start, perhaps, with the likes of garlic king prawns in butter, white wine and chilli, or classic Peking duck pancakes with a julienne of spring onions, cucumber and hoi sin sauce. Main courses might include Shannon beef Wellington with a mushroom, button onion and Burgundy sauce; pan-fried herring fillets with mustard sauce; or roasted

Mediterranean vegetable tarte Tatin with baked camembert, charlotte potatoes and pesto dressing.

Desserts are hand-crafted by Linda O'Neill, a former member of Ireland's Panel of Chefs: choose from individual sticky lemon and raspberry pudding with sauce anglaise; or honeycomb and amaretto cheesecake finished with a tuile biscuit.

**Open** Tue eve-Sun Closed: Mon & Tue L (ex BH) **Bar Meals** L served Wed-Sat 12-2.30, Sun 12-3.30 D served Mon-Sat 6.30-9.30 **Restaurant** L served Wed-Sat 12-2.30, Sun 12-3.30 D served Mon-Sat 6.30-9.30 ⊕ FREE HOUSE ◪ Marstons, guest ales ♂ Thatchers. ♈ 19 **Facilities** Garden Parking

Save on Hotels. Book at theAA.com/hotel

LEICESTERSHIRE 287 ENGLAND

## MOUNTSORREL
Map 11 SK51

### The Swan Inn ★★★★ INN

10 Loughborough Rd LE12 7AT
☎ 0116 230 2340 ▤ 0116 237 6115
e-mail: swan@jvf.co.uk
dir: *On A6 between Leicester & Loughborough*

Originally two 17th-century terraced cottages, this Grade II listed free house stands on the banks of the River Soar in pretty Mountsorrel, midway between Leicester and Loughborough. Expect to find exposed beams, flagstone floors and roaring winter log fires in the cosy bar and dining areas, and a secluded riverside garden for summer sipping. Cask-conditioned beers from Theakstons and Ruddles and fine wines accompany Thai chicken pasta, pheasant with mushrooms, Madeira and cream, and locally farmed Charolais sirloin steak with pepper sauce. Light lunches and snacks include sandwiches and salads. There is a luxury apartment available.

**Open** all wk 12-2.30 5.30-11 (Sat 12-11 Sun 12-3 7-10.30) **Bar Meals** L served all wk 12-2 D served Mon-Sat 6.30-9.30 Av main course £8 **Restaurant** L served all wk 12-2 D served Mon-Sat 6.30-9.30 Fixed menu price fr £10.90 Av 3 course à la carte fr £18 ⊕ FREE HOUSE ◀ Black Sheep Bitter, Theakston's XB, Old Peculier, Ruddles County, Abbot Ale. **Facilities** Dogs allowed Garden Parking **Rooms** 1

## MOWSLEY
Map 11 SP68

### PICK OF THE PUBS

### The Staff of Life ♥

*See Pick of the Pubs on opposite page*

## NETHER BROUGHTON
Map 11 SK62

### The Red House ♥

23 Main St LE14 3HB
☎ 01664 822429 ▤ 01664 823805
e-mail: bernie@mulberrypubco.com
dir: *M1 junct 21A, A46. Right onto A606. Or take A606 from Nottingham*

The Red House is a fine mixture of a 300-year-old village pub (with log fires in winter) and light, contemporary design. The lounge bar opens into an airy restaurant, and a conservatory area overlooks the outdoor bar, terrace and courtyard grill. Immaculate gardens include a small play area and a permanent marquee for weddings, parties and corporate functions. Dishes range from a selection of sandwiches or hot dishes like Guinness and beef sausages with mash and stout gravy in the bar, to roast rump of English lamb, pea mash and confit carrots in the restaurant. An ideal spot for walking, fishing and bird-watching.

**Open** all wk Mon-Thu 7-3 5-11 (Fri-Sun all day) **Bar Meals** L served Mon-Sat 12-3 D served Mon-Sat 5-7.30 Av main course £9.95 food served all day **Restaurant** L served Mon-Sat 12-3, Sun 12-5 D served Mon-Sat 5-9.30 booking required Av 3 course à la carte fr £25 food served all day ⊕ MULBERRY PUB (UK) PLC ◀ Guinness, Belvoir Brewery Cask, Greene King IPA, Ö Jacques. ♥ 20 **Facilities** Children's menu Children's portions Play area Dogs allowed Garden Parking

## NEWTOWN LINFORD
Map 11 SK50

### PICK OF THE PUBS

### The Bradgate ♥

37 Main St LE6 0AE
☎ 01530 242239 ▤ 01530 249391
e-mail: john@thebradgate.co.uk
dir: *M1 junct 22, A50 towards Leicester 1.5m. At 1st rdbt left towards Newton Linford 1.5m, at end of road turn right 0.25m. Pub on right*

Long a favourite with locals and walkers, both as a watering hole and for fine dining. A recent makeover has left the pub with a modern, natural look, partly owing to the extensive use of light wood bar, flooring and furniture, and off-white walls. The food is very much in keeping, meeting the demand for style and innovation on the plate. Start with spiced crab cake, green onion risotto and sweet chilli oil; follow with braised pork with fondant potato and summer cabbage and light apple and white wine sauce; or roast scallops with pak choi and sweet potato; and finish with warm pear galette and almond and Armagnac ice cream. The pub is family friendly with a children's menu and a large play area. Dogs on a lead are welcome in the beer garden.

**Open** all wk winter: 11.30-3 5.30-11 (Sun 12-9) summer: all day, every day ◀ Tiger, Beacon, Original, Guest ales. ♥ 10 **Facilities** Play area Family room Garden Parking

## OADBY
Map 11 SK60

### PICK OF THE PUBS

### Cow and Plough ♥

Gartree Rd, Stoughton Farm LE2 2FB
☎ 0116 272 0852 ▤ 0116 272 0852
e-mail: info@steaminbilly.co.uk
dir: *3m Leicester Station A6 to Oadby. Turn off to Spire Hospital, pub 0.5m beyond*

Formerly a Victorian dairy farm, this much-loved free house dates back to 1989, when licensee Barry Lount approached the owners of Stoughton Grange Farm, who were then in the process of opening the farm to the public. The farm park attraction has since closed, but the Cow and Plough continues to prosper, hosting functions and events such as beer and cider festivals in the former farm buildings. The pub also brews its own award-winning Steamin' Billy beers, named after the owners' Jack Russell terrier. The interior is decorated with historic inn signs and brewing memorabilia, providing a fascinating setting in which to enjoy food from the regularly-changing menus. Typical choices include ham hock and smoked chicken terrine with apple and pear chutney, followed by chicken and mushroom pie with creamy mash; venison with Dijon mash and juniper sauce; and pan-fried halibut with wilted spinach and lemon hollandaise, with vanilla pannacotta and pecan pie with toffee sauce among the pudding choices.

**Open** all day all wk **Bar Meals** L served all wk 12-2.30 D served all wk 6-9 Av main course £6 **Restaurant** L served all wk 12-2.30 D served all wk 6-9 booking required Fixed menu price fr £9.95 Av 3 course à la carte fr £12.95 ⊕ FREE HOUSE ◀ Steamin' Billy Bitter, Steamin' Billy Skydiver, London Pride, Abbeydale, Batemans Mild. ♥ 10 **Facilities** Children's portions Family room Dogs allowed Garden Parking

## OLD DALBY
Map 11 SK62

### PICK OF THE PUBS

### The Crown Inn ♥

Debdale Hill LE14 3LF ☎ 01664 823134
e-mail: oldcrown@castlerockbrewery.co.uk
web: www.crownolddalby.co.uk
dir: *A46 turn for Willoughby/Broughton. Right into Nottingham Ln, left to Old Dalby*

A classic creeper-covered, country pub dating from 1509, set in extensive gardens and orchards, with small rooms, all with open fires. The new owners have returned the pub to its former glory - traditional with a contemporary feel. They place a strong emphasis on fresh seasonal produce: if the food doesn't all come from Leicestershire, the county's suppliers are nonetheless wholeheartedly supported. Expect dishes like pan-fried sea bass with lemon and crayfish risotto, or oven roasted rack and braised shoulder of lamb with minted pea purée.

*continued on page 288*

**OLD DALBY** *continued*

There's a good choice of real ales to help wash down a meal, or to enjoy without food: Castle Rock Hemlock and Harvest Pale are among the selection.

*The Crown Inn*

**Open** all wk noon-close Closed: Mon L ◼ Castle Rock Hemlock, Beaver, Harvest Pale, 3 Guest Ales ♻ Stowford Press. ♟ 10 **Facilities** Family room Dogs allowed Garden Parking

---

### REDMILE                        Map 11 SK73

## Peacock Inn ★★★★ INN

**Church Corner, Main St NG13 0GA**
☎ 01949 842554    📄 01949 843746
**e-mail:** reservations@thepeacockinnredmile.co.uk
**web:** www.thepeacockinnredmile.co.uk
**dir:** *From A1 take A52 towards Nottingham. Turn left, follow signs for Redmile & Belvoir Castle. In Redmile at x-rds turn right. Pub at end of village*

Set beside the Grantham Canal in the Vale of Belvoir, this 16th-century stone-built pub is only two miles from the picturesque castle. The inn has beamed ceilings, cosy open fires and warm and friendly atmosphere. It also has a local reputation for good quality food and real ales, and offers a relaxed setting for wining and dining. The menus are based on local seasonal produce; try torched goat's cheese, apple compote, dressed leaves; steak pudding with chunky chips; wild mushroom risotto; lemon posset, kiwi, and fruit sorbet. There are charming guest rooms if you would like to stay over.

**Open** all day all wk **Bar Meals** L served all wk 12-2.30 D served all wk 6-9 **Restaurant** D served all wk 6-9 ⊕ CHARLES WELLS ◼ Young's Bitter, Bombardier. **Facilities** Children's portions Dogs allowed Garden Parking **Rooms** 10

---

### SADDINGTON                     Map 11 SP69

## The Queens Head

**Main St LE8 0QH** ☎ 0116 240 2536
**dir:** *Between A50 & A6 S of Leicester, NW of Market Harborough*

A traditional prize-winning English pub with terrific views from the restaurant and garden over the Saddington Reservoir. The inn specialises in real ale and good food, with four specials boards to supplement the evening menu. Foil-cooked cod fillet, roast Barbary duck, lamb shank with garlic mash, steak and ale pie, monkfish medallions with Parma ham, and pan-fried tuna steak with sweet pepper and oyster sauce guarantee something for everyone.

**Open** all wk noon-11 (Sun noon-10) ◼ Everards Tiger Best & Beacon Bitter, guests. **Facilities** Garden Parking

---

### SILEBY                          Map 11 SK61

## The White Swan ♟

**Swan St LE12 7NW** ☎ 01509 814832    📄 01509 815995
**dir:** *From Leicester A6 towards Loughborough, turn right for Sileby; or take A46 towards Newark-on-Trent, turn left for Sileby*

Behind the unassuming exterior of this 1930s building, you'll find a free house of some character, with a book-lined restaurant and a homely bar with an open fire. A wide selection of home-made rolls, baguettes and snacks is on offer; menus change twice weekly, and there are blackboard specials, too. Typical main course choices include baked pheasant with chestnut and cranberry stuffing; plaice with prawns in garlic butter; and roast lamb with garlic and rosemary. Tuesdays and Wednesdays are special curry nights.

**Open** Tue-Sun L Closed: 1-7 Jan, (Sun eve & Mon, May-Sep Sun L) **Bar Meals** L served Tue-Sun 12-1 D served Tue-Sat 7-8.30 Av main course £8 **Restaurant** L served Sun 12-1 D served Tue-Sat 7-8.30 Fixed menu price fr £8 Av 3 course à la carte fr £16 ⊕ FREE HOUSE ◼ Marston's Pedigree, Tetley's Cask, Ansells, Fuller's London Pride ♻ Old English. ♟ 8 **Facilities** Garden Parking

---

### SOMERBY                         Map 11 SK71

## Stilton Cheese Inn ♟

**High St LE14 2QB** ☎ 01664 454394
**dir:** *From A606 between Melton Mowbray & Oakham follow signs to Pickwell & Somerby. Enter village, 1st right to centre, pub on left*

This attractive 17th-century inn enjoys a good reputation for its food, great selection of real ales, wine and malt whiskies. Built from mellow local sandstone, it stands in the centre of the village surrounded by beautiful countryside: nearby is Melton Mowbray famous for its pork pies and Stilton cheese, hence the pub's name. An interesting range of food from the regularly-changing specials board includes home-made Stilton and cranberry parcels; monkfish and crayfish tails thermidor; game pie; and butternut squash ravioli.

---

*Stilton Cheese Inn*

**Open** all wk 12-3 6-11 (Sun 7-11) **Bar Meals** L served all wk 12-2 D served Mon-Sat 6-9, Sun 7-9 Av main course £8.95 **Restaurant** L served all wk 12-2 D served Mon-Sat 6-9, Sun 7-9 ⊕ FREE HOUSE ◼ Grainstore Ten Fifty, Brewster's Hophead, Belvoir Star, Tetley's Cask, Marston's Pedigree ♻ Old Rosie, Westons Scrumpy, Bounds Brand. ♟ 15 **Facilities** Children's menu Children's portions Family room Garden Parking

---

### STATHERN                        Map 11 SK73

### PICK OF THE PUBS

## Red Lion Inn ◉ ♟

**Red Lion St LE14 4HS**
☎ 01949 860868    📄 01949 861579
**e-mail:** info@theredlioninn.co.uk
**dir:** *From A1 (Grantham), A607 towards Melton, turn right in Waltham, right at next x-rds then left to Stathern*

Whatever the season, there are treats to be enjoyed at the Red Lion Inn: Pimms on the terrace or Saturday barbecues in the summer, or mulled wine in winter, with chestnuts roasted on the open fires. The pub is located in the beautiful the Vale of Belvoir and comprises a stone-floored bar, a comfortable lounge with plenty of reading material, an elegant dining room and an informal dining area. Menus change daily in accordance with locally supplied produce and the menus offer a mixture of classic pub food and innovative country cooking. Typical dishes are Red Lion fish and chips with tartare sauce and mushy peas; and roast partridge with chestnut cabbage, caramelised pear, bread sauce and game chips. In collaboration with its sister pub, The Olive Branch at Clipsham, Red Olive Foods provides preserves, wholesale wines, hampers and speciality dishes, available to purchase from the pubs. Outside catering can also be arranged.

**Open** 12-3 6-11 (Fri-Sat 12-11, Sun 12-7) Closed: Sun eve **Bar Meals** L served Tue-Sat 12-2, Sun 12-3 booking required D served Tue-Thu 5.30-9, Fri 5.30-9.30, Sat 7-9.30 booking required Av main course £13.50 **Restaurant** L served Tue-Sat 12-2, Sun 12-3 booking required D served Tue-Thu 5.30-9, Fri 5.30-9.30, Sat 7-9.30 booking required Fixed menu price fr £10 Av 3 course à la carte fr £21.50 ⊕ RUTLAND INN COMPANY LTD ◼ Grainstore Red Lion Ale, Brewster's Marquis, London Pride ♻ Aspall, Sheppy. ♟ 8 **Facilities** Dogs allowed Garden Parking

## THORPE LANGTON     Map 11 SP79

### The Bakers Arms ▼

**Main St LE16 7TS** ☎ **01858 545201** 🖹 **01858 545924**
**dir:** *Take A6 S from Leicester then left signed 'The Langtons', at rail bridge continue to x-rds. Straight on to Thorpe Langton. Pub on left*

Set in a pretty village, this thatched pub offers plenty of period charm, with an enthusiastic following. The modern pub food is one of the key attractions, with the menu changing from week to week. Expect dishes like duet of salmon and monkfish with prawn jus or lamb fillet with white onion sauce and pea mash. An intimate atmosphere is created with low beams, rug-strewn quarry-tiled floors, large pine tables, and open fires. The area is popular with walkers, riders and mountain bikers.

**Open** 6.30-11 (12-2.30 wknds) Closed: 1-7 Jan, Sun eve-Mon **Restaurant** L served Sat-Sun 12-2.30 booking required D served Tue-Sat 6.30-9.15 booking required Av main course £14 Av 3 course à la carte fr £23 ⊕ FREE HOUSE ◀ Langton Brewery, Bakers Dozen Bitter. ▼ 9 **Facilities** Garden Parking

## WELHAM     Map 11 SP79

### The Old Red Lion ▼

**Main St LE16 7UJ** ☎ **01858 565253**
**e-mail:** redlion@king-henrys-taverns.co.uk
**dir:** *NE of Market Harborough take B664 to Weston by Welland. Left to Welham*

This old country pub is part of the King Henry's Taverns group. It was once a coaching inn, and the small area opposite the main bar was originally the archway where the coaches would swing in to offload their weary passengers. In winter the leather chesterfields around the log fires create a cosy feel, while in summer take an evening stroll along one of the many footpaths and bridleways. The menu goes in for traditional pub grub, burgers, curries, and vegetarian dishes. For those with a larger appetite it offers the Mary Rose Special, a 16oz T-bone steak.

**Open** all day all wk noon-11 ◀ Greene King IPA, Marstons Pedigree, Guinness. ▼ 15 **Facilities** Play area Family room Parking

## WOODHOUSE EAVES     Map 11 SK51

### The Wheatsheaf Inn ★★★ INN ▼

**Brand Hill LE12 8SS** ☎ **01509 890320**
**e-mail:** richard@wheatsheafinn.net
**dir:** *M1 junct 22, follow Quorn signs*

Around the turn of the 19th century, when local quarrymen wanted somewhere to drink, they built themselves The Wheatsheaf. It's what locals call a Dim's Inn, a succession of pubs run by three generations of the Dimblebee family. With a good selection of real ales, the chalk board always has fresh fish dishes such as grilled sea bass fillets on roasted Mediterranean vegetables with a basil dressing. Other tempting choices might be braised pheasant in red wine and redcurrant, and Spanish style pork in tomato sauce with chorizo and black olives. Three modern en suite bedrooms are available.

**Open** Mon-Sun Closed: Sun eve in winter **Bar Meals** L served Mon-Fri 12-2, Sat 12-2.30, Sun 12-3.30 D served all wk 6.30-9.15 Av main course £10 **Restaurant** L served Mon-Fri 12-2, Sat 12-2.30, Sun 12-3.30 D served all wk 6.30-9.15 Av 3 course à la carte fr £18 ⊕ FREE HOUSE ◀ Greene King Abbot Ale, Draught Burton Ale, Timothy Taylor Landlord, Adnams Broadside, Tetley Smooth, guest ale. ▼ 16 **Facilities** Children's portions Dogs allowed Garden Parking **Rooms** 2

## LINCOLNSHIRE

### ALLINGTON     Map 11 SK84

### The Welby Arms ★★★★ INN ▼

**The Green NG32 2EA**
☎ **01400 281361** 🖹 **01400 281361**
**dir:** *From Grantham take either A1 N, or A52 W. Allington 1.5m*

A creeper-covered inn overlooking the village green, the Welby Arms has a traditional country pub aspect. It is popular with travellers on the A1 as it also provides overnight accommodation. An excellent choice of real ales is offered alongside home-cooked food. Bar snacks take in home-made beef burgers, baguettes and chilli, and there is a full restaurant menu. Specials include steak and kidney pudding or monkfish wrapped in Parma ham with king prawns.

**Open** all wk 12-3 6-11 (Sun 12-10.30) **Bar Meals** L served Mon-Sat 12-2, Sun 12-8.30 D served Mon-Sat 6-9 **Restaurant** L served Mon-Sun 12-2, Sun 12-8.30 booking required D served Mon-Sat 6-9, booking required ⊕ ENTERPRISE INNS ◀ John Smith's, Interbrew Bass, Timothy Taylor Landlord, Jennings Cumberland Ale, Badger Tanglefoot, Adnams Broadside ♂ Stowford Press. ▼ 22 **Facilities** Children's menu Children's portions Garden Parking **Rooms** 3

### ASWARBY     Map 12 TF03

### The Tally Ho Inn

**NG34 8SA** ☎ **01529 455170**
**e-mail:** info@thetallyhoinn.com
**dir:** *3m S of Sleaford on A15 towards Bourne/ Peterborough*

Built from sturdy old pillars and beams and exposed stonework, this handsome, award-winning inn is located on the Aswarby Estate and has strong connections with major hunts and other field sports. The old English garden, complete with fruit trees, overlooks the estate parkland and grazing sheep. Favourite dishes at lunch and dinner include suet pudding with braised beef and mushrooms, and lamb and Stilton casserole. Baguettes and toasted sandwiches are also served at lunchtime.

**Open** noon-2.30 5.30-11 (Tue 6-11 Sun noon-4) Closed: Tue L **Bar Meals** L served Mon-Sat 12-2.30, Sun 12-3.30 D served Mon-Sat 6-9.30 ⊕ FREE HOUSE ◀ Timothy Taylor Landlord, Abbot Ale, Guest Ales ♂ Westons Organic. **Facilities** Children's portions Play area Garden Parking

### BARNOLDBY LE BECK     Map 17 TA20

### The Ship Inn

**Main Rd DN37 0BG** ☎ **01472 822308** 🖹 **01472 823706**
**e-mail:** johnlinecaughtgy@aol.com
**dir:** *M180 junct 5, A18 past Humberside Airport. At Laceby Junction rdbt (A18 & A46) straight over follow Skegness/Boston signs. Approx 2m turn left signed Waltham & Barnoldby le Beck*

Set in a picturesque village just five miles from Grimsby, this 300-year-old inn specialises in fresh seafood brought in daily by its own fishing boats. The bar is filled with maritime bric-a-brac, and there's a beautiful garden outside. The line-caught fish options, such as plaice fillet with cheese, cherry tomato and herb crust, are supplemented by a range of freshly-made sandwiches, as well as hot dishes such as the Ship's special beef and ale pie, or mushroom and pepper stroganoff.

**Open** all wk 12-3 6-12 **Bar Meals** L served all wk 12-2 D served all wk 6.30-9.30 booking required Av main course £15 **Restaurant** L served all wk 12-2 booking required D served all wk 6.30 booking required Av 3 course à la carte fr £25 ⊕ INNOVATIVE SIGHT LTD ◀ Black Sheep Best, Tetley's Smooth, Boddingtons, Guinness, Tom Woods Bomber County. **Facilities** Children's portions Garden Parking

## BELCHFORD　　　　　Map 17 TF27

### The Blue Bell Inn

**1 Main Rd LN9 6LQ** ☎ **01507 533602**
dir: *Off A153 between Horncastle & Louth*

Located on the Viking Way in the heart of the Lincolnshire
Wolds, this welcoming free house is run by husband and
wife team Darren and Shona Jackson. Inside, expect
comfy armchairs and chalkboard menus, well kept real
ales and a wide selection of wines. Tempting lunchtime
ciabatta rolls come with Kettle chips, salad and home-
made coleslaw, whilst hot dishes range from spiced lamb
shank in white wine to twice-baked Stilton soufflé and
Waldorf salad.

**Open** Tue-Sun L Closed: 2nd & 3rd wk Jan, Sun eve-Mon
**Bar Meals** L served Tue-Sun 12-2 D served Tue-Sat
6.30-9 **Restaurant** L served Tue-Sun 12-2 D served Tue-
Sat 6.30-9 ⊕ FREE HOUSE ◀ Black Sheep, Timothy Taylor
Landlord, guest ale. **Facilities** Garden Parking

## BOURNE　　　　　Map 12 TF02

### The Wishing Well Inn

**Main St, Dyke PE10 0AF**
☎ **01778 422970** 🖷 **01778 394508**
**e-mail:** wishingwell@hotmail.com
dir: *Take A15 towards Sleaford. Inn in next village*

This Lincolnshire village free house started life in 1879
as a one-room pub called the Crown. Several extensions
have since been sympathetically executed with recycled
stone and timbers; the well that gives the pub its name,
previously in the garden, is now a feature of the smaller
dining room. Loyal customers return again and again to
enjoy a comprehensive menu of traditional favourites in
the warm and welcoming atmosphere. Outside, an
attractive beer garden backs onto the children's play
area.

**Open** all wk 11-3 5-11 (Fri-Sat 11-mdnt Sun & summer
all wk 11-11) **Bar Meals** L served Mon-Thu 12-2.30, Fri-
Sun 12-9 D served Mon-Thu 5.30-9, Fri-Sun 12-9 ⊕ FREE
HOUSE ◀ Greene King Abbot Ale, Spitfire, 3 guest ales.
**Facilities** Play area Dogs allowed Garden Parking

## BRIGG　　　　　Map 17 TA00

### The Jolly Miller

**Brigg Rd, Wrawby DN20 8RH** ☎ **01652 655658**
dir: *1.5m E of Brigg on A18, on left*

Popular country inn a few miles south of the Humber
Estuary. The pleasant bar and dining area are traditional
in style, and there's a large beer garden. The menu offers
a good range of food: tuck into a chip butty; vegetable
burger bap; home-made curry; or steak with onion rings.
Puddings include hot chocolate fudge cake and banana
split. Play area and children's menu. Coach parties
accepted with advanced booking.

**Open** all wk ◀ Guinness, John Smith's Extra Smooth, 2
guest ales. **Facilities** Play area Garden Parking

## CONINGSBY　　　　　Map 17 TF25

### The Lea Gate Inn

**Leagate Rd LN4 4RS**
☎ **01526 342370** 🖷 **01526 345468**
**e-mail:** theleagateinn@hotmail.com
**web:** www.the-leagate-inn.co.uk
dir: *Off B1192 just outside Coningsby*

The oldest licensed premises in the county, dating from
1542, this was the last of the Fen Guide Houses that
provided shelter before the treacherous marshes were
drained. The oak-beamed pub has a priest's hole and a
very old inglenook fireplace among its features. The same
family have been running the pub for over 25 years. Both
the bar and restaurant serve food and offer seasonal
menus with lots of local produce (including game in
season) and great fish choices, such as freshwater trout
and lobster.

**Open** all wk 11.30-3 6-11 (Sun 12-10.30) **Bar Meals** L
served Mon-Sat 11.30-2.15, Sun 12-9 D served Mon-Sat
6-9 Av main course £9 **Restaurant** L served Mon-Sat
11.30-2.15, Sun 12-9 D served Mon-Sat 6-9 Av 3 course
à la carte fr £20 ⊕ FREE HOUSE ◀ Theakston's XB,
Bombardier, guest ales. **Facilities** Children's menu Play
area Garden Parking

## DONINGTON ON BAIN　　　　　Map 17 TF28

### The Black Horse Inn ★★★ INN

**Main Rd LN11 9TJ** ☎ **01507 343640** 🖷 **01507 343640**
**e-mail:** mike@blackhorse-donington.co.uk
dir: *Telephone for directions*

Ideal for walkers, this old-fashioned country pub is set in
a small village in the heart of the Lincolnshire Wolds on
the Viking Way. A large grassed area surrounded by trees
is ideal for enjoying a drink or dining alfresco on sunny
days. Dining options include the dining room, the Blue
Room, and the Viking Snug. There are eight spacious
bedrooms if you would like to stay over.

**Open** all wk ◀ John Smith's, Greene King, Theakstons.
**Facilities** Dogs allowed Garden Parking **Rooms** 8

## FROGNALL　　　　　Map 12 TF11

### The Goat

**155 Spalding Rd PE6 8SA** ☎ **01778 347629**
**e-mail:** graysdebstokes@btconnect.com
dir: *A1 to Peterborough, A15 to Market Deeping, old A16
to Spalding, pub approx 1.5m from A15 & A16 junct*

Families are welcome at this cosy, friendly country free
house, which has an open fire, large beer garden and
plenty to amuse the children. Main courses include beef
stroganoff; pork in sweet and sour sauce; leek and
mushroom pie; warm bacon and Stilton salad; and home-
made prawn curry. Beer is taken seriously, with five
different guest ales each week and regular beer festivals
throughout the year. There's a good choice of ciders too,
such as Weston's Old Rosie, Broadoak Moonshine and
Thatchers Cheddar Valley.

**Open** all wk 11.30-3 6-11.30 (Sun noon-11) Closed: 25
Dec, 1 Jan **Bar Meals** L served Mon-Sat 12-2 booking
required D served Mon-Sat 6.30-9.30, Sun 12-9 booking
required **Restaurant** L served Mon-Sat 12-2, Sun 12-9
booking required D served Mon-Sat 6.30-9.30, Sun 12-9
booking required ⊕ FREE HOUSE ◀ Guest ales: Elgoods,
Batemans, Abbeydale, Nethergate, Hopshackle
♻ Westons Old Rosie, Broadoak Moonshine, Thatchers
Cheddar Valley. **Facilities** Children's menu Children's
portions Play area Family room Garden Parking

## GREATFORD          Map 12 TF01

# The Hare and Hounds NEW

**Main St PE9 4QA ☎ 01778 560332**
**e-mail:** agdixey@hotmail.co.uk
**dir:** From A16 at West Deeping turn into Kings St, N towards Bourne. In 2.5m 2nd left signed Greatford. 0.5m. Pub at W end of Main St

The stone-built south Lincolnshire village of Greatford is the location for this lovely old-world pub, with its stone fireplaces, wooden beams and traditional sofas. It is also where Andrew and Gemma Dixey have built a reputation for their home-made pub food, friendly atmosphere and variety of beers such as Digfield Shacklebush. Bar snacks include the pub's own crisps, filled baps, soups and pasta dishes, all home made from scratch, with main courses like landlord's beef 'n' ale casserole which comes with a complimentary side order, or Thai green chicken curry. The pub also offers a peaceful summer beer garden and a small a caravan and camping site.

**Open** Tue 6-11 Wed-Fri 12-2 6-11 Sat 12-3 6-11 Sun 12-6 Closed: Sun eve, Mon, Tue L **Bar Meals** L served Tue-Fri 12-2, Sat 12-2.30, Sun 12-4 D served Tue-Sat 6-9 Av main course £4.50 **Restaurant** L served Tue-Fri 12-2, Sat 12-2.30, Sun 12-4 D served Tue-Sat 6-9 Fixed menu price fr £11.50 Av 3 course à la carte fr £15 ⊕ FREE HOUSE ◀ Black Sheep, Digfield Shacklebush, Elgood's Cambridge Bitter, Guinness ♂ Jollydale, Thatchers Gold, Thatchers Katy. **Facilities** Children's menu Children's portions Play area Garden Parking

## HOUGH-ON-THE-HILL          Map 11 SK94

# The Brownlow Arms ★★★★★ INN ⊛

**High Rd NG32 2AZ ☎ 01400 250234  ▤ 01400 251993**
**e-mail:** armsinn@yahoo.co.uk
**web:** www.thebrownlowarms.com
**dir:** Take A607 (Grantham to Sleaford road). Hough-on-the-Hill signed from Barkston

In the heart of a picturesque village, this 17th-century stone inn is named after former owner Lord Brownlow and still looks like a well-tended country house. Enjoy a glass of real ale in the friendly bar while perusing the menu. Modern classic dishes includes pan-fried rib-eye steak, cracked black peppercorns, chopped shallots, Armagnac and cream, and fillet of salmon, new season asparagus and lemon hollandaise. Alfresco dining can be enjoyed on the landscaped terrace. Take advantage of one of the four en suite double bedrooms.

**Open** Tue-Sat 6pm-11pm, Sun L Closed: 25-27 Dec, 1-20 Jan, 1wk Sep, Mon, Sun eve **Restaurant** L served Sun 12-2.15 booking required D served Tue-Sat 6.30-9.30 booking required ⊕ FREE HOUSE ◀ Timothy Taylor Landlord, Marston's Pedigree. **Facilities** Garden Parking **Rooms** 4

## KIRTON IN LINDSEY          Map 17 SK99

# The George

**20 High St DN21 4LX ☎ 01652 640600**
**e-mail:** enquiry@thegeorgekirton.co.uk
**dir:** From A15 take B1205, turn right onto B1400

Extensively restored in a modern traditional style by Glen and Neil McCartney, The George is an 18th-century former coaching inn offering locally brewed Bateman's ales and seasonally changing menus. From traditional Lincolnshire sausages with mash and gravy in the bar, the choice extends to beef stroganoff, braised lamb shank with mint pea sauce and rib-eye steak with peppercorn sauce. For pudding, indulge in sticky toffee pudding. A children's menu is available. Lincoln and The Wolds are within easy reach.

**Open** all wk 12-2 5-11 (Sun 11-3) **Bar Meals** Av main course £7.95 food served all day **Restaurant** Fixed menu price fr £9.95 food served all day ⊕ FREE HOUSE ◀ Batemans XB. **Facilities** Children's menu Children's portions Play area Garden

## LINCOLN          Map 17 SK97

# Pyewipe Inn

**Fossebank, Saxilby Rd LN1 2BG**
**☎ 01522 528708  ▤ 01522 525009**
**e-mail:** enquiries@pyewipe.co.uk
**dir:** From Lincoln on A57 past Lincoln/A46 Bypass, pub signed in 0.5m

First licensed in 1778, the Pyewipe (local dialect for lapwing) stands in four acres alongside the Roman-built Fossedyke Navigation. From the grounds there's a great view of nearby Lincoln Cathedral. All food is bought locally and prepared by qualified chefs. With a selection of menu boards to choose from, expect shank of lamb on a root vegetable mash with rosemary and red wine jus; or Mediterranean vegetable and feta cheese filo parcel in a sun-blushed tomato sauce. There is a beer garden where you can enjoy your meal or one of the regularly beers such as Everards Tiger.

**Open** all day all wk 11-11 **Bar Meals** Av main course £10.50 food served all day **Restaurant** Av 3 course à la carte fr £18.50 food served all day ⊕ FREE HOUSE ◀ Timothy Taylor Landlord, Greene King Abbot Ale, Shepherds Neame Spitfire, Everards Tiger. **Facilities** Dogs allowed Garden Parking

---

# The Victoria ♥

**6 Union Rd LN1 3BJ ☎ 01522 541000**
**e-mail:** jonathanjpc@aol.com
**dir:** From city outskirts follow signs for Cathedral Quarter. Pub 2 mins' walk from all major up-hill car parks

Situated right next to the Westgate entrance of the Castle and within a stone's throw of Lincoln Cathedral, a long-standing drinkers' pub with a range of real ales, including six changing guest beers, ciders and perries, as well as two beer festivals a year. As well as the fantastic views of the castle, the pub also offers splendid meals made from exclusively home-prepared food including hot baguettes and filled bacon rolls, Saturday breakfast and Sunday lunches. House specials include sausage and mash, various pies, chilli con carne and home-made lasagne.

**Open** all day all wk 11-mdnt (Fri-Sat 11-1am) ◀ Timothy Taylor Landlord, Batemans XB, Castle Rock Harvest Pale, guest ales ♂ Westons. ♥ 10 **Facilities** Play area Dogs allowed Garden Parking

## PICK OF THE PUBS

# Wig & Mitre ♥

**32 Steep Hill LN2 1LU**
**☎ 01522 535190  ▤ 01522 532402**
**e-mail:** email@wigandmitre.com
**dir:** At top of Steep Hill, adjacent to cathedral & Lincoln Castle car parks

This reassuringly civilised free house has been owned and operated by the same family since 1977. Standing on the Pilgrim Way in the heart of medieval Lincoln, the building is a mix of the 14th and 16th centuries with some more recent parts, too. There's never any music, but you will find a reading room, and real ales like Black Sheep and Batemans XB are on tap. The food service runs from 8.30am to around midnight daily throughout the year, with a comprehensive breakfast menu served until noon. Hot and cold sandwiches are amongst the lighter options, which also include a minute fillet au poivre with vegetables and potato. Daily specials might begin with roast plum tomato soup with balsamic and basil oil, followed by stuffed roast chicken thigh with tarragon mousse, herb mash and buttered beans. Round things off, perhaps, with lemon posset and blueberry compote.

**Open** all day all wk 8.30am-mdnt **Bar Meals** L served all wk 8-11 D served all wk 8-11 Av main course £13.50 **Restaurant** L served all wk 8-11 booking required D served all wk 8-11 booking required Fixed menu price fr £17.50 Av 3 course à la carte fr £20.20 ⊕ FREE HOUSE ◀ Black Sheep Special, Batemans XB, Youngs London Gold. **Facilities** Children's portions Dogs allowed

## LITTLE BYTHAM — Map 11 TF01

### The Willoughby Arms ♟

**Station Rd NG33 4RA** ☎ 01780 410276
**e-mail:** info@willoughbyarms.co.uk
**dir:** *B6121 (Stamford to Bourne road), at junct follow signs to Careby/Little Bytham, inn 5m on right*

Originally built as the booking office and waiting room for Lord Willoughby's private railway line, this 150 year-old traditional stone, beamed free house is popular with locals and travellers alike. Recently refurbished the pub has a fresher look whilst retaining its traditional charms. Expect a good selection of real ales - including several from local micro-breweries - with great, home-cooked food available every lunchtime and evening. As well as sea bass with cherry tomato sauce, or spicy king prawn curry, expect a range of simple but delicious pub food. There is a large beer garden with stunning views to enjoy on warmer days.

**Open** all day all wk noon–11 **Bar Meals** L served Mon-Sat 12-2, Sun 12-4 D served all wk 6-9 Av main course £8 ⊕ FREE HOUSE ◀ White Hart, Batemans XB, Absolution Ŏ Old Rosie. ♟ 10 **Facilities** Children's menu Children's portions Dogs allowed Garden Parking

## LOUTH — Map 17 TF38

### Masons Arms

**Cornmarket LN11 9PY**
☎ 01507 609525 ▤ 0870 7066450
**e-mail:** info@themasons.co.uk
**dir:** *In town centre*

This Grade II listed building, located in the heart of Georgian Louth, dates back to 1725. In the days when it was known as the Bricklayers Arms, the local Masonic lodge met here. The real ale award-winning Market Bar is for beer lovers, while the 'upstairs' restaurant offers an à la carte menu where you might find honey roast ham, fried egg and home-made chips; steak and kidney pie; and cauliflower cheese.

**Open** all wk ◀ Abbeydale Moonshine, Marston's Pedigree, Batemans XB Bitter, XXXB, 2 guest ales.

## MARKET RASEN — Map 17 TF18

### The Black Horse Inn ♟

**Magna Mile LN8 6AJ**
☎ 01507 313645 ▤ 01507 313645
**e-mail:** reedannam@aol.com
**dir:** *In village on A631, between Louth & Market Rasen*

A strong suite of mostly Lincolnshire micro-brewery beers welcomes visitors to this village inn at the heart of the Lincolnshire Wolds. Comfy contemporary furnishings and open fires blend easily with displays recalling 101 Squadron, based at nearby Ludford Magna airfield in WW2. Diners can enjoy an eclectic menu of home-made, locally sourced meals: perhaps a salad of local smoked eel with apple, walnut and lemon dressing or ragout of hare (a tomato and red wine based stew finished with

chocolate) followed by a chocolate, prune and Armagnac torte with crème fraîche.

**Open** 12-2.30 6-10 Closed: 2wks Jan, Sun eve-Mon **Bar Meals** L served Tue-Sat 12-2.30, Sun 12-3 D served Tue-Sat 6-10 Av main course £10 **Restaurant** L served Tue-Sat 12-2.30, Sun 12-3 D served Tue-Sat 6-10 Av 3 course à la carte fr £15.40 ⊕ FREE HOUSE ◀ Tom Woods Best, Great Newsome, Pricky Back Otchan, Poachers Monkey Hanger Ŏ Westons Scrumpy, Skidbrooke Cyder. ♟ 13 **Facilities** Children's portions Garden Parking

## NEWTON — Map 12 TF03

### The Red Lion

**NG34 0EE** ☎ 01529 497256
**dir:** *10m E of Grantham on A52*

Dating from the 17th century, the Red Lion is particularly popular with walkers and cyclists, perhaps because the flat Lincolnshire countryside makes for easy exercise. Low beams, exposed stone walls and an open fire in the bar help to create a very atmospheric interior. Popular dishes include haddock in beer batter, lemon sole with parsley butter sauce, breadcrumbed scampi, and home-made steak and ale pie. The carvery serves cold buffets on weekdays, hot ones on Friday and Saturday evenings, and Sunday lunchtime.

**Open** 12-3 6-11 Closed: Sun eve & Mon eve **Bar Meals** Av main course £12 **Restaurant** Av 3 course à la carte fr £20 ⊕ FREE HOUSE **Facilities** Dogs allowed Garden Parking

## PARTNEY — Map 17 TF46

### Red Lion Inn

**PE23 4PG** ☎ 01790 752271 ▤ 01790 753360
**e-mail:** enquiries@redlioninnpartney.co.uk
**dir:** *On A16 from Boston, or A158 from Horncastle*

This peaceful village inn at the foot of the Lincolnshire Wolds is warmly welcoming, so walkers and cyclists take refreshment here between visits to the nearby nature reserves and sandy beaches. Two real ales are always on tap, with ciders, lagers, and a good choice of wines too. The pub also has an excellent reputation for good home-cooked food: starters such as breaded butterfly prawns; main courses of beef casserole and Stilton cheese; and specials such as oven-baked fresh trout.

**Open** all wk 12-2 6-11 **Bar Meals** L served Mon-Sat 12-2, Sun 12-9 D served Mon-Sat 6-9.30 Av main course £7.50 **Restaurant** L served Mon-Sat 12-2, Sun 12-9 D served Mon-Sat 6-9.30 ⊕ FREE HOUSE ◀ Black Sheep, Guinness, Tetley's, Guest ales Ŏ Westons' 1st Quality Draught. **Facilities** Children's portions Garden Parking

## RAITHBY — Map 17 TF36

### Red Lion Inn

**PE23 4DS** ☎ 01790 753727
**dir:** *A158 from Horncastle, right at Sausthorpe, left to Raithby*

Traditional beamed black-and-white village pub, parts of which date back 300 years. Log fires provide a warm welcome in winter. A varied menu of home-made dishes includes sea bass with lime stir fry vegetables, roast guinea fowl with tomato, garlic and bacon, and medallions of beef with peppercorn sauce. Meals can be taken in the garden in the warmer months.

**Open** all wk 12-2 6-11 (Mon 6-11) **Bar Meals** L served Tue-Sun 12-2 D served Tue-Sun 7-8.30 **Restaurant** L served Tue-Sun 12-2 D served Tue-Sun 7-8.30 ⊕ FREE HOUSE ◀ Theakston, Dixons. **Facilities** Children's menu Children's portions Garden Parking

## SKEGNESS — Map 17 TF56

### Best Western Vine Hotel ★★★ HL ♟

**Vine Rd, Seacroft PE25 3DB**
☎ 01754 763018 & 610611 ▤ 01754 769845
**e-mail:** info@thevinehotel.com
**dir:** *In Seacroft area of Skegness. S of town centre*

Substantially unchanged since 1770, the Vine is the second oldest building in Skegness. Set amid two acres of gardens, the ivy-covered hotel was bought by the brewer Harry Bateman in 1927. This charming hostelry offers comfortable accommodation and a fine selection of Bateman's own ales. The bar menu ranges from soup or a simple sandwich to bistro-style salads and substantial mixed grills; there's a traditional Sunday carvery, too.

**Open** all wk ◀ Bateman's XB & XXXB, Valiant, Black Sheep, Dixon's ale. ♟ 8 **Facilities** Dogs allowed Garden Parking **Rooms** 25

## SOUTH RAUCEBY — Map 11 TF04

### PICK OF THE PUBS

### The Bustard Inn & Restaurant ◉ ♟

**44 Main St NG34 8QG** ☎ 01529 488250
**e-mail:** info@thebustardinn.co.uk
**dir:** *A15 from Lincoln. Right onto B1429 for Cranwell, 1st left after village, straight across A17*

This attractive stone free house was built in 1860 by the owners of nearby Rauceby Hall, who demolished a former hostelry to make way for a new south gate. According to legend, England's last great bustard had been shot locally a few years earlier, hence the inn's unusual name. Since buying the pub in 2006, Alan and Liz Hewitt have renovated the building to bring out its best features, especially the courtyard, old brewhouse and the ornate oriel window overlooking the beer garden. In the bar a pint of the whimsically named Cheeky Bustard might accompany a Bustard ploughman's with pork pie, terrine, cheeses and pickles, or a 100 per cent Lincolnshire beef burger.

Save on Hotels. Book at **theAA.com/hotel**

**LINCOLNSHIRE** 293 ENGLAND

Meanwhile, an à la carte restaurant meal could begin with Parma ham and goat's cheese salad, followed by roast guinea fowl with leek and pasta ribbons. Warm treacle sponge with crème anglaise rounds things off nicely.

Open 12-3 5.30-11 (Sun 12-3.30) Closed: Sun eve, Mon Bar Meals L served Tue-Sat 12-2.30, Sun 12-3 D served Tue-Sat 6-9.30 Av main course £10 Restaurant L served Tue-Sat 12-2.30, Sun 12-3 D served Tue-Sat 6-9.30 Av 3 course à la carte fr £33 ⊕ FREE HOUSE ◀ Bateman's GHA, Guinness, Cheeky Bustard, Guest ale. ♀ 12 Facilities Children's portions Garden Parking

## Blue Cow Inn & Brewery

High St NG33 5QB ☎ 01572 768432 ▤ 01572 768432
e-mail: enquiries@bluecowinn.co.uk
dir: Between Stamford & Grantham on A1

Low beams, pillars, flagged floors and dressed-stone walls characterise this partly medieval building that has been a pub for over 400 years. Cracking log fires take the edge off the fenland breezes; any remaining chill may be generated by the pub's ghosts – a lady and a dog. Licensee Simon Crathorn brews his own award-winning beers here; just ask if you would like to see the brewery. The inn has a colourful patio beer garden for warm evenings.

Open all day all wk 11-11 Bar Meals Av main course £7.50 food served all day Restaurant Fixed menu price fr £10 Av 3 course à la carte fr £20 food served all day ⊕ FREE HOUSE Facilities Children's menu Children's portions Family room Dogs allowed Garden Parking

## The George of Stamford ★★★ HL ⊛ ♀

71 St Martins PE9 2LB
☎ 01780 750750 ▤ 01780 750701
e-mail: reservations@georgehotelofstamford.com
dir: From Peterborough take A1 N. Onto B1081 for Stamford, down hill to lights. Hotel on left

A walled monastery garden, log fires and oak-panelled restaurant are all part of the traditional charm at this magnificent 16th-century coaching inn. Two doors near the entrance, marked 'London' and 'York', open into the panelled rooms once used by passengers awaiting the

coaches that changed horses in the hotel's cobbled courtyard. Despite the essentially traditional style, today's visitors will appreciate the up-to-date comfort, cuisine and service. Various menus are available: head for the York Bar for soup, sandwiches, and a substantial ploughman's with Dickinson and Morris pork pie and Colston Basset Stilton. Meanwhile, in the bistro-style restaurant the food ranges from smoked duck salad with orange and honey mustard dressing; to pan-fried bream with courgette rösti, confit tomato and parsley oil; and pea and basil risotto with sunblushed tomatoes and basil crisps. The hotel has 47 individually designed, well-equipped bedrooms.

Open all day all wk 11-11 (Sun 12-11) Bar Meals L served all wk 11.30-2.30 Av main course £7.85 Restaurant L served all wk 12-2.30 (Garden Lounge all wk 12-11) booking required D served all wk 7-10.30 booking required Fixed menu price fr £20.75 Av 3 course à la carte fr £42 food served all day ⊕ FREE HOUSE ◀ Adnams Broadside, Ruddles Bitter, Grainstore Brewery ♂ Aspall Suffolk Cider. ♀ 15 Facilities Dogs allowed Garden Parking Rooms 47

## The Tobie Norris ♀ NEW

12 Saint Pauls St PE9 2BE ☎ 01780 482256
e-mail: info@tobienorris.com
dir: From A1 to Stamford on A6121, which becomes West St, then East St. After right bend turn right into Saint Pauls St

Dating back to 1280 when it was a built as a medieval hall, 12 St Pauls Street has only been a pub since 2006. Named after a bell founder who lived in the property in the 16th century, The Tobie Norris has won awards for its renovation and the seven rooms set across three floors have been sympathetically restored. This free house pub offers a fine range of real ales and one of them is always White Hart, brewed by the pub's own Ufford Ales brewery six miles away. The kitchen specialises in stone-baked pizzas, cooked in specially imported Italian ovens, and you can choose your own toppings – anything from flaked duck breast to Ufford Ale meatballs. There is also a full menu of seasonal Italian-inspired specials and typical dishes include buffalo mozzarella and aubergine ragu; linguine fruits de mer, and Stilton and black pudding burgers.

Open all day all wk Bar Meals L served Mon-Fri 12-2.30, Sat-Sun 12-3 D served Mon Thu 6-9 Av main course £10 ⊕ FREE HOUSE ◀ Ufford Ales White Hart, Adnams Bitter, Guest ales ♂ Aspalls, Jollydale. ♀ 18 Facilities Dogs allowed Garden

## The Ship Inn

154 Reservoir Rd PE11 4DH
☎ 01775 680547 ▤ 01775 680541
e-mail: shipsurfleet@hotmail.com
dir: Off A16 (Spalding to Boston). Follow tourist signs towards Surfleet Reservoir then The Ship Inn signs

A fenland pub by the lock gates controlling the Rivers Glen and Welland, and Vernatti's Drain. Dating from only 2003, it occupies the footprint of an earlier hostelry, which the drainage-fixated Vernatti built in 1642. The bar is panelled in hand-crafted oak, while upstairs is the restaurant overlooking the marshes. Locally sourced food includes Whitby scampi; home-made pies; roast rib of Lincolnshire beef; and pan-fried salmon in the restaurant.

Open all wk 11-3 5-mdnt (Sat-Sun 11am-mdnt) ◀ Hydes Smooth, local micro-breweries. Facilities Dogs allowed Parking

## The Jenny Wren Inn

East Ferry Rd DN17 3AS ☎ 01724 784000
e-mail: info@jennywreninn.co.uk
dir: Telephone for directions

It's easy to imagine an 18th-century farmer, tankard in hand, in front of the open fire looking forward to his simple supper in this beamed, wood-panelled former farmhouse. Fast forward to what, for him, would be an unimaginable choice: a pint of Theakston's or Tom Wood, with Atlantic wholetail scampi; beer-battered haddock and chips; Lincolnshire sausages with mash and onion gravy; or home-braised lamb shank in red wine. Specials include line caught fish and the pub's calamari is renowned. The River Trent flows passed the front.

Open all wk Mon-Thu 11.30-3 4.30-10.30 Fri-Sun 11.30-10.30 Bar Meals L served Mon-Thu 12-2, Fri-Sun 12-9 booking required D served Mon-Thu 5.45-9, Fri-Sun 12-9 booking required Av main course £10 food served all day Restaurant L served Mon-Thu 12-2, Fri-Sun 12-9 booking required D served Mon-Thu 5.45-9, Fri-Sun 12-9 booking required Fixed menu price fr £9.95 Av 3 course à la carte fr £20 ⊕ FREE HOUSE ◀ Old Speckled Hen, IPA Bitter, Theakstons, Tom Wood. Facilities Children's menu Children's portions Dogs allowed Garden Parking

## The Penny Farthing Inn ★★★★ INN NEW

4 Station Rd LN4 3SA
☎ 01526 378359 ▤ 01526 378915
dir: From Sleaford take A153, left onto B1189. At junct with B1191 follow signs for Timberland

Located just outside Lincoln in a charming village, this popular and friendly pub is worth noting if you're looking for a comfortable and informal inn as a base from which *continued*

**TIMBERLAND *continued***

to explore the city and cathedral. En suite rooms are well appointed and equipped with flat-screen TV and Wi-fi, and the seasonal dinner menu is worth staying in for. Follow duck rillette with a watercress and rocket salad and plum chutney, with roast pork belly with fennel, bacon and cider jus, and baked chocolate tart with vanilla ice cream.

**Open** all day all wk **Bar Meals** L served all wk 12-6 D served all wk 12-9 **Restaurant** L served all wk 12-9 booking required D served all wk 12-9 booking required Fixed menu price fr £9.75 Av 3 course à la carte fr £20 FREE HOUSE Spitfire, John Smith's, Timothy Taylor Landlord, Bombardier. **Facilities** Children's portions Dogs allowed Garden Parking **Rooms** 7

**WOODHALL SPA** Map 17 TF16

## Village Limits Country Pub, Restaurant & Motel

**Stixwould Rd LN10 6UJ ☎ 01526 353312**
**e-mail:** info@villagelimits.co.uk
**dir:** *At rdbt on main street follow Petwood Hotel signs. Motel 500yds past Petwood Hotel*

The pub and restaurant are situated in the original part of the building, so expect bare beams and old world charm. Typical meals, championing the ingredients of many local Lincolnshire suppliers, include chicken and avocado salad; or smoked trout and salmon pâté; followed by home-made steak and ale pie; or slow roast belly pork with plum and apple sauce. Finish with bread and butter pudding. There's a good choice of real ales to wash it all down.

**Open** 11.30-3 6.30-11 Closed: Mon L **Bar Meals** L served Tue-Sun 11.30-2 booking required D served all wk 6.30-9 booking required **Restaurant** L served Tue-Sun 11.30-2 booking required D served all wk 6.30-9 booking required FREE HOUSE Batemans XB, Tetley's Smooth Flow, Highwood Tom Wood's Best, Fulstow IPA, Dixon's Major Bitter. **Facilities** Children's portions Garden Parking

**WOOLSTHORPE** Map 11 SK83

**PICK OF THE PUBS**

## The Chequers Inn ★★★★ INN

**Main St NG32 1LU ☎ 01476 870701**
**e-mail:** justinnabar@yahoo.co.uk
**dir:** *Approx 7m from Grantham. 3m from A607. Follow heritage signs to Belvoir Castle*

Modern style and traditional features rub along happily together in this atmospheric inn just a stone's throw from Belvoir Castle. The interior is warmed by five real fires, and there are further delights outside, including a cricket pitch, pétanque, and castle views from the mature garden. For refreshment, the fully-stocked bar meets every whim and taste, from ales to single malts. You can eat here too if you like, or try the Bakehouse Restaurant, which contains the oven from the pub's previous incarnation as the village bakery, built in 1646. Expect sophisticated pub food along the lines of winter broth of braised lamb and pearl barley, or risotto of king prawn and deep fried ginger to start, followed by loin of venison, blue cheese polenta, curly kale and peppered sauce; or red Thai vegetable curry with jasmine rice. Pub classics include beer-battered haddock, hand-cut chips and home-made tartare sauce; and David Cox of Stathern sausages, mash and onion gravy. Comfortable bedrooms can be found in the former stable block.

**Open** all wk Mon-Fri 12-3 5.30-11 (all day Sat-Sun) Closed: 25 eve & 26 eve Dec, 1 Jan eve **Bar Meals** L served Mon-Sat 12-2.30, Sun 12-4 D served Mon-Sat 6-9.30, Sun 6-8.30 Av main course £10 **Restaurant** L served Mon-Sat 12-2.30, Sun 12-4 D served Mon-Sat 6-9.30, Sun 6-8.30 Fixed menu price fr £16.50 Av 3 course à la carte fr £24.50 FREE HOUSE Woodforde's Wherry, Batemans ales Aspall, Old Rosie Scrumpy. 25 **Facilities** Children's menu Children's portions Family room Dogs allowed Garden Parking **Rooms** 4

# LONDON

**E1**

## Town of Ramsgate PLAN 2 F4

**62 Wapping High St E1W 2NP ☎ 020 7481 8000**
**dir:** *0.3m from Wapping tube station & Tower of London*

A 500-year-old pub close to The City, decorated with bric-a-brac and old prints. Judge Jeffries was caught here while trying to flee the country and escape the kind of justice he dealt out. Press gangs used to work the area, imprisoning men overnight in the cellar. The owners continue to serve a good selection of real ales and up to 13 wines by the glass. The bar food offers good value for money, and can be enjoyed on the decked terrace overlooking the River Thames.

**Open** all day all wk noon-mdnt (Sun noon-11) **Bar Meals** L served all wk 12-9 D served all wk 12-9 Av main course £8.50 food served all day FREE HOUSE Adnams, Youngs, Fuller's London Pride Brothers Pear Cider. 13 **Facilities** Dogs allowed Garden

**E8**

## The Cat & Mutton PLAN 2 F4

**76 Broadway Market, Hackney E8 4QJ**
**☎ 020 7254 5599**
**e-mail:** catandmutton@yahoo.co.uk
**web:** www.catandmutton.co.uk
**dir:** *Telephone for directions*

A fixture in London's East End since the mid-1700s, when it was an ale house for cattle and sheep drovers, this once run-down street corner boozer was revamped and reinvented as a gastro-pub in 2003. At scrubbed tables in trendy, gentrified surroundings, order mussels with smoked haddock and bacon, or a ploughman's slate at lunch, with inventive evening extras taking in peppered venison steak with potato pancake and port jus. The bar serves good ales and up to 12 wines by the glass.

***The Cat & Mutton***

**Open** all day all wk noon-11 (Fri-Sat noon-1am) Closed: 25-26 Dec **Bar Meals** L served Mon-Fri 12-3 D served Mon-Sat 6.30-10 booking required Av main course £12 **Restaurant** L served Mon-Sat 12-3, Sun 12-5 D served Mon-Sat 6-10 booking required Fixed menu price fr £12.50 Av 3 course à la carte fr £25 SEAMLESS LTD Adnams Bitter, Shepherd Neame Spitfire, Staropramen Westons. 12 **Facilities** Children's portions Dogs allowed

**E9**

**PICK OF THE PUBS**

## The Empress of India PLAN 2 F4

**130 Lauriston Rd, Victoria Park E9 7LH**
**☎ 020 8533 5123 020 8533 4483**
**e-mail:** info@theempressofindia.com
**dir:** *From Mile End Station turn right onto Grove Rd, leads onto Lauriston Rd*

This archetypal East End pub was built a few years after Queen Victoria became Empress of India, and has in its time been a nightclub, a print works and, more recently, a floristry training school. The beautifully styled interior includes a carpet with the pub's name woven into it. The bar serves classic cocktails, draught beers and fine wines from around the globe. Modern British food, served from the open kitchen, offers options throughout the day, including breakfast, lunch, dinner, bar snacks, kids' menu, afternoon tea and a feast menu. Sunday lunchtime brings the likes of roast sirloin of Angus beef and all the trimmings - Yorkshire pudding, horseradish cream and seasonal vegetables - or whole roasted free-range Devonshire bronze chicken from the rotisserie with pigs in blankets, thyme stuffing and bread sauce. Rare breed meats, poultry and game are spit roasted daily; and shellfish figures prominently – pint o' prawns and Colchester oysters.

**Open** all wk 9-11 (Sun 9-10.30) Closed: 25-26 Dec ROCHE COMMUNICATIONS Amstell, Bitburger. 30

## E14

### PICK OF THE PUBS

**The Grapes**  PLAN 2 G4

76 Narrow St, Limehouse E14 8BP
☎ 020 7987 4396  📠 020 7531 9264
dir: Telephone for directions

Charles Dickens once propped up the bar here, and so
taken was he by its charms that the pub appears, thinly
disguised, as the Six Jolly Fellowship Porters in his
novel Our Mutual Friend. While the novelist might still
recognise the interior, the surroundings have changed
dramatically with the development of Canary Wharf and
the Docklands Light Railway. However, old-fashioned
values are maintained by the pulling of superb cask
conditioned ales in the atmospheric bar downstairs,
while in the tiny upstairs restaurant only the freshest
seafood is served. This is a fish lover's paradise, with a
menu that includes sea bass, monkfish, Dover sole and
bream, all available with a range of different sauces.
Nonetheless meat lovers and vegetarians should not be
deterred from experiencing this evocative slice of old
Limehouse; traditional roasts are served on Sundays,
and sandwiches and salads are always available.

**Open** all day all wk noon-11 (Mon-Wed noon-3
5.30-11) Closed: 25-26 Dec, 1 Jan **Bar Meals** L served
Mon-Sat 12-2.30, Sun 12-3.30 D served Mon-Sat
7-9.30 Av main course £7.95 **Restaurant** L served
Mon-Fri 12-2.30 booking required D served Mon-Sat
7-9.30 booking required Av 3 course à la carte fr £25
◀ Adnams, Marstons Pedigree, Timothy Taylor
Landlord. **Facilities** Dogs allowed

### PICK OF THE PUBS

**The Gun** ◉ ♟  PLAN 2 G4

27 Coldharbour, Docklands E14 9NS
☎ 020 7515 5222  📠 020 7515 4407
e-mail: info@thegundocklands.com
dir: From South Quay DLR, east along Marsh Wall to
mini rdbt. Turn left, over bridge then 1st right

Destroyed by fire several years ago, this Grade II listed
18th-century pub re-opened in 2004 following
painstaking restoration work. It stands on the banks of
the Thames in an area once home to the dockside iron
foundries which produced guns for the Royal Navy
fleets. The Gun itself used to shelter smugglers — a spy
hole on the secret circular staircase was used when
looking out for the 'revenue men'. Excellent real ales
are backed by popular international beers at the bar,
which can also seat 40 for food; a back bar has two
snugs and two private dining rooms, while a fabulous
riverside terrace accommodates up to 50. Bar snacks
include Welsh rarebit; salt and pepper squid; and hot
pig (crispy pork belly) with apple sauce. A concise
selection of larger plates may include ox cheeks with
mashed potato and onion jus, or pie of the week.

**Open** all wk 11am-mdnt (Sun 11-11) Closed: 25-26
Dec ⊕ FREE HOUSE ◀ Guinness, London Pride,
Adnams, Greene King. ♟ 22 **Facilities** Garden

## EC1

### PICK OF THE PUBS

**The Bleeding Heart
Tavern** ◉ ♟  PLAN 1 E4

19 Greville St EC1N 8SQ
☎ 020 7242 8238  📠 020 7831 1402
e-mail: bookings@bleedingheart.co.uk
dir: Close to Farringdon tube station, at corner of
Greville St & Bleeding Heart Yard

Standing just off London's famous Leather Lane, and
dating from 1746, when Holborn had a boozer for every
five houses and inns boasted that their customers
could be 'drunk for a penny and dead drunk for
twopence'. It traded until 1946, was a grill for 52
years, and reopened as The Tavern Bar in 1998. Today
this Tavern offers traditional real ales and a light
lunchtime menu if you're pressed for time. Downstairs,
the warm and comforting dining room features an open
rotisserie and grill serving free-range organic British
meat, game and poultry alongside an extensive wine
list. Typical menu choices might start with mackerel
and whisky pâté as a prelude to braised beef in
Adnams Ale with dumplings, or spit-roast suckling pig
with sage apple and onion stuffing and crushed garlic
potatoes. Desserts include steamed chocolate pudding,
treacle tart and a jam roly-poly.

**Open** all day 7am-11pm Closed: BHs, 10 days at Xmas,
Sat-Sun **Bar Meals** Av main course £8.95 food served
all day **Restaurant** L served Mon-Fri 12-2.30 booking
required D served Mon-Fri 5.30-11 booking required Av
3 course à la carte fr £19.50 ⊕ FREE HOUSE
◀ Adnams Southwold Bitter, Broadside, Fisherman,
Mayday ○ Aspall. ♟ 17

### PICK OF THE PUBS

**Coach & Horses** ♟  PLAN 1 E5

26-28 Ray St, Clerkenwell EC1 3DJ ☎ 020 7278 8990
e-mail: info@thecoachandhorses.com
dir: From Farringdon tube station right onto Cowcross
St. At Farringdon Rd turn right, after 500yds left onto
Ray St. Pub at bottom of hill

On this spot once stood Hockley-in-the-Hole bear
garden, a popular entertainment venue in Queen
Anne's day. Nearly two centuries later, in about 1855,
this now classic Victorian London pub was built to
serve the myriad artisans, many of them Italian, who
populated this characterful area. What is now the

public bar used to be a sweet shop, people lived in the
beer cellars, and there was a secret passage to the
long-buried River Fleet. Unsurprisingly there are a few
ghosts, including an old man and a black cat. Among
the reasonably priced dishes, look for herring roes on
toast; black pudding hash with fried egg, plus these
examples from a dinner menu: braised cuttlefish on
toast; venison pie with mash; sea bream with roasted
salsify, fennel, chervil and cucumber; cassoulet; and
Jerusalem artichoke risotto. Over the road is the
original Clerk's Well, from which this district takes its
name.

**Open** all wk noon-11 (Sat 6-11 Sun noon-5) Closed: 24
Dec-1st Mon in Jan, BH's **Bar Meals** L served Mon-Fri &
Sun 12-3 D served Mon-Sat 6-10 Av main course
£12.50 **Restaurant** L served Mon-Fri & Sun 12-3 D
served Mon-Sat 6-10 Av 3 course à la carte fr £20
⊕ PUNCH PUBS ◀ Timothy Taylor Landlord, Adnams
Bitter, London Pride ○ Burrow Hill Farm. ♟ 19
**Facilities** Dogs allowed Garden

### PICK OF THE PUBS

**The Eagle** ♟  PLAN 1 E4

159 Farringdon Rd EC1R 3AL ☎ 020 7837 1353
dir: Angel/Farringdon tube station. Pub at north end of
Farringdon Rd

The Eagle, which opened in 1990, was a front-runner in
the new breed of stylish eating and drinking
establishments that we now know as gastro-pubs.
Farringdon Road was more downbeat in those days but
Clerkenwell is quite a trendy district now. The Eagle is
still going strong, despite considerable competition, and
remains one of the neighbourhood's top
establishments. The airy interior includes a wooden-
floored bar and dining area, a random assortment of
furniture, and an open-to-view kitchen that produces a
creatively modern, daily-changing menu which revels
in cosmopolitan flavours. Typical of the range are
smoked haddock and chorizo soup, with tomato, fennel,
chilli and potato; bifeana — marinated rump steak
sandwich; and pork and cockles Alentejo style (smoked
paprika, cloves, garlic and white wine). The tapas
selection includes oak-smoked salmon and horseradish
mousse. Lemon and almond cake with mascarpone and
berries is typical of the desserts.

**Open** all day Closed: BHs (not Good Fri eve) (1wk
Xmas), Sun eve **Bar Meals** L served Mon-Fri 12.30-3,
Sat-Sun 12.30-3.30 D served Mon-Sat 6.30-10.30 Av
main course £10 ⊕ FREE HOUSE ◀ Wells Eagle IPA,
Bombardier ○ Westons. ♟ 15 **Facilities** Children's
portions Dogs allowed

**EC1** *continued*

## PICK OF THE PUBS

### The Jerusalem Tavern    PLAN 1 F4

**55 Britton St, Clerkenwell EC1M 5NA**
☎ 020 7490 4281
**e-mail:** thejerusalemtavern@gmail.com
**dir:** *100mtrs NE of Farringdon tube station; 300mtrs N of Smithfield*

This historic tavern is named after the Priory of St John of Jerusalem, founded in 1140. The tavern can be traced back to the 14th century, having occupied several sites in the area including part of St John's Gate. The current premises date from 1720 although the frontage dates from about 1810, when it was a workshop for Clerkenwell's various watch and clock craftsmen. A fascinating and wonderfully vibrant corner of London, it has only recently been 'rediscovered', centuries after Samuel Johnson, David Garrick and the young Handel used to drink here. Its dark, dimly-lit Dickensian bar, with bare boards, rustic wooden tables, old tiles, candles, open fires and cosy corners, is the perfect film set – which is what it has been on many occasions. A classic pub in every sense, it's open every weekday and offers the full range of bottled beers from St Peter's Brewery (which owns it), as well as a familiar range of pub fare, including game pie, risotto, sausage and mash and various roasts.

**Open** all day 11-11 Closed: 25 Dec-1 Jan, Sat-Sun **Bar Meals** L served Mon-Fri 12-3 Av main course £8 ⊕ ST PETER'S BREWERY ◀ St Peter's (complete range) ♻ Aspall. **Facilities** Dogs allowed

## PICK OF THE PUBS

### The Peasant ⚐    PLAN 1 D3

**240 Saint John St EC1V 4PH**
☎ 020 7336 7726    ▤ 020 7490 1089
**e-mail:** eat@thepeasant.co.uk
**dir:** *Exit Angel & Farringdon Rd tube station. Pub on corner of Saint John St & Percival St*

In 2009 Gregory and Patrick Wright celebrated ten years of running their 1860-built, award-winning Clerkenwell gastro-pub. Grade II listing acknowledges the many original Victorian gin palace features, such as the lovingly restored mahogany horseshoe bar, inlaid mosaic floor, and the period chandeliers in the upstairs restaurant. There's a fabulous conservatory too. An extensive range of pumped and bottled beers, including Belgian Trappist monk brews, is supplemented by Thatchers and Aspall real ciders and a good wine list. In the bar, cult band posters and old speedway billboards on the walls, you might opt for dressed Dorset crab with bacon croquettes; and swede and butternut squash pie, while the circus art-themed restaurant offers sirloin with crispy bone marrow, potato galette, spinach and morel essence; and pan-fried pollock fillet with saffron mash, clams and mussels. While up there, see the extraordinary Heath Robinsonesque, 1910 coffee maker, rescued from a Spitalfields café.

**Open** all day all wk Closed: 24 Dec-2 Jan **Bar Meals** L served all wk 12-11 D served all wk 12-11 Av main course £9.50 food served all day **Restaurant** L served Tue-Fri 12-3 D served Tue-Sat 6-11, Sun 12-9 Fixed menu price fr £35 Av 3 course à la carte fr £30 ⊕ FREE HOUSE ◀ Bombardier, Dekonick Belgian Ale, Crouch Vale, Brewers Gold, Staropramen ♻ Thatchers Pear & Katy, Aspall. ⚐ 15 **Facilities** Children's portions Dogs allowed Garden

---

### The Well    PLAN 1 F5

**180 Saint John St, Clerkenwell EC1V 4JY**
☎ 020 7251 9363    ▤ 020 7404 2250
**e-mail:** drink@downthewell.co.uk
**dir:** *Farringdon tube station left to junct, left onto St John, pub on corner on right*

A gastro-pub in trendy Clerkenwell offering a regularly changing, modern European lunch and dinner menu, an extensive wine selection, and lots of draught and bottled beers. The lower ground features a leather-panelled aquarium bar with exotic tropical fish in huge tanks. From the appealing menu, start with celeriac and black truffle oil soup or crayfish tails with avocado and shellfish cream; followed by roasted sea bream fillet with wild mushroom risotto or rabbit and whole grain mustard pie with creamed cauliflower.

**Open** all wk ◀ San Miguel, Paulaner, Red Stripe, Kronenbourg, Guinness.

---

### Ye Olde Mitre ⚐    PLAN 1 E4

**1 Ely Court, Ely Place, By 8 Hatton Garden EC1N 6SJ**
☎ 020 7405 4751
**dir:** *From Chancery Lane tube station exit 3 walk downhill to Holborn Circus, left into Hatton Garden. Pub in alley between 8 & 9 Hatton Garden*

Curiously, this quirky old pub (founded in 1546), hidden down a City alleyway off Hatton Gardens, is part of Cambridgeshire; the Bishops of Ely once held sway at their palace here. Elizabeth 1st danced Maypole around the cherry tree preserved in the bar; modern merrymakers can enjoy a choice of at least five real ales, quaffed in the magnificently wood-panelled rooms. Food is forthright 'British Tapas' of toasted sandwiches, pork pies, scotch eggs, sausages, pickled eggs and gherkins, available from 11.30am to 9pm. The pub is closed at weekends.

**Open** all day Closed: 25 Dec, 1 Jan, BH, Sat-Sun (ex 1st wknd Aug 12-5) **Bar Meals** food served all day ⊕ FULLER SMITH & TURNER ◀ Gales Seafarer, Fullers London Pride, Deuchars IPA, Adnams Broadside, guest ales. ⚐ 8 **Facilities** Dogs allowed Garden

---

**EC2**

### Old Dr Butler's Head ⚐    PLAN 1 F4

**Mason's Av, Coleman St, Moorgate EC2V 5BT**
☎ 020 7606 3504    ▤ 020 7600 0417
**e-mail:** olddoctorbutlers@shepherdneame.co.uk
**dir:** *Telephone for directions*

Dr Butler was Court Physician to King James 1st; his sometimes questionable cures included a 'medicinal ale', sold through his chain of alehouses of which this is the sole survivor, rebuilt after the Great Fire of 1666. Pub lunches are served in the Dickensian gas-lit bar, while upstairs, the Chop House restaurant offers a lunchtime menu featuring favourites such as pan-fried pork fillet and cod and chips, complementing the Shepherd Neame real ales and an extensive wine list. In common with many City pubs, Dr Butler's is closed at weekends.

**Open** all day Closed: Sat-Sun **Bar Meals** L served all wk 12-3 **Restaurant** L served all wk 12-3 booking required ⊕ SHEPHERD NEAME ◀ Shepherd Neame Spitfire, Bishops Finger Master Brew, Shepherd Neame Best. ⚐ 12

---

**EC4**

### The Black Friar ⚐    PLAN 1 F3

**174 Queen Victoria St EC4V 4EG** ☎ 020 7236 5474
**dir:** *Opposite Blackfriars tube station*

Located on the site of Blackfriar's monastery, where Henry VIII dissolved his marriage to Catherine of Aragon and separated from the Catholic church. The pub has made several TV appearances because of its wonderful Art Nouveau interior. It is close to Blackfriars Bridge and station and gets very busy with after-work drinkers. A traditional-style menu includes steak and ale pie, sausage and mash, and sandwiches, all washed down with a pint of Sharp's Doom Bar or St Austell Tribute.

**Open** all day all wk 10am-11pm (Thu-Fri 10am-11.30pm Sun noon-10.30) Closed: 25 Dec ◀ Fuller's London Pride, Adnams, Timothy Taylor, St Austell Tribute, Sharp's Doom Bar ♻ Westons Organic. ⚐ 14 **Facilities** Garden

---

### ⓞ The Old Bank of England    PLAN 1 E4

**194 Fleet St EC4A 2LT** ☎ 020 7430 2255
**e-mail:** oldbankofengland@fullers.co.uk
**dir:** *Pub by Courts of Justice*

This magnificent building previously housed the Law Courts' branch of the Bank of England. Set between the site of Sweeney Todd's barbershop and his mistress' pie shop, it stands above the original bank vaults and the tunnels in which Todd butchered his unfortunate victims. Aptly, there's an extensive range of speciality pies including game, brandy and redcurrant; and lamb and red pepper, but other treats include roasted lemon and thyme chicken breast on a pearl barley broth; and caramelised onion and olive puff pastry tart.

**Open** all day Closed: BH's, Sat-Sun **Bar Meals** L served Mon-Fri 12-8 D served Mon-Fri 12-8 Av main course £10 ⊕ FULLER SMITH TURNER PLC ◀ London Pride, ESB, Chiswick, Discovery, Seasonal. **Facilities** Garden

## PICK OF THE PUBS

### The White Swan ◉ ♀　　PLAN 1 E4

**108 Fetter Ln, Holborn EC4A 1ES**
☎ 020 7242 9696 ▤ 020 7404 2250
e-mail: info@thewhiteswanlondon.com
dir: *Nearest tube: Chancery Lane. From station towards St Paul's Cathedral. At HSBC bank left into Fetter Lane. Pub on right*

Transformed from the old Mucky Duck pub, this is now a handsome, traditional city watering hole. Downstairs is the wood-panelled bar serving a range of real ales, lagers and ten wines by the glass. Upstairs is a mezzanine area and a beautifully restored dining room with mirrored ceiling and linen-clad tables. Of course, this being the ever busy City, eating can be a rushed business. No problem, the weekday Express Menu delivers two courses in one hour - in at twelve, out at one. Fish comes fresh from Billingsgate market each morning, including the pub menu's sardines on toast with a tomato and herb sauce, alongside pork and herb sausages, colcannon and onion gravy; and Jerusalem artichoke risotto. The Dining Room menu lists additional temptations such as lobster and mushroom tortellini, followed by poached Icelandic cod with squid, with lemon posset and blueberries to finish.

**Open** 11-12 (Fri 11-1am) Closed: 25-26 Dec, 1 Jan, Sat-Sun & BH's **Bar Meals** L served Mon-Fri 12-3 D served Mon-Fri 6-10 Av main course £10 **Restaurant** L served Mon-Fri 12-3 booking required D served Mon-Fri 6-10 booking required Fixed menu price fr £23 Av 3 course à la carte fr £23 ⊕ ETM GROUP ◧ London Pride, Guinness, San Miguel, Adnams. ♀ 10

---

N1

## PICK OF THE PUBS

### The Barnsbury ♀　　PLAN 2 F4

**209-211 Liverpool Rd, Islington N1 1LX**
☎ 020 7607 5519 ▤ 020 7607 3256
e-mail: info@thebarnsbury.co.uk
dir: *Telephone for directions*

The Barnsbury, a 'free house and dining room' in the heart of Islington, is a welcome addition to the London scene. It's a gastro-pub where both the food and the prices are well conceived – and its walled garden makes it a secluded and sought-after summer oasis for alfresco relaxation. At least two guest ales are backed by an in-depth wine list. The food is cooked from daily supplies of fresh ingredients which have been bought direct from the market, itemised in refreshingly concise terms on the menu. Weekday lunches range from oysters to mushroom tagliatelle or lamb shank shepherd's pie. The à la carte dinner choice is also a no-nonsense selection of the day's produce: grilled sardines, caponata and basil oil could be your starter. Pork fillet with sweet potato purée and caramelised apples gives a flavour of the half dozen main course options. There has been a change of hands.

---

Open all day all wk noon-11 (Sun noon-10.30) Closed: 25-26 Dec, 1 Jan **Bar Meals** L served Mon-Fri 12-3 Av main course £8 **Restaurant** L served Sat-Sun 12-4 D served all wk 6.30-10 Av 3 course à la carte fr £26 ⊕ FREE HOUSE ◧ guest ales ♂ Stowford Press. ♀ 12 **Facilities** Dogs allowed Garden

---

### The Compton Arms　　PLAN 2 F4

**4 Compton Av, Off Canonbury Rd N1 2XD**
☎ 020 7359 6883
e-mail: andard07@btinternet.com
dir: *Telephone for directions*

George Orwell was once a customer at this peaceful pub, 'a country pub in the city', on Islington's back streets. The late 17th-century building has a rural feel, and is frequented by a mix of locals, actors and musicians. One local described it as 'an island in a sea of gastro-pubs'. Expect real ales from the hand pump, and good value steaks, mixed grills, big breakfasts and Sunday roasts. The bar is busy when Arsenal are at home. Now under new ownership.

**Open** all day all wk Closed: 25 Dec afternoon **Bar Meals** L served Mon-Fri 12-2.30 D served Mon-Fri 6-8.30 Av main course £8 ⊕ GREENE KING ◧ Greene King IPA, Abbot Ale, guest ale. **Facilities** Dogs allowed Garden

---

### The Crown ♀　　PLAN 2 F4

**116 Cloudsley Rd, Islington N1 0EB** ☎ 020 7837 7107
e-mail: crown.islington@fullers.co.uk
dir: *From tube station take Liverpool Rd, 6th left into Cloudesley Sq. Pub on opposite side of Square*

A lovely Grade II listed Georgian building in the Barnsbury village conservation area of Islington, this pub boasts one of only two remaining barrel bars in London. It has a shaded outdoor area for good weather and a roaring log fire for winter. The pub specialises in quality gastro-pub food, along with Fullers beers. The daily changing menu offers mezze-style options such as houmous and flatbread or various platters to share, and main meals along the lines of fishcakes or steak and ale pie.

**Open** all day all wk Closed: 25 Dec **Bar Meals** L served Mon-Fri 12-3, Sat 12-5, Sun 12-9 D served Mon-Sat 6-10 Av main course £10.50 ⊕ FULLERS BREWERY ◧ Fuller's London Pride, Organic Honeydew, ESB, London Porter, Peroni ♂ Aspall. ♀ 10 **Facilities** Children's portions Dogs allowed Garden

---

## PICK OF THE PUBS

### The Drapers Arms ◉ ♀　　PLAN 2 F4

**44 Barnsbury St N1 1ER** ☎ 020 7619 0348
e-mail: nick@thedrapersarms.com
dir: *Turn right from Highbury & Islington station, 10 mins along Upper St. Barnsbury St on right opposite Shell service station*

First established by the Drapers' Livery Company in 1830, the current owners Nick Gibson and Ben Maschler have focussed on creating a community pub

---

with honest, authentic food and drink. Led by Karl Goward, the kitchen brigade produces simple, no-nonsense classic British dishes that make the best of seasonal ingredients. Starters like smoked haddock and bacon chowder, or middle white pork, pigeon and foie gras terrine might herald gutsy main course dishes that range from braised lamb, chick peas, tomato and watercress to baked crab, chopped egg, parsley and breadcrumbs. Desserts include bread and butter pudding with rum and raisin ice cream; and blood orange posset. The downstairs open plan bar is illuminated by large picture windows, its unfussy interior furnished with a mix of squashy sofas and solid wooden tables. For a more contemplative pint, retire to the secluded and peaceful garden.

**Open** all day all wk **Bar Meals** L served Mon-Sat 12-3, Sun 12-4 D served all wk 6-11 food served all day **Restaurant** L served Mon-Sat 12-3, Sun 12-4 D served all wk 6-11 Av 3 course à la carte fr £25 ⊕ FREE HOUSE ◧ Harveys Wandle, Bitburger, Staropramen ♂ Aspall, Stowford Press, Thatchers. ♀ 18 **Facilities** Children's menu Dogs allowed Garden

---

## PICK OF THE PUBS

### The Duke of Cambridge ♀　　PLAN 2 F4

**30 Saint Peter's St N1 8JT**
☎ 020 7359 3066 ▤ 020 7359 1877
e-mail: duke@dukeorganic.co.uk
dir: *Telephone for directions*

A beacon in the gastro-pub world, with an extraordinary commitment to sourcing sustainable, ethically-produced food approved by The Soil Association and Marine Conservation Society and with minimal environmental impact. Owner Geetie Singh's dedication to the Green cause ensures that even the pub's electricity is produced on-site from wind and solar power. Beers from local micro-breweries and organic wines go hand-in-hand with a remarkable menu that changes twice daily, the team of chefs ever-ready to utilise the freshest seasonal produce. A spring starter could be marinated Alham Wood mozzarella with asparagus, little gem salad and pesto whilst a summer main may be sardines with lentils and braised radicchio with mint and anchovy salsa. Puddings include lavender crème brûlée, perhaps enjoyed with a farm cider from Dunkertons.

**Open** all day all wk Closed: 24-26 & 31 Dec, 1 Jan **Bar Meals** L served Mon-Fri 12.30-3, Sat-Sun 12.30-3.30 D served Mon-Sat 6.30-10.30, Sun 6.30-10 Av main course £15 **Restaurant** L served Mon-Fri 12.30-3, Sat-Sun 12.30-3.30 booking required D served Mon-Sat 6.30-10.30, Sun 6.30-10 booking required ⊕ FREE HOUSE ◧ Pitfield SB Bitter & Eco Warrior, St Peter's Best Bitter, East Kent Golding, Shoreditch Stout ♂ Westons, Dunkertons, Luscombe Draft. ♀ 12 **Facilities** Children's portions Dogs allowed

**N1** *continued*

## The House ⚑     PLAN 2 F4

**63-69 Canonbury Rd N1 2DG**
☎ 020 7704 7410 📄 020 7704 9388
e-mail: info@inthehouse.biz
dir: *Telephone for directions*

This successful gastro-pub has featured in a celebrity cookbook and garnered plenty of praise since it opened its doors a few years ago. Situated in Islington's prestigious Canonbury district, expect a thoroughly modern menu at lunch and dinner. Enjoy roast salmon, red onion and basil risotto at lunchtime; or a starter of half dozen Colchester rock oysters and Cabernet Sauvignon dressing from the à la carte menu. Main courses include confit duck leg with warm Asian salad and hoi sin dressing; and traditional favourites like The House shepherd's pie.

**Open** all day 10-11 Closed: Mon L (ex BH) **Bar Meals** Av main course £15 **Restaurant** L served Tue- Fri 12-3, Sat-Sun 10-4 D served all wk 6-10.30 Fixed menu price fr £10 Av 3 course à la carte fr £25 ⊕ PUNCH TAVERNS ◀ Adnams, Guinness ⚬ Aspall. ⚑ 8 **Facilities** Dogs allowed Garden

## The Northgate ⚑     PLAN 2 F4

**113 Southgate Rd, Islington N1 3JS**
☎ 020 7359 7392 📄 020 7359 7393
dir: *Nearest tube stations: Old Street & Angel. (7 mins from bus 21/76/141 from Old Street & 5 mins on bus 38/73 from Angel)*

This popular pub was transformed from a run-down community local into a friendly modern establishment serving excellent food. There's a regular guest beer, two real ales, and a good mix of draught lagers and imported bottled beers. The menu changes daily, and might include smoked haddock fishcake, slow-roast tomatoes with lemon butter; roast confit duck leg, mustard mash and Savoy cabbage; and roast aubergine, goats' cheese and onion tart with mixed leaves.

**Open** all wk 5-11 (Fri-Sat noon-mdnt Sun noon-10.30) Closed: 24-26 Dec, 1 Jan ◀ IPA, Fuller's London Pride, Guest ales. ⚑ 18 **Facilities** Dogs allowed Garden

### N6

## PICK OF THE PUBS

## The Flask ⚑     PLAN 2 E5

**Highgate West Hill N6 6BU** ☎ 020 8348 7346
e-mail: theflaskhighgate@london-gastros.co.uk
dir: *Nearest tube: Archway/Highgate*

A school in Georgian times, this iconic building in the leafy urban village of Highgate matured last century into a watering hole favoured by luminaries such as Sir John Betjeman and TS Elliot. The pub shelters a number of small rooms served by two bars, one of which is listed and includes the original bar sash windows which are raised at opening time. Fullers draught beers and a speciality list of Belgian and worldwide bottled ales divert from the select gastro-

pub menu which boasts starters including pork and apricot terrine, toast and cornichons, or a crayfish, crème fraîche and rocket sandwich with chips. Mains run to Gloucester Old Spot pressed belly, poached loin, crackling, redcurrant spinach and celeriac purée or shepherd's pie with buttered hispi and gravy, finishing with desserts like prune and walnut steamed pudding with cardamom custard. Traditional Sunday roast dinners are a firm favourite. A large outdoor seating area at the front of the pub is extremely popular on summer days.

**Open** all day all wk 12-11 (Sun 12-10.30) **Bar Meals** L served Mon-Fri 12-3, Sat-Sun 12-5 D served Mon-Fri 6-10, Sat-Sun 6-9.30 Av main course £10 ⊕ FULLERS ◀ Fuller's London Pride, ESB, Discovery ⚬ Aspall. ⚑ 13 **Facilities** Dogs allowed Garden

### N19

## The Landseer     PLAN 2 E5

**37 Landseer Rd N19 4JU** ☎ 020 7263 4658
e-mail: info@thelandseer.wanadoo.co.uk
dir: *Nearest tube stations: Archway & Tufnell Park*

Leather sofas, chunky farmhouse-style tables and much indoor greenery characterise this airy gastro-pub. This is an ideal spot to relax with the weekend papers, or while away an evening with one of the pub's extensive library of board games. Snack from the bar, brunch or tapas menu, indulge in chargrilled meat or fish steaks, or claim a classic sea bass with braised fennel; Sunday roasts are a major draw here. In warmer weather, enjoy a meal or a drink on the spacious patio.

**Open** all day all wk noon-mdnt (Mon-Tue & Sun noon-11) Closed: 25 Dec, 1 Jan **Bar Meals** L served Mon-Fri 12-3, Sat-Sun all day D served Mon-Fri 12-3, Sat-Sun all day Av main course £12 **Restaurant** L served Mon-Fri 12-3, Sat-Sun all day booking required D served Mon-Fri 12-3, Sat-Sun all day booking required ⊕ FREE HOUSE ◀ Staropramen, guest ales ⚬ Brothers Pear Cider, Aspall. **Facilities** Children's portions Play area Dogs allowed

### NW1

## The Chapel ⚑     PLAN 1 B4

**48 Chapel St NW1 5DP**
☎ 020 7402 9220 📄 020 7723 2337
e-mail: thechapel@btconnect.com
dir: *By A40 Marylebone Rd & Old Marylebone Rd junct. Off Edgware Rd by tube station*

There's an informal atmosphere at this bright and airy Marylebone gastro-pub with stripped floors and pine furniture. The open-plan building derives its name from nothing more than its Chapel Street location, but it enjoys one of the largest gardens in central London with seating for over 60 customers. Fresh produce is delivered daily, and served in starters like broccoli and watercress soup, and mains such as pan-roasted chicken breast with sautéed ratte potatoes. A children's menu is also available.

**Open** all day all wk Closed: 25-26 Dec, 1 Jan, Etr **Bar Meals** Av main course £12 **Restaurant** L served Mon-Sat 12-2.30, Sun 12.30-3 D served all wk 7-10 Av 3 course à la carte fr £25 ⊕ GREENE KING ◀ Greene King IPA, St Edmunds ⚬ Aspall. ⚑ 15 **Facilities** Children's menu Children's portions Dogs allowed Garden

## PICK OF THE PUBS

## The Engineer ⚑     PLAN 2 E4

**65 Gloucester Av, Primrose Hill NW1 8JH**
☎ 020 7722 0950 📄 020 7483 0592
e-mail: info@the-engineer.com
dir: *Telephone for directions*

Situated in a residential part of Primrose Hill close to Camden Market, this unassuming street corner pub is worth seeking out. Built by Isambard Kingdom Brunel in 1841, it attracts a discerning dining crowd who relish its imaginative and well-prepared food and friendly, laid-back atmosphere. Inside it is fashionably rustic, with a spacious bar area, sturdy wooden tables with candles, simple decor and changing art exhibitions in the restaurant area. A walled, paved and heated garden to the rear is extremely popular in fine weather. The regularly-changing menu features an eclectic mix of inspired home-made dishes using organic and free-range meats. Typical starters could be sugar-cured venison with beetroot and horseradish remoulade; and sardine escabeche with almonds and caper berries. For a main course look out for the roasted label anglais chicken supreme with aubergine parmigiana and spinach. Dessert of stem ginger and white chocolate cheesecake with berries could be followed by a delightful hand-crafted tea from the Rare Tea Company in Primrose Hill.

**Open** all day all wk 9am-11pm (Sun & BH 9am-10.30pm) **Bar Meals** Av main course £15 food served all day **Restaurant** L served Mon-Fri 12-3, Sat-Sun 12.30-4 booking required D served Mon-Sat 7-11, Sun & BH 7-10.30 booking required Av 3 course à la carte fr £22 ⊕ MITCHELLS & BUTLER ◀ Erdinger, Bombardier, Staropramen, St Peters. ⚑ 19 **Facilities** Children's menu Children's portions Family room Dogs allowed Garden

## The Globe ⚑     PLAN 1 B4

**43-47 Marylebone Rd NW1 5JY**
☎ 020 7935 6368 📄 020 7224 0154
e-mail: globe.1018@thespiritgroup.com
dir: *At corner of Marylebone Rd & Baker St, opposite Baker St tube station*

The Globe Tavern is contemporaneous with the adjoining Nash terraces and the Marylebone Road itself. The first omnibus service from Holborn stopped here, and the Metropolitan Railway runs beneath the road outside. Built in 1735, the pub retains much of its period character, and the owners proudly serve traditional English fare. A good choice of real ales is offered alongside dishes such as posh bacon and eggs; city deli salad; and 8oz Aberdeen Angus burger.

Save on Hotels. Book at **theAA.com/hotel**

**LONDON** 299 **ENGLAND**

Open all day all wk 10am-11pm (Fri-Sat 10am-11.30pm, Sun noon-10.30) Closed: 25 Dec, 1 Jan ◼ Scottish Courage Best, Bombardier, Young's, IPA, Old Speckled Hen, occasional guest ales. ☐ 17

## PICK OF THE PUBS

### The Lansdowne      PLAN 2 E4

**90 Gloucester Av, Primrose Hill NW1 8HX**
☎ **020 7483 0409**
e-mail: info@thelansdownepub.co.uk
dir: *From Chalk Farm underground station cross Adelaide Rd, turn left up bridge approach. Follow Gloucester Ave for 500yds. Pub on corner*

In 1992, Amanda Pritchett started The Lansdowne as one of the earliest dining pubs in Primrose Hill. Stripping the pub of its fruit machines, TVs and jukebox, she brought in solid wood furniture and back-to-basics decor; today, it blends a light, spacious bar and outdoor seating area with a slightly more formal upper dining room. All that apart, however, its success depends on the quality of its cooking. All food is freshly prepared on the premises, using organic or free-range ingredients wherever possible, and portions are invariably generous. The seasonal menu offers spiced red lentil soup with Greek yoghurt; home-cured bresaola with rocket, capers and parmesan; pan-fried sardines on toast with watercress; confit pork belly with prunes, potatoes and lardons; poached sea trout with crushed herb potatoes; polenta with roast pumpkin, buffalo mozzarella and walnut. There has been a recent change of hands.

Open all day all wk noon-11 (Sun noon-10.30) **Bar Meals** L served Mon-Sat 12-10, Sun 12.30-9 D served Mon-Sat 12-10, Sun 12.30-9 food served all day **Restaurant** L served Mon-Sat 12-10, Sun 12.30-9 D served Mon-Sat 12-10, Sun 12.30-9 food served all day ⊕ FREE HOUSE ◼ Bombardier ⚬ Cornish Orchards, Aspall. **Facilities** Dogs allowed

### The Prince Albert      PLAN 2 E5

**163 Royal College St NW1 0SG**
☎ **020 7485 0270** 📄 **020 7713 5994**
e-mail: info@princealbertcamden.com
dir: *From Camden tube station follow Camden Rd. Right onto Royal College St, 200mtrs on right*

Standing solidly behind the picnic tables in its small, paved courtyard, The Prince Albert's welcoming interior features polished wooden floors and bentwood furniture. Twenty wines by the glass team with Adnam's Broadside and Black Sheep bitters at the bar, whilst menu choices include roast butternut squash penne with goat's cheese and sprout tops; Charolais beef burger with aged Cheddar on ciabatta; and sausages and mash with caramelised onion jus.

Open all day all wk noon-11 (Sun 12.30-10.30) Closed: 25-30 Dec **Bar Meals** L served Mon-Sat 12-3, Sun 12.30-6 D served Mon-Sat 6-10 **Restaurant** L served Mon-Sat 12-3, Sun 12.30-6 D served Mon-Sat 6-10 ⊕ FREE HOUSE ◼ Black Sheep, Adnams Broadside, Hoegaarden, Staropramen, Kirin Ichiban ⚬ Brothers. ☐ 20 **Facilities** Dogs allowed Garden

### The Queens  ☐     PLAN 2 E4

**49 Regents Park Rd, Primrose Hill NW1 8XD**
☎ **020 7586 0408**
e-mail: thequeens@geronimo-inns.co.uk
dir: *Nearest tube - Chalk Farm*

In one of London's most affluent and personality-studded areas, this Victorian pub looks up at 206ft-high Primrose Hill from a beautiful balcony. Main courses may include seared calves' liver with bacon and sage mash, roast vegetable Yorkshire pudding, smoked chicken with mango and mange-tout peas, and whole roasted plaice with prawns and pancetta. On Sundays there's a selection of roasts. Beers include Youngs and guests. Recent change of hands.

Open all day all wk 11-11 (Sun noon-10.30) Closed: 25 Dec **Bar Meals** L served Mon-Fri 10-3, Sat 10-5, Sun 10-8 D served Mon-Sat 7-10 **Restaurant** L served Mon-Fri 10-3, Sat 10-5, Sun 10-8 D served Mon-Sat 7-10 ⊕ GERONIMO INN LTD ◼ Young's Bitter & Special, Deuchars IPA. ☐ 12 **Facilities** Dogs allowed

### NW3

### Ø The Holly Bush  ☐     PLAN 2 E5

**Holly Mount, Hampstead NW3 6SG**
☎ **020 7435 2892** 📄 **020 7431 2292**
e-mail: info@hollybushpub.com
dir: *Nearest tube: Hampstead. Exit tube station onto Holly Hill, 1st right*

The Holly Bush was once the home of English portraitist George Romney and became a pub after his death in 1802. The building has been investigated by 'ghost busters', but more tangible 21st-century media celebrities are easier to spot. Depending on your appetite, the menu offers snacks and starters - Colchester rock oysters, Dorset clam chowder, and Lincolnshire Farmhouse meat loaf. Main dishes might include Orkney Angus rump steak with creamy rosemary potatoes or monkfish cheek, herb and cuttlefish risotto, including vegetarian options.

Open all day all wk noon-11 (Sun noon-10.30) Closed: 1 Jan ◼ Harveys Sussex Best, Adnams Broadside, Fuller's London Pride, Brakspear Bitter, Hook Norton Old Hooky. ☐ 10 **Facilities** Dogs allowed

### Spaniards Inn  ☐     PLAN 2 E5

**Spaniards Rd, Hampstead NW3 7JJ** ☎ **020 8731 8406**
dir: *Nearest tube: Golders Green*

Believed to be the birthplace of highwayman Dick Turpin, this former tollhouse is a famous landmark beside Hampstead Heath. Named after two brothers who fought a fatal duel in 1721, it was mentioned by Bram Stoker in *Dracula*, and is still much frequented by celebrities. Traditional British fare is on offer, such as fish and chips, sausage and mash, and steamed steak and kidney pudding. In summer the stone flagged courtyard provides a shady retreat.

Open all day all wk 12-11 (Sun 10-11) ◼ Fuller's London Pride, Adnams Best, Oakhams JHB, guest ales ⚬ Westons Vintage, Aspall. ☐ 16 **Facilities** Dogs allowed Garden Parking

### NW5

### Dartmouth Arms  ☐     PLAN 2 E5

**35 York Rise NW5 1SP** ☎ **020 7485 3267**
e-mail: info@darmoutharms.co.uk
dir: *5 min walk from Hampstead Heath*

Comedy nights, regular quizzes and themed food nights (perhaps steak or mussels) are popular fixtures at this welcoming pub close to Hampstead Heath. As well as a good range of beers and ciders, food choices include a home-cooked breakfast, brunch menu, traditional and 'posh' sandwiches. A seasonal menu offers 'small plates' of maybe rillettes of pork, or Serrano ham with bread and oil; and 'big plates' of coq au Riesling with mash; and salmon and dill patties on ciabatta with chips. Desserts and cheeses are displayed on the specials boards.

Open all day all wk 11-11 (Sun 11-10.30) **Bar Meals** Av main course £10 food served all day **Restaurant** Fixed menu price fr £15 Av 3 course à la carte fr £18 food served all day ⊕ INDEPENDANT ◼ Adnams, Fuller's London Pride, Titanic Stout ⚬ Westons, Dunkertons, Brook Farm. ☐ 10 **Facilities** Children's menu Children's portions Dogs allowed

## PICK OF THE PUBS

### The Junction Tavern  ☐     PLAN 2 E5

**101 Fortess Rd NW5 1AG**
☎ **020 7485 9400** 📄 **020 7485 9401**
dir: *Between Kentish Town & Tufnell Park tube stations*

This friendly local, halfway between Kentish Town and Tufnell Park underground stations, is handy for Camden and the green spaces of Parliament Hill and Hampstead Heath. The pub specialises in real ales, with five real ale pumps on the bar – Sambrook's Wandle included. Regular beer festivals celebrate the amber liquid, when enthusiasts in the conservatory or large heated garden choose from a range of up to 50 beers hooked to a cooling system and served straight from the cask. The seasonal menus change daily to offer an interesting choice at lunch and dinner: pig's head terrine with piccalilli; razor clams, chorizo, spring onion, chilli and garlic; lemon sole with saffron mash; pea risotto and marinated artichokes; roast rib of beef, roast vegetables and Yorkshire pudding. Finish with rhubarb and custard; or passionfruit Pavlova.

Open all day all wk noon-11 (Sun noon-10.30) Closed: 24-26 Dec, 1 Jan **Bar Meals** L served Mon-Fri 12-3, Sat-Sun 12-4 D served Mon-Sat 6.30-10.30, Sun 6.30-9.30 Av main course £14 **Restaurant** L served Mon-Fri 12-3, Sat-Sun 12-4 booking required D served Mon-Sat 6.30-10.30, Sun 6.30-9.30 booking required ⊕ ENTERPRISE INNS ◼ Sambrook's Wandle Ale, Guest ales ⚬ Westons Organic. ☐ 11 **Facilities** Dogs allowed Garden

## NW5 continued

### The Lord Palmerston 🍷     PLAN 2 E5

**33 Dartmouth Park Hill Park NW5 1HU**
☎ **020 7485 1578**
e-mail: lordpalmerston@geronimo-inns.co.uk
dir: *From Tufnell Park Station turn right. Up Dartmouth Park Hill. Pub on right, on corner of Chetwynd Rd*

Stylishly revamped London pub in the Dartmouth Park conservation area. It has two open fires in winter and fully opening windows in summer, plus a large front terrace and rear garden for dining. Food is taken seriously, with dishes ranging from crisp fried salt and pepper squid, with tomato and sweet chilli salsa, to a dry-aged British Rib eye steak, with asparagus flan, hand cut chips and 'maitre d'hotel' butter. Saturday brunch is served from noon until 4pm, when the fish finger baguette and pea purée may prove too tempting.

**Open** all day all wk 12-11 (Sun 12-10.30) **Bar Meals** L served Mon-Fri 12-3, Sat 12-4, Sun 12-5 booking required D served Mon-Sat 6.30-10, Sun 6-8.30 booking required Av main course £10 ⊕ GERONIMO INNS LTD ◀ Adnams Best, Bombardier, Sharp's Doom Bar, Twickenham Naked Ladies ○ Aspall. 🍷 24 **Facilities** Dogs allowed Garden

---

### PICK OF THE PUBS

### The Vine     PLAN 2 E5

**86 Highgate Rd NW5 1PB**
☎ **020 7209 0038** 🖷 **020 7209 9001**
e-mail: info@thevinelondon.co.uk
dir: *Telephone for directions*

The look of an Edwardian London pub on the outside belies the contemporary decor on the inside, with its copper bar, wooden floors, huge mirrors and funky art. Comfy leather sofas and an open fire make for a relaxed atmosphere. The Vine is billed as a bar, restaurant and garden, and the latter is a great asset – fully covered for year round use and popular for wedding receptions. Two dramatically decorated rooms are also available upstairs for private meetings or dinner parties. Lunchtime dishes range from antipasti or tuna carpaccio to start; to main courses such as caciucco de pesce – prawns, mussels, langoustines, baby octopus and squid in a chick pea stew with grilled garlic bread. The Italian flavours are particularly pronounced in a range of stone-baked pizzas, which can be ordered to take away and include a children's margherita. Cidre Breton competes with Brakspear Oxford Gold and Ringwood Old Thumper ales at the bar.

**Open** all day all wk 11am-mdnt Closed: 26 Dec **Bar Meals** L served all wk 12-3 D served all wk 6-10 Av main course £11.50 **Restaurant** L served all wk 12-3 D served Sun-Mon 6-10, Fri-Sat 6-10.30 Av 3 course à la carte fr £22 ⊕ FREE HOUSE ◀ Old Thumper, Oxford Gold, Staropramen ○ Cidre Breton. **Facilities** Dogs allowed Garden

---

## NW6

### The Salusbury Pub and     PLAN 2 D4
### Dining Room 🍷

**50-52 Salusbury Rd NW6 6NN** ☎ **020 7328 3286**
e-mail: thesalusbury@london.com
dir: *100mtrs left from Queens Park tube & train station*

Gastro-pub with a lively and vibrant atmosphere, offering a London restaurant-style menu without the associated prices. The award-winning wine list boasts more than a hundred wines including mature offerings from the cellar. The owners are appreciated by a strong local following for continuity of quality and service. Example dishes are roast sea bream with Roman artichokes, leg of duck confit with lentils and cotechino, and Angus rib-eye steak. The pub was closed for refurbishment but reopened in May 2010.

**Open** all day 12-11 (Thu-Sat 12-12, Sun 12-10.30) Closed: 25-26 Dec & 1 Jan, Mon lunch ◀ Broadside, Bitburger, Guinness, Staropramen ○ Aspall. 🍷 13 **Facilities** Family room Dogs allowed

---

## NW8

### PICK OF THE PUBS

### The Salt House 🍷     PLAN 2 D4

**63 Abbey Rd, St John's Wood NW8 0AE**
☎ **020 7328 6626**
e-mail: salthousemail@majol.co.uk
dir: *Turn right outside St Johns Wood tube. Left onto Marlborough Place, right onto Abbey Rd, pub on left*

Describing itself as a mere scuttle from The Beatles' famous Abbey Road zebra crossing, this 18th-century inn promises a two-fold commitment to good food: to source excellent ingredients and to home cook them. With the exception of the odd bottle of ketchup, everything – including bread, buns and pasta – is made on site. Meats are accredited by the Rare Breed Survival Trust, and most fish served has been caught by Andy in Looe. Representative starters are Thai-style fishcake with lemon aïoli, and pork pâté, with apple jelly and toast. Main courses include comfort dishes such as beer-battered fish and chips with pea purée, and pork and leek sausages with mustard mash. Warm pear and almond tart with Chantilly cream is a nice finish, or look to the cheeseboard for three varieties served with grapes, crackers and home-made chutney. A function room can be hired for larger parties, while outside heaters allow for alfresco dining even when the weather is inclement.

**Open** all day all wk 12-11 (Sat 12-12, Sun 12-11) **Bar Meals** food served all day ⊕ GREENE KING ◀ Abbot Ale, Guinness ○ Aspall. 🍷 14 **Facilities** Family room Dogs allowed

---

## NW10

### William IV Bar &     PLAN 2 D4
### Restaurant

**786 Harrow Rd NW10 5JX**
☎ **020 8969 5944** 🖷 **020 8964 9218**
e-mail: williamivw10@yahoo.co.uk
dir: *Nearest tube: Kensal Green*

The William IV is a large rambling gastro bar encompassing five distinct spaces, including a relaxed sofa area where people can chill out away from the music-orientated bar. Modern European food, hugely influenced by Spain, has starters of sautéed potatoes in rich spicy tomato sauce; rice dishes with chicken, chorizo sausages and roasted peppers; meat dishes such as chicken livers pan-fried with spring onions, ginger and Oloroso sherry; and desserts such as crema Catalana, and tarta de Santiago (almond tart) with ice cream.

**Open** all day all wk 12-11 (Sat-Sun noon-1am) Closed: 25 Dec, 1 Jan ◀ Fuller's London Pride, guest ales. **Facilities** Dogs allowed Garden

---

## SE1

### The Anchor 🍷     PLAN 1 F3

**Bankside, 34 Park St SE1 9EF**
☎ **020 7407 1577 & 7407 3003** 🖷 **020 7407 7023**
dir: *Telephone for directions*

In the shadow of the Globe Theatre, this historic pub lies on one of London's most famous tourist trails. Samuel Pepys supposedly watched the Great Fire of London from here in 1666, and Dr Johnson was a regular, with Oliver Goldsmith, David Garrick and Sir Joshua Reynolds. The river views are excellent, and inside are black beams, old faded plasterwork, and a maze of tiny rooms. A varied menu includes fish and chips, pan-fried halibut with olives, and cod in crispy bacon served on wilted spinach.

**Open** all wk Closed: 25 Dec ◀ Courage Directors, Greene King IPA, Adnams Broadside, Bombardier, guest ales. 🍷 14 **Facilities** Garden

---

### PICK OF THE PUBS

### The Anchor & Hope ◉◉     PLAN 1 E2

**36 The Cut SE1 8LP**
☎ **020 7928 9898** 🖷 **020 7928 4595**
e-mail: anchorandhope@btconnect.com
dir: *Nearest tube: Southwark & Waterloo*

It has picked up a long list of accolades for its excellent cooking, but The Anchor and Hope remains a down-to-earth and lively place with a big bar; children, parents, and dogs with owners are all welcome. In fine weather, pavement seating allows you to watch the world go by as you enjoy a pint, or one of the wines sold by the glass. The wine list is notable for its straightforward approach to prices as many half bottles can be bought for half the cost of full ones – appreciated by the pub's faithful diners. A heavy curtain separates the bar from the dining area which has an open kitchen. The short menu, too, is refreshingly unembroidered. Expect robust, gutsy dishes along the lines of pig's head in vinaigrette; kippers from Orkney, grilled; venison faggot and mash; braised Hereford beef shin, lentils and relishes. You could finish with a rhubarb queen of puddings.

**Open** all day Closed: BH, Xmas, New Year, Mon L **Bar Meals** L served Tue-Sat 12-2.30, Sun 2pm fixed time D served Mon-Sat 6-10.30 Av main course £13.50 **Restaurant** Fixed menu price fr £30 Av 3 course à la carte fr £24 ⊕ FREE HOUSE ◀ Bombardier, Youngs Ordinary, IPA, Erdinger, Kirin, Red Stripe. **Facilities** Dogs allowed Garden

## The Bridge House Bar &      PLAN 1 G2
## Dining Rooms ♈

**218 Tower Bridge Rd SE1 2UP**
☎ 020 7407 5818   ▤ 020 7407 5828
e-mail: the-bridgehouse@tiscali.co.uk
dir: *5 min walk from London Bridge/Tower Hill tube stations*

The nearest pub to Tower Bridge, this 19th-century pub has great views of the Thames, the Gherkin and the rest of the City's ever-changing skyline. It comprises a bar, dining room and café, plus facilities for private functions. Adnams real ales are always accompanied by a guest. All food is home-made and produce purchased at the local markets. Typical dishes are sausages, mash and onion gravy; rib-eye and sirloin steaks; and home-made lamb burger with grilled tomatoes and peppercorn sauce. Specials might include corn-fed chicken salad or rabbit casserole.

**Open** all day all wk Closed: 25-26 Dec **Bar Meals** L served all wk 12-4 D served all wk 5.30-10.30 Av main course £7.50 **Restaurant** L served all wk 12-4 D served all wk 5.30-10.30 Fixed menu price fr £12.50 Av 3 course à la carte fr £15 ⊕ ADNAMS ◀ Adnams Best Bitter, Adnams Broadside, Adnams Explorer, guest ale. ♈ 32 **Facilities** Children's menu Children's portions Family room

## PICK OF THE PUBS

## The Fire Station ♈      PLAN 1 D2

**150 Waterloo Rd SE1 8SB** ☎ 020 7620 2226
e-mail: firestation.waterloo@marstons.co.uk
dir: *Turn right at exit 2 of Waterloo Station*

Close to Waterloo, and handy for the Old Vic Theatre and Imperial War Museum, this remarkable conversion of an early-Edwardian fire station has kept many of its former trappings intact. The rear dining room faces the open kitchen, and the menu offers gastro-pub favourites like collar of ham, mint and pea risotto, or vegetable curry with rice. The handy location means it can get very busy, but the friendly staff cover the ground with impressive speed.

**Open** all day all wk 9am-mdnt (Sun 10am-mdnt) Closed: 1 Jan **Bar Meals** L served Mon-Sat 9am-12am, Sun 10am-12am D served Mon-Sat 9am-12am, Sun 10am-12am food served all day **Restaurant** L served all wk 12-3 D served all wk 5-10.45 ⊕ MARSTONS ◀ Fuller's London Pride, Brakspear, Ringwood. ♈ 8

## PICK OF THE PUBS

## The Garrison ♈      PLAN 1 G2

**99-101 Bermondsey St SE1 3XB**
☎ 020 7407 3347   ▤ 020 7407 1084
e-mail: info@thegarrison.co.uk
dir: *From London Bridge tube station, E towards Tower Bridge 200mtrs, right onto Bermondsey St. Pub in 100mtrs*

A friendly neighbourhood gastro-pub, transformed a few years ago from a typical 'Sarf London' boozer. It may still look rather ordinary from the outside, but the cleverly restyled interior, with its delightful hotch-potch of decorative themes, is French brasserie à la Bermondsey. Antique odds and ends, including mismatched chairs and tables, add to the quirky charm. The place bounces with life from breakfast through to dinner and beyond, when the downstairs room doubles as a mini-cinema. Breakfast could be smoked haddock, poached egg, potato pancake and hollandaise; or perhaps porridge with seasonal fruit; at lunchtime or in the evening there's fricassée of guinea fowl and fresh tagliatelle; pan-roast sea bream with ratatouille; English lamb gigot with root vegetable purée; and wild mushroom and pea risotto. To drink are real ales from Adnams, Breton cider and a good few wines by the glass.

**Open** all day all wk 8am-11pm (Fri 8am-mdnt, Sat 9am-mdnt, Sun 9am-10.30pm) Closed: 25 & 26 Dec **Bar Meals** L served Mon-Fri 12-3, Sat-Sun 12.30-4 booking required D served Mon-Sat 6-10, Sun 6-9.30 booking required Av main course £14 **Restaurant** L served Mon-Fri 12-3, Sat-Sun 12.30-4 booking required D served Mon-Sat 6-10, Sun 6-9.30 booking required Fixed menu price fr £14 Av 3 course à la carte fr £24 ⊕ FREE HOUSE ◀ Adnams, Franziskaner, Staropramen ○ Thatchers Pear Cider, Cidre Breton. ♈ 17

## The George Inn      PLAN 1 G3

**77 Borough High St SE1 1NH**
☎ 020 7407 2056   ▤ 020 7403 6956
e-mail: 7781@greeneking.co.uk
dir: *From London Bridge tube station, take Borough High St exit, left. Pub 200yds on left*

The only remaining galleried inn in London and now administered by the National Trust. This striking black and white building may have numbered one William Shakespeare among its clientele, and Dickens mentioned it in *Little Dorrit* - his original life assurance policy is displayed along with 18th-century rat traps. The honestly-priced pub grub includes hot and cold sandwiches, salads and Wiltshire ham, duck egg and chips; and salmon and broccoli fishcakes.

**Open** all day all wk 11-11 (Sun noon-10.30) Closed: 25-26 Dec **Bar Meals** L served Mon-Sun 12-9 food served all day **Restaurant** booking required food served all day ⊕ GREENE KING ◀ Greene King Abbot Ale, George Inn Ale, IPA, Old Speckled Hen, Royal London, guest ale ○ Aspall. **Facilities** Garden

⑥ ## The Market Porter ♈      PLAN 1 F3

**9 Stoney St, Borough Market, London Bridge SE1 9AA**
☎ 020 7407 2495   ▤ 020 7403 7697
dir: *Close to London Bridge Station*

Situated in the middle of bustling Borough Market, this traditional tavern is friendly and always bustling. You will find rustic wooden floors and traditional decor after a recent refurbishment. The pub was used as a location in *Lock, Stock and Two Smoking Barrels* and *Only Fools and Horses*. The exceptional choice of real ales is the draw here with beers changing up to nine times a day. It is matched by a menu that includes sandwiches, bar snacks, bangers and mash, fish and chips and specials like baked chicken fillet with cep sauce and creamed cabbage mash. Early morning opening.

**Open** all day all wk **Bar Meals** L served Sun-Fri 12-3 **Restaurant** L served Mon-Fri 12-3, Sat-Sun 12-5 booking required ⊕ FREE HOUSE ◀ Harveys Best, wide selection of international ales. ♈ 10

## The Old Thameside ♈      PLAN 1 F3

**Pickford's Wharf, Clink St SE1 9DG**
☎ 020 7403 4243   ▤ 020 7407 2063
dir: *Telephone for directions*

Just two minutes' walk from Tate Modern, the Millennium Bridge and Shakespeare's Globe, this former spice warehouse is also close to the site of England's first prison, the Clink. The pub features a large outdoor seating area that overhangs the River Thames, and the friendly staff are always happy to point bewildered tourists in the right direction! Traditional pub fare includes fish and chips, sausage and mash, curries and vegetarian pies.

**Open** all wk Closed: 25 Dec ◀ Fuller's London Pride, Adnams Bitter, Landlords Ale. ♈ 10 **Facilities** Garden

### SE5

## The Sun and Doves ♈      PLAN 2 F3

**61-63 Coldharbour Ln, Camberwell SE5 9NS**
☎ 020 7733 1525
e-mail: mail@sunanddoves.co.uk
dir: *On corner of Caldecot Rd & Coldharbour Ln*

Recognized for food, drink and art, this attractive Camberwell venue mixes private views with wine tastings, jazz, film and music evenings. As London pubs go, it has a decent sized garden, planted in Mediterranean style, plus a paved patio where you can enjoy a pint or a choice of cocktails. The menu at this community pub is stylishly simple, with great brunches all weekend and wonderful Sunday roasts representing excellent value. Other choices range from toasted triple deck sandwiches to slow roasted belly pork with braised lentils and salsa verde.

**Open** all day all wk Closed: 25-26 Dec **Bar Meals** Av main course £9 food served all day **Restaurant** Av 3 course à la carte fr £18 food served all day ◀ Old Speckled Hen, Ruddles, Bombardier, Adnams Best Wandle ○ Hogans Draught. ♈ 8 **Facilities** Children's portions Dogs allowed Garden

## SE10

### *The Cutty Sark Tavern* ☂    PLAN 2 G3

**4-6 Ballast Quay, Greenwich SE10 9PD**
☎ **020 8858 3146**
dir: *Nearest tube: Greenwich. From Cutty Sark ship follow river towards Millennium Dome (10 min walk)*

Originally the Union Tavern, this 1695 waterside pub was renamed when the world famous tea-clipper was dry-docked upriver in 1954. Inside, low beams, creaking floorboards, dark panelling and from the large bow window in the upstairs bar, commanding views of the Thames, Canary Wharf and the Millennium Dome. Well-kept beers, wines by the glass and a wide selection of malts are all available, along with bangers and mash, seafood, vegetarian specials and Sunday roasts. Busy at weekends, especially on fine days.

**Open** all wk ◀ Fuller's London Pride, St Austells Tribute, Adnams Broadside. ☂ 8 **Facilities** Garden

### PICK OF THE PUBS

### Greenwich Union Pub    PLAN 2 G3

**56 Royal Hill SE10 8RT** ☎ **020 8692 6258**
e-mail: pub@meantimebrewing.com
dir: *From Greenwich DLR & main station exit by main ticket hall, turn left, 2nd right into Royal Hill. Pub 100yds on right*

Comfortable leather sofas and flagstone floors help to keep the original character of this refurbished pub intact. Interesting beers (including chocolate and raspberry!), lagers and even freshly-squeezed orange juice, along with a beer garden make this a popular spot. The food is an eclectic range of traditional and modern dishes drawn from around the world. Everything is freshly prepared and sourced locally where possible; for example the fish comes straight from Billingsgate Market. The lunch menu might include risotto of beetroot and parmesan, mackerel escabeche, or steak and Meantime London Stout pie. Try tempting bar snacks in the evening like crispy squid and home-made cocktail sauce, Spanish tortilla, or home-made Scotch egg and curry mayo. For heartier dishes expect slow roast shoulder of lamb, braised celeriac and mustard parsley crust. The Meantime Brewing Co., which brews the beers on offer, was the only UK brewery to win awards at the 2004 Beer World Cup.

**Open** all day all wk noon-11 (Sun noon-10.30)
**Bar Meals** food served all day **Restaurant** food served all day ⊕ FREE HOUSE ◀ Helles, Kolher, Wheat Stout, London Pale Ale ♂ Sheppys, Aspall. **Facilities** Dogs allowed Garden

### PICK OF THE PUBS

### North Pole Bar &    PLAN 2 G3
### Restaurant ☂

***See Pick of the Pubs on opposite page***

## SE21

### *The Crown & Greyhound* ☂    PLAN 2 F2

**73 Dulwich Village SE21 7BJ**
☎ **020 8299 4976**   📠 **020 8693 8959**
dir: *Nearest tube: North Dulwich*

With a tradition of service and hospitality reaching back to the 18th century, the Crown and Greyhound counts Charles Dickens and John Ruskin amongst its celebrated patrons. Modern day customers will find three bars and a restaurant in the heart of peaceful Dulwich Village. The weekly-changing menu might feature bean cassoulet with couscous, or an 8oz Angus burger with Cheddar cheese and potato wedges. There are daily salads, pasta and fish dishes, too. Recent change of hands.

**Open** all day all wk 11-11 (Thu-Sat 11-12 Sun 11-10.30)
**Bar Meals** food served all day ⊕ MITCHELLS & BUTLERS ◀ Fuller's London Pride, Harveys Sussex Best, guest ales ♂ Aspall, Westons Organic. ☂ 15 **Facilities** Family room Dogs allowed Garden

## SE22

### PICK OF THE PUBS

### Franklins ◉ ☂    PLAN 2 F2

**157 Lordship Ln, Dulwich SE22 8HX** ☎ **020 8299 9598**
e-mail: info@franklinsrestaurant.com
dir: *0.5m S from East Dulwich station along Dog Kennel Hill & Lordship Lane*

A good selection of real ales, ciders and lagers awaits visitors to this neighbourhood pub, whose AA Rosette restaurant interior has been stripped back, its brick walls exposed and floors bared, then furnished with smartly clothed tables. The bar, though, has a more traditional feel. The daily changing menu is available for both lunch and dinner, and there is a good-value, weekday set lunch (except bank holidays and in December), priced for two or three courses. Shellfish lovers may wish to start with Colchester native or rock oysters; other possibilities are fennel and rocket soup; salt beef fritters and pickled cucumber; and quail and celeriac remoulade. Main courses include tongue with beetroot and onions; rabbit with turnips, leeks and bacon; plaice with capers and brown butter; and kohlrabi with white beans, wild mushrooms and goat's curd. Traditional savouries Welsh rarebit, Scotch woodcock and black pudding on toast are a feature.

**Open** all day all wk Closed: 25-26 & 31 Dec, 1 Jan
**Bar Meals** Av main course £15 food served all day
**Restaurant** Fixed menu price fr £13.50 Av 3 course à la carte fr £20 food served all day ⊕ FREE HOUSE ◀ Whitstable Bay Organic Ale, Guinness, Meantime Pale Ale, Shepherd Neame's Orginal Porter, Harveys ♂ Westons, Aspalls, Biddendens. ☂ 13 **Facilities** Children's portions Dogs allowed

## SE23

### *The Dartmouth Arms* ☂    PLAN 2 F2

**7 Dartmouth Rd, Forest Hill SE23 3HN**
☎ **020 8488 3117**
e-mail: mail@thedartmoutharms.com
dir: *800mtrs from Horniman Museum on South Circular Rd*

The long-vanished Croydon Canal once ran behind this transformed old pub, and you can still see the towpath railings at the bottom of the car park. Smart bars serve snacks, traditional real ales, continental lagers, cocktails, coffees and teas, while the restaurant might offer devilled ox kidneys with black pudding or smoked haddock tart for starters, and mains might be pork belly with cannellini beans or scallops with cauliflower purée and crispy pancetta.

**Open** all wk Closed: 25-26 Dec, 1 Jan **Bar Meals** Av main course £10 food served all day **Restaurant** L served Mon-Sat 12-3.30, Sun 12-10 D served Mon-Sat 12-10.30, Sun 12-10 Av 3 course à la carte fr £15 ⊕ ENTERPRISE INNS ◀ Fuller's London Pride, Timothy Taylor Landlord, Adnams Broadside. ☂ 10 **Facilities** Garden Parking

## SW1

### *The Albert* ☂    PLAN 1 D2

**52 Victoria St SW1H 0NP**
☎ **020 7222 5577 & 7222 7606**
e-mail: thealbert.westminster@thespiritgroup.com
dir: *Nearest tube - St James Park*

Built in 1854, this Grade II Victorian pub is named after Queen Victoria's husband, Prince Albert. The main staircase is decorated with portraits of British Prime Ministers, from Salisbury to Blair, and the pub is often frequented by MPs. To make sure they don't miss a vote, there's even a division bell in the restaurant. The pub was the only building in the area to survive the Blitz of WWII, with even its old cut-glass windows remaining intact. The traditional menu includes a carvery, buffet, a selection of light dishes and other classic fare.

**Open** all day all wk 8-11pm (Sun 11am-10.30pm) Closed: 25 Dec, 1 Jan ◀ Bombardier, Courage Directors, London Pride, John Smith's, Greene King IPA, plus 2 guest ales. ☂ 14

# PICK OF THE PUBS

## North Pole Bar & Restaurant

SE10 PLAN 2 G3

**131 Greenwich High Rd,
Greenwich SE10 8JA**
☎ **020 8853 3020** 📠 **020 8853 3501**
**e-mail:**
natalie@northpolegreenwich.com
**dir:** *From Greenwich rail station turn right,
pass Novotel. Pub on right (2 min walk)*

Built in 1833, the pub's name reflects the Victorian obsession with polar exploration. The building was converted in 1998 to the stylish venue that it is today, offering a complete night out under one roof. Guests might begin the evening with a signature cocktail in the bar, then climb the spiral staircase to the stylish Piano Restaurant, where the resident pianist tinkles away on the ivories from Thursday to Sunday evenings. If at this point you happen to look up and see goldfish swimming around in the chandeliers, don't worry: they're for real, and nothing to do with

anything that you may have drunk earlier. In the basement you'll find the South Pole club, where you can dance until 2am – and, to complete the picture, there's also a terrace, which makes an ideal spot for a glass of Pimms on a summer's evening.

An extensive bar menu is available daily from noon until 10.30pm (8pm on Fridays and Saturdays). Choices include light bites such as breaded prawns with basil mayonnaise; stuffed vine leaves with rice, raisins and spices; and mini duck cracker spring rolls with hoi sin dipping sauce. A selection of salads, wraps and baguettes also cater for smaller appetites.

Meanwhile, the Piano Restaurant menu offers a range of hot dishes from mushroom risotto; or home-made North Pole burger with chips and salad; to sausage and mash with onion gravy; or crispy scampi tails with chips, salad and tartare sauce. Follow on with ice cream, or a selection of English cheeses served with grapes and walnut bread. Sundays bring roast dinners in the restaurant and live jazz, funk and Latin music downstairs. Lager lovers might like to know that the beers here include Staropramen.

**Open** all day all wk noon–2am
**Bar Meals** L served all wk 12-10 D served all wk 12-10 Av main course £7 food served all day **Restaurant** L served Sat-Sun 12-5 D served all wk 6-10.30 booking required Fixed menu price fr £19.95 Av 3 course à la carte fr £25 food served all day ⊕ FREE HOUSE ◀ Guinness, IPA, Staropramen, Peroni ⚬ Aspall. ♟ 9
**Facilities** Children's menu Dogs allowed Garden

## SW1 continued

### The Buckingham Arms ♥ PLAN 1 D2

62 Petty France SW1H 9EU ☎ 020 7222 3386
e-mail: buckinghamarms@youngs.co.uk
dir: Nearest tube: St James's Park

Known as the Black Horse until 1903, this elegant,
Young's pub is situated close to Buckingham Palace.
Retaining its old charm, this friendly pub is popular with
tourists, business people and real ale fans alike. With its
etched mirrors, the long bar offers a good range of simple
pub food, including the 'mighty' Buckingham burger,
nachos with chilli, chicken ciabatta and old favourites
like ham, egg and chips.

Open all day 11-11 (Sat noon-6, Sun noon-6 summer)
Closed: Sun (winter) Bar Meals L served all wk 12-3 D
served Mon-Fri 3-8, Sat-Sun 3-5 ⊕ YOUNG & CO
BREWERY PLC ◀ Youngs Bitter, Special & Winter
Warmer, Bombardier. ♥ 15 Facilities Dogs allowed

### The Clarence ♥ PLAN 1 D3

55 Whitehall SW1A 2HP
☎ 020 7930 4808 📄 020 7321 0859
dir: Between Big Ben & Trafalgar Sq

This apparently haunted pub, situated five minutes' walk
from Big Ben, the Houses of Parliament, Trafalgar Square
and Buckingham Palace, has leaded windows and
ancient ceiling beams from a Thames pier. Typical of the
menu choice are sausage and mash; pesto penne pasta
with brie or chicken; and pie of the day. Daily specials are
available. The pub has a friendly atmosphere and is
handy for the bus and tube.

Open all wk Closed: 25 Dec ◀ Bombardier, Fuller's London
Pride, Youngs, Adnams Broadside & guest ale. ♥ 17

### The Grenadier ♥ PLAN 1 B2

18 Wilton Row, Belgravia SW1X 7NR ☎ 020 7235 3074
dir: From Hyde Park Corner along Knightsbridge, left into
Old Barracks Yd, pub on corner

Regularly used for films and television series, the ivy-clad
Grenadier stands in a cobbled mews behind Hyde Park
Corner, largely undiscovered by tourists. Famous patrons
have included King George IV and Madonna! Outside is
the remaining stone of the Duke's mounting block. Expect
traditional favourites on the blackboard, and keep an eye
out for the ghost of an officer accidentally flogged to
death for cheating at cards.

Open all wk ◀ Fuller's London Pride, Wells Bombardier,
Timothy Taylor Landlord, Shepherd Neame Spitfire. ♥ 10
Facilities Dogs allowed

---

### PICK OF THE PUBS

### Nags Head PLAN 1 B2

53 Kinnerton St SW1X 8ED ☎ 020 7235 1135
dir: Telephone for directions

With a frontage like a Dickens shop and an unspoilt
interior, the award-winning Nags Head may not be
London's smallest pub, but it's certainly compact and
bijou. Located in a quiet mews near Harrods, its front
and back bars, connected by a narrow stairway, boast
wooden floors, panelled walls, and low ceilings. It was
built in the early 19th century to cater for the footmen
and stable hands who looked after the horses in these
Belgravia mews. The walls are covered with photos,
drawings, mirrors and more: there are military hats and
model aeroplanes too. There is a cosy, easy atmosphere
here along with a bar that is only waist high. The full
Adnams range is served, along with a good value menu
that includes sandwiches; a help-yourself salad bar; a
daily roast; and traditional pub favourites like
shepherd's pie and real ale sausages and mash.

Open all day all wk Bar Meals Av main course £7.50
food served all day Restaurant Fixed menu price fr
£7.50 food served all day ⊕ FREE HOUSE ◀ Adnams
Best, Broadside, Fisherman, Regatta ♻ Aspalls.
Facilities Dogs allowed

### The Wilton Arms PLAN 1 B2

71 Kinnerton St SW1X 8ED
☎ 020 7235 4854 📄 020 7235 4895
e-mail: wilton@shepherd-neame.co.uk
dir: Between Hyde Park Corner & Knightsbridge tube
stations

Its name is a reference to the 1st Earl of Wilton, but this
early 19th-century hostelry is known locally as The Village
Pub. In summer it is distinguished by its fabulous flower-
filled baskets and window boxes. High settles and
bookcases create individual seating areas in the air-
conditioned interior, and a conservatory covers the old
garden. Shepherd Neame ales accompany traditional pub
fare: sausage, egg and chips; traditional fish and chips;
and the house speciality - salt beef doorstep with
horseradish and mustard dressing.

Open all day all wk Closed: BHs Bar Meals L served Mon-
Fri 12-4, Sat 12-3 D served Mon-Fri 6-9.30 Av main
course £6.95 ⊕ SHEPHERD NEAME ◀ Spitfire, Holsten,
Orangeboom, Bishops Finger.

### SW3

### The Admiral Codrington ♥ PLAN 1 B2

17 Mossop St SW3 2LY
☎ 020 7581 0005 📄 020 7589 2452
e-mail: admiral.codrington@333holdingsltd.com
dir: Nearest tube stations: South Kensington & Sloane
Square. Telephone for detailed directions

The local nickname for this smart and friendly gastro-pub
is, inevitably, The Cod. Although this old Chelsea boozer
was given a complete makeover that resulted in a stylish

---

new look when it re-opened, it still retains a relaxed and
homely feel. The modern British menu runs to
caramelised red onion soup; pumpkin and ricotta ravioli;
confit Norfolk port belly; and organic Loch Duart salmon
and crab cake. Also look out for the 21-day and 35-day
aged steaks. A good proportion of the well-chosen wines
are available by the glass.

Open all day all wk 11.30am-mdnt (Fri-Sat 11.30am-
1am, Sun noon-10.30) ◀ Guinness, Black Sheep, Spitfire.
♥ 20 Facilities Garden

---

### PICK OF THE PUBS

### The Builders Arms ♥ PLAN 1 B1

13 Britten St SW3 3TY ☎ 020 7349 9040
e-mail: buildersarms@geronimo-inns.co.uk
dir: From Sloane Square tube station down Kings Rd. At
Habitat turn right onto Chelsea Manor St, at end turn
right onto Britten St, pub on right

Just off Chelsea's famous Kings Road, a three-storey
Georgian back-street pub built by the same crew that
constructed St Luke's church over the way. Inside,
leather sofas dot the spacious informal bar area, where
your can enjoy a pint of Cornish Coaster or London
Pride. A brief, daily changing menu offers a good
choice of modern English food with a twist, but if
further ideas are needed, consult the specials board
and dine in the restaurant. Starters on the main menu
might include mackerel and dill fishcake with spicy
tomato ketchup; mussels and clams with cider, red
onion and cream sauce; and sautéed chicken livers
with smoked Black Forest bacon and broad beans.
Typical main courses are baked codling fillet with
Parmentier potatoes and mustard lentils; pan-fried sea
bass with caramelised shallot and gremolata; and
courgette, sun-blushed tomato and feta risotto. There
are more than 30 bins, with French producers just
about taking the lead, plus 16 wines by the glass.
When the sun shines the outdoor terrace is highly
popular.

Open all wk Closed: 25 Dec ◀ Adnams, London Pride,
Sharp's Cornish Coaster ♻ Aspall. ♥ 16 Facilities Dogs
allowed

---

### PICK OF THE PUBS

### The Coopers of PLAN 1 B1
### Flood Street ♥

87 Flood St, Chelsea SW3 5TB
☎ 020 7376 3120 📄 020 7352 9187
e-mail: coopersarms@youngs.co.uk
dir: From Sloane Square tube station, straight onto
Kings Rd. Approx 1m W, opposite Waitrose, turn left.
Pub half way down Flood St

A quiet backstreet Chelsea pub close to the Kings Road
and the river. Celebrities and the notorious rub
shoulders with the aristocracy and the local road
sweeper in the bright, vibrant atmosphere, while the
stuffed brown bear, Canadian moose and boar bring a
character of their own to the bar. Food is served here

and in the quiet upstairs dining room, with a focus on meat from the pub's own organic farm. The fresh, adventurous menu also offers traditional favourites that change daily: seared king scallops and chorizo; grilled chicken, bacon, avocado and sunblushed tomato salad might precede chargrilled harissa lamb steak with Moroccan vegetable couscous; bangers and mash with onion gravy; and ricotta and spinach tortellini. Good staff-customer repartee makes for an entertaining atmosphere. Recent change of hands.

**Open** all day all wk 11-11 (Sun 12-10.30) **Bar Meals** L served Mon-Fri 12-3, Sat 12-10, Sun 12-9 D served Mon-Fri 5-10 **Restaurant** L served Mon-Fri 12-3, Sat 12-10, Sun 12-9 D served Mon-Fri 5-10 ⊕ YOUNG & CO BREWERY PLC ◀ Youngs Special, Youngs Bitter, Wells Bombardier, Guinness. ☗ 15 **Facilities** Children's portions Dogs allowed Garden

---

### The Cross Keys ☗      PLAN 2 E3

**1 Lawrence St, Chelsea SW3 5NB**
☎ 020 7349 9111   📄 020 7349 9333
**e-mail:** sophia@thexkeys.co.uk
**dir:** *From Sloane Square walk down Kings Rd, left onto Old Church St, then left onto Justice Walk, then right*

New faces behind the scenes have overseen pioneering developments at this long-established Chelsea pub, once the haunt of JMW Turner, Whistler and DG Rossetti, with 'Tabletap' self-service beer fonts at some tables and an innovative retractable roof over the restaurant area; ideal for a hot summer's day. The new menus see diners tucking in to an ever-evolving bill-of-fare, maybe beef carpaccio or scallop and chorizo starters, with sea bass fillet or Wagyu burger and truffle fries to follow.

**Open** all day all wk Closed: 23-29 Dec, 1-4 Jan & BH **Bar Meals** L served Mon-Fri 12-3, Sat-Sun 12-10.30 D served Mon-Fri 6-10, Sat-Sun 12-10.30 **Restaurant** L served all wk12-3 D served all wk 6-10.30 ⊕ FREE HOUSE ◀ Directors, Guinness, Coors Light, Tiger ♂ Symonds. ☗ 11 **Facilities** Children's portions Dogs allowed

---

### The Pig's Ear ☗      PLAN 2 E3

**35 Old Church St SW3 5BS**
☎ 020 7352 2908   📄 020 7352 9321
**e-mail:** thepigsear@hotmail.co.uk
**dir:** *Telephone fo directions*

An award-winning gastro-pub off the King's Road, specialising in traditional beers and continental cuisine, with food sourced from top quality suppliers. The lunch menu offers spinach and potato gnocchi with wild mushrooms, parmesan and truffle oil; and Angus rib-eye steak with French fries, leaf salad and café de Paris butter. In the Blue Room, main courses might include roast Berkshire grouse with parsnip purée, Agen prunes, game crisps and blackberries, or braised lamb shank with spiced pardina lentils.

**Open** all wk ◀ Pigs Ear, Caledonian Deuchars IPA, Guinness. ☗ 10

---

### SW4

### The Coach & Horses ☗      PLAN 2 E3

**173 Clapham Park Rd SW4 7EX**
☎ 020 7622 3815   📄 020 7622 3832
**e-mail:** coach@coachandhorsesclapham.com
**dir:** *5 mins walk from Clapham High Street & Clapham Common tube station*

This traditional London pub has recently been renovated. It offers an extensive choice of well-kept real ales, real ciders and fresh, simply cooked food using free-range produce. Aberdeen Angus burgers; wild mushroom risotto, and beer battered pollack with hand-cut chips are typical dishes. The pub is family friendly, and dogs are made welcome with water bowls and rawhide chews. Thursday night is quiz night and there is live acoustic music on a Friday.

**Open** all day all wk noon-11 (Fri-Sat noon-1am, Sun noon-10.30) Closed: 1 Jan ◀ Timothy Taylor Landlord, Adnams Broadside, Hop Back Summer Lightning, Sharp's Doom Bar, Caledonian Deuchars IPA ♂ Westons Stowford Press, Thatchers. ☗ 8 **Facilities** Dogs allowed Garden

---

### The Windmill on the Common ☗      PLAN 2 E2

**Clapham Common South Side SW4 9DE**
☎ 020 8673 4578   📄 020 8675 1486
**e-mail:** windmillhotel@youngs.co.uk
**dir:** *5m from London, just off South Circular 205 at junct with A24 at Clapham*

Crackling open fires in winter and soft leather sofas make this pub a popular place for friends to meet. The original part of the building was known as Holly Lodge and at one time was the property of the founder of Young's Brewery. The Windmill today offers a varied menu with something for all tastes and appetites: 'Young's own famous pies' including steak and ale or chicken, leek and ham; fresh fish, grilled or in Young's beer batter; or sausage of the day.

**Open** all day all wk Mon-Sat 11am-mdnt Sun noon-10pm **Bar Meals** noon-10pm **Restaurant** noon-10pm ⊕ YOUNG & CO BREWERY PLC ◀ Young's SPA & PA ♂ Rekorderlig, Koppaberg. **Facilities** Garden Parking

---

### SW6

### PICK OF THE PUBS

### The Atlas ☗      PLAN 2 D3

**16 Seagrave Rd, Fulham SW6 1RX**
☎ 020 7385 9129   📄 020 7386 9113
**e-mail:** theatlas@btconnect.com
**dir:** *2 mins walk from West Brompton tube station*

This is one of only a handful of London pubs to have a walled garden. Located in a fashionable part of town where a great many pubs have been reinvented to become trendy diners or restaurants, here is a traditional local that remains true to its cause. The spacious bar area – split into eating and drinking

---

sections – attracts what in rural enclaves would be quaintly referred to as outsiders, but to be a local here you can come from Chelsea, Hampstead or Hammersmith. Lunch might feature starters such as courgette, chilli and potato soup, and pork terrine with home-made fruit chutney. Tempting mains continue the European influences in dishes such as grilled Italian sausages, mash and red onion marmalade; roasted cod fillet with chorizo, chickpeas, coriander and gazpacho salsa. Real ales for the current season are listed on the menu along with the ales about to arrive.

**Open** all day all wk Closed: 24 Dec-1 Jan **Bar Meals** L served Mon-Fri 12-2.30, Sat 12-4, Sun 12-10 D served Mon-Sat 6-10, Sun 12-10 Av main course £11 ⊕ FREE HOUSE ◀ Fuller's London Pride, Caledonian Deuchars IPA, Timothy Taylor Landlord, guest ale. ☗ 15 **Facilities** Garden

---

### PICK OF THE PUBS

### The White Horse ☗      PLAN 1 A1

**1-3 Parson's Green, Fulham SW6 4UL**
☎ 020 7736 2115
**e-mail:** info@whitehorsesw6.com
**dir:** *140mtrs from Parson's Green tube*

This coaching inn has stood on this site since at least 1688, and has advanced impressively since then, with its polished mahogany bar and wall panels, open fires and contemporary art on the walls. A large modern kitchen is behind the imaginative, good value meals served in the bar and Coach House restaurant. For lunch, you might try basil-infused seared tuna with Greek salad, or pork sausages with mash, summer cabbage and beer onion gravy. In the evening there might be seared turbot with summer vegetable and black-eye bean broth, or chowder of gurnard, conger eel and smoked bacon. Every dish from the starters through to the desserts comes with a recommended beer or wine, and the choice of both is considerable. In fact the 2-day beer festival held annually in November with over 300 beers waiting to be sampled is a magnet for lovers of real ale and European beers.

**Open** all day all wk ◀ Adnams Broadside, Harveys Sussex Best Bitter ♂ Aspall. ☗ 20 **Facilities** Dogs allowed Garden

---

### SW7

### The Anglesea Arms ☗      PLAN 1 A1

**15 Selwood Ter, South Kensington SW7 3QG**
☎ 020 7373 7960
**e-mail:** enquiries@angleseaarms.com
**dir:** *Telephone for directions*

Feeling like a country pub in the middle of South Kensington, the interior has barely changed since 1827, though the dining area has been tastefully updated with panelled walls and leather-clad chairs, plus there's outside seating. Lunch and dinner menus place an emphasis on quality ingredients, fresh preparation and *continued*

## SW7 continued

cosmopolitan flavours. From the menu expect perhaps goat's cheese, spinach and fig tart; crispy fried baby squid with risotto nero; wild boar and apple sausages with mash, braised red cabbage and shallot gravy; pan-fried skate wing with hand-cut chips, watercress and aïoli; followed by rum pannacotta with rhubarb compôte. Sunday lunches are popular, booking is advisable.

**Open** all day all wk Closed: 25-26 Dec **Bar Meals** L served Mon-Fri 12-3, Sat-Sun 12-5 D served Mon-Fri 6-10, Sat 6-10, Sun 6-9.30 Av main course £5 **Restaurant** L served Sat-Sun 12-5 booking required D served Mon-Fri 6.30-10, Sat 6-10, Sun 6-9.30 Fixed menu price fr £12.95 Av 3 course à la carte fr £24.95 ⊕ CAPITAL PUB COMPANY ◄ Fuller's London Pride, Adnams Bitter, Broadside, Sambrooks Wandle, Sharp's Doom Bar Ò Symonds. ♀ 18 **Facilities** Children's portions Dogs allowed Garden

### SW8

## The Masons Arms ♀      PLAN 2 E3

**169 Battersea Park Rd SW8 4BT**
☎ 020 7622 2007   020 7622 4662
e-mail: masons.arms@london-gastros.co.uk
dir: *Opposite Battersea Park BR Station*

This Fuller's gastro-pub breaks the mould, with live jazz, blues or folk at weekends adding a new dimension to the indoor-outdoor choice of where to eat and sup. Worn wooden floors, friendly, professional staff and a welcoming atmosphere, all equally suited for a quiet romantic dinner or a family outing. Food - British, with Italian and Asian influences, the menu changes daily – is freshly prepared in an open kitchen, a touch of theatre whilst awaiting perhaps squid stuffed with feta and chilli.

**Open** all day all wk noon-11 (Fri noon-mdnt Sun noon-10.30) Closed: 25 Dec **Bar Meals** L served Mon-Fri 12-3, Sat 12-4, Sun 12-5 D served Mon-Sat 6-10, Sun 6-9 Av main course £12 **Restaurant** L served Mon-Fri 12-3, Sat 12-4, Sun 12-5 D served Mon-Sat 6-10, Sun 6-9 Av 3 course à la carte fr £20 ⊕ FULLERS ◄ London Pride, Peroni, Staropramen, Fuller's Organic Honey dew. ♀ 12 **Facilities** Dogs allowed Garden

### SW10

### PICK OF THE PUBS

## The Chelsea Ram ♀      PLAN 2 E3

**32 Burnaby St SW10 0PL** ☎ 020 7351 4008
e-mail: bookings@chelsearam.co.uk
dir: *Telephone for directions*

A popular neighbourhood corner gastro-pub and friendly local, The Chelsea Ram is located close to Chelsea Harbour and Lots Road, a little off the beaten track. There is a distinct emphasis on fresh produce in the monthly-changing menu, which includes fish and meat from Smithfield Market. Start with goat's cheese, spring onion and spinach tart; steamed Shetland mussels; or 'London cured' smoked salmon plate. Among the main courses might be slow braised pork

belly and crackling; 'retro' chicken Kiev; or roasted butternut risotto, sage and walnut pesto. Finish with a traditional apple and pear crumble, or puff pastry mille feuille, toffee bananas, rum cream and chocolate and sea salt sauce. If you haven't a sweet tooth then a selection of English cheeses, wheat wafers, red grapes and home-made chutney will appeal. A stone's throw from the Kings Road, it is the ideal place to refuel after a shopping spree, or relax with a pint at the end of the day.

**Open** all day all wk **Bar Meals** L served all wk 12-3 D served all wk 6.30-10 Av main course £13 **Restaurant** L served all wk 12-3 D served all wk 6.30-10 Av 3 course à la carte fr £25 ⊕ YOUNG & CO BREWERY PLC ◄ Young's Bitter, Bombardier, Guinness, Peroni. ♀ 14 **Facilities** Children's portions Dogs allowed

### PICK OF THE PUBS

## The Hollywood Arms ♀      PLAN 1 A1

**45 Hollywood Rd SW10 9HX** ☎ 020 7349 7840
e-mail: hollywoodarms@youngs.co.uk
dir: *1 min from Chelsea & Westminster Hospital, 200mtrs down Hollywood Rd on right towards Fulham Rd*

This listed building is one of Chelsea's hidden treasures. The interior has been elegantly refurbished, augmenting its original charm with rich natural woods, pastel shades and modern fabrics. The large upstairs lounge has elegant mouldings around the ceiling and large open fires at each end, with the bar centred on its length; four huge picture windows make the ambience light and airy. The ground floor pub and restaurant retains much of its traditional atmosphere. Here the chefs lovingly create menus from scratch using high quality ingredients; some, such as cheeses and cured meats, have won national or international recognition. Small plates will produce Rannoch Smokery smoked goose breast, or salt and pepper squid, while main courses offer the home-made half-pound beefburger and chips, Welsh lamb cutlets, or Muffs of Bromborough Old English herb sausages. Award-winning Burtree House Farm puddings are among the desserts.

**Open** all day all wk noon-11.30 (Thu-Sat noon-mdnt Sun noon-10.30) ◄ Guinness. ♀ 12 **Facilities** Dogs allowed

### PICK OF THE PUBS

## Lots Road Pub and      PLAN 2 E3
## Dining Room ♀

**114 Lots Rd, Chelsea SW10 0RJ** ☎ 020 7352 6645
e-mail: lotsroad@foodandfuel.co.uk
dir: *5-10 mins walk from Fulham Broadway Station*

Located just off the bustling King's Road, opposite the entrance to Chelsea Harbour, the Lots Road is a real star of the gastro-pub scene, appealing to well-heeled locals for the relaxing vibe and a daily menu that lists

imaginative, modern pub food. Expect a smart, comfortable, well-designed space, which segues smoothly between jaunty bar area and the more secluded dining area. Slate grey and cream walls and wooden tables create a light, pared-down feel, and attentive staff are set on making you feel comfortable. There's real ales, an excellent wine list, and cocktails both quirky and classic. Food takes in a mix of seasonal pub classics and more innovative dishes, perhaps pumpkin and ginger soup; or steamed Isle of Lewis mussels, white wine, garlic and shallots, followed by lamb shoulder shepherd's pie and curly kale; root vegetable and butter bean lasagne and French beans; then a pudding of sticky toffee pudding with honey pot ice cream; or chocolate mousse tart and orange syrup. Don't miss Saturday brunch and the Sunday family roasts.

**Open** all day all wk 11-11 (Sun noon-10.30) **Bar Meals** L served Mon 12-3, Tue-Sat 12-4, Sun 12-5 D served Mon-Sat 6-10, Sun 6-9.30 Av main course £10.50 **Restaurant** L served Mon 12-3, Tue-Sat 12-4, Sun 12-5 D served Mon-Sat 6-10, Sun 6-9.30 ⊕ FOOD AND FUEL ◄ Sharp's Doom Bar, Bombardier, IPA, Guinness. ♀ 24 **Facilities** Children's menu Children's portions Dogs allowed

## The Sporting Page ♀      PLAN 1 A1

**6 Camera Place SW10 0BH**
☎ 020 7349 0455   020 7352 8162
e-mail: sportingpage@foodandfuel.co.uk
dir: *Nearest tube - Sloane Square or South Kensington*

A small whitewashed pub happily tucked away between the King's and Fulham Roads. Its smart interior of varnished pine and rosewood and sporting murals makes it easy to unwind there after a day's work. The popular modern British menu includes traditional comfort food such as Cumberland sausage and mash, cheese and bacon burger, and beer battered haddock and chips. Despite its side street location, there's seating for 60 outside.

**Open** all wk Closed: 25-26 Dec ◄ Wells Bombardier, Fuller's London Pride. ♀ 12 **Facilities** Dogs allowed Garden

### SW11

## The Castle ♀      PLAN 2 E3

**115 Battersea High St SW11 3HS** ☎ 020 7228 8181
e-mail: thecastlebattersea@youngs.co.uk
dir: *Approx 10min walk from Clapham Junction*

Built in the mid-1960s to replace an older coaching inn, this ivy-covered pub tucked away in 'Battersea Village', has rugs and rustic furnishings on bare boards inside, and an outside enclosed patio garden. A typical menu offers fresh salmon and dill fishcakes; Cajun chicken sandwich; organic lamb steak; and fresh swordfish steak with avocado salsa.

**Open** all day all wk noon-11 (Fri-Sat noon-mdnt Sun noon-10.30) ◄ Youngs Original, Youngs Special, Guest Ales. ♀ 14 **Facilities** Dogs allowed Garden Parking

Save on Hotels. Book at **theAA.com/hotel**

**LONDON** 307 **ENGLAND**

## PICK OF THE PUBS

### The Fox & Hounds ⚑     PLAN 2 E3

**66 Latchmere Rd, Battersea SW11 2JU**
☎ **020 7924 5483** 📠 **020 7738 2678**
e-mail: foxandhoundsbattersea@btopenworld.com
dir: *From Clapham Junction exit onto High St turn left,
through lights into Lavender Hill. After post office, left
at lights. Pub 200yds on left*

Just like the Queen Vic in *EastEnders*, this is one of
those archetypal Victorian corner pubs that London still
has in abundance. The style is simple, imparting the
convivial feel of a true neighbourhood local, with bare
wooden floors, an assortment of furniture, walled
garden, extensive patio planting and a covered and
heated seating area. Locals head here for the good
selection of real ales, among them Wandle from
Sambrook's Battersea brewery, and an international
wine list. Fresh ingredients are delivered daily from the
London markets, enabling the Mediterranean-style
menu and specials to change accordingly; all prepared
in the open-to-view kitchen. So, you might start with
traditional onion soup; smoked salmon salad with
grilled asparagus and baby beets; or roasted artichoke
with tomato, Parma ham and pesto. Follow with
sautéed king prawns; pan-roasted red snapper; grilled
Italian sausages; or slow-cooked oxtail. A traditional
British lunch is served on Sundays.

**Open** noon-3 5-11 (Mon 5-11 Fri-Sat noon-11 Sun
noon-10.30) Closed: 24 Dec-1 Jan, 2nd Mon Aug, Mon L
**Bar Meals** L served Fri 12.30-3, Sat 12.30-4, Sun
12.30-10 D served all wk 6-10 Av main course £12.50
⊕ FREE HOUSE ◀ Caledonian Deuchars IPA, Harveys
Sussex Best Bitter, Fuller's London Pride, St Austell
Tribute. ⚑ **14 Facilities** Children's portions Dogs
allowed Garden

---

### SW13

### *The Bull's Head* ⚑     PLAN 2 D3

**373 Lonsdale Rd, Barnes SW13 9PY**
☎ **020 8876 5241** 📠 **020 8876 1546**
e-mail: jazz@thebullshead.com
dir: *Telephone for directions*

Facing the Thames and established in 1684, the Bull's
Head has become a major venue for mainstream modern
jazz and blues. Indeed, this is the 50-year anniversary of
jazz at the pub. Nightly concerts draw music lovers from
far and wide, helped in no small measure by some fine
cask-conditioned ales. Traditional home-cooked meals
are served in the bar, with dishes ranging from haddock
and crab to a variety of roasts and pies. Popular home-
made puddings. A Thai menu is available throughout the
pub in the evening.

**Open** all day all wk noon-mdnt Closed: 25 Dec ◀ Young's
Special, Bitter, Winter Warmer, Bombardier, Ramrod,
Guinness. ⚑ **32 Facilities** Family room Dogs allowed
Garden

## PICK OF THE PUBS

### The Idle Hour ⚑     PLAN 2 D3

**62 Railway Side, Barnes SW13 0PQ** ☎ **020 8878 5555**
e-mail: theidlehour@aol.com
dir: *From Mortlake High St (A3003) into White Hart Ln.
5th left into Railway Side (at rail crossing). Pub just
past school*

Built as a pub in 1864, this Victorian free house went
through a number of guises before becoming the Idle
Hour ten years ago. Though hidden away down an
alleyway, the pub is noted for its cosy atmosphere with
plenty of fresh flowers, candles, and clocks that tell the
wrong time. As the name suggests, this is just the spot
for whiling away an afternoon, while the stunning
secluded garden is ideal for alfresco summer dining.
The weekday menu changes regularly and features
some traditional choices alongside more adventurous
dishes. Typical starters include home-made mixed
mushroom and herb soup; and grilled halloumi with
chickpea salsa and harissa. Main course options might
include seared sea bass fillets on Puy lentils with
sweet potato; organic tagliatelle with lemon, peas,
cream and parmesan; or Moroccan-style organic lamb
shank with couscous and spicy tomato sauce. The
dessert menu features apple and pear crumble with
vanilla custard.

**Open** all wk 5-mdnt (Sat-Sun noon-mdnt) **Bar Meals** L
served Sat-Sun 1-9 D served all wk 7-10 **Restaurant** L
served Sat-Sun 1-9 D served all wk 7-10 Av 3 course à la carte fr £18.20 ⊕ FREE HOUSE
◀ Adnams, Harveys Sussex. ⚑ **10 Facilities** Dogs
allowed Garden

---

### SW15

## PICK OF THE PUBS

### The Spencer Arms ⚑     PLAN 2 D3

**237 Lower Richmond Rd, Putney SW15 1HJ**
☎ **020 8788 0640** 📠 **020 8788 2216**
e-mail: info@thespencerarms.co.uk
dir: *Corner of Putney Common & Lower Richmond Rd,
opposite Old Putney Hospital*

The Spencer Arms, now under new ownership, was
transformed a few years into an attractive and cosy
gastro-pub with a large sunlit bar area and dining room,
and a relaxed fireside area with leather banquettes, all
done out in pastels and dark wood. Enjoy one of the real
ales or ciders, or one of the eleven wines by the glass
while choosing your meal. On offer are daily-changing
lunch and dinner menus which incorporate the very best
ingredients sourced from a wide variety of creditable
suppliers. Kick off with perhaps tomato and basil soup,
steamed mussels with white wine, parsley and garlic, or
a crayfish cocktail, then choose chicken, leek, bacon and
tarragon open pie; confit of duck with braised flageolets
à la crème with dauphinoise potatoes; luxury smoked
haddock and salmon fish pie; or a salad of grilled Rosary
goat's cheese, pine nuts and roasted peppers. Children
have their own menu. Parking might be a bit tricky.

**Open** all day all wk 10-mdnt Closed: 25 Dec, 1 Jan
**Bar Meals** L served Mon-Sat 12-3, Sun 12-9 booking
required D served Mon-Sat 6-10, Sun 12-9 booking
required Av main course £11.95 **Restaurant** L served
Mon-Sat 12-3, Sun 12-9 booking required D served
Mon-Sat 6-10, Sun 12-9 booking required Av 3 course
à la carte fr £23.45 ⊕ FREE HOUSE ◀ Guinness,
Fuller's London Pride, Sharp's Doom Bar, Heineken,
Peroni ☼ Aspalls Draught, Peronelle's Blush, Westons
Organic. ⚑ **11 Facilities** Children's menu Children's
portions Dogs allowed Garden

---

### SW18

## PICK OF THE PUBS

### The Alma Tavern     PLAN 2 E3

**499 Old York Rd, Wandsworth SW18 1TF**
☎ **020 8870 2537**
e-mail: alma@youngs.co.uk
dir: *Opposite Wandsworth town rail station*

This Young's pub, just a stone's throw from
Wandsworth Town Station, is a classic example of
Victorian pub architecture. The carefully restored
building boasts shiny green tiles on its outside walls,
and a second floor dome that makes it one of the Old
York Road's most distinctive landmarks. Once inside,
the buzzing central bar gives way to a large and airy
dining room, with rustic tables and open French doors
that lead into a secluded dining courtyard. The bar
menu features delights such as pork pie with balsamic
baby onions; Welsh rarebit; and herb crust mussels
and fries. The main menu continues the eclecticism in
dishes such as mixed nut coated canon of lamb, pear
chutney, grilled artichoke and Rosary goat's cheese;
and home-cured salmon with golden beetroot and
crème fraîche terrine. The pub is an established
watering hole for rugby internationals at Twickenham,
and has long associations with local rugby teams too.

**Open** all day all wk **Bar Meals** L served Mon-Sat
12-10.30, Sun 12-9.30 D served Mon-Sat 12-10.30,
Sun 12-9.30 Av main course £11.50 food served all day
**Restaurant** L served Mon-Fri 12-4, Sat 12-10.30, Sun
12-9.30 D served Mon-Fri 6-10.30, Sat 12-10.30, Sun
12-9.30 ⊕ YOUNG & CO BREWERY ◀ Youngs Bitter,
Youngs Special, Youngs Winter Warmer, Youngs guest/
seasonal ales. **Facilities** Children's portions Dogs
allowed

## PICK OF THE PUBS

### The Cat's Back     PLAN 2 D3

**86-88 Point Pleasant, Putney SW18 1NN**
☎ **020 8877 0818 & & 8874 2937**
e-mail: info@catsback.co.uk
dir: *2 min walk from Wandsworth Park, by river*

Some years ago, just before the landlord went on
holiday, the pub cat disappeared, causing much
concern among the regulars. A month later, after mine
host's return, in strolled the wayward feline, prompting
him to write a notice reading, somewhat prosaically,

*continued*

**SW18 continued**

"The cat's back". Much relief all round. Built in 1865 for lightermen on the Thames and Wandle, this vestige of a once-busy riverside stands defiant among blocks of new apartments. Its eccentricity is exemplified by an old globe-topped petrol pump on the pavement, dodgy Victorian photographs, a Calypso fruit machine (one old penny a go), Barbie dolls in glass cases and more. The bar offers a wide range of tempting food including lamb stew; Cumberland sausages and mash; cheese ravioli; spaghetti Bolognese; beef stroganoff; and vegetarian spring rolls. Food is also served in the ornate first-floor dining room. Live music, from jazz to West African, can break out spontaneously.

**Open** all day all wk 11am-mdnt (Fri-Sat 11am-2am) **Bar Meals** L served all wk 11-10 D served all wk 11-10 food served all day **Restaurant** L served Sun 12-5 booking required D served all wk 6.30-10 booking required ⊕ FREE HOUSE ◀ Guinness, Stella, Staropramen Ö Biddenden. **Facilities** Dogs allowed Garden

## PICK OF THE PUBS

### The Earl Spencer ⬗     PLAN 2 D2

**260-262 Merton Rd, Southfields SW18 5JL**
☎ 020 8870 9244   📄 020 8877 2828
**e-mail:** theearlspencer@hotmail.com
**dir:** *Exit Southfields tube station, down Replingham Rd, left at junct with Merton Rd, to junct with Kimber Rd*

A rare mix of community and gastro-pub only 10 minutes from the Wimbledon Tennis Centre. Edwardian pubby grandeur, log fires and polished wood furnishings offer a relaxed, informal atmosphere, whilst a good selection of wines and real ales draws in a dedicated bunch of regulars. It's child-friendly too, something of a rarity in establishments where food is taken seriously. The emphasis is on fresh cooking (even the bread is home baked) with an international cast of chefs; the menu changes daily and reflects seasonal produce. Kick in with poached salted ox tongue, lentils and green sauce or Normandy oysters, shallot vinegar and lemon before progressing to neck end of pork, root vegetable mash, buttered kale, cider and mustard, or whole lemon sole accompanied by ratte potatoes, braised leeks, chives and vermouth. Round off with Bramley apple and blackberry crumble or prune and Armagnac iced parfait. Events are catered for in a large, self-contained function suite, or simply unwind with a beer on the front patio.

**Open** all wk Mon-Thu 11am-11pm (Fri-Sat 11am-mdnt Sun noon-10.30pm) Closed: 25 Dec **Bar Meals** L served Mon-Sat 12.30-3, Sun 12.30-4 D served Mon-Sat 7-10.30, Sun 7-9.30 Av main course £12 ⊕ ENTERPRISE INNS ◀ Guinness, Hook Norton, Fuller's London Pride, Sharp's Doom Bar Ö Aspalls. ⬗ 17 **Facilities** Dogs allowed Garden

### The Old Sergeant ⬗     PLAN 2 D2

**104 Garrett Ln, Wandsworth SW18 4DJ**
☎ 020 8874 4099   📄 020 8874 4099
**dir:** *Telephone for directions*

One of the first pubs bought by Young's in the 1830s. Traditional, friendly and oozing with character, The Old Sergeant enjoys a good reputation for its beers and pub grub. Tuck into a full English breakfast while watching the rugby on the big screen, or scan the frequently changing specials list for something more considered. Burgers, bangers and mash, fish and chips – all have a place here alongside the great selection of world beers on tap. Recent change of hands.

**Open** all wk Mon-Wed 12-11 (Thu-Sat 12-2 Sun 12-10.30) ⊕ YOUNG & CO BREWERY PLC ◀ Youngs Ordinary, Youngs Special. ⬗ 12 **Facilities** Dogs allowed Garden

### The Roundhouse ⬗     PLAN 2 E3

**2 Northside, Wandsworth Common SW18 2SS**
☎ 020 7326 8580
**e-mail:** roundhouse@sabretoothvintners.com
**dir:** *Telephone for directions*

Sambrook's Brewery in Battersea furnishes this pub with its Wandle and Junction ales, the former named after a nearby river and the latter for the famous station at Clapham. The young brewery's crafted ales fit well with the Roundhouse, which has undergone a renaissance in name, decor and management in recent years. But the ambience of a friendly local has been preserved, with a round black walnut bar, open kitchen, eclectic art on the walls, daily-changing menus and those lip-smacking Sambrook's ales.

**Open** all day all wk **Bar Meals** L served Fri, Sat, Sun 12-4 D served all wk 6-10 Av main course £10 **Restaurant** L served Fri, Sat, Sun 12-4 D served all wk 6-10 ⊕ FREE HOUSE ◀ Wandle, Junction Ö Westons Organic. ⬗ 15 **Facilities** Children's portions Dogs allowed Garden

### The Ship Inn ⬗     PLAN 2 E3

**Jew's Row SW18 1TB**
☎ 020 8870 9667   📄 020 8874 9055
**e-mail:** drinks@theship.co.uk
**dir:** *Wandsworth Town BR station nearby. On S side of Wandsworth Bridge*

Situated next to Wandsworth Bridge on the Thames, the Ship exudes a lively, bustling atmosphere. The saloon bar and extended conservatory area lead out to a large beer garden, and in the summer months an outside bar is open for business. There is a popular restaurant, and all-day food is chosen from a single menu, with the emphasis on free-range produce from the landlord's organic farm. Expect the likes of lamb cutlets, chargrilled marlin fillet, shepherds pie, and peppers stuffed with hazelnuts and goat's cheese.

**Open** all wk ◀ Youngs: PA, SPA, Waggle Dance, Winter Warmer, Youngs Limited Edition seasonal ales. ⬗ 15 **Facilities** Dogs allowed Garden

---

### SW19

### The Brewery Tap ⬗     PLAN 2 D2

**68-69 High St, Wimbledon SW19 5EE** ☎ 020 8947 9331
**e-mail:** thebrewerytap@hotmail.com
**dir:** *Nearest tube station: Wimbledon*

A small, cosy one room pub, big on sports like football, rugby and cricket. It is also the closest pub to the Wimbledon tennis championships. Breakfast is served until 12.30pm, and snacks take in wooden platters, sandwiches and salad bowls. More substantial lunches are hot salt beef, and bangers and mash (with veggie sausage alternative). The only evening food is tapas on Wednesday. Special events are held for Burns' Night, Bastille Day etc.

**Open** all day all wk noon-11 (Fri-Sat noon-mdnt, Sun noon-10.30) **Bar Meals** L served all wk 12-2.30 D served Fri-Sun 7-10 Av main course £9 ⊕ ENTERPRISE INNS ◀ Fuller's London Pride, Deuchars, Guest ales Ö Aspalls. ⬗ 14 **Facilities** Dogs allowed

---

### W1

### The Argyll Arms ⬗     PLAN 1 C4

**18 Argyll St, Oxford Circus W1F 7TP** ☎ 020 7734 6117
**dir:** *Nearest tube - Oxford Circus*

A tavern has stood on this site since 1740, but the present building is mid-Victorian and is notable for its stunning floral displays. The interior is divided into 'snugs' by wood and etched glass partitions dating from the late 1800s. There's a popular range of sandwiches and the hot food menu might offer vegetarian moussaka, beef and Guinness pie, chicken and leek pie, haddock and lasagne.

**Open** all day all wk 10am-11pm (Fri-Sat 10am-11.30pm) Closed: 25 Dec ◀ Fuller's London Pride, Timothy Taylor Landlord, guest ales Ö Aspall, Westons Organic. ⬗ 15

### French House ⬗     PLAN 1 D4

**49 Dean St, Soho W1D 5BG**
☎ 020 7437 2477   📄 020 7287 9109
**e-mail:** fhrestaurant@aol.com
**dir:** *Telephone for directions*

For 21 years Lesley Lewis has run this historic pub, patronised by General de Gaulle during the Second World War, and later by Dylan Thomas, Francis Bacon, Dan Farson and many other louche Soho habitués. Only half pints of beer are served in the tiny bar. In the small upstairs restaurant regular appearances are made by fillet steak with béarnaise sauce; Loch Duart salmon; smoked haddock cake; marinated poussin; snails; and pumpkin ravioli.

**Open** all day all wk noon-mdnt (Sun noon-10.30) Closed: 25 Dec **Bar Meals** L served Mon-Sat 12-4 Av main course £7.50 **Restaurant** L served Mon-Sat 12-4 booking required D served Mon-Sat 5.30-11 booking required Av 3 course à la carte fr £30 ⊕ FREE HOUSE ◀ Budvar, Kronenbourg, Leffe, Guinness Ö Cidre Breton. ⬗ 22 **Facilities** Children's portions

## W2

### The Cow     PLAN 2 D4

89 Westbourne Park Rd W2 5QH
☎ 020 7221 5400 ☐ 020 7727 8687
e-mail: office@thecowlondon.co.uk
dir: Telephone for directions

A gastro-pub popular with the Notting Hill glitterati, The Cow has a bustling downstairs bar and a tranquil first-floor dining room. 'Eat heartily and give the house a good name' is the sound philosophy of The Cow, which specialises in oysters and Guinness. Try a bowl of whelks and winkles, whole cracked Dorset crab and a oli, or Aberdeen Angus fore rib in the bar. Go upstairs for starters like sautéed squid, lime, coriander and star anise, followed by fillet of bream, broccoli, cockles and brown shrimp, or côte de boeuf, dauphinoise potatoes, watercress and béarnaise sauce.

Open all wk Closed: 25 Dec Bar Meals L served Mon-Fri 12-3.30, Sat 12-10.30, Sun 12-10 D served Mon-Fri 6-10.30, Sat 12-10.30 Sun 12-10 Restaurant L served Sat-Sun 12-3.30 booking required D served all wk 7-10.30 booking required ⊕ FREE HOUSE ◀ Fuller's London Pride, Guinness, Courage Directors Bitter, De Konick.

### The Prince Bonaparte     PLAN 2 D4

80 Chepstow Rd W2 5BE ☎ 020 7313 9491
e-mail: princebonaparte@realpubs.co.uk
dir: Nearest tube: Notting Hill Gate

A first-generation gastro-pub where Johnny Vaughan filmed the Strongbow ads. Renowned for its bloody Marys, good music and quick, friendly service, the pub proves popular with young professionals and has DJ nights on Fridays and Saturdays. The building is Victorian, with an airy and open plan interior. Typical meals include sausages and mash, tomato and mozzarella bruschetta and sea bass with spinach, and can be enjoyed with one of 13 wines served by the glass or a guest ale.

Open all day all wk Bar Meals L served Mon-Fri 12-3.30, Sat 12-4.30, Sun 12-9 booking required D served Mon-Sat 6-10.30 booking required Restaurant L served all wk 12-3.30 booking required D served all wk 6-10.30 booking required ⊕ REAL PUBS ◀ Sharp's Doom Bar, 2 guest ales Ŏ Aspalls. ☗ 13 Facilities Children's portions Dogs allowed

### The Westbourne ☗     PLAN 2 D4

101 Westbourne Park Villas W2 5ED
☎ 020 7221 1332 ☐ 020 7243 8081
dir: On corner of Westbourne Park Rd & Westbourne Park Villas

Bare floorboards and a long green and zinc bar characterise this classic Notting Hill gastro-pub, much favoured by its bohemian and celebrity clientele. The popular terrace is a sun trap in summer and heated in winter, attracting many locals and visitors to enjoy good food and drinks in a unique atmosphere. Daily-changing imaginative dishes are listed on a large blackboard

above the bar, using fresh ingredients from leading independent suppliers. Dishes might include Gloucester Old Spot pork loin chop with chorizo and black cabbage.

Open Mon eve-Sun Closed: 24 Dec-2 Jan, Mon L Bar Meals 12.30-3.30, 6.30-10 ⊕ FREE HOUSE ◀ Leffe, Hoegaarden, Flowers, Deuchars, Staropramen Ŏ Breton. ☗ 10 Facilities Children's portions Dogs allowed Garden

## W4     Map 6 TQ27

### PICK OF THE PUBS

### The Devonshire ◉ ☗     PLAN 2 C3

126 Devonshire Rd, Chiswick W4 2JJ
☎ 020 7592 1360 ☐ 020 7592 1603
e-mail: thedevonshire@gordonramsay.com
dir: 150yds off Chiswick High Rd. 100yds from Hogarth rdbt & A4

A laid back and unpretentious gastro-pub located in a leafy district of Chiswick, The Devonshire was formerly known as the Manor Tavern, and is now part of Gordon Ramsay Holdings. Its transformation into an attractive, light and airy bar and restaurant happened a few years back returning it to its former glory. Expect high ceilings, large windows, original fireplaces and the restoration of its unique wood panelling and façade as well as an attractive landscaped garden to the rear of the pub. It serves an interesting mix of modern British and Mediterranean dishes, and changes daily depending on the fresh produce currently available. You can whet your appetite with rabbit terrine with pear chutney, or warm mushroom and Cheddar tart from the bar menu before launching in to the menu proper. A typical three courses might comprise swede and honey soup with pressed ham hock, or warm salad of quail and cured pork belly; followed by Gloucester pork sausages with champ and red onion gravy, or pan-fried sea bass with clams in a white bean winter broth; and cranberry and clementine shortcake to finish. Children are made to feel welcome with a secure garden to play in, plus books, crayons and games to keep them entertained.

Open all day all wk Mon-Sat 12-11 (Sun 12-10.30) Bar Meals L served Mon- Fri 12-3, Sat 12-4, Sun 12-9 booking required D served all wk 6-10 booking required Restaurant L served Mon-Fri 12-3, Sat 12-4, Sun 12-9 booking required D served all wk 6-10 booking required ⊕ GORDON RAMSAY HOLDINGS LTD ◀ London Pride, Guinness, Caledonian Deuchars IPA. ☗ 12 Facilities Dogs allowed Garden

### The Pilot ☗     PLAN 2 C3

56 Wellesley Rd W4 4BZ ☎ 020 8994 0828
e-mail: thepilot@london-gastros.co.uk
dir: Nearest tube station: Gunnersbury

A friendly pub and eating house, The Pilot has a simple, understated style with local artwork displayed on the walls, and a relaxed atmosphere. The large rear garden comes into its own during the barbecue season, serving unusual cuts of meat such as alligator and bison as well as traditional beef. Throughout the year, dishes from the

daily-changing menu take full advantage of seasonal produce. A function room is available in the garden, away from the main building.

Open all wk Closed: 25-26 Dec ◀ Staropramen, Fuller's London Pride, Guinness, Peroni. ☗ 14 Facilities Dogs allowed Garden

### PICK OF THE PUBS

### The Swan ☗     PLAN 2 C3

1 Evershed Walk, 119 Acton Ln W4 5HH
☎ 020 8994 8262 ☐ 020 8994 9160
e-mail: theswanpub@btconnect.com
dir: Pub on right at end of Evershed Walk

A friendly gastro-pub, The Swan is much appreciated by locals for its international range of beers and cosmopolitan atmosphere. A pub for all seasons, it has a welcoming wood-panelled interior and a large lawned garden and patio area for outdoor refreshments. Good food is at the heart of the operation, and you can sit and eat wherever you like. The menu of modern, mostly Mediterranean cooking has a particular Italian influence, and vegetarians are not forgotten. Start with perhaps grilled quail and pomegranate salad; or Harira – Moroccan lamb and chickpea soup with saffron, ginger and coriander. Mains might be roast guinea fowl with Savoy cabbage, sultanas, chestnuts, pancetta, and parsnip purée; or oxtail Milanese. Still have an appetite, then finish off with apple and date crumble with ice cream, or tiramisu? Real ales in season are listed on the menu along with the next guest ale.

Open all wk 5-11.30 (Sat noon-11.30, Sun noon-10.30) Closed: 23 Dec-2 Jan, Etr Bar Meals L served Sat 12.30-3, Sun 12.30-4 D served Sun-Thu 6-10, Fri-Sat 6-10.30 ⊕ FREE HOUSE ◀ Fuller's London Pride, Guinness, Harvey's Sussex Best Ŏ Westons Organic. ☗ 12 Facilities Dogs allowed Garden

## W5

### The Red Lion ☗     PLAN 2 C3

13 St Mary's Rd, Ealing W5 5RA ☎ 020 8567 2541
dir: Nearest tube: South Ealing

The pub opposite the old Ealing Studios, the Red Lion is affectionately known as the 'Stage Six' (the studios have five), and has a unique collection of film stills celebrating the Ealing comedies of the 50s. Sympathetic refurbishment has broadened the pub's appeal, and the location by Ealing Green has a leafy, almost rural feel, plus there's an award-winning walled garden. Pub food ranges through oysters, burgers, bangers and mash, and fillet steak.

Open all day all wk 11-11 (Thu-Sat 11am-mdnt, Sun 12-11) ◀ Fuller's London Pride, Chiswick & ESB, 2 guest ales. ☗ 10 Facilities Dogs allowed Garden

## W5 continued

### The Wheatsheaf ♥ — PLAN 2 C4

**41 Haven Ln, Ealing W5 2HZ** ☎ 020 8997 5240
**e-mail:** wheatsheaf@fullers.co.uk
**dir:** *1m from A40 junct with North Circular*

Just a few minutes from Ealing Broadway, this large Victorian pub has a rustic appearance inside. Ideal place to enjoy a big screen sporting event and a drink among wooden floors, panelled walls, beams from an old barn, and real fires in winter. Fullers beers and traditional pub grub that includes Cumberland sausages and mash; home-made fish pie; platters to share; Fuller's beer battered cod and hand cut chips; and spaghetti carbonara. There is a quiz night on Mondays.

**Open** all day all wk noon-11 (Sun noon-10.30)
**Bar Meals** L served Mon-Thu 12-3, Fri-Sat 12-10, Sun 12-8 D served Mon-Thu 6-10, Fri-Sat 12-10, Sun 12-8 Av main course £8 ⊕ FULLER SMITH TURNER PLC ◀ Fuller's London Pride, Discovery, Chiswick, seasonal ales ♻ Aspall Suffolk Draught. ♥ 13 **Facilities** Children's portions Dogs allowed Garden

---

### W6

## PICK OF THE PUBS

### Anglesea Arms ⊛ ♥ — PLAN 2 D3

**35 Wingate Rd W6 0UR** ☎ 020 8749 1291
**dir:** *Telephone for directions*

A traditional corner pub close to Ravenscourt Park tube station, and walkable from Goldhawk Road and Hammersmith. It's whispered that the Great Train Robbery was hatched here back in the 1960s, but who knows. Today, real fires and a relaxed atmosphere are the attraction, together with a terrace where drinks and food can be served. Behind the Georgian façade ales are dispensed from breweries as far apart as Suffolk and Cornwall, and the place positively hums with people eagerly seeking out the highly reputable food. Simple yet robust dishes are served in the sky-lit dining area behind the bar, with views to the open kitchen. A light meal option could be the feta, squash and thyme tart chosen from the list of starters. Main courses step up a gear with dishes such as poached skate wing with artichokes barigoules and aïoli, or salt marsh lamb breast and cutlet teamed with sprouting broccoli and parsnip purée. To finish you could try the Yorkshire rhubarb and mascarpone Pavlova.

**Open** all day all wk 11-11 (Sun noon-10.30) Closed: 25-27 Dec ◀ Fuller's London Pride, Timothy Taylor Landlord, Ringwood Fortyniner, St Austell Tribute, Adnams East Green ♻ Westons Organic. ♥ 20 **Facilities** Dogs allowed Garden

---

## PICK OF THE PUBS

### The Dartmouth Castle ♥ — PLAN 2 D3

**26 Glenthorne Rd, Hammersmith W6 0LS**
☎ 020 8748 3614 ▤ 020 8748 3619
**e-mail:** dartmouth.castle@btconnect.com
**dir:** *Nearest tube station: Hammersmith. 100yds from Hammersmith Broadway*

George and Richard Manners took over the Dartmouth Castle in Hammersmith a couple of years ago. While their aim is to keep the place very much a pub - somewhere to relax over a pint or two - the food is proving an even greater attraction. The monthly changing menu ranges from imaginative sandwiches (grilled chicken, pancetta, avocado and tomato) to dishes such as Caldeirada fish stew; salmon and dill fishcakes, sautéed spinach and paprika hollandaise; grilled rib-eye with roast new potatoes, rocket and salsa verde. Vegetarian aren't forgotten either, with maybe bruschetta di pomodoro – grilled Pugliese bread with tomato, basil and garlic. Typical desserts are pear and almond tart with vanilla ice cream, and tiramisu. The range of beers includes at least two real ales on tap at any one time, and there's a good wine list with 15 available by the glass. Facilities extend to a beer garden and function room.

**Open** all day all wk noon-11 (Sun noon-10.30) Closed: Etr, 23 Dec-2 Jan & 2nd Mon Aug **Bar Meals** L served Mon-Fri 12-3, Sat 12-10, Sun 12-9.30 D served Mon-Fri 6-10, Sat 12-10, Sun 12-9.30 Av main course £11 ⊕ FREE HOUSE ◀ Fuller's London Pride, guest ales ♻ Aspalls. ♥ 15 **Facilities** Dogs allowed Garden

---

### The Stonemasons Arms ♥ — PLAN 2 D3

**54 Cambridge Grove W6 0LA**
☎ 020 8748 1397 ▤ 020 8846 9636
**e-mail:** stonemasonsarms@london-gastros.co.uk
**dir:** *Hammersmith tube. Walk down King St, 2nd right up Cambridge Grove, pub at end*

Fascinating menu options make this imposing corner pub, just a short hop from Hammersmith tube station, well worth finding; charcuterie plate to share and braised hare with crushed truffle potatoes all tantalise the tastebuds, enhancing the popularity of the pub with local residents and business people alike. During warmer months a decking area can be used for alfresco dining, and there's a secluded, intimate restaurant area. The pub carries an ever-changing display of works by a local artist, whilst the upstairs function room doubles as a tiny (and free) cinema on Sunday afternoons.

**Open** all day all wk 11-11 (Sun noon-10.30) **Bar Meals** L served Mon-Fri 12-3, Sat 12-10, Sun 12-9.30 D served Mon-Fri 6-10, Sat 12-10, Sun 12-9.30 **Restaurant** L served Mon-Fri 12-3, Sat 12-10, Sun 12-9.30 D served Mon-Fri 6-10, Sat 12-10, Sun 12-9.30 ⊕ FULLERS ◀ Fuller's London Pride & Organic Honeydew, Guinness ♻ Symonds Founder Reserve. ♥ 20 **Facilities** Children's portions Garden

---

### W8

### The Churchill Arms ♥ — PLAN 2 D3

**119 Kensington Church St W8 7LN** ☎ 020 7727 4242
**e-mail:** churchill@fullers.co.uk
**dir:** *Off A40 (Westway). Nearest tube: Notting Hill Gate*

Thai food is the speciality at this traditional 200-year-old pub with strong emphasis on exotic chicken, beef, prawn and pork dishes. Try Kaeng Panang curry with coconut milk and lime leaves, or Pad Priew Wan stir-fry with sweet and sour tomato sauce. Oriental feasts notwithstanding, the Churchill Arms has many traditional British aspects including oak beams, log fires and an annual celebration of Winston Churchill's birthday.

**Open** all day all wk 11-11 (Tue-Sat 11am-mdnt, Sun 12-10.30) Closed: 25 Dec eve ◀ Fuller's London Pride, ESB, Chiswick Bitter. ♥ 25 **Facilities** Dogs allowed Garden

---

### The Scarsdale ♥ — PLAN 2 D3

**23A Edwardes Square, Kensington W8 6HE**
☎ 020 7937 1811 ▤ 020 7938 2984
**dir:** *Exit Kensington High Street Station, turn left, 10 mins along High St. Edwardes Sq next left after Odeon Cinema*

A 19th-century, free-standing local with a stone forecourt enclosed by railings, just off Kensington High Street. The Frenchman who developed the site was supposedly one of Bonaparte's secret agents. There's so much about this place, not least its intriguing mix of customers, that ensures you don't forget which part of London you are in. The food is modern European and highly praised, but the stupendous Bloody Marys are the real talking point.

**Open** all day all wk noon-11 (Sun noon-10.30) Closed: 25-26 Dec ◀ London Pride, Old Speckled Hen, Young's, Greene King IPA, Bombardier, Shepherd Neame Spitfire. ♥ 20 **Facilities** Dogs allowed Garden

---

### The Windsor Castle ♥ — PLAN 2 D4

**114 Campden Hill Rd W8 7AR** ☎ 020 7243 8797
**dir:** *From Notting Hill Gate, take south exit towards Holland Park, left onto Campden Hill Rd*

Established in 1845, this pub takes its name from the royal castle, which could once be seen from the upper-floor windows. Unchanged for years, it boasts oak panelling and open fires, and is reputedly haunted by the ghost of Thomas Paine, author of *The Rights of Man*. A good variety of food is offered on a regularly changing menu – perhaps oven-baked camembert with rosemary and garlic; a wide selection of sausages accompanied by mash and red onion gravy; honey-roast pork belly with colcannon.

**Open** all day all wk noon-11 (Sun noon-10.30) ◀ Staropramen, Timothy Taylor Landlord, Fuller's London Pride, Greene King Abbot Ale, Paulaner ♻ Westons Old Rosie Scrumpy. ♥ 10 **Facilities** Dogs allowed Garden

## W9

### The Waterway PLAN 2 D4

**4 Formosa St W9 2JU**
**☎ 020 7266 3557 📠 020 7266 3547**
**e-mail:** info@thewaterway.co.uk
**dir:** *From Warwick Ave tube, up Warwick Ave, turn left at Formosa St, pub is No. 54*

Trendy Maida Vale restaurant and bar in a canalside setting with a large decking area where popular barbecues are held. In colder weather, the bar is a great place to relax with its comfy sofas and open fires. There is a good choice of drinks, including cocktails and champagne by the glass, plus Burt's hand-fried potato chips. The restaurant menu offers a choice of modern European food – goat's cheese beignets with artichokes and chorizo; chargrilled squid with chilli sauce; wild mushroom and herb risotto.

**Open** all day all wk noon-11pm (Sat 10.30am-11pm Sun 11am-10.30pm) **Bar Meals** L served all day D served all day food served all day **Restaurant** L served Mon-Fri 12-3.30, Sat-Sun 12-4 D served Mon-Sat 6.30-10.30, Sun 6.30-10 ENTERPRISE Guinness, Hoegaarden, Fuller's London Pride Aspalls. 16
**Facilities** Children's menu Dogs allowed Garden

## W10

### PICK OF THE PUBS

### The Fat Badger PLAN 2 D4

**310 Portobello Rd W10 5TA ☎ 020 8969 4500**
**e-mail:** hellen@thefatbadger.com
**dir:** *Nearest tube: Ladbroke Grove*

Notting Hill's Portobello Road is famous for its antique shops and Saturday street market. Right at its heart is this former drinking pub, which once had a reputation for loud music but is now reborn as the place to relax with good beers and hearty food. Steve Ham and Bob Taylor took it over a couple of years ago and are building the pub's reputation for a friendly reception and comfortable surroundings. The wood-floored bar has plenty of tables and chairs to choose from and offers snacks such as Falmouth Bay rock oysters. The emphasis of the main menu is firmly on 'best of British' produce – including cuts of meat that have fallen from favour, fresh fish from day-boats, and regional ingredients from carefully chosen suppliers. Among the starters may be found crubbeens with sauce gribiche, and grilled mackerel with ginger dressing. Pork and prune pie or poached smoked haddock are typical main course options.

**Open** all day all wk 12-11 (Fri 12-12, Sat 11.30am-mdnt, Sun 11.30am-10.30pm) **Bar Meals** L served Mon-Fri 12-3.30, Sat-Sun 12-5 D served Mon-6.30-9, Tue-Thu 6.30-10, Fri-Sat 6.30-10.30, Sun 6.30-9 ENTERPRISE INNS Butcombe Bitter, guest ales.
**Facilities** Children's portions Dogs allowed

### *The North Pole* PLAN 2 D4

**13-15 North Pole Rd W10 6QH**
**☎ 020 8964 9384 📠 020 8960 3774**
**e-mail:** northpole@massivepub.com
**dir:** *Right from White City tube station, past BBC Worldwide, turn right at 2nd lights, 200yds on right. 10 mins walk*

This trendy modern gastro-pub with large windows and bright decor was formerly owned by Jade Jagger. Its name could be considered appropriate given that it's just five minutes' walk from BBC Worldwide. Expect leather sofas, armchairs, daily papers, real ales, a good range of wines by the glass, cocktails and a lively atmosphere in the bar. Menus show real awareness of today's dietary requirements, with vegetarian and gluten-free options among the eclectic mix of snacks, favourites, great burgers and platters to share.

**Open** all day all wk 11am-11.30pm (Sun 12-10.30) Kronenbourg, Guinness, Kronenbourg Blanc. 14
**Facilities** Dogs allowed

## W11

### Portobello Gold PLAN 2 D4

**95-97 Portobello Rd W11 2QB ☎ 020 7460 4900**
**e-mail:** reservations@portobellogold.com
**dir:** *From Notting Hill Gate Tube Station, follow signs to Portobello Market*

This quirkily stylish Notting Hill pub cum brasserie retains its powerful appeal with a programme of live music, an internet café and monthly art exhibitions in the Gold Gallery. Add to this an eclectic range of beers, great wines and cocktails, and funky international menus for a winning package. Food is served in the bar or tropical-style conservatory, and seafood is a speciality, particularly oysters. Booking is essential. Children portions are available, and for the very young, puréed fresh food can be prepared.

**Open** all day all wk **Bar Meals** L served all day D served all day Av main course £8 food served all day **Restaurant** Fixed menu price fr £11 Av 3 course à la carte fr £21 food served all day ENTERPRISE Guinness, Fuller's London Pride, Harveys Sussex Ales, Leffe, Meantime, Freedom Thatchers Gold, Katy, Spartan. 18 **Facilities** Children's portions Dogs allowed

## W14

### PICK OF THE PUBS

### The Cumberland Arms PLAN 2 D3

**29 North End Rd, Hammersmith W14 8SZ**
**☎ 020 7371 6806 📠 020 7371 6848**
**e-mail:** thecumberlandarmspub@btconnect.com
**dir:** *From Kensington Olympia, exit station, turn left, at Hammersmith Rd right, at T-junct (North End Rd) left, 100yds, pub on left*

A popular gastro-pub close to Olympia, the Cumberland has an attractive blue-painted façade with gold lettering and impressive floral displays in season. Pavement benches and tables help alleviate the pressure inside, where mellow furniture and stripped floorboards characterise its interior. Friendly staff, an affordable wine list and well-kept ales are the draw for those seeking after-work refreshment, but it is also a great place for flavoursome plates of unpretentious Mediterranean-style food offered from a monthly-changing menu. Hearty dishes range through bruschetta al pomodoro – grilled Pugliese bread with vine tomatoes and basil; orecchiette with purple-sprouting broccoli, chilli, anchovy, garlic and olive oil; and Catalan chicken with sultanas, pine nuts, almonds and tomatoes. Even the sandwiches, if that's all you have time for, are a cut above the rest: mozzarella with slow roast tomatoes and pesto, for example, or grilled chicken with pancetta and avocado salsa. There's a canapé menu too.

**Open** all day all wk noon-11 (Sun noon-10.30 Thu-Fri noon-mdnt) Closed: 23 Dec-2 Jan **Bar Meals** Av main course £13.50 **Restaurant** L served Mon-Sat 12-3, Sun 12.30-9.30 D served all wk 6-10 Fixed menu price fr £7 THE PURPLE TIGER Fuller's London Pride, Exmoor Gold, Sharp's Doom Bar, Staropramen. 16
**Facilities** Children's portions Dogs allowed Garden

### The Havelock Tavern PLAN 2 D4

**57 Masbro Rd, Brook Green W14 0LS ☎ 020 7603 5374**
**e-mail:** enquiries@thehavelocktavern.co.uk
**dir:** *Nearest tubes: Shepherd's Bush & Olympia*

Despite being a gastro-pub for nearly fifteen years, the Havelock is still run very much as a boozer – no table bookings are taken and prices represent excellent value. It is popular with both lunchtime and evening customers who want a tasty plate of food before returning to work or home. They can choose between the likes of deep-fried monkfish cheeks and tiger prawns, with sweet chilli dipping sauce; and slow roast belly of pork with dauphinoise potatoes.

**Open** all day all wk 11-11 (Sun 12-10.30) Closed: 5 days at Xmas & Etr Sun **Bar Meals** L served Mon-Sat 12-2.30, Sun 12.30-3 D served Mon-Sat 7-10, Sun 7.30-9.30 FREE HOUSE Fullers London Pride, Sharp's Doom Bar, Sambrook's Wandle Hogan's. 11
**Facilities** Children's portions Dogs allowed Garden

## WC1

### PICK OF THE PUBS

### The Bountiful Cow ♥     PLAN 1 E4

51 Eagle St, Holborn WC1R 4AP
☎ 020 7404 0200 📄 020 7404 8737
e-mail: manager@roxybeaujolais.com
dir: *230mtrs NE from Holborn tube station, via Procter St. Walk through 2 arches into Eagle St. Pub between High Holborn & Red Lion Square*

Roxy Beaujolais, proprietor of the ancient Seven Stars a few blocks away, devotes this neon-signed, 1960s street-corner pub to beef, particularly the finest steaks and Bountyburgers. Her architect husband Nathan Silver's traditional oak-floored interior is best described as funky bistro meets trendy saloon, aided by dozens of pictures glorifying cows and beef. Five cuts feature on the menus: onglet/flank (for sandwiches), rib-eye, sirloin, fillet and T-bone, all aged many weeks in-house and cooked to your exact requirements. If steak's not for you, there's chicken pie; dill-cured herring; and couscous with roast vegetables. The Almost Free Lunch deal (12-3, Monday-Saturday) involves a changing menu of dishes such as eggs Benedict; corned beef hash and mild chilli mole at 'a trifling price', provided you buy an alcoholic or soft drink, such as an Adnams real ale, cider, a glass of wine, or Roxy's 'perfect' dry martini.

**Open** all day Closed: BHs, Sun **Bar Meals** Av main course £11 food served all day **Restaurant** Fixed menu price fr £5.50 food served all day ⊕ FREE HOUSE ◀ Adnams Best, Adnams Broadside, Dark Star Best, Hophead, guest ales ⊙ Aspall. ♟ 14

### PICK OF THE PUBS

### The Lamb ♥     PLAN 1 E4

94 Lamb's Conduit St WC1N 3LZ ☎ 020 7405 0713
e-mail: lambwc1@youngs.co.uk
dir: *Russell Square, turn right, 1st right, 1st left, 1st right*

This building was first recorded in 1729, was 'heavily improved' between 1836-1876, and frequented by Charles Dickens when he lived nearby in Doughty Street (now housing the Dickens Museum). This really is a gem of a place, with its distinctive green-tiled façade, very rare glass snob screens, dark polished wood, and original sepia photographs of music hall stars who performed at the nearby Holborn Empire. The absence of television, piped music and fruit machines allows

conversation to flow, although there is a working polyphon. Home-cooked bar food includes a vegetarian corner (vegetable curry, or burger), a fish choice including traditional fish and chips; and steaks from the griddle, plus pies and baked dishes from the stove. Favourites are steak and ale pie (called the Celebration 1729 pie); sausage and mash; liver and bacon; and fried egg and chips. For something lighter, try a ploughman's or a vegetable samosa with mango chutney. Recent change of hands.

**Open** all day all wk noon-11 (Thu-Sat noon-mdnt, Sun noon-10.30) **Bar Meals** L served all wk 12-9 D served all wk 12-9 food served all day ⊕ YOUNG & CO BREWERY PLC ◀ Youngs (full range). ♟ 11 **Facilities** Garden

## WC2

### The George ♥ NEW     PLAN 1 E4

213 Strand WC2R 1AP ☎ 020 7353 9638
e-mail: enquiries@georgeinthestrand.com
dir: *Opposite Royal Courts of Justice*

Facing the Royal Courts of Justice, The George was built as a coffee house in 1723, although the black and white façade is late Victorian. Once regulars included Horace Walpole and Samuel Johnson, today mingle with judges, barristers and court reporters over a pint of Sharp's Doom Bar or Black Sheep, a lunchtime salad, an open sandwich or hot wrap. For something more substantial, try roast poussin; bangers and mash; leek and mushroom Stilton pie; herb-battered cod and chips; the famous lunchtime roast carvery or traditional Irish stew.

**Open** all day all wk Closed: 25-26 Dec **Bar Meals** L served all wk 12-5 D served Mon-Sat 5-9 Sun 5-8 Av main course £8.50 **Restaurant** L served Mon-Fri 12-3 D served pre-booked only booking required Fixed menu price fr £8.95 ⊕ FREE HOUSE ◀ Sharp's Doom Bar, Hogsback TEA, Sussex Best, Sambrooks Wandle, Black Sheep ⊙ Aspalls, Suffolk Cider. ♟ 12 **Facilities** Dogs allowed

### The Lamb and Flag ♥     PLAN 1 D3

33 Rose St, Covent Garden WC2E 9EB
☎ 020 7497 9504
dir: *Leicester Square, Cranbourne St exit, turn left into Garrick St, 2nd left*

Licensed during the reign of Elizabeth I, The Lamb and Flag exudes a strong atmosphere, with low ceilings, wood panelling and high-backed settles both striking features of the bar. In 1679 the poet Dryden was almost killed in a nearby alley. These days office workers and Covent Garden tourists throng the surrounding streets. Typical examples of the hot food served upstairs include Cumberland sausages, chips and beans; and roast beef, pork, lamb or chicken. There is a courtyard to enjoy in fine weather.

**Open** all day all wk 11-11 (Fri-Sat 11am-11.30pm, Sun 12-10.30) Closed: 25 Dec **Bar Meals** L served Mon-Fri 12-3, Sat-Sun 12-5 Av main course £6.95 ⊕ FREE HOUSE ◀ Courage Best, Directors, Young's PA, Young's Special, Wells Bombardier, Harveys Best. ♟ 9

### PICK OF THE PUBS

### The Seven Stars     PLAN 1 E4

53 Carey St WC2A 2JB ☎ 020 7242 8521
e-mail: roxy@roxybeaujolais.com
dir: *From Temple N via The Strand & Bell Yard to Carey St. From Holborn SE via Lincoln's Inn Fields & Searle St to Carey St*

Chef, cookbook writer and broadcaster Roxy Beaujolais, and her architect husband Nathan Silver, own this survivor of the Great Fire of London in 1666 (they also own the beef-oriented Bountiful Cow off High Holborn). The Royal Courts of Justice are over the road and it doesn't take too many judges, barristers and other members of the legal profession taking much-needed breathers here to fill the compact and bijou, but essentially unadulterated interior. Although there are plenty of pubs in the area, the reason they come here is to enjoy a good pint and one of Roxy's chicken, rabbit or game pies; merguez sausages with cracked wheat; garlic chilli prawns; or field mushrooms and pancetta on focaccia bread. Even if you don't need the loo, pretend you do for the pleasure of navigating the narrow Elizabethan stairs. Beers come from Adnams, Dark Star and guest breweries, plus ciders from Aspall and Westons.

**Open** all day all wk 11-11 (Sat noon-11, Sun noon-10.30) Closed: 25-26 Dec, 1 Jan, Good Fri, Etr Sun **Bar Meals** L served Mon-Fri 12-3, Sat-Sun 12-9 D served Mon-Fri 5.30-9, Sat-Sun 12-9 Av main course £10 **Restaurant** Av 3 course à la carte fr £18 ⊕ FREE HOUSE ◀ Adnams Best, Adnams Broadside, Dark Star Best, Hophead, guest ales ⊙ Aspalls, Weston Organic Pear.

### The Sherlock Holmes ♥ NEW     PLAN 1 D3

10 Northumberland St WC2N 5DB
☎ 020 7930 2644 📄 020 7839 0263
e-mail: 7967@greeneking.co.uk
dir: *From Charing Cross tube station exit onto Villiers St. Through 'The Arches' (runs underneath Charing Cross station) straight across Craven St into Craven Passage to Northumberland St*

Painted black with etched glass windows and colourful hanging baskets, this traditional corner pub is chock-full of Holmes memorabilia, including photographs of Conan Doyle, mounted pages from manuscripts, and artefacts and pieces recording the adventures of the Master etective. There's even a replica of Holmes' and Watson's tting room and study adjacent to the restaurant. Even e menu is themed and offers traditional pub food.

**pen** all day all wk Closed: 25-26 Dec **Bar Meals** Av main ourse £7.45 food served all day **Restaurant** booking quired booking required Fixed menu price fr £9.25 food erved all day ⊕ Greene King ◀ Sherlock Holmes Ale, bbot Ale, Old Speckled Hen ὃ Aspalls. 🍷 14 **acilities** Garden

## GREATER LONDON

### CARSHALTON Map 6 TQ26

### *reyhound Hotel* 🍷

High St SM5 3PE
☎ 020 8647 1511 📠 020 8647 4687
**-mail:** greyhound@youngs.co.uk
**ir:** *5 mins walk from Carshalton rail station (20 min by ail from Victoria Station)*

tanding directly opposite the ponds in Carshalton Park, his distinctive former coaching inn has a welcoming fire n the bar in winter months. Records dating back to 1706 how that the white-painted building was formerly a entre for cock-fighters and race-goers. Today's visitors vill find an interesting range of filled ciabattas and nacks, together with more substantial options like ome-made steak and kidney pudding; and hake fillet in oung's beer batter, hand cut chips and mushy peas.

**pen** all wk ◀ Youngs Special, Winter Warmer, PA, Vaggle Dance. 🍷 17 **Facilities** Parking

### CHELSFIELD Map 6 TQ46

**PICK OF THE PUBS**

### The Five Bells 🍷 NEW

**BR6 7RE ☎ 01689 821044 📠 01689 891157**
**dir:** *From M25 junct 4 take A224 towards Orpington. In approx 1m turn right into Church Rd. Pub on left*

Conveniently located just inside the M25 at Junction 4, The Five Bells is situated in a village in a protected conservation area. A Grade II-listed building dating from 1668, it gets its name from the magnificent St Martin of the Tours church just up the road. There are two bars, with the dog-friendly front 'public bar' boasting an original inglenook fireplace. The larger bar also houses the restaurant area and leads to the patio and extensive garden which comes complete with a swing park area for the children. In the kitchen, chef Chris Miller offers a seasonal menu to complement the choice of real ales and wines. As well as sandwiches and pizzas, chef's specials might include roasted duck breast with slow braised cabbage, farmhouse potatoes and red wine jus; and roasted cod with chive mash, grilled asparagus and cherry tomatoes.

**Open** all day all wk **Bar Meals** L served all wk 12-3 D served Thu-Sat 6.30-9 Av main course £6 **Restaurant** L served all wk 12-3 D served Thu-Sat 6.30-9 Fixed menu price fr £8.50 Av 3 course à la carte fr £17 ⊕ ENTERPRISE INNS ◀ Courage Best, Sharp's Doom Bar, Guinness. 🍷 13 **Facilities** Children's menu Children's portions Play area Dogs allowed Garden Parking

## MERSEYSIDE

### BARNSTON Map 15 SJ28

### Fox and Hounds 🍷

**Barnston Rd CH61 1BW**
**☎ 0151 648 7685 📠 0151 648 0872**
**e-mail:** ralphleech@hotmail.com
**dir:** *M53 junct 4 take A5137 to Heswall. Right to Barnston on B5138. Pub on A551*

The pub, located in a conservation area, was built in 1911 on the site of an alehouse and barn. Its Edwardian character has been preserved in the pitch pine woodwork and leaded windows. Incredible collections of 1920s/1930s memorabilia include ashtrays, horse brasses, police helmets and empty whisky cases. Real ales and 12 wines by the glass are served alongside dishes such as starters of potted shrimps; and southern fried chicken goujons; plus various platters with a seasonal salad; sandwiches and baguettes. Sunday roasts, daily specials and desserts are posted on the chalkboard.

**Open** all wk 11-11 (Sun noon-10.30) **Bar Meals** L served Mon-Sat 12-2, Sun 12-2.30 booking required Av main course £6.25 ⊕ FREE HOUSE ◀ Websters, Theakston's Best, Old Peculier, 3 guest ales. 🍷 12
**Facilities** Children's portions Family room Dogs allowed Garden Parking

### BROMBOROUGH Map 15 SJ38

### Dibbinsdale Inn ★★★★ INN NEW

**Dibbinsdale Rd, ☎ 0151 334 9818 📠 0151 334 0097**
**e-mail:** dibbinsdaleinn.wirral@thwaites.co.uk
**dir:** *M53 junct 5, A41 towards Birkenhead. In 2m left towards Bromborough rail station. Through 2 sets of lights. 2nd right into Dibbinsdale Rd. Inn 600yds on left*

When it bought this urban-fringe pub a few years ago, Thwaites Brewery gave it the contemporary exterior and striking interior you see today. No prizes for guessing whose cask ales are sold, although there are guests too. Sourcing from carefully chosen suppliers, the kitchen creates an ever-changing menu featuring traditional Cheshire pork sausages with creamy mash and onion gravy; chicken tikka masala; and tagliatelle with creamed forest mushrooms. If you would like to explore the area or play golf, comfortable bedrooms are available.

**Open** all day all wk **Bar Meals** Av main course £7.50 food served all day **Restaurant** Fixed menu price fr £4.50 food served all day ⊕ SHIRE ◀ Thwaites cask ales, Lancaster Bomber, Guinness ὃ Kingston Press. **Facilities** Children's menu Children's portions Garden Parking **Rooms** 12

### HIGHTOWN Map 15 SD30

### The Pheasant Inn 🍷

**20 Moss Ln L38 3RA ☎ 0151 929 2106**
**dir:** *From A565 take B5193, follow signs to Howtown*

Surrounded by fields and nearby golf courses, this former alehouse is just minutes from Crosby Beach, where sculptor Antony Gormley's 100 cast-iron figures gaze out to sea. An original brick in the restaurant wall is dated 1719, when the pub was called the Ten Billets Inn. In the bar these days you'll find Timothy Taylor Landlord alongside Aspall's ciders. On the fixed-price menu are chilli con carne on rice with crème fraîche, tomato salsa and crispy tortillas; and spicy crumbled chicken supreme, chips and minted cucumber and yoghurt dip. There are grill nights and fish supper wine and dine nights to enjoy.

**Open** all day all wk noon-11pm (Sun noon-10.30pm) **Bar Meals** food served all day **Restaurant** Fixed menu price fr £6.50 Av 3 course à la carte fr £16 food served all day ⊕ MITCHELLS & BUTLERS ◀ Timothy Taylor Landlord ὃ Aspall Draught & Organic. 🍷 30 **Facilities** Children's menu Garden Parking

### LIVERPOOL Map 15 SJ39

### Everyman Bistro

**9-11 Hope St L1 9BH**
**☎ 0151 708 9545 📠 0151 703 0290**
**e-mail:** bistro@everyman.co.uk
**dir:** *In front of Metropolitan Cathedral. Bistro in basement of Everyman Theatre*

Celebrating 40 years in business, this is a favourite haunt of Liverpool's media, academic and theatrical fraternity - Bill Nighy and Julie Walters started out in the theatre above. But you don't need to write erudite leader columns, wear a mortar board, or worry about saying 'Macbeth' out loud to enjoy dishes from the twice-daily changing menus, such as Greek lamb with rice and

*continued*

**LIVERPOOL** *continued*

marinated feta; Aberdeen Angus beef provençal; aubergine and sunblush tomato risotto; followed by apple and almond Eve's pudding. Enjoy your meal with a pint of Black Sheep, continental beers or from the selection of wines.

**Open** noon-mdnt (Fri-Sat noon-2am) Closed: Sun & BH **Bar Meals** food served all day **Restaurant** food served all day ⊕ FREE HOUSE ◀ Cains Bitter, Black Sheep, Derwent Pale Ale, Copper Dragon, Timothy Taylor Landlord.

## NORFOLK

### BAWBURGH — Map 13 TG10

## PICK OF THE PUBS

### Kings Head ♀

*See Pick of the Pubs on opposite page*

### BINHAM — Map 13 TF93

## Chequers Inn

**Front St NR21 0AL ☎ 01328 830297**
e-mail: steve@binhamchequers.co.uk
dir: *On B1388 between Wells-next-the-Sea & Walsingham*

The Chequers is home to the Front Street Brewery, but even though they brew their own beer they still have regular Norfolk/East Anglian guest ales, and a large selection of bottled beers such as Old Tom. The pub has been owned by a village charity since the 1640s, and was originally a trade hall. Many stones from the nearby Binham Priory were used in its construction. The daily changing menu offers dishes such as Norfolk duck pâté, fresh lobster thermidor and plum crumble.

**Open** all wk 11.30-2.30 6-11 (Fri-Sat 11.30-2.30 6-11.30 Sun noon-2.30 7-11) **Bar Meals** L served all wk 12-2 D served all wk 6-9 ⊕ FREE HOUSE ◀ Binham Cheer 3.9%, Callums Ale 4.3%, Unity Strong 5%, Seasonal specials, micro-brewery on site. **Facilities** Children's menu Children's portions Garden Parking

### BLAKENEY — Map 13 TG04

## PICK OF THE PUBS

### The Blakeney White Horse ♀

*See Pick of the Pubs on page 316*

## The Kings Arms ♀

**Westgate St NR25 7NQ**
**☎ 01263 740341  🖹 01263 740391**
e-mail: kingsarmsnorfolk@btconnect.com
dir: *From Holt or Fakenham take A148, then B1156 for 6m to Blakeney*

A Grade II listed free house close to the North Norfolk coastal path, it's an ideal base for walks or a ferry trip to the nearby seal colony. Hosts Marjorie and Howard Davies

settled here after long and successful showbiz careers, with their son Nic now handling the day-to-day running of the pub. An excellent selection of real ales is backed by menus featuring locally-caught fish and seasonal seafood — crab in summer and mussels in winter — together with game, home-made lasagne and steaks.

**Open** all day all wk **Bar Meals** Av main course £7.50 food served all day ⊕ FREE HOUSE ◀ Greene King Old Speckled Hen, Woodforde's Wherry Best Bitter, Marston's Pedigree, Adnams Best Bitter. ♀ 10 **Facilities** Children's menu Children's portions Play area Family room Dogs allowed Garden Parking

### BLICKLING — Map 13 TG12

## PICK OF THE PUBS

### The Buckinghamshire Arms

**Blickling Rd NR11 6NF ☎ 01263 732133**
e-mail: bucksarms@tiscali.com
dir: *A410 from Cromer exit at Aylsham onto B1354, follow Blickling Hall signs*

One of Norfolk's most beautiful inns, 'The Bucks' stands by the gates of the National Trust's Blickling Hall. A late 17th-century coaching inn, it is said to be haunted by Anne Boleyn's ghost, who wanders in the adjacent courtyard and charming garden. The lounge bar and restaurant, with their solid furniture and wood-burning stoves, have plenty of appeal. Meals can be taken in either, with menus offering fresh local food served in both traditional and modern styles. Dishes from the dinner menu include starters of sweet red onion and goat's cheese tartlet, and duo of potted brown shrimp and smoked salmon mousse. Robust main courses often feature Gunton Park venison or Norfolk-reared Red Poll beef; the traditional fish pie with spinach is topped with creamy mature Cheddar mash. Vegetarians may select the home-made lasagne of aubergine, spinach and mushroom, with a sun-blushed tomato salad and French fries. The Victorian cellar houses real ales from Norfolk's Wolf Brewery and Adnams in Suffolk.

**Open** all day all wk 11-11 Closed: 25 Dec **Bar Meals** L served Mon-Fri 12-2, Sat-Sun 12-2.30 booking required D served all wk 6.45-9 booking required Av main course £9.95 **Restaurant** L served Mon-Fri 12-2, Sat-Sun 12-2.30 booking required D served all wk 6.45-9 booking required ⊕ FREE HOUSE ◀ Adnams Bitter & Regatta, Woodforde's Wherry, Nelson's Revenge, Wolf Coyote Bitter ♉ Aspall, Norfolk. **Facilities** Children's portions Garden Parking

### BRANCASTER STAITHE — Map 13 TF74

## PICK OF THE PUBS

### The White Horse ★★★ HL ◉◉ ♀

**PE31 8BY ☎ 01485 210262  🖹 01485 210930**
e-mail: reception@whitehorsebrancaster.co.uk
dir: *A149 (coast road), midway between Hunstanton & Wells-next-the-Sea*

Overlooking the creeks, marshes and sandbars of a National Nature Reserve, the glass-screened viewing balcony edging the sundeck terrace is the place to head for to view inspiring sunsets over the head of The Wash. Equally inspiring is the extensive, daily-changing restaurant menu at this two AA Rosette inn, where alfresco dining in the sunken garden is a popular warm-weather option, accompanied by Brancaster Best bitter. Inside, scrubbed pine tables and high-backed settles help to create a welcoming atmosphere for diners eager to sample the freshest seafood, including seasonal shellfish gathered from the Staithe at the foot of the inn's garden. Look forward to grilled whole skate wing with warm charred chorizo and semi-dried tomato and grain mustard dressing, or pan-seared fillets of brill with spring onion mash and crayfish tails; meat-lovers can tuck in to pan-fried best end of local lamb with braised shoulder. Tastefully furnished en suite bedrooms look out over the Norfolk Coast AONB.

**Open** all day all wk 9am-11pm (Sun 9am-10.30pm) **Bar Meals** L served all wk 11-9 D served all wk 11-9 Av main course £8.95 food served all day **Restaurant** L served all wk 12-2 booking required D served all wk 6.30-9 booking required Av 3 course à la carte fr £26.50 ⊕ FREE HOUSE ◀ Adnams Best Bitter, Fuller's London Pride, Woodforde's Wherry, Brancaster Best, guest ales ♉ Aspall. ♀ 16 **Facilities** Children's menu Children's portions Dogs allowed Garden Parking **Rooms** 15

### BRISLEY — Map 13 TF92

## The Brisley Bell Inn & Restaurant ★★★ INN

**The Green NR20 5DW ☎ 01362 668686**
e-mail: info@brisleybell-inn.co.uk
dir: *On B1145, between Fakenham & East Dereham*

Enjoying an isolated position adjacent to the village, the patio of this attractive 16th-century warm brick-built pub overlooks the largest piece of common land in Norfolk, amounting to some 200 acres. Inside you'll find a small refurbished bar serving reliable ales, with old beams, large brick fireplace and exposed brick walls. There's a separate neatly laid-up dining room, and a wide-ranging menu that takes in bar snacks, fresh locally-sourced game, steaks, daily fish specials, and popular Sunday roasts. If you would like to stay over to explore the area, then there are newly decorated bedrooms available.

*continued on page 316*

# PICK OF THE PUBS

## Kings Head ♥

**BAWBURGH**  Map 13 TG10

**Harts Ln NR9 3LS ☎ 01603 744977**
e-mail:
anton@kingshead-bawburgh.co.uk
**dir:** *From A47 W of Norwich take B1108 W*

Standing opposite the village green, with the River Yare flowing close by, the 17th-century Kings Head has been in the hands of Pam and Anton Wimmer for more than twenty years. The pub is big on traditional charm with solid oak beams, bulging walls, wooden floors, comfy leather seating and pine dining furniture, making it the perfect place to be after a day exploring the delights of nearby Norwich, either warming yourself by the woodburners, or whiling away the evening on the south-facing patio, or out in the landscaped garden. As a free house it serves real ales from East Anglia, as well as Aspall cider from the Suffolk village of that name.

Monthly menus and daily changing specials firmly rooted in local markets offer a wide choice of modern British, European and oriental dishes, as well as pub classics. The pub has a list of VIPs (Very Important Producers) who provide produce for them; it also quoted the miles travelled. Recent menus include starters of home-made black pudding scotch egg; and deep-fried Norfolk rabbit with home-made ketchup; main courses of free-range mutton and rosemary sausages with rosemary mash; slow-roasted Swannington pork belly with spiced Bramley apple purée, cider sauce, bubble and squeak, black pudding and crackling; and pan-fried sea trout with local samphire, brown shrimp nut butter and warm potato and sorrel salad. Roast meats on Sundays are all served with seasonal vegetables, Yorkshire pudding and goose-fat roast potatoes.

The dessert list might feature custard tart with poached rhubarb, saffron syrup and rhubarb ripple ice cream; or home-made halva, mixed nut baklava with pistachio and cardamom kulfi. Bar snacks and nibbles include somebody called Jonny's home-made crumpets,

and smoked Dapple cheese and Marmite on toast. Take home some fish and chips - wrapped in proper paper!

**Open** all day Closed: 25-27 Dec eve, 1 Jan eve, Mon **Bar Meals** L served Tue-Sat 12-2, Sun 12-4 booking required D served Tue-Sat 5.30-9 booking required Av main course £9.95 **Restaurant** L served Tue-Sat 12-2, Sun 12-4 booking required D served Tue-Sat 5.30-9 booking required Av 3 course à la carte fr £20 ⊕ FREE HOUSE ◀ Adnams Best, Adnams Broadside, Woodforde's Wherry, Norfolk Nog ♻ Aspall, Aspall Blush. ♟ 14 **Facilities** Children's menu Dogs allowed Garden Parking

# PICK OF THE PUBS

## The Blakeney White Horse 🍷

**BLAKENEY**　　　　Map 13 TG04

4 High St NR25 7AL
☎ 01263 740574　📠 01263 741303
e-mail: info@blakeneywhitehorse.co.uk
dir: *From A148 (Cromer to King's Lynn road) onto A149 signed to Blakeney*

A short stroll from the quayside in this gem of a coastal village stands the 17th-century White Horse. Set around the old courtyard and stables of a former coaching inn, this traditional brick-and-flint building is tucked away in the cluster of narrow streets lined with flint-built fishermen's cottages winding down to a small tidal harbour, with fabulous views over creeks, Glaven Valley estuary and vast marshes of sea lavender, samphire and mussel beds. Inside, the bar, dining room and airy conservatory are tastefully decorated in creams and darkwood with soft lamplight, and the informal bar is adorned with local artwork.

The inn has a deserved reputation for its food, with lobster, crab and mussels sourced from local fishermen, meat and game from nearby Holkham Estate, and soft fruit, salads and vegetables from small farms and suppliers. At lunch, tuck into locally smoked prawns, deep-fried soft herring roes on toast, a ploughman's featuring Binham Blue and Ellie Betts' cheese and home-made pickles, smoked haddock and crayfish kedgeree and home-made fish pie, as well as a selection of granary bread sandwiches.

From the evening carte, choose grilled sardines with toasted ciabatta, gazpacho sauce and pea shoots, pork rillettes with spiced chutney and toast, or roast red pepper, monks beard, red onion, parmesan and duck egg frittata. Moving on to main courses and you might find fresh Morston mussels à la marinière, confit duck leg with lyonnaise potatoes, Savoy cabbage, chestnuts and bacon, or Arthur Howell's rib-eye steak, fondant potato, red kale and the pub's own black pudding. A 80-bin wine list, 35 of which are available by the glass, and real ales from Adnams and Woodforde's complete the picture.

**Open** all day all wk 10.30am-11pm Closed: 25 Dec **Bar Meals** L served all wk 12-2.15 booking required D served Thu-Sun 6-9, Fri-Sat 6-9.30 booking required **Restaurant** ⊕ FREE HOUSE ◀ Adnams Bitter, Woodforde's Wherry, Adnams Broadside, Yetmans ♂ Aspall. 🍷 35 **Facilities** Children's menu Family room Dogs allowed (daytime only) Garden Parking

Save on Hotels. Book at **theAA.com/hotel**

**NORFOLK** 317 **ENGLAND**

**RISLEY** *continued*

pen noon-3 6-11 (Sat 11-11 Sun noon-10.30) Closed:
Mon **Bar Meals** L served Tue-Sun 12-2.30 D served Tue-
Thu & Sun 6-8, Fri-Sat 6-9 Av main course £5.95
**Restaurant** L served Tue-Sun 12-2.30 D served Tue-Thu
& Sun 6-8, Fri-Sat 6-9 booking required Av 3 course à la
carte fr £16 ⊕ FREE HOUSE ◀ Greene King IPA, Abbot,
Olde Trip, OSU, Guinness ♻ Aspall. **Facilities** Children's
menu Children's portions Garden Parking **Rooms** 3

---

### BURNHAM MARKET     Map 13 TF84

## PICK OF THE PUBS

## The Hoste Arms ★★★ HL ◉◉ �

*See Pick of the Pubs on page 318*

---

### BURNHAM THORPE     Map 13 TF84

## PICK OF THE PUBS

## The Lord Nelson �

**Walsingham Rd PE31 8HN**
☎ 01328 738241   📄 01328 738241
e-mail: simon@nelsonslocal.co.uk
web: www.nelsonslocal.co.uk
**dir:** *B1355 (Burnham Market to Fakenham road), pub
9m from Fakenham & 1.75m from Burnham Market.
Pub near church opposite playing fields*

Opposite the delightful village cricket ground and
bowling green, this pub started life in 1637 as The
Plough. It was renamed The Lord Nelson in 1798, to
honour Horatio Nelson who was born in the village.
Visitors today can soak up an atmosphere that has
changed little over the past 370 years; you can even sit
on Nelson's high-backed settle. Drinks are served from
the taproom, with real ales drawn straight from the
cask. In the cosy bar you can also partake in unique
rum-based tipples such as Nelson's Blood. The kitchen
aims to cook dishes with balance between flavours, so
that the quality of the ingredients shines. Lamb shank
with rosemary sauce and sea bass with white wine
sauce on bacon and leek mash are typical choices, with
seasonal specialities such as Brancaster mussels and
Cromer crab. Children will enjoy the huge garden.

---

**Open** noon-3 6-11 (Jul-Aug noon-11pm) Closed: Mon eve
(ex school hols) **Bar Meals** L served all wk 12-2.30 D
served Tue-Sun 6-9 Av main course £11.95 **Restaurant** L
served all wk 12-2.30 D served Tue-Sun 6-9 booking
required Av 3 course à la carte fr £19.50 ⊕ GREENE KING
◀ Greene King Abbot Ale & IPA, Woodforde's Wherry,
Nelson's Blood Bitter. � 14 **Facilities** Children's menu
Play area Dogs allowed Garden Parking

---

### CLEY NEXT THE SEA     Map 13 TG04

## PICK OF THE PUBS

## The George Hotel �

**High St NR25 7RN**
☎ 01263 740652   📄 01263 741275
e-mail: info@thegeorgehotelatcley.co.uk
**dir:** *On A149 through Cley next the Sea, approx 4m
from Holt*

Located near the sea and marshes, The George is
stands on historic Cley's winding High Street. The beer
garden backs onto the marshes, from where you can
see Cley's famous mill, while the lovely oak-floored bar
provides a year-round welcome. You can snack in the
lounge bar or dine in the light, painting-filled
restaurant. At lunchtime the menu runs from
sandwiches (hot chicken, avocado, crispy bacon and
red pesto mayonnaise; or brie, smoked ham and fresh
mango) to starters and light meals such as warm pan-
fried chicken liver, duck liver and rocket salad with
balsamic dressing; or hearty main courses - perhaps
home-made steak, kidney and suet pudding. Dinner
brings starters of roast parsnip and honey soup laced
with cream, followed by braised pork belly with spiced
red cabbage, wilted spinach and honey glaze. Seafood
is a real strength.

**Open** all day all wk 11-11 ◀ Greene King IPA, Abbot
Ale, Yetmans ales, Adnams Broadside, Woodforde's
Wherry ♻ Aspall. � 8 **Facilities** Family room Dogs
allowed Garden Parking

---

### COLTISHALL     Map 13 TG21

## Kings Head

**26 Wroxham Rd NR12 7EA** ☎ 01603 737426
e-mail: contact@kingsheadcoltishall.co.uk
**dir:** *A47 (Norwich ring road) onto B1150 to North
Walsham at Coltishall. Right at petrol station, follow to
right past church. Pub on right by car park*

Standing on the banks of the River Bure, this 17th-
century free house is right in the heart of the Norfolk
Broads. Hire cruisers are available at nearby Wroxham,
and fishing boats can be hired at the pub. If you prefer to
stay on dry land you'll find a warm welcome at the bar,
with a range of real ales that includes Adnams Bitter,
Directors and Marston's Pedigree. There's an inviting
menu, too, served in both the bar and the restaurant.

---

**Open** all wk 11-3 6-12 Closed: 26 Dec **Bar Meals** L
served all wk 12-2 booking required D served all wk 6-7
booking required Av main course £9.50 **Restaurant** L
served all wk 12-2 booking required D served all wk 6-9
booking required Av 3 course à la carte fr £25 ⊕ FREE
HOUSE ◀ Adnams Bitter, Directors, Marston's Pedigree,
Fuller's London Pride. **Facilities** Children's
menu Children's portions Parking

---

### DEREHAM     Map 13 TF91

## Yaxham Mill ★★★★ INN �

**Norwich Rd, Yaxham NR19 1RP**
☎ 01362 851182   📄 01362 691482
e-mail: yaxhammill@hotmail.co.uk
**dir:** *From Norwich take A47 towards Swaffham. At East
Dereham take B1135. Yaxham 2m*

A converted windmill in the middle of open Norfolk
countryside and dating back to 1810. The miller's house
and chapel were transformed into a restaurant and bar.
Menus cater for all tastes, with grilled lemon sole, minted
lamb steak, sweet and sour chicken, and chilli con carne
among other dishes. Home-made pies, including steak
and kidney and cottage, are something of a speciality.

**Open** all wk ◀ Bombardier, Youngs, 2 guest ales. � 8
**Facilities** Garden Parking **Rooms** 12

---

### EAST RUDHAM     Map 13 TF82

## PICK OF THE PUBS

## The Crown Inn � NEW

**The Green PE31 8RD** ☎ 01485 528530
e-mail: reception@crowninnnorfolk.co.uk
**dir:** *On A148, 6m from Fakenham on King's Lynn road*

Part of TV chef Chris Coubrough's thriving Flying Kiwi
mini-empire of pubs along the Norfolk coast, the
revamped Crown at East Rudham opened its doors in
2008 and business has been brisk ever since. Smack
beside the A148 and overlooking the village green, it
draws the crowds for its charming, spruced-up interior,
which successfully blends traditional period features (low
beams, rug-strewn wooden floor, open log fires) with
contemporary comforts — cool Farrow & Ball colours, high-
backed leather chairs at scrubbed tables, shelves of
books, fresh flowers and chunky church candles. Equally
bang up-to-date is the food, with the short, daily printed
menus listing good modern British dishes prepared from
fresh Norfolk produce. Tuck into sharing slate of antipasti,
or start with braised ham hock terrine with piccalilli, then
follow with roast duck with cabbage and bacon hash,
onion jam and balsamic jus, or seared salmon with
smoked haddock and leek chowder and parmesan,
leaving room for sticky ginger cake with walnut ice cream.
Expect decent lunchtime sandwiches and proper kids'
food on daughter Lily Coubrough's menu.

**Open** all day all wk **Bar Meals** L served all wk 12-2.30
D served all wk 6.30-9.30 Av main course £10.95
⊕ FLYING KIWI INNS ◀ Adnams Explorer, Broadside,
Flying Kiwi Homebrew ♻ Aspall. **Facilities** Children's
menu Children's portions Dogs allowed

# PICK OF THE PUBS

## The Hoste Arms ★★★HL 🌸🌸 🍷

**BURNHAM MARKET**    Map 13 TF84

**The Green PE31 8HD**
☎ 01328 738777    📄 01328 730103
**e-mail:** reception@hostearms.co.uk
**dir:** *Signed off B1155, 5m W of Wells-next-the-Sea*

Situated on the village green in one of Norfolk's best known villages, this former coaching inn is just a stone's throw from stunning beaches and walks along the north Norfolk coast. Built as a manor house in 1550, The Hoste Arms has been an inn since 1720. Over the centuries it has also been a courthouse and livestock market - not to mention a spell as a Victorian brothel. It was rescued by Paul and Jeanne Whittome in

1989 after 130 years of decline, and is now a beautifully presented hotel with striking interior design and 35 stylish bedrooms. The bar retains a traditional feel with its lively atmosphere and open log fire; there's also a pretty walled garden tucked behind the Moroccan-themed terrace, as well as a relaxed conservatory where you can chill out and read the papers over a cappuccino.

Expect to dine well in one of the six restaurant areas: lunchtime choices include a range of soups, salads and sandwiches, with plenty of local seafood supplemented by a range of hot dishes. The dinner menu might begin with toasted goat's cheese with a marinated vegetable and rocket salad; or shredded duck and Oriental vegetable tart. Follow up with mixed seafood, garlic and parsley stew; wild mushroom, spinach and mascarpone risotto with shaved Parmesan; or braised ox cheeks with sautéed mushrooms, horseradish mash and crispy pancetta. The pudding menu ranges from espresso tart with coffee

sauce and vanilla ice cream to elderflower crème brûlée with coconut shortbread and lime sorbet.

As well as a great choice of real ales, including the best from Woodforde's and Greene King Breweries, the cellar houses over 100 fine wines in a temperature-controlled environment.

**Open** all wk **Bar Meals** L served all wk 12-2 D served all wk 6-9 Av main course £14 **Restaurant** L served all wk 12-2 booking required D served all wk 6-9 booking required Fixed menu price fr £23.50 FREE HOUSE 🍺 Woodforde's Wherry Best, Greene King Abbot Ale, Nelson's Revenge. 🍷 16
**Facilities** Children's menu Dogs allowed Garden Parking **Rooms** 35

Save on Hotels. Book at **theAA.com/hotel**

NORFOLK 319 ENGLAND

## EAST RUSTON — Map 13 TG32

### The Butchers Arms

**Oak Ln NR12 9JG ☎ 01692 650237**
dir: *From A149 SE of North Walsham follow signs for Briggate, Honing & East Ruston. Oak Ln off Off School Rd*

Originally three terraced cottages built in the early 1800s, the middle one of which was a butcher's shop. Today it's a quintessential beamed village pub, without jukebox or pool table; you'll just find 'Mavis', a 1954 Comma fire engine, parked outside. Landlady Julie Gollop takes pride in creating a welcoming atmosphere, offering a good choice of real ales from local breweries, and serving traditional home-cooked favourites such as liver and bacon casserole, or roast pork and apple sauce. There is a beer garden and vine-covered patio for summer dining.

Open 12-2.30 6.30-11 Closed: Mon Jan & Feb Bar Meals L served all wk 12-2 D served all wk 7-8.30 Av main course £6.95 Restaurant L served all wk 12-2 D served all wk 7-8.30 Fixed menu price fr £6.95 Av 3 course à la carte fr £16 ⊕ FREE HOUSE ◀ Adnams, Woodforde's, Old Speckled Hen, Greene King IPA. Facilities Children's menu Children's portions Dogs allowed Garden Parking Notes ⊛

## EATON — Map 13 TG20

### The Red Lion ⬤

**50 Eaton St NR4 7LD**
**☎ 01603 454787 📠 01603 456939**
e-mail: redlioneaton@hotmail.co.uk
dir: *Off A11, 2m S of Norwich city centre*

This heavily-beamed 17th-century coaching inn has bags of character, thanks to its Dutch gables, panelled walls and inglenook fireplaces. The covered terrace enables customers to enjoy one of the real ales or sample the extensive wine list outside during the summer months. The extensive lunch menu offers everything from steak and kidney suet pudding to grilled red snapper fillets with mango and sweet chilli salsa; or Swannington baked gammon with a Cumberland sauce.

Open all day all wk ◀ Old Speckled Hen, Courage Directors, Greene King IPA, Adnams Bitter, Woodforde's Wherry, Fuller's London Pride. ⬤ 10 Facilities Garden Parking

## ERPINGHAM — Map 13 TG13

### PICK OF THE PUBS

### The Saracen's Head

**NR11 7LZ ☎ 01263 768909 📠 01263 768993**
e-mail: saracenshead@wolterton.freeserve.co.uk
dir: *From A140, 2.5m N of Aylsham, left through Erpingham, pass Spread Eagle on left. Through Calthorpe bear left (do not follow road to Aldborough), straight on to pub*

The privately owned Saracen's Head is deep among the fields down country lanes — and you do find yourself wondering why there's a pub in such a lonely spot. The answer is that it was once a coach house, built in Tuscan farmhouse style in 1806 for neighbouring Wolterton Hall. Its arty, parlour room atmosphere is the legacy of the former owner, who has now been succeeded by Tim and Janie Elwes. You may eat in one of the bars, where Suffolk and Norfolk real ales are on hand pump, or in the restaurant, where a sample three-course meal might comprise grilled halloumi on lavender (a local crop) croute with sun-blushed tomatoes; roast Norfolk pheasant with Calvados and cream; or baked Cromer crab with apple and sherry; and poached pears in spicy red wine. For a really quiet drink or meal, sit out in the sheltered courtyard garden.

Open all wk 11.30-3 6-11 (Sun noon-3 7-10.30) Closed: 25 Dec Bar Meals L served 12.30-2 booking required Restaurant L served 12.30-2 booking required D served 7.30-9 booking required ⊕ FREE HOUSE ◀ Adnams Best Bitter, Woodforde's Wherry. Facilities Children's menu Children's portions Garden Parking

## FAKENHAM — Map 13 TF92

### The Wensum Lodge Hotel

**Bridge St NR21 9AY**
**☎ 01328 862100 📠 01328 863365**
e-mail: enquiries@wensumlodge.fsnet.co.uk
dir: *In town centre*

Idyllically located by the River Wensum just three minutes walk from Fakenham, this lovely pub has a stream flowing through its garden and offers guests free fishing on the river. The building dates from around 1700, and was originally the grain store for the adjoining mill. Fine ales are complemented by home-cooked food prepared from locally supplied ingredients, with baguettes, jacket potatoes and an all-day breakfast on the light bite menu and a carte menu for heartier fare. An ideal base for cycling, bird-watching, fishing and horse-racing.

Open all wk ⊕ FREE HOUSE ◀ Greene King Abbot Ale & IPA, Old Mill Bitter. Facilities Garden Parking

### The White Horse Inn ★★★★ INN

**Fakenham Rd, East Barsham NR21 0LH**
**☎ 01328 820645 📠 01328 820645**
e-mail: whitehorse@norfolkinns.co.uk
dir: *1.5m N of Fakenham on minor road to Little Walsingham*

Ideally located for birdwatching, walking, cycling, fishing, golf and sandy beaches, this refurbished 17th-century inn offers en suite rooms and a characterful bar with log-burning inglenook. Good range of beers and malt whiskies. Fresh ingredients are assured in daily specials, with fish especially well represented. Typical choices include chicken breast stuffed with Stilton, peppered mackerel fillets, sweet and sour pork, and venison steak. There is also a grill menu. Birdwatching tours can be arranged.

Open all wk ◀ Adnams Best, Adnams Broadside, Tetley, Wells Eagle IPA. Facilities Garden Parking Rooms 3

## GREAT RYBURGH — Map 13 TF92

### The Blue Boar Inn ⬤

**NR21 0DX ☎ 01328 829212**
e-mail: blueboarinn@ryburgh.co.uk
dir: *Off A1067 4m S of Fakenham*

James and Melinda Lee have put a great deal of effort into restoring this rambling 17th-century coaching inn with its beamed ceilings and inglenook fireplace. A large magnolia tree ushers you into the whitewashed listed building, which stands opposite the round towered Saxon church of St Andrew. Adnams supplies real ales alongside David Winter ales. Local produce features strongly on the extensive chalkboard menu, and typical dishes include Norfolk beef and ale pie; locally smoked Scottish salmon; and braised Ryburgh sausages.

Open 11.30-2.30 6.30-11.30 Closed: Tue Bar Meals L served Wed-Mon 11.30-2.30 D served Wed-Mon 6.30-10.30 Av main course £9.95 Restaurant L served Wed-Mon 11.30-2.30 D served Wed-Mon 6.30-10.30 Av 3 course à la carte fr £20 ⊕ FREE HOUSE ◀ Adnams Bitter, Winters Golden, Winters Revenge, Guinness, Staropramen. ⬤ 8 Facilities Children's menu Children's portions Play area Family room Dogs allowed Garden Parking

## HEVINGHAM — Map 13 TG12

### Marsham Arms Freehouse ⬤

**Holt Rd NR10 5NP ☎ 01603 754268**
e-mail: nigelbradley@marshamarms.co.uk
dir: *On B1149 N of Norwich airport, 2m through Horsford towards Holt*

Built as a roadside hostel for poor farm labourers by Victorian philanthropist and landowner Robert Marsham. Some original features remain, including the wooden beams and large open fireplace. There is a spacious garden with paved patio and dedicated family room. A good range of fresh fish dishes includes cod, haddock, sea bass, herrings and crab. With a popular 'help yourself' salad bar, other main courses might include braised beef with red wine and cranberry; locally sourced roast pheasant; and steaks. Look out for the monthly wine appreciation evenings.

Open all day all wk Bar Meals L served all wk 12-2.30 D served all wk 6-9.30 Restaurant L served all wk 12-2.30 D served all wk 6-9.30 ⊕ FREE HOUSE ◀ Adnams Best, Woodforde's Wherry Best Bitter, Mauldens, Worthington, Broadside ○ Aspall. Facilities Children's menu Children's portions Play area Family room Dogs allowed Garden Parking

# PICK OF THE PUBS

## Walpole Arms

**ITTERINGHAM** Map 13 TG13

**NR11 7AR**
☎ 01263 587258  📠 01263 587074
**e-mail:**
goodfood@thewalpolearms.co.uk
**web:** www.thewalpolearms.co.uk
**dir:** *From Aylsham towards Blickling. After Blickling Hall take 1st right to Itteringham*

Formerly owned by Robert Horace Walpole, a direct descendant of Britain's first prime minister, the Walpole Arms has been a pub since 1836. Today it is both a real pub and a dining destination. Operated by Fine Country Inns, a family business headed by Alan and Cheryl Sayers, the Walpole's team of highly experienced individuals includes an ex-producer of TV's *Masterchef* programme. So expect to find a dozen wines served by the glass,

as well as Adnams Broadside and Woodforde's Wherry Best on tap.

The kitchen team uses the best seasonal and local produce to create thoroughly modern dishes. Both restaurant and oak-beamed bar offer a daily changing three-course carte; children are welcome and have their own menu to choose from. Bar snacks comprise the likes of Cheddar ploughman's with Norfolk Dapple, home-made pickles and apple salad, and corned beef hash cake with a fried egg.

For those with a hearty appetite, the carte will not disappoint. Typical starters include terrine of chicken, ham and pepper with cherry tomato salad, and warm potato salad with feta, fennel, parsley and black olives. Main course choices are equally well considered: confit of Gressingham duck with borlotti beans, chorizo, fennel and tomato; locally caught sea bass with saffron mash, baked tomato and gazpacho salsa; and open butternut squash ravioli with ricotta, spinach and amaretti. Desserts are traditional and

modern at the same time: Italian chocolate and almond torte with crème fraîche and tipsy cherries typifies the kitchen's approach.

Extensive gardens to the front and rear of the vine-covered terrace encourage relaxation on summer days. Locals and visitors alike enjoy the informal quiz evening in the bar every Wednesday.

**Open** all wk noon-3 6-11 (Sun noon-4) Closed: 25 Dec **Bar Meals** L served all wk 12-2 D served all wk 6-9.30 **Restaurant** L served Thu-Sun 12-2 D served Thu-Sun 6-9.30 ⊕ FREE HOUSE ⬛ Adnams Broadside & Bitter, Woodforde's Wherry Best Bitter, guest ales ♂ Aspalls. ♀ 12 **Facilities** Children's menu Play area Dogs allowed Garden Parking

## HEYDON — Map 13 TG12

### Earle Arms ♀

**The Street NR11 6AD ☎ 01263 587376**
**e-mail:** haitchy@aol.com
**dir:** Signed between Cawston & Corpusty on B1149 (Holt
to Norwich road)

Horse-racing memorabilia adorn the walls of this 16th-
century free house situated in this pretty privately-owned
village. One of the two rooms offers service through a
hatch to the tables in the pretty back garden. Heydon
itself is often used as a film location, and stars of stage
and screen have enjoyed a high quality menu that
includes wild mushroom risotto with dressed salad, and
fillet of sole with herb butter, or Swannington pork and
black pepper sausages.

**Open** 12-3 6-11 Closed: Mon **Bar Meals** L served Tue-Sun
12-2 booking required D served Tue-Sun 7-9 booking
required Av main course £9 **Restaurant** L served Tue-Sun
12-2 booking required D served Tue-Sun 7-9 booking
required Av 3 course à la carte fr £25 ⊕ FREE HOUSE
◀ Adnams, Woodforde's Wherry, Black Sheep. ♀ 16
**Facilities** Children's portions Dogs allowed Garden
Parking

## HOLKHAM — Map 13 TF84

### PICK OF THE PUBS

### Victoria at Holkham ★★ SHL ◉◉ ♀

**Park Rd NR23 1RG**
**☎ 01328 711008 ▤ 01328 711009**
**e-mail:** victoria@holkham.co.uk
**dir:** On A149, 3m W of Wells-next-the-Sea

The Victoria stands at the gates of landlord Tom Coke's
Palladian ancestral home, Holkham Hall, just minutes
from the golden sands of Holkham Beach. Its opulent,
colonial-style interior is full of furniture and
accessories from Rajahstan and other exotic places.
Outside is a courtyard where summer barbecues are
popular. Tom Coke would argue that the Victoria's
main attraction is what he calls 'some of the most
consistently good food in North Norfolk'. Key words here
are fresh, local and seasonal, whether it be shellfish,
fish or samphire from the north Norfolk coast, beef
from farms on the Holkham estate, organic chickens
from a tenant farmer, venison from the herd of fallow
deer or, in the winter, wild game from family shoots.
Perhaps choices might be pumpkin and truffle risotto;
slow braised beef with pomme purée; or Holkham
venison with braised red cabbage; and chilled vanilla
rice pudding with stewed English plums.

**Open** all day all wk 11-11 **Bar Meals** L served all wk
12-2.30 **Restaurant** L served all wk 12-2.30 booking
required D served Sun-Thu 7-9, Fri-Sat 7-9.30 booking
required ⊕ HOLKHAM ESTATE ◀ Adnams Best,
Woodforde's Wherry, guest ale ♂ Aspall. ♀ 12
**Facilities** Children's menu Children's portions Play
area Dogs allowed Garden Parking **Rooms** 10

## HORSEY — Map 13 TG42

### Nelson Head

**The Street NR29 4AD ☎ 01493 393378**
**dir:** On B1159 (coast road) between West Somerton &
Sea Palling

Located on a National Trust estate, which embraces
nearby Horsey Mere, this 17th-century inn will, to many,
epitomise the perfect country pub. It enjoys the tranquility
of a particularly unspoilt part of the Norfolk coast -
indeed, the Broads are ½ mile away and glorious beaches
only a mile - and the sheltered gardens look out towards
the dunes and water meadows. Haddock and chips,
cottage pie and a selection of vegetarian choices are
among the dishes available. Local beers are Woodforde's
Wherry and Nelson's Revenge.

**Open** all day all wk **Bar Meals** L served all wk 12-2.30 D
served all wk 6-8.30a Av main course £7.95 **Restaurant** L
served all wk 12-2.30 D served all wk 6-8.30 ⊕ FREE
HOUSE ◀ Woodforde's Wherry, Nelson's Revenge
♂ Stowford Press. **Facilities** Children's menu Play area
Family room Garden Parking

## HORSTEAD — Map 13 TG21

### Recruiting Sergeant ♀

**Norwich Rd NR12 7EE ☎ 01603 737077**
**dir:** On B1150 between Norwich & North Walsham

Matthew and Nicola Colchester have developed an
enviable local reputation for food at this award-winning
colour-washed brick and flint free house. Fresh local
produce is the foundation of their ever-changing menu,
which might include steamed steak and kidney pudding;
baked red mullet with garlic king prawns; or leek and
Roquefort tart on a bed of dressed leaves. The sheltered
rear patio and lawned garden are ideal for alfresco
summer dining.

**Open** all day all wk 11-11 (Sun noon-10.30) **Bar Meals** L
served Mon-Sat 12-2, Sun 12-9 booking required D
served Mon-Sat 6-9, Sun 12-9 booking required Av main
course £8 **Restaurant** L served Mon-Sat 12-2, Sun 12-9
booking required D served Mon-Sat 6-9, Sun 12-9
booking required Av 3 course à la carte fr £20 ⊕ FREE
HOUSE ◀ Adnams, Woodforde's, Greene King Abbot Ale,
Scottish Courage ♂ Aspall. ♀ 10 **Facilities** Children's
menu Children's portions Dogs allowed Garden Parking

## HUNSTANTON — Map 12 TF64

### The King William IV 🅰 ★★★★ INN ♀

**Heacham Rd, Sedgeford PE36 5LU**
**☎ 01485 571765 ▤ 01485 571743**
**e-mail:** info@thekingwilliamsedgeford.co.uk
**dir:** From A149 turn right at lights in Heacham onto
B1454. Pub 2m in village

Tucked away in the village of Sedgeford and conveniently
close to the north Norfolk coastline, this extensively
refurbished and extended free house has been an ale
house since 1836. It has winter log fires and a covered
alfresco dining area for warmer months. Appetising
salads and baguettes will fill the odd corner, whilst
choices like Snettisham Park venison; or parmesan
crusted sea bass in pesto sauce cater for larger
appetites.

**Open** all day 11-11 (Sun 12-10.30) Closed: Mon L (ex BH)
**Bar Meals** L served Tue-Sat 12-2, Sun 12-2.30 booking
required D served all wk 6.30-9 booking required
**Restaurant** L served Tue-Sat 12-2, Sun 12-2.30 booking
required D served all wk 6.30-9 booking required ⊕ FREE
HOUSE ◀ Woodforde's Wherry, Adnams Bitter, Greene
King Abbot Ale, Old Speckled Hen, guest ale. ♀ 9
**Facilities** Children's menu Children's portions Dogs
allowed Garden Parking **Rooms** 9

## HUNWORTH — Map 13 TG03

### The Hunny Bell ♀ NEW

**The Green NR24 2AA ☎ 01263 712300**
**e-mail:** hunnybell@animalinns.co.uk
**dir:** From Holt take B1110. 1st right to Hunworth

The traditional beamed main bar and cosy snug at this
whitewashed 18th-century inn have been carefully
restored to blend historic character with modern
amenities. East Anglian ales and cider accompany a
menu where traditional favourites feature heavily: suet
crust steak and kidney pie; home-cooked ham, eggs and
chips; and apple and rhubarb crumble are typical
choices. Outside, there's a new terrace overlooking the
green, as well as a charming old-world English garden.

**Open** all wk noon-3 6-11 **Bar Meals** L served all wk
12-2.30 D served all wk 6-9 Av main course £7.50
**Restaurant** L served all wk 12-2.30 D served all wk 6-9
Fixed menu price fr £15 Av 3 course à la carte fr £27
⊕ ANIMAL INNS ◀ Woodforde's Wherry, Adnams, Greene
King, Elgoods ♂ Aspall. ♀ 10 **Facilities** Children's
menu Children's portions Dogs allowed Garden Parking

## ITTERINGHAM — Map 13 TG13

### PICK OF THE PUBS

### Walpole Arms ◉ ♀

*See Pick of the Pubs on opposite page*

## KING'S LYNN · Map 12 TF62

### The Stuart House Hotel, Bar & Restaurant ★★★ HL

35 Goodwins Rd PE30 5QX
☎ 01553 772169 📠 01553 774788
e-mail: reception@stuarthousehotel.co.uk
web: www.stuarthousehotel.co.uk
dir: *Follow signs to town centre, pass under Southgate Arch, immediate right, in 100yds turn right*

Situated within its own grounds, this hotel and bar is a short walk from Kings Lynn's historic town centre. Cask conditioned East Anglian ales and traditional dishes are served in the bar, and there is a separate restaurant offering a carte menu and daily specials. A programme of events includes regular live music, murder mystery dinners and an annual beer festival. The patio and beer garden are perfect places to relax in warmer months.

Open all wk 5-11 **Bar Meals** D served all wk 6-9.30 **Restaurant** D served all wk 7-9.30 ⊕ FREE HOUSE ◄ Adnams, Woodforde's, Greene King, Oakham JHB, Timothy Taylor Landlord. **Facilities** Play area Garden Parking **Rooms** 18

## LARLING · Map 13 TL98

### PICK OF THE PUBS

### Angel Inn ♥

NR16 2QU ☎ 01953 717963 📠 01953 718561
dir: *5m from Attleborough, 8m from Thetford. 1m from station*

Ideally situated for visiting the Brecks or walking in Thetford Forest, this 17th-century former coaching inn has been run by three generations of the Stammers family for more than 80 years. There's a homely, local feel to the heavily-beamed public bar, whilst the lounge bar has wheel-back chairs, an oak settle, winter log fires and a collection of more than 100 water jugs. There are five real ales available plus four guests including a mild. The extensive menus feature local ingredients wherever possible, with lighter options ranging from freshly-made sandwiches or jacket potatoes to ploughman's, burgers and salads. Main dishes include a substantial mixed grill; local farmed trout with parsley butter; and broccoli and cream cheese bake topped with sliced potatoes and melted cheese. Camping and caravan pitches are available just across the road in Angel meadow, and each August the Angel hosts Norfolk's largest outdoor beer festival.

---

Open all day all wk 10am-mdnt **Bar Meals** L served Sun-Thu 12-9.30, Fri-Sat 12-10 booking required D served Sun-Thu 12-9.30, Fri-Sat 12-10 booking required Av main course £9.95 food served all day **Restaurant** L served Sun-Thu 12-9.30, Fri-Sat 12-10 booking required D served Sun-Thu 12-9.30, Fri-Sat 12-10 booking required food served all day ⊕ FREE HOUSE ◄ Adnams Bitter, Hop Back, Caledonian Deuchars IPA, Timothy Taylor Landlord, Mauldons Ŏ Aspall. ♥ 10 **Facilities** Children's menu Children's portions Play area Garden Parking

## LETHERINGSETT · Map 13 TG03

### The Kings Head ♥ NEW

Holt Rd NR25 7AR ☎ 01263 712691
e-mail: thebar@kingsheadnorfolk.co.uk
dir: *On A148 just before entering Holt. Pub on corner*

Part of the small, Norfolk-based Flying Kiwi group, the Kings Head offers a homely mix of original features and modern-day comfort in both the bar and restaurant. Fresh, locally sourced ingredients are the foundation of main course offerings like pan-roasted rack of lamb, and roasted squash and garlic risotto. The light lunch menu includes a smoked salmon and dill mayonnaise baguette, washed down with a pint of Flying Kiwi Homebrew maybe? The enormous garden has a large play castle to keep the children entertained.

Open all day all wk **Bar Meals** L served all wk 12-2.30 D served all wk 6.30-9.30 Av main course £10.95 ⊕ FLYING KIWI INNS ◄ Adnams Broadside, Flying Kiwi Homebrew Ŏ Aspall. ♥ 13 **Facilities** Children's menu Children's portions Play area Family room Dogs allowed Garden Parking

## LITTLE FRANSHAM · Map 13 TF91

### The Canary and Linnet

Main Rd NR19 2JW ☎ 01362 687027
dir: *On A47 between Dereham & Swaffham*

A pretty, former blacksmith's cottage fulfilling the key requirements of a traditional English country pub - low ceilings, exposed beams and an inglenook fireplace. Its sign once showed footballers in Norwich City (Canaries) and Kings Lynn (Linnets) strips, but now features two birds in a cage. Food offered throughout the bar, conservatory restaurant and garden includes steak and ale pie, medallions of pork in Stilton sauce, and seared Cajun spiced swordfish steak with lime and coriander dressing.

Open all wk noon-3 6-11 (Sun noon-3 6.30-10.30) **Bar Meals** L served all wk 12-2 booking required D served all wk 6-9 booking required **Restaurant** L served all wk 12-2 D served all wk 6-9 ⊕ FREE HOUSE ◄ Greene King IPA, Adnams Bitter, Wolf Ŏ Aspall. **Facilities** Children's menu Dogs allowed Garden Parking

## LITTLE WALSINGHAM · Map 13 TF93

### The Black Lion Hotel ♥

Friday Market Place NR22 6DB
☎ 01328 820235 📠 01328 821407
e-mail: lionwalsingham@btconnect.com
dir: *From King's Lynn take A148 & B1105. Or from Norwich take A1067 & B1105*

Parts of this former coaching inn date from 1310, when they were built to accommodate Edward III on his numerous pilgrimages to the shrine at Walsingham (the hotel's name comes from his wife's coat of arms). The friendly bar is warmed by a fire in winter, and the menu offers something for every taste: light options include soup and filled baps, while a full meal could feature goat's cheese melt, followed by mixed grill, and hot crumble or pie of the day.

Open all wk noon-3 6-mdnt (Sat noon-mdnt) **Bar Meals** ▶ served all wk 12-2 D served all wk 7-9 Av main course £6 **Restaurant** L served all wk 12-2 D served all wk 7-9 booking required Av 3 course à la carte fr £15 ⊕ ENTERPRISE INNS ◄ Woodforde's Wherry, Black Sheep Special, Woodforde's Nelson's Revenge, Tetley's. ♥ 8 **Facilities** Children's portions Dogs allowed Garden

## MARSHAM · Map 13 TG12

### The Plough Inn ♥

Norwich Rd NR10 5PS
☎ 01263 735000 📠 01263 735407
e-mail: enq@ploughinnmarsham.co.uk
web: www.ploughinnmarsham.co.uk
dir: *On A140, 10m N of Norwich*

A warm welcome is assured at this 18th-century countryside inn, ideally located for the North Norfolk coast and the Broads. The pumps serve both real ales and ciders, while menus based on local and seasonal produce include traditional favourites such as home-made fish cakes; rolled sirloin of beef with Stilton fritter; venison and steak suet pudding; chef's signature dish of slow-roasted belly of Blythburgh pork; and a carvery on Sunday. A specials board proffers fresh fish; gluten- and wheat-free meals are also a speciality.

Open all wk 12-2.30 6-11 (all day Sat in summer) **Bar Meals** L served all wk 12-2.30 D served all wk 6-9 ⊕ FREE HOUSE ◄ IPA, Adnams, John Smith's Ŏ Aspall. ♥ 10 **Facilities** Children's menu Children's portions Garden Parking

# PICK OF THE PUBS

## The Mad Moose Arms

**2 Warwick St NR2 3LB**
☎ **01603 627687**   📄 **01508 494946**
**e-mail:** madmoose@animalinns.co.uk
**web:** www.themadmoose.co.uk
**dir:** *1m from A11*

A warm neighbourhood pub, the result of a stunning refit that created a decidedly stylish ground floor bar, all vibrant red walls, exposed brickwork and gleaming wood. Locals and regular visitors know they can expect Norfolk real ales - Woodforde's Wherry and Wolf's Straw Dog - and a bar menu offering a variety of interesting sandwiches with skinny fries and green salad; light meals and salads; and main dishes such as Kerelan tiger prawns and green mango curry; 28-day matured Dedham Vale 8oz rib-eye steak; and spicy bean cakes with yam chips.

On the first floor is the elegant, AA two-Rosette, 1Up restaurant with chandeliers, sea-green drapes, and a feature wall depicting a fairytale forest – the fine dining part of the operation. Confident and ambitious cooking is typified by starters of warm pigeon breast, sweet red onions, sauté back bacon with a poached raisin and herb reduction; fillets of east coast mackerel, green beans, beetroot purée and sauté potato vinaigrette; or potted Suffolk pork, capers, cornichons, celeriac remoulade and toasted brioche. To follow: daube de boeuf, bacon lardons, baby onions, glazed carrots and horseradish mash; slow roasted pork belly and cheek, risotto balls, red cabbage, butternut squash and Madeira jus; pan roasted fillet of line-caught cod, white beans, salsify, chorizo and crispy leeks; wild mushroom and Jerusalem artichoke millefeuille, sweet potato purée and leafy salad.

Among the desserts consider dark chocolate terrine, glazed bananas, praline anglaise and licquorice ice cream; warm ginger and sesame dacquoise, vanilla poached rhubarb and fresh rhubarb sorbet. There is a stylish outdoor patio for alfresco dining in warmer weather.

**Open** all day all wk noon-mdnt Closed: 25 Dec **Bar Meals** L served Mon-Fri 12-2, Sat-Sun 12-9 D served Mon-Fri 6-10, Sat-Sun 12-9 Av main course £7.50 **Restaurant** L served Sun 12-3 booking required D served Mon-Sat 7-9.30 booking required Av 3 course à la carte fr £25 🍺 Woodforde's Wherry, Straw Dog. ♟ 9 **Facilities** Garden

## MUNDFORD     Map 13 TL89

### Crown Hotel

Crown Rd IP26 5HQ
☎ 01842 878233   🖷 01842 878982
e-mail: info@the-crown-hotel.co.uk
dir: *A11 to Barton Mills junct, then A1065 to Brandon & onto Mundford*

Built in 1652, the Crown has been many things - a famous hunting lodge; the local magistrates' court; even a doctors' waiting room. Its most unusual feature, in these pancake-flat parts, is that it is set into a hill! Traditional food, home-cooked is served in the bars and the restaurant; perhaps steak and ale pie or Jimmy Butler's slow roasted pork belly with apple, brandy sauce, baked apple and dauphinoise potatoes. In addition to the real ales and wines, there is a choice of over 50 malt whiskies.

**Open** all day all wk **Bar Meals** L served all wk 12-3 D served all wk 6.30-10 **Restaurant** L served all wk 12-3 D served all wk 6.30-10 booking required ⊕ FREE HOUSE ◀ Courage Directors, Marston Pedigree, Greene King IPA, Woodforde's Wherry, guest ales. **Facilities** Children's portions Dogs allowed Garden Parking

## NORWICH     Map 13 TG20

### Adam & Eve ♞

Bishopsgate NR3 1RZ
☎ 01603 667423   🖷 01603 667438
e-mail: theadamandeve@hotmail.com
dir: *Telephone for directions*

Norwich's oldest pub, the Adam & Eve has been serving ale since 1249, when it was the lodging house for craftsmen building the Anglican cathedral next door. These days it remains a traditional pub undisturbed by TV or games machines, and counts a few ghosts among its regulars. Decked with award-winning flowers in summer, it offers real ales and plenty of traditional, home-made food with the likes of steak and kidney pudding, and pork ribs with chips and salad.

**Open** all day all wk 11-11 (Sun noon-10.30) Closed: 25-26 Dec, 1 Jan **Bar Meals** L served Mon-Sat 12-7, Sun 12-5 Av main course £7.95 ⊕ ENTERPRISE INNS ◀ Adnams Bitter, Theakston Old Peculier, Wells Bombardier, Mauldons Moletrap ♂ Aspall. ♞ 11 **Facilities** Parking

---

## PICK OF THE PUBS

### The Mad Moose Arms ◉◉ ♞

*See Pick of the Pubs on page 323*

---

### Ribs of Beef ♞

24 Wensum St NR3 1HY
☎ 01603 619517   🖷 01603 625446
e-mail: roger@cawdron.co.uk
dir: *From Tombland (in front of cathedral) turn left at Maids Head Hotel. Pub 200yds on right on bridge*

Once used by the Norfolk wherry skippers, this welcoming riverside pub is still popular among boat owners cruising The Broads. Its structure incorporates remnants of the original 14th-century building, which was destroyed in the Great Fire in 1507. The pub is famous for its range of cask ales, excellent wines and traditional English food using locally sourced produce. The menu offers a wide range of tempting sandwiches and baguettes, burgers and jacket potatoes, while larger appetites should be satisfied with dishes such as beef and ale stew; salmon and dill fishcakes; or chilli con carne. Sit outside on the jetty in the warmer months.

**Open** all day all wk 11-11 (Fri-Sat 11am-1am) **Bar Meals** L served Mon-Fri 12-2.30, Sat-Sun 12-5 Av main course £6.45 ⊕ FREE HOUSE ◀ Woodforde's Wherry, Adnams Bitter, Elgoods Mild, Oakham JHB, Fullers London Pride ♂ Kingfisher Norfolk Cider. ♞ 9 **Facilities** Children's menu Children's portions Family room

## REEPHAM     Map 13 TG12

### The Old Brewery House Hotel ★★ HL

Market Place NR10 4JJ
☎ 01603 870881   🖷 01603 870969
e-mail: manager.oldbreweryhouse@ohiml.com
dir: *Off A1067 (Norwich to Fakenham road), B1145 signed Aylsham*

A grand staircase, highly polished floors and wooden panelling characterise this fine hotel, originally built as a private residence in 1729. It became a hotel in the 1970s, retaining many of its Georgian features. Alongside the real ales and fine wines, there's a bar menu of freshly produced dishes. Recent change of hands.

**Open** all day all wk Sun-Thu 8-12 (Fri-Sat 8-1) **Bar Meals** L served all wk 12-2.30 D served all wk 6.30-9 ⊕ FREE HOUSE ◀ IPA, Abbot Ale, London Pride, Directors. **Facilities** Children's menu Dogs allowed Garden Parking **Rooms** 23

## RINGSTEAD     Map 12 TF74

## PICK OF THE PUBS

### The Gin Trap Inn ★★★★ INN ◉ ♞

*See Pick of the Pubs on opposite page*

---

## SALTHOUSE     Map 13 TG04

### The Dun Cow

Coast Rd NR25 7XG ☎ 01263 740467
dir: *On A149 (coast road). 3m E of Blakeney, 6m W of Sheringham*

Overlooking some of the country's finest freshwater marshes, the front garden of this attractive pub is inevitably popular with birdwatchers and walkers. The bar area was formerly a blacksmith's forge, and many original 17th-century beams have been retained. Children are welcome, but there's also a walled rear garden reserved for adults. The menu includes snacks, pub staples like burgers and jacket potatoes, and main courses like gammon steak, pasta and meatballs, plaice and chips, and lasagne.

**Open** all wk ◀ Greene King IPA & Abbot Ale, Adnams Broadside. **Facilities** Family room Dogs allowed Garden Parking

## SNETTISHAM     Map 12 TF63

## PICK OF THE PUBS

### The Rose & Crown ★★ HL ◉ ♞

Old Church Rd PE31 7LX
☎ 01485 541382   🖷 01485 543172
e-mail: info@roseandcrownsnettisham.co.uk
dir: *10m N from King's Lynn on A149 signed Hunstanton. Inn in village centre between market square & church*

With its rose-covered façade, the 14th-century whitewashed Rose & Crown is everything you'd expect from a North Norfolk village inn - twisting passages and hidden corners, low ceilings and old beams, uneven pamment floors, log fires, excellent beers and an informal atmosphere. The pretty walled garden was once the village bowling green. Each of the three convivial bars has its own character - and characters! The single menu allies traditional pub favourites with more exotic dishes, all prepared to a high standard and using, wherever possible, locally supplied produce. Beef, for example, comes from cattle that grazed the nearby salt marshes; fishermen still in their waders deliver Brancaster mussels and Thornham oysters; and strawberries and asparagus are grown all around. Typical dishes lying behind the AA Rosette award are seared Norfolk pigeon breast, roast beetroot and Jerusalem artichoke; and crispy pork belly, caramelised plum, soy glaze. Stylish bedrooms offer excellent accommodation.

**Open** all day all wk **Bar Meals** L served Mon-Fri 12-2, Sat-Sun 12-2.30 booking required D served Sun-Thu 6-9, Fri-Sat 6-9.30 booking required Av main course £13 **Restaurant** L served Mon-Fri 12-2, Sat-Sun 12-2.30 booking required D served Sun-Thu 6-9, Fri-Sat 6-9.30 booking required Av 3 course à la carte fr £25 ⊕ FREE HOUSE ◀ Adnams Bitter & Broadside, Interbrew Bass, Fuller's London Pride, Greene King IPA. ♞ 12 **Facilities** Children's menu Children's portions Play area Family room Dogs allowed Garden Parking **Rooms** 16

# PICK OF THE PUBS

## The Gin Trap Inn ★★★★INN 🌹 ♇

RINGSTEAD                     Map 12 TF74

**6 High St PE36 5JU ☎ 01485 525264**
**e-mail:** thegintrap@hotmail.co.uk
**web:** www.gintrapinn.co.uk
**dir:** *A149 from King's Lynn towards Hunstanton. In 15m turn right at Heacham for Ringstead*

Set in a tranquil village a few miles inland from Hunstanton and the bird-rich marshes of the North Norfolk coast, this 17th-century former coaching inn is now very much a charming, modern-day gastro-pub. Once festooned with old gin traps and farm implements (hence the name), the rustic bar has a relaxed and friendly atmosphere, exposed brickwork and beams, and blazing log-burning stove for warmth throughout the winter, plus an intimate dining room and modern conservatory, and a pretty garden for summer alfresco drinking and dining. Walkers pop in for drinks and a meal to fortify them on their way, and dogs are very welcome - landlords Steve Knowles and Cindy Cook have two great danes.

Food is taken very seriously, and the snacks board includes local mussels in season and a selection of hand-cut sandwiches including some based on speciality breads, such as ciabatta and focaccia. The menu is available throughout the pub and makes good use of local seasonal produce, from organic meats reared at Courtyard Farm in the village, and mussels and oyster delivered daily in season from nearby Thornham.

Typically, start with six Thornham oysters, served on ice with shallot and red wine vinegar dressing, or ham hock terrine with pear and walnut chutney and home-baked bread, then move on to pot-roasted lamb shoulder with pearl barley and winter vegetable broth; sea bass with celeriac and parsley purée, creamed leeks and red wine gravy; or confit Courtyard Farm organic saddleback pork belly with wholegrain mustard velouté. Desserts range from dark chocolate tart with milk chocolate sorbet to banana and rum parfait, and orange scented rice pudding with roast pears. There are three individually appointed bedrooms available.

**Open** all day all wk 11.30am-11pm (11.30-2.30 6-11 in winter) **Bar Meals** L served Mon-Fri 12-2, Sat-Sun 12-2.30 D served Sun-Thu 6-9, Fri-Sat 6-9.30 Av main course £12 **Restaurant** L served Mon-Fri 12-2, Sat-Sun 12-2.30 D served Sun-Thu 6-9, Fri-Sat 6-9.30 Av 3 course à la carte fr £24 ⊞ FREE HOUSE ◀ Adnams Best, Woodforde's Wherry, guest ales ♂ Aspall. ♇ 9 **Facilities** Children's menu Dogs allowed Garden Parking **Rooms** 3

# PICK OF THE PUBS

## The Wildebeest Arms

**STOKE HOLY CROSS**  Map 13 TG20

**82-86 Norwich Rd NR14 8QJ**
☎ 01508 492497  📄 01508 494946
**e-mail:** wildebeest@animalinns.co.uk
**web:** www.thewildebeest.co.uk
**dir:** *From A47 take A140, left to Dunston. At T-junct turn left, Wildebeest Arms on right*

Worth the short drive south of Norwich, this charming village local has been tastefully modernised, taking on a modern rustic chic look. Thick, chunky wooden tables, wooden floors and oak beams, vases of fresh lilies, potted plants, crackling log fires and yellow rag-washed walls create a good first impression. What is striking is the quirky collection of African tribal art, which adds a touch of exoticism, with colourful masks, primitive instruments, large carved hippos and a giraffe, and various spears and bold rugs.

Although the emphasis has been placed firmly on delivering great food, drawing discerning Norwich diners, all are welcome to pop in for a pint of Adnams and a decent glass of wine (16 are available by the glass).

The kitchen takes a modern approach – underpinned by a classical French theme – on the appealing carte and lunch and dinner menu du jour offers. From the latter, kick off with roast vine tomato and red pepper soup, or dill and lime cured gravad lax with smoked mackerel cake, blood orange salad and horseradish cream, and follow with chargrilled chicken breast with sautéed potatoes, chorizo and mushroom jus, or butternut squash, leek and parmesan risotto. Pudding choice may include raspberry and almond Bakewell tart, and Bramley apple crumble with vanilla ice cream.

Alternatively, look to the carte for confit duck and pancetta cake with roasted sweet glazed figs, followed by sea bass with saffron potatoes and dill velouté, or lamb rump with red wine jus, with frozen ginger parfait with poached rhubarb and rhubarb jelly, or a taster of Norfolk Binham Blue cheese for pudding. There is stylish outdoor seating to enjoy in warmer weather. The perfect retreat from the hustle and bustle of Norwich.

**Open** all wk Closed: 25-26 Dec
**Bar Meals** L served all wk 12-2.30 D served all wk 6-9 Av main course £14
**Restaurant** L served all wk 12-2.30 booking required D served all wk 6-9 booking required Fixed menu price fr £14.95 Av 3 course à la carte fr £22.50 ⊕ FREE HOUSE 🛢 Adnams ᷁ Aspall. 🍷 16 **Facilities** Garden Parking

# PICK OF THE PUBS

## Chequers Inn A ★★★★ INN ☙

**THOMPSON**  Map 13 TL99

**Griston Rd IP24 1PX**
☎ **01953 483360**  📄 **01953 488092**
**e-mail:**
richard@thompsonchequers.co.uk
**web:** www.thompsonchequers.co.uk
**dir:** *Between Watton & Thetford off A1075*

Like its namesakes elsewhere, this delightful 17th-century free house takes its name from the chequered cloth used for counting money, wages and rents in medieval times. Manorial courts, held here from at least 1724, dealt with rents, letting of land, and petty crime.

Today, the whitewashed building with its low-slung thatched roof stands hidden amongst the trees on the edge of Thompson village. Original features include exposed beams and timbers, whilst old farming memorabilia hangs from the walls.

Food is served seven days a week from a varied selection of menus and specials boards. Eat in the bar for pub favourites such as gammon steak with egg or pineapple; deep-fried cod and chips; and home-made vegetable curry. In the evenings, restaurant choices might include double lamb chops topped with cheese and mushrooms; stuffed chicken breast with smoked salmon; butternut squash and goat's cheese lasagne; and home-made mushroom and sweet pepper Stroganoff. Round things off with home-made desserts like treacle and almond tart, or opt for a selection of English and continental cheeses served with grapes, celery and biscuits.

If you're tempted to stay awhile, three purpose-built guest rooms adjacent to the inn make The Chequers an ideal base for exploring the heart of Norfolk on local walks, or the Peddars Way National Trail. Alternatively, the eight-mile Great Eastern Pingo Trail follows a succession of shallow depressions in the ground that were formed during the last Ice Age. These shallow pools are now home to many uncommon plants, insects and amphibians.

Dogs are welcome in the large rear garden, which offers picnic tables and children's play equipment, as well as extensive views over the surrounding countryside.

**Open** all wk 11.30-3 6.30-11
**Bar Meals** L served all wk 12-2 D served all wk 6.30-9 Av main course £8
**Restaurant** L served all wk 12-2 D served all wk 6.30-9 Av 3 course à la carte fr £22 ⊕ FREE HOUSE ◀ Fuller's London Pride, Adnams Best, Wolf Best, Greene King IPA, Woodforde's Wherry Best Bitter. ☙ 8 **Facilities** Children's menu Play area Dogs allowed Garden Parking **Rooms** 3

## STOKE HOLY CROSS | Map 13 TG20

### PICK OF THE PUBS

### The Wildebeest Arms ⊚⊚ ♀

*See Pick of the Pubs on page 326*

## STOW BARDOLPH | Map 12 TF60

### PICK OF THE PUBS

### The Hare Arms ♀

PE34 3HT ☎ 01366 382229 📠 01366 385522
e-mail: trishmc@harearms222.wanadoo.co.uk
dir: *From King's Lynn take A10 to Downham Market. After 9m village signed on left*

Trish and David McManus have been licensees at this attractive ivy-clad pub for over 30 years. The pub was built during the Napoleonic wars and takes its name from the surrounding estate, ancestral home of the Hare family since 1553. The Hare has preserved its appeal and become deservedly popular. The L-shaped bar and adjoining conservatory are packed with decades-worth of fascinating bygones; the cat warms itself by the fire and peacocks wander around outside. An extensive menu of regular pub food is supplemented by daily specials, including local smoked sprats with horseradish dip; luxury fish pie; popular steak and peppercorn pie; and Jeff Sargeant's sausages with chive mash. The silver service restaurant offers a carte menu in the evening with a range of steaks, and dishes such as beef fillet medallions in a creamy smoked paprika, red pepper and garlic sauce; and guinea fowl with pork, apple and raisin stuffing and Calvados sauce. Vegetarians are well catered for.

**Open** all wk 11-2.30 6-11 (Sun noon-10.30) Closed: 25-26 Dec **Bar Meals** L served Mon-Sat 12-2, Sun 12-10 D served Mon-Sat 6.30-10, Sun 12-10 **Restaurant** D served Mon-Sat 7-9 booking required Fixed menu price fr £15 Av 3 course à la carte fr £28 ⊕ GREENE KING ◀ Greene King Abbot Ale, IPA & Old Speckled Hen, St Edmunds, guest ale ♂ Aspall. ♀ 9 **Facilities** Children's menu Children's portions Family room Garden Parking

## SWANTON MORLEY | Map 13 TG01

### *Darbys Freehouse*

1&2 Elsing Rd NR20 4NY
☎ 01362 637647 📠 01362 637928
e-mail: louisedarby@hotmail.co.uk
dir: *From A47 (Norwich to King's Lynn) take B1147 to Dereham*

Built in the 1700s as a large country house, then divided into cottages in the late 19th century. In 1987, after the village's last traditional pub closed, it was converted into the pub you see today, while retaining its old beams and inglenooks. Traditional pub food includes steak and mushroom pudding, braised lamb shank, chargrilled pork loin, scampi, beer-battered haddock, steaks, curries and a vegetarian selection. Children have their own menu and a play area.

**Open** all wk 11.30-3 6-11 (Sat 11.30-11, Sun 12-10.30). Food served all day Sat-Sun ◀ Woodforde's Wherry, Adnams Broadside & Best, 2 guest ales. **Facilities** Play area Family room Dogs allowed Garden Parking

## THOMPSON | Map 13 TL99

### PICK OF THE PUBS

### Chequers Inn ◮ ★★★★ INN ♀

*See Pick of the Pubs on page 327*

## THORNHAM | Map 12 TF74

### PICK OF THE PUBS

### Lifeboat Inn ★★ HL ⊚ ♀

Ship Ln PE36 6LT ☎ 01485 512236 📠 01485 512323
e-mail: reception@lifeboatinn.co.uk
dir: *A149 from Hunstanton for approx 6m. 1st left after Thornham sign*

The Lifeboat is a 16th-century inn overlooking Thornham Harbour and the salt marshes. Its original character has been retained, and inside, the warm glow of paraffin lamps enhances the welcoming atmosphere, while the adjoining conservatory is renowned for its ancient vine and adjacent walled patio garden. The best available fish and game feature on the frequently changing menus; baked fillet of salmon in filo, for example, or smoked haddock fishcakes; or try the lamb cutlets or fillet of beef with horseradish mash. Nearby is Thornham Beach, Blakeney, Cley, Sandringham and Nelson's birthplace at Burnham Thorpe.

**Open** all day all wk **Bar Meals** food served all day **Restaurant** D served all wk 7-9.30 booking required ⊕ MAYPOLE GROUP PLC ◀ IPA, Abbot, Wherry, Adnams, guest ales. ♀ 10 **Facilities** Children's menu Children's portions Play area Dogs allowed Garden Parking **Rooms** 13

### PICK OF THE PUBS

### The Orange Tree ♀

High St PE36 6LY ☎ 01485 512213 📠 01485 512424
e-mail: email@theorangetreethornham.co.uk
dir: *Telephone for directions*

This contemporary country pub, recently taken over by Mark and Joanna Goode, stands by the ancient Peddar's Way in a lovely coastal village. Head chef Philip Milner was named Great British Seafood Pub Chef of the Year 2010 for his wild sea bass and Norfolk razor clams signature dish. He changes his menus frequently, according to the season, while his specials vary from day to day. Along with a good choice of real ales, bar snacks include chargrilled Sandringham (the Royal Estate supplies most of the meats) Red Poll steak burger; and chilli tikka masala. Naturally, the seafood on the main menu is the best, such as pan-fried red snapper with Brancaster mussels and chorizo paella; and baked barracuda. Other tempting possibilities are Moroccan spiced lamb rump; corn-fed chicken and mushroom pie; and portobello mushroom Wellington. Two large gardens and a children's play area add extra family appeal.

*The Orange Tree*

**Open** all day all wk **Bar Meals** food served all day **Restaurant** food served all day ⊕ PUNCH TAVERNS ◀ Woodforde's Wherry, Adnams Best Bitter, Broadside ♂ Aspall. ♀ 10 **Facilities** Children's menu Play area Dogs allowed Garden Parking

## TITCHWELL | Map 13 TF74

### PICK OF THE PUBS

### Titchwell Manor Hotel ★★★ HL ⊚⊚ ♀

PE31 8BB ☎ 01485 210221 📠 01485 210104
e-mail: margaret@titchwellmanor.com
dir: *A149 between Brancaster & Thornham*

In a stunning location on Norfolk's north coast and run by the Snaith family for 20 years, this Victorian manor has been tastefully updated with a light, modern decor. Expect to find a contemporary-styled lounge, an informal bar with stripped wooden floors, and a light and airy conservatory restaurant. From its pretty walled garden the sea views are glorious, and its proximity lends a major influence to the menus. The cooking is skilled and interesting, using local and seasonal ingredients to produce imaginative and well-presented dishes with starters such as Brancaster oysters, and confit duck leg. Mains include oriental pork casserole; fish, chips and mushy peas; chicken pie, mash and leeks; and smoked red pepper pastry ratatouille; and a desserts could be a tempting sticky toffee pudding and Earl Grey prunes. Families are welcome (children have their own interesting menu) and stylish rooms are uncluttered, warmly decorated and split between the inn and a converted barn set around a courtyard.

**Open** all day all wk **Bar Meals** food served all day **Restaurant** food served all day ⊕ FREE HOUSE ◀ Greene King IPA, Abbot. ♀ 8 **Facilities** Children's menu Dogs allowed Garden Parking **Rooms** 26

# PICK OF THE PUBS

## The Crown ♇

### WELLS-NEXT-THE-SEA
Map 13 TF94

**The Buttlands NR23 1EX**
☎ **01328 710209**  📄 **01328 711432**
**e-mail:**
reception@crownhotelnorfolk.co.uk
**dir:** *10m from Fakenham on B1105*

Overlooking the tree-lined green known as The Buttlands, the striking contemporary decor and furnishings of this 17th-century former coaching inn blend effortlessly with its old-world charm. Beneath the bar's ancient beams, East Anglian ales and Aspall real cider accompany from the bar menu dishes such as smoked salmon with pickled beetroot; and chicken breasts on roast root vegetables. Whether you eat here, more formally in the restaurant, in the new, warm and cheerful Orangery, or

outside with its great views, the main menu features traditional favourites, the best of modern British cuisine, and dishes influenced by the cooking of the Pacific Rim. Starters include kipper and whisky pâté, and warm leek and pepper tart. Always likely to go down well are the traditional, represented by roast rack of lamb with roast vegetables and potatoes with tapenade jus; and pork and leek sausages with grain mustard mash and onion gravy.

Flag-waving for the modern British selection are sun-blushed tomato, mozzarella and basil-stuffed chicken breast on herb-crushed potato and roast red onion; and seared sea bream with orange and fennel salad. Finally, market fish in Thai watermelon curry with fragrant rice and coriander yoghurt conveys the flavour of the Far East. Try also a sampler of European and Asian appetizers served on a tile. Seafood specials are always available. Typical desserts are vanilla and star anise crème brûlée with rhubarb compote, and lemon and almond tart with butterscotch sauce.

The wine list prefers the personal, hands-on producer, rather than the big brands. Indeed, a good few are available by the glass and there are a few half-bottles.

**Open** all day all wk **Bar Meals** L served all wk 12-2.30 D served all wk 6.30-9.30 Av main course £11.95 **Restaurant** D served all wk 7-9 booking required ⊕ FREE HOUSE ◀ Adnams Bitter, Woodforde's Wherry, guest ale ♂ Aspall. ♇ 14 **Facilities** Children's menu Dogs allowed Garden Parking

# PICK OF THE PUBS

## Wiveton Bell

**WIVETON**  Map 13 TG04

**Blakeney Rd NR25 7TL**
☎ **01263 740101**
e-mail: enquiries@wivetonbell.co.uk
dir: *1m from Blakeney. Wiveton Rd off A149*

The classically elegant, 18th-century Bell overlooks Wiveton's green and church, just a mile from wild, bird-abundant salt marshes. The interior is clean (in the design sense, of course) with earthy heritage-coloured walls, greyish woodwork, stripped beams, chunky tables and oak-planked floors. Further character is provided by the bold, contemporary oil paintings by local artists that line the walls of the cosy bar, where Adnams Broadside, Woodforde's Wherry and Yetman's Holt beers, premium draught lager and a carefully selected wine list hold sway.

If it's chilly outside, head for the tables close to the inglenook fireplace and mingle with the locals. To avoid a crush at the bar on busy summer days, a serving hatch delivers drinks to the sheltered, south-facing rear garden, lit in the evening by candlelight to ensure maximum enjoyment of starlit skies. Chef Jamie Murch's extensive seasonal menu is bolstered by adventurous specials that make good use of local fish, game and much more, and one glance at the menu should provide a strong clue as to why the Bell has earned an AA Rosette.

As well as classic bistro favourites, there's always a daily fish special. Begin then, in the airy, book-lined conservatory restaurant, with tempura tiger prawns with ginger, chilli and coriander dipping sauce or pea, mint and mascarpone risotto. Follow with smoked Norfolk Dapple cheese burger with hand-cut chips and home-made relish; penne pasta with wild mushroom and pancetta; chicken korma with onion bahji; or slow roast Briston pork belly with whole grain mash and Bramley

apple jus. For dessert, choose from apple, pear and sultana crumble, banoffee cheesecake and raspberry coulis, and bread and butter pudding.

**Open** all day all wk Closed: 25 Dec **Bar Meals** L served all wk 12-2.15 booking required D served all wk 6-9 booking required **Restaurant** L served all wk 12-2.15 booking required D served all wk 6-9 booking required
⊕ FREE HOUSE ◀ Woodforde's Wherry, Adnams Broadside, Yetmans
Ô Stowford Press. ♑ 17
**Facilities** Children's menu Dogs allowed Garden Parking

## PICK OF THE PUBS

### Three Horseshoes

**NR23 1NL** ☎ **01328 710547**

*dir: From Wells A149 to Cromer, then right onto B1105 to Warham*

This gem of a pub first opened its doors in 1725. Its rambling old rooms, including a gas-lit main bar, are stone floored with scrubbed wooden tables; a grandfather clock ticks away in one corner, and a curious green and red dial in the ceiling turns out to be a rare example of Norfolk Twister, an ancient pub game. Vintage posters, clay pipes, photographs and memorabilia adorn the walls, while down a step are old one-arm bandits. Woodforde's Norfolk Wherry and guest ales are served from the cask through a hole in the bar wall. Home-made soups, pies and puddings dominate the menu, so start with beef and onion soup; or cheesy mushroom bake; follow with game and wine pie; or seafood and salmon pie; and end with chocolate syrup sponge; or bread and butter pudding. A no-chips policy applies, incidentally. Outside is a beer garden and covered courtyard.

**Open** all wk 12-2.30 6-11 **Bar Meals** L served all wk 12-1.45 D served all wk 6-8.30 Av main course £7.80 ⊕ FREE HOUSE ◀ Greene King IPA, Woodforde's Wherry ♂ Whin Hill Cider. **Facilities** Children's portions Family room Dogs allowed Garden Parking **Notes** ☺

## PICK OF THE PUBS

### The Crown ♥

*See Pick of the Pubs on page 329*

### The Wheatsheaf

**Manor Farm, Church Rd NR25 6NX** ☎ **01263 822110**
*dir: 2m inland from Sheringham on A148, turn opp Sheringham Park*

Formerly known as the 'old manor farmhouse', this charming building was converted to a pub over 20 years ago and retains many original features. Sample one of the real ales from Woodforde's or Nelson's Revenge and relax in refurbished bar, one of the restaurants or the large garden. All food is made on the premises using fresh local produce. From the bar menu, dishes might include prime beef lasagne or steak and kidney suet pudding, while typical choices from the restaurant menu are minted lamb meatballs with tomato sauce; and local rabbit casseroled in wine and herbs.

**Open** 11.30-3 6.30-11.30 Closed: Mon **Bar Meals** L served all wk 12-2 D served all wk 6.30-9 Av main course £12 **Restaurant** L served all wk 12-2 D served all wk 6.30-9 ⊕ FREE HOUSE ◀ Woodforde's Wherry Best Bitter, Nelson's Revenge, Norfolk Nog, Greene King IPA, guest ales ♂ Aspall. **Facilities** Children's menu Children's portions Play area Dogs allowed Garden Parking

### Fishermans Return

**The Lane NR29 4BN** ☎ **01493 393305**
e-mail: fishermansreturn@yahoo.co.uk
web: www.fishermans-return.com
*dir: 8m N of Great Yarmouth on B1159*

Long beaches and National Trust land are within 300 metres of this 350-year-old brick and flint pub – and it's dog-friendly too, making it an ideal spot to finish a walk. Behind the bar are Woodforde's Wherry, Norfolk Nog and guest ales. Menus include popular favourites, from toasted sandwiches to cottage pie. But look to the daily-changing blackboard for fish and seafood specials, when freshly caught sea bass and mackerel may be on offer.

**Open** all wk **Bar Meals** L served all wk 12-2.30 D served all wk 6-9 Av main course £9 **Restaurant** L served all wk 12-2.30 D served all wk 6-9 ⊕ FREE HOUSE ◀ Woodforde's Wherry, Norfolk Nog, Guest Ales ♂ Westons Stowford Press, Old Rosie Scrumpy. **Facilities** Children's menu Play area Family room Dogs allowed Garden Parking

## PICK OF THE PUBS

### Wiveton Bell ◉ ♥

*See Pick of the Pubs on opposite page*

### The Fur & Feather Inn ♥

**Slad Ln NR13 6HQ** ☎ **01603 720003** 📠 **01603 722266**
*dir: From A1151 (Norwich to Wroxham road), follow brown signs for Woodforde's Brewery. Pub next to Brewery*

This idyllic country pub is ideal for real ale lovers: Woodforde's Brewery is next door, and of course the ales are offered here, straight from the cask. The pub was originally two farm cottages, and now boasts three cosy bar areas and a smart restaurant where you can enjoy steak and ale pie, home baked ham, and goat's cheese,

pepper and tomato lasagne, for example, followed by pannacotta and Norfolk honey or a baked vanilla cheesecake maybe.

**Open** all wk ◀ Woodforde's Wherry, Sundew, Norfolk Nog, Nelsons Revenge, Adnam's Reserve. ♥ 10 **Facilities** Garden Parking

# NORTHAMPTONSHIRE

### The Olde Coach House Inn ♥

**CV23 8UN** ☎ **01788 890349** 📠 **01788 891541**
e-mail: info@oldecoachhouse.co.uk
*dir: M1 junct 18 follow A361/Daventry signs. Village on left*

A carefully modernised former farmhouse with lots of different eating and drinking areas, at least three real ales, a good choice of wines, friendly staff, and plenty of seating outside. The handsome creeper-clad stone inn is furnished with all manner of chairs, squashy leather sofas, pale wooden tables, large mirrors, hunting scenes, an original old stove, and fresh flowers. Dining here is popular too: expect the likes of smoked pigeon breast with herb croûte; meat and fish grazing boards; and lemon tart with raspberry sorbet.

**Open** all wk Mon-Fri noon-3 5.30-11 (Sat-Sun all day) **Bar Meals** L served Mon-Sat 12-2.30, Sun 12-8 D served Mon-Sat 6-9.30, Sun 12-8 booking required Av main course £8.95 **Restaurant** L served Mon-Sat 12-2.30, Sun 12-8 D served Mon-Sat 6-9.30, Sun 12-8 booking required Av 3 course à la carte fr £22.95 ⊕ CHARLES WELLS ◀ Everards Tiger, Youngs, Wells Bombardier, Old Hooky. ♥ 12 **Facilities** Children's menu Children's portions Play area Dogs allowed Garden Parking

### The Old Crown ♥

**1 Stoke Rd NN7 2JN** ☎ **01604 862268**
e-mail: bex@theoldcrownashton.co.uk
*dir: M1 junct 15. 1m from A508 from Roade*

A well-appointed homely village local in the small rural community of Ashton. A pub for over 300 years old; its pretty, sheltered gardens are a popular choice for summer dining, or settle in to the beamed bar room and look forward to choosing from the well thought out, balanced menus while sipping a pint of a weekly-changing guest ale. Perhaps kick in with a spicy lamb and coriander samosa prior to a dish of twice cooked pig's cheek with parsnip mash, red wine and smoky bacon, or a fillet of salmon with prawn, crab, tomato and basil linguini. There are regular events held throughout the year such as the village garden party.

**Open** Tue-Fri noon-3 6-11 (Sat noon-11.30 Sun noon-10.30) Closed: Mon **Bar Meals** L served Tue-Fri 12-3, Sat 12-9.30, Sun 12-6 D served Tue-Fri 6-9.30, Av main course £9 **Restaurant** Av 3 course à la carte fr £24 ⊕ CHARLES WELLS ◀ IPA Eagle, Youngs Directors. ♥ 10 **Facilities** Children's portions Dogs allowed Garden Parking

# PICK OF THE PUBS

## The Queen's Head 🍷

**BULWICK** **Map 11 SP99**

**Main St NN17 3DY ☎ 01780 450272**
**e-mail:**
queenshead-bulwick@tiscali.co.uk
**dir:** *Just off A43, between Corby & Stamford*

Probably a pub since the 17th century, parts of this stone-built free house date back to 1400. The portrait on the sign board outside is that of Katherine of Braganza, the Portuguese wife of Charles II, who had a thing about very elaborate hairstyles.

Overlooking the village church, the pub is a warren of small rooms with exposed wooden beams, four open fireplaces and flagstone floors. Relax by the fire or on the patio with a pint of real ale from the local Oakham or Rockingham breweries. Local shoots supply seasonal game such as teal, woodcock and partridge, and other ingredients often include village-grown fruit and vegetables brought in by customers and friends.

Lunchtime brings a good selection of sandwich and snacks, and main dishes that have helped the pub to attract a string of awards, such as roast monkfish with saffron and mussel risotto; and braised shoulder of Cornish lamb with mash, fine green beans and caramelised grelot onion sauce. Starters on the evening menu include potato, spinach, parsley and garlic soup; and oak-smoked salmon with shaved fennel, lemon and rocket. Among the mains are Warwickshire Wizzer pork sausages with mash and white onion and grainy mustard sauce; slow-cooked belly of Suffolk free-range pork with cannellini bean and chorizo cassoulet; whole local roast wood-pigeon rubbed in garlic, sage and rosemary wrapped in prosciutto; roast monkfish with saffron and mussel potato; and poached potato gnocchi with minted, creamed leeks, broad beans and parmesan.

Typical desserts include warm apricot and almond tart with Dorset clotted cream; and artisan cheeses with biscuits, celery and quince jelly. The menu is backed by a comprehensive wine list.

Now under new ownership, The Queen's Head also has a new outdoor oven for outside dining.

**Open** all day 12-11 Closed: Mon **Bar Meals** L served Tue-Sun 12-2.30 booking required D served Tue-Sat 6-9.30 booking required **Restaurant** L served Tue-Sun 12-2.30 booking required D served Tue-Sat 6-9.30 booking required Fixed menu price fr £12.50 FREE HOUSE Elland, Rockingham Ales, Newby Wyke, Thornbridge, Oakham. 🍷 9 **Facilities** Dogs allowed Garden Parking

# PICK OF THE PUBS

## The Collyweston Slater ★★★★ INN

**COLLYWESTON**            Map 11 SK90

**87-89 Main Rd PE9 3PQ**
☎ **01780 444288**
e-mail: info@collywestonslater.co.uk
dir: *4m SW of Stamford, A43. 2m off A1 junct*

Set in the heart of the village, this traditional coaching inn dates from the 17th century and was enlarged in the 1970s to incorporate the adjoining terraced houses. The building was later transformed by a major renovation that created a light, welcoming and relaxed interior. Although Collyweston slate is a limestone, the Romans discovered that it splits along natural cleavage lines just like the real thing. As well as being used on the pub's roof, it also appears inside, where it offsets the original oak timbering to give the modern interior a convincing rustic look.

After taking over the business in 2009, head chef Dameon Clarke introduced a bar menu that's strong on pies. There's a choice of several distinctive fillings, and all come with minted pease pudding and roasted sweet potato chips. But if pies aren't for you, the bar choice also includes a range of interesting sandwiches such as salt beef and piccalilli on rye bread; and main course dishes like salmon and cod fishcakes with mango chilli sauce.

Alternatively, head for the two AA-Rosetted restaurant, where the short, frequently-changing menus make the most of seasonal produce. Here, you might start with truffle risotto with truffle pearls and Parmesan shavings, or local game terrine with Cumberland jelly, marinated beetroot and crispy quail egg. Main course choices include breaded herb plaice with fricassee of scallops and cauliflower purée; fillet of beef with cottage pie, Jerusalem artichoke and buttered spinach; and spiced duck breast with plum sauce. Round things off with a choice of desserts such as chocolate tart with mascarpone sorbet, or plum crumble with vanilla ice cream.

Overnight guests have a choice of four rooms and one luxury suite with a double jacuzzi.

**Open** all day all wk Closed: 25 Dec, 2 Jan **Bar Meals** Av main course £8.50 food served all day **Restaurant** L served all wk 11.30-3 D served all wk 6-9.30 Av 3 course à la carte fr £27 ◀ Tiger, Bitter, Original Bitter, Sunchaser, Beacon. **Facilities** Garden Parking **Rooms** 5

## BULWICK
Map 11 SP99

### PICK OF THE PUBS

## The Queen's Head ♀

*See Pick of the Pubs on page 332*

## CASTLE ASHBY
Map 11 SP85

### The Falcon ★★★ INN NEW

**NN7 1LF** ☎ **01604 696200** 📠 **01604 696673**
**e-mail:** 6446@greeneking.co.uk
**dir:** *From A428 follow Castle Ashby signs. Inn in village centre*

A world away from the hustle and bustle of daily life, the 16th-century Falcon Inn is set in the idyllic hamlet of Castle Ashby, home to the Marquis of Northampton's family for over four centuries. The bar menu offers pub classics and lighter snacks, whilst restaurant choices include venison haunch with beetroot pesto sauce and pancetta, and baked squash with pistachio and redcurrant couscous. Some of the inn's fifteen en suite bedrooms are dog friendly.

**Open** all day all wk **Bar Meals** L served all wk 12-3 D served all wk 6-9 Av main course £9.95 food served all day **Restaurant** L served all wk 12-3 booking required D served all wk 6-9 booking required Av 3 course à la carte fr £21 ⊕ GREENE KING ◀ Greene King IPA.
**Facilities** Children's menu Children's portions Dogs allowed Garden Parking **Rooms** 15

## CHACOMBE
Map 11 SP44

### PICK OF THE PUBS

## George and Dragon

**Silver St OX17 2JR**
☎ **01295 711500** 📠 **01295 710516**
**e-mail:** georgeanddragonchacombe@googlemail.com
**dir:** *M40 junct 11, A361 (Daventry road). Chacombe 1st right*

An attractive, honey-stoned, 16th-century pub tucked away beside the church in a pretty village protected by Conservation Area status. There's a welcoming feel to the three comfortable bars, where the traditional atmosphere is upheld by an abundance of low beams, simple wooden chairs and settles, log fires (which really are lit), and warm terracotta decor. The blackboards list an interesting selection of food, from sandwiches and baked butternut squash or jacket potatoes (filled with flaked tuna and lemon mayonnaise, prawns with a lime dressing), to favourites and specials: you'll find fish pie at lunchtime, along with fish and chips; pork and apple burgers; root vegetable bake; smoked duck salad; and warm bacon and green leaf salad. In the evening, the menu lists starters like goat's cheese and caramelised pears; with such main dishes as smoked salmon and avocado salad; steak and Everard Tiger beer pie; and wild mushroom risotto.

**Open** all day all wk noon-11 **Bar Meals** L served Mon-Thu 12-9, Fri-Sat 12-9.30, Sun 12-7 booking required D served Mon-Thu 12-9, Fri-Sat 12-9.30, Sun 12-7 booking required Av main course £9 food served all day **Restaurant** L served Mon-Thu 12-9, Fri-Sat 12-9.30, Sun 12-7 booking required D served Mon-Thu 12-9, Fri-Sat 12-9.30, Sun 12-7 booking required Av 3 course à la carte fr £20 food served all day ⊕ EVERARDS ◀ Everards Tiger, Everards Beacon, Guest ales.
**Facilities** Children's menu Children's portions Garden Parking

## CLIPSTON
Map 11 SP78

### The Bulls Head ♀

**Harborough Rd LE16 9RT**
☎ **01858 525268** 📠 **01858 525268**
**e-mail:** clipstonhead1@aol.co.uk
**dir:** *On B4036 S of Market Harborough*

American airmen once pushed coins between the beams as a good luck charm before bombing raids, and the trend continues with foreign paper money pinned all over the inn. In addition to its good choice of real ales, the pub has an amazing collection of over 500 whiskies. The menu includes shark steaks, whole sea bass, hot toddy duck, and steak pie.

**Open** all wk 11.30-2.30 6-mdnt (Fri-Sat 11.30-2 Sun noon-mdnt) ◀ Tiger, Beacon, guest, seasonal ales. ♀ 14
**Facilities** Dogs allowed Garden Parking

## COLLYWESTON
Map 11 SK90

### PICK OF THE PUBS

## The Collyweston Slater ★★★★ INN ◉◉ ♀

*See Pick of the Pubs on page 333*

## CRICK
Map 11 SP57

### The Red Lion Inn

**52 Main Rd NN6 7TX**
☎ **01788 822342** 📠 **01788 822342**
**e-mail:** ptm180@tiscali.co.uk
**dir:** *From M1 junct 18, 0.75m E on A428, follows signs for Crick from new rdbt*

A thatched, stone-built coaching inn dating from the 17th century, with beams and open fires, and easily accessible from the M1. The Marks family, landlords here for many years, give their regulars and visitors exactly what they want - a friendly atmosphere, real ales and traditional food. The daily home-made steak pie is a lunchtime favourite, while fillet and sirloin steaks are a speciality in the evening. Fish eaters will find trout, stuffed lemon sole, salmon and seafood platter.

**Open** all wk 11-2.30 6.15-11 (Sun noon-3 7-11)
**Bar Meals** L served all wk 12-2 D served Mon-Sat 6.30-9 Av main course £6.60 ⊕ WELLINGTON PUB COMPANY ◀ Wells Bombardier, Greene King Old Speckled Hen, Deuchars IPA, guest ale. **Facilities** Dogs allowed Garden Parking

## FARTHINGHOE
Map 11 SP53

### The Fox ♀ NEW

**Baker St NN13 5PH** ☎ **01295 713965**
**e-mail:** enquiries@foxatfarthinghoe.co.uk
**dir:** *Follow A422, midway between Banbury & Brackley*

After being derelict for five years, this Charles Wells pub reopened in 2009 to bring its customers fresh, locally sourced food with friendly service, well kept beers and a relaxing atmosphere. In practice this translates as a straightforward menu offering fresh sandwiches; charcuterie, seafood and vegetarian deli boards; plaice dieppoise; game casserole; chicken supreme; loin of pork; and liver and bacon. There is even a take out menu. Ladies' Night on Wednesdays means three courses and a glass of wine for £15.

**Open** all day all wk **Bar Meals** L served all wk 12-2.30 booking required D served all wk 6-9.30 booking required Av main course £12 **Restaurant** L served all wk 12-2.30 booking required D served all wk 6-9.30 booking required Av 3 course à la carte fr £12 ⊕ CHARLES WELLS ◀ Youngs, Bombardier, Erdinger. ♀ 12
**Facilities** Children's portions Garden Parking

## FARTHINGSTONE
Map 11 SP65

### PICK OF THE PUBS

## The Kings Arms

**Main St NN12 8EZ**
☎ **01327 361604** 📠 **01327 361604**
**e-mail:** paul@kingsarms.fsbusiness.co.uk
**dir:** *M1 junct 16, A45 towards Daventry. At Weedon take A5 towards Towcester. Right signed Farthingstone*

This 300-year-old stone free house is tucked away in perfect walking country, close to the National Trust's Elizabethan mansion at Canon's Ashby. Paul and Denise Egerton grow their own salads and herbs in the pub's exceptional garden, which is full of interesting recycled items as well as decorative trees and shrubs. Gardening clubs visit because of its originality. This is the place to enjoy alfresco dining on warmer days with red kites and buzzards overhead – but, in winter, real fires signal the warmth of the welcome. The Kings Arms is mainly a drinker's pub, with up to five real ales and Weston's Old Rosie cider at the bar, but Paul and Denise offer a short menu at weekend lunchtimes. Expect Loch Fyne fish platters; pork and plum casserole with rice and salad; Kings Arms fish cakes and salad; and beef in Guinness with mashed potato. Baguettes, cheese platters and home-made soup are also available to fill the odd corner.

**Open** 7-11.30 (Sat-Sun 12-3.30 7-11.30) Closed: Mon **Bar Meals** L served Sat-Sun 12-2 Av main course £8.25 ⊕ FREE HOUSE ◀ Thwaites Original, Adnams, St Austell Tinners, Young's Bitter, Hoggleys Northamptonshire Bitter Ö Westons Old Rosie.
**Facilities** Children's portions Family room Dogs allowed Garden Parking **Notes** ◉

Save on Hotels. Book at **theAA.com/hotel**

**NORTHAMPTONSHIRE** 335 **ENGLAND**

## FOTHERINGHAY — Map 12 TL09

### PICK OF THE PUBS

### The Falcon Inn ◉ ☉

**PE8 5HZ** ☎ **01832 226254** 🖨 **01832 226046**
e-mail: info@thefalcon-inn.co.uk
dir: *N of A605 between Peterborough & Oundle*

First the history: it was in this sleepy village that
Richard III was born in 1452, and 115 years later Mary,
Queen of Scots was beheaded. The attractive 18th-
century, stone-built pub stands in gardens redesigned
by award-winning landscape architect Bunny
Guinness. It's a real local, the Tap Bar regularly used
by the village darts team, their throwing arms
lubricated by pints of Fool's Nook and Westons Organic
Vintage real cider. The menus in both the bar and
charming conservatory restaurant rely extensively on
locally sourced ingredients, offering pan-fried salmon
with tagliatelle and shellfish broth; crisp pork belly
with sage and onion rösti; corn-fed chicken breast with
bubble and squeak; and spinach, feta and tomato
cannelloni. For dessert, there's vanilla pannacotta with
caramelised pineapple and coconut sorbet; pannetone
bread and butter pudding with Dorset clotted cream;
and local cheeses. About fourteen wines and
Champagnes are available by the glass.

**Open** all day all wk noon–11 **Bar Meals** L served Mon-
Sat 12-2.15, Sun 12-3 D served Mon-Sat 6.15-9.15,
Sun 6.15-8.30 Av main course £7.50 **Restaurant** L
served Mon-Sat 12-2.15, Sun 12-3 D served Mon-Sat
6.15-9.15, Sun 6.15-8.30 Av 3 course à la carte fr
£22 ⊕ FREE HOUSE ◀ Greene King IPA, Fool's Nook,
Fuller's London Pride, Guest ales ♂ Westons Organic
Vintage. ☉ 14 **Facilities** Children's menu Children's
portions Dogs allowed Garden Parking

## GRAFTON REGIS — Map 11 SP74

### *The White Hart* ☉

**Northampton Rd NN12 7SR** ☎ **01908 542123**
e-mail: alan@pubgraftonregis.co.uk
dir: *M1 junct 15 onto A508 between Northampton &
Milton Keynes*

A friendly village with approximately 96 residents is home
to the White Hart, a thatched, stone-built property dating
from the 16th century. In 1464 Edward IV married
Elizabeth Woodville in this historic place. The pub has
been owned by the same family for 12 years and Alan,
one of the owners, is chef. Menus change frequently
according to available produce. There are always at least
three home-made soups, specials, fresh fish of the day,
and dishes such as mature Welsh fillet steak, or roast
chicken with creamy garlic mushroom sauce.

**Open** 12-2.30 6-11 Closed: Mon ◀ Greene King, Abbot
Ale, IPA. ☉ 14 **Facilities** Garden Parking

## GREAT OXENDON — Map 11 SP78

### PICK OF THE PUBS

### The George Inn ☉

**LE16 8NA** ☎ **01858 465205** 🖨 **01858 465205**
e-mail: info@thegeorgegreatoxendon.co.uk
dir: *A508 towards Market Harborough*

Original beams, old photographs and a lovely log fire
lend charm to this country dining pub. Parts of the inn
are up to 600 years old, and the building is said to
have accommodated soldiers after the battle of
Naseby. Today the George has a county-wide reputation
for excellent food and service, but customers are still
welcome to call in for a pint of Black Sheep or Stowford
Press cider. Three dining areas comprise the cosy
restaurant, a conservatory overlooking award-winning
gardens, and a patio. Owner David Dudley and his son
Philip offer lunchtime sandwiches, as well as light
bites that include home-made soup with rustic bread;
twice-baked cheese soufflé; and smoked Scottish
salmon and Norwegian prawn salad. Dinner in the
restaurant might begin with black pudding on a rösti
with smoked bacon and poached egg; continuing,
perhaps, with Gressingham duck, gratin potatoes,
nutty Dutch cabbage and Cointreau sauce. The wine
list provides useful notes.

**Open** Mon-Sat 12-3 5.30-11 (Sun 12-3) Closed: 25
Dec, Sun eve **Bar Meals** L served all wk 12-2 D served
Mon-Sat 6-9.30 Av main course £12.95 **Restaurant** L
served all wk 12-2 D served Mon-Sat 6-9.30 ⊕ FREE
HOUSE ◀ Batemans guest ale, Adnams Bitter, Timothy
Taylor Landlord, Black Sheep ♂ Stowford Press. ☉ 10
**Facilities** Children's portions Garden Parking

## HARRINGTON — Map 11 SP78

### PICK OF THE PUBS

### The Tollemache Arms ☉

**49 High St NN6 9NU** ☎ **01536 710469**
e-mail: markandjo@tollemacheharrington.com
dir: *6m from Kettering, off A14 junct 3. Follow signs
for Harrington*

A refurbished, thatched and whitewashed 16th-century
pub that retains its traditional charm, with open fires in
winter and panoramic views from the large garden. It's
named after the Reverend Tollemache, whose
replacement managed to acquire it, then closed it on
Sundays in the hope of boosting his congregation!
Among the variety of meals on the all-day bar are beer-
battered fish and chips; steak and Guinness pudding;
and chicken in a basket. Also available all day is the
seasonal restaurant menu, which might lead you to
start with crayfish stir-fry; sautéed chicken livers; or
Stilton, apple and pine-nut salad. It may then steer you
towards slow-braised lamb shank; roast poussin; pan-
fried sea bass; or vegetable pudding. Bombardier, Eagle
IPA and two weekly guest real ales are served in the bar,
and the wine list offers fifteen by the glass in three
different sizes. Saturday brunch is held once a month.

**Open** all day all wk noon-11 (Sun noon-10.30)
**Bar Meals** L served all wk 12-9.30 D served all wk
12-9.30 Av main course £8 food served all day
**Restaurant** L served all wk 12-9.30 D served all wk
12-9.30 Av 3 course à la carte fr £20 food served all
day ⊕ CHARLES WELLS ◀ Bombardier, Eagle IPA,
Guest ales. ☉ 15 **Facilities** Children's menu Children's
portions Garden Parking

## KETTERING — Map 11 SP87

### *The Overstone Arms* ☉

**Stringers Hill, Pytchley NN14 1EU**
☎ **01536 790215** 🖨 **01536 791098**
dir: *1m from Kettering, 5m from Wellingborough*

The 18th-century coaching inn is at the heart of the
village and has been home to the Pytchley Hunt, which
over the years has attracted many royal visitors. Years
ago guests would travel up from London, staying here or
at Althorp Hall, mainly for the hunting. Despite its rural
location, the pub is just a mile from the busy A14. Home-
made pies, grilled trout, steaks, lasagne and curry are
typical dishes.

**Open** all wk ◀ Greene King, Marston's Pedigree,
Interbrew Bass, Adnams Bitter, Abbot Ale, Spitfire, IPA,
Pedigree. ☉ 8 **Facilities** Garden Parking

## NORTHAMPTON — Map 11 SP76

### The Fox & Hounds ☉

**Main St, Great Brington NN7 4JA**
☎ **01604 770651** 🖨 **01604 770164**
e-mail: althorpcoachinginn@btconnect.com
web: www.althorp-coaching-inn.co.uk
dir: *From A428 pass main gates of Althorp House, left
before rail bridge. Great Brington 1m*

A 16th-century coaching inn on the Althorp Estate, the
Spencer ancestral home and close to the final resting
place of Diana, Princess of Wales. A brick and cobbled
courtyard is surrounded by stable rooms, and the
enclosed flower garden is a wonderfully peaceful spot in
which to sample one of the twelve real ales. A cellar
restaurant specialises in traditional English cooking.
Beef from the owner's farm and other local produce
appear in dishes such as Bucky-bred sirloin steak; and
roasted supreme of guinea fowl.

*continued*

**NORTHAMPTON** *continued*

**Open** all day all wk 11-11 **Bar Meals** L served all wk 12-3 D served Sun-Thu 6.30-9.30. Fri-Sat 6.30-10 Av main course £9 **Restaurant** L served all wk 12-3 D served Sun-Thu 6.30-9.30. Fri-Sat 6.30-10 Av 3 course à la carte fr £17.50 ⊕ FREE HOUSE ◗ Greene King IPA, Fuller's London Pride, Abbot Ale, Cottage Puffing Billy, Tunnell Parish Ale, 5 guest ales ♂ Farmhouse, Thatchers Heritage. ♀ 10 **Facilities** Children's menu Children's portions Dogs allowed Garden Parking

---

**OUNDLE** Map 11 TL08

## The Chequered Skipper

**Ashton PE8 5LD ☎ 01832 273494**
**e-mail:** enquiries@chequeredskipper.co.uk
**dir:** *A605 towards Dundle, at rdbt follow signs to Ashton. 1m turn left into Ashton, pub in village*

At the heart of the Rothschild's glorious model village, all stone and thatch cottages nestling around the village green, the thatched, open-plan pub has a contemporary feel, with stone and oak flooring and an unusual flagstone bar top. Using the best of local produce with suppliers listed on the menu, beer-battered haddock and home-made stone-baked pizzas are available in the bar, while the restaurant menu might include slow braised belly of pork in Aspall's cider with demerara-glazed beetroot. On tap are local Rockingham and Oakham ales - don't miss the annual beer festivals.

**Open** all wk 11.30-3 6-11 (Sat 11.30-11 Sun 11.45-11) ◗ Rockingham Ale, Oakham Ale. **Facilities** Dogs allowed Garden Parking

## The Montagu Arms ♀

**Barnwell PE8 5PH ☎ 01832 273726 ▤ 01832 275555**
**e-mail:** ianmsimmons@aol.com
**dir:** *Off A605 opposite Oundle slip road*

One of Northamptonshire's oldest inns, the Montagu Arms was originally three cottages dating from 1601, housing the workmen building the nearby manor house. The inn has a large garden, well equipped for children's play, and overlooks the brook and village green of the royal village of Barnwell. An extensive menu serving the bar and restaurant ranges through snacks and sharing platters, and dishes such as Rutland sausages and mash, stuffed chicken, and crispy fish pie.

**Open** all wk ◗ Digfield Ales, Adnams Broadside, Hop Back Summer Lightning, Fuller's London Pride, Oakham Ale, JHB. ♀ 14 **Facilities** Play area Garden Parking

---

**SIBBERTOFT** Map 11 SP68

## PICK OF THE PUBS

## The Red Lion ♀

*See Pick of the Pubs on opposite page*

---

**STOKE BRUERNE** Map 11 SP74

## The Boat Inn

**NN12 7SB ☎ 01604 862428 ▤ 01604 864314**
**e-mail:** info@boatinn.co.uk
**web:** www.boatinn.co.uk
**dir:** *In village centre, just off A508 or A5*

This busy free house is set on the banks of the Grand Union Canal, just across the lock from the National Waterways Museum. Run by the same family since 1877, the pub has cosy bars, open fires and flagstone floors beneath its thatched roof. The all-day bar menu begins with traditional breakfasts, and continues with hot baguettes, burgers, main courses and desserts. You will find dishes like braised lamb shank and beef fillet medallions on the Woodwards Restaurant menu. Boat trips can be arranged on the pub's own narrowboat.

**Open** all day all wk 9.30am-11pm (Sun 9.30am-10.30pm) **Bar Meals** L served all wk 9.30am-9.30pm D served all wk 9.30am-9.30pm Av main course £8 food served all day **Restaurant** L served Tue-Sun 12-2 booking required D served all wk 7-9 booking required Fixed menu price fr £14.95 Av 3 course à la carte fr £18 ⊕ FREE HOUSE ◗ Banks Bitter, Marstons Pedigree, Frog Island Best, Marstons Old Empire, Wychwood Hobgoblin ♂ Thatcher's Traditional. **Facilities** Children's menu Children's portions Dogs allowed Garden Parking

---

**TOWCESTER** Map 11 SP64

## The Saracens Head ♀ NEW

**219 Watling St NN12 8BX**
**☎ 01327 350414 ▤ 01327 359879**
**e-mail:** saracenshead.towcester@greeneking.co.uk
**dir:** *From M1 junct 15A, A43 towards Oxford. Take A5 signed Towcester*

This imposing building dates back over 400 years, and is featured in Charles Dickens' first novel, *The Pickwick Papers*. The same home comforts that Dickens enjoyed when visiting Towcester have been updated to modern standards, and discerning guests will find excellent service in the restored hotel. Main menu choices include guinea fowl stuffed with pancetta; baked salmon fillet with a tomato, pepper and white wine Provençale sauce; and Mediterranean vegetable lasagne with a dressed salad.

**Open** all day all wk **Bar Meals** L served all wk 12-5 D served all wk 5-10 booking required Av main course £9 food served all day **Restaurant** L served all wk 12-5 D served all wk 5-10 booking required Av 3 course à la carte fr £17 food served all day ⊕ GREENE KING OLD ENGLISH INNS ◗ Abbot Ale, IPA, Guest ale. ♀ 13 **Facilities** Children's menu Children's portions Garden Parking

---

**WADENHOE** Map 11 TL08

## PICK OF THE PUBS

## The King's Head ♀

**Church St PE8 5ST ☎ 01832 720024**
**e-mail:** info@kingsheadwadenhoe.co.uk
**dir:** *From A605, 3m from Wadenhoe rdbt. 2m from Oundle*

A haven for travellers since the 17th century, The King's Head is a stone-built partially thatched inn situated at the end of a quiet country lane. Extensive gardens overlook the tranquil River Nene; here, customers can sit and watch the boats pass by as they enjoy a pint of Barnwell bitter. The warm, welcoming interior has quarry-tiled and bare-boarded floors, heavy oak-beamed ceilings, pine furniture and open log fires. Indeed, the pub has lost none of its old world charm but offers most modern facilities. You can challenge the locals to a game of Northamptonshire skittles – if you dare! The lunchtime menu offers sandwiches, and pies such as beef and ale or roast chicken and mushroom; light bites take the form of sausages and mash, or home-made burger with Cheddar cheese and hand-cut chips. In the evening you can dine regally on fresh mussels cooked in white wine and cream, followed by pan-fried calves' liver on creamy mash.

**Open** all day 11-11 (Sun noon-10, winter 11-2.30 5.30-11 Sun noon-6) Closed: Sun eve in winter **Bar Meals** Av main course £8.95 food served all day **Restaurant** Av 3 course à la carte fr £19.85 food served all day ⊕ FREE HOUSE ◗ Kings Head Bitter, Barnwell Bitter, ♂ Westons Stowford Press. ♀ 15 **Facilities** Children's portions Dogs allowed Garden Parking

---

**WESTON** Map 11 SP54

## PICK OF THE PUBS

## The Crown

*See Pick of the Pubs on page 338*

# PICK OF THE PUBS

## The Red Lion 🍷

SIBBERTOFT                Map 11 SP68

**43 Welland Rise LE16 9UD**
☎ **01858 880011**
**e-mail:** andrew@redlionwinepub.co.uk
**dir:** *From Market Harborough take A4304, through Lubenham, left through Marston Trussell to Sibbertoft*

Wine is the special passion of owner Andrew Banks at this friendly 300-year-old free house. Over 200 bins appear on the ever-growing wine list, and twenty are served by the glass. Additionally all the wines can be bought at take-home prices – so having tasted a wine you can avoid the guesswork in a supermarket. When choosing a wine for dinner, allow time to absorb the useful guidelines on twinning food types with grape varieties; you'll also enjoy the humorous quotations, which reveal truths every wine lover will recognise.

"The list is my passion and I will always be around to discuss it with you," says Andrew. He is also developing fun and informative dinners during which his customers can listen to wine makers and suppliers.

The pub offers an appealing blend of contemporary and classic décor, with oak beams, leather upholstery and a smartly turned-out dining room. In fine weather, meals are served in the quiet garden, which is a favourite with local walkers and cyclists; there's also an outdoor play area for children.

The same monthly-changing menu is served in all the pub's eating areas; local and seasonal produce is used wherever possible. The list of lunchtime snacks runs from home-made soup of the day to faggot with fries and mushy peas. Freshly made baguettes or sandwiches include melting brie and bacon, and hot beef and horseradish fillings.

A typical dinner could start with a sharing platter of battered jalapeños, crunchy chicken fillets, mild chillies with cream cheese, warm olives and crusty bread. Meat from nearby farms butchered by Joseph Morris appears in main courses such as slow-roasted pork belly with white onion and mustard sauce; and mature rib-eye steak with crosscut fries. Date and sticky toffee pudding accompanied by one of Andrew's 'stickies' (dessert wines) makes for a happy ending.

**Open** 12-2 6.30-11 Closed: Mon & Tue L, Sun eve **Bar Meals** L served Wed-Sun 12-2 booking required D served Mon-Sat 6.30-9.30 booking required Av main course £10 **Restaurant** L served Wed-Sun 12-2 booking required D served Mon-Sat 6.30-9.30 booking required Fixed menu price fr £9.95 Av 3 course à la carte fr £16 ⊕ FREE HOUSE ◄ Adnams, Timothy Taylor Landlord, Black Sheep Ŏ Samuel Smiths Reserve. 🍷 20 **Facilities** Children's menu Play area Garden Parking

# PICK OF THE PUBS

## The Crown

**WESTON**      Map 11 SP54

**Helmdon Rd NN12 8PX**
☎ **01295 760310**   📠 **01295 760310**
**e-mail:** info@thecrownweston.co.uk
**dir:** *Accessed from A43 or B4525*

Following the brutal murder of his children's nanny at his London house in 1974, Lord Lucan was never seen again. Or was he? Some say he had a pint the following day in this attractive 16th-century inn, but we'll probably never know for sure. What is certain is that the inn has been serving ales since the reign of Elizabeth I, the first recorded owner being All Souls College, Oxford. Latest in a long line is Robert Grover, who took over in 2003 and who has ensured ever since that his pub features prominently in the life of the community by providing excellent beers, welcoming staff and a friendly atmosphere.

Seasonal menus, a selection of freshly made snacks at lunchtime, and traditional roasts on Sundays have proved particular hits all year round. A typical evening menu might start with cumin roasted butternut squash soup; chicken liver and pistachio terrine with toasted ciabatta; and grilled brie wrapped in Black Forest ham with cranberry sauce. Follow these with a main course such as pork sausages with buttered mash and onion gravy; duck confit with dauphinoise potatoes and a creamy redcurrant sauce; chicken, leek and bacon pie; saffron and pea risotto with parmesan and rocket; or rump steak with chips and a creamy pepper sauce. Round off with green tea crème brûlée, chocolate brownie with vanilla ice cream, or a plate of English cheeses with oatcakes and sweet chilli and tomato chutney. Smaller portions for children are available.

Robert organises regular curry nights and other occasions. Wines are reasonably priced, from the unashamedly gluggable to sophisticated gems from top producers, with seven by the glass. Nearby attractions include Sulgrave Manor, the ancestral home of George Washington, and Silverstone racing circuit.

**Open** all wk 6-11.30 (Fri-Sat noon-3.30 6-11.30 Sun noon-3.30 7-11) Closed: 25 Dec **Bar Meals** L served Fri-Sun 12-2.30 D served Tue-Sat 6-9.30 Av main course £8.95 ⊕ FREE HOUSE ◀ Greene King IPA , Hook Norton Best, Black Sheep, Landlord, Reservoir Hogs.
**Facilities** Family room Dogs allowed Garden Parking

# PICK OF THE PUBS

## The Wollaston Inn

**WOLLASTON**  Map 11 SP96

**87 London Rd NN29 7QS**
☎ **01933 663161**
**e-mail:** info@wollaston-inn.co.uk
**web:** www.wollaston-inn.co.uk
**dir:** *From Wellingborough, onto A509 towards Wollaston. After 2m, over rdbt, then immediately left. Inn at top of hill*

Back in the late Sixties and early Seventies, when this was the Nags Head, the late John Peel was the resident Sunday night DJ here. Renowned for his love of live music, he attracted artists of the calibre of Rod Stewart and Led Zeppelin to this simple village pub. Then in 2003, Chris Spencer took over, reinvented it as a restaurant within a pub and gave it a name that immediately conferred on it a status perhaps formerly missing. If the name change was, dare it be suggested, cosmetic, he backed it up with a loving restoration of the 350-year-old

building's interior to provide a commendable backdrop to soft Italian leather sofas, casual tables and chairs, ambient lighting and gentle background music.

The menus are prepared every day from only fresh ingredients and everything, from the bread and infused oils to the ice creams and rich, dark Belgian chocolate truffles, is made on the premises. The daytime menu is served until 7pm; this is the one for antipasti, soup, burgers and club sandwiches, while the evening carte moves with the seasons to offer starters like warm pigeon breast salad with soft boiled quail's egg and beetroot and new potato salad; terrine of guinea fowl and ham hock with sultana and sweet wine compote with thyme jelly and brioche; poached duck egg with minted peas and Jerusalem artichoke, hollandaise sauce and potato crisps; or maybe butternut squash and roasted red pepper cannelloni with chargrilled aubergine terrine and salad. Mains might include herb crusted pork tenderloin with crispy pork belly and dauphinoise potatoes, apple purée and buttered vegetables; roast pavé of Wield Wood venison, creamed celeriac, buttered savoy

cabbage, pancetta crisp and rosemary jus; Bowland Farm beef blade – served braised, pudding and chargrilled, with horseradish mash, roast parsnips and carrots, parsley and shallot salad. The fresh seafood menu is available all day and changes following daily deliveries from the markets. Ask for the all-day bar menu if you want fresh sandwiches and other snacks. A traditional Sunday lunch menu is served alongside the seafood and bar versions until 5pm. An extensive wine list recommends what to drink with your food, while the bar stocks draught Burton Bitter, Marstons and a good selection of bottled beers

**Open** all day all wk **Bar Meals** food served all day **Restaurant** food served all day ⊕ FREE HOUSE ◀ Burton Bitter, Marstons, Guinness, guest ales. ⏺ 12 **Facilities** Garden Parking

## WOLLASTON — Map 11 SP96

### PICK OF THE PUBS

### The Wollaston Inn ♥

*See Pick of the Pubs on page 339*

## NORTHUMBERLAND

## ALNWICK — Map 21 NU11

### The Masons Arms

Stamford, Nr Rennington NE66 3RX
☎ 01665 577275 📄 01665 577894
e-mail: bookings@masonsarms.net
web: www.masonsarms.net
dir: *NE of Alnwick on B1340, 0.5m past Rennington*

A tastefully modernised 200-year-old coaching inn, known by the local community as Stamford Cott. It is a useful staging post for visitors to Hadrian's Wall, Lindisfarne and the large number of nearby golf courses. There is a great range of beers to enjoy, including Farne Island and Secret Kingdom. The substantial home-cooked food is available in the bar and the restaurant, and is made using the best of local produce. Typical examples include lemon sole with prawns and parsley sauce, or Northumbrian game casserole.

**Open** all wk noon-2 6.30-11pm (Sun noon-2 6.30-10.30pm) **Bar Meals** L served all wk 12-2 D served all wk 6.30-9 Av main course £9.50 ⊕ FREE HOUSE ◀ John Smiths, Theakston Best, Secret Kingdom, Gladiator, Farne Island. **Facilities** Children's menu Children's portions Family room Garden Parking

## BELFORD — Map 21 NU13

### Blue Bell Hotel

Market Place NE70 7NE
☎ 01668 213543 📄 01668 213787
e-mail: enquiries@bluebellhotel.com
dir: *Off A1, 15m N of Alnwick , 15m S of Berwick-upon-Tweed*

A touch of old-world charm with modern day comforts permeates this 17th-century coaching inn on the A1 London to Edinburgh route, and there are spectacular views across the hotel gardens to Belford church. The menu takes its cue from the best of country kitchens, and choices from the menu might include favourites like darne of salmon, rump steak or chicken supreme.

*Blue Bell Hotel*

**Open** all day all wk 11am-mdnt **Bar Meals** L served all wk 12-2.30 D served all wk 6-9 **Restaurant** L served Sun 12-2.30 booking required D served all wk 6-9 booking required ⊕ FREE HOUSE ◀ Calders, Tetleys Smooth, Black Sheep, Guinness. **Facilities** Children's menu Children's portions Play area Garden Parking

## BLANCHLAND — Map 18 NY95

### The Lord Crewe Arms ♥

DH8 9SP ☎ 01434 675251 📄 01434 675337
e-mail: lord@crewearms.freeserve.co.uk
dir: *10m S of Hexham via B6306*

Set amongst the honey coloured buildings in the heart of the village, this 12th-century free house is one of England's oldest inns. Once the private chapel of the abbot of Blanchland Abbey, it was a significant location in the first Jacobite Rebellion in 1715. Its antique furniture, blazing log fires and flagstone floors make for an atmospheric setting. The wide-ranging bar and restaurant menus offer sandwiches and salads, as well as main course dishes like breast of chicken stuffed with mango and brie, and oat rolled salmon fishcakes.

**Open** all day all wk 11-11 (Sun noon-10.30) **Bar Meals** L served all wk 12-2 D served all wk 7-9 Av main course £8 food served all day **Restaurant** D served all wk 7-9.15 booking required Fixed menu price fr £15 Av 3 course à la carte fr £25 food served all day ⊕ FREE HOUSE ◀ Black Sheep, John Smith's, Guinness, Theakston. ♥ 10 **Facilities** Children's menu Family room Dogs allowed Garden Parking

## CARTERWAY HEADS — Map 19 NZ05

### PICK OF THE PUBS

### The Manor House Inn ♥

DH8 9LX ☎ 01207 255268
dir: *A69 W from Newcastle, left onto A68 then S for 8m. Inn on right*

A small family-run free house in an elevated position on the A68, overlooking open moorland and the stunning Derwent valley. Built around 1760, this completely refurbished inn is an ideal base for exploring Northumberland's rolling hills and beautiful beaches; for a city visit, Newcastle and Durham are both a short drive away. The stone-walled bar, with log fires, low-beamed ceiling and massive timber support, serves five real ales all year, among which are Courage

Directors and Workie Ticket from the Mordue brewery in North Shields. The bar and lounge are good for a snack, while the restaurant is divided into two dining areas, the larger of which welcomes families with children. The focus on fresh local produce is typified by dishes such as Cumberland sausage and mash; prime rib-eye steak; and fish pie. The specials board is aptly named, bringing you wild African kudu; pan-fried swordfish; and even braised squirrel.

**Open** all day all wk 11-11 (Sun noon-10.30) **Bar Meals** food served all day **Restaurant** food served all day ⊕ FREE HOUSE ◀ Theakstons Best, Mordue Workie Ticket, Greene King Ruddles County, Courage Directors, Old Speckled Hen Ò Westons Old Rosie Scrumpy. ♥ 8 **Facilities** Children's menu Children's portions Dogs allowed Garden Parking

## CHATTON — Map 21 NU02

### The Percy Arms Hotel

Main Rd NE66 5PS ☎ 01668 215244 📄 01668 215277
dir: *From Alnwick take A1 N, then B6348 to Chatton*

Traditional 19th-century former coaching inn, situated in the heart of rural Northumberland. Expect a warm, traditional pub welcome, as well as a selection of fine beers, wines and tempting food. Bar menu includes Aberdeen Angus steaks, deep-fried haddock, steak and kidney pie and a wide selection of fish and seafood dishes. Bar games include snooker, pool and darts, but those who wish to can still enjoy a quiet pint in comfort.

**Open** all wk **Bar Meals** L served all wk 12-3 booking required D served all wk 6-9 booking required Av main course £7.95 **Restaurant** L served all wk 12-3 booking required D served all wk 6-9 booking required ⊕ JENNINGS BROTHERS PLC ◀ Jennings Cumberland Cream, guest ales. **Facilities** Garden Parking

## CORBRIDGE — Map 21 NY96

### The Angel of Corbridge ♥

Main St NE45 5LA ☎ 01434 632119 📄 01434 633496
e-mail: info@theangelofcorbridge.com
dir: *0.5m off A69, signed Corbridge*

Stylish 18th-century coaching inn overlooking the River Tyne. Relax with a pint and the daily papers in the wood-panelled lounge, attractive split-level lounge bar, or the refurbished bar, and enjoy a home-made dish or two in the new oak-beamed restaurant hung with local artists' work. Plenty of choices on the menu range from starters of chilled poached salmon, to mains of stir-fried beef fillet, and sweets such as chocolate brownie with deep-fried vanilla ice cream.

**Open** all day all wk Closed: 25 Dec **Bar Meals** D served except Sun Av main course £9.95 food served all day **Restaurant** D served except Sun Av 3 course à la carte fr £20 food served all day ⊕ FREE HOUSE ◀ Timothy Taylor Landlord, local ales. **Facilities** Children's menu Children's portions Garden Parking

# PICK OF THE PUBS

## The Pheasant Inn ★★★★INN

**FALSTONE**                    Map 21 NY78

**Stannersburn NE48 1DD**
☎ 01434 240382   📠 01434 240382
**e-mail:** enquiries@thepheasantinn.com
**dir:** A69, B6079, B6320, follow signs for
Kielder Water

Dating from 1624, this traditional
country inn was originally a large
farmstead. For over 380 years, one room
of the sprawling stone-walled building
was used as a locals' bar, but its
permanent change of use came in the
mid-1970s, when some of the farm
buildings were also converted into
bedrooms. Robin, Irene and Walter
Kershaw took over the business in 1985
and, since then, they have continually
improved and upgraded the buildings
whilst retaining the rustic atmosphere.
Old photos around the walls record local
people engaged in long-abandoned
trades and professions.

The Kershaws' cooking is fresh,
generous and flavoursome, producing
wholesome traditional English fare.
Meals may be taken alfresco beside the
stream in the pretty grassed courtyard,
or in the oak-beamed restaurant with its
cottage-style furnishings and warm
terracotta walls. The bar menu changes
daily according to season, whilst the
restaurant menu starters could embrace
smoked Scottish salmon, or a filo pastry
basket with mildly curried vegetables.
Main courses from the blackboard might
include sirloin steak with green
peppercorn sauce, or pan-fried
marinated chicken with honey-roasted
peppers. Vegetarian and salad choices
will also be available. Raspberry crème
brûlée and tuile basket with ice cream
and summer fruits are typical desserts.

Nearby Kielder Water is the largest
artificial lake in Europe, and the new
26-mile track around its shores is a
magnet for walkers, cyclists and sailors.
There's also Hadrian's Wall, some of
England's least spoilt countryside and
coastline, and sights such as Alnwick
Castle and Gardens. Eight en suite
bedrooms provide guests with stunning
views over the surrounding countryside.

**Open** 12-3 6.30-11 Closed: 25-27 Dec,
Mon-Tue (Nov-Mar) **Bar Meals** L served
Mon-Sat 12-2.30 Av main course £9.95
**Restaurant** L served Mon-Sat 12-2.30
booking required D served Mon-Sat
6.30-8.30 booking required Av 3 course
à la carte fr £22 ⊕ FREE HOUSE
🍺 Timothy Taylor Landlord, Wylam Gold,
Wylam Rocket, Wylam Red Kite, Wylam
Angel. **Facilities** Children's menu Play
area Family room Dogs allowed Garden
Parking **Rooms** 8

## CRASTER
Map 21 NU21

### Cottage Inn

**Dunstan Village NE66 2UD**
☎ 01665 576658   📄 01665 576788
**e-mail:** enquiries@cottageinnhotel.co.uk
**dir:** NW of Howick to Embleton road

Set in six acres of woodland, in an Area of Outstanding
Natural Beauty, this 18th-century inn lies in a hamlet
close to the coast. Nearby is Dunstanburgh Castle, one of
Northumberland's great historic landmarks. Inside is a
beamed bar, together with a restaurant, conservatory and
patio. One menu serves all and includes the ever-popular
Craster kippers, steak and game pie, venison sausages,
and vegetable risotto. Local ingredients are used
wherever possible.

**Open** all wk ◀ Mordue, Tetley's, Farne Island, Black
Sheep, Timothy Taylor Landlord. **Facilities** Play area
Garden Parking

### Jolly Fisherman Inn

**Haven Hill NE66 3TR** ☎ 01665 576461
**e-mail:** muriel@silk8234.fsnet.co.uk
**dir:** Exit A1 at Denwick, follow Dunstanburgh Castle signs

The first landlord, in 1847, was a fisherman - presumably
a jovial fellow. The pub stands right by the water in this
tiny fishing village, world-renowned for its Craster
kippers. The menu is not extensive, but it makes full use
of the sea's bounty with home-made crabmeat soup with
whisky and cream; special recipe kipper pâté; fresh or
oak-smoked salmon sandwiches; lite bites includes
stottie cake pizza. Finish off with a home-made sweet of
the day, details of which are chalked on the board.
Nearby Dunstanburgh Castle is worth a visit.

**Open** all day all wk 11-11 (all day at wknds & summer)
**Bar Meals** L served all wk 11-2.30 ⊕ PUNCH TAVERNS
◀ Black Sheep, John Smith's, Mordue Workie Ticket.
**Facilities** Dogs allowed Garden Parking **Notes** ⊛

## ETAL
Map 21 NT93

### Black Bull

**TD12 4TL** ☎ 01890 820200   📄 07092 367733
**dir:** Off A697, left at junct for 1m then left into Etal

The Black Bull stands by the ruins of Etal Castle, not far
from the River Till, with the grand walking country of the
Cheviots on the doorstep. The only thatched pub in
Northumberland, it serves traditional pub food such as
mince and dumpling with potatoes and vegetables; or
home-made steak and ale pie. Lighter options include
soup, sandwiches, and toasted teacakes.

**Open** 12-3 6-11 (Summer 11-11) Closed: Tue (winter)
**Bar Meals** food served all day **Restaurant** food served
all day ⊕ PUBMASTER ◀ Deuchars, John Smith's Smooth.
**Facilities** Children's menu Garden Parking

## FALSTONE
Map 21 NY78

### PICK OF THE PUBS

### The Pheasant Inn ★★★★ INN

*See Pick of the Pubs on page 341*

## GREAT WHITTINGTON
Map 21 NZ07

### PICK OF THE PUBS

### Queens Head Inn ♀

**NE19 2HP** ☎ 01434 672267   📄 01434 672267
**dir:** Turn off A69 towards Jedburgh, then N on A68. At
rdbt take 3rd exit onto B6318, 1st left signed Great
Whittington

At the heart of Hadrian's Wall country this old pub/
restaurant, once a coaching inn, radiates a welcoming
atmosphere in comfortable surroundings of beamed
rooms, oak settles and open fires. In addition to real
ales there are eleven wines by the glass. Menus
combine the best of local and European ingredients,
without losing touch with the classics. Expect starters
like tempura of black pudding with a beetroot and red
onion relish and crisp salad. Follow that with a main
course such as pork tenderloin on an orange and onion
marmalade with black pudding fritters and cider and
sage jus. Traditional desserts include old favourites
like sticky toffee pudding, bread and butter pudding,
and baked vanilla cheesecake.

**Open** all wk ◀ Farne Island, Auld Hemp, Nels Best.
♀ 11 **Facilities** Garden Parking

## HALTWHISTLE
Map 21 NY76

### Milecastle Inn

**Military Rd, Cawfields NE49 9NN** ☎ 01434 321372
**e-mail:** clarehind@aol.com
**dir:** From A69 into Haltwhistle. Pub approx 2m at
junct with B6318

This friendly inn sits close to Hadrian's Wall, and there
are good views of some of the best bits of this
fascinating landmark from the garden. Inside you'll find
exposed stone walls, polished brasses open fires and,
possibly, the resident ghost. A blackboard menu above
the fireplace offers a changing selection of home-cooked
food. Typical dishes include game pie; venison casserole;
Whitby scampi; lasagne; and pheasant in garlic and
Madeira.

**Open** all day noon-11 (noon-3 6-10 Nov-Mar) Closed: Sun
eve in Jan-Mar **Bar Meals** L served all wk 12-2.30 winter,
12-8.45 summer D served all wk 6-8.30 winter, 12-8.45
summer **Restaurant** L served all wk 12-2.30 winter,
12-8.45 summer D served all wk 6-8.30 winter, 12-8.45
summer ⊕ FREE HOUSE ◀ Big Lamp, Prince Bishop,
Carlsberg-Tetley, Castle Eden. **Facilities** Children's
menu Children's portions Garden Parking

## HAYDON BRIDGE
Map 21 NY86

### The General Havelock Inn ♀

**Ratcliffe Rd NE47 6ER**
☎ 01434 684376   📄 01434 684283
**e-mail:** info@generalhavelock.co.uk
**dir:** On A69, 7m W of Hexham

Built in around 1766, this riverside free house is named
after a 19th-century British Army officer. The pub, with
its restaurant in a converted barn overlooking the River
Tyne, is a favourite with show business personalities.
Local ingredients are the foundation of the menus, which
include smoked haddock risotto with poached egg;
chargrilled chicken with roast Mediterranean vegetables;
and roast duck breast on apple mash. Look out for the
range of gins, including a locally distilled one.

**Open** 12-2.30 7-mdnt Closed: Mon **Bar Meals** L served
12-2 D served 7-9 Av main course £8.50 **Restaurant** L
served 12-2 booking required D served 7-9 booking
required Av 3 course à la carte fr £21 ⊕ FREE HOUSE
◀ Hesket Newmarket Helvellyn Gold, Wylam Magic, High
House Nel's Best, Durham Brewery Magus, Allendale Best
Bitter. ♀ 15 **Facilities** Children's portions Dogs allowed
Garden

## HEDLEY ON THE HILL
Map 19 NZ05

### PICK OF THE PUBS

### The Feathers Inn ♀

*See Pick of the Pubs on opposite page*

## HEXHAM
Map 21 NY96

### PICK OF THE PUBS

### Battlesteads Hotel & Restaurant

*See Pick of the Pubs on page 344*

# PICK OF THE PUBS

## The Feathers Inn ♀

**HEDLEY ON THE HILL**            Map 19 NZ05

**NE43 7SW**
☎ **01661 843607**    🖷 **01661 843607**
**e-mail:** info@thefeathers.net
**web:** www.thefeathers.net
**dir:** *Telephone for directions*

From its hilltop position, this small stone-built free house overlooks the splendid adventure country of the Cheviots. The three-roomed pub is well patronised locally, but strangers are frequently charmed by its friendly and relaxed atmosphere. Old oak beams, coal fires and rustic settles set the scene, and there's a good selection of traditional pub games like shove ha'penny and bar skittles. The stone walls are decorated with local photographs of rural life.

Award-winning chef Rhian Cradock puts on a spectacular menu that changes everyday. The freshest of local ingredients – including game from local shoots, rare breed local cattle and longhorn beef – are used to create great British classics as well as regional dishes from the North East. Expect starters such as Jerusalem artichoke soup and home-made bread, or home-made black pudding with poached free-range egg and devilled gravy. Main course options might include Cranston's Cumberland sausage with creamy mashed potatoes and real ale gravy; Northumbrian leek, sweet potato and Doddington's cheese pie with creamy mash; or poached smoked North Shields haddock with heritage new potatoes. Leave room for desserts like pink rhubarb crumble with vanilla custard; and blood orange jelly with local cream. You can enjoy one of the great selection of cask ales beside a real open fire and dip into one of the many cookery books that spill over the place.

The Feathers is the perfect location to enjoy a relaxing afternoon lunch with beautiful Northumbrian views, or meet with friends for an intimate dinner. Families are welcome, and a small side room can be booked in advance if required.

**Open** all wk (Tue-Sat 12-11, Mon 6-10.30, Sun 12-10.30) Closed: No food served 1st 2wks Jan
**Bar Meals** L served Tue-Sat 12-2, Sun 12-2.30 booking required D served Mon 6-8, Tue-Sat 6-8.30 booking required Av main course £10 ⊕ FREE HOUSE
🍺 Mordue Workie Ticket, Fuller's London Pride, Northumberland Pit Pony, Orkney Red McGreggor, Hadrian Gladiator, Wylam Red Kite, Consett Red Dust
Ö Westons 1st Quality, Westons Old Rosie. ♀ **Facilities** Parking

# PICK OF THE PUBS

# Battlesteads Hotel & Restaurant

**HEXHAM**  Map 21 NY96

**Wark NE48 3LS**
☎ **01434 230209**  📄 **01434 230039**
**e-mail:** info@battlesteads.com
**web:** www.battlesteads.com
*dir: 10m N of Hexham on B6320 (Kielder road)*

Built as a farmhouse in 1747, this family-run hotel stands just a few miles north of Hadrian's Wall. Battlesteads became a temperance hotel in the early 20th century, and still offers a great range of organic soft drinks and ginger beer from Fentimans of Newcastle. Nowadays, following a major renovation, cask ales like Durham Magus, Wylam Gold Tankard and Durham White Velvet are also available, together with a decent wine list. Flower tubs and hanging baskets greet travellers in the

summer, whilst in winter a cosy wood-burning stove warms the wood-panelled bar with its comfy leather settees. There's an 80-seater restaurant, and a sunny conservatory that leads out to the secret walled beer garden.

Tasteful decor reflects the flavoursome modern British menu, which includes a smattering of international choices for those with more cosmopolitan tastes. Constantly changing menus include prime local ingredients for freshness and flavour, with free-range eggs, seasonal game, and locally reared lamb and beef. Fish and seafood come from North Shields Fish Quay, with oak-smoked duck, chicken and salmon from Bywell Smokery. Fresh vegetables and herbs are grown in the hotel garden, and vegetarian choices are always available.

The seasonal menu changes throughout the week, featuring starters such as goat's cheese and red onion confit tart on dressed leaves, and devilled kidneys and mushrooms on buttery toast. Moving on, typical main courses include herb-crusted rack of Northumbrian lamb with creamy mash and mange tout;

pan-fried sea bass fillets on a fennel, orange and pomegranate salad with heritage new potatoes; and roast vegetable linguine in rich tomato sauce with fresh Parmesan and garlic sourdough. Round things off with sticky toffee pudding, millionaire's sundae, or the award-winning whisky and marmalade bread and butter pudding.

**Open** all day all wk **Bar Meals** L served all wk 12-3 booking required D served all wk 6.30-9.30 booking required **Restaurant** L served all wk 12-3 booking required D served all wk 6.30-9.30 booking required Fixed menu price fr £18.50 🍺 FREE HOUSE ◀ Wylam Gold Tankard, Black Sheep Special, Durham White Velvet, Durham Magus, Black Sheep Bitter Ö Thatchers Gold. **Facilities** Dogs allowed Garden Parking

Save on Hotels. Book at **theAA.com/hotel**

**NORTHUMBERLAND** 345 | ENGLAND

## PICK OF THE PUBS

### Dipton Mill Inn ☻

**Dipton Mill Rd NE46 1YA ☎ 01434 606577**
**e-mail:** ghb@hexhamshire.co.uk
**dir:** *2m S of Hexham on HGV route to Blanchland, B6306, Dipton Mill Rd*

A former farmhouse, with the millstream running right through the gardens, the pub has recently celebrated its rebuilding 400 years ago. It is surrounded by farms and woodland with footpaths for pleasant country walks, and there is Hadrian's Wall and an assortment of other Roman sites in the area to explore. The Dipton Mill is home to Hexhamshire Brewery ales, including Devil's Water and Old Humbug. Food is served evenings and lunchtimes and all dishes are freshly prepared from local produce where possible. Start with home-made soup, such as carrot and celery served with a warm roll, followed by hearty dishes like mince and dumplings, lamb leg steak in wine and mustard sauce, or tomato, bean and vegetable casserole. Traditional desserts include bread and butter pudding or syrup sponge and custard. Salads, sandwiches and ploughman's are also always available.

**Open** noon-2.30 6-11 (Sun noon-3) Closed: 25 Dec, Sun eve **Bar Meals** L served all wk 12-2 D served Mon-Sat 6.30-8 ⊕ FREE HOUSE ◀ Hexhamshire Shire Bitter, Old Humbug, Devil's Water, Devil's Elbow, Whapweasel ♂ Westons Old Rosie. ☻ 17 **Facilities** Children's portions Garden Notes ⊛

### Miners Arms Inn

**Main St, Acomb NE46 4PW ☎ 01434 603909**
**e-mail:** info@theminersacomb.com
**dir:** *17m W of Newcastle on A69. 2m W of Hexham*

Situated close to Hadrian's Wall in a peaceful location, this welcoming family-run village pub with open hearth fire dates from 1746. Pride is taken in the range and quality of the ales - there are always three award-winning ales and special bitters are introduced every weekend - and in the good home-cooked food. Menus feature leek and potato soup; steak, ale and mushroom pie; chilli beef; and venison casserole. Sunday lunches are especially popular. There is a pleasant beer garden, and families are welcome.

**Open** all wk Mon-Fri 5-mdnt (Sat-Sun noon-mdnt) **Bar Meals** L served Sat 12-2.30 booking required D served Thu-Sat 5-8.30 booking required **Restaurant** L served Sun 12-2.30 booking required D served Thu-Sat 5-8.30 booking required ⊕ FREE HOUSE ◀ Wylam Bitter, Pilsner Urquell, Mordue, Yates Bitter ♂ Wylam Perry's Farmhouse Cider. **Facilities** Dogs allowed Garden

### Rat Inn ☻

**NE46 4LN ☎ 01434 602814**
**e-mail:** info@theratinn.com
**dir:** *2m from Hexham, Bridge End (A69) rdbt, take 4th exit signed Oakwood. Inn 500yds on right*

Set in the picturesque hamlet of Anick, The Rat has spectacular views across Hexham and the Tyne Valley. A classic country pub with a stunning summer garden and log fires in winter, it offers a classy selection of traditional food cooked to order using local ingredients. Examples include pigeon and black pudding salad followed by herb-crusted rack of lamb with courgettes provençale and dauphinoise potatoes. Excellent real ales.

**Open** all wk noon-3 6-close (Sat-Sun & Summer noon-close) **Bar Meals** L served Tue-Sat 12-2, Sun 12-3 booking required D served Tue-Sat 6-9 booking required **Restaurant** L served Tue-Sat 12-2, Sun 12-3 booking required D served Tue-Sat 6-9 booking required ⊕ FREE HOUSE ◀ John Smith's, Guinness, Bass, Deuchars IPA ♂ Farmhouse Cider. ☻ 8 **Facilities** Children's portions Garden Parking

| LONGFRAMLINGTON | Map 21 NU10 |

## PICK OF THE PUBS

### The Anglers Arms

*See Pick of the Pubs on page 346*

| LONGHORSLEY | Map 21 NZ19 |

### Linden Tree ★★★★ HL ⊛⊛

**Linden Hall NE65 8XF**
**☎ 01670 500033 📠 01670 500001**
**e-mail:** lindenhall@macdonald-hotels.co.uk
**dir:** *Off A1 on A697, 1m N of Longhorsley*

This popular pub was originally two large cattle byres. It takes its name from the linden trees near Linden Hall, the impressive Georgian mansion (now hotel) in whose grounds it stands. The brasserie-style menu might include a ham and pease pudding sandwich; a traditional Caesar salad; home-made Craster kipper pâté with brown bread, butter and lemon; spaghetti carbonara; and (from its Taste of Northumberland selection) home-made steak and suet pudding.

**Open** all wk Mon-Sat 11am-11pm (Sun 11am-10.30pm) ◀ Worthington, Greene King IPA, Caffreys, Guinness. **Facilities** Play area Garden Parking **Rooms** 50

| LOW NEWTON BY THE SEA | Map 21 NU22 |

### The Ship Inn

**The Square NE66 3EL ☎ 01665 576262**
**e-mail:** forsythchristine@hotmail.com
**dir:** *NE from A1 at Alnwick towards Seahouses*

The beach is only a stroll away from this pretty inn, which overlooks the green. Low Newton was purpose-built as a fishing village in the 18th century and remains wonderfully unspoilt. Bustling in summer and a peaceful retreat in winter, The Ship offers plenty of fresh, locally caught fish and free-range meats, along with interesting vegetarian food and old fashioned puddings. The pub now has its own micro-brewery, so expect some cracking real ales.

**Open** all wk **Bar Meals** L served all wk 12-2.30 D served all wk 7-8 (some seasonal variations, please telephone for details) booking required ⊕ FREE HOUSE ◀ Micro-brewery - Sea Coal, Dolly Day Dream, Sea Wheat, Ship Hop Ale, Sandcastles at Dawn. **Facilities** Dogs allowed Garden **Notes** ⊛

| MILFIELD | Map 21 NT93 |

### The Red Lion Inn NEW

**Main Rd NE71 6JD ☎ 01668 216224**
**dir:** *On A697, 9m S of Coldstream (6m N of Wooler)*

A solid, four-square stone building originating 300 years ago as a sheep drover's pub, later a stagecoach inn on the old road between Newcastle and Edinburgh, then popular with WW2 fighter pilots who were based nearby. It's a great community pub, with leek-growers discussing their secrets over excellent guest beers. Visitors heading for the nearby battle site of Flodden Field (AD1513) rest here to enjoy an enticing, solid range of pub food including locally made Northumbrian sausages, saddle of rabbit and sea trout fishcakes.

**Open** all wk all day Etr-Oct (Oct-Etr 11-2 6-9, all day Sat-Sun) **Bar Meals** Av main course £9 food served all day ⊕ SCOTTISH & NEWCASTLE ◀ Greene King IPA, Theakston Best, Guinness. **Facilities** Children's menu Children's portions Garden Parking

*See advert on page 347*

# PICK OF THE PUBS

## The Anglers Arms

**LONGFRAMLINGTON**  Map 21 NU10

**Weldon Bridge NE65 8AX**
☎ **01665 570271 & 570655**
e-mail:
johnyoung@anglersarms.fsnet.co.uk
*dir: From N, 9m S of Alnwick right Weldon
Bridge sign. From S, A1 to by-pass Morpeth,
left onto A697 for Wooler & Coldstream. 7m,
left to Weldon Bridge*

Open log fires are a welcoming treat on winter days at this former coaching inn, which has commanded the picturesque Weldon Bridge over the River Coquet since the 1760s. The interior is full of nice little touches such as antiques and quaint bric-a-brac, whilst the walls are covered with pictures and fishing memorabilia. Timothy Taylor Landlord and Theakstons Best Bitter are amongst the ales on offer to accompany a range of popular bar meals, where main course choices include traditional cod and chips with mushy peas; Northumbrian sausage on bacon and onion bubble and squeak; and a sizzling oriental platter with braised rice and prawn crackers.

Outside, there's plenty of space for alfresco summer dining in the carefully-tended half-acre of garden, which also includes a children's play park. But for more style and a different set of options, the pub's own Pullman railway carriage provides an unusual restaurant experience. Silver service comes as standard here, and you can choose from starters like chef's own soup of the day, and scallop and bacon salad with cherry tomatoes and rocket on a garlic crouton. Moving on to the main course, the alternatives include pan-fried duck breast with honey roasted parsnips and sweet potatoes; oven-baked stuffed peppers with a brie and basil crust; and grilled salmon fillet with new potatoes, baby corn, green beans, rocket and chilli sauce. Turn to the blackboard for a range of daily-changing desserts to complete your meal, or opt for a selection of English and continental cheeses served with celery and apple.

The Anglers Arms is ideally situated for visiting Alnwick Castle, Cragside and Hadrian's Wall; or you can fish with a day permit on the inn's own mile stretch of the River Coquet.

**Open** all day all wk 11-11 (Sun 12-10.30) **Bar Meals** Av main course £9 food served all day **Restaurant** Av 3 course à la carte fr £30 food served all day ⊕ FREE HOUSE ◙ Timothy Taylor Landlord, Old Speckled Hen, Abbot Ale, Theakstons Best Bitter. **Facilities** Play area Family room Garden Parking

## NETHERTON — Map 21 NT90

### he Star Inn

E65 7HD ☎ 01669 630238
ir: 7m from Rothbury

his place is a real find - owned by the same family since
917, and situated in superb remote countryside, the
tar retains many period features. The bar is a bit like
omeone's living room, comfortable and quiet, with no
uit machines or piped music — no food is served and
here's nothing fancy about it - just cask ales in the peak
f condition, served from a hatch in the entrance hall.

pen 7.30-11 Closed: Mon, Thu ⊕ FREE HOUSE
Camerons Strongarm. Facilities Parking Notes ☺

## NEWTON-ON-THE-MOOR — Map 21 NU10

### PICK OF THE PUBS

### The Cook and Barker
### Inn ★★★★ INN ⬤

NE65 9JY ☎ 01665 575234 ▤ 01665 575887
e-mail: info@cookandbarkerinn.co.uk
dir: 0.5m from A1 S of Alnwick

From its elevated position in a picturesque village this
traditional country inn commands outstanding views of
the Cheviot Hills and the Northumbrian coast. The Cook
and Barker is a long-established family business fun
by Phil Farmer, who has set his sights well above the
conventional 'pub grub with rooms'. To this end, highly
skilled kitchen staff strive to prepare quality dishes
that give value for money, while the front-of-house
team looks after guests with expertise and finesse. A
good choice of real ales is backed by a dozen wines
served by the glass. Food can be served in the
restaurant, bar, snug or lounge. A late spring menu
featured dishes such as roasted vine tomato soup;
terrine of wild boar with red onion marmalade; crab
and ginger fishcakes with buttered spinach and chips;

baked artichokes with goat's cheese, pine kernels and
a crisp vegetable spring roll; and Moroccan lamb
shank with prunes, cinnamon and star anise with
lentils and minted couscous. There are 18 smartly
furnished en suite bedrooms if you would like to stay
over.

Open all day all wk 12-11 Bar Meals food served all
day Restaurant L served Mon-Sat 12-2, Sun all day
booking required D served Mon-Sat 7-9, Sun all day
booking required ⊕ FREE HOUSE ◀ Timothy Taylor
Landlord, Theakstons Best Bitter, Fuller's London Pride,
Batemans XXXB, Black Sheep. ⬤ 12
Facilities Children's menu Family room Garden Parking
Rooms 18

## ROWFOOT — Map 21 NY66

### The Wallace Arms

NE49 0JF ☎ 01434 321872 ▤ 01434 321872
dir: Telephone for directions

The pub was rebuilt in 1850 as the Railway Hotel at
Featherstone Park station, when the now long-closed
Haltwhistle-Alston line (today's South Tyne Trail) was
engineered. It changed to the Wallace Arms in 1885.
Sample menu includes modestly-priced haddock fillet in
beer batter, salmon fillet in lemon and tarragon sauce,
steak and ale pie, grilled sirloin steak, and smoked
haddock and prawn pasta. There are light snacks,
burgers and sandwiches, if you prefer.

Open all wk ◀ Hook Norton Old Hooky, Young's Special,
Greene King IPA, Greene King Abbot Ale, Jennings
Cumberland Ale. Facilities Garden Parking

## SEAHOUSES — Map 21 NU23

### PICK OF THE PUBS

### The Olde Ship Inn ★★★★ INN ⬤

9 Main St NE68 7RD
☎ 01665 720200 ▤ 01665 721383
e-mail: theoldeship@seahouses.co.uk
dir: Lower end of main street above harbour

This stone-built free house sits comfortably above the
bustling old harbour of Seahouses, and reflects the
fishing heritage of this tiny port. Built as a farm
around 1745, The Olde Ship has been in the present
owners' family for 100 years. These days it is now a
residential inn with a long established reputation for
good food and drink in relaxing surroundings. The main
saloon bar, with its wooden floor made from pine ships'
decking, offers a selection of real ales. The inn's
corridors and boat gallery are an Aladdin's cave of
antique nautical artefacts and seafaring mementoes.
Popular bar foods include locally caught seafood,
freshly made sandwiches and home-made soups. In
the evenings, starters like home-made meat loaf
herald main course options that include gamekeeper's
casserole in red wine gravy, and lemon sole grilled in
butter. The tastefully decorated bedrooms are well
appointed, and some have views to the bird and seal
sanctuary on the Farne Islands.

Open all day all wk 11-11 (Sun noon-11) Bar Meals L
served all wk 12-2.30 D served all wk 7-8.30 (no D late
Nov-late Jan) booking required Av main course £10
Restaurant L served Sun 12-2 booking required D
served all wk 7-8.30 (no D late Nov-late Jan) booking
required Av 3 course à la carte fr £20 ⊕ FREE
HOUSE ◀ Black Sheep, Theakstons, Best Scotch,
Ruddles. ⬤ 10 Facilities Family room Garden Parking
Rooms 18

## SLAGGYFORD — Map 18 NY65

### The Kirkstyle Inn NEW

**CA8 7PB ☎ 01434 381559**
*dir: Just off A689, 6m N of Alston*

With enviable views of the South Tyne river, the Kirkstyle takes its name from the stile into the adjacent churchyard. A real log fire heats the pub in winter, but there's a warm welcome here all the year round. Beers include real ale from local breweries including Yates' Bitter and in summer a special Kirkstyle ale is available. Expect lunchtime snacks and specials, including local sausages served with local honey mustard and either eggs and hand-cut chips, or mash and gravy. This dog-friendly pub is handy for both the Pennine Way and the South Tyne trail.

**Open** all wk noon-3 6-11 Closed: Mon in winter **Bar Meals** L served all wk 12-2 D served Mon-Sat 6-8.30 Av main course £7.95 **Restaurant** L served all wk 12-2 D served Mon-Sat 6-8.30 Av 3 course à la carte fr £18.95 ⊕ FREE HOUSE ◀ Kirkstyle Ale, Yates Bitter, Guinness. **Facilities** Children's portions Dogs allowed Garden Parking

## WARDEN — Map 21 NY96

### The Boatside Inn ♀

**NE46 4SQ ☎ 01434 602233**
**e-mail:** sales@theboatsideinn.com
**web:** www.theboatsideinn.com
*dir: Off A69 W of Hexham, follow signs to Warden Newborough & Fourstones*

The name of this stone-built country free house harks back to the days when a rowing boat ferried people across the river before the bridge was built. Standing beneath Warden Hill at the confluence of the North and South Tyne rivers, the Boatside welcomes children, walkers and cyclists; the inn also has fishing rights on the river. Main course options include mince and leek dumplings; vegetarian Wellington; and steamed halibut with lemon and parsley butter.

**Open** all day all wk 11-11 (Sun 11-10.30) **Bar Meals** L served Mon-Sat 11-9, Sun 12-8 D served Mon-Sat 11-9, Sun 12-8 Av main course £8.95 food served all day **Restaurant** L served Mon-Sat 12-2.30, Sun 12-8 D served Mon-Sat 6-9, Sun 12-8 ⊕ FREE HOUSE ◀ Black Sheep, John Smith's, Mordue, Wylam. ♀ 15 **Facilities** Children's menu Children's portions Dogs allowed Garden Parking

## WARENFORD — Map 21 NU12

### PICK OF THE PUBS

### The White Swan

**NE70 7HY ☎ 01668 213453**
**e-mail:** dianecuthbert@yahoo.com
*dir: 100yds E of A1, 10m N of Alnwick*

This 200-year-old coaching inn stands near the original toll bridge over the Waren Burn. Formerly on the Great North Road, the building is now just a stone's throw from the A1. Inside, you'll find thick stone walls and an open fire for colder days; in summer, there's a small sheltered seating area, with further seats in the adjacent field. The Dukes of Northumberland once owned the pub, and its windows and plasterwork still bear the family crests. Visitors and locals alike enjoy the atmosphere and Northumbrian dishes: try Seahouses kippers with creamy horseradish sauce; venison pudding with lemon suet crust and fresh vegetables; or roast pork hock with wine and herbs. Vegetarians are well catered for, with interesting dishes like beetroot and potato gratin; artichoke and leek pancakes; and celeriac pan Haggarty with fresh tomato sauce.

**Open** all day all wk noon-mdnt **Bar Meals** L served all wk 12-3 D served all wk 6-9 Av main course £7.75 **Restaurant** L served all wk 12-3 D served all wk 6-9 Av 3 course à la carte fr £22.50 ⊕ FREE HOUSE ◀ Black Sheep, John Smith's. **Facilities** Children's menu Children's portions Dogs allowed Garden Parking

## WHALTON — Map 21 NZ18

### PICK OF THE PUBS

### Beresford Arms

**NE61 3UZ ☎ 01670 775225**
**e-mail:** nixon_100@hotmail.co.uk
*dir: 5m from Morpeth town centre on B6524*

This ivy-covered coaching inn continues to maintain its country pub atmosphere, while at the same time conveying a modern feel. It lies in the picturesque village of Whalton, popular with cyclists and walkers enjoying the delights of nearby Kielder Forest and Northumberland National Park. Set opposite the village hall, it also provides a welcome focus for village life. Start with a pint of Bombardier while perusing the menu. Your meal could start with home-made soup, or prawn and avocado salad with Marie Rose sauce; follow with grilled Wallington Hall rib-eye steak with tomato, mushrooms, onion rings and chips; and finish with a crumble.

**Open** all wk Mon-Sat 12-2 6-9 (Sun 12-4) **Bar Meals** L served Mon-Sat 12-2, Sun 12-4 D served Mon-Sat 6-9 **Restaurant** L served Fri-Sat 12-2, Sun 12-4 D served Fri-Sat 6-9 ⊕ ENTERPRISE ◀ Bombardier, Directors, John Smith's. **Facilities** Children's menu Garden Parking

## NOTTINGHAMSHIRE

## BEESTON — Map 11 SK53

### Victoria Hotel ♀

**Dovecote Ln NG9 1JG**
**☎ 0115 925 4049 ▤ 0115 922 3537**
**e-mail:** hopco.victoriabeeston@btconnect.com
*dir: M1 junct 25, A52 E. Turn right at Nurseryman PH, right opp Rockaway Hotel into Barton St 1st left, next to railway station*

The Victoria dates from 1899 when it was built next to Beeston Railway Station, and the large, heated patio garden is still handy for a touch of train-spotting. It offers an excellent range of traditional ales (up to 14 at a time), continental beers and lagers, traditional ciders, a good choice of wines by the glass and single malt whiskies. Home-cooked dishes on the menu might includ wild boar liver pâté; braised spiced meatballs; roast guinea fowl supreme; cottage pie; or Dartmouth Smokehouse kiln-roasted trout fillets. There are always plenty of vegetarian options available. Check out the dates for beer festivals throughout the year.

**Open** all day all wk 10.30am-11pm (Sun 12-11) Closed: 26 Dec **Bar Meals** L served Sun-Tue 12-8.45, Wed-Sat 12-9.30 Av main course £8.95 food served all day **Restaurant** L served Sun-Tue 12-8.45, Wed-Sat 12-9.30 booking required food served all day ⊕ FREE HOUSE ◀ Batemans XB, Castle Rock Harvest Pale, Castle Rock Hemlock, Everards Tiger, 6 guest ales ☼ Thatchers Traditional, Broadoak Medium, Biddendens Bushels. ♀ 25 **Facilities** Dogs allowed Garden Parking

## BINGHAM — Map 11 SK73

### The Chesterfield ♀

**Church St NG13 8AL ☎ 01949 837342**
**e-mail:** eat@thechesterfield.co.uk
*dir: 6m E of Nottingham, Bingham off A52 & A46 junct. Pub just off market square*

One of the earliest buildings in the centre of this small market town, the Chesterfield has been refurbished in contemporary style. The pub now features a stylish bar and gastro-style restaurant, as well as a private dining room and garden. Lunchtime brings snacks and sandwiches, plus a traditional Sunday roast. Typical restaurant choices include rack of lamb with apricots and cheese; seared fresh salmon salad; and grilled halloumi with couscous and curry sauce.

**Open** all wk ◀ Timothy Taylor Landlord, Marston Pedigree, Wells Bombardier, Shepherd Neame Spitfire, Fuller's London Pride. ♀ 12 **Facilities** Garden Parking

Save on Hotels. Book at theAA.com/hotel

NOTTINGHAMSHIRE 349 ENGLAND

## BLIDWORTH
Map 16 SK55

### Fox & Hounds 🍷

**Blidworth Bottoms NG21 0NW ☎ 01623 792383**
e-mail: info@foxandhounds-pub.com
dir: *Right off B6020 between Ravenshead & Blidworth*

A traditional country pub, extensively refurbished a few years ago to create attractive surroundings in which to eat and drink. It was probably built as a farmhouse in the 19th century, when Blidworth Bottoms was a thriving community, with shops and a post office. A reputation for good pub food comes from dishes such as steak and ale pie; Mediterranean chicken; blackened salmon in Cajun spices; home-made vegetarian cottage pie; and hot chilli con carne.

**Open** all day all wk 11.30am-11.30pm (Fri-Sat 11.30am-mdnt) **Bar Meals** L served all wk 11.30-9 D served all wk 11.30-9 food served all day ⊕ GREENE KING ◀ H&H Cask Bitter, Old Speckled Hen, Olde Trip H&H, seasonal guest ales. 🍷 9 **Facilities** Children's menu Play area Dogs allowed Garden Parking

## CAUNTON
Map 17 SK76

### PICK OF THE PUBS

### Caunton Beck 🍷

**NG23 6AB ☎ 01636 636793 📠 01636 636828**
e-mail: email@cauntonbeck.com
dir: *6m NW of Newark on A616 to Sheffield*

Like its sister establishment, the Wig and Mitre in Lincoln, this civilised village pub-restaurant opens daily for breakfast and carries on serving food after 10pm. It is built around a beautifully restored 16th-century cottage with herb gardens and a colourful rose arbour that reflects a tradition started by the vicar of Caunton, Samuel Reynolds Hole. Real ales complement a worthy international wine list, including a wide choice by the glass. The extensive breakfast menu features Bucks Fizz and a selection of Champagnes alongside more traditional teas and coffees, whilst the main menu changes with the seasons. To start you might choose roast halloumi and tomato salad with warm ciabatta, followed by grilled Atlantic cod with a crab and coriander tartare. Chilled lemon and raspberry tart is a typical dessert. A sandwich and light meal menu is also available, with home-made fudge on offer.

**Open** all day all wk 8am-mdnt **Bar Meals** L served all wk 8-11 D served all wk 8-11 Av main course £13.50 food served all day **Restaurant** L served all wk 8-11 booking required D served all wk 8-11 booking required Fixed menu price fr £11 Av 3 course à la carte fr £13.50 food served all day ⊕ FREE HOUSE ◀ Batemans GHA, Marston's Pedigree, Black Sheep, Guinness Ò Thatchers. 🍷 34 **Facilities** Children's portions Dogs allowed Garden Parking

## CAYTHORPE
Map 11 SK64

### Black Horse Inn

**NG14 7ED ☎ 0115 966 3520**
dir: *12m from Nottingham off A612 towards Southwell*

Old-fashioned hospitality is guaranteed in this small, beamed country pub which has been run by the same family for three generations. It has its own brewery, producing Caythorpe Dover Beck bitter (named after the stream that runs past the pub), a coal fire in the bar, and delicious home-cooked food prepared from seasonal ingredients. Fresh fish dishes such as mussels or fish and chips are a speciality; other choices might include fresh asparagus or a generous mixed grill. Good local walks.

**Open** noon-2.30 6-11 (Sun noon-5 8-10.30) Closed: Mon L (ex BH) & every 3rd Tue L **Bar Meals** L served Tue-Sat 12-1.45 booking required D served Tue-Sat 6.30-8.30 booking required Av main course £8.50 **Restaurant** L served Tue-Sat 12-1.45 booking required D served Tue-Fri 6.30-8.30 booking required ⊕ FREE HOUSE ◀ Greene King Abbot Ale, Dover Beck Bitter, Batemans XB, Adnams Ò Westons Stowford Press. **Facilities** Dogs allowed Garden Parking **Notes** ⊜

## COLSTON BASSETT
Map 11 SK73

### PICK OF THE PUBS

### The Martin's Arms

*See Pick of the Pubs on page 350*

## EDWINSTOWE
Map 16 SK66

### Forest Lodge ★★★★ INN 🍷

**4 Church St NG21 9QA**
**☎ 01623 824443 📠 01623 824686**
e-mail: audrey@forestlodgehotel.co.uk
web: www.forestlodgehotel.co.uk
dir: *A614 towards Edwinstowe, turn onto B6034. Inn opposite church*

Sympathetically restored by the Thompson family over the past six years, including accommodation, this 18th-century coaching inn stands right on the edge of Sherwood Forest opposite the church where Robin Hood reputedly married Maid Marion. Five cask ales are always on tap in two beamed bars, both warmed by open fires. An impressive baronial-style dining hall is an ideal setting for appetising plates of wholesome fare such as moules marinières; baked salmon; gammon with egg and pineapple; and the famous beefsteak pie with shortcrust pastry.

*Forest Lodge*

**Open** all wk 11.30-3 5.30-11 (Fri 11.30-3 5-11, Sun noon-3 6-10.30) Closed: 1 Jan **Bar Meals** L served all wk 12-2 booking required D served all wk 6-9 booking required **Restaurant** L served all wk 12-2 booking required D served all wk 6-9 booking required ⊕ FREE HOUSE ◀ Bombardier, Kelham Island Pale Rider, Kelham Island Easy Rider, Acorn Pale Ale, Eagle IPA. 🍷 8 **Facilities** Children's menu Children's portions Dogs allowed Garden Parking **Rooms** 13

## ELKESLEY
Map 17 SK67

### Robin Hood Inn

**High St DN22 8AJ ☎ 01777 838259**
e-mail: a1robinhood@aol.com
dir: *5m SE of Worksop off A1 towards Newark-on-Trent*

Parts of this unassuming village inn date back to the 14th century. Ceilings and floors are deep red, while the green walls are adorned with pictures of food. The comprehensive choice is served in both the bar and restaurant, and includes a fixed price menu, carte and daily specials board. Typical dishes are grilled breast of chicken, roast red peppers, chorizo and spiced plum tomato; and roasted peppered Barnsley chop, steamed greens, mint and caper gravy.

**Open** 11.30-2.30 6-11 Closed: Sun eve & Mon **Bar Meals** L served Tue-Sun 12-2 D served Tue-Sat 6-8 Av main course £10 **Restaurant** L served Tue-Sun 12-2 D served Tue-Sat 6-9 Av 3 course à la carte fr £15 ⊕ ENTERPRISE INNS ◀ John Smith's Extra Smooth, Black Sheep Best Bitter, guest ale. **Facilities** Children's portions Play area Dogs allowed Garden Parking

# PICK OF THE PUBS

## The Martin's Arms

**COLSTON BASSETT**  Map 11 SK73

**School Ln NG12 3FD**
☎ **01949 81361**  📄 **01949 81039**
e-mail: martins_arms@hotmail.co.uk
**dir:** Off A46 between Leicester & Newark

There's a strong commitment to local produce and the environment at this award-winning 18th-century inn. Good quality organic food comes from artisan suppliers in the surrounding Vale of Belvoir; apples and rhubarb grow in the pub's own garden, whilst drinks bottles and other packaging are either re-used or recycled. The listed building stands right at the heart of the village beside a market cross dating back to 1257, and its period furnishings, hunting prints, and winter fires in the Jacobean fireplace give the place a real country house feel. The acre of landscaped grounds backs on to National Trust land, and includes a herb garden and well-established lawns.

As a free house, the inn can offer an impressive range of real ales, including Black Sheep Best, Bateman's and Timothy Taylor Landlord; plus soft drinks like Belvoir elderflower pressé and organic ginger beer.

Regional ingredients are a feature of appetising and inventive dishes in both the bar and the restaurant, with preserves, sauces and desserts all freshly made on site. Local Colston Basset Stilton and Melton Mowbray pork pies are a feature of the lunchtime ploughman's, whilst the range of hot and cold sandwiches are made with the pub's own home-baked bread. Three-course appetites might start with red pepper and feta cheese terrine, or Serrano ham with asparagus, duck egg and smoked hollandaise. Main course choices include aubergine, goat's cheese and cherry tomato tart with red pepper coulis; grilled salmon with cauliflower and saffron purée, creamed leeks and wholegrain mustard; and game pie with mashed potato and braised red cabbage. Among the desserts is date and walnut pudding with butterscotch and condensed milk ice cream. More than 30 wines are grouped by dryness, richness, softness, heartiness and other essential qualities.

**Open** all wk noon-3.30 6-11 Closed: 25 Dec eve **Bar Meals** L served Mon-Sat 12-2, Sun 12-2.30 D served Mon-Sat 7-9.30 Av main course £14
**Restaurant** L served all wk 12-2 booking required D served Mon-Sat 7-9.30 booking required Fixed menu price fr £15.95 Av 3 course à la carte fr £25 ◀ Marston's Pedigree, Interbrew Bass, Greene King Abbot Ale, Timothy Taylor Landlord, Black Sheep Best, Batemans, IPA, London Pride.
**Facilities** Family room Garden Parking

Save on Hotels. Book at **theAA.com/hotel**

NOTTINGHAMSHIRE 351 ENGLAND

## FARNDON
Map 17 SK75

### PICK OF THE PUBS

## The Farndon Boathouse ♥

**Riverside NG24 3SX**
☎ 01636 676578  📠 01636 673911
**e-mail:** info@farndonboathouse.co.uk
**dir:** From Newark-on-Trent take A46 to Farndon x-rds, turn right, continue to river. Boathouse on riverside

Clad in wood, with chunky exposed roof trusses, stone floors, warehouse-style lighting, and an abundance of glass, this modern bar and eatery, in the style of an old boathouse, sits wonderfully well on the banks of the River Trent. Just how well you'll realise if you approach from the river in your cruiser, or watch a sunset through the extensively glazed frontage of the bar and restaurant. The food philosophy champions local sourcing and home preparation, with home-smoked meats, fish, spices and cheeses, for example, and herbs and leaves grown in the kitchen garden. Reasonably priced dishes include pan-roasted fillet of Scotch beef with balsamic roasted shallot and pan-fried foie gras; slow-cooked pork belly with pancetta and apple potato cake; spiced bouillabaisse; and lamb's lettuce with potato gnocchi, tomato sauce and shallots. Cask-conditioned real ales change frequently, and live music is played every Sunday evening.

**Open** all day all wk 10am-11pm **Bar Meals** L served Mon-Fri 12-2.30, Sat-Sun 12-3 D served all wk 6-9.30 Av main course £11 **Restaurant** L served Mon-Fri 12-2.30, Sat-Sun 12-3 D served all wk 6-9.30 Fixed menu price fr £12 Av 3 course à la carte fr £27 ⊕ FREE HOUSE ◀ Black Sheep, Caythorpe Dover Beck, One Swallow. ♥ 46 **Facilities** Children's menu Children's portions Garden Parking

## HALAM
Map 17 SK65

### PICK OF THE PUBS

## The Waggon and Horses

**The Turnpike, Mansfield Rd NG22 8AE**
☎ 01636 813109  📠 01636 816228
**e-mail:** info@thewaggonathalam.co.uk
**dir:** From A614 at White Post Farm rdbt follow signs to Farnsfield. In Halam, pub on right

Halam's dapper village local shines like a beacon in the Nottinghamshire countryside, drawing diners from far and wide for chef-patron Roy Wood's inventive pub food. The smartened-up open-plan bar and dining room ooze charm and character with heavy oak beams, chunky tables on wooden or tiled floors, and a wealth of cricketing memorabilia. Sup a pint of Thwaites Wainwright while perusing the day's chalkboard menu. Expect a modern approach to classic pub dishes which make good use of local seasonal ingredients: black pudding and Stilton salad; or pan-fried liver with onions and bacon. Alternatively lunchtime and early evening specials may include smoked mackerel and horseradish cream; cottage pie; or goat's cheese and beetroot bruschetta. Not only do you eat and drink well

here, but you do so in the relaxed knowledge that Roy and his wife Laura have worked with the CarbonNeutral Company in their effort to operate the pub as a carbon-neutral business.

**Open** 11.45-3 5.45-10 Closed: Sun eve & Mon **Bar Meals** L served Tue-Sat 11.45-2 booking required D served Tue-Sat 5.45-8 booking required Av main course £13 **Restaurant** L served Tue-Sun 11.45-2 booking required D served Tue-Sun 5.45-8 booking required Fixed menu price fr £15 Av 3 course à la carte fr £24 ⊕ THWAITES ◀ Thwaites Bomber, Smooth & Wainwright. **Facilities** Children's portions Parking

## HARBY
Map 17 SK87

## Bottle & Glass ♥

**High St NG23 7EB** ☎ 01522 703438  📠 01522 703436
**e-mail:** email@bottleandglassharby.com
**dir:** S of A57 (Lincoln to Markham Moor road)

Much more ancient than it appears, Edward the First's wife Queen Eleanor reputedly died here in 1290. This compact, convivial free-house, rich with flagged floors and heavy beams, strives successfully to offer great food and fine beers to locals and diners wise enough to seek out this tranquil village at the edge of the Vale of Trent. The sunny terrace is a good base at which to chow down on a comprehensive, seasonally adjusted menu that may feature roast rump of lamb on lovage mash or roast chicken breast with asparagus spears and wild mushroom sauce. An appropriate wine is suggested with each dish, whilst early-birds can enjoy a breakfast break here.

**Open** all day all wk 11am-11pm **Bar Meals** Av main course fr £13 Av 3 course à la carte fr £20 food served all day **Restaurant** Fixed menu price fr £13 Av 3 course à la carte fr £20 food served all day ⊕ FREE HOUSE ◀ Young's Bitter, Young's Gold, Black Sheep, Guinness ♂ Thatchers Gold. ♥ 34 **Facilities** Children's portions Dogs allowed Garden Parking

## KIMBERLEY
Map 11 SK44

## The Nelson & Railway Inn

**12 Station Rd NG16 2NR**
☎ 0115 938 2177  📠 0115 938 2179
**dir:** 1m N of M1 junct 26

The landlord of more than 30 years gives this 17th-century pub its distinctive personality. Next door is the Hardy & Hanson brewery that supplies many of the beers, but the two nearby railway stations that once made it a railway inn are now sadly derelict. A hearty menu of pub favourites includes soup, ploughman's, and hot rolls, as well as grills and hot dishes like home-made steak and kidney pie; gammon steak; and mushroom stroganoff.

**Open** all day all wk 11am-mdnt ◀ Hardys, Hansons Best Bitter, Cool & Dark, Olde Trip, Morlands, Ruddles. **Facilities** Family room Dogs allowed Garden Parking

## LAXTON
Map 17 SK76

## The Dovecote Inn ♥

**Cross Hill NG22 0SX** ☎ 01777 871586
**e-mail:** dovecote_inn@btconnect.com
**dir:** Exit A1 at Tuxford through Egmanton to Laxton

Like most of the village of Laxton, this family-run, 18th-century pub is Crown Estate property belonging to the Royal Family. Outside is a delightful beer garden with views of the church. The interior includes a bar and three cosy wining and dining rooms. Here the seasonal, home-cooked dishes could include Lancashire hot pot; slow roast pork belly; fish pie; and Whitby scampi. The village still practises the Medieval strip field farming method — there is a visitor centre in the pub car park.

**Open** all wk 11.30-3 6.30-11 (Sun noon-10.30) **Restaurant** L served Mon-Sat 2-2, Sun 12.30-6 booking required D served Mon-Sat 6.30-9.30 booking required ⊕ FREE HOUSE ◀ Mansfield Smooth, John Smith's Smooth, Black Sheep, Greene King Old Speckled Hen, Adnams. ♥ 9 **Facilities** Children's menu Children's portions Garden Parking

## MORTON
Map 17 SK75

### PICK OF THE PUBS

## The Full Moon Inn ♥

*See Pick of the Pubs on page 352*

*See Pick of the Pubs on page 352*

## NOTTINGHAM
Map 11 SK53

## Cock & Hoop

**25 High Pavement NG1 1HE**
☎ 0115 852 3231  📠 0115 852 3236
**e-mail:** drink@cockandhoop.co.uk
**dir:** Follow tourist signs for 'Galleries of Justice'. Pub opposite

Tasteful antiques, a real fire, a cellar bar and some striking bespoke artwork characterize this traditional Victorian alehouse. It stands opposite the Galleries of Justice, where Lord Byron is said to have watched hangings from his lodgings above the pub.

**Open** all wk Closed: 25-26 Dec ◀ Deuchars IPA, Cock & Hoop, London Pride, Timothy Taylor Landlord, Old Speckled Hen. **Facilities** Family room Dogs allowed

# PICK OF THE PUBS

## The Full Moon Inn ♀

---

**MORTON**                     Map 17 SK75

**Main St NG25 0UT**
☎ **01636 830251**   📠 **01636 830554**
**e-mail:** info@thefullmoonmorton.co.uk
**dir:** *Newark A617 to Mansfield. Past Kelham, turn left to Rolleston & follow signs to Morton*

William and Rebecca White have transformed this friendly free house from a dark and dated pub into one that is light, comfortable and contemporary. They've exposed the old beams and brickwork from the original 18th-century cottages, and used reclaimed panels, furniture and new carpets to help create a destination pub in this Trent-side hamlet. Year-round appeal includes a charming garden for the summer, and two roaring log fires for the winter. Five

hand pulls prove that William takes his real ales very seriously – and the respectable wines are fairly priced, with many served by the glass.

Rebecca is in charge of a kitchen where the emphasis is on farm-fresh food, mostly sourced locally, with a set menu running alongside the pub menu at lunchtime and in the evenings. There's plenty on offer, beginning with a full breakfast menu that features a local feast of bacon and black pudding from Porters, bangers from Gonalston and bread from Atherleys. At lunchtime the emphasis changes: expect filled rustic baguettes and free range omelettes, as well as soups, salads, burgers and hot dishes.

The evening menu offers starters that range from bread, dips and mixed olives, to black pudding and bacon with poached egg and mustard dressing. Follow through with wholetail scampi, salad and chips; stuffed corn-fed chicken breast with potato purée, pesto and steamed vegetables; or lentil and roast squash pie with creamed leeks

and chips. On Friday and Saturday nights the set menu is replaced with a specials board featuring fish chosen by a local fishmonger and only chalked up after he's delivered it. There's plenty here to keep children occupied too, with a designated indoor play area, an outdoor castle and a sand pit, while dogs are also welcome.

**Open** all wk fr 10.30am
**Bar Meals** L served all wk 12-2.30 booking required D served all wk 6-9.30 booking required Av main course £10
**Restaurant** L served all wk 12-2.30 booking required D served all wk 6-9.30 booking required Fixed menu price fr £16 Av 3 course à la carte fr £22
🍺 FREE HOUSE 🛢 Bombardier, Dover Beck, Moonshine, guest ales. ♀ 8
**Facilities** Children's menu Play area Family room Dogs allowed Garden Parking

**NOTTINGHAM** *continued*

## Fellows Morton & Clayton

**54 Canal St NG1 7EH**
☎ 0115 950 6795   📠 0115 953 9838
**e-mail:** office@fellowsmortonandclayton.co.uk
**dir:** *Telephone for directions*

Surrounded by the impressive Castle Wharf complex, with a cobbled courtyard overlooking the Nottingham canal, FMC was converted from a former warehouse in 1979. The pub is a regular Nottingham in Bloom award winner. Inside, the giant plasma screen shows all the major sporting events. So there is no need to miss a goal while tucking into the likes of chicken club sandwich; bangers and mash, home-made burgers, or a sirloin with all the trimmings.

**Open** all day all wk **Bar Meals** L served Mon-Sun 10-3 D served Thu-Sun 3-9 Av main course £8 **Restaurant** L served Fri 12-2 Fixed menu price fr £10.95 Av 3 course à la carte fr £13.95 ⊕ ENTERPRISE INNS ◀ Timothy Taylor Landlord, Fuller's London Pride, Nottingham EPA, Deuchars IPA, Mallard Bitter. **Facilities** Children's portions Garden Parking

### PICK OF THE PUBS

## Ye Olde Trip to Jerusalem ♟

**1 Brewhouse Yard, Castle Rd NG1 6AD**
☎ 0115 947 3171
**e-mail:** 4925@greeneking.co.uk
**dir:** *In town centre*

Castle Rock, upon which stands Nottingham Castle, is riddled with caves and passageways cut into the sandstone. The builders of this unusual pub made the most of this, incorporating some of the caves into the design of the inn, one of Britain's oldest, founded in 1189AD. The name recalls that soldiers, clergy and penitents gathered here before embarking on the Crusade to The Holy Land – doubtless they drank to their quest at the castle's beer-house before their trip to Jerusalem. Centuries of service and piecemeal renovations over the years give the Trip instant appeal, from the magpie collection of furnishings in the warren of rooms to the unique Rock Lounge (look for the Ring the Bull game), spooky alcoves (several ghosts here) and quirks such as the cursed galleon and the fertility chair. Beers from the Nottingham Brewery feature strongly, accompanying a reliable menu of old favourites (sausage and mash, steak and ale pie) and innovative new bites (cauliflower and Cheddar cheese tart).

**Open** all day all wk 11am-11pm (Fri-Sat 11am-mdnt) **Bar Meals** D served all wk 11-8 Av main course £7 food served all day ⊕ GREENE KING ◀ Ye Olde Trip Ale, Nottingham Brewery guest ales, Greene King IPA, Abbot Ale, Old Speckled Hen 🍏 Aspall. ♟ 13 **Facilities** Garden

---

**RUDDINGTON**   Map 11 SK53

## Three Crowns ♟

**23 Easthorpe St NG11 6LB** ☎ 0115 921 3226
**e-mail:** simon@nottinghamthai.co.uk
**dir:** *A60 towards Loughborough. Right at 1st lights into Ruddington, right & right again, pub 500yds on left*

A modern pub with an authentic Thai restaurant next door, where traditionally attired waitresses from the Land of Smiles glide between the tables. Lunchtime pub snacks include baguettes, omelettes, burgers, traditional pies and Thai stir-fries. The restaurant serves pork, chicken, beef, duck, fish and seafood curries of various strengths, and other Thai dishes, as well as steaks. Traditional roasts and other non-Thai meals are served on Sundays.

**Open** all wk ◀ Adnams, Nottingham Brewery, Timothy Taylor Landlord, Cottage Brewery, guest ales. ♟ 18 **Facilities** Dogs allowed

---

**THURGARTON**   Map 17 SK64

## The Red Lion

**Southwell Rd NG14 7GP** ☎ 01636 830351
**dir:** *On A612 between Nottingham & Southwell*

This 16th-century inn was originally the alehouse for the monks at the nearby Thurgarton Priory, and in 1936 it was the scene of the murder of the landlady by her niece. Today the pub is a peaceful haven offering a delightful tree-shaded terraced beer garden and inside a warren of rooms with original beams and welcoming open fires. Pub food can be enjoyed in the bar, restaurant or garden. Main courses include Cajun chicken; cod, prawn and salmon crumble; beef lasagne; or a variety of steaks. For a lighter option, try a one of the many salads on offer.

**Open** all wk 11.30-2.30 6.30-11 (Sat-Sun & BH 11.30-11) **Bar Meals** L served all wk 12-2 D served Sun-Fri 6.30-9, Sat 6.30-9.30 Av main course £9.50 **Restaurant** L served all wk 12-2 D served Sun-Fri 6.30-9, Sat 6.30-9.30 ⊕ FREE HOUSE ◀ Black Sheep, Blue Monkey, Bass. **Facilities** Children's menu Children's portions Garden Parking

---

**TUXFORD**   Map 17 SK77

## The Mussel & Crab ♟

**Sibthorpe Hill NG22 0PJ** ☎ 01777 870491
📠 01777 872302
**e-mail:** musselandcrab1@hotmail.com
**dir:** *From Ollerton/Tuxford junct of A1& A57. N on B1164 to Sibthorpe Hill. Pub 800yds on right*

Beautifully fresh fish and seafood dominate the menu at this quirky pub with a multitude of rooms, all decked out in inimitable style. The piazza room is styled as an Italian courtyard, with murals by artist Tony Cooke; the beamed restaurant is big on rustic charm; and the gents' toilets is brightened with a tank of fish! Countless blackboards offer ever-changing dishes such as Isle of Shuna mussels; pan fried red mullet; or Cromer crab, plus some fish you have never tasted as well as non-fishy dishes like pork fillet or beef Wellington.

**Open** all wk 11-3 6-11 **Bar Meals** L served Mon-Sat 11-2.30, Sun 11-3 booking required D served Mon-Sat 6-10, Sun 6-9 booking required Av main course £10 **Restaurant** L served Mon-Sat 11-2.30, Sun 11-3 booking required D served Mon-Sat 6-10, Sun 6-9 booking required Av 3 course à la carte fr £25 ⊕ FREE HOUSE ◀ Tetley Smooth, Tetley Cask, Guinness. ♟ 16 **Facilities** Children's menu Family room Dogs allowed Garden Parking

### OXFORDSHIRE

**ABINGDON**   Map 5 SU49

## The Merry Miller ♟

**Cothill OX13 6JW** ☎ 01865 390390   📠 01865 390040
**e-mail:** rob@merrymiller.co.uk
**dir:** *1m from Marcham interchange on A34*

Any inventory of the Merry Miller must include its wealth of risqué prints. Despite the beams, flagstones and stripped pine tables, the interior of this 17th-century former granary is more redolent of Tuscany - which at least ensures that the pasta dishes feel at home! But lunch could just as easily be a club sandwich or seafood salad bowl, whilst evening diners might choose roasted Gressingham duck; or tomato, goat's cheese and Puy lentil tartlettes.

**Open** all wk ◀ Greene King IPA, Old Speckled Hen. ♟ 15 **Facilities** Dogs allowed Garden Parking

# PICK OF THE PUBS

## The Boar's Head ★★★★INN  ♟

**ARDINGTON**      Map 5 SU48

**Church St OX12 8QA**
☎ **01235 833254**   🖹 **01235 833254**
**e-mail:** info@boarsheadardington.co.uk
**web:** www.boarsheadardington.co.uk
**dir:** *Off A417 E of Wantage, next to village church*

Ardington and its twin community, Lockinge, lie within the estate laid out in the 19th century by Lord Wantage, who would no doubt be delighted that it remains very much as he left it. The half-timbered Boar's Head has been serving the local community for over 150 years, today as pub, first-class restaurant and provider of three attractive en suite guest rooms, converted from the original barns and outbuildings. Its scrubbed pine tables, candles, fresh flowers and blazing log fires create just the atmosphere that so many pubgoers love.

Local breweries, including Best Mates (in Ardington itself), Butts and West Berkshire, are given a good share of the bar action. Everything, from bread to ice cream, and from pasta to pastries, is made on the premises. In the two-AA Rosette restaurant, the regularly changing menu is well known for its fish specialities, featuring whatever is sent up daily from Cornish ports.

A typical meal might begin with scallop tempura with chilli jam or artichoke velouté; to be followed by roast tranche of Newlyn cod with red wine vinaigrette and wild garlic; roast squab pigeon with black pudding and port wine sauce; or roast rack of spring lamb with herb crust and garlic confit. Finish with a praline soufflé and iced nougat, or toffee banana croustade with vanilla ice cream. The seven-course tasting menu is good value at £39.50.

Ardington is surrounded by footpaths and cycle routes winding through nearby villages and running up to the ancient Ridgeway. Golfers will find several excellent courses nearby, while fly-fishers can obtain a day-pass for the area's well-stocked trout lakes.

**Open** all wk **Bar Meals** L served all wk 12-2 D served all wk 7-9.30 Av main course £12.50 **Restaurant** L served all wk 12-2 D served all wk 7-9.30 🛢 FREE HOUSE ◀ West Berkshire Brewery Dr Hexter's, Butts Brewery, Barbus Barbus, Best Mates Brewery, Ardington Ale ⚘ Stowford Press. **Facilities** Garden Parking **Rooms** 3

Save on Hotels. Book at theAA.com/hotel

OXFORDSHIRE 355 ENGLAND

## ADDERBURY
Map 11 SP43

### Red Lion ★★★ INN ⚲

The Green OX17 3LU
☎ 01295 810269  ▤ 01295 811906
e-mail: 6496@greeneking.co.uk
dir: Off M40, 3m from Banbury

A fine stone-built coaching inn on the Banbury to Oxford road, overlooking the village green. Established in 1669, the Red Lion was once known as the King's Arms, and had a tunnel in the cellar used by Royalists in hiding during the Civil War. Enter the rambling, beamed interior to find daily newspapers, real ales, good wines, accommodation and a varied menu, with plenty of fish choices like home-made Thai salmon fish cakes, chargrilled tuna steaks, and salmon steak parcels.

Open all day all wk 7am-11pm (Sat 8am-11.30pm, Sun 9am-11pm) ⚫ Greene King IPA, Abbot Ale, Old Speckled Hen, Guest. ⚲ 11 Facilities Garden Parking Rooms 12

## ARDINGTON
Map 5 SU48

### PICK OF THE PUBS

### The Boar's Head ★★★★ INN ◉◉ ⚲

*See Pick of the Pubs on opposite page*

## BAMPTON
Map 5 SP30

### The Romany

Bridge St OX18 2HA ☎ 01993 850237
e-mail: theromanyinnbampton@yahoo.co.uk
dir: Telephone for directions

This 18th-century building of Cotswold stone was a shop until 20 years ago. Now a pretty inn and with a new landlord, The Romany counts a beamed bar, log fires and intimate dining room among its many charms. The choice of food ranges from bar snacks and bar meals to a full carte restaurant menu, with home-made specials like lasagne, chicken Romany, or chilli and chips. There is a good range of vegetarian choices. Regional singers provide live entertainment a couple of times a month.

Open all day all wk 12-12 Bar Meals L served all wk 12-2 D served all wk 6-9 Av main course £4.50 Restaurant L served all wk 12-2 D served all wk 6-9 Fixed menu price fr £6.50 ⊞ PUNCH ⚫ Hooky Bitter, London Pride, guest ales ○ Westons Stowford Press. Facilities Children's menu Children's portions Play area Garden

## BANBURY
Map 11 SP44

### The Wykham Arms ⚲

Temple Mill Rd, Sibford Gower OX15 5RX ☎ 01295 788808
e-mail: info@wykhamarms.co.uk
dir: Between Banbury & Shipston-on-Stour off B4035. 15m S of Stratford-upon-Avon

This thatched, Cotswold-stone inn with intimate beamed rooms and lovely views was originally part of William of Wykham's estate, hence the name. Along with well kept ales and a good wine list, there is a bar menu also available on the patio and garden, plus a full dining menu. Locally sourced ingredients lie behind the dishes, including breast of corn-fed chicken in smoked bacon with leek, potato and flageolet bean ragout; confit of Warwickshire pork belly with bubble and squeak and shallot cream sauce; and pavé of Shetland salmon with red wine risotto and fennel compote.

*The Wykham Arms*

Open 12-2.30 6-11 Closed: Mon Bar Meals L served Tue-Sat 12-3 Sun 12-3 D served Tue-Sat 6-9.30 Av main course £10 Restaurant L served Tue-Sat 12-3 Sun 12-3 D served Tue-Sat 6-9.30 Av 3 course à la carte fr £25 ⊞ FREE HOUSE ⚫ Hook Norton Best, Guinness, St Austell Tribute, Adnams Broadside, Fuller's London Pride. ⚲ 20 Facilities Children's portions Family room Dogs allowed Garden Parking **See advert below**

## BANBURY *continued*

### Ye Olde Reindeer Inn

**47 Parsons St OX16 5NA ☎ 01295 264031**
**e-mail:** tonypuddifoot@aol.com
**dir:** *1m from M40 junct 11, in town centre just off market square*

The oldest pub in Banbury, the Reindeer dates back to 1570. During the Civil War, Oliver Cromwell met his men here in the magnificent Globe Room, which still has its original panelling. A great range of cask ales is kept (usually 5 at any one time) and a large selection of malt whiskies. Mulled wines are another house speciality. Menu favourites are bubble and squeak with honey roast ham, baked beans and fried egg; Yorkshire pudding filled with sausage, onion and gravy; home-made beef and Hooky ale pie.

**Open** all day all wk **Bar Meals** L served Mon-Sat 11-2.30 Av main course £6 **Restaurant** Fixed menu price fr £8 Av 3 course à la carte fr £12 ⊕ HOOK NORTON BREWERY ◀ Hook Norton, Best, Hook Norton Haymaker, Old, 12 Days, Dark & Gold. **Facilities** Children's menu Children's portions Family room Dogs allowed Garden Parking

**BARNARD GATE**     Map 5 SP41

### PICK OF THE PUBS

### The Boot Inn

**OX29 6XE ☎ 01865 881231**
**e-mail:** info@theboot-inn.com
**dir:** *Off A40 between Witney & Eynsham*

The Boot is renowned for its celebrity boot collection – the Bee Gees, George Best and Jeremy Irons to name a few. Exposed beams, stone-flagged floors and two fabulous open fires set the scene at the inn, which is surrounded by beautiful countryside on the edge of the Cotswolds, near the ancient village of Eynsham, a few miles west of Oxford. There is a pleasant garden for summer use, a welcoming bar and secluded dining areas. Beers from well-known and reliable brewers are on tap, and the wine list would satisfy the most cosmopolitan of oenophiles. The lunch menu offers salads, doorstop sandwiches and a selection from the chargrill: burgers, sausages and steaks. Dinner options are along the lines of confit pork belly with Lyonnaise potatoes and balsamic roasted beetroot; ale battered fish with hand-cut chips; and butternut squash and feta cheese risotto.

**Open** all wk Mon-Sat 12-3 6-11 (Sun all day) **Bar Meals** L served Mon-Sat 12-2.30, Sun 12-10 D served Mon-Sat 7-9.30, Sun 12-10 **Restaurant** L served Mon-Sat 12-2.30, Sun 12-10 D served Mon-Sat 7-9.30, Sun 12-10 ⊕ CHARLES WELLS ◀ Youngs, Charles Wells Eagle IPA, guest ales. **Facilities** Children's portions Garden Parking

**BECKLEY**     Map 5 SP51

### The Abingdon Arms

**High St OX3 9UU ☎ 01865 351311    📄 01865 358502**
**e-mail:** chequers89@hotmail.com
**dir:** *M40 junct 8, follow signs at Headington rdbt for Beckley*

Expect a warm welcome at this cosy, traditional pub set in a pretty village to the north of Oxford. It has been smartly

updated, and good food is also helping to put it on the map, backed by excellent beers from Brakspear. A range of sandwiches and bar snacks is available at lunchtime, while dinner could feature whole grilled sea bass; liver and bacon; or a chicken and ham pie. There are opportunities for many pleasant walks in the area. Recent change of hands.

**Open** all wk **Bar Meals** L served Mon-Fri 12-3, Sat 12-9.30, Sun 12-6 D served Mon-Fri 6-9.30, Sat 12-9.30 **Restaurant** L served Mon-Fri 12-3, Sat 12-9.30, Sun 12-6 D served Mon-Fri 6-9.30, Sat 12-9.30 Fixed menu price fr £9 Av 3 course à la carte fr £20 ⊕ BRAKSPEAR ◀ Brakspear Bitter, Brakspear Special, Brakspear guest, Hobgoblin, Marston Pedigree. **Facilities** Children's menu Children's portions Play area Garden Parking

**BLACK BOURTON**     Map 5 SP20

### PICK OF THE PUBS

### The Vines

**Burford Rd OX18 2PF**
**☎ 01993 843559    📄 01993 840080**
**e-mail:** info@vineshotel.com
**web:** www.vinesblackbourton.co.uk
**dir:** *From A40 Witney, take A4095 to Faringdon, then 1st right after Bampton to Black Bourton*

A beautiful Cotswold village within easy reach of Burford, Witney and the Thames Path is the setting for The Vines, a traditional stone-built inn with an elegant, contemporary feel and surrounded by delightful gardens. The BBC's *Real Rooms* team famously designed and transformed the restaurant and bar, so expect a surprisingly stylish interior for a Cotswold pub, with murals, wooden floors, big plants in pots, and leather sofas fronting open log fires. Relax with a pint of Hooky or linger over lunch or dinner; the menus listing an imaginative choice of modern British dishes with an international twist, all freshly prepared using locally sourced produce. Typical examples from the carte include lime and coriander chicken with coconut milk; baked halibut with seafood and cream sauce; rib-eye steak with tomato, mushrooms and chips and either a red wine, mushroom or pepper sauce. In addition, there's a good-value light bites menu, decent Sunday roasts, and a raft of Old and New World wines by the glass. On sunny days, dine alfresco on the sun-trap patio or play a nostalgic game of Aunt Sally.

**Open** all wk Mon-Fri eve only (Sat-Sun L & D) Closed: Mon-Fri L **Bar Meals** L served Sat-Sun 12-2 D served Mon-Sat 6-9 Sun 7-9 Av main course £7.80 **Restaurant** L served Sat-Sun 12-2 D served Mon-Sat 6-9 Sun 7-9 Av 3 course à la carte fr £17.50 ⊕ FREE HOUSE ◀ Old Hooky, Tetley Smooth. **Facilities** Children's menu Children's portions Garden Parking

**BLOXHAM**     Map 11 SP43

### The Elephant & Castle

**OX15 4LZ ☎ 0845 873 7358**
**e-mail:** bloxhamelephant1@btconnect.com
**dir:** *M40 junct 11, pub just off A361, in village centre. 3m from Banbury*

The arch of this family-run 15th-century Cotswold-stone coaching inn used to straddle the former Banbury to Chipping Norton turnpike. At night the gates of the pub were closed, and no traffic could get over the toll bridge. Locals play Aunt Sally or shove-ha'penny in the big wood-floored bar, whilst the two-roomed lounge boasts a bar-billiards table and a large inglenook fireplace. The menu offers favourites like roast chicken breast with stuffing, crispy battered cod and lasagne verdi, and the bar serves seasonal and guest ales.

**Open** all wk 10-3 5-12 (Fri 10-3 5-2am, Sat 10am-2am, Sun 10am-mdnt) **Bar Meals** L served Mon-Sat 12-2 Av main course £6 **Restaurant** L served Mon-Sat 12-2 ⊕ HOOK NORTON BREWERY ◀ Hook Norton Best Bitter, Hook Norton seasonal ales, guest ales ◑ Westons Old Rosie Scrumpy. **Facilities** Children's menu Children's portions Family room Dogs allowed Garden Parking

**BRIGHTWELL BALDWIN**     Map 5 SU69

### PICK OF THE PUBS

### *The Lord Nelson Inn* ❦

*See Pick of the Pubs on page 358*

**BRIGHTWELL-CUM-SOTWELL**     Map 5 SU59

### The Red Lion **NEW**

**The Street OX10 0RT ☎ 01491 837373**
**e-mail:** enquiries@redlion.biz
**dir:** *From A4130 (Didcot to Wallingford road) follow Brightwell-cum-Sotwell signs. Pub in village centre*

A picture-postcard thatched and timbered 16th-century village pub that's not only pretty but also a cracking community local, playing host to charity quiz nights, French and painting classes, various cuisine nights and an annual festival. Hearty, traditional pub food is freshly prepared from local produce. Look to the chalkboard for their famous short-crust pastry pie, lamb ragout, home-made fishcakes, and the popular ginger pudding, then wash it down with a pint of West Berkshire Good Old Boy. Don't miss the Sunday roast lunches.

**Open** all wk 12-3 6-11 **Bar Meals** L served all wk 12-2 D served all wk 6.30-9 Av main course £9 **Restaurant** L served all wk 12-2 D served all wk 6.30-9 Av 3 course à la carte fr £14 ⊕ FREE HOUSE ◄ Good Old Boy, Hoppit, Brightwell Gold ♻ Stowford Press, Tutts Clump. **Facilities** Children's menu Children's portions Dogs allowed Garden Parking

*See advert below*

## Saye and Sele Arms ♀

**Main Rd OX15 5ED ☎ 01295 263348**
e-mail: mail@sayeandselearms.co.uk
dir: *3m from Banbury Cross*

Five minutes' walk from this pretty, 16th-century free house is Broughton Castle, home to Lord and Lady Saye and Sele, a barony going back to 1447. Adnams and Sharp's are the pub's resident beers, plus two changing guests and real ciders. Chef/proprietor Danny McGeehan's 'wholesome proper pies' are always on the menu, as are grilled sirloin steak, poached salmon, jumbo sausages, lean ham and eggs; and Danny's souffléd bread and butter pudding to finish. The garden and garden furniture have recently been refurbished.

**Open** 11.30-2.30 7-11 (Sat 11.30-3 7-11 Sun 12-5) Closed: 25 Dec, Sun eve **Bar Meals** L served Mon-Sat 12-2 booking required D served Mon-Sat 7-9.30 booking required Av main course £13 **Restaurant** L served Mon-Sat 12-2, Sun 12-3 booking required D served Mon-Sat

7-9.30 booking required Av 3 course à la carte fr £25 ⊕ FREE HOUSE ◄ Adnams Southwold, Sharp's Doom Bar, 2 guest ales ♻ Westons Stowford Press, Thatchers Dry. ♀ 8 **Facilities** Children's portions Garden Parking

## The Chequers ♀

**OX14 3DP ☎ 01865 407771  ▤ 01865 407771**
e-mail: enquiries@thechequers-burcot.co.uk
dir: *On A415 (Dorchester to Abingdon road) between Clifton Hampden & Dorchester*

Once a staging post for barges on the Thames, this 400-year-old thatched and timber framed pub now combines the best of old and new. On winter days the blazing fire surrounded by sofas is the favoured spot, especially for toasting marshmallows; in summer, the enclosed beer garden takes precedence. The food is serious, pubby home cooking: think pan-fried field mushrooms in garlic and herb butter on toast to start; followed by slow roasted lamb shank with mint and redcurrant gravy. To accompany the food, try one of 12 wines served by the glass or a guest ale.

**Open** all day all wk 12-11 (Sun 12-4) **Bar Meals** L served all wk 12-3 D served Mon-Sat 6.30-9.30 Av main course £13.50 **Restaurant** L served all wk 12-3 booking required D served Mon-Sat 6.30-9.30 booking required Av 3 course à la carte fr £25 ⊕ FREE HOUSE ◄ Young's, guest ales ♻ Westons Stowford Press. ♀ 12 **Facilities** Children's menu Children's portions Garden Parking

### PICK OF THE PUBS

## The Inn for All Seasons ★★★ RR ♀

*See Pick of the Pubs on page 359*

### PICK OF THE PUBS

## The Lamb Inn ★★★ SHL ◉◉

**Sheep St OX18 4LR ☎ 01993 823155  ▤ 01993 822228**
e-mail: info@lambinn-burford.co.uk
web: www.cotswold-inns-hotels.co.uk/lamb
dir: *M40 junct 8, follow A40 & Burford signs, 1st turn, down hill into Sheep St*

Descriptive phrases such as 'a charming old inn' may not always be fully deserved, but there's no questioning its appropriateness for The Lamb. Built in 1420 as weavers' cottages, it has a welcoming atmosphere in the bar, with its stone-flagged floor, log fire, fine wines and traditional real ales. Throughout, the inn combines old world charm with stylish interiors. The spacious, two-AA Rosette restaurant looks out to a walled cottage garden through mullioned windows. The regularly-changing menus present contemporary English cooking based entirely on local produce. Extensive lunch and dinner options include starters of smoked haddock risotto with poached egg, or ham hock terrine with piccalilli, and main courses such as roasted pheasant and mushroom risotto from the game board, or grilled lemon sole with new potatoes and citrus butter. Pistachio crème brûlée with chocolate cookies makes a fitting finish. Children are well catered for with their own menu, everything home made by the chef with the same degree of dedication to his craft.

**Open** all day all wk **Bar Meals** L served all wk 12-2.30 D served all wk 6.30-9.30 Av main course £13.50 **Restaurant** L served all wk 12-2.30 D served all wk 7-9.30 Av 3 course à la carte fr £35 ⊕ FREE HOUSE ◄ Hook Norton Best, Brakspear. **Facilities** Children's menu Children's portions Dogs allowed Garden **Rooms** 17

---

# *The Red Lion*

Brightwell-cum-Sotwell, Oxfordshire OX10 0RT
Tel: 01491 837373   Email: enquiries@redlion.biz
Web: www.redlion.biz

A traditional 16th century village pub situated in the centre of the beautiful Oxfordshire village of Brightwell-cum-Sotwell. Serving typical pub fare, all our food is home cooked using local produce where possible. Menu includes Liver and Bacon, Steak and Kidney Pie, Goats Cheese and Red Onion Tart, and delicious home made puddings including Apple Crumble, Sticky Toffee Pudding or Spotted Dick. Traditional Sunday lunch is freshly cooked, using local meat. Very friendly pub, children and dogs welcome. Four local real ales always available. CAMRA Pub of the Year for South Oxfordshire 2009.

# PICK OF THE PUBS

## The Lord Nelson Inn ♟

**BRIGHTWELL BALDWIN**     Map 5 SU69

**OX49 5NP** ☎ **01491 612497**
**e-mail:** ladyhamilton1@hotmail.co.uk
**dir:** *Off B4009 between Watlington & Benson*

Originally constructed as a thatched cottage, later additions to this 300 year-old stone-built inn include 18th-century gables and a quaint veranda facing the village church. In Nelson's day the pub was simply known as the Admiral Nelson; but when, in 1797, the great man was elevated to the peerage, the pub's name was elevated too. For more than a century after that, villagers slaked their thirst here until, in 1905, the inn was closed following complaints about over-indulgent estate workers. That could have been the end of the

story – but, a generation later, the building was bought by a couple who just liked the look of it. They gave it a complete makeover, and the Lord Nelson finally re-opened on Trafalgar Day, 1971.

Now full of fresh flowers, candlelight and a splendid inglenook fireplace, it's just the place to relax after a country walk or a day at the office. And, during the summer, the pretty terraced garden with its weeping willow is popular for alfresco eating and drinking.

All the food is freshly cooked, using local produce where possible. The house menu begins with a complimentary basket of bread and olives. Starters might include home-made smoked haddock and salmon fishcake with watercress and sweet chilli dressing, or French black pudding with smoked bacon and apple salad. For light main course options, try a smoked salmon and prawn platter, or the house special salad of mixed leaves, asparagus spears, tuna and boiled egg. Other main courses include half a slow-roast duck with orange sauce, and leek and morel

mushroom risotto topped with Parmesan shavings.

Look out for red kites while you're in the area; the RSPB reintroduced them onto the nearby Chiltern escarpment in the early 1990s.

**Open** all wk 12-3 6-11 (Sun 12-10.30)
**Bar Meals** L served Mon-Sat 12-3, Sun 12-10.30 D served Mon-Sat 6-11, Sun 12-10.30 Av main course £12
**Restaurant** L served Mon-Sat 12-2.30, Sun 12-2.30 D served Mon-Sat 6-10, Sun 7-9.30 Av 3 course à la carte fr £20 ◗ West Berkshire Brewery, Brakspear, John Smiths, Black Sheep. ♟ 20 **Facilities** Garden Parking

# PICK OF THE PUBS

## The Inn for All Seasons ★★★ RR 🍷

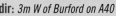
BURFORD

**BURFORD**                    Map 5 SP21

**The Barringtons OX18 4TN**
☎ 01451 844324    📠 01451 844375
e-mail: sharp@innforallseasons.com
dir: *3m W of Burford on A40*

The inn's humble beginnings were as two quarry cottages, where Cotswold stone was brought to the roadside destined for buildings such as Blenheim Palace and St Paul's cathedral. So ale was probably dispensed to thirsty workers from the day the cottages were built; their transition to a coaching inn was inevitable. Certainly stagecoach travellers between London and West Wales in the 18th century would have been gasping for refreshment by the time they reached Burford. The New Inn, as it was then, was one of three coaching inns at which they could have stopped, all owned by the Barrington

Park Estate. It remained estate-owned until the 1950s when, along with the nearby garage, it was bought by Shell. Then in 1964 it was sold to a couple who had worked on the film *A Man For All Seasons* (hence the inn's name). In the mid-1980s the Sharp family took over and have been here ever since. Within its solid Cotswold stone walls is a treasure trove of ancient oak beams, inglenooks and coaching age memorabilia, giving it that true country pub feel. Guest ales always include a Wychwood from nearby Witney.

Matthew Sharp is a classically trained chef with a string of prestigious postings behind him. He selects only the best of everything for his British Continental cuisine, including game from the estate. And he knows all the right people in Brixham to guarantee a daily supply of excellent fish for dedicated seafood menus featuring the likes of a pair of red mullet lightly pan-fried; seared scallops with crisp smoked streaky bacon; and whole cock crabs freshly cooked and served with garlic mayonnaise. Meat lovers will not be disappointed with choices such as grilled sirloin of Aberdeen Angus beef with fat chips; and roasted rump of Cornish lamb with dauphinoise potatoes.

There are 10 traditional country-style bedrooms available. Look out for the history of the piece of shrapnel that hangs over the fireplace!

**Open** all day all wk **Bar Meals** L served all wk 11-2.30 D served all wk 6.30-9.30 Av main course £12.50 **Restaurant** L served all wk 11-2.30 D served all wk 6.30-9.30 booking required Fixed menu price fr £19.50 Av 3 course à la carte fr £24.50 🍺 Wadworth 6X, Interbrew Bass, Wychwood, Badger, Sharp's Doom Bar 🍏 Stowford Press, Westons Organic. 🍷 16
**Facilities** Children's menu Play area Dogs allowed Garden Parking **Rooms** 10

## CASSINGTON                              Map 5 SP41

### The Chequers Inn ♥ NEW

**6 The Green OX29 4DG ☎ 01865 882620**
**dir:** *From Oxford take A40 towards Witney. Right to Cassington*

Turn off the busy A40, and you'll find this imposing Cotswold stone inn next to the church at the end of the village road. The refurbished interior is cosy yet stylish, with polished flagstone floors, winter log fires and wooden furniture adorned by pretty candles. Freshly-prepared bar meals include charcuterie platters, a vegetarian meze, a range of pizzas, and summer house special of seafood platter, whilst halibut with apple and parmesan rösti is characteristic of the regularly changing carte. There is a beautiful orangery, perfect for private parties and functions.

**Open** all wk Mon-Fri 11.30-3.30 5.30-close (Sat-Sun all day in summer) **Bar Meals** L served Mon-Fri 12-2.30 (Sat-Sun 12-3) D served all wk 6.30-9.30 Av main course £8 **Restaurant** L served Mon-Fri 12-2.30 (Sat-Sun 12-3) D served all wk 6.30-9.30 ⊕ YOUNGS ◀ Youngs Bombardier. ♥ 10 **Facilities** Children's menu Children's portions Dogs allowed Garden Parking

## CHADLINGTON                             Map 10 SP32

### The Tite Inn

**Mill End OX7 3NY ☎ 01608 676475  ▤ 01608 676475**
**dir:** *2m S of Chipping Norton & 7m N of Burford*

Seventeenth-century Cotswold-stone free house where, in 1642, Royalist troops sank a few stiffeners before the Battle of Edgehill nearby. Situated in the beautiful countryside of the Cotswolds, the inn has a traditional, warm welcoming feel, with an open fire, flagstone floor and oak topped bar. The restaurant area is separate and the menu offers the finest range of home reared South Devon cross beef from fillet steak to burgers. Expect warm duck salad with redcurrant sauce, or pan fried scallops in lemon butter; followed by grilled ginger and coriander marinated tuna, or pan fried sirloin steak with peppercorn sauce.

**Open** 11-3 6-11 (Sun 12-3 7-10.30) Closed: Mon (ex BH) ◀ Sharp's, Timothy Taylor Landlord ☼ Westons Stowford Press. **Facilities** Dogs allowed Garden Parking

## CHALGROVE                               Map 5 SU69

## PICK OF THE PUBS

### The Red Lion Inn

**The High St OX44 7SS ☎ 01865 890625**
**e-mail:** raymondsexton@btinternet.com
**web:** www.redlionchalgrove.co.uk
**dir:** *B480 from Oxford ring road, through Stadhampton, left then right at mini-rdbt. At Chalgrove Airfield right into village*

A traditional village high street pub owned by head chef Raymond Sexton, and his wife and head pastry chef, Suzanne. Their surname is handily appropriate for one of the country's only two pubs owned by a parish church. You have a choice of where to eat: at one of the many tables in the bar, in the restaurant, or in the front or rear garden. The half-dozen main courses include fillet of halibut with linguine in rich shellfish bisque; chargrilled medallions of pork on creamy mash with three-mustard sauce; and home-made butternut squash, goat's cheese and rosemary ravioli with pine-nut and rocket pesto, backed by daily specials, including fresh whole lobster Thermidor; and pork and leek sausages with mash and red onion gravy. Sandwiches and side orders are also available at lunchtime. Real ales are supplied by Adnams, Fuller's and Timothy Taylor, and ciders by Aspall and Westons.

*The Red Lion Inn*

**Open** all wk 11.30-3 6-mdnt (Sat 11.30-3 6-1am Sat 11.30am-1am Sun 11.30am-mdnt in summer) **Bar Meals** L served Mon-Sat 12-2, Sun 12-3 D served Mon-Sat 6-9 Av main course £12 **Restaurant** L served Mon-Sat 12-2, Sun 12-3 D served Mon-Sat 6-9 Av 3 course à la carte fr £25 ⊕ FREE HOUSE ◀ Fuller's London Pride, Adnams Best, Timothy Taylor Landlord, guest ale ☼ Aspall, Westons Stowford Press. **Facilities** Children's menu Children's portions Play area Dogs allowed Garden

## CHARLBURY                               Map 11 SP31

## PICK OF THE PUBS

### The Bull Inn ♥

**Sheep St OX7 3RR ☎ 01608 810689**
**e-mail:** info@bullinn-charlbury.com
**dir:** *M40 junct 8, A40, A44 follow Woodstock/Blenheim Palace signs. Through Woodstock take B4437 to Charlbury, pub at x-rds in town*

The mellow stone frontage of this fine 16th-century free house presides over Charlbury's main street, within easy reach of Woodstock, Blenheim Palace and other Cotswold attractions. The beamed interior is full of period character, and log fires burn in the inglenook fireplaces in winter. The traditional bar with wooden floors serves ales by reliable brewers from the Cotswolds and neighbouring counties. A tastefully furnished lounge and dining room add to the relaxing space, while outside the vine-covered terrace is a delightful spot to sit and enjoy a drink or a meal in summer. Food is served in both the bar and restaurant, with menus to match your chosen venue. The bar menu, for example, features a full range of favourites: chicken liver pâté; vegetarian lasagne verde; crispy duck pancakes; and, at the top end, sirloin steak with garlic butter and cracked black pepper. Look to the seasonal blackboard specials for further options.

**Open** 12-2.30 6-11 Closed: Sun eve & Mon **Bar Meals** L served Tue-Fri 12-2, Sat-Sun 12-2.30 D served Tue-Sat 7-9 Av main course £11 **Restaurant** L served Tue-Fri 12-2, Sat-Sun 12-2.30 booking required D served Tue-Sat 7-9 booking required Av 3 course à la carte fr £22 ⊕ FREE HOUSE ◀ Wye Valley, Wickwar, Goffs Loddon. ♥ 10 **Facilities** Children's portions Garden Parking

## CHECKENDON                              Map 5 SU68

### The Highwayman ⊛

**Exlade St RG8 0UA ☎ 01491 682020**
**dir:** *On A4074 (Reading to Wallingford road)*

This early 17th-century listed inn has been beautifully restored and refurbished. The emphasis in the character bar is on wooden floors and open fireplaces, while the exterior has plenty of seating for fine days to enjoy a pint of Loddon Ferryman's Gold. The famous Maharajah's Well nearby is surrounded by numerous walks in the glorious Chiltern beechwoods. Eggs Benedict, trio of Cumberland sausages on bubble and squeak, and a superb list of local cheeses are typical examples from the inviting menu.

**Open** all wk 11.30-3 5.30-11 ◀ Fuller's London Pride, Loddon Ferryman's Gold, Butlers Brewers, guest ale. **Facilities** Dogs allowed Garden Parking

## CHINNOR                                 Map 5 SP70

## PICK OF THE PUBS

### The Sir Charles Napier ⊛⊛ ♥

**Spriggs Alley OX39 4BX**
**☎ 01494 483011  ▤ 01494 485311**
**dir:** *M40 junct 6 to Chinnor. Turn right at rdbt, up hill to Spriggs Alley*

Elegant red kites soar over this sublime flint-and-brick dining inn, enviably located amidst the beech woods of the high Chilterns. Making the most of this secluded locale, seasonal forays to the hedgerows and woods (customers can join in) produce herbs, fungi and berries used in the inventive menus, whilst the plump local game finds its way into some of the extraordinary AA 2-Rosette winning dishes here. Diners distribute themselves amidst a most eclectically furnished suite of rooms; Michael Cooper's memorable sculptures not the least of such, joining comfy sofas set near warming winter log fires. Oxtail croquette with sauce gribiche gives a flavour of things to come; wood pigeon with pearl barley risotto and morel sauce or Stonor Park venison cottage pie with chestnut purée, choucroute and redcurrant jus for example, accompanied by a choice from over 200 wines. Digestive time may be spent appreciating the superb grounds, where more sculptures are displayed.

**Open** noon-4 6-mdnt (Sun noon-6) Closed: 25-26 Dec, Mon, Sun eve **Bar Meals** L served Tue-Fri 12-2.30 D served Tue-Fri 6.30-9 Av main course £11.50 **Restaurant** L served Tue-Sat 12-2.30, Sun 12-3.30 booking required D served Tue-Sat 6.30-10 booking required Fixed menu price fr £14.50 Av 3 course à la carte fr £34.50 ⊕ FREE HOUSE ◀ Wadworth 6X, Wadworth IPA. ♥ 12 **Facilities** Children's menu Children's portions Dogs allowed Garden Parking

CHIPPING NORTON                        Map 10 SP32

### The Chequers ♥

Goddards Ln OX7 5NP
☎ 01608 644717   📠 01608 646237
e-mail: info@chequers-pub.com/webmail
dir: In town centre, next to theatre

Log fires, low ceilings and soft lighting make for a cosy atmosphere in the bar of this popular 16th-century inn. By contrast, the courtyard restaurant is wonderfully light and airy. Well-kept Fullers ales, good wines and decent coffee are served along with freshly prepared contemporary dishes. Look for starters like wild mushroom risotto; and mains including baked cod in parma ham with sun-dried tomato and pine nut couscous, and chicken stir-fry with cashew nuts.

**Open** all day all wk 11am-11pm (Fri-Sat 11am-mdnt Sun 11am-10.30pm) Closed: 25 Dec **Bar Meals** L served Mon-Sat 12-2.30, Sun 12-4 D served Wed-Sun 6-9.30 Av main course £9 **Restaurant** L served Mon-Sat 12-2.30, Sun 12-4 D served Wed-Sun 6-9.30 ⊕ FULLERS BREWERY ◀ Fuller's Chiswick Bitter, London Pride & ESB, Organic Honeydew, Fullers Special Ale. ♥ 12 **Facilities** Children's menu Children's portions Dogs allowed

CHISELHAMPTON                         Map 5 SU59

## PICK OF THE PUBS

### Coach & Horses Inn ★★★ INN ♥

Watlington Rd OX44 7UX
☎ 01865 890255   📠 01865 891995
e-mail: enquiries@coachhorsesinn.co.uk
dir: From Oxford on B480 towards Watlington, 5m

A young girl killed during the Civil War is believed to haunt this delightful 16th-century inn. Set in peaceful countryside on the old Roman road Icknield Street, the inn, as the name attests, once provided hospitality for the stage coaches travelling from Birmingham to London. Inside you'll find roaring log fires, quaint beams and an old bread oven. Start with deep fried

whitebait or grilled goats' cheese salad; followed by slow roasted half shoulder of English lamb; or grilled free range pork fillet. The daily specials fish board could include fillet of sea bass with freshwater crayfish tails and a champagne sauce. Grills, poultry and game are also perennial favourites. There are nine chalet-style en suite bedrooms available, all with lovely rural views.

**Open** all day all wk **Bar Meals** L served Mon-Sat 12-2 booking required Av main course £12 **Restaurant** L served all wk 12-2 booking required D served Mon-Sat 7-9.30 booking required Av 3 course à la carte fr £20 ⊕ FREE HOUSE ◀ Hook Norton Best, London Pride, Old Hooky. ♥ 10 **Facilities** Garden Parking **Rooms** 9

CHRISTMAS COMMON                      Map 5 SU79

### The Fox and Hounds ♥

OX49 5HL ☎ 01491 612599
e-mail: hello@thetopfox.co.uk
dir: M40 junct 5, 2.5m to Christmas Common, on road towards Henley

Renovations have transformed this charming 500-year-old inn into a stylish dining pub with an immaculate interior, a large restaurant complete with open-plan kitchen, and four cosy bar areas. Changing special and an imaginative menu that places a clear emphasis on quality ingredients, local where possible. Recent change of hands.

**Open** all day all wk Mon-Sat noon-11 (Sun noon-10.30) Closed: 25-26 Dec eve, 1 Jan eve, BHs eve **Bar Meals** L served Mon-Fri 12-2, Sat 12-3, Sun 12-4 D served Mon-Thu 7-9, Fri-Sun 7-9.30 **Restaurant** L served Mon-Fri 12-2, Sat 12-3, Sun 12-4 D served Mon-Thu 7-9, Fri-Sun 7-9.30 ⊕ Brakspear ◀ Brakspear Bitter, seasonal ales. ♥ 14 **Facilities** Children's portions Dogs allowed Garden Parking

CHURCH ENSTONE                        Map 11 SP32

## PICK OF THE PUBS

### The Crown Inn ♥

Mill Ln OX7 4NN ☎ 01608 677262
dir: Off A44, 15m N of Oxford

Award-winning chef Tony Warburton runs this stone-built 17th-century free house on the eastern edge of the Cotswolds with his wife Caroline. During the summer season you can while away the long evenings eating or drinking in the quiet and secluded rear garden, which is sheltered from the wind but enjoys the best of the late sunshine. Inside you'll find a traditional rustic bar with an open fire, a spacious slate floored conservatory, and a richly decorated beamed dining room. All meals are prepared on the premises using fresh produce, including pork, beef and game from the local farms and estates. Starters may include venison terrine with plum chutney, or avocado and prawn salad with honey and lime dressing. Main course choices range from roast loin of pork with Bramley apple sauce,

and fillet of Cornish hake with black olive crust to fettuccini with mushrooms, spinach pesto and cream. A home-made dessert such as bread and butter pudding will round things off nicely.

**Open** all wk noon-3 6-11 (Sun noon-4) Closed: 26 Dec, 1 Jan **Bar Meals** L served all wk 12-2 D served Mon-Sat 7-9 Av main course £10.95 food served all day **Restaurant** L served all wk 12-2 D served Mon-Sat 7-9 Fixed menu price fr £17.95 Av 3 course à la carte fr £21 food served all day ⊕ FREE HOUSE ◀ Hook Norton Best Bitter, Timothy Taylor Landlord, Wychwood Hobgoblin. ♥ 8 **Facilities** Children's portions Dogs allowed Garden Parking

CLIFTON                               Map 11 SP43

### Duke of Cumberland's Head

OX15 0PE ☎ 01869 338534   📠 01869 338643
e-mail: info@thecliftonduke.com
dir: A4260 from Banbury, then B4031 from Deddington. 7m from Banbury

Built in 1645, this thatched and beamed stone pub was named to honour Rupert of the Rhine, whose forces fought for his uncle, Charles I, at the nearby Battle of Edge Hill; important strategic decisions may well have been made around the pub's inglenook fireplace. Today it offers a choice of real ales, two dining rooms, and a wonderful garden in summer. The menu is based on traditional pub favourites like sausages and mash, with changing chef's specials and a large selection of fish and game in season.

**Open** all wk 11-3 6-11 Closed: 25 Dec **Bar Meals** L served Mon-Sat 12-2.30, Sun 12-3 D served Mon-Thu 6.30-9, Fri-Sat 6.30-9.30 Av main course £10 **Restaurant** L served Mon-Sat 12-2.30, Sun 12-3 D served Mon-Thu 6.30-9, Fri-Sat 6.30-9.30 Fixed menu price fr £10 ⊕ CLIFTON PUBLIC HOUSE MANAGEMENT LTD ◀ Hook Norton, Adnams, Deuchars, Black Sheep, Cotswold Ales ♂ Stowford Press. **Facilities** Dogs allowed Garden Parking

CUMNOR                                Map 5 SP40

## PICK OF THE PUBS

### Bear & Ragged Staff ♥

*See Pick of the Pubs on page 362*

# PICK OF THE PUBS

## Bear & Ragged Staff ♀

**CUMNOR**  Map 5 SP40

**28 Appleton Rd OX2 9QH**
☎ 01865 862329  📄 01865 862048
e-mail:
enquiries@bearandraggedstaff.com
**dir:** *A420 from Oxford, right onto B4017
signposted Cumnor*

This solid, stone-built dining pub has a long and robust history. The name is taken from the family crest of the renowned Earls of Warwick; the mistress of one such influential courtier is reputed to haunt the 16th century part of the inn. Whilst visiting soldiers billeted here during the Civil War, Richard Cromwell, Lord Protector of England in the 1650s, allegedly chiselled away the Royal Crest that once gleamed from the lintel above one of the doors in the bar, and Sir Walter Scott mentions the Cumnor Bear and Ragged Staff in his novel *Kenilworth*.

Set in typically tranquil Oxfordshire countryside, the chefs here take full advantage of the fresh, seasonal game available from the bevy of local estates and shoots; the surrounding woods and farmland teem with pheasant, partridge, deer, muntjac, rabbit, duck and pigeon, for instance. The food is best described as hearty, country-style cooking, and casseroles, stews and pub classics, such as bangers and mash and other staple comfort food will always be found on the menus, which change every three months.

Base yourself in one of the traditional bar rooms, all dressed stone and warmed by cracking log fires, relax on the flagged patio or head for the comfortably stylish restaurant and contemplate a solid menu which may run to chargrilled venison steak, hand-cut chips, mixed leaf salad and redcurrant jus; or chicken with butternut, red pepper and spinach risotto with basil oil and toasted pine nuts. Snack-starters ooze character, try pigeon breast with smoked bacon, brown cap mushrooms and a devilled cream sauce, whilst the cheese board is awash with the best modern British offerings including Cornish Yarg and Derbyshire Sage. A tight, popular bin of wines and a brace of real ales complete the picture.

**Open** all day all wk **Bar Meals** L served Mon-Fri 12-2.30, Sat 12-3, Sun 12-2.30 D served all wk 6.30-9.30 Av main course £10 **Restaurant** L served Mon-Fri 12-2.30, Sat 12-3, Sun 12-6 D served all wk 6.30-9.30 Fixed menu price fr £6.95 Av 3 course à la carte fr £23 ⊕ GREENE KING ◼ IPA, Abbot Ale. ♀ 14 **Facilities** Children's menu Play area Dogs allowed Garden Parking

Save on Hotels. Book at **theAA.com/hotel**

**OXFORDSHIRE** 363 **ENGLAND**

**CUMNOR** *continued*

### The Vine Inn

**11 Abingdon Rd OX2 9QN**
☎ 01865 862567 🖹 01865 862567
*dir: A420 from Oxford, right onto B4017*

An old village pub whose name, when you see the frontage, needs no explanation. In 1560, the suspicious death of an Earl's wife in Cumnor Place first had people asking 'Did she fall, or was she pushed?'. A typical menu here could include lamb shank with a red wine and mint sauce, pan-fried fillet steak with brandy and mushroom sauce, and the day's fresh fish. There's also a good range of snacks. Children love the huge garden.

**Open** all wk 🍺 Adnams Bitter, Tetley Bitter, Hook Norton, guest ales. **Facilities** Play area Dogs allowed Garden Parking

| **CUXHAM** | **Map 5 SU69** |
|---|---|

### The Half Moon 🍷

**OX49 5NF** ☎ 01491 614151
e-mail: info@thehalf-moon.com
*dir: M40 junct 6 follow Watlington signs. Right at T-junct, 2nd right to Cuxham. Across rdbt, Pub in 1m on right, just past Cuxham sign*

Eilidh Ferguson grows the vegetables and salad leaves that end up on the dining plates at this 16th-century thatched pub. Her partner and chef Andrew Hill smokes the salmon and prepares the game from surrounding farms. Typically, you could expect dishes such as duck hearts on toast; fried Harlesford Farm organic mutton with bubble and squeak; roast chicken with Caesar salad; grilled dab with caper butter; mutton pie; and vegetable meze. Enjoy a pint of Brakspear Ordinary or Westons cider in the large beer garden in summer.

**Open** noon-3 6-11 (Sat noon-11 Sun noon-5) Closed: Mon ex BH Sun eve (winter) 🍺 Brakspear Ordinary Ò Westons Organic. 🍷 8 **Facilities** Dogs allowed Garden Parking

| **DEDDINGTON** | **Map 11 SP43** |
|---|---|

### PICK OF THE PUBS

### Deddington Arms ★★★ HL ◉ 🍷

**Horsefair OX15 0SH**
☎ 01869 338364 🖹 01869 337010
e-mail: deddarms@oxfordshire-hotels.co.uk
*dir: M40 junct 11 to Banbury. Follow signs for hospital, then towards Adderbury & Deddington, on A4260*

This historic old coaching inn has been welcoming travellers since the 16th century. It overlooks the picturesque market square in Deddington, one of the gateways to the Cotswolds, and offers innovative, freshly prepared food served in friendly surroundings. Good quality ales and an international wine list add to the experience. Settle in the oak beamed bar with its flagstone floors and cosy fireplace for a bar snack, or move to the elegant restaurant where a meal might begin with pan-fried pigeon breast with apple fritters

and Irish cider jus, followed by roasted rump of lamb with basil mash, Puy lentils and paysanne vegetables. A tempting dessert menu might offer espresso ice cream parfait with bitter chocolate sorbet, and there's also an enticing selection of traditional cheeses. Accommodation includes 27 en suite bedrooms with cottage suites and four-poster luxury.

**Open** all day all wk Mon-Sat 11am-mdnt (Sun 11-11) **Bar Meals** L served all wk 12-2.30 D served all wk 6.30-9.30 **Restaurant** L served all wk 12-2.30 D served all wk 6.30-9.30 ⊕ FREE HOUSE 🍺 Black Sheep, Adnams, 2 Guest ales Ò Stowford Press. 🍷 8 **Facilities** Children's menu Children's portions Parking Rooms 27

### The Unicorn Inn 🍷

**Market Place OX15 0SE** ☎ 01869 338838
e-mail: robbie@theunicorninn.net
*dir: 6m S of Banbury on A4260*

Populated by friendly locals and smiling staff, visitors feel welcome too in this Grade II listed 17th-century coaching inn overlooking the market square. Exposed beams and an open fire characterise the bar which serves award-winning cask ales and a large selection of wines by the glass. For warmer days the tranquility of the secret walled garden is much enjoyed by couples and families alike. The restaurant offers excellent home-cooked food, using locally sourced fresh produce. The menu includes traditional pub favourites which compliment the more contemporary dishes. Fresh fish deliveries six days per week make seafood a particular strength. Children have their own menu and dietary requirements are catered for.

**Open** all day all wk 11-11 (Fri-Sat 11am-12.30am, Sun noon-10.30) 🍺 Hook Norton, Bombardier, Youngs Special, Guest Ale. 🍷 10 **Facilities** Dogs allowed Garden Parking

| **DORCHESTER (ON THAMES)** | **Map 5 SU59** |
|---|---|

### Fleur De Lys

**9 High St OX10 7HH**
☎ 01865 340502 🖹 01865 341360
e-mail: info@fleurdorchester.co.uk
*dir: Telephone for directions*

Dating from around 1525, this lovely old pub is located on the High Street of the picturesque village. It has retained much of its original character with a pretty garden and cosy bar and dining room. Locally sourced

produce is used in dishes such as smooth chicken liver parfait with honey fig compote; scallop, black pudding and pancetta salad; chicken; lemon and pea risotto; and pan-fried calves' liver with creamy mash, caramelised onions, roasted apple, all made in-house. Vegetarian options might include Vegetable Wellington, while bar snacks offer a pint of prawns with garlic mayonnaise.

**Open** all wk noon-3 6-12.30am (Sat-Sun all day) Closed: Winter 3-6 **Bar Meals** L served all wk 12-2.30 booking required D served all wk 6.30-9.30 booking required Av main course £6.95 **Restaurant** L served all wk 12-2.30 booking required D served Mon-Sat 6.30-9.30 booking required ⊕ FREE HOUSE 🍺 Brakspear, Hooky, Guinness, guest beer Ò Stowford Press. **Facilities** Children's portions Dogs allowed Garden Parking

### PICK OF THE PUBS

### The George ★★ HL

**25 High St OX10 7HH**
☎ 01865 340404 🖹 01865 341620
e-mail: georgedorchester@relaxinnz.co.uk
*dir: From M40 junct 7, A329 S to A4074 at Shillingford. Follow Dorchester signs. From M4 junct 13, A34 to Abingdon then A415 E to Dorchester*

The George stands at the centre of the picturesque village of Dorchester-on-Thames, opposite the famous Dorchester Abbey and museum. A 15th-century coaching inn, believed to be one of the oldest public houses in Britain, its welcoming atmosphere has attracted the likes of DH Lawrence in the past. Oak beams and inglenook fireplaces characterise the interior, while the elevated restaurant offers a secret garden with waterfall. The Potboys bar is a traditional taproom – just the spot to enjoy a pint of Brakspear while tucking into a grilled rump steak in a mushroom sauce flambéed in brandy; or a lamb shank braised in red wine and rosemary and served with parsnip purée, red cabbage and roasted vegetables. If you're just passing through at lunchtime, stop by for a fresh baguette, a ploughman's, or bangers and mash with red onion gravy. Expect crumbles, cheesecakes and ice creams on the dessert list. There was a change of hands in 2009.

**Open** all wk 11am-mdnt **Bar Meals** L served all wk 12-3 D served all wk 6-9 Av main course £8 **Restaurant** L served all wk 12-3 booking required D served all wk 6-9 booking required Fixed menu price fr £12.95 Av 3 course à la carte fr £15 ⊕ CHAPMANS GROUP 🍺 Wadworth 6X, Brakspear Ò Upton. **Facilities** Children's menu Children's portions Garden Parking **Rooms** 17

**DORCHESTER (ON THAMES)** *continued*

## PICK OF THE PUBS

### The White Hart ★★★ HL ⊛ ♈

**High St OX10 7HN**
☎ **01865 340074** 📠 **01865 341082**
e-mail: whitehart@oxfordshire-hotels.co.uk
dir: *A4074 (Oxford to Reading), 5m from M40 junct 7/*
*A329 to Wallingford*

If this picture-perfect hotel looks familiar, that could
be because it has played a starring role in the TV series
*Midsomer Murders*. Set seven miles from Oxford in
heart of historic Dorchester-on-Thames, it has
welcomed travellers for around 400 years, and the bars
attract locals, residents and diners alike. There is a
great choice of real beers available. Log fires and
candlelight create an intimate atmosphere for the
enjoyment of innovative dishes prepared from fresh
ingredients. A good-value fixed-price lunch is available
Monday to Saturday, with a choice of three starters,
mains and desserts. The carte menu doubles your
choice and includes imaginative dishes such as
pumpkin risotto or Thai-style fish cakes, followed by
roasted loin of pork with braised red cabbage,
caramelised apple and sweet potato crisps; fish and
chips in beer batter with crushed minted peas and
hand cut chips; or grilled peppered rump steak. Recent
change of hands.

**Open** all day all wk Mon-Sat 11-12 (Sun 11-11)
**Bar Meals** L served all wk 12-2.30 D served all wk
6.30-9.30 **Restaurant** L served all wk 12-2.30 D served
all wk 6.30-9.30 ⊕ FREE HOUSE ◀ Adnams, Black
Sheep. ♈ 12 **Facilities** Children's portions Parking
**Rooms** 26

---

### EAST HENDRED    Map 5 SU48

### The Wheatsheaf ♈

**Chapel Square OX12 8JN**
☎ **01235 833229** 📠 **01235 821521**
e-mail: info@thewheatsheaf.org.uk
dir: *2m from A34 Milton interchange*

Formerly used as a courthouse, this 16th-century pub
stands in a pretty village close to the Ridgeway path.
Spit-roasts and barbecues are popular summer features
of the attractive front garden, which overlooks the village.
Bar meals include baguettes; a venison burger with hand
cut chips; and classic Greek salad with French bread. The
restaurant menu might offer twice-baked Cheddar,
Stilton and spinach soufflé, followed by noisette of lamb
with mint and blackcurrant jus and dauphinoise
potatoes.

**Open** all wk ◀ IPA, 2 guest ales. ♈ 8 **Facilities** Family
room Dogs allowed Garden Parking

---

### FARINGDON    Map 5 SU29

## PICK OF THE PUBS

### The Lamb at Buckland ♈

**Lamb Ln, Buckland SN7 8QN** ☎ **01367 870484**
e-mail: enquiries@thelambatbuckland.co.uk
dir: *Just off A420, 3m E of Faringdon*

The Lamb, with its display of ovine artefacts, enjoys a
village location on the fringe of the Cotswolds in the
Vale of the White Horse. Dating from the 18th century,
the pub changed ownership at the end of 2009 when it
was taken over by husband and wife Richard and
Shelley Terry and Christopher Green. All three are
trained chefs, but you'll find Shelley running front of
house while the two men work in the kitchen. The trio
are united in their objective: to proffer good food in a
pub atmosphere, with relaxed and friendly service. To
this end local producers of both ales and food are
called upon to stock the bar and larder. Typical dishes
plucked from the new menu might be pan-fried breast
of pigeon with soused winter vegetables; pan-roasted
fillet of Kelmscott pork with leeks, prunes and
pancetta; and rice pudding with poached apples for
dessert.

**Open** all wk 11.30-3 6-11 Closed: Sun eve, Mon
**Bar Meals** L served Tue-Sat 12-2, Sun 12-3 booking
required D served Tue-Sat 7-9 booking required
**Restaurant** L served Tue-Sat 12-2, Sun 12-3 booking
required D served Tue-Sat 7-9 booking required ⊕ FREE
HOUSE ◀ Brakspear Bitter, Ramsbury Gold, West Berks
Good Old Boy. ♈ 12 **Facilities** Children's portions Dogs
allowed Garden Parking

---

## PICK OF THE PUBS

### The Trout at Tadpole
### Bridge ★★★★ INN ◀ ♈

**Buckland Marsh SN7 8RF** ☎ **01367 870382**
e-mail: info@troutinn.co.uk
dir: *From A420 (between Oxford & Swindon) take A417*
*into Faringdon, onto A4095 signed Bampton, pub*
*approx 2m*

In a classic 'Wind in the Willows' setting on the River
Thames, just twenty minutes from Oxford, this 17th-
century free house offers log fires, cask ales, and a
kitchen that makes good use of the best local
ingredients. The building, once a riverside toll house,
has been completely refurbished and now offers six
luxurious bedrooms. Having run several fine-dining
restaurants, owners Gareth and Helen Pugh take food
seriously, without marginalising the locals who come in
every night for the fine range of regional beers. Yet the
couple also understand that families need toys and a
decent children's menu. Typical menu choices include
confit of duck leg with black pudding mash and red
onion gravy; spinach and gruyère cheese Wellington
with pepper sauce; and whole crayfish with citrus
mayonnaise. The Trout was chosen as the AA's Pub of
the Year for England in 2009-2010.

---

**Open** 11.30-3 6-11 Closed: 25-26 Dec, Sun eve (Nov-
Apr) **Bar Meals** L served all wk 12-2 booking required D
served all wk 7-9 booking required Av main course
£13.95 **Restaurant** L served all wk 12-2 booking
required D served all wk 7-9 booking required Av 3
course à la carte fr £30 ⊕ FREE HOUSE ◀ Ramsbury
Bitter, Youngs PA Bitter, White Horse ♻ Stowford Press.
♈ 12 **Facilities** Children's menu Children's portions
Dogs allowed Garden Parking **Rooms** 6

---

### FIFIELD    Map 10 SP21

### Merrymouth Inn

**Stow Rd OX7 6HR** ☎ **01993 831652** 📠 **01993 830840**
e-mail: tim@merrymouthinn.fsnet.co.uk
dir: *On A424 between Burford & Stow-on-the-Wold*

A beautifully restored Cotswold inn dating back to the
13th century. At that time it was owned by the monks of
nearby Bruern Abbey, to which hitherto undiscovered
underground passages are said to lead. A blackboard of
fresh fish, vegetarian and other daily specials includes
such dishes as a warm salad of scallops and bacon and
gilt head sea bream with fennel and tomato. Home-made
puddings include raspberry marshmallow meringue.

**Open** all wk Closed: Sun eve in Winter ◀ Hook Norton
Best Bitter, Adnams Broadside. **Facilities** Dogs allowed
Garden Parking

---

### FRINGFORD    Map 11 SP62

### The Butchers Arms

**OX27 8EB** ☎ **01869 277363**
e-mail: butcherarms@aol.com
dir: *4m from Bicester on A4421 towards Buckingham*

The landlord tells us that the village of Fringford is
Candleford in *Lark Rise to Candleford*, and that the
Butchers Arms was Flora Thompson's workplace. This
pretty, creeper clad pub offers a good selection of fresh
fish and other seafood, including mussels, crab and king
prawns, as well as liver, bacon and onions, peppered
fillet steak, half a roast duck, and steak and kidney pie.
Pumps display Adnams Broadside labels. From the patio
watch the cricket during the summer.

**Open** all wk ◀ Adnams Broadside, Hooky Bitter, Old
Speckled Hen. **Facilities** Dogs allowed Parking

## FULBROOK Map 10 SP21

### The Carpenters Arms NEW

**Fulbrook Hill OX18 4BH**
**01993 823275 01993 823275**
**e-mail:** info@carpentersarmsfulbrook.com
**dir:** *From rdbt on A40 at Burford take A361 signed Chipping Norton. Pub on right 150mtrs from mini rdbt just after bridge*

To the delight of local Burford residents, chef-patron Paul Griffith has returned to the pub he firmly put on the Cotswold culinary map a couple of years back. The 17th-century stone pub oozes charm and character; the warren of cosy, beautifully decorated and furnished rooms draw a cosmopolitan crowd for the civilised atmosphere and Paul's modern British cooking. Look to the chalkboard and perhaps find spiced pumpkin soup, baked scallops with garlic butter and gruyère cheese, cod in beer batter with fat chips, and warm chocolate and orange tart.

**Open** 11.30-3.30 6-11 Closed: 25-26 Dec, Sun eve, Mon **Bar Meals** L served all wk 12-3 booking required D served all wk 6-9.30 booking required Av main course £14 **Restaurant** L served all wk 12-3 booking required D served all wk 6-9.30 booking required Fixed menu price fr £10 Av 3 course à la carte fr £27 GREENE KING Greene King IPA, Abbot Ale. 10 **Facilities** Children's portions Dogs allowed Garden Parking

## FYFIELD Map 5 SU49

**PICK OF THE PUBS**

### The White Hart

*See Pick of the Pubs on page 366*

## GORING Map 5 SU68

**PICK OF THE PUBS**

### Miller of Mansfield ★★★★★ RR

**High St RG8 9AW 01491 872829 01491 873100**
**e-mail:** reservations@millerofmansfield.com
**dir:** *From Pangbourne take A329 to Streatley. Right on B4009, 0.5m to Goring*

Highly rated as a restaurant with rooms, the Miller of Mansfield nonetheless remains a focal point for the village. It welcomes local and visiting real ale drinkers, and wine lovers who must choose between 15 served by the glass; indeed, refreshments extend to triple-certified origin coffees and organic teas. The beautiful old building, an 18th-century coaching inn in an Area of Outstanding Natural Beauty, has been stylishly renovated and includes sumptuous accommodation with distinctive and individual style. The kitchen focuses on freshness of ingredients, so expect seasonality in its take on modern British cooking. Product suppliers are carefully selected, and just about everything that can be is home made, including bread and pastries, hand-rolled pasta, sorbets and ice creams, jams and jellies. So each dish is awash with flavours: lemon and dill scented goat's cheesecake; baked Turkish aubergine; and fresh crayfish, crab, chilli, garlic and parsley linguini are just a selection. Yet you can order triple-cooked hand-cut chips on their own – ample demonstration of the lack of ostentation within this welcoming hostelry.

**Open** all day all wk 8am-11pm **Bar Meals** L served all wk 12-10 D served all wk 12-10 food served all day **Restaurant** L served all wk 12-4.30 D served all wk 6.30-10 booking required FREE HOUSE Good Old Boy, Rebellion IPA, Organic Jester. **Facilities** Dogs allowed Garden Parking **Rooms** 13

## GREAT TEW Map 11 SP42

**PICK OF THE PUBS**

### The Falkland Arms

**OX7 4DB 01608 683653 01608 683656**
**e-mail:** falklandarms@wadworth.co.uk
**dir:** *Off A361, 1.25m, signed Great Tew*

This 500-year-old inn takes its name from Lucius Carey, 2nd Viscount Falkland, who inherited the manor of Great Tew in 1629. Nestling at the end of a charming row of Cotswold stone cottages, the Falkland Arms is a classic: flagstone floors, high-backed settles and an inglenook fireplace characterise the intimate bar, where a huge collection of beer and cider mugs and jugs hangs from the ceiling. Home-made specials such as spiced lamb burger with salsa and sautéed potatoes; or smoked haddock kedgeree topped with a poached egg supplement the lunchtime menu of filled baguettes and ploughman's; these can be enjoyed in the bar or the pub garden. In the evening, booking is essential for dinner in the small dining room. Expect a pint of shell-on prawns with crusty bread; Falkland Arms fish pie; or whole roasted partridge with Puy lentils and roast vegetables. Being a genuine English pub, clay pipes and snuff are always on sale.

**Open** all wk Mon-Fri 11.30-3 6-11 (Sat 11.30-mdnt Sun noon-10.30) **Bar Meals** L served Mon-Fri 12-2.30, Sat-Sun 12-9.30 D served Mon-Fri 6-9.30 Av main course £9.95 **Restaurant** D served Mon-Sat 6-9 booking required WADWORTH & CO LTD Wadworth 6X, Henry's IPA, Horizon, guest ales Westons Traditional Scrumpy. 18 **Facilities** Children's portions Dogs allowed Garden

## HAILEY Map 11 SP31

### Bird in Hand

**Whiteoak Green OX29 9XP**
**01993 868321 01993 868702**
**e-mail:** welcome@birdinhandinn.co.uk
**dir:** *From Witney N onto B4022 through Hailey to Whiteoak Green for 5m. At Charlbury S onto B4022 for 5m*

Set in the Oxfordshire countryside just outside the village of Hailey, this classic Cotswold stone inn is Grade II listed and dates from the 16th century. The beamed interior has huge inglenook fireplaces, with log fires in winter. The food in the restaurant ranges from devilled lambs' kidneys on toast, to roast partridge, braised red cabbage, fondant potato and bread sauce; or orecchiette pasta, grilled artichokes and white wine.

**Open** all day all wk **Bar Meals** L served Mon-Sat 12-2.30, Sun 12-3 D served Mon-Sat 6.30-9.30, Sun 6-9 Av main course £7.50 **Restaurant** L served Mon-Sat 12-2.30, Sun 12-3 D served Mon-Sat 6.30-9.30, Sun 6-9 Fixed menu price fr £15 Av 3 course à la carte fr £20 FREE HOUSE Ramsbury Stowford Press. 10 **Facilities** Children's menu Children's portions Dogs allowed Garden Parking

## HAMPTON POYLE Map 11 SP51

### The Bell ★★★★★ INN NEW

**OX5 2QD 01865 376242**
**e-mail:** contactus@thebelloxford.co.uk
**dir:** *From N: exit A34 signed Kidlington, over bridge. At mini rdbt turn right, left to Hampton Poyle (before slip road to rejoin A34). From Kidlington: at Oxford rd rdbt (junct of A4260 & A4165), take Bicester Rd (Sainsbury's on left & towards A34). Left to Hampton Poyle*

This newly-opened dining inn with boutique-style rooms nestles close to the Cherwell to the north of Oxford, where the old village pub was updated with a contemporary restaurant, blending easily with the historic heart of the inn with its limestone flagged floors and oak beams. An eye-catching feature is a wood-burning oven where some dishes from the open kitchen are prepared, including memorable rustic pizzas and Thai seafood curry with trout dumplings. A short, top quality wine list and cask ales set the seal on the experience.

**Open** all wk (all day Sat-Sun) **Bar Meals** L served Mon-Fri 12-2.30, Sat-Sun all day D served Mon-Fri 6-9.30, Sat-Sun 6-10 Av main course £11 food served all day **Restaurant** L served Mon-Fri 12-2.30, Sat-Sun all day D served Mon-Fri 6-9.30, Sat-Sun 6-10 Av 3 course à la carte fr £30 FREE HOUSE Fuller's London Pride, Wadworth Stowford Press. **Facilities** Dogs allowed Garden Parking **Rooms** 9

# PICK OF THE PUBS

## The White Hart 🍷

**FYFIELD** Map 5 SU49

**Main Rd OX13 5LW ☎ 01865 390585**
**e-mail:** info@whitehart-fyfield.com
**dir:** *6m S of Oxford just off A420 (Oxford to Swindon road)*

Now a beautiful, country free house pub and restaurant, the 15th-century White Hart was built for a chantry priest and five almsmen to live in. By 1548, however, chantries had been abolished and it was sold to St John's College, Oxford, whose tenants converted it into a drinking establishment, inserting a floor between the ground and the roof of the hall.

In the 1960s the college removed the floor to reveal the original arch-braced roof again in all its glory; this grand space with soaring eaves and beams, huge stone-flanked windows and flagstones, overlooked by a minstrels' gallery, is now the main restaurant. From the low-ceilinged bar to the manor house runs a tunnel that priests probably used as an escape route during the Dissolution of the Monasteries between 1536 and 1541.

Owners Mark and Kay Chandler are steadfast in their pursuit of fresh, seasonal food from trusted local suppliers and their own garden. Mark changes his menus daily to offer twice baked Cornish Yarg and spinach soufflé, sharing boards of fish (delivered daily from Brixham, although Mark catches crayfish locally in the summer), antipasti and mezze; roast rack of Cotswold lamb, sweetbreads, broad beans, samphire, dauphinoise; roasted fillet of cod with haricot bean cassoulet, clams, chorizo, chilli and thyme; and potato and rosemary ravioli with wild mushrooms. For pudding try lemon balm crème brûlée with vanilla shortbread; or sticky toffee pudding with home-made butterscotch ice cream. Set two- and three-course lunches are another attraction.

With over 50 wines on the list, 16 of which are sold by the glass, there's something for everyone. A good range of cask-conditioned ales always includes something from Hook Norton; the others change after each barrel. Among occasional events are an August Bank Holiday beer festival, and regular themed evenings.

**Open** noon-3 5.30-11 (Sat noon-11 Sun noon-10.30) Closed: Mon ex BH
**Bar Meals** L served Tue-Sat 12-2.30, Sun 12-4 booking required D served Tue-Sat 7-9.30 booking required Av main course £15 **Restaurant** L served Tue-Sat 12-2.30, Sun 12-4 booking required D served Tue-Sat 7-9.30 booking required Fixed menu price fr £15 Av 3 course à la carte fr £24.50 🍺 FREE HOUSE ◀ Hooky Bitter, Doom Bar, Hullabaloo, Guest ales ♻ Thatchers Cheddar Valley. 🍷 16
**Facilities** Children's menu Play area Garden and terrace Parking

Save on Hotels. Book at **theAA**.com/hotel

**OXFORDSHIRE** 367 **ENGLAND**

---

**HENLEY-ON-THAMES**　　　　　**Map 5 SU78**

## PICK OF THE PUBS

## The Cherry Tree Inn ♀

**Stoke Row RG9 5QA**
☎ 01491 680430　📠 01491 682168
e-mail: info@thecherrytreeinn.com
**dir:** *B481 towards Reading & Sonning Common 2m,*
*follow Stoke Row sign*

There's a confident blend of ancient and modern inside
this 400-year-old listed building. Originally three flint
cottages, the Cherry Tree has been comprehensively refitted, mixing the original flagstone floors, beamed
ceilings and fireplaces with contemporary decor, strong
colours and comfortable modern furnishings. The
contemporary theme continues throughout the pub,
which offers Brakspear real ales, fine malt whiskies
and over 40 different wines, including 12 served by the
glass. Service is informal, with a variety of classic
European dishes prepared from fresh local ingredients.
Lunchtime choices include grilled focaccia with goat's
cheese, peppers and pesto; as well as more substantial
dishes like belly of pork with black pudding and creamy
mash. À la carte options range from chargrilled rib-eye
steak, to grilled squid and chorizo salad. Outside, the
large south-facing garden is perfect for alfresco
summer dining.

**Open** all wk Mon-Sun noon-11 **Bar Meals** L served all
wk 12-3 D served all wk 7-10 **Restaurant** L served all
wk 12-3 D served all wk 7-10 ⊕ BRAKSPEAR
◀ Brakspear Bitter, Brakspear Organic, Douvel, Orval,
Erdinger ♂ Westons. ♀ 12 **Facilities** Children's menu
Dogs allowed Garden Parking

## PICK OF THE PUBS

## The Five Horseshoes

**Maidensgrove RG9 6EX**
☎ 01491 641282　📠 01491 641086
e-mail: admin@thefivehorseshoes.co.uk
**dir:** *From Henley-on-Thames take A4130, in 1m take*
*B480 to right, signed Stonor. In Stonor left, through*
*woods, over common, pub on left*

This traditional 16th-century pub enjoys far-reaching
views across the surrounding countryside from its two
large beer gardens. Once inside, old pub games, log
fires, heavy beams and brasses set the scene; there
are two snug bar areas serving real ales, wines and
champagnes by the glass, as well as a large
conservatory restaurant. Food focuses on the freshest
produce, locally sourced where possible, and the menu
begins with wild mushroom and sherry soup; home
smoked rainbow trout; and wood pigeon salad. Other
choices include roast haunch of Muntjac for two; and
ox cheek and oyster pudding; plus pub favourites such
as doorstep sandwiches, and prime minced beef of
venison burger. Puddings range from apricot soufflé to
steamed ginger pudding with butterscotch sauce.
Walkers, cyclists and dogs are all welcome in this Area
of Outstanding Natural Beauty. Summer weekend
barbecues and bank holiday hog roasts are held in one
of the gardens. Change of hands in 2009.

**Open** all wk noon-3.30 6-11 (Sat noon-11 Sun noon-6)
**Bar Meals** L served Mon-Fri 12-2.30, Sat 12-3, Sun
12-4 booking required D served Mon-Sat 6.30-9.30 Av
main course £12 **Restaurant** L served Mon-Fri 12-2.30,
Sat 12-3, Sun 12-4 booking required D served Mon-Sat
6.30-9.30 booking required Fixed menu price fr £10.95
Av 3 course à la carte fr £22 ⊕ BRAKSPEAR
◀ Brakspear Ordinary, Oxford Gold.
**Facilities** Children's portions Dogs allowed Garden
Parking

## The Little Angel ♀ NEW

**Remenham Ln RG9 2LS** ☎ 01491 411008
e-mail: enquiries@thelittleangel.co.uk
**dir:** *From Henley-on-Thames take A4130 (White Hill)*
*towards Maidenhead. Pub on left*

The River Thames flows sedately under Henley's old
bridge just 100 yards from this stylishly decorated pub,
marked with a plaque denoting that it's of special
historic and architectural interest. Modern English
cooking will be enjoyed by those whose fancy steers them
towards paupiettes of sole with crab and sun-blushed
tomato mousse; chicken in white wine and tarragon
sauce; and risotto Milanese with squid. Sunday
lunchtimes can be pretty busy, but food is served until
4pm. There are cocktails every Friday and live music
evenings.

**Open** all day all wk Closed: 1 Jan **Bar Meals** Av main
course £9 food served all day **Restaurant** L served Mon-
Fri 12-3, Sat-Sun all day booking required D served Mon-
Fri 7-11, Sat-Sun all day booking required Fixed menu
price fr £13.50 Av 3 course à la carte fr £25
⊕ BRAKSPEAR ◀ Brakspear, Oxford Gold Organic,
seasonal ales, Guinness. ♀ 11 **Facilities** Children's
portions Dogs allowed Garden Parking

*See advert on page 368*

## PICK OF THE PUBS

## WhiteHartNettlebed ♀

**High St, Nettlebed RG9 5DD**
☎ 01491 641245　📠 01491 649018
e-mail: info@whitehartnettlebed.com
**dir:** *On A4130 between Henley-on-Thames &*
*Wallingford*

Royalist and parliamentary soldiers made a habit of
lodging in local taverns during the English Civil War;
this 15th-century inn reputedly billeted troops loyal to
the King. During the 17th and 18th centuries the area
was plagued by highwaymen, including the notorious
Isaac Darkin, who was eventually caught, tried and

hung at Oxford Gaol. These days the beautifully
restored property is favoured by a stylish crowd who
appreciate the chic bar and restaurant. Heading the
beer list is locally-brewed Brakspear backed by popular
internationals and a small selection of cosmopolitan
bottles. A typical three-course meal selection could
comprise sweet potato and gruyère tartlet with rocket;
spinach, feta and cumin spanakopita with
babaganouche; and lemon and thyme pannacotta with
red wine poached pear. Recent change of hands.

**Open** all day all wk 11am-11pm (Sun 11am-10pm)
**Bar Meals** L served Mon-Sat 12-3, Sun 12-8 booking
required D served Mon-Sat 6-10 booking required
**Restaurant** L served Mon-Sat 12-3, Sun 12-8 booking
required D served Mon-Sat 6-10 booking required
⊕ BRAKSPEAR ◀ Brakspear, Guinness. ♀ 12
**Facilities** Children's menu Children's portions Play
area Family room Dogs allowed Garden Parking

---

**HOOK NORTON**　　　　　**Map 11 SP33**

## PICK OF THE PUBS

## The Gate Hangs High

**Whichford Rd OX15 5DF** ☎ 01608 737387
e-mail: gatehangshigh@aol.com
**dir:** *Off A361 SW of Banbury*

This rural pub is set amid beautiful countryside near
the mystical Rollright Stones and Hook Norton, where
the cask-conditioned, dry-hopped ales served here are
brewed. It is on the old drovers' road from Wales to
Banbury and a tollgate that once stood outside was
said to hang high enough for small creatures to pass
under, although owners of larger beasts had to pay. In
the low-beamed bar, polished horse brasses reflect the
glow from the candles, pretty wall lights and roaring
log fire. Now under new management, the food is
described as 'a return to good old fashioned cooking.'
Start perhaps with home-made chicken liver and
brandy pâté, and follow with oven roasted rack of lamb
with creamed potatoes, or trio of sausages with mash.
Menu choices are further extended by the fresh fish
boards.

**Open** all wk Closed: 25 Dec eve **Bar Meals** L served
Mon-Fri 12-2.30, Sat-Sun 12-9.30 D served Mon-Fri
6-9.30, Sat-Sun 12-9.30 Av main course £4.50
**Restaurant** L served Mon-Fri 12-2.30, Sat-Sun 12-9.30
D served Mon-Fri 6-9.30, Sat-Sun 12-9.30 Fixed menu
price fr £9.95 ⊕ HOOK NORTON BREWERY ◀ Hook
Norton - Best, Old Hooky, Gold ♂ Stowford Press.
**Facilities** Children's portions Dogs allowed Garden
Parking

# The Little Angel

Henley On Thames, Remenham Lane, Henley On Thames, Berks RG9 5EJ
**Tel:** 01491 411 008
**E-mail:** enquiries@thelittleangel.co.uk   **Web:** www.thelittleangel.co.uk

"When entering The Little Angel, those paying their inaugural visit might be pleasantly surprised by not only the unique style and sophisticated ambience of this historic pub but at its size and clever use of space. From the outside, this lovely, traditional white pub, a stones throw from Henley Bridge and the river Thames is perfectly positioned in every respect and with its interior showing you a modern, creative and comfortable personality – it has something for everyone.

This is a foodhouse pub but is still a great pub with well kept real Ales. A beautiful and tempting bar with comfy chairs and a welcoming smile, The Little Angel is a draw for locals and visitors afar and is not to be missed on any of the many annual social events throughout Henley's calendar (during Henley Royal Regatta, Music & Arts Festival in June/July to the huge 80's Rewind Festival in August). The pub is firmly established as a main destination for corporate and private groups and individuals to meet, eat, drink and be seen throughout the year.

It is unique in its positioning and is garnering an increasing following for excellent food (emphasis heavily on local, fresh and seasonal produce), service and flexibility and is as happy catering for wedding receptions as it is a quiet lunch or dinner for two. Being open all day, every day (even Christmas Day) with seasonally changing menus of locally sourced produce; it is perfect for any occasion.

On a summer's day, there's no better place to be than in the large patio garden, enjoying a three course lunch, or maybe a jug of Pimms, whilst watching the quintessential English cricket game on the Henley lawns.

Those that know The Little Angel have seen it evolve over the years and are loyal to it. This is a smooth operation that adds that special touch!"

Save on Hotels. Book at theAA.com/hotel

OXFORDSHIRE 369 ENGLAND

## HOOK NORTON continued

### Sun Inn ▼

**High St OX15 5NH** ☎ **01608 737570** 📠 **01608 737570**
e-mail: thesuninnhooky@hotmail.co.uk
dir: 5m from Chipping Norton, 8m from Banbury, just
off A361

Set in picturesque Hook Norton, this welcoming Cotswold
stone inn is just a 10 minute walk from the Hook Norton
Brewery – ideal if you're planning a tour! Inside you'll
find oak beams, flagstones, an inglenook fireplace and
plenty of Hook Norton ales on tap. Food runs from
sandwiches and British classics to more poised offerings
such as cured haunch of smoked wild boar with
parmesan, rocket and truffle oil followed by honey-glazed
ham hock with roasted garlic and parsley mash and
Meaux mustard sauce.

**Open** all wk 11-3 6-12 (Sun 12-12) 🍺 Hook Norton Best
Bitter, Old Hooky, Hooky Gold, seasonal ales ♂ Westons
Organic. ▼ 8 **Facilities** Dogs allowed Garden Parking

### KELMSCOTT    Map 5 SU29

## The Plough Inn

**GL7 3HG** ☎ **01367 253543**
dir: From M4 junct 15 onto A419 towards Cirencester then
right onto A361 to Lechlade. A417 towards Faringdon,
follow signs to Kelmscott

Dating from 1631, this attractive Cotswold stone inn
stands on the Thames Path midway between Radcot and
Lechlade, making it a haven for walkers and boaters. It's
also just a short walk from Kelmscott Manor, once home
to William Morris. Exposed stone walls and flagstone
floors set the scene for real ales and an extensive, hearty
menu. Dishes range from braised lamb shank with port,
red berry and rosemary sauce to Chinese duck with hoi
sin noodles and pak choi.

**Open** all day all wk **Bar Meals** L served all wk 12-3 D
served all wk 6-10 **Restaurant** L served all wk 12-3 D
served all wk 6-10 ⊕ FREE HOUSE 🍺 Thames Tickler,
Dirty Tackle, Timothy Taylor, Old Lech ♂ Thatchers Gold.
**Facilities** Children's menu Children's portions Dogs
allowed Garden

### KINGHAM    Map 10 SP22

## The Kingham Plough NEW

**The Green OX7 6YD** ☎ **01608 658327**
e-mail: book@thekinghamplough.co.uk
dir: From Chipping Norton, take B4450 to Churchill. Take
2nd right to Kingham, left at T junct in Kingham. Pub
on right.

Situated on the village green The Kingham Plough was
extensively refurbished in 2007. This quintessential
Cotswold inn has a relaxing bar where you can enjoy a
drink and daily changing bar snacks like Cotswold rarebit
and sourdough soldiers, and potted rabbit. In the
restaurant chef/proprietor Emily Watkins, who worked at
The Fat Duck, changes the short menu daily to
accommodate the deliveries from local farms, small

holdings and game estates. Expect dishes like Cornish
lemon sole with twice baked wild garlic mousse and sea
beet, Hampshire Down hogget with pearl barley and
spring vegetable stew, or Alan's asparagus mousse. Look
out for A Taste of the Cotswolds menu along with other
events such as the annual farmers' market, quiz nights
and food tasting evenings.

**Open** all day all wk Closed: 25 Dec **Bar Meals** L served all
wk 12-9.30 D served all wk 12-9.30 Av main course £7
food served all day **Restaurant** L served Mon-Sat 12-2
(Sun 12-2.30) D served Mon-Sat 7-9 Av 3 course à la
carte fr £30 ⊕ FREE HOUSE 🍺 Cotswold Premium, Hook
Norton, Mad Goose, Hereford Pale Ale, Cotswold Wheat
Beer ♂ Stowford Press. **Facilities** Children's
menu Children's portions Dogs allowed Garden Parking

### LEWKNOR    Map 5 SU79

## The Leathern Bottel ▼

**1 High St OX49 5TW** ☎ **01844 351482**
dir: 0.5m from M40 junct 6 north or south

Run by the same family for more than 25 years, this
16th-century coaching inn is set in the foothills of the
Chilterns. Walkers with dogs, families with children,
parties for meals or punters for a quick pint are all made
equally welcome. In winter there's a wood-burning stove,
a good drop of Brakspears ale, tempting specials and a
quiz on Sunday. Summer is the time for outdoor eating,
the children's play area, Pimm's and Morris dancers.

**Open** all wk Closed: 25-26 Dec 🍺 Brakspear Ordinary,
Special. ▼ 12 **Facilities** Play area Family room Dogs
allowed Garden Parking

### LOWER SHIPLAKE    Map 5 SU77

### PICK OF THE PUBS

## The Baskerville Arms ★★★★ INN ▼

**See Pick of the Pubs on page 370**

### LOWER WOLVERCOTE    Map 5 SP40

### PICK OF THE PUBS

## The Trout Inn ▼

**195 Godstow Rd OX2 8PN** ☎ **01865 510930**
dir: From A40 at Wolvercote rdbt (N of Oxford) follow
signs for Wolvercote, through village to pub

An old riverside inn on the banks of the Isis, as the
Thames is known here. It was built around 1133 as a
hospice to serve Godstow Nunnery, the ruins of which
are on the opposite bank. With stone walls, slate roof,
leaded windows, great oak beams, flagged floors and
ancient fireplaces glowing in winter, it is arguably
Oxford's most atmospheric inn. Many drinkers are
happy just to sit on the terrace and watch the fast
flowing waters while enjoying a pint of Brakspear's
Oxford Gold. The menu tempts, though, with Italian
flavours predominant. It kicks off with sharing plates
of garlic pizzette, and starters such as arancini risotto

balls with zucchini, red peppers, ham, provolone
cheese and tomato salsa. Then there are salads,
pastas, stone-baked pizzas and meats from the stove,
grill or rotisserie. So will it be linguini with crab and
tiger prawns, perhaps, quattro formaggi with red onion
marmalade, or Venetian calves' liver? Tough choices…

**Open** all day all wk **Bar Meals** Av main course £12 food
served all day **Restaurant** Av 3 course à la carte fr £22
food served all day ⊕ FREE HOUSE 🍺 Brakspear Oxford
Gold, Paulaner, Timothy Taylor Landlord, Adnams Best
Bitter ♂ Aspall Suffolk Draught. ▼ 21 **Facilities** Garden
Parking

### MARSTON    Map 5 SP50

## Victoria Arms ▼

**Mill Ln OX3 0PZ** ☎ **01865 241382**
e-mail: kyffinda@yahoo.co.uk
dir: From A40 follow signs to Old Marston, sharp right
into Mill Lane, pub in lane 500yds on left

Friendly country pub situated on the banks of the River
Cherwell, occupying the site of the old Marston Ferry that
connected the north and south of the city. The old
ferryman's bell is still behind the bar. Popular
destinations for punters, and fans of TV sleuth Inspector
Morse, as the last episode used this as a location. Typical
menu includes lamb cobbler, steak and Guinness pie,
spicy pasta bake, battered haddock, and ham off the
bone.

**Open** all wk Closed: Oct-Apr afternoons 🍺 Henrys IPA,
Wadworth 6X, JCB, guest ales. ▼ 15 **Facilities** Family
room Dogs allowed Garden Parking

### MIDDLETON STONEY    Map 11 SP52

## Best Western Jersey Arms
## Hotel ★★ HL ▼

**OX25 4AD** ☎ **01869 343234** 📠 **01869 343565**
e-mail: jerseyarms@bestwestern.co.uk
dir: 3m from junct 9/10 of M4. 3m from A34 on B430

This charming family-run free house was built as an ale
house in the 13th century, on what used to be the estate
of Lord Jersey. The cosy bar offers a good range of
popular bar food with the extensive menu supplemented
by daily blackboard specials. Start with warm salad of
duckling and brie with redcurrant sauce, or smoked
salmon; then try the slow roasted shoulder of Oxfordshire
pork; or the salmon and coriander fishcakes; followed by
bread and butter pudding with custard.

**Open** all wk **Bar Meals** L served all wk 12-2 D served all
wk 6.30-9 Av main course £8.95 **Restaurant** L served all
wk 12-2 booking required D served all wk 6.30-9 booking
required Av 3 course à la carte fr £24 ⊕ FREE HOUSE
🍺 Interbrew Flower. ▼ 9 **Facilities** Children's menu
Garden Parking **Rooms** 20

# PICK OF THE PUBS

## The Baskerville Arms ★★★★INN ♟

**LOWER SHIPLAKE**     Map 5 SU77

**Station Rd RG9 3NY** ☎ **0118 940 3332**
**e-mail:** enquiries@thebaskerville.com
**dir:** *Just off A4155, 1.5m from Henley*

This appealing pub stands on the popular Thames Path, close to Shiplake station and just a few minutes from historic Henley-on-Thames. Brick-built on the outside, modern-rustic within, it boasts an attractive garden where summer Sunday barbecues are a common fixture. Walkers remove their muddy boots at the door before heading to the bar, where pints of Loddon Hoppit, brewed two miles away, are served with welcoming smiles. Also on tap are Fuller's and Timothy Taylor, backed by Pilsner Urquell, reckoned by many to be one of the best Czech lagers available today. The wine list extends to 50 bins, and owner Allan Hannah betrays his origins with his range of 35 malt whiskies.

Variety and choice for the customer is a top priority here, as witnessed by different menus covering lunch, set lunch, set evening, à la carte, Sunday lunch and children's choices; a bar snacks blackboard menu has recently been added too, proffering home-made scotch pies, Cornish pasties, pork pies and scotch eggs. The objective is to serve really good food at a reasonable price in a relaxed and unpretentious atmosphere. Modern British describes the Head Chef Marc Price's approach, with continental and eastern influences. All produce is delivered daily, and all dishes, including the bread, are prepared on the premises and cooked to order; organic, sustainably sourced ingredients travel as few miles as possible, and a special fish menu runs throughout the summer months.

Lunchtime open sandwiches include the Baskerville special: grilled chorizo, chicken, cheese, lettuce and tomato. Alternatively you could dive into a plate of pan-fried red tilapia fillet with lemon braised fennel and shallots. A typical evening choice could start with wild rabbit, pork and cranberry terrine with apple and pear chutney; and follow with slow-cooked free range pork belly complete with crackling and black pudding. Booking essential during Henley Regatta in early July.

**Open** all wk 11.30-2.30 6-11 (Sun noon-5) Closed: 1 Jan **Bar Meals** L served Mon-Sat 11.30-2, Sun 12-4 D served Mon-Thu 6-9.30, Fri-Sat 6-10 Av main course £11 **Restaurant** L served Mon-Sat 11.30-2, Sun 12-4 booking required D served Mon-Thu 6-9.30, Fri-Sat 6-10 booking required Fixed menu price fr £15 Av 3 course à la carte fr £25 ⊕ ENTERPRISE INNS ◀ London Pride, Loddon Hoppit, Timothy Taylor Landlord. ♟ 12 **Facilities** Children's menu Play area Dogs allowed Garden Parking **Rooms** 4

# PICK OF THE PUBS

# The Black Boy Inn ♀

**OX15 4HH**
☎ **01295 722111**   📠 **01295 722978**
**e-mail:** info@blackboyinn.com
**web:** www.blackboyinn.com
**dir:** *From Banbury take A4260 to Adderbury. After Adderbury turn right signed Bloxham. Onto Milton Road to Milton. Pub on right*

A splendid 16th-century building set back from the road on the edge of picturesque Milton, the pub's name is thought to be associated with the dark-skinned Charles II, sometimes referred to as 'the black boy'; other popular theories naturally include a reference to the slave trade.

The charming interior has solid pine furniture that's entirely in keeping with the 400-year-old building, and the long room has a real wood stove at one end and a comfortable dining room at the other; in between is the bar, from which extends a conservatory-style dining room overlooking a gravelled courtyard. Outside, the patio and a lovely half-acre garden offer plenty of seating and space for children to run around. A rotating list of guest ales and a selection of wines by the glass ensure that drinkers can enjoy the relaxed and informal atmosphere of this quintessentially English free house.

Meanwhile, head chef Kevin Hodgkiss uses fresh, seasonal ingredients to produce modern British food, including plenty of pub classics; fish pie topped with buttered mash, and pan-fried liver and bacon with a rich shallot sauce. On the main menu, starters like pan-fried scallops with slow roasted pork belly and pea purée, or trout gravadlax with chilli and basil, served on fennel and radicchio salad, are followed main courses that include honey roasted Gressingham duck breast with buttered spring greens, pan-fried potato cake and a red wine shallot dressing, or mini rack of lamb with buttered runner beans, crushed new potatoes and thyme jus. Desserts are excellent: try the white chocolate croissant bread and butter pudding with vanilla anglaise and praline ice cream. Plenty of fresh salads and interesting sandwiches complete the choice.

**Open** all wk 12-3 5.30-11.30 (Sat-Sun noon-11.30) **Bar Meals** L served Mon-Sat 12-2.30, Sun 12-3 D served Mon-Sat 6.30-11 booking required **Restaurant** L served Mon-Sat 12-2.30, Sun 12-3 D served Mon-Sat 6.30-11 booking required 🛢 FREE HOUSE ◀ Adnams, Abbot Ale, rotating guest ales ♨ Aspall. ♀ 8 **Facilities** Play area Dogs allowed Garden Parking

# PICK OF THE PUBS

## The Crown Inn

**PISHILL**  Map 5 SU78

**RG9 6HH** ☎ **01491 638364**
e-mail:
enquiries@thecrowninnpishill.co.uk
web: www.thecrowninnpishill.co.uk
dir: *On B480 off A4130, 8m NW of Henley-on-Thames*

As it is bound to come up in conversation, perhaps we should first deal with the name of the village. Old maps show a second 's' in Pishill, which is why some people insist on separating the two syllables. Furthermore, in pre-combustion engine days waggon drivers would stop at the inn for a swift half after the stiff, six-mile climb from Henley-on-Thames, and their horses would relieve themselves while their masters were inside. (Quite why the

horses waited so long isn't recorded.) On the other hand, maybe the word evolved from Peashill, because peas used to be grown round here. Take your pick, depending on whether Great Aunt Gertrude is with you.

This pretty, 15th-century brick and flint coaching inn contains a priest's hole (reputably the largest in the country), which was used extensively when Henry VIII was busy persecuting Catholics. Indeed, one of the many clerics who were smuggled in from the big house at nearby Stonor met a sticky end while hiding out at The Crown and his ghost still haunts the pub on the anniversary of his death.

The bar is supplied by mostly local breweries, including Marlow. The menus and specials are revised daily, typically to provide medallions of beef tenderloin on rösti potato with wild mushrooms and port sauce; whole grilled lemon sole with herb butter and seasonal vegetables; breast of chicken stuffed with brie and wrapped in smoked bacon; and wild mushroom and spinach risotto.

On a fine day, enjoy the picturesque gardens overlooking the valley and watch the red kites circling overhead. In winter experience the warmth and cosy atmosphere of the three log fires.

**Open** all wk 11.30-3 6-11 (Sun noon-3 7-10) Closed: 25-26 Dec
**Bar Meals** L served all wk 12-2.30 D served all wk 7-9.30 **Restaurant** L served all wk 12-2.30 D served all wk 7-9.30 ⊕ FREE HOUSE ◼ Brakspears, West Berkshire Brewery, Loddon Brewery, Marlow Brewery, Hidden Brewery. **Facilities** Dogs allowed Garden Parking

# PICK OF THE PUBS

## The Royal Oak ♉

**RAMSDEN**  Map 11 SP31

**High St OX7 3AU**
☎ **01993 868213**  📠 **01993 868864**
**dir:** *From Witney take B4022 towards Charlbury, then right before Hailey, through Poffley End*

Standing opposite the church in the pretty Cotswold village of Ramsden, this 17th-century former coaching inn was once a stopping off point for the London to Hereford stagecoach. These days the inn is more popular with walkers eager to explore the lovely surrounding countryside. Whether you are walking or not, the inn makes a fine place to stop for refreshment, and its old beams, warm fires and stone walls provide a very cosy welcome.

The Royal Oak is a free house with beers sourced from local breweries, such as Hook Norton Best, and Purity's UBU from neighbouring Warwickshire. Somerset's

Original Cider Company furnishes the bar with its Pheasant Plucker cider, alongside Weston's Old Rosie. The wine list has over 200 wines, specialising in those from Bordeaux and Languedoc, with 30 of them served by the glass.

The main menu, built on the very best of fresh local and seasonal ingredients, regularly features a pie of the week topped with puff pastry, and there are other pub favourites such as chilli con carne with rice and tortillas; home-made beef burgers served with toasted ciabatta roll, salad garnish and French fries; and traditional Aberdeen Angus steak and kidney suet pudding. Aberdeen Angus beef is also available in the form of sirloin and rump steaks, cooked to your liking on the char-grill. The Gymkhana Club curry is based on a traditional Sri Lankan recipe, served with rice and pickles. Fresh crab and smoked salmon fishcakes come with a piquant tomato and sweet pepper sauce. Another alternative is fresh pennoni pasta with a wild mushroom truffle sauce, garnished with shiitake mushrooms and fresh parmesan. Every Thursday evening there is a special offer of steak, with a glass of wine and dessert included.

**Open** all wk 11.30-3 6.30-11 (Sun 12-3 7-10.30) Closed: 25 Dec **Bar Meals** L served all wk 11.30-2 D served all wk 7-10 Av main course £12 **Restaurant** L served all wk 11.30-2 D served all wk 7-10 Fixed menu price fr £14 Av 3 course à la carte fr £26 ⊕ FREE HOUSE ◀ Hook Norton Old Hooky, Best, Adnams Broadside, Youngs Special, Hook Norton Bitter, Purity UBU ♂ Old Rosie, Pheasant Plucker. ♉ 30 **Facilities** Dogs allowed Garden Parking

| MILTON | Map 11 SP43 |
|---|---|

## PICK OF THE PUBS

### The Black Boy Inn ⚲

*See Pick of the Pubs on page 371*

| MURCOTT | Map 11 SP51 |
|---|---|

## PICK OF THE PUBS

### The Nut Tree Inn ⊚⊚ ⚲

**Main St OX5 2RE ☎ 01865 331253**
dir: *M40 junct 9, A34 towards Oxford. Left onto B4027 signed Islip. At Red Lion turn left. Right signed Murcott, Fencott & Charlton-on-Otmoor. Pub on right in village*

This thatched 15th-century free house is a traditional village local, standing in four acres overlooking the village pond. You can stop here for a relaxing pint of Vale Hadda's Winter Solstice at the end of a hard day's work – but step into the restaurant, and you'll discover great modern British food and attentive service. Mike North grew up locally and always dreamed of owning The Nut Tree. In 2006 he made those dreams a reality when he and his fiancée Imogen bought the pub with its oak beams, wood-burning stoves and unusual carvings. At the bar and in the garden, the chalkboard menu might include daily soups; sandwiches on home-made bread; and a hot dish such as smoked salmon and scrambled eggs. A typical restaurant selection starts with pavé of Nut Tree smoked Orkney salmon, followed by roast saddle of lamb with grilled polenta and butternut squash purée, and rounded off with Yorkshire rhubarb trifle.

**Open** all day Closed: Mon **Bar Meals** L served Tue-Sat 12-2.30, Sun 12-3 D served Tue-Sat 7-9 (Sun 6.30-8 (summer)) Av main course £7.50 **Restaurant** L served Tue-Sat 12-2.30, Sun 12-3 booking required D served Tue-Sat 7-9 booking required Fixed menu price fr £15 Av 3 course à la carte fr £32 ⊕ FREE HOUSE ◼ Hook Norton, Vale Hadda's Winter Solstice, Fuller's London Pride, Brains Rev James, Wickwar Bob. ⚲ 16 **Facilities** Children's portions Dogs allowed Garden Parking

| OXFORD | Map 5 SP50 |
|---|---|

## PICK OF THE PUBS

### The Anchor

**2 Hayfield Rd, Walton Manor OX2 6TT**
**☎ 01865 510282**
dir: *A34 (Oxford ring road N), exit Peartree rdbt, 1.5m then right at Polstead Rd, follow road to bottom, pub on right*

Built in 1937, The Anchor has been a local institution for decades. Especially popular with the well-heeled locals of leafy North Oxford, it's off the beaten track – but, for all that, remains firmly on the map for its well-kept real ales and carefully chosen wines! The relaxed

and comfortable surroundings extend to log fires, daily newspapers, a weekly coffee morning and monthly book club. Lunchtime specials include rabbit ballottine with truffled lentils and soft boiled egg, and whole roast wood pigeon with pancetta, mushrooms, spinach and shallots. On the main menu, devilled lamb's kidneys with creamed spinach and toast might herald a main course of taleggio, mushroom and Swiss chard tart with beetroot and potato salad. Vanilla pannacotta with poached rhubarb is a typical dessert. There's a garden for alfresco dining, and major sporting events are shown in the Oak Bar.

**Open** all day all wk Closed: 25 & 26 Dec **Bar Meals** L served all wk 12-2.30 D served all wk 6-9.30 Av main course £12 **Restaurant** L served all wk 12-2.30 booking required D served all wk 6-9.30 booking required Av 3 course à la carte fr £25 ⊕ WADWORTH ◼ Wadworth 6X, Henrys IPA, Bishops Tipple ⚬ Westons Stowford Press. **Facilities** Children's menu Children's portions Dogs allowed Garden Parking

### The Oxford Retreat ⚲ NEW

**1-2 Hythe Bridge St OX1 2EW ☎ 01865 250309**
e-mail: info@theoxfordretreat.com
dir: *In city centre. 200mtrs from rail station towards centre*

Set at the heart of the University city and right next to the Isis, the decked, tree-shaded waterside garden is the place to be seen at this chic boutique pub, an imposing, gabled building where cocktails are de rigueur and diners can look forward to wild boar bangers and mash or marinated wood pigeon from an eclectic, finely tuned menu prepared in the open kitchen. In winter huddle round the log fire with a real ale, a cosy retreat from the dreaming spires.

**Open** all day all wk **Bar Meals** L served Mon-Fri 12-3, Sat-Sun all day D served Mon-Fri 6-10, Sat-Sun all day (pizzeria open 10pm-3am) Av main course £10 **Restaurant** L served Mon-Fri 12-3, Sat-Sun all day D served Mon-Fri 6-10, Sat-Sun all day (pizzeria open 10pm-3am) Av 3 course à la carte fr £25 ⊕ FREE HOUSE ◼ Fuller's London Pride, Guinness, Staropramen ⚬ Westons Organic. ⚲ 10 **Facilities** Children's portions Garden

### Turf Tavern

**4 Bath Place, off Holywell St OX1 3SU ☎ 01865 243235**
e-mail: 8004@greeneking.co.uk
dir: *Telephone for directions*

A jewel of a pub, and consequently one of Oxford's most popular. It's not easy to find either as it is approached through hidden alleyways, which, if anything, adds to its allure. Previously called the Spotted Cow, it became the Turf in 1842 probably in deference to its gambling clientele; it has also had brushes with literature, film and politics. It's certainly one of Oxford's oldest, with some 13th-century foundations and a 17th-century low-beamed front bar. Three beer gardens help ease overcrowding, but the eleven real ales and reasonably priced pub grub keep the students, locals and visitors flowing in.

**Open** all day all wk Closed: 25-26 Dec, 1 Jan **Bar Meals** Av main course £8 food served all day ⊕ GREENE KING ◼ Traditional ales, changing daily ⚬ Westons Old Rosie Scrumpy. **Facilities** Dogs allowed Garden

| PISHILL | Map 5 SU78 |
|---|---|

## PICK OF THE PUBS

### The Crown Inn

*See Pick of the Pubs on page 372*

| RAMSDEN | Map 11 SP31 |
|---|---|

## PICK OF THE PUBS

### The Royal Oak ⚲

*See Pick of the Pubs on page 373*

| ROKE | Map 5 SU69 |
|---|---|

### *Home Sweet Home* ⚲

**OX10 6JD ☎ 01491 838249   ▤ 01491 835760**
dir: *Just off the B4009 from Benson to Watlington, signed on B4009*

Long ago converted from adjoining cottages by a local brewer, this pretty 15th-century inn stands in a tiny hamlet surrounded by lovely countryside. Oak beams and the large inglenook fireplace dominate a friendly bar with an old-fashioned feel. Starters might include spicy nachos topped with cheese for two to share; while main courses run to Cornish crab fishcakes with home-made tartare sauce; or calves' liver and bacon with an onion gravy. Extensive Sunday menu.

**Open** all wk Closed: 25-26 Dec ◼ Black Sheep, Loddon Brewery ales- Hoppit & Branoc. ⚲ 10 **Facilities** Dogs allowed Garden Parking

| SHIPTON-UNDER-WYCHWOOD | Map 10 SP21 |
|---|---|

## PICK OF THE PUBS

### The Shaven Crown Hotel

**High St OX7 6BA ☎ 01993 830330**
e-mail: relax@theshavencrown.co.uk
dir: *On A361, halfway between Burford & Chipping Norton opposite village green & church*

As its name suggests, the Shaven Crown has a monastic past: it was built by the monks of Bruern Abbey as a hospice for the poor. Following the Dissolution of the monasteries, Elizabeth I used it as a hunting lodge before giving it to the village in 1580, when it became the Crown Inn. It was not until 1930 that a brewery with a touch of humour changed the name to reflect the hairstyle favoured by monks. A 700-year-old honey-coloured Cotswold stone building set around a medieval courtyard, its interior is brimming with original features. Oxfordshire ales and light meals are served in the Monk's Bar, while the restaurant offers a more serious style of dining. Begin with drinks in the impressive Great Hall, then settle down to starters of deep-fried brie with raspberry coulis, followed perhaps by venison steak with wild mushroom and chive sauce. Fresh fish is delivered daily. Outside is an enclosed courtyard and a tree-dotted lawned area.

**Open** all wk 11-3 6-11 (Sat-Sun 11-11) **Bar Meals** L served Mon-Fri 12-2, Sat-Sun 12-9.30 D served Mon-Fri 6-9.30, Sat-Sun 12-9.30 Av main course £11.95 **Restaurant** L served Mon-Fri 12-2, Sat-Sun 12-9.30 D served Mon-Fri 6-9.30, Sat-Sun 12-9.30 Av 3 course à la carte fr £23 ⊕ FREE HOUSE ◀ Hook Norton Ales, Wye Valley, Goffs, Cottage Brewery ♻ Westons Stowford Press. **Facilities** Children's menu Children's portions Dogs allowed Garden Parking

---

### SHUTFORD     Map 11 SP34

#### PICK OF THE PUBS

## The George & Dragon ♀

*See Pick of the Pubs on page 377*

---

### SOUTH MORETON     Map 5 SU58

## The Crown Inn ♀

**High St OX11 9AG ☎ 01235 812262** e-mail: dallas.family@ntlworld.com dir: *From Didcot take A4130 towards Wallingford. Village on right*

Friendly village pub located midway between Wallingford and Didcot. It prides itself on its home-prepared food, and has real ale on tap. Families are welcome and customers come from far and wide. During the summer the garden is very popular. Dishes include steaks, shoulder of lamb, fresh battered haddock, and salmon fillet hollandaise.

**Open** noon-3 6-11pm (Fri noon-3 6-mdnt Sat noon-mdnt Sun noon-5) Closed: 1 Jan, Sun eve ◀ Wadworth 6X, Henrys IPA. ♀ 12 **Facilities** Family room Dogs allowed Garden Parking

---

### SOUTH STOKE     Map 5 SU58

## The Perch and Pike ★★★ INN

**RG8 0JS ☎ 01491 872415 📄 01491 871001** e-mail: info@perchandpike.co.uk dir: *On Ridgeway Hiking Trail. 1.5m N of Goring & 4m S of Wallingford on B4009*

The Perch and Pike, just two minutes' walk from the River Thames, was the village's foremost beer house back in the 17th century. There is a welcoming atmosphere in the original pub and in the adjoining barn conversion, which houses the 42-seater restaurant. Food ranges from a selection of salads, baguettes and ploughman's to the likes of parcel of nile perch baked in foil; chestnut mushroom and beetroot stroganoff; and pan-fried lamb steak with roasted red peppers and chilli butter. There are four comfortable rooms available.

---

**Open** all wk 11.30-3 5.30-11 (Sat-Sun 11.30-11) **Bar Meals** L served Mon-Sat 12-2.30 booking required D served Mon-Sat 7-9.30 booking required Av main course £9 **Restaurant** L served Sun 12-2.30 booking required D served Mon-Sat 7-9.30 booking required Av 3 course à la carte fr £24 ⊕ BRAKSPEAR ◀ Brakspear ales. **Facilities** Children's portions Dogs allowed Garden Parking **Rooms** 4

---

### STANTON ST JOHN     Map 5 SP50

## The Talkhouse

**Wheatley Rd OX33 1EX ☎ 01865 351648 📄 01865 351085** e-mail: talkhouse@fullers.co.uk dir: *Village signed from Oxford ring road*

First recorded as a pub in 1783, the Talkhouse comprises three bar and dining areas, all with a Gothic look and a welcoming atmosphere. A recently refurbished thatched property, it offers a good range of cask ales. Various bar meals (shepherd's pie, sausage and mash) are supplemented by a carte menu.

**Open** all day all wk noon-11pm (Sun noon-10.30pm) ◀ London Pride, ESB, Discovery, Guinness. **Facilities** Dogs allowed Garden Parking

---

### STOKE ROW     Map 5 SU68

#### PICK OF THE PUBS

## Crooked Billet ♀

*See Pick of the Pubs on page 378*

---

### SWALCLIFFE     Map 11 SP33

## Stag's Head ♀

**OX15 5EJ ☎ 01295 780232 📄 01295 788977** dir: *6m W of Banbury on B4035*

This friendly, 600 year-old thatched village inn enjoys picture postcard looks and a pretty village setting. It seems that Shakespeare used to drink here, until he was barred! Blending a traditional pub feel with a family-friendly environment, the Stag also offers a beautiful terraced garden and play area. Freshly prepared dishes include goat's cheese tart with chips or salad; moules marinière with chorizo and crusty bread; and Oxfordshire liver and bacon with red wine and onion gravy. Look out for the landlord's own paintings of local scenes.

**Open** Tue-Sun Closed: Mon ◀ Adnams Bitter, Deuchars IPA, Wye Valley IPA, Badgers Gold, St Austell Tribute. ♀ 8 **Facilities** Play area Dogs allowed Garden

---

### SWERFORD     Map 11 SP33

#### PICK OF THE PUBS

## The Mason's Arms ◉ ♀

**Banbury Rd OX7 4AP ☎ 01608 683212 📄 01608 683105** e-mail: admin@masons-arms.com dir: *Between Banbury & Chipping Norton on A361*

A 300-year-old, stone-built former Masonic lodge, this award-winning pub in the Cotswolds has a formidable reputation for its food. Owners Bill and Charmaine Leadbeater have refurbished the interior, added a new dining room and remodelled the gardens, but retained its traditional, informal feel. 'Bill's Food' and 'Bill's Specials' menus confirm his supremacy in the kitchen and these range from pan-fried fillet of West Coast gurnard, minestrone of vegetables and fresh parsley, to 18-hour shoulder of Old Spot pork, chorizo and olive mash, tea-soaked sultanas and rich gravy. His specials include chargrilled Cornish shark steak with tomato and onion salsa, rocket oil, or 28 day hung Exmoor rib-eye steak with fries, beetroot relish and rocket. Bakewell tart with raspberry compote and clotted cream and lemon and orange posset are typical desserts. There is also a tempting children's menu. The bar dispenses well kept Hook Norton real ales and offers an extensive wine list.

**Open** all wk 10-3 6-11 Closed: 25-26 Dec **Bar Meals** L served Mon-Sat 12-2 booking required D served Mon-Sat 7-9 booking required Av main course £10 **Restaurant** L served Mon-Sat 12-2, Sun 12-3.30 booking required D served all wk 7-9 booking required Fixed menu price fr £15 Av 3 course à la carte fr £25 ⊕ FREE HOUSE ◀ Hook Norton Best, Theakstons Best. ♀ 20 **Facilities** Children's menu Garden Parking

---

### SWINBROOK     Map 5 SP21

#### PICK OF THE PUBS

## The Swan Inn ★★★★ INN ◉ NEW

**OX18 4DY ☎ 01993 823339 📄 01993 823167** e-mail: swaninnswinbrook@btconnect.com dir: *A40 towards Cheltenham, left towards Swinbrook, pub 1 mile before Burford*

With the Kings Head at nearby Bledington (see entry) thriving, owners Archie and Nicola Orr-Ewing took on the lease of this dreamy, wisteria-clad stone pub from Dowager Duchess of Devonshire, the last surviving Mitford sister, in 2007. Hidden in the Windrush Valley in timeless Swinbrook, The Swan is the perfect English country pub – it stands by the River Windrush near the village cricket pitch and overlooks rolling unspoilt Cotswold countryside. It gets even better inside, the two cottagey front rooms, replete with worn flagstones, crackling log fires, low beams and country furnishings, leading through to a cracking bar and classy conservatory extension. First-class pub food ranges from simple bar snacks like mushrooms on toast with watercress salad to pressed wild rabbit terrine; potted

*continued*

**SWINBROOK** *continued*

Cornish crab; brill with tomato, haricot bean, chorizo and clam stew; roast haunch of roe deer with tarragon jus; and apple tarte Tatin with toffee apple ice cream. You won't want to leave, so book one of the stunning en suite rooms in the newly restored barn and enjoy a riverside walk into Burford.

**Open** all wk open all day Sat-Sun (spring/summer/autumn) Closed: 25 Dec **Bar Meals** L served all wk 12-2 booking required D served all wk 7-9 booking required Av main course £14 **Restaurant** L served all wk 12-2 booking required D served all wk 7-9 booking required ⊕ FREE HOUSE ◀ Hook Norton, Wadworths, Cottage, Stroud, Vale Brewery ♨ Stowford Press, Westons Organic. **Facilities** Children's portions Dogs allowed Garden Parking **Rooms** 6

---

### SYDENHAM
Map 5 SP70

#### PICK OF THE PUBS

### The Crown Inn

Sydenham Rd OX39 4NB ☎ 01844 351634
*dir: M40 junct 6 take B4009 towards Chinnor. Left onto A40. At Postcombe turn right to Sydenham*

In a small village below the scarp slopes of the Chilterns, this pretty 16th-century inn shows how careful refurbishment can successfully incorporate both traditional and modern styles. Old photographs, for example, hang contentedly alongside contemporary paintings. The menu is short – barely a dozen items are featured – but expect good things of those that are, such as main courses of slow-roasted Moroccan spiced lamb shank with baked potato mash; barbecued Jack Daniel's-glazed rack of pork ribs; grilled Cornish sea bass fillet with king prawn, ginger, chilli and spring onion salsa; and spinach and wild mushroom risotto. In the bar, a pint of Brakspear would go well with a ploughman's, omelette, baguette or pizza. Treasure Hunts starting and finishing at The Crown take you through some of the prettiest villages in this part of Oxfordshire.

**Open** 12-3 5.30-11 (Sat noon-11 Sun noon-3) Closed: 1 wk Jan, 1 wk Aug, Sun eve, Mon **Bar Meals** L served Tue-Sun 12-2.30 D served Tue-Sat 7-9.30 **Restaurant** L served Tue-Sun 12-2.30 D served Tue-Sat 7-9.30 ⊕ THE SYDENHAM PUB CO ◀ Brakspear, London Pride, Guinness, guest ale ♨ Stowford Press. **Facilities** Children's portions Dogs allowed Garden

---

### TADMARTON
Map 11 SP33

### The Lampet Arms ★★★ GA

Main St OX15 5TB ☎ 01295 780070 📄 01295 788066
*dir: Take B4035 from Banbury to Tadmarton, 5m*

A Victorian-style free house offering well-kept ales, ciders and hearty home cooking. Located between Banbury and Shipston-on-Stour, the pub is named after Captain Lampet, the local landowner who built it; he mistakenly believed he could persuade the council to have the

railway line redirected through the village, thereby increasing trade. Typical menu choices include steaks; chicken Kiev; steak and ale pie; chilli con carne; sandwiches and baguettes. Four spacious, thoughtfully equipped bedrooms are in a converted coach house.

**Open** all day all wk **Bar Meals** D served all wk 7-9 Av main course £7.50 **Restaurant** D served all wk 7-9 ⊕ FREE HOUSE ◀ Hook Norton, Theakstons, Guinness, John Smith's. **Facilities** Children's menu Children's portions Dogs allowed Garden Parking **Rooms** 4

---

### TETSWORTH
Map 5 SP60

### The Old Red Lion ♥

40 High St OX9 7AS ☎ 01844 281274
*dir: Oxford Service area, turn right onto A40. At T-junct turn left then right onto A40 signed Stokenchurch, via Milton Common to Tetsworth*

This pink-washed pub, now under new ownership, is right on the village green, which conveniently has a large enclosed children's play area. In the bar real ales change seasonally and food can be enjoyed in Nemards restaurant behind the bar, or in the quieter Library. Dishes might be beef and ale pie; liver, onions and bacon; jumbo cod and chips; sticky toffee pudding; banana and toffee sponge; and home-made fruit crumble. There is also a Sunday carvery with three meats to choose from.

**Open** all wk 12-3 5.30-11 **Bar Meals** L served all wk 12-2.30 D served all wk 6-9 Av main course £6.99 **Restaurant** L served all wk 12-2.30 D served all wk 6-9 ⊕ FREE HOUSE ♥ 8 **Facilities** Children's portions Dogs allowed Garden Parking

---

### TOOT BALDON
Map 5 SP50

#### PICK OF THE PUBS

### The Mole Inn ◉◉ ♥

OX44 9NG ☎ 01865 340001 📄 01865 343011
e-mail: info@themoleinn.com
*dir: 5m SE from Oxford city centre off B480*

Just five miles from the city of Oxford, this stone-built, Grade II-listed country pub has been extensively renovated and its reputation continues to grow, due in no small measure to the efforts of award-winning chef/host Gary Witchalls and wife Jenny. Inside, a great deal of care and attention has been lavished on this classic old local, and now customers can relax in black leather sofas amid stripped beams and solid white walls. The dining areas are equally impressive with their intimate lighting and terracotta floors. Gary's menu changes frequently and draws plenty of foodies from nearby Oxford and further afield, tempted by dishes such as open beef Wellington with crispy shallots and horseradish creamed potatoes; tiger prawn and baby squid Thai red curry; and seared sea bass with lightly curried pine nuts, raisin and lentil dressing, spinach and potato mousseline.

**Open** all day all wk 12-12 (Sun 12-11) Closed: 25 Dec **Restaurant** L served Mon-Sat 12-2.30, Sun 12-4 booking required D served Mon-Sat 7-9.30, Sun 6-9 booking required ⊕ FREE HOUSE ◀ Hook Norton, London Pride, Spitfire, Guinness. ♥ 11 **Facilities** Children's portions Garden Parking

---

### WANTAGE
Map 5 SU38

### The Hare

Reading Rd, West Hendred OX12 8RH
☎ 01235 833249 📄 01235 833268
*dir: At West Hendred on A417 between Wantage & Didcot*

A late 19th-century inn mid-way between Wantage and Didcot, modernised in the 1930s by local brewers, Morland. The building's exterior features a colonial-style veranda and colonnade, while inside are original wood floors, beams and an open fire. Steaks, the house speciality, can be cut to any size to order. Jackets, baguettes, sandwiches and salads at lunchtime are superseded by more adventurous fare in the evening – the fish mixed grill, for example, includes marlin and barramundi.

**Open** all day all wk **Bar Meals** L served all wk 12-2 served all wk 6-9.30 Av main course £8.95 **Restaurant** L served all wk 12-2 D served all wk 6-9.30 Av 3 course à la carte fr £20 ⊕ GREENE KING ◀ Morland Original, guest ales ♨ Stowford Press, St Heliers. **Facilities** Children's portions Dogs allowed Garden Parking

---

### WHEATLEY
Map 5 SP50

### Bat & Ball Inn

28 High St OX44 9HJ
☎ 01865 874379 📄 01865 873363
e-mail: info@batball.co.uk
*dir: Through Wheatley towards Garsington, turn left signed Cuddesdon*

No surprise that the bar here is packed to the gunnels with cricketing memorabilia, but the charm of this former coaching inn extends to beamed ceilings, flagstone floors and solid wood furniture warmed by an open log fire. The house ale 'LBW' is flanked by interesting and well-kept guests. A comprehensive menu, supplemented by daily specials, is likely to include the Bat burger, home made from fresh steak and with a choice of toppings; and slow-braised shoulder of lamb. Look out for clay pigeon shoots, pig roasts, steak nights and sausage and mash evenings. The pub is in an ideal spot for walkers.

**Open** all day all wk **Bar Meals** L served Mon-Fri 12-2.15, Sat-Sun all day booking required D served Mon-Fri 6-9.30, Sat-Sun all day booking required Av main course £10 **Restaurant** L served Mon-Fri 12-2.30, Sat-Sun all day booking required D served Mon-Fri 6-9.30, Sat-Sun all day booking required Av 3 course à la carte fr £20 ⊕ MARSTONS ◀ Marston's Pedigree, House LBW Bitter, Guinness ♨ Thatchers Gold. **Facilities** Children's menu Children's portions Dogs allowed Garden Parking

# PICK OF THE PUBS

## The George & Dragon ♟

**SHUTFORD**      Map 11 SP34

**Church Ln OX15 6PG ☎ 01295 780320**
**web:** www.thegeorgeanddragon.com
**dir:** *Take A422 from Banbury. After 4m turn*
*left at sign for Shutford, follow directly to*
*pub*

This pretty Cotswold stone country pub,
dating back to the 13th century, is
conveniently located at the start of the
popular Shutford Walk. It is a favourite
rest stop for ramblers who congregate in
the beer garden overlooking the
picturesque village. Legend has it that
several ghosts haunt the pub, and that
a secret tunnel links it to the manor
house.

The bar (where dogs are welcome, and
where in winter the locals play dominoes
by the roaring fire) is probably unique in
that it's actually twelve feet
underground; the pub is built into the
side of a hill, with the village church
directly above. That's surely something
to think about while ordering one of the
five real ales, or a refreshing glass of
wine.

Everything on the seasonal menus,
except for the locally baked bread, is
made from scratch; villagers bring in
game and vegetables from their
allotments. Look to the specials list first
to find a pan-fried fillet of sea bass with
sautéed fennel; or roasted breast and
confit leg of locally-shot duck with
wilted spinach. The à la carte menu will
tempt with seared calves' liver with
roast parsnip purée; guinea fowl terrine
with spiced apple and cider chutney;
and free-range chicken and thyme
hotpot. To finish, the treacle tart or dark
chocolate mousse cannot be resisted. If
you just want a bar snack before
heading off round the ancient tracks of
the Shutford Walk, try a soft bap stuffed
with double Gloucester and pickle or the
pie of the week with mash.

Alternatively, forget the walk and time
your visit for a Sunday – you'll be
choosing from the likes of breast of
Shutford pheasant sautéed with
chestnuts and rocket; roast rib of
Oxfordshire beef with roast potatoes and
mixed vegetables; and spiced apple and
raspberry crumble.

**Open** 12-2.30 5.30-11 (Sat noon-11 Sun
noon-10.30) Closed: Mon (ex BH)
**Bar Meals** L served Tue-Sat 12-2, Sun
12-2.30 D served Tue-Sat 6.30-9 Av
main course £8 **Restaurant** L served
Tue-Sat 12-2, Sun 12-2.30 D served
Tue-Sat 6.30-9 Fixed menu price fr £11
Av 3 course à la carte fr £22 ⊕ FREE
HOUSE ◼ Hooky Bitter, London Pride,
Old Peculier, Pedigree, Bombardier. ♟ 8
**Facilities** Dogs allowed Garden

# PICK OF THE PUBS

## Crooked Billet ♀

**STOKE ROW**        Map 5 SU68

**RG9 5PU**
☎ **01491 681048**   📄 **01491 682231**
web: www.thecrookedbillet.co.uk
dir: *From Henley towards Oxford on A4130.
Left at Nettlebed for Stoke Row*

Dating from 1642, this charmingly rustic pub was once the haunt of highwayman Dick Turpin who, when forced to hide here from local law enforcers, whiled away the hours by courting the landlord's daughter, Bess. Tucked away down a single track lane in deepest Oxfordshire, the pub is now a popular hideaway for the well-heeled and the well known. Many of its finest features are unchanged, including the low beams, tiled floors and open fires that are so integral to its character. Famous customers, several of whom were introduced to the pub by the late

George Harrison, have included Kate Winslet, who famously held her first wedding reception here, *Eastenders* cast members, and Jeremy Paxman.

Menus are the work of award-winning chef/proprietor Paul Clerehugh. Local produce and organic fare are the mainstays of his kitchen, to the extent that he will even exchange a lunch or dinner for the locals' excess vegetables. A typical set lunch menu might start with chunky oxtail broth, followed by pan-fried sea bass, with a dessert such as Bakewell tart and custard or rich dark Belgian chocolate mousse. A la carte offerings include starters like crispy fried wild mushroom risotto cakes; and rabbit, smoked bacon and green peppercorn terrine. To follow, there's a good range of fish mains, including wild Anglesey bass fillet with garlic potato fondant, or sauté halibut with caramelised shallot. Other alternatives include slow-roast belly of Old Spot pork with crackling and roast Bramley; and spinach, ricotta and mild chilli filo parcel.

The pub hosts music nights, free wine tastings and other events, and also contributes some of its profit to the daily meals that it provides for a local primary school.

**Open** all wk noon-3 7-mdnt (Sat-Sun noon-mdnt) **Bar Meals** L served Mon-Fri 12-3, Sat-Sun all day booking required D served Mon-Fri 7-10, Sat-Sun all day booking required **Restaurant** L served Mon-Fri 12-3, Sat-Sun all day booking required D served Mon-Fri 7-10, Sat-Sun all day booking required Fixed menu price fr £13.95 ⊕ BRAKSPEAR ◼ Brakspear Bitter. ♀ 10 **Facilities** Garden Parking

## WITNEY — Map 5 SP31

### The Bell Inn

Standlake Rd, Ducklington OX29 7UP
☎ 01993 702514  📠 01993 706822
e-mail: danny@dpatching4.wanadoo.co.uk
dir: 1m S of Witney in Ducklington, off A415 (Abingdon Road)

Nearly 700 years have passed since the men building the adjacent church also erected their own living accommodation. Their hostel eventually became the Bell, and much extended over the years, it even embraces William Shepheard's former brewery, which closed in 1886. Today it is a popular, traditional village local, with many original features - and a collection of some 500 bells. Home-made pies, stews and burgers are a speciality.

Open all wk Closed: 25-26 Dec & 1 Jan ◀ Greene King, IPA & Old Speckled Hen, Morland Original, Guinness. Facilities Play area Garden Parking

### The Three Horseshoes ♥

78 Corn St OX28 6BS ☎ 01993 703086
e-mail: thehorseshoeswitney@hotmail.co.uk
web: www.horseshoeswitney.co.uk
dir: From Oxford on A40 towards Cheltenham take 2nd turn to Witney. At rdbt take 5th exit to Witney. Over flyover, through lights. At next rdbt take 5th exit into Corn St. Pub on left

This traditional family-run pub sits on Witney's original main street. Built of Cotswold stone, the historic Grade II listed building has a charming interior with stone walls, low ceilings, wood and flagstone floors, and blazing log fires in winter. Dishes include native fish stew and saffron potatoes; goat's cheese risotto with slow roasted tomato and herb oil; and Scotch beef bourguignon, horseradish mash and parsnip crisps. There's a steak night every Tuesday, plus all-day half price champagne and real ale on Thursdays (5-9pm).

Open all day all wk 11am-12.30am Bar Meals L served all wk 12-3 D served all wk 6-10 Av main course £12 Restaurant L served all wk 12-3 D served all wk 6-10 Fixed menu price fr £12 Av 3 course à la carte fr £14 ⊕ ADMIRAL TAVERNS ◀ White Horse, Ringwood Fortyniner, Wychwood Hobgoblin, Brakspears Bitter, Hook Norton ◌ Wychwood Green Goblin, Westons Stowford Press. ♥ 10 Facilities Children's portions Dogs allowed Garden

## WOODSTOCK — Map 11 SP41

### The King's Head ♥ NEW

11 Park Ln OX20 1UD ☎ 01993 812164
e-mail: mail@kingsheadwoodstock.co.uk
dir: Off A44, between Oxford & Chipping Norton. Turn left at pharmacy onto Park Lane

Close to the World Heritage Site of Blenheim Palace, this pub dates from 1801. To the front its cosy bar with original stone walls and open fireplace stocks at least two Oxfordshire ales; to the rear are a large dining room and attractive courtyard. Well-known locally for being a 'spud pub', it celebrates the best of British food by using as much local produce as possible. The ploughman's features Oxford Blue, while main dishes may include honey-roast Callow Farm ham with double egg and chips.

Open all day all wk Bar Meals booking required Av main course £9 food served all day Restaurant booking required Av 3 course à la carte fr £18 food served all day ⊕ PUNCH TAVERNS ◀ Brakspear, Hobgoblin, Hook Norton. ♥ 14 Facilities Children's menu Children's portions Dogs allowed Garden

## WOOLSTONE — Map 5 SU28

### The White Horse

SN7 7QL ☎ 01367 820726  📠 01367 820566
e-mail: whitehorseinnwoolstone@gmail.com
dir: Off A420 at Watchfield onto B4508 towards Longcot signed Woolstone

Unusual windows add to the appeal of this black-and-white-timbered, thatched, Elizabethan village pub. Upholstered stools line the traditional bar, where a fireplace conceals two priest holes, visible to those who don't mind getting their knees dirty. Lunchtime bar snacks include fajitas, burgers and fish and chips. An extensive menu of freshly prepared English and international dishes in the oak-beamed restaurant includes steak and ale pie, curries, steaks, fish pie and mushroom stroganoff.

Open Mon-Sun Closed: Sun eve ◀ Arkells, Guinness ◌ Stowford Press. Facilities Dogs allowed Garden Parking

## WYTHAM — Map 5 SP40

### PICK OF THE PUBS

### White Hart ♥

OX2 8QA ☎ 01865 244372
e-mail: whitehartwytham@btconnect.com
dir: Just off A34 NW of Oxford

In a sleepy hamlet west of Oxford, this Cotswold stone pub was featured in the Inspector Morse TV series. The pub is more smart gastro-pub than traditional village local, the bold interior blending flagged floors and big stone fireplaces with a contemporary, Mediterranean style. You can pop in for a pint of Hooky but this is predominantly a place to eat, and there's an extensive wine list. The eggs, chicken, pork and bacon are sourced from a farm less than a mile away, and all the meat is either free range or organic. The modern menu is supplemented by daily specials listing fresh fish and game dishes in season. In summer, dine alfresco on the Mediterranean-style terrace. Recent change of hands.

Open all wk Mon-Fri 12-4 6-11 (Sat-Sun noon-11) Bar Meals L served Mon-Sun 12-4 D served Mon-Fri 6-10, Sat-Sun 6-11 Restaurant L served Mon-Sun 12-4 D served Mon-Fri 6-10, Sat-Sun 6-11 ⊕ MITCHELL'S & BUTLER ◀ Hook Norton, Timothy Taylor Landlord. ♥ 15 Facilities Children's menu Garden Parking

## RUTLAND

## BARROWDEN — Map 11 SK90

### PICK OF THE PUBS

### Exeter Arms ♥

LE15 8EQ ☎ 01572 747247  📠 01572 747247
e-mail: enquiries@exeterarmrutland.co.uk
dir: From A47 turn at landmark windmill, village 0.75m S. 6m E of Uppingham & 17m W of Peterborough

This 17th-century pub-restaurant overlooks the green and duck pond in this pretty stone village not far from Rutland Water. With a half-acre garden for lazy summer days, it's a perfect country pub but it has been many other things in its long life, including a smithy, a dairy and a postal collection point. Ales brewed by the landlord in the barn next door rejoice in names such as Beech, Bevin, Hopgear, Owngear and Attitude Two. Lunchtime sandwiches may include hot sirloin beef, or open bacon with brie; for a larger affair, choose between the likes of smoked haddock with soft poached egg and spring onion mash; and Barrowden steak and ale puff pastry pie with hand-cut chips. Typical dinner menu choices could be filo basket filled with black pudding, Stilton and onion marmalade; and roast belly pork with roast roots, crackling and Bramley apple compôte.

Open 12-2.30 6-11 Closed: Sun eve, Mon L Bar Meals L served Tue-Sat 12-2 Av main course £11 Restaurant L served Sun 12-2 D served Tue-Sat 6.30-9 ⊕ FREE HOUSE ◀ Beech, Bevin, Owngear, Hopgear, Attitude Two. ♥ 10 Facilities Dogs allowed Garden Parking

---

## PICK OF THE PUBS

### The Olive Branch ★★★★ INN ⊛⊛ ⬤

**Main St LE15 7SH**
☎ 01780 410355   📠 01780 410000
e-mail: info@theolivebranchpub.com
dir: *2m off A1 at B664 junct, N of Stamford*

Saved from closing well before the continuing
decimation of Britain's pubs began in earnest, The
Olive Branch shows what can be done with careful
thought and determined effort. Outside, an attractive
front garden and terrace; inside, a beautifully
refurbished interior with bookshelves and an eclectic
mix of antique and pine furniture. The bar serves local
ales including Grainstore 1050, Olive Oil and Fenland,
and Sheppy's real cider. From the two-AA Rosette
kitchen come classics like Lincolnshire sausage, mash
and onion gravy, and fish pie with seasonal vegetables,
holding their own alongside jellied eel terrine (from a
winter menu); loin of swordfish, chorizo gnocchi,
Mediterranean vegetables tomato coulis; braised
shoulder of lamb, rosemary and cannellini bean
cassoulet; and vegetarian choices such as twice baked
cheese soufflé and walnut salad, wild mushroom and
white truffle conchiglie pasta. To follow: poached pear
millefeuille and pear sorbet; and chocolate fondant,
pistachio ice cream. Check out the good selection of
wines and interesting list of suggested beers with food.
Accommodation is available across the road at Beech
House.

**Open** all wk noon-3.30 6-11 (Fri-Sun noon-11) Closed:
25 Dec eve **Bar Meals** L served Mon-Fri 12-2, Sat 12-2
2.30-5.30, Sun 12-3 D served all wk 7-9.30 Av main
course £16.50 **Restaurant** L served Mon-Sat 12-2, Sun
12-3 booking required D served Mon-Sat 7-9.30, Sun
7-9 booking required Fixed menu price fr £20.50 Av 3
course à la carte fr £30 ⊕ RUTLAND INN COMPANY LTD
◀ Grainstore 1050 & Olive Oil, Fenland, Brewster's,
VPA, Ö Sheppy's Dabinett Apple, Oakwood Special.
⬤ 10 **Facilities** Children's menu Children's portions
Dogs allowed Garden Parking **Rooms** 6

---

### The White Horse Inn ★★★ INN ⬤

**Main St LE15 8PS** ☎ 01780 460221   📠 01780 460521
e-mail: info@whitehorserutland.co.uk
web: www.whitehorserutland.co.uk
dir: *From A1 take A606 signed Oakham & Rutland Water.
From Oakham take A606 to Stamford*

An ideal place to recharge your batteries following a walk
or cycle around Rutland Water, this former 17th-century
courthouse has lost none of its period charm. The open
fire, beamed bar and friendly staff are a recipe for total
relaxation. The home-made food starts with sandwiches,
home-made soup and baguettes and runs to hearty meals
such as leek and pumpkin soup followed by cajun spiced
chicken with sauté sweet peppers and soy, or whole
baked sea bass with parsley and lemon butter. Bedrooms
are available.

---

*The White Horse Inn*

**Open** all day all wk Closed: 25 Dec **Bar Meals** L served all
wk 12-9 D served all wk 12-9 Av main course £9.50 food
served all day **Restaurant** L served all wk 12-9 D served
all wk 12-9 Av 3 course à la carte fr £18 food served all
day ⊕ ENTERPRISE INNS ◀ John Smith's, Adnams Best
Bitter, Oakham Ales JHB, Timothy Taylor Landlord, Black
Sheep Bitter. ⬤ 10 **Facilities** Children's menu Children's
portions Dogs allowed Garden Parking **Rooms** 13

---

## PICK OF THE PUBS

### Fox & Hounds ⬤

**19, The Green LE15 8AP** ☎ 01572 812403
e-mail: sandra@foxandhoundsrutland.co.uk
dir: *Take A606 from Oakham towards Stamford, at
Barnsdale turn left, after 1.5m turn right towards
Exton. Pub in village centre*

A big and beautiful walled garden makes this former
coaching inn a perfect spot for a sunny day. The
imposing 17th-century building stands opposite the
green in the centre of Exton, a charming village with
countless stone and thatched cottages. The pub has a
reputation for good food and hospitality, and is an
ideal stopping-off point for those exploring the many
good walks in the surrounding area. Its menu is the
work of Italian chef/proprietor Valter Floris and his
team, and combines the best of traditional English and
Italian cuisine. In the evenings, there is an impressive
list of authentic, thin-crust pizzas. The main menu
features wood pigeon breast and red onion marmalade;
fillet of beef topped with Stilton and red wine sauce;
and fillet of sea bass with chargrilled vegetables. Good
beers include Oakham's Ales.

**Open** 11-3 6-11 Closed: Mon ex BH **Bar Meals** L served
all wk 12-2 D served Tue-Sat 6-9 Av main course £13
**Restaurant** L served all wk 12-2 D served Tue-Sat 6-9
⊕ FREE HOUSE ◀ Greene King IPA, Oakham ales,
Timothy Taylor Landlord, Grainstore 1050, Ö St Helier
Pear, Aspall. ⬤ 10 **Facilities** Children's menu
Children's portions Family room Dogs allowed Garden
Parking

---

### The Old Pheasant ⬤

**Main Rd LE15 9BP** ☎ 01572 822326   📠 01572 823316
e-mail: info@theoldpheasant.co.uk
dir: *On A47 between Leicester & Peterborough. Just
outside Uppingham*

The stuffed head of a wild boar presides over the bar of
this picture-perfect inn, which also features a smart
stone-walled restaurant complete with evocative relics o
farming history. Menus are constructed around quality
produce, locally sourced where possible. Seasonal game
from shoots is regularly featured, alongside trout from
nearby rivers. Try home-cured gravadlax, honey glazed
duck breast, and chocolate marquise, or an excellent
range of cheeses.

**Open** all wk Closed: 2-7 Jan ◀ Pheasant Ale, Timothy
Taylor Landlord, Fuller's London Pride, Everards Original,
Greene King Abbot Ale. ⬤ 8 **Facilities** Garden Parking

---

### Old White Hart ★★★★ INN ⬤

**51 Main St LE15 9LR**
☎ 01572 821703   📠 01572 821978
e-mail: mail@oldwhitehart.co.uk
dir: *From A6003 between Uppingham & Corby take B672
Pub on main street opp village green*

The honey-coloured sandstone cottages of rural
Lyddington surround this 17th-century free house
opposite the village green. It has retained its original
beamed ceilings, stone walls and open fires, and is
surrounded by well-stocked gardens. Aspall's cider sits
alongside a good choice of ales in the bar, while the
menu offers interesting, freshly prepared food – dishes
such as individual partridge and silverskin onion suet
pudding set this pub's food apart. Ten individually
decorated en suite bedrooms, with home-made sausages
for breakfast, complete the package.

**Open** all wk 12-3 6.30-11 (Sun 12-3 7-10.30) Closed: 25
Dec, 26 Dec eve **Bar Meals** L served Mon-Sat 12-2, Sun
12-2.30 booking required D served all wk 6.30-9 (Sun in
summer 7-9) booking required Av main course £12
**Restaurant** L served Mon-Sat 12-2, Sun 12-2.30 booking
required D served all wk 6.30-9 (Sun in summer 7-9)
booking required Fixed menu price fr £10.95 Av 3 course
à la carte fr £25 ⊕ FREE HOUSE ◀ Greene King IPA &
Abbot Ale, Timothy Taylor Landlord, Fuller's London Pride,
Timothy Taylor Golden Best Ö Aspall Suffolk Cider. ⬤ 10
**Facilities** Children's portions Play area Garden Parking
**Rooms** 10

---

## OAKHAM     Map 11 SK80

# Barnsdale Lodge Hotel ★★★ HL ⊛ ☼

**The Avenue, Rutland Water, North Shore LE15 8AH**
☎ 01572 724678 📄 01572 724961
e-mail: enquiries@barnsdalelodge.co.uk
dir: *A1 onto A606. Hotel 5m on right, 2m E of Oakham*

This former farmhouse has been in the proprietor's family since 1760 and is part of the adjoining Exton Estate. It overlooks Rutland Water in the heart of this picturesque little county. There's a cosy bar with comfortable chairs and a courtyard with outdoor seating. The bistro-style menu draws on local produce and offers dishes such as tiger prawns with Caesar salad followed by seared spring lamb rump with chorizo, new potatoes and pea and mint jus. Accommodation comprises 44 stylish en suite rooms.

**Open** all day all wk **Bar Meals** food served all day **Restaurant** L served 12-2.15 D served 7-9.30 ⊕ FREE HOUSE ◀ Rutland Grainstore, Tetley, Guinness. ☼ 15 **Facilities** Children's menu Children's portions Play area Dogs allowed Garden Parking **Rooms** 44

# The Grainstore Brewery

**Station Approach LE15 6RE**
☎ 01572 770065 📄 01572 770068
e-mail: grainstorebrewery.com
dir: *Next to Oakham rail station*

Founded in 1995, Davis's Brewing Company is housed in the three-storey Victorian grain store next to Oakham railway station. Finest quality hops and ingredients are used to make the beers that can be sampled in the pub's Tap Room. Food is wholesome and straightforward, with the ales playing an important part in recipes for steamed fresh mussels; Cheddar and ale soup; Quenby Hall Stilton and Rutland Panther pâté; and beef and Panther stew. A full diary of events includes live music and the annual August Bank Holiday beer festival.

**Open** all day all wk 11am-1am **Bar Meals** L served all wk 11-3 ⊕ FREE HOUSE ◀ Rutlands Panther, Triple B, Ten Fifty, Silly Billy, Rutland Beast, Nip, seasonal beers Ŏ Sheppy's. **Facilities** Dogs allowed Garden Parking

## SOUTH LUFFENHAM     Map 11 SK90

# The Coach House Inn

**3 Stamford Rd LE15 8NT**
☎ 01780 720166 📄 01780 720866
e-mail: thecoachhouse123@aol.com
dir: *On A6121, off A47 between Morcroft & Stamford*

Horses were once stabled here while weary travellers enjoyed a drink in what is now a private house next door. Now elegantly refurbished, it offers a comfortable 40-cover dining room and a cosy bar. A short, appealing menu in the Ostler's Restaurant might feature goat's cheese, poached pear and walnut tart, followed by fillet of beef with chicken liver pâté and rösti potatoes.

**Open** noon-2 5-11 (Sat all day) Closed: 25 Dec, 1 Jan, Sun eve, Mon morning **Bar Meals** L served Tue-Sat 12-2 booking required D served Mon-Sat 6.30-9 booking required Av main course £8 **Restaurant** L served Tue-Sun 12-2 booking required D served Mon-Sat 6.30-9 booking required Fixed menu price fr £12 Av 3 course à la carte fr £25 ⊕ FREE HOUSE ◀ IPA, Adnams, Timothy Taylor Landlord, Guinness Ŏ Aspall. **Facilities** Children's portions Dogs allowed Garden Parking

## STRETTON     Map 11 SK91

## PICK OF THE PUBS

# The Jackson Stops Inn

**Rookery Rd LE15 7RA** ☎ 01780 410237
dir: *1m off A1 (pass Little Chef). Follow Stretton sign at B668 for Oakham*

For those keen on tracking down uniquely named pubs, this is a winner. You can guarantee nowhere else will have acquired its name by virtue of an estate agent sign that once hung outside for so long that locals dispensed with the original moniker of The White Horse Inn! The long, low, stone-built partly thatched building actually dates from 1721, and has plenty of appealing features: stone fireplaces with log fires, exposed stone and quarry tiled floors, scrubbed wood tables and no fewer than four intimate dining rooms. In the timeless, black-beamed snug bar, you can order a pint of Adnams Bitter and play a rare pub game using old pennies – the traditional 'nurdling bench' is one of just two left in the country. For a snack, order a baguette or panini and create your own filling from interesting and mind-boggling list of 30 ingredients. For something more substantial, look to the main menu and specials board.

**Open** Tue-Sun L Closed: Sun eve, Mon ◀ Oakham Ales JHB, Aldershaws Old Boy, Adnams Broadside, Timothy Taylor Landlord, Hop Back Summer Lightning. **Facilities** Dogs allowed Garden Parking

# Ram Jam Inn

**The Great North Rd LE15 7QX**
☎ 01780 410776 📄 01780 410361
dir: *On A1 N'bound carriageway past B668, through service station into car park*

The inn was originally a humble ale house called the Winchelsea Arms, and belonged to the Earl of that title who lived nearby. It is thought that its current name stems from a home-brew invented by a resident publican during the 18th century, when the pub sign advertised 'Fine Ram Jam'. Sadly no recipe survives, so its ingredients remain a mystery. Today's informal café-bar and bistro, with a patio overlooking orchard and paddock, welcomes visitors with its comprehensive daily-changing menu.

**Open** all day all wk 7.30am-10pm (Sun 8.30am-6pm) Closed: 25 Dec ◀ John Smith's Smooth, Fuller's London Pride. **Facilities** Play area Garden Parking

## WING     Map 11 SK80

## PICK OF THE PUBS

# Kings Arms ★★★★ INN ⊛⊛ ☼

**Top St LE15 8SE** ☎ 01572 737634 📄 01572 737255
e-mail: info@thekingsarms-wing.co.uk
dir: *1m off B6003 between Uppingham & Oakham*

Dating from 1649, this attractive free house is run by David and Gisa Goss, whilst their son James looks after the kitchen. The bar, with its flagstone floors, low beamed ceilings, nooks, crannies and two open fires is the oldest part of the building, and offers a wide selection of traditional cask ales and guest beers. Popular bar meals and lunchtime sandwiches are supplemented by an à la carte menu and daily specials. A selection from the two-Rosetted main menu might begin with cold smoked Rutland trout, followed by a cannon of Melton lamb with crisp sweetbreads and fondant potatoes. Finish, perhaps, with lime and ginger Catalan crème brûlée. Eight spacious en suite letting rooms are set away from the pub with their own private entrance, and guests are welcome to use the large car park for light boats and motorised campers.

**Closed:** Sun eve, Mon, Tue L (Oct-Mar); Sun eve, Mon L (Apr-Sep) **Bar Meals** L served Tue-Sun 12-2.30 booking required D served Tue-Sat 6.30-8.30 booking required Av main course £9 **Restaurant** L served Tue-Sun 12-2.30 booking required D served Mon-Sat 6.30-8.30 booking required Av 3 course à la carte fr £25 ⊕ FREE HOUSE ◀ Shepherd Neame Spitfire, Grainstore Cooking, Bass Ŏ Sheppey's. ☼ 20 **Facilities** Children's portions Garden Parking **Rooms** 8

## SHROPSHIRE

### ADMASTON                                    Map 10 SJ61

## The Pheasant Inn at Admaston ♥

**TF5 0AD ☎ 01952 251989**
**e-mail:** info@thepheasantadmaston.co.uk
**web:** www.thepheasantadmaston.co.uk
**dir:** M54 junct 6 follow A5223 towards Whitchurch then
follow B5063 towards Shawbirch & Admaston. Pub is on
left of main rd

Once owned by the Great Western Railway, this lovely old
country pub dates from the 19th century and is renowned
for it well kept beers. Stylish interior decor and a real fire
add character to the dining areas, whilst the large
enclosed garden is ideal for families. Using the best of
local produce, expect pan-seared lambs' liver with crispy
bacon and home-grown sage and red wine gravy; roast
sea bass with prawn and cucumber butter; and broccoli,
leek and field mushroom pie. There is also a very good
'Little People's' menu.

**Open** all day all wk **Bar Meals** L served Mon-Sat 12-2,
Sun 12-7 booking required D served Mon-Fri 6-9, Sat all
day Av main course £10 ⊕ FREE HOUSE ◀ Shropshire
Gold, Greene King IPA, Shropshire Lad, Guinness. ♥ 10
**Facilities** Children's menu Children's portions Play area
Dogs allowed Garden Parking

### BASCHURCH                                   Map 15 SJ42

## The New Inn

**Church Rd SY4 2EF ☎ 01939 260335**
**e-mail:** bean.newinn@btconnect.com
**dir:** 8m from Shrewsbury, 8m from Oswestry

This stylishly modernised old whitewashed village pub
near the medieval church is a focal point for all things
Welsh Marches; with beers from nearby Oswestry's
Stonehouse brewery amongst five ales stocked, meats
from the village's Moor Farm or Shrewsbury's renowned
market, and cheeses from a Cheshire supplier. Chef-
patron Marcus and his team transform these into
tempting fare such as pan-fried pork tenderloin with
black pudding rösti, parsnip crisps and sage jus, or
home-cured salmon with beetroot and apple salsa.

**Open** all wk 11-3 6-11 (Sun 12-4 7-11) Closed: 26 Dec,
1 Jan **Bar Meals** L served all wk 12-2 D served all wk
6.30-9.30 **Restaurant** L served all wk 12-2 booking
required D served all wk 6.30-9.30 booking required
⊕ FREE HOUSE ◀ Greene King Abbot Ale, Banks Bitter,
Stonehouse Station, Hobsons Best Bitter ♂ Thatchers.
**Facilities** Children's portions Dogs allowed Garden
Parking

### BISHOP'S CASTLE                             Map 15 SO38

## PICK OF THE PUBS

## The Sun at Norbury ★★★★★ INN

**SY9 5DX ☎ 01588 650680**
**dir:** 10m from Church Stretton, 3m from Bishop's
Castle off A489

Time has stood still for centuries in this secret corner
of Shropshire. The Sun lies deep in the valley of the
Long Mynd, where you can discover the 'blue
remembered hills' that the poet A E Housman wrote
about in A Shropshire Lad. Enjoy a drink before dinner
in the delightful garden, then head indoors to the bar
with its wealth of unusual artefacts, the 18th-century
sitting room, or the elegant dining room. The chef/
proprietors Charles and Carol Cahan have established
a restaurant with a reputation for good, unpretentious
food produced from quality ingredients. Starters
include melon with grapes marinated in port wine;
followed by main course options like braised rainbow
trout with roasted almonds; roast Shropshire duck with
a rich morello cherry sauce; and fresh vegetable
roulade with béchamel sauce. This is glorious walking
and cycling countryside, so why not stay overnight in
one of the comfortable en suite guest rooms.

**Open** 7pm-11pm (Sun 12-3) Closed: Sun eve, Mon
**Bar Meals** L served Sat-Sun (summer) 12-2 D served
Tue-Sat 7-9 booking required Av main course £8
**Restaurant** L served Sun 12-2 booking required D
served Tue-Sat 7-9 booking required Fixed menu price
fr £15 Av 3 course à la carte fr £20 ◀ Wye Valley
Bitter, Woods Shropshire Lad ♂ Westons Stowford
Press. **Facilities** Children's portions Dogs allowed
Garden Parking **Rooms** 6

## The Three Tuns Inn ♥

**Salop St SY9 5BW ☎ 01588 638797**
**e-mail:** timce@talk21.com
**dir:** From Ludlow take A49 through Craven Arms, then left
onto A489 to Lydham, then A488 to Bishop's Castle

A traditional timber-framed town centre local established
in 1625, and a brewery since 1642. Today the wondrous
array of Three Tuns ales can be enjoyed more or less in
peace – there's no piped music or fruit machines, just
occasional live music or Morris dancing in the restored
function room. The public bar, snug bar and lounge bar
have been joined by a classy oak framed, glass sided
dining room. Menus seduce with spiced piri-piri chicken

salad; home-made pork and sage burger; and pecan and
bourbon tart.

**Open** all day all wk **Bar Meals** L served all wk 12-3 D
served all wk 7-9 Av main course £9.25 **Restaurant** L
served all wk 12-3 D served all wk 7-9 ⊕ FREE HOUSE
◀ Tuns XXX, Solstice, Scrooge, Clerics Cure, 1642. ♥ 12
**Facilities** Children's menu Children's portions Dogs
allowed Garden

### BRIDGNORTH                                  Map 10 SO79

## Halfway House Inn ★★★ INN ♥

**Cleobury Rd, Eardington WV16 5LS**
**☎ 01746 762670**  ▤ 01746 768063
**e-mail:** info@halfwayhouseinn.co.uk
**dir:** M54 junct 4, A442 to Bridgnorth. Or M5 junct 4, A491
towards Stourbridge. A458 to Bridgnorth. Follow tourist
signs on B4363

An original Elizabethan wall mural is a fascinating
feature of this former coaching inn, but the Halfway
House owes its current name to a visit in 1823 by
Princess Victoria and her entourage. (She was halfway
between Shrewsbury and Worcester.) The pub is renowned
for a good selection of real ales, 40 malts, around 100
wines, and locally sourced, home-cooked food. Dishes
range from bar snacks to braised beef in Guinness,
grilled local steaks and Astbury Falls rainbow trout. There
is plenty of accommodation available if you want to stay
over.

**Open** 5-11.30 (Fri & Sat 11am-11.30pm Sun 11-6)
Closed: Sun eve ex BH **Bar Meals** L served Fri-Sun 12-2 D
served Mon-Sat 6-9 Av main course £8.95 **Restaurant** D
served Mon-Sat 6-9 booking required Fixed menu price fr
£22.50 Av 3 course à la carte fr £19.95 ⊕ FREE HOUSE
◀ Holden's Golden Glow, Wood's Shropshire Lad,
Hobson's Town Crier, Draught Guinness ♂ Weston's
Stowford Export. ♥ 10 **Facilities** Children's menu
Children's portions Play area Garden Parking **Rooms** 10

## Pheasant Inn

**Linley Brook WV16 4TA ☎ 01746 762260**
**e-mail:** pheasant-inn@tiscali.co.uk
**dir:** From Bridgnorth take B4373 towards Broseley. At
junct of B4373 & Briton's Ln follow brown & white tourist
sign for pub. Pub in 400yds

Run by a husband and wife team for over 25 years, this is
a perfect, traditional country pub in a pretty location.
Birds in the garden and sheep in the adjacent fields
provide the soundtrack – piped music and gaming
machines have no place here. Open fires and wood
burners heat its two rooms, where locals play bar
billiards, dominoes and card games. Various small
breweries, usually local, furnish the two pumps, and
simple pub food is prepared by the landlord's wife: rump
steaks and gammon from a local butcher are popular, in
addition to home-made lasagne, curries, and at least one
vegetarian option. Local walks include one leading down
to the River Severn.

Open all wk 12-2 6.30-11 (12-3 Sat & Sun) **Bar Meals** L served all wk 12-2 D served all wk 7-9 Av main course £8 ⊞ FREE HOUSE ◀ Hobson Bitter, Hobson Town Crier, Wye Valley HPA, Salopian Shropshire Gold, Cannon Royall Arrowhead Ŏ Westons. **Facilities** Children's portions Garden Parking **Notes** ✆

---

| BURLTON | Map 15 SJ42 |

## PICK OF THE PUBS

### The Burlton Inn ★★★★ INN

SY4 5TB ☎ 01939 270284 ⊞
e-mail: enquiries@burltoninn.com
dir: *10m N of Shrewsbury on A528 towards Ellesmere*

Standing on the road between Shrewsbury and Ellesmere, this pretty old building has been transformed into a classy, contemporary interpretation of an 18th-century inn. There's a fresh looking dining area, a soft furnished space for relaxation, and a traditional bar - the perfect place to enjoy a pint of Robinson's Unicorn and other seasonal bitters. Behind the main building are en suite guest rooms and the newly-laid terrace, ideal for alfresco summer dining. Hosts Lindsay and Paul serve an appealing menu that begins with starters like tempura courgette flower with goat's cheese and soft herbs; and smoked ham hock soup with shiitake mushroom broth and a mirepoix of vegetables. Main course dishes such as spring pea risotto with toasted pine nuts, and roast gilt-head bream with steamed asparagus are representative choices. Home-made desserts include lychee and white peach parfait, and coffee crème brûlée.

**Open** all wk Mon-Sat noon-3 6-11 (Sun noon-5) Closed: 25 Dec **Bar Meals** L served Mon-Sat 12-2, Sun 12-3 D served Mon-Sat 6.30-9 Av main course £8.95 **Restaurant** L served Mon-Sat 12-2, Sun 12-3 booking required D served Mon-Sat 6.30-9 booking required Av 3 course à la carte fr £21 ● ROBINSONS ◀ Robinsons Unicorn, Cumbria Way, seasonal bitters Ŏ Stowford Press. **Facilities** Children's menu Children's portions Garden Parking **Rooms** 6

---

| BURWARTON | Map 10 SO68 |

## PICK OF THE PUBS

### The Boyne Arms ▾

Bridgnorth Rd WV16 6QH ☎ 01746 787214
e-mail: theboynearms@btconnect.com
dir: *On B4364 between Ludlow & Bridgnorth*

Set in the village of Burwarton amid idyllic Shropshire countryside, this Grade II listed Georgian former coaching inn is part of the Boyne estate, and has belonged to Lord Boyne's family for generations. It draws travellers and locals alike. A beautiful mature walled garden at the rear includes a children's playground, making it perfect for families. Four real ales plus a real cider are always on tap, and the wine list is extensive enough to suit most tastes and pockets. The stable bar with its wood burning stove and solid beams hosts games and functions, while the

tap room is the locals' favourite. The dining room is elegant with stiff white napery and attentive friendly service. Attractive plates of food, prepared by chef patron Jamie Yardley, combine fresh regional produce with classic French flavours. Expect dishes such as Burwarton trout en papillote followed by baked almond tart with cherry brandy ice cream; more simple fare such as steak and ale pie or ploughman's is also served.

*The Boyne Arms*

**Open** all wk all day (wknds only) **Bar Meals** L served Tue-Sat 12-2 D served Tue-Sat 6.30-9 Av main course £8 **Restaurant** L served Fri-Sun 12-2 D served Tue-Sat 6.30-9 Fixed menu price fr £13.95 Av 3 course à la carte fr £55 ⊞ FREE HOUSE ◀ Shropshire Lad, Bridgnorth Bitter, Town Crier, Queen Bee, Twisted Spire Ŏ Weston's Organic Scrumpy. ▾ 9 **Facilities** Children's menu Children's portions Play area Dogs allowed Garden Parking

---

| CHURCH STRETTON | Map 15 SO49 |

### The Bucks Head ★★★★ INN

42 High St SY6 6BX ☎ 01694 722898
e-mail: lnutting@btinternet.com
dir: *12m from Shrewsbury & Ludlow*

An original and listed part of this pub may have been built as a hunting lodge for the Marquis of Bath, and a tunnel is rumoured to run from the cellar under the beer garden. At the heart of the local community, the Bucks Head is known for its well kept Marston and guest ales, its steaks and specials board, and four nicely welcoming letting rooms. So bring your boots, ramble along the Long Mynd, and return to a sizzling rump steak and chips.

**Open** all day all wk **Bar Meals** L served all wk 12-2.30 D served all wk 6-9 **Restaurant** L served all wk 12-2.30 D served all wk 6-9 ● MARSTON'S PUB COMPANY ◀ Banks Original, Banks Bitter, Marston's Pedigree, Guinness, Guest Ale. **Facilities** Children's menu Children's portions Garden Parking **Rooms** 4

---

### The Royal Oak

Cardington SY6 7JZ
☎ 01694 771266 🖥 01694 771685
e-mail: inntoxicated@gmail.com
dir: *Turn right off A49 N of Church Stretton; 2m off B4371 (Church Stretton-Much Wenlock road)*

Said to be the oldest continuously licensed pub in the county, this 15th-century free house is set in a

conservation village surrounded by lovely countryside close to the South Shropshire hills. It has a low-beamed bar with a vast inglenook, and a comfortable beamed dining room. Four cask ales are served, along with home-cooked food. Typical specials may include rabbit in cider and bacon sauce; Moroccan lamb stew; and Thai cod and prawn fishcakes.

**Open** 12-2.30 (Sun 12-3.30) Tue-Wed 6.30-11 (Thu-Sat 6.30-mdnt Sun 7-mdnt) Closed: Mon (ex BH Mon L) **Bar Meals** L served Tue-Sat & BH Mon 12-2, Sun 12-2.30 D served Tue-Sat 6.30-9, Sun 7-9 **Restaurant** L served Tue-Sat & BH Mon 12-2, Sun 12-2.30 D served Tue-Sat 6.30-9, Sun 7-9 ⊞ FREE HOUSE ◀ Hobsons Best Bitter, Three Tuns XXX, Wye Valley Butty Bach, Bass, Six Bells 1859. **Facilities** Children's menu Garden Parking

---

| CLEOBURY MORTIMER | Map 10 SO67 |

## PICK OF THE PUBS

### The Crown Inn ★★★★ INN ▾

*See Pick of the Pubs on page 384*

---

| COCKSHUTT | Map 15 SJ42 |

### The Leaking Tap

Shrewsbury Rd SY12 0JQ
☎ 01939 270636 🖥 01939 270746
e-mail: lesley@theleakingtap.org
dir: *On A528 (Shrewsbury to Ellesmere road)*

Saved from closure in 2009 and now privately owned, this traditional old coaching inn is in the heart of beautiful Shropshire countryside on the road from Shrewsbury to Ellesmere. The Leaking Tap has a unique atmosphere and charm and features oak beams and log fires, along with a selection of ales and food cooked from local produce. Regularly changing lunchtime or evening menus are available and might include chicken breast wrapped in bacon in a brandy and Stilton sauce, or leek and parsnip cheese bake.

**Open** all wk 12-2 5.30-11.30 **Bar Meals** L served all wk 12-2 D served all wk 5.30-9.30 Av main course £5 **Restaurant** L served all wk 12-2 D served all wk 5.30-9.30 Fixed menu price fr £7.95 Av 3 course à la carte fr £18 ⊞ FREE HOUSE ◀ Worthington, Guest ales. **Facilities** Children's menu Children's portions Parking

---

| CRAVEN ARMS | Map 9 SO48 |

### The Sun Inn ▾

Corfton SY7 9DF ☎ 01584 861239
e-mail: normanspride@btconnect.com
dir: *On B4368, 7m N of Ludlow*

First licensed in 1613, this historic pub has a public bar with pool table, jukebox and dartboard, along with a lounge and restaurant. Landlord Norman Pearce brews the Corvedale ales in what was the pub's old chicken and lumber shed, using local borehole water; Mahoral cider, from just down the road, is another drinks option. Teresa Pearce uses local produce in a delicious array of

*continued on page 385*

# PICK OF THE PUBS

## The Crown Inn ★★★★ INN 🍷

**CLEOBURY MORTIMER** Map 10 SO67

**Hopton Wafers DY14 0NB**
**☎ 01299 270372 📠 01299 271127**
**e-mail:** desk@crownathopton.co.uk
**web:** www.crownathopton.co.uk
**dir:** *On A4117 8m E of Ludlow, 2m W of Cleobury Mortimer*

Virginia creeper covers the exterior of this 16th-century coaching inn so densely that your eyes have to search for the brickwork you know must be there. First time visitors to this part of Shropshire will avoid a verbal faux pas by knowing that Cleobury is pronounced Clibbery; the Mortimer bit comes from the great Norman family that established itself here in 1086.

The Crown has an enviable reputation for good food: whether traditional dish or adventurous house speciality, the ingredients are all sourced from regional producers and can all be experienced in each of the three eating areas: in the Shropshire Restaurant overlooking the countryside; in Poachers, with exposed beams, stonework and large inglenook fireplace; and in the Rent Room, just off the bar, which offers traditional pine kitchen style seating, daily menus, light bites and specials – ideal for walkers, cyclists and sightseers – and more of those rural views. The latter, by the way, was where local tenants paid their dues to the estate, which owned The Crown.

In Poachers, typical starters are grilled asparagus wrapped in Parma ham with mixed cress, rocket and hollandaise sauce; and salad of feta cheese, black olives, roasted bell peppers, herbs and balsamic dressing. Main courses include fillet of beef on beetroot risotto with a port reduction; leg of lamb steak with braised red cabbage and red wine sauce; and, as a special, medallions of monkfish with tiger prawns, couscous and dill. The wine list has been selected by a local merchant and includes a wide range of fine ports, Armagnacs and Cognacs.

Eighteen en suite bedrooms make The Crown an ideal choice for a short walking break in the lush surrounding farmland and wooded valleys. Special packages can be put together to cater for racegoers at Ludlow.

**Open** all wk **Barmeals** L served Mon-Fri 12.30-2, Sat 12-2.30, Sun 12-8 D served Mon-Fri 6-9, Sat 6-9.30, Sun 12-8 **Restaurant** L served 12.30-2, Sat 12-2.30, Sun 12-8 D served Mon-Fri 6-9, Sat 6-9.30, Sun 12-8 FREE HOUSE Timothy Taylor Landlord, Hobsons Best, Guest ales. 🍷 25 **Facilities** Childrens Menu Play area Dogs allowed Garden Parking **Rooms** 18

Save on Hotels. Book at theAA.com/hotel

SHROPSHIRE 385 ENGLAND

## RAVEN ARMS continued

additional dishes, served with up to six fresh vegetables and a choice of chips or new potatoes. The pub has historic connection with the transportation of criminals to Australia.

**Open** all wk 12-2.30 6-11 (Sun 12-3 7-11) **Bar Meals** L served all wk 12-2 D served all wk 6-9 Av main course £8.50 **Restaurant** L served all wk 12-2 D served all wk 6-9 ⊕ FREE HOUSE ◀ Corvedale Normans Pride, Dark & Delicious, Julie's Ale, Katie's Pride, Farmer Rays, Mahoral. ⓣ 10 **Facilities** Children's menu Children's portions Play area Dogs allowed Garden Parking

### CRESSAGE
Map 10 SJ50

## The Riverside Inn

Cound SY5 6AF ☎ 01952 510900 📄 01952 510926
dir: On A458 7m from Shrewsbury, 1m from Cressage

Originally a vicarage for St Peter's church in the village, the building also housed a girls' school and a railway halt before becoming a pub in 1878. A haven for fishermen, the inn sits in three acres of garden alongside the River Severn, offering customers delightful river views both outdoors and from a modern conservatory. Service with a smile delivers to the table wholesome plates of chicken carbonara; poached salmon and coriander; and Bakewell tart and a jug of cream. Their own brew, Riverside Inn Bitter, is available in the cosy bar.

**Open** all wk all day Sat-Sun May-Sep **Bar Meals** L served all wk 12-2.30 D served all wk 6.30-9.30 Av main course £11 **Restaurant** L served all wk 12-2.30 D served all wk 6.30-9.30 Av 3 course à la carte fr £19 ⊕ FREE HOUSE ◀ Riverside Inn Bitter, guest ales. **Facilities** Dogs allowed Garden Parking

### HODNET
Map 15 SJ62

## The Bear at Hodnet

TF9 3NH ☎ 01630 685214 📄 01630 685787
e-mail: reception@bearathodnet.co.uk
dir: At junct of A53 & A442 turn right at rdbt. Inn in village centre

Standing opposite Hodnet Hall Gardens, Allison and Ben Christie's 16th-century coaching inn is steeped in history, with original beams and fireplaces in the character bar, and secret passages leading to the parish church. Famous for medieval banquets in the newly refurbished hall, food in the bar takes in rare breed

meats (roast belly of Maynard's pork with sage and cider jus) and pub classics like ham, egg and chips, and liver and bacon with mash and onion gravy.

**Open** 11-11 Closed: Sun eve **Bar Meals** L served Mon-Sat 12-2.30 D served Mon-Sat 6-9.30 **Restaurant** L served all wk 12-2.30 D served Mon-Sat 6-9.30 ⊕ FREE HOUSE ◀ Theakston, Worthers, Guest ales, Shropshire Gold, Guinness ⓞ Stowford Press. **Facilities** Dogs allowed Garden Parking

### IRONBRIDGE
Map 10 SJ60

## The Malthouse ⓣ

The Wharfage TF8 7NH
☎ 01952 433712 📄 01952 433298
e-mail: enquiries@themalthouseironbridge.com
dir: Telephone for directions

An inn since the 1800s, the Malthouse is located in the village of Ironbridge next to the river, now a designated UNESCO World Heritage Site famous for its natural beauty and award-winning museums. Party menus are available for both the popular jazz bar and the restaurant, while the main menu ranges from lasagne or faggots to monkfish and pancetta baked and served with sweet chorizo, mussel and tomato cassoulet.

**Open** all wk ◀ Directors, Greene King IPA, Badger. ⓣ 10 **Facilities** Dogs allowed Garden Parking

### LLANFAIR WATERDINE
Map 9 SO27

### PICK OF THE PUBS

## The Waterdine

LD7 1TU ☎ 01547 528214
e-mail: info@waterdine.com
dir: 4.5m W of Knighton off B4355, turn right opposite Lloyney Inn, 0.5m into village, last on left opp church

There's an air of total peace and quiet, and there are fine views down the Teme Valley from this low, stone whitewashed pub, tucked away in a tiny hamlet smack on the border between England and Wales. The old parish church stands opposite, the Teme runs through the bottom of the garden, and chef-landlord Ken Adams proudly continues to provide sustenance and shelter for weary travellers at his 400-year-old former drover's inn. There are two dining rooms, the Garden Room looking out over the river, and the Taproom, tucked away in the oldest part of the building with heavy beams and a stone floor. Menus are based on home-grown and locally supplied organic produce (listed on the menu), so dishes like pheasant terrine with gooseberry marmalade; cream of wild mushroom soup; loin of Mortimer Forest roe deer, sliced beans, beetroot purée and dauphinoise potatoes are appropriately seasonal. Leave room to enjoy a dessert such as mulberry cheesecake, or warm plum tart with ginger cream.

**Open** 12-3 7-11 Closed: 1wk winter, 1wk spring, Sun eve & Mon (ex BH) **Bar Meals** L served Thu-Sun 12.15-1.30 booking required **Restaurant** L served Thu-Sun 12.15-1.30 booking required D served Tue-Sat 7-8.30 booking required Fixed menu price fr £32.50 ⊕ FREE HOUSE ◀ Wood Shropshire Legends, Parish Bitter, Shropshire Lad. **Facilities** Garden Parking

### LUDLOW
Map 10 SO57

## The Church Inn ★★★★ INN

Buttercross SY8 1AW
☎ 01584 872174 📄 01584 877146
dir: In town centre, behind Buttercross

The inn stands on one of the oldest sites in Ludlow, dating back some seven centuries, and through the ages has been occupied by a blacksmith, saddler, druggist and barber-surgeon. These days it enjoys a good reputation for providing a range of ales alongside traditional pub food, including cod in beer batter, locally made faggots, and three cheese pasta and broccoli bake. There are eight en suite bedrooms with televisions and tea-making facilities.

**Open** all wk **Bar Meals** L served Mon-Fri 12-2.30, Sat-Sun 12-3 D served Mon-Sat 6.30-9, Sun 6.30-8.30 ⊕ FREE HOUSE ◀ Hobsons Town Crier, Weetwood, Wye Valley Bitter, Ludlow Gold, Boilingwell Mild ⓞ Stowford, Aspall. **Facilities** Dogs allowed **Rooms** 8

### PICK OF THE PUBS

## The Clive Bar & Restaurant with Rooms
RR ⊛⊛ ⓣ

Bromfield SY8 2JR
☎ 01584 856565 & 856665 📄 01584 856661
e-mail: info@theclive.co.uk
web: www.theclive.co.uk
dir: 2m N of Ludlow on A49, between Hereford & Shrewsbury

This classy bar, restaurant and rooms is situated two miles north of Ludlow and was once home to Robert Clive, who laid the foundation of British rule in India, and his original coat of arms hangs in the oldest part of this unusual operation. For within this handsome Georgian house, which was built as a farmhouse in the 18th century, traditional and contemporary looks blend well. The bar is a bright modern area, with glass-topped tables and contemporary artwork, and leads to a more traditional space with beams and brick and stone walls where you can relax on sofas by an

*continued*

## LUDLOW continued

enormous fireplace. On warmer days, take your drinks out into the sheltered courtyard. Cooking is a happy mix of good British classics with Mediterranean touches, with the emphasis on quality local ingredients. From bar meals like cod and chips and hot filled baguettes, the choice extends to ham hock and rabbit confit terrine, smoked salmon and scrambled egg, lamb with minted polenta mash, Puy lentils and shallot sauce, and orange tart with chocolate sorbet. Fifteen stylish en suite bedrooms are simply furnished in a style that is more Scandinavian-inspired than English country.

*The Clive Bar & Restaurant With Rooms*
**Open** all day all wk Mon-Sat 11-11 (Sun 12-10.30)
Closed: 25-26 Dec **Bar Meals** L served Mon-Fri 12-3,
Sat-Sun 12-6.30 booking required D served Mon-Sat
6.30-10, Sun 6.30-9.30 booking required Av main
course £9.95 **Restaurant** L served all wk 12-3 booking
required D served Mon-Sat 6.30-10, Sun 6.30-9.30
booking required Av 3 course à la carte fr £25 ⊕ FREE
HOUSE ◀ Hobsons Best Bitter, Ludlow Gold Bitter,
Guinness ♂ Dunkertons Original, Mahoral Farm,
Thatchers Old Rascal Oak Aged. ♏ 9
**Facilities** Children's portions Garden Parking
Rooms 15

### PICK OF THE PUBS

## The Unicorn ♏

**Corve St SY8 1DU**
☎ 01584 873555 📄 01584 876268
**e-mail:** graham-unicorn@btconnect.com
**dir:** A49 to Ludlow. From town centre down Corve St towards river

This low, attractive, timber-framed building backs on to the once flood-prone River Corve. During the great flood of 1885 a photograph was taken of men sitting drinking around a table in the bar while water lapped the doorway. Apparently it wasn't unusual for empty beer barrels to float out of the cellar and down the river. These days, all is warm and dry: log fires in winter and the sunny riverside terrace in summer prove very appealing. The impressive food offerings run from sandwiches (brie and cranberry; home-cooked ham) to full meals such as home-made Shropshire pâté with sweet onion marmalade followed by the likes of fish pie – a house speciality – or braised local lamb shanks with proper gravy and fresh vegetables. For those seeking pub classics, there are home-made faggots, home-made rare breed steak burger and ale-battered

fish with home-made chips. Home-made desserts include sticky toffee pudding and dark chocolate torte.

**Open** all day all wk 11am-mdnt ◀ Ludlow Best Ale,
Butty Bach, Guinness. ♏ 15 **Facilities** Dogs allowed
Garden

### MADELEY — Map 10 SJ60

## All Nations Inn

**20 Coalport Rd TF7 5DP**
☎ 01952 585747 📄 01952 585747
**dir:** On Coalport Rd, overlooking Blists Hill Museum

Only three families have owned this friendly, largely unspoilt pub since it opened as a brewhouse in 1831. And a brewhouse it has remained. There's no jukebox, pool or fruit machine, although Six Nations rugby matches are shown on a TV perched on barrels. No restaurant either, but quality rolls and pork pies are available all day. From the outside seating area you can see Blists Hill Victorian Town open air museum.

**Open** all day all wk noon-mdnt ◀ Dabley Ale, Dabley
Gold, Coalport Dodger Mild, Guest ales. **Facilities** Dogs
allowed Garden Parking **Notes** ⊛

## The New Inn

**Blists Hill Victorian Town, Legges Way TF7 5DU**
☎ 01952 601018 📄 01785 252247
**e-mail:** sales@jenkinsonscaterers.co.uk
**dir:** Between Telford & Broseley

Here's something different - a Victorian pub that was moved brick by brick from the Black Country and re-erected at the Ironbridge Gorge Open Air Museum. The building remains basically as it was in 1890, and customers can buy traditionally brewed beer at five-pence farthing per pint - roughly £2.10 in today's terms - using pre-decimal currency bought from the bank. The mainly traditional menu includes home-made soup, steak and kidney pudding, and ham and leek pie. Tea and coffee are served from 10-2.30, and afternoon tea from 2.30-3.30.

**Open** all wk 10-4 winter, 10-5 summer Closed: 25 Dec, 1
Jan **Restaurant** L served all wk 12-2.30 ⊕ IRONBRIDGE
GEORGE MUSEUMS ◀ Banks Bitter, Banks Original,
Pedigree. **Facilities** Garden Parking

### MARTON — Map 15 SJ20

## The Lowfield Inn ♏ NEW

**SY21 8JX** ☎ 01743 891313
**e-mail:** lowfieldinn@tiscali.co.uk
**dir:** From Shrewsbury take B4386 towards Montgomery.
Through Westbury & Brockton. Pub on right in 13m just
before Marton

With pubs continuing to close, this pub is a surprise - it's only four years old! Built on the site of its demolished predecessor, there is a relaxed and informal feel here with mix and match tables and chairs, comfy sofas and walls displaying local art. This country pub on the Shropshire/Powys border serves locally brewed real ales and ciders, wines from all over the world, and locally

sourced, modern British food typified by chicken dhansak, kedgeree; pan-fried sea bass; Cumberland sausages; and butternut squash, red onion and spinach lasagne. There are fantastic views from the large garden.

**Open** all day all wk **Bar Meals** Av main course £10.50
food served all day **Restaurant** Fixed menu price fr £15
Av 3 course à la carte fr £18.45 food served all day
⊕ FREE HOUSE ◀ Three Tuns XXX, Three Tuns 1642,
Monty's Moonrise, Monty's Mojo, Wood's Shropshire Lad
♂ Inch's Stonehouse, Weston Old Rosie. ♏ 18
**Facilities** Children's menu Children's portions Dogs
allowed Garden Parking

## The Sun Inn ♏

**SY21 8JP** ☎ 01938 561211
**e-mail:** suninnmarton@googlemail.com
**dir:** On B4386 (Shrewsbury to Montgomery road), in centre
of Marton opp village shop

This classic stone free house dating back to 1760 is surrounded by glorious Shropshire countryside. Guest ales from Monty's and Six Bells await in the bar, while all food on the bar and restaurant menus is home made and cooked to order. Fish delivered fresh from Newlyn supplements local game in dishes such as Talley Mountain goat's cheese with fresh fig and honey tart; roast partridge with pear in ginger wine; and fillet of hake with spinach and cheese sauce.

**Open** 12-3 7-mdnt Closed: Sun eve, Mon, Tue L
**Bar Meals** L served Wed-Sat 12-2.30 booking required D
served Tue-Fri from 7pm booking required Av main course
£8 **Restaurant** L served Wed-Sun 12-2.30 booking
required D served Tue-Sat from 7pm booking required Av
3 course à la carte fr £25 ⊕ FREE HOUSE ◀ Hobsons
Best Bitter, Worthington Creamflow, Guest ales. ♏ 8
**Facilities** Children's portions Garden Parking

### MUCH WENLOCK — Map 10 SO69

## The George & Dragon

**2 High St TF13 6AA** ☎ 01952 727312
**e-mail:** thegeorge.dragon@btinternet.com
**dir:** On A458 halfway between Shrewsbury & Bridgnorth

Oozing history, charm and character, the George & Dragon is an oak-beamed 17th-century inn at the heart of Much Wenlock. Sited next to the market square, Guildhall and ruined priory, the inn welcomes everyone, from locals to celebrities — John Cleese, Tony Robinson, Jenifer Jones and George Cole are among those who have popped in for refreshment. Run by locals Bev and James, the cask ales are well kept, and home-cooked traditional food includes filled jackets, faggots in gravy, cottage pie, and beef lasagne.

**Open** all day all wk 11-11 (Fri-Sat 11am-mdnt Sun
11am-11pm) **Bar Meals** L served all wk 12-2.30 D served
Mon-Tue, Thu-Sat 6-9 Av main course £6.95 **Restaurant** L
served all wk 12-2.30 D served Mon-Tue, Thu-Sat 6-9
⊕ PUNCH RETAIL ◀ Greene King Abbot Ale, Wadworth 6X,
Tribute, guest ales ♂ Westons Organic.
**Facilities** Children's menu Children's portions Dogs
allowed

Save on Hotels. Book at **theAA.com/hotel**

**SHROPSHIRE** 387 **ENGLAND**

## Longville Arms ♀

**Longville in the Dale TF13 6DT**
☎ **01694 771206** 📠 01694 771742
**dir:** *From Shrewsbury take A49 to Church Stretton, then B4371 to Longville*

Prettily situated in an Area of Outstanding Natural Beauty in Shropshire, ideally placed for walking and touring, this welcoming country inn is now under new ownership. Solid elm or cast-iron-framed tables, oak panelling and wood-burning stoves are among the features that help to generate a warm, friendly ambience. Favourite main courses on the bar menu and specials board include steak and ale pie, mixed fish platter, and a range of steaks. Portions can be adapted for children and they have their own menu. There is a tethering facilities for horses and dogs are welcome.

**Open** all day all wk **Restaurant** L served Sun & BH 12-2.30 D served Fri-Sat & BH 6.30-9.30 ⊕ FREE HOUSE ◀ Local guest ales. ♀ 10 **Facilities** Children's menu Children's portions Play area Dogs allowed Garden Parking

## The Talbot Inn ★★★ INN

**High St TF13 6AA** ☎ **01952 727077** 📠 01952 728436
**e-mail:** the_talbot_inn@hotmail.com
**dir:** *M54 junct 4, follow Ironbridge Gorge Museum signs, then Much Wenlock signs. Much Wenlock on A458, 11m from Shrewsbury, 9m from Bridgnorth*

Dating from 1360, the Talbot was once a hostel for travellers and a centre for alms giving. The delightful courtyard was used in the 1949 Powell and Pressburger film *Gone to Earth.* Daily specials highlighted on the varied menu may include steak and kidney pie, baked sea bass, Shropshire pie and cod mornay.

**Open** all day all wk 11am-2am **Bar Meals** L served all wk 12-2.30 D served Mon-Sat 6-9, Sun 6-8.30 ⊕ FREE HOUSE ◀ Bass, Guest Ales. **Facilities** Children's portions Garden Parking **Rooms** 6

**PICK OF THE PUBS**

## Wenlock Edge Inn ♀

**Hilltop, Wenlock Edge TF13 6DJ**
☎ **01746 785678** 📠 01746 785285
**e-mail:** info@wenlockedgeinn.co.uk
**dir:** *4.5m from Much Wenlock on B4371*

Originally a row of 17th-century quarrymen's cottages, this inn perches at one of the highest points of Wenlock

Edge's dramatic wooded ledge. The cosy interior contains a small country-style dining room and several bars, one with a wood-burning stove. Outside, a furnished patio takes full advantage of the views stretching across Apedale to Caer Caradoc and the Long Mynd. It even has its own fish pond from the Wenlock Edge fresh water spring. Traditional British pub food is served alongside Hobsons real ales, continental lagers and a good choice of wine by the glass. Local and regional produce is used and favourite dishes include local steaks with chunky hand-cut chips and home-made pies. There is also a daily fish board and special fish nights with specialities such as lobster and beer-battered scallops.

**Open** all day all wk Mon-Sun 11-11 **Bar Meals** L served all wk 12-3 D served all wk 6-9 food served all day **Restaurant** L served all wk 12-3 D served all wk 6-9 food served all day ⊕ FREE HOUSE ◀ Hobsons Best & Town Crier, Three Tuns, Enville Ale Ò Thatchers Gold. ♀ 8 **Facilities** Children's portions Dogs allowed Garden Parking

**MUNSLOW** Map 10 SO58

**PICK OF THE PUBS**

## The Crown Country Inn ★★★★ INN ◎◎

*See Pick of the Pubs on page 388*

**NORTON** Map 10 SJ70

**PICK OF THE PUBS**

## The Hundred House Hotel ★★ HL ◎◎ ♀

*See Pick of the Pubs on page 389*

**OSWESTRY** Map 15 SJ22

## The Bradford Arms ★★★★ INN

**Llanymynech SY22 6EJ**
☎ **01691 830582** 📠 01691 839009
**e-mail:** robinbarsteward@tesco.net
**web:** www.bradfordarmshotel.com
**dir:** *5.5m S of Oswestry on A483 in Llanymynech*

Close to Powis and Chirk Castles on the Welsh border in an Area of Outstanding Natural Beauty, this coaching inn offers newly refurbished rooms and above average eating

in its spotless, quietly elegant bar and dining rooms. Arrive early to ensure a seat and then tuck into, say, Cajun chicken salad followed by lamb casserole, with home-made treacle tart for dessert. Good lunchtime sandwiches, traditional Sunday roasts, and Black Sheep Best on tap are other plus points. Once the coaching inn on the Earl of Bradford's estate, it is ideally situated for golfing, fishing and walking.

**Open** all wk 11.30-3 6-mdnt **Bar Meals** L served all wk 11.30-2 Av main course £8.95 **Restaurant** L served all wk 11.30-2 D served all wk 6.30-9 Fixed menu price fr £7.95 ⊕ FREE HOUSE ◀ Black Sheep Best, Tetley Smooth, Guinness, 2 Guest ales Ò Olde English. **Facilities** Children's menu Children's portions Dogs allowed Garden Parking **Rooms** 5

**PAVE LANE** Map 10 SJ71

## The Fox ♀

**TF10 9LQ** ☎ **01952 815940** 📠 01952 815941
**e-mail:** fox@brunningandprice.co.uk
**dir:** *1m S of Newport, just off A41*

A big Edwardian-style pub, with a mix of private corners and sunny spacious rooms, all wrapped around a busy central bar. There's a large south-facing terrace with views over wooded hills. In addition to light bites and sandwiches, the comprehensive menu could include mushroom and Shropshire Blue soup; Wenlock Edge air-dried Shropshire ham and fig salad; Shropshire rabbit pie; artichoke heart tortelloni with watercress, caper and parmesan pesto. There is a good variety of real ales on offer.

**Open** all day all wk noon-11 (Sun noon-10.30) **Bar Meals** Av main course £10.95 food served all day **Restaurant** food served all day ⊕ BRUNNING & PRICE ◀ Timothy Taylor Landlord, Woods Shropshire Lad, Thwaites Original, Titanic Mild, Hobsons Golden Glow. **Facilities** Dogs allowed Garden Parking

**PICKLESCOTT** Map 15 SO49

## Bottle & Glass Inn

**SY6 6NR** ☎ **01694 751345**
**dir:** *Exit A49 at Dorrington (between Shrewsbury & Church Stretton)*

The hamlet of Pickelscott lies in the northern foothills of the Long Mynd, or Mountain. The landlord of this 16th-century pub, who has been here for 30-odd years, occasionally hears the ghost of a wooden-legged predecessor tap-tapping around, somehow upsetting the pub's electrics. A typical starter is Roquefort-stuffed pear with green mayonnaise: homity pie; game and red wine casserole; and haddock with cheese sauce on spinach are among the main courses. Recent change of hands.

**Open** all wk 12-3 6-12 (Sat-Sun noon-mdnt) **Bar Meals** L served all wk 12-2.30 D served all wk 6.30-9 **Restaurant** L served all wk 12-2.30 D served all wk 6.30-9 ⊕ FREE HOUSE ◀ Hobsons, Three Tuns XXX, Wye Valley Butty Bach Ò Stowford Press. **Facilities** Dogs allowed Parking

# PICK OF THE PUBS

## The Crown Country Inn ★★★★ INN 🌹🌹

MUNSLOW      Map 10 SO58

**SY7 9ET ☎ 01584 841205**
e-mail: info@crowncountryinn.co.uk
dir: *On B4368 between Craven Arms & Much Wenlock*

The Grade II listed Crown has stood in a lovely setting below the rolling hills of Wenlock Edge in the Vale of the River Corve since it was built in Tudor times. The impressive, three-storey building was formerly a Hundred House, where courts dished out punishment to local miscreants – including, perhaps, the black-clothed Charlotte whose ghost is sometimes seen in the pub. The main bar retains its sturdy oak beams, flagstone floors and prominent inglenook fireplace, whilst free house status means Mahoral Farm ciders and a good range of local beers, including Holden's Black Country Bitter, are served.

Owners Richard and Jane Arnold have a strong commitment to good food. In fact, Richard is not only head chef but has also been a Master Chef of Great Britain for more than a decade. Meals are served in the main bar, the Bay dining area, and the Corvedale Restaurant. He acquires his top quality local produce from trusted sources and is proud to feature it in his dishes, many of which can be either starter or main course. These include pressed local ham hock and herb terrine with home-made sweet chilli jam; crostini of black pudding and tomato fondue with Wenlock Edge dry cure bacon; and fresh basil pesto risotto with roasted vegetables and melted goat's cheese.

Other main course options might encompass crisp roast belly pork with buttered cabbage and smoked bacon; crispy sage and Parmesan risotto cakes with onion marmalade and port wine syrup; or smoked haddock kedgeree with poached eggs. The cheeseboard lists ten English and Welsh cheeses, while for something sweet there's rich chocolate and orange tart with vanilla poached satsuma and clotted cream. Three large en suite bedrooms are located in a converted Georgian stable block.

**Open** Tue-Sat 12-3.30 6.45-11 (Sun 12-3.30) Closed: Xmas, Sun eve, Mon **Bar Meals** L served Tue-Sun 12-2 booking required D served Tue-Sat 6.45-8.45 booking required Av main course £9 **Restaurant** L served Tue-Sun 12-2 booking required D served Tue-Sat 6.45-8.45 booking required Av 3 course à la carte fr £25 🛢 FREE HOUSE ◀ Holden's Black Country Bitter, Holden's Golden Glow, Holden's Special Bitter, Three Tuns Brewery XXX ♻ Mahoral. **Facilities** Play area Garden Parking **Rooms** 3

# PICK OF THE PUBS

## The Hundred House Hotel ★★HL

**NORTON**　　　　　Map 10 SJ70

**Bridgnorth Rd TF11 9EE**
☎ **01952 580240** 📠 **01952 580260**
**e-mail:**
reservations@hundredhouse.co.uk
**web:** www.hundredhouse.co.uk
**dir:** *On A442, 6m N of Bridgnorth, 5m S of Telford centre*

In medieval times, England was divided into areas called hundreds. Their affairs were administered by hundred houses, which is what the 14th-century, half-timbered, thatched barn outside this hotel used to be, while opposite are the remnants of the old stocks and whipping post where offenders were punished.

The mainly Georgian hotel has been lovingly run by the Phillips family for more than a quarter of a century and the minute you push through the swing doors with stained-glass panels stating 'Temperance Hall', you realise they have created somewhere special. Downstairs is an amazing interconnecting warren of lavishly decorated bars (where All Seasons bitter comes from the Wem Brewery) and dining rooms with old quarry-tiled floors, exposed brickwork, beamed ceilings and oak panelling. Baskets of pumpkins and marrow lurk in corners at harvest time; in December you might find a basket of huge decorated onions, while herbs hang from the beams to dry. Look out too for the display of AA Rosette plates, one for each of the last thirteen years.

Younger son Stuart Phillips continues to head kitchen operations, producing new dishes such as home-made sausage of the month; Thai green chicken curry; tapas for two; and beef and venison pie, as well as pub favourites like steak and kidney pie. The Brasserie/Bar serves sophisticated dishes like black bean and spiced broccoli tortilla, as well as chargrills and lasagne, while a sample carte lists roast rack of Shropshire lamb with houmous, ginger and sweet pepper; grilled beef fillet with smoked bacon, blue cheese risotto and beef jus; fish of the day; and roast butternut squash with sweet pepper chutney and mushroom and chestnut filo. Daily specials might include venison casserole with herb dumplings and damson cheese; and chicken gumbo with steamed rice. For budding cooks there are master chef school classes available.

**Open** all day all wk 11-11 Closed: 25-26 Dec eve **Bar Meals** L served all wk 12-2.30 D served all wk 6-9.30 Av main course £10 **Restaurant** L served all wk 12-2.30 D served all wk 6-9.30 Fixed menu price fr £13 Av 3 course à la carte fr £30 ⊕ FREE HOUSE ◀ Heritage Bitter, Shropshire Stout, All Seasons Bitter. ♀ 10 **Facilities** Children's menu Garden Parking **Rooms** 10

## SHIFNAL
Map 10 SJ70

### Odfellows Wine Bar ♥

**Market Place TF11 9AU**
☎ 01952 461517 📄 01952 463855
**e-mail:** reservations@odley.co.uk
**dir:** M54 junct 4, 3rd exit at rdbt, at next rdbt take 3rd
exit, past petrol station, round bend under rail bridge.
Bar on left

Quirky, popular wine bar owned by Odley Inns, which
explains the 'od' spelling. The bar and outdoor area
serves regional real ales and ciders, as well as the great
wine selection and eleven by the glass. The carefully
prepared food, served in an elevated dining area and
attractive conservatory, is ethically sourced from local
suppliers. Seasonal menus might offer sautéed chorizo
and quails' eggs on French toast; Arabian lamb with
couscous; a skillet of Odfellows spicy chilli; and free-
range chicken and ham pie. There is live music every
Sunday.

**Open** all day all wk noon-mdnt Closed: 25-26 Dec, 1 Jan
**Bar Meals** L served all wk 12-2.30 Av main course £6
**Restaurant** L served all wk 12-2.30 D served all wk 6-10
Av 3 course à la carte fr £23 ⊕ FREE HOUSE ◀ Salopian,
Wye Valley, Holdens, Ludlow Gold, Three Tuns
Ö Thatchers, Westons. ♥ 11 **Facilities** Children's
menu Children's portions Garden Parking

## SHREWSBURY
Map 15 SJ41

### The Armoury ♥

**Victoria Quay, Victoria Av SY1 1HH**
☎ 01743 340525 📄 01743 340526
**e-mail:** armoury@brunningandprice.co.uk
**dir:** Telephone for directions

The converted Armoury building makes an impressive,
large scale pub, just over the bridge on the opposite bank
of the river from the new Theatre Severn. Large warehouse
windows and huge bookcases dominate the interior of the
bar and restaurant area. There is a comprehensive menu
accompanied by a great range of real ales and
comprehensive wine list. Typical dishes are pan-fried sea
bass fillets, chorizo, new potatoes and salad; beef and
ale pie; and Welsh lamb sausages, buttered mash, roast
root vegetables and mint gravy.

**Open** all day all wk Closed: 25-26 Dec **Bar Meals** food
served all day **Restaurant** food served all day
⊕ BRUNNING & PRICE ◀ Roosters APA, Salopian
Shropshire Gold, Deuchars IPA, Woods Shropshire Lad,
Three Tuns Steamer Ö Stowford Press, Ludlow Cider.
**Facilities** Children's portions Dogs allowed

## PICK OF THE PUBS

### The Mytton & Mermaid
Hotel ★★★ HL ⊛⊛ ♥

**Atcham SY5 6QG** ☎ 01743 761220 📄 01743 761292
**e-mail:** reception@myttonandmermaid.co.uk
**dir:** From M54 junct 7 signed Shrewsbury, at 2nd rdbt
take 1st left signed Ironbridge/Atcham. In 1.5m hotel
on right after bridge

Dating from 1735, this Grade II listed, ivy-clad hotel
stands opposite Attingham Park (National Trust) and
enjoys spectacular views over the River Severn.
Tastefully decorated throughout, the interior recalls the
atmosphere of its coaching days and there's a relaxed
gastro-pub feel about the place, especially in Mad
Jack's Bar, which is named after a colourful local
squire and features a wood floor, scrubbed tables,
comfy sofas and an open log fire. Here you can quaff a
pint of local Shropshire Gold and tuck into some
interesting dishes from the seasonal modern British
menu (two AA Rosettes). Top-notch Shropshire
ingredients are used wherever possible in dishes like
Attingham Park venison with girolle and tarragon jus,
and Wenlock Edge pork and sage sausages with mash,
apple chutney and lentil gravy. The menu may also list
scallops with celeriac purée; sea bass with crab, lemon
and chilli linguini; pan-fried Wrekin pheasant with
bread sauce, braised leeks, roasted shallots and pan
jus; and sticky ginger pudding.

**Open** all day all wk 7am-11pm Closed: 25 Dec
**Bar Meals** L served Mon-Sat 12-2.30, Sun 12-9 D
served Mon-Sat 6.30-10, Sun 12-9 Av main course £12
**Restaurant** L served Mon-Sat 12-2.30, Sun 12-9
booking required D served Mon-Sat 7-10, Sun 12-9
booking required Fixed menu price fr £24.95 Av 3
course à la carte fr £29.95 ⊕ FREE HOUSE
◀ Shropshire Lad, Shropshire Gold, Hobsons Best.
♥ 12 **Facilities** Children's menu Garden Parking
**Rooms** 18

### The Plume of Feathers

**Harley SY5 6LP** ☎ 01952 727360 📄 01952 728542
**e-mail:** feathersatharley@aol.com
**dir:** Telephone for directions

Nestling under Wenlock Edge, this 17th-century inn has
stunning views across the valley. Look for the Charles I
oak bedhead, full size cider press and inglenook fireplace.
Food reflects the seasons, with a changing fish menu; bar
meals such as Shropshire baked ham with egg and chips;
and restaurant dishes such as lamb en croûte stuffed
with wild mushroom and leek gratin, with oxtail gravy; or
pan-fried duck breast with black cherry sauce.

**Open** all wk ◀ Worthingtons, Guinness, Directors, guest
ales. **Facilities** Play area Garden Parking

## STOTTESDON
Map 10 SO68

### Fighting Cocks

**1 High St DY14 8TZ** ☎ 01746 718270 📄 01746 718270
**e-mail:** sandrafc_5@hotmail.com
**dir:** 11m from Bridgnorth off B4376

An unassuming 18th-century building, the pub was first
licensed in 1850 and called the Cock Inn until the 1980s.
It once reputedly brewed an ale containing chicken for
monks at the village church; called cock ale, it was also
served to travellers along with chicken jelly. Today's food,
including all pâtés, pies and puddings, is home made
and rather more appealing. Live music, open mic nights
with curries, quizzes, firework displays and hog roasts for
charity can all be enjoyed at this lively local.

**Open** all wk 6-mdnt (Fri 5pm-1am Sat noon-mdnt Sun
noon-10.30) **Bar Meals** L served Sat-Sun 12-2.30 booking
required Av main course £9 **Restaurant** L served Sat-Sun
12-2.30 booking required D served Mon-Sat 7-9 booking
required ⊕ FREE HOUSE ◀ Hobsons Best, Hobsons Town
Crier, Hobsons Mild, Wye Valley HPA, Wye Valley Bitter
Ö Stowford Press, Flagon. **Facilities** Children's menu
Garden Parking

## UPPER AFFCOT
Map 9 SO48

### The Travellers Rest Inn ♥

**SY6 6RL** ☎ 01694 781275 📄 01694 781555
**e-mail:** travellersrestinn@live.co.uk
**dir:** on A49, 5m S of Church Stretton

Locals and passing trade enjoy the friendly atmosphere.
This traditional south Shropshire inn is located on the
A49 between Church Stretton and Craven Arms. The
traditional food suits the appetite and the pocket, and is
served until 9pm. Expect to see starters of smoked
mackerel or prawn cocktail, traditional mains like steak
or chilli con carne, and spotted Dick or treacle sponge.
The ales range from Wood Shropshire Lad to Hobsons
Best.

**Open** all day all wk 11.30am-mdnt **Bar Meals** L served all
wk 12-9 D served all wk 12-9 Av main course £9 food
served all day **Restaurant** L served all wk 12-9 D served
all wk 12-9 Fixed menu price fr £4.95 Av 3 course à la
carte fr £9 food served all day ⊕ FREE HOUSE ◀ Wood
Shropshire Lad, Wood Shropshire Lass, Wood Parish,
Hobsons Best. ♥ 12 **Facilities** Children's menu Children's
portions Garden Parking

## WELLINGTON
Map 10 SJ61

### The Old Orleton Inn ★★★★★ INN ♥
NEW

**Holyhead Rd TF1 2HA** ☎ 01952 255011
**e-mail:** aapub@theoldorleton.com
**dir:** From M54 junct 7 take B5061 (Holyhead Rd), 400yds
on left on corner of Haygate Rd & Holyhead Rd

Recently revamped in a contemporary style, this 17th-
century former coaching inn overlooks the famous Wrekin
Hill and provides a chic and comfortable base for walking

Save on Hotels. Book at **theAA.com/hotel**

SHROPSHIRE – SOMERSET 391 **ENGLAND**

and exploring the Shropshire countryside. The old and new blend effortlessly throughout the rambling building, no more so than in the 10 individual boutique style bedrooms. Local Hobson ales and modern British food have found favour with local drinkers and diners. Lunch in the brasserie offers club sandwiches, light bites like crayfish and prawn pancakes, and salad platters, with evening dishes taking in venison with port and liquorice sauce, and sea bass with crab butter.

**Open** noon-3 5-11 Closed: 1st 2wks Jan, Sun eve **Bar Meals** L served Mon-Sat 12-2.30 (Sun 12-4) D served Mon-Sat 6-9.30 Av main course £14 **Restaurant** L served Mon-Sat 12-2.30 (Sun 12-4) booking required D served Mon-Sat 6-9.30 booking required Av 3 course à la carte fr £26 ⊕ FREE HOUSE ◼ Hobsons Best, Hobsons Town Crier ♙ Stowford Press. ♟10 **Facilities** Garden Parking **Rooms** 10

## WENTNOR
*Map 15 SO39*

## The Crown Inn

SY9 5EE ☎ 01588 650613 ▤ 01588 650436
**e-mail:** crowninn@wentnor.com
**dir:** *From Shrewsbury A49 to Church Stretton, follow signs over Long Mynd to Asterton, right to Wentnor*

Winter walkers warm up beside wood-burning stoves in this inviting 16th-century timbered inn deep in the Shropshire Hills, whilst summer visitors relax on the covered decking, indulging in Three Tuns bitter and gazing at the Long Mynd's lofty ridge. Its homely atmosphere, enhanced by beams, wood burners and horse brasses, makes eating and drinking here a pleasure. Meals are served in the bar or separate restaurant. Typical daily changing, traditional home-made dishes include at least three vegetarian options, or spoil yourself with a famous Crown Pie.

**Open** all wk noon-3 6-11 (Sat noon-mdnt Sun noon-10) Closed: 25 Dec **Bar Meals** L served Mon-Fri 12-2 D served Mon-Fri 6-9 Av main course £7.95 **Restaurant** L served Sat-Sun 12-9 D served Sat-Sun 12-9 Av 3 course à la carte fr £15 ⊕ FREE HOUSE ◼ Hobsons, Old Speckled Hen, Three Tuns, Wye Valley ♙ Westons Scrumpy. **Facilities** Children's menu Children's portions Play area Garden Parking

## WHITCHURCH
*Map 15 SJ54*

## Willeymoor Lock Tavern ♟

Tarporley Rd SY13 4HF ☎ 01948 663274
**dir:** *2m N of Whitchurch on A49 (Warrington to Tarporley road)*

A former lock keeper's cottage idyllically situated beside the Llangollen Canal, and near the Sandstone Trail and the Bishop Bennett Way. Low-beamed rooms are hung with a novel teapot collection; there are open log fires and a great range of real ales. Deep-fried fish and a choice of grills rub shoulders with traditional steak pie, chicken curry and vegetable chilli. Other options include salad platters, children's choices and gold rush pie for dessert.

**Open** all wk 12-2.30 6-11 (Sun 12-2.30 6-10.30) Closed: 25 Dec **Bar Meals** L served all wk 12-2 D served all wk 6-9 Av main course £7.50 **Restaurant** L served all wk 12-2 D served all wk 6-9 ⊕ FREE HOUSE ◼ Abbeydale, Moonshine, Weetwood, Oakham JHB, Best & Eastgate, Timothy Taylor Landlord, Greene King IPA, Old Speckled Hen. ♟9 **Facilities** Children's menu Play area Garden Parking **Notes** ☻

## WISTANSTOW
*Map 9 SO48*

## PICK OF THE PUBS

## The Plough ♟

SY7 8DG ☎ 01588 673251
**e-mail:** richardsys@btconnect.com
**dir:** *1m N of Craven Arms. Turn off A49 to Wistanstow*

Beers don't have to travel far to end up being drawn through century-old hand-pumps in the simply furnished bar of this traditional country pub. Located next to the award-winning Wood Brewery, it is effectively the brewery tap, serving Parish Bitter, Shropshire Lad and Wood's other real ales. An ethically sourced menu includes the ever-popular fish and chips (made with Wood's beer batter, of course); Shropshire sirloin and gammon steaks; and scampi, as well as children's choices. The specials board changes regularly and might feature home-made curries (try the fish cooked in coconut milk and turmeric; or spicy lamb and spinach); and farmhouse pork, bacon and cheese pie. Local faggots, omelettes and baguettes appear on the lunchtime menu. On Sundays, as well as the regular menus, there are traditional beef, pork or free-range chicken roasts. Take your drinks and meals out to the patio and beer garden on fine days.

**Open** all wk noon-2.30 5-mdnt (Sun noon-11) **Bar Meals** L served all wk 12-2 D served all wk 6.30-9 ⊕ WOOD BREWERY ◼ Wood's Shropshire Lad, Parish, Pot O' Gold ♙ Stowford Press. ♟9 **Facilities** Children's menu Children's portions Dogs allowed Garden Parking

## WOORE
*Map 15 SJ74*

## Swan at Woore

Nantwich Rd CW3 9SA ☎ 01630 647220
**dir:** *A51 (Stone to Nantwich road). 10m from Nantwich*

Refurbished 19th-century dining inn by the A51 near Stapeley Water Gardens. Four separate eating areas lead off from a central servery. Daily specials boards supplement the menu, which might include crispy confit of duck, slow roast knuckle of lamb, roasted salmon on vegetable linguine, or red onion and garlic tarte Tatin. There's a separate fish menu, offering grilled red mullet fillets, perhaps, or seared tuna on roasted sweet peppers.

**Open** all day all wk noon-11 ◼ Wells Bombardier, Boddingtons. **Facilities** Dogs allowed Garden Parking

## SOMERSET

## APPLEY
*Map 3 ST02*

## The Globe Inn ♟

TA21 0HJ ☎ 01823 672327
**e-mail:** globeinnappley@btconnect.com
**dir:** *From M5 junct 26 take A38 towards Exeter. Village signed in 5m*

Known for its large collection of Corgi and Dinky cars, Titanic memorabilia, old advertising posters and enamel signs, this Grade II listed inn dates back 500 years and is hidden in a maze of lanes on the Somerset-Devon border. Its smart beer gardens have lovely views over rolling hills, and it makes a perfect refreshment stop for walkers and cyclists. Food-wise, local seasonal produce is used in dishes like salmon and pollack fishcake to start followed by Spanish style fish and chorizo stew or pan-fried duck breast with plum sauce. Tempting filled baguettes and favourites such as ham, egg and chips are also available.

**Open** Tue-Sun Closed: Mon (ex BH) **Bar Meals** L served Tue-Sun 12-2 booking required D served Tue-Sun 7-9.30 booking required Av main course £8 **Restaurant** L served Tue-Sun 12-2 booking required D served Tue-Sun 7-9.30 booking required Fixed menu price fr £10 Av 3 course à la carte fr £25 ⊕ FREE HOUSE ◼ Exmoor Ales, Appleys Ale, Doom Bar, Tribute, Cotleigh Harrier ♙ Thatchers Gold. ♟8 **Facilities** Children's menu Children's portions Play area Garden Parking

## ASHCOTT
*Map 4 ST43*

## The Ashcott Inn ♟

50 Bath Rd TA7 9QQ
☎ 01458 210282 ▤ 01458 210282
**dir:** *M5 junct 23 follow signs for A39 to Glastonbury*

Dating back to the 16th century, this former coaching inn has an attractive bar with beams and stripped stone walls, as well as quaint old seats and an assortment of oak and elm tables. Outside is a popular terrace and a delightful walled garden. A straightforward menu offers 'Home Favourites' such as Cumberland sausages, pasta carbonara, Spanish omelette and steak baguette, while poultry and seafood choices include chicken provençal, tuna steak with salad, or chicken tikka masala. Vegetarians may enjoy mushroom stroganoff with gherkins and capers, or Stilton and walnut salad.

**Open** all wk ◼ Otter. ♟12 **Facilities** Play area Dogs allowed Garden Parking

## ASHCOTT *continued*

# Ring O'Bells ♥

**High St TA7 9PZ ☎ 01458 210232**
**e-mail:** info@ringobells.com
**dir:** *M5 junct 23 follow A39 & Glastonbury signs. In Ashcott turn left, at post office follow church & village hall signs*

A free house successfully run by the same family for 23 years. Parts of the building date from 1750, so the traditional village pub interior has beams, split-level bars, an old fireplace and a collection of bells and horse brasses. Local ales and ciders are a speciality, while all food is made on the premises. Look to the good value specials board for Moroccan spiced king prawns; lamb's liver in a piquant sauce; and steamed pear pudding with chocolate custard.

**Open** all wk noon-3 7-11 (Sun 7-10.30pm) Closed: 25 Dec **Bar Meals** L served all wk 12-2 D served all wk 7-10 Av main course £9 **Restaurant** L served all wk 12-2 D served all wk 7-10 Av 3 course à la carte fr £17 ⊕ FREE HOUSE ◀ guest ales ♡ Wilkins Farmhouse Cider. ♥ 8 **Facilities** Children's menu Children's portions Play area Dogs allowed Garden Parking

---

**ASHILL**                                      Map 4 ST31

# Square & Compass

**Windmill Hill TA19 9NX ☎ 01823 480467**
**e-mail:** squareandcompass@tiscali.co.uk
**dir:** *Exit A358 at Stewley Cross service station onto Wood Rd. 1m to pub in Windmill Hill*

There's a warm, friendly atmosphere at this traditional, family-owned country pub, beautifully located overlooking the Blackdown Hills in the heart of rural Somerset. Lovely gardens make the most of the views, and the bar area features hand-made settles and tables. There is a good choice of home-cooked food (prepared in the state-of-the-art large kitchen). Dishes might include sweet and sour pork, lambs' kidneys braised with sherry and Dijon mustard, and mixed grill. The barn next door was built by the owners from reclaimed materials for use as a wedding and village events venue.

**Open** all wk 12-3 6.30-late **Bar Meals** L served all wk 12-2 D served all wk 6.30-late Av main course £10 **Restaurant** L served all wk 12-2 D served all wk 6.30-late Av 3 course à la carte fr £15 ⊕ FREE HOUSE ◀ Exmoor Ale & Gold Moor Withy Cutter, Wadworth 6X, Branscombe Bitter, WHB, HSD. **Facilities** Children's menu Children's portions Dogs allowed Garden Parking

---

**AXBRIDGE**                                    Map 4 ST45

# Lamb Inn

**The Square BS26 2AP**
**☎ 01934 732253** ▤ 01934 733821
**dir:** *10m from Wells & Weston-Super-Mare on A370*

Parts of this rambling 15th-century inn were once the guildhall, but it was licensed in 1830 when the new town hall was built. Standing across the medieval square from King John's hunting lodge, the pub's comfortable bars have log fires; there's also a skittle alley and large terraced garden. Snacks and pub favourites support contemporary home-made dishes like pan-fried salmon in cheese and chive coating; and Mediterranean roasted vegetable pancakes in Stilton sauce.

**Open** all wk ◀ Butcombe, Butcombe Gold, guest ales ♡ Thatchers. **Facilities** Garden

---

**BABCARY**                                     Map 4 ST52

# Red Lion ♥

**TA11 7ED ☎ 01458 223230** ▤ 01458 224510
**e-mail:** redlionbabcary@btinternet.com
**dir:** *Please telephone for directions*

The Red Lion is a beautifully refurbished, stone-built free house, with rich, colour-washed walls, heavy beams and simple wooden furniture setting the tone in the friendly bar, whilst French doors lead out into the garden from the restaurant. Granary sandwiches, ciabattas and hot pub favourites like fish pie and honey-glazed Somerset ham, egg and chips are served in the bar. In the restaurant, expect slow roasted pork belly with celeriac purée; butternut squash and sage risotto; and free range duck breast with wild mushroom cream sauce.

**Open** all wk **Bar Meals** L served all wk 12-2.30 D served Mon-Sat 7-9.30 Av main course £11.75 **Restaurant** L served all wk 12-2.30 D served Mon-Sat 7-9.30 Av 3 course à la carte fr £27.50 ⊕ FREE HOUSE ◀ Teignworthy Reel Ale, O'Hanlons, Otter, Bath Ales. ♥ 12 **Facilities** Play area Dogs allowed Garden Parking

---

**BATH**                                        Map 4 ST76

## PICK OF THE PUBS

# The Hop Pole ♥

**7 Albion Buildings, Upper Bristol Rd BA1 3AR**
**☎ 01225 446327**
**e-mail:** hoppole@bathales.co.uk
**dir:** *On A4 from city centre towards Bristol. Pub opposite Royal Victoria Park*

Opposite the Royal Victoria Park and just off the canal path, this is a great spot for quaffing summer ales. One of just ten pubs belonging to Bath Ales, a fresh young micro-brewery, the beers rejoice in names such as Gem, Spa, Wild Hare and Barnstormer. Described as a country pub in the heart of a city, The Hop Pole has a stripped-down, stylish interior, and the lovingly restored, spacious beer garden to the rear is complete with patio heaters and pétanque pitch. The atmospheric old skittle alley has been transformed into a large restaurant, which can accommodate coach parties if pre-booked. Home-cooked food ranges from imaginative bar snacks and sandwiches through to full meals. Children are served smaller portions from the main menu. You could start with pork and foie gras sausage roll with piccalilli before moving on to a slowly braised chuck and shin steak stew, mash and onion gravy, or basil risotto and buffalo mozzarella. Monday night is quiz night and breakfast/brunch is now served on Saturdays and Sundays from 9.30am.

**Open** all day all wk noon-11 (Fri-Sat noon-mdnt) **Bar Meals** L served Mon-Sat 12-2, Sun 12-3 D served Mon-Sat 6-9 Av main course £10 **Restaurant** L served Mon-Sat 12-2, Sun 12-3 D served Mon-Sat 6-9 ◀ Bath Ales: Gem, Spa, Barnstormer, Festivity, Wild Hare. ♥ 14 **Facilities** Children's menu Children's portions Garden

---

## PICK OF THE PUBS

# King William ♥

**36 Thomas St BA1 5NN ☎ 01225 428096**
**e-mail:** info@kingwilliampub.com
**dir:** *At junct of Thomas St & A4 (London Rd), on left from Bath towards London. 15 mins walk from Bath Spa main line station*

A short stroll from the city centre, this 19th-century pub has gone from strength to strength over the past six years under the ownership of Charlie and Amanda Digney. What was once a run-down old boozer with an image problem is now a smart and stylish gastro-pub. It now offers the best of everything: real ales from local micro-breweries, organic cider, and 14 wines served by the glass. Occupying a corner site just off the London Road, it has a cosy snug in the cellar and an elegant upstairs restaurant to showcase the couple's passion for good food. Meat and poultry are free range or organic, and seafood arrives daily from the Cornish coastline. The menu might include chicken, bacon and rocket salad with herb mayonnaise, followed by braised oxtail, sweet onions and horseradish mash. Finish with Seville orange marmalade bread and butter pudding.

**Open** noon-3 5-close (Sat-Sun noon-close) Closed: Mon L **Bar Meals** L served Tue-Sun 12-3 D served all wk 6-10 Av main course £16 **Restaurant** L served Sat-Sun 12-3 booking required D served Wed-Sat 6-10 booking required ⊕ FREE HOUSE ◀ Lady of the Lake, Danish Dynamite, Otter Ale, Dorset Gold, Palmers 200 ♡ Pheasant Plucker, Westons Organic, Orchard Pig. ♥ 14 **Facilities** Children's portions Dogs allowed

---

## PICK OF THE PUBS

# The Marlborough Tavern ◉ ♥

**35 Marlborough Buildings BA1 2LY ☎ 01225 423731**
**e-mail:** joe@marlborough-tavern.com
**dir:** *200mtrs from W end of Royal Crescent, on corner of Marlborough Buildings. 10m from M4 junct 18*

Revamped from a dreary boozer to a contemporary dining pub in 2006, this 18th-century corner pub stands just a stone's throw from Bath's famous Royal Crescent. Foot-weary from the city's tourist trail, customers seek rest and refreshment in the rustic-chic bars or the attractive courtyard garden. Since acquiring the freehold in 2009, Joe Cussens has added Timothy Taylor and Otter ales to the cellar, and upped the number of wines sold by the glass to 23. The classy menu delivers gutsy, full-flavoured dishes prepared from local seasonal and organic produce; you'll find a full list of suppliers on the back of the menu. These top-class ingredients translate to imaginative dinner specials such as a starter of smoked fillet of lamb

Save on Hotels. Book at theAA.com/hotel

SOMERSET 393 ENGLAND

served with butternut and fennel seed purée, dressed with cuttlefish salsa verde; and a main course T-bone steak from Cotmarsh Farm in Hereford, served with slow-roast tomato, hand-cut chips, and a brandy and peppercorn sauce.

**Open** all day all wk noon-11 (Fri-Sat noon-12.30am) Closed: 25 Dec **Bar Meals** Av main course £12 **Restaurant** L served Mon-Sat 12.30-2.30, Sun 12.30-4 booking required D served Mon-Sat 6-9.30, Sun 6-9 booking required Av 3 course à la carte fr £27 ⊕ FREE HOUSE ◀ Butcombe Bitter, Timothy Taylor Landlord, Otter Beer Ö Westons Organic. ♀ 23 **Facilities** Children's portions Dogs allowed Garden

## The Old Green Tree ♀

12 Green St BA1 2JZ ☎ 01225 448259
**dir:** In town centre

Loved for its faded splendour, this 18th-century, three-roomed, oak-panelled pub has a dim and atmospheric interior and a front room decorated with World War II Spitfires. Food ranges from pub basics like soup and bangers and mash ('probably the best sausages in Bath') through to smoked duck and poached apple salad; or mussels in white wine and cream sauce. Great for real ales, German lager, malt whiskies and real coffee.

**Open** all wk Closed: 25 Dec ◀ Spire Ale, Brand Oak Bitter, Pitchfork, Mr Perrretts Stout & Summer Lightning. ♀ 12 **Notes** ⊕

## Pack Horse Inn

Hods Hill, South Stoke BA2 7DU
☎ 01225 832060 📠 01225 830075
**e-mail:** info@packhorseinn.com
**dir:** 2.5m from Bath city centre, take A367 (A37). Take B3110 towards Frome. Take South Stoke turn on right

This country inn maintains a tradition of hospitality that dates back to the 15th century. It was built by monks to provide shelter for pilgrims and travellers, and still has the original bar and inglenook fireplace. Outside an extensive garden overlooks the surrounding countryside. All the meals are home made, from sandwiches and snacks to main courses of spinach, pea and forest mushroom risotto; Normandy chicken, or pepper smoked mackerel fillet with horseradish sauce.

**Open** all wk ◀ Butcombe Bitter, 6X, London Pride.
**Facilities** Dogs allowed Garden

## The Raven

7 Queen St BA1 1HE ☎ 01225 425045
**e-mail:** enquiries@theravenofbath.co.uk
**dir:** Between Queen Sq & Milsom St

Real ale lovers flock to this traditional, family-owned free house, set in two Georgian townhouses on a quiet cobbled street in the centre of Bath. Two hundred ales have been served in the last year alone, including the exclusively brewed Raven and Raven's Gold. And what better accompaniment for your pint than a home-made pie with mash or chips, and gravy? Puddings are along

the lines of spotted Dick, lemon sponge and sticky toffee pudding.

**Open** all wk 11.30-11.30 Closed: 25-26 Dec ◀ Raven, Raven's Gold Ö Stowford Press.

## The Star Inn

23 Vineyards BA1 5NA ☎ 01225 425072
**e-mail:** landlord@star-inn-bath.co.uk
**dir:** On A4, 300mtrs from centre of Bath

One of Bath's oldest pubs and of outstanding historic interest, the Star was first licensed in 1760. Set amid glorious Georgian architecture, it is an impressive building in its own right, with original features including 19th-century Gaskell and Chambers bar fittings, a barrel lift from the cellar, and even complimentary pinches of snuff found in tins in the smaller bar! Long famous for its pints of Bass served from the jug, these days Abbey Ales from Bath's only brewery are also popular. Fresh filled rolls are available and free snacks on Sundays.

**Open** all wk noon-2.30 5.30-mdnt (Fri noon-2.30 5.30-1am Sat noon-1am Sun noon-mdnt) ⊕ PUNCH TAVERNS ◀ Bellringer, Bass, Bath Star, Doom Bar Ö Hells Bells. **Facilities** Dogs allowed

### BAWDRIP                    Map 4 ST33

## The Knowle Inn

TA7 8PN ☎ 01278 683330
**e-mail:** peter@matthews3.wanadoo.co.uk
**dir:** M5 junct 23 or A39 from Bridgwater towards Glastonbury

A mile off the M5, this 16th-century pub nestles beneath the Polden Hills on the edge of the Somerset levels – a great place for walking and cycling. A true community pub, with live music, skittles and darts, it also specialises in fresh seafood, with sea bass and John Dory often among the catch delivered from Plymouth. A full range of sandwiches and light meals is backed by pub favourites such as home-made lasagne, home-cooked ham, and the butcher's choice mixed grill. A Mediterranean-style garden, complete with fish pond, is ideal for summer alfresco meals.

**Open** all day all wk **Bar Meals** L served all wk 11-3 D served all wk 6-9 Av main course £12 **Restaurant** L served all wk 11-3 D served all wk 6-9 Av 3 course à la carte fr £17 ⊕ ENTERPRISE INNS ◀ Otter, Champflower Ale, Revival, Somerland Gold Ö Thatchers. **Facilities** Children's menu Children's portions Dogs allowed Garden Parking

### BECKINGTON                    Map 4 ST85

## Woolpack Inn ★★★ INN ♀

BA11 6SP ☎ 01373 831244 📠 01373 831223
**e-mail:** 6534@greeneking.co.uk
**dir:** Just off A36 near junct with A361

Standing in the middle of the village, this charming, stone-built coaching inn dates back to the 1500s. Inside there's an attractive, flagstone floor in the bar and

outside at the back, a delightful terraced garden. The lunch menu offers soup and sandwich platters, and larger dishes such as home-made sausages and mash; fresh herb and tomato omelette; steak and ale pie; and beer-battered cod and chips. Some of these are also listed on the evening bar menu. Eleven en suite bedrooms, including one four poster room and one family room, are available.

**Open** all day all wk 11am-11pm (Sun 11am-10pm) **Bar Meals** L served Mon-Sat 12-2.30, Sun 12-3 booking required D served Mon-Sat 6-10, Sun 6-9 booking required Av main course £7 **Restaurant** L served Mon-Sat 12-2.30, Sun 12-3 booking required D served Mon-Sat 6-10, Sun 6-9 booking required Fixed menu price fr £20 Av 3 course à la carte fr £25.50 ⊕ OLD ENGLISH INNS & HOTELS ◀ Greene King IPA, Abbot Ale, guest ale Ö Moles Black Rat. ♀ 14 **Facilities** Children's menu Children's portions Dogs allowed Garden Parking **Rooms** 11

### BICKNOLLER                    Map 3 ST13

## The Bicknoller Inn

32 Church Ln TA4 4EL ☎ 01984 656234
**e-mail:** james_herd@sky.com
**dir:** Telephone for directions

A 16th-century thatched country inn set around a courtyard with a large garden under the Quantock Hills. Inside you'll find traditional inglenook fireplaces, flagstone floors and oak beams, as well as a theatre-style kitchen and restaurant. Meals range from sandwiches and pub favourites like hake in beer batter (priced for an 'adequate' or 'generous' portion), to the full three courses with maybe smoked salmon; chicken supreme cooked in red wine, and warm treacle tart.

**Open** all wk noon-3 6-11 (Fri-Sun all day) Closed: Mon L ex BH ◀ Palmers Copper, Palmers IPA, Palmers Gold, guest ales Ö Thatchers Traditional. **Facilities** Play area Dogs allowed Garden Parking

### BLAGDON                    Map 4 ST55

## The New Inn ♀

Church St BS40 7SB
☎ 01761 462475 📠 01761 463523
**e-mail:** newinn.blagdon@tiscali.co.uk
**dir:** From Bristol take A38 S then A368 towards Bath, through Blagdon left onto Church Ln, past church on right

A lovely old country pub in the village of Blagdon at the foot of the Mendips, the New Inn offers open fires, traditional home-cooked food, and magnificent views across fields to Blagdon Lake. The menu is locally sourced, and ranges through snacks, salads and main meals such as brewer's beef (the meat marinated in Wadworth bitter); deep-fried breaded plaice, with chips, jacket or baby potatoes; and vegetable risotto served with a side salad.

**Open** all wk ◀ Wadworth 6X, Henry's IPA, JCB, Guinness. ♀ 16 **Facilities** Dogs allowed Garden Parking

## BLUE ANCHOR · Map 3 ST04

# The Smugglers ⌕

**TA24 6JS ☎ 01984 640385**
**e-mail:** info@take2chefs.co.uk
**dir:** *Off A3191, midway between Minehead & Watchet*

'Fresh food, cooked well' is the simple philosophy at this friendly 300-year-old inn, standing just yards from Blue Anchor's sandy bay with a backdrop of the Exmoor Hills. Food, using fresh produce locally sourced, can be enjoyed in the Cellar Bar or the Dining Room. Sandwiches, filled jacket potatoes, pizzas, wraps, pastas, grills, salads, speciality sausages and fish and seafood are available. Specials might include cider and honey marinated leg of lamb with roasted garlic mash. In fine weather diners eat in the large walled garden, where children can enjoy the animals at the nearby farm and the bouncy castle. The pub now also offers a take-away menu.

**Open** Mon-Fri noon-3 6-11 (Sat-Sun 12-11) Closed: Nov-Etr, Sun eve, Mon-Tue **Bar Meals** L served all wk 12-2.15 D served all wk 6-9 Av main course £8.95 **Restaurant** L served all wk 12-2.15 D served all wk 6-9 ⊕ FREE HOUSE ◀ Smuggled Otter, Otter Ale, John Smith's Ò Western Traditional. ⌕ 8 **Facilities** Children's menu Children's portions Play area Dogs allowed Garden Parking

## BRADFORD-ON-TONE · Map 4 ST12

# White Horse Inn

**Regent St TA4 1HF ☎ 01823 461239**
**e-mail:** glenwhitehorse@googlemail.com
**dir:** *N of A38 between Taunton & Wellington*

Dating back over 300 years, this stone-built inn stands opposite the church in the heart of a delightful thatched village. Very much a community pub, it has a bar area, restaurant, skittle alley, garden and patio. Real ales brewed in the south west include guests, and home-cooked food favours tried and tested popular dishes, with fish a speciality: deep-fried brie; garlic mushrooms; Thai green curry; seafood pie; black grape cheesecake; and warm dark chocolate fudge cake. Jamming sessions take place two nights every week.

**Open** all day all wk **Bar Meals** L served all wk 12-2 D served all wk 6-9 Av main course £5 **Restaurant** L served all wk 12-2 D served all wk 6-9 Fixed menu price fr £9.50 Av 3 course à la carte fr £16.70 ⊕ ENTERPRISE INNS ◀ Cotleigh Tawney, John Smith's, Whitbread Best, Sharp's Doom Bar, Exmoor ale, guest ales. **Facilities** Children's menu Children's portions Dogs allowed Garden Parking

## CATCOTT · Map 4 ST33

# The Crown Inn ⌕ NEW

**1 The Nydon TA7 9HQ ☎ 01278 722288**
**e-mail:** catcottcrownin@aol.com
**dir:** *M5 junct 23, A39 towards Glastonbury. Turn left to Catcott*

Perhaps 400 years old, this low-beamed, flagstone-floored pub in the Somerset levels originated as a beer house serving local peat-cutters. The winter log fire takes the chill off Bristol Channel winds; in summer the half-acre beer garden is great for families and sun worshippers. The obliging cooks here experiment with

prime Somerset produce, creating specials like Calypso pork (with a ginger and pear sauce) to try alongside firm pubby favourites, helped along by cask ales from regional micro-breweries.

*The Crown Inn*

**Open** 12-2.30 6-late Closed: Mon L **Bar Meals** L served Tue-Sun 12-2 (booking advisable Sun) D served all wk 6-9 Av main course £7.95 **Restaurant** L served Tue-Sun 12-2 (booking advisable Sun) D served Sun-Thu 6-9, Fri-Sat 6-9.30 (booking advisable Fri-Sat) Fixed menu price fr £9.95 Av 3 course à la carte fr £17.95 ⊕ FREE HOUSE ◀ Butcombe, Sharp's Doom Bar Ò Ashton Press. ⌕ 10 **Facilities** Children's menu Children's portions Play area Dogs allowed Garden Parking

*See advert below*

# PICK OF THE PUBS

## The Hunters Rest ★★★★ INN 🍷

**CLUTTON**          Map 4 ST65

**King Ln, Clutton Hill BS39 5QL**
☎ **01761 452303** 📠 **01761 453308**
**e-mail:** info@huntersrest.co.uk
**web:** www.huntersrest.co.uk
**dir:** *On A37 follow signs for Wells through Pensford, at large rdbt left towards Bath, 100mtrs right into country lane, pub 1m up hill*

The breathtaking views from this popular free house over the Cam Valley to the Mendip Hills, and across the Chew Valley to Bristol, are well worth a visit on their own account. The pub was originally built around 1750 as a hunting lodge for the Earl of Warwick; but, when the estate was sold in 1872, the building became a tavern serving the growing number of coal miners working in the area. Mining has finished now and the inn has been transformed into an attractive place to eat and stay, with its five well-appointed bedrooms, including some four-poster suites.

Paul Thomas has been running The Hunters Rest for over 20 years, and has established a great reputation for a warm welcome and good home-made food. He offers a range of real beers like Butcombe and Bath Gem, as well as a reasonably priced wine list, with a good choice by the glass.

The menu includes a selection of salads, ploughman's and bakehouse rolls with fillings like cold roast beef and horseradish; and Norwegian prawns with coleslaw. Giant filled pastries, or oggies, might come with chicken and wholegrain mustard; or mixed smoked fish with Cheddar sauce. Other hot dishes include Somerset faggots with onion gravy; vegetarian lasagne; lamb's liver and bacon with onions; and daily fresh Brixham fish choices from the blackboard. There's a children's menu, too, plus popular puds such as tarte au citron with blackberry ice cream; and maple and walnut cheesecake.

In summer you can sit out in the landscaped grounds and watch the miniature railway take customers on rides around the garden, while in winter you can cosy up to the crackling log fires.

**Open** all wk noon-3 6-11 (Fri-Sun noon-11) **Bar Meals** L served Mon-Thu 12-3, Fri-Sun 12-10 D served Mon-Thu 6-10, Fri-Sun 12-10 Av main course £9.50 **Restaurant** Av 3 course à la carte fr £20 ⊕ FREE HOUSE ◄ Butcombe, Bath Gem, Otter Ale ♻ Broadoak Thatchers. 🍷 10 **Facilities** Children's menu Play area Family room Dogs allowed Garden Parking **Rooms** 5

## CHEW MAGNA — Map 4 ST56

### PICK OF THE PUBS

### The Bear and Swan ♥

**South Pde BS40 8SL ☎ 01275 331100**
**e-mail:** bearandswan@fullers.co.uk
**dir:** *A37 from Bristol. Turn right signed Chew Magna onto B3130. Or from A38 turn left on B3130*

An early 18th-century, oak-beamed pub with a Victorian frontage, beyond which lies a light, fresh-feeling interior with scrubbed wooden floorboards, and a hotchpotch of reclaimed tables and chairs. Real ales include Fuller's London Pride and Seafarers, real ciders come from around and about and the wines have been well selected. The restaurant offers a daily menu and a carte with good choices of fish, game, seafood, meats and vegetarian dishes. A lunchtime bar meal could involve seafood bake; gammon with double egg and fries; or cheese and tomato omelette, while if you're eating in the restaurant, you might start with steamed mussels, chorizo, coriander and lime; or smoked duck with fresh fig salad in balsamic syrup. Options then could be roast sirloin of beef, Yorkshire pudding and red wine gravy; smoked haddock baked with herb crust and mashed potatoes; or grilled vegetable risotto and halloumi cheese. Desserts are all freshly made.

**Open** all day Closed: 25 Dec, Sun eve **Bar Meals** L served all wk 12-2.30 D served Mon-Sat 6.30-9.30 Av main course £8 **Restaurant** L served all wk 12-2.30 booking required D served Mon-Sat 6.30-9.30 booking required Av 3 course à la carte fr £24 ⊕ FULLERS ◼ London Pride, Seafarers Ale ♻ Scrumpy, Ashton Press. ♥ 12 **Facilities** Children's portions Dogs allowed Garden Parking

## CHISELBOROUGH — Map 4 ST41

### The Cat Head Inn ♥

**Cat St TA14 6TT ☎ 01935 881231**
**e-mail:** info@thecatheadinn.co.uk
**dir:** *1m off A303, take slip road to Crewkerne (A356)*

This creeper-clad hamstone pub was converted from a farmhouse in 1896. Today, the flagstone floors, open fires and contemporary artefacts create a unique atmosphere inside, while outside you will find an award-winning beer garden and play area. Sup real ales or local ciders while browsing the menu, with lunchtime options like scampi and chips, steak or salads like smoked chicken and pine nut, to evening dishes of crispy duck with scrumpy sauce, or saddle of rabbit with mustard and thyme.

**Open** all wk noon-3 6.30-11 Closed: 25 Dec eve, Sun eve ◼ Butcombe, Otter, Old Speckled Hen, Tribute, London Pride ♻ Thatchers Cheddar Valley, Katy. ♥ 8 **Facilities** Play area Dogs allowed Garden

## CHURCHILL — Map 4 ST45

### The Crown Inn

**The Batch BS25 5PP ☎ 01934 852995**
**dir:** *From Bristol take A38 S. Right at Churchill lights, left in 200mtrs, up hill to pub*

At the base of the Mendip Hills, this gem of a pub was originally a coaching stop on the old Bristol to Exeter route. Constantly changing local brews are tapped straight from the barrel in the two rustic bars, where you'll find open fires, flagstone floors and stone walls. Freshly prepared food is served at lunchtime only, with options such as sandwiches, filled jacket potatoes, sausages and mash and pork casserole. There are beautiful gardens for outdoor eating in the summer.

**Open** all day all wk 11-11 (Fri 11-mdnt) **Bar Meals** L served all wk 12-2.30 Av main course £5.50 ⊕ FREE HOUSE ◼ Palmers IPA, Draught Bass, P G Steam, Butcombe, Batch Bitter ♻ Thatchers. **Facilities** Children's portions Dogs allowed Garden Parking **Notes** ⊛

## CLAPTON-IN-GORDANO — Map 4 ST47

### PICK OF THE PUBS

### The Black Horse ♥

**Clevedon Ln BS20 7RH ☎ 01275 842105**
**e-mail:** theblackhorse@talktalkbusiness.net
**dir:** *M5 junct 19, 3m to village. 2m from Portishead, 10m from Bristol*

The pretty, whitewashed Black Horse was built in the 14th century and at one time what is now the small Snug Bar was the village lock up, as the surviving bars on one of the windows testify. The traditional bar features low beams, flagstone floors, wooden settles and old guns above the big open fireplace. The kitchen in this listed building is tiny, which limits its output to traditional pub food served lunchtimes only (and not at all on Sundays). The repertoire includes hot and cold filled baguettes; beef cooked in Guinness; corned beef hash; and Moroccan lamb tagine, as well as seasonal specials. The large rear garden includes a children's play area, and there's a separate family room.

**Open** all day all wk **Bar Meals** L served Mon-Sat 12-2 ◼ Courage Best, Wadworth 6X, Shepherd Neame Spitfire, Butcombe Best, Exmoor Gold ♻ Thatchers Dry, Moles Black Rat. ♥ 8 **Facilities** Play area Family room Dogs allowed Garden Parking

## CLUTTON — Map 4 ST65

### PICK OF THE PUBS

### The Hunters Rest — INN ♥

*See Pick of the Pubs on page 395*

## COMBE HAY — Map 4 ST75

### PICK OF THE PUBS

### The Wheatsheaf Inn ♥

*See Pick of the Pubs on page 398*

## CONGRESBURY — Map 4 ST46

### The Ship and Castle ★★★★ INN ♥ NEW

**High St BS49 5JA ☎ 01934 833535**
**e-mail:** info@shipandcastle.com
**dir:** *M5 junct 21, A370 towards Bristol for 4m. Pub in village centre at lights*

New life has been breathed into this 500-year-old inn close to Bristol Airport and the M5, with six boutique-style bedrooms opening in 2009, and a stylish refurbishment of the cosy bar and dining areas. Expect to find log fires in old stone fireplaces, fat church candles on chunky tables, deep sofas to sink into, Greene King ales on handpump and seasonal menus that champion local produce. Try the seafood chowder, followed by braised lamb shank, and chocolate brownie with clotted cream.

**Open** all day all wk **Bar Meals** L served all wk 12-6 D served all wk 6-9.30 Av main course £7 food served all day **Restaurant** L served all wk 12-6 D served Mon-Sat 6-9.30 Fixed menu price fr £12 Av 3 course à la carte £25 food served all day ⊕ GREENE KING ◼ Greene King IPA, Abbot Ale, Old Speckled Hen ♻ Stowford Press, Aspall. ♥ 12 **Facilities** Children's menu Children's portions Dogs allowed Garden Parking **Rooms** 6

### The White Hart Inn ♥

**Wrington Rd BS49 5AR ☎ 01934 833303**
**e-mail:** murat@simplywhitehart.co.uk
**dir:** *From M5 junct 21, A370 through Congresbury, right towards Wrington. Inn 2.3m*

A handy M5 pit-stop a short drive from junction 21, this charming dining pub has a secluded garden with views of the Mendip Hills, and the beamed bars are country-cosy with log fires in stone inglenooks. Refuel with simple, honest food such as steak and Badger ale pie, venison with blackberry and Stilton sauce, or a lunchtime brie and bacon baguette, washed down with a pint of Tanglefoot. The gin list is impressive and don't miss the Turkish night – music and belly dancers.

**Open** all wk 12-3 6-11.30 (Fri-Sun 12-11.30) Closed: 25 Dec **Bar Meals** booking required booking required Av main course £8 food served all day **Restaurant** booking required booking required Fixed menu price fr £13 Av 3

Save on Hotels. Book at **theAA.com/hotel**

SOMERSET 397 ENGLAND

course à la carte fr £20 food served all day ⊕ HALL & WOODHOUSE ◀ Badger, Tanglefoot, Pickled Partridge ♂ Westons Stowford Press, Thatchers Gold. ♀ 8
**Facilities** Children's menu Children's portions Play area Dogs allowed Garden Parking

### CORTON DENHAM      Map 4 ST62

## PICK OF THE PUBS

## The Queens Arms ♀

**DT9 4LR ☎ 01963 220317**
e-mail: relax@thequeensarms.com
dir: *From A30 (Sherborne) take B3145 signed Wincanton. Approx 1.5m left at red sign to Corton Denham. 1.5m, left down hill, right at bottom into village. Pub on left*

A past AA Pub of the Year, The Queens Arms luxuriates in its location in a secluded village tucked away in the rolling hills of the Somerset/Dorset border. Fiercely dedicated to supporting local producers, Rupert and Victoria Reeves seek out the finest farmhouse ciders (using apples such as slack-ma-girdle) and offer eager locals and guests a choice of beers from micro-breweries such as Moor, a Somerset favourite. The owners of this stone built, classically appointed dining inn champion low food miles and animal welfare; pork is from their own (beer fed!) pigs, poultry and eggs via their own free-range chickens. Menus offer huge variety: perhaps start with local shot hare rillettes with grape chutney and crisp rye bread or braised leek and quail's egg tart with hollandaise sauce before really tucking into pork belly stuffed with apricot with crushed new potatoes and braised red cabbage or pan-fried hake wrapped in home-cured smoked bacon with celeriac chips.

**Open** all wk 11-3 6-11 (Sat-Sun, BH, Xmas wk 11-11) **Bar Meals** L served Mon-Sat 12-3, Sun 12-4 D served Mon-Sat 6-10, Sun 6-9.30 Av main course £10.50 **Restaurant** L served Mon-Sat 12-3, Sun 12-4 D served Mon-Sat 6-10, Sun 6-9.30 Av 3 course à la carte fr £23 ⊕ FREE HOUSE ◀ Moor Revival, Abbeydale Riot, changing guests ♂ Thatchers Cheddar Valley, Hecks, Wilkins. **Facilities** Children's menu Children's portions Dogs allowed Garden Parking

### CRANMORE      Map 4 ST64

## Strode Arms

**BA4 4QJ ☎ 01749 880450**
dir: *S of A361, 3.5m E of Shepton Mallet, 7.5m W of Frome*

Just up the road from the East Somerset Railway, this rambling old coaching inn boasts a splendid front terrace overlooking the village duck pond. Spacious bar areas are neatly laid out with comfortable country furnishings and warmed by winter log fires; the perfect setting to enjoy a pint of Bishop's Tipple. The bar menu features filled baguettes and pub favourites like Wiltshire ham, eggs and chips. Meanwhile, restaurant diners might choose roast guinea fowl; or bubble and squeak with asparagus.

**Open** all wk 11.30-3 6-11 **Bar Meals** L served all wk 12-2 D served Mon-Sat 6-9 **Restaurant** L served all wk 12-2 D served Mon-Sat 6-9 ⊕ WADWORTH ◀ Henry's IPA, Wadworth 6X, JCB, Bishop's Tipple. ♀ 7
**Facilities** Children's menu Children's portions Family room Dogs allowed Garden Parking

### CREWKERNE      Map 4 ST40

## The George Inn ★★★ INN ♀

**Market Square TA18 7LP**
☎ 01460 73650   📠 01460 72974
e-mail: georgecrewkerne@btconnect.com
web: www.thegeorgehotelcrewkerne.co.uk
dir: *Telephone for directions*

The George has been welcoming travellers in the heart of Crewkerne since the 16th century, though the present hamstone building dates from 1832. Thatchers ciders sit alongside four real ales and three lagers in the bar, while the kitchen produces an array of popular dishes for bar snacks (cheese on toast; toasted sandwiches) and 'serious nosh' (giant Yorkshire pudding and chips; large battered cod; Mediterranean Wellington for vegetarians). Thirteen comfortable en suite bedrooms await replete diners.

**Open** all day all wk **Bar Meals** L served all wk 12-2 D served all wk 7-9 Av main course £7.95 **Restaurant** L served all wk 12-2 D served all wk 7-9 Av 3 course à la carte fr £16 ⊕ FREE HOUSE ◀ Old Speckled Hen, Doom Bar, Tribute, Boddington's ♂ Thatchers Dry, Thatchers Gold. ♀ 8 **Rooms** 13

## The Manor Arms

**North Perrott TA18 7SG**
☎ 01460 72901   📠 01460 74055
e-mail: themanorarms@hotmail.co.uk
dir: *From A30 (Yeovil/Honiton) take A3066 towards Bridport. North Perrott 1.5m*

On the Dorset-Somerset border, this 16th-century Grade II listed pub and its neighbouring hamstone cottages overlook the village green. The popular River Parrett trail runs by the door. The inn, now under new ownership, has been lovingly restored and an inglenook fireplace, flagstone floors and oak beams are among the charming

features inside. With ales like Exmoor and Thatchers Gold cider, expect simple traditional food such as grilled steaks and chicken dishes, with bar snacks like sandwiches, baguettes and jacket potatoes.

**Open** all wk noon-11 **Bar Meals** L served all wk 12-2.30 D served all wk 6.30-9 Av main course £7 **Restaurant** L served all wk 12-2.30 D served all wk 6.30-9 Fixed menu price fr £10 ◀ ENTERPISE INNS ◀ Butcombe, Sharp's Doom Bar, Exmoor ♂ Thatchers Gold. **Facilities** Children's menu Children's portions Dogs allowed Garden Parking

### CROSCOMBE      Map 4 ST54

## The Bull Terrier ★★★ INN ♀

**Long St BA5 3QJ ☎ 01749 343658**
e-mail: barry.vidler@bullterrierpub.co.uk
dir: *Halfway between Wells & Shepton Mallet on A371*

First licensed in 1612, this unspoiled village free house is one of Somerset's oldest pubs. The building itself dates from the late 15th century, though the fireplace and ceiling in the inglenook bar are later additions. Formerly known as the 'Rose and Crown', the name in 1976. One menu is offered throughout, including whitebait; hot smoked mackerel with horseradish; and ginger chicken or lamb steak. Accommodation consists of two brightly decorated bedrooms.

**Open** all wk **Bar Meals** L served all wk 12-2 D served all wk 7-9 Av main course £6.95 **Restaurant** L served all wk 12-2 D served all wk 7-9 ⊕ FREE HOUSE ◀ Butcombe, Courage Directors, Marston's Pedigree, Greene King Old Speckled Hen, Ruddles County ♂ Thatchers Cheddar Valley, Thatchers Gold. ♀ 8 **Facilities** Family room Dogs allowed Garden Parking **Rooms** 2

### DINNINGTON      Map 4 ST41

## Dinnington Docks

**TA17 8SX ☎ 01460 52397   📠 01460 52397**
e-mail: hilary@dinningtondocks.co.uk
dir: *S of A303 between South Petherton & Ilminster*

Formerly known as the Rose & Crown, this traditional village pub on the old Fosse Way has been licensed for over 250 years and has no loud music, pool tables or fruit machines to drown out the conversation. Inside you will find pictures, signs and memorabilia of its rail and maritime past. Good quality cask ales and farmhouse cider are served, and freshly prepared food including the likes of crab cakes, Greek salad, faggots, snapper, steak, and lamb shank for two. It is located in an ideal place for cycling and walking.

**Open** all wk 11.30-3.30 6-mdnt (all day Sat-Sun) **Bar Meals** L served all wk 12-2 D served all wk 7-9 Av main course £3.95 food served all day **Restaurant** L served all wk 12-2 D served all wk 7-9 food served all day ⊕ FREE HOUSE ◀ Butcombe Bitter, guest ales ♂ Burrow Hill, Stowford Press, Thatchers Gold. **Facilities** Children's menu Children's portions Play area Family room Dogs allowed Garden Parking

# PICK OF THE PUBS

## The Wheatsheaf Inn 🍷

**COMBE HAY** Map 4 ST75

**BA2 7EG**
☎ 01225 833504  📠 01225 833504
e-mail: info@wheatsheafcombehay.com
dir: *From Bath take A369 (Exeter road) to Odd Down, left at park towards Combe Hay. 2m to thatched cottage, turn left*

A pretty white painted free house, nestling on a peaceful hillside just off the A367 south of Bath and close to the route of the former Somerset Coal Canal. The canal and the railway have come and gone, but the valley and its people survive; in fact, a newspaper recently named Combe Hay as one of England's most desirable villages.

The Wheatsheaf was originally built as a farmhouse in 1576, and parts of the present building date back to the 16th century. It began opening its doors as a public house in the 18th century, and has been welcoming locals and travellers alike ever since. Today, real ales, local cider and an amazing European wine list (thanks to the passion of the owner) are available in the stylishly decorated, rambling bar with its massive wooden tables, sporting prints and open fires. The building is decorated with flowers in summer, when the gorgeous south-facing garden makes an ideal spot for alfresco dining.

The daily menus feature ploughman's lunches and an impressive selection of freshly cooked hot dishes. Lunch or dinner might begin with Brixham crab, lemongrass and ginger risotto; terrine of Creedy Carver duck and Sandridge streaky, with Cumberland jam; or seared Lulworth Bay scallops, black pudding and cauliflower purée. Follow with Wheatsheaf chicken and mushroom pie with spring greens; rump of spring lamb, braised belly, gribiche and garlic purée; or sweet peppered loin of Sandridge Farm pork, ham hock hash and spring onions. Don't miss dessert options like vanilla and rhubarb crème brûlée; milk chocolate and honeycomb mousse; Valrhona chocolate fondant, malted milk ice cream; or Alphanso Mando rice pudding with mango sorbet. Polite dogs are welcome to join the pub's own spaniels, Milo and Brie.

**Open** Tue-Sun Closed: 25-26 Dec & 1st 2wks Jan, Sun eve, Mon (ex BH)
**Bar Meals** L served Tue-Sun 12-2.30 D served Tue-Sun 6.30-9.30 Av main course £14 **Restaurant** L served Tue-Sun 12-2.30 D served Tue-Sun 6.30-9.30 ⊕ FREE HOUSE ◀ Butcombe Bitter, Bath Ales ♂ Cheddar Valley Cider, Ashton Press. ♀ 13
**Facilities** Children's menu Dogs allowed Garden Parking

## DITCHEAT
Map 4 ST63

### PICK OF THE PUBS

### The Manor House Inn ♥

BA4 6RB ☎ 01749 860276  📠 0870 286 3379
e-mail: landlord@manorhouseinn.co.uk
dir: *From Shepton Mallet take A371 towards Castle Cary, in 3m turn right to Ditcheat*

About 150 years ago this delightful 17th-century free house, constructed from Ditcheat red brick, belonged to the lord of the manor and was known as the White Hart. It's tucked away in a charming Mendip village offering easy access to the Royal Bath and West showground, and the East Somerset steam railway. Inside you'll find roaring log fires in winter and flagstone floors, with the bar serving Butcombe Bitter and regular guest ales, local cider, apple brandies and up to nine wines by the glass. Menus are seasonal; you may find starters such as fresh beetroot, pine nuts and goat's cheese risotto, or tempura prawns with lemongrass, chilli and soya dressing. Main courses may proffer venison rump on buttered Savoy cabbage with new potatoes, Chantenay carrots and a port and blackcurrant sauce; or braised rabbit in a grain mustard and brandy sauce. Choose a home-made dessert from the board in the restaurant.

**Open** all day all wk 11.30-3 5.30-11 (Fri-Sun noon-mdnt) **Bar Meals** L served Mon-Sat 12-2.30, Sun 12-5 D served Mon-Thu 6.30-9, Fri-Sat 6.30-9.30 Av main course £8.95 **Restaurant** L served Mon-Sat 12-2.30, Sun 12-5 booking required D served Mon-Thu 6.30-9, Fri-Sat 6.30-9.30 booking required Av 3 course à la carte fr £22.50 ⊕ FREE HOUSE ◀ Butcombe, John Smiths's, guest ales ♂ Ashton Press, Natch. ♥ 9 **Facilities** Children's portions Dogs allowed Garden Parking

## DUNSTER
Map 3 SS94

### PICK OF THE PUBS

### The Luttrell Arms ★★★ HL

High St TA24 6SG
☎ 01643 821555  📠 01643 821567
e-mail: info@luttrellarms.fsnet.co.uk
dir: *From A39 (Bridgewater to Minehead), left onto A396 to Dunster (2m from Minehead)*

Built in the 15th-century as a guest house for the Abbots of Cleeve, this beguiling hotel has retained all its atmospheric charms. Open fires and oak beams make the bar a welcoming place in winter, while the bedrooms are period pieces complete with leather armchairs and four-poster beds. A rib-sticking wild venison casserole with ale and horseradish sauce is just the thing for a chilly day, while in the more formal restaurant you could tuck into smoked haddock fishcakes, followed by wild pigeon and mushroom parcels with cider jus. Desserts include sticky ginger parkin with vanilla-steeped pineapple and ginger ice cream in the restaurant, and clotted cream rice pudding in the bar. Locally brewed beers and cider and

a good value wine list makes staying the night an appealing option, especially since the murmuring of ghostly monks is rumoured to cure even the most stubborn insomnia.

**Open** all wk 8am-11pm **Bar Meals** L served all wk 11.30-3, all day summer D served all wk 7-10 **Restaurant** L served Sun 12-3 booking required D served all wk 7-10 booking required ⊕ FREE HOUSE ◀ Exmoor Gold Fox, Guest ale ♂ Cheddar Valley Cider. **Facilities** Children's menu Children's portions Family room Dogs allowed Garden **Rooms** 28

## EAST COKER
Map 4 ST51

### PICK OF THE PUBS

### The Helyar Arms ★★★★ INN ◉

Moor Ln BA22 9JR
☎ 01935 862332  📠 01935 864129
e-mail: info@helyar-arms.co.uk
dir: *3m from Yeovil. Take A57 or A30, follow East Coker signs*

Reputedly named after Archdeacon Helyar, a chaplain to Queen Elizabeth I, this Grade II listed building dates back in part to 1468. Log fires warm the old world bar in this charming inn, where Butcombe, Black Sheep and Hobgoblin ales are backed by Stowford Press and Taunton Traditional ciders. There's a skittle alley, comfortable accommodation and a separate restaurant occupying an original apple loft. The kitchen makes full use of local produce, including wood pigeon, rabbit, venison, pheasant and fish from the south Devon coast. There's plenty of choice from sandwiches and lighter bites to starters such as chicken liver parfait with carrot and orange marmalade; and salmon gravadlax with horseradish. For a main course there could be home-made lasagne; roast corn-fed chicken with Lyonnaise potatoes, cabbage, bacon and tarragon sauce; or tartlet of baby red mullet with leeks and caviar cream. Succulent steaks can be cut to order and grilled. All puddings are home made, and coffees and teas come with home-made petits fours.

**Open** all wk **Bar Meals** L served all wk 12-2.30 D served all wk 6.30-9.30 Av main course £7 **Restaurant** L served all wk 12-2.30 D served all wk 6.30-9.30 Av 3 course à la carte fr £25 ⊕ PUNCH TAVERNS ◀ Butcombe Bitter, Black Sheep, Hobgoblin ♂ Stowford Press, Taunton Traditional. **Facilities** Family room Dogs allowed Garden Parking **Rooms** 6

## EXFORD
Map 3 SS83

### PICK OF THE PUBS

### The Crown Hotel ★★★ HL ◉ ♥

*See Pick of the Pubs on page 400*

## FAULKLAND
Map 4 ST75

### Tuckers Grave

BA3 5XF ☎ 01373 834230
dir: *From Bath take A36 towards Warminster. Turn right on A366, through Norton St Philip towards Faulkland. In Radstock, left at x-rds, pub on left*

Tapped ales and farm cider are served at Somerset's smallest pub, a tiny atmospheric bar with old settles. Lunchtime sandwiches and ploughman's lunches are available, and a large lawn with flower borders makes an attractive outdoor seating area. The grave in the pub's name is the unmarked one of Edward Tucker, who hung himself here in 1747.

**Open** 11.30-3 6-11 (Sun noon-3 7-10.30) Closed: 25 Dec, Mon L ⊕ FREE HOUSE ◀ Interbrew Bass, Butcombe Bitter ♂ Cheddar Valley, Farmhouse Gold. **Facilities** Family room Garden Parking **Notes** ◉

## FRESHFORD
Map 4 ST76

### The Inn at Freshford ♥

BA2 7WG ☎ 01225 722250  📠 01225 723887
dir: *1m from A36 between Beckington & Limpley Stoke*

With its 15th-century origins, and log fires adding to its warm and friendly atmosphere, this popular inn in the Limpley Valley has extensive gardens and is an ideal base for walking, especially along the Kennet & Avon Canal. The à la carte menu changes weekly to show the range of food available, and a daily specials board and large children's menu complete the variety. Typical home-made dishes are pâtés, steak and ale pie, lasagne and desserts; a nice selection of fish dishes includes fresh local trout.

**Open** all wk ◀ Butcombe Bitter, Courage Best, guest ale. ♥ 12 **Facilities** Dogs allowed Garden Parking

# PICK OF THE PUBS

## The Crown Hotel ★★★HL 🌸 ♟

**EXFORD**     Map 3 SS83

**TA24 7PP**
☎ **01643 831554**   📄 **01643 831665**
**e-mail:** info@crownhotelexmoor.co.uk
**web:** www.crownhotelexmoor.co.uk
*dir: From M5 junct 25 follow Taunton signs. Take A358 then B3224 via Wheddon Cross to Exford*

The family-run 17th-century Crown Hotel was the first purpose-built coaching inn on Exmoor, strategically sited between Taunton and Barnstaple. This venerable establishment, surrounded by beautiful countryside and moorland, is located in a pretty village in three acres of gardens and woodland, through which runs a fast-flowing trout stream. Not surprisingly, outdoor pursuits around here include walking, hunting, horse-riding and shooting. Perhaps this is why the Crown is a pet-friendly establishment, with reasonable rates for dogs and horses staying overnight.

The cosy country bar remains very much the social heart of the village, many of whose patrons enjoy the Exmoor Ales from Wiveliscombe just down the road. Welcoming log fires are lit in the lounge and bar in winter, and lovely water and terrace gardens are idyllic places to relax in summer.

In the kitchen, quality ingredients are sourced locally where possible and cooked to order. The hotel's day menu is served from noon and throughout the afternoon: sandwiches and baguettes; baked potatoes brimming with tuna mayo, prawns and marie rose or coronation chicken; or Exmoor venison burger, sweetcorn and tomato chutney; and light meals such as warm chicken, chorizo and pine nut salad with pesto dressing. Served in the bar you'll find such dishes as halloumi, sun-blushed tomato and basil brochetta followed by sesame encrusted salmon teryaki with soy noodles, bean sprouts, stir-fried vegetables and lemon and ginger sauce. Organic meats include sausages, lamb and pork, represented in dishes such as beef and Exmoor Ale pie in all-butter shortcrust pastry, or roasted spring lamb rump niçoise with sauté fine beans, sun-blushed tomatoes, parisienne potatoes, anchovies and salsa verdi.

If you plump for a restaurant meal and a tastefully decorated room for the night, a feast certainly awaits: a starter of roast wood pigeon with braised celery heart and Puy lentils could be followed by poached brill with wilted pak choy, white asparagus, violet potatoes and truffle dressing. An orange-scented crème caramel with mango sorbet and shortbread biscuit will round things off nicely, before you retire to the lounge for coffee and home-made petits fours.

**Open** all day all wk noon-11pm
**Bar Meals** L served all wk 12-2.30 D served all wk 5.30-9.30 Av main course £10.50 **Restaurant** D served all wk 7-9 Av 3 course à la carte fr £35 🍺 FREE HOUSE 🍺 Exmoor Ale, Exmoor Gold, Guest ales 🍏 Thatchers Gold, Cornish Rattler. ♟ 10 **Facilities** Dogs allowed Garden Parking **Rooms** 16

## FROME                                    Map 4 ST74

### PICK OF THE PUBS

### The Horse & Groom ⚑

**East Woodlands BA11 5LY ☎ 01373 462802**
**e-mail:** kathybarrett@btconnect.com
**web:** www.horseandgroom.care4free.net
**dir:** *A361 towards Trowbridge, over B3092 rdbt, take immediate right towards East Woodlands, pub 1m on right*

Located at the end of a single track lane, this attractive 17th-century building is adorned with colourful hanging baskets in summer and surrounded by lawns fronted by severely pollarded lime trees. The bar, furnished with pine pews and settles on a flagstone floor and a large inglenook fireplace, offers shove ha'penny, cribbage, dominoes and a selection of daily newspapers for your diversion. There's also a carpeted lounge, including three dining tables in addition to the conservatory-style garden room with 32 covers. A great choice of drinks includes smoothies and milkshakes, and designated drivers are provided with free soft drinks. The lunch and bar menu is offered at lunchtime along with baguettes, salads and daily specials. In the evening, the bar and baguette menus are complemented by a full carte served in all areas. Typical dishes are smoked salmon roulade followed by peppered venison with Cumberland sauce.

**Open** all wk Mon-Sat 11.30-2 6.30-11 (Sun 12-2 7-10.30) **Bar Meals** food served all day ⊕ FREE HOUSE ◀ Wadworth 6X, Butcombe Bitter, Timothy Taylor Landlord, Blindmans Brewery, Blindmans Buff, Yeovil Star Gazer ☼ Stowford Press, Westons Bounds Scrumpy, Westons Old Rosie. ⚑ 9 **Facilities** Dogs allowed Garden Parking

## HASELBURY PLUCKNETT              Map 4 ST41

### PICK OF THE PUBS

### The White Horse at Haselbury ⚑

**North St TA18 7RJ ☎ 01460 78873**
**e-mail:** haselbury@btconnect.com
**dir:** *Just off A30 between Crewkerne & Yeovil on B3066*

Set in the peaceful village of Haselbury Plucknett, the building started life as a rope works and flax store, later becoming a cider house. Its interior feels fresh and warm, but retains the original character of exposed stone and open fires. Patrick and Jan Howard

---

have run the hostelry for over ten years, with the explicit promise to provide the best food, service and value for money possible. This is confirmed by the lunchtime set menu served from Tuesday to Saturday, when vegetable soup could be followed by poached smoked hake with creamy spinach sauce, and rounded off with spiced fruit sponge and brandy sauce. However, an excellent selection of fish specials may tempt: lemon baked salmon fillet with lobster sauce; or fillet of cod baked with a pesto crust perhaps. The eclectic carte also includes pork and three mustard stroganoff, and roasted breast of Aylesbury duck with plum sauce. Enjoy your meal with a glass of Otter ale, Burrows Hill cider or one of the ten wines by the glass.

**Open** noon-2.30 6.30-11 Closed: Sun eve, Mon **Bar Meals** L served Tue-Sun 12-2 D served Tue-Sat 6.30-9.30 Av main course £8 food served all day **Restaurant** L served Tue-Sun 12-2 D served Tue- Sat 6.30-9.30 Fixed menu price fr £12.95 Av 3 course à la carte fr £18 ⊕ FREE HOUSE ◀ Palmers IPA, Otter Ale ☼ Thatchers Dry, Burrow Hill. ⚑ 10 **Facilities** Children's menu Children's portions Garden Parking

## HINTON BLEWETT                    Map 4 ST55

### Ring O'Bells ⚑

**BS39 5AN ☎ 01761 452239   📠 01761 451245**
**e-mail:** jonjenssen@btinternet.com
**dir:** *11m S of Bristol on A37 towards Wells. Turn right from either Clutton or Temple Cloud to Hinton Blewett*

On the edge of the Mendips, this 200-year-old inn describes itself as the 'archetypal village green pub' and offers good views of the Chew Valley. An all-year-round cosy atmosphere is boosted by a log fire in winter, and a wide choice of real ales. There's always something going on, whether it's a tour of the brewery or pig racing night! Good value dishes include home-made fishcakes, steaks, and braised beef and Butcombe in a giant Yorkshire pudding. Baguettes, sandwiches, jacket potatoes and ploughman's also available.

**Open** all wk Mon-Thu 12-3 5-11 (all day Fri-Sun) **Bar Meals** L served all wk 12-2 D served all wk 6.30-9 booking required Av main course £7.95 **Restaurant** L served all wk 12-2 D served all wk 6.30-9 booking required ⊕ BUTCOMBE ◀ Butcombe, Fuller's London Pride, Butcombe Gold, Gem, Guest ales. ⚑ 8 **Facilities** Dogs allowed Garden Parking

## HINTON ST GEORGE                  Map 4 ST41

### PICK OF THE PUBS

### The Lord Poulett Arms ⚑

**High St TA17 8SE ☎ 01460 73149**
**e-mail:** reservations@lordpoulettarms.com
**dir:** *2m N of Crewkerne, 1.5m S of A303*

This elegantly restored 17th-century thatched free house stands in a street of golden hamstone buildings in one of Somerset's loveliest villages. The dining room has real fires in open fireplaces, whilst the bar features bare flagstones and boarded floors, furnished with a

---

mixture of chairs complemented by old oak and elm tables. Most of the food is locally sourced: free-range meat comes from the Somerset/Dorset border, and many of the herbs are home-grown in the pub garden. The lunch menu offers a daily gourmet baguette, backed up by light meals such as chicken in spicy black bean and ginger sauce, and sticky lamb with apricot and chickpea tagine. Evening starters might feature Jerusalem artichoke soup, followed by roast Tewkesbury chicken supreme marinated in garlic and rosemary. In summer, enjoy a drink under the wisteria-shaded pergola or dine in the wild flower meadow.

**Open** all day all wk noon-11 Closed: 26 Dec, 1 Jan **Bar Meals** L served all wk 12-2.30 booking required D served all wk 7-9.15 booking required Av main course £8 food served all day **Restaurant** L served all wk 12-2.30 booking required D served all wk 7-9.15 booking required Av 3 course à la carte fr £24 ⊕ FREE HOUSE ◀ Hopback, Branscombe, Cotleigh, Archers, Otter ☼ Thatchers Gold, Burrows Hill. ⚑ 14 **Facilities** Children's portions Dogs allowed Garden Parking

## HOLCOMBE                          Map 4 ST64

### The Holcombe Inn ⚑

**Stratton Rd BA3 5EB**
**☎ 01761 232478   📠 01761 233737**
**e-mail:** bookings@holcombeinn.co.uk
**dir:** *On A367 to Stratton-on-the-Fosse, take concealed left turn opposite Downside Abbey signed Holcombe, take next right, pub 1.5m on left*

This country inn boasts a large garden with views of nearby Downside Abbey and the Somerset countryside. The lunch menu runs to various filled pitta, panini and ciabatta sandwiches, while the evening choice is supplemented by a specials board: start with pigeon breast salad or smoked salmon rillettes; and move on to marinated leg of lamb with salsa verde and potato cake; or stuffed pork fillet with black pudding and grain mustard sauce, served with herb mash.

**Open** all wk 11.30-11.30 (Sat 11.30-2.30 6.30-11 Sun noon-3 6.45-10.30) Closed: Sun eve & Mon in winter **Bar Meals** L served all wk 12-2 D served Mon-Sat 7-9, Sun 7-8.30 **Restaurant** L served all wk 12-2 D served Mon-Sat 7-9, Sun 7-8.30 ⊕ FREE HOUSE ◀ Otter Ale, Guinness, guest bitter ☼ Thatchers Old Rascal. ⚑ 17 **Facilities** Children's menu Children's portions Dogs allowed Garden Parking

## ILCHESTER                         Map 4 ST52

### Ilchester Arms ⚑

**The Square BA22 8LN**
**☎ 01935 840220   📠 01935 841353**
**e-mail:** mail@ilchesterarms.com
**dir:** *From A303 take A37 signed Ilchester/Yeovil, left at 2nd Ilchester sign. Hotel 100yds on right*

An elegant Georgian fronted house with lots of character, this establishment was first licensed in 1686; attractive features include open fires and a secluded garden. Between 1962 and 1985 it was owned by the man who *continued*

## ILCHESTER continued

developed Ilchester cheese, and its association with good food continues: chef proprietor Brendan McGee takes pride in producing modern British dishes with the likes of pheasant supreme over braised red cabbage; roast saddle of rabbit with crispy pancetta; and golden Thai vegetable parcels.

**Open** all day all wk 7am–11pm Closed: 26 Dec **Bar Meals** L served Mon-Sat 12-2.30 D served Mon-Sat 7-9 Av main course £6.50 **Restaurant** L served all wk 12-2.30 D served Mon-Sat 7-9 Av 3 course à la carte fr £35 ⊕ FREE HOUSE ◀ Butcombe, Flowers IPA, Bass, local ales ♂ Thatchers Gold, Thatchers Pear. ♥ 14 **Facilities** Children's menu Children's portions Play area Family room Garden Parking

### ILMINSTER      Map 4 ST31

### New Inn ★★★★ INN ♥

**Dowlish Wake TA19 0NZ ☎ 01460 52413**
**dir:** *From Ilminster follow Kingstone & Perry's Cider Museum signs, in Dowlish Wake follow pub signs*

Deep in rural Somerset, you'll find this 350-year-old stone-built pub tucked away in the village of Dowlish Wake, close to Perry's thatched cider mill. Inside there are two bars with wood-burning stoves and a restaurant, and outside there is a large secluded beer garden. The menu of home-cooked food features local produce in dishes such as Perry's pork steak, with a rich cider, apple and cream sauce; and Aunt Sally's home-made apple pie. Four en suite bedrooms are available in an annexe.

**Open** all wk ◀ Butcombe Bitter, Poachers Bitter, Otter Ale ♂ Thatcher's Gold. ♥ 10 **Facilities** Dogs allowed Garden Parking **Rooms** 4

### KILVE      Map 3 ST14

### The Hood Arms ♥

**TA5 1EA ☎ 01278 741210 📠 01278 741477**
**e-mail:** info@thehoodarms.com
**dir:** *From M5 junct 23/24 follow A39 to Kilve. Village between Bridgwater & Minehead*

This traditional, family-run 17th-century coaching inn is set among the Quantock Hills and provides thirsty walkers with real ales in the charming beamed bar or large garden with lovely views. A good range of fresh fish dishes can be found on the menu along with the inn's famous beef and ale pie and succulent steaks. Meals can be enjoyed with one of 12 wines served by the glass.

**Open** all day all wk **Bar Meals** L served all wk 12-2 D served all wk 6-9 Av main course £8.95 **Restaurant** L served all wk 12-2 D served all wk 6-9 Av 3 course à la carte fr £15.95 ⊕ FREE HOUSE ◀ Guinness, Otter Head, Palmers Copperdale, Fullers London Pride, Guest ales ♂ Thatchers Gold. ♥ 12 **Facilities** Children's menu Children's portions Play area Family room Dogs allowed Garden Parking

### KINGSDON      Map 4 ST52

### Kingsdon Inn ♥

**TA11 7LG ☎ 01935 840543**
**e-mail:** enquiries@kingsdoninn.co.uk
**dir:** *A303 onto A372, right onto B3151, right into village, right at post office*

Once a cider house, the three charmingly decorated, saggy-beamed rooms in this pretty thatched pub create a relaxed and friendly feel. Stripped pine tables and cushioned farmhouse chairs are judiciously placed throughout, and there are enough open fires to keep everywhere well warmed. Traditional country cooking includes pheasant, venison and other game in season; lambs' liver, bacon and onion gravy, or walnut, leek and Stilton pie and salad. There is always a wide selection of guest beers provided by local micro-breweries as well as more traditional ales.

**Open** all wk noon-3 6-11 (Sun noon-3 7-10.30) **Bar Meals** L served all wk 12-2 booking required D served all wk 6.30-9 booking required Av main course £11.50 ⊕ FREE HOUSE ◀ Butcombe Cask, Otter Cask, Guest ale ♂ Burrow Hill. ♥ 10 **Facilities** Garden Parking

### LANGLEY MARSH      Map 3 ST02

### The Three Horseshoes

**TA4 2UL ☎ 01984 623763**
**e-mail:** mark_jules96@hotmail.com
**dir:** *M5 junct 25 take B3227 to Wiveliscombe. Turn right up hill at lights. From square, turn right, follow Langley Marsh signs, pub in 1m*

This handsome 17th-century red sandstone pub has had only four landlords during the last century. It remains a free house, with traditional opening hours, child-free bars and a good choice of ales straight from the barrel. The landlord's wife prepares home-cooked meals, incorporating local ingredients and vegetables from the pub garden. Typical specials include halibut steak baked with tomatoes and wine, and pheasant breast with smoked bacon and cranberries. There's an enclosed garden with outdoor seating.

**Open** noon-2.30 7-11 Closed: Sun eve, Mon, Tue-Wed D **Bar Meals** L served Thu-Sun 12-1.45 D served Tue-Sat 7-9 ⊕ FREE HOUSE ◀ Palmer IPA, Otter Ale, Exmoor Ale, Cotleigh 25. **Facilities** Garden Parking

### LANGPORT      Map 4 ST42

### The Old Pound Inn ★★★ INN

**Aller TA10 0RA ☎ 01458 250469 📠 01458 250469**
**e-mail:** oldpoundinn@btconnect.com
**dir:** *2.5m N of Langport on A372. 8m SE of Bridgwater on A372*

Dating from 1571, the Old Pound Inn was built as a cider house and retains plenty of historic character with oak beams, open fires and a garden that used to be the village pound. It's a friendly pub with a good reputation

Save on Hotels. Book at theAA.com/hotel

SOMERSET 403 ENGLAND

or its real ale and home-cooked food, but also provides
unction facilities for 200 with its own bar. There is also
skittle alley, plus accommodation including a four-
oster bedroom.

Open all wk 11.30-2.30 5-11 (Sat 11.30-mdnt Sun noon-
0) **Bar Meals** L served all wk 12-2 D served all wk 6-9
Av main course £9 **Restaurant** D served Fri-Sun 6-9
FREE HOUSE ◀ Tribute, Sharp's, Cotleigh,
ranscombe, Glastonbury, Teignworthy Ö Thatchers Gold.
**Facilities** Children's menu Children's portions Dogs
allowed Garden Parking **Rooms** 8

## Rose & Crown

Huish Episcopi TA10 9QT ☎ 01458 250494
dir: M5 junct 25, A358 towards Ilminster. Left onto A378.
Village in 14m (1m from Langport). Pub near church in
village

This traditional, family-run inn (also known as Eli's) has
no bar, just a flagstone taproom lined with casks of ales
and farmhouse ciders, an upright piano and some fairly
basic seating. Folk music and storytelling evenings are a
regular feature, while the home-made food includes
sandwiches, soups, jacket potatoes, pork cobbler and
cottage pie. Vegetarian meals are always available,
along with puddings like apple crumble. Burrow Hill
Farmhouse cider available.

Open all wk 11.30-3 5.30-11 (Fri-Sat 11.30-11.30 Sun
noon-10.30) **Bar Meals** L served all wk 12-2 D served
Mon-Sat 5.30-7.30 Av main course £6.90 FREE HOUSE
◀ Teignworthy Reel Ale, Mystery Tor, Hop Back Summer
Lightning, Butcombe Bitter, Summathat Ö Burrow Hill
Farmhouse. ♀ 5 **Facilities** Play area Family room Dogs
allowed Garden Parking **Notes** ⊜

### LEIGH UPON MENDIP                  Map 4 ST64

## The Bell Inn ♀

BA3 5QQ ☎ 01373 812316   📄 01373 812434
e-mail: rodcambourne@aol.com
dir: From Frome take A37 towards Shepton Mallet. Turn
right, through Mells, on to Leigh upon Mendip

The Bell was built in the early 16th century to house
workers constructing the village church, and Pilgrims
used to stop here en route to Glastonbury. There is a bar
with two inglenook fireplaces, a 30-seat restaurant, a
skittle alley/function room and a large garden with
children's play equipment. Snacks and meals are served
(mussels with Thai curry, lamb stew and dumplings). A
three-mile walk around the lanes starts and finishes at
the pub.

Open all wk ◀ Wadworth 6X, Butcombe Bitter,
Wadworths JCB, Henrys IPA, Bishops Tipple. ♀ 12
**Facilities** Play area Family room Dogs allowed Garden
Parking

### LONG SUTTON                        Map 4 ST42

## PICK OF THE PUBS

### The Devonshire
### Arms ★★★★ INN ⊛ ♀

TA10 9LP ☎ 01458 241271   📄 01458 241037
e-mail: mail@thedevonshirearms.com
dir: Exit A303 at Podimore rdbt onto A372. Continue for
4m, left onto B3165

A fine-looking, stone-built former hunting lodge on a
pretty village green. Step through its imposing portico,
decorated with the Devonshire family crest, to discover
unexpectedly contemporary styling complementing the
large open fire and other original features.
Refreshments come in the form of increasingly popular
regional brews and ciders, and the pub is also
renowned for its daily changing menu based whenever
possible on locally sourced produce. Maybe try the
Cornish mussels steamed in Burrow Hill cider, garlic,
chilli and thyme; or Dorset crab crème brûlée, followed
by spicy pork stew with apricots and walnuts; or
Quantock duck confit with mash and mixed vegetables.
Desserts may include chocolate clafoutis with praline
ice cream; and ginger sticky toffee pudding with lime
leaf ice cream. Your can drink and dine alfresco in the
courtyard, large walled garden or overlooking the green
at the front. To complete the picture, nine en suite
bedrooms, each with wide-screen TV, are designed in a
fresh modern style, and benefit from the personal touch
of hosts Philip and Sheila Mepham.

Open all wk noon-3 6-11 Closed: 25-26 Dec, 1 Jan
**Bar Meals** L served all wk 12-2.30 booking required D
served all wk 7-9.30 booking required Av main course
£10 **Restaurant** D served all wk 7-9.30 booking
required Av 3 course à la carte fr £26 FREE HOUSE
◀ Bath Spa, Cheddar Potholer, Moor Revival, Moor
Merlins Magic Ö Burrow Hill, Olde Harry's. ♀ 10
**Facilities** Children's menu Play area Dogs allowed
Garden Parking **Rooms** 9

### LOVINGTON                          Map 4 ST53

## PICK OF THE PUBS

## The Pilgrims ★★★★ INN ♀

BA7 7PT ☎ 01963 240597
e-mail: jools@thepilgrimsatlovington.co.uk
dir: A303 onto A37 to Lyford, right at lights, 1.5m to
The Pilgrims on B3153

With disarming honesty, owners Sally and Jools
Mitchison admit that The Pilgrims will never be pretty
from the outside. Step inside, however, and it's another
story. Wicker and leather seating characterise the bar,
and locals' pewter mugs hang ready for the next pint of
Cottage ale, brewed just around the corner, or a real
cider. 'Local' is a much-used word here; herbs and
vegetables are grown in the pub's own garden, and
every effort is made to source produce nearby,
especially cheeses. Starters and light lunches include
'pilgrims on horseback' – seared hand-dived scallops

from Lyme Bay on Ashley's black pudding and mashed
potato; and cauliflower pannacotta with balsamic
glazed shallots. After an evening meal comprising West
Country mussels cooked in cider, leeks and garlic;
Cornish hake with Puy lentils; and Jools' glazed lemon
tart, one of the five highly individual king size guest
rooms may beckon.

Open noon-3 7-11 Closed: Oct, Sun eve, Mon, Tue L
**Bar Meals** L served Wed-Sun 12-2.30 D served Tue-Sat
7-9 Av main course £12 **Restaurant** L served Wed-Sun
12.30-2.30 D served Tue-Sat 7-9 booking required Av 3
course à la carte fr £30 FREE HOUSE ◀ Cottage
Brewing Champflower Ö Burrow Hill, Orchard Pig. ♀ 12
**Facilities** Children's portions Dogs allowed Garden
Parking **Rooms** 5

### LOWER LANGFORD                     Map 4 ST46

## The Langford Inn ★★★★ INN ♀ NEW

BS40 5BL ☎ 01934 863059   📄 01934 863539
e-mail: langfordinn@aol.com
dir: M5 junct 21, A370 towards Bristol. At Congresbury
turn right onto B3133 to Lower Langford. Village on A38

With a reputation for great hospitality and service, a
display of local memorabilia jollies up the oak-beamed
bar and lounge of this traditional, stone-built country
pub in a village nudging the Mendip Hills. Butcombe
beers come from nearby Wrington. The extensive seasonal
menus uses local produce as much as possible and
might include sizzling beef with oyster sauce; chicken
curry masala; fisherman's pie; and mushroom stroganoff.
On the daily changing specials board: scallops and black
pudding; Barbary duck breast; and fish chowder. Two
converted 17th-century barns house seven en suite
bedrooms.

Open all day all wk **Bar Meals** L served 12-9 Av main
course £9 food served all day **Restaurant** L served 12-9 D
served Fri-Sat 12-9.30 Fixed menu price fr £7.95 Av 3
course à la carte fr £15 food served all day BRAINS
◀ Butcombe, Brains SA, Guinness Ö Thatchers Gold,
Thatchers Katy. ♀ 24 **Facilities** Children's menu
Children's portions Dogs allowed Garden Parking
**Rooms** 7                       *See advert on opposite page*

---

**LOWER VOBSTER**                    Map 4 ST74

## PICK OF THE PUBS

Vobster Inn                    INN ◎◎ ♀

*See Pick of the Pubs on opposite page*

---

**MARTOCK**                    Map 4 ST41

## The Nag's Head Inn

**East St TA12 6NF ☎ 01935 823432**
dir: *Telephone for directions*

This 200-year-old former cider house is set in a lovely
hamstone street in a picturesque south Somerset village.
The large rear garden is partly walled and has pretty
borders and trees. Local real ales, wines and food are
served in both the public and lounge bars, where crib,
dominoes, darts and pool are available. The pub also has
a skittle alley and a decked smoking area.

**Open** all wk noon-3 6-11 (Fri-Sun noon-mdnt)
◖ Guinness, Worthington, Toby. **Facilities** Family room
Dogs allowed Garden Parking

---

**MILVERTON**                    Map 3 ST12

## PICK OF THE PUBS

The Globe                    INN ♀

*See Pick of the Pubs on page 406*

---

**MONTACUTE**                    Map 4 ST41

## The Kings Arms Inn ♀

**49 Bishopston TA15 6UU ☎ 01935 822255**
e-mail: info@thekingsarmsinn.co.uk
dir: *From A303 onto A3088 at rdbt signed Montacute.
Hotel in village centre*

The hamstone-built, freshly refurbished Kings Arms has
stood in this picturesque village, at the foot of Mons
Acutus (thus, supposedly, Montacute) since 1632. Along
with cask ales and fine wines, you can eat in the fire-
warmed bar or lounge, in the large beer garden, or in the
restaurant. Starters include deep-fried whitebait, or duck
and orange pâté, with main courses of chicken supreme
with bacon, mushroom and shallot cream sauce; or
battered cod and chips. A bar favourite is the succulent
salt beef sandwich. There are plenty of events to watch
out for.

**Open** all wk noon-3 6-11.30 (Sun noon-3 Oct-Feb)
**Bar Meals** L served all wk 12-3 D served all wk 6-9 Av
main course £4.75 **Restaurant** D served all wk 6-9
booking required Fixed menu price fr £15 ⊕ GREENE KING
◖ Ruddles County, Abbot Ale, Old Speckled Hen ♂ Aspall.
♀ 10 **Facilities** Dogs allowed Garden Parking

---

## The Phelips Arms

**The Borough TA15 6XB ☎ 01935 822557**
e-mail: phelipsarmsmontacute@talktalk.net
dir: *From Cartgate rdbt on A303 follow signs for
Montacute*

A 17th-century listed ham stone building overlooking the
village square and close to historic Montacute House
(NT). The emphasis is on the well kept Palmers beers and
quality of the food, and everything is prepared on the
premises using the best local and West Country produce.
The menu features dishes such as home-made steak and
ale pie, stuffed oven-cooked pork belly with pear and
apple jus; followed by rhubarb crumble or strawberry
Pavlova.

**Open** all wk noon-2.30 6-11 Closed: 25 Dec **Bar Meals** L
served all wk 12-2 D served all wk 6.30-9 Av main course
£7.25 **Restaurant** L served all wk 12-2 booking required
D served all wk 6.30-9 booking required Fixed menu price
fr £9.95 ⊕ PALMERS ◖ Palmers IPA & 200 Premium Ale,
Copper Ale ♂ Thatchers Gold. **Facilities** Children's
menu Children's portions Dogs allowed Garden Parking

---

**NORTH CURRY**                    Map 4 ST32

## The Bird in Hand ♀

**1 Queen Square TA3 6LT ☎ 01823 490248**
dir: *M5 junct 25, A358 towards Ilminster, left onto A378
towards Langport. Left to North Curry*

Cheerful staff provide a warm welcome to this friendly
300-year-old village inn, which boasts large inglenook
fireplaces, flagstone floors, exposed beams and studwork.
The place is very atmospheric at night by candlelight,
and blackboard menus feature local produce including
vegetarian options and steak dishes, while the constantly
changing seafood is supplied by a Plymouth fishmonger.

**Open** all wk ⊕ FREE HOUSE ◖ Badger Tanglefoot, Exmoor
Gold, Otter Ale, Cotleigh Barn Owl, Hop Back
Thunderstorm, Butcombe Gold, Teignworthy Old Moggie
♂ Parsons Farm. ♀ 9 **Facilities** Dogs allowed Parking

---

**NORTON ST PHILIP**                    Map 4 ST75

## PICK OF THE PUBS

## George Inn ♀

**High St BA2 7LH ☎ 01373 834224**
e-mail: georgeinn@wadworth.co.uk
dir: *From Bath take A36 to Warminster, after 6m take
A366 on right to Radstock, village 1m*

With more than 700 years under its belt, this Grade
I-listed building is one of the country's oldest
continuously licensed inns. Just over a decade ago, the
Wadworth brewery meticulously restored it, and during
the process uncovered medieval wall paintings, now
preserved. Other noteworthy features are the stone-
slated roof, massive doorway, cobbled courtyard and
impressive timbered galleries. There are two menus,
one in the bar, the other in the beamed restaurant;
typical dishes include hearty soups; home-made pâtés;

---

and queen scallops with lime and chorizo to start;
among the mains are steak and ale pie; pork tenderloin
medallions with brandy and wild mushroom cream;
rack of lamb with apricot and leeks; fresh sea bass
with Parma ham; and roasted vegetable and feta filo
pastry purse. For pudding, try the mixed berry
cheesecake; or chocolate and chilli bread and butter
pudding. Outside you can eat in the ancient and
atmospheric courtyard and from the beer garden watch
cricket on the Mead.

*George Inn*

**Open** all day all wk **Bar Meals** L served Mon-Fri
12-2.30 D served Mon-Thu 6-9, Fri 6-9.30 Av main
course £8.50 **Restaurant** L served Mon-Fri 12-2.30,
Sat-Sun 12-9 booking required D served Mon-Thu 7-9,
Fri 7-9.30, Sat-Sun 12-9 booking required Av 3 course
à la carte fr £24 ⊕ WADWORTH ◖ Wadworth 6X, Henrys
IPA, Wadworth Bishops Tipple, JCB. ♀ 32
**Facilities** Children's portions Dogs allowed Garden
Parking

---

**NUNNEY**                    Map 4 ST74

## The George at Nunney

**Church St BA11 4LW**
**☎ 01373 836458   📠 01373 836565**
e-mail: info@thegeorgeatnunney.co.uk
dir: *0.5m N off A361, Frome/Shepton Mallet*

Fraser Carruth and head chef Wayne Carnegie took over
The George in mid-2008 and rapidly established it as a
hub of the village's lively community. Sited in a classic
English village complete with moated castle ruins, the
rambling inn serves a choice of real ales, ciders and
imported beers in the comfortable beamed bar. Lunch
and dinner menus change weekly. A typical selection
could comprise smoked mackerel pâté topped with
Norwegian prawns; a Harmony Farm steak from the grill;
Sunday rare roast sirloin of Scottish beef; and meringue
glacé with pineapple and caramel sauce.

**Open** all wk 12-3 6-11 (Sun 7-10.30) **Bar Meals** L served
all wk 12-2 D served all wk 7-9 Av main course £9.75
**Restaurant** L served all wk 12-2 D served all wk 7-9
booking required Av 3 course à la carte fr £38.75 ⊕ FREE
HOUSE ♂ Stowford Press. **Facilities** Dogs allowed Garden
Parking **Rooms** 9

# PICK OF THE PUBS

## Vobster Inn ★★★★ INN 🌹🌹 🍷

　Map 4 ST74

**BA3 5RJ**
☎ 01373 812920 📄 01373 812247
e-mail: info@vobsterinn.co.uk
dir: *4m W of Frome*

Set in four acres of glorious countryside in the pretty hamlet of Lower Vobster, this long stone building dates back to the 17th century, though there was probably an inn here even before that. It is believed the inn originated a century before that and was used by James II and his army of Royalists prior to the battle of Sedgemoor in 1685.

Raf and Peta Davila have been making their mark here ever since they arrived, a process that includes being awarded two AA Rosettes for the quality of their food and ingredients. The simple bar menu makes choosing easy with inexpensive suggestions such as fried whitebait with aioli; seared beef sandwich, granary bloomer, goat's cheese glaze and caramelized onions; and grilled mushrooms with smoked ham and Welsh rarebit.

On the main menu you'll find echoes of Raf's origins on Galicia's wild coast, including a selection of Spanish cured and smoked meats with salad, olives, houmous and crusty bread. Typical among the mains options are fillet of West Country beef and oyster pie, goose fat chips and purple sprouting broccoli, and pot-roasted boned quail, ox tongue, Puy lentils, roast garlic and foie gras.

Fish lovers will want to see what has come up fresh from St Mawes in Cornwall: fillet of bass, perhaps, with crushed herb potatoes, beetroot syrup, olive oil, tomato and olive dressing, or pan-fried monkfish, crayfish ravioli, vegetable spaghetti and red pepper relish. All desserts are home made, with choices like apple tart with spiced fruit ice cream and Catalan crème brûlée with black cracked pepper strawberries and orange and mango sorbet. Children are particularly welcome and have their own menu, plus there is a great cheese menu too. Three individually furnished bedrooms are available.

**Open** 12-3 6.30-11 Closed: Sun eve **Bar Meals** L served all wk 12-2 booking required D served Mon-Sat 6.30-9 booking required Av main course £10 **Restaurant** L served all wk 12-2 booking required D served Mon-Sat 6.30-9 booking required Av 3 course à la carte fr £25 🛢 FREE HOUSE
🍺 Butcombe Blonde, Butcombe Bitter
👌 Ashton Press, Orchard Pig. 🍷 10
**Facilities** Children's menu Family room Garden Parking **Rooms** 3

# PICK OF THE PUBS

## The Globe ★★★ INN ♟

**MILVERTON** Map 3 ST12

**Fore St TA4 1JX ☎ 01823 400534**
**e-mail:** info@theglobemilverton.co.uk
**dir:** *On B3187*

The Globe is a free house that is clearly very much part of the village and local community, thanks to husband and wife team, Mark and Adele Tarry. They've been presiding over this old coaching inn for five years, its clean-lined, contemporary interior sitting comfortably within the Grade II-listed structure. Local artists display their paintings on the walls of the restaurant and bar area, whilst a wood-burning stove and an open air courtyard provide for all seasons. One of Mark's passions is local ales; Exmoor and Cotleigh are the regulars, while guest ales come from other Somerset brewers such as Quantock and Yeovil. Sheppy's local cider and English wines are also available.

An extensive menu ranges from traditional steak and kidney pie and home-made burgers at lunchtime, to the main menu with slow-roasted Gloucester Old Spot belly pork, and a wide selection of fish specials, among them sea trout, scallops and River Fowey mussels. Everything is home made, including the bread. For a quick and easy lunch option there are baguettes and ciabattas with fillings like Parma ham, brie and rocket; and roasted vegetables with feta cheese.

The kitchen uses West Country produce extensively in the production of sea bass fillets with chorizo pesto and rocket; chargrilled rib-eye steak with brandy and green peppercorn sauce and home-made fat chips; roasted Barbary duck breast with celeriac purée and spiced orange sauce; and wild mushroom and gruyère cheese tart with red onion jam. Home-made (with a little help from Mark's mum) desserts include classic crème brûlée; mascarpone and Amaretto tiramisu; and lemon tart with raspberry cream. There is a carefully thought out children's menu too.

Stay over in one of the comfortable bedrooms because Milverton is a good base from which to explore the Quantock Hills and Exmoor.

**Open** noon-3 6-11 (Fri-Sat noon-11.30) Closed: Sun eve, Mon L **Bar Meals** L served Tue-Sun 12-2 D served Mon-Sat 6.30-9 booking required Av main course £7.95 **Restaurant** L served Tue-Sun 12-2 D served Mon-Sat 6.30-9 booking required Av 3 course à la carte fr £25 ⊕ FREE HOUSE ◀ Exmoor Ale, Cotleigh 25, Butcombe Bitter, Guest ales ♂ Thatchers, Sheppys. ♟ 8 **Facilities** Children's menu Parking **Rooms** 2

Save on Hotels. Book at theAA.com/hotel

SOMERSET 407 ENGLAND

## OAKHILL — Map 4 ST64

### The Oakhill Inn ★★★★ INN ¶ NEW

Fosse Rd BA3 5HU ☎ 01749 840442
e-mail: info@theoakhillinn.com
dir: On the A367 between Radstock & Shepton Mallet

The Oakhill is a spacious but cosy country inn with warming winter fires and comfy sofas, and a newly landscaped garden for the warmer weather with views of the village and Mendip Hills. The inn helps to support the county's increasingly prolific brewing industry by serving at least four real ales from local micro-breweries, and Somerset ciders too. Lunch or dinner might be duck breast with sherry and orange sauce; braised brisket with roast root vegetables; fresh beer-battered haddock with triple-cooked chips; and Jerusalem artichoke gratin with mixed nut crumble and Yorkshire blue cheese. Five refurbished en suite rooms are now available.

Open all wk Mon-Fri noon-3 5-11 (Sat-Sun all day) Bar Meals L served all wk 12-3 booking required D served all wk 5-9.30 booking required Av main course £11 ⊕ FREE HOUSE ◀ Sharp's Doom Bar, Butcombe ⱷ Orchard Pig, Pheasant Plucker. Facilities Children's menu Children's portions Dogs allowed Garden Parking Rooms 5

## OVER STRATTON — Map 4 ST41

### The Royal Oak

TA13 5LQ ☎ 01460 240906
e-mail: info@the-royal-oak.net
dir: Exit A303 at Hayes End rdbt (South Petherton). 1st left after Esso garage signed Over Stratton

Blackened beams, flagstones, log fires, pews and settles set the scene in this welcoming old thatched inn built from warm ham stone. Expect real ales served in the bar, including Tanglefoot from the Badger Brewery in Blandford Forum. Dishes ranging from beer battered haddock and chips with home-made tartare sauce to supreme of chicken in an apricot, ginger and white wine sauce. Added attractions are the beer garden, children's play area and barbecue.

Open Tue-Sun Closed: Mon Bar Meals L served Tue-Sun 12-2 booking required D served Tue-Sun 6-9 booking required Restaurant L served Tue-Sun 12-2 booking required D served Tue-Sun 6-9 booking required ⊕ HALL & WOODHOUSE ◀ Badger Best, Tanglefoot, Sussex Best Bitter. Facilities Play area Family room Dogs allowed Garden Parking

## PITNEY — Map 4 ST42

### The Halfway House ¶

TA10 9AB ☎ 01458 252513
dir: On B3153, 2m from Langport & Somerton

This pub is largely dedicated to the promotion of real ale, and there are always six to ten available in tip-top condition, including Cotleigh Tawny Ale and Teignworthy. This delightfully old-fashioned rural pub has three homely rooms boasting open fires, books and games, but no music or electronic games. Home-cooked meals (except Sundays when it is too busy with drinkers) include soups, local sausages, sandwiches and a good selection of curries and casseroles.

Open all wk 11.30-3 5.30-11 (Fri-Sat 5.30-mdnt Sun noon-3 7-11) Closed: 25 Dec Bar Meals L served Mon-Sat 12-2.30 D served Mon-Sat 7-9.30 ⊕ FREE HOUSE ◀ Butcombe Bitter, Teignworthy, Otter Ale, Cotleigh Tawny Ale, Hop Back Summer Lightning ⱷ Kingston Black, Burrow Hill, Wilkins Medium. ¶ 8 Facilities Play area Dogs allowed Garden Parking

## PORLOCK — Map 3 SS84

### The Bottom Ship

Porlock Weir TA24 8PB ☎ 01643 863288
e-mail: info@thebottomship.co.uk
dir: Telephone for directions

At the water's edge on the southern bank of the Bristol Channel, this thatched pub's outside seats offer superb views over to south Wales, but there's plenty of space inside if the weather is inclement. Exmoor ales are the mainstay in the beamed bar, with a couple of real ciders also on tap. Home-made food using fresh local produce includes most pub favourites, from deep-fried whitebait to steak and ale pie. Children have their own menu and dogs are welcome.

Open all day all wk Bar Meals L served all wk 12-3 D served all wk 5.30-8.30 ⊕ FREE HOUSE ◀ Exmoor Ale, Exmoor Stag, Otter Bright, Proper Job, St Austell IPA ⱷ Pear & Apple Rattler, Cheddar Valley. Facilities Children's menu Children's portions Dogs allowed Garden Parking

### The Ship Inn

High St TA24 8QD ☎ 01643 862507
e-mail: enquiries@shipinnporlock.co.uk
dir: A358 to Williton, then A39 to Porlock. 6m from Minehead

Many travellers have been welcomed to this 13th-century inn, one of the oldest on Exmoor, including Wordsworth, Coleridge and even Nelson's press gang. Nestling at the foot of Porlock's notorious hill, where Exmoor tumbles into the sea, its thatched roof and traditional interior provide an evocative setting for a meal, drink or overnight stay. Regularly changing menus include ploughman's, light bites and dishes such as sausage and mash and beer battered cod and chips. There's a beer garden with children's play area.

Open all day all wk Bar Meals L served all wk 12-2.30 D served all wk 6-9 booking required Av main course £7 Restaurant L served all wk 12-2.30 D served all wk 6-9 booking required Av 3 course à la carte fr £10.50 ⊕ FREE HOUSE ◀ Tribute, Exmoor Ale, Otter, Proper Job, Tawny ⱷ Cheddar Valley, Thatchers. Facilities Children's menu Children's portions Play area Dogs allowed Garden Parking

## RODE — Map 4 ST85

### The Mill at Rode ¶

BA11 6AG ☎ 01373 831100 📠 01373 831144
e-mail: info@themillatrode.co.uk
dir: 6m S of Bath

A magnificent, multi-storeyed Georgian woollen mill straddling the mill-race beside the river Frome in the rural hinterland south of Bath. The dining-terrace overhangs the rushing waters, a great location in which to indulge in local beers or select from the West Country based menu; perhaps locally cured boiled bacon with pease pudding or loin of Somerset pork stuffed with black pudding, finishing with local cheeses or ices. A children's playroom offers grown-ups the chance of escape and a peaceful chinwag.

Open all day all wk noon-11 Closed: 25 Dec Bar Meals L served all wk 12-7 booking required D served all wk 7-10 booking required Av main course £10 food served all day Restaurant L served all wk 12-7 booking required D served all wk 7-10 booking required food served all day ⊕ FREE HOUSE ◀ Butcombe Bitter, Pedigree, Guinness, Guest ales ⱷ Black Rat, Inch's Stonehouse. ¶ 35 Facilities Children's menu Children's portions Play area Family room Garden Parking

## RUDGE — Map 4 ST85

### The Full Moon at Rudge ★★★ INN

BA11 2QF ☎ 01373 830936 📠 01373 831366
e-mail: info@thefullmoon.co.uk
dir: From A36 (Bath to Warminster road) follow Rudge signs

Strategically placed at the crossing of two old drove roads, this inn enjoys great views of Westbury White Horse. The venerable 16th-century building had been sympathetically updated and retains its small, stone-floored rooms furnished with scrubbed tables. Modern British cooking is the watchword with menus changing to reflect the seasons. Lamb chump chop with bubble and squeak and a rosemary jus or simple steak and kidney pie are examples of the fare. There are 17 comfortable bedrooms if you would like to stay over.

Open all day all wk 11.30-11 (Sun noon-10.30) ◀ Butcombe Bitter, John Smith's, Potholer ⱷ Stowford Press, Thatchers Cheddar Valley. Facilities Dogs allowed Garden Parking Rooms 17

## SHEPTON BEAUCHAMP — Map 4 ST41

### Duke of York ¶

North St TA19 0LW ☎ 01460 240314
e-mail: sheptonduke@tiscali.co.uk
dir: M5 junct 25 Taunton or A303

In the lovely village of Shepton Beauchamp is this 17th-century free house, run by husband and wife team Paul and Hayley Rowlands, and Purdy, the 'famous' pub dog. The bar stocks some good West Country real ales and the restaurant has a varied menu. Local chargrilled steaks
*continued*

**SHEPTON BEAUCHAMP** *continued*

and fresh fish from Bridport, as well as a selection of pub classics such as lamb moussaka and trio of lamb chops on minted creamed potato and redcurrant and port sauce, shows the style. Food and drink can also be enjoyed in the pub garden.

**Open** all day Closed: Mon L **Bar Meals** L served Tue-Sun 12-2 D served Tue-Sat 6.45-9 booking required **Restaurant** L served Tue-Sun 12-2 D served Tue-Sat 6.45-9 booking required ⊕ FREE HOUSE ◀ Teignworthy Reel Ale, Otter Bright ○ Thatchers Gold. � 9 **Facilities** Children's menu Children's portions Family room Dogs allowed Garden Parking

---

| **SHEPTON MALLET** | Map 4 ST64 |

## PICK OF THE PUBS

## The Three Horseshoes Inn ★★★★ INN ⊛ �

*See Pick of the Pubs on opposite page*

## PICK OF THE PUBS

## The Waggon and Horses �

**Frome Rd, Doulting Beacon BA4 4LA**
☎ 01749 880302
e-mail: dawncorp@yahoo.co.uk
dir: *1.5m N of Shepton Mallet at x-roads with Old Wells-Frome road, 1m off A37*

This rural coaching inn is a pretty, whitewashed building with leaded windows. The pub, which has views over Glastonbury, is set in a large garden and a flower-filled paddock and drinks and meals can be enjoyed outside in fine weather. Other attractions include the upstairs skittle alley, which together with a small bar, is available for hire. A varying range of real beers, a good choice of wines by the glass and cider are served alongside traditional home-made dishes. Expect the likes of fresh battered cod with chips; steak and ale pie; tarragon chicken with a creamy sauce, and home-made faggots. A great range of desserts includes raspberry cheesecake, spotted Dick, pineapple upside down pudding and apple crumble.

**Open** all wk Mon-Fri 12-2.30 6-11 (Sat-Sun & Summer) all day **Bar Meals** L served Mon-Sat 12-2.30, Sun 12-3 D served Mon-Sat 6-9, Sun 6-8 **Restaurant** L served Mon-Sat 12-2.30, Sun 12-3 D served Mon-Sat 6-9, Sun 6-8 ⊕ PUNCH TAVERNS ◀ Wadworth 6X, Butcombe ○ Natch. � 12 **Facilities** Children's menu Children's portions Dogs allowed Garden Parking

---

| **SHEPTON MONTAGUE** | Map 4 ST63 |

## PICK OF THE PUBS

## The Montague Inn �

**BA9 8JW** ☎ 01749 813213 📄 01749 813213
e-mail: themontagueinn@aol.com
dir: *From Wincanton & Castle Cary turn right off A371*

Hidden down winding country lanes close to Castle Cary, this comfortably refurbished, 18th-century stone-built village inn nestles in rolling unspoilt Somerset countryside on the edge of sleepy Shepton Montague. Tastefully decorated throughout, with the homely bar featuring old dark pine and an open log fire, and a cosy, yellow-painted dining room, the focus and draw of this rural dining pub is the careful sourcing of local foods from artisan producers and John McGeevor's imaginative seasonal menus. Expect to find cask ales from Cottage Brewery, salads, fruit and vegetables from local farms, and free range eggs from Blackacre Farm. This translates to lunchtime dishes like pork and chicken terrine with home-made chutney; twice-baked Cheddar cheese, spinach and leek soufflé; and open home-made focaccia bread with Serrano ham, mozzarella and pesto. Evening specials might include pork belly with basil and sage faggot, black pudding potato cake and cider and thyme sauce. Puddings include a classic apple tarte Tatin and Bailey's and chocolate cheesecake. The attractive rear terrace with rural views is perfect for summer sipping.

**Open** noon-3 6-11.30 Closed: Mon, Sun eve **Bar Meals** L served Tue-Sun 12-2.30 booking required D served Tue-Sat 7-9.30 booking required **Restaurant** L served Tue-Sun 12-2.30 booking required D served Tue-Sat 7-9.30 booking required Fixed menu price fr £12.50 Av 3 course à la carte fr £24 ⊕ FREE HOUSE ◀ Bath Ale, Wadworth 6X, Strongarm, Guest ales ○ Local cider, Thatchers Gold, Westons Organic. **Facilities** Children's portions Family room Dogs allowed Garden Parking

---

| **SPARKFORD** | Map 4 ST62 |

## The Sparkford Inn

**High St BA22 7JH** ☎ 01963 440218 📄 01963 440358
e-mail: sparkfordinn@sparkford.fsbusiness.co.uk
dir: *Just off A303, 400yds from rdbt at Sparkford*

A 15th-century former coaching inn with beamed bars and a fascinating display of old prints and photographs. It is set in an attractive garden just off the A303 between Wincanton and Yeovil. The restaurant offers a popular lunchtime carvery, light meals and a full evening menu, featuring steaks from the grill. Dishes include marinated Cajun chicken breast; smoked haddock and bacon au gratin; and bean, celery and coriander chilli.

**Open** all wk ◀ Marstons Pedigree, Banks Bitter, guest ales. **Facilities** Play area Dogs allowed Garden Parking

---

| **STANTON WICK** | Map 4 ST66 |

## PICK OF THE PUBS

## The Carpenters Arms �

*See Pick of the Pubs on page 41 ▶*

---

| **STOGUMBER** | Map 3 ST03 |

## The White Horse

**High St TA4 3TA** ☎ 01984 656277
e-mail: info@whitehorsestogumber.co.uk
dir: *From Taunton take A358 to Minehead. In 8m left to Stogumber, 2m into village centre. Right at T-junct & right again. Pub opp church*

Nestling between the Quantock Hills and Exmoor in an Area of Outstanding Natural Beauty, with the West Somerset Steam Railway only a mile away. The dining room of this traditional free house was once the historic village's Market Hall and Reading Room. Home-cooked menus change daily; typical dishes are smoked salmon tartare with cucumber salad, followed by pan-fried pheasant breast with caramelised apple and cider. The courtyard garden is a perfect place to sample one of the local ales.

**Open** all day all wk 11-11 (Sun 12-11) **Bar Meals** L served all wk 12-2 D served all wk 7-9 **Restaurant** L served all wk 12-2 D served all wk 7-9 ⊕ FREE HOUSE ◀ Cotleigh Tawny Bitter, Local West Country, Proper Job, Guest ales ○ Thatchers Cheddar Valley. **Facilities** Children's menu Family room Dogs allowed Garden Parking

---

| **STOKE ST GREGORY** | Map 4 ST32 |

## Rose & Crown

**Woodhill TA3 6EW** ☎ 01823 490296
e-mail: info@browningpubs.com
dir: *M5 junct 25, A358 towards Langport, left at Thornfalcon, left again, follow signs to Stoke St Gregory*

Run by the same family for over 30 years, this pub enjoys a well deserved reputation for good food, local produce and a warm reception. A chatty newsletter gives diary dates and reminders of special offers such as fish on Fridays, charity events, and take-away dishes at reduced cost. Following a fire in 2008, internal changes have been introduced gradually and focus on maximising customer comfort. The menu is particularly warming with the likes of pan-fried squid and chorizo; and pork tenderloin marinated in Somerset brandy.

*continued on page 41 ▶*

# PICK OF THE PUBS

## The Three Horseshoes Inn ★★★★INN

**Batcombe BA4 6HE**
☎ 01749 850359   📄 01749 850615
e-mail:
info@thethreehorseshoesinn.com
dir: *Take A359 from Frome to Bruton. Batcombe signed on right. Pub by church*

Tucked away down a web of country lanes in the very rural Batcombe Vale, this honey-coloured stone inn enjoys a peaceful position and the lovely rear garden overlooks the old parish church.

The long and low-ceilinged main bar has exposed stripped beams, deep window seats, a huge stone inglenook with log fire, and is warmly and tastefully decorated, with terracotta walls hung with old paintings, creating a relaxed and homely atmosphere. From gleaming handpumps on the bar come foaming pints of Butcombe and locally brewed Cheddar Potholer. Menus draw on the wealth of fresh seasonal produce available locally, with brasserie-style lunches taking in local pigeon breast with crispy ham and green pea vinaigrette; local sausages with mash and onion gravy; calves' liver on creamed potatoes with home-cured bacon and sage; and cassolette of shellfish and white fish.

Choice at dinner extends to Coln Valley oak-smoked salmon with lemon and capers and Bagborough Farm goats' cheese with sun-blushed tomato pesto for starters, with the likes of whole Cornish plaice, slow-braised shoulder of organic Somerset lamb, fillet of West Country beef, and local free-range chicken with crispy bacon and bread sauce to follow. Desserts include sticky toffee pudding with butterscotch sauce and vanilla ice cream; classic treacle sponge with lemon zest, ginger and 'real English' custard; and local and continental cheeses with celery, biscuits and home-made chutney. The wines are reasonably priced, with a more or less equal split between European and New World. There are three stylishly decorated letting bedrooms here.

**Open** all wk Mon-Sat 12-3 6-11 (Sun 12-3 6-10.30) **Bar Meals** L served Mon-Sun 12-2 booking required D served Mon-Sun 7-9.30 booking required Av main course £11 **Restaurant** L served Mon-Sun 12-2 booking required D served Mon-Sat 7-9.30 booking required Av 3 course à la carte fr £22 ⊕ FREE HOUSE 🍺 Butcombe Bitter, Moor Revival, Cheddar Potholer ♂ Orchard Pig, Butcombe Blond, Ashton Press. ♟ 8 **Facilities** Children's menu Dogs allowed Garden Parking **Rooms** 3

# PICK OF THE PUBS

## The Carpenters Arms ♟

**STANTON WICK**     Map 4 ST66

**BS39 4BX**
☎ 01761 490202   📄 01761 490763
**e-mail:** carpenters@buccaneer.co.uk
**web:** www.the-carpenters-arms.co.uk
**dir:** *A37 to Chelwood rdbt, then A368. Pub 8m S of Bath*

Overlooking the Chew Valley, the hamlet of Stanton Wick provides a tranquil and picturesque setting for the Carpenters Arms. Formerly a row of miners' cottages, this delightful, stone-built free house is straight out of Central Casting's book of quintessential English pubs, plus combining the old with the new with the comfort and refinement expected by today's travellers. Outside is a landscaped patio for alfresco drinks or meals, while behind the flower-

bedecked façade lies a comfortable bar with low beams, a chatty, music-free atmosphere, and real ales, including Butcombe Bitter from Wrington, not far away.

Seasonal and local produce is a priority, so menus and daily specials change regularly to make the best of what's available, as well as (say the owners) to keep the chefs on their toes! There are certainly dishes to suit most tastes: among them you may see lightly fried fishcake with lime and coriander mayonnaise; lamb steak marinated in garlic and rosemary on sautéed potatoes; honey and thyme glazed pork belly on onion mash and braised cabbage; and seared calves' liver, mash and onion gravy. Vegetarians could well be tempted by goat's cheese pannacotta, oven dried tomato and basil salsa; and roasted butternut squash and leek risotto with chilli and tarragon oil.

Puddings will sure to tempt, perhaps glazed lemon tart and blackcurrant sorbet; and steamed orange sponge

pudding with custard. Lighter snacks include baguettes and sandwiches. To complement the food, the extensive wine list combines New and Old World favourites.

**Open** all day all wk 11-11 (Sun 12-10.30) Closed: 25-26 Dec
**Bar Meals** L served Mon-Sat 12-2, Sun 12-9 booking required D served Mon-Thu 6-9.30, Fri-Sat 6-10, Sun 12-9 booking required Av main course £13.95
**Restaurant** L served Mon-Sat 12-2, Sun 12-9 booking required D served Mon-Thu 6-9.30, Fri-Sat 6-10, Sun 12-9 booking required Av 3 course à la carte fr £26 ⊕ FREE HOUSE ◀ Butcombe Bitter, Sharp's Doom Bar, Otter Ale. ♟ 10
**Facilities** Children's menu Garden Parking

Save on Hotels. Book at theAA.com/hotel

SOMERSET 411 ENGLAND

**STOKE ST GREGORY** *continued*

Open all wk 11-3 6-11 **Bar Meals** L served all wk 12-2 booking required D served all wk 7-9 booking required Av main course £7 **Restaurant** L served all wk 12-2 booking required D served all wk 7-9 booking required Fixed menu price fr £10.50 ⊕ FREE HOUSE ◼ Exmoor Fox, Stag, Butcombe, Otter Ale, Exmoor Ale, guest ales Ö Thatchers Gold, Local Country Cider. **Facilities** Children's menu Children's portions Garden Parking

## TAUNTON Map 4 ST22

### The Hatch Inn ★★★ INN ▾

**Village Rd, Hatch Beauchamp TA3 6SG**
☎ 01823 480245
e-mail: jamie@thehatchinn.co.uk
dir: *M5 junct 25, S on A358 for 3m. Left to Hatch Beauchamp, pub in 1m*

This father and daughter-run pub prides itself on its friendly atmosphere and the quality of its beers and wines. Wholesome home-made food is served, prepared from West Country produce, with a good choice of snacks and meals served in the both the bar and restaurant. A children's menu is also offered. B&B accommodation is available to those who plan to stay over and explore this delightful corner of Somerset.

Open Mon eve-Sun Closed: Mon L, D Oct-Feb ◼ Exmoor Ale, Sharp's Doom Bar, Cotleigh Ö Thatchers Stowford Press. ▾ 8 **Facilities** Dogs allowed Parking **Rooms** 5

## PICK OF THE PUBS

### Queens Arms ▾

**Pitminster TA3 7AZ**
☎ 01823 421529 ▤ 01823 451068
e-mail: enquiries@queensarms-taunton.co.uk
dir: *4m from town centre. On entering Corfe, turn right signed Pitminster. 0.75m, pub on left*

This ancient building was once a mill and even gets a mention in the Domesday Book of 1086. Situated in the heart of Pitminster, its present day incarnation is as a stylish country pub that combines the traditional welcome of a classic country inn with a touch of continental sophistication. Oak and slate floors and roaring log fires in winter add to the appeal, while in summer the patio garden is the perfect spot for a cold drink or after-dinner coffee. The chef uses only the finest locally produced ingredients, with fish delivered daily from Brixham. Meat and game are produced in Somerset, and the vegetables are grown locally. Starters such as fresh mussels cooked with cream, onions and garlic might be followed by oven roasted duck breast with olive oil mash, a selection of vegetables and hoi sin sauce. There is an extensive and impressive wine list.

Open 12-3 6-12 Closed: Sun eve & Mon **Bar Meals** L served Tue-Sun 12-3 booking required D served Tue-Sat 6-10 booking required Av main course £9.50 **Restaurant** L served Tue-Sun 12-3 booking required D served Tue-Sat 6-11 booking required Fixed menu price fr £9.95 Av 3 course à la carte fr £20 ⊕ ENTERPRISE INNS ◼ Otter Ale, Exmoor Ale, Sharp's Doom Bar Ö Thatchers Gold. ▾ 10 **Facilities** Children's menu Children's portions Dogs allowed Garden Parking

## TINTINHULL Map 4 ST41

## PICK OF THE PUBS

### The Crown and Victoria Inn ★★★★ INN ⊛ ▾ NEW

**14 Farm St BA22 8PZ**
☎ 01935 823341 ▤ 01935 825786
e-mail: info@thecrownandvictoria.co.uk
dir: *Next to the National Trust gardens at Tintinhull House*

In a lovely rural setting amidst spacious countryside and sweeping willow trees, this 300-year-old building is now a friendly family-orientated pub with a peaceful beer garden. Mark Hilyard and Isabel Thomas have worked wonders since taking it over in 2006. Along with award-winning beers and a good selection of wines, the locally sourced food, much of it organic, has built up a following of its own. Typical dishes on the extensive menu might include grilled Dorset Down Barnsley lamb chop with nettle and mint sauce, spiced Puy lentils and mash; beer-battered Cornish hake with triple cooked chips, tartare sauce and mushy peas; or pan-fried Creedy Carver duck breast served with rösti potatoes, buttered spinach and Madeira jus. Finish with galette of rhubarb, vanilla yoghurt mousse and pannacotta ice cream or treacle tart with crème Anglaise. The five spacious bedrooms complete the package.

Open all wk 10-4 5.30-late **Bar Meals** L served all wk 12-2.30 D served all wk 6.30-9.30 **Restaurant** L served all wk 12-2.30 D served all wk 6.30-9.30 booking required ⊕ FREE HOUSE ◼ Butcombe, Cheddar Ales, Sharp's Doom Bar, Cotleigh, Yeovil Ales Ö Ashton Press. ▾ 10 **Facilities** Children's menu Children's portions Dogs allowed Garden Parking **Rooms** 5

## TRISCOMBE Map 4 ST13

## PICK OF THE PUBS

### The Blue Ball ▾

**TA4 3HE** ☎ 01984 618242 ▤ 01984 618371
e-mail: info@blueballinn.co.uk
dir: *From Taunton take A358 past Bishops Lydeard towards Minehead*

A public house since 1608, The Blue Ball is hidden away down a narrow lane in the Quantock Hills. Beneath the A-frame wooden ceilings of the converted 18th-century thatched barn you'll find solid beech furniture and log fires, as well as windows that offer superb southerly views to the Brendon Hills. A range of West Country ales including Cotleigh Tawny, Exmoor Gold and Otter Head accompanies a solid selection of hot and cold sandwiches like Exmoor blue cheese with home-made red onion marmalade; and north Atlantic prawns with lime crème fraîche. Other light bites range from cauliflower cheese to smoked salmon with pickled gherkin, caper berries and brown bread. Typical main meals are a trio of sausages with creamy mash and red onion gravy; kipper kedgeree; and Thai yellow potato and spinach curry with naan bread and Basmati rice.

Open all day noon-3.30 6.30-11 (Fri-Sat 12-11 Sun 12-9) Closed: 25-26 Dec eve, 1 Jan eve **Bar Meals** L served Mon-Sat 12-2.30, Sun 12-6 D served all wk 7-9.30 Av main course £6.50 **Restaurant** L served Tue-Sat 12-2.30, Sun 12-6 booking required D served Tue-Sun 7-9.30 booking required Av 3 course à la carte fr £25 ⊕ PUNCH TAVERNS ◼ Cotleigh Tawny, Exmoor Gold & Stag, St Austell, Tribute, Otter Head Ale. ▾ 11 **Facilities** Dogs allowed Garden Parking

## WASHFORD Map 3 ST04

### The Washford Inn

**TA23 0PP** ☎ 01984 640256
e-mail: washfordinn@mail.com
dir: *Telephone for directions*

A pleasant family inn located beside Washford Station, a stop on the West Somerset Railway between Minehead and Bishop's Lydeard - the longest privately-owned line in Britain. A service runs all year, using both diesel and nostalgic old steam locos. A good range of beers and a simple menu of proven pub favourites such as omelette and chips, grilled steaks, and all-day breakfast. Chicken, sausages or pizzas for young trainspotters.

Open all wk all day from end of May ◼ Adnams Broadside, Spitfire, Old Speckled Hen. **Facilities** Play area Family room Dogs allowed Garden Parking

## WATERROW Map 3 ST02

## PICK OF THE PUBS

### The Rock Inn ★★★★ INN ▾

*See Pick of the Pubs on page 412*

## WELLS Map 4 ST54

### The City Arms ▾

**69 High St BA5 2AG** ☎ 01749 673916
e-mail: cityofwellspubcoltd@hotmail.com
dir: *On corner of Queen St & Lower High St*

Steeped in history, the building was once the city gaol (Judge Jeffreys passed sentence here) and original features include barred windows, a solitary cell, chains and locks. The pub offers traditional standards of quality and service, and its choice of seven real ales, draught ciders and menus of fresh local produce. The restaurant, completely refurbished in 2009 with a jazz/blues theme, serves a tapas-style menu (Thursday-Sunday) with dishes such as cured meats with olives, roasted artichoke hearts and aïoli. There are monthly live music evenings.

Open all wk 9am-11pm (Fri-Sat 9-mdnt Sun 10am-11pm) **Bar Meals** Av main course £6.25 food served all day **Restaurant** L served all wk 12-3 booking required D served all wk 6-10.30 booking required Av 3 course à la carte fr £17.95 food served all day ⊕ FREE HOUSE ◼ Butcombe, Sharp's, Potholer, Barbus, Hedge Monkey, George Best Ö Ashton Press, Aspall. ▾ 10 **Facilities** Children's menu Children's portions Family room Dogs allowed Garden

# PICK OF THE PUBS

## The Rock Inn ★★★★INN ⚲

**TA4 2AX**
☎ 01984 623293   📄 01984 623293
e-mail: lnp@rockinn.co.uk
web: www.rockinn.co.uk
dir: *From Taunton take B3227. Waterrow approx 14m W. Or from M5 junct 27, A361 towards Tiverton, then A396 N, right to Bampton, then B3227 to Waterrow*

Halfway between Wiveliscombe and Bampton on the B3227, The Rock Inn is on the southern fringe of the Exmoor National Park and only half an hour drive from the sea. Set in a lovely green valley beside the River Tone, this 400-year-old black and white inn was once a smithy, partly carved from the rock face, some of which is still visible behind the bar. Enjoy a pint of local real ale and cider or one of the nine wines by the glass.

Everything served here is freshly sourced, prepared and cooked to order and you can eat in the bar, where dogs are welcome, or in the bistro-style restaurant. Ever-changing blackboard menus feature the best and most succulent cuts of West Country meat (Aberdeen Angus beef comes from the Rock's own farm two miles away), locally caught fish daily from Brixham, and indulgent puddings.

Lunch could extend to prawn cocktail or pan-fried wood pigeon breasts with black pudding and leaf salad, followed by steak and kidney pie or home-cooked ham, local free-range eggs and home-made chips. Dinner options are more extensive, with typical starters of smoked haddock and prawn gratin, or Thai crab cakes, bean sprout and pak choi salad with sweet chilli dressing. For a main course, choose from Fitzhead venison steak, dauphinoise potato, red wine and port sauce, or fillet of Brixham cod, crushed new potatoes, langoustine, prawns and mussels. And finally, the puddings - try baked lemon cheesecake or pannacotta and gin-poached plums.

Miles of wonderful walking and fishing country make this region much cherished by outdoor types. Stop off for a night or two in one of the cosy bedrooms.

**Open** all wk **Bar Meals** L served all wk 12-2.30 D served all wk 6.30-9.30 Av main course £11 **Restaurant** L served all wk 12-2.30 D served all wk 6.30-9.30 Av 3 course à la carte fr £20 ⊕ FREE HOUSE ◾ Cotleigh Tawny, Exmoor Gold, Otter Ale, Cotleigh Barn Owl, Exmoor Antler ⚬ Sheppy's. ⚲ 9 **Facilities** Children's menu Dogs allowed Parking **Rooms** 8

Save on Hotels. Book at theAA.com/hotel

SOMERSET 413 ENGLAND

## PICK OF THE PUBS

### The Fountain Inn & Boxer's Restaurant ♥

**1 Saint Thomas St BA5 2UU**
☎ 01749 672317  📠 01749 670825
e-mail: eat@fountaininn.co.uk
dir: *In city centre, at A371 & B3139 junct. Follow signs for The Horringtons. Inn on junct of Tor St & Saint Thomas St*

Built during the 16th century to house the builders working on nearby Wells Cathedral, the award-winning Fountain Inn & Boxer's Restaurant has earned a well-deserved reputation for good food and exciting wine. A family-run business since Adrian and Sarah Lawrence took over in 1981, the front of house is now managed by their eldest daughter Kateley (who was born at the pub!) and her husband Andrew Kinnersley. Head chef Julie Pearce uses the finest local produce to create an impressive selection of quality home-cooked food for both the bar and the restaurant. Lunchtime favourites might include doorstep sandwiches with dressed salad and hand-cut chips; or oven-baked goat's cheese in Parma ham with tomato salad. Among the restaurant mains, try roasted cod with pesto and creamy leek mash; roast guinea fowl with chestnut and sage stuffing; or filo parcel with chargrilled Mediterranean vegetables, basil pesto and Greek salad.

**Open** all wk Mon-Sat noon-2.30 6-11 (Sun 7-11) Closed: 25-26 Dec **Bar Meals** L served all wk 12-2 D served all wk 6-9 **Restaurant** L served all wk 12-2 D served all wk 6-9 ⊕ PUNCH ◀ Butcombe Bitter, Sharp's Doom Bar. ♥ 23 **Facilities** Children's menu Children's portions Parking

### WEST BAGBOROUGH          Map 4 ST13

### The Rising Sun Inn ♥

**TA4 3EF** ☎ 01823 432575
e-mail: jon@risingsuninn.info
dir: *Telephone for directions*

Following a devastating fire in 2002, The Rising Sun was rebuilt around the original 16th-century cob walls and

magnificent door, and the craftsmen-led reincarnation is both bold and smart. Local ales are served and a good choice of food at lunch and dinner, with choices such as ham and black pudding terrine topped with a quail's egg; warm chicken and bacon salad; pan fried calves' liver with coarse grain mash and caramelised onion juices; and whole lemon sole with crayfish tails.

**Open** all wk **Bar Meals** L served all wk 12-2 D served all wk 6.30-9.30 Av main course £10.95 **Restaurant** L served all wk 12-2 D served all wk 6.30-9.30 Av 3 course à la carte fr £25 ⊕ FREE HOUSE ◀ Exmoor Ale, Butcombe, Taunton Castle. **Facilities** Children's portions Dogs allowed

### WEST CAMEL          Map 4 ST52

## PICK OF THE PUBS

### The Walnut Tree ★★ HL ◉ ♥

**Fore St BA22 7QW**
☎ 01935 851292  📠 01935 851292
e-mail: info@thewalnuttreehotel.com
dir: *Off A303 between Sparkford & Yeovilton Air Base*

A smartly modernised and extended village inn located half a mile off the A303 between Sparkford and Ilchester, and named after the magnificent walnut tree that stands in the pretty, shrub-filled garden. A popular pit-stop for weary A303 travellers, the friendly, family-run inn is also a favoured refreshment stop among walkers exploring the Leyland Trail that passes through the village. Oak and flagstone floors, red leather chairs and black beams set the relaxing scene in the contemporary-styled bar for a pint of Otter Ale and dish from the lunch menu, perhaps lamb casserole or steak and kidney pie. The imaginative evening menu, served in the Rosewood Restaurant, changes with the seasons and may offer rib-eye steak with pepper sauce; rump of lamb with red wine and rosemary sauce; wild sea bass with lemon butter sauce; and venison with bubble-and-squeak and red wine and redcurrant sauce. The 13 bedrooms are well appointed and individually decorated.

**Open** all wk 11-3 5.30-11 Closed: 25-26 Dec, 1 Jan **Bar Meals** L served all wk 12-2 D served all wk 6-9 Av main course £11 **Restaurant** L served all wk 12-2 booking required D served all wk 6-9 booking required Av 3 course à la carte fr £31.50 ⊕ FREE HOUSE ◀ Otter Ale, Bitter. ♥ 9 **Facilities** Children's portions Garden Parking **Rooms** 13

### WEST HUNTSPILL          Map 4 ST34

## PICK OF THE PUBS

### Crossways Inn

**Withy Rd TA9 3RA** ☎ 01278 783756
e-mail: crossways.inn@virgin.net
dir: *On A38 3.5m from M5*

The Crossways Inn, now under new ownership, is a 17th-century coaching inn that forms an integral part of village life. There is a good choice of real ales and ciders to enjoy, and food is prepared from locally sourced produce wherever possible. Starters include deep fried Somerset brie with home-made red pepper and onion chutney; and button mushrooms, smoky bacon lardons cooked in garlic white wine sauce. Main dishes run along the lines of pie of the day; chilli con carne; faggots and mash; pan-fried cod and garlic prawns; and roasted vegetable and four cheese pasta bake. There are plenty of steaks, light bites and Sunday roasts too. The inn has a family room, skittle alley and secluded garden.

**Open** all day all wk Closed: 25 Dec **Bar Meals** food served all day **Restaurant** food served all day ⊕ FREE HOUSE ◀ Fuller's London Pride, Exmoor Stag, Cotleigh Snowy, Butcombe ♂ Thatchers Gold, Thatchers Dry. **Facilities** Children's menu Children's portions Play area Family room Dogs allowed Garden Parking

# PICK OF THE PUBS

## White Hart ★★★★ INN ☙

**West St TA4 2JP**
☎ **01984 623344** 📠 **01984 624748**
**e-mail:** reservations@
whitehartwiveliscombe.co.uk
**web:** www.whitehartwiveliscombe.co.uk
**dir:** *M5 junct 26. Pub in town centre*

Located at the foot of the Brendon Hills and nearby Quantocks, The White Hart offers an attractive gateway to Exmoor. Facing the square in Wiveliscombe, this former coaching inn dates back some 350 years. Now completely transformed after a major renovation, it offers high standards and modern comforts, whilst still retaining its traditional appeal.

Wiveliscombe has been described as Somerset's capital of brewing and, with its rich history dating back over two hundred years, it is now home to both the Cotleigh and Exmoor Breweries. Both companies' products are regularly on offer in the vibrant, friendly bar, beside a variety of other regional and award-winning guest ales.

Meanwhile, head chef Dave Gaughan's reputation for high quality, freshly cooked food using locally sourced produce has led to a number of prestigious accolades for his pub classics, such as fresh battered Brixham pollock and home-made chips; organic roasted vegetable lasagne with salad and garlic bread; and a choice of ploughman's with home-made bread, chutney and salad. Other favourites include starters like slow roasted organic tomato and basil soup with home-made bread; and honey roast ham with local free range poached egg, home-made bruschetta and spicy chutney. Main course dishes like grilled Exe Valley trout with local organic herbs, sautéed potatoes and local organic salad; Gloucester Old Spot pork belly in local cider sauce with apple mash and seasonal organic vegetables; or oven roasted rack of local lamb with creamy minted new potatoes; might precede profiteroles with strawberry cream filling and warm chocolate sauce; or summer pudding with ginger crème fraîche.

Each of the sixteen en suite bedrooms has its own individual character, with a blend of original and contemporary features.

**Open** all day all wk 10.30am-11pm (Fri-Sat 10am-mdnt) **Bar Meals** L served Mon-Sat 12-2, Sun 12-2.30 booking required D served all wk 6.30-9 booking required Av main course £6.95 **Restaurant** L served Mon-Sun 12-2, Sun 12-2.30 booking required D served all wk 6.30-9 booking required Fixed menu price fr £11.95 ⊕ FREE HOUSE ◀ Cotleigh, Exmoor Fox, Sharp's Doom Bar, Cotleigh Harrier, Taunton Gold, Yeovil Stargazer ♂ Rattler. ☙ 8 **Facilities** Children's menu Dogs allowed Garden Parking **Rooms** 16

Save on Hotels. Book at theAA.com/hotel

SOMERSET 415 ENGLAND

## WEST MONKTON
Map 4 ST22

### PICK OF THE PUBS

## The Monkton Inn

**Blundells Ln TA2 8NP ☎ 01823 412414**
web: www.themonkton.co.uk
dir: *M5 junct 25 to Taunton, right at Creech Castle for 1m, left into West Monkton*

Here is a village pub that, since 2006, has been completely rejuvenated with landlords Eddie Street and Guy Arnold in charge. A significant sum of money has been invested in refurbishing the interior and kitchen, and adding a stylish patio area. A mission statement requires staff to greet customers within 30 seconds of entering, to "go the extra mile", and to have fun at work. Hear, hear! By serving freshly prepared, reasonably priced food they have built a loyal following, while taking good care of the drinks-only community too. Lunch and dinner menus change daily, which makes for a great many possibilities. Randomly selected are starters of pineapple ring filled with prawn salad; melon slice topped with Black Forest ham; main courses of fresh tagliatelle tossed in home-made pesto; a trio of local sausages served on colcannon mash; and desserts such as strawberry and white chocolate cheesecake; and blueberry and Drambuie crème brûlée.

**Open** noon-3 6-11 (Sat-Sun noon-11) Closed: Sun eve, Mon L **Bar Meals** L served Tue-Sun 12-2 Av main course £9 **Restaurant** L served Tue-Sun 12-2 D served Mon-Sat 6.30-9.30 booking required Fixed menu price fr £15 Av 3 course à la carte fr £19 ⊕ ENTERPRISE INNS ◀ Butcombe Bitter, Cotleigh Tawny Exmoor Ale, Exmoor Gold. **Facilities** Children's portions Play area Garden Parking

## WHEDDON CROSS
Map 3 SS93

## The Rest and Be Thankful Inn ★★★★ INN �}

**TA24 7DR ☎ 01643 841222 📄 01643 841813**
e-mail: stay@restandbethankful.co.uk
dir: *5m S of Dunster*

An early 19th-century coaching inn, nearly 1,000 feet up in Exmoor National Park's highest village, where years ago travellers were grateful for a break. Old world charm blends with friendly hospitality in the bar and spacious restaurant, where log fires burn in winter and home-cooked food is served. Relax with a pint of Proper Job

while choosing from the small but perfectly formed menu, which includes specials and vegetarian options. Typical dishes may include grilled goat's cheese with West Country chutney; game cobbler; smoked haddock gratin; and delicious Somerset farmhouse ice creams. Comfortable accommodation is available.

*The Rest and Be Thankful Inn*

**Open** all wk 10-3 6-close **Bar Meals** L served all wk 12-2 D served all wk 7-9 booking required **Restaurant** L served all wk 12-2 booking required D served all wk 7-9 booking required ⊕ FREE HOUSE ◀ Exmoor Ale, Proper Job, Tribute, Guinness, Sharps Own Ŏ Thatchers Gold, Rattler. �} 9 **Facilities** Children's menu Children's portions Garden Parking **Rooms** 8

## WIVELISCOMBE
Map 3 ST02

### PICK OF THE PUBS

## White Hart ★★★★ INN �}

*See Pick of the Pubs on opposite page*

## WOOKEY
Map 4 ST54

## The Burcott Inn

**Wells Rd BA5 1NJ ☎ 01749 673874**
e-mail: ian@burcottinn.co.uk
dir: *2m from Wells on B3139*

The 300-year-old stone building is set on the edge of a charming village with views of the Mendip Hills from the large garden. The inn features low beamed ceilings, a flagstone floor, log fires and a copper topped bar. Meals are served in the restaurant, and snacks and daily specials in the bar alongside quality local ales. Typical dishes include steaks with a choice of sauces, pan-fried chicken goujons in an apricot and Stilton cream sauce; and home-made steak and ale pie.

**Open** all wk 11.30-2.30 6-11 (Sun 12-3 7-10.30) Closed: 25-26 Dec, 1 Jan **Bar Meals** L served all wk 12-2 D served Tue-Sat 6.30-9 Av main course £8.45 **Restaurant** L served all wk 12-2 D served Tue-Sat 6.30-9 Av 3 course à la carte fr £18 ⊕ FREE HOUSE ◀ Teignworthy Old Moggie, RCH Pitchfork, Hop Back Summer Lightning, Cotleigh 25, Cheddar Potholer. **Facilities** Children's menu Children's portions Family room Garden Parking

## YARLINGTON
Map 4 ST62

## The Stags Head Inn

**Pound Ln BA9 8DG ☎ 01963 440393 📄 01963 440393**
e-mail: mrandall1960@tiscali.co.uk
dir: *Exit A303 at Wincanton onto A37 signed Castle Carey. In 3m turn left signed Yarlington, take 2nd right into village. Pub opposite church*

Halfway between Wincanton and Castle Cary lies this completely unspoilt country inn with flagstones, real fires and no electronic intrusions. A sample menu includes slow-roasted lamb shank on creamed mash with redcurrant and rosemary; haddock fillet in beer batter; or chargrilled rump steak with chips, onion rings and mushrooms. Burgers and light bites also available.

**Open** Tue-Sun L Closed: 25 Dec, Sun (eve), Mon ◀ Greene King, IPA, Bass, Guinness, guest ales Ŏ Inch's. **Facilities** Dogs allowed Garden Parking

## YEOVIL
Map 4 ST51

## The Masons Arms ★★★★ INN �}

**41 Lower Odcombe BA22 8TX**
**☎ 01935 862591 📄 01935 862591**
e-mail: paula@masonsarmsodcombe.co.uk
dir: *A3088 to Yeovil, right to Montacute, through village, 3rd right after petrol station to Lower Odcombe*

This was a traditional cider house comprising three cottages, with a small parlour where thirsty masons from the local quarry were served. Built of the self-same hamstone, with four thatched 'eyebrows' above the upper windows, it dates back to the 16th century. In the bar, sample a pint from the pub's own micro-brewery – will it be Odcombe No 1 or Odcombe Roly-Poly? Proprietors Drew and Paula Read have built strong green credentials, recycling anything and everything and growing many of their own vegetables and fruit. The wine list reflects this commitment, with choices that range from organic or vegetarian to biodynamic or fair-traded. Drew also runs the kitchen, producing freshly prepared dishes for seasonal and daily changing à la carte menus. On the winter menu you're likely to find pub grub along the lines of game casserole with herb dumplings, while the carte may offer roasted leg of lamb in Thai massaman curry. The comfortable en suite letting rooms are set back from the road and overlook the garden.

**Open** all wk noon-3 6-mdnt **Bar Meals** L served all wk 12-2 booking required D served all wk 6.30-9.30 booking required Av main course £8 **Restaurant** L served all wk 12-2 booking required D served all wk 6.30-9.30 booking required Av 3 course à la carte fr £25 ⊕ FREE HOUSE ◀ Odcombe No1, Odcombe Spine, Odcombe Roly Poly, Odcombe Winters Tail, Odcombe Half Jack Ŏ Thatchers Gold, Thatchers Heritage. �} 8 **Facilities** Children's menu Children's portions Dogs allowed Garden Parking **Rooms** 6

## STAFFORDSHIRE

### ALSTONEFIELD — Map 16 SK15

## PICK OF THE PUBS

### The George ▾

**DE6 2FX ☎ 01335 310205**
**e-mail:** emily@thegeorgeatalstonefield.com
**dir:** 7m N of Ashbourne, signed Alstonefield to left off A515

The nearby valley is a famous haunt for ramblers and many seek well-earned refreshment at this friendly 18th-century coaching inn. Run by three generations of the same family, the current landlady warmly welcome all-comers, as long as muddy boots are left at the door. The appeal of this fine pub, other than the wonderful location and welcome, includes the cracking range real ales and wines by the glass, and the fantastic home-cooked food. The emphasis is on seasonal, regional and traditional dishes: at lunch start with smoked mackerel pâté; or ham hock and parsley terrine with piccalilli; followed by beer battered haddock fillet, pea purée and chips; and lemon possett with lemon sorbet. By night, tuck into oven baked breaded goat's cheese, sweet poached pear, leaf and walnut salad; pan-fried chicken breast, lentils, cherry tomatoes and creamed mushrooms; followed by warm bitter chocolate sponge pudding with vanilla bean and praline ice cream. There is a farm shop and wedding venue in the Grade II listed coach house.

**Open** all wk Mon-Fri 11.30-3 6-11 (Sat 11.30-11 Sun 12-9.30) Closed: 25 Dec **Bar Meals** L served all wk 12-2.30 booking required D served Mon-Sat 7-9, Sun 6.30-8 booking required Av main course £10 **Restaurant** L served all wk 12-2.30 booking required D served Mon-Sat 7-9, Sun 6.30-8 booking required Av 3 course à la carte fr £25 ⊕ MARSTONS ◀ Marston's Bitter & Pedigree, Jennings Cumberland Ale, Brakspear Oxford Gold, Guest ale ♂ Thatchers. ▾ 10 **Facilities** Children's portions Dogs allowed Garden Parking

### ALTON — Map 10 SK04

## Bulls Head Inn

**High St ST10 4AQ ☎ 01538 702307 📄 01538 702065**
**e-mail:** janet@thebullsheadalton.co.uk
**dir:** M6 junct 14, A518 to Uttoxeter. Follow Alton Towers signs. Onto B5030 to Rocester, then B5032 to Alton. Pub in village centre

Traditional beers and home cooking are provided in the heart of Alton, less than a mile from Alton Towers theme park. Oak beams and an inglenook fireplace set the scene for the old world bar, the cosy snug and the country-style restaurant. Menus offer the likes of sirloin steak, deep fried breaded plaice, lasagne verde, steak, ale and mushroom pie, and hunter's chicken.

**Open** all wk 11am-11pm **Bar Meals** L served all wk 12-2 D served all wk 6-9.30 **Restaurant** L served all wk 12-2 D served all wk 6-9.30 ⊕ FREE HOUSE ◀ Guest ales. **Facilities** Parking

### ANSLOW — Map 10 SK22

## The Burnt Gate Inn ▾

**Hopley Rd DE13 9PY ☎ 01283 563664**
**e-mail:** info@burntgate.co.uk
**dir:** From Burton take B5017 towards Abbots Bromley. At top of Henhurst Hill turn right Inn on Hopley Rd, 2m from town centre

Selective contemporary updating has nicely enhanced this well-favoured country dining pub, originally two cottages and a farmhouse parts of which are up to 300 years old, whilst retaining the traditional elements of oak-floored bar and open fires. The enthusiastic owners are committed to offering menus to cater for particular diets, so coeliacs and vegans will find a hearty welcome alongside diners enjoying the comprehensive choice of dishes such as cheese and apple pie or hand-made roasted and sundried tomato risotto Kiev.

**Open** all day all wk Closed: 31 Dec **Bar Meals** L served Mon-Thu 12-2.30, Fri-Sat 12-9, Sun 12-4 D served Mon-Thu 6-9, Fri-Sat 12-9 Av main course £6 **Restaurant** L served Mon-Thu 12-2.30, Fri-Sat 12-9, Sun 12-4 D served Mon-Thu 6-9, Fri-Sat 12-9 Fixed menu price fr £10 Av 3 course à la carte fr £20 ⊕ FREE HOUSE ◀ Pedigree, guest ales. ▾ 12 **Facilities** Children's menu Dogs allowed Parking

### BURTON UPON TRENT — Map 10 SK22

## Burton Bridge Inn ▾

**24 Bridge St DE14 1SY ☎ 01283 536596**
**dir:** Telephone for directions

A former coaching inn, the Burton Bridge is the oldest pub in Burton, and has its own brewery at the back in an old stable block. The old-fashioned interior has oak panelling, feature fireplaces, and a distinct lack of electronic entertainment. There is also thought to be a resident ghost. A full range of Burton Bridge ales is available on tap and the menu offers straightforward dishes. A skittle alley is also available for hire.

**Open** all wk 11.30-2.15 5-11 (Sun noon-2 7-10.30) ◀ Burton Bridge - Gold Medal Ale, Festival Ale, Golden Delicious, Bridge Bitter. ▾ 15 **Facilities** Dogs allowed Garden **Notes** ⊛

### CAULDON — Map 16 SK04

## Yew Tree Inn

**ST10 3EJ ☎ 01538 308348 📄 01782 212064**
**dir:** Between A52 & A523. 4.5m from Alton Towers

The Yew Tree is so well known that people come from all over the world to see it. The pub dates back 300 years and has plenty of character and lots of fascinating artefacts, including Victorian music boxes, pianolas, grandfather clocks, a crank handle telephone, and a pub lantern. A varied snack menu offers locally made, hand-raised pork pies, sandwiches, baps, quiche and desserts, and can be washed-down with a pint of Burton Bridge.

**Open** all wk 10.30-2.30 6-12 (Sun 12-3 7-12) ⊕ FREE HOUSE ◀ Burton Bridge, Bass, Rudgate Ruby Mild. **Facilities** Family room Dogs allowed Parking **Notes** ⊛

### CHEADLE — Map 10 SK04

## The Queens At Freehay

**Counslow Rd, Freehay ST10 1RF**
**☎ 01538 722383 📄 01538 723748**
**dir:** 4m from Alton Towers

Very much a family-run establishment, the pub dates from the 18th century and has a pretty setting surrounded by mature trees and garden. The interior is refreshingly modern in style, with elegant tables and chairs. The pub has established a good reputation for food, and dishes from the menu are supplemented by chef's specials from the fish or meat boards. Expect home-made beef and merlot pie; Moroccan lamb tagine; and fish and chips. Children have their own menu.

**Open** all wk noon-3 6-11 (Sun noon-4 6.30-11) Closed: 25-26, 31 Dec-1 Jan ◀ Draught Burton, Peakstones Alton Abbey. **Facilities** Garden Parking

### COLTON — Map 10 SK02

## PICK OF THE PUBS

### The Yorkshireman ▾

See Pick of the Pubs on opposite page

### ECCLESHALL — Map 15 SJ82

## The George ▾

**Castle St ST21 6DF ☎ 01785 850300 📄 01785 851452**
**e-mail:** vicki@slatersales.co.uk
**dir:** From M6 junct 14 take A5013 to Eccleshall (6m)

A 17th-century former coaching inn, The George has been in the Slater's hands for over 20 years. It's the brewery tap for the other part of the family business – the micro-brewery a few miles away in Stafford where the owners' son produces award-winning ales. The traditional bar features a large open fireplace, and proffers a good selection of malt whiskies and wines in addition to the family brews. A wide variety of dishes, including Wexford mushroom crostini and Eccleshall-reared lamb steak, can be eaten either in the bar or in the appealing restaurant.

**Open** all day all wk Mon-Thu 11am-1.30am (Fri-Sat 11am-2.30am Sun noon-mdnt) Closed: 25 Dec **Bar Meals** food served all day **Restaurant** food served all day ⊕ FREE HOUSE ◀ Slaters Ales. ▾ 18 **Facilities** Children's menu Dogs allowed Parking

### HOPEDALE — Map 16 SK15

## PICK OF THE PUBS

### The Watts Russell Arms ▾

See Pick of the Pubs on page 418

# PICK OF THE PUBS

## The Yorkshireman 🍷

**COLTON**          **Map 10 SK02**

**Colton Rd WS15 3HB ☎ 01889 583977**
e-mail:
theyorkshireman@btconnect.com
dir: *10m from Stafford*

Originally serving Rugeley station on the West Coast main line, this was formerly the Railway Tavern. Long before it was given its current identity (by a landlord from Yorkshire, believe it or not) it was known colloquially as "Wilf and Rosa's", the lady in question, or at least so today's owners, John and Jo Ashmore, have been told, being quite a character, "a wild-haired woman who enjoyed a good night!" Rugeley attracted attention in other ways too: it once had a notorious serial-murdering doctor, who poisoned many of his patients, and (unwittingly) provided Blythe's Brewery just up the road at Hamstall Ridware

with the name for one of its beers, Palmer's Poison, sold in the bar. Curled up on his bed in the corner of the bar, completely untroubled by thoughts of wild-haired women or murderous medics, is Dahl, the pub's lazy greyhound, known to occasionally lift his head in welcome, mostly, it must be said, to other well-behaved dogs.

The kitchen tries to source as much produce as possible from around the area, availability being reflected in the modestly priced, daily changing menu. You can start with a Yorkshireman deli board - ideal for sharing - and for a main course you will often find Staffordshire-reared steak with hand-cut chips, onion rings, sautéed mushrooms and grilled tomatoes; tandoori-marinated loin of Gloucester Old Spot pork on a tomato and fennel curry with cardamom; and fresh linguine tossed with tomatoes, olives, mushrooms and rocket topped with mozzarella. Freshly cut sandwiches are served on locally baked granary or white bread, and weekend specials often include fresh fish collected from the local market.

There's no specific children's menu, but smaller portions of adult dishes are available. Several of the wines are priced below £15, which is good to find these days.

**Open** all wk noon-2.30 5.30-11 (Sat noon-11pm Sun noon-6)
**Bar Meals** L served Mon-Sat 12-2.30, Sun 12-6 D served Mon-Fri 6-9.30, Sat 6-11 food served all day **Restaurant** L served Mon-Sat 12-2.30, Sun 12-6 booking required D served Mon-Sat 6-9.30 booking required Av 3 course à la carte fr £15 ⊕ FREE HOUSE ◀ Local Blythe Brewery ♂ Stowford Press. 🍷 10 **Facilities** Dogs allowed Garden Parking

# PICK OF THE PUBS

## The Watts Russell Arms

**HOPEDALE**  Map 16 SK15

**Hopedale DE6 2GD** ☎ **01335 310126**
**e-mail:** contact@wattsrussell.co.uk
**web:** www.wattsrussell.co.uk
**dir:** *Take A515 N towards Buxton. In 6.5m left to Alstonefield & Mildale. Cross River Dove, take left fork to Mildale. 1.5m to pub*

Husband and wife team Bruce and Chris Elliott run this picture-postcard pub, originally a homestead dating from the 17th century. Later it became a beer-house called the New Inn, which was renamed in 1851 in honour of the wife of Jesse Watts-Russell; her family owned Ilam Hall down the road, the surviving part of which is now a Youth Hostel. Perhaps the dear lady wasn't that grateful, as her ghost reputedly still roams the area.

Dogs are welcome in the terraced gardens and courtyard, while the cosy interior is welcoming for all the family, with a bar made from old oak barrels. Here Chris holds sway, serving perfectly kept pints of Timothy Taylor Landlord, Black Sheep or the guest ale, single malts from a selection of fifteen, or eight wines by the glass. In the kitchen, Bruce prepares everything from scratch, using mostly locally supplied produce and ingredients – nothing comes from a packet or a tin. Salt beef is cured on the premises, and dishes such as hand-rolled six-hour pork allow the kitchen time to cater for special dietary demands. Occasionally neighbours supply herbs and vegetables, and even unusual donations such as giant puffballs will go straight on the menu.

At lunchtime there are tempting sandwiches, wraps, soups, hand-made pizzas and hot plates such as beef chilli, while typical evening selections could comprise Irish onion soup; lobby (Staffordshire's own beef and vegetable casserole); and vegetarian dishes, of which there are usually at least three, such as vegetable whim, reflecting the latest neighbourly donation. Popular Sunday lunches include prime topside of beef served pink, and leg of lamb slow-roasted with garlic, rosemary and orange. Once a month, Bruce hosts an evening devoted to food from other countries. A short walk from the pub is the River Dove and the beginning of Dovedale, one of the country's most beautiful walks.

**Open** 12-2.30 6.30-10.30 (Sat 12-11, Sun 12-9) Closed: Mon eve
**Bar Meals** L served Mon-Fri 12-2, Sat-Sun 12-4 D served Tue-Sat 7-9, Sun 6-8 booking required Av main course £9.50
**Restaurant** Av 3 course à la carte fr £20 ⊕ FREE HOUSE ◂ Timothy Taylor Landlord, Black Sheep Best, guest ales. ♟ 8 **Facilities** Dogs allowed Garden Parking

Save on Hotels. Book at **theAA.com/hotel**

**STAFFORDSHIRE** 419 **ENGLAND**

## LEEK
Map 16 SJ95

### Three Horseshoes Inn ★★★ HL ⚙ 🏆

Buxton Rd, Blackshaw Moor ST13 8TW
☎ 01538 300296 📠 01538 300320
e-mail: enquiries@threeshoesinn.co.uk
dir: On A53, 3m N of Leek

A family-run inn and country hotel in the Peak National
Park, the Three Horseshoes offers breathtaking views
from the attractive gardens. Inside this creeper-covered
inn, the main bar features wood fires in the winter, with a
good selection of real ales. Visitors can choose from
traditional decor and roast meats in the bar carvery, the
relaxed atmosphere of the brasserie or Kirks Restaurant.
Using the best of local produce, expect dishes like
Packington pork fillet ballantine, Thai duck curry, and
steak and kidney pie. Delicious afternoon teas also
available.

**Open** all day all wk **Bar Meals** Av main course £8.80 food
served all day **Restaurant** L served Sun 12.15-1.30
booking required D served Mon-Sat 6.30-9 booking
required Fixed menu price fr £15.45 Av 3 course à la carte
fr £20 ⊕ FREE HOUSE ◀ Theakstons XB Courage
Directors, Morland Old Speckled Hen, John Smith's. 🏆 12
**Facilities** Children's menu Children's portions Play area
Garden Parking **Rooms** 26

## NORBURY JUNCTION
Map 15 SJ72

### The Junction Inn

ST20 0PN ☎ 01785 284288
dir: From M6 junct 14 take A5013 for Eccleshall, left at
Great Bridgeford onto B5405 towards Woodseaves, left
onto A519 towards Newport, left for Norbury Junction

Not a railway junction, but a beautiful stretch of
waterway where the Shropshire Union Canal meets the
disused Newport arm. The inn's large beer garden gives a
ringside view of everything happening on the canal, as
well as hosting summer BBQs. Food ranges from
baguettes to specials such as home-made rabbit stew
with fresh crusty bread; traditional belly pork with black
pudding; and bangers and mash with onion gravy.
Disabled access at both front and rear.

**Open** all day all wk 11am-11pm (Fri-Sat 11am-mdnt Sun
noon-11pm) Closed: afternoon in winter **Bar Meals** L
served Mon-Fri 12-2.45, Sat-Sun all day D served Mon-Fri
6-8.45, Sat-Sun all day ⊕ FREE HOUSE ◀ Banks Mild,
Banks Bitter, Junction Ale, guest ales.
**Facilities** Children's menu Play area Family room Dogs
allowed Garden Parking

## STAFFORD
Map 10 SJ92

### PICK OF THE PUBS

### The Holly Bush Inn 🏆

See Pick of the Pubs on page 420

---

### PICK OF THE PUBS

### The Moat House ★★★★ HL ⚙ 🏆

Lower Penkridge Rd, Acton Trussell ST17 0RJ
☎ 01785 712217 📠 01785 715344
e-mail: info@moathouse.co.uk
dir: M6 junct 13 towards Stafford, 1st right to Acton
Trussell

A Grade II listed mansion dating back to the 14th
century, standing on a mound, scheduled as an Ancient
Monument, beside the Staffordshire and Worcestershire
Canal. Inside are oak beams and an inglenook
fireplace, the stylish Brasserie Bar, and the
Conservatory Restaurant. The food, for which the AA
has awarded two Rosettes, is listed on a variety of
menus offering, for example, beef tomato and buffalo
mozzarella salad with crushed basil and extra virgin
olive oil; 28-day, dry-aged Staffordshire sirloin steak
with thick-cut chips, onion rings, field mushroom,
tomato and a pepper sauce; free-range Tamworth pork
cutlet with mashed potatoes, mustard carrots and
cider velouté; and seared fillet of salmon served on a
bed of wilted spinach with a sauce vièrge and new
potatoes. Quality bedrooms, conference facilities and
corporate events are big attractions, and with four
honeymoon suites, two with four-posters, the Moat
House is a popular venue for weddings.

**Open** all day all wk Mon-Sun 10am-11pm Closed: 25
Dec **Bar Meals** L served all wk 12-2.15 D served Sun-
Fri 6-9.30 **Restaurant** L served all wk 12-2 booking
required D served all wk 6.30-9.30 booking required
⊕ FREE HOUSE ◀ Old Speckled Hen, Greene King IPA,
Guinness. 🏆 16 **Facilities** Children's menu Children's
portions Family room Garden Parking **Rooms** 41

## STOCKTON BROOK
Map 16 SJ95

### The Hollybush 🏆 NEW

1 Stanley Rd ST9 9NL ☎ 01782 502116
e-mail: mail@thehollybush.info
dir: Just off A53 between Stoke-on-Trent & Leek

The chic yet cosy interiors of this attractive canalside pub
are an effortless blend of stone, whitewash, pine and
leather. Watch the chefs at work in their open kitchen
whilst waiting for contemporary dishes like lemon and
thyme glazed spit chicken with red wine jus, or goat's
cheese and shallot tarte Tatin with red pepper dressing.
The beautifully landscaped gardens are just the place to
sit and relax on warm summer days.

---

Open all day all wk Closed: 1 Jan **Bar Meals** L served
Mon-Fri 12-3, Sat 12-9.30, Sun 12-8 D served Mon-Fri
5.30-9 Av main course £9 **Restaurant** L served Mon-Fri
12-3, Sat 12-9.30, Sun 12-8 booking required D served
Mon-Fri 5.30-9 booking required ⊕ MOYO LTD
◀ Wadworth 6X, Hancocks HB. 🏆 12 **Facilities** Children's
menu Children's portions Garden Parking

## STOURTON
Map 10 SO88

### The Fox Inn

Bridgnorth Rd DY7 5BL
☎ 01384 872614 & 872123 📠 01384 877771
e-mail: fox-inn-stourton@dial.pipex.com
dir: 5m from Stourbridge town centre. On A458
(Stourbridge to Bridgnorth road)

The Fox is a late 18th-century inn on an estate once
owned by Lady Jane Grey. In the forty years Stefan Caron
has been running it, he has built up an undeniable
reputation for quality and value for money, but his
customers are also attracted by its warm atmosphere and
historic surroundings, with many original features still in
place. There's also a large garden, complete with weeping
willow, gazebo and attractive patio area. The inn has a
civil ceremony licence.

**Open** all wk 10.30-3 5-11 (Sat-Sun 10.30am-11pm)
**Bar Meals** L served Mon-Sat 12-2.30 D served Tue-Sat
7-9.30 **Restaurant** L served Tue-Sat 12-2.30 D served
Tue-Sat 7-9.30 booking required ⊕ FREE HOUSE
◀ Bathams Ale, Hereford Pale Ale, Boddingtons,
Guinness. **Facilities** Children's menu Children's portions
Garden Parking

## TAMWORTH
Map 10 SK20

### The Globe Inn ★★★ INN

Lower Gungate B79 7AT
☎ 01827 60455 📠 01827 63575
e-mail: info@theglobetamworth.com
dir: Telephone for directions

A popular meeting place in the 19th century, the Globe
was rebuilt in 1901. More recently, the building has been
extended and refurbished to offer 18 en suite bedrooms,
though retaining the elegant carved bar and fireplaces
that reflect its period character. A range of light meals,
salads and hot paninis liven up the snack menu, whilst
main dishes include poached smoked haddock with
Charlotte potatoes, and a 3 course Sunday lunch for only
£7.95, booking required.

**Open** all day all wk 11-11 (Thu-Sat 11am-mdnt Sun 11-4
7-11) Closed: 25 Dec, 1 Jan **Bar Meals** L served all wk
11-2 D served Mon-Sat 6-9 Av main course £6
**Restaurant** L served all wk 11-2 D served Mon-Sat 6-9
⊕ FREE HOUSE ◀ Bass, Worthington.
**Facilities** Children's menu Children's portions Parking
**Rooms** 18

# PICK OF THE PUBS

## The Holly Bush Inn ♉

**STAFFORD**      Map 10 SJ92

**Salt ST18 0BX**
☎ **01889 508234**   📄 **01889 508058**
**e-mail:** geoff@hollybushinn.co.uk
**web:** www.hollybushinn.co.uk
**dir:** *Telephone for directions*

The inn is situated in the village of Salt, probably a settlement originating from the Saxon period due to its sheltered position and proximity to the river Trent. Believed to be only the second pub in the country to receive, back in Charles II's reign, a licence to sell alcohol, although the building itself possibly dates from as long ago as 1190. And when landlord Geoff Holland's son became a joint licensee at the age of 18 years and 6 days, he was the youngest person ever to be granted a licence.

The pub's comfortably old-fashioned interior contains all the essential ingredients: heavy carved beams, open fires, attractive prints and cosy alcoves. In the kitchen there's a strong commitment to limiting food miles by supporting local producers, and to ensuring that animals supplying meat have lived stress-free lives.

The main menu features traditional dishes such as steak and kidney pudding; battered cod with mushy peas; and mixed grill, but also included are the still-traditional-but-less-well-known, such as braised venison with chestnuts; and slow-cooked lamb and barley stew. The specials board changes every session, but will usually include Staffordshire oatcakes stuffed with bacon and cheese; hand-made pork, leek and Stilton sausages with fried eggs and chips; and a roast meat, perhaps topside of beef; or ham with sweet Madeira gravy.

The evening specials board may offer home-smoked fillet of Blythe Field trout with creamy horseradish sauce; warm pan-fried duck and pear salad; Scottish mussels steamed with cider and cream; rabbit casserole with dumplings; or slow-cooked mutton with caper sauce.

Cheeses are all hand-made to old English recipes, while seasonal puddings include the unquestionably traditional bread and butter pudding, and apple crumble with cinnamon and nutmeg dusting. Handmade pizzas are cooked in a wood-fired brick oven; in addition to the usual favourites, try the surf and turf, or seafood special.

**Open** all wk 12-11 (Sun 12-10.30)
**Bar Meals** Av main course £10.50 food served all day **Restaurant** food served all day ⊕ FREE HOUSE ◀ Adnams, Pedigree, guest ales. ♉ 12
**Facilities** Children's menu Garden Parking

# PICK OF THE PUBS

## The Crown Inn ♟

**WRINEHILL**  Map 15 SJ74

**Den Ln CW3 9BT**
☎ 01270 820472   📄 01270 820547
**e-mail:** mark_condliffe@hotmail.com
**dir:** *Village on A531, 1m S of Betley. 6m S of Crewe; 6m N of Newcastle-under-Lyme*

Landlord Charles Davenhill is reputedly the longest-serving licensee in Staffordshire; he and his wife Sue have owned this 19th-century free house for more than thirty years. In 2001 they were joined by their daughter Anna and husband Mark Condliffe, so The Crown is now a family-run, traditional country inn serving a good line-up of regular and guest beers. Sit beneath exposed oak beams in the open plan interior, the roaring open fire in the large inglenook fireplace a welcome presence on cold nights.

Food is a major part of the pub's success, famed locally not just for the generosity of its portions, but also for its consistent quality. The seasonal menus offer a wide range of dishes, with at one end of the scale a simple jacket potato filled with cheese and coleslaw, and at the other an 8oz fillet steak with all the usual accoutrements. In between comes a veritable roll-call of meat, fish and vegetarian dishes, including baked swordfish steak in a marinade of orange juice, fresh ginger, garlic and soy sauce; sizzling strips of duck breast in plum, spring onion and fresh ginger sauce; smoked salmon and haddock fishcakes; and sea bass fillets baked in olive oil with Chardonnay, caper and fresh parsley cream.

The vegetarian selection – aubergine and mozzarella with fresh basil, tomato and pine kernels; and burritos filled with courgettes, mushrooms, baby corn and peppers, for example – is driven by Sue and Anna's own dietary preferences. Or for something lighter, how about a soft floury bap filled with brie, cranberry sauce and toasted almonds? From the sweet menu, try sugared waffle with home-made toffee sauce and ice cream; or Belgian chocolate bombe with cream. Children have their own menu.

**Open** all wk noon-3 6-11 (Sun noon-4 6-10.30) Closed: 25-26 Dec
**Bar Meals** L served Mon-Sat 12-2, Sun 12-3 D served Mon-Fri 6.30-9.30, Sat 6-10, Sun 6-9 Av main course £9
🛢 FREE HOUSE ◀ Marstons Pedigree & Bitter, Cumberland Ale, Sneck Lifter, guest ales. ♟ 10 **Facilities** Children's menu Garden Parking

## TATENHILL      Map 10 SK22

### Horseshoe Inn ♈

**Main St DE13 9SD ☎ 01283 564913**
dir: *From A38 at Branston follow signs for Tatenhill*

Probably five to six hundred years old, this historic pub retains much original character, including evidence of a priest's hiding hole. In winter, log fires warm the bar and family area. In addition to home-made snacks like chilli con carne, and Horseshoe brunch, there are sizzling rumps and sirloins, chicken curry, moussaka, battered cod with chips and mushy peas, and a pasta dish of the week. And specials too - beef bourguignon, or steak and kidney pudding, for instance.

**Open** all day all wk 11am-11pm (Thu-Sat 11am-11.30pm) ◄ Marstons Pedigree. ♈ 14 **Facilities** Play area Family room Dogs allowed Garden Parking

## TUTBURY      Map 10 SK22

### Ye Olde Dog & Partridge Inn ♈

**High St DE13 9LS ☎ 01283 813030   📄 01283 816159**
dir: *On A50 NW of Burton-on-Trent, signed from A50 & A511*

A magnificent, medieval half-timbered marvel in a picturesque Staffordshire village, close to the castle and the famous River Dove. The heavily beamed interior shelters discrete nooks and alcoves where may be enjoyed a menu which covers the whole gamut, from old standards to inventive new twists: a teriyaki turf and surf or scallops with chilli jam for example, seen off with a lemon and almond tart and a good list of wines.

**Open** all day all wk **Bar Meals** L served all wk 12-10 Av main course £9 food served all day **Restaurant** L served all wk 12-10 Fixed menu price fr £9 food served all day ⊕ PUNCH PUB COMPANY ◄ Marston's Pedigree, Courage Director's. ♈ 12 **Facilities** Children's menu Children's portions Family room Garden Parking

## WETTON      Map 16 SK15

### Ye Olde Royal Oak

**DE6 2AF ☎ 01335 310287**
e-mail: royaloakwetton@live.co.uk
dir: *A515 towards Buxton, left in 4m to Manifold Valley-Alstonfield, follow signs to Wetton*

The stone-built inn dates back over 400 years and features wooden beams recovered from oak ships at Liverpool Docks. It was formerly part of the Chatsworth Estate, and the Tissington walking and cycling trail is close by. Guest ales are served along with dishes such as home-made soup; large battered cod; and treacle sponge. Separate vegetarian and children's menus are available. The pub's moorland garden includes a campsite with showers and toilets.

**Open** 12-2 7-closing Closed: Mon-Tue in winter **Bar Meals** L served Wed-Sun 12-2 D served Wed-Sun 7-9 Av main course £8 ⊕ FREE HOUSE ◄ Hartington, Old Speckled Hen. **Facilities** Children's menu Family room Dogs allowed Garden Parking

## WOODSEAVES      Map 15 SJ72

### The Plough Inn

**Newport Rd ST20 0NP ☎ 01785 284210**
dir: *From Stafford take A5013 towards Eccleshall. Turn left onto B4505. Woodseaves at junct with A519. 5m from Eccleshall on A519 towards Newport*

Now under new ownership, this mid-18th century country pub was built for workers constructing the nearby canal. The Plough has fires in winter and pretty hanging baskets in the summer. There's a good selection of real ales, and the welcoming new owners are locals and are proud to return the pub back to its traditional roots, serving home cooked, traditional pub dishes.

**Open** all wk Mon 5-11 Tue-Thu 12-3 5-11 (Fri-Sat noon-mdnt Sun noon-10.30pm, all day BHs) **Bar Meals** L served 12-3 D served 5-8.30 Av main course £6 **Restaurant** L served Sat-Sun 12-8.30 Av 3 course à la carte fr £11 ⊕ FREE HOUSE ◄ Banks Bitter, Banks Mild, Pedigree, Jennings, Cumberland Ale ♻ Thatchers Gold. **Facilities** Children's menu Children's portions Garden Parking

## WRINEHILL      Map 15 SJ74

### PICK OF THE PUBS

**The Crown Inn ♈**

*See Pick of the Pubs on page 421*

### The Hand & Trumpet ♈

**Main Rd CW3 9BJ ☎ 01270 820048   📄 01270 821911**
e-mail: hand.and.trumpet@brunningandprice.co.uk
dir: *M6 junct 16, A351, follow Keele signs, 7m, pub on right in village*

A relaxed country pub, The Hand & Trumpet has a comfortable interior with original floors, old furniture, open fires and rugs. A deck to the rear overlooks the sizeable grounds, which include a large pond. Six cask ales including guests and over 70 malt whiskies are served, along with a locally sourced menu. Braised lamb shoulder with honey roasted vegetables, rosemary and redcurrant gravy, or wild mushroom, celeriac, leek and thyme pie are typical dishes.

**Open** all day all wk 11.30-11 (Sun 11.30-10.30) Closed: 25 Dec **Bar Meals** L served all wk 12-10 D served all wk 12-10 Av main course £11.95 food served all day ⊕ FREE HOUSE ◄ Deuchars IPA, Hawkshead Lakeland Gold, Guest ales ♻ Thatchers Gold. ♈ 12 **Facilities** Children's portions Dogs allowed Garden Parking

## SUFFOLK

### ALDEBURGH      Map 13 TM45

### The Mill Inn ★★★ INN

**Market Cross Place IP15 5BJ ☎ 01728 452563**
e-mail: peeldennisp@aol.com
dir: *Follow Aldeburgh signs from A12 on A1094. Pub last building on left before sea*

A genuine fisherman's inn located less than 100 metres from the seafront, and a short walk from the town and bird sanctuaries. Seafood bought fresh from the fishermen on the beach is a speciality here, backed by pub favourites such as sirloin steak, ham and eggs, and lamb shank. Well-kept Adnams Bitter, Broadside, Regatta and Fisherman can all be enjoyed at this favourite haunt of the local lifeboat crew. There are four bedrooms available, some with sea views.

**Open** all wk 11-11 ◄ Adnams Bitter, Broadside, Regatta & Fisherman, OLD ♻ Aspall. **Facilities** Dogs allowed Garden **Rooms** 4

### ALDRINGHAM      Map 13 TM46

### The Parrot and Punchbowl Inn & Restaurant

**Aldringham Ln IP16 4PY ☎ 01728 830221**
dir: *On B1122, 1m from Leiston, 3m from Aldeburgh, on x-rds to Thorpeness*

Originally called The Case is Altered, it became the Parrot in 1604 and as such enjoyed considerable notoriety, particularly during the 17th century, as the haunt of Aldringham's smuggling gangs. Don't ask if there's any contraband rum on offer; just study the menu and try and decide between slowly braised lamb's liver with onion and bacon and mashed potato; steak and kidney pie with short crust pastry top; or pan seared duck breast with a raspberry jus. 'Parrot sandwiches' are generously overfilled.

**Open** all wk 12-2.30 6-11 **Bar Meals** L served all wk 12-2 D served all wk 6.30-9 Av main course £6.95 **Restaurant** L served all wk 12-2 booking required D served all wk 6.30-9 booking required Fixed menu price fr £8.95 Av 3 course à la carte fr £18 ⊕ ENTERPRISE INNS ◄ Adnams, guest ale ♻ Aspall. **Facilities** Children's portions Play area Family room Dogs allowed Garden Parking

Save on Hotels. Book at **theAA**.com/hotel

SUFFOLK 423 ENGLAND

---

### BARNBY
Map 13 TM49

## PICK OF THE PUBS

## The Swan Inn

**Swan Ln NR34 7QF**
☎ **01502 476646** 🖷 **01502 585539**
*dir: Just off A146 between Lowestoft & Beccles*

Behind the distinctive pink-painted façade of this warm and friendly free house, just to the south of the Norfolk Broads, is one of Suffolk's foremost fish restaurants. Donald and Michael Cole own it - their family have been wholesale fish merchants since grandfather set up the business in 1936. Although not immediately apparent externally, the property dates from 1690; obvious signs, like low beams, you'll find in the rustic restaurant, along with nautical memorabilia displayed in tribute to Lowestoft's brave fishermen. The menu, which lists some 80 seafood dishes, starts with smoked sprats (which you can eat whole); smoked trout pâté; and Italian seafood salad; and mains such as grilled turbot; monkfish tails in garlic butter; and crab gratin. The Swan has its own smokehouse, one of just three remaining in what was once one of Britain's busiest fishing ports. Anyone preferring meat has a choice of steaks and a few other dishes.

**Open** all wk ⊕ FREE HOUSE ◀ Interbrew Bass, Adnams Best, Broadside, Greene King Abbot Ale, IPA, guest ales. **Facilities** Play area Garden Parking

---

### BRANDESTON
Map 13 TM26

## PICK OF THE PUBS

## The Queens Head ⊜

**The Street IP13 7AD** ☎ **01728 685307**
e-mail: thequeensheadinn@btconnect.com
*dir: From A14 take A1120 to Earl Soham, then S to Brandeston*

Originally four cottages, the pub has been serving ale to the villagers of Brandeston since 1811. In the 17th century the Witch Finder General terrorised the population in the village and as a consequence an elderly and unpopular vicar was accused of being in league with the devil, and hanged; and romantic heroine Margaret Catchpole - horse thief, smuggler and convict - is said to have buried contraband in the pond in front of her Brandeston home. The pub has a large open bar which allows drinkers and diners to mix, and good use is made of the huge garden in summer. Exceptional local food, Adnams ales and wines are served, with award-winning dishes like pigeon and smoked bacon pâté with celeriac coleslaw and warm brioche; steamed hake, confit potato and pesto roasted vegetables; toffee and banana crumble with banana ice cream. Some starters came be served as a main course, for example tiger prawns, coconut and coriander broth and glass noodles.

---

**Open** noon-3 5-mdnt (Sun noon-5) Closed: Sun eve **Bar Meals** L served all wk 12-2 booking required D served Mon-Sat 6.30-9 booking required Av main course £10 **Restaurant** L served all wk 12-2 booking required D served Mon-Sat 6.30-9 booking required ⊕ ADNAMS ◀ Adnams Broadside & Bitter, Explorer, seasonal ales Ò Aspall. **Facilities** Children's menu Children's portions Dogs allowed Garden Parking

---

### BURY ST EDMUNDS
Map 13 TL86

## The Linden Tree

**7 Out Northgate IP33 1JQ** ☎ **01284 754600**
e-mail: lindentree@live.com
*dir: Opposite railway station*

Built to serve the railway station, this is a big, friendly Victorian pub, with stripped pine bar, dining area, conservatory and charming garden. The family-orientated menu ranges from beef curry, home-made pies, and liver and bacon, to crab thermidor, fresh sea bass, and mushroom and lentil moussaka. Youngsters will go for the burgers, scampi, or pork chipolatas. Freshly filled ciabattas at lunchtime.

**Open** all wk noon-11 (Fri-Sat 11-11 Sun noon-10) Closed: 25 Dec **Bar Meals** L served Mon-Fri 12-2.30, Sat-Sun all day D served Mon-Fri 6-9.30, Sat-Sun all day **Restaurant** L served Mon-Fri 12-2.30, Sat-Sun all day booking required D served Mon-Fri 6-9.30, Sat-Sun all day booking required ⊕ GREENE KING ◀ Greene King, IPA & Old Speckled Hen, guest Ò Aspall. **Facilities** Children's menu Children's portions Play area Dogs allowed Garden

---

## The Nutshell

**17 The Traverse IP33 1BJ** ☎ **01284 764867**
*dir: Telephone for directions*

Unique pub measuring just 15ft by 7ft, and said to be Britain's smallest, although somehow more than 100 people and a dog managed to fit inside in the 1980s. The bar's ceiling is covered with paper money, and there have been regular sightings of ghosts around the building, including a nun and a monk who apparently weren't praying! No food is available, though the pub jokes about its dining area for parties of two or fewer.

**Open** all day all wk ⊕ GREENE KING ◀ Greene King IPA, Abbot Ale, guest ales. **Facilities** Dogs allowed **Notes** ⊜

---

## The Old Cannon Brewery ★★★ INN ☉

**86 Cannon St IP33 1JR** ☎ **01284 768769**
e-mail: info@oldcannonbrewery.co.uk
web: www.oldcannonbrewery.co.uk
*dir: From A14 (junct 43) follow signs to Bury St Edmunds town centre, at 1st rdbt take 1st left onto Northgate St, then 1st right onto Cadney Ln, left at end onto Cannon St, pub 100yds on left*

Two giant stainless steel brewing vessels dominate the bar of the only independent brewpub in Bury St Edmunds. In true brasserie style, the Brewery Kitchen serves 'cannon fodder', freshly prepared from great local produce. Slow cooked wild rabbit; Norfolk mussels à la

---

marinière; the pub's own sausages; and parsnip fritters with sweet and sour sauce are typical choices, with Thai dishes regularly appearing on the specials board. Overnight guests are catered for in the converted Brewery Rooms, just across the courtyard from the bar.

*The Old Cannon Brewery*

**Open** all wk noon-3 5-11 (Sat noon-11 Sun & BHs noon-10.30) Closed: 25-26 Dec, 1 Jan **Restaurant** L served Tue-Sun 12-3 booking required D served Tue-Sat 6-11 booking required Av 3 course à la carte fr £20 ⊕ FREE HOUSE ◀ Old Cannon Best Bitter, Old Cannon Gunner's Daughter, Old Cannon Blonde Bombshell, Adnams Bitter, seasonal Old Cannon ales, guest ales Ò Aspall. ☉ 12 **Facilities** Garden Parking **Rooms** 5

---

## The Three Kings ★★★★ INN ☉

**Hengrave Rd, Fornham All Saints IP28 6LA**
☎ **01284 766979**
e-mail: thethreekings@keme.co.uk
*dir: Bury St Edmunds (2m), A14 junct 42 (1m)*

A 17th-century coaching inn with a pretty village setting, the Three Kings features wood panelled bars, a conservatory, restaurant and courtyard. The Saturday night menu offers an elegant à la carte dining experience in additional to traditional bar food of burgers, beer battered fish and chips, and spicy vegetable chilli. There is also a popular Sunday roast carvery, for which booking is advised. Nine comfortable en suite bedrooms are available in converted outbuildings.

**Open** all day all wk noon-12 **Bar Meals** L served Mon-Fri 12-2, Sat-Sun 12-2.30 D served Sun-Mon 6-8, Tue-Sat 5.30-9 ⊕ GREENE KING ◀ Greene King IPA, Abbot, guest ales ☉ 14 **Facilities** Children's menu Garden Parking **Rooms** 9

## BUTLEY
Map 13 TM35

### The Butley Oyster ☐ NEW

**Woodbridge Rd IP12 3NZ** ☎ **01394 450790**
**e-mail:** info@snape-golden-key.co.uk
**dir:** On B1084 (Woodbridge to Orford road)

This informal inn received some overdue TLC in 2009, enhancing the welcome whilst retaining the essential, timeless character of the village local it truly is. Adnams beers from the coast a few miles away, live music and community events draw in dedicated regulars and a growing fan base for its hearty pub grub; sweet potato and spinach curry to shepherds pie, sarnies and ploughmans, all created from locally sourced seasonal produce.

**Open** 11-3 6-11 (Sat 11-11) (Sun 11-7 (winter)) 11-11 (summer) Closed: Mon in Nov-Feb **Bar Meals** L served Mon-Fri 12-2, Sat 12-3, Sun 12-6 booking required D served Mon-Sat 6.30-9 booking required Av main course £10 **Restaurant** Av 3 course à la carte fr £21 ⊕ ADNAMS ◀ Adnams Bitter, Broadside, Explorer ⓒ Aspall. ☐ 9 **Facilities** Children's portions Dogs allowed Garden Parking

## CAVENDISH
Map 13 TL84

### Bull Inn

**High St CO10 8AX** ☎ **01787 280245**
**e-mail:** knaffton@aol.com
**dir:** A134 (Bury St Edmunds to Long Melford), then right at green, pub 3m on right

A Victorian pub set in one of Suffolk's most beautiful villages, with an unassuming façade hiding a splendid 15th-century beamed interior. Expect a good atmosphere and decent food, with the daily-changing blackboard menu listing perhaps curries, shank of lamb, fresh fish and shellfish, and a roast on Sundays. Enjoy food and drink outside in the pleasant garden.

**Open** all wk 11-3 6.30-11 **Bar Meals** L served all wk 12-3 D served all wk 6.30-9 Av main course £8.95 **Restaurant** L served all wk 12-3 D served all wk 6.30-9 Av 3 course à la carte fr £10.95 ⊕ ADNAMS ◀ Adnams Bitter, Broadside, Nethergate Suffolk County ⓒ Aspall. **Facilities** Children's menu Children's portions Dogs allowed Parking

## CHILLESFORD
Map 13 TM35

### The Froize Inn ⊛ ☐

**The Street IP12 3PU** ☎ **01394 450282**
**e-mail:** dine@froize.co.uk
**dir:** On B1084 between Woodbridge (8m) & Orford (3m)

This free house and restaurant is housed in a former gamekeeper's cottage, a distinctive red-brick building dating from around 1490, set on the site of Chillesford Friary. It is a thoroughly traditional pub with a modern dining room championing East Anglian growers and suppliers. The menu offers rustic English and French dishes, with plenty of fresh seafood in summer and game in winter. It stands on the popular Suffolk Coastal Path.

**Open** Tue-Sun Closed: Mon **Restaurant** L served Tue-Sun 12-2 booking required D served Thu-Sat from 7pm booking required Fixed menu price fr £13.50 Av 3 course à la carte fr £22.50 ⊕ FREE HOUSE ◀ Adnams ⓒ Aspall. **Facilities** Garden Parking

## CRATFIELD
Map 13 TM37

### The Poacher NEW

**Bell Green IP19 0BL** ☎ **01986 798206**
**e-mail:** cratfieldpoacher@yahoo.co.uk
**dir:** From Halesworth take B1117 towards Eye. At Laxfield turn right, follow Cratfield signs (3m). Or, from Diss, take A143 towards Bungay. Right at Harleston onto B1123 towards Halesworth. Through Metfield, 1m, turn right & follow Cratfield signs (2m)

Off the beaten track in a sleepy village deep in rural Suffolk countryside, the 350-year-old Poacher is an attractive longhouse featuring some beautiful exterior plasterwork pargeting. Equally charming and unspoilt inside, with low beams, tiled floors and a welcoming atmosphere, the pub is the hub of the community, hosting musical evenings, bridge and book clubs, and bank holiday classic car rallies. Cracking beers from Adnams and Earl Soham breweries, local Aspall cider and home-cooked food, especially the haddock and chips, complete the pleasing picture at this proper village local.

**Open** noon-2.30, 6-mdnt (all day Sat-Sun) Closed: Mon, Tue L **Bar Meals** L served 12-2.30 (all day Sat-Sun) D served 6-9 (all day Sat-Sun) Av main course £7.50 **Restaurant** L served 12-2.30 (all day Sat-Sun) D served 6-9 (all day Sat-Sun) Fixed menu price £8.50 Av 3 course à la carte fr £11.95 ⊕ FREE HOUSE ◀ Adnams, Brewers Gold, Oakham JHB, Earl Soham Victoria, Earl Soham Mild ⓒ Aspall (draught and bottled). **Facilities** Children's menu Children's portions Dogs allowed Garden Parking

## DENNINGTON
Map 13 TM26

### The Queens Head

**The Square IP13 8AB** ☎ **01728 638241**
**e-mail:** queenshead123@yahoo.co.uk
**dir:** From Ipswich A14 to exit for Lowestoft (A12). then B1116 to Framlingham then follow signs to Dennington

It may be refurbished, but this 500-year-old inn retains bags of old world charm including open fires, a resident ghost, a coffin hatch and a bricked-up tunnel to the neighbouring church. Locally brewed Aspall cider is available alongside real ales from Elgoods, Adnams and Mauldons. The menu centres around fresh food made with local produce and ingredients - perhaps cottage pie or fillet of plaice parcels.

**Open** all wk Closed: 25-26 Dec ◀ Adnams, Elgoods, Mauldons ⓒ Aspall. **Facilities** Garden Parking

## DUNWICH
Map 13 TM47

### The Ship Inn ★★ SHL ⊛

**Saint James St IP17 3DT**
☎ **01728 648219** 🖨 **01728 648675**
**e-mail:** info@shipatdunwich.co.uk
**web:** www.shipatdunwich.co.uk
**dir:** N on A12 from Ipswich through Yoxford, right signed Dunwich

The once-thriving medieval port of Dunwich has long since been claimed by the sea, but thankfully this old smugglers' haunt looks invulnerable. As one would expect, fresh fish usually features on the daily-changing menu, including plaice, mackerel, prawns, scampi and fishcakes, as do steak and ale pie; lamb, pea and mint casserole; and jam roly poly. In fine weather you can eat in the garden then slip down to the beach, two minutes away.

**Open** all day all wk 11am-11pm (Sun noon-10.30pm) **Bar Meals** L served all wk 12-3 D served all wk 6-9 ⊕ FREE HOUSE ◀ Adnams ⓒ Aspall. **Facilities** Children's menu Family room Dogs allowed Garden Parking **Rooms** 20

## EARL SOHAM
Map 13 TM26

### Victoria

**The Street IP13 7RL** ☎ **01728 685758**
**dir:** From A14 at Stowmarket take A1120 towards Yoxford

This friendly, down to earth free house is a showcase for Earl Soham beers, which for many years were produced from a micro-brewery behind the pub. Some nine years ago the brewery moved to the Old Forge building opposite the village green, where production still continues. The Victoria offers traditional home-cooked pub fare, including ploughman's, jacket potatoes, macaroni cheese, and smoked salmon salad. Heartier meals include a variety of casseroles and curries, followed by home-made desserts. A specials board and vegetarian dishes add to the choices.

**Open** all wk 11.30-3 6-11 **Bar Meals** L served all wk 12-2 D served all wk 7-10 Av main course £8.50 ⊕ FREE HOUSE ◀ Earl Soham Victoria Bitter, Albert Ale, Brandeston Gold, Earl Soham Porter ⓒ Aspall. **Facilities** Children's portions Dogs allowed Garden Parking

## EYE — Map 13 TM17

### The White Horse Inn ★★★★ INN

Stoke Ash IP23 7ET ☎ 01379 678222 📠 01379 678800
e-mail: mail@whitehorse-suffolk.co.uk
dir: On A140 between Ipswich & Norwich

A 17th-century coaching inn set amid lovely Suffolk countryside. The heavily-timbered interior accommodates an inglenook fireplace, two bars and a restaurant. There are eleven spacious motel bedrooms in the grounds, as well as a patio and secluded grassy area. An extensive menu is supplemented by lunchtime snacks, grills and daily specials from the blackboard. Try pan fried lamb's liver and crispy bacon; Cantonese style lemon chicken; or lamb and mint burger.

**Open** all day all wk 7am-11pm (Sat 8am-11pm Sun 8am-10.30pm) **Bar Meals** Av main course £9.95 food served all day **Restaurant** food served all day ⊕ FREE HOUSE ◀ Adnams, Greene King Abbot Ō Aspall.
**Facilities** Children's menu Children's portions Garden Parking **Rooms** 11

## FRAMLINGHAM — Map 13 TM26

### The Station Hotel

Station Rd IP13 9EE ☎ 01728 723455
e-mail: framstation@btinternet.com
dir: Bypass Ipswich towards Lowestoft on A12. Approx 6m left onto B1116 towards Framlingham

Built as part of the local railway in the 19th century, The Station Hotel has been a pub since the 1950s, outliving the railway which closed in 1962. You will find scrubbed tables and an eclectic mix of furniture. During the last decade it has established a fine reputation for its gutsy and earthy food, such as home-cured meats, pies and suet puddings. Try ales such as Earl Soham Victoria and Albert and Mild, supplied by the Earl Soham brewery.

**Open** all wk noon-2.30 5-11 (Sun noon-3 7-10.30)
**Bar Meals** L served all wk 12-2 D served Sun-Thu 6.30-9, Fri-Sat 6.30-9.30 booking required ⊕ FREE HOUSE ◀ Earl Soham Victoria, Albert & Mild, Veltins, Crouch Vale, Guinness Ō Aspall. **Facilities** Family room Dogs allowed Garden Parking

## FRAMSDEN — Map 13 TM15

### The Dobermann Inn

The Street IP14 6HG ☎ 01473 890461
dir: S off A1120 (Stowmarket to Yoxford road) 10m from Ipswich on B1077 towards Debenham

Previously The Greyhound, the pub was renamed by its current proprietor, a prominent breeder and judge of Dobermanns. The thatched roofing, gnarled beams, open fire and assorted furniture reflect its 16th-century origins. Food ranges from sandwiches, ploughman's and salads to main courses featuring game from a local estate when in season, and plenty of fish choices. Reliable favourites include sirloin steak with sautéed mushrooms, and chicken and mushroom pie. Vegetarians can feast on mushroom stroganoff or spicy nut loaf.

**Open** noon-3 7-11 Closed: 25-26 Dec, Sun eve, Mon
**Bar Meals** L served Tue-Sun 12-2 D served Tue-Sat 7-9 ⊕ FREE HOUSE ◀ Adnams Bitter & Broadside, Mauldons Moletrap Bitter, Adnams Old WA Ō Aspall, Bitburger.
**Facilities** Garden Parking **Notes** ⊛

## GREAT BRICETT — Map 13 TM05

### PICK OF THE PUBS

### Red Lion

Green Street Green IP7 7DD
☎ 01473 657799 📠 01473 658492
e-mail: janwise@fsmail.net
dir: 4.5m from Needham Market on B1078

This charming 17th-century building may look like a traditional village pub and it was, arguably, just another hostelry until Jan Wise came along and turned it into East Anglia's only vegetarian pub. She has a fixed rule: nothing is served that means killing an animal, so there's no Sunday carvery, no mixed grill, no scampi in a basket. Wanting to 'celebrate the fantastic flavours that only vegetables can provide', Jan uses her 30 years' experience as a vegetarian caterer to create internationally-inspired starters such as dim sum, nachos or houmous, perhaps followed by oyster mushroom, leek and pine nut parcel; roasted vegetable and brie tart; or African sweet potato stew. She's back on more familiar territory with her desserts, which typically include chocolate brownies, rhubarb crumble and summer pudding. Not only is it advisable to book especially at weekends, you'll also need a healthy appetite. Special diets catered for.

**Open** all wk 12-3 6-11 Closed: Mon **Bar Meals** L served Tue-Sun 12-2 D served Tue-Sat 6-9 Av main course £8.90 ⊕ GREENE KING ◀ Greene King IPA, Old Speckled Hen Ō Aspall. **Facilities** Children's menu Children's portions Play area Dogs allowed Garden Parking

## GREAT GLEMHAM — Map 13 TM36

### The Crown Inn ⊛

IP17 2DA ☎ 01728 663693
e-mail: crown-i.cottle@btconnect.com
dir: A12 (Ipswich to Lowestoft), in Stratford-St-Andrew left at Shell garage. Pub 1.5m

A warm welcome, open fires and excellent food and ales make this cosy 17th-century village pub an appealing prospect. Set in Great Glemham, it overlooks the Great Glemham Estate, where some of the fine produce is sourced, and is within easy reach of the Suffolk Heritage Coast. You can eat in the extensively renovated bars with their wooden pews, sofas and inglenook fireplace, and large flower-filled garden. Smoked haddock and pea fishcake with lemon crème fraîche, and slow-roasted belly pork with crunchy crackling and dauphinoise potatoes might appear on the menu.

**Open** 11.30-3 6.30-11.30 Closed: Mon (ex BH)
**Bar Meals** L served Tue-Sun 11.30-2.30 booking required D served Tue-Sun 6.30-9 booking required Av main course £10 ⊕ FREE HOUSE ◀ Adnams Bitter, Tribute, Hobgoblin, Old Ale Ō Aspall. **Facilities** Children's menu Children's portions Dogs allowed Garden Parking

## HALESWORTH — Map 13 TM37

### PICK OF THE PUBS

### The Queen's Head ⴵ

The Street, Bramfield IP19 9HT ☎ 01986 784214
e-mail: qhbfield@aol.com
dir: 2m from A12 on A144 towards Halesworth

A lovely old building in the centre of Bramfield on the edge of the Suffolk Heritage Coast near historic Southwold. The enclosed garden, ideal for children, is overlooked by the thatched village church which has an unusual separate round bell tower. The pub's interior welcomes with scrubbed pine tables, exposed beams, a vaulted ceiling in the bar and enormous fireplaces. In the same capable hands for over 13 years, the landlord enthusiastically supports the 'local and organic' movement – reflected by the menu which proudly names the farms and suppliers from which the carefully chosen ingredients are sourced. Local produce notwithstanding, there's a definite cosmopolitan twist in dishes such as organic dates wrapped in British bacon; and free-range pork chop with Chinese spice sauce. Vegetarian options are a definite strength, and children love the locally-made burgers and sausages. Amanda's home-made desserts tempt with options such as steamed orange and ginger pudding; or a gluten-free Pavlova with cream, fresh mango and raspberry sauce. She also makes jams, chutney and cakes to take home.

**Open** all wk 11.45-2.30 6.30-11 (Sun noon-3 7-10.30) Closed: 26 Dec **Bar Meals** L served all wk 12-2 D served Mon-Fri 6.30-9.15, Sat 6.30-10, Sun 7-9 Av main course £10.95 ⊕ ADNAMS ◀ Adnams Bitter, Broadside Ō Aspall. ⴵ 8 **Facilities** Children's portions Family room Dogs allowed Garden Parking

## HITCHAM
Map 13 TL95

### The White Horse Inn ♀

The Street IP7 7NQ ☎ 01449 740981 📠 01449 740981
e-mail: lewis@thewhitehorse.wanadoo.co.uk
dir: *13m from Ipswich & Bury St Edmunds, 7m Stowmarket, 7m Hadleigh*

There's a warm, friendly atmosphere at this family-run free house. Parts of the Grade II listed building are estimated to be around 400 years old, and make a perfect setting for traditional pub games and regular live entertainment. Freshly-prepared meals are served in the bar and restaurant and, in summer, the beer garden is open for barbecues.

**Open** all wk 12-3 6-11 **Bar Meals** L served all wk 12-2.30 D served all wk 6-9 **Restaurant** L served all wk 12-2.30 D served all wk 6-9 booking required ⊕ FREE HOUSE ◀ IPA, Adnams Best Bitter, Rattlesden Best, Stowmarket Porter, Adnams Fisherman ♂ Aspall. **Facilities** Children's menu Children's portions Dogs allowed Garden Parking

## HOLBROOK
Map 13 TM13

### The Compasses ♀

Ipswich Rd IP9 2QR
☎ 01473 328332 📠 01473 327403
e-mail: compasses.holbrook@virgin.net
dir: *From A137 S of Ipswich, take B1080 to Holbrook, pub on left. From Ipswich take B1456 to Shotley. At Freston Water Tower right onto B1080 to Holbrook. Pub 2m right*

Holbrook is bordered by the rivers Orwell and Stour, and this traditional country pub, which dates from the 17th century, is on the Shotley peninsula. A good value menu includes ploughman's, salads and jacket potatoes; pub favourites such as chilli con carne or chicken with cashew nuts; and a fish selection including seafood lasagne. Party bookings are a speciality, and look out for Wine of the Week deals. Pensioners' weekday lunches complete this pub's honest offerings.

**Open** 11.30-2.30 6-11 (Sun noon-3 6-10.30) Closed: 26 Dec-1 Jan, Tue eve **Bar Meals** L served all wk 12-2.15 booking required D served Wed-Mon 6-9.15 booking required Av main course £8.95 **Restaurant** L served all wk 12-2.15 booking required D served Wed-Mon 6-9.15 booking required ⊕ PUNCH TAVERNS ◀ Greene King IPA, Adnams Bitter ♂ Aspall. ♀ 12 **Facilities** Children's menu Children's portions Play area Garden Parking

## HONEY TYE
Map 13 TL93

### The Lion ♀

CO6 4NX ☎ 01206 263434 📠 01206 263434
e-mail: enquiries@lionhoneytye.co.uk
dir: *On A134 midway between Colchester & Sudbury*

A traditional country dining pub, located in an Area of Outstanding Natural Beauty, The Lion has low-beamed ceilings and an open log fire inside, plus a patio with tables and umbrellas for outside eating and drinking. The menu offers a good choice of fish (pan seared mackerel

fillets with warm horseradish potato salad), pub favourites (chargrilled gammon steak with fried egg and chips), and main dishes such as pressed pork belly and apple terrine.

**Open** all wk 11.30-3 6-11 (Sun noon-10) **Bar Meals** L served Mon-Sat 12-2, Sun 12-8 D served Mon-Sat 6-9, Sun 12-8 **Restaurant** L served Mon-Sat 12-2, Sun 12-8 D served Mon-Sat 6-9, Sun 12-8 ◀ Greene King IPA, guest ale. ♀ 9 **Facilities** Children's menu Children's portions Garden Parking

## HOXNE
Map 13 TM17

### The Swan ♀

Low St IP21 5AS ☎ 01379 668275
e-mail: info@hoxneswan.co.uk
dir: *Telephone for directions*

This 15th-century Grade II listed lodge, reputedly built for the Bishop of Norwich, has large gardens running down to the River Dove, with a vast willow tree. Inside, the restaurant and front bar boast a 10ft inglenook fireplace, ornate beamed ceilings and old planked floors. Food ranges from lunchtime snacks like deep fried blanchbait or twice baked goats' cheese souffle, to a weekly changing lunch and dinner menu. Traditional dishes include slow-roast belly pork with black pudding on a bed of apricot, bacon and savoy cabbage with a cider jus, or beer-battered cod, served with chips and mushy peas. Good vegetarian choices include, sweet potato, red lentil and baby new potato creamy coconut curry with rice.

**Open** all wk **Bar Meals** L served all wk 12-2 booking required D served all wk 6.30-9 booking required Av main course £7.50 **Restaurant** L served all wk 12-2 booking required D served all wk 6.30-9 booking required Av 3 course à la carte fr £9.95 ⊕ ENTERPRISE INNS ◀ Adnams Best Bitter, 4 other real ales ♂ Aspall. ♀ 9 **Facilities** Children's portions Dogs allowed Garden Parking

## ICKLINGHAM
Map 13 TL77

### The Plough Inn ♀

The Street IP28 6PL
☎ 01638 711770 📠 01638 583885
e-mail: info@ploughpubinn.co.uk
dir: *Telephone for directions*

This old, flint-built village pub is part of the Iveagh Estate and was refurbished to provide space for 50 diners. All the food is cooked on the premises by chef -proprietor Rocke, while his wife Sue manages front of

house. Among the numerous fish dishes are Thai seared salmon fillet with coconut noodles; and grilled red snapper fillets a Rougay sauce. Other main courses include lamb shank braised in red wine port with mushroom risotto; home-made lamb and coriander burger; and steak and kidney pie. Accompany your meal with one of the real ales on offer or some wine; there are 27 by the glass to choose from.

**Open** all day all wk Closed: 25-26 Dec, 1 Jan **Bar Meals** Av main course £9.95 food served all day **Restaurant** Av 3 course à la carte fr £21 food served all day ⊕ FREE HOUSE ◀ IPA, Woodforde's Wherry, London Pride, Adnams. ♀ 27 **Facilities** Garden Parking

---

### The Red Lion ♀

The Street IP28 6PS ☎ 01638 711698
dir: *A1101 from Bury St Edmunds, 8m. In Icklingham, pub on main street on left*

A sympathetically restored, 16th-century thatched country inn set back from the road behind a grassed area with flower beds and outdoor furniture. The interior, glowing by candlelight in the evening, features exposed beams, a large inglenook fireplace, wooden floors, and antique furniture.

**Open** all wk Closed: 25 Dec ◀ Greene King Abbot Ale & IPA, Morlands Old Speckled Hen. ♀ 15 **Facilities** Garden Parking

## IXWORTH
Map 13 TL97

### Pykkerell Inn

38 High St IP31 2HH
☎ 01359 230398 📠 01359 234019
dir: *On A143 from Bury St Edmunds towards Diss*

This former coaching inn, now with a new licensee, dates back to 1530 and still retains most of its original beams, inglenook fireplace and other features in the lounge and public bars: it is surrounded by Grade I listed buildings too. The extensive menu includes starters such as whitebait; battered king prawns; and moules marinière; and mains of lasagne verdi; beef and kidney suet pudding; and lamb shank with minted gravy. Traditional pub food predominates at lunchtime, plus there is a fish dish specials board to look out for.

**Open** all day all wk **Bar Meals** L served Mon-Fri 12-2 booking required D served all wk 5-9 booking required Av main course £8 **Restaurant** L served Mon-Fri 12-2, Sat-Sun 12-4 booking required D served all wk 5-9 booking required ⊕ GREENE KING ◀ Greene King IPA, Abbot Ale, Old Speckled Hen ♂ Aspall. **Facilities** Children's menu Children's portions Dogs allowed Garden Parking

# PICK OF THE PUBS

## The Angel ★★★★RR ✿ ♟

**LAVENHAM** Map 13 TL94

**Market Place CO10 9QZ**
☎ 01787 247388 📠 01787 248344
**e-mail:** angel@maypolehotels.com
**web:** www.maypolehotels.com
**dir:** *7m from Sudbury on A1141 between Sudbury & Bury St Edmunds*

Good food, comfortable rooms and a friendly atmosphere await you in the heart of England's finest medieval village. The Angel, which overlooks the market place and famous timbered Guildhall, was first licensed in 1420. Believed to be Lavenham's oldest Inn, it was originally a 'high hall' house, and smoke from a central fire would drift out through vents in the roof. The ventilation improved in around 1500, when two wings with brick chimneys were added to the building, along with a first-floor solar room, which is now the residents' lounge. Renovations over the years have revealed a rare Tudor shop

window, which has been preserved for all to see, and in 1990 the owners created the present open plan ground floor layout. Nevertheless, the historic character of this famous inn can still be seen in the beamed dining room and adjoining bar, with its huge inglenook fireplace and attractive plasterwork.

All food is prepared on the premises from fresh ingredients by chefs Mike, Andy and Eva, whose consistent high standards have earned an AA rosette every year since 1995. The menus cater for diets of all kinds, and the vegetarian options and seasonal game are particularly popular. Expect starters like Thai-style chicken and crayfish salad, and duck and orange parfait with toast. Main courses might take in Lancashire hot-pot; pork, cider and apple casserole; or smoked haddock with Welsh rarebit topping and spring onion mash. You could finish with a selection of English cheeses, or perhaps pear and ginger steamed pudding with custard.

The en suite bedrooms are full of character, with old beams and sloping floors — perfect for lingering in this fabulous medieval setting and exploring the unspoilt Suffolk villages and surrounding countryside.

**Open** all wk Mon-Sat 11-11 Sun 12-10.30 **Bar Meals** L served all wk 12-2.15 booking required D served all wk 6.45 - 9.15 booking required Av main course £9.95 **Restaurant** L served all wk 12-2.15 booking required D served all wk 6.45-9.15 booking required Av 3 course à la carte fr £27.50 ⊕ FREE HOUSE 🍺 Adnams Bitter, Nethergate, Greene King IPA, Ŏ Aspalls. ♟ 9 **Facilities** Children's menu Dogs allowed Garden Parking **Rooms** 8

# PICK OF THE PUBS

## The Ship Inn ♉

**LEVINGTON**  Map 13 TM23

**Church Ln IP10 0LQ**
☎ 01473 659573  📄 01473 659151
**dir:** *Off A14 towards Felixstowe. Nr Levington Marina*

The Ship Inn stands within sight of the Orwell estuary and the Suffolk marshes, where the hulks of beached sailing vessels were broken up for their precious beams. Indeed, the timbers of this part-14th-century thatched inn are impregnated with the salt of the sea, and ghosts of bygone smugglers still occupy the many nooks and crannies.

Families are welcome to enjoy the estuary views outside on the attractive front seats, or install themselves on the rear patio adorned with hanging and potted plants. The interior walls and surfaces, however, are so full of seafaring pictures, maritime lamps, compasses, curiosities and keepsakes that it's deemed an unsafe environment for children.

Adnams ales and Aspall cider are hand-pulled in the bar, both produced in the same county. Whichever tipple you prefer, settle back and enjoy it as you read old newspaper cuttings on the walls about contraband turning up here, closely followed by the excise men.

Under new management since 2010, the style of service is informal, friendly and attentive. The menu changes daily, and focuses on executing a select number of dishes well. Starters may include sauté of tiger prawns, sweet chilli and garlic butter on a bed of fregola pasta. Main courses have fish options such as roast whole lemon sole; griddled fillet of mackerel; or a smoked haddock, cod and salmon fish pie. Meats vary from sautéed liver with bacon, to venison and red wine sausages. Desserts are variations on familiar themes: mixed fruit crumble tart with crème anglaise; and vanilla pannacotta with blackberry compôte. Vegetarians will enjoy Stilton and leek tart with endive salad, followed by butternut squash and sage risotto with parmesan.

Afterwards you can stroll to the Levington marina to admire other people's boats, or step out for a longer walk along the estuary foreshore.

**Open** all wk Mon-Fri 11.30-3 6-11, Sat 11.30-11, Sun 12-10.30 Closed Dec 25-26, Dec-Jan seasonal times **Bar Meals** L served Mon-Sat 12-2, Sun 12-3 D served Mon-Sat 6.30-9.30 Av main course £12 **Restaurant** Av 3 course à la carte fr £24 ⊞ Adnams 🍺 Adnams Best, Broadside, guest ale 🍎 Aspall. ♉ 10 **Facilities** Dogs allowed Garden Parking

## KETTLEBURGH    Map 13 TM26

### The Chequers Inn

IP13 7JT
☎ 01728 723760 & 724369    📠 01728 723760
e-mail: info@thechequers.net
dir: *From Ipswich A12 onto B1116, left onto B1078 then right through Easton*

The Chequers is set in beautiful countryside on the banks of the River Deben. The landlord serves a wide range of cask ales, including two guests. In addition to snack and restaurant meals, the menu in the bar includes local sausages and ham with home-produced free-range eggs. The riverside garden can seat up to a hundred people.

**Open** all wk ◼ Greene King IPA, Black Dog Mild, 3 guest ales ♻ Aspall. **Facilities** Play area Dogs allowed Garden Parking

## LAVENHAM    Map 13 TL94

### PICK OF THE PUBS

### The Angel ★★★★ RR ◉ ♈
*See Pick of the Pubs on page 427*

## LAXFIELD    Map 13 TM27

### The Kings Head ♈

Gorams Mill Ln IP13 8DW ☎ 01986 798395
e-mail: bob-wilson5505@hotmail.co.uk
dir: *On B1117*

Beautifully situated overlooking the river, the garden of this thatched 16th-century alehouse was formerly the village bowling green. Beer is still served straight from the cask in the original tap room, whilst high-backed settles and wooden seats add to the charming atmosphere. Traditional home-cooked dishes complement the à la carte menu and chef's specials and, on warmer evenings, the rose gardens and arbour are perfect for alfresco dining.

**Open** all wk ◼ Adnams Best & Broadside, Adnams seasonal, guest ales ♻ Aspall. ♈ 8 **Facilities** Play area Family room Dogs allowed Garden Parking

## LEVINGTON    Map 13 TM23

### PICK OF THE PUBS

### The Ship Inn ♈
*See Pick of the Pubs on opposite page*

## LIDGATE    Map 12 TL75

### PICK OF THE PUBS

### The Star Inn

The Street CB8 9PP
☎ 01638 500275    📠 01638 500275
e-mail: tonyaxon@aol.com
dir: *From Newmarket clocktower in High St follow signs towards Clare on B1063. Lidgate 7m*

This pretty, pink-painted Elizabethan building is made up of two cottages with gardens front and rear; inside, two traditionally furnished bars with heavy oak beams, log fires and pine furniture lead into the dining room. Yet the Star's quintessentially English appearance holds a surprise, for here you'll find a renowned Spanish restaurant offering authentic Mediterranean cuisine. No mere gastro-pub, The Star provides an important meeting place for local residents. It's also popular with Newmarket trainers on race days, and with dealers and agents from all over the world during bloodstock sales. The menu offers appealingly hearty food: starters like Piquillo peppers and cod brandade; clams and artichokes; and paella Valenciana. English tastes are also catered for, with dishes such as warm chicken liver salad; venison steaks in port; and pigs' cheeks. There's an extensive wine list, too.

**Open** noon-3 6-mdnt Closed: 25-26 Dec, 1 Jan, Mon **Bar Meals** L served Tue-Sat 12-3 booking required D served Tue-Sat 7-10 booking required Av main course £16.95 **Restaurant** L served Tue-Sun 12-3 booking required D served Tue-Sat 7-10 booking required Fixed menu price fr £10 Av 3 course à la carte fr £15 ⊕ GREENE KING ◼ Greene King IPA, Ruddles County, Abbot Ale. **Facilities** Children's portions Garden Parking

## MELTON    Map 13 TM25

### Wilford Bridge ♈

Wilford Bridge Rd IP12 2PA
☎ 01394 386141    📠 01394 386141
e-mail: wilfordbridge@debeninns.com
dir: *From A12 towards coast, follow signs to Bawdsey & Orford, cross rail lines, next pub on left*

Just down the road from the famous Sutton Hoo treasure ship, Mike and Anne Lomas have been running the free house at Wilford Bridge for the last 18 years. As a former West End chef, Mike specialises in classic English dishes, especially seafood dishes; look out for local game,

mussels and sprats in season, as well as crab, lobster, cod, salmon, trout, sea bass and others as available. At the bar, guest ales supplement the regular choice of beers.

*Wilford Bridge*

**Open** all day all wk **Bar Meals** Av main course £9.95 food served all day **Restaurant** Av 3 course à la carte fr £19.95 food served all day ⊕ FREE HOUSE ◼ Adnams Best, Broadside, John Smiths, Guest ales ♻ Aspall. ♈ 9 **Facilities** Children's menu Dogs allowed Garden Parking

## MILDENHALL    Map 12 TL77

### PICK OF THE PUBS

### The Olde Bull Inn ★★★ HL ◉ ♈

The Street, Barton Mills IP28 6AA
☎ 01638 711001    📠 01638 712003
e-mail: bookings@bullinn-bartonmills.com
dir: *Off A11 between Newmarket & Mildenhall, signed Barton Mills*

The Olde Bull Inn stands just off the A11 on the Cambridge/Suffolk border. Rich in history and looking much the same as it did when it was built as a coaching inn in the 17th century, the pub is a popular pit-stop for travellers heading for Norwich or the Norfolk coast. Beautifully refurbished in contemporary style a few years ago, it's full of the charm and character associated with scrubbed pine tables and reclaimed oak flooring. Gleaming hand-pumps dispense tip-top East Anglian ales, so order a pint of Brandon's and settle by the fire to peruse menus of AA Rosette standard food. Everything is freshly prepared on the premises, so stay in the bar for chicken and bacon melt; Whitby scampi; or the Olde Bull curry — be it chicken or vegetarian. Alternatively move to the Oak Room restaurant if you want to linger over three courses; here you can follow Bottisham smoked salmon with baked Lowestoft cod, and finish with Shaun's apple crumble. Why not relax in one of the well-appointed, individually designed bedrooms?

*continued*

## MILDENHALL *continued*

**Open** all day all wk 8am-11pm **Bar Meals** L served all wk 12-9 D served all wk 12-9 Av main course £10 food served all day **Restaurant** L served Sun 12-3 D served all wk 6-9 ⊕ FREE HOUSE ◀ Adnams Broadside, Greene King IPA, Brandon Brewery Rusty Bucket, Humpty Dumpty, Wolf ♂ Aspall. ₱ 8
**Facilities** Children's menu Children's portions Family room Garden Parking **Rooms** 14

---

### MONKS ELEIGH      Map 13 TL94

#### PICK OF THE PUBS

### The Swan Inn ⓖⓖ

**The Street IP7 7AU ☎ 01449 741391**
e-mail: carol@monkseleigh.com
dir: *On B1115 between Sudbury & Hadleigh*

Sited in a beautiful Suffolk village near the historical town of Lavenham, one of England's best-preserved medieval wool towns; Wolves' Wood, an RSPB reserve, is also close by. With its magnificent open fireplace, the main restaurant in this thatched free house may once have been used as the local manorial court. The pub welcomed its first customers in the 16th century when the interior would have been open to the roof; evidence of the former smokehole can still be seen. Other historical features include original wattle and daub exposed during renovation work; part has been preserved behind a glass panel. Expect to find game in season, locally picked vegetables, and fresh fish from the Suffolk coast. Starters like pan-fried scallops with crispy sage leaves may precede main course options such as Italian-style sweet and sour duck leg, or spicy Moroccan chicken breast; puddings such as iced brandy mousse complete the meal nicely.

**Open** noon-2.30 7-11 Closed: 25-26 Dec, 2wks in summer, Sun eve & Mon **Bar Meals** L served Tue-Sun 12-2 D served Tue-Sat 7-9 Av main course £12 **Restaurant** L served Tue-Sun 12-2 D served Tue-Sat 7-9 Fixed menu price fr £13.75 Av 3 course à la carte fr £25 ⊕ FREE HOUSE ◀ Greene King IPA, Adnams Bitter, Broadside ♂ Aspall, Thatchers Katy.
**Facilities** Children's portions Garden Parking

---

### NAYLAND      Map 13 TL93

#### PICK OF THE PUBS

### Anchor Inn

**26 Court St CO6 4JL**
**☎ 01206 262313 🖷 01206 264166**
e-mail: enquiries@anchornayland.co.uk
dir: *Follow A134 Colchester to Sudbury for 3.5m through Gt Horkesley, bottom of hill turn right to Nayland, Horkesley Road. Pub on right after bridge*

Nestling on the banks of the River Stour, this 15th-century free house is reputedly the last remaining place from which press-gangs recruited their 'volunteers'. Visitors are welcome to wander around the adjoining Anchor Inn Heritage Farm, which provides the

kitchen with most of its daily requirements. The farm is run on traditional lines, with working Suffolk Punch horses helping produce good old-fashioned food in the time-honoured way – this farm-kitchen relationship helped win a prestigious green award. From the smokehouse comes the platter of smoked fish, meats and cheeses served with home-baked bread rolls. Specials, such as steamed venison and Guinness pudding or rolled fillet of lamb, follow seasonal availability. But the Anchor is not just about food; the traditional bar is warmed by roaring fires in winter, where ales from Greene King and Adnams are drawn, and wines include an award-winner from a vineyard just three miles away.

**Open** all wk 11-3 5-11 (all day spring and summer) **Bar Meals** L served Mon-Fri 12-2, Sat 12-2.30, Sun 12-3 D served Mon-Fri 6.30-9, Sat 6.30-9.30, Sun 5-8.30 Av main course £14 **Restaurant** L served Mon-Fri 12-2, Sat 12-2.30, Sun 12-3 D served Mon-Fri 6.30-9, Sat 6.30-9.30, Sun 5-8.30 Av 3 course à la carte fr £12.95 ⊕ FREE HOUSE ◀ Adnams, IPA, Mild, Local ales. **Facilities** Children's menu Garden Parking

---

### ORFORD      Map 13 TM45

### Jolly Sailor Inn ★★★ INN ₱

**Quay St IP12 2NU ☎ 01394 450243 🖷 0870 128 7874**
e-mail: hello@thejollysailor.net
web: www.thejollysailor.net
dir: *On B1084 E of Woodbridge, Orford signed from A12 approx 10m*

The sheltered anchorage protected by Orford Ness's shingle bank draws yachtsmen to moor and landlubbers to dream of long-gone smuggling practices here on the Suffolk coast. This timber-framed 16th century quayside inn relies on local fishermen's catches – maybe skate wing, lobster or roasted cod will feature - to complement the hearty, red-blooded pub fare of roasts, sausages and hams or a brace of inventive vegetarian options. Sup Adnams beers in the orchard with great views to the saltings and marshes where avocets nest. If you want to stay over there are three recently refurbished en suite rooms available.

**Open** all wk 11-3 6-mdnt (Sat 11am-1am Sun noon-11 summer all wk 11am-mdnt ) **Bar Meals** L served Mon-Fri 12-3, Sat-Sun 11-11 D served Mon-Fri 6-9.30, Sat-Sun 11-11 **Restaurant** L served Mon-Fri 12-3, Sat-Sun 11-11 D served Mon-Fri 6-9.30, Sat-Sun 11-11 ⊕ ADNAMS ◀ Adnams Bitter, Broadside, Explorer ♂ Aspall. ₱ 14
**Facilities** Children's menu Children's portions Play area Family room Dogs allowed Garden Parking **Rooms** 3

### King's Head

**Front St IP12 2LW ☎ 01394 450271**
e-mail: ian_thornton@talk21.com
dir: *From Woodbridge follow signs for Orford Castle on B1084. Through Butley & Chillesford on to Orford*

An inn with a smuggling history, The King's Head stands on the old market square, a short walk from the quay. The atmospheric interior includes a beamed bar serving Adnams ales, and a wood-floored restaurant offering plenty of local produce. Typical starters include garlic mushrooms, whitebait, and smoked mackerel, followed perhaps by 'boozy beef' (made with Adnams ale); cod in beer batter; or vegetable stir fry. Bar snacks include sandwiches, burgers and things with chips.

**Open** all wk ◀ Adnams Bitter, Adnams Broadside, Adnams Regatta, Adnams Tally Ho, Adnams Explorer. **Facilities** Dogs allowed Garden Parking

---

### REDE      Map 13 TL85

### The Plough ₱

**IP29 4BE ☎ 01284 789208**
dir: *On A143 between Bury St Edmunds & Haverhill*

This picture-postcard, half-thatched, 16th-century pub has an old plough outside. The building has a cream exterior and restored beams, with a fresh, open feel to the interior. Light snacks in the form of carpaccio of wild boar or dressed Cromer crab are backed by an adventurous array of blackboard-listed dishes such as grilled sea bass with a cream and bacon sauce, and wild woodpigeon with lentils, alongside more traditional dishes. Menus change with the seasons and availability of fresh local produce. The bar serves a range of ales and up to ten wines by the glass.

**Open** all wk **Bar Meals** L served all wk 12-2 D served Mon-Sat 6-9 **Restaurant** L served all wk 12-2 D served Mon-Sat 6-9 ⊕ ADMIRAL TAVERNS ◀ Greene King IPA, Abbot Ale, London Pride, Adnams. ₱ 10 **Facilities** Garden Parking

---

### ST PETER SOUTH ELMHAM      Map 13 TM38

#### PICK OF THE PUBS

### Wicked at St Peter's Hall ₱

**NR35 1NQ ☎ 01986 782288**
e-mail: mail@wickedlygoodfoodltd.co.uk
dir: *From A143/A144 follow brown signs to St Peter's Brewery*

This magnificent 13th-century moated hall is now home to one of Suffolk's most unusual and romantic pub/restaurants. The building was enlarged in 1539 using materials salvaged from nearby Flixton Priory, and the stunning conversion features period furnishings that make the most of original stone floors, Gothic windows and lofty ceilings. St Peter's brewery was established in 1996 in an adjacent range of former agricultural buildings, and now produces traditional ales as well as some more unusual varieties

ke honey porter and fruit beer. The full range of cask
nd bottled beers is available alongside Aspall cider in
he bar. Locally sourced free range and organic produce
s the mainstay of the menus, which range through
ishes like crayfish, lemon thyme and spring onion
isotto; rosemary and garlic studded braised shoulder
f lamb with rich red wine and Madeira jus; and lemon
art with Grand Marnier ice cream. There are often
pecial dining events such as Tapas Evening.

pen noon-3 6-11 (Sun noon-4) Closed: 1-12 Jan, Mon
ar Meals L served Tue-Sat 12-3 booking required Av
ain main course £8.95 Restaurant L served Sun 12-4
ooking required D served Tue-Sat 6-10 booking
equired Av 3 course à la carte fr £24 ⊕ ST PETER'S
BREWERY ◀ Golden Ale, Organic Ale, Grapefruit ale,
ream Stout, Organic Best Bitter ♂ Aspall. ♀ 12
acilities Children's portions Garden Parking

## SIBTON                            Map 13 TM36

### ibton White Horse Inn ★★★★ INN ♀
### EW

alesworth Rd IP17 2JJ ☎ 01728 660337
mail: info@sibtonwhitehorseinn.co.uk
r: From A12 at Yoxford take A1120 signed Sibton &
easonhall (ignore all Sibton signs). Turn right opposite
easeys (butcher), signed White Horse/Pouy Street/
alpole. 1m to inn

dden away on the edge of a pretty Suffolk village, this
6th-century free house incorporates stone floors,
xposed brickwork and ships' timbers believed to have
ome from Woodbridge shipyard. Neil and Gill Mason are
ommitted to producing high quality food from fresh local
gredients — and, to prove it, they grow many of their
egetables in the raised beds behind the pub. Dishes like
ek and wild mushroom suet pudding, and pan-roasted
ythburgh pork chop with mustard mash are typical
hoices.

pen 12-2.30 6.30-11 (winter) 6-11 (summer) Sun
2-3.30 Closed: 26-27 Dec, Mon L Bar Meals L served
ue-Sat 12-2, Sun 12-2.30 booking required D served all
k 7-9 booking required Av main course £12
estaurant L served Tue-Sat 12-2, Sun 12-2.30 booking
equired D served Mon-Sat 7-9 booking required Av 3
ourse à la carte fr £24 ⊕ FREE HOUSE ◀ Adnams Bitter,
reene King Abbot Ale, Woodforde's Wherry ♂ Aspall. ♀ 9
acilities Children's portions Dogs allowed Garden
arking Rooms 6

*See advert on page 432*

## SNAPE                              Map 13 TM35

### PICK OF THE PUBS

## The Crown Inn ♀

**Bridge Rd IP17 1SL ☎ 01728 688324**
e-mail: snapecrown@tiscali.co.uk
dir: *A12 N to Lowestoft, right to Aldeburgh, then right
again in Snape at x-rds by church, pub at bottom of hill*

First-time visitors to this 15th-century former
smugglers' inn are often astonished by the adjoining
smallholding where a veritable menagerie of livestock
is lovingly reared by mine-hosts Teresa and Garry Cook.
It pays not to become too attached however, as these
are destined for the table at this marvellously
atmospheric pub (no gaming machines or background
music here), with abundant old beams, log fire, brick
floors and, around the large inglenook, a very fine
double Suffolk settle. Fish from Orford fishermen and
locally raised beef feature in the strong British menus,
with daily specials adding to the tally: commence with
Orford kipper pâté with horseradish and granary toast
before tackling ham hock and macaroni cheese; Crag
Farm limousine minced beef cottage; or Campsea Ashe
pheasant with Puy lentils, smoked bacon and baby
onions. Afters may offer coconut meringue with
passionfruit curd, all helped along with Adnams beers
or a choice from 12 wines by the glass. There is a
spacious garden for summer dining.

Open all wk Bar Meals L served all wk 12-2.30 booking
required D served all wk 6-9.30 booking required Av
main course £11 Restaurant L served all wk 12-2.30
booking required D served all wk 6-9.30 booking
required Av 3 course à la carte fr £20 ⊕ ADNAMS
◀ Adnams Best, Broadside, Old Ale, Regatta, Explorer
♂ Aspall. ♀ 12 Facilities Children's portions Dogs
allowed Garden Parking

### PICK OF THE PUBS

## The Golden Key ♀

**Priory Ln IP17 1SQ ☎ 01728 688510**
e-mail: info@snape-golden-key.co.uk
dir: *Telephone for directions*

This award-winning village pub dates back to the
1600's and some aspects of the interior recall those
days, particularly the fabulous fireplaces beside which
winter visitors warm by grand log fires. There's a
cottagey feel to the place, with a run of rooms and
alcoves popular both with locals enjoying the Adnams
beers and discerning diners who travel far to sample
the well-balanced menu that draws strongly on ultra-
local produce. Fish is fresh daily from nearby Aldeburgh
beach; organic vegetables come from the parson's
garden, game from a nearby shoot and lamb from a
neighbouring farm. Few other pubs will offer starters
such as terrine of pigeon, woodcock, quail and
pistachio nut with beetroot chutney before hitting you
with venison casserole or slow-braised shoulder of Alde
Valley lamb stuffed with spinach, garlic and pine nuts.
The wine list stretches to 43 bins; on good days enjoy
such outside beside the boules pitch.

Open all wk 12-3 6-11 (Sat 12-4 6-11 Sun 12-4 7-11)
Bar Meals L served Mon-Sat 12-2, Sun 12-2.30
booking required D served Mon-Sat 6.30-9, Sun 7-9
booking required Av main course £12 Restaurant L
served Mon-Sat 12-2, Sun 12-2.30 booking required D
served Mon-Sat 6.30-9, Sun 7-9 booking required Av 3
course à la carte fr £23 ⊕ ADNAMS ◀ Adnams Bitter,
Broadside, Explorer, Old, Oyster Stout ♂ Aspall. ♀ 15
Facilities Children's portions Dogs allowed Garden
Parking

## Plough & Sail ♀

**Snape Maltings IP17 1SR**
**☎ 01728 688413  📠 01728 688930**
e-mail: ploughandsail@debeninns.co.uk
dir: *Snape Maltings on B1069 S of Snape. Signed from
A12*

A pink, pantiled old inn at the heart of the renowned
Snape Maltings complex, handy for the cultural and
shopping opportunities here and close to splendid coastal
walks. The interior is a comfy mix of dining and avant
garde destination pub; local ales and a good bin of wines
accompany a solid menu, featuring an Orford smoked fish
platter or slow roast belly of pork with Suffolk cider apple
chutney, finishing with baked pear stuffed with honey
and walnuts, plus a wide range of starters, nibbles and
sandwiches.

Open all day wk Bar Meals L served all wk 12-2.30 all
day summer D served all wk 6-9 all day summer Av main
course £9 Restaurant L served all wk 12-2.30 all day
summer D served all wk 6-9 all day summer Av 3 course
à la carte fr £18 ⊕ FREE HOUSE ◀ Adnams Broadside,
Adnams Bitter, Explorer, Woodforde's Wherry ♂ Aspall
Suffolk Cyder. ♀ 10 Facilities Children's menu Children's
portions Dogs allowed Garden Parking

## SOUTHWOLD                         Map 13 TM57

### PICK OF THE PUBS

## The Crown Hotel ★★ HL ◉ ♀

**The High St IP18 6DP**
**☎ 01502 722275  📠 01502 727263**
e-mail: crown.hotel@adnams.co.uk
dir: *A12 onto A1095 to Southwold. Into town centre,
pub on left*

Once a posting inn dating from 1750, this pub, wine
bar, eatery and small hotel is now the flagship
operation for Adnams Brewery, so expect plenty of
excellent ales on tap. The whole place buzzes with lively
informality as waiting staff attend to customers
installed on green leather cushioned settles or at the
green-washed oak-panelled bar. It's a popular place,
especially in summer when customers can enjoy a pint
or a meal outside. The high standard of cooking is
recognised with an AA rosette. The seaside location
brings impressive seafood options such as pan-fried
North Sea plaice, crushed celeriac, spring cabbage and
pickled mushrooms, or home-made fish pie with a
cheesy mash top and greens. Other options might
include curried Suffolk mutton with braised rice,

*continued on page 433*

# SIBTON WHITE HORSE INN
## Suffolk

Sibton is set in the heart of the Suffolk countryside, yet just five miles from the A12 and only ten miles from the Heritage coast. Here you will find the White Horse, built during the sixteenth century, it's a rather fascinating pub, definitely one of those pubs that are a joy to discover.

Off the beaten track with the sound of bird song rather than traffic, and a somewhat feeling of time standing still, the White Horse is the perfect place to drink, eat or stay overnight. Whatever the reason for your visit you will find the hospitality friendly and relaxed, from the welcoming ambience to the attentive service.

Call the White Horse a gastro pub and you won't be thanked. Neil and Gill Mason have painstakingly maintained all the traditions of this wonderful country pub and yes it's a foodie heaven, but drinkers and guests don't miss out either.

Enter the pub to be surprised, no gimmicks here, just pure origins of years gone by. The pub has many areas in which to enjoy real ales, fine wines and of course some great food. The bar with its charming raised gallery has a real pubby atmosphere where locals and travellers engage, and then there is an elegant dining room with its heavily beamed low ceiling and a secluded courtyard that is reminiscent of a Mediterranean garden in the summertime.

Housed in an adjacent converted building are six most comfortable rooms, well appointed and offering the comforts expected of a four star silver rated inn. With ample parking, many rooms overlook the green and the fields beyond.

The White Horse was awarded 'Suffolk's Best Food Pub' in both 2008 and 2009, the only pub to have won this prestigious accolade twice.

Sibton White Horse Inn. Halesworth Road, Sibton,
Nr Saxmundham, Suffolk. IP17 2JJ.
Tel: 01728 660337. Email: info@sibtonwhitehorseinn.co.uk
www.sibtonwhitehorseinn.co.uk

Save on Hotels. Book at **theAA.com/hotel**

SUFFOLK 433 ENGLAND

## SOUTHWOLD *continued*

mango chutney and raita, or Suffolk rose veal, tomato and lemon stew with herb dumpling. Excellent puddings include rhubarb and custard trifle. The Crown's bedrooms have been built around twisting corridors and staircases.

**Open** all wk 8am-11pm (Sun 8am-10.30pm) Apr-Sep **Bar Meals** L served Sun-Fri 12-2, Sat 12-2.30 (12-3 summer) D served Sun-Fri 6-9, Sat 6-9.30 (5.30-9.30 summer) Av main course £15 ⊕ ADNAMS ◼ Adnams Ales ♻ Aspall. ⚑ 20 **Facilities** Children's menu Children's portions Dogs allowed Parking **Rooms** 14

### PICK OF THE PUBS

## The Randolph

**41 Wangford Rd, Reydon IP18 6PZ**
☎ **01502 723603** ▤ **01502 722194**
e-mail: reception@therandolph.co.uk
dir: *A1095 from A12 at Blythburgh 4m, Southwold 9m from Darsham train station*

This grand, late-Victorian, family-run pub, hotel and restaurant was built by Southwold brewery Adnams, and is named after Sir Winston Churchill's father. It is a fifteen minute stroll from the centre of picturesque Southwold and is the perfect place for exploring the Suffolk Heritage Coast. The traditional bar has contemporary furnishings including high-backed chairs and comfortable sofas. The same brewer's beers are sold today, alongside real cider from another Suffolk maker, Aspall. Sandwiches and lighter meals are served in the traditional bar, whereas in the large dining area the cooking style is modern British. Locally sourced ingredients produce dishes such as Italian meatballs with linguine; crispy hoi sin pork salad; Suffolk chicken with chestnut and mushroom; Sri Lankan salmon, mussel and prawn curry with fragrant rice and cucumber sambal; steamed venison suet pudding; pan-fried fillet of sea bass; and Tuscan vegetable and white bean stew. To one side of the building lies a large enclosed garden.

**Open** all day all wk **Bar Meals** L served all wk 12-2 D served all wk 6.30-9 Av main course £12.50 **Restaurant** L served all wk 12-2 D served all wk 6.30-9 Fixed menu price fr £15.95 ⊕ ADNAMS PLC ◼ Adnams Bitter, Adnams Broadside, Explorer, Old Ale ♻ Aspall. **Facilities** Children's menu Children's portions Dogs allowed Garden Parking

### STANTON            Map 13 TL97

## *The Rose & Crown*

**Bury Rd IP31 2BZ** ☎ **01359 250236**
dir: *On A413 from Bury St Edmunds towards Diss*

Three acres of landscaped grounds surround this 16th-century coaching inn. Curl up on one of the comfy sofas in the split-level bar for a pint of locally brewed Adnams Broadside, before perusing a menu that offers the likes of seared scallop, chorizo and black pudding salad; glazed

pork loin chops; and sea bass with crayfish and saffron risotto. The adjoining Cobbled Barn is a popular spot for weddings and parties.

**Open** all wk ◼ Greene King IPA, Adnams Broadside, Guinness. **Facilities** Play area Garden Parking

### STOKE-BY-NAYLAND            Map 13 TL93

### PICK OF THE PUBS

## The Angel Inn ⚑

**C06 4SA** ☎ **01206 263245** ▤ **01206 264145**
e-mail: info@theangelinn.net
dir: *From Colchester take A134 towards Sudbury, 5m to Nayland. Or from A12 between juncts 30 & 31 take B1068, then B1087 to Nayland*

Set in a landscape immortalised in the paintings of local artist, John Constable, The Angel is a 16th-century inn with beamed bars, log fires and a long tradition of hospitality. The relaxed, modern feel extends to the air-conditioned conservatory, the patio and sun terrace. Tables for lunch and dinner may be reserved in The Well Room, which has a high ceiling open to the rafters, a gallery leading to the pub's accommodation, rough brick and timber studded walls, and the well itself, fully 52 feet deep. Eating in the bar, by comparison, is on a strictly first-come, first-served basis but the same menu is served throughout. Main courses offer a range of meat, seafood and vegetarian options, typically including griddled whole plaice served with salad and French fries. There is an extensive wine list. Recent change of hands.

**Open** all day all wk Mon-Sat 11-11 (Sun 11-10.30) **Bar Meals** L served Mon-Sat 12-2.30, Sun 12-7.30 D served Mon-Sat 12-2.30, Sun 12-7.30 **Restaurant** L served Mon-Sat 12-2.30, Sun 12-7.30 D served Mon-Sat 6-9.15, Sun 12-7.30 ⊕ FREE HOUSE ◼ Adnams Best, 2 Guest ales ♻ Aspall. ⚑ 9 **Facilities** Children's menu Family room Dogs allowed Garden Parking

### PICK OF THE PUBS

## The Crown ★★★ SHL ◉◉ ⚑

**C06 4SE** ☎ **01206 262001** ▤ **01206 264026**
e-mail: info@crowninn.net
dir: *Exit A12 signed Stratford St Mary/Dedham. Through Stratford St Mary 0.5m, left, follow signs to Higham. At village green turn left, left again 2m, pub on right*

Tucked away in the beautiful Box Valley, close to the timeless villages of Lavenham, Kersey and Long Melford, this classy 16th-century inn has been stylishly updated and extended, with 11 boutique bedrooms added in late 2008. The contemporary bar and dining areas are informal and decked out in smart soft furnishings and relaxing pastel colours — the glass wine cellar-cum-shop catches the eye and offers some cracking wines to take away. Wherever possible, local produce underpins dishes on the monthly-changing modern British menu, all of them freshly prepared using top-notch local ingredients. Lunch brings full meals or light options such as deep-fried chilli and salt

squid. An evening meal might take in pork, rabbit, prune and pistachio terrine; rump steak with thick-cut chips and cauliflower cheese; and banana tarte Tatin with home-made sticky toffee pudding ice cream. Look to the chalkboard for the daily fish selection, perhaps grilled lemon sole with cherry vine tomatoes and herb oil. Every dish is given a wine match and a decent selection of ales sits alongside a superb wine list.

**Open** all day all wk 7.30am-11pm (Sun 8am-10.30pm) Closed: 25-26 Dec **Bar Meals** L served Mon-Sat 12-2.30, Sun 12-9 D served Mon-Thu 6-9.30, Fri-Sat 6-10, Sun 12-9 Av main course £13.95 **Restaurant** L served Mon-Sat 12-2.30, Sun 12-9 D served Mon-Thu 6-9.30, Fri-Sat 6-10, Sun 12-9 ⊕ FREE HOUSE ◼ Adnams Best Bitter, Brewers Gold, Woodforde's Wherry, guest ales ♻ Aspall. ⚑ 32 **Facilities** Children's menu Children's portions Dogs allowed Garden Parking **Rooms** 11

### STOWMARKET            Map 13 TM05

### PICK OF THE PUBS

## The Buxhall Crown ⚑

**Mill Rd, Buxhall IP14 3DW** ☎ **01449 736521**
e-mail: thebuxhallcrown@hotmail.co.uk
dir: *3m from Stowmarket and A14*

A 17th-century building, The Buxhall Crown has a classic old bar with intimate corners and an open fire, and a second bar with a lighter, more modern feel. The owners and staff pride themselves on the friendly family feel of the pub, and the high quality of the food they serve. Dishes are prepared from locally sourced produce, and breads, biscuits, ice creams and sorbets are all freshly made on the premises. Anything from a bar snacks to a full four-course meal is catered for, and the menu changes regularly to suit the weather and the availability of ingredients. Venison loin carpaccio, juniper and cranberry wine reduction, Roquefort salad; oxtail and barley stew with honey and black pepper roast parsnips; steak and kidney pie, pink fir apple potatoes and seasonal vegetables; mulled poached pear with warm cardamom rice pudding; and white chocolate and Bailey's bread and butter pudding with espresso sorbet all appeared on a winter menu.

**Open** noon-3 7-11 (Sat noon-3 6.30-11) Closed: 25 & 26 Dec, Sun eve & Mon **Bar Meals** L served Tue-Sun 12-2 D served Tue-Fri 7-9.30, Sat 6.30-9.30 Av main course £10 **Restaurant** L served Tue-Sun 12-2 D served Tue-Fri 7-9.30, Sat 6.30-9.30 Fixed menu price fr £10 Av 3 course à la carte fr £18 ⊕ GREENE KING ◼ Greene King IPA, Olde Trip, Old Speckled Hen, Guest Ale ♻ Aspall. ⚑ 12 **Facilities** Children's portions Dogs allowed Garden Parking

# PICK OF THE PUBS

## The Westleton Crown ★★★HL

**WESTLETON**    Map 13 TM46

**The Street IP17 3AD**
☎ **01728 648777**    📄 **01728 648239**
e-mail: info@westletoncrown.co.uk
web: www.westletoncrown.co.uk
dir: *A12 N, turn right for Westleton just after Yoxford. Hotel opposite on entering Westleton*

Over the years this attractive brick-built pub has evolved into a well-appointed inn, combining historic character with contemporary charm. Standing opposite the parish church in a peaceful village close to the RSPB's Minsmere Reserve, it provides a comfortable base for exploring Suffolk's glorious Heritage Coast. Guests have stayed on this site since the 12th century, when a priest in charge of Sibton Abbey lived here and took in travellers; later, in the 17th century, it became a thriving coaching inn. On winter days you'll find three crackling log fires, local real ales including Adnams Bitter and Brandeston Gold, and a good list of wines (with 11 available by the glass).

There's also an extensive menu that includes innovative daily specials and classic dishes with a twist, all freshly prepared from the best local produce available. You can eat in the cosy bar, the elegant dining room, or the light and airy garden room. Sandwiches are made with a choice of The Crown's own breads, and served with sea-salted crisps and a dressed salad.

More substantial appetites might choose from starters like terrine of Blythburgh ham and duck liver pâté with green bean salad and a artichoke purée; or tempura of tiger prawns with chilli dipping sauce and garlic aïoli. Follow up with main course choices such as roast loin of lamb with goat's cheese and lavender; beer-battered haddock and hand-cut chips; or baked baby leek and parmesan loaf with mint crushed potato and rocket and tomato salad. Save some space for accomplished desserts like rhubarb and ginger crumble tart with natural yogurt sorbet, and caramelised pineapple and star anise tarte Tatin with coconut ice cream. There is a separate vegetarian menu.

Retire to one of the 34 comfortable, individually styled and refurbished bedrooms, complete with flat screen TV. Outside, the large terraced gardens are floodlit in the evening.

**Open** all day all wk 7am-11pm (Sun 7.30am-10.30pm) **Bar Meals** L served all wk 12-2.30 D served all wk 7-9.30 Av main course £12 food served all day **Restaurant** L served all wk 12-2.30 D served all wk 7-9.30 Av 3 course à la carte fr £25 ⊕ FREE HOUSE ◀ Adnams Bitter, Purity UBU, Green Jack, Brandeston Gold ⌾ Aspall. ♀ 11 **Facilities** Children's menu Dogs allowed Garden Parking **Rooms** 34

Save on Hotels. Book at theAA.com/hotel

SUFFOLK 435 ENGLAND

## STRADBROKE — Map 13 TM27

### The Ivy House ☂

**Wilby Rd IP21 5JN ☎ 01379 384634**
e-mail: stensethome@aol.com
dir: Telephone for directions

A Grade II listed thatched pub just off the main street in Stradbroke. The comfortable bar offers real ales and wine from Adnams wine cellar. The remodelled restaurant has beech tables and chairs and white china. The weekly-changing menu makes good use of local and seasonal produce, some grown on the premises. Typical dishes include skate wing cooked in caper butter with Norfolk samphire, or roast loin of local venison with aromatic braised red cabbage and celeriac. In warmer weather you can sit outside at the front or in the garden.

Open all wk Restaurant L served all wk 12-2 booking required D served all wk 6.30-9 booking required ⊕ FREE HOUSE ◀ Adnams, Woodforde's, Buffy's ♂ Aspall. ☂ 12 Facilities Dogs allowed Garden Parking

## SWILLAND — Map 13 TM15

### Moon & Mushroom Inn ☂

**High Rd IP6 9LR ☎ 01473 785320**
e-mail: nikki@ecocleen.fsnet.co.uk
dir: Take B1077 (Westerfield road) from Ispwich. Approx 6m right to Swilland

This 300-year-old free house has a reputation as 'the pub that time passed by', and the owners intend to keep it that way. Winter fires, good company and a extensive choice of East Anglian ales straight from the barrel all play their part. Steaks and fish and chips with mushy peas are staples, while ever popular are beef in ale with dumplings; pan-fried partridge breast; shoulder of lamb; and a good vegetarian selection. Food and drink can be enjoyed in the garden in warmer months.

Open Tue-Sun L & Mon L Closed: Sun eve & Mon eve Bar Meals L served all wk 12-2 D served Tue-Sat 6-9 Av main course £9.95 Restaurant L served all wk 12-2 D served Tue-Sat 6-9 ⊕ FREE HOUSE ◀ Nethergate Suffolk County, Woodforde's Wherry, Buffy's Hopleaf, Wolf Ale, Golden Jackal, Lavender Honey ♂ Aspall. ☂ 10 Facilities Children's portions Dogs allowed Garden Parking

## THORPENESS — Map 13 TM45

### The Dolphin Inn ☂

**Peace Place IP16 4NA ☎ 01728 454994**
e-mail: dolphininn@hotmail.co.uk
dir: A12 onto A1094 & follow Thorpeness signs

Just a short stroll from the beach, this traditional free house has an inviting, pine-furnished interior and a kitchen that also supplies preserves, pies and pastries to the attached village store. The bar dispenses real ales from independent local producers and has developed an excellent wine list. Prepared from local, usually organic, ingredients, dishes from the daily changing menu might

be soft-poached egg with grilled lamb chops and Niçoise salad; beer-battered hake and chips; linguine with pancetta, chilli and clams; and grilled vegetable and emmental tart. Barbecued fish and meats are served in the huge garden in summer.

Closed: Sun eve & Mon in winter Bar Meals L served all wk 12-2.30 booking required D served all wk 6.30-9.30 booking required Av main course £11 Restaurant L served all wk 12-2.30 booking required D served all wk 6.30-9.30 booking required Fixed menu price fr £16.50 Av 3 course à la carte fr £20 ⊕ FREE HOUSE ◀ Adnams Best, Adnams Broadside, Rusty Bucket, Nautilus, Mid Summer Gold ♂ Aspall. ☂ 16 Facilities Children's menu Children's portions Dogs allowed Garden Parking

## TOSTOCK — Map 13 TL96

### Gardeners Arms

**IP30 9PA ☎ 01359 270460**
e-mail: brandon@brandonmchaledesigns.com
dir: A14 follow signs to Tostock, turn at slip road through Beyton. Left at T-junct over A14 turn left into Tostock. 1st right to end of road, pub on right

Parts of this charming pub, at the end of the village green, near the horse chestnut tree, date back 600 years. The basic bar menu - salads, grills, ploughman's, sandwiches, toasties, etc - is supplemented by specials boards offering six starters and 12 main courses in the evening. Look out for lamb balti, Thai king prawn green curry, steak and kidney pie, and chicken and Stilton roulade. There's a large grassy garden.

Open 11.30-3 7-11 (Fri-Sat 11.30-3 7-12) Closed: Mon L ◀ Greene King IPA, Greene King Abbot, Greene King seasonal ales. Facilities Dogs allowed Garden Parking

## WALBERSWICK — Map 13 TM47

### PICK OF THE PUBS

### The Anchor ◉ ☉ ☂

**Main St IP18 6UA**
☎ 01502 722112   📠 01502 724464
e-mail: info@anchoratwalberswick.com
dir: From A12 turn at B1387. Follow signs for Walberswick. Continue on Main St, pub on right

Just a stones skim from the golden sands of Walberswick beach, this lovingly renovated Arts and Crafts style inn makes the most of its village setting and draws in appreciative locals to enjoy Mark Dorber's great range of real ales and bottle conditioned beers. So dedicated is he to the noble hop that Mark runs a monthly beer course here, tutored by a commercial brewer; there's a great wine list, too. Sophie Dorber oversees the food side here, earning an AA Rosette award for her creative, modern dishes which draw heavily on locally sourced produce, with a distinct nod to denizens of the surf. The bar menu stretches to roast cod with Puy lentils, leeks and salsa verde; 'Mostly smoked' platter of Lowestoft red herring, smoked fish terrine and smoked salmon and duck confit with chorizo and cannellini bean stew. The specials board

changes twice daily to make the most of Suffolk's bountiful larder: the inn's wildflower meadow is a great place to indulge in a picnic from The Anchor's kitchen.

Open all day all wk Bar Meals L served all wk 12-3 D served all wk 6-9 Restaurant L served all wk 12-3 booking required D served all wk 6-9 booking required ◀ Adnams Bitter, Broadside, Seasonal, Meantime Helles, Meantime Pale Ale, Bitburger ♂ Aspall. ☂ 22 Facilities Children's menu Children's portions Family room Dogs allowed Garden Parking

### PICK OF THE PUBS

### Bell Inn ☂

**Ferry Rd IP18 6TN ☎ 01502 723109**
e-mail: thebell@adnams.co.uk
dir: From A12 take B1387, follow to beyond village green, bear right down track

The inn dates back 600 years and is located near the village green, beach and the ancient fishing harbour on the River Blyth. The large garden has beach and sea views, while the building's great age is evident from the interior's low beams, stone-flagged floors, high wooden settles and open fires. Adnams furnishes the bar with Broadside and Spindrift among others, while Suffolk cyder maker Aspall is also well represented. (Aspall has spelt its cyder with a 'y' since the 1920s, reputedly to reflect the refined quality of the family firm's multi-award-winning product.) Food is all home cooked with local produce featuring strongly, particularly fresh fish. Specialities include starters of locally smoked sprats or Suffolk smokies — flaked smoked haddock in a creamy cheese sauce — both served with granary toast and a salad garnish. There are non-fish dishes too, like baked Suffolk ham or lamb burger in toasted ciabatta.

Open all wk Mon-Thu 11-3 6-11 (Fri-Sat 11-11 Sun 11-10.30 Summer all day) Bar Meals L served all wk 12-2 D served all wk 6-9 ⊕ ADNAMS ◀ Adnams Bitter, Broadside, Explorer, Spindrift ♂ Aspall. ☂ 15 Facilities Children's menu Family room Dogs allowed Garden Parking

## WESTLETON — Map 13 TM46

### PICK OF THE PUBS

### The Westleton Crown ★★★ HL ◉ ◉ ☂

*See Pick of the Pubs on page 434*

## WHEPSTEAD — Map 13 TL85

### The White Horse ▼ NEW

**Rede Rd IP29 4SS ☎ 01284 735760**
**dir:** *From Bury St Edmunds take A143 towards Haverhill. Left onto B1066 to Whepstead. In Whepstead right into Church Hill, leads into Rede Rd*

Built in the 17th century as a farmhouse and extended by the Victorians, this refurbished free house offers a series of cosy rooms adorned with curios and artworks. The open fire and comfortable wooden chairs make you feel instantly at home, whilst nostalgic touches like the Tuck Shop appeal to adults and children alike. Along with real ales and ciders, fresh, locally sourced ingredients drive the menu: expect smoked haddock Florentine with cream and wilted spinach, and braised local pork with dates and juniper berries. There is a new regional menu and local fish in Adnams Broadside batter and hand-cut chips on Wednesdays and Thursdays.

**Open** 11.30-3 7-11 Closed: 25-26 Dec, Sun eve **Bar Meals** L served all wk 12-2 D served Mon-Sat 7-9.30 Av main course £9.95 **Restaurant** L served all wk 12-2 D served Mon-Sat 7-9.30 Av 3 course à la carte fr £22 ⊕ FREE HOUSE ◄ Adnams Bitter, Adnams Broadside, Guest Ale ◑ Aspall. ▼ 10 **Facilities** Children's portions Dogs allowed Garden Parking

# SURREY

## ABINGER — Map 6 TQ14

# PICK OF THE PUBS

## The Stephan Langton

*See Pick of the Pubs on page 438*

See Pick of the Pubs on page 438

### The Volunteer ▼

**Water Ln, Sutton RH5 6PR**
**☎ 01306 730798 🖹 01306 731621**
**dir:** *Between Guildford & Dorking, 1m S of A25*

Enjoying a delightful rural setting with views over the River Mole, this popular village pub was originally farm cottages and first licensed about 1870. An ideal watering hole for walkers who want to relax over a pint in the attractive pub garden. Typical fish dishes include lobster thermidor, Mediterranean squid pasta and fillet of sea bass, while Thai coconut chicken, partridge with red wine and junipers and fillet of braised beef on fennel feature among the meat dishes.

**Open** all day all wk 11.30-11 (Sat 11-11 Sun noon-11) Closed: 25 Dec ◄ Badger Tanglefoot, King & Barns Sussex, plus guest ales ◑ Stowford Press. ▼ 9 **Facilities** Dogs allowed Garden Parking

## ALBURY — Map 6 TQ04

### *The Drummond Arms Inn* ★★★ INN ▼

**The Street GU5 9AG**
**☎ 01483 202039 🖹 01483 205361**
**e-mail:** drummondarms@aol.com
**dir:** *6m from Guildford*

Triple gables at the second-floor level add an interesting architectural twist to this village pub, set in an attractive garden overlooking the River Tillingbourne. The menu offers sandwiches, old favourites (fish and chips; sausage and mash), and regular main courses such as braised lamb shank, or chicken New Yorker (with barbecue sauce and mozzarella cheese); fish dishes feature strongly. There is also a choice of daily specials.

**Open** all day all wk 11-11 (Fri-Sat 11-mdnt, Sun noon-10.30) ◄ Courage Best, London Pride, Shere Drop. ▼ 8 **Facilities** Family room Dogs allowed Garden Parking **Rooms** 9

### William IV

**Little London GU5 9DG ☎ 01483 202685**
**web:** www.williamivalbury.com
**dir:** *Just off A25 between Guildford & Dorking. Near Shere*

This quaint country pub is just a stone's throw from Guildford yet deep in the heart of the Surrey Hills conservation area. It is great walking and riding country, and the attractive garden is ideal for post-ramble relaxation. A choice of cask ales and a daily changing blackboard menu of proper home-cooked pub food are all part of the appeal. Home-produced, free-range, rare-breed pork variously features, alongside steak and chips and battered cod all served in a calm, relaxed atmosphere.

**Open** all wk 11-3 5.30-11 (Sat 11-11, Sun noon-11) Closed: 25 Dec **Bar Meals** L served all wk 12-2 booking required D served Mon-Sat 7-9 booking required ⊕ FREE HOUSE ◄ Flowers IPA, Hogs Back, Surrey Hills Brewery ◑ Westons Stowford Press, Bounds Brand Scrumpy. **Facilities** Children's portions Dogs allowed Garden Parking

## BETCHWORTH — Map 6 TQ25

### The Red Lion ★★★ INN ▼

**Old Rd, Buckland RH3 7DS**
**☎ 01737 843336 🖹 01737 845242**
**e-mail:** info@redlionbetchworth.co.uk
**dir:** *Telephone for directions*

The family-run Red Lion dates back to 1795 and is set in 18 acres with a cricket ground, a 230-year-old wisteria and rolling countryside views, all just 15 minutes from Gatwick Airport. A vaulted cellar accommodates a function room, and six en suite bedrooms are available in a separate self-contained block. The menu offers a pie of the week; perhaps from the specials menu there could be Mediterranean salmon; pan-fried mackerel; or Kashmiri rack of lamb. The area is ideal for walkers.

**Open** all day all wk 11am-11.30pm (Fri-Sat 11am-mdnt) **Bar Meals** L served Sun-Fri 12-2.30, Sat 12-4 **Restaurant** L served Mon-Fri 12-2.30, Sat-Sun 12-4 D served Mon-Thu 6.30-9, Fri-Sat 6.30-9.30, Sun 6.30-8 ⊕ PUNCH TAVERNS ◄ Fuller's London Pride, Adnams Broadside, Adnams Bitter ◑ Kopparberg. ▼ 9 **Facilities** Children's menu Children's portions Dogs allowed Garden Parking **Rooms** 6

## BLACKHEATH — Map 6 TQ04

### *The Villagers Inn*

**Blackheath Ln GU4 8RB ☎ 01483 893152**
**e-mail:** info@thevillagersinn.co.uk
**dir:** *Telephone for directions*

More than a hundred years old, this free house stands on the edge of Blackheath, a natural woodland area of several square miles in the heart of Surrey. A menu of traditional pub food includes steak and kidney pie, chicken pie, and fillet steak. A covered patio extends the opportunity for alfresco dining. Real ales are represented by London Pride, Surrey Hill Shere Drop and Weltons Horsham Best.

**Open** all wk 12-3 6-11 (Sun 12-11) ◄ Surrey Hill Shere Drop, Weltons Horsham Best, Sussex Best, London Pride, guest ale ◑ Stowford Press. **Facilities** Play area Dogs allowed Garden Parking

# The Bat and Ball Freehouse

*Bat and Ball Lane, Boundstone, Farnham, Surrey GU10 4SA*
*www.thebatandball.co.uk*

*Tel: 01252 792108*
*E-mail: info@thebatandball.co.uk*

The Bat and Ball Freehouse nestles in the bottom of the Bourne valley in Boundstone near Farnham. Over 150 years old, the Pub has a relaxed, rural feel, surrounded by woodland and wildlife, and is the focal point of 5 footpaths which connect to local villages. Customers can eat or drink throughout the Pub, patio area and the large south-facing garden (which backs onto the Bourne stream and has a popular children's play structure). All the food is cooked in-house and this is very much a pub that serves restaurant quality food and not a restaurant that sells beer! The bar area has both a traditional and modern style to it to provide for our differing customer tastes, both young and old, and we have a tempting selection of 6 well-kept Cask Ales.

# PICK OF THE PUBS

## The Stephan Langton

**ABINGER** Map 6 TQ14

**Friday St RH5 6JR**
☎ 01306 730775 & 01306 737129
e-mail: iinfo@stephanlangtonpub.co.uk
dir: *Exit A25 between Dorking & Guildford at Hollow Lane, W of Wootton. 1.5m then left into Friday St. At end of hill right at pond*

Undulating mixed woodland surrounds this secluded hamlet at the base of Leith Hill, which is nothing more than a tranquil hammer pond and a handful of stone and timber cottages. This is prime Surrey walking country and a popular pit-stop is The Stephan Langton, a 1930s building named after the first archbishop of Canterbury, who was supposedly born in Friday Street. He helped draw up the Magna Carta and a copy of the Odocument is pinned to a wall in the rustic, bare-boarded bar.

Equally unpretentious is the adjoining dining room, with its cream-washed walls, simple wooden tables and chairs, and open fires. Having conquered Leith Hill, the highest summit in south-east England, relax on the sun-trap patio and savour a thirst-quenching pint of locally-brewed Hog's Back TEA or Shere Drop.

Peruse the short, inviting menu that hits the spot with lunchtime sandwiches and starters like smoked chicken and leek risotto and local smoked trout with potato scones, mixed leaves and walnut pesto dressing. Typical hearty main dishes take in grilled cod with Tuscan bean broth; beef slow-braised in beer with root vegetables, bashed neeps and tatties; seared venison with roasted beetroot, local watercress and crème de cassis jus; and thyme and sage roasted rack of lamb with sweet potato gratin, cavalo nero and red wine jus. Changing daily specials make the most of local produce, much of it sourced from the surrounding Wooton Estate.

New owners Mathew Granger and Marissa Waters took over the pub in November 2009 and are gradually upgrading the place and developing the food side of the operation.

**Open** all wk 11-3 5-10.30 (Sat 11-11 Sun 12-9) **Bar Meals** L served Tue-Sat 12-2.30, Sun 12-4 booking required D served Tue-Sat 6.30-9.30 booking required Av main course £10 **Restaurant** L served Tue-Sat 12-2.30, Sun 12-4 booking required D served Tue-Sat 6.30-9.30 booking required Av 3 course à la carte fr £25 ⊕ FREE HOUSE ◀ Fuller's London Pride, Hog's Back TEA, Shere Drop ♻ Aspall, Old Rosie Scrumpy. **Facilities** Dogs allowed Garden Parking

Save on Hotels. Book at **theAA.com/hotel**

SURREY 439 ENGLAND

## BRAMLEY
Map 6 TQ04

### Jolly Farmer Inn ☕

**High St GU5 0HB** ☎ 01483 893355 📠 01483 890484
e-mail: enquiries@jollyfarmer.co.uk
dir: *From Guildford take A281 (Horsham road). Bramley 3.5m S of Guildford*

The family that own this friendly 16th-century free house (for nearly 40 years) have a passion for cask ales, and you'll always find up to eight real ales and six lagers, as well as an impressive range of Belgian bottled beers. All meals are freshly cooked to order: expect the likes of smoked haddock fishcakes; pork tenderloin with Lyonnaise potatoes, green beans and sweet plum sauce; or home-made duck and Cognac sausages with buttered mash and red wine jus on the specials board, alongside old favourites such as salmon fillet en croute.

**Open** all day all wk 11-11 **Bar Meals** L served all wk 12-2.30 D served all wk 6-9.30 Av main course £11 **Restaurant** L served all wk 12-2.30 D served all wk 6-9.30 Av 3 course à la carte fr £18.75 ⊕ FREE HOUSE ◄ 8 continually changing cask ales Ö Westons Stowford Press. ☕ 16 **Facilities** Children's menu Dogs allowed Garden Parking

## CHIDDINGFOLD
Map 6 SU93

### The Crown Inn ★★★★★ INN

**The Green GU8 4TX** ☎ 01428 682255 📠 01428 685736
e-mail: enquiries@thecrownchiddingfold.com
dir: *On A283 between Milford & Petworth*

Historic inn, dating back over 700 years, with lots of charming features, including ancient panelling, open fires, distinctive carvings, huge beams, and eight comfortable bedrooms. Reliable food ranges from pork and leek sausages served with mash and onion gravy or home made chicken and mushroom pie on the bar menu; to monkfish wrapped in Parma ham served with confit tomato and pepper salad or cumin spiced rump of lamb on butternut squash with spinach and a rosemary jus on the à la carte.

**Open** all day all wk **Bar Meals** L served Mon-Sat 12-2.30, Sun 12-3 booking required D served Mon-Sat 6.30-10, Sun 6.30-9.30 booking required **Restaurant** L served Mon-Sat 12-2.30, Sun 12-3 booking required D served Mon-Sat 6.30-10, Sun 6.30-9.30 booking required ⊕ FGH INNS ◄ London Pride, Moon Dance, Crown Bitter, Summer Lightning. **Facilities** Children's menu Children's portions Dogs allowed Garden **Rooms** 8

## CHURT
Map 5 SU83

### PICK OF THE PUBS

### Pride of the Valley ☕

**Tilford Rd GU10 2LH**
☎ 01428 605799 📠 01428 605875
e-mail: reservations@prideofthevalleyhotel.com
dir: *4m from Farnham on outskirts of Churt. 3m from Haslemere*

A comfortable country house hotel distinguished by some fine Art Nouveau touches and wonderful wood panelling. Once a watering hole for former Prime Minister David Lloyd George, who retired locally, the Pride of the Valley is set in some of Surrey's best countryside, close to Devil's Jumps beauty spot and Frensham Common with its sculpture park spread across hillsides, vales and woodlands. The owner is an enthusiastic supporter of the local Hogs Back Brewery and maintains a first class wine list, all of which complements a regularly refreshed menu reflecting seasonal, locally sourced produce. A typical day may find roast breast of pigeon, foie gras tortellini, caramelised apples and a red wine reduction, or pan fried fillet of brill, fricassee of baby potatoes, smoked bacon and broad beans, finishing off with rhubarb crème brûlée or citrus parfait with tequila jelly.

**Open** all wk **Bar Meals** L served Mon-Sat 12-2.30, Sun 12-3 D served all wk 6.30-9.30 Av main course £11 **Restaurant** L served Tue-Sun 12-2.30 booking required D served Tue-Sun 6.30-9.30 booking required Av 3 course à la carte fr £27.50 ⊕ FREE HOUSE ◄ Hogs Back TEA, Hogs Back Bitter, Ringwood Fortyniner. ☕ 8 **Facilities** Children's portions Dogs allowed Garden Parking

## CLAYGATE
Map 6 TQ16

### Swan Inn & Lodge ☕

**2 Hare Ln KT10 9BS** ☎ 01372 462582
e-mail: info@swaninn.net
web: www.theswanlodge.net
dir: *At Esher/Oxshott junct of A3 take A244 towards Esher. Right at 1st lights, pub 300yds on right*

Rebuilt in 1905 overlooking the village green and cricket pitch, yet barely 15 miles from Charing Cross. There's an attractively furnished Continental-style bar and a Thai restaurant offering nearly 75 starters, soups, curries, stir-fries, and seafoods. The Thai menu is available at lunchtime and in the evenings, as are calamari, Cajun

chicken burgers, scampi, roast beef and lamb, and paninis. Dishes of the day appear on the specials board. Recent change of hands.

**Open** all day all wk noon-11 **Bar Meals** L served Mon-Sat 12-10, Sun 12-6 D served Mon 3-8, Tue-Sat 5-10 food served all day ⊕ WELLINGTON PUB COMPANY ◄ London Pride, Old Speckled Hen, Woodforde's Wherry Ö Aspall. ☕ 8 **Facilities** Children's menu Play area Family room Dogs allowed Garden Parking

## COBHAM
Map 6 TQ16

### The Cricketers

**Downside KT11 3NX**
☎ 01932 862105 📠 01932 868186
e-mail: info@thecricketersdownside.co.uk
dir: *M25 junct 10, A3 towards London. 1st exit signed Cobham. Straight over 1st rdbt, right at 2nd. In 1m right opposite Waitrose into Downside Bridge Rd*

Traditional, family-run pub, parts of which date back to 1540, with beamed ceilings and log fires. The inn's charming rural setting makes it popular with walkers, and the pretty River Mole is close by. The main menu offers dishes like best end of lamb served with herb crust, ratatouille and rosemary jus; or confit duck leg served with mashed potato, Savoy cabbage with raisins, honey and port sauce.

**Open** all day all wk **Bar Meals** L served Mon-Sat 12-3, Sun 12-8 D served Mon-Sat 6.30-9.30, Sun 12-8 Av main course £10 ◄ Old Speckled Hen, London Pride, IPA. **Facilities** Children's portions Play area Dogs allowed Garden Parking

### The Old Bear ◎◎ ☕ NEW

**River Hill KT11 3DX** ☎ 01932 862116 📠 01932 868416
e-mail: info@theoldbearcobham.co.uk
dir: *M25 junct 10, A3 towards London. Take A245 signed Cobham. Straight on at 1st rdbt, 2nd exit at next rdbt. Pub on left after Waitrose*

An early-Georgian pub within a medieval frame, lovingly refurbished as a comfy, characterful village inn with all the trimmings: log fire, beams, polished floorboards and a pleasant country garden and terrace. Head chef Nathan Green has gained two AA Rosettes for his acclaimed menu of starters including sautéed ox heart with chestnut mushrooms and mains across the board of surf, turf and game; perhaps chargrilled octopus with chorizo and chick pea salad. Great beers, too, and some classic bins, including rare boutique wines by the glass.

**Open** all wk 11-3 5-12 **Bar Meals** L served all wk 12-3 D served all wk 6-10 Av main course £16 **Restaurant** L served all wk 12-3 D served all wk 6-10 Fixed menu price fr £15.50 ⊕ REVIVE PUBS ◄ Doom Bar, Black Sheep, Hobgoblin, Greene King IPA. ☕ 13 **Facilities** Children's portions Dogs allowed Garden Parking

## COLDHARBOUR · Map 6 TQ14

### PICK OF THE PUBS

### The Plough Inn

**Coldharbour Ln RH5 6HD**
☎ 01306 711793 📠 01306 710055
e-mail: ploughinn@btinternet.com
dir: *M25 junct 9, A24 to Dorking. A25 towards Guildford. Coldharbour signed from one-way system*

It's easy to live the high life here; the highest point in south-eastern England is a pleasant stroll from this, the highest pub in the region. Leith Hill has long drawn out walkers, cyclists and country lovers from London to take the airs; earlier visitors were perhaps less fastidious - a well-worn smugglers' route from the coast to London once passed its door, which probably explains why the resident ghost is a matelot. Another high point of The Plough is its own micro-brewery, from the vessels of which are decanted Tallywhacker Porter and Crooked Furrow bitter, whilst a Kentish cider adds to the tempting range. Long-term, painstaking refurbishment of this handsome, beamed 17th century former coaching inn has produced a comfy, family-friendly place with grand winter fires and a pretty garden. Food is firmly traditional British, with a signature dish of steamed bacon, onion and sage suet pudding with mash and veg a great favourite. Ramblers may revive themselves with parsnip and parmesan roulade or good old-fashioned fish and chips before retiring with a rich steamed figgy fruit pudding.

**Open** all day all wk 11.30am-mdnt (Fri-Sat 11.30-1am) Closed: 25 Dec **Bar Meals** L served Mon-Fri 12-2.30, Sat-Sun 12-3 D served Mon-Sat 6.30-9.30, Sun 6.30-9 Av main course £11 **Restaurant** L served Mon-Fri 12-2.30, Sat-Sun 12-3 booking required D served Mon-Sat 6.30-9.30, Sun 6.30-9 booking required Av 3 course à la carte fr £21 ⊕ FREE HOUSE ◀ Crooked Furrow, Leith Hill Tallywhacker, Ringwood Old Thumper, Timothy Taylor Landlord, Shepherd Neame Best Bitter ○ Biddenden Scrumpy. **Facilities** Children's menu Children's portions Dogs allowed Garden Parking

## COMPTON · Map 6 SU94

### The Withies Inn

**Withies Ln GU3 1JA** ☎ 01483 421158 📠 01483 425904
dir: *Telephone for directions*

Set amid unspoiled country on Compton Common just below the Hog's Back, this low-beamed 16th-century pub has been carefully modernised to incorporate a small restaurant. There is also a splendid garden where meals can be served under the pergola. Snacks available in the bar range from sandwiches and jackets to fisherman's broth or a seafood platter. In the restaurant seasonal specialities include game and lobster, alongside dishes of roasted rack of lamb, calves' liver, or steaks from the chargrill.

**Open** 11-3 6-11 (Fri 11-11) Closed: Sun eve **Bar Meals** L served all wk 12-2.30 D served Mon-Sat 7-10 Av main course £6 **Restaurant** L served all wk 12-2.30 D served Mon-Sat 7-10 Av 3 course à la carte fr £30 ⊕ FREE HOUSE ◀ TEA, Adnams, Young's. **Facilities** Dogs allowed Garden Parking

## DUNSFOLD · Map 6 TQ03

### The Sun Inn ♥

**The Common GU8 4LE**
☎ 01483 200242 📠 01483 201141
e-mail: suninn@dunsfold.net
dir: *A281 through Shalford & Bramley, take B2130 to Godalming. Dunsfold on left after 2m*

A traditional 500-year-old family-run inn in a chocolate box village, set opposite the cricket green and village pond. Inside the welcome is warm, with blazing fires and an array of real ales including Adnams and Harveys. Home-made food, using produce from the inn's own vegetable garden, includes carrot, ginger and lime soup; smoked mackerel and caper pâté; a choice of burgers hand made from locally sourced meat accompanied by a topping of your choosing; aubergine, pine nut and spinach filo pie; and beer-battered cod fillet. There is a great menu for children too. Enjoy the quiz every Sunday evening.

**Open** all wk 11-3 5-mdnt (Fri-Sun 11am-1am) **Bar Meals** L served all wk 12-2.30 D served Tue-Sat 7-9.15, Sun 6-8.30 Av main course £8.95 **Restaurant** L served all wk 12-2.30 D served Tue-Sat 7-9.15, Sun 7-8.30 ⊕ PUNCH TAVERNS ◀ Harveys Sussex, Adnams, Old Speckled Hen, Tribute, Guinness ○ Westons Old Rosie. ♥ 10 **Facilities** Children's menu Children's portions Dogs allowed Garden Parking

## EAST CLANDON · Map 6 TQ05

### The Queens Head ♥ NEW

**The Street GU4 7RY** ☎ 01483 222332
e-mail: mark.williams@redmistleisure.co.uk
dir: *4m E of Guildford on A246. Signed*

Nestling in the Surrey Hills just a short step from the North Downs Way, this handsome brick-built village pub is a haven for ramblers and locals seeking the best local produce. Beer is courtesy of the nearby Surrey Hills Brewery whilst the specials board announces the latest finds that the inventive chefs have discovered round the way; hand-made Surrey pork and herb sausages with buttered kale will revive after a winter walk, or share a charcuterie platter, including smoked venison and duck breast, in the tree-shaded garden.

**Open** all wk noon-3 6-11 (Sat noon-11 Sun noon-9) **Bar Meals** L served Mon-Sat 12-2.30, Sun 12-8 booking required D served Mon-Thu 6-9, Fri-Sat 6-9.30, Sun 12-8 booking required Av main course £12 **Restaurant** L served Mon-Sat 12-2.30, Sun 12-8 booking required D served Mon-Thu 6-9, Fri-Sat 6-9.30, Sun 12-8 booking required Fixed menu price fr £12 Av 3 course à la carte fr £23 ⊕ FREE HOUSE ◀ Shere Drop, TEA, Oxford Gold, Spitfire. ♥ 13 **Facilities** Children's menu Children's portions Dogs allowed Garden Parking

## EFFINGHAM · Map 6 TQ15

### The Plough

**Orestan Ln KT24 5SW**
☎ 01372 458121 📠 01372 458121
dir: *Between Guildford & Leatherhead on A246*

The Plough provides a peaceful retreat in a rural setting close to Polesden Lacy National Trust property. It is located on a no-through road in a picturesque village and has a good crowd of regulars. The pub has a reputation for well kept ales and freshly prepared food at reasonable prices. The monthly changing menu, backed up by daily specials, might offer salad of soused sardines, baby pepper and ricotta; and beef bourguignon, deep fried cauliflower with horseradish and chive mash. All puddings are home made.

**Open** all wk 11.30-3 5.30-11 (Sun noon-3 7-10.30) Closed: 25-26 Dec & 1 Jan eve **Bar Meals** L served all wk 12-2.30 booking required D served Mon-Sat 7-10, Sun 7-9 booking required Av main course £11.95 **Restaurant** L served all wk 12-2.30 booking required D served Mon-Sat 7-10, Sun 7-9 booking required Av 3 course à la carte fr £5.95 ⊕ YOUNG & CO BREWERY PLC ◀ Youngs IPA, Special, Winter Warmer, Bombardier, Courage Directors. **Facilities** Children's portions Garden Parking

## EGHAM · Map 6 TQ07

### The Fox and Hounds ♥

**Bishopgate Rd, Englefield Green TW20 0XU**
☎ 01784 433098 📠 01784 438775
e-mail: thefoxandhounds@4cinns.co.uk
dir: *From village green left into Castle Hill Rd, then right into Bishopsgate Rd*

The Surrey border once ran through the centre of this pub on the edge of Windsor Great Park, convenient for walkers and riders. Features include a large garden, handsome conservatory and weekly jazz nights. Menus offer a range of daily-changing fish specials as well as dishes like orange and sesame chicken fillets on coriander and lime noodles, or roast pork with grain mustard glaze and parmesan crisps.

**Open** all wk ◀ Hogs Back Brewery Traditional English Ale, Brakspears Bitter. ♥ 8 **Facilities** Dogs allowed Garden Parking

## ELSTEAD · Map 6 SU94

### The Woolpack

**The Green, Milford Rd GU8 6HD** ☎ 01252 703106
e-mail: info@woolpackelstead.co.uk
dir: *A3 S, take Milford exit, follow signs for Elstead on B3001*

Now under new ownership, The Woolpack was originally a wool exchange dating back to the 17th century. The surrounding common land attracts ramblers galore, especially at lunchtime. In the carpeted bar, weaving shuttles and other remnants of the wool industry make

Save on Hotels. Book at theAA.com/hotel

SURREY 441 ENGLAND

ppealing features, as do the open log fires, low beams, igh-backed settles, window seats and spindle-backed hairs. A good range of cask-conditioned beers is offered.

pen all wk noon-3 5.30-11 (Sat-Sun noon-11) ar Meals L served Mon-Sat 12.2.30, Sun 12-4 D served on-Sat 7-9.30 Restaurant L served Mon-Sat 12.2.30, un 12-4 D served Mon-Sat 7-9.30 ⊕ PUNCH TAVERNS ◀ Greene King Abbot Ale, Hobgoblin, Deuchars, Spitfire, ondon Pride ♂ Old English. Facilities Children's nenu Children's portions Family room Dogs allowed arden Parking

## FARNHAM — Map 5 SU84

### PICK OF THE PUBS

## The Bat & Ball Freehouse ?

**15 Bat & Ball Ln, Boundstone GU10 4SA**
☎ **01252 792108**
e-mail: info@thebatandball.co.uk
dir: From A31 Farnham bypass follow signs for Birdworld. Left at Bengal Lounge into School Hill. At top over staggered x-rds into Sandrock Hill Rd. After 0.25m left into Upper Bourne Lane, signed

Tucked down a lane in a wooded valley south of Farnham, this 150-year-old inn is not that easy to find, but well worth hunting out. Hops for the local breweries in Farnham and Alton were grown in the valley, and originally the hop pickers were paid in the building that eventually became the pub. An enterprising tenant grasped the business opportunity that presented itself, and began to provide the pickers with ale, relieving them of some of their hard earned cash in the process! Very much a community pub, the interior features terracotta floors, oak beams, a roaring fire on colder days, and plenty of cricketing memorabilia. The lovely garden has a terrace with vine-topped pergola and a children's play fort. Expect six regularly changing cask-conditioned ales, a range of quaffable wines, and home-cooked food at reasonable prices. Starters and light meals might include a choice of avocado and crab claw meat with a lemon and dill mayonnaise; a platter of dips with olives, prosciutto ham, sundried tomatoes and breads to share; or deep-fried whitebait with home-made tartare sauce; while for a main course the cassoulet of guinea fowl, bacon and Toulouse sausage; home-made corned beef hash topped with poached eggs; grilled sea bass fillet; and Moroccan mixed bean and aubergine tagine served with herbed couscous and mint yoghurt dip are typical of the flavoursome dishes on offer. There's live music on the last Sunday of the month, and a Beer, Cider and Music Festival every June.

Open all day all wk 11-11 (Sun noon-10.30)
Bar Meals L served Mon-Sat 12-2.15, Sun 12-3 booking required D served Mon-Sat 7-9.30, Sun 6-8.30 booking required Av main course £10.50 ⊕ FREE HOUSE ◀ Youngs Bitter, Tongham TEA, Triple fff, Harvey's Sussex Bitter. ♀ 8 Facilities Children's menu Children's portions Play area Family room Dogs allowed Garden Parking

**See advert on page 437**

## FOREST GREEN — Map 6 TQ14

### PICK OF THE PUBS

## The Parrot Inn ?

**RH5 5RZ** ☎ **01306 621339** 📠 **01306 621255**
e-mail: drinks@theparrot.co.uk
dir: B2126 from A29 at Ockley, signed Forest Green

Nestling opposite the village green and cricket pitch in a rural hamlet, this attractive 17th-century building is in many ways the archetypal English inn. But in addition to the expected oak beams and huge fire, it has its own butchery, charcuterie and farm shop. The owners have a farm just a couple of miles away where they raise shorthorn cattle, Middle White pigs, Dorset sheep and Black Rock hens. The pub makes its own sausages, preserves and chutneys, and much of the menu uses these home-grown or home-made products. The dishes blend modern, traditional and European influences: baked Pisley Farm duck egg with creamed wild mushrooms and thyme, for example, followed by guinea fowl breast, celeriac and spinach dauphinoise with a bordelaise sauce. Not to be forgotten is a good range of real ales, which can be enjoyed in the bar or one of the four pub gardens.

Open all day all wk Bar Meals L served Mon-Sat 12-3, Sun 12-5 D served Mon-Sat 6-10 Av main course £12 Restaurant L served Mon-Sat 12-3, Sun 12-5 booking required D served Mon-Sat 6-10 booking required Av 3 course à la carte fr £20 ⊕ FREE HOUSE ◀ Ringwood Best, Youngs PA, Timothy Taylor Landlord, Ringwood Old Thumper, Dorking Brewery DB1. ♀ 14 Facilities Dogs allowed Garden Parking

## GUILDFORD — Map 6 SU94

## The Keystone ?

**3 Portsmouth Rd GU2 4BL** ☎ **01483 575089**
e-mail: drink@thekeystone.co.uk
dir: From Guildford rail station turn right. Cross 2nd pedestrian crossing, follow road downhill. past Savills Estate Agents. Pub 200yds on left

Once a run-down boozer, Mark and Kath Eleveld have transformed The Keystone into a stylish and modern town centre pub. From its outdoor seating areas to the wooden floors and leather sofas in the bar, it has a stylish, well-kept feel. Themed nights and live music are just some of things to look out for. Along with real ales and cider, and interesting cocktails, expect fairly priced, modern pub food including award-winning pies, bangers and mash, steak and chips and chilli con carne. On the special's

*The Keystone*

board you might find pan-fried fillets of sea bass with ratatouille.

Open all day all wk noon-11 (Fri-Sat noon-mdnt Sun noon-5) Closed: 25-26 Dec, 1 Jan Bar Meals L served all wk 12-3 D served Mon-Thu 6-9 Av main course £8 ◀ Black Sheep, 6X ♂ Westons Organic. ♀ 10 Facilities Children's portions Garden

## HASCOMBE — Map 6 TQ03

## The White Horse ?

**The Street GU8 4JA** ☎ **01483 208258** 📠 **01483 208200**
e-mail: pub@whitehorsehascombe.co.uk
dir: From Godalming take B2130. Pub on left 0.5m after Hascombe

Surrounded by picturesque walking country, this 16th-century building is unmissable in summer thanks to its flower-filled garden. A pristine, traditional interior with fine beers, popular family room and ample outdoor seating are three of its selling points; another is the high standard of its food. All meat is from organic pedigree breeds. A meal might include linguini with basil pesto and parmesan shavings followed by roasted best end of lamb with rosemary sauce. In addition the inn hosts food evenings as well as live music indoors and outdoors.

Open all day all wk Bar Meals Av main course £12 food served all day Restaurant Fixed menu price fr £14 Av 3 course à la carte fr £25 food served all day ⊕ PUNCH TAVERNS ◀ Harveys, Tribute, Altons Pride, Guest ales ♂ Old Rosie, Green Goblin, Koppaberg Pear. ♀ 11 Facilities Children's menu Children's portions Play area Family room Dogs allowed Garden Parking

## HASLEMERE — Map 6 SU93

## The Wheatsheaf Inn ★★★ INN

**Grayswood Rd, Grayswood GU27 2DE**
☎ **01428 644440** 📠 **01428 641285**
e-mail: thewheatsheaf@aol.com
web: www.thewheatsheafgrayswood.co.uk
dir: Exit A3 at Milford, A286 to Haslemere. Grayswood approx 7.5m N

A stunning display of hanging baskets takes the eye at this friendly, award-winning village inn set in the tranquil Surrey Hills; the magnificent viewpoint at Black Down, beloved of Alfred, Lord Tennyson, is nearby. You may be tempted to book B&B here by this or by the inviting menus of classics and specials - pan-fried pigeon

continued

## HASLEMERE *continued*

breasts on spinach, roasted fennel and couscous or home-made South Downs beef lasagne might feature – before relaxing with Sharp's Doom Bar beer in the peaceful garden.

*The Wheatsheaf Inn*

**Open** all wk 11-3 6-11 (Sun noon-3 7-10.30) **Bar Meals** L served all wk 12-2 booking required D served all wk 7-9.45 booking required Av main course £10.95 **Restaurant** L served all wk 12-2 booking required D served all wk 7-9.45 booking required ⊕ FREE HOUSE ◀ London Pride, Sharp's Doom Bar, Abbot Ale Hip Hop ♻ Thatchers. **Facilities** Children's menu Children's portions Dogs allowed Garden Parking **Rooms** 7

---

| **HINDHEAD** | Map 6 SU83 |

### Devil's Punchbowl Inn ♟

**London Rd GU26 6AG**
☎ **01428 606565** ▤ 01428 605713
e-mail: hotel@punchbowlhotels.co.uk
dir: *A3 N of Hindhead, opp National Trust car park for Devils Punch Bowl*

The hotel, which dates from the early 1800s, stands 900ft above sea level with wonderful views as far as London on a clear day. The 'punchbowl' is a large natural bowl in the ground across the road. The menu, while not large, has something for everybody, with chilli con carne, steak and Guinness pie, Surrey shepherds pie, sausage and mash, and hand-made burger with chunky chips.

**Open** all wk ◀ Bass, 6X, Tetleys, Bombardier. ♟ 15 **Facilities** Family room Garden Parking

---

| **LEIGH** | Map 6 TQ24 |

### The Plough ♟

**Church Rd RH2 8NJ** ☎ 01306 611348 ▤ 01306 611299
e-mail: sarah@theploughleigh.wanadoo.co.uk
dir: *Telephone for directions*

This white-painted, featherboarded, family-run country pub stands on the village green opposite the church. The low beams (it's OK, they're padded) in the lounge bar date from the late 15th century; the public bar, where you can play traditional pub games, is positively new by comparison, being only 111 years old. There is a bar menu, special boards and an à la carte in the small restaurant. Food runs from jacket potatoes and salads to braised lamb shank in redcurrant and mint gravy; and sea bass fillet with Champagne and asparagus sauce. Popular destination with walkers.

---

**Open** all wk 11-11 (Sun noon-11) **Bar Meals** food served all day **Restaurant** food served all day ⊕ HALL & WOODHOUSE ◀ Badger Best, Tanglefoot, Sussex Bitter. ♟ 11 **Facilities** Children's menu Children's portions Dogs allowed Garden Parking

---

| **LINGFIELD** | Map 6 TQ34 |

### PICK OF THE PUBS

### Hare and Hounds

**Common Rd RH7 6BZ** ☎ 01342 832351
e-mail: info@hareandhoundspublichouse.co.uk
dir: *From A22 follow signs for Lingfield Racecourse into Common Rd*

An 18th-century country pub close to Lingfield Park racecourse, the Hare and Hounds has great charm and character. Enjoy the relaxing atmosphere by the fire, the candlelit snug or just propping up the bar with a pint of Ruddles County. The pub has a good name for its modern and classic food. The owners have worked in the UK and France and developed some great seasonal recipes. Using local suppliers of produce where possible, the dinner menu may start with cauliflower velouté, almond croquette and curry oil; followed by stuffed smoked rabbit, cavalo nero, spaetzel and pistachio; or whole grilled sea bass, confit fennel, tomato and saffron dressing. Desserts run along the lines of baked lemon tart with blackcurrant jam and vanilla ice cream; and hot chocolate fondant, pistachio ice cream and caramelised nuts. The blackboard menu could offer honey roast ham, pickled pineapple and fried egg; or pan-fried beef bavette, fat chips and béarnaise sauce. Head for the split-level decked garden for a drink in the sun.

**Open** all day Closed: 1-5 Jan, Sun eve **Bar Meals** L served Mon-Sat 12-2.30 D served Mon-Sat 7-9.30 Av main course £10 **Restaurant** L served Mon-Sat 12-2.30 D served Mon-Sat 7-9.30 Av 3 course à la carte fr £25 ⊕ PUNCH TAVERNS ◀ Greene King IPA, Flowers Original, Guinness, London Pride, Ruddles County ♻ Stowford Press. **Facilities** Children's portions Dogs allowed Garden Parking

---

| **LONG DITTON** | Map 6 TQ16 |

### The Ditton ♟

**64 Ditton Hill Rd KT6 5JD** ☎ 020 8339 0785
e-mail: goodfood@theditton.co.uk
dir: *Telephone for directions*

Whilst at heart this rambling village pub remains a community local with beers from the likes of Sharp's and Young's, the main ambience leans towards a contemporary dining pub where families are particularly welcome. Light bites and ciabattas take the edge off an appetite, or stick with solid pub favourites like bangers 'n' mash or beef, ale and root vegetable stew. Also here is Long's Brasserie with more continental styled cuisine. The barbecue menu draws the crowds to the large garden on warm summer days.

---

**Open** all day all wk noon-11 **Bar Meals** L served all wk 12-9 D served all wk 12-9 Av main course £7 food served all day **Restaurant** L served Wed-Sun 12-9 booking required D served Wed-Sat 12-9 booking required Fixed menu price fr £15 Av 3 course à la carte fr £20 ⊕ ENTERPRISE INNS ◀ Bombardier, Youngs, Tanglefoot, Sharp's Doom Bar. ♟ 10 **Facilities** Children's menu Children's portions Play area Dogs allowed Garden Parking

---

| **MICKLEHAM** | Map 6 TQ15 |

### King William IV ♟

**Byttom Hill RH5 6EL** ☎ 01372 372590
dir: *From M25 junct 9, A24 signed to Dorking, pub just before Mickleham*

The former ale house, built in 1790 for workers on Lord Beaverbrook's estate, has a panelled snug and larger back bar with an open fire, cast iron tables and grandfather clock. The terraced garden, ideal for summer dining, offers panoramic views of the Mole Valley. The chef proprietor serves good food alongside real ales, with specials such as roast pheasant breast with red wine jus, and seared king scallops on crayfish in tomato sauce. An ideal location for outstanding local walks.

**Open** all wk Closed: 25 Dec ◀ Hogs Back TEA, Adnams Best, guest ales ♻ Stowford Press. ♟ 11 **Facilities** Garden Parking

---

### The Running Horses ♟

**Old London Rd RH5 6DU**
☎ **01372 372279** ▤ 01372 363004
e-mail: info@therunninghorses.co.uk
dir: *1.5m from M25 junct 9. Off A24 between Leatherhead & Dorking*

The Running Horses, now under new ownership, has been welcoming travellers for more than 400 years and has a history of sheltering highwaymen. It stands amid Natural Trust countryside close to Box Hill. The interior resonates with history, right down to the bare beams and real fires. Menus might offer salmon and smoked haddock fishcakes; garden pea and baby spinach risotto; sautéed steak and onion baguette; potted game and mushroom rillettes; and shellfish bisque with chive crème fraîche.

**Open** all wk 11.30-11 (Sun noon-10.30) Closed: 25-26 Dec, 31 Dec-1 Jan eve **Bar Meals** L served Mon-Fri 12-2.30, Sat-Sun 12-3 D served Mon-Sat 7-9.30, Sun 6.30-9 Av main course £11 **Restaurant** L served Mon-Fri 12-2.30, Sat-Sun 12-3 booking required D served Mon-

Sat 7-9.30, Sun 6.30-9 booking required Av 3 course à la carte fr £32 ⊕ FREE HOUSE ◀ Fuller's London Pride, Young's Bitter, HSB, Chiswick Ö Aspall. ₹ 9
**Facilities** Children's portions Dogs allowed Garden

## NEWDIGATE　　　　　　　Map 6 TQ14

### The Surrey Oaks

**Parkgate Rd RH5 5DZ**
☎ 01306 631200 ▤ 01306 631200
**e-mail:** ken@surreyoaks.co.uk
**dir:** From A24 follow signs to Newdigate, at T-junct turn left, pub 1m on left

Picturesque oak-beamed pub located one mile outside the village of Newdigate. Parts of the building date back to 1570, and it became an inn around the middle of the 19th century. There are two bars, one with an inglenook fireplace, as well as a restaurant area, patio and beer garden with boules pitch. The great selection of beers are mainly from micro-breweries. A typical specials board features Barnsley lamb chop with minted gravy, or grilled plaice with parsley butter. This family-friendly pub also has a children's menu and play area.

**Open** all wk 11.30-2.30 5.30-11 (Sat 11.30-3 6-11 Sun noon-10.30) **Bar Meals** L served Mon-Sat 12-2, Sun 12-2.30 D served Tue-Sat 6.30-9.30 Av main course £8 **Restaurant** L served Mon-Sat 12-2, Sun 12-2.30 D served Tue-Sat 6.30-9.30 Av 3 course à la carte fr £15.50 ⊕ ADMIRAL TAVERNS ◀ Harveys Sussex Best, Surrey Hills Ranmore Ale, rotating guest ales Ö Moles Black Rat, Weston's Country Perry. **Facilities** Children's menu Children's portions Play area Dogs allowed Garden Parking

## OCKHAM　　　　　　　　Map 6 TQ05

### The Black Swan ₹ NEW

**Old Ln KT11 1NG** ☎ 01932 862364
**e-mail:** theblackswan@geronimo-inns.co.uk
**dir:** M25 junct 10, A3 towards Guildford. Approx 2m turn left to Ockham

Pubs with this name tend to get called the Mucky Duck, but after Geronimo Inns bought this one locals became more respectful. Inside are rough sawn timbers, wooden rafters, unusual antique furnishings, great beers and wine, and good food at affordable prices. Using the best of local produce, dishes include Dexter rump or sirloin steak with hand-cut chips, field mushroom and peppercorn sauce; prawn and salmon penne pasta with white wine sauce; and aubergine and vegetable stack with tomato sauce.

**Open** all day all wk **Bar Meals** Av main course £8.50 food served all day **Restaurant** L served Mon-Thu & Sat 1-3, Fri 12-3, Sun 12-6 D served all wk 6-8 Av 3 course à la carte fr £18 ⊕ FREE HOUSE ◀ Shere Drop, Doom Bar, Bitburger, Guinness Ö Aspall. ₹ 28 **Facilities** Children's menu Children's portions Dogs allowed Garden Parking

## OCKLEY　　　　　　　　Map 6 TQ14

### PICK OF THE PUBS

## Bryce's at The Old School House ◉ ₹

**RH5 5TH** ☎ 01306 627430 ▤ 01306 628274
**e-mail:** fish@bryces.co.uk
**dir:** 8m S of Dorking on A29

Formerly a boarding school, this Grade II listed building dates back to 1750 and was bought by Bill Bryce nearly 20 years ago. He's passionate about fresh fish and offers a huge range, despite the location in rural Surrey. It's more of a restaurant than a pub, although there is a bar with its own interesting menu (duo of herring rollmops and jellied eels with horseradish mayonnaise; grilled whole sardines). The dishes on the restaurant menu are nearly all fish, with some non-fish daily specials. Options to start include warm crab and crayfish tart; herb-crumbed skate nobs on egg noodles with honey and hoi sin sauce. Main course examples are fillets of plaice on a warm salad of leeks, mushroom and kale; and Cajun spiced salmon on Puy lentils and caramelised Asian onions. Desserts such as steamed syrup pudding with spiced rum anglaise complete a rewarding experience.

**Open** noon-3 6-11 Closed: 25-26 Dec, 1 Jan, (Sun pm Nov, Jan-Feb) **Bar Meals** L served all wk 12-2.30 D served all wk 6-9.30 Av main course £10 **Restaurant** L served all wk 12-2.30 D served all wk 7-9.30 Fixed menu price fr £14 ⊕ FREE HOUSE ◀ London Pride, Horsham Bitter, John Smith's Smooth. ₹ 15 **Facilities** Children's portions Dogs allowed Parking

### The Kings Arms Inn ₹

**Stane St RH5 5TS** ☎ 01306 711224
**e-mail:** enquiries@thekingsarmsockley.co.uk
**dir:** From M25 junct 9 take A24 through Dorking towards Horsham, A29 to Ockley

The many charms of this heavily-beamed 16th-century inn include welcoming log fires, a priest hole, a friendly ghost, and an award-winning garden. Set in the picturesque village of Ockley and overlooked by the tower of Leith Hill, it's an ideal setting in which to enjoy a pint and home-cooked food. Using the best of local produce where possible, expect dishes like braised ham hock; rabbit and chicken casserole; pan-fried calves' liver with crispy bacon or confit of Gressingham duck leg. Puddings might include the chef's cheesecake of the day; baked lemon custard tart with stewed raspberries, or the cheese plate with local cheeses.

**Open** all wk noon-2.30 5-11 **Bar Meals** L served all wk 12-2.30 D served all wk 6-9.30 Av main course £10 **Restaurant** L served all wk 12-2.30 D served all wk 6-9.30 Av 3 course à la carte fr £25 ⊕ CROSSOAK INNS ◀ Horsham Best, Doom Bar Ö Stowford Press. ₹ 10 **Facilities** Children's menu Children's portions Garden Parking

## PIRBRIGHT　　　　　　Map 6 SU95

### The Royal Oak ₹

**Aldershot Rd GU24 0DQ** ☎ 01483 232466
**dir:** M3 junct 3, A322 towards Guildford, then A324 towards Aldershot

A genuine old world pub specialising in real ales (up to nine at any time), and well known for its glorious prize-winning garden. The Tudor cottage pub has an oak church door, stained glass windows and pew seating, and in winter there are welcoming log fires in the rambling bars. The menu may include smoked salmon and pesto, braised lamb shoulder, steak and ale pie, and penne pasta Alfredo, along with various specials.

**Open** all wk ◀ Flowers IPA, Hogs Back Traditional English Ale, Bass Ringwood Ale, Abbots Ales, Old Speckled Hen. ₹ 18 **Facilities** Dogs allowed Garden Parking

## RIPLEY　　　　　　　　Map 6 TQ05

### PICK OF THE PUBS

## The Talbot Inn ★★★★ INN ◉ ₹

**High St GU23 6BB**
☎ 01483 225188 ▤ 01483 211332
**e-mail:** info@thetalbotinn.com
**dir:** Telephone for directions

One of England's finest 15th-century coaching inns, The Talbot is said to have provided the stage for Lord Nelson and Lady Hamilton's love affair in 1798. Recently refurbished, but retaining its impressive historic features, the cosy beamed bar boasts open fires and real ales. In contrast, the chic dining room has a copper ceiling and modern glass conservatory extension. Good food blends pub classics like fish and chips or local sausages and mash with more innovative dishes like venison loin with chestnut purée and spiced pears, or brill paupiettes with creamed leeks and shellfish sauce. Finish with hot apple and rhubarb crumble and crème Anglaise. The 39 stylish bedrooms are smart and contemporary, ranging from beamed rooms in the inn to new-build rooms overlooking the garden. The pub is conveniently positioned just 20 minutes from Heathrow and Gatwick International airports.

**Open** all day all wk noon-11 (Sun noon-10) **Bar Meals** D served Mon-Sat 6-11, Sun 6-8.30 booking required Av main course £10 food served all day **Restaurant** L served all wk 12-3 booking required D served Mon-Sat 6-9.30 booking required Av 3 course à la carte fr £25 ⊕ MERCHANT INNS ◀ Shere Drop, IPA, Abbot Ale Ö Stowford Press. ₹ 27 **Facilities** Children's menu Dogs allowed Garden Parking **Rooms** 39

# PICK OF THE PUBS

## The Inn @ West End 🍷

**WEST END**      Map 6 SU96

**42 Guildford Rd GU24 9PW**
☎ **01276 858652**
e-mail: greatfood@the-inn.co.uk
web: www.the-inn.co.uk
dir: *On A322 towards Guildford. 3m from M3 junct 3, just beyond Gordon Boys rdbt*

Very much a destination gastro-pub, there's still room here for locals to pop in for a pint of Timothy Taylor Landlord or Black Sheep bitter and not feel out of place at the bar or enjoying a fine evening on the clematis-dressed terrace overlooking the garden and boules pitch. In just ten years, Gerry and Ann Price have created an establishment to match the most hyped restaurants in London, out-manoeuvring many of these with their regular specialist evenings featuring innovative fish, game and cooking-style presentations.

You'll find an open-plan, modern interior, with wooden floors, yellow walls, tasteful check fabrics, crisp linen-clothed tables in the dining area, an open fire, daily papers and magazines in the bar, and a relaxed and informal atmosphere. The kitchen makes good use of home-grown herbs, vegetables and pigs, and locally sourced ingredients, game shot by Gerry (the pub has its own game room and plucking machine), and fresh fish collected from the south coast in the pub's own chiller van.

An enthusiastic team of six chefs work their magic on an eye-opening menu of modern British cuisine. Luscious starters include strips of marinated game with a pomegranate and satsuma dressing or goujons of fresh British fish with tartare sauce, rouille and aioli. These serve to prepare you for mains of slowly braised game casserole in a redcurrant, herb and wine jus with red cabbage and dauphinoise potatoes; home raised saddleback pork loin with creamy potatoes, roasted winter vegetables and trotter jus, or maybe wild mushroom, chestnut and caramelised onion stroganoff with curly kale and wild rice. A final flourish could be South African vinegar pudding with boozy raisins and crème anglaise or an assault on the exceptional cheeseboard. Gerry's a respected oenophile, reflected in the remarkable list of bins (15 by the glass) that reaches into the hundreds.

**Open** all wk **Bar Meals** L served all wk 12-2.30 D served all wk 6-9.30 Av main course £6.50 **Restaurant** L served all wk 12-2.30 booking required D served all wk 6-9.30 booking required Fixed menu price fr £12.25 Av 3 course à la carte fr £30 ⊕ ENTERPRISE ◾ Timothy Taylor Landlord, Fuller's London Pride, Exmoor. 🍷 15 **Facilities** Dogs allowed Garden Parking

Save on Hotels. Book at theAA.com/hotel

SURREY – SUSSEX, EAST 445 ENGLAND

## SOUTH GODSTONE — Map 6 TQ34

# Fox & Hounds

Tilburstow Hill Rd RH9 8LY ☎ 01342 893474
dir: 4m from M25 junct 6

A pub since 1601, although parts of this old building date back to 1368. There's a large inglenook in the restaurant, and a real fire in the lower bar. If you're fond of fish it might lead to baked mackerel with rhubarb; monkfish medallions with cherry tomato beurre blanc; or dressed crab salad. Alternatives include beef Wellington; slow-roast gammon hock on pear, Stilton and sage mash; and rabbit pie. Outside, the large garden offers rural views.

Open all day all wk noon-11 (25 Dec noon-2)
Bar Meals food served all day Restaurant food served all day ⊕ GREENE KING ◀ All Greene King.
Facilities Children's menu Dogs allowed Garden Parking

## STAINES — Map 6 TQ07

# The Swan Hotel ♥

The Hythe TW18 3JB
☎ 01784 452494 ▤ 01784 461593
e-mail: swanhotel@fullers.co.uk
dir: Just off A308, S of Staines Bridge. 5m from Heathrow

This 18th-century inn stands just south of Staines Bridge and was once the haunt of river bargemen who were paid in tokens which could be exchanged at the pub for food and drink. It has a spacious, comfortable bar, and a menu based on traditional home-cooked food. Examples range from sausage and mash; pot-roast lamb shank; and steak and ale pie, to seafood risotto or vegetarian noodle bowl.

Open all wk 11-11 ◀ Fuller's London Pride, ESB, Discovery. ♥ 10 Facilities Dogs allowed Garden

## WEST END — Map 6 SU96

### PICK OF THE PUBS

# The Inn @ West End ♥

**See Pick of the Pubs on opposite page**

## WEST HORSLEY — Map 6 TQ05

### PICK OF THE PUBS

# The King William IV ♥

83 The Street KT24 6BG
☎ 01483 282318 ▤ 01483 282318
e-mail: kingbilly4th@aol.com
dir: On The Street off A246 (Leatherhead to Guildford)

Fresh flowers, welcoming staff and hand written specials boards greet you at this pretty village local. Named in honour of the monarch who relaxed England's brewing laws, the business was started by a miller, Edmund Collins, who knocked two cottages together to create an ale house. Fortunately, many of

the original Georgian features have been preserved, augmented by open winter fires and an airy conservatory restaurant. Today it's popular with walkers, not least for the large garden and terrace to the rear, with colourful tubs and floral baskets. Beers include Shere Drop and Courage Directors, with a dozen wines offered by the glass. The well-priced menu ranges over reliable choices of sandwiches, salads, burgers and jacket potatoes, backed up with hot choices like King Billy's curry and lamb's liver with smoked bacon and creamy mash. Leave room for dessert; apple, raisin and cinnamon crumble is a typical choice.

Open all day all wk 11.30am-mdnt (Sun noon-10.30)
Bar Meals L served all wk 12-3 D served Mon-Sat 6.30-9.30 Av main course £6.95 Restaurant L served all wk 12-3 D served Mon-Sat 6.30-9.30 Fixed menu price fr £8.50 Av 3 course à la carte fr £16.95
⊕ ENTERPRISE INNS ◀ Shere Drop, Courage Best, Courage Directors. ♥ 12 Facilities Children's menu Children's portions Family room Dogs allowed Garden Parking

## WITLEY — Map 6 SU93

# The White Hart

Petworth Rd GU8 5PH ☎ 01428 683695
e-mail: thewhitehartwitley@yahoo.co.uk
dir: From A3 follow signs to Milford, then A283 towards Petworth. Pub 2m on left

A delightfully warm and welcoming pub, built in 1380 as a hunting lodge for Richard II; the white hart became his personal emblem. Licensed since 1700, the three log fires, oak beams, Shepherd Neame ales and hearty portions of good value home-cooked food continue to attract. Soups, sandwiches, salads and pastas make a light lunch; steak and kidney pudding, venison casserole, and sausages and mash are some of the main course options. Families and dogs welcome.

Open 11-3 5.30-11 (Sat 11-11 Sun noon-6) Closed: Sun eve ◀ Shepherd Neame Master Brew, Spitfire, Guinness, seasonal ale. Facilities Play area Dogs allowed Garden Parking

## SUSSEX, EAST

## ALCISTON — Map 6 TQ50

### PICK OF THE PUBS

# Rose Cottage Inn ♥

BN26 6UW ☎ 01323 870377 ▤ 01323 871440
e-mail: ian@alciston.freeserve.co.uk
dir: Off A27 between Eastbourne & Lewes

This traditional Sussex pub, with roses round the door, is situated in a cul-de-sac village below the South Downs. Ramblers will find it a good base for long walks in unspoilt countryside, especially along the old traffic-free coach road to the south. The inn has been in the same family for over 40 years, and is well known for its good, 'fresh daily' home-cooked food. This includes the

best local meats, poultry and game, served in rambling dining rooms, in the bar or in the patio garden. The local butcher's sausages and steaks are particularly good. From the choices on the restaurant menu you might opt for confit of duck with Chinese spices; one of the chargrilled Sussex steaks; pan-fried Gressingham duck breasts with home-made cherry brandy sauce; or Moroccan style Firle partridge tagine with chickpeas, apricots and chilli. Lunchtime eating is primarily casual, with booking necessary only in the restaurant.

Open all wk 11.30-3 6.30-11 Closed: 25-26 Dec
Bar Meals L served all wk 12-2 D served all wk 7-9.30 Av main course £10 Restaurant L served all wk 12-2 booking required D served all wk 12-2 booking required Av 3 course à la carte fr £17.50 ⊕ FREE HOUSE ◀ Harveys Best, Dark Star ♂ Biddenden. ♥ 8 Facilities Dogs allowed Garden Parking

## ALFRISTON — Map 6 TQ50

# George Inn

High St BN26 5SY ☎ 01323 870319
e-mail: info@thegeorge-alfriston.com
dir: Telephone for directions

Splendid 14th-century, Grade II listed flint and half-timbered inn set in a magical South Downs village. The George boasts heavy oak beams, an ancient inglenook fireplace and a network of smugglers' tunnels leading from its cellars. The team of three chefs create delights such as seared salmon with lime hollandaise; marinated rump of lamb with herb and garlic sauce, or guinea fowl with port, thyme and wild mushrooms; follow with molten chocolate cake with black cherry and cream; or carrot and orange cake with vanilla ice cream.

Open all day all wk Closed: 25-26 Dec Bar Meals food served all day Restaurant booking required booking required food served all day ⊕ GREENE KING ◀ Greene King IPA, Abbot Ale, 2 guests. Facilities Children's menu Children's portions Dogs allowed Garden

# The Sussex Ox ♥

Milton St BN26 5RL ☎ 01323 870840
e-mail: mail@thesussexox.co.uk
dir: Off A27 between Wilmington & Drusillas. Follow brown signs to pub

Drink deeply of old Sussex here, with the wonderful, match-boarded old bar rooms, wood and sealed-brick floors oozing character and a lawned beer garden looking out to that famous Sussex character, the Long Man of Wilmington. Dine in the bar, the Garden Room, or the more formal Dining Room; the daily-changing menu relies on the best local materials; perhaps slow-roast belly of pork with apple and sausage cassoulet or local game mixed grill with a red wine sauce. Bar snacks and Sussex Cheddar ploughman's are also available, perhaps washed down with the pub's own Oxhead Bitter from Dark Star Brewery or any of 17 wines by the glass.

*continued*

**ALFRISTON** *continued*

**Open** all wk 11.30-3 6-11 Closed: 25-31 Dec **Bar Meals** L served all wk 12-2 booking required D served all wk 6-9 booking required Av main course £9.50 **Restaurant** L served all wk 12-2 booking required D served all wk 6-9 booking required Av 3 course à la carte fr £20 ⊞ FREE HOUSE ◀ Harveys Best, Dark Star Oxhead, Golden Gate, Hop Back Summer Lightning, Crouch Vale Brewers Gold ♂ Westons Perry. ♟ 17 **Facilities** Children's portions Family room Dogs allowed Garden Parking

---

### ASHBURNHAM PLACE      Map 6 TQ61

## Ash Tree Inn

**Brownbread St TN33 9NX** ☎ **01424 892104**
**dir:** *From Eastbourne take A271 at Boreham Bridge towards Battle. Next left, follow pub signs*

The Ash Tree is a friendly old pub with three open fires, plenty of exposed beams and a traditional local atmosphere. With a great choice of real ales, bar food includes ploughman's, salads and sandwiches, while the restaurant serves steaks, local lamb, steak and ale pie, or salmon in a variety of sauces. Daily specials chalked on the blackboard add to the choice, and there's always a roast on Sundays.

**Open** noon-4 7-11 (Sat-Sun 11.30am-mdnt) Closed: Mon **Bar Meals** L served Tue-Sun 12-3 booking required D served Tue-Sun 7-9 booking required **Restaurant** L served Tue-Sun 12-3 booking required D served Tue-Sun 7-9 booking required ⊞ FREE HOUSE ◀ Harveys Best, Greene King Old Speckled Hen, Brakspear Bitter, guest ales. **Facilities** Dogs allowed Garden Parking

---

### BERWICK      Map 6 TQ50

### PICK OF THE PUBS

## The Cricketers Arms ♟

**BN26 6SP** ☎ **01323 870469** 📠 **01323 871411**
**e-mail:** pbthecricketers@aol.com
**dir:** *Off A27 between Polegate & Lewes, follow signs for Berwick Church*

A traditional flint and stone cottage pub in beautiful gardens close to many popular walks, including the South Downs Way running along the crest of the chalk scarp to the south. In the 16th century it was two farmworkers' cottages, then an alehouse for 200 years. Harvey's of Lewes, Sussex's oldest brewery, bought it around 50 years ago and turned it into a 'proper' pub. Three beamed, music-free rooms with stone floors and open fires are simply furnished with old pine furniture. Home-made food includes starters such as duck and pistachio terrine, and crayfish tail cocktail. Sharing options include the popular Spanish platter, with Serrano ham, Gran Vera chorizo, salchichon sausage, manchego cheese, olives and sun-blushed tomatoes. Main courses include fresh haddock in beer batter, and pork and herb sausages. Nearby is Charleston Farmhouse, the country rendezvous of the London writers, painters and intellectuals known as the Bloomsbury Group, and scene of an annual literary festival.

**Open** all wk Closed: 25 Dec **Bar Meals** L served Mon-Sun 12-2.15 (Etr-Sep 12-9) booking required D served Mon-Sun 6-9 (Etr-Sep 12-9) booking required Av main course £9 food served all day ⊞ HARVEYS OF LEWES ◀ Harveys Best Bitter, Pale, Armada ♂ Thatchers. ♟ 12 **Facilities** Children's portions Family room Dogs allowed Garden Parking

---

### BLACKBOYS      Map 6 TQ52

## The Blackboys Inn ♟

**Lewes Rd TN22 5LG**
☎ **01825 890283** 📠 **01825 890283**
**e-mail:** blackboys-inn@btconnect.com
**dir:** *From A22 at Uckfield take B2102 towards Cross in Hand. Or from A267 at Esso service station in Cross in Hand take B2102 towards Uckfield. Village in 1.5m at junct of B2102 & B2192*

An eye-catching, part-weatherboarded 14th century rural retreat, named after the apprentices to local charcoal-burners who ended each day sooty and thirsty. Much rustic character is retained, together with contemporary comforts, whilst outside are rambling grounds and an orchard. Vegetables come from the inn's market garden, game from local shoots and estates and fish from Rye and Hastings. Keep an eye out for scallops and black pudding with pea and red onion purée or pigeon breasts on a bed of lentils with Chianti sauce. There is a fabulous function room available.

**Open** all day all wk noon-mdnt **Bar Meals** L served Mon-Fri 12-3, Sat 12-10, Sun 12-9 D served Sun-Mon 6-9, Tue-Sat 6-10 Av main course £8.50 **Restaurant** L served Mon-Fri 12-3, Sat 12-10, Sun 12-9 D served Sun-Mon 6-9, Tue-Sat 6-10 Av 3 course à la carte fr £25 ⊞ HARVEYS OF LEWES ◀ Harveys Sussex Best Bitter, Sussex Hadlow, Sussex XXXX Old Ale, seasonal. ♟ 15 **Facilities** Children's portions Dogs allowed Garden Parking

---

### BRIGHTON & HOVE      Map 6 TQ30

## The Basketmakers Arms

**12 Gloucester Rd BN1 4AD**
☎ **01273 689006** 📠 **01273 682300**
**e-mail:** bluedowd@hotmail.co.uk
**dir:** *From Brighton station main entrance 1st left (Gloucester Rd). Pub on right at bottom of hill*

This Victorian corner pub in the North Laine area of the city has had the same landlord for 23 years. At least eight real ales are offered, 90-100 malt whiskies and a large selection of vodkas and gins. All the food is made on the premises from locally sourced produce, organic where possible. The home-made burgers, including a veggie version, are famously local, plus there is at least one seafood special per day with fish sourced straight from the local fishermen.

**Open** all day all wk 11-11 (Fri-Sat 11am-mdnt Sun noon-11) **Bar Meals** L served Mon-Thu 12-8.30, Fri-Sat 12-6, Sun 12-5 D served Mon-Thu 12-8.30, Fri-Sat 12-6, Sun 12-5 Av main course £7.50 food served all day ⊞ FULLERS BREWERY ◀ Fuller's HSB, Butser Bitter, London Pride, ESB & Discovery, seasonal ales. **Facilities** Dogs allowed

---

## The Chimney House ♟

**28 Upper Hamilton Rd BN1 5DF** ☎ **01273 556708**
**e-mail:** info@chimneyhousebrighton.co.uk
**dir:** *Telephone for directions*

This is primarily a family-friendly pub serving the local community, but word of mouth has spread its popularity beyond the neighbourhood. In addition to reliable Harveys ales, the food is fresh, seasonal, and bought locally if possible. You'll find different menus for lunch and dinner; children have their own selections, and Sunday roasts feature prime Sussex pork, lamb and beef. Choices in the evening might include wood pigeon salad; Jerusalem artichoke risotto; and grilled Dover sole with lemon and sorrel sauce.

**Open** noon-3 5-11 (Sat noon-11 Sun noon-8) Closed: 25 Dec 1 Jan, Mon **Bar Meals** L served Tue-Fri 12-2.30, Sat 12-4, Sun 12-6 D served Tue-Sat 6-9.45 Av main course £9 **Restaurant** L served Tue-Fri 12-2.30, Sat 12-4, Sun 12-6 booking required D served Tue-Sat 6-9.45 booking required Av 3 course à la carte fr £20 ⊞ FREE HOUSE ◀ Harvey's Sussex Best Bitter, Guinness, Staropramen, Kirin Ichiban ♂ Aspall, Westons. ♟ 22 **Facilities** Children's menu Children's portions Dogs allowed

---

### PICK OF THE PUBS

## The Greys

**105 Southover St BN2 9UA** ☎ **01273 680734**
**e-mail:** chris@greyspub.com
**dir:** *0.5m from St Peters Church in Hanover area of Brighton*

Painted an eye-catching turquoise and described by the landlord as a 'shoebox', The Greys delights in its role as a thriving community pub in the bohemian area of Hanover in central Brighton. A compact back-street local, stripped wood and flagstone floors and timber panelled walls give the sense of a country pub in the town, and with the wood-burning stove glowing in the fireplace, there is no finer place to relax with a pint of Harveys bitter or a Breton cider. There is a great selection of Belgian beers, too, and annual Sussex and Belgian beer festivals. Former Claridge's chef Roz Batty tantalises the tastebuds with an eclectic, ever-changing menu based on local, seasonal produce, so expect anything from pig's ear goujons with sweet chilli sauce to baked herb polenta with roast red onion, field mushroom, Swiss chard and walnut dressing. The Greys is also known for its live country/folk/bluegrass music on Monday nights, featuring many leading artistes.

**Open** 4-11 (Sat noon-mdnt Sun noon-11) **Bar Meals** L served Tue-Thu & Sat 6-9 Av main course £10 **Restaurant** L served Sun 12-4.30 D served Tue-Thu & Sat 6-9 Av 3 course à la carte fr £20 ⊞ ENTERPRISE INNS ◀ Timothy Taylor Landlord, Harveys Best Bitter ♂ Stowford Press, Westons Organic, Cidre Breton. **Facilities** Dogs allowed Parking

## The Market Inn ★★ INN

**1 Market St BN1 1HH**
☎ 01273 329483 📠 01273 777227
e-mail: marketinn@reallondonpubs.com
dir: *In The Lanes area, 50mtrs from junct of North St & East St*

Set in the historic Lanes area, this lively Victorian corner pub has had the same landlord for over 22 years. This inn is located a short walk from the Brighton Pavilion, seafront and pier. A traditional English menu is served all day along with local and regional ales, and a wide list of international wines. All the food is made on the premises from locally sourced produce. If you would like to stay over and enjoy this famous seaside city, there are two attractively decorated en suite rooms available, with a separate guest entrance.

**Open** all wk 11-11 (Fri-Sat 11am-mdnt Sun noon-10.30) **Bar Meals** L served Mon-Sat 11-9, Sun 12-6 D served Mon-Sat 11-9, Sun 12-6 Av main course £8 food served all day ⊕ SCOTTISH COURAGE ◀ Harveys, Wells Bombardier, Spitfire. **Facilities** Children's portions Dogs allowed **Rooms** 2

### CHAILEY　　　　Map 6 TQ31

## The Five Bells Restaurant and Bar

**East Grinstead Rd BN8 4DA**
☎ 01825 722259 📠 01825 723368
e-mail: info@fivebellschailey.co.uk
dir: *5m N of Lewes on A275*

With origins in the 15th century and serving ale since the 17th, this country pub cum wine bar cum smart restaurant has many original features, including a large inglenook fireplace. It's handy for Sheffield Park, the Bluebell Railway, Plumpton racecourse and walks around Chailey. The highly qualified kitchen team create modern European dishes rooted in English tradition from fresh, organic and free-range ingredients – maybe vegetable pakora followed by grilled sea bream with mussel and saffron cream sauce. Friday evenings host live jazz, and in summer the large bar terrace and secluded restaurant garden come into their own.

**Open** noon-3 6-11 (Sun-Mon noon-3) Closed: Sun & Mon eve **Bar Meals** L served all wk 12-2.30 D served Tue-Thu 6-9, Fri-Sat 6-9.30 Av main course £9.95 **Restaurant** L served all wk 12-2.30 D served Tue-Thu 6-9, Fri-Sat 6.9.30 ⊕ ENTERPRISE INNS ◀ Harvey's Best, Youngs Special Ö Stowford Press. **Facilities** Children's menu Dogs allowed Garden Parking

### CHIDDINGLY　　　　Map 6 TQ51

## The Six Bells

**BN8 6HE** ☎ 01825 872227
dir: *E of A22 between Hailsham & Uckfield. Turn opp Golden Cross PH*

Inglenook fireplaces and plenty of bric-a-brac are to be found at this large free house which is where various veteran car and motorbike enthusiasts meet on club

nights. The jury in the famous Onion Pie Murder trial sat and deliberated in the bar before finding the defendant guilty. Exceptionally good value bar food includes French onion soup; hock of ham, French bread and beans; chilli con carne; steak and kidney pie; ravioli with a spicy sauce; and lentil, leek and mushroom loaf. Enjoy the fortnightly popular folk and blues evenings.

**Open** all wk 10-3 6-11 (Fri-Sun all day) **Bar Meals** L served all wk 12-2.30 (Fri-Sun all day) D served all wk 6-10 (Fri-Sun all day) Av main course £6 **Restaurant** L served all wk 12-2.30 (Fri-Sun all day) D served all wk 6-10 (Fri-Sun all day) ⊕ FREE HOUSE ◀ Courage Directors, Harveys Best. **Facilities** Family room Dogs allowed Garden Parking

### COOKSBRIDGE　　　　Map 6 TQ41

## PICK OF THE PUBS

## The Rainbow Inn ♥

**Resting Oak Hill BN8 4SS**
☎ 01273 400334 📠 01273 401667
e-mail: enquires@rainbowsussex.co.uk
dir: *3m outside Lewes on A275 towards Haywards Heath*

Built of brick and flint and making the most of its tree-sheltered corner site, the 17th-century Rainbow boasts a sun-trap enclosed rear terrace and grassy beer garden with views to the South Downs; the pub is right on the edge of the newly designated South Downs National Park. It has seen use as a film location, but its starring role remains that of a warm and welcoming country local with a huge reputation as a destination dining pub. On cooler days, head inside and cosy-up by the blazing fire in the rustic bar, where regulars chinwag over pints of their favourite tipple Harvey's Bitter, or guests such as beers from Sussex's Dark Star brewery. Spreading from this heart of the pub are three warmly decorated dining areas, all sporting wooden floors, an eclectic mix of tables and chairs, tasteful artwork, all creating a most relaxing atmosphere. There's an impressive menu, complemented by busy chalk-boards with specials drawing on produce with a very local pedigree: game from the enclosing Conyboro Estate, fresh fish from Newhaven, meats from nearby Holmansbridge and lamb from Ditchling. Commence with a warm salad of quail eggs, black pudding, pancetta and raspberry vinaigrette before settling in with cider braised pork belly, root vegetable mash and spiced sausage and pearl barley casserole; seafood connoisseurs will enjoy pan roasted fillet of haddock, dill and vermouth borlotti beans and crab bisque. A comprehensive wine list is tilted to old world standards, but with a good nod to new world bins. If you're celebrating or looking for intimate spaces, then upstairs are two charming little private dining rooms.

**Open** all day all wk noon-11 **Bar Meals** L served all wk 12-3 D served all wk 6.30-10 Av main course £7 **Restaurant** L served all wk 12-3 D served all wk 6.30-10 Fixed menu price fr £12.50 Av 3 course à la carte fr £30 ⊕ STERLING PUB COMPANY ◀ Harveys Best Bitter, Guinness, Dark Star Ö Stowford Press. ♥ 10 **Facilities** Children's menu Children's portions Dogs allowed Garden Parking

### COWBEECH　　　　Map 6 TQ61

## PICK OF THE PUBS

## The Merrie Harriers ♥

**BN27 4JQ** ☎ 01323 833108 📠 01323 833108
e-mail: ben@sussexcountrytaverns.co.uk
dir: *Off A271, between Hailsham & Herstmonceux*

The striking appearance of this Grade II listed, white clapboarded village inn, built in 1624 continues inside, with a wealth of oak beams and huge inglenook fireplace taking centre stage. Outside, the terrace overlooks an acre of the Weald where the pub's tug-of-war team practices – members have represented England; here too is the home allotment where much fresh produce is grown to enhance the daily-changing menu which relies heavily on local organic raw materials whenever possible. Guests sampling the ever-reliable Harvey's beers or 10 wines by the glass can cast their gaze on a menu boasting pan-fried pigs' cheeks with The Merrie Harriers chilli relish and toasted baguette starter, leading to a mains choice featuring roast cod with Jerusalem artichoke mash, steamed spinach and lemon oil or twice-cooked Sussex pork belly, Lyonnaise potatoes, fine beans and apple sauce.

**Open** all wk Mon-Thurs 11.30-3 6-12 (Fri-Sun all day) **Bar Meals** L served all wk 12-2.30 D served all wk 6.30-9 **Restaurant** L served all wk 12-2.30 D served all wk 6.30-9 ⊕ FREE HOUSE ◀ Harveys, Timothy Taylor, W J King Ö Stowford Press. ♥ 10 **Facilities** Children's menu Children's portions Dogs allowed Garden Parking

### DANEHILL　　　　Map 6 TQ42

## PICK OF THE PUBS

## The Coach and Horses ♥

**RH17 7JF** ☎ 01825 740369 📠 01825 740369
dir: *From East Grinstead, S through Forest Row on A22 to junct with A275 (Lewes road), right on A275, 2m to Danehill, left onto School Lane, 0.5m, pub on left*

The cough of a distant steam engine on the Bluebell Railway may drift across the lovely countryside in which The Coach and Horses is set. The Victorian landed gentry hereabouts built an alehouse and stabling to serve local estates; from this has developed a welcoming food-oriented pub which also strives successfully to be the village local. It's a popular place to sit in the tranquil gardens (one is 'adults only') and drink in both local beers and views to Ashdown Forest and the South Downs; inside, vaulted ceilings, panelling and stone and wood flooring add to the charm. The menu is strong on surf, turf and game, with fish fresh daily from Seaford, pheasant, rabbit and venison from local estates and lamb from a neighbouring farm. Typical choices may be smoked Rye Bay whiting and saffron tagliatelle with sweet chilli and parmesan, or slow-braised Ashdown venison with confit celeriac, baby turnips and mashed potatoes.

*continued*

**DANEHILL** *continued*

**Open** all wk 11.30-3 6-11 (Sat-Sun 12-11) Closed: 26 Dec **Bar Meals** L served all wk 12-2, Sat-Sun 12-2.30 D served Mon-Fri 7-9, Sat 7-9.30 Av main course £12 **Restaurant** L served all wk 12-2, Sat-Sun 12-2.30 D served Mon-Fri 7-9, Sat 7-9.30 Av 3 course à la carte fr £24 ⊕ FREE HOUSE ◀ Harveys Best & Old Ale, Hepworth, WJ King & Co, Dark Star ♻ Stowford Press, Black Rat Scrumpy. ⬤ 8 **Facilities** Children's menu Children's portions Play area Dogs allowed Garden Parking

---

### DITCHLING                           Map 6 TQ31

## PICK OF THE PUBS

### The Bull ★★★★ INN ⬤

*See Pick of the Pubs on opposite page*

---

### EAST CHILTINGTON              Map 6 TQ31

## The Jolly Sportsman ⬤

**Chapel Ln BN7 3BA ☎ 01273 890400** 🖶 **01273 890400**
**e-mail:** thejollysportsman@mistral.co.uk
*dir: From Lewes take A275, left at Offham onto B2166 towards Plumpton, take Novington Ln, after approx 1m left into Chapel Ln*

Secluded and romantic, this sympathetically upgraded dining inn is tucked away down a quiet no-through road surrounded by downland. The bar retains some of the character of a Victorian ale house, with guest ales, unusual bottled beers, selection of malts and cocktails on offer. The dining room strikes a cool, modern pose; a terrace with Moroccan-tiled tables overlooks the garden. Typical carte dishes are soused mackerel with new potato salad; rump of Ditchling lamb with mash and buttered kale; and tarte Tatin with vanilla ice cream. Fixed price lunch, dinner, Sunday lunch and children's menus are also available.

**Open** all wk (Sat all day) Closed: 25-26 Dec **Bar Meals** L served Mon-Sat 12.15-2.30, Sun 12.15-3 D served Mon-Thu & Sun 7-9.30, Fri-Sat 7-10 Av main course £12 **Restaurant** L served Mon-Sat 12.15-2.30, Sun 12.15-3 booking required D served all wk 7-9.30, Fri-Sat 7-10, Sun 7-9 booking required Fixed menu price fr £12 Av 3 course à la carte fr £25 ⊕ FREE HOUSE ◀ Dark Star Hophead, Guest ales ♻ Gwynt-y-draig. ⬤ 14 **Facilities** Children's menu Children's portions Play area Dogs allowed Garden Parking

---

### FLETCHING                          Map 6 TQ42

## PICK OF THE PUBS

### The Griffin Inn ⬤

**TN22 3SS ☎ 01825 722890** 🖶 **01825 722810**
**e-mail:** info@thegriffininn.co.uk
*dir: M23 junct 10 to East Grinstead, then A22, then A275. Village signed on left, 15m from M23*

Few pubs can boast the view that guests at The Griffin enjoy from the huge, landscaped gardens here; across towards Ashdown Forest, the Sussex Downs and the

Ouse Valley, whilst steam buffs will delight in the proximity of the Bluebell Railway. This imposing Grade II listed inn has served lucky villagers for four centuries; it effortlessly oozes charm with its beams, panelling, settles, log fires and bar groaning beneath handpumps dispensing the best of local ales, and a generous wine list. Walkers and cyclists arriving to join destination diners will revel in the terrific menu which absorbs the freshest of local produce; venison, beef and game from local farms, sea fish from Rye and greens from Fletching's own market gardens. On offer may be squid, parsley and cannelloni bean stew; country terrine of rabbit, pigeon breast and pork with peach chutney; beer-battered Rye Bay cod, tartare, minted peas and home-made chips, ending with Chocolate nemesis with griottine cherries!

**Open** all wk noon-11 Closed: 25 Dec **Bar Meals** L served Mon-Fri 12-2.30, Sat-Sun 12-3 D served all wk 7-9.30 Av main course £17.50 **Restaurant** L served Mon-Fri 12-2.30, Sat-Sun 12-3 booking required D served Mon-Sat 7-9.30 booking required Fixed menu price fr £31.50 Av 3 course à la carte fr £30 ⊕ FREE HOUSE ◀ Harvey Best, Kings of Horsham, Hepworths. ⬤ 16 **Facilities** Children's menu Children's portions Play area Dogs allowed Garden Parking

---

### GUN HILL                            Map 6 TQ51

## PICK OF THE PUBS

### The Gun Inn ⬤

**TN21 0JU ☎ 01825 872361**
**e-mail:** enquiries@thegunhouse.co.uk
*dir: 5m S of Heathfield, 1m off A267 towards Gun Hill. 4m off A22 between Uckfield & Hailsham*

A lovely old building and former courthouse set in delightful East Sussex countryside, with extensive views from a pretty terrace and garden. Wood dominates the interior, with beams, a beautiful wooden floor, and lots of hideaway places for quiet eating and drinking. A separate panelled dining room with a stunning fireplace is ideal for private parties. Three deli board selections can be shared by a gathering of friends - the fish board, for example, includes anchovies, prawn cocktail, cured salmon crostini, marinated squid and rolled mop herrings. A winter menu might include home-made game terrine with red onion chutney; locally reared Limousin rib-eye steak with chunky chips; Harvey's beer battered hake, chips and mushy peas; braised lamb shank with tomato and rosemary sauce; and warm chocolate fondant and honeycomb ice cream. The Old Coach House behind The Gun has been transformed into a farmer's market offering a wide selection of fresh local fruits and vegetables, organic foods, fish and meats.

**Open** noon-3 6-11 (Sat-Sun noon-11) **Bar Meals** L served Mon-Sat 12-3, Sun 12-8 D served Mon-Sat 6-9.30, Sun 12-8 Av main course £8 **Restaurant** L served Mon-Sat 12-3, Sun 12-8 D served Mon-Sat 6-9.30, Sun 12-8 Fixed menu price fr £10 Av 3 course à la carte fr £22 ⊕ FREE HOUSE ◀ Harveys, Guinness, Youngs ♻ Biddenden. ⬤ 14 **Facilities** Children's menu Play area Dogs allowed Garden Parking

---

### HARTFIELD                           Map 6 TQ43

## Anchor Inn

**Church St TN7 4AG ☎ 01892 770424**
*dir: On B2110*

A 14th-century inn at the heart of Winnie the Pooh country, deep within the scenic Ashdown Forest. Inside are stone floors enhanced by a large inglenook fireplace. Sandwiches and salads are among the bar snacks, while for something more substantial you could try whole Dover sole; grilled pork loin on a bed of spaghetti; or medallions of beef fillet. Puddings include crème brûlée, and chocolate and ginger torte with whiskey cream.

**Open** all day all wk **Bar Meals** L served all wk 12-2 booking required D served all wk 6-10 booking required **Restaurant** L served all wk 12-2 booking required D served all wk 6-10 booking required ⊕ FREE HOUSE ◀ Harveys Sussex Best Bitter, Larkins. **Facilities** Family room Dogs allowed Garden Parking

---

## PICK OF THE PUBS

### The Hatch Inn ⬤

*See Pick of the Pubs on page 450*

---

### ICKLESHAM                           Map 7 TQ81

## The Queen's Head ⬤

**Parsonage Ln TN36 4BL**
**☎ 01424 814552** 🖶 **01424 814766**
*dir: Between Hastings & Rye on A259. Pub in village on x-rds near church*

Full of exposed oak beams, this award-winning 17th-century tile-hung pub enjoys a magnificent view across the Brede valley to Rye. The traditional atmosphere has been preserved, with vaulted ceilings, large inglenook fireplaces, church pews, old farm implements, and a bar from the old Midland Bank in Eastbourne. A great fund-raiser for local and national charities, landlord Ian Mitchell keeps his customers happy with at least six real ales and a menu of home-made pies, curries, all-day breakfasts and grills. Gardens include a new play area for children, and a boules pitch for mum and dad.

**Open** all wk 11-11 (Sun 11-10.30) **Bar Meals** L served Mon-Fri 12-2.30, Sat-Sun 12-9.30 D served Mon-Fri 6-9.30, Sat-Sun 12-9.30 Av main course £8.95 ⊕ FREE HOUSE ◀ Rother Valley Level Best, Greene King Abbot Ale, Harveys Best, Dark Star, Ringwood Fortyniner ♻ Biddenden, Westons Old Rosie. **Facilities** Children's menu Children's portions Play area Garden Parking

# PICK OF THE PUBS

## The Bull ★★★★INN ♛

**DITCHLING** Map 6 TQ31

**2 High St BN6 8TA**
☎ **01273 843147** 📠 **01273 843147**
**e-mail:** info@thebullditchling.com
**web:** www.thebullditchling.com
**dir:** *S on M23/A23 5m. N of Brighton follow signs to Pyecombe/Hassocks then signs to Ditchling, 3m*

Low timber beams, open fires and deep leather sofas characterise this stylishly-converted free house in the heart of Ditchling village. The Bull is one of the oldest buildings in the village, and has been welcoming travellers and locals for over 500 years. It dates from 1563, when it was used as an overnight resting place for the monks who kept a medicinal herb garden on what is now the village green. Beer was brewed here until 1861, in a brew house attached to the main building. The pub then saw a succession of lively owners, and had an uncertain future until Dominic and Vanessa Worrall rescued it in 2003. Now, real ale lovers can quaff four top-notch beers, including the local Harveys Best, leaving wine drinkers to enjoy 18 regularly-changing wines by the glass.

The Bull offers affordable daily-changing menus with gourmet British food and lighter vegetarian fare, all cooked to order. A grazing board menu of dishes to share helps to fill the odd corners, with a choice of traditional roasts on Sundays. There's also a dedicated menu for children. 'Small plates' include choices like mackerel fillet with pea and mint crushed new potatoes; marinated pigeon with mango salad and raspberry dressing; and courgette, aubergine and pesto tartlet with red pepper coulis. 'Large plates' range from roasted winter vegetable crumble with pistachio crust to venison haunch with sauté sweet potatoes and red wine jus. Round things off with chocolate and orange cheesecake, or pear and cardamom tarte Tatin.

Eat and drink wherever you like – on farmhouse chairs at scrubbed wooden tables in the bar; in the cosy snug; or soak up the views of the South Downs from the terrace and large garden. There are four individually-designed bedrooms available.

**Open** all day all wk 11-11 (Sun noon-10.30) **Bar Meals** L served Mon-Fri 12-2.30, Sat 12-3, Sun 12-9 D served Mon-Fri 6-9.30, Sat 6-9.30, Sun 12-9 🍺 FREE HOUSE 🛢 Harveys Best, Timothy Taylor Landlord, Hop Back Summer Lightning, Dark Star. ♛ 18 **Facilities** Children's menu Play area Dogs allowed Garden Parking **Rooms** 4

# PICK OF THE PUBS

## The Hatch Inn ♥

**HARTFIELD**                    Map 6 TQ43

**Coleman's Hatch TN7 4EJ**
☎ 01342 822363   📄 01342 822363
**e-mail:** nickad@bigfoot.com
**dir:** *A22, 14m, left at Forest Row rdbt, 3m to Colemans Hatch, right by church. Straight on at next junct, pub on right*

This picturesque 15th-century free house stands on the northern fringes of Ashdown Forest just a mile or so from Poohsticks Bridge, immortalised in A.A. Milne's *Winnie the Pooh* stories. Reputedly dating from 1430, the building was converted in the 18th century from three cottages, probably used by workers at the local water-driven hammer mill. The pub is named after one of the hatches, or gates, into Ashdown Forest, and at one time is thought to have been a smugglers' haunt with links to the notorious Captain Kidd. There are two large beer gardens for alfresco summer dining, one of which enjoys views out over the forest.

Quality ingredients are sourced locally, and head chef Greg Palmer produces exciting menus that include a good selection of light bites and traditional dishes. Lunchtime sandwiches are made using locally-baked malt crunch or thick sliced 'Village Bakery' bread, with fillings like brie and apple, and crayfish tail with Marie Rose sauce. More substantial appetites might choose from home-made steak, Guinness and field mushroom pie with creamed potatoes and fresh vegetables; or traditional hot chicken Caesar salad with crispy bacon, warmed Parmesan croutons and Caesar dressing.

Booking is essential in the evenings, when you might be tempted by starters like chicken liver parfait with warmed French toasts and home-made grape chutney, or seared tuna loin with fresh pineapple salsa and sweet basil oil dressing. Follow on with main course options such as locally-reared new season lamb with dauphinoise potatoes and a port and redcurrant reduction; or leek, garden peas and spinach risotto, finished with white wine, cream and Parmesan shavings. For dessert, try fresh treacle tart with vanilla custard or cream; or Cointreau and orange panacotta with a compote of berries.

**Open** all wk 11.30-3 5.30-11 (Sat-Sun all day) Closed: 25 Dec
**Bar Meals** L served all wk 12-2.15 D served Mon-Thu 7-9.15, Fri-Sat 7-9.30 booking required **Restaurant** L served all wk 12-2.15 D served Mon-Thu 7-9.15, Fri-Sat 7-9.30 ⊕ FREE HOUSE ◀ Harveys, Fuller's London Pride, Larkins, Harvey's Old. ♥ 10
**Facilities** Play area Dogs allowed Garden

Save on Hotels. Book at **theAA.com/hotel**

**SUSSEX, EAST** 451 | ENGLAND

## KINGSTON (NEAR LEWES) — Map 6 TQ30

### The Juggs ▮

**The Street BN7 3NT ☎ 01273 472523** 📄 **01273 483274**
e-mail: juggs@shepherd-neame.co.uk
dir: *E of Brighton on A27*

Named after the women who walked from Brighton with baskets of fish for sale, this rambling, tile-hung 15th-century cottage, tucked beneath the South Downs, offers an interesting selection of freshly-cooked food. The area is ideal for walkers, and families are very welcome.

**Open** all day all wk 11am-11pm (Sun 11am-10.30pm) ◀ Shepherd Neame Spitfire, Best, Bishops Finger, Seasonal. **Facilities** Family room Dogs allowed Garden Parking

## MAYFIELD — Map 6 TQ52

### PICK OF THE PUBS

### The Middle House ▮

*See Pick of the Pubs on page 452*

## OFFHAM — Map 6 TQ41

### The Blacksmiths Arms ★★★★ INN ▮

**London Rd BN7 3QD ☎ 01273 472971**
e-mail: blacksmithsarms@shineadsl.co.uk
dir: *2m N of Lewes on A275*

An attractive, mid-18th-century free house in an Area of Outstanding Natural Beauty that now has national park status. A hostelry since it was built, with charming accommodation available, today's ales hale from Harvey's and log fires still burn in the inglenook. Bernard and Sylvia Booker aim to provide high quality dishes using the best of local produce, sustainably sourced and simply presented. The seafood platter; Bernard's own steak and kidney pie; and Newhaven whole grilled plaice 'on the bone' all meet these worthy objectives.

**Open** 12-3 6.30-10.30 Closed: Mon **Bar Meals** L served Tue-Sun 12-2 Av main course £5.50 **Restaurant** L served Tue-Sun 12-2 booking required D served Tue-Sun 6.30-9 booking required Fixed menu price fr £10.95 Av 3 course à la carte fr £21 ⊕ FREE HOUSE ◀ Harveys Ales, Bitburger. ▮ 10 **Facilities** Children's portions Garden Parking **Rooms** 4

## RINGMER — Map 6 TQ41

### The Cock ▮

**Uckfield Rd BN8 5RX**
**☎ 01273 812040** 📄 **01273 812040**
e-mail: matt@cockpub.co.uk
web: www.cockpub.co.uk
dir: *On A26 approx 2m N of Lewes just outside Ringmer*

Built in the 16th century, The Cock takes its name from a bygone era when a spare horse (the cock horse) was kept to help another horse pull its heavy load to the top of a steep hill. Original oak beams, flagstone floors and a blazing fire in the inglenook set a cosy scene. Harveys ales and guest beers accompany the extensive menu of favourites and specials among which dishes of Sussex lamb chops, venison rump, and smoked haddock may be found.

**Open** all wk 11-3 6-11.30 (Sun 11-11) Closed: 26 Dec **Bar Meals** L served Mon-Sat 12-2, Sun 12-9.30 D served Mon-Sat 6-9.30, Sun 12-9.30 Av main course £9.50 **Restaurant** L served Mon-Sat 12-2, Sun 12-9.30 booking required D served Mon-Sat 6-9.30, Sun 12-9.30 booking required Av 3 course à la carte fr £13.40 ⊕ FREE HOUSE ◀ Harveys Sussex Best Bitter, Sussex XXXX Old Ale, Fuller's London Pride, Dark Star Hophead ⊙ Thatchers Gold. ▮ 9 **Facilities** Children's portions Play area Dogs allowed Garden Parking

## RUSHLAKE GREEN — Map 6 TQ61

### PICK OF THE PUBS

### Horse & Groom

**TN21 9QE ☎ 01435 830320** 📄 **01435 830310**
e-mail: chappellhatpeg@aol.com
dir: *Telephone for directions*

An appealing pub-restaurant at the edge of the enormous green that gives the village its name. Residents have supped here for over 230 years and the pub retains much rustic character, with heavy beams, hearth, lots of brass and copper and a cosy Gun Room restaurant replete with many antique firearms, whilst outside a huge garden offers a grand prospect over the pretty East Sussex countryside. Drinkers delight in Shepherd Neame's best ales whilst diners are rewarded by a fulfilling standard menu featuring braised steak and onion suet pudding with red wine, real ale and herbs, complemented by daily specials with a strong nod to the nearby fishing town of Hastings and its seasonal catches, perhaps fresh-dressed crab or plump English Channel cod. Local lamb is a favourite with many; try a half-shoulder slowly braised with a herb crust served with pan roast redcurrant gravy.

**Open** all wk 11.30-3 6-11 (Sun all day) **Bar Meals** L served Mon-Fri 12-2.15, Sat-Sun 12-2.30 booking required D served all wk 7-9.30 booking required Av main course £8 **Restaurant** L served Mon-Fri 12-2.15, Sat-Sun 12-2.30 booking required D served all wk 7-8.30 booking required Av 3 course à la carte fr £24 ⊕ SHEPHERD NEAME ◀ Master Brew, Spitfire, Kent Best, Late Red, Bishop's Finger. **Facilities** Children's portions Dogs allowed Garden Parking

## RYE — Map 7 TQ92

### The Globe Inn ▮

**10 Military Rd TN31 7NX ☎ 01797 227918**
e-mail: info@theglobe-inn.com
dir: *M20 junct 11 onto A2070 & A259*

A small, informal free house, now with a new owner, just outside the ancient town walls. An absence of gaming machines, jukeboxes and TV screens encourages even husbands and wives to talk to each other over their drinks, or while they enjoy their contemporary food in the modern, wood-floored bar and restaurant area. Using local produce, dishes might include the likes of oak-smoked kipper, poached egg, spiced spinach and tomato vinaigrette, followed by braised lamb shank shepherd's pie, or chilli, mushroom, feta and saffron risotto.

**Open** 12-3.30 6-11 (all day BHs) Closed: Mon, Sun eve **Bar Meals** L served all wk 12-3 D served Tue-Sat 6-9 booking required Av main course £7.50 **Restaurant** L served all wk 12-3 D served Tue-Sat 6-9 booking required Fixed menu price fr £10 Av 3 course à la carte fr £20 ⊕ FREE HOUSE ◀ ESB, Harveys, Star's. ▮ 10 **Facilities** Children's portions Dogs allowed Garden Parking

# PICK OF THE PUBS

# The Middle House ♀

**MAYFIELD**       Map 6 TQ52

**High St TN20 6AB**
☎ **01435 872146**   📠 **01435 873423**
e-mail: kirsty@middle-house.com
web: www.middlehousemayfield.co.uk
dir: *E of A267, S of Tunbridge Wells*

This Grade I listed, 16th-century village inn dominates Mayfield's High Street. Described as 'one of the finest examples of a timber-framed building in Sussex', it has survived since 1575, when it was built for Sir Thomas Gresham, Elizabeth I's Keeper of the Privy Purse and founder of the London Stock Exchange. A private residence until the 1920s, the entrance hall features a large ornate wooden carved fireplace by master carver Grinling Gibbons; records show it originally came from the Royal College of Physicians in London.

A family-run business from start to finish, the Middle House is owned by

Monica and Bryan Blundell; their son Darren is general manager, while son-in-law Mark is the head chef.

Well known for good, hand-made food, the kitchen uses meats, poultry, game and vegetables from local farms and producers. The bar menu consists of over 40 dishes including traditional classics such as Thai chicken curry; home-made sausages of the day; and cold cuts with bubble and squeak. Fresh salads, vegetarian options and a children's healthy eating menu are augmented by lunchtime offerings of ploughman's, baguettes, ciabattas and a 'ladies lunch menu' for the smaller appetite; fresh fish and daily specials are displayed on blackboards around the huge working fire.

The beautiful oak-panelled restaurant, which incorporates a private chapel, offers a weekly-changing carte with over twenty main courses to choose from. Expect starters of smoked chicken mousse; tempura battered fillets of grey mullet; and roasted butternut squash, pine nut and thyme ravioli. Meaty main courses will probably include Highfield Farm fillet or rib-eye steaks; roasted half shoulder of lamb; and Mayfield pheasant breast with bacon and chestnut farce en croûte. South coast skate wing, brill, bass and cod are

typical of the fish choices, while desserts follow traditional lines. Head outside to the lovely garden with sun parasols in warmer weather.

**Open** all wk **Bar Meals** L served Mon-Fri 12-2, Sat-Sun 12-2.30 D served Mon-Sat 6.30-9.30, Sun all day **Restaurant** L served Tue-Sun 12-2 booking required D served Tue-Sat 6.30-9 booking required ⊕ FREE HOUSE ◧ Harveys Best, Greene King Abbot Ale, Black Sheep Best, Theakston Best, Adnams Bitter ♂ Thatchers Gold. ♀ 9 **Facilities** Children's menu Play area Garden Parking

Save on Hotels. Book at **theAA.com/hotel**

**SUSSEX, EAST** 453 **ENGLAND**

## PICK OF THE PUBS

### Mermaid Inn ★★★ HL ◉ ♟

Mermaid St TN31 7EY
☎ 01797 223065 📄 01797 225069
e-mail: info@mermaidinn.com
dir: *A259, follow signs to town centre, then into Mermaid St*

Destroyed by the French in 1377 and rebuilt in 1420 (on foundations dating back to 1156), the Mermaid is steeped in history and stands among the cobbled streets of Rye. Once famous for its smuggling associations, the infamous Hawkhurst Gang used to meet here, it remains strong on romantic, old-world appeal, with beams hewn from ancient ships' timbers, antique furnishings, linenfold panelling, and huge fireplaces carved from French stone ballast rescued from the harbour. There is also a priest's hole in the lounge bar. Food is served in the bar and atmospheric restaurant, and in the summer you can relax under sunshades on the patio. Bar food ranges from sandwiches or salmon and pea fishcakes, to steak and kidney pudding, smoked fish chowder, and confit duck salad with chilli dressing. Bedrooms ooze character and include eight four-poster rooms – book the Elizabethan Chamber, an impressive panelled room with a magnificent carved four-poster bed.

**Open** all wk noon-11 **Bar Meals** L served all wk 12-2.30 D served all wk 6-9 Av main course £9 **Restaurant** L served all wk 12-2.30 booking required D served all wk 7.30-9.30 booking required Fixed menu price fr £24 Av 3 course à la carte fr £41 ⊕ FREE HOUSE ◖ Greene King Old Speckled Hen, Fuller's London Pride, Harveys. ♟ 15 **Facilities** Children's menu Children's portions Garden Parking **Rooms** 31

## PICK OF THE PUBS

### The Ypres Castle Inn ♟

*See Pick of the Pubs on page 454*

*See Pick of the Pubs on page 454*

### SHORTBRIDGE     Map 6 TQ42

## PICK OF THE PUBS

### The Peacock Inn ♟

TN22 3XA ☎ 01825 762463 📄 01825 762463
e-mail: enquiries@peacock-inn.co.uk
dir: *Just off A272 (Haywards Heath to Uckfield road) & A26 (Uckfield to Lewes road)*

Mentioned in Samuel Pepys' diary, this traditional inn dates from 1567 and is full of old world charm, both inside and out. Today it is renowned for its food (created by no fewer than three chefs), and also the resident ghost of Mrs Fuller. The large rear patio garden is a delightful spot in summer. Food choices include toasted ciabatta and toasted foccacia with a variety of fillings. For the hungry there are starters such as chicken and duck liver pâté, or crayfish tails and smoked salmon, followed by seafood crêpe, pan-fried sea bass fillets; steak, Guinness and mushroom pie or

fillet steak with garlic and Stilton butter. For the non-meat eaters there's Mediterranean vegetable and mozzarella tartlet, or vegetarian tagine. Look out for chefs' specials.

**Open** all wk Mon-Fri 11-3 6-11 (Sat-Sun all day) Closed: 25-26 Dec **Bar Meals** L served all wk 11-3 D served all wk 6-9.30 **Restaurant** L served all wk 11-3 D served all wk 6-9.30 ⊕ FREE HOUSE ◖ Harveys Best Bitter, Fuller's London Pride, Marlets. ♟ 8 **Facilities** Dogs allowed Garden Parking

### THREE LEG CROSS     Map 6 TQ63

### The Bull

Dunster Mill Ln TN5 7HH
☎ 01580 200586 📄 01580 201289
e-mail: enquiries@thebullinn.co.uk
dir: *From M25 exit at Sevenoaks toward Hastings, right at x-rds onto B2087, right onto B2099 through Ticehurst, right for Three Legged Cross*

The Bull started life as a 14th-century Wealden hall house, reputedly one of the oldest dwelling places in the country, and is set in a hamlet close to Bewl Water. The interior features oak beams, inglenook fireplaces, quarry tiled floors, and a mass of small intimate areas in the bar. The extensive gardens are popular with families who enjoy the duck pond, petanque pitch, aviary and children's play area. Menus offer pub favourites ranging from freshly baked baguettes and bar snacks to hearty dishes full of comfort, such as bangers and mash and treacle tart.

**Open** all wk noon-mdnt Closed: 25-26 Dec eve **Bar Meals** L served Mon-Fri 12-2.30, Sat 12-3, Sun 12-8 D served Mon-Sat 6.30-9, Sun 6.30-8 **Restaurant** L served Mon-Fri 12-2.30, Sat 12-3, Sun 12-8 D served Mon-Sat 6.30-9, Sun 6.30-8 ⊕ FREE HOUSE ◖ Harveys, Sussex Best, Harveys Armada, Timothy Taylor, 1066, Guest ales Ö Stowford Press. **Facilities** Play area Dogs allowed Garden Parking

### UPPER DICKER     Map 6 TQ50

### The Plough

Coldharbour Rd BN27 3QJ ☎ 01323 844859
dir: *Off A22, W of Hailsham*

A 17th-century former farmhouse which has been a pub for over 200 years, and now comprises two bars and two restaurants. Excellent wheelchair facilities, a large beer garden and a children's play area add to the appeal, and the Plough is also a handy stop for walkers. Expect such fish dishes as Sussex smokie or prawn, brie and broccoli bake, while other options include duck breast in spicy plum sauce, veal in lemon cream, or lamb cutlets in redcurrant and rosemary.

**Open** all day all wk 11am-11pm (Sun noon-10.30pm) ◖ Shepherd Neame Spitfire Premium Ale, Best, Kent Best. **Facilities** Play area Family room Dogs allowed Garden Parking

### WADHURST     Map 6 TQ63

## PICK OF THE PUBS

### The Best Beech Inn

Mayfield Ln TN5 6JH ☎ 01892 782046
dir: *7m from Tunbridge Wells. On A246 at lights turn left onto London Rd (A26), left at mini rdbt onto A267, left then right onto B2100. At Mark Cross signed Wadhurst, 3m on right*

The unusually-named Best Beech Inn is going from strength to strength. The inn dates back to 1680, and has been sympathetically refurbished in recent years to preserve the essentially Victorian character of its heyday. The result is a place bursting with personality, characterised by comfy chairs, exposed brickwork and open fireplaces. Ideally situated near the Kent and Sussex border, in an Area of Outstanding Natural Beauty, the inn includes a fine à la carte restaurant offering excellent European cuisine with a French influence. For those who prefer a more informal atmosphere, there is the bar bistro with a comprehensive menu available from the blackboard. Dinner could begin with pork rillette and apricot chutney, move on to bouillabaisse with saffron new potatoes, and finish with tarte au chocolate, marmalade syrup and vanilla ice cream.

**Open** all day all wk Mon-Sat noon-11pm (Sun noon-10.30) **Bar Meals** L served Mon-Sat 12-2.30, Sun 12-4 booking required D served Mon-Sat 6-9.30 booking required **Restaurant** L served Mon-Sat 12-2.30, Sun 12-4 booking required D served Mon-Sat 6-9.30 booking required ⊕ SHEPHERD NEAME ◖ Kent Best, Master Brew. **Facilities** Children's portions Family room Dogs allowed Garden Parking

### WARBLETON     Map 6 TQ61

### The War-Bill-in-Tun Inn

Church Hill TN21 9BD
☎ 01435 830636 📄 01435 830636
e-mail: whitton@thewarbillintun.wanadoo.co.uk
dir: *From Hailsham take A267 towards Heathfield. Turn right for village. 15m from Hailsham*

A 400-year-old smugglers' haunt, famously frequented by the Beatles in the 1960s when visiting their manager, Brian Epstein, who lived half a mile away. Family run, this heart-warmingly ancient hostelry lives up to its motto: 'Difficult to find, impossible to forget'. Owner Bryan Whitton aims to offer good food and friendly service along traditional lines, with dishes such as deep-fried whitebait; Barnsley chop with mint gravy; deep-fried breaded seafood platter; and a range of fresh salads.

**Open** all wk ⊕ FREE HOUSE ◖ Harveys Best, Bishop's, Finger, Tanglefoot, Spitfire Smooth. **Facilities** Dogs allowed Garden Parking

# PICK OF THE PUBS

## The Ypres Castle Inn ♍

**RYE**                    Map 7 TQ92

**Gun Garden TN31 7HH**
☎ **01797 223248**
**e-mail:** info@yprescastleinn.co.uk
**web:** www.yprescastleinn.co.uk
**dir:** *Behind church & adjacent to Ypres Tower*

Friday night is music night at this white weather boarded free house, when the pub comes alive with a varied programme of contemporary rock, jazz and blues bands. Known locally as 'The Wipers', the pub has been providing hospitality to the people of Rye for centuries; originally built in 1640, it stands close to Rye harbour and was once the haunt of smugglers.

Nowadays, the colourful art and interior furnishings give the building a warm and friendly atmosphere, and the large garden offers outdoor eating and relaxation during the summer months.

There are delightful views of the nearby Ypres Tower and the River Rother, where the working fishing fleet brings home Rye Bay scallops and most of the seafood offered in the restaurant. Other local produce on the ever-changing menu includes Winchelsea pork, and ham cooked in local cider.

Lunchtime brings daily soups, as well as a selection of freshly-baked filled baguettes served with crisps and a salad garnish. The range of hot dishes includes Ypres fish cakes with potato salad; creamy butternut squash risotto; and Romney Marsh lamb burger with chips, salad and minted yoghurt.

In the evenings, dinner might begin with avocado, crevette and crayfish tail salad; or an antipasti platter of cured meats, mozzarella, olives and toasted French bread; followed, perhaps, by herb crusted cod fillet with creamed leeks and roasted new potatoes; sirloin steak with horseradish mash, wilted spinach, tomato and shallot red wine sauce; or bell pepper with roasted vegetable couscous, goat's cheese and new potatoes. A choice of desserts from the blackboard will round off your meal. Booking is advisable in the summer and at weekends.

**Open** all day all wk **Bar Meals** L served all wk 12-3 D served Mon-Sat 6-9 Av main course £12 **Restaurant** L served all wk 12-3 D served Mon-Sat 6-9 booking required Av 3 course à la carte fr £20 ⊕ FREE HOUSE ◼ Harveys Best, Adnams Broadside, Wells Bombardier, Timothy Taylor Landlord, Fuller's London Pride Ö Biddenden Bushels. ♍ 12 **Facilities** Children's menu Garden

# PICK OF THE PUBS

## The Lamb Inn 🍷

WARTLING      Map 6 TQ60

**BN27 1RY ☎ 01323 832116**
web: www.lambinnwartling.co.uk
dir: *A259 from Polegate to Pevensey rdbt. Take 1st left to Wartling & Herstmonceux Castle. Pub 3m on right*

This family-run, classic country pub and restaurant was built in 1526, although it did not begin dispensing ale until 1640. Since then it has provided a welcome rest stop to everyone from 18th-century smugglers to today's birdwatchers, walkers and locals who enjoy the nearby Pevensey Levels and surrounding East Sussex countryside. Draw up one of the comfortable cream sofas to the fire and, as your well-behaved dog settles down at your feet, enjoy a real ale from Sussex breweries or a glass of wine.

Aside from liquid refreshment, the pub is well known for its food. Everything is made on the premises, including the bread, and, as far as possible, makes use of top quality produce sourced locally from places like Chilley Farm, which specialises in raising Gloucester Old Spot pigs, Southdown and Kent Cross lamb, and Sussex beef without additives and in unhurried fashion. Fish makes the short journey from Hastings and Newhaven to become house specialities, offered daily on the specials board.

The menu offers plenty of variety, so that a meal might begin with grilled king scallops and bacon with Parmesan crumbs; salad of roasted beetroot, bacon and Stilton with pesto; or chicken liver mushroom and brandy pâté with melba toast and cornichons, followed by cassoulet of duck, bacon and sausages with borlotti beans and tomato sauce; Sussex beef braised with bacon, red wine and mushrooms with grain mustard mash; or Chilley Farm boneless pork loin chops, black pudding and apple mash.

Traditional home-made desserts are represented by orange and Cointreau cheesecake or nectarine Eton Mess. Look out for year round events and special nights.

**Open** all wk Tue-Sat 11-3 6-11 (Sun 12-3) Closed: Sun eve, Mon
**Bar Meals** L served Tue-Sun 12-2.15 booking required D served Tue-Sat 7-9 booking required Av main course £9.99
**Restaurant** L served Tue-Sun 12-2.15 booking required D served Tue-Sat 7-9 booking required Fixed menu price fr £11.95 Av 3 course à la carte fr £22.95
🛢 FREE HOUSE 🍺 Harveys, guest beers ♨ Stowford Press. 🍷 8
**Facilities** Children's menu Dogs allowed Garden Parking

# PICK OF THE PUBS

## The Dorset Arms

**TN7 4BD**
☎ **01892 770278** 📄 **01892 770195**
e-mail: pete@dorset-arms.co.uk
**dir:** *4m W of Tunbridge Wells on B2110 between Groombridge & Hartfield*

Set on the borders of Kent and Sussex, this white weather-boarded inn is ideally situated for exploring Ashdown Forest, the setting for Winnie the Pooh's immortal exploits. The pub is named after the arms of the Sackville family – once the Earls of Dorset – of nearby Buckhurst Park, and it has been an inn since the 18th century. Three hundred years earlier it was known as Somers, an open-halled farmhouse with earth floors, and the building still retains many historic features.

There are massive wall and ceiling beams in the restaurant, an oak-floored bar, a huge open fireplace, and an old ice-house buried in the hillside at the back. The prize-winning beers come from Harveys of Lewes, and there is an extensive wine list.

The food offered ranges through bar snacks and daily specials to a full à la carte restaurant, and the ingredients are locally sourced and cooked to order. The lunchtime snack menu features light meals, sandwiches and jacket potatoes, whilst four blackboards of daily specials might include crispy duck breast with stuffing and plum sauce; salmon fishcakes with chilli dip, salad and chips; lamb's liver casserole with bacon and onions; or creamy chicken and mushroom pie.

Typical choices from the main menu begin with red onion and goat's cheese tart with balsamic dressing, followed by pan-seared venison in rich Cumberland sauce. Desserts include bread and butter pudding; forest fruit crème brûlée; and chocolate fudge brownie with ice cream. The pub is a popular

venue for local fishing and cricket teams, and holds regular quiz nights and music evenings.

**Open** all wk 11.30-3 6-11 (all day Sat-Sun) **Bar Meals** L served Tue-Sun 12-2, all day Sat-Sun D served Tue-Sat 7.30-9, all day Sat-Sun **Restaurant** L served Tue-Sun 12-2, all day Sat-Sun D served Tue-Sat 7.30-9, all day Sat-Sun ⊕ HARVEYS OF LEWES 🍺 Harveys Sussex Best, seasonal ales. **Facilities** Dogs allowed Garden Parking

## WARTLING                    Map 6 TQ60

### PICK OF THE PUBS

## The Lamb Inn ♥

*See Pick of the Pubs on page 455*

## WILMINGTON                 Map 6 TQ50

## The Giants Rest

**The Street BN26 5SQ**
☎ 01323 870207   🖃 01323 870207
**e-mail:** abecjane@aol.com
**dir:** *2m from Polegate on A27 towards Brighton*

With the famous chalk figure of the Long Man of
Wilmington standing guard opposite, this family-owned,
Victorian free house is admirably committed to home-
prepared, seasonal food. Sit at a pine table, play a game
or puzzle, and order roast chicken and leek pie; beef in
Guinness with rosemary dumplings; hake with coriander,
spring onion and chilli fishcakes; or halloumi warm salad.
There are daily specials too. In warmer months, food can
be enjoyed outside with a pint of Summer Lightning.

**Open** all wk 11am-3 6-11pm (Sat-Sun all day)
**Bar Meals** L served Mon-Fri 11.30-2, Sat-Sun all day
booking required D served Mon-Fri 6.30-9, Sat-Sun all
day booking required Av main course £9.50 **Restaurant** L
served Mon-Fri 11.30-2, Sat-Sun all day booking required
D served Mon-Fri 6.30-9, Sat-Sun all day booking
required ⊕ FREE HOUSE ◀ Harveys Best, Timothy Taylor
Landlord, Summer Lightning, Harveys Best ⁷ Stowford
Press. **Facilities** Children's portions Dogs allowed Garden
Parking

## WINCHELSEA                 Map 7 TQ91

## *The New Inn* ♥

**German St TN36 4EN** ☎ 01797 226252
**dir:** *Telephone for directions*

Elegant Winchelsea has seen much change over the
centuries, not least the sea's retreat that ended its days
as a thriving seaport. The 18th-century New Inn has
witnessed change of a far more beneficial nature and is
known today for its comfort, hospitality and excellent
cuisine. Chalkboard specials include lobster tails with
chips and salad, Rye Bay lemon sole, and chicken Kiev.
The lovely walled garden is a delight on a sunny day.

**Open** all wk ◀ Morlands Original, Abbots Ale, Greene
King IPA, Old Speckled Hen. ♥ 10 **Facilities** Family room
Dogs allowed Garden Parking

## WITHYHAM                    Map 6 TQ43

### PICK OF THE PUBS

## The Dorset Arms

*See Pick of the Pubs on opposite page*

---

### SUSSEX, WEST

## AMBERLEY                    Map 6 TQ01

## Black Horse

**High St BN18 9NL** ☎ 01798 831700
**dir:** *Telephone for directions*

A beautiful South Downs village setting for this lively
17th-century tavern. Look out for the display of sheep
bells donated by the last shepherd to have a flock on the
local hills. Food is served in the large restaurant and bar
or in the beer garden complete with pond, and there's
plenty of choice for everyone, including a children's menu.
Great beer, good local walks, and nice views of the South
Downs. Dogs (on leads) are welcome in the bar.

**Open** all day all wk **Bar Meals** L served all wk 12-3 D
served Mon-Thu 6-8.30, Fri-Sat 6-9.30, Sun 12-8 Av main
course £10 **Restaurant** L served Sun only booking
required D served Mon & Wed-Thu 6-8.30, Fri-Sat 6-9.30,
Sun 12-8 booking required ⊕ ADMIRAL TAVERNS
◀ Greene King IPA, Harveys Sussex, Guest ale.
**Facilities** Children's menu Dogs allowed Garden

## The Bridge Inn

**Houghton Bridge BN18 9LR** ☎ 01798 831619
**e-mail:** bridgeamberley@btinternet.com
**web:** www.bridgeinnamberley.com
**dir:** *5m N of Arundel on B2139. Next to Amberley main
line station*

Standing alongside the River Arun at the mid-point of the
South Downs Way National Trail, this traditional free
house dates from 1650. The pretty pub garden and patio
are summer favourites, whilst the candle-lit bar and log
fires come into their own on cold winter evenings.
Drinkers will find Westons ciders and a good range of real
ales, whilst other chalkboard specials and an extensive
range of pub classics sustain the heartiest appetites.

**Open** all day all wk noon-11 (Sun noon-10.30) **Bar
Meals** L served Mon-Fri 12-2.30, Sat-Sun 12-4 D served
Mon-Sat 6-9, Sun 5.30-8 ⊕ FREE HOUSE ◀ Harveys
Sussex, Skinners Betty Stogs, Hopback Summer
Lightning, Sharps Cornish Coaster ⁷ Westons Stowford
Press, Westons Old Rosie. **Facilities** Children's
menu Children's portions Dogs allowed Garden Parking

---

## ASHURST                     Map 6 TQ11

### PICK OF THE PUBS

## The Fountain Inn ♥

**BN44 3AP** ☎ 01403 710219
**e-mail:** fountainashurst@aol.com
**dir:** *On B2135 N of Steyning*

The South Downs loom as the southern horizon visible
from the pretty gardens - there's a great duck pond, too
- of this 16th century Sussex inn where Paul McCartney
once played; he filmed his *Wonderful Christmas Time*
video here back in 1979. A huge brick chimneystack
vents the capacious inglenook, just one of the period
features that run to flagstone floors, wonky walls, rustic
furnishings and old beams whilst, for the sporty, a
traditional skittles alley is a must. Local beers from
Harveys and other regional breweries accompany the
good, solid pub food that attracts walkers, cyclists and
locals. At lunchtime there are ploughman's, salads,
freshly cut sandwiches, and Sussex smokie - smoked
haddock and prawns in a cheese sauce. The menu runs
to favourites like steak, mushroom and ale pie as well
as chunky steaks, chicken breast or perhaps a choice
of fresh fish straight from the English Channel; or
maybe try the tempting apple and Calvados sausages.

**Open** all day all wk 11.30am-11pm (Sun noon-
10.30pm) **Bar Meals** L served Mon-Sat 11.30-2.30, Sun
12-3 D served Mon-Sat 6-9.30, Sun 6-8.30
**Restaurant** L served Mon-Sat 11.30-2.30, Sun 12-3 D
served Mon-Sat 6-9.30, Sun 6-8.30 ⊕ FREE HOUSE
◀ Harveys Sussex, Fuller's London, Seasonal ales,
Guest ales ⁷ Stowford Press. ♥ 11 **Facilities** Dogs
allowed Garden Parking

## BALCOMBE                    Map 6 TQ33

## The Cowdray ♥

**RH17 6QD** ☎ 01444 811280
**e-mail:** alexandandy@hotmail.co.uk
**dir:** *From M23 junct 10a take the B2036 towards
Balcombe*

Just a mile from Junction 10a of the M23, this once run-
down village boozer has been transformed into a cosy
dining pub. Expect wood floors, a fresh, crisp decor, and a
pub menu that's a cut above average. Alex and Andy
Owen, who previously worked for Gordon Ramsay,
specialise in sourcing their ingredients within Sussex,
and produce everything in-house except bread and ice
cream. Follow honey-roast pigeon and quail with slow-
cooked Sussex pork belly or the fish of the day.

**Open** all wk noon-3 5.30-11 Closed: 25 Dec eve, 1 Jan eve
**Bar Meals** L served Mon-Sat 12-3, Sun 12-4 D served
Mon-Thu 6-9, Fri-Sat 6-10 Av main course £12.95
**Restaurant** L served Mon-Sat 12-3, Sun 12-4 booking
required D served Mon-Thu 6-9, Fri-Sat 6-10 booking
required Fixed menu price fr £14.95 Av 3 course à la carte
fr £25 ⊕ GREENE KING ◀ Morland Original, IPA,
Guinness. ♥ 11 **Facilities** Children's portions Play area
Family room Dogs allowed Garden Parking

## BARNHAM — Map 6 SU90

## The Murrell Arms ♀

**Yapton Rd PO22 0AS ☎ 01243 553320**
*dir: From Brighton follow A27 through Arundel for 2m, left at The Oaks, follow road to end. Turn right at The Olive Branch*

Built in 1750 as a farmhouse, this attractive white-painted pub became an inn shortly after the railway station opened over 100 years later. Lavish window boxes and hanging baskets make a real splash in the summer, and, with the briefest of menus at the lowest of prices, there's no more affordable place to sit down for a ploughman's, bacon hock with new potatoes and green beans, or cockles and mussels, washed down with a reliable pint of Fuller's.

**Open** all wk 11-2.30 5.30-11 (Sat 11-11 Sun noon-10.30) **Bar Meals** L served all wk 12-2 D served all wk 6-9 Av main course £3.75 ⊕ FULLERS BREWERY ◀ Fuller's London Pride, ESB & Butser Best - Horndean Special Brew. ♀ 15 **Facilities** Play area Dogs allowed Garden Parking **Notes** ⊕

## BURGESS HILL — Map 6 TQ31

## The Oak Barn ♀

**Cuckfield Rd RH15 8RE**
**☎ 01444 258222   📄 01444 258388**
**e-mail:** enquiries@oakbarnrestaurant.co.uk
**web:** www.oakbarnrestaurant.co.uk
*dir: Telephone for directions*

After being lovingly restored using salvaged timbers from wooden ships, this 250-year-old barn has been transformed into a popular pub-restaurant. Brimming with charm and atmosphere, the interior is rich in acres of oak flooring, authentic wagon wheel chandeliers, and fine stained glass. Lofty raftered ceilings, a galleried restaurant, and leather chairs fronting a huge fireplace are an idyllic setting for supping a pint of Harveys and tucking into steamed steak and kidney pudding; roasted fillet of halibut; and rhubarb crème brûlée. Outside is an enclosed courtyard with water features.

**Open** all day all wk 10am-11pm (Sun 11-11) **Bar Meals** L served all wk 12-2.30 D served all wk 6-9.30 Av main course £8.95 **Restaurant** L served all wk 12-2.30 booking required D served all wk 6-9.30 booking required Fixed menu price fr £10.95 Av 3 course à la carte fr £25 ⊕ FREE HOUSE ◀ Guinness, Harveys. ♀ 8 **Facilities** Children's portions Garden Parking

## BURPHAM — Map 6 TQ00

### PICK OF THE PUBS

## George & Dragon ◉

**BN18 9RR ☎ 01903 883131**
**e-mail:** sara.cheney@btinternet.com
*dir: Off A27 1m E of Arundel, signed Burpham, 2.5m pub on left*

Tucked away down a long 'no through road', Burpham looks across the Arun valley to the mighty Arundel Castle. There are excellent riverside and downland walks on the doorstep of this 300 year-old free house, and walkers and their dogs are welcome in the bar. Step inside and you'll find beamed ceilings and modern prints on the walls, with worn stone flags on the floor. The original rooms have been opened out to form a large space that catches the late sunshine, but there are still a couple of alcoves with tables for an intimate drink. You'll also discover a small bar hidden around a corner. This is very much a dining pub, attracting visitors from far and wide. The à la carte menu and specials board offer a good choice of dishes between them: for starters you could try ravioli of braised oxtail or assiette of trout. Main courses might include orange-roasted partridge with thyme fondant root vegetables, or cannon of lamb with white and black pudding. There are tables outside, ideal for whiling away an afternoon or evening in summer, listening to the cricket being played on the green.

**Open** all wk Mon-Sun 12-3 6-11 **Bar Meals** L served Mon-Fri 12-2, Sat-Sun 12-3 booking required D served Mon-Sun 6.30-9 booking required Av main course £13.95 **Restaurant** L served Mon-Fri 12-2, Sat-Sun 12-3 booking required D served Mon-Sun 6.30-9 booking required Av 3 course à la carte fr £24.95 ⊕ FREE HOUSE ◀ Arundel Ales and guest ales, Sharp's Doom Bar, Betty Stogs, Dark Star ♂ Thatchers Gold. **Facilities** Children's menu Dogs allowed Garden Parking

## BURY — Map 6 TQ01

## The Squire & Horse ♀

**Bury Common RH20 1NS**
**☎ 01798 831343   📄 01798 831904**
**e-mail:** squireandhorse@btconnect.com
*dir: On A29, 4m S of Pulborough, 4m N of Arundel*

The original 16th-century building was extended a few years ago, with old wooden beams and country fireplaces

throughout. All the food is freshly cooked to order and sourced locally wherever possible. With the head chef originating from Australia there are innovative dishes on offer here. These could include barbecued barracuda fillet on a bed of prawn risotto, or calves' liver with bacon and red wine glaze. Thai food is a speciality too. You can also dine outside in the stylish seating area. There is a members dining club to join with discounts throughout the year.

**Open** all wk 11-3 6-11 **Bar Meals** L served all wk 12-2 D served all wk 6-9 **Restaurant** L served all wk 12-2 D served all wk 6-9 ⊕ FREE HOUSE ◀ Greene King IPA, Harveys Sussex, guest ales. ♀ 10 **Facilities** Children's menu Garden Parking

## CHARLTON — Map 6 SU81

### PICK OF THE PUBS

## The Fox Goes Free ♀

*See Pick of the Pubs on page 460*

## CHICHESTER — Map 5 SU80

## Crown and Anchor ♀

**Dell Quay Rd PO20 7EE ☎ 01243 781712**
**e-mail:** crown&anchor@thespiritgroup.com
*dir: Take A286 from Chichester towards West Wittering, turn right for Dell Quay*

Nestling at the foot of the Sussex Downs with panoramic views of Chichester harbour, this unique hostelry dates in parts to the early 18th century when it also served as a custom house for the old port. It has a superb terrace overlooking the quay for alfresco dining. Menu choices include fish (battered to order) and chips, grilled steaks, and steak and ale pie.

◀ Bombardier, Theakstons, Guinness. ♀ 17 **Facilities** Dogs allowed Garden Parking

### PICK OF THE PUBS

## The Earl of March ◉◉◉ ♀ **NEW**

**Lavant Rd, Lavant PO18 0BQ ☎ 01243 533993**
*dir: On A286, 1m N of Chichester*

Run by former Ritz Hotel executive head chef Giles Thompson, this 'country plush-style' (sumptuous leather sofas, open wood fire) pub restaurant has Goodwood, the Earl of March's family home, for a near neighbour. Back in the 18th century, as The Bat and Ball, it served stagecoaches on the main Chichester to Midhurst road, and it's easy to understand how, in 1803, the poet and composer William Blake came to write the words to 'Jerusalem' here, as he looked out over the South Downs. It didn't take Giles long to receive an AA Rosette for his cooking, all prepared from fresh, regional and local ingredients whenever possible. This 'localness' is amply demonstrated by a starter of Tangmere red pepper mousse with grilled Sussex halloumi cheese; and main courses of grilled Rother Valley sirloin steak; and Southdown lamb

Save on Hotels. Book at **theAA.com/hotel**

**SUSSEX, WEST** 459 ENGLAND

cutlets with sweetbreads. Specials change to reflect what is best, natural/wild and seasonal.

**Open** all day all wk **Bar Meals** L served all wk 12-2.30 (winter) 12-9 (summer) D served all wk 12-9 (summer) Av main course £9 **Restaurant** L served all wk 12-2.30 (winter) booking required D served all wk 5.30-9.30 (winter) 12-9 (summer) booking required Av 3 course à la carte fr £15 ⊕ ENTERPRISE INNS ◀ Summer Lightning, Harveys, Fuller's London Pride, Ringwood ○ Stowford Press. ☕ 16 **Facilities** Children's menu Children's portions Dogs allowed Garden Parking

## PICK OF THE PUBS

## Royal Oak Inn ★★★★★ INN ◉ ☕

**Pook Ln, East Lavant PO18 0AX** ☎ **01243 527434**
**e-mail:** enquiries@royaloakeastlavant.co.uk
**web:** www.royaloakeastlavant.co.uk
**dir:** A286 from Chichester signed Midhurst, 2m then right at mini-rdbt, pub over bridge on left

Just outside Chichester in the picturesque village of East Lavant, this coaching inn offers a friendly welcome, real ales and award-winning food all within easy reach of rolling Sussex downland. The Royal Oak was a regular pub for many years, but has been exceptionally well converted to offer stylish, sleekly furnished guest accommodation complete with state of the art entertainment systems. The brick-lined restaurant and bar achieve a crisp, rustic brand of chic: details include fresh flowers, candles, and wine attractively displayed in alcoves set into the walls; Arundel ale and Gospel Green champagne cider are among the thirst-quenchers on offer. Favourite starters include confit duck and ham hock terrine, and roast beetroot and goat's cheese tarte Tatin. Main courses range from pan-fried fillet of turbot with crayfish and sage risotto; to duo of Sussex pork, with pan-roasted fillet and twice-cooked belly served with dauphinoise potatoes, curly kale and pickled pear.

**Open** all day all wk 7am-11.30pm Closed: 25 Dec **Bar Meals** food served all day **Restaurant** L served all wk 12-3.30 booking required D served all wk 6-11 booking required ⊕ FREE HOUSE ◀ Ballards, HSB, Sussex, Arundel ○ Gospel Green Champagne Cider. ☕ 16 **Facilities** Children's portions Garden Parking **Rooms** 8

---

**CHILGROVE** Map 5 SU81

### PICK OF THE PUBS

## The Fish House ★★★★★ RR ◉◉ ☕

**High St PO18 9HX** ☎ **01243 519444**
**e-mail:** info@thefishhouse.co.uk
**dir:** On B2141 between Chichester & Petersfield

Low ceilings, beams, an Irish marble-topped bar, a 300-year-old French fireplace and decorative brickwork combine with leather sofas in this wisteria-covered building. Why the name? Well, there's the Fish Bar, with its local beers and ciders, the show-stopping oyster counter, and there are the fish tanks, through which you can see the chefs preparing their organically sourced modern classics and innovative world dishes. In the restaurant, holder of two AA Rosettes, John Holt paintings adorn the walls, the furniture is hand made, and contrasting linen and drapes set off the oak and limestone floor. Here, main courses include crab risotto; Cornish brill with herb tagliatelle; skate wing with mash and caper beurre noisette; and pork belly with king scallops, apples and bok choi. On Sundays The Fish House serves its well known roasts until 4pm. The 200-plus wines are stored in wine caves for guests' inspection.

**Open** all day all wk **Bar Meals** L served all wk 12-2.30 D served all wk 6-10 Av main course £15 **Restaurant** L served all wk 12-2.30 booking required D served all wk 6-10 booking required Fixed menu price fr £17.50 Av 3 course à la carte fr £45 ⊕ FREE HOUSE ◀ Black Sheep, Harveys Best ○ Westons Organic. ☕ 24 **Facilities** Children's menu Children's portions Dogs allowed Garden Parking **Rooms** 15

---

**COMPTON** Map 5 SU71

## Coach & Horses

**The Square PO18 9HA** ☎ **023 9263 1228**
**dir:** On B2146 S of Petersfield, to Emsworth, in centre of Compton

A very pretty Downland village is the setting for this 16th-century pub, a popular spot for walkers and cyclists. The front bar features two open fires and a bar billiards table, while the restaurant is in the oldest part of the pub, with many exposed beams. Up to five guest beers from independent breweries are usually available, plus Stowford Press and Thatchers ciders. There is an extensive menu of home-cooked dishes, all made to order.

---

**Open** all wk 11.30-3 6-11 **Bar Meals** L served all wk 12-2 D served all wk 7-9 Av main course £8.35 **Restaurant** L served all wk 12-2 booking required Av 3 course à la carte fr £25 ⊕ FREE HOUSE ◀ Fuller's ESB, Ballard's Best, Dark Star Golden Gate, Oakleaf Brewery Nuptu'ale, Dark Star Hophead ○ Stowford Press, Thatchers. **Facilities** Children's portions Dogs allowed

---

**DUNCTON** Map 6 SU91

## The Cricketers

**GU28 0LB** ☎ **01798 342473**
**e-mail:** info@thecricketersduncton.co.uk
**dir:** On A285, 3m from Petworth, 8m from Chichester

Dating back to the 16th century, this attractive white-painted pub is situated in spectacular South Downs walking country. The inn, little changed over the years, is named to commemorate its one-time owner John Wisden, the first-class cricketer and creator of the famous sporting almanac. The menu offers good hearty meals like rabbit casserole with cider, apple and mustard; and Barnsley lamb chop in red wine gravy. Children are welcome in the dining areas and gardens, with a menu catering to younger tastes.

**Open** all day all wk **Bar Meals** L served Mon-Fri 12-2.30, Sat-Sun 12-6 D served Mon-Fri 6-9, Sat-Sun 12-9 **Restaurant** L served Mon-Fri 12-2.30, Sat-Sun 12-6 D served Mon-Fri 6-9, Sat-Sun 12-9 ⊕ FREE HOUSE ◀ Betty Stogs, Horsham Best, Arundel Gold, Guest ale ○ Thatchers Heritage, Thatchers Draught. **Facilities** Children's menu Play area Dogs allowed Garden Parking

---

**EAST ASHLING** Map 5 SU80

## Horse and Groom ★★★★ INN

**East Ashling PO18 9AX**
☎ **01243 575339** 📠 **01243 575560**
**e-mail:** info@thehorseandgroomchichester.co.uk
**dir:** 3m from Chichester on B1278 between Chichester & Rowland's Castle. 2m off A27 at Fishbourne

Located at the foot of the South Downs, this is good walking country, and there's plenty to do within easy reach of this substantially renovated 17th-century inn. The flagstone floor and beamed bar is cosy, with a working range at one end and an open fire at the other. The underground cellar keeps ales at a constant temperature, and there are bar snack, blackboard and full carte menus. Dishes include favourites such as

***continued on page 461***

# PICK OF THE PUBS

## The Fox Goes Free ♍

---

**CHARLTON**        Map 6 SU81

**PO18 0HU**
☎ **01243 811461** 🖷 **01243 811712**
e-mail: enquiries@thefoxgoesfree.com
web: www.thefoxgoesfree.com
dir: *A286, 6m from Chichester towards Midhurst. 1m from Goodwood racecourse*

Nestling in unspoilt countryside, this lovely old brick and flint free house was a favoured hunting lodge of William III. With its three huge fireplaces, old pews and brick floors, the 15th-century building simply exudes charm and character. The pub, which hosted the first Women's Institute meeting in 1915, lies close to the rambling Weald and Downland open-air museum, where fifty historic buildings from around southern England have been reconstructed to form a unique collection. Goodwood estate is also close by, and the Fox attracts many a punter during the racing season and the annual Festival of Speed.

Away from the high life, you can watch the world go by from the solid timber benches and tables to the front, or relax under the apples trees in the lawned rear garden. Lest all this sounds rather fancy, you'll find The Fox is a friendly and welcoming drinkers' pub. A good selection of real ales includes the eponymous Fox Goes Free bitter, and eating here is not prohibitive either.

Everything is home made and, whether you're looking for a quick bar snack or something more substantial, the daily changing menus offer something for every taste. Chilli con carne with rice, lasagne with chips and salad, honey-roast ham and eggs are some of the lighter meals.

À la carte choices may start with fried pizza dough topped with guacamole, buffalo mozzarella and baby red peppers; or chicken liver parfait with apple chutney and toast. Continue with meat and fish main courses such as chicken breast stuffed with banana; pork chop with bubble and squeak; and grilled John Dory or Torbay sole. Inviting vegetarian options may include baked brie and tomato tart with rocket and pesto, or pea, rocket and parmesan risotto. Salads can be prepared for both small and large appetites.

**Open** all day all wk 11-11 (Sun noon-11) Closed: 25 Dec eve **Bar Meals** L served Mon-Fri 12-2.30, Sat-Sun 12-10 booking required D served Mon-Fri 6.30-10, Sat-Sun 12-10 booking required Av main course £9.50 **Restaurant** L served all wk 12-2.30 booking required D served all wk 6.30-10 booking required Fixed menu price fr £14.50 Av 3 course à la carte fr £23 ⊕ FREE HOUSE ◼ Ballards Best, The Fox Goes Free, Harveys Sussex ♍ 9 **Facilities** Children's menu Dogs allowed Garden Parking

Save on Hotels. Book at theAA.com/hotel

SUSSEX, WEST 461 ENGLAND

## EAST ASHLING *continued*

cheese-topped smoked haddock with spinach; steak and Guinness pie; or lamb cutlets. The enclosed garden is great place for alfresco eating in warmer weather. There are eleven spacious rooms available if you would like to stay over.

**Open** noon-3 6-11 (Sun noon-6) Closed: Sun eve **Bar Meals** L served all wk 12-2.15 D served Mon-Sat 6.30-9.15 Av main course £4.95 **Restaurant** L served all wk 12-2.15 D served Mon-Sat 6.30-9.15 booking required Av 3 course à la carte fr £9.95 ⊕ FREE HOUSE ◀ Youngs, Harveys, Summer Lightning, Hop Head Ⓞ Stowford Press. **Facilities** Children's menu Children's portions Dogs allowed Garden Parking **Rooms** 11

### EAST DEAN                           Map 6 SU91

## PICK OF THE PUBS

## The Star & Garter ⚑

PO18 0JG ☎ 01243 811318  ▤ 01243 811826 e-mail: thestarandgarter@hotmail.com **dir:** *On A286 between Chichester & Midhurst. Exit A286 at Singleton. Village in 2m*

Close to Goodwood racecourse and motor racing venues, the pub is located in the pretty downland village of East Dean just above the village pond. It was built as a pub around 1740 from traditional Sussex napped flint; outside are a large well sheltered stone-paved patio, an original well and attractive lawned gardens. The interior has been opened out to give a light and airy atmosphere, with original brickwork, oak flooring, antique panelling, scrubbed tables and a wood-burning stove. In the bar you'll find three real ales served from the barrel alongside two ciders, various lagers and more than ten wines by the glass. Locally renowned for its excellent selection of fish and shellfish, the menu also includes fine meat and vegetarian dishes. Expect the likes of roast wild duck with a Bramley apple compôte and fondant potatoes; and organic brie and roasted red pepper tart. Desserts are home made – try the chocolate and ginger baked cheesecake.

**Open** all wk **Bar Meals** L served all wk 12-2.30 D served all wk 4.30-11 Av main course £10 food served all day **Restaurant** L served all wk 12-2.30 booking required D served all wk 6.30-10 booking required Av 3 course à la carte fr £27.50 food served all day ◀ Ballards Best, Guinness, Arundel Castle, Gold Ⓞ Westons 1st Quality, Aspall. ⚑ 11 **Facilities** Children's menu Children's portions Dogs allowed Garden Parking

### ELSTED                              Map 5 SU81

## PICK OF THE PUBS

## The Three Horseshoes

GU29 0JY ☎ 01730 825746 **dir:** *A272 from Midhurst towards Petersfield, after 2m left to Harting & Elsted, after 3m pub on left*

Tucked below the steep scarp slope of the South Downs in the peaceful village of Elsted, this 16th-century former drovers' ale house is one of those quintessential English country pubs that Sussex specialises in, full of rustic charm. Expect unspoilt cottagey bars, worn stone-flagged floors, low beams, latch doors, a vast inglenook, and a motley mix of antique furnishings. On fine days the extensive rear garden, with roaming chickens and stunning southerly views, is hugely popular. Tip-top real ales, including Bowman's from across the Hampshire border, are drawn from the cask, and a daily-changing blackboard menu offers classic country cooking. Starters such as devilled kidneys or potted shrimps are followed by main courses likely to include venison; stalked locally and hung by the landlord, it may be served roasted with a redcurrant sauce reduction. Game such as pheasant is abundant in season; alternatively fish of the day comes with dauphinoise potatoes.

**Open** all wk **Bar Meals** L served all wk 12-2 D served Mon-Sat 6.30-9, Sun 7-8.30 Av main course £10 **Restaurant** L served all wk 12-2 D served Mon-Sat 6.30-9, Sun 7-8.30 Av 3 course à la carte fr £25.30 ⊕ FREE HOUSE ◀ Flowerpots Ale, Ballard's Best, Fuller's London Pride, Timothy Taylor Landlord, Hop Back Summer Lightning, Bowman Ales Wallops Wood. **Facilities** Dogs allowed Garden Parking

### FERNHURST                          Map 6 SU82

## The Red Lion ⚑

The Green GU27 3HY ☎ 01428 643112  ▤ 01428 643939 **dir:** *Just off A286 midway between Haslemere & Midhurst*

Renowned for its warm welcome and friendly atmosphere, this attractive 16th-century inn with oak beams and open fires is set in its own lovely gardens on the village green. The good choice of beers includes Fuller's ESB, Chiswick and London Pride along with seasonal guest ales. Freshly cooked, traditional English food is offered from a regularly changing specials menu featuring the likes of rabbit casserole; steak and kidney pudding; and sautéed calves' liver with a brandy and peppercorn sauce.

**Open** all wk 11.30am-11pm (closed Mon-Thu 3-5) **Bar Meals** L served all wk 12-2.30 D served all wk 6-9.30 **Restaurant** L served all wk 12-2.30 D served all wk 6-9.30 ⊕ FULLER SMITH TURNER PLC ◀ Fuller's ESB, Chiswick, London Pride, Guest Ale. ⚑ 8 **Facilities** Children's menu Children's portions Dogs allowed Garden Parking

### GRAFFHAM                           Map 6 SU91

## PICK OF THE PUBS

## The Foresters Arms ⚑

The Street GU28 0QA ☎ 01798 867202 e-mail: info@forestersgraffham.co.uk **dir:** *Telephone for directions*

A country pub at the foot of the South Downs, the Foresters is ideally placed for refreshments before racing at Goodwood or polo at Cowdray Park. A large garden is well furnished with picnic benches, parasols and boules pitch. In the bar you'll find old beams and a large smoke-blackened fireplace, as well as a great real ale choice likely to embrace Ballards, Hogsback, Sharps and Youngs – a pint of Midhurst Mild makes a refreshing change, or there are nine wines served by the glass. Freshly prepared food uses local produce where possible, but no corners are cut in the pub's objective to offer the best in quality and value: a prawn, crab and smoked salmon cheesecake with cucumber dressing, followed by slow-roast belly pork with smoked bacon rösti and braised carrots are two examples from the credit crunch menu. Otherwise chef's specials include the likes of moules marinière; and pan-fried pavé of New Zealand stone bass.

**Open** all wk 11am-2.30 6-late (all day in summer) **Bar Meals** L served all wk 12-2.15 booking required D served all wk 6.15-9.15 booking required Av main course £10 **Restaurant** L served all wk 12-2.15 booking required D served all wk 6.15-9.15 booking required ⊕ FREE HOUSE ⚑ 9 **Facilities** Children's menu Children's portions Dogs allowed Garden Parking

### HALNAKER                           Map 6 SU90

## PICK OF THE PUBS

## The Anglesey Arms at Halnaker ⚑

*See Pick of the Pubs on page 462*

# PICK OF THE PUBS

## The Anglesey Arms at Halnaker

**HALNAKER**      Map 6 SU90

**PO18 0NQ**
☎ 01243 773474   📄 01243 530034
e-mail: angleseyarms@aol.com
web: www.angleseyarms.co.uk
dir: *From centre of Chichester 4m E on A285
(Petworth road)*

Standing in two acres of landscaped grounds on the Goodwood Estate, this charmingly old-fashioned Georgian inn is a country local with a separate dining room. Whether you pop in for a quick drink or a full meal, you'll find a warm welcome in the wood-floored bar, with Bowman Swift One and Young's Bitter amongst the hand-pulled ales; cider drinkers are offered Stowford Press, and the extensive wine list includes unusual wines from small vineyards.

Hand-cut sandwiches, ploughman's with unpasteurised cheese, local sausages, and other traditional pub favourites will fill the odd corner, or you could sample something from the à la carte menu. The kitchen team makes skilful use of meat from fully traceable and organically raised animals, as well as locally-caught fish from sustainable stocks. The Anglesey has built a special reputation for its steaks, cut from British beef and hung for at least 21 days. The Estate's Home Farm supplies additional meats, while vegetables come from Wayside Organics. The area is noted for shooting, so game birds and venison are also available in season.

Dinner might begin with home-made Selsey crab pâté with brown toast; Anglesey game terrine and chutney; or organic Roquefort and baby fig salad with truffle dressing. Main course options include venison fillet with parsnip mash, winter greens and port wine sauce; duck confit with champ, red wine and thyme jus; and wild mushroom pasta. Home-made puddings like pannacotta with stewed rhubarb or chocolate mousse with poppy seed biscuits round off the meal nicely, or you might choose hand-made cheeses with water biscuits and home-made chutney.

**Open** all wk 11-3 5.30-11 (Sat-Sun 11-11) **Bar Meals** L served Mon-Sat 12-2.30, Sun 12-4 D served Mon-Sat 6.30-9.30 Av main course £10 **Restaurant** L served Mon-Sun 12-2.30, Sun 12-4 booking required D served Mon-Sat 6.30-9.30 booking required Av 3 course à la carte fr £24 ⊕ PUNCH TAVERNS ◀ Young's Bitter, Bowman Swift One, Black Sheep Bitter Ö Stowford Press. ♀ 14 **Facilities** Dogs allowed Garden Parking

Save on Hotels. Book at **theAA.com/hotel**

**SUSSEX, WEST** 463 **ENGLAND**

## HEYSHOTT — Map 6 SU81

### PICK OF THE PUBS

## Unicorn Inn

**GU29 0DL** ☎ **01730 813486** 📠 **01730 814896**
e-mail: unicorninnheyshott@hotmail.co.uk
dir: *Telephone for directions*

A free house dating from 1750, brimming with rural charm, and with good views from the beautiful, south-facing rear gardens. The bar, with beams and large log fire, is part of the original building, and very atmospheric it is too. The pub is within the South Downs National Park, and it's a fair bet that you'll share floorspace with walkers and cyclists (and, of course, some locals) detouring from the South Downs Way, thirstily knocking back a pint of Horsham Best Bitter or London Pride. The subtly lit, cream-painted restaurant is also in perfect historical tune. Locally sourced food is important, with fish arriving daily from Selsey – try plaice fillets stuffed with prawn and cod in white wine sauce. Lamb fillet is served with rosemary and redcurrant sauce; béarnaise, peppercorn or garlic butter will adorn your sirloin steak; and leek and goat's cheese tart comes with new potatoes and salad.

**Open** 11.30-3 6-11 (Sun 12-4) Closed: Sun eve & Mon **Bar Meals** L served Tue-Sat 12-2, Sun 12-2.30 booking required D served Tue-Sat 7-9 booking required **Restaurant** L served Tue-Sat 12-2, Sun 12-2.30 booking required D served Tue-Sat 7-9 ⊕ FREE HOUSE ◖ Horsham Best Bitter, Fuller's London Pride ♻ Stowford Press. **Facilities** Children's portions Dogs allowed Garden Parking

## HORSHAM — Map 6 TQ13

## The Black Jug ♀

**31 North St RH12 1RJ**
☎ **01403 253526** 📠 **01403 217821**
e-mail: black.jug@brunningandprice.co.uk
dir: *Telephone for directions*

This busy town centre pub is close to the railway station and popular with Horsham's well-heeled. Here you'll find a congenial atmosphere with friendly staff, an open fire, large conservatory and courtyard garden. Meals are freshly prepared using local ingredients wherever possible; light bites include wild garlic, parma ham and parmesan risotto, or rump steak sandwich with fried onions, whilst larger appetites might go for smoked haddock and salmon fishcakes or steak and ale pie with chips and peas.

**Open** all day all wk 11.30am-11pm (Sun 12-10.30) **Bar Meals** L served Mon-Sat 12-10, Sun 12-9.30 booking required D served Mon-Sat 12-10, Sun 12-9.30 booking required Av main course £11.50 food served all day **Restaurant** L served Mon-Sat 12-10, Sun 12-9.30 booking required D served Mon-Sat 12-10, Sun 12-9.30 booking required food served all day ⊕ BRUNNING & PRICE ◖ Harveys, Deuchars IPA, Guest Ales. ♀ 20 **Facilities** Children's portions Dogs allowed Garden

## KINGSFOLD — Map 6 TQ13

## The Dog and Duck

**Dorking Rd RH12 3SA** ☎ **01306 627295**
e-mail: info@thedogandduck.fsnet.co.uk
dir: *On A24, 3m N of Horsham*

A 16th-century, family-run country pub with a very large garden, children's play equipment and a summer ice cream bar. The pub has been steadily building a reputation for wholesome home-made food, such as liver and bacon, breaded plaice with prawns, chicken curry, chilli con carne and lasagne. It hosts many events, including quizzes, darts evenings, a big beer festival and fundraising activities.

**Open** all wk Mon-Thu 12-3 6-11 (Fri 12-3 6-12 Sat noon-mdnt Sun noon-10pm) **Bar Meals** L served 12-2.30 (3pm Sun) booking required D served 6-9 booking required Av main course £9.75 **Restaurant** L served 12-2.30 (3pm Sun) booking required D served 6-9 booking required Fixed menu price fr £10 ⊕ HALL & WOODHOUSE ◖ King & Barnes Sussex, Badger Best, seasonal variations, guest ales ♻ Stowford Press. **Facilities** Children's menu Children's portions Play area Dogs allowed Garden Parking

## KIRDFORD — Map 6 TQ02

### PICK OF THE PUBS

## The Half Moon Inn

*See Pick of the Pubs on page 464*

## LAMBS GREEN — Map 6 TQ23

## The Lamb Inn ♀

**RH12 4RG**
☎ **01293 871336** & **871933** 📠 **01293 871933**
e-mail: lambinnrusper@yahoo.co.uk
dir: *6m from Horsham between Rusper & Faygate. 5m from Crawley*

The Lamb remains an unchanged traditional country pub, with a patio to side and front, a bar with inglenook fire, and a conservatory. A good selection of real ales is sourced from local micro-breweries, and as much local produce as possible is used in the kitchen – everything on the menu from starters to puddings is home made. Ploughman's with Tremains organic Cheddar; Lydling Farm gammon and chips; and three Sussex sausages with mash give a flavour of the menu.

**Open** all wk Mon-Thu 11.30am-3 5.30-11pm (Fri-Sat 11.30am-11pm Sun noon-10.30pm) Closed: 25-26 Dec **Bar Meals** L served Mon-Thu 12-2, Fri-Sat 12-9.30, Sun 12-9 D served Mon-Thu 6.30-9.30, Fri-Sat 12-9.30, Sun 12-9 Av main course £11 **Restaurant** L served Mon-Thu 12-2, Fri-Sat 12-9.30, Sun 12-9 D served Mon-Thu 6.30-9.30, Fri-Sat 12-9.30, Sun 12-9 ⊕ FREE HOUSE ◖ Kings Old Ale, Weltons Old Cocky, Langham LSD, Dark Star Hop Head, Dark Star Best ♻ Stowford Press, Biddenden Cider, Rekorderlig. ♀ 12 **Facilities** Children's menu Children's portions Family room Dogs allowed Parking

## LICKFOLD — Map 6 SU92

### PICK OF THE PUBS

## The Lickfold Inn ♀

**GU28 9EY** ☎ **01798 861285**
e-mail: lickfold@evanspubs.co.uk
dir: *From A3 take A283, through Chiddingfold, 2m on right signed 'Lurgashall Winery', pub in 1m*

In the capable hands of Camilla Hansen and Mark Evans, this thriving free house dates back to 1460. Period features include an ancient timber frame with attractive herringbone-patterned bricks, and a huge central chimney. Inside are two restaurant areas with oak beamed ceilings, and a cosy bar dominated by a large inglenook fireplace, Georgian settles and moulded panelling. Look for the recurring garlic motif, reflecting the village's Anglo-Saxon name, 'leac fauld', which means an enclosure where garlic grows. The pub is heavily food oriented, offering tempting lunchtime sandwiches, Sunday roasts, and seasonal dishes complemented by a choice of well-kept real ales and a comprehensive wine list. Expect Lickfold Inn fish pie; grilled aubergine with spinach and ricotta; and roast guinea fowl in bacon with potato rösti and redcurrant sauce. The large courtyard and rambling terraced gardens are ideal for alfresco dining. Fifty per cent of the pub's profits go to a children's hospice.

**Open** all day all wk noon-11 Closed: 25 Dec **Bar Meals** L served Mon-Sat 12-9.45, Sun 12-8.45 food served all day **Restaurant** food served all day ⊕ FREE HOUSE ◖ Hogs Back TEA, Guinness, Langham. ♀ 12 **Facilities** Children's menu Dogs allowed Garden Parking

## LODSWORTH — Map 6 SU92

### PICK OF THE PUBS

## The Halfway Bridge Inn ♀

*See Pick of the Pubs on page 465*

# PICK OF THE PUBS

# The Half Moon Inn

**KIRDFORD**  Map 6 TQ02

**RH14 0LT** ☎ **01403 820223**
**web:** www.halfmoonkirdford.co.uk
**dir:** *Off A272 between Billingshurst &
Petworth. At Wisborough Green follow
Kirdford signs*

Set directly opposite the church in this
quiet unspoilt Sussex village near the
River Arun, this picturesque, red-tiled
16th-century village inn is covered in
climbing roses. A bit off the beaten
track, the pub is made up of cottages
that were once craftsmen's workshops.

Although drinkers are welcome, The Half
Moon is mainly a dining pub. The
interior consists of an attractive bar
with adjoining wooden-floored
restaurant area. The furniture and
paintings charmingly reflect the oak
beams, tiled floors, open fireplaces and
log fires in winter.

The chef serves honest wholesome food,
locally sourced from healthy well-reared
stock. The à la carte and daily set
menus reflect the best of the season's
ingredients. Lunch choices from the
menu might include starters like
roasted pepper and goat's cheese salad;
chicken and pistachio terrine; tian of
crayfish and tartare of salmon; or
charcuterie of smoked meats. These
might be followed by rump of lamb with
redcurrant and mint jus; veal chop with
Calvados and fresh apple sauce; or fillet
of turbot with wild mushroom and white
wine sauce. Lunchtime snacks reflect
the seasons, for example salads in
summer and hotpots in winter. At
dinner, the menu is broadly similar,
although the atmosphere changes, with
candlelight, linen tablecloths and
polished glassware. Private dining is
available.

Well-tended gardens at the front and
rear are an added draw in the summer,
and a pamphlet featuring local country
walks is available. Look out for the
monthly themed music-to-dine-to
evenings. There are also a number of
cycle routes in the area if you want to
work up an appetite.

**Open** 11-3 6-11 Closed: Sun eve, Mon
eve **Bar Meals** L served all wk 12-2.30
D served Tue-Sat 6-9.15 ☎ Local ale,
Ballards. **Facilities** Children's portions
Garden Parking

# PICK OF THE PUBS

## The Halfway Bridge Inn ♛

**LODSWORTH**  Map 6 SU92

**Halfway Bridge GU28 9BP**
☎ **01798 861281**
e-mail: enquiries@halfwaybridge.co.uk
web: www.halfwaybridge.co.uk
dir: *Between Petworth & Midhurst, next to
Cowdray Estate & Golf Club on A272*

Right at the heart of the 2010-created South Downs National Park, the inn stands half-way between Midhurst (voted 'the most pleasant town in England') and the popular antique emporia of Petworth (with its fabulous National Trust-owned country mansion). Add to these a network of great walking trails, the Cowdray Park polo ground and the splendid scenery of the South

Downs, little wonder that guests chose to stay over at the gabled inn's accommodation, created from stables around a 250 year old equine yard.

The Halfway Bridge is a cunning mix of traditional pub and contemporary dining inn; log fires, beams, blackened iron stove and wooden floors recall its days as a coaching inn whilst modern touches added by Paul and Sue Carter add an airy, cutting-edge atmosphere. An inspiring choice of real ales guarantees that locals and visitors seeking a short interlude will find a great welcome, whilst the hugely appealing menu, enhanced by specials each day on a chalkboard, offers a particularly wide range of options, matched by a connoisseurs wine list.

Open the proceedings with pigeon breast with a mushroom soufflé served with a black pepper cream or pan-seared scallops and belly of pork with mixed spice fruit compote before indulging in steak, ale and Stilton pie with celeriac mashed potato and a red wine jus, turn to the sea for grilled whole sea bass with roasted cherry tomatoes, parsnip and swede purée with a dill cream sauce, or succumb to the

appeal of roasted butternut squash stuffed with almond and sweet potato mousse with julienne vegetables and a chervil cream sauce. Squeeze in a home-made ice cream or sorbet before rewarding yourself with a seat in the peaceful patio and garden.

**Open** all wk Mon-Sat 11-11, Sun 12-10.30 Closed: 25 Dec **Bar Meals** L served all wk 12-2.30 D served all wk 6.30-9.15 **Restaurant** L served all wk 12-2.30 D served all wk 6.30-9.15 ⊕ FREE HOUSE ◧ Skinners Betty, Sharp's Doom Bar, Langhams Halfway to Heaven. ♛ 12 **Facilities** Children's menu Dogs allowed Garden Parking

## LODSWORTH continued

### PICK OF THE PUBS

## The Hollist Arms ⟨glass⟩

**The Street GU28 9BZ** ☎ **01798 861310**
e-mail: george@thehollistarms.co.uk
**dir:** *0.5m between Midhurst & Petworth, 1m N of A272, adjacent to Country Park*

The Hollist Arms, a pub since 1823, is full of traditional charm and character. The 15th-century building overlooks a lawn where a grand old tree stands ringed by a bench. Step through the pretty entrance porch and you'll find open fires in winter, leather sofas and a blissful absence of fruit machines. The atmospheric dining room has a popular window table, but if that's occupied you can head for the snug or one of a number of small intimate rooms in which to drink or eat with family and friends. All the dishes served here are prepared by chefs using traditional methods and fresh local ingredients whenever possible. Summer sees everyone heading for the wonderful garden and terraced area clutching pints of Horsham Best or Stowford Press cider. Well behaved children and dogs are welcome, all looked after by smiling staff who contribute greatly to this hostelry's warm and friendly ambience.

**Open** all day all wk 11am–11pm **Bar Meals** L served all wk 12–9 booking required D served all wk 12–9 booking required Av main course £8.50 food served all day **Restaurant** L served all wk 12–9 booking required D served all wk 12–9 booking required Fixed menu price fr £12 food served all day ⊕ FREE HOUSE ◀ Langham, Timothy Taylor Landlord, Horsham Best ♂ Stowford Press. ⟨glass⟩ 9 **Facilities** Children's menu Children's portions Dogs allowed Garden Parking

### LURGASHALL                    Map 6 SU92

## The Noah's Ark

**The Green GU28 9ET** ☎ **01428 707346**
e-mail: amy@noahsarkinn.co.uk
**dir:** *B2131 from Haslemere follow signs to Petworth/ Lurgashall. A3 from London towards Portsmouth. At Milford take A283 signed Petworth. Follow signs to Lurgashall*

In a picturesque village beneath Blackdown Hill, this attractive 16th-century inn overlooks the cricket green. The revitalised interior is full of warmth thanks to the charm of old beams, a large inglenook fireplace, and the enthusiasm of its owners. Ales include a regularly changing guest, and traditional British food with a contemporary twist uses ingredients carefully sourced from the best local suppliers: crab and leek tartlet or Sussex beef carpaccio may precede main courses such as roast guinea fowl with marquis potatoes, or whole grilled lemon sole.

**Open** all wk 11–3.30 5.30–11 (all day Sat-Sun) **Bar Meals** L served all wk 12–2.30 booking required D served all wk 7–9.30 booking required **Restaurant** L served all wk 12–2.30 booking required D served all wk 7–9.30 booking required ⊕ GREENE KING ◀ Greene King IPA , Abbot, Guest ale ♂ Stowford Press. **Facilities** Children's portions Family room Dogs allowed Garden Parking

### MAPLEHURST                    Map 6 TQ12

## The White Horse ⟨glass⟩

**Park Ln RH13 6LL** ☎ **01403 891208**
**dir:** *5m SE of Horsham, between A281 & A272*

In the tiny Sussex hamlet of Maplehurst, this traditional rural pub offers a break from modern life: no music, no fruit machines, no cigarette machines — just hearty home-cooked pub food and an enticing range of local brews served over what is reputedly the widest bar counter in Sussex. Sip a pint of Harveys Best, Welton's Pride & Joy, or Dark Star Espresso Stout whilst admiring the rolling countryside from the large, quiet, south-facing and child-friendly garden. Village-brewed cider is a speciality.

**Open** all wk 12–2.30 6–11 (Sun 12–3 7–11) **Bar Meals** L served all wk 12–2 D served all wk 6–9 Av main course £6 ⊕ FREE HOUSE ◀ Harvey's Best, Welton's Pride & Joy, Dark Star Espresso Stout, King's Red River, Station Pullman ale ♂ Local cider, JB Cider. ⟨glass⟩ 11 **Facilities** Children's menu Children's portions Play area Family room Dogs allowed Garden Parking **Notes** ⊛

### MIDHURST                    Map 6 SU82

## The Angel Hotel ★★★ HL

**North St GU29 9DN** ☎ **01730 812421**   ▤ **01730 815928**
e-mail: info@theangelmidhurst.co.uk
**dir:** *Telephone for directions*

An imposing and well-proportioned late-Georgian façade hides the true Tudor origins of this former coaching inn. Its frontage overlooks the town's main street, while at the rear attractive gardens give way to meadowland and the ruins of Cowdray Castle. A reliable pint of Fuller's could be followed by dinner in the new Bentley's Grill, where a range of the finest Argentinian steaks can be cut to suit appetites large and small. A total refurbishment has created 15 boutique bedrooms with every modern convenience.

**Open** all day all wk **Bar Meals** L served all wk 12–2 D served all wk 7–10 Av main course £10.95 **Restaurant** L served all wk 12–2 D served all wk 7–10 Fixed menu price fr £25 Av 3 course à la carte fr £30 ⊕ FREE HOUSE ◀ Fuller's HSB, Best, London Pride, Guinness ♂ Aspall. **Facilities** Children's menu Children's portions Garden Parking **Rooms** 15

### NUTHURST                    Map 6 TQ12

### PICK OF THE PUBS

## Black Horse Inn

**Nuthurst St RH13 6LH** ☎ **01403 891272**
e-mail: enquiries@theblackhorseinn.com
**dir:** *4m S of Horsham, off A281, A24 & A272*

Under the management of Matt Henwood and Zoe Brittain since mid-2009, the Black Horse's 18th-century features — stone-flagged floors, exposed wattle and daub walls, inglenook fire — have been combined with touches of contemporary style to create a truly

relaxing dining pub. The lovely old building, half masked by impressive window boxes in summer, was originally part of a row of workers' cottages on the Sedgwick Park estate; it was first recorded as an inn in 1817. Today the award-winning hostelry's real ales and ciders are backed by a concise but complete menu of dishes from the kitchen. Lunch sees a range of open sandwiches competing with classic hot plates (Sussex bangers and mash) and specials (pan-fried salmon with creamed leeks and new potatoes). In the evening expect more complex fare such as rump of lamb provençale; or loin of pork with roast peppers. Home-made puddings follow simple but classic lines such as vanilla crème brûlée. On sunny days you can sit out on the terraces at the front and rear, or take drinks across the stone bridge over a stream into the delightful back garden.

**Open** all wk all day Sat-Sun & BHs **Bar Meals** L served all wk 12–2.30 booking required D served all wk 6–9.30 booking required Av main course £11.50 **Restaurant** L served all wk 12–2.30 booking required D served all wk 6–9.30 booking required Fixed menu price fr £9.50 Av 3 course à la carte fr £14.50 ⊕ FREE HOUSE ◀ Harveys Sussex, W J King, Fuller's London Pride, Hepworths, guest ales ♂ Westons Stowford Press. **Facilities** Children's menu Children's portions Dogs allowed Garden Parking

### OVING                    Map 6 SU90

## The Gribble Inn ⟨glass⟩

**PO20 2BP** ☎ **01243 786893**   ▤ **01243 786893**
**dir:** *From A27 take A259. After 1m left at rdbt, 1st right to Oving, 1st left in village*

Named after local schoolmistress Rose Gribble, the inn retains all of its 16th-century charm. You'll find large open fireplaces, wood burners, low beams and no background music at this peaceful hideaway. In short, here are ideal conditions in which to quietly sup any of the eight real ales from the on-site micro-brewery; takeaway polypins are also sold. A daily-changing chalk board menu displays traditional pub food with a twist, such as pigeon fajitas; venison sausages with colcannon mash; and seafood from Selsey.

**Open** all wk 11–3 5.30–11 (Fri-Sun 11–11) **Bar Meals** L served all wk 12–2 D served all wk 6.30–9.30 Av main course £9.95 **Restaurant** L served all wk 12–2 booking required D served all wk 6.30–9.30 booking required ⊕ HALL & WOODHOUSE ◀ Gribble Ale, Reg's Tipple, Badger First Gold, Pigs Ear, Fuzzy Duck ♂ Stowford Press. ⟨glass⟩ 20 **Facilities** Children's menu Children's portions Family room Dogs allowed Garden Parking

Save on Hotels. Book at theAA.com/hotel

SUSSEX, WEST 467 ENGLAND

## PETWORTH
Map 6 SU92

### The Black Horse

Byworth GU28 OHL ☎ 01798 342424

dir: A285 from Petworth, 2m, turn right signed Byworth, pub 50yds on right

An unspoilt 16th-century village pub, once part of the old tanneries, The Black Horse retains a rustic feel with exposed beams, flagstone floors, pew seating, scrubbed wooden tables, period photographs and open fires. It is a great place for enjoying a glass of well kept ale. The former kitchen has been transformed into a snug dining area including the original Aga, whilst the large garden offers views to the South Downs. Expect lunchtime baguettes, jacket potatoes, light dishes and ploughman's, and in the evening maybe seared king scallops with crispy bacon and aged balsamic reduction, followed by honey and mustard glazed pork steak with oven roasted vegetables.

Open all day all wk 11-11 (Sun 12-11) **Bar Meals** L served all wk 12-3 D served Mon-Thu 6-9, Fri-Sat 6-9.30 **Restaurant** L served all wk 12-3 booking required D served Mon-Thu 6-9, Fri-Sat 6-9.30 booking required ⊕ FREE HOUSE ◀ Fuller's London Pride, TEA, Flowerpots, Hophead. **Facilities** Children's menu Dogs allowed Garden Parking

### PICK OF THE PUBS

### The Grove Inn

Grove Ln GU28 0HY ☎ 01798 343659

e-mail: steveandvaleria@tiscali.co.uk

dir: On outskirts of town, just off A283 between Pullborough & Petworth. 0.5m from Petworth Park

A 17th-century free house a stone's throw south of historic Petworth. Idyllically sited, it nestles in beautiful gardens with views to the South Downs; a patio area with shady pergola is ideal for alfresco drinks. Inside is a bar with oak-beamed ceilings and large fireplace, while the conservatory restaurant is the place to sample a seasonal menu revised every six to eight weeks. The pub is hosted by a husband and wife partnership: Valeria looks after front of house, warmly welcoming locals and visitors alike, while husband Stephen runs the kitchen operation. His simple objective is to serve quality dishes at prices that do not detract from their enjoyment. Typical starters include deep fried calamari with garlic mayonnaise; followed by South Downs venison fillet medallions with port jus; or poached smoked haddock topped with cheese sauce and a poached egg. Expect desserts along the lines of toffee and banana pancake with vanilla ice cream or rhubarb crumble.

Open Tue-Sat 12-3 6-11 (Sun 12-3) Closed: Sun eve & Mon (ex BH) **Bar Meals** L served Tue-Sun 12-2.30 D served Tue-Sat 6-9.15 Av main course £13.95 **Restaurant** L served Tue-Sun 12-2.30 D served Tue-Sat 6-9.15 Fixed menu price fr £15.95 Av 3 course à la carte fr £28 ⊕ FREE HOUSE ◀ Youngs, Betty Stogs, Sharp's Doom Bar, Halfway to Heaven. **Facilities** Children's portions Dogs allowed Garden Parking

## POYNINGS
Map 6 TQ21

### PICK OF THE PUBS

### Royal Oak Inn ☗

*See Pick of the Pubs on page 468*

## ROWHOOK
Map 6 TQ13

### PICK OF THE PUBS

### The Chequers Inn ◉ ☗

RH12 3PY ☎ 01403 790480   📠 01403 790480

e-mail: thechequersrowhook@googlemail.com

dir: Off A29 NW of Horsham

A white-washed 15th-century inn in the small hamlet of Rowhook in West Sussex, The Chequers is full of character, with 'mind your head' original beams, flagstones, open fires and real ales with 30 wines by the glass. Master Chef Tim Neal offers a good choice of food and produce can be sourced as locally as the pub's own raised beds or local shoots. In the restaurant, typical starters might be risotto of natural smoked haddock and butternut squash with parmesan and olive oil, or terrine of smoked ham hock and foie gras with organic fig relish. Mains could include slow-braised British pork belly with home-made black pudding, apple and celeriac purée, or peppered breast of duck with vanilla roasted rhubarb, buttered greens and cocotte potatoes. The bar menu takes in ploughman's, a range of baked ciabattas and hot specials such as Harveys beer battered haddock with chunky chips and mushy peas.

Open 11.30-3.30 6-11.30 Closed: 25 Dec, Sun eve **Bar Meals** L served all wk 12-2 booking required D served Mon-Fri 7-9 booking required Av main course £8.50 **Restaurant** L served all wk 12-2 booking required D served Mon-Sat 7-9 booking required Fixed menu price fr £12.30 Av 3 course à la carte fr £30 ⊕ FREE HOUSE ◀ Harvey's Sussex Ale, Fuller's London Pride, Guest ale ♂ Thatchers Gold. ☗ 30 **Facilities** Children's portions Dogs allowed Garden Parking

## RUDGWICK
Map 6 TQ03

### The Fox Inn ☗

Guildford Rd, Bucks Green RH12 3JP
☎ 01403 822386   📠 01403 823950

e-mail: seafood@foxinn.co.uk

dir: On A281 midway between Horsham & Guildford

'Famous for Fish!' is the claim of this attractive 16th-century inn, a message borne out by the extensive menu. Food offered includes all-day breakfast and afternoon tea, while the bar menu focuses on seafood, from fish and chips to the huge fruits de mer platter. Dishes include Foxy's famous fish pie; roasted cod loin with chorizo; and hand-made Cumberland sausage on Stilton mash. A horse is apparently walked through the pub each Christmas day!

Open all wk ◀ King & Barnes Sussex, Badger Tanglefoot, Fursty Ferret. ☗ 8 **Facilities** Play area Dogs allowed Garden Parking

## SHIPLEY
Map 6 TQ12

### PICK OF THE PUBS

### The Countryman Inn ☗

*See Pick of the Pubs on page 469*

### George & Dragon ☗

Dragons Green RH13 8GE ☎ 01403 741320

e-mail: marlenegrace@googlemail.com

dir: Signed from A272 between Coolham & A24

Set amid beautiful Sussex countryside, this 17th-century cottage is a haven of peace and quiet, especially on balmy summer evenings when the garden is a welcome retreat. Its interior is all head-banging beams and inglenook fireplaces, with an excellent choice of real ales at the bar. Food-wise, expect pub classics such as local ham with egg and chips or a Yorkshire pudding filled with sausage, mash and gravy. Shipley is famous for its smock mill. The pub now has new landlords.

Open all wk 12-3 6-11 (all day Sat-Sun) **Bar Meals** L served all wk 12-2 booking required D served Tue-Sun 6-9 booking required **Restaurant** L served all wk 12-2 booking required D served Tue-Sun 6-9 booking required ⊕ HALL & WOODHOUSE ◀ Badger Best, Sussex Best, Hall and Woodhouse Fursty Ferret & Pickled Partridge, Guest ale ♂ Westons Stowford Press. ☗ 8 **Facilities** Children's portions Play area Family room Dogs allowed Garden Parking

## SINGLETON
Map 5 SU81

### The Partridge Inn ☗

PO18 0EY ☎ 01243 811251

e-mail: info@thepartrdigeinn.co.uk

dir: Telephone for directions

Back in the 16th century, this inn (formerly called the Fox and Hounds) was part of a huge hunting park owned by the Fitzalan Earls of Arundel. Today, it is popular with walkers enjoying the rolling Sussex countryside and visitors to Goodwood for motor and horse-racing. A menu of classic pub fare runs from sandwiches (prawn and crayfish; tarragon chicken) to ham, egg and chips, terrine of duck and pheasant with red onion marmalade or whitebait with tartare sauce.

Open all wk all day Sat-Sun **Bar Meals** L served all wk 12-2, Sat-Sun 12-3 D served all wk 6-9, Fri-Sat 6-9.30 Av main course £12.50 **Restaurant** L served all wk 12-2, Sat-Sun 12-3 booking required D served all wk 6-9, Fri-Sat 6-9.30 booking required ⊕ ENTERPRISE INNS ◀ London Pride, Harvey's Sussex, Summer Lightening ♂ Stowford Press. ☗ 10 **Facilities** Children's menu Children's portions Dogs allowed Garden Parking

# PICK OF THE PUBS

## Royal Oak Inn ♀

**POYNINGS**        Map 6 TQ21

**The Street BN45 7AQ**
☎ **01273 857389**   📠 **01273 857202**
e-mail: ropoynings@aol.com
**dir:** *N on A23 just outside Brighton, take
A281 signed Henfield & Poynings, then follow
signs into Poynings*

There has been a 'Royal Oak' on this
site, tucked away in a fold of the South
Downs below the Devil's Dyke, since the
1880s. The present business has been
owned and operated by Paul Day and
Lewis Robinson since 1996, and regular
visitors have witnessed an ongoing
refurbishment programme over the last
couple of years. The eye-catching
window blinds and cream-painted
exterior draw customers into a building
with solid oak floors, where old beams
hung with hop bines blend effortlessly
with contemporary decor and comfy
sofas.

In the bar, Sussex-bred Harveys real
ales sit alongside offerings from
Sharps, and a decent wine list that
includes new and old world wines with
up to 14 available by the glass. The
menu changes seasonally, utilising
local produce to offer a range of options
that will suit most appetites. Sandwich
platters might feature fillings such as
Springs' locally smoked salmon and
mascarpone, or brie, apple and spinach
with walnut dressing on warm whole
ciabattas with a helping of potato
chips.

Moving up the scale, again changing
regularly, good old-fashioned pub
classics like deep-fried fish of the day
with tartare sauce, chunky chips and
mushy peas; or home-roasted gammon
with sauté potatoes and free-range
eggs; rub shoulders with more
ambitious international twists.
Starters, for instance might feature
salmon, ginger and lime cakes with
curly kale and mango salsa, or leek and
gorgonzola tartlet with dressed mixed
leaves and sun-blush tomatoes. Main
course options might include wild
mushroom and green pea risotto with

parmesan shavings, and slow roasted
lamb shank with sweet potato mash
and honey glazed parsnips. Local beef
from the pedigree Sussex herd from the
neighbouring farm is featured on the
menus whenever it is available.
Puddings can be served with hand
made ice cream from a local dairy herd.
In summer months the barbecue menu
is very popular as are the winter themed
menu events.

**Open** all day all wk 11-11 (Sun noon-
10.30) **Bar Meals** Av main course £11
food served all day **Restaurant** food
served all day 🍺 FREE HOUSE
🍺 Harveys Best, Sharp's Doom Bar
🍎 Westons Herefordshire Country
Perry. ♀ 14 **Facilities** Children's menu
Play area Dogs allowed Garden Parking

# PICK OF THE PUBS

## The Countryman Inn 🍷

**Countryman Ln RH13 8PZ**
☎ **01403 741383** 📄 **01403 741115**
**e-mail:**
countrymaninn@btinternet.com
**web:** www.countrymanshipley.co.uk
**dir:** *From A272 at Coolham into Smithers Hill Ln. 1m to junct with Countryman Ln*

This traditional rural free house with its open log fires, cosy bar and a large restaurant has been run by the Vaughan family since 1986. The inn stands close to the small village of Shipley, and is surrounded by 3,500 acres of farmland owned by the Knepp Castle Estate. The area is managed largely for nature conservation and low intensity meat production, with fallow deer, Tamworth pigs, Exmoor ponies and longhorn cattle roaming free.

In fine weather, the inn's garden is a great place to enjoy the open-air kitchen and barbecue in the company of the birds that are attracted by the estate's wild grasses. Local produce is used wherever possible, and free-range meat and vegetables from local farms make their appearance on the menu alongside home-grown herbs, fresh fish from Shoreham and Newhaven, and local game in season.

Day-to-day menus change frequently, though pub classics such as Cumberland sausages and mash; and home-made fishcakes are usually available alongside lunchtime baguettes, ploughman's and summer salads. Typical starters like smoked salmon with brown bread and butter; and Sussex pâté with toasted rustic bread; herald main course choices that might include slow-roast shoulder of minted lamb with mashed potato and creamed leeks; or roasted vegetable and goat's cheese bake. Amongst the appetising desserts, you might find crème brûlée, or steamed chocolate pudding. The restaurant is not suitable for very young children.

Shipley's historic eight-sided smock mill, which is the fictional home of the BBC's *Jonathan Creek*, is just a mile's walk along a woodland bridle path from the pub.

**Open** all wk 10-4 6-11
**Bar Meals** L served all wk 11.30-3.30 D served all wk 6-10 **Restaurant** L served all wk 11.30-3.30 D served all wk 6-10
🌐 FREE HOUSE 🛢 Harveys, London Pride, Dark Star 🍶 Thatchers Gold. 🍷 18
**Facilities** Dogs allowed Garden Parking

## SLINDON
Map 6 SU90

### The Spur ♀

**BN18 0NE** ☎ **01243 814216** 🖹 **01243 814707**
**dir:** *Off A27 on A29 outside Slindon*

Set just outside the village of Slindon on top of the rolling
South Downs, this 17th-century pub is a an ideal
stopping-off point on a day out in the country. It has been
praised for its friendly atmosphere and for generous
portions of food. The interior includes an open-plan bar
and restaurant, warmed by crackling log fires. If you book
in advance you can use the skittle alley, or enjoy a game
of pool or other pub games.

**Open** all wk 11.30-3 6-11 (Sun noon-3 7-10.30)
**Bar Meals** L served all wk 12-2 D served Sun-Tue 7-9,
Wed-Sat 7-9.30 Av main course £12 **Restaurant** L served
all wk 12-2 booking required D served Sun-Tue 7-9, Wed-
Sat 7-9.30 booking required Av 3 course à la carte fr £20
⊕ FREE HOUSE ◄ Sharp's Doom Bar, Directors
Ò Thatchers Gold. ♀ 10 **Facilities** Dogs allowed Garden
Parking

## SOUTH HARTING
Map 5 SU71

### The Ship Inn

**GU31 5PZ** ☎ **01730 825302**
**dir:** *From Petersfield take B2146 towards Chichester.
Inn in 5m*

A 17th-century inn made from a ship's timbers, hence
the name. There is a great selection of real ales and
Thatchers Gold cider available. Home-made pies are a
feature, and other popular dishes include fish pie, mussel
chowder, calves' liver, rack of lamb, ham and asparagus
mornay, and Hungarian goulash, all washed down with a
pint of Palmer IPA. A range of vegetarian dishes and bar
snacks is also available.

**Open** all day all wk 11.30-11 (Sun noon-11) **Bar Meals** L
served all wk 12-2.30 D served Mon & Wed-Thu 7-9, Fri-
Sat 7-9.30 Av main course £8.95 **Restaurant** L served
Mon-Sat 12-2.30, Sun 12-6 D served Mon & Wed-Sat 7-9
Av 3 course à la carte fr £20 ⊕ FREE HOUSE ◄ Palmer
IPA, Dark Star Brewery Hophead, Ballards Wassail,
Palmers Copper Ale Ò Thatchers Gold.
**Facilities** Children's menu Children's portions Dogs
allowed Garden Parking

## STEDHAM
Map 5 SU82

### Hamilton Arms/Nava Thai Restaurant ♀

**Hamilton Arms School Ln GU29 0NZ**
☎ **01730 812555** 🖹 **01730 817459**
**e-mail:** hamiltonarms@hotmail.com
**web:** www.thehamiltonarms.co.uk
**dir:** *Off A272 between Midhurst & Petersfield*

Standing opposite the village common amid beautiful
South Downs countryside, this whitewashed free house is
one of the first country pubs to serve authentic Thai food.
It's also the home of the Mudita Trust, dedicated to
helping abused and underprivileged children in Thailand.

The extensive menu encompasses everything from soups
and starters to curries, seafood and vegetarian fare, and
a takeaway service is also available. There's a patio to
enjoy on warmer days while sipping a pint from the good
range of real ales.

*Hamilton Arms/Nava Thai Restaurant*

**Open** all day Closed: Mon (ex BH) **Bar Meals** L served
Tue-Sun 12-2.30 D served Tue-Sun 6-10 Av main course
£8.50 **Restaurant** L served Tue-Sun 12-2.30 D served
Tue-Sun 6-10 booking required Fixed menu price fr £24
Av 3 course à la carte fr £22 ⊕ FREE HOUSE ◄ Fuller's
London Pride, Fuller's HSB, Wadworth 6X, Alton Pride,
Ò Westons Vintage, Stowford Press. ♀ 8
**Facilities** Children's menu Children's portions Play area
Dogs allowed Garden Parking

## SUTTON
Map 6 SU91

### The White Horse Inn NEW

**The Street RH20 1PS**
☎ **01798 869221** 🖹 **01798 869221**
**e-mail:** mail@whitehorse-sutton.co.uk
**dir:** *From Petworth follow signs for roman villa then to
Sutton village*

Set in the beautiful village of Sutton in the heart of the
Sussex countryside, what was once a run-down boozer
was transformed into a smart pub when new owners took
over in 2008. Local suppliers and local produce are used
as much as possible on the modern menu which is
complemented by local ales and a good selection of
wines. Dishes include halibut fillet with lemon and
coriander butter, Sussex Down rump of lamb on roasted
vegetable medley, and steak and ale pie.

**Open** all wk 11-3 6-11 **Bar Meals** L served all wk
11.30-2.30 D served all wk 6.30-9.30 Av main course £8
**Restaurant** L served all wk 11.30-2.30 booking required
D served all wk 6.30-9.30 booking required Fixed menu
price fr £12 Av 3 course à la carte fr £22 ⊕ ENTERPRISE
INNS ◄ Sharp's Doom Bar, Harveys, Adnams, London
Pride Ò Stowford Press. **Facilities** Children's portions
Dogs allowed Garden Parking

## TILLINGTON
Map 6 SU92

### The Horseguards Inn ★★★★ INN ◉ ♀ NEW

**GU28 9AF** ☎ **01798 342332** 🖹 **01798 345126**
**e-mail:** info@thehorseguardsinn.co.uk
**dir:** *From Petworth towards Midhurst on A272. In 1m
turn right signed Tillington. Inn 300mtrs up hill opposite
church*

Set at the foot of the South Downs and overlooking the
Rother valley, this 300 year-old inn stands on the
perimeter of the National Trust's Petworth Park. Menus
change daily and with the seasons, but South Downs
hare suet pudding with roasted roots, and herb crumbled
haddock with crushed potatoes, leeks and hollandaise
sauce are typical choices. Three bright, airy bedrooms
and a secluded garden provide a quiet, homely location
for an overnight stay.

**Open** all day all wk **Bar Meals** L served Mon-Fri 12-2.30,
Sat 12-3, Sun 12-4 D served Mon-Sat 6.30-9 Av main
course £14 **Restaurant** L served Mon-Fri 12-2.30, Sat
12-3, Sun 12-4 booking required D served Mon-Sat
6.30-9 booking required Av 3 course à la carte fr £22
⊕ ENTERPRISE INNS ◄ Harveys Sussex Best, Skinners
Betty Stogs, Staropramen, Guinness Ò Stowford Press.
♀ 11 **Facilities** Children's menu Children's portions Dogs
allowed Garden **Rooms** 3

## TROTTON
Map 5 SU82

### PICK OF THE PUBS

### The Keepers Arms ◉ ♀

**GU31 5ER** ☎ **01730 813724**
**e-mail:** nick@keepersarms.co.uk
**dir:** *5m from Petersfield on A272, pub on right just
after narrow bridge*

This charming 17th-century free house is tucked onto a
hillside just above the river Rother, in an Area of
Outstanding Natural Beauty. A log fire provides a warm
welcome in the lovely, low-ceilinged bar, and the
stylish dining room is also a treat with its warm
colours, modern oak dining tables, comfortable
upholstered chairs and tartan fabrics. By day, there are
fabulous views over the South Downs. Food is taken
seriously, with real efforts made to source local and
seasonal produce. Blackboard menus offer pub
favourites such as chargrilled sirloin steak and chips
or Cumberland sausages and mash, while the
frequently changing à la carte menu features starters
such as warm salad of wild rabbit or carpaccio of
yellowfin tuna with soy vinaigrette, followed by slow-
roasted pork belly with seared scallops and cauliflower
purée or poached turbot with crab and coriander ravioli
and pak choi. As well as taking meals in the bar or
dining room, you can sit outside on the sun terrace
with those great views.

Save on Hotels. Book at theAA.com/hotel

SUSSEX, WEST 471 ENGLAND

Open all wk 12-3.30 6-11 **Bar Meals** L served all wk 12-2 D served all wk 7-9.30 **Restaurant** L served all wk 12-2 D served all wk 7-9.30 ⊕ FREE HOUSE ◖ Dark Star Hophead, Ringwood Best, Ballards Best, Ringwood Fortyniner, Otter Ale ☼ Old English. ♀ 8 **Facilities** Children's portions Dogs allowed Garden Parking

## WALDERTON    Map 5 SU71

### The Barley Mow ♀

**PO18 9ED ☎ 023 9263 1321   📠 023 9263 1403**
e-mail: info@thebarleymowpub.co.uk
dir: *B2146 from Chichester towards Petersfield. Turn right signed Walderton, pub 100yds on left*

Popular with walkers, cyclists and and horse-riders out exploring the Kingley Vale nature reserve, this ivy-clad 18th-century pub was used by the local Home Guard as its HQ in World War II; it's famous locally for its skittle alley. The secluded, stream-bordered garden is a real sun trap, perfect for a pint of Fortyniner; in winter months the log fires crackle. The menu covers the usual favourites such as steak and Guinness pie; home-cooked lasagne; and ham, egg and chips. Look out for jazz and country folk nights.

Open all wk 11-3 6-11 (Sun 12-10.30) **Bar Meals** L served Mon-Sat 12-2.30 (Sun all day) D served all wk 6-9.30 Av main course £7.50 **Restaurant** L served all wk 12-2.30 D served all wk 6-9.30 ⊕ FREE HOUSE ◖ Ringwood Old Thumper & Fortyniner, Fuller's London Pride, Harveys Best ☼ Stowford Press. ♀ 10 **Facilities** Children's menu Children's portions Dogs allowed Garden Parking

## WARNHAM    Map 6 TQ13

### *The Greets Inn*

**47 Friday St RH12 3QY**
**☎ 01403 265047   📠 01403 265047**
dir: *Off A24 N of Horsham*

A fine Sussex hall house dating from about 1350 and built for Elias Greet, a local merchant. A magnificent inglenook fireplace and low beams will be discovered in the flagstone-floored bar. There is a rambling series of dining areas where diners can sample the wares of the kitchen team. Look out for some good pasta and fish dishes.

Open all wk ◖ Interbrew, Greene King IPA, Fuller's London Pride, Abbot Ale. **Facilities** Dogs allowed Garden Parking

## WARNINGLID    Map 6 TQ22

### The Half Moon ♀

**The Street RH17 5TR ☎ 01444 461227**
e-mail: info@thehalfmoonwarninglid.co.uk
dir: *1m from Warninglid/Cuckfield junct of A23 & 6m from Haywards Heath*

This picture perfect Grade II listed building dates from the 18th century and has been sympathetically extended to preserve its traditional feel. Enjoy a pint of Harveys or a real cider while perusing the menu in this picturesque pub with its friendly atmosphere. The menu offers snacks, specials and pub classics. Try beer-battered halloumi with tomato fondue and pea purée at lunchtime, or guinea fowl, pork and apricot terrine followed by confit pork belly with creamed leeks, black pudding and mash in the evening.

Open all wk 11.30-2.30 5.30-11 (Sun 11.30-11) **Bar Meals** L served Mon-Sat 12-2, Sun 12-3 D served Mon-Sat 6-9.30 Av main course £12 **Restaurant** L served Mon-Sat 12-2, Sun 12-3 booking required D served Mon-Sat 6-9.30 booking required ⊕ FREE HOUSE ◖ Harveys Sussex, Black Sheep, Ringwood Best, Dark Star, Harvey's Old Ale ☼ Westons Stowford Press, Sheppy's Dabinett, Oakwood Special. ♀ 12 **Facilities** Children's portions Dogs allowed Garden Parking

## WEST CHILTINGTON    Map 6 TQ01

### The Queens Head

**The Hollow RH20 2JN**
**☎ 01798 812244   📠 01798 815039**
e-mail: enquiries@thequeenshead.info
dir: *Telephone for directions*

The pub is named after Anne of Cleves who was given an estate nearby in her divorce settlement. This is a textbook country pub, from its beams, low ceilings and open fire to the bar serving a good selection of well-kept real ales. The building is mostly 17th-century country, and houses two bars plus a restaurant. Meals range from traditional beer battered cod and chips to spicy Thai green chicken curry. Home-made pies are a speciality and come with a dizzying choice of fillings, from liver and onion to red lentil and pepper.

Open all day all wk noon-11 (Mon 5-11 ex BHs noon-11 Sun noon-10.30) **Bar Meals** L served Tue-Sat 12-2.30, Sun & BH 12-4 D served Tue-Sat 6-9.30 Av main course £11.60 **Restaurant** L served Tue-Sat 12-2.30, Sun & BH 12-4 D served Tue-Sat 6-9.30 Av 3 course à la carte fr £21.55 ⊕ ENTERPRISE INNS PLC ◖ Harveys Sussex Best Bitter, Fuller's London Pride, Ballards Best Bitter, Itchen Valley Godfathers, Langhams Halfway to Heaven. **Facilities** Children's portions Dogs allowed Garden Parking

## WINEHAM    Map 6 TQ22

### The Royal Oak ♀

**BN5 9AY ☎ 01444 881252**
e-mail: theroyaloakwineham@sky.com
dir: *Wineham between A272 (Cowfold to Bolney) & B2116 (Hurst to Henfield)*

After dispensing ale straight from the barrels for more than two centuries, this delightful 14th-century half-timbered cottage still retains its traditional, unspoilt character. It is a true rural alehouse - so expect rustic furnishings, and food like venison sausage toad-in-the-hole; cauliflower cheese; steak and ale pie; and home-made soups. Snacks of potted and smoked mackerel, and ploughman's on a wooden board are served weekdays, with roasts on Sundays. Outside, the extensive gardens are ideal for summer drinking.

Open all wk 11-2.30 5.30-close (Sat 11-3.30 6-close Sun noon-4 7-10.30) **Bar Meals** L served Mon-Sat 12-2.30, Sun 12-3 booking required D served Mon-Sat 7-9.30 booking required **Restaurant** L served Mon-Sat 12-2.30, Sun 12-3 booking required D served Mon-Sat 7-9.30 booking required ⊕ FREE HOUSE ◖ Harveys Sussex Best Bitter, Guest ales ☼ Thatchers Gold. ♀ 20 **Facilities** Children's portions Dogs allowed Garden Parking

## WISBOROUGH GREEN    Map 6 TQ02

### Cricketers Arms ♀

**Loxwood Rd RH14 0DG ☎ 01403 700369**
e-mail: craig@cricketersarms.com
dir: *On A272 between Billingshurst & Petworth. In centre of Wisborough Green turn at junct next to village green, pub 100yds on right*

A traditional village pub dating from the 16th century with oak beams, wooden floors and open fires. Fans of extreme sports should be aware that the Cricketers is the home of the British Lawn Mower Racing Association. Alongside real ales there are thirty wines by the glass in the bar, with a menu ranging from snacks to three course meals and Sunday roasts, with plenty of specials. Typical dishes include steak pie, sea bass in a prawn and oyster sauce, game dishes in season, and 'mega' salads. Thursday is live music night.

Open all day all wk **Bar Meals** L served Mon-Fri 12-2, Sat-Sun 12-2.30 D served Mon-Thu 6.30-9, Fri-Sat 6.30-9.30, Sun 6.30-8.30 **Restaurant** L served Mon-Fri 12-2, Sat-Sun 12-2.30 D served Mon-Thu 6.30-9, Fri-Sat 6.30-9.30, Sun 6.30-8.30 ⊕ ENTERPRISE INNS ◖ Harveys Sussex, Fuller's London Pride, Swift One. ♀ 30 **Facilities** Children's menu Children's portions Dogs allowed Garden Parking

## TYNE & WEAR

### NEWCASTLE UPON TYNE
Map 21 NZ26

## Shiremoor House Farm ♥

**Middle Engine Ln, New York NE29 8DZ**
☎ **0191 257 6302** 📠 **0191 257 8602**
**dir:** *Telephone for directions*

A swift pint of Jarrow River Catcher or Mordue Workie Ticket in New York? Since that's the name of the village, it's eminently feasible at this popular North Tyneside pub, brilliantly converted from an old farm. Particularly appealing is the glazed former granary where a wide range of traditional, home cooked pub food is served, from a daily changing blackboard menu - perhaps steak, ale and mushroom casserole; fillet of salmon with prawn and dill sauce; and sizzling strips of chicken with sweet chilli sauce. The fish on the menus has been caught and landed locally.

**Open** all day all wk **Bar Meals** L served all wk 11-10 D served all wk 11-10 Av main course £8.50 food served all day ⊕ FREE HOUSE ◀ Timothy Taylor Landlord, Mordue Workie Ticket, Theakston BB, John Smith's, Jarrow River Catcher. ♥ 12 **Facilities** Children's menu Family room Garden Parking

### TYNEMOUTH
Map 21 NZ36

## Copperfields ★★★ HL

**Grand Hotel, Hotspur St NE30 4ER**
☎ **0191 293 6666** 📠 **0191 293 6665**
**e-mail:** info@grandhotel-uk.com
**dir:** *On NE coast, 10m from Newcastle upon Tyne*

The bar is at the rear of the imposing Grand Hotel, where Stan Laurel and Oliver Hardy always stayed when they played Newcastle's Theatre Royal. Worth a visit for the great views up and down the coast, as well as an extensive bar menu that includes home-made ham, leek and Cheddar clanger (a steamed pudding); smokie fish pie; sticky chilli belly pork; Mexican beefburger; and riccia pasta ribbons. A blackboard lists daily specials.

**Open** all wk ◀ Bass '9', Black Sheep, Durham Brewery ales. **Facilities** Parking **Rooms** 45

### WHITLEY BAY
Map 21 NZ37

## The Waterford Arms ♥

**Collywell Bay Rd, Seaton Sluice NE26 4QZ**
☎ **0191 237 0450**
**e-mail:** les47@bt.connect.com
**dir:** *From A1 N of Newcastle take A19 at Seaton Burn then follow signs for A190 to Seaton Sluice*

The building dates back to 1899 and is located close to the small local fishing harbour, overlooking the North Sea. Splendid beaches and sand dunes are within easy reach, and the pub is very popular with walkers. Seafood dishes are the speciality, including seared swordfish, lemon sole, halibut, crab-stuffed plaice, and the famously large portions of fish and chips.

**Open** all wk noon-11.30 (Thu-Sat noon-mdnt Sun noon-10.30) **Bar Meals** Av main course £6.95 **Restaurant** L served Mon-Sat 12-9, Sun 12-4 booking required D served Mon-Sat 12-9, Sun 12-4 booking required Fixed menu price fr £6.95 food served all day ⊕ PUNCH ◀ Tetleys, John Smith's, Scotch, Guinness. ♥ 9 **Facilities** Children's menu Parking

## WARWICKSHIRE

### ALCESTER
Map 10 SP05

### PICK OF THE PUBS

## The Holly Bush

**37 Henley St B49 5QX**
☎ **01789 762482** & **0788 4342363**
**e-mail:** thehollybushpub@btconnect.com
**dir:** *M40 junct 15 for Warwick/Stratford, take A46 to Stratford*

Tracey-Jane Deffley has transformed the 17th-century Holly Bush from a one-bar boozer to a thriving pub serving great ales and delicious food. Find it between Alcester's parish church and historic town hall, and watch out for regular live music nights as well as beer festivals in June and October. At other times you can still sample eight real ales, as well as Hogans local cider. Traditional and contemporary food is freshly prepared using seasonal ingredients that include herbs, tomatoes and vegetables from the pub's allotment garden. Lunchtime sandwiches, salads and pasta are supported by hot dishes like pan-fried lamb's liver with spring onion mash, whilst evening choices might include braised Warwickshire lamb shank with roasted roots and herb mash; or Mediterranean rösti with vine tomatoes and tarragon dressing. This is a cracking town centre pub run with passion and panache – and there's a great garden, too.

**Open** all day all wk noon-mdnt (Fri-Sat noon-1am) **Bar Meals** L served Mon-Sat 12-2.30, Sun 12-4 D served Tue-Sat 7-9.30 **Restaurant** L served Mon-Sat 12-2.30, Sun 12-4 D served Tue-Sat 7-9.30 ⊕ FREE HOUSE ◀ Sharp's Doom Bar, Black Sheep, Purity Gold, Purity Mad Goose, Uley Bitter ♂ Local farm cider, Hogans. **Facilities** Children's portions Dogs allowed Garden Parking

### ALDERMINSTER
Map 10 SP24

### PICK OF THE PUBS

## The Bell ♥

**CV37 8NY** ☎ **01789 450414** 📠 **01789 450998**
**e-mail:** info@thebellald.co.uk
**dir:** *On A3400 3.5m S of Stratford-upon-Avon*

An 18th-century coaching inn whose interior blends modern touches with traditional charms. The spacious conservatory restaurant overlooks a delightful old courtyard with views of the Stour Valley beyond. A good selection of starters and 'little dishes' could include antipasti grazing platters, (either vegetarian or continental meats); or something more substantial like swordfish, spring onion and dill fishcake, with home-made tartare sauce; followed by marinated goat's cheese with poached fig salad, green beans, sun blush tomatoes and lambs lettuce; or thyme roasted chicken breast with lemon and pea risotto with juniper berries and a shallot and port sauce. Those fond of fresh fish should keep an eye on the blackboard menu.

**Open** 11.30-2.30 6-11 (Fri-Sat 11.30-11 Sun noon-4.30) Closed: Sun eve **Bar Meals** L served Mon-Fri 12-2, Sat 12-2.30, Sun 12-3 booking required D served Mon-Thu 7-9, Fri-Sat 6-9 booking required Av main course £14.50 **Restaurant** L served Mon-Fri 12-2, Sat 12-2.30, Sun 12-3 booking required D served Mon-Thu 7-9, Fri-Sat 6-9 booking required ⊕ FREE HOUSE ◀ Hook Norton, Lady Godiva, Alscot Ale ♂ Hogans Cider. ♥ 14 **Facilities** Children's menu Children's portions Dogs allowed Garden Parking

### ALVESTON
Map 10 SP25

### PICK OF THE PUBS

## The Baraset Barn ♥

*See Pick of the Pubs on opposite page*

# PICK OF THE PUBS

## The Baraset Barn 🍷

**ALVESTON**  Map 10 SP25

**1 Pimlico Ln CV37 7RF**
☎ **01789 295510** 📠 **01789 292961**
e-mail: barasetbarn@lovelypubs.co.uk

This converted old barn is now a light, modern gastro-pub with a dramatic interior styled from granite, pewter and oak. Baraset Barn is one of a select group established in 1995 by visionary operators Paul Salisbury and Paul Hales, who now have six quality dining destinations in the area. The building oozes continental style, whilst retaining a traditional warm welcome. Original flagstones, redolent of the barn's 200-year history, contrast with the glass-fronted kitchen that introduces a stylish, up-to-the-minute visual appeal. Stone steps lead from the bar to the main dining area with its brick walls and high oak beams, whilst the open mezzanine level makes for a perfect vantage point. There's also a luxurious lounge with comfortable sofas for whiling away a relaxing morning coffee with the papers.

The chef uses only the finest ingredients; fresh herbs are imported from France, and the best meat and vegetables ensure top quality fare at all times. The crowd-pleasing menu successfully blends classic British dishes with an eclectic Mediterranean choice, offering sharing plates of rustic breads, roast garlic and pomodoro alongside conventional starters like egg florentine, wilted spinach and hollandaise; bucatini carbonara with smoked haddock, cream, egg and bacon; or spiced crab and prawn cocktail, guacamole, tomato and melba toast. Follow on with medallions of beef fillet with shiitake mushrooms, yuzu sauce and wasabi mash; ostrich steak wrapped in serrano ham, orange, pomegranate and rocket; or something tempting from the fish boards.

Leave room for one of the tempting desserts — chilled melon soup with vanilla pannacotta, raspberry ripple Eton mess, or sticky toffee pudding with butterscotch sauce and clotted cream ice cream are typical choices. The continental-style patio garden is just right for summer alfresco dining and sipping champagne.

**Open** all day 11am-mdnt Closed: 25 Dec & 1 Jan, Sun eve, Mon (Jan-Feb) **Bar Meals** L served all wk 12-2.30 D served Mon-Sat 6.30-9.30 Av main course £16 **Restaurant** L served Mon-Sat 12-2.30, Sun 12-3.30 booking required D served Mon-Sat 6.30-9.30 booking required Fixed menu price fr £12.50 Av 3 course à la carte fr £25 🍺 UBU. 🍷 12 **Facilities** Dogs allowed Garden Parking

## ARDENS GRAFTON     Map 10 SP15

### PICK OF THE PUBS

### The Golden Cross

**Wixford Rd B50 4LG**
☎ 01789 772420   📠 01789 773697
**e-mail:** info@thegoldencross.net
**dir:** Telephone for directions

Inside this beautiful 18th-century building you'll find a rug-strewn bar with flagstone floors, massive beams and open fires. Wells Bombardier and Purity Brewing ales are amongst the beers on offer here, together with regular guest ales. The light, airy dining room presents a complete contrast, with its soft pastel decor and elegant plaster ceiling. The same menu is served throughout the pub; traditional favourites are always available, and the blackboards reflect an ever-changing selection of specials. Starters from the main menu include leek and goat's cheese tart with roasted cherry tomatoes and herb salad, and char-grilled chicken and bacon salad. Main course choices are just as appealing; choose sage gnocchi with roasted butternut squash, spinach, wild mushrooms and parmesan cream, or cider roasted pork loin chop with black pudding mash, baked apple and creamed cabbage. For warmer days there's a large safe garden which also boasts a covered, heated patio. Thursday night is song and steak night – both local.

Open all wk May–Sep noon-3 5-11 **Bar Meals** L served all wk 12-3 D served all wk 5-9.30 **Restaurant** L served all wk 12-3 D served all wk 5-9.30 ⊕ CHARLES WELLS ◖ Wells Bombardier, Purity Brewing, Guest ales ♉ Thatchers Heritage. **Facilities** Children's menu Children's portions Garden Parking

## BARFORD     Map 10 SP26

### PICK OF THE PUBS

### The Granville @ Barford ♟

*See Pick of the Pubs on page 476*

## BROOM     Map 10 SP05

### Broom Tavern

**High St B50 4HL** ☎ 01789 773656   📠 01789 773656
**e-mail:** webmaster@broomtavern.co.uk
**dir:** N of B439 W of Stratford-upon-Avon

Once a haunt of William Shakespeare, this 16th-century brick and timber inn is smartly furnished, with a large beer garden where barbecues are held in summer. Very much at the heart of village life, it is home to the Broom Tavern Golf Society, and fun days, charity events and outings are a feature. The menu offers a large selection of vegetarian dishes and seafood specials, which can be accompanied with a good choice of ales.

Open all wk noon-3 5.30-11 **Bar Meals** L served all wk 12-2.30 D served all wk 6-9 Av main course £8.25 **Restaurant** L served all wk 12-2.30 booking required D served all wk 6-9 booking required ⊕ PUNCH TAVERNS ◖ Greene King IPA, Black Sheep, Timothy Taylor Landlord, Wells Bombardier, Hook Norton. **Facilities** Dogs allowed Garden Parking

## EDGEHILL     Map 11 SP34

### The Castle Inn

**OX15 6DJ** ☎ 01295 670255   📠 01295 670521
**e-mail:** info@thecastle-edgehill.com
**dir:** M40 junct 11 then A422 towards Stratford-upon-Avon. 6m to Upton House, next right, 1.5m to Edgehill

A fascinating property, the inn was built as a copy of Warwick Castle in 1742 to commemorate the centenary of the Battle of Edgehill, and stands on the summit of Edgehill, 700 feet above sea level. It opened on the anniversary of Cromwell's death in 1750, was first licensed in 1822, and acquired by Hook Norton a hundred years later. Bar snacks, sandwiches, hot platters and steaks are served.

Open all wk ◖ Hook Norton Best, Old Hooky & Generation Hooky Dark, guest ales. **Facilities** Garden Parking

## ETTINGTON     Map 10 SP24

### The Chequers Inn NEW

**91 Banbury Rd CV37 7SR** ☎ 01789 740387
**e-mail:** hello@the-chequers-ettington.co.uk
**dir:** Take A422 from Stratford-upon-Avon towards Banbury. Ettington in 5m, after junction with A429

This sumptuously appointed country dining inn is like a miniature Versailles with its subtle French decor and beautiful tapestries, but with a welcome for all, from nobility to locals seeking good British beers and great

...ood. Cooking style is modern European with a nod to traditional English staples, Sunday roasts and a very popular fish night each month – catch the red snapper with babaganouh and couscous with lemon and mint dressing. The grassy beer garden looks out over tranquil Warwickshire farmland.

Open noon-3 5-11 (Sat noon-11 Sun noon-6) Closed: Sun eve, Mon **Bar Meals** L served Tue-Sat 12-2.30 (Sun 12.30-3.30) booking required D served Tue-Sat 6.30-9.30 booking required Av main course £12 **Restaurant** L served Tue-Sat 12-2.30 (Sun 12.30-3.30) booking required D served Tue-Sat 6.30-9.30 booking required Av 3 course à la carte fr £24 ⊕ INDEPENDENT ◀ Hooky Gold, Tetley, JW Lees, Guest ales ♂ Stowford Press, Hogans. **Facilities** Children's menu Children's portions Dogs allowed Garden Parking

*See advert on opposite page*

## The Houndshill

Banbury Rd CV37 7NS
☎ 01789 740267 📠 01789 740075
dir: *On A422 SE of Stratford-upon-Avon*

Family-run inn situated at the heart of England, making it a perfect base for exploring popular tourist attractions such as Oxford, Blenheim, Stratford and the Cotswolds. The pleasant tree-lined garden is especially popular with families. Typical dishes range from poached fillet of salmon, and faggots, mash and minted peas, to supreme of chicken and ham and mushroom tagliatelle. Alternatively, try cold ham off the bone or home-made steak and kidney pie.

Open all wk Closed: 25-28 Dec ◀ Hook Norton Best, Spitfire. **Facilities** Play area Dogs allowed Garden Parking

### FARNBOROUGH — Map 11 SP44

## PICK OF THE PUBS

## The Inn at Farnborough ♥

OX17 1DZ ☎ 01295 690615
e-mail: enquiries@innatfarnborough.co.uk
dir: *M40 junct 11 towards Banbury. Right at 3rd rdbt onto A423 signed Southam. 4m & onto A423. Left onto single track road signed Farnborough. Approx 1m turn right into village, pub on right*

An ale house for at least 200 years, this Grade II listed 16th-century property enjoys a picturesque setting in a National Trust village. It was formerly known as the Butcher's Arms, having once belonged to the butcher on the Farnborough Estate. Original features include a

fine inglenook fireplace; at the bar there's a good choice of real ales, Hogan's cider, and plenty of wines served by the glass. The menu is concise, but the kitchen's focus on quality ingredients ensures that all tastes and appetites are catered for. Starters include home-cured bresaola with lemon and thyme dressing. Main courses embrace chargrilled steer's liver and bacon with herb mash and sage gravy; chicken and coconut curry with coriander and fragrant rice; and braised Aberdeenshire oxtail 'off the bone' with parsnip mash. Look for the fixed-price menu of one to three courses which changes according to season and availability.

Open all wk 10-3 6-11 (Sat-Sun all day) Closed: 25 Dec **Bar Meals** L served all wk 12-3 booking required D served all wk 6-10 booking required Av main course £10 **Restaurant** L served all wk 12-3 booking required D served all wk 6-10 booking required Fixed menu price fr £10.95 Av 3 course à la carte fr £22 ⊕ FREE HOUSE ◀ Marstons Pedigree, London Pride, Bombardier ♂ Hogan's Ciders, Local. ♥ 14 **Facilities** Children's menu Play area Dogs allowed Garden Parking

### GREAT WOLFORD — Map 10 SP23

## PICK OF THE PUBS

## The Fox & Hounds Inn

CV36 5NQ ☎ 01608 674220
e-mail: enquiries@thefoxandhoundsinn.com
dir: *Off A44 NE of Moreton-in-Marsh*

This unspoilt village hostelry nestles in Warwickshire's glorious countryside on the edge of the Cotswolds. Among the excellent ales on offer are some from the county's Purity Brewing Company, to be supped at leisure whilst enjoying the quintessential English inn ambience – old settles, Tudor inglenook fireplaces and solid ceiling beams adorned with jugs or festooned with hops. The busy kitchen uses fresh local produce such as Dexter beef and seasonal game from local shoots, herbs and vegetables from the garden, and locally gathered mushrooms; only fresh fish comes from further afield, with deliveries from Scotland and Cornwall. Sausages, bacon, chutneys and pickles are all prepared on site – even the bread is baked using fresh yeast and organic flour milled in the Cotswolds. A typical selection from the menu could include Windrush goats' cheese and beetroot salad; Kitebrook lamb loin with home-made black pudding, celeriac purée and braised Puy lentils; and honey and lavender crème brûlée.

Open 12-2.30 6-11.30 (Sun 12-10.30) Closed: 1st 2wks Jan, Mon **Bar Meals** L served Tue-Sun 12-2 D served Tue-Sat 6.30-9 ⊕ FREE HOUSE ◀ Hook Norton Best, Purity, guest ales ♂ Stowford Press. **Facilities** Dogs allowed Garden Parking

### HATTON — Map 10 SP26

## The Case is Altered

Case Ln, Five Ways CV35 7JD ☎ 01926 484206
dir: *Telephone for directions*

This traditional whitewashed free house proudly carries the standard for the old style of pub with great charm and character. It serves no food and does not accept children or dogs. That aside, it's a thoroughly welcoming spot for adults who appreciate the pleasures of a quiet pint. Greene King beers have a strong presence, and there is always a local and national guest ale to sup while enjoying lively conversation or just appreciating the atmosphere.

Open all wk noon-2.30 6-11 (Sun 12-2 7-10.30) ⊕ FREE HOUSE ◀ Greene King IPA, Wye Vally Butty Bach, 2 Guest ales. **Facilities** Parking **Notes** ⊗

### ILMINGTON — Map 10 SP24

## PICK OF THE PUBS

## The Howard Arms ♥

*See Pick of the Pubs on page 477*

### LAPWORTH — Map 10 SP17

## PICK OF THE PUBS

## The Boot Inn ♥

Old Warwick Rd B94 6JU
☎ 01564 782464 📠 01564 784989
e-mail: bootinn@hotmail.com
dir: *Telephone for directions*

Beside the Grand Union Canal in the unspoilt village of Lapworth, this lively and convivial 16th-century former coaching inn is well worth seeking out. Apart from its smart interior with its soft modern furnishings complementing the old world feel, the attractive garden is a great place to relax on warm days, while a canopy and patio heaters make it a comfortable place to sit even on cooler evenings; barbecues are a speciality. But the main draw is the modern brasserie-style food, with wide-ranging menus that deliver home-produced dishes. A selection from the menu might include marinated gravadlax salmon with dill and lemon crème fraîche; crispy oriental duck salad; calves' liver, smoked bacon, cabbage and chive beurre blanc; and lasagne of sweet potato, spinach and goat's cheese lasagne.

Open all day all wk 11-11 (Thu-Sat 11am-mdnt Sun 11-10.30) **Bar Meals** L served all wk 12-2.30 D served Mon-Fri 7-9.30, Sat 6.30-9.30, Sun 7-9 Av main course £12 **Restaurant** L served all wk 12-2.30 D served Mon-Fri 7-9.30, Sat 6.30-9.30, Sun 7-9 Fixed menu price fr £12.50 Av 3 course à la carte fr £20 ⊕ FREE HOUSE ◀ Fuller's London Pride, Hobgoblin, Purity UBU. ♥ 9 **Facilities** Children's menu Children's portions Dogs allowed Garden Parking

# PICK OF THE PUBS

## The Granville @ Barford 🍷

**BARFORD**  Map 10 SP26

**52 Wellesbourne Rd CV35 8DS**
☎ 01926 624236  📄 01926 624806
**e-mail:** info@granvillebarford.co.uk
**dir:** *1m from M40 junct 15. Take A429 signed Stow. Located at furthest end of Barford village*

Owned and run by Val Kersey since 2007, this comfortable dining pub stands in the heart of Shakespeare country. The impressive brick building, which dates back to Georgian times, was named after the Reverend Edward Granville, vicar of neighbouring Wasperton. In those days the pub was one of a dozen drinking establishments in Barford, but today the stylish décor and warm, friendly service has made the Granville a firm favourite with locals and visitors alike. Relax on the leather sofas in the lounge with a drink - a pint of Hooky or Purity perhaps, or choose from the manageable wine list that embraces Europe, South America and South Africa.

The Granville's ever-changing seasonal menus offer varied, interesting choices and value for money. Everything on your plate is home-made from local produce delivered daily, except for the rustic bread, which arrives every morning from a neighbouring village. The lunchtime offering ranges from doorstep sandwiches served with salad garnish and red cabbage coleslaw, to large starters like The Granville's duck liver, brandy and orange pâté with red onion marmalade and melba toast, chef's home-made fish cake served on a bed of leaves with lemon mayonnaise. A three course evening meal might begin with classic loin of pork slow roasted with creamy mash and honey roasted vegetables, topped with cider apple sauce and crackling. Main course options include pie of the day (with a short crust case and puff pastry lid) served with creamy mash; pan-fried chicken breast stuffed with wild mushrooms with fondant potato and Café Parisien sauce; salmon, crayfish and haddock pie with cheesy potato topping, or roasted vegetable tarte Tatin with fresh goat's cheese and leaf salad. Round things off with chocolate brownie and vanilla ice cream; or profiteroles and warmed chocolate orange sauce. Enjoy alfresco dining in the spacious patio garden.

**Open** Mon-Thu noon-3 5.30-11 (Fri noon-3, 5-11.30, Sat noon-11.30, Sun noon-11) **Bar Meals** L served Mon-Fri 12-2.30 D served Mon-Fri 6-9 Sat 12-10, Sun 12-5 **Restaurant** L served Mon-Fri 12-2.30 D served Mon-Fri 6-9 Sat 12-10, Sun 12-5 ⊕ ENTERPRISE INNS PLC 🍺 Hooky Bitter, Purity Gold, Purity UBU. 🍷 17 **Facilities** Dogs allowed Garden Parking

# PICK OF THE PUBS

## The Howard Arms ♟

**ILMINGTON**       Map 10 SP24

**Lower Green CV36 4LT**
☎ 01608 682226 📄 01608 682874
**e-mail:** info@howardarms.com
**web:** www.howardarms.com
**dir:** *Off A429 or A3400, 9m from Stratford-upon-Avon*

The 17th-century Cotswold stone inn is a rambling building with five arched windows overlooking the pretty village green. Centuries of connections with one of England's most illustrious families who resided at nearby Foxcote House confirm the historical credentials of this Cotswold gem. The flagstoned bar and open-plan dining room create a civilised look without sacrificing period charm, and it is all imbued with an informal atmosphere. The breadth of choice among pumps and bottles in the bar nevertheless indicates a serious approach to meeting the wide and various demands of today's sophisticated palates. Half a dozen award-winning ales feature famous names such as Goat's Milk and Hook Norton, while wine drinkers will need to ponder carefully before choosing from a list of over thirty served by the glass.

Equally serious are the inn's efforts to source excellent ingredients for the kitchen – neighbours are encouraged to exchange their excess vegetables. Many of the suppliers are named on the menu; while mulling it over you can warm to the task ahead with large green olives stuffed with feta cheese. Why not begin with pressed jellied chicken and wild mushroom terrine, or twice-baked Red Leicester cheese soufflé? Howard's favourite main dishes include calves' liver, smoked bacon, and truffle oil mash; and rigatoni pasta, dolcelatte cheese, spinach and roast tomatoes. Alternatively a steak from the grill cooked to your liking will be served with red chard and chips. And so to desserts: will it be the Howard's sticky toffee pudding, or the steamed syrup sponge with custard? Or a plate of fine cheeses perhaps, which feature three locally-made specialities and a 'guest'.

In the menu's small print you'll read light-hearted warnings such as 'fish contain bones' and 'puddings contain calories'. Oh, and for those who like too much information, the menu is printed on paper made from recycled elephant poo.

**Open** all day all wk Closed: 25 Dec eve, 26 Dec eve **Bar Meals** L served Mon-Sat 12-2.30, Sun 12-4 booking required D served Mon-Sat 6.30-9.30 booking required **Restaurant** L served Mon-Sat 12-2.30, Sun 12-4 booking required D served Mon-Sat 6.30-9.30 booking required Fixed menu price fr £16 Av 3 course à la carte fr £18 🍷 FREE HOUSE ◀ Everards Tiger Best, Hook Norton Gold, Purity Brewing UBU, Bard's Brewery Nobel Fool, Timothy Taylor Landlord, Black Sheep Bitter. ♟ 32 **Facilities** Dogs allowed Garden Parking

## LONG ITCHINGTON — Map 11 SP46

### The Duck on the Pond ☂

**The Green CV47 9QJ**
☎ 01926 815876 ▤ 01926 815766
dir: *On A423 in village centre, 1m N of Southam*

Children will be delighted to discover that the name of this attractive village inn does indeed indicate the presence of a pond complete with drakes and mallards. Winter fires light an intriguing interior, crammed with fascinating bric-a-brac, while the menu offers a selection of pub favourites, including battered fish; gammon; and steaks, as well as vegetarian choices like aubergine and walnut bake or spinach and ricotta cannelloni. For dessert choose the home made apple pie or meringue.

**Open** Winter 12-3 6-11 (Summer noon-mdnt) Closed: Mon (ex BH) **Bar Meals** L served all wk 12-2.30 **Restaurant** L served all wk 12-2.30 D served Sat-Sun 6-9 (Summer 12-9) ⊕ CHARLES WELLS ◀ Wells Bombardier, Young's Best, Guinness, Eagle IPA. ☂ 15
**Facilities** Children's menu Children's portions Garden Parking

## MONKS KIRBY — Map 11 SP48

### The Bell Inn

**Bell Ln CV23 0QY** ☎ 01788 832352 ▤ 01788 832352
e-mail: belindagb@aol.com
dir: *Village off B4455 (Fosse Way)*

The Spanish owners of this quaint, timbered inn, once a Benedictine priory gatehouse and then a brewhouse cottage, describe it as "a corner of Spain in the heart of England". The pine bar top came from a tree grown in Leire churchyard nearby. Mediterranean and traditional cuisine play an important role on the extensive menu. Enjoy a glass of Ruddles while taking you time to make your choices. Fillet steak Rossini; tuna à la Carzuela; lobster mornay; and beef stroganoff all make a showing.

**Open** Tue-Sun Closed: 26 Dec, 1 Jan, Mon ⊕ FREE HOUSE ◀ Boddingtons, IPA, Ruddles. **Facilities** Garden Parking

## NAPTON ON THE HILL — Map 11 SP46

### The Bridge at Napton

**Southam Rd CV47 8NQ** ☎ 01926 812466
e-mail: info@thebridgeatnapton.co.uk
dir: *At Bridge 111 on Oxford Canal on A425, 2m from Southam & 1m from Napton on the Hill*

This is an ideal place to moor the narrow boat, though travellers by car or bike are equally welcome. Built as a stabling inn at Bridge 111 on the Oxford canal, the pub has a restaurant, three bars and a large garden, plus its own turning point for barges. There are some excellent ales, and food choices range from Aberdeen Angus beefburger with chips to the likes of honey-roasted belly pork with caramelised onions.

**Open** noon-3 6-11 (Sun noon-8) Closed: Mon (ex BH & summer school hols) ◀ Guinness, John Smith's, Black Sheep, Guest ales. **Facilities** Play area Family room Dogs allowed Garden Parking

## OXHILL — Map 10 SP34

### The Peacock ☂ NEW

**Main St CV35 0QU** ☎ 01295 688060
e-mail: info@thepeacockoxhill.co.uk
dir: *From Stratford-upon-Avon take A422 towards Banbury. Turn right to Oxhill*

Meander down leafy lanes between Stratford and Banbury to locate Oxhill and this 16th-century stone-built pub. Recently spruced up and successfully combining traditional old-world charm with a contemporary feel, it focuses on sourcing local meats and vegetables from local farms and the seasonal menus and chalkboard specials have found favour with local diners. Typical choices may include smoked salmon ravioli with pesto cream, slow-roasted Paddock Farm pork belly with cider gravy, and zesty lemon bread and butter pudding.

**Open** all day all wk noon-11 **Bar Meals** Av main course £8.95 food served all day **Restaurant** L served Mon-Sat 12-2.30, Sun 12-8 booking required D served Mon-Sat 6-9.30, Sun 12-8 booking required Fixed menu price fr £12.50 ◀ Timothy Taylor Golden Best, Peacock Bitter, Butty Bach, HPA, Dorothy Goodbody ♂ Weston's Old Rosie, Thatchers Gold, Rattler. ☂ 10 **Facilities** Children's menu Children's portions Dogs allowed Garden Parking

## PRESTON BAGOT — Map 10 SP16

### The Crabmill ☂

**B95 5EE** ☎ 01926 843342 ▤ 01926 843989
e-mail: thecrabmill@lovelypubs.co.uk
dir: *M42 junct 8, A3400 towards Stratford-upon-Avon. Take A4189 Henley-in-Arden lights. Left, pub 1.5m on left*

The name is a reminder that crab apple cider was once made at this 15th-century hostelry, which is set in beautiful rural surroundings. Restored to create an upmarket venue, the pub has a light, open feel. Even the menu seems fresh and stylish, with dishes ranging from a lunchtime croque monsieur or panini, to evening dishes such as smoked haddock and leek fishcake with poached egg, hollandaise and chips; or pork escalope stuffed with sage wrapped in Serrano ham, with lemon roasted new potatoes and gremolata

**Open** all day 11-11 Closed: 25 Dec, Sun eve **Bar Meals** L served Mon-Fri 12-2.30, Sat 12-3, Sun 12-3.30 D served all wk 6.30-9.30 Av main course £12.95 **Restaurant** Fixed menu price fr £10 ⊕ FREE HOUSE ◀ Wadworth 6X, Tetleys, Greene King Abbot Ale. ☂ 9 **Facilities** Children's menu Children's portions Dogs allowed Garden Parking

## PRIORS MARSTON — Map 11 SP45

### The Hollybush Inn ☂

**Hollybush Ln CV47 7RW** ☎ 01327 260934
e-mail: enquiries@hollybushatpriorsmarston.co.uk
dir: *From Southam A425, off bypass, 1st right, 6m to Priors Marston. Left after war memorial, next left, 150yds left again*

Set in the beautiful village of Priors Marston in the heart of Warwickshire, the Hollybush, now under new ownership, was a farmhouse that started selling beer in 1927 and became fully licensed twenty years later. With its large fireplace burning brightly, it's a warm hub of village social activity with a very relaxed atmosphere; people can eat and/or drink wherever they choose. The menus range from a hot buffet at lunchtime five days, a traditional roast lunch on Sundays to a comprehensive main menu selection. Perhaps a starter of warm goat's cheese, toasted pine nut and spiced beetroot salad; or Welsh rarebit and a poached egg; followed by confit of duck leg, creamy garlic mash and cassoulet; or slow braised lamb shank with leek and smoked bacon mash, with rosemary and redcurrant sauce. Desserts could include a trio of chocolate mocha pot, lemon posset and crème brûlée. Smaller portions can be ordered for most of the grown-up dishes.

**Open** all wk Mon-Fri 12-3 5.30-11 (Sat-Sun 12-11) **Bar Meals** L served all wk 12-2.30 booking required D served Mon-Sat 6.30-9.30 booking required Av main course £9 **Restaurant** L served Mon-Sat 12-2.30, Sun 12-4 D served Mon-Sat 6-9.30, Sun 12-4 ⊕ PUNCH TAVERNS ◀ Hook Norton, Fullers, Old Speckled Hen ♂ Stowford Press. ☂ 12 **Facilities** Children's portions Dogs allowed Garden Parking

## RATLEY — Map 11 SP34

### The Rose and Crown

**OX15 6DS** ☎ 01295 678148
e-mail: k.marples@btinternet.com
dir: *Follow Edgehill signs, 7m N of Banbury (13m SE of Stratford-upon-Avon) on A422*

Following the Battle of Edgehill in 1642, a Roundhead was discovered in the chimney of this 12th-century pub and beheaded in the hearth. His ghost reputedly haunts the building. Enjoy the peaceful village location and the traditional pub food, perhaps including beef and ale pie, scampi and chips, chicken curry and the Sunday roast, plus vegetarian options.

**Open** Mon eve-Sun Closed: Mon L **Bar Meals** L served Tue-Sun 12-2.30 booking required D served Mon-Sat 6.30-9 booking required Av main course £9.95 ◀ Wells Bombardier, Eagle IPA, Greene King Old Speckled Hen, Guest ale. **Facilities** Family room Dogs allowed Garden Parking

Save on Hotels. Book at theAA.com/hotel

WARWICKSHIRE 479 ENGLAND

### PICK OF THE PUBS

## The Stag at Redhill

Alcester Rd B49 6NQ
☎ 01789 764634  📠 01789 764431
e-mail: info@thestagatredhill.co.uk
web: www.thestagatredhill.co.uk
dir: On A46 between Stratford-upon-Avon & Alcester

The Stag was originally Stratford's courthouse and jail
in the 17th century; a cell door and windows in cast
iron have been preserved. Today it's a family-run
business, satisfying popular demand for Greene King,
Abbot and guest ales such as Ruddles Best. Food
service begins with breakfast from 7.30am. From
Monday to Saturday you may be tempted by the
'Staggeringly Great Credit Crunch Lunch'. Wednesday
night is pie night, Friday night is grill night, and
Sunday sees the popular carvery in full swing.

**Open** all day all wk 7am-11pm **Bar Meals** L served all
wk 12-5 D served all wk 5-9 food served all day
**Restaurant** L served all wk 12-5 D served all wk 5-9
food served all day ⊕ GREENE KING ◀ Greene King IPA,
Abbot Ale, Old Speckled Hen, Ruddles, Morland Original
Ö Stowford Press. **Facilities** Children's menu Garden
Parking

*See advert below*

### PICK OF THE PUBS

## Golden Lion ★★★ HL

Easenhall CV23 0JA
☎ 01788 832265  📠 01788 832878
e-mail: reception@goldenlionhotel.org
dir: From Rugby take A426, take 1st exit Newbold road
B4112. Through Newbold. At Harborough Parva follow
brown sign, turn left, pub in 1m

In 1931, Herbert and Alice Austin came to this
charming 16th-century free house, with low oak-
beamed ceilings and narrow doorways. Eighty years
later, the third generation of Austins, James and
Claudia, run an award-winning restaurant, and are
now looking to the future with their twenty-bedroom
hotel. You'll find real ales such as Young's Bitter and
Well's Bombardier in the wattle-and-daub-walled bar,
winter fires and an extensive wine list, as well as
excellent food and service. Lunchtime offers almost a
dozen varieties of sandwich, baguette and
ploughman's; as well as chicken jalfrezi; steak and
Stilton pie; and Mediterranean vegetable tartlet. In the
evening the menu may feature Thai salmon fishcakes;
slow-braised lamb shank; local sausages with lamb's
liver; and tournedos Rossini. Desserts include banoffee
pie with ice cream, and lemon tart with berry compote.
The pub is set amidst idyllic countryside in one of
Warwickshire's best-kept villages.

**Open** all day all wk 11-11 (Sun noon-11) **Bar Meals** L
served Mon-Sat 12-2, Sun 12-2.30 D served Mon-Sat
4.30-9.30, Sun 3-8.45 Av main course £10.95
**Restaurant** L served Mon-Sat 12-2, Sun 12-2.30 D
served Mon-Sat 4.30-9.30, Sun 3-8.45 Av 3 course à la
carte fr £20 ⊕ FREE HOUSE ◀ Guinness, 2 real ales,
Youngs, Directors. **Facilities** Garden Parking **Rooms** 20

## Old Smithy ♀

1 Green Ln, Church Lawford CV23 9EF ☎ 02476 542333
e-mail: smithy@king-henry-taverns.co.uk
dir: From Rugby take A428 (Lawford Rd) towards
Coventry. Turn right to Church Lawford

Anyone asked to draw their idyllic 'roses round the door'
village pub might produce something looking like the Old
Smithy. As with all King Henry's Taverns pubs, the menu
features a huge choice of traditional favourites, such as
gammon steak, fish and seafood, to haddock in batter;
chicken dishes, and a selection for those with larger
appetites, including Brontosaurus lamb shank.
Vegetarians will welcome a six-way choice, including
tomato and basil penne pasta. If you 'dine after nine' any
night there is a special deal of free wine.

**Open** all day all wk noon-11 **Bar Meals** Av main course
£3 food served all day **Restaurant** Fixed menu price fr
£3.50 food served all day ⊕ FREE HOUSE ◀ Guinness,
IPA, Marstons Pedigree. ♀ 16 **Facilities** Children's
menu Children's portions Play area Family room Garden
Parking

## The Bell at Salford Priors ♀ NEW

Evesham Rd WR11 8UU ☎ 01789 772112
e-mail: info@thebellatsalfordpriors.com
dir: From A46 (Bidford Island) towards Salford Priors.
Through village. Pub on left

Situated in a picturesque area, this country pub serves
Wye Valley and Wickwar real ales and Weston's Old Rosie
scrumpy. The frequently-changing, simply written menu
uses quality local ingredients and offers starters of
antipasti; and pear and walnut salad; followed by beef
and winter vegetable stew; hand-carved ham, free-range
egg and chips; Ragley Estate topside of beef; hand-
battered fish with hand-cut chips; and Mediterranean
vegetable Tatin with melted brie. Roasts are served all
day on Sundays. A new beer garden should now be open.

*continued*

**SALFORD PRIORS** *continued*

**Open** all day all wk **Bar Meals** food served all day **Restaurant** L served Mon-Fri 12-3, Sat-Sun all day booking required D served Mon-Fri fr 6, Sat-Sun all day booking required ⊕ ENTERPRISE INNS ◀ Wye Valley HPA, Sharp's Doom Bar, Wickwar Bob ♂ Westons Old Rosie. ⚑ 10 **Facilities** Children's portions Dogs allowed Garden Parking

### SHIPSTON ON STOUR    Map 10 SP24

## The Cherington Arms ⚑

Cherington CV36 5HS ☎ 01608 686233
**dir:** *12m from Stratford-upon-Avon. 14m from Leamington & Warwick. 10m from Woodstock. 4m from Shipston on Stour*

An attractive 17th-century inn with exposed beams and Cotswold stone walls, stripped wood furniture and roaring log inglenook fire. The carte menu might announce crab fishcakes with mango and chilli salsa; or breast of chicken stuffed with sun-dried tomato and cream pesto, all washed down with a pint of Hook Norton. There's also a snack menu and specials board. Outside there are large riverside gardens with a mill race, ideal for alfresco dining. Horse riders and walkers are welcome.

**Open** all wk ◀ Hook Norton Best Bitter, guest ales ♂ Stowford Press. ⚑ 11 **Facilities** Dogs allowed Garden Parking

### PICK OF THE PUBS

## The Red Lion ★★★★ INN ◉ ⚑

Main St, Long Compton CV36 5JS
☎ 01608 684221 ▤ 01608 684968
**e-mail:** info@redlion-longcompton.co.uk
**web:** www.redlion-longcompton.co.uk
**dir:** *On A3400 between Shipston on Stour & Chipping Norton*

Originally built as a coaching inn in 1748, the Red Lion has seen many changes over the years. The bar with its high backed settles, oak beams and winter log fires oozes charm, but visitors can also eat in the restaurant area, sit out in the garden, or take a leisurely lunch on the pretty, flower-bordered patio. The menu and blackboards cater for all tastes, beginning with interesting sandwiches like smoked salmon, crushed black pepper and fresh lemon on granary bread. Serious diners might start with baked camembert studded with garlic and thyme, before moving on to

spiced duck breast with braised red cabbage, beetroot and port jus. Raspberry and almond trifle laced with rum and served with sablé biscuits provides a fresh, contrasting finish. Children have their own menu. Five elegant en suite bedrooms feature such modern luxuries as Egyptian cotton bed linen, fluffy towels and flat-screen televisions.

**Open** all wk Mon-Thu 10-2.30 6-11 (Fri-Sun all day) **Bar Meals** L served Mon-Thu 12-2.30, Fri-Sun 12-9.30 D served Mon-Thu 6-9, Fri-Sun 12-9.30 Av main course £19.95 **Restaurant** L served Mon-Thu 12-2.30, Fri-Sun 12-9.30 D served Mon-Thu 6-9, Fri-Sun 12-9.30 Fixed menu price fr £11.95 ⊕ FREE HOUSE ◀ Hook Norton Best, Adnams, Timothy Taylor. ⚑ 11 **Facilities** Children's menu Children's portions Play area Dogs allowed Garden Parking **Rooms** 5

## White Bear Hotel ⚑

High St CV36 4AJ ☎ 01608 661558
**e-mail:** whitebearshipston@hotmail.com
**dir:** *From M40 junct 15, follow signs to Stratford-upon-Avon, then take A3400 to Shipston on Stour*

Open fires and wooden settles give the refurbished bars of this Georgian hotel a comfortable, timeless appeal. You'll find a range of real ales and keg beers, with up to ten wines available by the glass. The restaurant with its crisp white tablecloths makes dining a delicious experience: starters like pan-fried kidneys with black pudding precede main course options that include rack of lamb; and haddock with spinach and Welsh rarebit. There are live music and comedy nights. Now with a new landlord.

**Open** all day all wk **Bar Meals** L served all wk 9-9 D served all wk 9-9 Av main course £9 food served all day **Restaurant** L served all wk 9-9 D served all wk 9-9 food served all day ⊕ PUNCH TAVERNS ◀ London Pride, Deuchars IPA, Hooky Bitter, 6x, Adnams, 3 guest ♂ Scrumpy, Old Rosie. ⚑ 10 **Facilities** Children's menu Children's portions Play area Dogs allowed Garden Parking

### SHREWLEY    Map 10 SP26

### PICK OF THE PUBS

## The Durham Ox Restaurant and Country Pub ⚑

Shrewley Common CV35 7AY ☎ 01926 842283
**e-mail:** enquiries@durham-ox.co.uk
**dir:** *M40 junct 15 onto A46 towards Coventry. 1st exit signed Warwick, turn left onto A4177. After Hatton Country World, pub signed 1.5m*

An award-winning pub/restaurant in a peaceful village just four miles from Warwick and Leamington. Warm and inviting, its old beams, roaring fire and traditional hospitality combine with a city chic that give it a competitive edge. Success is in no small measure due to the restaurant, where Master Chef Simon Diprose prepares impressive, seasonally changing classic and contemporary dishes. A meal might consist of deep-

fried Boursin with ratatouille and basil sorbet; roast fillet of five-spice salmon with sweetcorn, pak choi and coriander dressing; and hot chocolate and Snickers fondant with vanilla ice cream. For more examples of his style, consider roast vegetables with North African spices, couscous and yoghurt dressing; and fresh plaice fillet in crispy Cajun coating with buttered peas and chunky chips. Children are offered penne pasta, and home-made fishcakes from their own menu. Extensive gardens incorporate a safe children's play area.

**Open** all wk 11-11 (Sun 12-10) **Bar Meals** L served Mon-Fri 12-2.30, Sat 12-9.30, Sun 12-6.30 D served Mon-Fri 6-9.30 ⊕ GREENE KING ◀ Ruddles, IPA, guest ales ♂ Stowford Press. ⚑ 21 **Facilities** Play area Dogs allowed Garden Parking

### STRATFORD-UPON-AVON    Map 10 SP25

## The Dirty Duck

Waterside CV37 6BA ☎ 01789 297312
**dir:** *Telephone for directions*

Frequented by members of the Royal Shakespeare Company from the nearby theatre, this traditional, partly Elizabethan inn has a splendid raised terrace overlooking the River Avon. In addition to the interesting range of real ales, a comprehensive choice of food is offered. Light bites, pastas, salads and mains at lunchtime, plus pub classics and 'make it special' dishes at night, from rustic sharing bread with herbs, garlic and olives to roast rack of lamb.

**Open** all day all wk 11am-mdnt (Sun 11am-10.30pm) ◀ Morland Old Speckled Hen, Greene King IPA ♂ Stowford Press. **Facilities** Dogs allowed Garden

### PICK OF THE PUBS

## The Fox & Goose Inn ⚑

CV37 8DD ☎ 01608 682293 ▤ 01608 682293
**e-mail:** manager@foxandgoosearmscote.co.uk
**dir:** *1m off A3400, between Shipston on Stour & Stratford-upon-Avon*

Located in Armscote, a beautiful village south of Stratford-upon-Avon, The Fox & Goose was formerly two cottages and a blacksmith's forge. The inn was given a total refurbishment a few years ago, and the result is stylish and utterly distinctive. It includes a smart dining room and cosy bar with lots of squishy velvet cushions, an open fire, flagstone floors and piles of reading matter to enjoy while supping a local guest ale. A glass (or bottle) of bubbly is a must if your visit coincides with champagne happy hour in the early evening from Monday to Saturday. For more solid sustenance, look to the country-style menu: chicken and bacon salad with honey mustard dressing could be followed by the popular Fox & Goose grill: rib-eye, gammon, sausage, egg, mushroom, tomato and chips. Out in the garden there's a large grassy area, decking with 20 seats for dining under the vines, and lovely countryside views.

Save on Hotels. Book at theAA.com/hotel

WARWICKSHIRE 481 ENGLAND

Open all day all wk **Bar Meals** booking required booking required Av main course £5.95 food served all day **Restaurant** Fixed menu price fr £12 Av 3 course à la carte fr £35 food served all day ⊕ FREE HOUSE ◼ local guest ales ♻ Westons, Thatchers Gold. ☂ 10 **Facilities** Children's menu Children's portions Dogs allowed Garden Parking

## The One Elm ☂

Guild St CV37 6QZ ☎ 01789 404919
e-mail: theoneelm@peachpubs.com
dir: In town centre

Standing on its own in the heart of town, the One Elm has two dining rooms: downstairs is intimate, even with the buzzy bar (serving well kept ales — including local Purity Gold and UBU) close by, while upstairs feels grander. The menu features salmon and smoked salmon fishcake; honey roast Barbary duck breast and roasted aubergine, marinated tofu and Moroccan couscous as well as other main courses. The deli board offers all-day nuts and seeds, cheeses, charcuterie and antipasti. The secluded terrace induces a feeling of being abroad.

Open all day all wk Mon-Wed 11-11 Thu 11am-11.30pm Fri-Sat 11am-mdnt Sun 11-10.30 Closed: 25 Dec **Bar Meals** L served all wk 12-6 D served 12-2.30, 6-10 Av main course £7 food served all day **Restaurant** L served all wk 12-6 booking required D served all wk 12-2.30, 6-10 booking required Av 3 course à la carte fr £26 food served all day ⊕ PEACH PUB CO ◼ UBU Purity, Purity Gold, Bombardier. ☂ 8 **Facilities** Children's portions Dogs allowed Garden Parking

### STRETTON ON FOSSE    Map 10 SP23

## The Plough Inn ☂

GL56 9QX ☎ 01608 661053
e-mail: saraval@aol.com
dir: From Moreton-in-Marsh, 4m on A429 N. From Stratford-upon-Avon, 10m on A429 S

A classic award-winning village pub built from mellow Cotswold stone, The Plough has the requisite exposed beams and real fire, plus a friendly resident cat, Alfie, to add to the welcome. Four real ales are usually on tap, ciders include Black Rat from Moles, and there's a good range of wines too. It's a family-run affair, with French chef and co-owner Jean-Pierre in charge of the kitchen; so expect traditional French dishes on the specials board. Entertainment on Sunday evenings ranges from quizzes to folk music.

Open 11.30-2.30 6-11.30 (Sun noon-3) Closed: 25 Dec eve, Sun eve **Bar Meals** L served all wk 12-2 D served Mon-Sat 7-9 Av main course £10 ⊕ FREE HOUSE ◼ Hook Norton, Ansells Mild, Spitfire, Purity, local ales ♻ Old Katy, Black Rat, Thatchers Traditional. ☂ 9 **Facilities** Children's portions Play area Garden Parking

### TEMPLE GRAFTON    Map 10 SP15

## The Blue Boar Inn

B49 6NR ☎ 01789 750010 🖷 01789 750635
e-mail: info@theblueboar.co.uk
dir: From A46 (Stratford to Alcester) turn left to Temple Grafton. Pub at 1st x-rds

The oldest part of the inn is 17th century, and has been an alehouse since that time. The restaurant features a 35-foot glass-covered well, home to a family of koi carp, from which water was formerly drawn for brewing. There are four open fires in the bar and restaurant areas, and a patio garden with views of the Cotswold Hills. A menu of traditional dishes is served, with variety provided by daily specials prepared from local produce, game in particular.

Open all day all wk ◼ Marstons Banks Original, Pedigree, Guinness ♻ Thatchers Gold. **Facilities** Garden Parking

### WARWICK    Map 10 SP26

## The Rose & Crown ☂

30 Market Place CV34 4SH
☎ 01926 411117 🖷 01926 492117
e-mail: roseandcrown@peachpubs.com
dir: M40 junct 15 follow signs to Warwick. Pass castle car park entrance up hill to West Gate, left into Bowling Green St, 1st right

Stylish gastro-pub located in the centre of Warwick with large leather sofas in the bar, a good choice of real ales and wines by the glass. Breakfast, lunch and dinner are served in the vibrant red restaurant. The deli board is a popular feature, with nuts and seeds, cheese, charcuterie, antipasti, fish and bread. Mains take in free range coq au vin, Porterhouse steak, roast hake, and sausage of the week.

Open all day all wk 8am-11pm (Fri-Sat 8am-mdnt) Closed: 25 Dec ◼ Black Sheep, London Pride, Old Hooky. ☂ 8 **Facilities** Dogs allowed

### WELFORD-ON-AVON    Map 10 SP15

## PICK OF THE PUBS

### The Bell Inn ☂

Binton Rd CV37 8EB
☎ 01789 750353 🖷 01789 750893
e-mail: info@thebellwelford.co.uk
dir: Please telephone for directions

Well placed for visiting Shakespeare's Stratford and the glorious Cotswold countryside, The Bell is a classic 17th-century inn, replete with exposed beams, stone-flagged floors, antique oak and pine furnishings, three open log fires, and a host of interesting features. Legend has it that William Shakespeare contracted fatal pneumonia after stumbling home from here in the pouring rain. Expect a warm welcome from Colin and Teresa Ombler, five real ales on handpump, including Purity Pure Gold and UBU (brewed along the road in Great Alne), and an extensive modern pub menu that makes good use of top-notch produce from local

suppliers, who are listed in the menu. Food is taken seriously here and The Bell draws a loyal dining clientele. Start with seafood and saffron risotto or sardines with pepper and tomato salsa, move on to a classic lasagne; salmon and dill fishcakes; steak and red wine pie; or lamb curry; then round off with chocolate brioche bread-and-butter pudding. In summer, dine alfresco in the award-winning garden.

Open all wk Sat 11.30-11 Sun noon-10.30 **Bar Meals** L served Mon-Fri 11.30-2.30, Sat 11.30-3, Sun all day booking required D served Mon-Thu 6-9.30, Fri-Sat 6-10, Sun all day booking required Av main course £12.25 **Restaurant** L served Mon-Sat 11.30-2.30, Sun all day booking required D served Mon-Thu 6-9.30, Fri-Sat 6-10, Sun all day booking required Fixed menu price fr £12.25 Av 3 course à la carte fr £20 ⊕ ENTERPRISE INNS ◼ Hook Norton (various), Flowers Original, Hobsons Best, Wadworth 6X, Flowers Best, Purity Gold, UBU. ☂ 14 **Facilities** Children's menu Children's portions Dogs allowed Garden Parking

### WITHYBROOK    Map 11 SP48

## The Pheasant ☂

Main St CV7 9LT ☎ 01455 220480 🖷 01455 221296
e-mail: thepheasant01@hotmail.com
web: www.thepheasanteatinghouse.com
dir: 7m from Coventry

This popular 17th-century free house stands beside the brook where withies were once cut for fencing. An inglenook fireplace, farm implements and horse-racing photographs characterise the interior. Under the same ownership since 1981, the pub has a varied menu with a wealth of choices. Alongside a blackboard of specials, a typical menu includes chef's curry; steak, ale and mushroom pie; venison pie; and braised pheasant. Outside, the benches overlooking the Withy Brook can accommodate 100 people.

Open all wk 11-3 6-11.30 (Sun & BH 11-11) Closed: 25-26 Dec (unless falling at wknd) **Bar Meals** L served Mon-Sat 12-2, Sun 12-9 booking required D served Mon-Sat 6-10, Sun 12-9 booking required Av main course £11.75 **Restaurant** L served Mon-Sat 12-2, Sun 12-9 booking required D served Mon-Sat 6-10, Sun 12-9 booking required ⊕ FREE HOUSE ◼ Courage Directors, Theakstons Best, John Smith's Smooth, Theakstons Dark, Youngs Bitter. ☂ 12 **Facilities** Children's menu Children's portions Garden Parking

## WOOTTON WAWEN
Map 10 SP16

### PICK OF THE PUBS

### The Bulls Head ♥

**Stratford Rd B95 6BD** ☎ **01564 792511**
dir: *On B3400, 4m N of Stratford-upon-Avon, 1m S of Henley-in-Arden*

Non-locals may like to know that the village name is pronounced Woot'n Worn. Ideally placed for touring and exploring the lovely landscapes of Warwickshire and the Cotswolds, The Bulls Head is one of several notable buildings; now in new ownership. Originally two separate cottages, it displays a stone with the date 1317, and the bar and snug areas feature beams, leather sofas, open fires and old church pews. Banks beers are on offer along with guest ales. The same tone and style are maintained in the magnificent 'great hall' restaurant, with its vaulted ceiling and yet more exposed beams. Outside, you'll find a lawned garden and paved patio surrounded by mature trees. Dogs are welcome.

**Open** all day all wk **Bar Meals** Av main course £11.50 **Restaurant** L served Mon-Sat 12-2.30, Sun 12-4 D served all wk 6-9.30 ⊕ Billesley Pub Company ◀ Marston's Pedigree, Banks Bitter, Banks Original plus guest ales. ♥ 10 **Facilities** Dogs allowed Garden Parking

## WEST MIDLANDS

### BARSTON
Map 10 SP27

### PICK OF THE PUBS

### The Malt Shovel at Barston ◉

**Barston Ln B92 0JP**
☎ **01675 443223** ▤ **01675 443223**
web: www.themaltshovelatbarston.com
dir: *M42 junct 5, take turn towards Knowle. 1st left on Jacobean Ln, right at T-junct (Hampton Ln). Sharp left into Barston Ln. Restaurant 0.5m*

Natural wood and pastel colours characterise the interiors of this stylishly converted early 20th century mill building. The bar is cosy and relaxed with winter log fires, and the restaurant is housed in an adjacent converted barn. Now, the Malt Shovel is a bustling, award-winning free house with modern soft furnishings and interesting artefacts. Food is cooked to order, with imaginative, modern British dishes making the best of seasonal ingredients. The seafood menu

includes Scottish halibut with elderflower roasted parsnips, asparagus and smoked ham, and pan-fried sea bass with Mediterranean vegetables and goat's cheese. Alternatives might be braised lamb shank with cardamom infused carrots and damson jus; or Malaysian spiced trio of pumpkin, steamed lime rice and cashew nuts. The tempting desserts range from Eton Mess with cassis soaked raspberries, to dark chocolate delice with hazelnut praline and pear compote. There's a super rear garden for summer alfresco dining.

**Open** all day all wk **Bar Meals** L served Mon-Sat 12-2.30, Sun 12-4 booking required D served Mon-Sat 6-9.30 booking required Av main course £12.95 **Restaurant** L served Sun 12-4 booking required D served Mon-Sat 7-9.30 booking required Fixed menu price fr £21.95 Av 3 course à la carte fr £20 ⊕ FREE HOUSE ◀ Tribute, Brew XI, Timothy Taylor Landlord. **Facilities** Garden Parking

## BIRMINGHAM
Map 10 SP08

### The Peacock ♥

**Icknield St, Forhill, nr King's Norton B38 0EH**
☎ **01564 823232** ▤ **01564 829593**
dir: *Telephone for directions*

Despite its out of the way location, at Forhill just outside Birmingham, the Peacock keeps very busy serving traditional ales and a varied menu, (booking essential). Chalkboards display the daily specials, among which you might find braised partridge on a bed of pheasant sausage and mash, whole sea bass with crab, grilled shark steak with light curry butter, pan-fried sirloin steak with mild mushroom and pepper sauce, or lamb fillet with apricot and walnut stuffing. Several friendly ghosts are in residence, and one of their tricks is to disconnect the taps from the barrels. Large gardens with two patios.

**Open** all wk ◀ Hobsons Best Bitter, Theakstons Old Peculier, Enville Ale. ♥ 20 **Facilities** Garden Parking

### Penny Blacks ♥ NEW

**132-134 Wharfside St, The Mailbox B1 1XL**
☎ **0121 632 1460** ▤ **0121 632 1463**
e-mail: info@penny-blacks.com
dir: *In Mailbox district in city centre. Nearest station: Birmingham New Street*

Part of the regenerated Mailbox area of Birmingham, a short walk from the National Indoor Arena and Symphony Hall, this large city centre bar has a traditional pub feel with a warm and welcoming atmosphere. With five to seven real ales on tap and a vast range of wines, it has become a popular meeting place for locals and tourists alike. The bar menu is a mix of pub classics and modern British dishes, from pie or sausages with a choice of mash, to steaks, fish and chips and vegetarian options. There is also a restaurant and wine bar.

**Open** all day all wk Closed: 25-26 Dec, 1 Jan **Bar Meals** L served Mon-Thu 10-10, Fri-Sat 10am-10.30pm, Sun 10-8.30 D served Mon-Thu 10-10, Fri-Sat 10am-10.30pm, Sun 10-8.30 Av main course £10 food served all day ⊕ CROPTHORNE INNS ◀ Wyre Piddle, Hook Norton, St Austell, Church End. ♥ 15 **Facilities** Children's portions Dogs allowed Garden

## CHADWICK END
Map 10 SP27

### PICK OF THE PUBS

### The Orange Tree ♥

*See Pick of the Pubs on opposite page*

## HAMPTON IN ARDEN
Map 10 SP28

### PICK OF THE PUBS

### The White Lion

**10 High St B92 0AA** ☎ **01675 442833**
e-mail: info@thewhitelioninn.com
dir: *Opposite church*

This charming village inn is situated at the heart of the picturesque village of Hampton in Arden, yet is in close proximity to major road, rail and air links. Originally a farmhouse, this 17th-century timber-framed village pub has been licensed since at least 1836. In the Front Bar (no fancy names here!) locals tell tales they've probably told each other many times before over pints of Black Sheep and Adnams; in the comfortable Lounge Bar there are open fires and traditional bar food is served. Daily changing menus in the restaurant feature modern English cuisine, including starters of Parma ham, basil pesto, sun-blushed tomato and mozzarella bruschetta; and smoked salmon, dill and sweet mustard dressing. Main courses might be braised lamb shank in red wine with garlic and thyme; pan-fried duck breast on braised red cabbage and orange with blackberry and port jus; and chargilled chicken supreme and confit chicken leg with red wine, bacon and mushroom sauce. Children have plenty of choice and there are roasts on Sundays.

**Open** all wk noon-12.30am (Sun noon-10.30) **Bar Meals** L served all wk 12-2.30 D served all wk 6.30-9.30 ⊕ PUNCH TAVERNS ◀ Brew XI, Black Sheep, Adnams, guest ale Ò Thatchers Gold. **Facilities** Garden Parking

# PICK OF THE PUBS

## The Orange Tree ♥

**CHADWICK END**     Map 10 SP27

**Warwick Rd B93 0BN ☎ 01564 785364**
**e-mail:** theorangetree@lovelypubs.co.uk
**dir:** *3m from Knowle towards Warwick*

One of a small and select chain of comfy, chic pubs in the West Midlands owned by Paul Salisbury and Paul Hales, The Orange Tree is a destination dining pub that ticks all the right boxes. Chunky wooden furniture, airy interiors dappled with prints on thick walls supporting old beams; all meld easily with a labyrinth of more traditional rustic, pubby corners with leather sofas in quiet alcoves, log fires pushing out the calories, antiquey mirrors and colourwashed walls creating a great ambience.

The dining experience is summed up as 'simple but up-to-the-minute' and encapsulates a good range of comfort foods such as pizzas and pastas from the stone-fired ovens together with modern European and global dishes. Think as an appetiser a plate of sake-cured salmon with pickled ginger, wasabi crème fraîche and lime, or cauliflower and cumin fritters with parsley houmous and lime. Fresh made pizzas that draw appreciative comments include tuna, olives and crayfish tails whilst pastas flavoured with orecchiette duck ragu and pangrattato are an eye-opener. From the stove comes suckling pig with bubble and squeak, truffle oil and honey-roast apple or rosemary roast cod with pancetta and a Tuscan bean stew.

Steamed treacle, lemon and ginger pudding could follow, all accompanied by a carefully selected bin of wines. Summer diners can indulge in a feast on the sunny patio or amidst landscaped gardens in the tranquil Warwickshire countryside.

**Open** all day all wk 11-11 Closed: 25 Dec **Bar Meals** L served all wk 12-2.30 D served all wk 6-9.30 Av main course £8.95 **Restaurant** L served all wk 12-2.30 booking required D served all wk 6-9.30 booking required Fixed menu price fr £12.50 Av 3 course à la carte fr £20 ⊕ FREE HOUSE ◀ IPA, London Pride, UBU ⚬ Olde English. ♥ 10 **Facilities** Play area Dogs allowed Garden Parking

## OLDBURY — Map 10 SO98

### PICK OF THE PUBS

### Waggon & Horses

17a Church St B69 3AD ☎ 0121 552 5467
e-mail: andrew.gale.17a@hotmail.com
dir: Telephone for directions

Tucked away in the remnants of the old town centre
and popular with shoppers and office workers, the
Waggon & Horses is a Grade II-listed Victorian pub and
firmly on CAMRA's National Inventory of Historic Pub
Interiors. Come to see the ornate tiled walls, the lovely
copper-panelled ceiling, the fine Holts Brewery etched
windows, and the huge tie collection in the splendid
back bar. The side room has big old tables and high-
backed settles, where you can also enjoy freshly-cooked
traditional pub food, perhaps faggots and mash, pork
and leek sausages, lasagne, chilli, fish and chips, and
a good selection of vegetarian dishes. Ale drinkers can
sup contentedly as the choice is good, including Brains
Rev James, Enville White, Salopian Shropshire Gold and
three guest ales.

Open all wk (ex Sun eve in Winter) Closed: Sun eve in
Winter Bar Meals L served Mon-Sat 12-2.30 D served
Tue-Sat 5.30-7.30 Av main course £4.95 ⊕ S A BRAIN
◀ Enville White, Brains, 3 guest ales ♂ Rev James,
Salopian Shropshire Gold. Facilities Children's portions
Family room Parking

## SEDGLEY — Map 10 SO99

### PICK OF THE PUBS

### Beacon Hotel & Sarah Hughes Brewery

129 Bilston St DY3 1JE
☎ 01902 883380 📄 01902 884020
dir: Telephone for directions

Little has changed in 150 years at this beautifully
restored traditional brewery tap and tower brewery,
which still retain their Victorian atmosphere. The rare
snob-screened island bar serves a simple taproom, with
its old wall benches and a fine blackened range, a super
cosy snug replete with a green-tiled marble fireplace,
dark woodwork, velvet curtains and huge old tables, and
a large smoke-room with an adjoining, plant-festooned
conservatory. Proprietor John Hughes reopened the
adjoining Sarah Hughes Brewery in 1987, 66 years after
his grandmother became the licensee. Like the pub, it
remains totally unchanged and on a tour of the brewery
you can see the original grist case and rare open-topped
copper that add to the Victorian charm and give unique
character to the brews. Flagship beers are Sarah Hughes
Dark Ruby, Surprise and Pale Amber, with seasonal
bitter also available. Food in the pub is limited to filled
cob rolls.

Open all wk noon-2.30 5.30-11 (Sat-12-3 6-11 Sun 12-3
7-10.30) Bar Meals food served all day ⊕ SARAH
HUGHES BREWERY ◀ Sarah Hughes Dark Ruby, Surprise
& Pale Amber, plus guest, seasonal ales. Facilities Play
area Family room Garden Parking Notes ⊛

## SOLIHULL — Map 10 SP17

### The Boat Inn ♥

222 Hampton Ln, Catherine-de-Barnes B91 2TJ
☎ 0121 705 0474 📄 0121 704 0600
dir: Telephone for directions

Village pub with a small, enclosed garden located right
next to the canal in Solihull. Real ales are taken seriously
and there are two frequently changing guest ales in
addition to the regulars. There is also a choice of 14
wines available by the glass. Fresh fish is a daily option,
and other favourite fare includes chicken cropper,
Wexford steak, and beef and ale pie.

Open all wk ◀ Bombardier, Greene King IPA, 2 guest
ales. ♥ 14 Facilities Family room Garden Parking

## WEST BROMWICH — Map 10 SP09

### The Vine

Roebuck St B70 6RD ☎ 0121 553 2866
e-mail: bharat@thevine.co.uk
dir: 0.5m from M5 junct 1. 2m from town centre

Well-known, family-run business renowned for its
excellent curries and cheap drinks. Since 1978 the
typically Victorian alehouse has provided the setting for
Suresh 'Suki' Patel's eclectic menu. Choose from a
comprehensive range of Indian dishes (chicken balti,
lamb saag), a barbecue menu and Thursday spit roast,
offered alongside traditional pub fare. The Vine boasts
the Midlands' only indoor tandoori barbeque, plus it is a
stone's throw from The Hawthorns, West Bromwich
Albion's football ground.

Open all wk (all day Fri-Sun) Bar Meals L served Mon-Fri
12-2, Sat-Sun 12-3 D served Mon-Fri 5.30-10.30 Av main
course £4.95 Restaurant L served Sat-Sun 1-10.30 D
served Sat-Sun 1-10.30 Fixed menu price fr £4.95 Av 3
course à la carte fr £15 ⊕ FREE HOUSE ◀ Banks Mild,
Brew XI, John Smith's. Facilities Garden

## WIGHT, ISLE OF

## ARRETON — Map 5 SZ58

### The White Lion

PO30 3AA ☎ 01983 528479
e-mail: chrisandkatelou@hotmail.co.uk
dir: B3056 (Newport to Sandown road)

Expect a genuinely hospitable welcome at this 300-year-
old former coaching inn sited in an outstandingly
beautiful conservation area. Oak beams, polished brass
and open fires set the cosy tone inside, while a safe
outside seating area enjoys views of the Arreton scenery.
Well-kept ales and pub grub are served all day, ranging
from traditional snacks to specials such as slow-roasted
pork ribs, nasi goreng and lamb shanks.

The White Lion

Open all day all wk Bar Meals Av main course £8.95 food
served all day Restaurant Fixed menu price fr £10 food
served all day ⊕ ENTERPRISE INNS ◀ Badger Best,
Fuller's London Pride, Timothy Taylor Landlord, John
Smith's Smooth, Flowers Best ♂ Stowford Press.
Facilities Children's menu Children's portions Play area
Family room Dogs allowed Garden Parking

## BEMBRIDGE — Map 5 SZ68

### The Crab & Lobster Inn ★★★★ INN ♥

32 Forelands Field Rd PO35 5TR
☎ 01983 872244 📄 01983 873495
e-mail: info@crabandlobsterinn.co.uk
dir: From Bembridge village, 1st left after Boots onto
Forelands Rd to Windmill Hotel. Left onto Lane End
Rd, 2nd right onto Egerton Rd, left onto Howgate Rd &
immediately right onto Forelands Field Rd

Originally a fisherman's cottage, this refurbished, award-
winning beamed pub sits just yards from the popular 65-
mile coastal path. A raised deck and patio area offer
superb sea views. Locally caught seafood is one of the
pub's great attractions; typical choices include a pint of
prawns; lobster salad; home-made crab cakes; and
seafood platters. For meat eaters there are pub classics
such as steaks or ham, egg and chips. The bar serves a
range of ales and 12 wines by the glass. The bedrooms
are light and airy, and some have stunning views.

Open all wk summer 11-11 (Sun 11-10.30) winter 11-3
6-11 (Sun 6-10.30) Bar Meals L served all wk 12-2.30
booking required D served Sun-Thu 6-9, Fri-Sat 6-9.30
booking required Av main course £9 Restaurant L served
all wk 12-2.30 (summer Sat-Sun & BHs 2.30-5.30 limited
menu) booking required D served Sun-Thu 6-9, Fri-Sat
6-9.30 booking required ⊕ ENTERPRISE INNS ◀ Sharp's
Doom Bar, Goddards Fuggle-Dee-Dum, Greene King IPA,
John Smith's. ♥ 12 Facilities Children's menu Children's
portions Dogs allowed Garden Parking Rooms 5

### The Pilot Boat Inn ♥

Station Rd PO35 5NN ☎ 01983 872077 & 874101
dir: On corner of harbour at bottom of Kings Rd

Just a stone's throw from Bembridge harbour, this
strikingly designed free house enjoys a strong local
following, whilst being handy for yachtsmen and
holidaymakers. Owners Nick and Michelle Jude offer an
attractive menu of traditional favourites, including cod in
beer batter with chips and peas; and bangers and mash
with red wine and onion gravy. There's also a children's

menu, together with specials like vegetable balti with rice; and chunky lamb stew and mash.

**Open** all day all wk 11-11 (Wed 11am-mdnt Fri 11am-late Sat 11am-11.30pm Sun noon-11) London Pride, Guinness, guest ale. 8 **Facilities** Dogs allowed Parking

## The Windmill Inn ★★★★ INN NEW

1 Steyne Rd PO35 5UH
☎ 01983 872875 01983 874760
e-mail: enquiries@windmill-inn.com
dir: *From Sandown take B3395 (Sandown Rd) Straight on at rdbt into Steyne Rd in Bembridge. Inn on right*

A short walk from the water in the quiet village of Bembridge, the Windmill offers a relaxing place to chat and look at paintings by local artists depicting amusing village scenes and yachts in the harbour. Enjoy food all day, from a light snack of chicken liver pâté with red onion marmalade, to a main meal of home-made curry; or fresh lobster and fish from the blackboard. Try a pint of Fuggle-Dee-Dum from Goddards in Ryde. If you want to explore the island, why not stay over in one of the recently renovated guest rooms.

**Open** all day all wk **Bar Meals** Av main course £9 food served all day **Restaurant** Av 3 course à la carte fr £20 food served all day FREE HOUSE Ringwood Best, Goddards Fuggle-Dee-Dum, Goddards Special Bitter, Greene King IPA Stowford Press. 12
**Facilities** Children's menu Children's portions Play area Dogs allowed Garden Parking **Rooms** 14

### BONCHURCH　　　　Map 5 SZ57

## The Bonchurch Inn

Bonchurch Shute PO38 1NU
☎ 01983 852611 01983 856657
e-mail: gillian@bonchurch-inn.co.uk
dir: *Off A3055 in Bonchurch*

In its quiet, off the road location, this small family-run free house inn lies tucked away in a secluded Dickensian-style courtyard. You won't be disturbed by juke boxes or gaming machines, for little has changed here since this former coaching inn and stables was granted its first licence in the 1840s. Food is available lunchtime and evenings in the bar; choices range from sandwiches and ploughman's to plenty of fresh fish dishes, juicy steaks and Italian specialities.

**Open** all wk 11-3 6.30-11 Closed: 25 Dec **Bar Meals** L served all wk 12-2 D served all wk 6.30-9 booking required Av main course £9 **Restaurant** D served all wk 7-8.45 booking required FREE HOUSE Courage Directors, Best. **Facilities** Children's portions Family room Dogs allowed Garden Parking

### COWES　　　　Map 5 SZ49

## The Folly

Folly Ln PO32 6NB ☎ 01983 297171
dir: *Telephone for directions*

Reached by land and water, and very popular with the boating fraternity, the Folly is one of the island's more unusual pubs. Timber from an old sea-going French barge was used in the construction, and wood from the hull can be found in the bar. The menus are wide ranging with something for everyone. Dishes might include pan-seared Barbury duck breast; butternut squash, spinach, lentil and spicy coconut curry; plus there's 'Sharers' such as an antipasti board and a cheese fondue.

**Open** all day all wk **Bar Meals** L served all wk 12-5 D served all wk 5-10 Av main course £8.50 food served all day **Restaurant** L served all wk 12-5 D served all wk 5-10 food served all day GREENE KING Greene King IPA, Old Speckled Hen, Goddard's Best Bitter Aspall. 11
**Facilities** Children's menu Children's portions Dogs allowed Garden Parking

### FRESHWATER　　　　Map 5 SZ38

## PICK OF THE PUBS

## The Red Lion

Church Place PO40 9BP
☎ 01983 754925 01983 754483
dir: *In Freshwater follow signs for parish church*

The yachting fraternity from nearby Yarmouth harbour are amongst those who beat a path to the door of this charming inn, close to the church in the pretty village centre. Its origins go back to the 11th century, although today's climber-clad building is clearly more recent. A garden at the rear is well furnished with hardwood chairs and tables, and a canvas dome comes into its own for candlelit alfresco dinners. The bar is comfortable with settles and chairs around scrubbed pine tables, the log fire burns throughout the winter, and peace and quiet is preferred to music as regulars settle down with a pint of Goddards bitter. Much of the produce used in Lorna Mence's filling meals comes from the Island and is detailed on the daily-changing blackboard menu. Added to this is the ultra-traditional British pub bar food at its best; think smoked haddock kedgeree, chicken and asparagus pie or calves' liver with bacon and onion gravy, with apple pie or sticky toffee pudding before you admit defeat.

**Open** all wk 11.30-3 5.30-11 (Sun noon-3 7-10.30) **Bar Meals** L served all wk 12-2 booking required D served all wk 6.30-9 booking required Av main course £10.50 **Restaurant** L served all wk 12-2 booking required D served all wk 6.30-9 booking required Av 3 course à la carte fr £20 ENTERPRISE INNS Interbrew Flowers Original, Spitfire, Goddards, Wadworth 6X. **Facilities** Dogs allowed Garden Parking

### GODSHILL　　　　Map 5 SZ58

## PICK OF THE PUBS

## The Taverners

High St PO38 3HZ ☎ 01983 840707
dir: *Please telephone for directions*

Islanders Roger Serjent and Lisa Choi are so committed to genuinely local, seasonal food that a large sign outside their convivial hostelry asks local farmers and growers to bring in their produce. And it works – village gardeners supply fruit and vegetables; meat, poultry, eggs and dairy produce all come from within a couple of miles' radius, whilst fish and seafood arrives from nearby Ventnor and Bembridge. Not to be left out, Roger and Lisa have put in their own vegetable beds, planted fruit trees, and built a chicken run. Amongst the simple, rustic, dishes emerging from the kitchen, you might expect Brownrigg Farm chicken and mushroom pie with swede purée and red cabbage; whole local plaice with new potatoes, spinach, lemon and caper butter; and lentil faggots with onion gravy, roasted carrots and potato purée. There's a good choice of real ales and a robust range of sandwiches and bar snacks, too.

**Open** all day all wk Closed: 1st 2wks Jan **Bar Meals** L served all wk 12-3 D served all wk summer 6-9.30, Mon-Sat winter 6-9 Av main course £10 **Restaurant** L served all wk 12-3 booking required D served Sun-Thu 6-9, Fri-Sat 6-9.30 booking required Av 3 course à la carte fr £21 PUNCH Undercliff, London Pride, John Smith's, Taverners Own, Sharp's Doom Bar, Black Sheep Stowford Press, Old Rosie. **Facilities** Children's menu Children's portions Family room Dogs allowed Garden Parking

### NINGWOOD　　　　Map 5 SZ38

## Horse & Groom NEW

Main Rd PO30 4NW ☎ 01983 760672 01983 874760
e-mail: info@horse-and-groom.com
dir: *On A3054 (Yarmouth to Newport road)*

A couple of miles west of Yarmouth, this large family pub is a landmark on the Newport road. There's a nice garden with a large children's play area, and four-footed family members are also welcome on the stone and wood floored indoor areas. Food is served daily from noon until 9pm, and the offering ranges from baguettes and light bites to pub favourites like braised lamb shank; battered fish and chips; and Mediterranean vegetable lasagne.

**Open** all day all wk **Bar Meals** L served all wk 12-9 booking required D served all wk 12-9 booking required Av main course £9 food served all day ENTERPRISE INNS Ringwood, Goddards. 16 **Facilities** Children's menu Children's portions Play area Dogs allowed Garden Parking

### NITON
Map 5 SZ57

## Buddle Inn ?

**St Catherines Rd PO38 2NE** ☎ 01983 730243
**dir:** *Take A3055 from Ventnor. In Niton take 1st left signed 'to the lighthouse'*

A stone's throw from the English Channel one way and the Coastal Path the other, this 16th-century, former cliff-top farmhouse is one of the island's oldest hostelries. Popular with hikers and ramblers (and their muddy boots and dogs), the interior has the full traditional complement - stone flags, oak beams and large open fire, as well as great real ales on tap. Hearty home-made food is served, along with specials like fresh lemon sole with hot crab, and chargrilled duck breast with plum sauce.

**Open** all day all wk 11-11 (Fri-Sat 11-mdnt Sun noon-10.30) **Bar Meals** L served all wk 12-2.45 (all day from Etr) D served all wk 6-9 (all day from Etr) Av main course £8.95 food served all day **Restaurant** L served all wk 12-2.45 D served all wk 6-9 ⊕ ENTERPRISE INNS ◀ Adnams, Buddle Best, London Pride ♂ Stowford Press. ♥ 8 **Facilities** Children's menu Children's portions Family room Dogs allowed Garden Parking

### NORTHWOOD
Map 5 SZ49

## Travellers Joy

**85 Pallance Rd PO31 8LS** ☎ 01983 298024
**e-mail:** tjoy@globalnet.co.uk
**dir:** *Telephone for directions*

Ruth, Derek and Andy run this 300-year-old alehouse, just a little way inland from Cowes. They keep eight real ales on hand pump all year round. Don't expect dishes described on the menu as 'drizzled' or 'pan-roasted' here because the food is home cooked and uncomplicated but with all the trimmings – Travellers grill; home-made cheese quiche with chips or salad; jumbo battered cod; corned beef, eggs, chips and beans; and children's meals. Outside is a pétanque terrain, pets' corner and play area.

**Open** all wk **Bar Meals** L served all wk 12-2 D served all wk 6.30-9.30 Av main course £6.95 ⊕ FREE HOUSE ◀ Goddards Special Bitter, Courage Directors, Ventnor Golden Bitter, Deuchars IPA, St Austell Tribute. **Facilities** Children's menu Children's portions Play area Family room Dogs allowed Garden Parking

### ROOKLEY
Map 5 SZ58

## *The Chequers*

**Niton Rd PO38 3NZ** ☎ 01983 840314 🖷 01983 840820
**e-mail:** richard@chequersinn-iow.co.uk
**dir:** *Telephone for directions*

Horses in the neighbouring riding school keep a watchful eye on comings and goings at this 250-year-old family-friendly free house. In the centre of the island, surrounded by farms, the pub has a reputation for good food at reasonable prices. Fish, naturally, features well, with sea bass, mussels, plaice, salmon and cod usually

available. Other favourites are mixed grill, pork medallions, T-bone steak, and chicken supreme with BBQ sauce and cheese.

**Open** all wk ◀ John Smith's, Courage Directors, Best, Wadworth 6X, 3 guest ales. **Facilities** Play area Family room Dogs allowed Garden Parking

### SEAVIEW
Map 5 SZ69

## The Boathouse ? Ⓤ NEW

**Springvale Rd PO34 5AW**
☎ 01983 810616 🖷 01983 874760
**e-mail:** info@theboathouseiow.co.uk
**dir:** *From Ryde take A3055. Left onto A3330, left into Puckpool Hill. Pub 0.25m on right*

This tastefully refurbished pub stands in a spectacular setting overlooking the Solent on a popular seafront promenade. Now under new ownership, the Boathouse offers real ales, an extensive wine list, and exciting specials boards that make the most of freshly-landed local fish. Other choices include lunchtime baguettes, as well as hot dishes like gammon ham, free range eggs and chips, and tagliatelle with creamy leek and wild mushroom sauce.

**Open** all wk 9-3 6-11 (Sat-Sun 9am-10.30pm) all day everyday May-Sep **Bar Meals** L served May-Sep 12-9.30, Oct-Apr 12-2.30 D served May-Sep 12-9.30, Oct-Apr 6-9.30 Av main course £12 **Restaurant** L served May-Sep 12-9.30, Oct-Apr 12-2.30 D served May-Sep 12-9.30, Oct-Apr 6-9.30 ⊕ PUNCH TAVERNS ◀ Ringwood Best, Sharp's Doom Bar, Bass, Greene King IPA ♂ Stowford Press. ♥ 11 **Facilities** Children's menu Children's portions Dogs allowed Garden Parking **Rooms** 4

### PICK OF THE PUBS

## The Seaview Hotel & Restaurant ★★★ HL ◎◎

***See Pick of the Pubs on opposite page***

### SHALFLEET
Map 5 SZ48

### PICK OF THE PUBS

## The New Inn ?

**Mill Ln PO30 4NS** ☎ 01983 531314 🖷 01983 531314
**e-mail:** info@thenew-inn.co.uk
**dir:** *6m from Newport to Yarmouth on A3054*

This is one of the island's best-known dining pubs, and its location on the National Trust-owned Newtown River estuary makes it an absolute mecca for yachties. Its name reflects how it rose phoenix-like from the charred remains of an older inn, which burnt down in 1743; original inglenook fireplaces, flagstone floors and low-beamed ceilings give it bags of character. The waterside location helps explain its reputation for excellent seafood dishes, with lobster and cracked local crab usually featuring on the specials carte; other fish options may include grilled fillets of hake or pollock, and whole mackerel. For meat lovers there are local hand-made sausages with mash; prime steaks;

and gammon with double egg and chips. The excellent vegetarian section of the menu may offer mushroom gnocchi with parsley and walnut cream sauce. At the bar you'll find Goddards Special and Greene King among others, and over 60 worldwide wines comprise one of the island's most extensive selections.

*The New Inn*

**Open** all day all wk **Bar Meals** L served all wk 12-2.30 booking required D served all wk 6-9.30 booking required Av main course £10 **Restaurant** L served all wk 12-2.30 booking required D served all wk 6-9.30 booking required Av 3 course à la carte fr £22.50 ⊕ ENTERPRISE INNS ◀ Interbrew Bass, Goddards Special Bitter, Greene King IPA, Marston's Pedigree. ♥ 11 **Facilities** Children's menu Children's portions Dogs allowed Garden Parking

### SHORWELL
Map 5 SZ48

### PICK OF THE PUBS

## The Crown Inn ?

**Walkers Ln PO30 3JZ**
☎ 01983 740293 🖷 01983 740293
**e-mail:** pamela@notjust.org.uk
**dir:** *Turn left at top of Carisbrooke High Street, Shorwell approx 6m*

Set in a pretty village in picturesque West Wight, with thatched cottages, a small shop, three manor houses, and the church opposite. In summer, arum lilies decorate the garden stream, and a Wendy house, slide and swings keep youngsters amused. The building dates in part from the 17th century, and different floor levels attest to many alterations. Log fires, antique furniture, and a friendly female ghost who disapproves of card playing, complete the picture of this traditional family-run pub. Beers on tap include an island brew, locally sourced lamb, beef, game in winter and fish in summer. Tempting pub grub menus and an award-winning specials board offer cottage pie, steak and kidney pie, crown of pheasant or lamb tagine. Fish lovers may strike lucky with a seafood platter, fish pie, crab and prawn gratin, or sea bass.

**Open** all day all wk **Bar Meals** L served all day 12-9 booking required D served all day 12-9 booking required Av main course £8.95 food served all day **Restaurant** L served all day 12-9 booking required D served all day 12-9 booking required food served all day ⊕ ENTERPRISE INNS ◀ Goddards (local), Ringwood Fortyniner, Ringwood Best, Sharp's Doom Bar, Adnams Broadside ♂ Stowford Press. ♥ 12 **Facilities** Children's menu Children's portions Play area Family room Dogs allowed Garden Parking

# PICK OF THE PUBS

## The Seaview Hotel & Restaurant ★★★HL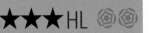

**SEAVIEW**  Map 5 SZ69

**High St PO34 5EX**
☎ 01983 612711  📄 01983 613729
**e-mail:** reception@seaviewhotel.co.uk
**dir:** *B3330 (Ryde to Seaview road), left via Puckpool along seafront road, hotel on left*

In a sailing-mad village, whose name means what it says on the tin, is this rather special establishment. Its quiet location just a short stroll from the seafront means that from selected vantage points, particularly The Terrace, it too enjoys fantastic views of the Solent. Watch ships pass, porpoises dive, seagulls glide, Seaview Mermaid yachts sail and dinghies occasionally capsize.

In the Pump Bar, real ales from Goddard's Brewery in Ryde are complemented by an extensive menu of traditional and innovative dishes, including an array of locally caught fresh fish specials. The Front Bar, modelled on a naval wardroom, is home to a magnificent collection of naval pictures, photographs, lobster pots, oars, masts and other nautical artefacts – apparently one of the most extensive private collections to be found on the Island.

The hotel offers a choice of dining venues (with two AA Rosettes); there's the small Victorian dining room, and the more contemporary Sunshine restaurant and conservatory. Both offer the same menu, which reflects the hotel's close relationship with Wight farmers and fishermen, and ensures that the chefs are always working with the very best that this small, but bounteous 148 square miles can produce.

Give your tastebuds a treat with hot crab ramekin, or broccoli soup with creamed goat's cheese and fresh chives. For a main course, ask what Captain Stan of Bembridge has brought in as catch of the day; or choose local free-range chicken with white bean and chunky winter vegetable broth. Highland cattle from the hotel's own farm guarantee fine steaks; rosemary- and thyme-braised beef; and cottage pie. The latest addition to the many stylish bedrooms is the converted Old Bank into three family suites.

**Open** all wk **Bar Meals** L served all wk 12-2.30 D served all wk 6.30-9.30 Av main course £10.50 **Restaurant** L served all wk 12-2 (summer), Sat-Sun 12-2 (winter) booking required D served all wk 6.30-9.30 booking required Av 3 course à la carte fr £28 ⊕ FREE HOUSE ◀ Goddards, Ventnor Bitter, Guest ale. **Facilities** Dogs allowed **Rooms** 28

## VENTNOR — Map 5 SZ57

### The Spyglass Inn ♟

**The Esplanade PO38 1JX**
☎ 01983 855338 📠 01983 855220
**e-mail:** info@thespyglass.com
**dir:** Telephone for directions

For centuries this area was a haunt of smugglers, and echoes of these activities can be seen in the huge collection of nautical memorabilia on the walls of this famous 19th-century inn. It has a superb position, right at the end of Ventnor Esplanade. Much of the food here is, naturally, fish, with home-made fish chowder, Ventnor crab and lobster, but other dishes might include several varieties of pie; local sausages; or ham and leek bake.

**Open** all day all wk 10.30am–11pm ◀ Ventnor Golden, Goddards Fuggle-Dee-Dum, Yates Undercliff Experience, Ringwood Best, Ringwood Fortyniner. ♟ 8 **Facilities** Family room Dogs allowed Garden Parking

---

### WILTSHIRE

### ALDBOURNE — Map 5 SU27

### The Crown Inn ★★★★ INN ♟

**The Square SN8 2DU** ☎ 01672 540214
**e-mail:** gant11@hotmail.co.uk
**dir:** M4 junct 15, N on A419, signed to Aldbourne

Overlooking the village square and duck pond, the Crown is a spick-and-span 18th-century inn with a cosy, traditional beamed bar and a comfortable, wooden-floored dining room. Very much the village inn, smartly refurbished and with local Ramsbury Gold on tap, it offers a good selection of home-cooked dishes, from soup and sandwiches to Sunday roasts and a popular tapas menu, and four comfortable, well decorated bedrooms. The courtyard is a pleasant spot for summer sipping.

**Open** all wk noon–3 6–11 (Sat-Sun noon–11) **Bar Meals** L served Mon-Sat 12-3, Sun 12-4 D served Mon-Sat 6-9 **Restaurant** L served Mon-Sat 12-3, Sun 12-4 D served Mon-Sat 6-9 ⊕ ENTERPRISE INNS ◀ Spitfire Shepherds Neame, Ramsbury Gold Ŏ Westons Stowford Press. ♟ 8 **Facilities** Children's menu Play area Dogs allowed Garden Parking **Rooms** 4

---

### ALDERBURY — Map 5 SU12

### The Green Dragon ♟

**Old Rd SP5 3AR** ☎ 01722 710263
**dir:** 1m off A36 (Southampton to Salisbury road)

There are fine views of Salisbury Cathedral from this 15th-century pub, which is probably named after the heroic deeds of Sir Maurice Berkeley, the Mayor of Alderbury, who slew a green dragon in the 15th century. Dickens wrote *Martin Chuzzlewit* here, and called the pub the Blue Dragon. An interesting and daily changing menu features home-made meat and vegetarian dishes using locally sourced produce.

**Open** all wk ◀ Badger First Gold, Tanglefoot, Fursty Ferret Ŏ Stowford Press. ♟ 14 **Facilities** Dogs allowed Garden Parking

---

### AXFORD — Map 5 SU27

## PICK OF THE PUBS

### Red Lion Inn

*See Pick of the Pubs on opposite page*

---

### BARFORD ST MARTIN — Map 5 SU03

### Barford Inn

**SP3 4AB** ☎ 01722 742242 📠 01722 743606
**e-mail:** thebarfordinn@btconnect.com
**dir:** On A30 5m W of Salisbury 1.5m from Wilton

There was a change of management at this 16th-century former coaching inn five miles outside Salisbury, but the welcoming lounge, lower bar area and intimate snug have greeted visitors for generations. During World War II the Wiltshire Yeomanry dedicated a tank to the pub, known then as The Green Dragon. Meals are served in the bar or restaurant, and in warmer months in the garden or patio area. Alongside ploughman's, hot baguettes, jackets and sandwiches, you'll find gammon steak, sausage and mash, beef stroganoff or grilled sea bass fillet.

**Open** all day all wk ◀ Badger Dorset Best, Fursty Ferret, Festive. **Facilities** Dogs allowed Garden Parking

---

### BOX — Map 4 ST86

### The Northey ♟

**Bath Rd SN13 8AE** ☎ 01225 742333
**e-mail:** thenorthey@ohhcompany.co.uk
**dir:** 4m from Bath on A4 towards Chippenham. Between M4 juncts 17 & 18

A former station hotel, this stylishly transformed pub is now a favourite in the area for eating, drinking and listening to the soothing tones of Sinatra and Fitzgerald. Designed throughout by owner Sally Warburton, the interior makes good use of wood and flagstone flooring, high-backed oak chairs, leather loungers and handcrafted tables around the bar, where inviting sandwiches, ciabattas and Italian platters hold sway.

The main menu ranges from Thai green chicken curry to pork and goose casserole. There is also takeaway fish and chips and monthly live music evenings.

**Open** all day all wk Bar Meals L served all wk 11-6 D served all wk 6-10 Av main course £7 food served all day **Restaurant** L served all wk 11-6 D served all wk 6-10 Fixed menu price fr £12 Av 3 course à la carte fr £20 food served all day ⊕ WADWORTH ◀ Wadworth 6X, IPA, Malt 'n' Hops, Old Father Timer Ŏ Stowford Press. ♟ 10 **Facilities** Children's menu Children's portions Dogs allowed Garden Parking

---

### The Quarrymans Arms ♟

**Box Hill SN13 8HN** ☎ 01225 743569
**dir:** Telephone for directions

When Brunel built his Great Western Railway, he tunnelled through the solid limestone beneath this 300-year-old pub. The display of quarrying memorabilia is a legacy. There are great views from the restaurant of the valley, abundantly marked with marked paths and trails. In addition to regulars like spaghetti carbonara; home-made faggots; and Thai chicken curry, see if pheasant casserole; line-caught wild sea bass; or sizzling stir-fry are on as specials. Some good West Country real ales, ciders and wines, and over 50 malts are available.

**Open** all day all wk 11am-11.30pm **Bar Meals** L served all wk 11-3 booking required D served all wk 6-last booking booking required Av main course £6.50 **Restaurant** L served all wk 11-last booking booking required D served all wk 6-last booking booking required Fixed menu price fr £8.50 Av 3 course à la carte fr £20 ⊕ FREE HOUSE ◀ Butcombe Bitter, Wadworth 6X, Moles Best, Local guest ales Ŏ Stowford Press, Black Rat. ♟ 13 **Facilities** Children's menu Children's portions Family room Dogs allowed Garden Parking

---

### BRADFORD-ON-AVON — Map 4 ST86

### The Dandy Lion ♟

**35 Market St BA15 1LL**
☎ 01225 863433 📠 01225 869169
**e-mail:** Dandylion35@aol.com
**dir:** Telephone for directions

Over the years this property has been a boot and shoe shop, a medicine and wine shop, and a grocery shop, but the spirit of the original 18th century inn lives on through its well-kept ales and continental lagers, together with a mix of traditional English and rustic European food. The café-bar menu offers grazing boards ideal for sharing, and hot-filled flatbreads alongside old comforts like beer battered hake, chips and peas. A meal in the air-conditioned restaurant could start with goat's cheese fondue, cherry burst tomatoes, balsamic glaze with tortilla chips; then followed by home-made steak and 6X pie with creamy mash and seasonal vegetables. Desserts are also home made and are shown on the blackboard.

**Open** all wk 11-3 6-11 (Fri-Sat 11-11 Sun 11.30-10.30) **Bar Meals** L served all wk 12-2.30 D served all wk 6-9 **Restaurant** D served Fri-Sat 7-9.30 booking required ⊕ WADWORTH ◀ Wadworth 6X, Henrys IPA, Wadworth Seasonal, Wadworth Horizon Ŏ Stowford Press, Westons Organic. ♟ 21 **Facilities** Children's portions Dogs allowed

# PICK OF THE PUBS

# Red Lion Inn

**AXFORD**  Map 5 SU27

**SN8 2HA**
☎ **01672 520271**
**e-mail:** info@redlionaxford.com
**dir:** *M4 junct 15, A246 Marlborough centre. Follow Ramsbury signs. Inn 3m*

For over 400 years, this eye-catching old inn has welcomed travellers on lanes threading along the Kennet valley just outside the stirring Georgian town of Marlborough. From the flower-bedecked terrace (perfect for alfresco summer dining), divine views percolate to the river and this most peaceful stretch of countryside. It's located in the North Wessex Downs AONB and close to the popular walks in the remarkable, ancient Savernake Forest; ample opportunity to work up an appetite to sate at one of Wiltshire's finest dining inns.

Tables and chairs cunningly constructed from half-barrels and squashy, all-too comfortable sofas dot the timeworn parquet flooring of the convivial bar, all beams and boards focussed on a huge inglenook fireplace. Elsewhere, brick and flint feature walls are the backdrop for the well-appointed lounges and Garden Restaurant, offering a choice of dining areas. Settle in with a vintage from the extensive wine list or a glass of own-label Axford Ale from the nearby Ramsbury micro-brewery and consider a menu which is strong on seasonal game and fish dishes with a contemporary European flavour.

Start with smoked trout fillet with horseradish cream and tomato fondue or perhaps a carpaccio of venison with celeriac remoulade. Mains that make the most of Wiltshire's larder include fricassee of partridge with brandy Madeira and wild mushrooms or confit of slowly braised crisp belly pork with a sauté of scallops, baby prawns and lemon butter sauce. Vegetarian options include home-made caramelised onion and fig tart with smoked Cheddar and tomato. Completing the calorie top-up is a daily-changing dessert choice.

**Open** 12-3 6-11 Closed: 1st 2wks Jan, Sun eve, Mon **Bar Meals** L served Tue-Sat 12-2 D served Tue-Fri 6-9 Av main course £12 **Restaurant** L served Tue-Sun 12-2 D served Tue-Sun 6-9 Fixed menu price fr £20 Av 3 course à la carte fr £30 ⊕ FREE HOUSE ◖ Axford Ale, Ramsbury Gold, Guest ales ♂ Stowford Press. **Facilities** Garden Parking

# PICK OF THE PUBS

## The Tollgate Inn ★★★★INN   ♟

**Holt BA14 6PX**
☎ 01225 782326   📄 01225 782805
e-mail: alison@tollgateholt.co.uk
dir: *M4 junct 18, A46 towards Bath, then A363 to Bradford-on-Avon, then B3107 towards Melksham, pub on right*

This 16th-century free house was formerly a weaving shed and Baptist chapel. As with many old buildings it has a chequered history, and some of the building was knocked down when the nearby Kennet and Avon Canal was cut in the early 19th century.

The bar serves a rotating selection of guest ales, mostly from small West Country micro-breweries, and diners can eat in a small adjoining room with a wood-burning stove and country-style decoration. The restaurant proper is up wooden stairs in what was originally the chapel for the weavers working below.

Regular customers are attracted by modern British cooking with Mediterranean influences, with locally sourced ingredients whenever possible. Hand-reared beef comes from nearby Broughton Gifford; lamb from Limpley Stoke; and pork from Woolley Farm. Village shoots provide the game, whilst vegetables are grown in the surrounding farms.

Set lunches are available from Tuesday to Saturday, and there's a traditional Sunday lunchtime menu, too. Typical choices begin with roasted tomato soup with basil pesto; followed by smoked salmon kedgeree with poached egg; and concluding with crêpe Suzette with orange and Grand Marnier sauce. On the à la carte menu, starters like pan-fried scallops on spiced lentils with chilli oil; and chicken liver parfait with home-made chutney and toasted brioche; herald main course dishes such as roasted chicken breast on apple mash with Stowford Press cider sauce; and whole grilled Torbay sole with wilted spinach and sautéed potatoes.

The well-established garden and terrace is a tranquil place to eat when the weather permits. Four luxuriously furnished en suite bedrooms make the Tollgate an ideal touring base for nearby attractions such as Bath, Lacock Abbey and Castle Combe.

**Open** 11.30-3 5.30-11 (Sun 11.30-3) Closed: Mon **Bar Meals** L served Tue-Sun 12-2 D served Tue-Sat 7-9 Av main course £13.50 **Restaurant** L served Tue-Sun 12-2 D served Tue-Sat 7-9 Fixed menu price fr £10.95 Av 3 course à la carte fr £24 ⊕ FREE HOUSE ◼ Tunnel Vision, Moles Best, Sharp's Own, Tor, York Ales, Sharp's Doom Bar ♂ Thatchers Scrumpy, Stowford Press, Bee Sting Pear. ♟ 10 **Facilities** Garden Parking **Rooms** 4

Save on Hotels. Book at **theAA.com/hotel**

**WILTSHIRE** 491 **ENGLAND**

## PICK OF THE PUBS

### The Kings Arms ♟

Monkton Farleigh BA15 2QH ☎ 01225 858705
e-mail: enquiries@kingsarms-bath.co.uk
dir: Off A363 (Bath to Bradford-on-Avon road), follow
brown tourist signs to pub

Dating back to the 11th century, this historic Bath
stone building is situated in an attractive village just
outside Bradford-on-Avon. Conversion into an alehouse
took place in the 17th century, but original features
remain, including the mullioned windows, flagged
floors and a vast inglenook - said to be the largest in
Wiltshire - in the medieval-style Chancel restaurant,
which is hung with tapestries and pewter plates. The
Bar and Garden menu offers light lunches such as
Bath sausages, spring onion and smoked bacon mash;
steak frites; three-egg omelette (with various fillings)
and chips; and wild mushroom, spinach and
asparagus lasagne. From the à la carte menu come
main dishes such as duck breast with balsamic glaze,
mascarpone and almond dauphinoise; game casserole
with herb dumplings; brochette of sirloin steak and
tiger prawns (known as the 'Trawler and Tractor'),
while specials may include roast poussin with smoked
bacon, parsley mash and Cheddar cheese sauce; pork
schnitzel with sesame-fried potatoes and dolcelatte
cheese sauce; and chicken piri piri sizzle with white
and wild rice.

**Open** all wk 12-3 6-11 (Sat-Sun 12-11.30) **Bar Meals** L
served Mon-Fri 12-3, Sat 12-10. Sun 12-9 D served
Mon-Fri 6-10, Sat 12-10, Sun 12-9 ⊕ PUNCH TAVERNS
◄ Butcombe Bitter, Tribute, guest ale. ♟ 8
**Facilities** Dogs allowed Garden Parking

### The Swan ★★★★ INN

1 Church St BA15 1LN
☎ 01225 868686 ▤ 01225 868681
e-mail: theswan-hotel@btconnect.com
dir: From train station turn left, over bridge, on left
adjacent to river

Smack beside the medieval bridge that spans the River
Avon, the Swan is a striking, 15th-century honey-stoned
inn that is appointed with style and flair. Bar and dining
areas exude an elegant, contemporary feel, with rugs on
stripped boards and flagged floors and comfy sofas
fronting blazing log fires. Modern touches extend to the
short menus, from a lunchtime deli board to braised lamb
shank on buttered mash with mint and port gravy; or

aubergine rolls stuffed with spinach, onion, garlic and
feta, dauphinoise potatoes and roasted pine nut dressing.
There is a very good children's menu too. A sunny terrace
and comfortable accommodation complete the picture.

**Open** all day all wk 7am-11pm (Sun 7am-10.30pm)
**Bar Meals** L served all wk 12-2.30 booking required D
served Mon-Sat 6.30-9.30, Sun 6.30-8.30 booking
required Av main course £12 **Restaurant** L served all wk
12-2.30 booking required D served Mon-Sat 6.30-9.30,
Sun 6.30-8.30 booking required Fixed menu price fr £10
Av 3 course à la carte fr £20 ⊕ GREENE KING ◄ Old
Speckled Hen, Olde Trip Ō Stowford Press.
**Facilities** Children's menu Children's portions Garden
Parking **Rooms** 12

## PICK OF THE PUBS

### The Tollgate Inn ★★★★ INN ⊛⊛ ♟

**See Pick of the Pubs on opposite page**

### BRINKWORTH                    Map 4 SU08

## PICK OF THE PUBS

### The Three Crowns ♟

SN15 5AF ☎ 01666 510366
dir: From Swindon take A3102 to Wootton Bassett, then
B4042, 5m to Brinkworth

For over 200 years the village green-side pub has been
serving the needs of locals and travellers to
Brinkworth, on the lip of Daunsey Vale which catches
the eye from the garden room, patio and secluded beer
garden. In winter, a welcoming log fire burns in the
lounge. The Drinkers' Bar is dominated by two giant
forge bellows and a wheelwright's bellow, all now
converted into tables; settle there for a pint of
Wadworth 6X or Abbey Ales Bellringer, and perhaps a
game of cribbage or chess. The remarkable menu
changes frequently, depending largely upon just what
can be sourced that morning from local suppliers and
markets. Together with good old English steaks and
home-made pies, there's always the chance of the
exotic here; 'A Taste of the Wild' features marinated
kangaroo, venison and ostrich meats, or maybe steam-
fried strips of crocodile finished with lime, fresh ginger
and coconut milk is to your taste. Wild boar, great fish
dishes, good vegetarian options and an 80-bin wine
list ensure a satisfying visit for all.

**Open** all day all wk 10am-mdnt Closed: 25-26 Dec
**Bar Meals** L served Mon-Sat 12-2, Sun 12-9 D served
Mon-Sat 12-2, Sun 12-9 Av main course £10.50
**Restaurant** L served Mon-Sat 12-2, Sun 12-9 D served
Mon-Sat 6-9.30, Sun 12-9 Av 3 course à la carte fr £25
⊕ ENTERPRISE INNS ◄ Wadworth 6X, Greene King IPA,
Abbey Ales Bellringer, London Pride Ō Stowford Press.
♟ 27 **Facilities** Children's menu Children's portions
Play area Dogs allowed Garden Parking

### BROAD CHALKE                    Map 5 SU02

### The Queens Head Inn

1 North St SP5 5EN ☎ 01722 780344  & 0870 770 6634
dir: A354 from Salisbury towards Blandford Forum, at
Coombe Bissett right towards Bishopstone, pub in 4m

Attractive 15th-century-inn with friendly atmosphere and
low-beamed bars, once the village bakehouse. On sunny
days, enjoy the flower-bordered courtyard, whilst in colder
weather the low beams and wood burner in the bar
provide a cosy refuge. Menus include light snacks such
as sandwiches, ploughman's lunches and home-made
soups, as well as more substantial main courses:
perhaps grilled trout with almonds, sirloin steak with a
choice of vegetables, or wild game casserole.

**Open** all wk noon-3 6-11.30 (Fri-Sat 6-mdnt Sun noon-
10.30) ◄ Badgers Best, Badger Tanglefoot, Hopping Hare
Ō Stowford Press. **Facilities** Family room Dogs allowed
Garden Parking

### BURCOMBE                    Map 5 SU03

### The Ship Inn ♟

Burcombe Ln SP2 0EJ
☎ 01722 743182 ▤ 01722 743182
e-mail: theshipburcombe@mail.com
dir: In Burcombe, off A30, 1m from Wilton & 5m W of
Salisbury

A 17th-century village pub with low ceilings, oak beams
and a large open fire. In summer the riverside garden is a
great place to enjoy a leisurely meal in the company of
the resident ducks. Seasonal menu examples include
warm chorizo sausage and new potato salad; wild
mushroom tartlet with a parmesan glaze; pan fried duck
breast, gratin dauphinoise and mange-tout; and pan-
fried sea bass fillet with red Thai mussel noodles. Daily
changing specials, sandwiches and light bites are also
available.

*continued*

## BURCOMBE *continued*

**Open** all wk 11-3 6-11 **Bar Meals** L served all wk 12-2.30 D served all wk 6-9 Av main course £9 **Restaurant** L served all wk 12-2.30 D served all wk 6-9 Av 3 course à la carte fr £25 ◀ Wadworth 6X, Ringwood Best, Butcombe. ♀ 9 **Facilities** Children's menu Children's portions Dogs allowed Garden Parking

### BURTON · Map 4 ST87

## The Old House at Home ★★★★★ INN ♀

**SN14 7LT** ☎ **01454 218227**
**e-mail:** office@ohhcompany.co.uk
**dir:** On B4039 NW of Chippenham

This ivy-clad stone pub has beautiful landscaped gardens and a waterfall, and inside, low beams and an open fire. Overseen by the same landlord for some twenty years, the crew here are serious about food. The kitchen offers a good fish choice, vegetarian and pasta dishes, and traditional pub meals. Favourites include a wide choice of steaks; rack of lamb; kedgeree; or lamb's liver and bacon.

**Open** all day all wk **Bar Meals** L served all wk 12-2.30 D served all wk 6.30-10 **Restaurant** L served all wk 12-2.30 D served all wk 6.30-10 ⊕ FREE HOUSE ◀ Maiden Voyage, Doom Bar, Wadworth Ale ♂ Stowford Press. ♀ 12 **Facilities** Dogs allowed Garden Parking **Rooms** 6

### COLLINGBOURNE DUCIS · Map 5 SU25

## The Shears Inn ♀

**The Cadley Rd SN8 3ED** ☎ **01264 850304**
**e-mail:** info@theshears.co.uk
**dir:** On A338 NW of Andover & Ludgershall

A traditional country inn dating from the 18th century, The Shears was once – as its name suggests - a shearing shed for market-bound sheep. The original part of the building is thatched. Inside there are wooden and slate floors, low beamed ceilings and large fireplace; the bar has sofa seating and tables, and leads to the terrace. Now a thriving country inn, the inn serves pub classics and modern British dishes such as mackerel tartare with radish, blood orange and pork crackling, followed by pan-fried breast and confit leg of duck with curly kale and glazed carrots.

**Open** 11-3 6-11 (Sat 11-11 summer, Sun fr noon) Closed: Sun eve **Bar Meals** L served Mon-Sat 12-2, Sun 12-3.30 D served all wk 6-9.30 Av main course £9 **Restaurant** L served Mon-Sat 12-2, Sun 12-3.30 booking required D served Mon-Fri 7-9.15, Sat-Sun 7-9.30 booking required Av 3 course à la carte fr £27 ⊕ BRAKSPEAR ◀ Brakspear Bitter, Hobgoblin, guest ales. ♀ 12 **Facilities** Children's portions Dogs allowed Garden Parking

### CORSHAM · Map 4 ST87

## PICK OF THE PUBS

## The Flemish Weaver ♥

**63 High St SN13 0EZ** ☎ **01249 701929**
**dir:** Next to town hall on Corsham High St

Standing opposite the historic Corsham Court, this stone-built town centre inn takes its name from a nearby row of original Flemish weavers' cottages. Drinkers and diners are all welcome to enjoy the winter log fires and candlelit interior - though it's advisable to book a table. Thatchers Gold and Stowford Press ciders complement a good range of real ales, some of which are served straight from the barrel. There's also an extensive wine list, with many choices available by the glass. Menus are changed daily, and you might start with hand-crumbed Somerset brie and cranberry compote before making the choice between tagliatelle in dolcelatte cream sauce with spinach and toasted pine nuts; and cod with leek and potato gratin. Typical desserts include bread and butter pudding laced with Bailey's; and summer fruits and jelly terrine. Enjoy them in the large outdoor eating area on warmer days.

**Open** 11-3 5.30-11 (Sun noon-3) Closed: Sun eve ◀ Bath Spa, Doom Bar, Bath Gem, Bob, HPA Wye Valley, Hook Norton ♂ Thatchers Gold, Stowford Press. ♀ 10 **Facilities** Dogs allowed Garden Parking

### CORTON · Map 4 ST94

## PICK OF THE PUBS

## The Dove Inn ★★★ INN ◉

**BA12 0SZ** ☎ **01985 850109** 🖷 **01985 851041**
**e-mail:** info@thedove.co.uk
**dir:** A36 (Salisbury towards Warminster), in 14m turn left signed Corton & Boyton. Cross rail line, right at T-junct. Corton approx 1.5m, turn right into village

Tucked away in a lovely Wiltshire village near the River Wylye, this thriving traditional pub is a haven of tranquility. A striking central fireplace is a feature of the refurbished bar, and the spacious garden is the perfect spot for barbecues or a drink on long summer days. The award-winning menu is based firmly on West Country produce, with many ingredients coming from within just a few miles. Popular lunchtime bar snacks give way to a full evening carte featuring a classy but hearty take on pub food. A typical starter of fat scallops is served with confit duck leg and a chilli and ginger dressing. For the healthy appetite, a whole roast partridge could come next, accompanied by local bacon, sautéed onions and wild mushrooms. A sticky toffee date pudding with home-made custard is a crowd-pleasing dessert. Five en suite bedrooms arranged around a courtyard make The Dove an ideal touring base – Bath, Salisbury and Stonehenge are all close by.

**Open** all wk noon-3 6-11.30 **Bar Meals** L served all wk 12-3 D served all wk 7-9.30 Av main course £14 **Restaurant** L served all wk 12-3 D served all wk 7-9.30 Av 3 course à la carte fr £25.30 ⊕ FREE HOUSE ◀ London Pride, Sharp's Doom Bar, GFB ♂ Stowford Press. **Facilities** Dogs allowed Garden Parking **Rooms** 5

### DEVIZES · Map 4 SU06

## The Bear Hotel ★★★ HL ♀

**The Market Place SN10 1HS**
☎ **01380 722444** 🖷 **01380 722450**
**e-mail:** info@thebearhotel.net
**dir:** In town centre, follow Market Place signs

Dating from at least 1559, this old coaching inn lists Judge Jeffreys, George III and Harold Macmillan amongst its notable former guests. Right in the centre of Devizes, it has plentiful old beams, log fires and fresh flowers inside. Outside is a courtyard for sunny days. A meal might include chicken terrine with hazelnut dressing, followed by cider braised pork belly with glazed apple and braised fennel. Music fans should check out the weekly jazz sessions in the cellar.

**Open** all day all wk 9.30am-11pm Closed: 25-26 Dec **Bar Meals** L served Mon-Sun 11.30-2.30 D served all wk 7-9.30 Av main course £6 **Restaurant** L served Sun 12-2.30 D served Mon-Sat 7-9.45 Fixed menu price fr £16.50 Av 3 course à la carte fr £25 ⊕ WADWORTH ◀ Wadworth 6X, Wadworth IPA, Old Timer, Malt & Hops, Wadworths Strong in the Arm, Horizon, seasonal ales. ♀ 15 **Facilities** Children's menu Children's portions Dogs allowed Garden Parking **Rooms** 25

## The Raven Inn ♀

**Poulshot Rd SN10 1RW**
☎ **01380 828271** 🖷 **01380 828271**
**dir:** A361 from Devizes towards Trowbridge, left at Poulshot sign

A characterful half-timbered 18th-century pub in an attractive village - an easy walk to the Kennet and Avon Canal and the towpath by the famous Caen Hill flight of locks. The weekly-changing menu, which changes weekly, is a mixture of modern pub classics and restaurant dishes. From burgers, pizzas and fish and chips to confit of duck, slow roasted belly pork and pan fried venison, everyone should find something to suit their palate and budget. The pub is dog friendly and there are plenty of local walks to build up a healthy appetite.

**Open** 11.30-2.30 6.30-9 (Sun 12-3 7-10.30) Closed: Mon ◀ Wadworth 6X, Wadworth IPA, Summersault, Wadworth Old Timer ♂ Stowford Press. ♀ 8 **Facilities** Dogs allowed Garden Parking

| DONHEAD ST ANDREW | Map 4 ST92 |
| --- | --- |

## PICK OF THE PUBS

### The Forester ?

**Lower St SP7 9EE ☎ 01747 828038**
**e-mail:** possums1@btinternet.com
**dir:** *4.5m from Shaftesbury off A30 towards Salisbury*

The Forester is a lovely old country pub located in the Donheads close to Wardour Castle in beautiful walking country. Traditional in style, it has warm stone walls, a thatched roof, original beams and an inglenook fireplace. An extension provides a restaurant and a restaurant/meeting room, with double doors opening on to the lower patio area. The garden and large terrace are furnished with hardwood chairs and tables as well as bench seating. The restaurant has a good reputation for its freshly cooked meals and specialises in Cornish seafood, with deliveries five times a week. These quality ingredients are treated with a mix of traditional and cosmopolitan flavours to create dishes such as classic eggs Benedict with Serrano ham; and fritto misto of Cornish fish with aïoli and fries. Events such as 'An evening in Provence' may offer tarte au pissaladière, followed by Marseille bouillabaisse or venison bourguignon, with crêpe Suzette to finish.

**Open** noon-2 6.30-11 Closed: Sun eve **Bar Meals** L served all wk 12-2 booking required D served Mon-Sat 7-9 booking required Av main course £10.50 **Restaurant** L served all wk 12-2 D served Mon-Sat 7-9 booking required Fixed menu price fr £17.50 Av 3 course à la carte fr £25 ⊕ FREE HOUSE ◀ Ringwood, Butcombe, Butts, Otter ☾ Stowford Press, Ashton Press. ♟ 15 **Facilities** Children's menu Children's portions Dogs allowed Garden Parking

| EAST KNOYLE | Map 4 ST83 |
| --- | --- |

## PICK OF THE PUBS

### The Fox and Hounds ?

*See Pick of the Pubs on page 494*

| EBBESBOURNE WAKE | Map 4 ST92 |
| --- | --- |

## PICK OF THE PUBS

### The Horseshoe

**Handley St SP5 5JF ☎ 01722 780474**
**dir:** *Telephone for directions*

A genuine old English pub, The Horseshoe dates from the 17th century. The original building has not changed much, except for a necessary conservatory extension to accommodate more diners, and there's a pretty, flower-filled garden. Beyond the climbing roses are two rooms filled with simple furniture, old farming implements and country bygones, linked to a central servery where cask-conditioned ales are dispensed straight from their barrels. Good value bar food is freshly prepared from local produce; favourites include the home made pies. There are some great home-made desserts: seasonal fruit crumble, Bakewell tart, and crème brûlée among them.

**Open** all wk Closed: 26 Dec, Sun eve & Mon L **Bar Meals** L served Tue-Sat 12-2 booking required D served Tue-Sat 7-9 booking required **Restaurant** L served Sun 12-2.30 D served Tue-Sat 7-9 booking required ⊕ FREE HOUSE ◀ Otter Best bitter, Bowmans Swift One, Palmers Copper ☾ Hecks Farm Cider, Thatchers Gold. **Facilities** Children's portions Play area Dogs allowed Garden Parking

| FONTHILL GIFFORD | Map 4 ST93 |
| --- | --- |

### The Beckford Arms ♟ NEW

**SP3 6PX ☎ 01747 870385**
**e-mail:** info@beckfordarms.com
**dir:** *From A303 (E of Wincanton) take turn to Fonthill Bishop. At T-junct in village turn right, 1st left signed Fonthill Gifford & Tisbury. Through Fonthill Estate arch (lake on left) to pub*

Arrive in grand style at this Georgian coaching inn through the Triumphal Arch on the edge of the 10,000-acre Fonthill Estate. The new owners have given the inn an extensive but sympathetic refurbishment. The parquet-floored bar serves interesting real ales and ciders; the restaurant's glass wall opens on to the terrace. Menus change daily: try a simple pork pie with house chutney; day-boat-landed fish; roast onglet with mash, bone marrow and shallots; or twice-baked goat's cheese soufflé. The large garden is "ridiculously pretty", but then the owners are ex-Soho House.

**Open** all day all wk **Bar Meals** L served all wk 12-3 D served all wk 6-9.30 Av main course £12 **Restaurant** L served Mon-Sat 12-2.30, Sun 12-3 D served all wk 6-9.30 Av 3 course à la carte fr £22 ⊕ FREE HOUSE ◀ Butcombe, Keystone Large One, Piddle's Jimmy Riddle, Erdinger Wheat, Veltins ☾ Ashton Press, Weston's Organic, Sheppy's. ♟ 12 **Facilities** Children's menu Children's portions Play area Dogs allowed Garden Parking

*See advert below*

# PICK OF THE PUBS

# The Fox and Hounds ♀

**EAST KNOYLE**                    Map 4 ST83

**The Green SP3 6BN**
☎ 01747 830573   📠 01747 830865
e-mail:
pub@foxandhounds-eastknoyle.co.uk
web:
*www.foxandhounds-eastknoyle.co.uk*
dir: *1.5m off A303 at the A350 turn off,
follow brown signs*

The very name Blackmore Vale quickens
the heart of countryside lovers. This
partly thatched and half-timbered,
rustic old inn makes the most of its
location in a timeless village on a
greensand ridge, with exceptional views
from the patio beer garden and nearby
East Knoyle village green across these
Wiltshire and Dorset boundary-lands,
where Sir Christopher Wren was born
and the family of Jane Seymour (Henry
VIII's third wife) were based.

The engaging exterior is well matched
by the atmospheric interior, with lots of
flagstone flooring, wood-burning fires
and restful stripped wood furniture,
where locals eager to partake of
Somerset cider or select local ales from
ultra-reliable micro-breweries such as
Butcombe, Hopback and the historic
Palmers of Bridport rub shoulders with
diners keen to make the acquaintance
of the eclectic menu.

Good, wholesome pub grub like a
traditional ploughman's with Somerset
cheddar and brie, a meat lasagne or
scampi and chips share the board with
venison haunch steak with port and
redcurrant sauce; prawn and smoked
salmon risotto; or belly pork on a
Spanish casserole of chorizo, butter
beans and red peppers. Vegetarians can
look forward to Moroccan vegetable
tagine with fruited couscous, or sweet
onion, ricotta and parmesan tart.

Stone-baked pizzas baked in a clay oven
add to the fray, whilst afters include the
enchantingly-named chocolate lumpy
bumpy and cream or Bramley apple

sultana and cinnamon pie. Blackboard
menus will add another dimension to
this choice, dependant entirely on the
availability of the freshest local fare;
catch of the day is a local favourite.

**Open** all wk 11.30-3 5.30-11
**Bar Meals** L served all wk 12-2.30 D
served all wk 6-9 Av main course £10
**Restaurant** L served all wk 12-2.30
D served all wk 6-9 ⊕ FREE HOUSE
🍺 Durdle Door, Butcombe, Copper Ale,
Summer Lightning ♂ Thatchers Cheddar
Valley. ♀ 15 **Facilities** Children's menu
Dogs allowed Garden Parking

Save on Hotels. Book at **theAA.com/hotel**

**WILTSHIRE** 495 **ENGLAND**

| GREAT BEDWYN | Map 5 SU26 |

## PICK OF THE PUBS

# The Three Tuns ♥

**High St SN8 3NU** ☎ **01672 870280**
e-mail: jan.carr2@btinternet.com
dir: *Off A4 between Marlborough & Hungerford*

Just a short walk from the bustling Kennet and Avon Canal, boaters join a dedicated local trade basking in the warmth of the huge inglenook fire or chilling out in the attractive beer garden. Based on the old village bakery – the bread oven is a restaurant feature – trading started in 1756; the cellar was also the village morgue and unquiet spirits are rumoured to be abroad! This great community pub (with a renowned Sunday meat raffle) overflows with a cornucopia of rustic artefacts and continues to shine, with rare local beers a perfect accompaniment to the enticing menu created largely from Wiltshire goodies; what the owners casually refer to as 'peasant food'. The rillette of pork served with ciabatta starter is a good entrée before pushing out the boat with, perhaps, home-made salmon fishcakes served on a bed of buttered leeks with fresh tomato and basil sauce and shoestring fries, or local rabbit Normandy style cooked in cider – the landlord knows his stuff here, he was gamekeeper to the Prince of Wales. Rarely have peasants been so well-catered for!

**Open** 12-3 6-11 (Sun 12-6) **Closed:** Sun eve
**Bar Meals** L served Mon-Sat 12-2, Sun 12-2.30 D served Mon-Sat 7-9 Av main course £12 **Restaurant** L served Mon-Sat 12-2, Sun 12-2.30 D served Mon-Sat 7-9 ⊕ FREE HOUSE ◀ Ramsbury Gold, Three Tuns Bitter, local guest ales. ♥ 9 **Facilities** Children's menu Children's portions Dogs allowed Garden Parking

| GREAT CHEVERELL | Map 4 ST95 |

## PICK OF THE PUBS

# The Bell Inn ♥

**High St SN10 5TH** ☎ **01380 813277**
e-mail: gary06weston@aol.com
dir: *From Salisbury take A360 towards Devizes, through West Lavington, 1st left after black & yellow striped bridge onto B3098. Right to Great Cheverell*

This former coaching inn on the northern edge of Salisbury Plain is famous for its television appearance on *Location, location, location.* Sit by the log fire in the 18th-century bar and browse through the daily papers, or get involved with the varied programme of entertainment. Doom Bar and 6X are among the ales on offer, and home-cooked West Country food is served in the elegantly styled restaurant. The imaginative and varied menu makes use of top-quality ingredients which you'll find in starters such as Arbroath smokie tarte; pan-fried scallops; and mussels in a creamy white wine sauce. Main courses extend to wild venison with braised red cabbage, and calves' liver topped with crispy bacon; traditional comforts such as olde English

bangers and mash, and home-cooked chicken curry also have a place on the menu. The sunny, secluded garden is set in tranquil surroundings with lots of wooden benches and a patio area, enjoyed by families and locals long into the evening.

**Open** all wk **Bar Meals** L served all wk 12-2.30 D served all wk 6-9 Av main course £9.50 **Restaurant** L served all wk 12-2.30 D served all wk 6-9 ⊕ FREE HOUSE ◀ 6X, IPA, Doom Bar, guest ale Ö Stowford Press. ♥ 16 **Facilities** Children's menu Children's portions Dogs allowed Garden Parking

| GREAT HINTON | Map 4 ST95 |

## PICK OF THE PUBS

# The Linnet ♥

**BA14 6BU** ☎ **01380 870354** 🖹 **01380 870354**
dir: *Just off A361 (Devizes to Trowbridge road)*

This attractive village inn was built as a woollen mill, being converted to the New Inn after The Great War. Its present name dates from the 1970's - the then-owner was a keen ornithologist! Today's multi award-winning team continue to excel in the quality and variety of the menus they create, promising 'something you wouldn't normally eat at home' using the freshest local produce and making everything on the premises, right down to the bread, pasta and sausages. With a set lunch menu including delicacies such as rabbit, pistachio and bacon terrine or mutton shepherd's pie, the evening carte expands to include a fine range of modern and classic British and European dishes; vegetarians may be tempted by butternut squash risotto cakes with parmesan polenta chips and roast tomato sauce. Steaks are a speciality here too, including local venison. In summer there are seats on the large front patio area.

**Open** 11-2.30 6-11 **Closed:** 25-26 Dec, 1 Jan, Mon **Bar Meals** L served Tue-Sat 12-2, Sun 12-2.30 booking required D served Sun, Tue-Thu 6.30-9, Fri-Sat 6.30-9.30 booking required Av main course £9 **Restaurant** L served Tue-Sat 12-2, Sun 12-2.30 booking required D served Tue-Sun 6.30-9 booking required ⊕ WADWORTH ◀ Wadworth 6X, Henrys IPA Ö Stowford Press. ♥ 11 **Facilities** Children's portions Dogs allowed Garden Parking

| GRITTLETON | Map 4 ST88 |

## The Neeld Arms

**The Street SN14 6AP**
☎ **01249 782470** 🖹 **01249 782168**
e-mail: neeldarms@zeronet.co.uk
dir: *Telephone for directions*

This 17th-century Cotswold stone pub stands at the centre of a pretty village in lush Wiltshire countryside. Quality real ales and freshly prepared food are an equal draw to diners who will eagerly tuck in to lamb shanks, home-made steak and kidney pie or sausage and mash. Children are welcome and the small garden is especially popular for alfresco eating in fine weather.

**Open** all wk ◀ Wadworth 6X, Buckleys Best, Brakspear Bitter, IPA. **Facilities** Dogs allowed Garden Parking

| HANNINGTON | Map 5 SU19 |

## The Jolly Tar ♥

**Queens Rd SN6 7RP**
☎ **01793 762245** 🖹 **01793 765159**
e-mail: jolly.tar@sky.com
dir: *M4 junct 15, A419 towards Cirencester. At Bunsdon/ Highworth sign follow B4109. Towards Highworth, left at Freke Arms, follow Hannington & Jolly Tar pub signs*

Old timbers, a log fire and locally brewed Arkells ales make this pretty inn an appealing prospect, now with new owners. Although it's a fair old trek to the sea, there is a connection - the marriage of a lady from a local land-owning family to a 19th-century battleship captain. The traditional and cosy bar and restaurant are comfortably furnished and the ideal place to relax with a drink or a meal. All food is home cooked and freshly prepared with daily seasonal changes to the menu.

**Open** all wk 12-3 6-11 **Bar Meals** Av main course £9 **Restaurant** L served all wk 12-2 booking required D served all wk 6.30-9 booking required ⊕ ARKELLS ◀ Arkells 3B, Noel Ale, Kingsdown. ♥ 9
**Facilities** Children's menu Play area Family room Garden Parking

| HEYTESBURY | Map 4 ST94 |

## PICK OF THE PUBS

# The Angel Coaching Inn ♥

*See Pick of the Pubs on page 496*

# PICK OF THE PUBS

## The Angel Coaching Inn ♉

**HEYTESBURY**  Map 4 ST94

**High St BA12 0ED**
☎ 01985 840330  📠 01985 840931
e-mail: admin@angelheytesbury.co.uk
dir: *From A303 take A36 towards Bath, 8m, Heytesbury on left*

Although this 16th-century inn by the River Wylye is essentially a dining pub, it's one that retains the traditional charm and character of a coaching inn past. Original features and modern comforts blend well: the beamed bar, for instance, has scrubbed pine tables, sofas, warmly decorated walls and a wood-burning stove in an attractive fireplace. You may eat here, or in the restaurant, furnished with antiques and various objects of interest or, during the summer, in the secluded courtyard garden.

The head chef focuses on offering customers fresh, seasonal ingredients at wallet-friendly prices, local wherever possible.

Menus change daily to offer starters of trout roulade with cream cheese, spinach, lemon and rocket; and 'bang bang' hot smoked chicken with salad, baby gem, crispy pancetta, croutons and peanut dressing. Among a good selection of mains, look for baked fillet of cod with spiced aubergine, onion bhaji, spinach and light curry sauce; home-cooked ham with free-range eggs and chunky chips; and garlic-roasted vegetable cannelloni in slow-roasted tomato and basil sauce. Good friends may share crown of Creedy Carver duck with confit legs, potato rösti, Savoy cabbage, bacon and red wine. Cheese and ham ploughman's; eggs Benedict; and smoked trout with poached egg on toasted muffin are served at lunchtime only.

An interesting thing to do near here is to visit the abandoned village of Imber, although this is only possible when the

Army opens the access roads across Salisbury Plain. Then head back here for a pint of Morlands, or a glass of house wine from the extensive, carefully selected list.

**Open** all wk **Bar Meals** L served all wk 12-2.30 D served all wk 6.30-9.30 booking recommended Av main course £8 **Restaurant** L served all wk 12-2.30 booking recommended D served all wk 6.30-9.30 Av 3 course à la carte fr £20 ⊕ GREENE KING ◀ Morlands, Greene King IPA, 6X ♻ Stowford Press. ♉ 8 **Facilities** Dogs allowed Garden Parking

Save on Hotels. Book at **theAA.com/hotel**

WILTSHIRE 497 ENGLAND

## HINDON
Map 4 ST93

### PICK OF THE PUBS

## Angel Inn ♀

**High St SP3 6DJ ☎ 01747 820696**
e-mail: info@theangelathindon.com
dir: *1.5m from A303, on B3089 towards Salisbury*

An elegant gastro-pub where rustic charm meets urbane sophistication in a beautifully restored Georgian coaching inn. Outside is an attractive paved courtyard and garden furniture, where food can be served in fine weather. The interior is characterised by natural wood flooring, beams, large stone fireplace and comfortable leather seating. Behind the bar can be found Sharp's and Ringwood ales; pine country-style tables and chairs, together with the day's newspapers, lend a friendly and relaxed atmosphere. An eclectic mix of traditional and modern dishes characterise the brasserie-style menu, based on quality seasonal ingredients. Typical starters are twice baked Roquefort soufflé and wilted spinach; or chicken and port terrine with spiced apple chutney. The main courses could be confit saddle of rabbit with plum, ginger and anise; fish pie topped with Cheddar mash; pan-fried duck with colcannon and curly kale; and 8oz Ashdale 28-day matured fillet steak with béarnaise sauce. Desserts are on the blackboard, as are the day's set menu and specials.

**Open** all wk 11-11 (Sun noon-4) **Bar Meals** L served all wk 12-2.30 D served Mon-Sat 6-9.30 Av main course £7 **Restaurant** L served all wk 12-2.30 D served Mon-Sat 6-9.30 Fixed menu price fr £10 Av 3 course à la carte fr £18 ⊕ FREE HOUSE ◀ Sharp's, Ringwood, Timothy Taylor Landlord. ♀ 14 **Facilities** Children's portions Dogs allowed Garden Parking

### PICK OF THE PUBS

## The Lamb at Hindon ★★★★ INN ⊛ ♀

**High St SP3 6DP ☎ 01747 820573  📠 01747 820605**
e-mail: info@lambathindon.co.uk
dir: *From A303 follow signs to Hindon. At Fonthill Bishop right onto B3089 to Hindon. Pub on left*

A Lamb Inn was trading in this charming Wiltshire village 800 years ago; the current, wisteria smothered Georgian inn continues this selfless service to locals and visitors, who can enjoy a game of boules on the village green opposite. The interior of the stone-built inn is divided into several cosy areas and oozes old-world charm, with sturdy period furnishings, flagstone floors, terracotta walls hung with old prints and paintings, and a splendid old stone fireplace with a crackling log fire creates a warm, homely atmosphere, especially on cold winter nights. Where better to enjoy Wiltshire's largest selection of malt whiskies? The Scottish theme continues on the menu, which leads with a heady mix of local and Scottish produce; no surprise, then that mini Macsween haggis with neeps is a popular choice. A specials board is strong on the freshest fish, game and seasonal dishes, gaining the

chefs an AA Rosette for the quality and range of meals: haddock fillet with a prawn and herb risotto and rocket salad just one example to look out for. You can stay here too in one of 19 antique-rich bedrooms.

**Open** all day all wk 7.30am-mdnt **Bar Meals** L served all wk 12-2.30 D served all wk 6.30-9.30 booking required Av main course £10 **Restaurant** L served all wk 12-2.30 D served all wk 6.30-9.30 booking required Av 3 course à la carte fr £17 ⊕ BOISDALE ◀ Youngs Bitter, St Austell Tribute, Youngs London Gold Ŏ Stowford Press. ♀ 10 **Facilities** Children's menu Children's portions Family room Dogs allowed Garden Parking **Rooms** 19

## HORNINGSHAM
Map 4 ST84

### PICK OF THE PUBS

## The Bath Arms at Longleat ★★★★ GA ⊛⊛

**BA12 7LY ☎ 01985 844308  📠 01985 845187**
e-mail: enquiries@batharms.co.uk
dir: *Off B3092 S of Frome*

An impressive creeper-clad stone inn situated by one of the entrances to Lord Bath's Longleat Estate. Built in the 17th century, it became a public house with rooms in 1732 called the New Inn; it was later renamed the Weymouth Arms, and became the Marquess of Bath Arms in 1850. It has been comfortably refurbished and features two fine beamed bars with settles and old wooden tables, and a terracotta-painted dining room with an open fire. The Wessex Brewery furnishes the public bar with its much cherished Horningsham Pride ale, while most food is sourced within 50 miles of the pub. Simple menus focus on quality produce, with minimal use of foreign flavouring. The lunchtime menu has traditional favourites such as bangers and mash, but these belie the kitchen team's culinary expertise which has won two AA Rosettes — revealed in dinner dishes such as grilled fillet of mackerel with bacon and orange; and stuffed saddle of rabbit with rabbit 'shepherds' pie' and pickled vegetables.

**Open** all day all wk **Bar Meals** L served all wk 12-2.30 D served all wk 7-9 Av main course £9.50 **Restaurant** L served all wk 12-2.30 booking required D served all wk 7-9 booking required Av 3 course à la carte fr £29.50 ⊕ HILLBROOKE HOTELS ◀ Horningsham Pride, guest ales Ŏ Stowford Press. **Facilities** Children's menu Children's portions Dogs allowed Garden Parking **Rooms** 15

## HORTON
Map 5 SU06

## The Bridge Inn ♀

**Horton Rd SN10 2JS ☎ 01380 860273**
e-mail: bridge.innhorton@talktalkbusiness.net
dir: *A361 from Devizes, right at 3rd rdbt. Follow brown signs*

Built as a farm in about 1800, the buildings that are now the Bridge Inn were later used as a flour mill. Today, this attractive waterside pub boasts a cosy interior with open fires, and a delightful garden bordering the Kennet and Avon canal. The extensive menu ranges from freshly filled rolls and boatman's lunches to hot dishes like braised chicken breast with bacon and cheese sauce; mixed fish pie; pub favourite steak and 6X ale pie and Bargee's all-day breakfast. An ideal destination for boaters, cyclists, walkers and anglers.

**Open** 12-3 6-11 Closed: Mon ex BHs **Bar Meals** L served Tue-Sun 12-2 D served Tue-Sat 6-8.30 Av main course £6.95 **Restaurant** L served Tue-Sun 12-2 D served Tue-Sat 6-8.30 Fixed menu price fr £10.95 ⊕ WADWORTH ◀ Wadworth Henry's Original IPA, 6X, Old Father Timer, Horizon Ŏ Stowford Press. ♀ 10 **Facilities** Children's menu Children's portions Dogs allowed Garden Parking

## KILMINGTON
Map 4 ST73

## The Red Lion Inn

**BA12 6RP ☎ 01985 844263**
dir: *B3092 off A303 N towards Frome. Pub 2.5m from A303 on right on B3092 just after turn to Stourhead Gardens*

There's a good local pub atmosphere at this 14th-century former coaching inn, which once provided spare horses to assist coaches in the climb up nearby White Sheet Hill. Inside, you'll find flagstone floors, beams, antique settles and blazing log fires, and outside a large garden and a smoking shelter. Good value meals are served, such as home-made chicken casserole, vegetarian quiche, hunter's game pie, Cornish pasties, jacket potatoes and ploughman's.

**Open** all wk 11.30-2.30 6.30-11 (Sun noon-3 7-11) **Bar Meals** L served all wk 12-1.50 Av main course £6.95 ⊕ FREE HOUSE ◀ Butcombe Bitter, Jester, Guest ale Ŏ Thatchers Cheddar Valley, Ashton Press. **Facilities** Dogs allowed Garden Parking **Notes** ⊛

## LACOCK
Map 4 ST96

## The George Inn ♀

**4 West St SN15 2LH**
**☎ 01249 730263  📠 01249 730186**
e-mail: thegeorge01@btconnect.com
dir: *M4 junct 17 take A350, S, between Chippenham and Melksham*

Steeped in history and much used as a film and television location, this beautiful National Trust village includes an atmospheric inn. The George dates from 1361 and boasts a medieval fireplace, a low-beamed ceiling, mullioned *continued*

## LACOCK continued

windows, flagstone floors, plenty of copper and brass, and an old tread wheel by which a dog would drive the spit. Wide selection of steaks and flavoursome pies, and fish options include specials in summer; finish with home-made bread and butter pud.

**Open** all day all wk Thu-Sun 9am-11pm Closed: 25 Dec **Bar Meals** L served all wk 12-2 D served all wk 6-9 Av main course £9.95 **Restaurant** L served all wk 12-2 D served all wk 6-9 Av 3 course à la carte fr £19.95 ⊕ WADWORTH ◄ Wadworth 6X, Henrys IPA, J.C.B, Henrys Smooth ♂ Stowford. ☻ 9 **Facilities** Children's menu Children's portions Play area Dogs allowed Garden Parking

## Red Lion Inn ☻

1 High St SN15 2LQ ☎ 01249 730456 📄 01249 730766
e-mail: redlionlacock@wadworth.co.uk
dir: *Just off A350 between Chippenham & Melksham. Follow Lacock signs*

This historic 18th-century inn has kept its original features intact, from the large open fireplace to the flagstone floors and Georgian interior. Wadworth ales and a varied wine list accompany the home-cooked meals and daily specials. Lunchtime menu offers sandwiches or organic baguettes, small plates like breaded whitebait, home comforts, and ploughman's boards, whilst more substantial evening dishes include goat's cheese and Cheddar terrine; braised shoulder of lamb, port and redcurrant sauce; beef and garlic casserole; and butternut squash and parmesan risotto.

**Open** all day all wk 11-11 (Sun 11-10.30) ◄ Wadworth 6X, Henrys IPA, seasonal ales ♂ Stowford Press, Thatchers Gold. ☻ 15 **Facilities** Dogs allowed Garden Parking

## The Rising Sun ☻

32 Bowden Hill SN15 2PP ☎ 01249 730363
e-mail: the.risingsun@btinternet.co.uk
dir: *Telephone for directions*

The pub is located close to the National Trust village of Lacock, on a steep hill, providing spectacular views over Wiltshire from the large garden. Beer festivals, live music, hog roasts and barbecues are a regular feature, and games and reading material are provided in the bar. Thai curries and stir-fries are popular options, alongside traditional liver, bacon and onions, steaks, and beef and Stilton pie. Enjoy a pint of Moles ale or Black Rat cider.

**Open** all wk noon-3 6-11 ◄ Moles Best, Molecatcher, Tap Bitter, Rucking Mole, guest ale ♂ Thatchers Gold, Black Rat. ☻ 10 **Facilities** Play area Dogs allowed Garden Parking

---

**LIMPLEY STOKE**  Map 4 ST76

## The Hop Pole Inn ☻

Woods Hill, Lower Limpley Stoke BA2 7FS
☎ 01225 723134 📄 01225 723199
dir: *Telephone for directions*

Set in the beautiful Limpley Stoke valley, the Hop Pole dates from 1580 and takes its name from the hop plant that still grows outside the pub. Eagle-eyed film fans may recognise it as the hostelry in the 1992 film *Remains of the Day*. A hearty menu includes Thai vegetable curry; home-made pies; fresh local trout; and steaks. Food can be enjoyed with one of the many ales, or one of 11 wines served by the glass.

**Open** all wk 11-2.30 6-11 (Sun noon-3 7-10.30) Closed: 25 Dec **Bar Meals** L served Mon-Sat 12-2, Sun 12-2.15 D served Mon-Thu 6-9, Fri-Sat 6-9.30, Sun 7-9 ⊕ FREE HOUSE ◄ Courage Best, Butcombe Bitter, Sharp's Doom Bar, Guest ales ♂ Ashton Press. ☻ 11 **Facilities** Children's menu Children's portions Family room Dogs allowed Garden Parking

---

**LITTLE CHEVERELL**  Map 4 ST95

## The Owl

Low Rd SN10 4JS ☎ 01380 812263
dir: *A344 from Stonehenge, then A360, after 10m left onto B3098, right after 0.5m. Pub signed*

Sit in the pretty garden after dark and you'll discover that this pub is aptly named. As well as the hoot of owls, woodpeckers can be heard in summer. A brook runs at the bottom of the garden and there are views of Salisbury Plain. The pub itself is cosy with oak beams and a fire in winter. Typical dishes include lasagne and Thai chicken curry.

**Open** all day noon-11 Closed: Sun fr 6pm & Mon fr 4pm **Bar Meals** L served all wk 12-9 D served all wk 12-9 Av main course £8.50 food served all day ⊕ ENTERPRISE INNS ◄ Sharp's Doom Bar, Timothy Taylor Landlord ♂ Thatchers Heritage. **Facilities** Children's portions Play area Dogs allowed Garden Parking

---

**LOWER CHICKSGROVE**  Map 4 ST92

### PICK OF THE PUBS

## Compasses Inn ★★★★ INN ◉ ☻

SP3 6NB ☎ 01722 714318
e-mail: thecompasses@aol.com
dir: *On A30 (1.5m W of Fovant) take 3rd right to Lower Chicksgrove. In 1.5m turn left into Lagpond Lane, pub 1m on left*

Standing amid rolling countryside in a tiny hamlet on the old drovers' track from Poole to Birmingham, this picture-perfect 14th-century thatched inn is bursting with character. An old cobbled path leads to the low latched door and the charming bar, with its worn flagstones, low old beams and stone walls. There's a large inglenook fireplace and intimate booth seating, with soft candlelight on winter evenings. Be sure to try

---

the food: the kitchen team have won an AA Rosette for the ever-changing range of freshly-made seasonal dishes featured on the blackboard menu. A goat's cheese filo parcel might herald Wiltshire venison steak with Bombay potatoes, before finishing with mixed berry iced parfait. The garden has a large grassed area with seats for forty people and some lovely views. Five bedrooms are available, providing an ideal base for exploring the beautiful surrounding countryside.

**Open** all wk noon-3 6-11 (Sun noon-3 7-10.30) Closed: 25-26 Dec **Bar Meals** L served all wk 12-2 D served all wk 6.30-9 Av main course £14 **Restaurant** Av 3 course à la carte fr £21 ⊕ FREE HOUSE ◄ Keystone Large One, Butcombe, Stonehenge Spire, Bristol Seven ♂ Stowford Press. ☻ 8 **Facilities** Children's menu Children's portions Dogs allowed Garden Parking **Rooms** 5

---

**MALMESBURY**  Map 4 ST98

### PICK OF THE PUBS

## The Horse & Groom Inn ☻

*See Pick of the Pubs on opposite page*

## The Smoking Dog

62 The High St SN16 9AT ☎ 01666 825823
e-mail: smokindog@sabrain.com
dir: *5m N of M4 junct 17*

A refined 17th-century stone-built pub, right in the heart of Malmesbury. Inside log fires and wooden floors make for a warm and cosy atmosphere. Local produce underpins an imaginative, ever-changing menu. Guest ales also change regularly, and there's also a selection of scrumpy ciders. A renowned beer and sausage festival over Whitsun weekend is the time to sample over 30 brews and 15 banger varieties.

**Open** all day all wk noon-11 (Fri-Sat noon-mdnt, Sun noon-10.30) **Bar Meals** L served Mon-Sat 12-2.30, Sun 12-3 D served Mon-Sat 6.30-9.30, Sun 6.30-8.30 **Restaurant** L served Mon-Sat 12-2.30, Sun 12-3 ⊕ S A BRAIN ◄ Reverend James, Butcombe Best, 3 guest bitters. **Facilities** Children's menu Children's portions Dogs allowed Garden

# PICK OF THE PUBS

## The Horse & Groom Inn ♆

**MALMESBURY**  Map 4 ST98

**The Street, Charlton SN16 9DL**
☎ **01666 823904**
**e-mail:** info@horseandgroominn.com
**web:** www.horseandgroominn.com
**dir:** *M4 junct 17 follow signs to Cirencester on A429. Through Corston & Malmesbury. Straight on at Priory rdbt, at next rdbt take 3rd exit to Cricklade, then to Charlton*

Fronted by a tree-sheltered lawn and surrounded by its own paddock, this 16th-century, Cotswold-stone coaching inn has all the charm and character you'd expect from original stone flags, open fires, solid oak tables and rug-strewn wooden floors. In the dog-friendly Charlton Bar, Greene King house beers are joined by a guest ale, while outside, there's plenty of space, including a lovely walled garden and separate play area.

Back inside, in the kitchen to be exact, almost all the ingredients come from within 40 miles of the pub, reflecting the loyalty of head chef Brian Soave and his team towards Wiltshire and its produce. Beef, for example, comes from Jesse Smith's, a local family butcher which recently celebrated its 200th anniversary. Their rib-eye steaks are hung for 28 days and are delivered on the bone when required; pork belly and bacon comes from nearby Bromham; free range chickens from a farm in Stroud; and lamb from the Cotswolds.

Once the chefs have worked their magic, these and all the other ingredients become the dishes for which the Horse & Groom is known. Sausage and mash, and home-made pies are among the traditional dishes, while the modern British are represented by free-range pork with black pudding and roasted garlic roulade wrapped in pancetta; diced breast of chicken with smoked bacon, leeks and tarragon casserole; and pan-fried Scottish beef liver with mash, sautéed spinach and red wine jus. Salads have their own section of the menu: listed are Chew Valley smoked trout with toasted almonds; and breast of chicken with sun-blushed tomatoes,

baby leaves, honey and mustard dressing. The wine list may not be that long, but it is comprehensive and offers a good number by the glass.

**Open** all wk 11-11 (Sun 11-10.30)
**Bar Meals** L served Mon-Sat 12-2.30 D served Sun-Thu 6.30-9, Fri-Sat 6.30-9.30 Av main course £11
**Restaurant** L served Mon-Sat 12-2.30, Sun 12-3 D served Sun-Thu 6.30-9, Fri-Sat 6.30-9.30 Av 3 course à la carte fr £25 ◼ Greene King IPA, Old Speckled Hen, guest ales ♂ Stowford Press. ♆
**Facilities** Children's menu Play area Dogs allowed Garden Parking

**MALMESBURY** *continued*

## PICK OF THE PUBS

### The Vine Tree ♥

**Foxley Rd, Norton SN16 0JP** ☎ **01666 837654**
**e-mail:** tiggi@thevinetree.co.uk
**dir:** *M4 junct 17, A429 towards Malmesbury. Turn left for village*

The Vine Tree used to be a mill, and workers apparently passed beverages out through front windows to passing carriages - an early drive-through it would seem. These days, it is well worth seeking out for its interesting modern pub food and memorable outdoor summer dining. In the central bar a large open fireplace burns wood all winter, and there's a wealth of old beams, flagstone and oak floors. Ramblers and cyclists exploring Wiltshire's charms are frequent visitors, and the inn is situated on the official county cycle route. Cooking is modern British in style, with menus changing daily in response to local produce availability. Dishes include salads, light bites and vegetarian options, local game and well-sourced fish and meats. Perhaps start with skewer of Moroccan chargrilled boned quail with minted couscous and tzatziki; followed by pan-fried wild sea bass from Looe, rustic ratatouille and cannellini beans. There are also great real ales and a terrific stock of wines with 40 by the glass. In addition to the suntrap terrace, there's a two-acre garden with two boules pitches.

**Open** all wk noon-3 6-12 (Sun noon-4 6-11)
**Bar Meals** L served Mon-Sat 12-2.30, Sun 12-3.30 D served Mon-Thu 7-9.30, Fri-Sat 7-10, Sun 7-9.30
**Restaurant** Av 3 course à la carte fr £25 ⊕ FREE HOUSE ◀ Tinners, Butcombe, Guest ales ♂ Stowford Press. ♥ 40 **Facilities** Children's menu Children's portions Play area Dogs allowed Garden Parking

---

### The Lamb Inn ★★★ INN ♥ NEW

**The Parade SN8 1NE**
☎ **01672 512668** ▤ **01672 512668**
**e-mail:** thelambinnmarlboro@fsmail.net
**dir:** *E along High St (A4) turn right into The Parade, pub 50yds on left*

A 17th-century coaching inn overlooking Marlborough's impressively wide main street offering plenty of traditional pub dishes and daily specials to enjoy in the bar or recently renovated former stables. Jackie and daughter Laura use prime ingredients - trout and crayfish come from the nearby River Kennet, meat from local butchers and locally shot game in season. Examples include home-made pork pie and steak, kidney and Wadworth 6X pie; duck confit with Seville orange sauce; and Sri Lankan butternut and cashew nut curry. Six en suite bedrooms complete the picture.

**Open** all day all wk **Bar Meals** L served all wk 12-2.30 booking required D served Mon-Thu 6.30-9 booking required ⊕ WADWORTH ◀ Wadworth 6X, Guest ales. ♥ 10 **Facilities** Children's portions Dogs allowed Garden **Rooms** 6

---

## PICK OF THE PUBS

### Vale of the White Horse Inn ♥

**SN16 9QY** ☎ **01666 860175**
**dir:** *On B4040 (3m W of Cricklade, 6m & E of Malmesbury)*

This eye-catching, beautifully restored inn overlooks its own lake. In summer, sitting out on the large raised terrace surrounded by rose beds, it's hard to think of a better spot. The lower ground floor originally provided stabling for horses, and nowadays the village bar still serves the local community well. Here you'll find a good selection of real ales, such as Three Castle Vale and Saxon Archer, and a range of sandwiches and simple bar meals. Upstairs, lunch and dinner are served in the stone-walled restaurant with its polished tables and bentwood chairs. The menus offer something for most tastes, with starters including home-smoked chicken and bacon salad with blue cheese dressing; braised lamb shank with spring onion mash; crispy confit five spice duck legs with garlic roasted potatoes; ale battered cod fillets, chips and crushed minted peas. Finish with home-made Bailey's bread and butter pudding and toffee ice cream; or crumble of the day with custard.

**Open** all day all wk 11-11 **Bar Meals** L served all wk 12-2.30 D served all wk 6-9.15 Av main course £10 **Restaurant** L served all wk 12-2.30 D served all wk 6-9.15 ⊕ FREE HOUSE ◀ Three Castle Vale Ale, Saxon Archer, Hancocks, Braydon Ales ♂ Stowford Press. ♥ 14 **Facilities** Children's menu Children's portions Family room Dogs allowed Garden Parking

---

## PICK OF THE PUBS

### The Malet Arms

**SP4 0HF** ☎ **01980 629279** ▤ **01980 629459**
**e-mail:** info@maletarms.com
**dir:** *8m N of Salisbury on A338, 2m from A303*

Off the beaten track, in a quiet village on the River Bourne, this 17th-century inn was originally built as a dwelling house. Much later it became The Three Horseshoes, named after a nearby smithy. An earlier Malet Arms, owned by lord of the manor Sir Henry Malet, closed in the 1890s and its name was transferred. It's not just the village that's quiet: the pub is too, as fruit machines and piped music are banned. There is a good range of real ales and all the food on the ever-changing blackboard menu is home cooked. Game is plentiful in season, often courtesy of the landlord who shoots pheasant and deer. The landlady makes all the puddings, often sourced from obscure old English recipes. In fine weather you can sit outside in the garden, where there is a children's play area. Dogs are also welcome.

---

**Open** all wk 11-3 6-11 (Sun 12-3 6-10.30) Closed: 25-26 Dec, 1 Jan **Bar Meals** D served all wk 6.30-10 booking required **Restaurant** D served all wk 6.30-10 booking required ◀ Ramsbury, Stonehenge, Triple fff, Palmers, Andwell ♂ Old Rosie, Stowford Press. **Facilities** Play area Dogs allowed Garden Parking

---

### The Radnor Arms

**SP5 4HS** ☎ **01722 329722**
**dir:** *From Salisbury ring road take A338 to Ringwood. Nunton signed on right*

A popular pub in the centre of the village dating from around 1750. In 1855 it was owned by the local multi-talented brewer/baker/grocer, and bought by Lord Radnor in 1919. Bar snacks are supplemented by an extensive fish choice and daily specials, which might include braised lamb shank, wild mushroom risotto, tuna with noodles, turbot with spinach or Scotch rib-eye fillet, all freshly prepared. Fine summer garden with rural views. Hosts an annual local pumpkin competition.

**Open** all wk 11-3.30 6-11.30 **Bar Meals** L served all wk 12-2 D served all wk 6-9 **Restaurant** L served all wk 12-2 D served all wk 6-9 ⊕ HALL & WOODHOUSE ◀ Badger Tanglefoot, Best, Hopping Hare ♂ Stowford Press. **Facilities** Children's portions Play area Family room Dogs allowed Garden Parking

---

## PICK OF THE PUBS

### The Wheatsheaf Inn ◉◉ ♥

**Wheatsheaf Ln SN16 9TB** ☎ **01666 577348**
**e-mail:** info@thecompletechef.co.uk
**dir:** *Off A419, 6m S of Cirencester, through waterparks, follow signs for Oaksey*

The inglenook fireplace, beams and flagstones in the bar of this traditional 14th-century Cotswold stone inn are complemented by the light and airy contemporary restaurant with its sisal carpet. Here, you'll find wooden tables and painted walls, decorated with wine racks and jars of preserved vegetables. The inn also has something rather bizarre - an 18th-century 'royal' coffin lid displayed above the open fireplace. Modern British pub food is the order of the day, with a keen eye on the seasons and local produce. Enjoy a pint of local ale or choose from the varied wine list as you order dishes like fish pie; or braised pork belly with cabbage

Save on Hotels. Book at **theAA.com/hotel**

**WILTSHIRE** 501 **ENGLAND**

and mustard mash; before finishing with chocolate fondant, vanilla ice cream and rum-soaked sultanas. Look out, too, for 'Britain's Best Burgers', as well as the fish and chip promotion on Monday evenings and Tuesday steak nights.

**Open** Tue-Sat 12-2 6-11 (Mon 6-11 Sun 12-6) Closed: Sun eve, Mon L **Bar Meals** L served Tue-Sun 12-2 D served Tue-Sat 6.30-9 Av main course £9.50 **Restaurant** L served Tue-Sun 12-2 D served Tue-Sat 6.30-9 Av 3 course à la carte fr £28 ⊕ FREE HOUSE ◀ Sharp's Doom Bar, Hook Norton, Bath Gem, Jouster, Butcombe Bitter. ♚ 9 **Facilities** Children's menu Children's portions Dogs allowed Garden Parking

---

**PEWSEY** Map 5 SU16

## The Seven Stars

**Bottlesford SN9 6LU**
☎ 01672 851325 📠 01672 851583
**e-mail:** info@thesevenstars.co.uk
**dir:** Off A345

This thatched 16th-century free house stands in a splendid seven acre garden. Its front door opens straight onto the low-beamed, oak-panelled bar, now tastefully refurbished. Expect well-kept ales and hearty meals such as cider-braised pork belly or sausage and mash, finish with raspberry cheesecake and shortbread, walk it off with a stroll in the garden.

**Open** noon-3 6-11 Closed: Mon & Tue L **Bar Meals** food served all day **Restaurant** food served all day ⊕ FREE HOUSE ◀ Wadworth 6X, Brakspear, Timothy Taylor Landlord, Guest ales ♙ Stowford Press, Lilleys Cider Barn, Apples & Pears. **Facilities** Children's menu Children's portions Dogs allowed Garden Parking

---

**PITTON** Map 5 SU23

### PICK OF THE PUBS

## The Silver Plough

**White Hill SP5 1DU**
☎ 01722 712266 📠 01722 712262
**e-mail:** thesilverplough@hotmail.co.uk
**dir:** From Salisbury take A30 towards Andover, Pitton signed. Approx 3m

Ambassadors lauding the archetypical English pub need look no further for inspiration than this bustling local at the heart of the thatched village of Pitton. Rustic, rural charm shines from the heavily beamed interior, with countless artefacts jostling for position, including 'lucky' antique glass rolling pins. Surrounded by the Salisbury Downs, the pub is a favourite with walkers and cyclists; the eye-catching carved bar sports locally brewed beers, popular with locals enjoying the skittles alley next to the snug. Equally enticing is the menu which is strong on local produce, much of it from the local Fjordling smokery where fish, game and chicken are enhanced prior to The Silver Plough's creative chefs working their magic. Smoked mackerel and home-made pies and puddings are well-

liked, or look for monkfish tails with king prawns and mussels in saffron sauce.

**Open** all wk 11-3 6-11 **Bar Meals** L served all wk 12-2 D served all wk 6-9 Av main course £10 **Restaurant** L served all wk 12-2 D served all wk 6-9 Av 3 course à la carte fr £25 ⊕ HALL & WOODHOUSE ◀ Badger Tanglefoot, Badger Gold, King Barnes Sussex, guest ale. **Facilities** Children's menu Children's portions Family room Dogs allowed Garden Parking

---

**RAMSBURY** Map 5 SU27

### PICK OF THE PUBS

## The Bell

**The Square SN8 2PE**
☎ 01672 520230 📠 01672 520832
**e-mail:** jeremy@thebellramsbury.com
**dir:** From Marlborough take A346 towards Swindon. Approx 0.5m turn right signed Ramsbury. Onto Poulton Hill, approx 1m, left, through Mildenhall to Ramsbury

The Bell, originally a 16th-century coaching inn, stands on ancient crossroads in the centre of the village, probably the site of a hostelry since medieval times. Head chef Paul Kinsey's passion for cooking stems from a training background in France and Hampshire, and two years working for celebrity chef, Antony Worrall-Thompson. Paul sources food from within Wiltshire or neighbouring Berkshire wherever possible, and delivers an impressive array of dishes. A typical meal might start with tian of crayfish with avocado and dressed leaves, or chicken liver parfait with fig chutney; continue with hand-made pork and leek sausages, mash and onion gravy; pan-fried sea bass with mussel, scallops and wilted spinach; or wild mushroom and blue cheese gnocchi. Finish with warm carrot cake with mascarpone and cinnamon ice cream; banana tarte Tatin with vanilla ice cream and spiced rum; or the cheese board of English cheeses. You could push the boat out and enjoy a 35 day aged rib eye steak with a glass of Ramsbury Gold or Bell Bitter.

**Open** 11-3 6-11 (Sun 11-3) Closed: 25 Dec, Sun eve (ex BH) **Bar Meals** L served Mon-Sat 12-2 D served Mon-Sat 7-9 Av main course £13 **Restaurant** L served all wk 12-2 booking required D served Mon-Sat 7-9 booking required Fixed menu price fr £15 Av 3 course à la carte fr £25 ⊕ FREE HOUSE ◀ Ramsbury Gold, Bell Bitter ♙ Black Rat. **Facilities** Children's portions Dogs allowed Garden Parking

---

**ROWDE** Map 4 ST96

### PICK OF THE PUBS

## The George & Dragon ★★★★ RR ⊛⊛ ♚

**High St SN10 2PN** ☎ 01380 723053
**e-mail:** thegandd@tiscali.co.uk
**dir:** 1m from Devizes, take A342 towards Chippenham

Winter log fires warm the panelled bars and dining room of this 15th-century free house, not far from the Caen Hill lock flight on the Kennet and Avon Canal. Real ales dispensed at the bar are several in number, while wine lovers will have nearly a dozen by the glass to choose from. Rooms are cosy, welcoming and full of character. Bearing witness to the pub's age, a Tudor rose is carved on one of the beams in the restaurant, where tables are replete with crisp white linen and glowing candles. The pub specialises in seafood delivered daily from St Mawes, so take your pick from the catch of the day on the blackboard. Starters are augmented by half a dozen dishes that can be served in starter or main course portions, such as smoked haddock and chive risotto, or chargrilled Scottish scallops with black pudding brochette. Meaty main events may include chicken breast parmigiana, or paillard of beef fillet with anchovy butter. Events throughout the year and comfortable accommodation complete the package.

**Open** Mon-Sun L Closed: Sun eve **Bar Meals** L served Mon-Sat 12-3, Sun 12-4 booking required D served Mon-Fri 7-10, Sat 6.30-10 booking required Av main course £10.50 **Restaurant** L served Mon-Sat 12-3, Sun 12-4 booking required D served Mon-Fri 7-10, Sat 6.30-10 booking required Fixed menu price fr £14.50 Av 3 course à la carte fr £30 ⊕ FREE HOUSE ◀ Butcombe Bitter, Sharp's Doom Bar, Bath Ales Gem, ESB, London Pride, Ringwood Fortyniner ♙ Ashton Press. ♚ 10 **Facilities** Children's menu Children's portions Dogs allowed Garden Parking **Rooms** 3

## SALISBURY — Map 5 SU12

### PICK OF THE PUBS

## The Haunch of Venison ♥

*See Pick of the Pubs on opposite page*

## The Wig and Quill ♥ NEW

**1 New St SP1 2PH ☎ 01722 335665**
**e-mail:** tricia@wigandquill.co.uk
**dir:** *On approach to Salisbury follow brown Old George Mall Car Park signs. Pub opposite car park*

New Street is very close to the cathedral, whose superlative spire soars skywards just behind this traditional city pub. In the roomy, beamed bar with its open fires, flagstone and wooden floored, enjoy a pint of Bishop's Tipple, Wadworth 6X or a guest cider. From the menu choose between Wiltshire minted lamb with new potatoes and salad; Scottish twin-tailed scampi with chips and peas; and home-made vegetarian lasagne. Lying behind is a sheltered courtyard garden. There are music and quiz nights, and winter mulled wine and chestnut evenings.

**Open** all wk 11-4 5-2.30am (Sat-Sun all day) **Bar Meals** L served all wk 12-3.30 D served all wk 6.30-8.45 Av main course £5.75 **Restaurant** L served all wk 12-3.30 D served all wk 6.30-8.45 Fixed menu price fr £7.95 Av 3 course à la carte fr £17.45 ⊕ WADWORTHS ◀ 6X, Bishops Tipple, IPA, Horizon, Guest ales ♂ Stowford Press, Westons, Guest ciders. ♥ 14 **Facilities** Children's menu Children's portions Dogs allowed Garden

## SEEND — Map 4 ST96

## Bell Inn

**Bell Hill SN12 6SA ☎ 01380 828338**
**e-mail:** fgfdevizes@aol.com
**dir:** *On A361 between Devices & Semington*

Oliver Cromwell and his troops reputedly enjoyed breakfast at this inn, quite possibly on 18 September 1645 when he was advancing from Trowbridge to attack Devizes Castle. Its other claim to fame is that John Wesley opened the chapel next door and preached against the 'evils' of drink outside the pub. The two-floor restaurant has lovely valley views and offers a lengthy list of dishes, from liver and bacon casserole to Highland sausages in whisky.

**Open** all wk 12-2.30 5.30-11.30 **Bar Meals** L served all wk 12-2.30 D served all wk 5.30-10 Av main course £4.95 **Restaurant** L served all wk 12-2.30 D served all wk 5.30-10 Av 3 course à la carte fr £18 ⊕ WADWORTH ◀ Wadworth 6X, Henry's IPA, Bishops Tipple ♂ Stowford Press. **Facilities** Children's menu Children's portions Play area Dogs allowed Garden Parking

## SEMINGTON — Map 4 ST86

## The Lamb on the Strand ♥

**99 The Strand BA14 6LL**
**☎ 01380 870263 & 870815  📄 01380 871203**
**e-mail:** lamb@cipubs.com
**dir:** *1.5m E on A361 from junct with A350*

An 18th-century farmhouse that later became a beer and cider house. Today it is a popular dining pub serving real ales such as Bath Gem and Moles Best, plus 15 wines by the glass. Expect starters of smoked salmon and pea risotto, and wild mushrooms and garlic on toast; followed by lamb, mint and chilli burger with chips; house speciality of slow roast local lamb for two; or pan-seared fillet of bream with sauce verte. Old favourites such as Downland Farm sausages and mash, and home-made steak and ale pie are sure to make an appearance. Take a look at the daily-changing chalkboard specials too.

**Open** noon-3 6.30-11 Closed: Sun eve, Mon **Bar Meals** L served all wk 12-2.30 D served Mon-Sat 6.30-9 Av main course £9 **Restaurant** L served all wk 12-2.30 D served Mon-Sat 6.30-9 Av 3 course à la carte fr £17 ⊕ FREE HOUSE ◀ Butcombe Bitter, Moles Best, Bath Gem, Guinness ♂ Scrumpy Jack. ♥ 15 **Facilities** Children's portions Dogs allowed Garden Parking

### PICK OF THE PUBS

## The Somerset Arms ★★★★ INN ♥ NEW

**Hight St BA14 6JR ☎ 01380 870067**
**dir:** *From Devizes towards Trowbridge on A361 (approx 8m) turn right at rdbt after rdbt junct with A350. Pub in village*

Following a period of closure, the doors of this old coaching inn finally re-opened in July 2009 with new owners and a swish new look. The spruced-up bar and lounge sport tiled floors, roaring log fires in brick fireplaces, squashy leather sofas, exposed beams, and warm heritage hues on the walls. Stylish design extends to the contemporary dining room, replete with modern light wood furniture and jazzy wall coverings, and upstairs to the three boutique style en suite bedrooms. Back in the bar, order a pint of Bath Gem and peruse the interesting short seasonal menu, which features locally-sourced meat and vegetables. Typical dishes include potted ham hock and pan-fried scallops with spinach and crab tortellini for starters, with main courses taking in pork loin with bubble-and-squeak, and rib-eye steak with all the trimmings. At lunchtime, tuck into a lamb and mint mayonnaise filled baguette, or a plate of gammon, egg and chips. Worth noting as it is strolling distance from the Kennet & Avon Canal and a handy stopover for Bath and Bradford-on-Avon.

**Open** all day all wk **Bar Meals** L served all wk 12-3 D served all wk 6.30-9 Av main course £7 **Restaurant** L served all wk 12-3 booking required D served Sun-Thu 6.30-9, Fri-Sat 6.30-9.30 booking required Av 3 course à la carte fr £20 ⊕ FREE HOUSE ◀ Gem, Summer Lightning, Golden Bolt, Danish Dynamite, Summerset ♂ Broadoak Perry, Cheddar Valley, Old Bristolian. ♥ 16 **Facilities** Children's menu Children's portions Family room Dogs allowed Garden Parking **Rooms** 3

## SHERSTON — Map 4 ST88

## The Rattlebone Inn ♥

**Church St SN16 0LR ☎ 01666 840871**
**e-mail:** eat@therattlebone.co.uk
**dir:** *M4 junct 17, A429 to Malmesbury. 2m after passing petrol station at Stanton St. Quentin, turn left signed Sherston*

Named after the legendary Saxon hero John Rattlebone, this lovely 16th-century pub boasts roaring winter fires and bags of character. A lively drinkers' pub serving real ales and organic cider, the Rattlebone also has a reputation for its country bistro menu. Expect locally sourced ingredients, summer spit roasts, and seasonal game, featuring dishes like venison marinated with port and juniper berries. The pub has two garden areas, two boules pistes and a well-used skittles alley.

**Open** all wk noon-3 5-11 (Fri noon-3 5-mdnt Sat noon-mdnt Sun noon-11) ◀ Youngs Bitter, Bombardier, St Austell Tribute ♂ Stowford Press, Westons Organic. ♥ 14 **Facilities** Dogs allowed Garden

## STOFORD — Map 5 SU03

## The Swan Inn ★★★★ INN ♥

**Warminster Rd SP2 0PR**
**☎ 01722 790236  📄 01722 444972**
**e-mail:** info@theswanatstoford.co.uk
**dir:** *From Salisbury take A36 towards Warminster. Stoford on right 4m from Wilton*

The Swan is a landmark coaching inn, close to the cathedral city of Salisbury, with attractive gardens overlooking the River Wylye to meadow and farmland. There is a welcoming log fire, great real ales, 30 wines by the glass and traditional home cooked food. Dishes might include slow braised duck, baby pearl onions, sautéed oyster mushrooms and Wiltshire bacon lardons; steamed Scottish rope mussels with a choice of sauce; and shredded smoked chicken and chorizo sausage linguine. As well as lovely riverside gardens, there are comfortable guest rooms available.

**Open** all day all wk 8am-11pm (Sun 8am-10.30pm) **Bar Meals** Av main course £11 food served all day **Restaurant** food served all day ⊕ ENTERPRISE INNS ◀ Hopback Odyssey, Timothy Taylor Landlord, Guest ale. ♥ 30 **Facilities** Children's portions Dogs allowed Garden Parking **Rooms** 9

# PICK OF THE PUBS

## The Haunch of Venison

**SALISBURY** Map 5 SU12

**1-5 Minster St SP1 1TB**
☎ **01722 411313**
**e-mail:** oneminsterst@aol.com
**dir:** *In city centre. Opposite Poultry Cross Monument, adjacent to market place*

Dating from 1320, this is probably Salisbury's oldest hostelry. Heavily beamed, it once housed craftsmen working on the cathedral spire, although it is closer to St Thomas's Church, whose clergy used to visit via a tunnel to avoid the unseemly goings on in some of the rooms. The arrangement of floor levels is supposed to reflect an ecclesiastical hierarchy, the so-called House of Lords room being for the higher orders. The bar has a small, intimate 'Horsebox', originally for ladies, which was reputedly used by Churchill and Eisenhower when planning the D-Day landings.

Charming details include what is believed to be the country's only surviving complete pewter bar top, as well as original gravity-fed spirit taps. Real ales served here are as local as you would wish, with Salisbury's Hop Back Brewery having a major presence. Which leads us nicely to another type of presence – the resident ghosts. Most talked about is the one-handed Demented Whist Player whose hand, severed for cheating at cards, was found mummified in the 19th century and is on display to this day; he is usually seen in the private bar, which has the only licensed landing in England. Another ghost, this time female, takes the form of the Grey Lady searching for her child; if seen, you may need to refer to the pub's list of 80 whiskies.

In the main dining room is a working fireplace dating back to 1588. Here, lunchtime sees fresh hot paninis and baguettes, backed by a short list of starters such as southern fried chicken goujons with aïoli, and main courses such as cold sausage platter with

dressed salad. In the evening, the menu continues to focus on quality of flavour at affordable prices: pan-fried foie gras with red onion marmalade could be followed by British pork spare rib chop with creamed leeks, pak choi, celeriac and apple potato rösti; or, of course, haunch of venison with garlic mash, braised spring onions and Savoy cabbage.

**Open** all day all wk 11-11 Closed: 25 Dec eve **Bar Meals** L served all wk 12-2.30 D served Sun-Wed 6-9.30 (Thu-Sat 6-10) **Restaurant** L served all wk 12-2.30 booking required D served Sun-Wed 6-9.30 (Thu-Sat 6-10) booking required ⊕ ENTERPRISE INNS
🍺 Courage Best, Summer Lightning, Greene King IPA, Hopback guest ale
Ö Stowford Press. ⬤ 13
**Facilities** Children's menu Dogs allowed

## STOURTON  Map 4 ST73

### PICK OF THE PUBS

### Spread Eagle Inn ★★★★ INN ⚑

**BA12 6QE** ☎ **01747 840587** 📠 01747 840954
**e-mail:** enquiries@spreadeagleinn.com
**dir:** N of A303 off B3092

Built at the beginning of the 19th century, this charming inn stands in the heart of the 2,650-acre Stourhead Estate, one of the country's most visited National Trust properties. Before or after a walk through the magnificent gardens and landscapes there is plenty on offer here, including locally produced beers and traditional food. Expect perhaps Wiltshire pasty with onion gravy and chips; lamb casserole and roasted root vegetables; and Old Spot sausages with bubble and squeak mash and sweet mustard sauce. The restaurant menu shifts things up a gear with breast of Gressingham duck with parsnip purée and apple sauce; escalope of cod with lentils and bacon; and chump of Cotswold lamb with spiced apricots and rosemary. The interior is smartly traditional, and in the bedrooms, antiques sit side by side with modern comforts. Recent change of hands.

**Open** all day all wk 9.30-11 ⊕ FREE HOUSE
◀ Kilmington, Butcombe, guest ales Ö Ashton Press.
⚑ 8 **Facilities** Garden Parking **Rooms** 5

## TOLLARD ROYAL  Map 4 ST91

### King John Inn ⚑

**SP5 5PS** ☎ **01725 516207**
**e-mail:** info@kingjohninn.co.uk
**dir:** On B3081 (7m E of Shaftesbury)

Named after one of King John's hunting lodges, this Victorian building dates from 1859, and was rescued from an advanced state of dereliction in 2008. The stylishly uncluttered interior boasts quarry-tiled floors and a solid oak bar complete with Belfast sink. The kitchen's output seeks the freshest of flavours from locally sourced produce. A typical meal might include celeriac and apple soup followed by whole grilled lemon sole with Jerusalem artichokes, new potatoes and steamed mussels.

**Open** all wk noon-3 6-11 **Bar Meals** L served Mon-Fri 12-2.30, Sat-Sun 12-3 booking required D served all wk 7-9.30 booking required Av main course £12 **Restaurant** L served Mon-Fri 12-2.30, Sat-Sun 12-3 booking required D served all wk 7-9.30 booking required ⊕ FREE HOUSE ◀ Ringwood Best, Fuller's London Pride, Summer Lightning, guest ales Ö Stowford Press. ⚑ 16 **Facilities** Children's portions Dogs allowed Garden Parking

## UPPER WOODFORD  Map 5 SU13

### The Bridge Inn ⚑

**SP4 6NU** ☎ **01722 782323**
**e-mail:** enquiries@thebridgewoodford.co.uk
**dir:** From Salisbury take A360. Turn right for Middle Woodford & Upper Woodford. (Village between A360 & A345 5m N of Salisbury)

Hidden away on a quiet lane beside the Wiltshire Avon just north of Salisbury, this charming pub has been completely refurbished to include a modern, theatre-style kitchen. As well as a riverside garden and winter fires, you'll find flowers and candles on the tables at any time of year. Seasonal menu choices might include pan-fried pigeon breast with bubble and squeak; butternut, pea and spinach risotto; smoked fish kedgeree with scrambled egg.

**Open** all wk 11-3 6-11 **Bar Meals** L served all wk 12-2.30 D served all wk 6-9 Av main course £9 **Restaurant** L served all wk 12-2.30 D served all wk 6-9 Av 3 course à la carte fr £25 ⊕ ENTERPRISE INNS ◀ Summer Lightning, Wadworth 6X, Ringwood Best. ⚑ 10 **Facilities** Children's menu Children's portions Dogs allowed Garden Parking

## UPTON LOVELL  Map 4 ST94

### Prince Leopold Inn ⚑

**BA12 0JP** ☎ **01985 850460**
**e-mail:** Princeleopoldinn@btconnect.com
**dir:** From Warminster take A36 after 4.5m turn left into Upper Lovell

Built in 1887 as the local shop, post office and store to service the then prosperous woollen industry, the inn's name was chosen to honour Prince Leopold who lived nearby. Possibly unique in England, the Mediterranean-style restaurant has an eye-level fireplace with a charcoal barbecue grill. Seafood features strongly on a wide ranging menu, offering brill fillet on champ mash with hollandaise sauce and thyme scented onions alongside Thai green chicken curry.

**Open** winter noon-3 7-11 (Sun noon-4 7-10.30) summer noon-11 Closed: winter Mon all day Tue L ◀ Ringwood Best, John Smith's, guest ales Ö Stowford Press. ⚑ 8 **Facilities** Dogs allowed Garden Parking

## WARMINSTER  Map 4 ST84

### PICK OF THE PUBS

### The Angel Inn ⚑

**Upton Scudamore BA12 0AG**
☎ **01985 213225** 📠 01985 218182
**e-mail:** mail@theangelinn.co.uk
**dir:** From Warminster take A350 towards Westbury or A36 towards Bath

The Angel is a restored 16th-century coaching inn located in a small village close to Warminster, so it's ideally placed for visits to Longleat, Stonehenge, Amesbury and the Cotswolds. Access to the pub is via a walled garden and terrace, where meals and drinks can be served in fine weather. Inside, open fires, natural wood flooring and guest ales create a welcoming atmosphere. Dishes from the lunch menu vary from traditional to modern – you might find, for example, a garlic roasted beetroot salad with quail's eggs, anchovy fritters and horseradish cream; and braised belly of pork on a cannellini bean and tomato salad. For dinner the eclectic range of flavours continues in such dishes as panaché of seafood in saffron consommé with julienne vegetables and garlic aïoli croûtons; and fresh linguini with butternut squash, sage, asparagus, black olives, cherry tomatoes and basil, finished with parmesan. You could finish with a trio of rice puddings with toasted plums. The Angel hosts four art exhibitions each year showcasing local artists.

**Open** all wk 11-3 6-11 ⊕ FREE HOUSE ◀ Wadworth 6X, Butcombe, John Smith's Smooth, Guest ales. ⚑ 10 **Facilities** Children's menu Children's portions Dogs allowed Garden Parking

### The Bath Arms

**Clay St, Crockerton BA12 8AJ**
☎ **01985 212262** 📠 01985 218670
**e-mail:** batharms@aol.com
**web:** www.batharmscrockerton.co.uk
**dir:** From Warminster on A36 take A350 towards Shaftesbury then left to Crockerton, follow signs for Shearwater

Set on the Longleat Estate close to the Shearwater Lake, this well-known free house attracts locals, walkers and tourists. The garden has been landscaped to provide a pleasant spot for outdoor drinking and dining, and the Garden Suite, with views across the lawn, provides additional seating on busy weekends. Expect stylish food

*continued on page 506*

# PICK OF THE PUBS

## The Pear Tree Inn ★★★★★ RR

**WHITLEY** Map 4 ST86

**Top Ln SN12 8QX**
☎ **01225 709131** 📠 **01225 702276**
**e-mail:**
peartreeinn@maypolehotels.com
**dir:** *A365 from Melksham towards Bath, at Shaw right onto B3353 into Whitley, 1st left in lane, pub at end*

This sublime, wisteria-clad stone pub surveys tranquil farmland between the Cotswolds and the Marlborough Downs, recalling its genesis as a yeoman's farmhouse centuries ago. Much rustic, rural character remains, from the flagstone floors to the grand open fires and eclectic collection of agricultural artefacts which engage the eye throughout. Like other establishments in the Maypole Group, it cares deeply about its real ales and a carefully selected worldwide wine list that features many by the glass.

The home-made food on its popular menu of hearty, traditional dishes has earned generous praise, not least from the AA, which has awarded two Rosettes for the obvious attention paid to the quality, selection and cooking of ingredients. Indeed, everything comes from locally based suppliers — meats from nearby farms and top quality fruit and vegetables from village growers - but some things have to come from further afield, such as the lemons from the Amalfi coast that provide the basis for the delicious lemon tart.

Taken in the characterful bar, airy restaurant or alfresco in the peaceful gardens, the fruits of the chefs' labours also extend to a modern fusion of British and European dishes; seared scallops on a fricassee of chopped chorizo, mushrooms and butternut squash or herb-crusted fillet of halibut with creamed Savoy cabbage explain the enduring appeal of the place.

Being close to Bath, Lacock Abbey and the remarkable Avebury stones, it's the ideal place for a short break in one of the eight designer bedrooms.

**Open** all day all wk breakfast - 11pm
**Bar Meals** L served all wk 12-2.30
D served all wk 6.30-9.30
**Restaurant** L served all wk 12-2.30 D served all wk 6.30-9.30 Fixed menu price fr £12.50 Av 3 course à la carte fr £25 ⊕ MAYPOLE GROUP LC ◀ Wadworth 6X, Sharps Doom Bar, London Pride ♂ Thatchers Gold. ♟ 8+
**Facilities** Children's menu Dogs allowed Garden Parking **Rooms** 8

## WARMINSTER *continued*

such as fillet of red mullet with cauliflower cheese and truffled celeriac or ribeye steak with rocket pesto and blue cheese fritters.

**Open** all wk **Bar Meals** L served all wk 12-2 D served all wk 6.30-9 **Restaurant** L served all wk 12-2 D served all wk 6.30-9 ⊕ FREE HOUSE ◀ Crockerton Classic, Naughty Ferrit, Guest ales. **Facilities** Play area Dogs allowed Garden Parking

### The George Inn ★★★★ INN ♉

**BA12 7DG** ☎ **01985 840396** 🖨 **01985 841333**
e-mail: info@the-georgeinn.co.uk
dir: *Telephone for directions*

A 17th-century coaching inn at the heart of the pretty village of Longbridge Deverill. Customers can enjoy a pint of real ale by the fire in the oak-beamed Longbridge bar, or sit outside in the two-acre garden on the banks of the River Wylye. Food is served in a choice of two restaurants, and there is a Sunday carvery in the Wylye Suite. Function facilities are available, plus accommodation in 12 en suite bedrooms.

**Open** all day all wk 11-11 (Sun noon-10.30) Closed: 25 Dec fr 3, 26 Dec (1 Jan open 11-3) **Bar Meals** L served Mon-Thu 12-2.30, Fri-Sat 12-9.30, Sun 12-9 D served Mon-Thu 6-9.30 **Restaurant** L served Mon-Thu 12-2.30, Fri-Sat 12-9.30, Sun 12-9 D served Mon-Thu 6-9.30 ⊕ POWDER TRAIN ◀ John Smith's, Wadworth 6X, Hobdens Doverills Advocat. ♉ 11 **Facilities** Children's menu Children's portions Play area Garden Parking **Rooms** 12

---

| WEST LAVINGTON | Map 4 SU05 |
|---|---|

### PICK OF THE PUBS

### The Bridge Inn ♉

**26 Church St SN10 4LD** ☎ **01380 813213**
e-mail: portier@btopenworld.com
dir: *Approx 7m S of Devizes on A360 towards Salisbury. On edge of village, beyond church*

The Bridge is an attractive food-led pub in a village setting on the edge of Salisbury Plain. Inside you'll find a beamed bar with a log fire and displays of local paintings for sale, while outside there is a large garden featuring a boule pitch. The pub is owned by Cyrille and Paula Portier; Cyrille, heading up the kitchen, brings a French influence to the menu, with dishes such as l'assiette de charcuterie for one or two to share; cassoulet with roast duck leg and sausage, or

soufflé with Emmental cheese and tomato pesto. Pub favourites offered from the specials board include soup of the day with crème fraîche and croutons; moules marinière; haddock in organic beer batter, or Wiltshire ham with organic free-range eggs and pommes frites. Annual events are now a regular feature at The Bridge, from Harvest Supper in September to the Charity Beer Festival over the August Bank Holiday weekend.

*The Bridge Inn*

**Open** noon-3 6.30-11 Closed: 2wks Feb, Sun eve & Mon **Bar Meals** L served Tue-Sun 12-2 booking required D served Tue-Sat 7-9 booking required **Restaurant** L served Tue-Sun 12-2 booking required D served Tue-Sat 7-9 booking required ⊕ ENTERPRISE INNS ◀ Wadworth Henry's IPA, Plain Ale Innocence, Sharp's Doom Bar. ♉ 12 **Facilities** Garden Parking

---

| WHITLEY | Map 4 ST86 |
|---|---|

### PICK OF THE PUBS

### The Pear Tree
### Inn ★★★★★ RR 🏵 🏵 ♉

**See Pick of the Pubs on page 505**

---

| WINTERBOURNE BASSETT | Map 5 SU07 |
|---|---|

### The White Horse Inn ♉

**SN4 9QB** ☎ **01793 731257** 🖨 **01793 739030**
e-mail: ckstone@btinternet.com
dir: *5m S of Swindon on A4361 (Devizes road)*

Just two miles north of the mysterious Avebury stone circle, this is an ideal base for walks on the historic Ridgeway path. Along with fine traditional ales from Wadworth Brewery, food is served in the bar and conservatory restaurant, as well as in the safe, lawned garden. Budget lunches and snacks are supported by a full menu and daily specials: look out for tiger prawn provençale; chicken Sorrento; or honey roasted vegetable Wellington.

**Open** all wk 11.30-3 6-11 **Bar Meals** L served all wk 12-2 D served all wk 6-7.30 Av main course £12 **Restaurant** L served all wk 12-2 D served all wk 6-9.30 Fixed menu price fr £6.25 Av 3 course à la carte fr £20 ⊕ WADWORTH ◀ Wadworth 6X, IPA, Hophouse Brews ♉ Stowford Press. ♉ 12 **Facilities** Children's menu Garden Parking

---

| WOODFALLS | Map 5 SU12 |
|---|---|

### The Woodfalls Inn ♉

**The Ridge SP5 2LN** ☎ **01725 513222** 🖨 **01725 513220**
e-mail: enquiries@woodfallsinn.co.uk
dir: *B3080 to Woodfalls*

Located on an old coaching route on the northern edge of the New Forest, The Woodfalls Inn has provided hospitality to travellers since the early Victorian era. A more recent extension accommodates a purpose built function suite, in addition to the bar areas, conservatory, lounge and restaurant. Home-made dishes include chicken curry, beef or vegetable lasagne, and steak and ale pie. There is also a comprehensive selection of grills. Recent change of hands.

**Open** all day all wk 11am-11pm (Sun noon-11pm) Closed: 1 Jan ◀ Ringwood Fortyniner, Best, 2 guest ales. ♉ 9 **Facilities** Dogs allowed Garden Parking

---

| WOOTTON RIVERS | Map 5 SU16 |
|---|---|

### PICK OF THE PUBS

### Royal Oak ♉

**SN8 4NQ** ☎ **01672 810322** 🖨 **01672 811168**
e-mail: royaloak35@hotmail.com
dir: *3m S from Marlborough*

Over the years this 16th-century thatched and timbered pub has expanded into the village farrier's yard and the bakery. Just 100 yards away are the Kennet and Avon Canal and the Mid-Wilts Way; the pub is also handy for exploring the ancient oaks of Savernake Forest. The interior is as charming as the setting, with low, oak-beamed ceilings, exposed brickwork and wide open fireplaces. In the bar you'll find Wadworth 6X and guest ales, including local Ramsbury Bitter. As well as the carte, snacks, sandwiches and meat, fish and poultry dishes, there are daily specials. To give you an idea of what may be available, items taken from a sample menu include pan-fried scallops with bacon and mushrooms, and Italian-style antipasti with olives as starters; and main meals of rich beef and Burgundy casserole with parsley dumplings; ratatouille topped with toasted brie; and grilled mackerel fillets with gooseberry sauce.

**Open** all wk noon-9.30 (all day Sun) **Bar Meals** Av main course £11.50 food served all day **Restaurant** Fixed menu price fr £12.50 Av 3 course à la carte fr £15 food served all day ⊕ FREE HOUSE ◀ Wadworth 6X, Guest ales inc local Ramsbury Bitter. ♉ 9 **Facilities** Children's menu Children's portions Family room Dogs allowed Garden Parking

## WYLYE
Map 4 SU03

### The Bell Inn ▾

High St BA12 0QP ☎ 01985 248338   📄 01985 248491
dir: *From Salisbury take A36 N'bound to Warminster,
then Wylye & A303 Honiton signed off A36. Follow signs
for Wylye*

There's a wealth of old oak beams, log fires and an
inglenook fireplace at this 14th-century coaching inn,
situated in the pretty Wylye valley. Owned by the Hidden
Brewery (located just two miles away in Dinton), and so
Hidden beers are available, but thankfully, not too well
hidden. Lunch and dinner menus feature mainly local
ingredients.

Open all wk ◗ Hidden Pint, Hidden Quest, Hidden
Oldsarum, Hidden Fantasy, Hidden Treasure, Hidden
Pleasure. ▾ 10 **Facilities** Dogs allowed Garden Parking

## WORCESTERSHIRE

### ABBERLEY
Map 10 SO76

### The Manor Arms at Abberley ★★★ INN ▾

WR6 6BN ☎ 01299 896507   📄 01299 896723
e-mail: info@themanorarms.co.uk
dir: *Signed from A443, Abberley B4202 towards Clows
Top, right at village hall*

Overlooking a picturesque valley in the historic village of
Abberley, this 300-year-old coaching inn has plenty of
original features, including oak beams and inglenook
fireplace. Food options range from bar snacks to a full à
la carte menu in the restaurant which overlooking the
valley. Typical choices include home-made chicken and
leek soup followed by duck breast with port and raspberry
sauce. Fish and chips are also available to take away on
Monday to Saturday evenings. Good choice of real ales
and comfortable accommodation are available.

Open noon-3 6-11.30 (Sat-Sun noon-11.30) Closed: Mon
L **Bar Meals** L served Tue-Sun 12-2.30 booking required
D served Mon-Sat 6-9 booking required Av main course
£7.95 **Restaurant** L served Tue-Sat 12-2.30, Sun 12-8 D
served Mon-Sat 6-9 Av 3 course à la carte fr £16
⊕ ENTERPRISE INNS ◗ Timothy Taylor, Fuller's London
Pride, Hereford HPA, Flowers IPA, Wye Valley Bitter, Guest
Ales ♻ Stowford Press. ▾ 15 **Facilities** Children's
menu Children's portions Dogs allowed Garden Parking
**Rooms** 10

## BECKFORD
Map 10 SO93

### The Beckford ★★★★ INN ▾

Cheltenham Rd GL20 7AN ☎ 01386 881532
e-mail: enquiries@thebeckford.com
web: www.thebeckford.com
dir: *On A46 (Evesham to Cheltenham road) 5m from M5
junct 9*

New owners took over this 18th-century former coaching
inn on the northern edge of Cotswolds in July 2009 and
have begun restyling and updating the bedrooms.
Contemporary-styled throughout, there's a relaxing bar
with five real ales on tap and a roaring log fire, an
*continued*

---

## The Beckford

*T*he Beckford Inn sits on the northern edge of the beautiful
Cotswolds, a stunning 18thC Coaching Inn set in open countryside
just off the A46.

Discover a beautiful new restaurant with great Chef's using the finest,
freshest local produce, even growing some of their own fruit & vegetables!

Relax in the lovely gardens or enjoy
the old pub bar with a roaring fire,
fine wines and real ales.   Stay longer
in rooms with lush new furnishings &
luxurious bathrooms.

*The Beckford Inn* is also a favourite
with business functions and
weddings.

Ideally situated close to Cheltenham
Race Course, Sudeley Castle and
even Stratford Upon Avon – all this
plus the warmest welcome in the
Cotswolds. Discover *The Beckford Inn*
today, ring 01386 881532.

The Beckford Inn, Cheltenham Road (A46), Beckford, Nr Tewkesbury GL20 7AN
Tel: 01386 881532 • Email: enquiries@thebeckford.com • Website: www.thebeckford.com

## BECKFORD *continued*

attractive formal dining room, and beautiful gardens for summer alfresco dining. Modern menus use local and home grown ingredients and list pub classics (beef and ale pie) alongside lamb loin with mint and redcurrant sauce and seared tuna with coriander salsa.

**Open** all day all wk **Bar Meals** L served Mon-Fri 12-2.30, Sat-Sun 12-9.30 D served Mon-Fri 6.30-9.30, Sat-Sun 12-9.30 Av main course £7 **Restaurant** L served Mon-Fri 12-2.30, Sat-Sun 12-9.30 D served Mon-Fri 6.30-9.40, Sat-Sun 12-9.30 Fixed menu price fr £20 Av 3 course à la carte fr £20 ⊕ FREE HOUSE ◀ London Pride, Greene King Abbot, St Austell, Tribute, Perscott Hill Climb, Timothy Taylor Landlord Ö Stowford Press. ♈ 22
**Facilities** Children's menu Children's portions Dogs allowed Garden Parking **Rooms** 13

*See advert on page 507*

---

| BEWDLEY | Map 10 SO77 |

## Little Pack Horse ♈

**31 High St DY12 2DH**
☎ 01299 403762 📄 01299 403762
**e-mail:** enquires@littlepackhorse.co.uk
**dir:** *From Kidderminster follow ring road & Safari Park signs. Then follow Bewdley signs over bridge, turn left, then right, right at top of Lax Ln. Pub in 20mtrs*

This historic timber-framed inn is warmed by cosy log fires and lit by candles at night. There are low beams, an elm bar, and a small outside patio for alfresco summer dining. Expect a great selection of real ales and ciders, and a menu built on local, seasonal produce. A meal might include fried whitebait and squid, followed by roast belly pork with apple and sage gravy. Home-made pies are a speciality, especially Desperate Dan cow pie.

**Open** all wk noon-2.30 6-11.30 (Sat-Sun noon-mdnt) **Bar Meals** food served all day **Restaurant** food served all day ⊕ PUNCH TAVERNS ◀ Wye Valley HPA, Dorothy Goodbody Golden Ale, Shepherd Neame Spitfire, Sharp's Doom Bar, Hobsons Best, St Austell Proper Job Ö Stowford Press, Westons Organic, Thatchers Katy. ♈ 10
**Facilities** Children's menu Children's portions Family room Dogs allowed Garden

---

### PICK OF THE PUBS

## The Mug House Inn & Angry Chef Restaurant ☆☆☆☆☆ INN ⊛ ♈

**12 Severnside North DY12 2EE**
☎ 01299 402543 📄 01299 402543
**e-mail:** drew@mughousebewdley.co.uk
**dir:** *A456 from Kidderminster to Bewdley. Pub in town on river*

Nestling beside the River Severn in picturesque Bewdley, this inn's riverside seating area is popular on warmer days. The unusual name dates back to the 17th century, when 'mug house' was a popular term for an alehouse. Nowadays you'll find at least two guest ales at the bar, alongside regulars such as Wye Valley and

Weston's scrumpy: the inn holds a beer festival each year. An extensive lunchtime bar menu includes Granny Clifford's home-made faggots with mash, onion gravy and mushy peas; a trio of choices for vegetarians may embrace mixed bean chilli in a garlic bread bowl, sprinkled with cheese and served with guacamole and sour cream. AA Rosette-standard carte options in the restaurant include lobster cooked direct from the tank; and poached monkfish wrapped in smoked salmon with pan-fried king prawns and a cream saffron sauce. Sweets offer comfort in abundance, with custard, cream or ice cream accompanying the likes of apple and sultana crumble and sticky toffee pudding. Accommodation is comfortable and thoughtfully furnished.

*The Mug House Inn & Angry Chef Restaurant*

**Open** all wk noon-11 **Bar Meals** L served Mon-Sat 12-2.30, Sun 12-5 Av main course £6.95 **Restaurant** L served Mon-Sat 12-2.30, Sun 12-5 D served Mon-Sat 6.30-9 booking required Fixed menu price fr £12.95 Av 3 course à la carte fr £25 ⊕ PUNCH TAVERNS ◀ Timothy Taylor Landlord, Wye Valley, Hereford Pale Ale, 2 guest ales Ö Westons Traditional Scrumpy. ♈ 9
**Facilities** Dogs allowed Garden **Rooms** 7

---

## Woodcolliers Arms ★★★ INN ♈

**76 Welch Gate DY12 2AU** ☎ 01299 400589
**e-mail:** roger@woodcolliers.co.uk
**dir:** *3m from Kidderminster. 2 mins walk from No 2 bus stop*

This family-run 18th-century inn stands close to the centre of Bewdley and just across the river from the Severn Valley steam railway. With a wide range of real ales on offer, ask the barman for a description of the week's ales and beers. Russian trained chef Boris Rumba serves a unique blend of pub favourites and authentic Russian dishes. The regularly changing menu might offer atbivnaya (pork loin steak cooked in batter and topped with sautéed shallots and mushrooms) and losos (roast salmon with white wine sauce), alongside traditional British pies or steak and chips. There are five generously-sized guest rooms.

**Open** all wk 5-12.30 (Sat 12.30pm-12.30am, Sun 12.30-11) **Bar Meals** L served Sat-Sun 12.30-3 D served all wk 6-9.30 booking required Av main course £10 **Restaurant** L served Sat-Sun 12.30-3 booking required D served all wk 6-9.30 booking required Av 3 course à la carte fr £15 ⊕ OLIVERS INNS LTD ◀ Ludlow Gold, Three Tuns 1642, Morland Original Ö Thatchers Gold, Thatchers Heritage. ♈ 24 **Facilities** Children's menu Children's portions Dogs allowed Garden Parking **Rooms** 5

---

| BRANSFORD | Map 10 SO75 |

## The Bear & Ragged Staff ♈

**Station road WR6 5JH**
☎ 01886 833399 📄 01886 833106
**e-mail:** mail@bear.uk.com
**dir:** *3m from Worcester or Malvern, clearly signed from A4103 or A449*

Set in glorious Worcestershire countryside, this lovely old pub was built in 1861 as an estate rent office. Today its reputation is founded on good food and beers like Hobsons twisted spire. A meal might take in sweet cured salmon with courgette carpaccio and caraway-scented olive oil, followed by breast of Gressingham duckling with port and cranberry sauce, with bread and butter pudding for dessert. Malvern and Worcester are just a few minutes' drive away.

**Open** all wk 11.30-2 6-11 Closed: 25 Dec eve, 1 Jan eve, Sun eve **Bar Meals** L served all wk 12 -2 D served Mon-Fri 6.30-9 Av main course £11 **Restaurant** L served all wk 12-2 D served Mon-Sat 6.30-9.30 Av 3 course à la carte fr £26 ⊕ FREE HOUSE ◀ Hobsons Twisted Spire, Fuller's London Pride. ♈ 10 **Facilities** Children's portions Dogs allowed Garden Parking

---

| BRETFORTON | Map 10 SP04 |

### PICK OF THE PUBS

## The Fleece Inn ♈

**The Cross WR11 7JE** ☎ 01386 831173
**e-mail:** nigel@thefleeceinn.co.uk
**dir:** *From Evesham follow signs for B4035 towards Chipping Campden. Through Badsey into Bretforton. Right at village hall, past church, pub in open parking area*

A quintessential English pub, owned by the National Trust – its first licensed property – and run with a love of tradition. The beautiful timbered building was originally a longhouse whose last private owner, Lola Taplin, died in front of the fire in the snug in 1977; she was a direct descendant of the man who built it. Having been part of Cotswold history for six centuries, the pub was nearly lost in a tragic fire in 2004; a massive renovation followed, when its features and integrity were restored. Real ale devotees will admire one of England's oldest pewter collections as they order a pint of Dog in the Fog, and cider lovers too over their Prior's Tipple. Families can enjoy the summer sunshine in the apple orchard while children use the play area. There are regular music evenings too. Typical dishes in

Save on Hotels. Book at theAA.com/hotel

WORCESTERSHIRE 509 ENGLAND

winter include creamy mushroom, herb and leek gratin; and pork belly slow-roasted in plum jerkum topped with roast pear and smoked apple wood cheese.

**Open** all wk 11-3 6-11 (11-11 in summer) **Bar Meals** L served Mon-Sat 12-2.30, Sun 12-4 D served Mon-Sat 6.30-9, Sun 6.30-8.30 ⊕ FREE HOUSE ◀ Buckle Street no 1 Bitter, Pig's Ear, Dog in the Fog, Pandora's Box ♖ Thatchers, Priors Tipple. ♛ 12 **Facilities** Children's menu Children's portions Play area Garden

---

### CLENT                    Map 10 SO97

## PICK OF THE PUBS

## The Bell & Cross ♛

Holy Cross DY9 9QL
☎ 01562 730319 🖹 01562 731733
dir: *Telephone for directions*

Roger Narbett is chef to the England football team, so you can be sure that the food at his award-winning 19th-century pub will be in the premier league. Recently refurbished, the building dates from the early 19th century. Head for the bar for traditional hand-pulled beers and an inviting log fire in winter, or the covered and heated patio for comfortable alfresco dining on cooler nights. Expect modern British food in a traditional setting; light bar lunches include a range of sarnies, pasta and risotto, as well as classic mains like beer battered fish and chips with tartare sauce; and Scotch steak pie with smashed neeps, mash and gravy. Evening dinner might kick off with fish cakes and white wine, prawn and chive sauce, followed by pot roasted belly pork with Savoy cabbage, leeks, crackling, griddled apple and Calvados. New York lemon curd cheesecake with honeycomb crisp is a typical dessert.

**Open** all wk noon-3 6-11 Closed: 25 Dec, 26 Dec eve, 31 Dec & 1 Jan eve **Bar Meals** L served all wk 12-2 D served Mon-Sat 6.30-9.15 booking required Av main course £10.95 **Restaurant** L served Mon-Sat 12-2, Sun 12-7 booking required D served Mon-Sat 6.30-9.15, Sun 12-7 booking required Fixed menu price fr £13.95 Av 3 course à la carte fr £27 ⊕ ENTERPRISE INNS ◀ Pedigree, Mild, Bitter, Timothy Taylor Landlord, Guest ales. ♛ 15 **Facilities** Children's menu Children's portions Dogs allowed Garden Parking

---

### CLOWS TOP                 Map 10 SO77

## PICK OF THE PUBS

## The Colliers Arms ♛

Tenbury Rd DY14 9HA ☎ 01299 832242
e-mail: thecolliersarms@aol.com
dir: *On A456.11 Pub 4m from Bewdley & 7m from Kidderminster*

Just a stones throw from the glades of Wyre Forest, this convivial country inn oozes character, with a great old tap room, comfy lounge and restaurant fusing seamlessly. From the outside patio and beer garden

you can enjoy the views of the largest Norman church in England at neighbouring Rock; closer to hand is the pub's own produce plot from which the chefs source most vegetables, fruits and herbs used in their oft-changing menu of modern British and dishes drawn from many other cuisines. Consider a starter of chicken, black pudding and tarragon terrine with grape jelly before launching into navarin of venison, rosemary and roots or baked salmon with Cheddar and spring onion mash dressed with chive butter sauce. A growing proportion of the food is sourced from local farms and estates; being at the heart of the slow-food, organic movement, this shines through in the excellent produce. In a similar vein, local breweries enjoy strong support at The Colliers, with beers from Hobsons a regular favourite.

**Open** noon-3 6-11 (Sat 11-11 Sun noon-4) Closed: Sun eve **Bar Meals** L served Mon-Fri 12-2, Sat 12-2.30, Sun 12-3 booking required D served Mon-Fri 6.30-9, Sat 6.30-9.30 booking required Av main course £9.95 **Restaurant** L served Mon-Fri 12-2, Sat 12-2.30, Sun 12-3 booking required D served Mon-Fri 6.30-9, Sat 6.30-9.30 booking required Fixed menu price fr £12.95 Av 3 course à la carte fr £14.50 ⊕ FREE HOUSE ◀ Hobsons Best, Town Crier, Guinness, Malvern Hills Black Pear, Wye Valley Butty Bach, guest ale ♖ Stowford Press. ♛ 14 **Facilities** Children's portions Dogs allowed Garden Parking

---

### DROITWICH                 Map 10 SO86

## PICK OF THE PUBS

## The Chequers ♛

Cutnall Green WR9 0PJ
☎ 01299 851292 🖹 01299 851744
dir: *Telephone for directions*

A display of football memorabilia on the bar wall reveals that this is the home of Roger Narbett, chef to the England football team. He runs The Chequers with his wife Joanne, retaining its charming and traditional village pub atmosphere with open fire, church panel bar and richly coloured furnishings after a recent makeover. A goodly range of real ales includes Hook Norton and Ruddles. Next to the bar is the modern country style Garden Room with warmly painted walls, a plush sofa and hanging tankards. Popular Sunday lunches here may start with cream of broccoli soup, continue with pot-roasted leg of Cornish lamb, and finish with crispy apple, mincemeat and cinnamon samosas with golden syrup. Children are well catered for, with their own menu or portions from the main menu. You'll also find light bites such as grilled skewered tiger prawns, mains like lemon thyme chicken breast with pumpkin, saffron and pea risotto, with pub classics such as slow-braised faggots with mushy peas and cheesy mash.

**Open** all wk 12-3 6-11 (Sun 12-4 6-10.30) Closed: 25 Dec, 1 Jan eve **Bar Meals** L served Mon-Sat 12-2, Sun 12-2.30 D served Mon-Sun 6.30-9.15 Av main course £11.50 **Restaurant** L served Mon-Sat 12-2, Sun 12-2.30 booking required D served Mon-Sun 6.30-9.15 booking required Av 3 course à la carte fr £17.50 ⊕ ENTERPRISE INNS ◀ Timothy Taylor, Enville Ale, Banks Bitter, Banks Mild, Hook Norton, Ruddles. ♛ 15 **Facilities** Children's menu Children's portions Family room Dogs allowed Garden Parking

---

## The Honey Bee ♛

Doverdale Ln, Doverdale WR9 0QB ☎ 01299 851620
e-mail: honey@king-henrys-taverns.co.uk
dir: *Website for directions*

'It's buzzin' at The Honey Bee but you won't get stung!' So say King Henry's Taverns, which owns this beekeeping-themed pub, with working beehives and a children's area containing an enormous beehive plaything. All the group's establishments offer a standard menu that covers most pub grub eventualities - steak and ale pie; whole roast chicken; pan-fried fillets of plaice; rump, fillet and rib steaks; lamb rogan josh; vegetarian balti; and broccoli and cream cheese bake.

**Open** all day all wk noon-10 **Bar Meals** food served all day **Restaurant** food served all day ⊕ KING HENRY TAVERNS ◀ Guinness, Greene King IPA, Marstons Pedigree. ♛ 15 **Facilities** Children's menu Children's portions Play area Family room Garden Parking

---

## The Old Cock Inn ♛

Friar St WR9 8EQ ☎ 01905 774233
dir: *M5 junct 5, A449 in Droitwich town centre opposite theatre*

Three stained-glass windows, rescued from a church destroyed during the Civil War, are a feature of this charming pub, first licensed during the reign of Queen Anne. The stone carving above the front entrance is believed to portray Judge Jeffreys, who presided over the local magistrates' court. A varied menu, including snacks and more substantial dishes - beer battered fish and chips, vegetarian risotto, and local sausages and mash - is supplemented by the daily specials.

**Open** 12-3 6-11 Closed: Sun eve **Bar Meals** L served all wk 12-2.30 D served all wk 6-9.30 Av main course £8 **Restaurant** L served all wk 12-2.30 D served all wk 6-9.30 ◀ Jennings Ales, 3 guest ales. ♛ 9 **Facilities** Children's menu Dogs allowed Garden

## FLADBURY · Map 10 SO94

### Chequers Inn ♥

**Chequers Ln WR10 2PZ** ☎ **01386 860276**
**e-mail:** chequersinn@btinternet.com
**dir:** Off A44 between Evesham & Pershore

The Chequers is a 14th-century inn with plenty of beams and an open fire, tucked away in a pretty village with views of the glorious Bredon Hills. Local produce from the Vale of Evesham provides the basis for home-cooked dishes offered from the monthly-changing menu, plus a choice of daily specials. There is also a traditional Sunday carvery. The pretty walled garden enjoys outstanding views, a great setting for drinking or dining, and the nearby River Avon is ideal for walking.

**Open** all wk 11.30-2.30 6-11 (Sun 11.30-3.30)
**Bar Meals** L served Mon-Sat 12-2 D served Mon-Sat 6-9 Av main course £6.95 **Restaurant** L served all wk 12-2 D served Mon-Sat 6-9 ⊕ ENTERPRISE INNS ◀ Purity, Bombardier Real Ales. ♥ 10 **Facilities** Children's menu Children's portions Garden Parking

## FLYFORD FLAVELL · Map 10 SO95

### PICK OF THE PUBS

### The Boot Inn ★★★★ INN ♥

**See Pick of the Pubs on opposite page**

## KEMPSEY · Map 10 SO84

### PICK OF THE PUBS

### Walter de Cantelupe Inn ★★★ INN

**See Pick of the Pubs on page 512**

## KINGTON · Map 10 SO95

### PICK OF THE PUBS

### The Red Hart

**Stratford Rd WR7 4DD** ☎ **01386 792559**
**e-mail:** redhartpub@yahoo.co.uk
**dir:** M5 junct 6, A4538. Then A422 towards Stratford-upon-Avon, approx 4m. From Redditch A441, right onto A422, approx 3m

This beautiful, easy-going country pub and restaurant was created from a derelict shell by a team of local craftsmen. The interior has been stripped to reveal its original looks, while some stunning contemporary touches have been added. The main bar is furnished in wine bar style, while the secondary bar area boasts deep leather sofas surrounding a log burner. The restaurant is also smart and full of atmosphere. You could start with duck and pork terrine with watercress and apple salad, and move on to lime crusted sea bass and Thai scented crab risotto; or crispy pork belly with leek and bacon mash, cider and vegetable jus. Lunch brings home-made soup, lasagne, baguettes and perhaps whole tail scampi and chips.

---

**Open** all wk Mon-Thu 12-3 (all day Fri-Sun)
**Bar Meals** L served Mon-Fri 12-2.30, Sat-Sun all day **Restaurant** L served Mon-Fri 12-2.30, Sat-Sun all day D served Mon-Sat 6-10.30, Sun 6-8 ⊕ MARSTONS ◀ Banks, Marstons, Cocker Hoop, Hobgoblin.
**Facilities** Children's menu Children's portions Dogs allowed Garden Parking

## KNIGHTWICK · Map 10 SO75

### PICK OF THE PUBS

### The Talbot ♥

**WR6 5PH** ☎ **01886 821235** 🖷 **01886 821060**
**e-mail:** admin@the-talbot.co.uk
**dir:** A44 (Leominster road) through Worcester, 8m W right onto B4197 at River Teme bridge

Annie Clift and her team have been running this late 14th-century coaching inn for over 25 years. Their unique style is firmly rooted in the traditions and produce of the Teme Valley; nearly everything is made in-house, including bread, preserves, black pudding, raised pies and so on. The inn has a large organic kitchen garden, which produces a wide range of salads, herbs and, of course, vegetables. The Talbot is also home to the Teme Valley Brewery, which uses locally-grown hops in a range of curiously named cask conditioned ales called This, That, T'Other and Wot. The bar menu offers ploughman's, filled rolls and hot dishes, whilst in the restaurant starters like cream of nettle soup with croutons might herald oxtail stew with creamy horseradish mash, or stuffed monkfish with bacon and warm spinach salad. Leave space for apricot bread and butter pudding. The pub hosts a produce market on the second Sunday of the month.

**Open** all day all wk 7.30am-11.30pm Closed: 25 Dec eve **Bar Meals** Av main course £11 food served all day **Restaurant** D served all wk 6.30-9 booking required Fixed menu price fr £32 Av 3 course à la carte fr £32 ⊕ FREE HOUSE ◀ Teme Valley This, That , T'Other & Wot, Hobsons Best Bitter Choice Ò Kingston Press, Kingston Rosy, Robinson's. ♥ 12 **Facilities** Children's portions Dogs allowed Garden Parking

---

## LOWER BROADHEATH · Map 10 SO85

### The Dewdrop Inn ★★★★ INN NEW

**Bell Ln WR2 6RR** ☎ **01905 640012** 🖷 **01905 640265**
**e-mail:** enquiries@thedewdrop-inn.co.uk
**dir:** From Worcester take A443 towards Kidderminster, left onto B4202 towards Martley. Left into Bell Ln on entering Lower Broadheath. Pub 400yds on left

Sir Edward Elgar hailed from Lower Broadheath; his birthplace museum is an easy stroll from this painstakingly refurbished country inn which reopened in 2009 under chef-patron Tim Hoare. Bar and restaurant meals take full advantage of the area's renowned meats – including a popular weekend carvery – and children are not forgotten, with child menus available and an adventure play area in the garden. B&B guests can enjoy breakfast in the lee of the pretty Malvern and Abberley Hills. All this and beer from the local St George's micro-brewery too!

**Open** all day all wk **Bar Meals** L served all wk 12-2.30 D served all wk 6-9.30 Av main course £8 **Restaurant** L served all wk 12-2.30 booking required D served all wk 6.30-9.30 booking required Fixed menu price fr £8.50 Av 3 course à la carte fr £25 ⊕ FREE HOUSE ◀ Fuller's London Pride, St George's, Guinness. **Facilities** Children's menu Children's portions Play area Garden Parking Rooms 7

## MALVERN · Map 10 SO74

### The Anchor Inn ♥

**Drake St, Welland WR13 6LN** ☎ **01684 592317**
**e-mail:** theanchor13@hotmail.com
**dir:** M50 junct 1, A38 follow signs for Upton upon Severn. Left onto A4104, through Upton upon Severn, 2.5m. Pub on right

The attractive 17th-century Anchor Inn has spectacular views of the Malvern Hills. There's a garden for warmer weather and a welcoming winter fire in the dining room. Fresh, quality food is cooked to order and dishes include pork loin stuffed with apple in Stilton sauce and steak and kidney pie. Themed menus and quiz nights feature regularly and the bar serves up to 20 wines by the glass. The inn has won awards from Britain in Bloom.

**Open** 12-3 6.45-11 Closed: Sun eve **Bar Meals** L served all wk 12-2 D served Mon-Sat 7-9 Av main course £9.99 **Restaurant** L served all wk 12-2 D served Mon-Sat 7-9 ⊕ FREE HOUSE ◀ Black Sheep, Woods, Hook Norton, Greene King, Malvern Hills Ò Kingston Press. ♥ 20 **Facilities** Children's portions Family room Garden Parking

### The Red Lion

**4 St Ann's Rd WR14 4RG** ☎ **01684 564787**
**e-mail:** johnholmes25@btintenet.com
**dir:** In town centre

An authentic Thai restaurant complete with chefs and waitresses from the Land of Smiles has been added to this thriving pub. The existing pub menu continues to be available, offering a wide choice of snacks, starters and main courses, all freshly cooked to order. Seafood is a particular speciality: try pan-fried king prawns. One of the main walking routes in the Malvern Hills runs right by, so expect plenty of ramblers.

**Open** all wk ◀ Marstons Bitter, 4 guest ales.
**Facilities** Garden

# PICK OF THE PUBS

## The Boot Inn ★★★★ INN 🍷

**FLYFORD FLAVELL**  Map 10 SO95

**Radford Rd WR7 4BS**
☎ 01386 462658  📠 01386 462547
**e-mail:** enquiries@thebootinn.com
**dir:** *From Worcester take A422 towards Stratford. Turn right to village*

A family-run, award-winning, traditional coaching inn, parts of which can be traced back to the 13th century. For evidence just look at the heavy beams and slanting doorways, and keep an eye out for the friendly ghost. It provides an ideal base for anyone wishing to explore Stratford-upon-Avon, The Cotswolds or the Malvern Hills. The large bar area is comfortable, the pool table and TV hived off to a separate room.

Traditional ales and an extensive wine list complement the varied and imaginative menus which change every six weeks. You can eat from the lunchtime sandwich and bar snack menu, from the extensive specials board, for which The Boot is renowned, or from the full carte menu. No matter which you choose, or indeed where — cosy public areas, attractive restaurant, light and airy conservatory or patio — only the best and freshest, mostly Worcestershire-sourced, produce is used.

A sample menu may include starters like avocado with melted Stilton on dressed leaves, or sticky chicken wings with sweet chilli; followed by a main course of smoked mackerel fillets with orange marmalade crust, or home-made cottage pie with cheesy mash and fresh vegetables. From the griddle expect the likes of sirloin, fillet, rib-eye or gammon steak; or perhaps a mixed grill.

Outside, front and back, are gardens and a shaded patio area especially suited to summer dining. The comfortable bedrooms in the converted coach house are furnished in antique pine and equipped with practical extras. All have modern bathrooms.

**Open** all wk noon-mdnt (25 Dec noon-2) **Bar Meals** L served all wk 12-2 D served all wk 6.30-10 Av main course £7.95 **Restaurant** L served all wk 12-2 D served all wk 6.30-10 Fixed menu price fr £9.50 Av 3 course à la carte fr £22 ⊕ PUNCH TAVERNS ◀ Old Speckled Hen, London Pride, John Smith's Tribute Ō Stowford Press. 🍷 8 **Facilities** Children's menu Dogs allowed (bar only) Garden Parking **Rooms** 5

# PICK OF THE PUBS

# Walter de Cantelupe Inn ★★★INN

**KEMPSEY** Map 10 SO84

**Main Rd WR5 3NA** ☎ **01905 820572**
**dir:** *4m S of Worcester city centre on A38.*
*Pub in village centre*

The inn commemorates a 13th-century Bishop of Worcester, who was strongly against his parishioners' habit of brewing and selling ales as a way to raise church funds, so its naming three centuries later was probably a bit of 16th-century irony on the part of the locals.

With its whitewashed walls bedecked with flowers, this privately owned and run free house dates in part from the 17th century. One of the bedrooms in the oldest part of the inn is said to be haunted. Outside, a walled and paved garden has been fragrantly planted with clematis, roses and honeysuckle, and its south-facing position can be a real sun-trap.

The menu is written up each day on a blackboard, with choices to appeal to both traditionalists and those seeking something more contemporary. You could begin with leek and potato soup with crusty bread; chicken liver pâté with Cantelupe chutney and toast, or Scottish smoked salmon with capers and lemon. Follow with baked sea bass with a lemon butter sauce; pan fried pork medallions with Tewksbury mustard cream sauce; wild mushroom, spinach and ricotta filo parcel; or beef and local ale pie with shortcrust pastry. Then you could finish with hot banana bread and butter pudding with chocolate sauce; or a plate of British cheeses (in good years grapes from the pub's own vines appear alongside).

Three or four cask ales are usually on offer, including Cannon Royal Brewery's Kings Shilling from nearby Uphampton. The pub's en suite accommodation is modelled on 'a friend's home' rather than a 'stereotypical motel'.

**Open** 12-2.30 6-11 (Sun 12-3 6-10.30)
Closed: 25-26 Dec, 1 Jan, Mon (ex BH)
**Bar Meals** L served Tue-Sat 12-2, Sun 12-3 D served Tue-Sat 6.30-9, Sun 6.30-8 Av main course £8
**Restaurant** L served Tue-Sat 12-2, Sun 12-3 D served Tue-Sat 6.30-9, Sun 6.30-8 ⊕ FREE HOUSE ◼ Timothy Taylor Landlord, Cannon Royal Kings Shilling, Mayfields Copper Fox ♻ Stowford Press.
**Facilities** Dogs allowed Garden Parking
**Rooms** 3

Save on Hotels. Book at **theAA.com/hotel**

**WORCESTERSHIRE** 513 **ENGLAND**

## MARTLEY
Map 10 SO76

## Admiral Rodney Inn ★★★★ INN

Berrow Green WR6 6PL ☎ 01886 821375
e-mail: rodney@admiral.fslife.co.uk
web: www.admiral-rodney.co.uk
dir: M5 junct 7, A44 signed Leominster. Approx 7m at
Knightwick right onto B4197. Inn 2m on left at Berrow
Green

This early 17th-century farmhouse/alehouse stands in
the heart of the countryside on the Worcester Way
footpath. The stylishly traditional interior includes a
split-level restaurant housed in an old barn. Traditional
pub fare includes gammon steak; ham with eggs and
chips; and a vegetarian choice that might include stuffed
butternut squash; all washed down with a pint of Wye
Valley Bitter. En suite bedrooms and a skittle alley are
also available.

Open all wk noon-3 5-11 (Mon 5-11 Sat noon-11 Sun
noon-10.30) Bar Meals L served Tue-Sat 12.30-2.30, Sun
12-3.30 D served all wk 6.30-9 Av main course £11
Restaurant L served Tue-Sat 12.30-2.30, Sun 12-3.30 D
served all wk 6.30-9 Fixed menu price fr £7.95 ⊕ FREE
HOUSE ◀ Wye Valley Bitter, HPA, local guest ales (Black
Pear, Malvern Hills Brewery, Kinver, Hobsons) ♂ Westons
Stowford Press, Robinsons Cask Cider.
Facilities Children's menu Dogs allowed Garden Parking
Rooms 3

## The Crown Inn

Berrow Green Rd WR6 6PA ☎ 01886 888840
e-mail: thecrowninnmartley@yahoo.co.uk
dir: 7m W of Worcester on B4204

A Victorian village pub with a large extension formed
from redundant outbuildings, the Crown was once the
scene of an unlikely gig by Eric Clapton. Set on the
Worcester Way, it is popular with walkers and locals. In
one bar is an open fire, Sky TV, pool table and jukebox,
while the other has dining tables and French windows to
the garden. Locally sourced, freshly cooked food runs
from steak and ale pie to Goan fish curry. There is also a
pizza and take away menu.

Open all wk noon-11 (Fri-Sat noon-mdnt Sun noon-
10.30) Bar Meals L served Mon-Fri 12-2.30, Sat-Sun
12-9 D served Mon-Fri 6-9, Sat-Sun 12-9 Av main course
£10 Restaurant L served Mon-Fri 12-2, Sat-Sun 12-9 D
served Mon-Sat 6-9 Av 3 course à la carte fr £20.05
⊕ MARSTONS ◀ Banks Bitter, Banks Mild.
Facilities Children's menu Children's portions Play area
Dogs allowed Garden Parking

## OMBERSLEY
Map 10 SO86

### PICK OF THE PUBS

## Crown & Sandys Arms ♥

Main Rd WR9 0EW ☎ 01905 620252
e-mail: enquiries@crownandsandys.co.uk
dir: 3m from Droitwich, off A449, 6m off junct 6 &
junct 5 of M5

After being closed for nearly a year for complete
refurbishment, this classy establishment run by
Richard and Rachael Everton reopened its doors in May
2009. The decor is bang up-to-date, yet the original
beams and fireplaces seem to blend effortlessly with
the trendy furnishings. Expect the same focus on well
kept real ales and ciders, a smoothly managed food
operation and excellent service. Regular 'wine dinners'
and themed evenings continue, complementing the
modern menus which burst with the latest flavours.
The full carte is backed by a weekly specials list, and
customers can choose between three dining areas: the
Orangery, the Bistro and the Bar. Starters may include
tian of smoked salmon with herb crème fraîche. Main
dishes offer favourites like pie of the day with triple-
cooked chips, and bangers and mash with sweet onion
and Worcestershire sauce gravy. Dishes from the
specials board may include roasted local venison with
dauphinoise potatoes and braised red cabbage, or
whole grilled mackerel or rainbow trout.

Open all day all wk 11-11 (Sun 11-10.30) Bar Meals L
served all wk 12-2.30 D served all wk 6-9.30 booking
required Av main course £9.95 Restaurant L served all
wk 12-2.30 booking required D served all wk 6-9.30
booking required Av 3 course à la carte fr £20 ⊕ FREE
HOUSE ◀ Wyre Valley H.P.A, Shropshire Lad, Hobsons
Twisted Spire ♂ Old English. ♥ 15 Facilities Children's
menu Children's portions Garden Parking

## PERSHORE
Map 10 SO94

## The Defford Arms ⋃ NEW

Upton Rd, Defford WR8 9BD ☎ 01386 750378
dir: From Pershore take A4104 towards Upton upon
Severn. Pub on left in village

Neil and Sue Overton, together with their son Les, bought
The Defford in 2007 and rescued it from dereliction. They
have worked hard to achieve the success of today's
drinking and eating pub, stocking Wye Valley real ales,
serving reasonably priced home-cooked food, and
welcoming all comers. As well as the usual lunchtime
quick bites (sandwiches, paninis, jackets), the properly,
hungry can tuck into pan-fried duck, faggots, or braised
lamb shank, followed by home-made apricot bread and
butter pudding with custard.

Open all wk noon-2 5-11 (Sat noon-mdnt Sun noon-9
Mon 5-9) Bar Meals L served Tue-Sun D served all wk
Restaurant L served Tue-Sun D served all wk ⊕ FREE
HOUSE ◀ Wye Valley Brewery ♂ Stowford Press.
Facilities Children's menu Children's portions Dogs
allowed Garden Parking Rooms 2

## POWICK
Map 10 SO85

## The Halfway House Inn

Bastonford WR2 4SL
☎ 01905 831098 📄 01905 831704
dir: From A15 junct 7 take A4440 then A449

This attractive Georgian property is just a few minutes'
drive from the picturesque spa town of Malvern. Situated
on the A449 between Worcester and Malvern, it is an
ideal stopping-off point for a great pint and traditional
home-cooked food served in the bar, restaurant or the
garden. Using local produce where possible and
specialising in seafood and steaks, choices range from
Herefordshire ribeye steak or surf and turf to grilled fillet
of sea bass on crushed potatoes with cherry tomatoes
and balsamic dressing.

Open noon-3 6-11 Closed: Mon L (ex BHs) Bar Meals L
served Tue-Sun 12-2 D served Tue-Sun 6-9 Av main
course £6 Restaurant L served Tue-Sun 12-2 D served
Tue-Sun 6-9 Fixed menu price fr £5 Av 3 course à la carte
fr £25 ⊕ FREE HOUSE ◀ Abbot Ale, St Georges Bitter,
Fuller's London Pride, Timothy Taylor ♂ Stowford Press.
Facilities Children's menu Children's portions Play area
Garden Parking

## STONEHALL
Map 10 SO84

## The Inn at Stonehall ◉

Stonehall Common WR5 3QG ☎ 01905 820462
e-mail: info@theinnatstonehall.com
dir: 2m from M5 junct 7. Stonehall Common 1.5m from St
Peters Garden Centre Norton

Known for many years as The Fruiterer's Arms, this pub
underwent a considerable transformation in 2007 when
Joanna Coull took over. It is now a modern gastro-pub
with a comfortable bar area, smart restaurant and
garden with breathtaking views. In the open kitchen,
Dwight Clayton produces well sourced modern British
cooking with a French influence, such as home-made
pork faggots with thyme sauce and dauphinoise
potatoes, and guinea fowl breast with smoked bacon and
pea risotto.

Open noon-5 6-11 (Sun 12-3) Closed: 26-30 Dec, 1-8
Jan, Sun eve & all day Mon Bar Meals L served Tue-Sat
12-2.30, Sun 12-3 Restaurant L served Tue-Sat 12-2.30,
Sun 12-3 D served Tue-Sat 6.30-9.30 Av 3 course à la
carte fr £22 ⊕ FREE HOUSE ◀ Malvern Hills, Black Pear
♂ Stowford Press. Facilities Children's menu Children's
portions Play area Dogs allowed Garden Parking

## TENBURY WELLS — Map 10 SO56

### PICK OF THE PUBS

### The Peacock Inn

**WR15 8LL** ☎ **01584 810506**
e-mail: info@the-peacock-at-boraston.co.uk
**dir:** *On A456 (Kidderminster to Tenbury Wells)*

A 14th-century coaching inn with a sympathetic extension overlooking the River Teme. A pleasant patio eating area means you can relax outside and enjoy the views over the valley in summer. The inviting bars and oak-panelled restaurant are enhanced by oak beams, dried hops and open log fires, while upstairs the ghost of Mrs Brown, a former landlady, does her best to make her presence felt. Produce from local markets and specialist suppliers is used for the menus, which cover an eclectic mix of reasonably priced dishes. The bar menu ranges from a three-egg omelette with choice of fillings and served with chips; to chilli con carne; or rendang pedis - a home-made Indonesian beef curry made to a traditional family recipe. Other main courses tend towards the more usual: spicy meatballs; wholetail scampi; creamy pasta bake; and barbecued chicken fillet are among the choices.

**Open** noon-3 6-11 Closed: Sun eve ⬛ Hobsons Best Bitter, Spitfire, guest ale ♻ Stowford Press, Westons Organic. **Facilities** Dogs allowed Garden Parking

## UPTON SNODSBURY — Map 10 SO95

### Bants ★★★★ INN ♟

**Worcester Rd WR7 4NN**
☎ **01905 381282** 🖹 **01905 381173**
e-mail: info@bants.co.uk
**dir:** *Exit M5 junct 6, follow Evesham signs. At 2nd rdbt left onto A422 towards Stratford. Bants 2m on left*

A 16th-century free house serving traditional ales, with real fires in winter warming an eclectic mix of ancient beams and modern furnishings, Bants takes its name from its owners, Sue and Steve Bant, who have been running the pub for nearly 25 years. Traditional dishes with a modern twist and are served in three lounge bars and the dedicated conservatory restaurant. The food has a high comfort factor: you may find slow cooked steak with Guinness or seafood and shellfish lasagne on the menu. There are eight en suite rooms available.

**Open** all wk **Bar Meals** Av main course £8 food served all day **Restaurant** Fixed menu price fr £15 Av 3 course à la carte fr £20 food served all day ⊕ FREE HOUSE ⬛ Guinness, London Pride, Cats Whiskas, Pettermans. ♟ 12 **Facilities** Children's menu Children's portions Dogs allowed Garden Parking **Rooms** 8

## YORKSHIRE, EAST RIDING OF

## BARMBY ON THE MARSH — Map 17 SE62

### The King's Head NEW

**High St DN14 7HT** ☎ **01757 630705** 🖹 **01757 630957**
e-mail: rainderpubcoltd@tiscali.co.uk
**dir:** *M62 junct 37 follow A614/Bridlington/York/Howden signs. Left at A63. At rdbt 1st exit onto A614/Booth Ferry Rd towards Goole. At rdbt 4th exit on B1228/Booth Ferry Rd. Left, through Asselby to Barmby on the Marsh*

Run by Tim and Darren Smith and their sister Katy, this traditional village free house's old-world charm remains intact following recent refurbishment. Using the best of local produce in the kitchen, book a table for a well presented three-course meal, such as pigeon breast marinated in red wine with rhubarb compote and Pontefract cake dressing; braised chicken, ham, leeks, cream and white wine with puff pastry lid; and home-made ice cream (including Horlicks). There is a home-made take-away deli menu available. Look out for themed nights.

**Open** Mon-Tue 5-11, Wed-Thu noon-2 5-11, Fri noon-2 5-mdnt, Sat noon-mdnt, Sun noon-11 Closed: Mon L, Tue L **Bar Meals** L served Wed-Fri 12-2, Sat-Sun all day D served Mon-Thu 5-8.30, Fri 5-9, Sat-Sun all day Av main course £4.50 **Restaurant** L served Wed-Fri 12-2, Sat-Sun all day booking required D served Mon-Thu 5-8.30, Fri 5-9, Sat-Sun all day booking required Av 3 course à la carte fr £11.50 ⊕ FREE HOUSE ⬛ Black Sheep Bitter, 3 Guest ales (changed weekly). **Facilities** Children's menu Children's portions Garden Parking

## BEVERLEY — Map 17 TA03

### White Horse Inn

**22 Hengate HU17 8BN** ☎ **01482 861973**
**dir:** *A1079 from York to Beverley*

Gas lighting, open fires, old cartoons and high-backed settles add to the charm of this classic 16th-century local. John Wesley preached in the back yard in the mid-18th century, and the pub's atmospheric little rooms arranged around the central bar are probably much as they were back then. Traditional bar food might include pasta dishes, fresh jumbo haddock, bangers and mash, and steak and ale pie. Toasted and plain sandwiches and daily specials also feature.

**Open** all day all wk 11am-11pm (Sun noon-10.30pm) ⬛ Samuel Smith Old Brewery Bitter, Sovereign Bitter. **Facilities** Play area Family room Garden Parking **Notes** ⊕

## DRIFFIELD — Map 17 TA05

### Best Western The Bell ★★★ HL ♟

**46 Market Place YO25 6AN**
☎ **01377 256661** 🖹 **01377 253228**
e-mail: bell@bestwestern.co.uk
**dir:** *Enter town from A164, right at lights. Car park 50yds on left behind black railings*

A delightful 18th-century coaching inn furnished with antiques, with an oak-panelled bar serving a good range of unusual cask beers (Falling Stones, Mars Magic, Tom Wood Shepherds Delight) and 300 whiskies. Food ranges through broiled salmon fillet cooked with red peppers, lemon, garlic and capers; roasted whole pork fillet coated with honey and Dijon mustard; and oven roasted breast of English duckling with spicy plum sauce. Fresh coffee is served in the mornings 9.30-11.30 with scones, jam and cream.

**Open** all day all wk Closed: 25 Dec, 1 Jan **Bar Meals** L served Mon-Sat 12-1.30 D served all wk 5-8.30 Av main course £8.50 **Restaurant** L served Sun 12-1.30 booking required D served Mon-Sat 6.30-8.30 booking required Av 3 course à la carte fr £18.50 ⊕ FREE HOUSE ⬛ Wold Top, Falling Stones, Mars Magic, Hambleton Stallion & Stud, Tom Wood Shepherds Delight. ♟ 10 **Facilities** Children's portions Parking **Rooms** 16

## FLAMBOROUGH — Map 17 TA27

### The Seabirds Inn ♟

**Tower St YO15 1PD** ☎ **01262 850242** 🖹 **01262 851874**
**dir:** *On B1255 E of Bridlington, 6m from train station*

Head westwards from famous Flamborough Head and you'll swiftly arrive at this 200-year-old village pub. Good eating is the emphasis here, with a daily changing specials board. Fresh fish dishes include grilled lemon sole and haddock fillet mornay; while meat options include steaks, gammon with egg or pineapple or both; and grilled butterfly chicken breast with garlic butter.

**Open** noon-3 6-11 Closed: Mon (winter) **Bar Meals** L served all wk 12-2 D served Sun-Fri 6-8.30, Sat 6-9.30 Av main course £6.95 **Restaurant** L served all wk 12-2 D served Sun-Fri 6-8.30, Sat 6-9.30 booking required Fixed menu price fr £10.95 Av 3 course à la carte fr £21 ⊕ FREE HOUSE ⬛ John Smith's, Interbrew, Boddingtons Bitter, Tetleys Creamflow. ♟ 9 **Facilities** Dogs allowed Garden Parking

## HOLME UPON SPALDING MOOR    Map 17 SE83

### Ye Olde Red Lion Hotel ♥

Old Rd YO43 4AD ☎ 01430 860220    📄 01430 861471

dir: Off A1079 (York to Hull road). At Market Weighton
take A614. Right at painted rdbt in village centre,
500yds, right then 1st left

A historic 17th-century coaching inn that once provided
hospitality for weary travellers who were helped across
the marshes by monks. It's still a great refuge, with a
friendly atmosphere, oak beams and a cosy fire. The
inspiring menu could include oven-baked duck breast
with star anise sauce, corn fed chicken coq-au-vin or
pan-seared sea bass with wilted greens and vièrge
sauce.

**Open** 11-3 5-11 (Mon 5-11) Closed: Mon until 5pm
◀ John Smith's, Black Sheep, Guinness. ♥ 9
**Facilities** Garden Parking

## HUGGATE    Map 19 SE85

### The Wolds Inn ★★★ INN

YO42 1YH ☎ 01377 288217

e-mail: huggate@woldsinn.freeserve.co.uk
dir: S off A166 between York & Driffield

Probably the highest inn on the Yorkshire Wolds, this
family-run hostelry is 16th century in origin, with tiled
roofs and white-painted chimneys, and a wood-panelled
interior with open fires and gleaming brassware. The
robust menu includes dishes such as steak pie, fillet of
plaice, chicken breast wrapped in bacon, grills, or a
selection of jackets, baguettes and sandwiches. For a
"mixed grill to remember", try the Wolds Topper.

**Open** noon-2 6-11 (Sun noon-10.30) (May-Sep Mon 6-11)
Closed: Mon (Oct-Apr ex BH) **Bar Meals** L served Tue-Sun
12-2 D served Tue-Sun 6-9 booking required Av main
course £8 **Restaurant** L served Tue-Sun 12-6 booking
required D served Tue-Sun 6-9 (May-Sep Mon 6-9)
booking required Av 3 course à la carte fr £20 ⊕ FREE
HOUSE ◀ Tetley Bitter, Timothy Taylor Landlord.
**Facilities** Children's menu Children's portions Garden
Parking **Rooms** 3

## KILHAM    Map 17 TA06

### The Old Star Inn

Church St YO25 4RG ☎ 01262 420619
e-mail: oldstarkilham@hotmail.com
dir: Between Driffield & Bridlington on A164. 6m from
Driffield. 9m from Bridlington

Easily accessible from Bridlington, Scarborough and the
Yorkshire Wolds this quaint pub is situated in the historic
village of Kilham. Here you'll find home-cooked food, a
good selection of real ales and a warm welcome. Food is
sourced from local suppliers, with particular attention to
reducing the travelling time of ingredients. Special diets
are catered for, and children have half price portions.
John Smith's is the resident beer, the three other pumps
operating a rotation of guest ales.

**Open** all wk 5-mdnt (Mon 6-mdnt, Fri noon-2 4-mdnt, Sat
noon-2.30 5.30-mdnt, Sun noon-10.30) Closed: Mon-Thu
L **Bar Meals** L served Fri-Sat 12-2, Sun 12-5 D served
Mon 6-8, Tue-Fri 5-8.30, Sat 5.30-8.30 Av main course
£8 **Restaurant** L served Sun 12-5 booking required
booking required D served Tue-Fri 5-8.30 Av 3 course à la carte fr £20 ⊕ FREE
HOUSE ◀ John Smith's Cask, Deuchars, Theakstons,
Black Sheep, Daleside, guest ales. **Facilities** Dogs
allowed Garden Parking

## LOW CATTON    Map 17 SE75

### The Gold Cup Inn ♥

YO41 1EA ☎ 01759 371354
dir: 1m S of A166 or 1m N of A1079, E of York

Solid tables and pews - reputedly made from a single oak
tree - feature in the restaurant of this 300-year-old,
family-run free house. There's a large beer garden, and
the adjoining paddock drops down to the River Derwent.
On the menu expect to find Stilton and apricot pâté with
oatcakes; mermaid's basket (seafood in filo); venison
steak, slowly braised in wine; half a crispy roast duckling
with cherry and brandy sauce; and spinach and cream
cheese cannelloni.

**Open** noon-2.30 6-11 (Sat-Sun noon-11) Closed: Mon L
**Bar Meals** L served Tue-Fri 12-2.30, Sat-Sun 12-6 D
served all wk 6-9 Av main course £9.50 **Restaurant** L
served Sun 12-8.30 booking required D served all wk 6-9
booking required Fixed menu price fr £12.95 Av 3 course
à la carte fr £18.20 ⊕ FREE HOUSE ◀ John Smith's,
Theakstons. ♥ 13 **Facilities** Children's menu Children's
portions Play area Dogs allowed Garden Parking

## LUND    Map 17 SE94

### The Wellington Inn ♥

19 The Green YO25 9TE
☎ 01377 217294    📄 01377 217192
e-mail: tellmemore@thewellingtoninn.co.uk
dir: On B1248 NE of Beverley

Nicely situated opposite the picture-postcard village
green, the Wellington Inn is popular with locals and
visitors alike, whether for a pint of real ale, a glass of
wine, or a plate of decent food. You can choose to eat
from the bar menu or from the carte. Expect baked fish,
prawn and fresh crab gratin; Godminster Cheddar and
cumin twice baked soufflé with beetroot chutney; calves'
liver, blue cheese and onion mash, and pancetta; and
wild mushroom risotto, pecorino, and white truffle oil.

**Open** 12-3 6.30-11 Closed: Mon L **Bar Meals** L served
Tue-Sun 12-2 D served Tue-Sat 6.30-9 Av main course
£12.95 **Restaurant** D served Tue-Sat 7-9 booking
required Av 3 course à la carte fr £28 ⊕ FREE HOUSE
◀ Timothy Taylor Landlord, Black Sheep Best, John
Smith's, Copper Dragon, regular guest ale. ♥ 11
**Facilities** Children's menu Children's portions Garden
Parking

## SOUTH CAVE    Map 17 SE93

### The Fox and Coney Inn ♥

52 Market Place HU15 2AT
☎ 01430 424336    📄 01430 421552
e-mail: foxandconey@mail.com
dir: 4m E of M62 on A63. 4m N of Brough mainline
railway

Right in the heart of South Cave, this family run pub
dates from 1739 and is probably the oldest building in
the village. The inn, which is handy for walkers on the
nearby Wolds Way, was known simply as The Fox until
William Goodlad added the Coney (rabbit) in 1788.
Sample starters such as smoked fishcakes or grilled field
mushroom with goat's cheese, before moving on to steak
and ale pie, pasta carbonara, Thai red curry or Toulouse
sausage. Vegetarians and other dietary requirements are
well catered for.

**Open** all wk 11.30-11 ◀ Timothy Taylor Landlord, John
Smith's, Theakston Cool Cask, Deuchars IPA, guest ales.
♥ 10 **Facilities** Family room Dogs allowed Garden Parking

## SOUTH DALTON    Map 17 SE94

### PICK OF THE PUBS

### The Pipe & Glass Inn ◉◉ ♥

*See Pick of the Pubs on page 516*

## SUTTON UPON DERWENT    Map 17 SE74

### St Vincent Arms ♥

Main St YO41 4BN ☎ 01904 608349
e-mail: enquiries@stvincentarms.co.uk
dir: From A64 follow signs for A1079. Turn right, follow
signs for Elvington on B1228. Through Elvington to
Sutton upon Derwent

The name comes from John Jervis, mentor to Admiral Lord
Nelson and created the first Earl of St Vincent in the 18th
century. This is a warm family-run pub with an old-
fashioned welcoming atmosphere, minus music or
gaming machines but plus great food and good selection
of beer. Food options include sandwiches, ciabatta,
salads, steaks and scampi at lunch, and in the evening
dishes such as chicken and ginger stir fry, smoked
haddock Florentine or fillet of beef stroganoff.

**Open** all wk 11.30-3 6-11 (Sun 12-3 6.30-10.30)
**Bar Meals** L served all wk 12-2 D served all wk 6.30-9.30
Av main course £11 **Restaurant** L served all wk 12-2 D
served all wk 6.30-9.30 ⊕ FREE HOUSE ◀ Timothy Taylor
Landlord, Fuller's ESB, Yorkshire Terrier, Wells
Bombardier, Fuller's London Pride, Old Mill Bitter, York
Brewery Terrier. ♥ 16 **Facilities** Garden Parking

# PICK OF THE PUBS

## The Pipe & Glass Inn

**SOUTH DALTON**  Map 17 SE94

**West End HU17 7PN** ☎ **01430 810246**
**e-mail:** email@pipeandglass.co.uk
**web:** www.pipeandglass.co.uk
**dir:** *Just off B1248 (Beverley to Malton road). 7m from Beverley*

James and Kate Mackenzie's part-15th, part 17th-century inn stands on the site of the original gatehouse to Dalton Hall, the family seat of Lord Hotham. The gatehouse was eventually replaced by the present building, part of which is 17th century, and it's where visitors to the big house would have stayed.

James and Kate have kept a country pub feel in the bar, where hand-pumps dispense Copper Dragon, Wold Top and Black Sheep real ales, and Westons Old Rosie cider. They've given the restaurant a more contemporary look; a large conservatory, which houses a magnificent 24-seater table, looks out over the garden, where there's also plenty of additional dining space.

James uses as much local and seasonal produce as possible for his regularly changing modern British menus, the nature of which can be conveyed by example starters of crispy fried wild rabbit rissoles with cockle and caper vinaigrette, sorrel and aged air-dried ham; and gratin of goat's cheese and marjoram with red chard, beetroot and walnut salad. Typical mains include fillet of English beef with watercress and shallot salad, Yorkshire Blue cheese fritter and hand-cut chips; venison and juniper suet pudding with wild mushrooms, braised butter Chantenay carrots, crispy smoked bacon and clapshot; and from the specials board, grilled fillet of North Sea mackerel with curried mussel broth and cumin parsnip crisps; Gloucester Old Spot pork chop with black pudding forcemeat, butternut squash purée and sage pesto.

For dessert, the temptation potential of sticky toffee pudding is raised even higher by the addition of wild prune and Armagnac ice cream, and walnut praline; slightly more prosaic perhaps, but just as delicious, is hot chocolate pudding with blood orange sorbet. The wines, including a selection of dessert wines, are sourced entirely from small producers.

**Open** noon-3 6.30-11 (Sun noon-10.30)
**Closed:** 2wks Jan, Mon (ex BH)
**Bar Meals** L served Tue-Sat 12-2, Sun 12-4 D served Tue-Sat 6.30-9.30
**Restaurant** L served Tue-Sat 12-2, Sun 12-4 booking required D served Tue-Sat 6.30-9.30 booking required ⊕ **FREE HOUSE** ◀ Wold Top, Copper Dragon, Black Sheep, Cropton, John Smiths ⵔ Old Rosie. ⵣ 15 **Facilities** Children's menu Garden Parking

Save on Hotels. Book at theAA.com/hotel

YORKSHIRE, NORTH 517 ENGLAND

# YORKSHIRE, NORTH

## AKEBAR
Map 19 SE19

### The Friar's Head ♥

Akebar Park DL8 5LY
☎ 01677 450201 & 450591  📠 01677 450046
e-mail: info@akebarpark.com
dir: From A1 at Leeming Bar onto A684, 7m towards Leyburn. Entrance at Akebar Park

A typical stone-built Dales pub at the entrance to a stunning, peaceful holiday park, The Friar's Head overlooks beautiful countryside and grounds, where bowls or croquet can be played on the lawn. The large south-facing conservatory dining room called The Cloister is a stunning feature, particularly by candlelight, with its stone flags, lush planting and fruiting vines. Hand-pulled local ales are served, and typical dishes include oak-smoked salmon with horseradish crème fraîche; and Yorkshire farmed venison steak, served pink, with onion marmalade, port wine sauce and game chips. Akebar Park has won the David Bellamy Gold Conservation Award.

**Open** all wk 10-3 6-11.30 (Fri-Sun 10am-11.30pm Jul-Sep) Closed: 25 Dec, 26 Dec eve & 1 Jan **Bar Meals** L served all wk 12-2.30 D served all wk 6-9.30 **Restaurant** L served all wk 12-2.30 booking required D served all wk 6-9.30 booking required ⊕ FREE HOUSE ◀ John Smith's & Theakston Best Bitter, Black Sheep Best, Timothy Taylor Landlord. ♥ 12 **Facilities** Children's portions Garden Parking

## APPLETON-LE-MOORS
Map 19 SE78

### The Moors Inn ♥

YO62 6TF ☎ 01751 417435
e-mail: enquiries@moorsinn.co.uk
dir: On A170 between Pickering & Kirbymoorside

Whether you're interested in walking or sightseeing by car, this inn, now under new ownership, is a good choice for its location and good home-cooked food. Set in a small moors village with lovely scenery in every direction, in summer you can sit in the large garden and enjoy the splendid views. Dishes include beef brisket, mash and red wine gravy, and twice baked sun blush tomato and Stilton soufflé, and in addition to hand-pumped Black Bull and Black Sheep, there is a selection of 50 malt whiskies and 11 wines by the glass.

**Open** all day all wk **Bar Meals** L served Mon-Sat 12.2.30 booking required D served Mon-Sat 5.30-9.30 booking required Av main course £11 **Restaurant** L served Mon-Sat 12-2.30, Sun 12-8 booking required D served Mon-Sat 5.30-9.30, Sun 12-8 booking required Av 3 course à la carte fr £22 ⊕ FREE HOUSE ◀ Black Sheep, Black Bull, Landlords ♂ Stowford Press. ♥ 11 **Facilities** Children's menu Children's portions Dogs allowed Garden Parking

## APPLETREEWICK
Map 19 SE06

### The Craven Arms

BD23 6DA ☎ 01756 720270
e-mail: thecravenarms@ukonline.co.uk
dir: From Skipton take A59 towards Harrogate, B6160 N. Village signed on right. Pub just outside village

Enjoy spectacular views of the River Wharfe and Simon's Seat from this 16th-century Dales pub, which was originally a farm and later used as a weaving shed and courthouse. The village stocks are still outside. The building retains its original beams, flagstone floors, gas lighting and magnificent fireplace. Ten cask beers are served all year round, and the menu changes frequently. A heather-thatched cruck barn to the rear serves as restaurant and function room.

**Open** all day all wk **Bar Meals** L served all wk 12-2.30 D served all wk 6.30-8.30 Av main course £10.95 **Restaurant** L served all wk 12-2.30 D served all wk 6.30-8.30 Fixed menu price fr £10.95 Av 3 course à la carte fr £25 ⊕ FREE HOUSE ◀ Hetton Cruck Barn Bitter, Hetton Pale Ale, Saltaire Raspberry Blonde, Moorhouses Blonde, Black Witch. **Facilities** Children's menu Children's portions Dogs allowed Garden Parking

## ASENBY
Map 19 SE37

### PICK OF THE PUBS

## Crab & Lobster ◎◎

Dishforth Rd YO7 3QL
☎ 01845 577286  📠 01845 577109
e-mail: reservations@crabandlobster.co.uk
web: www.crabandlobster.co.uk
dir: From A1(M) take A168 towards Thirsk, follow signs for Asenby

Amid seven acres of garden, lake and streams stands this unique 17th-century thatched pub and adjacent small hotel. It is an Aladdin's cave of antiques and artefacts from around the world. Equally famous for its innovative cuisine and special gourmet extravaganzas, the menus show influences from France and Italy, with occasional oriental spices too. Starters leave no doubt you are in seafood heaven: mussels mouclade, lightly curried cream and leeks; Colchester oysters can be served on ice with shallot vinegar, or with wasabi mayonnaise and chorizo. The theme continues into main courses with the likes of fillet of sea bream, braised baby gem, wild mushrooms, queenie scallops and pea velouté; and roast garlic lobster with scallops and king prawns. For those who prefer meat, the range

of locally-sourced ingredients will not disappoint: wood pigeon Wellington with celeriac purée; and roast pork tenderloin with confit of pork cheek, black pudding and apple stack.

**Open** all day all wk **Bar Meals** L served all wk 12-2.30 D served Sun- Mon 7-9, Sat 6.30-9.30 ⊕ FREE HOUSE ◀ John Smith's, Scots 1816, Golden Pippin, Guinness. **Facilities** Children's portions Garden Parking

## ASKRIGG
Map 18 SD99

### Kings Arms

Market Place DL8 3HQ
☎ 01969 650817  📠 01969 650597
dir: N off A684 between Hawes & Leyburn

At the heart of the Yorkshire Dales, Askrigg's pub was known as The Drovers in the TV series All Creatures Great and Small. Built in 1762 as racing stables and converted to a pub in 1860, today it boasts a good range of real ales and an extensive menu and wine list. Favourites are roasted rack of Dales lamb with a mustard and herb crust, beer-battered haddock fillet with chips, chicken breast with linguini, seared sea bass on fresh pasta with a shellfish nage, or grilled gammon steak with eggs or pineapple rings. Look our for the spectacular inglenook fireplace in the main bar.

**Open** all wk 10-3 6-mdnt (Sat-Sun 11am-mdnt) ◀ John Smith's, Black Sheep, Theakstons Best Bitter. **Facilities** Dogs allowed Garden

## AUSTWICK
Map 18 SD76

### The Game Cock Inn

The Green LA2 8BB ☎ 015242 51226
e-mail: richardlord495@hotmail.com
dir: Telephone for directions

Richard and Trish Lord offer a warm welcome to this award-winning pub, set in the limestone village of Austwick. There's a large garden and children's play area, with winter log fires in the cosy bar. Expect real ale, a range of malt whiskies, and an imaginative menu. Typical dishes include giant ham shank with mash and pickled red cabbage, whilst one of the regular French evenings might feature fresh Toulouse sausage on provençale couscous.

**Open** all wk ◀ Thwaites Best Bitter & Smooth, Warfsteiner. **Facilities** Play area Family room Garden Parking

# PICK OF THE PUBS

## The Black Bull Inn ♟

**BOROUGHBRIDGE**  Map 19 SE36

**6 St James Square YO51 9AR**
☎ **01423 322413**  📠 **01423 323915**
**web:** www.blackbullboroughbridge.co.uk
**dir:** *From A1(M) junct 48 take B6265
E for 1m*

Using a false name, highwayman Dick
Turpin stayed at this ancient inn which
stands in a quiet corner of the market
square and was one of the main
stopping points for travellers on the
long road between London and the
North. Today you have to turn off the
A1(M), but it's well worth it to discover
an inn built in 1258 that retains its
ancient beams, low ceilings and roaring
open fires, not to mention one that also
gives houseroom to the supposed ghosts
of a monk, a blacksmith, a cavalier and
a small boy.

Tony Burgess is the landlord and the
man responsible for high standards that
exclude anything electronic which
makes a noise. The hot and cold
sandwich selection in the bar is wide,
while in the dining room expect a good
choice of traditional pub food on menus
offering lamb shank on creamy mash in
port and honey gravy; salmon steak on
fried noodles with spicy oriental sauce;
Barnsley chop and other grills; and
Sizzlers, such as Mexican spiced
vegetables in a hot sweet salsa sauce;
and pan-fried duck breast topped with
peppers, mushrooms, bamboo shoots
and sweet and sour sauce.

Frequently changing blackboard
specials widen the choice to include
halibut steak with smoked salmon and
fresh prawns in white wine sauce; and
wild button mushroom ragout with
garlic slices and fresh salad. Possible
followers are apple pie and custard;
citrus lemon tart; or mixed ice creams,
brandy snaps and fruit purées.

In the bar, real ale drinkers will find
favourites from Timothy Taylor, Cottage
Brewery and Theakston's, while the wine
list shows all the signs of careful
compilation.

**Open** all day all wk 11-11 (Fri-Sat
11am-mdnt, Sun noon-11)
**Bar Meals** L served all wk 12-2 D served
all wk 6-9 Av main course £6.95 food
served all day **Restaurant** L served all
wk 12-2 booking required D served all
wk 6-9 booking required Av 3 course à
la carte fr £18.45 ⊕ FREE
HOUSE ◁▪ John Smiths, Timothy Taylor
Best Bitter, Cottage Brewing, Wells
Bombardier Premium Bitter, Theakston,
Guest ale. ♟ 11 **Facilities** Children's
menu Dogs allowed Parking

Save on Hotels. Book at theAA.com/hotel

YORKSHIRE, NORTH 519 ENGLAND

## AYSGARTH
Map 19 SE08

### PICK OF THE PUBS

## The George & Dragon Inn ⚑

**DL8 3AD** ☎ **01969 663358** 📠 **01969 663773**
e-mail: info@georgeanddragonaysgarth.co.uk
web: www.georgeanddragonaysgarth.co.uk
dir: *On A684 midway between Leyburn & Hawes. Pub
in village centre*

The George & Dragon Inn is a 17th-century Grade II
listed building in a superb location in the Yorkshire
Dales National Park, near the beautiful Aysgarth Falls.
The area is perfect for walking, touring and visiting
local attractions, including Forbidden Corner, the
Wensleydale Railway, and the cheese factory. The
owners are proud to continue a centuries-long tradition
of Yorkshire hospitality at the inn, with customers
keeping cosy in winter by the fireside, and in summer
enjoying their drinks and meals out on the furnished
flower-filled patio. Well-kept real ales are served, and
the inn has a great reputation for its traditional food
including steak pie and fish and chips. In the early
evening a fixed-price menu meets the needs of
ravenous walkers, while a broader à la carte choice
comes into force after 7pm. Choices could be home-
made chicken liver pâté with apple chutney;
Wensleydale pork sausages and mash; or braised pork
belly, mash, choucroute and cider reduction.

**Open** all wk **Closed:** 2wks Jan ⊕ FREE HOUSE ◀ Black
Sheep Best, Black Sheep Golden, John Smith's, John
Smith's Cask, Yorkshire Dales guest ♂ Thatchers Gold.
⚑ 16 **Facilities** Dogs allowed Garden Parking

## BAGBY
Map 19 SE48

## The Bagby Inn

Main St YO7 2PF ☎ 01845 597315
e-mail: thebagbyinn@hotmail.com
dir: *2m SE of Thirsk. Easily accessed from A19 & A170.
Follow signs for Bagby, Balk & Kilburn*

Yorkshire flavours predominate in this 18th century
whitewashed free house. New owners have reinstated the
pub as a hub for the local community, renaming it from
The Roebuck Inn, with a welcoming and friendly
atmosphere and a menu of great home-made food.
There's a good selection from the grill plus traditional
choices such as home-made steak and ale pie, lamb
Henry or beer-battered haddock with home-cut chips.
Finish with home-made fruit crumble and custard. Look
out for summer barbecues.

**Open** noon-3 5-11 (Fri 12-3 5-mdnt Sat noon-mdnt Sun
11am-11pm) **Closed:** Mon **Bar Meals** L served Tue-Sat
12-2.30, Sun 12-3.30 D served Tue-Sat 5.30-9 Av main
course £11.50 **Restaurant** L served Tue-Sat 12-2.30, Sun
12-3.30 D served Tue-Sat 5.30-9 Fixed menu price fr
£8.95 ⊕ FREE HOUSE ◀ John Smith's Cask, Black Sheep
Best, Theakstons Black Bull Cask, guest ales.
**Facilities** Children's menu Children's portions Dogs
allowed Garden Parking

## BILBROUGH
Map 16 SE54

### PICK OF THE PUBS

## The Three Hares Country Inn &
Restaurant

Main St YO23 3PH ☎ 01937 832128
dir: *Off A64 between A659 Tadcaster & A1237 York
junct*

This 18th-century country pub draws race-goers and
locals alike. A light and smartly turned-out brick-
walled dining room provides an elegant setting for the
food. On Sunday there's a traditional roast, and any
day of the week you'll find an excellent selection of real
ales, such as Copper Dragon. A heated terrace
completes the package.

**Open** all day **Closed:** Mon L **Bar Meals** L served Wed-
Sun booking required D served Tue-Sun booking
required Av main course £12 food served all day
**Restaurant** L served Wed-Sun booking required D
served Tue-Sun booking required Av 3 course à la carte
fr £25 food served all day ⊕ FREE HOUSE ◀ Copper
Dragon, Landlord, Tetley's Castle. **Facilities** Children's
portions Garden Parking

## BOROUGHBRIDGE
Map 19 SE36

### PICK OF THE PUBS

## The Black Bull Inn ⚑

*See Pick of the Pubs on opposite page*

## BREARTON
Map 19 SE36

### PICK OF THE PUBS

## Malt Shovel Inn ⚑

*See Pick of the Pubs on page 520*

## BROMPTON-BY-SAWDON
Map 17 SE98

## The Cayley Arms ⚑

YO13 9DA ☎ 01723 859372
e-mail: joannabou@hotmail.co.uk
dir: *On A170 in Brompton-by-Sawdon between Pickering
& Scarborough*

Named after pioneering aviator Sir George Cayley, this
pub stands in the heart of picturesque Brompton-by-
Sawdon. Its cosy log fire and friendly atmosphere have

been the centre of village life for over a century. All food
is sourced locally and specials include crab, lobster and
mussels. Chunky lunchtime sandwiches with home-made
crisps and hot baguettes are supplemented by hot dishes
such as warm chicken and bacon salad or fisherman's
pie. Outside is an award-winning garden and decked
area.

**Open** noon-3 5-close (Mon 6-close) **Closed:** Mon L
**Bar Meals** L served Tue-Sun 12-2 D served Mon-Sat 6-9
Av main course £8 **Restaurant** L served Tue-Sat 12-2 D
served Mon-Sat 6-9 ⊕ PUNCH TAVERNS ◀ Tetley Cask,
Black Sheep Cask. ⚑ 10 **Facilities** Children's
menu Children's portions Play area Dogs allowed Garden
Parking

## BROUGHTON
Map 18 SD95

### PICK OF THE PUBS

## The Bull ◎

**BD23 3AE** ☎ **01756 792065**
e-mail: enquiries@thebullatbroughton.com
web: www.thebullatbroughton.com
dir: *3m from Skipton on A59*

Tucked away off a busy main road, The Bull belongs to
another, less frantic era; the unhurried, relaxed
atmosphere of this Ribble Valley Inns dining pub eases
you seamlessly into this lost world. The setting helps,
of course; The Bull is part of the historic Broughton
Estate, 3,000 acres of prime Yorkshire turf owned by
the Tempest family for 900 years. The stunning
mansion is close by and the pedigree shorthorn cattle,
after which the pub is named, graze pastures skirting
the Aire Valley. Award winning chefs make the most of
the largesse offered by carefully selected producers
across Yorkshire and Lancashire; provenance and
traceability are key to the ingredients used in the
extensive, modern English menus here. How better to
start than with Hunter's parsnip soup with apple and
cumin cream, paving the way for Herdwick mutton
pudding, caper and parsley mash with black peas or
Wensleydale mature cheese and leek pie with sour
cream jackets and roasted beet salad. Finish with
frumenty (a traditional Yorkshire dessert), then relax
on the secluded patio with an local beer from Copper
Dragon or a refreshing Lancashire Sarsaparilla.

**Open** all day all wk Mon-Sat noon-11pm, Sun noon-
10.30pm **Closed:** 25 Dec **Bar Meals** Av main course
£15 **Restaurant** L served Mon-Sat noon-2, Sun noon-
8.30 D served Mon-Fri 6-9, Sat 5.30-9, Sun noon-8.30
⊕ FREE HOUSE ◀ Timothy Taylor, Copper Dragon,
Saltaire Raspberry Blonde. **Facilities** Children's menu
Dogs allowed Garden Parking

# PICK OF THE PUBS

## Malt Shovel Inn 🍷

**BREARTON**          Map 19 SE36

**HG3 3BX**
☎ **01423 862929**
e-mail: bleikers@
themaltshovelbrearton.co.uk
**dir:** *From A61 (Ripon/Harrogate) onto B6165
towards Knaresborough. Left & follow
Brearton signs. In 1m right into village*

With open winter fires, beamed ceilings
and flagstoned floors, the 16th-century
Malt Shovel exudes atmosphere and
character. The Bleiker family took over
in 2006 and it has been going from
strength to strength ever since. Swiss-
born Jürg is head chef and his wife
Jane, son D'Arcy and daughter-in-law
Anna run front-of-house. The bar is
created from old church panelling,
rediscovered fireplaces have been
brought back to life, and pianos
accompany D'Arcy and Anna, who are
also international opera soloists, and
their friends from Opera North on Opera
Nights.

There are several different eating areas:
The Monkey is one with the big open fire;
the opulent Red Room is where operatic
paraphernalia sits happily alongside
music scores; the elegant Green Room's
big, old tables are ideal for larger
parties; and then there's the
conservatory, a relatively recent
addition, with piano, ferns and lemon
tree.

Jürg specialises in fresh fish, classic
sauces and well-sourced local produce,
including organic vegetables, herbs,
eggs, lamb and pork from D'Arcy and
Anna's newly acquired smallholding.
Lunchtime starters and bar snacks
could include haddock smokie; devilled
kidneys; rösti with gruyère cheese and
home-cured pancetta; and Burgundy
snails with garlic butter.

Heading a recent list of main courses
was confit of duck with chips,
ratatouille and borlotti beans, followed
by, among others, slow-cooked belly
pork (locally hand-reared) and crackling
with bubble and squeak and Ampleforth
cider-enhanced gravy; fresh East Coast
haddock in Landlord beer batter with
mushy peas and tartare sauce; and

wiener schnitzel with capers, lemon,
anchovy and gratin dauphinoise. Try the
house speciality: mini oxtail and kidney
pudding with prime fillet béarnaise and
seared strips of rib on jasmine rice with
oyster and mint sauce – it's billed as "a
taste sensation". The local beers are
very well kept and there is a well
sourced wine list.

**Open** Wed-Sun L Closed: Mon-Tue, Sun
eve **Bar Meals** L served Wed-Sat 12-2,
Sun 12-3 booking required D served
Wed-Sat 6-9 booking required Av main
course £9.95 **Restaurant** L served Wed-
Sat 12-2, Sun 12-3 booking required D
served Wed-Sat 6-9 booking required Av
3 course à la carte fr £25 ⊕ FREE
HOUSE ◀ Black Sheep Best, Timothy
Taylor Landlord, Guest beer. 🍷 21
**Facilities** Garden Parking

## BURNSALL                    Map 19 SE06

### PICK OF THE PUBS

## The Red Lion ★★ HL ♀

**By the Bridge BD23 6BU**
☎ 01756 720204  📠 01756 720292
e-mail: redlion@daelnet.co.uk
dir: From Skipton take A59 E, take B6160 towards
Bolton Abbey, Burnsall 7m

This 16th-century ferryman's inn overlooks the River
Wharfe as it gently curves under a magnificent five-
arch bridge. Large gardens and terraces make it an
ideal spot for sunny days. The Grayshon family have
sympathetically upgraded the interior, retaining its
beamed ceilings and creaky sloping floors. The original
'one-up, one-down' structure, now the oak-panelled
and floored main bar, is the focal point of the hotel. Bar
food includes lunchtime sandwiches and light meals
such as ham hock terrine with shallot compote; and
shepherd's pie or pork belly with a spring vegetable and
smoked bacon jardinière in the evening. The main menu
ups the ante with the likes of Thai style fish fritters,
followed by oxtail and potato pie. If you are staying over
in one of the bedrooms look out for the horse trough – it
was easier to build the steps around it.

**Open** all day all wk **Bar Meals** L served Mon-Sat
12-2.30, Sun 12-9 D served all wk 7-9 ⊕ FREE HOUSE
◀ Timothy Taylor Golden Best, Theakston Best Bitter,
Copper Dragon. ♀ 14 **Facilities** Play area Family room
Dogs allowed Garden Parking **Rooms** 25

## BYLAND ABBEY                Map 19 SE57

### PICK OF THE PUBS

## Abbey Inn ◉ Ⓤ ♀

**Y061 4BD** ☎ 01347 868204
e-mail: info.appletreeinn@virgin.net
dir: From A19 Thirsk/York follow signs to Byland Abbey/
Coxwold

The ivy-clad Abbey Inn was built as a farmhouse in
1845 by Fr Alban Molyneux and a team of monks, using
'borrowed' stones from the ruined Cistercian monastery
just across the road. In July 2009 Melanie Drew took
over, and has great plans for the inn. There are three
dining rooms – Abbey Cider, Brown Brothers and Louis
Roederer. Melanie and her team take care of everything
front of house and she oversees the food with business
partner David. The food is described as 'crowd-
pleasing, modest and simple whilst remaining stylish
and full of flavour'. The best quality ingredients from
handpicked suppliers from Yorkshire and Lincolnshire
are used to create superb food, coupled with great
beers, fine wines and a warm, relaxed atmosphere. Pub
grub includes beef and cask ale hotpot pie or rare
breed sausages with wholegrain mustard mash. In the
dining room the menu might include a starter of
beetroot salmon gravadlax, followed by Byland Blue
cheese soufflé; pan-fried hake with seared scallop,
caviar and a mini fish pie; or braised thick flank of

'Tubby's' beef with roasted shallots and parsnip purée.
Beautiful bedrooms and a delightful shop complete the
package.

**Open** all day Wed-Mon Closed: 25-26 Dec, 1 Jan, Tue
**Bar Meals** booking required booking required Av main
course £12 food served all day **Restaurant** booking
required Av 3 course à la carte fr £18 food served all
day ⊕ FREE HOUSE ◀ Wold Top, Great Newsome, Tom
Woods, Hambleton, Rudcate. ♀ 13 **Facilities** Children's
portions Garden Parking **Rooms** 3

## CALDWELL                    Map 19 NZ11

## Brownlow Arms ♀ **NEW**

**DL11 7QH** ☎ 01325 718471  📠 01325 718471
e-mail: brownlowarms@mail.com
dir: From A1 at Scotch Corner take A66 towards Bowes.
Right onto B6274 to Caldwell. Or from A1 junct 56 take
B6275 N. 1st left through Mesonby to junct with B6274.
Right to Caldwell

Set in delightful, rolling countryside between Barnard
Castle and Darlington, fine food is to the fore at this
updated stone inn in tiny Caldwell. A blend of traditional
and modern rooms is the setting for unpicking a
phenomenal menu of game, fish, fowl and meat, pulling
out all the stops from Cajun salmon with sweet chilli
glaze through chicken in Cotherstone cheese on a bed of
leeks to wild boar sausage and black pudding in Madeira
sauce. With 10 wines by the glass, plenty more bins and
reliable Yorkshire real ales, time passes easily here.

**Open** all wk 5.30-10.30 (Sat-Sun noon-11) Closed: 25
Dec **Bar Meals** L served Sat-Sun all day fr 12 booking
required D served Mon-Fri 5.30-9, Sat-Sun 12-5 booking
required Av main course £8.50 **Restaurant** L served Sat-
Sun all day fr 12 booking required D served Mon-Fri
5.30-9, Sat-Sun 5-9.30 booking required Fixed menu
price fr £10.95 Av 3 course à la carte fr £24.95 ⊕ FREE
HOUSE ◀ Timothy Taylor Landlord, Black Sheep, John
Smith's, Guinness. ♀ 10 **Facilities** Children's
menu Children's portions Garden Parking

## CARTHORPE                   Map 19 SE38

### PICK OF THE PUBS

## The Fox & Hounds

**DL8 2LG** ☎ 01845 567433
dir: Off A1, signed on both N'bound & S'bound
carriageways

The Fox and Hounds has been serving its locals in the
sleepy village of Carthorpe for over 200 years. A family-
run pub with a warm welcome, Helen Taylor (whose
parents bought the pub in 1983) and her husband
Vincent take pride in the quality of their refreshments
and food, and have won many awards to prove it. Beers
include Black Sheep brewed nearby at Masham, while
the wine choice is plentiful and global in scope. The
restaurant was once the village smithy, and the old
anvil and other tools of the trade are still on display,
giving a nice sense of history to the place. The pub's
excellent reputation for food is built on named
suppliers and daily fresh fish deliveries; home-made
products such as jams and chutneys are available for
sale at the bar. A typical dinner choice could begin
with duck filled filo parcels, and continue with a
chicken breast stuffed with Coverdale cheese. A warm
chocolate, pear and almond tart brings a happy
conclusion.

**Open** all day Wed-Sun 12-3 7-11 Closed: 25-26 Dec
eve & 1st wk Jan, Mon **Bar Meals** L served Tue-Sat
12-2 D served Tue-Sat 7-9.30 ⊕ FREE HOUSE ◀ Black
Sheep Best, Worthington's Bitter ♂ Thatchers Gold.
**Facilities** Children's portions Parking

## CHAPEL LE DALE             Map 18 SD77

## The Old Hill Inn

**LA6 3A4** ☎ 015242 41256
dir: From Ingleton take B6255 4m, on right

Built as a farm, this inn dates in part to 1615 and once
served as a stopping place for drovers. These days it is
run by a family of chefs; three prepare the savoury dishes
and one, a pastry chef, is renowned for his spectacular
sugar sculptures. A meal might start with home-made
fish cakes, followed by lamb shank on boulangère
potatoes with a rich gravy, finishing with warm chocolate
pudding or blueberry tart. Lovely Dales views are offered,
with good walks from the pub.

**Open** Tue-Sun Closed: 24-25 Dec, Mon (ex BH)
**Bar Meals** L served Tue-Sat 12-2.30, Sun 12-3 booking
required D served Tue-Sun 6.30-8.45, Sat 6-8.45 booking
required **Restaurant** L served Tue-Sat 12-2.30, Sun 12-3
booking required D served Tue-Sun 6.30-8.45, Sat 6-8.45
booking required ⊕ FREE HOUSE ◀ Black Sheep Best &
Ale, Theakstons Best, Dent Aviator, Guest beer
♂ Thatchers Gold, Aspall. **Facilities** Children's
menu Children's portions Dogs allowed Garden Parking

## CLAPHAM
Map 18 SD76

### New Inn ?

**LA2 8HH** ☎ **01524 251203** 🖺 **01524 251496**
e-mail: info@newinn-clapham.co.uk
dir: *On A65 in Yorkshire Dales National Park*

Set in the charming village of Clapham beneath the
famous summit of Ingleborough in Three Peaks country,
this 18th-century inn offers a delightful blend of old and
new. The honest, wholesome food uses local produce,
particularly lamb and beef. Dishes range from a starter of
black pudding fritters with mustard sauce, to main
courses such as poached sea bream with caper butter;
risotto with wild mushrooms, smoked chicken and
chorizo; or crusty steak pie. Naturally, this is a popular
base for walking holidays.

**Open** all day all wk 11am-mdnt (Fri-Sat 11am-1am)
**Bar Meals** L served all wk 12-2 D served all wk 6.30-8.30
Av main course £10 **Restaurant** L served all wk 12-1.30
booking required D served all wk 6.30-8 booking required
Fixed menu price fr £25.60 Av 3 course à la carte fr £22
⊕ ENTERPRISE INNS ◀ Black Sheep Best, Timothy Taylor
Landlord, Copper Dragon Pippin, Copper Dragon Best,
Bowland Hen Harrier. ♀ 19 **Facilities** Children's menu
Dogs allowed Garden Parking

## COLTON
Map 16 SE54

### Ye Old Sun Inn ?

**Main St LS24 8EP** ☎ **01904 744261** 🖺 **01904 744261**
e-mail: info@yeoldsuninn.co.uk
dir: *3-4m from York, off A64*

Dating from the 18th-century, this whitewashed local
stands at the heart of the village with tables and chairs
on the lawn overlooking rolling countryside. The pub
prides itself on serving fine local food and ales –
restaurant-style dishes without the fuss. Ingredients are
locally sourced and mentioned on the menu and
everything is cooked from fresh. Typical dishes are lime
and ginger chicken, smoked venison and beetroot,
haddock with Yorkshire Blue cheese, and mixed bean
fricassee topped with a herb scone; all dishes come with
a wine recommendation.

**Open** 12-2.30 6-11 (Sun 12-10.30) Closed: 1-26 Jan, Mon
L **Bar Meals** L served Tue-Sat 12-2.30, Sun 12-7 booking
required D served Tue-Sat 6-9.30 booking required
⊕ FREE HOUSE ◀ Timothy Taylor Landlord, Timothy Taylor
Golden Best, Black Sheep, guest ale Ò Aspall. ♀ 18
**Facilities** Garden Parking

## CRAY
Map 18 SD97

### PICK OF THE PUBS

### The White Lion Inn ?

**Cray BD23 5JB** ☎ **01756 760262**
e-mail: admin@whitelioncray.com
dir: *B6265 from Skipton to Grassington, then B6160
towards Aysgarth. Or from Leyburn take A684 towards
Hawes. At Aysgarth take B6160 towards Grassington.
Cray in 10m*

Nestling beneath Buckden Pike, The White Lion is
Wharfedale's highest inn. It also boasts some
spectacular scenery, since it's set right at the heart of
the Yorkshire Dales. Indeed, the celebrated fell-walker
Wainwright once described this former drovers' hostelry
as a 'tiny oasis', a claim that's just as accurate today.
All the qualities of a traditional Yorkshire inn have
been maintained here, from warm hospitality to oak
beams, log fire and flagstone floors. A good choice of
hand-pulled real ales is offered and 20-plus malt
whiskies. You can eat and drink in the bar or dining
room, though the sight of the cascading Cray Gill,
which runs past the inn, is sure to entice children out
to the garden. Before or after a meal, you can also
make your way across the stepping-stones in the gill to
the open fells and many walks, long and short. In the
bar, lunchtime options include filled baguettes,
ploughman's, and plate-sized Yorkshire puddings with
a choice of fillings. Also available, lunchtime and
evenings, is a variety of substantial dishes such as
pork fillet in a honey and mustard cream sauce; whole
steamed Kilnsey trout, or steak and mushroom
casserole. A children's menu is also on offer.

**Open** all day all wk 10am-11pm **Bar Meals** L served all
wk 10-2 D served all wk 6-9 ⊕ FREE HOUSE ◀ Timothy
Taylor Golden Best, Copper Dragon Golden Pippin,
Copper Dragon 1816, John Smith's Cask Ò Stowford
Press. ♀ 9 **Facilities** Family room Dogs allowed Garden
Parking

## CRAYKE
Map 19 SE57

### PICK OF THE PUBS

### The Durham Ox ★★★★ 🅰 RR ?

**See Pick of the Pubs on opposite page**

## CROPTON
Map 19 SE78

### The New Inn

**YO18 8HH** ☎ **01751 417330** 🖺 **01751 417582**
e-mail: office@croptonbrewery.com
dir: *Telephone for directions*

Home of the award-winning Cropton micro-brewery, this
family-run free house on the edge of the North York Moors
National Park is popular with locals and visitors alike.
Meals are served in the restored village bar and in the
elegant Victorian restaurant: choices could include Whitby
cod with mushy peas and home-made chips; three cheese

and roasted vegetable frittata; an extensive range from the
grill; plus lunchtime sandwiches and ciabatta rolls.

**Open** all day all wk 11-11 (Sun 11-10.30) **Bar Meals** L
served all wk 12-2 D served all wk 6-9 ⊕ FREE HOUSE
◀ Cropton Two Pints, Monkmans Slaughter, Yorkshire
Moors Bitter, Honey Gold Bitter. **Facilities** Children's menu
Play area Family room Dogs allowed Garden Parking

## EAST WITTON
Map 19 SE18

### PICK OF THE PUBS

### The Blue Lion ?

**DL8 4SN** ☎ **01969 624273** 🖺 **01969 624189**
e-mail: enquiries@thebluelion.co.uk
dir: *From Ripon take A6108 towards Leyburn*

This former coaching inn has welcomed travellers since
the days when cattle drovers rested here on their
journey through glorious Wensleydale. Built towards the
end of the 18th century by the Marquis of Aylesbury, the
pub's stone façade can hardly have changed since it
first opened, while inside an extensive but sympathetic
refurbishment has created rural chic interiors with
stacks of atmosphere and charm. The bar with its open
fire and flagstone floor is a beer drinker's haven, where
the best of North Yorkshire's breweries present a
pleasant dilemma for the real ale lover. A blackboard
displays imaginative but unpretentious bar meals.
Diners in the candlelit restaurant can expect award-
winning culinary treats incorporating a variety of
Yorkshire ingredients. A fulfilling repast may comprise
slow-braised pig cheeks with red wine sauce, black
pudding, apple and parsnip purée; followed by sautéed
breast of free-range chicken with wild mushroom and
thyme tagliatelle; and treacle sponge with custard to
finish.

**Open** all day all wk 11-11 Closed: 25 Dec **Bar Meals** L
served all wk 12-2.15 D served all wk 7-9.30 Av main
course £16.50 **Restaurant** L served Sun 12-2.15 D
served all wk 7-9.30 Av 3 course à la carte fr £21.50
⊕ FREE HOUSE ◀ Black Sheep Bitter, Theakston Best
Bitter, Black Sheep Riggwetter, Worthingtons
Ò Thatchers Gold. ♀ 12 **Facilities** Children's portions
Dogs allowed Garden Parking

# PICK OF THE PUBS

## The Durham Ox ★★★★ A RR ☙

**CRAYKE**      Map 19 SE57

**Westway YO61 4TE**
☎ 01347 821506   🖷 01347 823326
e-mail: enquiries@thedurhamox.com
**dir:** *Off A19 from York to Thirsk, then to Easingwold. From market place to Crayke, turn left up hill, pub on right*

Comfy AA-rated accommodation in converted farm cottages and buildings around a secluded, flowery yard is the perfect excuse to linger at this 300-year old country inn which gained the accolade AA Pub of The Year (England) in 2007/8. The pretty pantiled pub and village are set in the beautiful Howardian Hills AONB and just a 20-minute drive from York, whilst Herriot country and the sublime Castle Howard are nearby. With flagstone floors, exposed beams, oak panelling and roaring fires in the main bar in winter, it ticks all the boxes on the 'traditional country pub' checklist.

The menus reveal that the eponymous ox was born in 1796 and grew to enormous proportions - five feet six inches tall, 11 feet from nose to tail, the same around its girth, and weighing 171 stone - little wonder the beast created such a sensation. Another claim to fame is that the hill outside the inn is reputedly the one the Grand Old Duke of York marched his men up and down. Whether you march in, arrive by helicopter or take a break on a ramble, the finest of Yorkshire welcomes awaits at this hilltop pub, with the White Rose County providing the real ales and the produce for many of the award-winning meals for which it has a national reputation; fish and game are particularly highly regarded.

Perhaps start the event with carpaccio of Mount Grace prime fillet of beef, progressing to roast saddle of Fountains Abbey venison with cabbage, celeriac, hedgerow sauce and potatoes of the day or steamed black bream with wilted pak choi, coriander, ginger, lemon grass and basmati rice before concluding with Conference pear parfait with almond tuiles. And Sundays simply wouldn't be Sundays without local roast sirloin of beef and, of course, Yorkshire pudding.

**Open** all wk 12-2.30 6-11 Closed: 25 Dec **Bar Meals** L served Mon-Sat 12-2.30, Sun 12-3 booking required D served Mon-Sat 6-9.30, Sun 6-8.30 booking required **Restaurant** L served Mon-Sat 12-2.30, Sun 12-3 booking required D served Mon-Sat 6-9.30, Sun 6-8.30 booking required Fixed menu price fr £12.95 ⊕ FREE HOUSE ◼ John Smiths, Theakstons, Timothy Taylor Landlord, Black Sheep Best. ☙ 10 **Facilities** Dogs allowed Garden Parking **Rooms** 5

# PICK OF THE PUBS

## The Plough Inn

**FADMOOR**      Map 19 SE68

**Main St YO62 7HY**
☎ **01751 431515**   📄 **01751 432492**
e-mail:
enquiries@theploughfadmoor.co.uk
**web:** www.theploughfadmoor.co.uk
**dir:** *1m N of Kirkbymoorside on A170 (Thirsk to Scarborough road)*

Dramatic views over Ryedale and the Wolds from this stylish country free house and restaurant on the village green will stay in the memory for a long time. Sympathetically restored a few years ago, the inn's mid-18th-century feel is strongly conveyed by low beamed ceilings, comfortable wall benches and winter log fires - just the place for a pint of guest ale, such as Sleck Dust from the Great Newsome brewery over near Hull.

Eat from the bar snack menu or carte in the bar area with its original Victorian tiled floor, or adjacent Coffee Lounge, Living Room or Snug. Head chef Neil Nicholson recently celebrated ten years here; he it is who creates the extensive and varied menus that rely heavily on local meats, vegetables, herbs and salad crops, and fish straight from East Coast quaysides. His wife Rachael looks after front of house, with a team of staff providing a level of service that encourages people to come back again and again.

Lunch and dinner menu starter options of pan-fried sweet potato and red chilli crab cakes, or deep-fried duck and pineapple spring rolls could be followed by roasted rack of Yorkshire lamb; a duet of sliced belly pork and black pudding; fresh Scottish salmon Thermidor; or a special, such as chilli con carne. Desserts made on the premises include almond meringue roulade; baked lemon curd cheesecake; and brandy snap basket filled with sliced banana. The Sunday lunch menu includes traditional roasts, but goes

beyond to include lamb and vegetable casserole, and mushroom and brie Wellington. The wine list has a good value house selection.

**Open** noon-2.30 6.30-11 (Sun noon-5) Closed: 25 Dec, 1 Jan, Mon-Tue (ex BH), Sun eve **Bar Meals** L served Wed-Sat 12-2, Sun 12-3.30 D served Wed-Sat 6.30-9 booking required Av main course £9.75 **Restaurant** L served Wed-Sat 12-2, Sun 12-3.30 D served Wed-Sat 6.30-9 booking required Fixed menu price fr £10 Av 3 course à la carte fr £23 🛢 FREE HOUSE 🍺 Black Sheep Best, John Smith's, Tetley Cask, Great Newsome Brewery's Sleck Dust, Guest ales Ö Stowford Press.
**Facilities** Children's menu Garden Parking

Save on Hotels. Book at **theAA.com/hotel**

**YORKSHIRE, NORTH** 525 **ENGLAND**

## EGTON — Map 19 NZ80

### PICK OF THE PUBS

## The Wheatsheaf Inn

YO21 1TZ ☎ 01947 895271
e-mail: info@wheatsheafegton.com
dir: Off A169 NW of Grosmont

This unassuming old pub sits back from the wide main road, so be careful not to miss it. The main bar is cosy and traditional, with low beams, dark green walls and comfy settles. There's a locals' bar too, but it only holds about twelve, so get there early. The pub is very popular with fishermen, as the River Esk runs along at the foot of the hill, and is a big draw for fly-fishers in particular. The menu offers white nut and artichoke heart roast with mushroom stroganoff, and chicken and smoked bacon puff pastry pie among others.

Open 11.30-3 5.30-11.30 (Sat 11.30-11.30 Sun 11.30-11) Closed: Mon Bar Meals L served Tue-Sun 12-2 D served Tue-Sat 6-9 ⊕ FREE HOUSE ◀ Black Sheep Bitter, Black Sheep Golden, John Smith's, Timothy Taylor Landlord, Guest Ales ⊘ Thatchers Gold. Facilities Dogs allowed Garden Parking

## EGTON BRIDGE — Map 19 NZ80

## Horseshoe Hotel

YO21 1XE ☎ 01947 895245
e-mail: paul@thehorseshoehotel.co.uk
dir: From Whitby take A171 towards Middlesborough. Village signed in 5m

An 18th-century country inn by the River Esk, handy for visiting the North Yorkshire Moors Railway. Inside are oak settles and tables, local artists' paintings and, depending on the weather, an open fire. Lunchtime bar food consists of sandwiches in granary bread and hot baguettes. The main menu includes starters like crab cakes with a sweet chilli dip, and mains like lasagne, scampi, or pie of the day. There is also a specials board.

Open all wk 11.30-3 6.30-11 (Sat 11.30-11 Sun noon-10.30) Bar Meals L served all wk 12-2 D served all wk 7-9 ⊕ FREE HOUSE ◀ John Smith's Cask, Durham, Black Sheep, guest ales. Facilities Family room Dogs allowed Garden Parking

## FADMOOR — Map 19 SE68

### PICK OF THE PUBS

## The Plough Inn

*See Pick of the Pubs on opposite page*

## GIGGLESWICK — Map 18 SD86

## Black Horse Hotel

32 Church St BD24 0BE
☎ 01729 822506 📄 01729 822506
e-mail: theblackhorse-giggle@tiscali.co.uk
dir: Telephone for directions

Set next to the church and behind the market cross in the 17th-century main street, this traditional free house is as charming as Giggleswick itself. Down in the warm and friendly bar you'll find a range of hand-pulled ales, with local guest beer sometimes available. The menu of freshly-prepared pub favourites ranges from hot sandwiches, home-made pizzas or giant filled Yorkshire puddings to main course dishes like traditional lamb hotpot or horseshoe of local gammon.

Open noon-2.30 5.30-11 (Sat-Sun noon-11) Closed: Mon L Bar Meals L served Tue-Sun 12-1.45 D served all wk 7-8.45 Av main course £8 Restaurant L served Sun only 12-1.45 booking required D served all wk 7-8.45 booking required ⊕ FREE HOUSE ◀ Carlsberg-Tetley Bitter, Timothy Taylor Landlord, John Smith's, Timothy Taylor Golden Best. Facilities Children's menu Children's portions Garden Parking

## GOATHLAND — Map 19 NZ80

## Birch Hall Inn

Beckhole YO22 5LE ☎ 01947 896245
e-mail: glenys@birchhallinn.fsnet.co.uk
dir: 9m from Whitby on A169

This delightful little free house, tucked away in a remote valley close to the North York Moors steam railway, has been in the same ownership for 25 years. With just two tiny rooms separated by a sweet shop, it offers an open fire in the main bar, well-kept local ales and a large garden with tempting views of the local walks. The simple menu features locally-baked pies, butties, home-made scones and buttered beer cake. Food and drink can be enjoyed in the garden in warmer months.

Open 11-3 7.30-11 (11-11 summer) Closed: Mon eve & Tue in winter Bar Meals food served all day ⊕ FREE HOUSE ◀ Black Sheep Best, Theakstons Black Bull, Cropton Yorkshire Moors Bitter, Daleside Brewery Legover, Durhams Black Velvet. Facilities Family room Dogs allowed Garden Notes ⊛

## GREAT AYTON — Map 19 NZ51

## *The Royal Oak* ★★★ INN ♥

123 High St TS9 6BW
☎ 01642 722361 📄 01642 724047
e-mail: info@royaloak-hotel.co.uk
dir: Telephone for directions

Real fires and a relaxed atmosphere are part of the attraction at this traditional 18th-century former coaching inn now corner pub, run by the Monaghan family since 1978. The public bar and restaurant retain many original features and offer a good selection of real ales, and an extensive range of food is available all day. There are five comfortable bedrooms if you would like to stay over.

Open all wk Closed: 25 Dec ◀ Theakstons, John Smith's Smooth, Directors. ♥ 10 Facilities Garden Rooms 5

## GREEN HAMMERTON — Map 19 SE45

## The Bay Horse Inn

York Rd YO26 8BN ☎ 01423 330338
e-mail: enquiry@bayhorsegreenhammerton.co.uk
dir: Telephone for directions

Over 200 years old and situated in a picturesque village in the vale of York, this family-run, former coaching inn's traditional bar has real fires and serves Timothy Taylor Landlord and Black Sheep real ales. Food is served in the bar and dining room, and the small garden and patio offer further seating. Locally sourced, home-made dishes include lasagne, omelettes, sausages with Yorkshire pudding and mash, and steak and Guinness pie. Tuesdays and Fridays are fish and chips nights, to eat in or take away.

Open 11.30-2.30 5.30-12 Closed: Sun eve Bar Meals L served all wk 12-2.30 D served Mon-Sat 6-9.30 Av main course £6.95 Restaurant L served all wk 12-2.30 D served Mon-Sat 6-9.30 Av 3 course à la carte fr £17 ⊕ GREENE KING ◀ Timothy Taylor, Black Sheep, Guest ale, Abbot Ale. Facilities Children's portions Dogs allowed Garden Parking

## GRINTON — Map 19 SE09

### PICK OF THE PUBS

## The Bridge Inn

*See Pick of the Pubs on page 526*

# PICK OF THE PUBS

## The Bridge Inn

**GRINTON**                    Map 19 SE09

**DL11 6HH**

☎ **01748 884224**

e-mail: atkinbridge@btinternet.com

web: www.bridgeinngrinton.co.uk

dir: *Exit A1 at Scotch Corner towards Richmond. In Richmond take A6108 towards Reeth, 10m*

Standing by the River Swale in the heart of the Yorkshire Dales National Park, this 13th-century, former coaching inn faces the parish church of St Andrew, known as the 'Cathedral of the Dales'. Careful renovation has protected the inn's beamed ceilings and open fires that help to declare its heritage. The bar stocks real ales from Jennings, and

guests from breweries such as Adnams, York and Caledonian, and there's also a fine cellar of wines handpicked by Andrew Atkin, your host.

Meals are served in the bar, games room and restaurant, over all of which resident chef John Scott is in charge, his menu inspired by carefully chosen seasonal local game, meats, fish and other produce, including herbs plucked from the garden. Hot and cold baguettes are served in the bar with a handful of chips.

In the restaurant, starters include black pudding spring rolls; savoury bread and butter pudding; and devilled whitebait. Typical main course choices include pan-fried breast of free-range chicken filled with Swaledale cheese, wrapped in bacon and served with cranberry and wine sauce; salmon steak baked with rosemary, lemon and garlic on roasted courgette and cherry tomatoes; and vegetarian cottage pie made with leeks, celery, lentils and mixed beans in

tomato sauce and topped with potato and cheese. The dessert menu includes three-chocolate brownie; Liz's meringues; and locally made Brymor ice cream.

Many visitors head for the Dales because they want to go walking, horse-riding, mountain biking or fishing, all of which are easy to do from here. Musician Night takes place every Thursday.

**Open** all day all wk **Bar Meals** Av main course £11.95 food served all day **Restaurant** Av 3 course à la carte fr £25 food served all day ⊕ JENNINGS BROTHERS PLC ◀ Cumberland Ale, Cocker Hoop, Deuchars IPA, Adnams, Yorkshire Terrier. **Facilities** Dogs allowed Garden Parking

Save on Hotels. Book at **theAA.com/hotel**

YORKSHIRE, NORTH 527 ENGLAND

## HAROME
Map 19 SE68

### PICK OF THE PUBS

## The Star Inn ⚛⚛ 🍷

**Y062 5JE** ☎ **01439 770397** 📠 **01439 771833**
e-mail: reservations@thestarinnatharome.co.uk
dir: *From Helmsley take A170 towards Kirkbymoorside 0.5m. Turn right for Harome*

A thatched 14th-century pub in a chocolate-box village on the edge of the North Yorkshire Moors, The Star Inn is widely regarded as one of the finest food pubs in the country, with several awards to its name. Produce sourced directly from nearby farms and estates, and fish and shellfish from Whitby and Hartlepool, are used to good effect in the regional menu. Dishes might include cassoulet of Hartlepool natural smoked haddock, creamed haricot beans and Wensleydale herb crust; and loin of milk-fed piglet with 24-hour braised belly, black pudding, Scotch egg, garden sage-scented apple purée and mulled Ampleforth cider. Recent additions have included a new dining area, a chef's table, a private dining room upstairs, a summer dining terrace and a kitchen garden, not to mention a new property with an indoor swimming pool and a 40-seater dining room within 200 yards of the inn.

**Open** 11.30-3 6-11 (Sun noon-11) Closed: 1 Jan, Mon L **Bar Meals** L served Tue-Sun 11.30-2 D served Mon-Sat 6-9.30 Av main course £18.20 **Restaurant** L served Tue-Sun 11.30-2 booking required D served Mon-Sat 6-9.30 booking required ⊕ FREE HOUSE ◀ Black Sheep Special, Copper Dragon, Hambleton Ales, John Smith's, Theakstons Best ♂ Stowford Press, Ampleforth. 🍷 24 **Facilities** Children's portions Garden Parking

## HAWES
Map 18 SD88

## The Moorcock Inn

**Garsdale Head LA10 5PU**
☎ **01969 667488** 📠 **01969 667488**
e-mail: admin@moorcockinn.com
dir: *On A684 5m from Hawes, 10m from Sedbergh at junct for Kirkby Stephen (10m). Garsdale Station 1m*

A heart-warming 18th-century hostelry in beautiful countryside, where weary walkers are welcomed with or without muddy boots and dogs. Inside there is a cosy traditional blend of original stonework and bright colours, furnished with comfy sofas and wooden chairs. Savour the pub's local ales, or one of the 50 malt whiskies, around the wood-burning stove, or enjoy the spectacular views from the garden. Traditional fare ranges from Whitby scampi; lamb and root vegetable hotpot; to steak, mushroom and ale pie.

**Open** all day all wk 11am-mdnt **Bar Meals** Av main course £7.50 food served all day **Restaurant** D served all wk 6.30-9 Av 3 course à la carte fr £17 ⊕ FREE HOUSE ◀ Black Sheep, Copper Dragon, Tetleys Cask, guest ales. **Facilities** Children's menu Children's portions Family room Dogs allowed Garden Parking

## HELMSLEY
Map 19 SE68

## The Crown Inn

**Market Square Y062 5BJ** ☎ **01439 770297**
e-mail: info@tchh.co.uk
dir: *Telephone for directions*

The family-run 16th-century inn overlooking Helmsley's beautiful square has been refurbished with style and taste, without losing the inn's historic charm. You can order a pint of Black Sheep and tuck into some fresh home-made food using local produce in the cosy bar and lounge, each warmed by an open log fire. Choose to stay to explore the North York Moors and visit nearby Castle Howard.

**Open** all day all wk 7.30am-11.30pm **Bar Meals** food served all day ⊕ FREE HOUSE ◀ Black Sheep, John Smith's Cask, Guest ale. **Facilities** Family room Dogs allowed Garden Parking

## HETTON
Map 18 SD95

### PICK OF THE PUBS

## The Angel ★★★★★ RR ⚛⚛ 🍷

**BD23 6LT** ☎ **01756 730263** 📠 **01756 730363**
e-mail: info@angelhetton.co.uk
dir: *A59 onto B6265 towards Grassington. Left at Rylstone Pond (signed) then left at T-junct*

Once a drovers' inn, this ancient Dales pub became a landmark gastro-pub when Denis and Juliet Watkins took the reins in 1985, and Juliet and her team have built on that success since Denis' death in 2004. The interior is all oak beams, nooks and crannies, and winter log fires; in summer you can sit on the flagged forecourt and enjoy views of Cracoe Fell. Chef Bruce Elsworth has stayed true to Denis' vision of 'good food and great value' with locally sourced meats, seasonal game and fresh Fleetwood fish the foundation of the varied menus. The brasserie blackboard menu might offer Goosnargh duck leg spring roll with plum sauce, ginger and coriander salad followed by mutton and ale pie, whilst à la carte diners might enjoy carpaccio of Yorkshire beef followed by halibut loin, confit fennel, curly kale, roasted butternut squash purée and crayfish butter sauce.

**Open** all wk Mon-Thu noon-3 6-11 Fri-Sun all day Closed: 25 Dec & 1wk Jan **Bar Meals** L served Mon-Sat 12-2.15, Sun all day D served all wk 6-9.30 (6-9 in winter) Av main course £14 **Restaurant** L served Sun 12-1.45 booking required D served Mon-Fri 6-9, Sat 6-9.30 booking required Fixed menu price fr £18.95 Av 3 course à la carte fr £25.95 ⊕ FREE HOUSE ◀ Black Sheep Bitter, Timothy Taylor Landlord, Hetton Pale Ale. 🍷 20 **Facilities** Children's menu Children's portions Garden Parking **Rooms** 5

## HOVINGHAM
Map 19 SE67

## The Malt Shovel

**Main St Y062 4LF** ☎ **01653 628264** 📠 **01653 628264**
e-mail: info@themaltshovelhovingham.co.uk
dir: *18m NE of York, 5m from Castle Howard*

Tucked away in the Duchess of Kent's home village, the stone-built 18th-century Malt Shovel offers a friendly atmosphere with well kept ales, good value food prepared from quality local ingredients. Popular options include Whitby wholetail scampi; local gammon with egg and chips; steak and ale pie; and chargrilled chicken. Fresh vegetables, hand-cut chips and daily specials board featuring perhaps pan-roasted pheasant on potato rösti, or braised ribs of beef in rich gravy, complete the picture. Hot or cold buffet is available by arrangement for walking parties, etc.

**Open** all wk 11.30-2 6-11 (winter), 11.30-2.30 5.30-11 (summer) **Bar Meals** L served Mon-Sat 11.30-2 (winter) 11.30-2.30 (summer), Sun 12-2.30 D served Mon-Sat 6-9 (winter) 5.30-9 (summer), Sun 5.30-8 Av main course £8.50 **Restaurant** L served Mon-Sat 11.30-2 (winter) 11.30-2.30 (summer), Sun 12-2.30 booking required D served Mon-Sat 6-9 (winter) 5.30-9 (summer), Sun 5.30-8 booking required Fixed menu price fr £8.75 ⊕ PUNCH TAVERNS ◀ Tetley's, Black Sheep, Guest Ale. **Facilities** Children's menu Children's portions Garden Parking

### PICK OF THE PUBS

## The Worsley Arms Hotel ★★★ HL 🍷

**Main St Y062 4LA**
☎ **01653 628234** 📠 **01653 628130**
e-mail: enquiries@worsleyarms.co.uk
dir: *On B1257 between Malton & Helmsley*

In 1841 Sir William Worsley thought he would turn the village of Worsley into a spa to rival Bath, and built a spa house and a hotel. However, he reckoned without the delicate nature of his guests who disliked the muddy track between the two. Inevitably the spa failed, but the hotel survived and, together with the separate pub, forms part of the Worsley family's historic Hovingham Hall estate, birthplace of the Duchess of Kent, and currently home to her nephew. You can eat in the restaurant or the Cricketer's Bar (the local team has played on the village green for over 150 years). Hambleton Stallion beer from nearby Thirsk is on tap, and food choices include seared Gressingham duck with celeriac and potato dauphinoise, Worsley Arms fishcakes with lemon fish cream, Waterford Farm sausages with mash and red onion confit, or rack of North Yorkshire lamb with fondant potato, roast garlic and fresh mint.

**Open** all day all wk 11-11 **Bar Meals** L served all wk 12-2 booking required D served all wk 6.30-9 booking required Av main course £11 **Restaurant** L served Sun 12-2 booking required D served all wk 6.30-9 booking required Fixed menu price fr £29.50 Av 3 course à la carte fr £23.50 ⊕ FREE HOUSE ◀ Tetleys, Hambleton Ales. 🍷 20 **Facilities** Dogs allowed Garden Parking **Rooms** 20

---

### HUBBERHOLME | Map 18 SD97

## The George Inn

**BD23 5JE** ☎ **01756 760223**
**dir:** *From Skipton take B6265 to Threshfield. B6160 to Buckden. Follow signs for Hubberholme*

To check if the bar is open, look for a lighted candle in the window. Another old tradition is the annual land-letting auction on the first Monday night of the year, when local farmers bid for 16 acres of land owned by the church. Stunningly located beside the River Wharfe, this pub has flagstone floors, stone walls, mullioned windows, an open fire and an inviting summer terrace. Lunches include Thai-style fishcakes and maybe a pint of Black Sheep; evening choices include steak and ale pie or chicken supreme.

**Open** noon-3 7-11 Closed: 1st 2wks Dec, Mon
**Bar Meals** L served Tue-Sun 12-2 D served Tue-Sun 7-8.30 booking required Av main course £9 ⊕ FREE HOUSE ◀ Black Sheep Special, Yorkshire Dales Brewery ♂ Thatchers Gold. **Facilities** Children's menu Garden Parking

---

### KILBURN | Map 19 SE57

## The Forresters Arms Inn

**YO61 4AH** ☎ **01347 868386**
**e-mail:** admin@forrestersarms.com
**dir:** *From Thirsk take A170, after 3m turn right signed Kilburn. At Kilburn Rd junct, turn right, Inn on left in village square*

A sturdy stone-built former coaching inn still catering for travellers passing close by the famous White Horse of Kilburn on the North York Moors. Next door is the famous Robert Thompson workshop; fine examples of his early work, with the distinctive mouse symbol on every piece, can be seen in both bars. Visiting coachmen would undoubtedly have enjoyed the log fires, cask ales and good food as much as today's visitors. Dishes include fish pie; honey mustard glazed belly pork; or sausage and mash.

**Open** all day all wk 9am-11pm **Bar Meals** L served all wk 12-2.30 booking required D served all wk 6-9 booking required Av main course £10 **Restaurant** L served all wk 12-2.30 booking required D served all wk 6-9 booking required Fixed menu price fr £10 ⊕ ENTERPRISE INNS ◀ John Smith's Cask, Guinness, Hambleton Bitter, Guest ales ♂ Symonds. **Facilities** Children's menu Children's portions Dogs allowed Garden Parking

---

### KIRBY HILL | Map 19 NZ10

## The Shoulder of Mutton Inn

**DL11 7JH** ☎ **01748 822772**
**e-mail:** info@shoulderofmutton.net
**dir:** *From A1 Scotch Corner junct take A66. Approx 6m follow signs for Kirby Hill on left*

A traditional ivy-clad 18th-century inn with panoramic views over Holmedale and beyond. Two open log fires burn

---

in the bar, adding to the enjoyment of a pint of Daleside or Copper Dragon. The separate stone-walled restaurant, replete with original beams and white linen, makes just the right kind of setting for renowned daily-changing home-cooked dishes. A typical selection could comprise warm kidney and bacon salad, followed by roast breast of duck on an apple compote, with a home-made pastry to round everything off.

**Open** all wk 6-11 (Sat-Sun noon-3 6-11) **Bar Meals** L served Sat-Sun 12-2 booking required D served Wed-Sun 6.30-9 booking required Av main course £10 **Restaurant** L served Sun 12-2 booking required D served Wed-Sun 6.30-9 booking required Av 3 course à la carte fr £25 ◀ Daleside, Black Sheep, Copper Dragon, Deuchars, Yorkshire Dales. **Facilities** Garden Parking

---

### KIRKBYMOORSIDE | Map 19 SE68

## PICK OF THE PUBS

## George & Dragon Hotel ♥

**17 Market Place YO62 6AA**
☎ **01751 433334** 📠 **0870 706 0004**
**e-mail:** reception@georgeanddragon.net
**dir:** *Just off A170 between Scarborough & Thirsk. In town centre*

A former cornmill, rectory and 17th-century coaching inn have been seamlessly combined to make this welcoming hotel in the heart of Kirkbymoorside. The beamed interior is full of character and comfy chairs. Visitors can sit by the log fire and sample hand-pulled real ales, wines by the glass and a choice of 30 malt whiskies. Food is served all day using fresh local produce, and includes a bar lunchtime menu, à la carte and specials board. Dishes range from pub food favourites like ploughman's or battered haddock to specials such as chicken on leek and bacon cream; pan-roasted breast of pheasant on potato rösti and cranberry gravy; or roast salmon with hollandaise sauce and fresh asparagus. A haven for real ale lovers, the bar offers guest ales alongside Copper Dragon.

**Open** all day all wk 10.30am-11pm **Bar Meals** Av main course £12 food served all day **Restaurant** Av 3 course à la carte fr £20 food served all day ⊕ FREE HOUSE ◀ Theakston XB, Tetley, Copper Dragon, Guest ale. ♥ 12 **Facilities** Children's menu Children's portions Dogs allowed Garden Parking

---

### KIRKHAM | Map 19 SE76

## PICK OF THE PUBS

## Stone Trough Inn ♥

**Kirkham Abbey YO60 7JS** ☎ **01653 618713**
**e-mail:** timstonetroughinn@live.co.uk
**dir:** *1.5m off A64, between York & Malton*

This free house has a great reputation for its friendliness, fine food and real ales. It stands high above Kirkham Priory and the River Derwent, and was sympathetically converted into licensed premises in the early 1980s from Stone Trough Cottage. The cottage

---

took its name from the base of a cross erected by a 12th-century French knight to commemorate a son killed in a riding accident. The cross has long since disappeared, but its hollowed-out base now stands at the entrance to the car park. A real fire, bare beams and wooden settles make for a pleasingly traditional interior. Food-wise there's a menu of serious intent that includes roast breast of guinea fowl with confit leg and a chanterelle sauce; whole grilled lemon sole with a shrimp beurre noisette dressing; and fillet of turbot with a basil and ginger sauce.

**Open** all day all wk 11-11 (Sun noon-11pm)
**Bar Meals** L served Mon-Thu 12-2.30, Fri-Sat 12-9.30, Sun 12-8 D served Mon-Thu 6-9.30 ⊕ FREE HOUSE ◀ Tetley Cask, Timothy Taylor Landlord, Black Sheep Best, York Brewery, Cropton Brewery, guest ales. ♥ 14 **Facilities** Dogs allowed Garden Parking

---

### KNARESBOROUGH | Map 19 SE35

## PICK OF THE PUBS

## The General Tarleton Inn ★★★★★ RR ◉◉ ♥

**See Pick of the Pubs on opposite page**

---

### LANGTHWAITE | Map 19 NZ00

## The Red Lion Inn ♥

**DL11 6RE** ☎ **01748 884218** 📠 **01748 884133**
**e-mail:** rlionlangthwaite@aol.com
**dir:** *Through Reeth into Arkengarthdale, 18m from A1*

The Red Lion is a traditional country pub owned by the same family for 45 years. It hosts two darts teams in winter, a quoits team in summer and bar snacks are served all year round. There are some wonderful walks in this part of the Dales and relevant books and maps are on sale. In the tiny snug there are photographs relating to the various films and TV programmes filmed at this unusually photogenic pub.

**Open** all wk 11-3 7-11 **Bar Meals** L served all wk 11-3 Av main course £3.50 ⊕ FREE HOUSE ◀ Black Sheep Bitter, Riggwelter, Worthington Cream Flow, Guinness ♂ Thatchers Gold. ♥ 9 **Facilities** Family room Garden Parking

---

# PICK OF THE PUBS

## The General Tarleton Inn ★★★★★ RR

### KNARESBOROUGH · Map 19 SE35

**Boroughbridge Rd, Ferrensby HG5 0PZ**
☎ **01423 340284** 📠 **01423 340288**
**e-mail:** gti@generaltarleton.co.uk
**web:** www.generaltarleton.co.uk
**dir:** *A1(M) junct 48 at Boroughbridge, take A6055 to Knaresborough. Inn 4m on right*

During the American War of Independence, Sir Banastre Tarleton was nicknamed "Butcher", a clue to his treatment of enemy troops. Even so, upon his return to England the name of this 18th-century coaching inn was changed in his honour.

Today it is known for its contemporary comforts and top-class dining, endorsed by two AA Rosettes. Step inside to find a lounge with large sofas, daily papers, magazines and a welcoming, low-beamed bar with log fires and cosy corners. The Bar Brasserie has the atmosphere of a traditional English pub, combined with stylish contemporary décor.

The Tarleton is the fine-dining restaurant, while eating is also possible in the Terrace Garden and covered courtyard. Menus entitled 'Food with Yorkshire Roots' change daily to reflect the pick of the crop or catch, thus the chef usually gets a call from fishing boat skippers returning to ports on both the east and west coasts. All those telephone calls are good news for seafood lovers: try Little Moneybags, the chef's signature dish of seafood parcels in lobster sauce, or his seafood Thermidor-fillets of salmon, haddock, cod, monkfish and prawns in brandy with mustard and cheese sauce.

Among the meats you'll find slow-braised shoulder of Dales lamb with crushed haricot beans, cracked coriander and confit garlic; chargrilled haunch of venison with mushrooms, roast shallots and pancetta in red wine sauce; and roast butternut, spinach and ricotta cannelloni. The children's menu of home-made dishes gets the culinary seal of approval from the owners' three offspring.

Proprietor John Topham is proud of his 150-bin cellar of wines from small producers, distinctive and exciting New World wines, and rare examples from the world's finest vineyards. The bedrooms are individually decorated and well equipped.

**Open** all wk 12-3 6-11
**Bar Meals** L served all wk 12-2 booking required D served all wk 6-9.15 booking required Av main course £13
**Restaurant** L served Sun 12-1.45 booking required D served Mon-Sat 6-9.15 booking required Av 3 course à la carte fr £28 ⊕ FREE HOUSE ◀ Black Sheep Best, Timothy Taylor Landlord. ♀ 11 **Facilities** Children's menu Garden Parking **Rooms** 14

## LASTINGHAM
Map 19 SE79

### Blacksmiths Arms

YO62 6TL ☎ 01751 417247 📠 01751 417247
e-mail: pete.hils@blacksmithslastingham.co.uk
dir: *7m from Pickering & 4m from Kirbymoorside. A170 (Pickering to Kirbymoorside road), follow Lastingham & Appleton-le-Moors signs*

This 17th-century pub stands opposite St Mary's Church (renowned for its Saxon crypt) in the National Park area. The stone-built free house retains its original low-beamed ceilings and open range fireplace, and outside there's a cottage garden and decked seating area. Home-cooked dishes prepared from locally supplied ingredients include lamb casserole served with Yorkshire pudding, and beer-battered jumbo cod. Enjoy the food with a pint of Theakstons Best Bitter or one of the guest ales.

**Open** all day Closed: Tue L (Nov-May) **Bar Meals** L served all wk (not Tue Nov-May) 12-5 D served all wk 6.30-8.45 Av main course £10 **Restaurant** L served all wk 12-5 (not Tue Nov-May) booking required D served all wk 6.30-8.45 booking required ⊕ FREE HOUSE ◀ Theakstons Best Bitter, 2 rotating guest ales. **Facilities** Children's menu Children's portions Family room Garden

## LEVISHAM
Map 19 SE89

### Horseshoe Inn ♀

Main St YO18 7NL ☎ 01751 460240 📠 01751 460052
e-mail: info@horseshoelevisham.co.uk
dir: *A169, 5m from Pickering. 4m, pass Fox & Rabbit Inn on right. In 0.5m left to Lockton. Follow steep winding road to village*

This spruced-up 16th-century inn sits at the head of a tranquil village on the edge of the North York Moors National Park. It makes an ideal pit-stop or base for walking, cycling and touring the moors – don't miss a trip on the nearby steam railway. Charles and Toby Wood have created an inviting atmosphere in the beamed bar, with its polished plank floor and roaring log fire, offering tip-top ales and hearty country cooking - maybe specials like loin of venison with dauphinoise potatoes or sea bass fillets with prawn and crayfish risotto, or steak and home-made chips.

**Open** all day all wk Closed: 25 Dec **Bar Meals** L served all wk 12-2 booking required D served all wk 6-8.30 booking required Av main course £11 **Restaurant** L served all wk 12-2 booking required D served all wk 6-8.30 booking required Av 3 course à la carte fr £19 ⊕ FREE HOUSE ◀ Black Sheep Best, Timothy Taylor Landlord, Crompton Brewery Yorkshire Moors, Yorkshire Warrior & Endeavour Ŏ Thatchers Gold. ♀ 12 **Facilities** Children's men Children's portions Dogs allowed Garden Parking

## LEYBURN
Map 19 SE19

### The Old Horn Inn

Spennithorne DL8 5PR ☎ 01969 622370
e-mail: desmond@furlong1706.fsbusiness.co.uk
dir: *From Leyburn on A684 approx 1.5m E. Turn right signed Spennithorne. From Bedale & A1 on A684 approx 9m W. Turn left signed Spennithorne*

Low beams and open log fires characterise this traditional 17th-century free house. The former farmhouse, which has been a pub for at least 100 years, is named after the horn that summoned the farmer's workers to lunch. Today's customers enjoy good food in the dining room. Expect local hog and hop sausages with mash and red onion marmalade; baked salmon with prawns and basil sauce; or roasted vegetable lasagne with garlic ciabatta bread.

**Open** Tue-Sun Closed: Mon (ex BH) ◀ Black Sheep Bitter & Special, John Smith's Cask, Worthington's Cream Flow. **Facilities** Dogs allowed Garden Notes ⊛

## PICK OF THE PUBS

### Sandpiper Inn

Market Place DL8 5AT
☎ 01969 622206 📠 01969 625367
e-mail: hsandpiper99@aol.com
dir: *From A1 take A684 to Leyburn*

Although it has been a pub for only 30 years, the building that houses the Sandpiper is the oldest in Leyburn, dating back to around 1640. Handy for Wensleydale and many other Yorkshire attractions, it has a beautiful summer garden. Inside is a bar and snug where you can enjoy a pint of Copper Dragon, or your pick from around 100 single malt whiskies. Chef/proprietor Jonathan Harrison will shortly be celebrating his tenth anniversary at the helm, during which time he has established an excellent reputation for preparing modern British food using the finest ingredients. So, head for the dining room to peruse the list of exciting and varied traditional and international dishes such as fillet of haddock wrapped in smoked salmon with roasted fennel, crispy duck leg with braised red cabbage, or Sandpiper fish pie. Lunch brings sandwiches such as the bookmaker (made with steak), or grilled chicken, beetroot and rocket. A Sunday lunch could begin with traditional fishcakes, to be followed by fillet of pork wrapped in Parma ham with roasted peppers and creamed pasta.

**Open** 11.30-3 6.30-11 (Sun noon-2.30 7-10.30) Closed: Mon & occasionally Tue **Bar Meals** L served all wk 12-2.30 **Restaurant** L served all wk 12-2.30 booking required D served all wk 6.30-9.30 booking required ⊕ FREE HOUSE ◀ Black Sheep Best, Black Sheep Special, Daleside, Copper Dragon, Archers. **Facilities** Children's menu Family room Dogs allowed Garden

## LITTON
Map 18 SD97

### Queens Arms ♀

BD23 5QJ ☎ 01756 770208
e-mail: info@queensarmslitton.co.uk
dir: *N of Skipton*

Surrounded by the beauty of the Yorkshire Dales, this is an ideal refreshment stop for everyone from walkers to potholers. This drover's inn dates from the 18th century and is full of original features including flagstones and beams. An open fire provides a warm winter welcome. The pub serves its own cask-conditioned ales, which are brewed on the premises, as well as fine wines and excellent home-cooked food made with ingredients from local farms.

**Open** noon-3 6.30-11.30 (Sun 7-11) Closed: Mon ◀ Litton Ale, Tetley Cask, guest ales Ŏ Stowford Press. ♀ 12 **Facilities** Family room Dogs allowed Garden Parking

## LONG PRESTON
Map 18 SD85

### Maypole Inn ♀

Maypole Green BD23 4PH
☎ 01729 840219 📠 01729 840727
e-mail: robert@maypole.co.uk
dir: *On A65 between Settle & Skipton*

Located at the edge of the Yorkshire Dales National Park, this inn has been welcoming visitors since 1695, when Ambrose Wigglesworth welcomed his first customers. Hand-drawn ales and traditional home cooking underpin the operation. Relax in the beamed dining room or cosy bars over a pint and a simple snack, sandwich, or cold platter; or try a hearty meal such as salmon and tuna fishcakes followed by local sausages or steak and ale pie. While outside seating provides great views of Long Preston Moor, the inn makes a good base for walking and cycling.

**Open** all day all wk **Bar Meals** L served Sun-Thu 12-9, Fri-Sat 12-9.30 food served all day **Restaurant** L served Mon-Fri 12-2.30, Sat-Sun all day D served Mon-Fri 6-9, Sat-Sun all day ⊕ ENTERPRISE INNS ◀ Timothy Taylor Landlord, Moorhouses Premier, Jennings, Cumberland, Copper Dragon, Bowland Beers Ŏ Westons 1st Quality, Westons Old Rosie. ♀ 11 **Facilities** Children's menu Children's portions Dogs allowed Garden Parking

Save on Hotels. Book at **theAA.com/hotel**

**YORKSHIRE, NORTH** 531 **ENGLAND**

## The Punch Bowl Inn ★★★★ INN ♀

DL11 6PF ☎ 01748 886233  📄 01748 886945
e-mail: info@pbinn.co.uk
dir: *A1 from Scotch Corner take A6108 to Richmond.
Through Richmond then right onto B6270 to Low Row*

Located in Swaledale with Wainwright's Coast to Coast
Walk on the doorstep, this stylish pub dates back to the
17th century. During a refurbishment a couple of years
ago, the bar and bar stools were hand-crafted by Robert
'The Mouseman' Thompson (see if you can spot the mice
around the bar). Typical food choices include pan-fried
mackerel with spiced lentils and spinach followed by
braised local lamb shank with redcurrant jus. Local cask
conditioned ales also feature. If you would like to stay
over for the Swaledale festivals in May and June, there
are stylish bedrooms available.

**Open** all day all wk 11am-mdnt Closed: 25 Dec
**Bar Meals** L served all wk 12-2 booking required D served
all wk 6.30-9 booking required Av main course £12.95
**Restaurant** L served all wk 12-2 booking required D
served all wk 6.30-9 booking required Av 3 course à la
carte fr £22.50 ⊕ FREE HOUSE ◀ Theakstons Best Bitter,
Black Sheep Best Bitter, Timothy Taylor's Landlord, Black
Sheep Riggwelter Ŏ Thatchers Gold. ♀ 13
**Facilities** Children's menu Children's portions Parking
**Rooms** 11

### PICK OF THE PUBS

## The Lister Arms ★★★★ INN ♀ NEW

BD23 4DB ☎ 01729 830330
e-mail: info@listerarms.co.uk
dir: *In town centre*

The Grade II-listed, ivy-clad coaching inn dates to the
1600s and stands on the village green in picture-
postcard Malham, just a short stroll beside the River
Aire to Malham's magnificent cove and limestone
pavement. Glorious Dales countryside and fabulous
walks (the Pennine Way cuts through the village)
surround the village, so explore and return at night in
winter to hunker down by the wood-burning stove in the
friendly, stone-walled bar or the cosy dining rooms. In
summer, spill out onto the cobbled terrace at the front
and refuel with a pint of Thwaites Lancaster Bomber
and hearty supper from the seasonal menu. Using local
suppliers, dishes range from starters of lamb faggot
with pea purée, root mash and mint gravy, or prawn

and smoked salmon timbale, to main courses like a
beef and ale shortcrust pastry pie, wild mushroom
risotto, and rib-eye steak with pepper sauce. In
addition, you'll find hot lunchtime sandwiches, roast
Sunday lunches, and nine refurbished en suite rooms,
with pretty fabrics, old pine and cast-iron beds, and
village or country views, plus activity breaks.

**Open** all day all wk **Bar Meals** L served Mon-Sat 12-3,
Sun all day D served Mon-Sat 6-9, Sun all day Av main
course £9.50 **Restaurant** L served Mon-Sat 12-3, Sun
all day D served Mon-Sat 6-9, Sun all day ⊕ THWAITES
INNS ◀ Thwaites Wainwright, Original, Bomber, Good
Elf, Nutty Black Ŏ Kingstone Press. ♀ 8
**Facilities** Children's menu Children's portions Dogs
allowed Garden Parking **Rooms** 9

## The Black Sheep Brewery

HG4 4EN
☎ 01765 680101  & 680100  📄 01765 689746
e-mail: sue.dempsey@blacksheep.co.uk
dir: *Off A6108, 9m from Ripon & 7m from Bedale*

The Black Sheep Brewery was founded in the early
nineties by Paul Theakston, of Masham's famous brewing
family. The complex boasts a visitor centre where you can
enjoy a 'shepherded' tour of the brewhouse, before
popping into the cosy bistro and 'baa...r' to sample the
ales. The beers also find their way into a range of hearty
dishes, including beer battered fish and chips and Black
Sheep ale sausages with mash.

**Open** all wk 10.30-4.30 (Thu-Sat 10.30-late)
**Bar Meals** food served all day **Restaurant** food served
all day ⊕ BLACK SHEEP BREWERY ◀ Black Sheep Best
Bitter, Riggwelter, Black Sheep Ale, Golden Sheep.
**Facilities** Children's menu Children's portions Family
room Garden Parking

## Kings Head Hotel ★★ HL ♀

Market Place HG4 4EF
☎ 01765 689295  📄 01765 689070
dir: *B6267 towards Masham, 7m from A1*

Overlooking Masham's large market square with its cross
and maypole, this tastefully renovated Georgian inn
boasts open fires in the public rooms and a pleasant
terrace for summer dining. Unwind over a pint of
Theakstons in the bar, or sample a range of traditional
and contemporary dishes in the wood panelled
restaurant. Options might include minted lamb shoulder

with creamy mash; chicken with thyme dumplings and
Savoy cabbage; and smoked salmon penne pasta.

**Open** all day all wk 10.30am-1am ◀ Theakstons Best
Bitter, Black Bull & Old Peculier, Theakstons XB, Black
Sheep. ♀ 14 **Facilities** Garden **Rooms** 27

## Black Swan Hotel

Market Place DL8 4NP
☎ 01969 622221  📄 01969 625086
dir: *Telephone for directions*

Backing onto Middleham Castle, home of Richard III, this
historic 17th-century pub is at the heart of Yorkshire's
racing country. Horses can be seen passing outside every
morning on their way to the gallops. The emphasis here is
on good food cooked by a skilled continental chef.
Choices run from bangers and mash to Kilnsey trout
roasted with parsley and thyme dressing. Fish and
seafood are a speciality.

**Open** all wk (all day summer & all wknds) **Bar Meals** L
served all wk 12-3 D served all wk 6-9.30 booking
required Av main course £6.95 **Restaurant** L served all
wk 12-3 D served all wk 6-9.30 booking required Av 3
course à la carte fr £20 ⊕ ENTERPRISE INNS ◀ John
Smith's, Theakstons Best Bitter, Old Peculier, Black
Sheep, Hambleton Stud. **Facilities** Children's
menu Children's portions Dogs allowed Garden

## The White Swan ♀

Market Place DL8 4PE
☎ 01969 622093  📄 01969 624551
e-mail: enquiries@whiteswanhotel.co.uk
dir: *From A1, take A684 towards Leyburn then A6108 to
Ripon, 1.5m to Middleham*

Middleham is within an hour's drive of five top
racecourses. No surprise then that this picturesque inn
overlooking the town's market square is steeped in the
history of the turf. A range of hand-pulled Yorkshire ales,
Thatchers cider and quality wines are served in the cosy
bar, all complementing classic brasserie cuisine: moules
marinières; home-made tagliatelle carbonara; chargrilled rib-eye steak with Café de Paris butter and home-
made chips. Desserts such as banoffee pie are all home
made too.

**Open** all day all wk 10.30am-11pm (mdnt at wknds)
**Bar Meals** Av main course £10.95 **Restaurant** L served
all wk 8am-9.30pm booking required D served all wk
8am-9.30pm booking required Fixed menu price fr £12.95
food served all day ⊕ FREE HOUSE ◀ Black Sheep Best,
John Smith's, Theakstons Ŏ Thatchers Gold. ♀ 9
**Facilities** Children's portions Family room Dogs allowed
Parking

## MIDDLESMOOR
Map 19 SE07

### Crown Hotel

**HG3 5ST** ☎ **01423 755204**
dir: *Telephone for directions*

Standing on a breezy 900ft hilltop with good views towards Gouthwaite Reservoir, the original building dates back to the 17th century. This pub is in an ideal spot for anyone following the popular Nidderdale Way. Visitors can enjoy a good pint of local beer by the cosy, roaring log fire, or in the sunny pub garden. A large selection of malt whisky is also on offer – for those who prefer something a little stronger.

**Open** all wk **Bar Meals** L served all wk 12-2 D served all wk 7-8.30 ⊕ FREE HOUSE ◀ Black Sheep Best, Guinness, Wensleydale Bitter. **Facilities** Dogs allowed Garden Parking

## MIDDLETON (NEAR PICKERING)
Map 19 SE78

### Fat Cactus @ The Middleton Arms

**Church Ln YO18 8PB** ☎ **01751 475444**
e-mail: themiddletonarms@aol.com
dir: *1m W of Pickering on A170*

Formerly known as the New Inn, the pub dates from the 17th century and retains much of its traditional charm. Chef proprietor Andy Green has rebranded the food side of the business, which now offers the Mexican-American flavours of a steak house and grill. So expect nachos, potato skins, melted cheese, sour cream, barbecue spare ribs, burgers, onion rings, sweet corn fritters and hand-cut chips. Top of the selections are rib-eye, sirloin or T-bone steaks cooked to your liking.

**Open** 6-11 (Sun noon-3 6-10.30) Closed: Mon **Bar Meals** Av main course £9 **Restaurant** D served Tue-Sun 6-9 ⊕ FREE HOUSE ◀ Timothy Taylor Landlord, John Smith's, Black Sheep, Camerons. **Facilities** Children's menu Children's portions Parking

## MOULTON
Map 19 NZ20

### Black Bull Inn

**DL10 6QJ** ☎ **01325 377289** ▤ **01325 377422**
e-mail: info@blackbullmoulton.com
dir: *1m S of Scotch Corner off A1, 5m from Richmond*

Old pews, settles and fresh flowers all lend character to this civilised free house. If you want more, try booking an evening table in 'Hazel', the pub's immaculate Pullman dining carriage that was built in 1932 for service on the Brighton Belle. The food is just as impressive, specialising in seafood. Lunchtime bar snacks include smoked salmon baguettes and Welsh rarebit with bacon, whilst evening choices range from wild bass on fennel purée to pan-fried liver with colcannon. Food and drink can be taken outside in warmer months.

**Open** noon-3 6-mdnt Closed: Sun eve **Bar Meals** L served Mon-Fri 12-2.30, Sat 12-2 Av main course £7 **Restaurant** L served Mon-Fri 12-2.30, Sun 12-4 booking required D served Mon-Thu 6.30-9.30, Fri-Sat 6.30-10 booking required Fixed menu price fr £16.95 Av 3 course à la carte fr £35 ⊕ FREE HOUSE ◀ Theakstons Best, John Smith's Smooth. **Facilities** Garden Parking

## MUKER
Map 18 SD99

### The Farmers Arms ♥

**DL11 6QG** ☎ **01748 886297** ▤ **01748 886375**
e-mail: dw.alderson@btconnect.com
dir: *From Richmond take A6108 towards Leyburn, turn right onto B6270*

The last remaining pub in the village of Muker, at the head of beautiful Swaledale, The Farmers Arms is understandably popular with walkers. A welcoming coal fire burns in the stone-flagged bar in cooler weather, while in summer the south facing patio is a relaxing place to sit and sup on a pint of Old Peculier. The award-winning ales are served along with good home-cooked food (the steak pie is a particular favourite). Dogs on leads are welcome in the bar.

**Open** all day all wk **Bar Meals** L served all wk 12-2.30 D served all wk 6-8.45 Av main course £9 ⊕ FREE HOUSE ◀ Theakstons Best, Old Peculier, John Smith's, Black Sheep, guest ales Ò Thatchers Gold. ♥ 9 **Facilities** Children's menu Children's portions Dogs allowed Garden Parking

## NUNNINGTON
Map 19 SE67

### The Royal Oak Inn ♥

**Church St YO62 5US**
☎ **01439 748271** ▤ **01439 748271**
dir: *Village centre, close to Nunnington Hall*

The sign on the front door says it all: 'Real ale, real food, real people'. This Grade II listed country inn welcomes with traditional decor, open fires in winter and fresh flowers in summer. Hearty home-cooked meals use locally reared meats, game from nearby estates, and fresh vegetables. Specials board examples are skate in black butter; pork fillet with cider and apple cream sauce; and sweet potato, carrot and Parlick Fell ewe's cheese tart.

**Open** 11.45-2.30 6.30-11 (Sun noon-2.30 7-11) Closed: Mon **Bar Meals** L served Tue-Sun 12-2 booking required Av main course £11.50 **Restaurant** D served Tue-Sun 6.30-9 ⊕ FREE HOUSE ◀ Black Sheep, Wold Top, John Smith's. ♥ 10 **Facilities** Children's menu Children's portions Dogs allowed Garden Parking

## OLDSTEAD
Map 19 SE57

### PICK OF THE PUBS

### The Black Swan ✩✩✩✩✩ RR ◉◉ ♥

*See Pick of the Pubs on opposite page*

## OSMOTHERLEY
Map 19 SE49

### PICK OF THE PUBS

### The Golden Lion

**6 West End DL6 3AA** ☎ **01609 883526**
e-mail: goldenlionosmotherley@yahoo.co.uk
dir: *Telephone for directions*

The Golden Lion is a cosy sandstone building of some 250 years standing. The atmosphere is warm and welcoming, with open fires and wooden flooring on one side of the downstairs area. Furnishings are simple with a wooden bar, bench seating and tables, whitewashed walls, mirrors and fresh flowers. The extensive menu ranges through basic pub grub to more refined dishes. The starters are divided between fish, soups, vegetarian, pastas and risottos, meat and salads, and might include smoked salmon; buffalo mozzarella with tomato and basil; spicy pork ribs; and avocado and king prawn salad. Mains are along the lines of grilled sea bass with new potatoes and peas; coq au vin; calves' liver with fried onions and mash; home-made beef burger with Mexican salsa; and spicy chilladas with fresh tomato sauce. Also interesting specials like pork stroganoff and rice, or lamb and feta lasagne. Sherry trifle, and bread and butter pudding with cream, are popular desserts.

**Open** 12-3 6-11 Closed: 25 Dec, Mon L, Tue L **Bar Meals** L served Wed-Sun 12-2.30 D served all wk 6-9 ⊕ FREE HOUSE ◀ Timothy Taylor Landlord, Yorkshire Dales Brewery, York Guzzler Ò Herefordshire Cider. **Facilities** Children's menu Dogs allowed Garden

### *Queen Catherine*

**7 West End DL6 3AG** ☎ **01609 883209**
e-mail: the_queen_catherine_hotel@hotmail.co.uk
dir: *Telephone for directions*

Nestling in the heart of a picturesque village, this traditional inn is believed to be the only one in Britain called 'Queen Catherine'. The name is a reference to Henry VIII's wife Catherine of Aragon, who reputedly left her horse and carriage here while sheltering from her husband in a nearby priory. There's no sense of menace around nowadays and visitors can enjoy comforting food, locally sourced where possible, such as crab-stuffed chicken breast, lamb shank with minted gravy and breaded Whitby scampi.

**Open** all wk ◀ Tetleys Smooth & Extra Cold, Tetleys Cask Bitter, guest ale. **Facilities** Dogs allowed

## PATELEY BRIDGE
Map 19 SE16

### PICK OF THE PUBS

### The Sportsmans Arms Hotel ♥

*See Pick of the Pubs on page 534*

# PICK OF THE PUBS

## The Black Swan at Oldstead ★★★★★ RR

### AA PUB OF THE YEAR FOR ENGLAND 2010-2011

**OLDSTEAD**  Map 19 SE57

near Coxwold YO61 4BL
☎ 01347 868387
e-mail:
enquiries@blackswanoldstead.co.uk
dir: *A1 junct 49, A168, A19 S. In 3m left for Coxwold, left for Byland Abbey, left for Oldstead. Pub on left*

The Black Swan, which dates from the 16th century, is owned and run by the Banks family, generations of whom have farmed in the village. It has a stunning location near Helmsley in the North York Moors National Park. The bar features a stone-flagged floor, an open log fire, antique furniture window seats, soft cushions and fittings by Robert 'Mousey' Thompson, in the 1930s a prolific maker of traditional handcrafted English oak furniture. Choice in here includes real ales, good wines by the glass, malt whiskies and vintage port, while food on offer changes with seasons and comes

mainly from local farms. Expect a light lunch of beer-battered haddock goujons with tartare sauce and dressed salad; parmesan risotto with tomato ragout, pak choi and tapenade, or indeed a pub classic, such as steak and chips; beef casserole; or salads and sandwiches.

The restaurant's comfortable, friendly feel is imparted by its oak floor, Persian rugs, antique furniture and soft light from traditional candles in old brass holders. On the menu are interesting starters of rabbit and vegetable soup; pan-fried mackerel with smoked eel remoulade; and ham hock and foie gras terrine with black pudding fritter. For a main course choose from fillet of turbot with beetroot risotto, red wine salsify and parsley and horseradish butter; shin of Aberdeen Angus beef with dauphinoise purée; or maybe free-range chicken breast with sage gnocchi, creamed Paris brown mushrooms, roast shallots and gem lettuce. Finish with a dessert that you won't find every day — baked Valrhona chocolate mousse with peanut butter ice cream and salted caramel, accompanied by a glass of equally hard to find Californian Elysium Black Muscat.

The superb newly appointed bedrooms are situated in a quiet south facing wing, each opening onto an individual terrace. They have solid oak floors and are furnished with quality antiques, stylish soft fabrics and paintings. Luxurious bathrooms include iron roll-top baths, walk-in wet-room shower areas and Moulton Brown toiletries. You are welcome to leave your vehicle in the car park while you are away on one of the walks which start from the pub — details are available at the bar.

**Open** noon-3 6-11 Closed: 1st 2wks Jan, Mon Tue & Wed L **Bar Meals** L served Thu-Sun 12-2 D served all wk 6-9 Av main course £12 **Restaurant** L served Thu-Sun 12-2 booking required D served all wk 6-9 booking required Av 3 course à la carte fr £32.50 ⊞ FREE HOUSE ◀ Black Sheep, Copper Dragon. ♟ 17 **Facilities** Children's menu Children's portions Garden Parking **Rooms** 4

# PICK OF THE PUBS

# The Sportsmans Arms Hotel ♀

**PATELEY BRIDGE**     Map 19 SE16

**Wath-in-Nidderdale HG3 5PP**
☎ **01423 711306**   📄 **01423 712524**
**dir:** *A59/B6451, hotel 2m N of Pateley
Bridge*

Wath is a conservation village,
picturesque and unspoilt, set in
beautiful Nidderdale, one of the loveliest
of the Yorkshire Dales. Ray and June
Carter have been running their 17th-
century restaurant, reached by a
packhorse bridge across the Nidd, for 30
years, although son Jamie and daughter
Sarah have leading roles too these days.
Enter the hallway and find open log
fires, comfortable chairs, a warm and
welcoming bar and a calm, softly lit
restaurant, dominated at one end by a
Victorian sideboard and substantial
wine rack.

As much of the food as possible is
locally sourced, but Ray has no qualms
about buying foreign produce if he
thinks it better. Fish arrives daily from
Whitby and other East Coast harbours
and will typically appear on the plate as
turbot with spinach and mousseline;
seared tuna with rocket salsa and Greek
salad; or maybe as lightly-cooked
halibut with beurre blanc glazed with
fresh Parmesan. Always a good choice
are the Nidderdale lamb, pork, beef,
fresh trout and game (season
permitting) from the moors. Best end of
Nidderdale lamb is perfectly
accompanied by creamy garlic mash,
natural jus and tomato concassée; and
chestnuts, cranberries and pancetta go
well with saddle of venison.

The wine list offers a wide selection of
styles and prices from traditional wine-
making areas, plus some new and
interesting examples. As well as fine
vintage ports, brandies and liqueurs, a
special interest in whiskies is shown
and some excellent Champagnes are
also available.

The Sportsmans Arms stands on the
53-mile, circular Nidderdale Way, hard
by the dam over the River Nidd (some
fishing rights belong to the hotel) that
creates Gouthwaite Reservoir.

**Open** all wk noon-2.30 6.30-11 Closed:
25 Dec **Bar Meals** L served all wk 12-2
D served all wk 7-9 **Restaurant** L served
Sun 12-2 D served Mon-Sat 7-9 🍺 FREE
HOUSE 🛢 Black Sheep, Worthingtons,
Timothy Taylor. ♀ 12 **Facilities** Garden
Parking

Save on Hotels. Book at **theAA.com/hotel**

YORKSHIRE, NORTH **535** ENGLAND

## PICK OF THE PUBS

### Fox & Hounds Country Inn ★★ HL ⊚

**Sinnington YO62 6SQ**
☎ 01751 431577   📠 01751 432791
e-mail: fox.houndsinn@btconnect.com
dir: *3m W of town, off A170 between Pickering & Helmsley*

This handsome 18th-century coaching inn lies in Sinnington, on a quiet road between Pickering and Kirkbymoorside. A gentle walk from the pub passes the village green to the pretty riverside where ducks swim in the shallows and an ancient packhorse bridge leads to more footpaths through the woods. Proprietors Andrew and Catherine Stephens and friendly efficient staff ensure a warm welcome. As you settle down with a pint of Theakstons or Black Sheep, you can relax and enjoy the oak-beamed ceilings, old wood panelling and open fires. The inn has ten well equipped en suite bedrooms, and a residents' lounge where guests can relax by the fire before dinner. The menu is full of locally farmed produce, and many of the starters are also available as main courses. Expect the likes of pan-crisp braised belly pork with ginger and honey noodles; Gressingham duck leg, roast beetroot and rocket; and Swaledale 'Old Peculiar' cheese soufflé.

**Open** all wk 12-2 6-11 (Sun 12-2 6-10.30) Closed: 25-26 Dec **Bar Meals** L served all wk 12-2 booking required D served all wk 6.30-9 booking required **Restaurant** L served all wk 12-2 booking required D served all wk 6.30-9 booking required ⊕ FREE HOUSE ◀ Theakstons Best, Black Sheep Special, Copper Dragon ♂ Thatchers Gold. **Facilities** Dogs allowed Garden Parking **Rooms** 10

### The Fox & Rabbit Inn ♥

**Whitby Rd, Lockton YO18 7NQ**
☎ 01751 460213   📠 01751 460052
e-mail: info@foxandrabbit.co.uk
dir: *From Pickering take A169 towards Whitby. Lockton in 5m*

Dating from the 18th century and originally known as Keld House, the pub sits at the edge of Dalby Forest with great views over the North York Moors. Brothers Charles and Toby Wood have been at the helm since 2004, and run a welcoming operation — lunch service has been extended to accommodate weary walkers, while over-60s

lunches and grill nights happen on Tuesdays. Order a Cropton ale and tuck in to plates of steak and Black Sheep ale pie, or braised lamb shank on creamy mash.

**Open** all day all wk Closed: 25 Dec **Bar Meals** L served all wk 12-4 D served all wk 5-8.30 Av main course £12 **Restaurant** L served all wk 12-4 D served all wk 5-8.30 Av 3 course à la carte fr £19 ⊕ FREE HOUSE ◀ Black Sheep Best, Timothy Taylor Landlord, Cropton Brewery Beers ♂ Thatchers Gold. ♥ 11 **Facilities** Children's menu Children's portions Dogs allowed Garden Parking

## PICK OF THE PUBS

### Nags Head Country Inn ★★★★ INN ⊚⊚ ♥

**YO7 4JG** ☎ 01845 567391   📠 01845 567212
e-mail: enquiries@nagsheadpickhill.co.uk
dir: *1m E of A1. 4m N of A1/A61 junct*

A magnificently traditional tap-room bar is a great opening gambit at this extended old coaching inn in a quiet Swale Valley village between the Dales and the Moors. Flagged and tiled floors, beams adorned with ties, wall benches and a magpie selection of tables and chairs tucked around open fires; racing prints and local snaps and a bar with wickets dispensing great Yorkshire beers tempts the passer-by to linger, whilst AA-listed accommodation allows an extended visit. A terrific menu is the icing on the cake here; a small but perfectly formed taproom menu offers cottage pie with cheese and leek mash or great pizzas and sandwiches. Move to the lounge or elegant restaurant and a worldly-wise choice is unleashed. Commence with wild rabbit and mushroom terrine with fig compote and Madeira jelly before upgrading to breasts of wood pigeon with winter greens, smoked bacon and prune sauce or poached North Sea halibut with caramelised endive and an olive oil sauce. Tempting, calorific puddings seal the deal.

**Open** all wk 11-11 (Sun 11-10.30) Closed: 25 Dec **Bar Meals** L served Mon-Sat 12-2, Sun 12-2.30 booking required D served Mon-Sat 6-9.30, Sun 6-9 booking required Av main course £11.95 **Restaurant** L served Mon-Sat 12-2, Sun 12-2.30 booking required D served Mon-Sat 6-9.30, Sun 6-9 booking required ⊕ FREE HOUSE ◀ Black Sheep Best, Old Peculier, Theakstons Best Bitter, Black Bull, York Brewery Guzzler ♂ Thatchers Gold. ♥ 8 **Facilities** Children's portions Garden Parking **Rooms** 15

### The Station Hotel

**TS15 0AE** ☎ 01642 700067
dir: *1.5m from A19*

'Hotel' by name only, this family-run and family-friendly village pub has been in the same hands for over 20 years. Offering fresh food at reasonable prices — even the chips are real and hand-cut — just about everything is home made from locally sourced produce and cooked to order. While the children enjoy the outdoor play area in the beer garden, parents can relax in front of the open fire and scan the extensive specials board over a pint of Black Sheep.

**Open** all wk 6-11.30 (Sat noon-2.30 6-11.30 Sun noon-4 6-11.30) **Bar Meals** L served Sat 12-2.30, Sun 12-4 booking required D served all wk Av main course £11 ⊕ FREE HOUSE ◀ Black Sheep Cask, Tetleys Smooth, Guinness, Timothy Taylor, Guest. **Facilities** Children's menu Children's portions Play area Garden Parking

## PICK OF THE PUBS

### Charles Bathurst Inn ★★★★ INN ♥

**Arkengarthdale DL11 6EN**
☎ 01748 884567   📠 01748 884599
e-mail: info@cbinn.co.uk
dir: *From A1 exit at Scotch Corner onto A6108, through Richmond, left onto B6270 to Reeth. At Buck Hotel right signed Langthwaite, pass church on right, inn 0.5m on right*

This enticing country inn stands on the flank of the most rugged and remote of the Yorkshire Dales, Arkengarthdale. Once at the heart of lead-mining country, this former miner's bunkhouse now caters for serious ramblers tackling The Pennine Way and the Coast-to-Coast route. Taking its name from the 18th-century lord of the manor and son of Oliver Cromwell's physician, roaring winter fires, low beamed rooms and antique pine furnishings offer escape from the rigours of the moors, whilst an AA rated range of 19 bedrooms may tempt other visitors to linger and enjoy the attractions of the area, including locations used in *All Creatures Great and Small*. The owners take particular pride on knowing the provenance of all their food, and the daily menu is written up on an imposing mirror hanging above a stone fireplace. Settle down with a pint of Landlord bitter and take the plunge with a

*continued*

**REETH** *continued*

goat's cheese pannacotta with beetroot carpaccio starter, the prelude to a main of wild duck breast, fondant potato, braised cabbage and orange sauce; the cooking style is a happy mix of old English and modern European. A decent bin of wines includes 12 by the glass

**Open** all wk 11am-mdnt Closed: 25 Dec **Bar Meals** L served all wk 12-2 booking required D served all wk 6.30-9 booking required Av main course £13.95 **Restaurant** L served all wk 12-2 booking required D served all wk 6.30-9 booking required Av 3 course à la carte fr £22.50 ⊕ FREE HOUSE ◀ Theakstons, Timothy Taylor Landlord, John Smith's Smooth, Black Sheep Best, Riggwelter. ☻ 12 **Facilities** Children's menu Children's portions Play area Garden Parking **Rooms** 19

## Laurel Inn

New Rd YO22 4SE ☎ 01947 880400
*dir: Telephone for directions*

Picturesque Robin Hood's Bay was once the haunt of smugglers who used a network of underground tunnels and secret passages to bring the booty ashore. Nowadays its the haunt of holidaymakers and walkers and the setting for this small, traditional pub which retains lots of character features, including beams and an open fire. The bar is decorated with old photographs, and an international collection of lager bottles.

**Open** all wk ⊕ FREE HOUSE ◀ Old Peculier, Theakstons Best, Deuchars IPA. **Facilities** Family room Dogs allowed **Notes** ⊛

## The Anvil Inn ☻

Main St YO13 9DY ☎ 01723 859896
e-mail: theanvilinnsawdon@btinternet.com
web: www.theanvilinnsawdon.co.uk
*dir: 1.5m N of Brompton-by-Sawdon, on A170 8m E of Pickering & 6m W of Scarborough*

Set on the edge of Dalby Forest, this is a walkers' and birdwatchers' paradise. It was a working forge for over 200 years until 1985; many artefacts remain, including the original furnace. An excellent range of local ales and ciders are always available. Local produce, nicely handled and well priced, appears in dishes such as beetroot cured

salmon with cucumber relish, herbed crème fraîche and red chard and rocket salad; or daube of beef, slow braised in red wine with shallot marmalade and buttery mash. Two self-catering cottages are available.

**Open** 12-2.30 6.30-11 Closed: 26 Dec & 1 Jan, Mon **Bar Meals** L served Tue-Sat 12-2, Sun 12-3 booking required D served Tue-Sat 6.30-9 booking required Av main course £13.75 **Restaurant** L served Tue-Sat 12-2, Sun 12-3 booking required D served Tue-Sat 6.30-9 booking required Av 3 course à la carte fr £24.50 ⊕ FREE HOUSE ◀ Daleside Blonde, Copper Dragon, Wold Top, Daleside Old Leg Over, Northumberland Brewery ☼ Stowford Press. ☻ 11 **Facilities** Children's portions Dogs allowed Garden Parking

## The Sawley Arms ☻

HG4 3EQ ☎ 01765 620642
e-mail: junehawes1@aol.co.uk
*dir: A1(M) junct 47, A59 to Knaresborough, B6165 to Ripley, A61 towards Ripon, left for Sawley. Or from Ripon B6265 towards Pateley Bridge, left to Sawley. Pub 1m from Fountains Abbey*

Just a mile from Fountains Abbey, this delightful 200-year-old pub was a frequent haunt of the late author and vet James Herriot. Run by the same owners for 41 years, it is big on old world charm and is surrounded by its own stunning award-winning gardens. The menu is modern British yet varied, with dishes ranging from salmon three ways to pork, sage and apricot cassoulet with cider, leeks, smoked bacon, mushrooms and cannelloni beans. Look out for various promotions and offers.

**Open** 11.30-3 6-10.30 Closed: 25 Dec, Mon eve in winter **Bar Meals** L served all wk 12-2.30 booking required D served all wk 6.30-9.30 booking required Av main course £10.45 **Restaurant** L served all wk 12-2.30 booking required D served all wk 6.30-9.30 booking required Av 3 course à la carte fr £16 ⊕ FREE HOUSE ◀ Theakston Best, John Smith's. ☻ 12 **Facilities** Children's portions Garden Parking

### PICK OF THE PUBS

## The Hare Inn ⊛ ☻

YO7 2HG ☎ 01845 597769
e-mail: info@thehareinn.co.uk
*dir: Telephone for directions*

Built in the 13th century and allegedly used as a brewhouse by the monks who built Rievaulx Abbey, the Hare also boasts a friendly ghost! Later, in the 17th century, ale was brewed here for local iron workers. Inside, you'll find low-beamed ceilings and flagstone floors, a wood-burning stove offering a warm welcome in the bar, and an old-fashioned kitchen range in the dining area. Eating here promises food of AA Rosette standard, with the kitchen ringing the changes according to availability of locally sourced ingredients.

The full à la carte menu is complemented by light lunch and early bird options, offering quality dining at value prices. A representative choice might start with roast goat's cheese in filo pastry with pine nuts and basil dressing; continuing with pan-fried breast of guinea fowl with tarragon mousse and wild mushrooms; and finishing with passionfruit crème brûlée.

**Open** Tue-Sun L Closed: Mon, Sun eve **Bar Meals** L served Tue-Sat 12-2, Sun 12-4 Av main course £14.50 **Restaurant** L served Tue-Sat 12-2, Sun 12-4 booking required D served Tue-Sat 6-9 booking required Av 3 course à la carte fr £35 ⊕ FREE HOUSE ◀ Black Sheep, Timothy Taylor Landlord, guest ales ☼ Thatchers. ☻ 10 **Facilities** Children's portions Garden Parking

## Golden Lion ☻

Duke St BD24 9DU ☎ 01729 822203 ▤ 01729 824145
e-mail: info@goldenlion.yorks.net
*dir: Telephone for directions*

This traditional Dales coaching inn has been the silent witness to incalculable comings and goings in Settle's market place since around 1640. Its cosy bars, open fire, commodious restaurant and comfy bedrooms often meet the needs of travellers on the spectacular Settle-Carlisle railway line. There is a good choice of beers and a strong emphasis on food prepared from fresh ingredients, with specials such as moules marinière, Moroccan lamb curry and vegetable stirfry.

**Open** all day all wk 11-11 (Sun noon-10.30) **Bar Meals** L served Mon-Fri 12-2.30 Sat 12-10, Sun 12-9.30 D served Mon-Thu 6-9.30, Fri 6-10, Sat 12-10, Sun 12-9.30 ⊕ DANIEL THWAITES PLS ◀ Thwaites Bitter, Bomber, Guest ales ☼ Kingston Press. ☻ 9 **Facilities** Parking

## Devonshire Arms

Grassington Rd, Cracoe BD23 6LA ☎ 01756 730237
e-mail: info@devonshirecrawe.co.uk
*dir: Telephone for directions*

This convivial, caringly renovated 17th-century inn was the original setting for the Rhylstone Ladies WI calendar. Conveniently located for the Three Peaks, it has excellent views of Rhylstone Fell. In the hands of experienced licensees, your will find character, quality and service here. A wide range of cask ales plus extensive wine list will wash down a menu that runs from local sausages with baby Yorkshire puddings and home-made gravy to fillet of monkfish finished with a grapefruit and star anise cream.

**Open** all wk **Bar Meals** L served Mon-Sat 12-2 D served Sun 12-7 Av main course £9 **Restaurant** L served Mon-Sat 12-2 booking required D served Sun 12-7 booking required Av 3 course à la carte fr £20 ⊕ Marstons ◀ Jennings, Jennings Cumberland, Pedigree. **Facilities** Children's menu Children's portions Play area Dogs allowed Garden Parking

Save on Hotels. Book at theAA.com/hotel

YORKSHIRE, NORTH 537 ENGLAND

## SNAINTON
Map 17 SE98

# Coachman Inn ☕

Pickering Road West YO13 9PL
☎ 01723 859231  📠 01723 850008
e-mail: info@coachmaninn.co.uk
web: www.coachmaninn.co.uk
dir: *5m from Pickering, off A170 onto B1258*

This imposing Grade II listed Georgian coaching inn was once the last staging post before Scarborough for the York mail. Food is served in the romantic candlelit restaurant, cosy lounge or rustic bar with its blazing log fire. Traditional beers and a wide selection of wines by the glass are available. Typical dishes include seared king scallops with crispy pancetta and artichoke purée followed by local calves' liver with a roasted shallot tart and pancetta jus. Outside is a large lawned area with flowers, trees and seating.

**Open** 12-3 6-11 Closed: Mon **Bar Meals** L served all wk 12-3 D served all wk 6.30-9 **Restaurant** L served all wk 12-3 booking required D served all wk 6.30-9 booking required Av 3 course à la carte fr £25 ⊕ FREE HOUSE ◀ John Smith's, Wold Top, Guinness. ☕ 15 **Facilities** Children's menu Garden Parking

## STARBOTTON
Map 18 SD97

# Fox & Hounds Inn ☕

BD23 5HY ☎ 01756 760269  & 760367
e-mail: starbottonfox@aol.com
dir: *Telephone for directions*

Situated in a picturesque limestone village in Upper Wharfedale in the heart of the Yorkshire Dales, this ancient pub was originally built as a private house, but has been a pub for more than 160 years. Make for the cosy bar, with its solid furnishings and flagstones, and enjoy a pint of Black Sheep or one of the ten wines served by the glass. The menu offers steak and ale pie, minted lamb shank, pork medallions in brandy and mustard sauce, and a selection of steaks.

**Open** noon-3 6-11 (Sun noon-3.30 5.30-10.30) Closed: 1-22 Jan, Mon **Bar Meals** L served all wk 12-2.30 D served Mon-Sat 6-9, Sun 5.30-8 Av main course £9 ⊕ FREE HOUSE ◀ Black Sheep, Timothy Taylor Landlord, Moorhouse, guest ales ↻ Thatchers Gold. ☕ 10 **Facilities** Garden Parking

## SUTTON-ON-THE-FOREST
Map 19 SE56

### PICK OF THE PUBS

# The Blackwell Ox
# Inn
INN ⊛ ☕

Huby Rd YO61 1DT
☎ 01347 810328  📠 01347 812738
e-mail: enquiries@blackwelloxinn.co.uk
dir: *A1237 onto B1363 to Sutton-on-the-Forest. Left at T-junct, 50yds on right*

Named after a magnificent beast weighing 2,278 pounds and slaughtered in 1779, some 40 years before the building, a house for a Mrs Mary Shepherd, was started. Today's Blackwell Ox blends modern elegance with period charm; visitors will find hand-pulled ales and an open fire in the bar, as well as a terrace for the warmer months. The chef believes in simple, honest cooking, and sources local North Yorkshire produce to create his dishes. Substantial 'knife and fork' sandwiches appear at lunchtime, alongside a short but well-considered menu that might include starters of duck scotch egg with warm bread and fruit chutney; sautéed mushrooms on toast with a soft poached egg; and seared pigeon breast with beetroot salsa. Half a dozen main courses may offer venison rack served pink; pheasant breast wrapped in bacon; and braised leek and blue cheese tart with grape and walnut salad. Just seven miles from the centre of York, the inn also offers comfortable, individually designed bedrooms.

**Open** all wk noon-3 5.30-11 (Sun noon-10.30) Closed: 25 Dec, 1 Jan **Bar Meals** L served all wk 12-2 D served all wk 6-9.30 Av main course £12.95 **Restaurant** L served all wk 12-2 D served all wk 6-9.30 Av 3 course à la carte fr £25 ⊕ FREE HOUSE ◀ Black Sheep, John Smith's Cask, Guinness, Timothy Taylor Landlord, Copper Dragon. ☕ 14 **Facilities** Children's menu Children's portions Garden Parking **Rooms** 7

## TERRINGTON
Map 19 SE67

# The Bay Horse Inn (The Storyteller Brewery) ☕ NEW

Main St YO60 6PP ☎ 01653 648416
e-mail: rob@thestorytellerb.plus.com
dir: *From Malton take unclassified road W (8m) through Coneysthorpe, pass turn for Castle Howard, through Ganthorpe & on to Terrington*

On the edge of the North York Moors in an unspoiled village, this 17th-century pub is home to The Storyteller Brewery, set up by landlord Robert Frankin in 2008. Expect to sup a tip-top pint of Genesis by the crackling log fire in the cosy lounge bar, or in the conservatory dining, which is adorned with old farm tools. If tempted to sample the Telltale ale, then accompany it with a plate of home-cooked food, perhaps the chicken and ham pie, or go the whole hog and order the sirloin steak, served with oven-roasted tomatoes and hand-cut chips.

**Open** Mon-Tue 5.30-11, Wed-Thu noon-2 5.30-11, Fri noon-3 5.30-11, Sat noon-11, Sun noon-7.30 Closed: Mon L, Tue L **Bar Meals** L served Wed-Sun 12-3 D served Wed-Sun 5.30-9 **Restaurant** L served Wed-Sun 12-3 D served Wed-Sat 5.30-9 booking required ⊕ THE STORYTELLER BREWERY ◀ Storyteller Genesis, 1402, Telltale. ☕ 8 **Facilities** Children's menu Children's portions Dogs allowed Garden Parking

## THORNTON LE DALE
Map 19 SE88

# The New Inn

Maltongate YO18 7LF ☎ 01751 474226
e-mail: enquire@the-new-inn.com
dir: *A64 N from York towards Scarborough. At Malton take A169 to Pickering. At Pickering rdbt right onto A170, 2m, pub on right*

An old Georgian coaching house dating back to 1720, this attractive family-run pub stands at the heart of a picturesque village complete with stocks and a market cross. The old world charm of the location is echoed inside the bar and restaurant, with real log fires and exposed beams. Enjoy well kept Theakston Black Bull and guest ales, bitters, lagers and wines and tuck into freshly cooked home-made burgers, steaks or a casserole of Whitby haddock, king prawns and asparagus.

**Open** all wk 12-2.30 5-11 (summer all day) **Bar Meals** L served Mon-Sat 12-2, Sun 12-2.30 booking required D served Mon-Sat 6-8.30, Sun 6.30-8.30 booking required **Restaurant** L served Mon-Sat 12-2, Sun 12-2.30 booking required D served Mon-Sat 6-8.30, Sun 6.30-8.30 booking required ⊕ SCOTTISH & NEWCASTLE ◀ Theakston Black Bull, guest ales. **Facilities** Children's menu Children's portions Dogs allowed Garden Parking

## THORNTON WATLASS
Map 19 SE28

### PICK OF THE PUBS

# The Buck Inn ★★★ INN
*See Pick of the Pubs on page 538*

## TOPCLIFFE
Map 19 SE37

# The Angel Inn ☕

YO7 3RW ☎ 01845 577237  📠 01845 578000
e-mail: kevin@topcliffeangelinn.co.uk
dir: *On A168(M), 3m from A1*

A refurbishment has given this old country inn a more contemporary feel, but with more than a nod to tradition. The restaurant has a good local reputation for creative dishes such as fillet of red mullet with warm potato, celeriac and beetroot salad; pheasant pot au feu with stuffed cabbage and spätzle; and, for two, seafood casserole under puff pastry.

**Open** all day all wk 9am-11pm (Fri-Sat 9am-mdnt) ◀ John Smith's, Black Sheep, Timothy Taylor. ☕ 8 **Facilities** Dogs allowed Garden Parking

# PICK OF THE PUBS

## The Buck Inn ★★★INN

**THORNTON WATLASS**  Map 19 SE28

**HG4 4AH**
☎ 01677 422461  📄 01677 422447
e-mail: innwatlass1@btconnect.com
dir: *From A1 at Leeming Bar take A684 to Bedale, then B6268 towards Masham. Village 2m on right, by cricket green*

A traditional, well run, friendly institution that has been in experienced hands of Michael and Margaret Fox for over 20 years, who have no trouble in maintaining its welcoming and relaxed atmosphere. The inn doesn't just overlook the village green and cricket pitch; players score four runs for hitting the pub wall, and six if the ball goes over the roof! Very much the quintessential village scene in beautiful Thornton Watlass, Bedale is where Wensleydale, gateway to the Yorkshire

Dales National Park, begins, and this glorious area is where much of the television programme *Heartbeat* was filmed.

There are three separate dining areas - the bar for informality, the restaurant for dining by candlelight, and on busy days the large function room is opened. The menu ranges from traditional, freshly prepared pub fare to exciting modern cuisine backed by daily changing blackboard specials. Typical bar favourites are Masham rarebit (Wensleydale cheese with local ale topped with bacon and served with pear chutney); steak and ale pie; oven-baked lasagne; lamb cutlets with rosemary and redcurrant sauce; and beer-battered fish and chips. Hearty and wholesome daily specials may take in seared scallops with frizzy salad and five spice sauce; prawn and crab tian with a herb and lemon mayonnaise; or smoked duck salad. Main courses include dishes like grilled smoked haddock with buttery mash, saffron cream and crisp onion rings; salmon fillet with buttered noodles and tomato

and garlic sauce; venison sausages with Lyonnaise potatoes and rosemary gravy; or pan-fried duck breast with stir fry vegetables and hoi sin sauce.

Beer drinkers have a choice of five real ales pulled from handpumps, including Masham-brewed Black Sheep, while whisky drinkers have a selection of some forty different malts to try, ideal when relaxing by the real coal fire, and there's live jazz music most Sunday lunchtimes. Cottage-style bedrooms provide a comfortable night's sleep.

**Open** all wk 11-mdnt Closed: 25 Dec eve **Bar Meals** L served Mon-Sat 12-2, Sun 12-3 D served all wk 6.30-9.30 **Restaurant** L served Mon-Sat 12-2, Sun 12-3 D served all wk 6.30-9.30 ⊕ FREE HOUSE ◀ Black Sheep Best, 3 guest ales Ö Thatchers Gold. **Facilities** Children's menu Play area Family room Dogs allowed Garden Parking **Rooms** 7

## WASS　　　　　Map 19 SE57

### PICK OF THE PUBS

*Wombwell Arms* 🍷

*See Pick of the Pubs on page 540*

## WEAVERTHORPE　　　　Map 17 SE97

### PICK OF THE PUBS

### The Star Country Inn

YO17 8EY ☎ 01944 738273 📠 01944 738273
e-mail: starinn.malton@btconnect.com
dir: *From Malton take A64 towards Scarborough. 12m, at Sherburn right at lights. Weaverthorpe 4m, inn opposite junct*

The Star is an ideal base for visiting local attractions such as Castle Howard, and the area is also popular with cyclists and bird-watchers. Situated in the village of Weaverthorpe in the heart of the Yorkshire Wolds, the 200-year-old inn has a rustic interior with large winter fires and a welcoming, convivial atmosphere. Owners Eddie and Benji are approaching their third anniversary in charge, during which time they have redecorated, installed new carpets and light fittings, replaced the windows, and restored the bar. Here Theakstons is the major real ale on tap, alongside beers from Wold Top and John Smith's. Food is fresh and locally sourced where possible, and pride is taken in everything from fresh-baked breads to home-made tomato ketchup. A meal might include roast pumpkin soup to start, fresh Whitby breaded scampi with hand-cut chips or Yorkshire beef and beer pie to follow, and a dessert from the blackboard.

**Open** all wk Mon-Thu 6-mdnt (Fri-Sun noon-2 6-mdnt) **Bar Meals** L served Fri-Sun 12-2 booking required D served all wk 6-9 booking required Av main course £8 **Restaurant** L served Fri-Sun 12-2 booking required D served all wk 6-9 booking required Fixed menu price fr £8 Av 3 course à la carte fr £15 ⊕ FREE HOUSE ◀ Bitter, John Smith's, Wold Top, Theakston. **Facilities** Children's menu Children's portions Garden Parking

## WEST BURTON　　　　Map 19 SE08

### Fox & Hounds

DL8 4JY ☎ 01969 663111 📠 01969 663279
web: www.fhinn.co.uk
dir: *A468 between Hawes & Leyburn, 0.5m E of Aysgarth*

In a beautiful Dales setting, The Fox and Hounds is a traditional pub, overlooking the village green, which has swings and football goals for children, and its own hidden waterfalls. A proper local, the pub hosts men's and women's darts teams and a dominoes team. In summer customers play quoits out on the green. Real ales, some from The Black Sheep Brewery down the road, and home-made food prepared from fresh ingredients are served. Dishes include chicken curry, steak and kidney pie, lasagne, steaks and other pub favourites.

*Fox & Hounds*

**Open** all day all wk **Bar Meals** L served all wk 12-2 D served all wk 6-8.30 Av main course £7.95 **Restaurant** L served all wk 12-2 booking required D served all wk 6-8.30 booking required ⊕ FREE HOUSE ◀ Black Sheep, John Smith's, Theakstons Best, Copper Dragon. **Facilities** Family room Dogs allowed Parking

## WEST TANFIELD　　　　Map 19 SE27

### PICK OF THE PUBS

### The Bruce Arms 🍷

Main St HG4 5JJ ☎ 01677 470325
e-mail: brucefarms1@btconnect.com
dir: *On A6108 between Ripon & Masham*

The Bruce Arms is an 1820 stone-built house situated in the heart of a pretty village that sits beside the River Ure on the edge of the Yorkshire Dales. The pub has seen a change of hands and the new owners, David Stead and Hugh Carruthers, experienced in the hospitality trade, are making their mark. Its bistro-style interior exudes charm with traditional exposed beams, log fires and candles on the tables. A good wine list, real ales and the new menus from Hugh using the best of local produce are proving a hit. A handy area for visiting the races at both Ripon and Thirsk, and visiting famous sights such as Fountains Abbey. This pub is one to watch.

**Open** 12-2.30 6-9.30 (Sun 12-3.30) Closed: Mon **Bar Meals** food served all day **Restaurant** food served all day ⊕ FREE HOUSE ◀ Black Sheep Bitter Ale, guest ales ♻ Aspall. 🍷 10 **Facilities** Dogs allowed Garden Parking

## WHASHTON　　　　Map 19 NZ10

### Hack & Spade

DL11 7JL ☎ 01748 823721
e-mail: info@hackandspade.com
dir: *From Scotch Corner A66 W towards Penrith for 5m. Left exit towards Ravensworth, follow for 2m. Left at x-rds for Whashton*

There are fantastic views over Holmedale and the surrounding area from this pub which sits amid rolling hills in the heart of North Yorkshire. Its name relates to the quarry that used to be opposite; nowadays it has been filled in to form part of the village green. The menu is built on local ingredients and is chalked on the board every day and might include local venison and Swaledale

lamb. Desserts are all home made including the ice cream.

**Open** all wk 6.30-11.30 **Restaurant** D served all wk 6.30-8.45 ⊕ FREE HOUSE ◀ John Smith's Smooth, Theakstons. **Facilities** Children's portions Parking

## WHITBY　　　　Map 19 NZ81

### The Magpie Café 🍷

14 Pier Rd YO21 3PU
☎ 01947 602058 📠 01947 601801
e-mail: ian@magpiecafe.co.uk
dir: *Telephone for directions*

More a licensed restaurant than a pub, the award-winning Magpie has been the home of North Yorkshire's best-ever fish and chips since the late 1930s. You could pop in for a pint of Cropton, but the excellent views of the harbour from the dining room, together with the prospect of fresh seafood, could prove too much of a temptation. Up to ten fish dishes are served daily, perhaps including Whitby cullen skink; and Scarborough woof (a type of catfish) with chips.

**Open** all day all wk Closed: 1-21 Jan **Bar Meals** L served all wk 11.30-9pm D served all wk 11.30-9pm Av main course £9 food served all day **Restaurant** Av 3 course à la carte fr £20 food served all day ⊕ FREE HOUSE ◀ Crompton, Scoresby Bitter, Tetley Bitter. 🍷 10 **Facilities** Children's menu Children's portions

## WIGGLESWORTH　　　　Map 18 SD85

### The Plough Inn

BD23 4RJ ☎ 01729 840243 📠 01729 840638
e-mail: plough.inn.wigglesworth@gmail.com
dir: *From A65 between Skipton & Long Preston take B6478 to Wigglesworth*

Dating back to 1720, the bar of this traditional country free house features oak beams and an open fire. There are fine views of the surrounding hills from the conservatory restaurant, where the pub's precarious position on the Yorkshire/Lancashire border is reflected in a culinary 'War of the Roses'. Yorkshire pudding with beef casserole challenges Lancashire hotpot and pickled red cabbage - the latest score is published beside the daily blackboard specials!

**Open** Tue-Sun Closed: Mon **Bar Meals** L served Tue-Sat 12-2, Sun 12-8.30 D served Tue-Sat 6-9, Sun 12-8.30 ⊕ FREE HOUSE **Facilities** Children's portions Parking

# PICK OF THE PUBS

## Wombwell Arms ♀

**WASS**        Map 19 SE57

**YO61 4BE**
☎ **01347 868280**
e-mail: wombwellarms@btconnect.com
web: www.wombwellarms.co.uk
dir: *From A1 take A168 to A19 junct. Take York exit, then left after 2.5m, left at Coxwold to Ampleforth. Wass 2m*

Ian and Eunice Walker run this character country pub on the southern edge of the North York Moors National Park. The surroundings are breathtaking, but function completely outweighed good views when it was built as a granary around 1620, using stones from the ruins of nearby Byland Abbey. It became an alehouse a couple of decades later.

There are two oak-beamed, flagstone-floored bars, one with a huge inglenook fireplace, the other with a wood-burning stove, and, in the latter, dogs are welcome to sprawl contentedly across the floor, while the human clientele — locals, walkers, cyclists and parents of students at nearby Ampleforth College — chat away over their glasses of wine and pints of Timothy Taylor Landlord, Theakston's Best or Old Peculier.

High quality, freshly prepared meals available in Poachers bar and the two restaurants are made from North Yorkshire produce as far as possible. Light lunches include filled ciabattas and granary bread sandwiches, salads, ploughman's and smoked salmon and scrambled eggs. On the easy-to-take-in menu appear starters of crab and ginger cakes with lime and chilli marmalade; and twice-baked cheese soufflé as starters; to follow could come grilled salmon fillet; smoked haddock risotto; roast Gressingham duck breast; Stilton chicken breast; Poacher's casserole; or open lasagne with flageolet beans. Then there are the Wombwell Classics of Wass steak, Guinness and mushroom pie; Masham pork and apple sausages; and real ale-battered haddock, chips and mushy peas.

Recent weekly specials included Yorkshire lamb casserole with parsley dumpling; South African beef sausage (boerewors); and liver and bacon. Children's lunches of home-made fish fingers, pizza Margherita, beef burger or pasta bolognaise with salad, all include a dessert of ice cream.

**Open** all wk noon-3 6-11 (Sat noon-11 Sun noon-4 6-10.30) **Bar Meals** L served Mon-Fri 12-2, Sat 12-2.30, Sun 12-3 D served Mon-Thu 6.30-9, Fri-Sat 6.30-9.30, Sun 6.30-8.30 Av main course £11 **Restaurant** L served Mon-Fri 12-2, Sat 12-2.30, Sun 12-3 booking recommended D served Mon-Thu 6.30-9, Fri-Sat 6.30-9.30 Sun 6.30-8.30 booking recommended Av 3 course à la carte fr £18 ⊕ FREE HOUSE ◂ Timothy Taylor Landlord, Best, Theakston Best, Theakston Old Peculier. ♀ 9
**Facilities** Children's menu Dogs allowed Garden Parking

## YORK                                Map 16 SE65

### PICK OF THE PUBS

## Blue Bell

**53 Fossgate YO1 9TF ☎ 01904 654904**
e-mail: robsonhardie@aol.com
**dir:** In city centre

Its narrow frontage makes it easy to miss, but don't walk past this charming pub – the smallest in York – which has been serving customers in the ancient heart of the city for 200 years. In 1903 it was given a typical Edwardian makeover, and since then almost nothing has changed - this includes the varnished wall and ceiling panelling, the two cast-iron tiled fireplaces, and the old settles. The layout is original too, with the taproom at the front and the snug down a long corridor at the rear, both with servery hatches. Quite fittingly, the whole interior is now Grade II listed. The only slight drawback is that the pub's size leaves no room for a kitchen, so don't expect anything more complicated than sandwiches. However, there's a good selection of real ales: no fewer than six are usually on tap, including rotating guests. The pub has won awards for its efforts in fund-raising.

**Open** all day all wk **Bar Meals** L served Mon-Sat 12-2.30 ⊕ PUNCH TAVERNS ◀ Deuchars IPA, Timothy Taylor Landlord, Adnams Bitter, Abbot Greene King, Tetleys Dark Mild ♂ Westons Traditional. **Facilities** Dogs allowed **Notes** ⊕

## Lysander Arms ♥

**Manor Ln, Shipton Rd YO30 5TZ ☎ 01904 640845**
e-mail: christine@lysanderarms.co.uk
**dir:** Telephone for directions

The Lysander Arms is a recently constructed pub built on the site of an old RAF airfield – hence the name – Lysander aircraft were stationed here during World War II. The contemporary feel of the pub's interior includes a long, fully air-conditioned bar with modern furnishings, brick-built fireplace and large-screen TV. Dishes on the summer menu include pan roasted calves liver; fish pie; veal escalope; mint crusted rack of lamb; and pan fried sea bass.

**Open** all day all wk **Bar Meals** L served all wk 12-2 D served all wk 5-9 Av main course £9 **Restaurant** L served all wk 12-2 D served all wk 5-9 ⊕ FREE HOUSE ◀ John Smith's Cask, John Smith's Smooth, Yorkshire Guzzler, Copper Dragon ♂ Koppaberg. ♥ 8 **Facilities** Children's menu Children's portions Play area Dogs allowed Garden Parking

## YORKSHIRE, SOUTH

### BRADFIELD                           Map 16 SK29

## The Strines Inn ♥

**Bradfield Dale S6 6JE ☎ 0114 2851247**
**dir:** N off A57 between Sheffield & Manchester

Overlooking Strines Reservoir and nestled amid the breathtaking moorland scenery of the Peak District National Park, this popular free house feels a world away from nearby Sheffield but is in fact within its border. Although it was built as a manor house in the 13th century, most of the present building is 16th century. It has been an inn since 1771. Traditional home-made fare ranges from giant Yorkshire puddings with a choice of fillings to pie of the day and grills. Look out for the peacocks in the garden.

**Open** all wk 10.30-3 5.30-11 (Sat-Sun 10.30am-11pm all day Apr-Oct) Closed: 25 Dec **Bar Meals** L served Mon-Fri 12-2.30 Sat-Sun 12-9 summer 12-9 D served Mon-Fri 5.30-9 Sat-Sun 12-9 summer 12-9 Av main course £8.70 ⊕ FREE HOUSE ◀ Marston's Pedigree, Kelham Island, Mansfield Cask, Bradfield Bitter, Old Speckled Hen. ♥ 10 **Facilities** Children's menu Children's portions Play area Dogs allowed Garden Parking

### CADEBY                              Map 16 SE50

### PICK OF THE PUBS

## Cadeby Inn

**Main St DN5 7SW ☎ 01709 864009**
e-mail: info@cadebyinn.co.uk
**dir:** Telephone for directions

This was a farmhouse before conversion into a picturesque whitewashed pub with stone-walled traditional bar; the restaurant is more contemporary, furnished with stylish yet comfortable chairs. Sandstone walls enclose the large front garden, while a patio and smaller garden lie to the rear; these are ideal places to relax with a pint from the local Wentworth brewery or a meal if the weather is warm enough. All dishes are freshly prepared on site from Yorkshire produce if possible; soups and stocks, sauces and desserts are all home made. The lunch menu offers interesting sandwiches such as chicken, bacon and poached egg; or steak and caramelised onion. Classic plates include game sausages; steak and ale pie; chicken chasseur; and tagliatelle carbonara. The à la carte menu may include roasted pheasant breasts, or pan-fried haunch of venison. Desserts range from individual fruit trifle to creamed rice pudding with spiced plums.

**Open** all wk noon-11 **Bar Meals** L served all wk 12-5.30 **Restaurant** L served Tue-Sat 12-2.30, Sun 12-8 D served Tue-Sat 5.30-9.30, Sun 12-8 Fixed menu price fr £9.95 Av 3 course à la carte fr £15 ⊕ FREE HOUSE ◀ John Smith's Cask, Black Sheep Best Bitter, Guinness. **Facilities** Children's menu Children's portions Garden Parking

### DONCASTER                           Map 16 SE50

## Waterfront Inn

**Canal Ln, West Stockwith DN10 4ET ☎ 01427 891223**
**dir:** From Gainsborough take either A159 N, then minor road to village. Or A631 towards Bawtry/Rotherham, right onto A161, then onto minor road

Built in the 1830s overlooking the Trent Canal basin and the canal towpath, the pub is now popular with walkers and visitors to the nearby marina. Real ales and good value food are the order of the day, including pasta with home-made ratatouille, broccoli and cheese bake, deep fried scampi, half honey-roasted chicken, and lasagne. The pub welcomes families and offers a children's menu and a play area.

**Open** noon-2.30 6-11 (Sat noon-11 Sun noon-9) Closed: Mon (ex BH) **Bar Meals** L served Tue-Sun, 12-2.30 D served Tue-Sun 6.30-9 Av main course £8.50 **Restaurant** L served Tue-Sun 12-2.30 D served Tue-Sun 6.30-9 Fixed menu price fr £8.50 ⊕ ENTERPRISE INNS ◀ John Smith's Cask, Greene King Old Speckled Hen ♂ Stowford Press. **Facilities** Children's menu Children's portions Play area Dogs allowed Garden Parking

### PENISTONE                           Map 16 SE20

### PICK OF THE PUBS

## Cubley Hall

***See Pick of the Pubs on page 542***

## The Fountain Inn Hotel ♥

**Wellthorne Ln, Ingbirchworth S36 7GJ**
**☎ 01226 763125   📠 01226 761336**
e-mail: enquiries@fountain-ingbirchworth.co.uk
**dir:** M1 junct 37, A628 to Manchester then A629 to Huddersfield

Parts of this former coaching inn date from the 17th century; it is attractively located by Ingbirchworth Reservoir in the foothills of the southern Pennines. The interior is cosy and stylish, the locals' bar has real log fires and traditional games, and the food focus is on quality with value for money: expect the likes of prawn cocktail, roast sirloin of local beef, and apple and blackberry crumble with custard. Garden with large decking and seating area.

**Open** all day all wk 11.30-11 **Bar Meals** food served all day **Restaurant** food served all day ⊕ INTREPID LEISURE ◀ Black Sheep, John Smith's Smooth, Timothy Taylor Landlord. ♥ 8 **Facilities** Children's menu Play area Garden Parking

# PICK OF THE PUBS

## Cubley Hall

**PENISTONE**                    Map 16 SE20

**Mortimer Rd, Cubley S36 9DF**
☎ 01226 766086   📠 01226 767335
**e-mail:** info@cubleyhall.co.uk
**dir:** *M1 junct 37, A628 towards Manchester, or M1 junct 35a, A616. Hall just S of Penistone*

If you see a lady dressed in Edwardian clothes wandering about, it might be Flo, or Florence Lockley to be precise, the resident ghost in this fine-looking free house. On the edge of the Peak District National Park, it was built as a farm in the 1700s, by Queen Victoria's reign and on into the 20th century it was a gentleman's residence, and from the 1930s to 1980, a children's home. Two years later it became a pub, and then in 1990 the massive, oak-beamed bar was converted into the restaurant and furnished with old pine tables, chairs

and church pews. In 1996, Cubley Hall was extended to incorporate the hotel, which was designed to harmonise with the original mosaic floors, ornate plaster ceilings, oak panelling and stained glass.

From the menu, there are plenty of snacks and light meals, such as creamy garlic mushrooms; pork and leek sausages with mash and rich onion gravy; sizzling platters of spicy chicken wings; pizzas and pastas; chargrills; and chicken fajitas. Main courses include chilli con carne with rice, sour cream and nachos; pie of the day with shortcrust pastry, salted steak fries and a panache of vegetables; pan-fried lamb's liver with onions and lardons; chicken breast marinated in cumin and coriander with steamed rice, sultanas, pine-nuts and natural yoghurt; breaded Whitby wholetail scampi with home-made tartare sauce; risotto with mixed beans, fresh herbs, parmesan and pesto; and seasonal salads. Blackboards offer ten daily specials, and children have their own menu. The hotel, particularly its garden pavilion, is a popular wedding venue.

**Open** all day all wk **Bar Meals** D served Mon-Fri until 9.30, Sat-Sun until 10 Av main course £7 food served all day **Restaurant** L served Sun 12.30-3.30 booking required D served Sun, last orders at 5.45 booking required Fixed menu price fr £9.75 ⊕ FREE HOUSE ◀ Tetley Bitter, Burton Ale, Greene King Abbot Ale, Young's Special.
**Facilities** Children's menu Play area Family room Garden Parking

## SHEFFIELD     Map 16 SK38

### PICK OF THE PUBS

## The Fat Cat

23 Alma St S3 8SA
☎ 0114 249 4801   📠 0114 249 4803
e-mail: info@thefatcat.co.uk
dir: Telephone for directions

This reputedly haunted three-storey, back street pub was built in 1832, and is Grade II listed. Beer-wise, it's hard to imagine anywhere better: a constantly changing range of guest beers from across the country, especially from micro-breweries, makes for a real ale heaven. Two hand-pumped ciders, unusual bottled beers and 21 country wines (the likes of elderberry and cowslip) are also sold, while the Kelham Island Brewery, owned by the pub, accounts for at least four of the ten traditional draught real ales on offer. The number of different beers sold since the concept was introduced now exceeds 4,500. The smart interior is very much that of a traditional, welcoming city pub; outside there's an attractive walled garden complete with Victorian-style lanterns, bench seating and shrubbery. Real fires in winter complete the cosy feel. Home-cooked food from a simple weekly menu is available except on Sunday evenings – nutty mushroom pie or Mexican chicken casserole. Look out for special events such as Monday curry night, beer and food evenings.

**Open** all wk noon-11 (Fri-Sat noon-mdnt) Closed: 25 Dec **Food** L served Mon-Fri 12-3, Sat 12-8, Sun 12-3 D served Mon-Fri 6-8 ⊕ FREE HOUSE ◀ Timothy Taylor Landlord, Kelham Island Bitter, Pale Rider, guest ales ♂ Stowford Press, Guest ciders. **Facilities** Children's portions Family room Dogs allowed Garden Parking

### PICK OF THE PUBS

## Kelham Island Tavern NEW

62 Russell St S3 8RW ☎ 0114 272 2482
e-mail: kelhamislandtav@aol.com
dir: Just off A61 (inner ring road). Follow brown tourist signs for Kelham Island

Anyone who doubts that pubs can be brought back from the brink should visit this survivor of Sheffield's industrial past. Having dodged the Luftwaffe's bombs and escaped demolition in the 1990s, this 1830s back-street pub was rescued in 2001 by Lewis Gonda and Trevor Wraith, who transformed a semi-derelict wreck into an award-winning 'small gem'. The real ale list is formidable: residents Barnsley Bitter, Brewers Gold and Farmers Blonde are joined by ten ever-changing guests, as well as Westons Old Rosie Scrumpy and Country Perry. No menus, just constantly updated blackboards, typically offering beef bourguignon; chicken fillet in mushroom and Stilton sauce; steak and ale pie; fish pie; butternut squash and ginger bake; broccoli and cheese pie; soups, pâtés and various bar snacks; and a small selection of desserts. The Kelham Island Museum round the corner in Alma Street tells the story of the city's industrial heritage.

**Open** all day all wk noon-11 (Sat-Sun noon-mdnt) **Bar Meals** L served Mon-Sat 12-3 Av main course £5 ⊕ FREE HOUSE ◀ Barnsley Bitter, Brewers Gold, Farmers Blonde, 10 changing guest ales ♂ Westons Old Rosie. **Facilities** Children's portions Family room Dogs allowed Garden

## TOTLEY     Map 16 SK37

### PICK OF THE PUBS

## The Cricket Inn ♥

Penny Ln, Totley Bents S17 3AZ ☎ 0114 236 5256
e-mail: info@brewkitchen.co.uk
dir: Follow A621 from Sheffield 8m. Turn right onto Hillfoot Rd, 1st left onto Penny Ln

Set in the picturesque landscape between Sheffield and Derbyshire, the Cricket Inn is a natural choice for sustenance after your ten-mile tramp or fell run, sitting by the fire or outside. Muddy running shoes, walking boots, children and dogs are all welcome. The pub is owned by the Thornbridge Brewery, so expect to find four of its ales on tap as well as a small selection of bottled Belgians. The building was originally a farmhouse which started selling beer to navvies building the Totley Tunnel on the nearby Sheffield to Manchester railway. It opened for business in its current guise in 2007 and today it's a forward-looking venture that links the innovative beers with great pub food. Fill the odd corner with flavoursome snacks like black pudding with sticky onion jam, or select from the likes of home-made fish cake, gammon steak and double fried egg, or Cricket Inn fish pie with Cheddar mash.

**Open** all wk 11-11 **Bar Meals** L served Mon-Fri 12-2.30, Sat-Sun all day D served Mon-Fri 5-8.30, Sat-Sun all day Av main course £12 **Restaurant** L served Mon-Fri 12-2.30, Sat-Sun all day D served Mon-Fri 5-8.30, Sat-Sun all day Av 3 course à la carte fr £16 ⊕ BREWKITCHEN LTD ◀ Wild Swan, Lord Marples, Jaipur. ♥ 10 **Facilities** Children's menu Children's portions Dogs allowed Garden Parking

## YORKSHIRE, WEST

## ADDINGHAM     Map 19 SE04

### PICK OF THE PUBS

## The Fleece ♥

154 Main St LS29 0LY ☎ 01943 830491
dir: Between Ilkley & Skipton

A 17th-century coaching inn popular with walkers, situated at the intersection of several well-tramped footpaths. Food and drink can be served on the front terrace in summer. At other times the stone-flagged interior welcomes with an enormous fireplace, wooden settles and a friendly bunch of locals. A pint of Copper Dragon might be all you're seeking, but if you feel peckish, be sure to consult the daily chalkboard. Much of the produce is local and organic, with beef and lamb coming from a nearby farm, surplus vegetables brought along by allotment holders, and seasonal game delivered straight from the shoot. Simple flavoursome dishes are the speciality here. The lunchtime offerings include sandwiches, omelettes and traditional plates such as roast local belly pork; half roast organic chicken; and Wharfedale braised lamb shank. For a full meal, choose from the likes of Shetland mussels or Manx queenie scallops to start, and pan-fried Gressingham duck breast or coq au vin to follow.

**Open** all wk noon-11 (Sun noon-10.30) **Bar Meals** L served Mon-Sat 12-2.15, Sun 12-8 D served Mon-Sat 6-9.15, Sun 12-8 booking required **Restaurant** L served Mon-Sat 12-2.15, Sun 12-8 booking required D served Mon-Sat 6-9.15, Sun 12-8 booking required Fixed menu price fr £29 ⊕ PUNCH TAVERNS ◀ Black Sheep, Copper Dragon, Timothy Taylor Landlord, Tetleys ♂ Stowford Press. ♥ 15 **Facilities** Children's menu Children's portions Dogs allowed Parking

## BRADFORD     Map 19 SE13

## New Beehive Inn

171 Westgate BD1 3AA
☎ 01274 721784   📠 01274 735092
e-mail: newbeehiveinn+21@btinternet.com
dir: A606 into Bradford, A6161 200yds B6144, left after lights, pub on left

Dating from 1901, this classic Edwardian inn retains its period atmosphere with separate bars and gas lighting. Outside, with a complete change of mood, you can relax in the Mediterranean-style courtyard. The pub offers a good range of unusual real ales and a selection of over 100 malt whiskies, served alongside some simple bar snacks.     *continued*

**BRADFORD** *continued*

**Open** all wk ⊕ FREE HOUSE ◀ Timothy Taylor Landlord, Kelham Island Bitter, Abbeydale Moonshine, Salamander Mudpuppy ♂ Westons Old Rosie. **Facilities** Family room Dogs allowed Garden Parking

---

### CLIFTON — Map 16 SE12

## The Black Horse Inn ◉ ♀

HD6 4HJ ☎ 01484 713862 📠 01484 400582
**e-mail:** mail@blackhorseclifton.co.uk
**dir:** *1m from Brighouse town centre. 0.5m from M62 junct 25*

The white-painted, 15th-century building was originally a farmhouse, which helps to explain why a six-inch layer of chicken droppings was found here during conversion in the 1970s. At the pub's heart is a well-kept bar serving traditional Yorkshire ales and a wide-ranging wine selection. Three separate dining areas provide a seasonal menu of locally sourced food, such as slow-braised lamb shank; pan-fried breast of chicken; beer-battered Whitby haddock; and leek and pea tartlet.

**Open** all day all wk noon-mdnt **Bar Meals** L served Mon-Sat 12-2.30, Sun 12-8 D served Mon-Sat 5.30-9.30, Sun 12-8 ⊕ FREE HOUSE ◀ Timothy Taylor Landlord, Black Horse Brew. ♀ 18 **Facilities** Garden Parking

*See advert on opposite page*

---

### EMLEY — Map 16 SE21

## The White Horse ♀ NEW

2 Chapel Ln HD8 9SP ☎ 01924 849823
**dir:** *M1 junct 38, A637 towards Huddersfield. At rdbt left onto A636, then right to Emley*

On the old coaching route to Huddersfield and Halifax, this 18th-century pub's bar is warmed by a working Yorkshire range; the restaurant has a fire too. Of the eight cask ales, four are permanent, four are ever-rotating guests, featuring micro-breweries and their own Ossett Brewery ales. Both the carte and blackboard specials show a fondness for fish, such as red snapper, sea bass, prawns and mussels. There's a lot more, including pan-fried pork tenderloin, braised lamb shank, venison and vegetarian options. The pub is popular with walkers and cyclists and locals, of course.

---

**Open** all wk Mon-Thu 4-11, Fri 3-11.30, Sat noon-11.30, Sun noon-11 **Bar Meals** L served Sat 12-5 D served Wed-Fri 4-6 Av main course £5 **Restaurant** L served Sun 12-5 booking required D served Wed-Sat 5-9 booking required Av 3 course à la carte fr £20 ⊕ OSSETT BREWERY PUB CO ◀ London Pride, Ossett Excelsior, Ossett Emley Cross, Ossett Pale Gold, Ossett Treacle Stout. ♀ 9
**Facilities** Children's portions Family room Dogs allowed Garden Parking

---

### HALIFAX — Map 19 SE02

### PICK OF THE PUBS

## The Old Bore ◉ ♀

Oldham Rd, Rishworth HX6 4QU ☎ 01422 822291
**dir:** *M62 junct 22, A672 towards Halifax, 3m on left after reservoir*

It may be known as the Old Bore, but there's nothing boring about this family-run 19th century converted coaching inn, which is packed with character. Flagged floors, oak beams, antique furniture and a wealth of interesting details make this a pub with old world charm. The bar is a popular haunt for locals and ale aficionados attracted by the well kept Black Sheep, Timothy Taylor Landlord and Bore Bitter. Owner Scott Hessel's restaurant CV means you can expect notable modern British food using seasonal produce from a network of committed suppliers. A typical three-courser might include braised pig's cheek, mash and caramelised apple followed by pheasant and partridge breasts with port flambéed grapes, braised red cabbage and gratin potatoes. Finish with rhubarb crumble or pineapple tarte Tatin with rum and raisin ice cream. A '2-4-1' lunch menu offers dishes such as dry-cured gammon and free-range eggs or fish and chips.

**Open** all wk noon-2.15 6-11 (Sun noon-11) **Bar Meals** L served Mon-Sat 12-2.15, Sun 12-8 D served Mon-Sat 6-9.30, Sun 12-8 booking required Av main course £11.95 **Restaurant** L served Mon-Sat 12-2.15, Sun 12-8 D served Mon-Sat 6-9.30, Sun 12-8 booking required Av 3 course à la carte fr £23 ⊕ FREE HOUSE ◀ Timothy Taylor, Black Sheep Best, Bore Bitter. ♀ 12
**Facilities** Children's menu Children's portions Dogs allowed Garden Parking

## The Rock Inn Hotel ♀

Holywell Green HX4 9BS
☎ 01422 379721 📠 01422 379110
**e-mail:** enquiries@therockhotel.co.uk
**dir:** *From M62 junct 24 follow Blackley signs, left at x-rds, approx 0.5m on left*

Substantial modern extensions have transformed this attractive 17th-century wayside inn into a thriving hotel and conference venue in the scenic valley of Holywell Green. All-day dining in the brasserie-style conservatory is truly cosmopolitan; kick off with freshly prepared parsnip and apple soup or crispy duck and seaweed, followed by liver and bacon, Thai-style steamed halibut, or vegetables jalfrezi. The bar serves a choice of beers and 14 wines by the glass.

---

**Open** all day all wk noon-11 **Bar Meals** L served Mon-Sat 12-2, Sun 12-8.30 D served Mon-Sat 6-9 Av main course £9.95 **Restaurant** L served Mon-Sat 12-2 D served Mon-Sat 5.30-9.30 Fixed menu price fr £15 Av 3 course à la carte fr £25 ⊕ FREE HOUSE ◀ Timothy Taylor Landlord, John Smith's. ♀ 14 **Facilities** Children's menu Children's portions Garden Parking

---

### PICK OF THE PUBS

### Shibden Mill Inn ★★★★ INN ♀

*See Pick of the Pubs on page 546*

---

### HAWORTH — Map 19 SE03

## The Old White Lion Hotel ★★★★ INN ♀

Main St BD22 8DU ☎ 01535 642313 📠 01535 646222
**e-mail:** enquiries@oldwhitelionhotel.com
**dir:** *A629 onto B6142, 0.5m past Haworth Station*

Set in the famous Brontë village of Haworth, this traditional family-run 300-year-old coaching inn looks down onto the famous cobbled Main Street. In the charming bar the ceiling beams are held up by timber posts. Bar food includes all the usual favourites plus a great selection of filled giant Yorkshire puddings. A meal in the candlelit restaurant might include king scallops with local bacon followed by crisp Barbary duck breast with port and cranberry sauce. If you would like to explore the area, why not stay over in the comfortable accommodation.

**Open** all wk 11-11 (Sun noon-10.30) **Bar Meals** L served Mon-Fri 12-2.30, Sat-Sun all day D served Mon-Fri 6-9.30, Sat-Sun all day Av main course £8.50 **Restaurant** L served Sun 12-2.30 booking required D served all wk 7-9.30 booking required Fixed menu price fr £17 Av 3 course à la carte fr £23.50 ⊕ FREE HOUSE ◀ Theakstons Best (Green Label), Tetley Bitter, John Smith's, Websters, guest beer. ♀ 9 **Facilities** Children's menu Children's portions Parking **Rooms** 15

---

### KIRKBURTON — Map 16 SE11

## The Woodman Inn ★★★★ INN ♀

Thunderbridge HD8 0PX
☎ 01484 605778 📠 01484 604110
**e-mail:** thewoodman@connectfree.co.uk
**dir:** *Approx 5m S of Huddersfield, just off A629*

Lovely old stone-built inn set in the wooded hamlet of Thunderbridge. One menu is offered throughout, but customers can eat in the bar downstairs or the more sophisticated ambience of the restaurant upstairs. Dishes include daily fresh fish (grilled brill with chilli), and the likes of wild boar and apple sausages. Wine is selected by the owners, whose family has been in the licensed trade since 1817. Accommodation is provided in adjacent converted weavers' cottages.

**Open** all day all wk 12-11 (Fri-Sat noon-mdnt Sun 12-10.30) **Bar Meals** food served all day **Restaurant** food served all day ⊕ FREE HOUSE ◀ Timothy Taylor Best Bitter, Black Sheep, guest ales ♂ Aspall. ♀ 13 **Facilities** Parking **Rooms** 12

# The Black Horse Inn

Clifton Village, Brighouse, West Yorkshire HD6 4HJ
Tel: 01484 713862   Fax: 01484 400582
E-mail: mail@blackhorseclifton.co.uk   Web: www.blackhorseclifton.co.uk

The Black Horse is a family owned village Inn, bubbling with country charm. It is located half a mile from junction 25 of the M62, but Clifton village is a real oasis and easily accessible. It has a great bar, an outstanding restaurant, fantastic function room, 21 individually designed boutique bedrooms and a lovely flower filled outdoor courtyard, perfect to relax and enjoy that well earned pint.

Luscious local food is at the heart of *The Black Horse Inn*, and the seasonal menu, sourced from Yorkshire's ambrosial larder, has won a loyal following. With great food comes great drink – cask conditioned ales such as championship bitter Timothy Taylor are served and also their own beer – *Black Horse Brew*, made exclusively for them by a small micro brewery from Sowerby Bridge; guest ales feature regularly too.

Why not take advantage of The Black Horse's 'Booze n Snooze' nights and enjoy a delicious combination of great food and drink, excellent service and first class accommodation.

# PICK OF THE PUBS

## Shibden Mill Inn ★★★★INN 🍷

**HALIFAX**                    Map 19 SE02

**Shibden Mill Fold HX3 7UL**
☎ **01422 365840** 📄 **01422 362971**
**e-mail:** enquiries@shibdenmillinn.com
**web:** www.shibdenmillinn.com
**dir:** *From A58 turn into Kell Ln. After 0.5m
left into Blake Hill*

"The mill wheel has long since been silent… The old order has changed and what was once a central place of business, is now one of pleasure, beer and boats." So said a member of the Halifax Antiquarian Society 100 years ago of this historic free house (although why the boats is a bit of a mystery). There had been a corn mill on this site, overlooking Red Beck, since the 14th century, until in 1845 it became a worsted mill. A disastrous fire in 1859, however, closed the business and in 1890 the mill was sold to a brewery, who filled in the mill pond, possibly to prevent water leaking into the local mine shafts; today this area is the inn's car park.

The pub's interior has been sympathetically renovated, while retaining much of the fabric, particularly in the log fire-warmed, oak-beamed bar and candlelit restaurant. Real ales include Shibden Ale and two guests, and the wine list has clearly been professionally compiled.

Here is a foretaste of a seasonal restaurant menu: starters of quail scotch eggs; miniature Wensleydale and spring onion pasty; and rolled and fried, crispy lamb breast. Main courses include crab and coriander croquettes; Lancashire hotpot; slow-cooked Asian-style pork belly; pan-fried sea bass; and spatchcock of whole spring chicken. Appearing on the favourites menu are Shibden Ale-battered cod; organic pork and leek sausages; and mozzarella and basil pesto sandwich. Typical desserts are twice-baked Belgian chocolate brownie, and Amaretto and marzipan cheesecake.

Many of the weekday dishes also feature on the Sunday menus as alternatives to the three roasts. Children like to tuck into haddock goujons or crispy chicken strips with potato wedges and peas. Eleven en suite bedrooms offer all you'd expect in the way of comfort and style.

**Open** all wk noon-2.30 5.30-11 (Sat-Sun noon-11) Closed: 25-26 Dec eve & 1 Jan eve **Bar Meals** L served Mon-Sat 12-2, Sun all day D served Mon-Sat 6-9.30 Av main course £12 **Restaurant** L served Sun 12-7.30 D served Fri-Sat 6-9.30 Fixed menu price fr £25 Av 3 course à la carte fr £30 ⊕ FREE HOUSE ◪ John Smiths, Theakston XB, Shibden Mill, 2 guest ales. 🍷 12 **Facilities** Children's menu Dogs allowed Garden Parking **Rooms** 11

Save on Hotels. Book at theAA.com/hotel

YORKSHIRE, WEST 547 ENGLAND

## LEDSHAM
Map 16 SE42

### The Chequers Inn

Claypit Ln LS25 5LP
☎ 01977 683135 📄 01977 680791
e-mail: cjwrath@btconnect.com
dir: Between A1(M) & A656 N of Castleford. 1m from
A1(M) junct 42

A quaint, creeper-clad inn located in an old estate
village, with low beams, wooden settles, and a history
traceable back to 1540. Ever since the lady of the manor
was offended by her over-indulgent farm workers over
60 years ago, the pub has been closed on Sundays. But
otherwise, you can tuck into peppered escalope of
venison, monkfish tail in pancetta, steak and mushroom
pie, steak sandwich, or smoked salmon crumble.

**Open** Mon-Sat Closed: Sun ◆ Theakston, John Smith's,
Timothy Taylor Landlord, Brown Cow, Golden Best. ♀ 10
**Facilities** Dogs allowed Garden Parking

## LEEDS
Map 19 SE23

### PICK OF THE PUBS

### The Cross Keys

107 Water Ln LS11 5WD ☎ 0113 243 3711
e-mail: info@the-crosskeys.com
dir: 0.5m from Leeds Station: right onto Neville St,
right onto Water Lane. Pass Globe Rd, pub on left

This cosy 19th century country inn seems out of place
in the heart of Leeds' modern city centre; in fact the
rustic log fires, beams and bare brick enhance the
pub's commitment to offering heart-warming,
traditional Yorkshire and British fare with a modern
twist to lucky patrons. Gastro-pub meets alehouse
here, with the best Yorkshire micro-brewery ales
rubbing shoulders with eclectic menu choices like
crispy pig's head, apple and salsify purée with roasted
barley starter leading into mains including rabbit
saddle with black pudding, roast garlic mash and
mustard sauce or bubble and squeak cake, deep-fried
duck egg, winter greens and home-made brown sauce.
Chef Brett Barnes ensures that only ethically-produced,
locally sourced ingredients make it into his kitchen,
whilst (hopefully) sunnier summer days will reveal a
lighter menu to reflect the season. A traditional
Yorkshire Sunday roast is always a good excuse to
leave behind the delights of shopping to relax on the
sun-trap courtyard patio.

**Open** all wk noon-11 (Fri-Sat noon-mdnt, Sun noon-
10.30) **Bar Meals** L served Mon-Sat 12-4, Sun 12-6 D
served Mon-Sat 6-10 **Restaurant** L served Mon-Sat
12-4, Sun 12-6 D served Mon-Sat 6-10 ⊕ FREE HOUSE
◆ Roosters, Duvel, Vedett, Kuppers Kolsche,
Timmermans Framboise ♂ Westons Organic, Westons
Medium Dry, Westons Pear. ♀ 13 **Facilities** Children's
menu Children's portions Dogs allowed Garden

### Whitelocks

Turks Head Yard, Briggate LS1 6HB
☎ 0113 245 3950 📄 0113 242 3368
e-mail: whitelocks@live.co.uk
dir: Next to Marks & Spencer in Briggate

First licensed in 1715 as the Turks Head, this is the
oldest pub in Leeds. Restoration has highlighted its
classic long bar with polychrome tiles, stained-glass
windows, advertising mirrors and a mid-Victorian-style
Top Bar known as Ma'Gamps. Food is along the lines of
home-made soup; roast of the day; ham, egg and chips;
home-made tray pie (steak; steak and Stilton or
vegetable); treacle sponge and apple pie. There is a
children's menu too. Guest ales are on a weekly rotation
– sometimes daily.

**Open** all wk 11-11 (Sun noon-6 winter Sun noon-10.30
summer) Closed: 25-26 Dec, 1 Jan **Bar Meals** food
served all day **Restaurant** booking required booking
required ⊕ CHENNEL & ARMSTRONG ◆ Theakston Best,
Old Peculier, John Smith's, Deuchars, Leeds & York
Brewery Ales, Guest ales. ♀ 16

## LINTHWAITE
Map 16 SE11

### The Sair Inn

Hoyle Ing HD7 5SG ☎ 01484 842370
dir: From Huddersfield take A62 (Oldham road) for 3.5m.
Left just before lights at bus stop (in centre of road) into
Hoyle Ing & follow sign

You won't be able to eat here, but this old hilltop ale
house has enough character in its four small rooms to
make up for that. Three are heated by hot (landlord Ron
Crabtree's word) Yorkshire ranges in winter. Ron has
brewed his own beers for 25 years and much sought after
they are by real ale aficionados. Imported German and
Czech lagers are available too. In summer the outside
drinking area catches the afternoon sun and commands
views across the Colne Valley.

**Open** all wk 5-11 (Sat noon-11 Sun noon-10.30) ⊕ FREE
HOUSE ◆ Linfit Special Bitter, Linfit Bitter, Linfit Gold
Medal, Autumn Gold, Old Eli ♂ Westons First Quality.
**Facilities** Dogs allowed **Notes** ⊛

## LINTON
Map 16 SE34

### The Windmill Inn

Main St LS22 4HT ☎ 01937 582209 📄 01937 587518
web: www.thewindmillinnwetherby.co.uk
dir: From A1 exit at Tadcaster/Otley junct, follow Otley
signs. In Collingham follow Linton signs

A coaching inn since the 18th century, the building
actually dates back to the 14th century, and originally
housed the owner of the long-disappeared windmill.
Stone walls, antique settles, log fires, oak beams and lots
of brass set the scene in which to enjoy good beers and
food prepared by enthusiastic licensees. Whether dining
in the bar or Pear Tree restaurant, expect the likes of
walnut, Stilton and fine bean salad, followed by a game
casserole of pheasant, partridge, wood pigeon and

grouse cooked with plums and raisins with creamy
tomato mash; or salmon fillet with dressed salad and
hollandaise. While you're there, ask to take a look at the
local history scrapbook.

*The Windmill Inn*

**Open** all wk 11-3 5.30-11 (Sat 11-11 Sun noon-10.30)
Closed: 1 Jan **Bar Meals** L served Mon-Fri 12-2, Sat
12-2.30, Sun 12-5.45 **Restaurant** L served Mon-Fri 12-2,
Sat 12-2.30, Sun 12-5.45 D served Mon-Tue 5.30-8.30,
Wed-Sat 5.30-9, Sun 12-5.45 ⊕ SCOTTISH COURAGE
◆ John Smith's, Theakston Best, Daleside, Greene King
Ruddles County. ♀ 12 **Facilities** Children's portions Dogs
allowed Garden Parking

## MARSDEN
Map 16 SE01

### The Olive Branch ★★★★ RR ⊛ ♀

Manchester Rd HD7 6LU ☎ 01484 844487
e-mail: eat@olivebranch.uk.com
dir: On A62 between Marsden & Slaithwaite, 6m from
Huddersfield

Set on a former packhorse route, this attractive moorland
inn has a strong reputation for its brasserie-style food.
The interior comprises a rambling series of rooms
warmed by real fires in winter. Expect modern French-
style cooking carried with flair and enthusiasm, and
fuelled by seasonal ingredients. The choice is wide, with
starters such foie gras and Armagnac terrine followed by
the likes of roast cod with lobster mash or confit duck leg
with red onion and sultana marmalade and red wine jus.
Locally brewed real ales are always available and can be
enjoyed on the sun deck in warmer weather. Three
designer bedrooms are available if you would like to stay
over.

**Open** all wk Mon-Sat 6.30-9.30 (Sun 12.30-9) Closed: 1st
2wks Jan **Bar Meals** Av main course £17.50 **Restaurant** D
served Mon-Sat 6.30-9.30, Sun 1-8 booking required
Fixed menu price fr £11.95 Av 3 course à la carte fr
£25.95 ⊕ FREE HOUSE ◆ Dogcross Bitter, Greenfield Red
Ale, Boddingtons. ♀ 12 **Facilities** Garden Parking
**Rooms** 3

# PICK OF THE PUBS

# The Three Acres Inn

**SHELLEY**  Map 16 SE21

**HD8 8LR**
☎ **01484 602606**  📄 **01484 608411**
e-mail: info@3acres.com
web: www.3acres.com
dir: *From Huddersfield take A629 then B6116, turn left for village*

Well into their fourth decade here, Brian Orme and Neil Truelove have built a reputation for good quality food, tasteful accommodation, and a welcoming atmosphere in this old drovers' inn. But the sheep farmers have long gone; today's visitors tend to visit the National Mining Museum and Yorkshire Sculpture Park, both five minutes' drive away, or they could be here for a Three Acres activity break, playing golf, clay pigeon shooting or wine tasting.

The inn's spacious interior is lavishly traditional — all rich reds, greens and yellows, exposed beams and large fireplaces. On summer evenings, sit out on the deck with a pint of Black Sheep (to remind you of the drovers), or a glass of wine.

The food, including plenty of fresh fish, is served in both bar and restaurant and successfully fuses traditional English with international influences. Starter firm favourites include potted shrimps with hot buttered soldiers and dressed watercress; and flash-grilled Loch Fyne queenies with White Orkney Cheddar and grain mustard. Among popular main courses are Borrobel Estate venison cottage pie with sweet potato chunky chips and buttered spring greens; roast breast of crispy Lunesdale duck with roast potatoes, orange and thyme stuffing, and spiced cranberry and orange sauce; and fresh Whitby haddock in Timothy Taylor beer batter with beef-dripping chips and mushy peas.

The three-course Sunday lunch menu offers seven or so choices at each stage, enabling you to begin with Parmesan waffles with baked plum tomato compote and rocket; ease into Hinchliffe's mature roast beef with Yorkshire pudding and horseradish sauce; and finish with Bakewell tart and Amaretto ice cream. A generous range of hot open and other sandwiches and light meals makes a great lunchtime choice. The views round here are fabulous.

**Open** all wk noon-2 6.30-9.30 Closed: 25-26 Dec eve, 1 Jan eve
**Bar Meals** food served all day
**Restaurant** food served all day 🏠 FREE HOUSE 🍺 Timothy Taylor Landlord, Black Sheep, Tetley's Smooth, Tetley's Bitter. **Facilities** Garden Parking

# PICK OF THE PUBS

## Ring O'Bells Country Pub & Restaurant

**THORNTON**          Map 19 SE03

**212 Hilltop Rd BD13 3QL**
☎ **01274 832296** 📄 **01274 831707**
e-mail: enquiries@theringobells.com
web: www.theringobells.com
dir: *From M62 take A58 for 5m, right onto A644. 4.5m follow Denholme signs, onto Well Head Rd into Hilltop Rd*

Thornton is the village where the Brontë Sisters, whose father was the rector, were born, christened and lived. Originally, the Ring O' Bells, high above the village, was a Wesleyan chapel overlooking the dramatic Yorkshire Pennines where, on a clear day, the views stretch for over 40 miles.

Ann and Clive Preston have successfully run the pub for over 18 years, and their cuisine, service and professionalism

have been recognised with accolades from the trade and visitors from far and wide. Their refurbishment of the bar and dining area in 2009 has done nothing to dilute its traditional, historical feel, enhanced by prints of the village in the 1920s on the wood-panelled walls, although contemporary art is displayed in the restaurant.

The fully air-conditioned Brontë restaurant, once two mill workers' cottages, now has a conservatory running its whole length that rewards diners with stunning valley views. Local farmers and suppliers of meat, fish, game and vegetables know that everything will be carefully prepared and cooked by a team of award-winning chefs, whose carte menu and daily specials board offer traditional British dishes with European influences.

Expect starters such as fresh Greenland prawns and home-made cocktail sauce; honeydew melon with fruit sorbet and strawberry and passion fruit syrup; and pan-fried mushrooms in garlic butter. Main courses may include steamed smoked haddock with poached egg,

crushed new potatoes, and wholegrain mustard and chive sauce; slow-cooked marinated belly pork and roasted pork fillet with black pudding mash and cider gravy; and award-winning shortcrust, puff pastry and herb suet pies. Imaginative vegetarian options are on the blackboard. Among the desserts, all made to order, are steamed roly-poly with vanilla custard, and espresso chocolate mousse with white chocolate pannacotta.

**Open** all wk 11.30-4 5.30-11.30 (Sat-Sun 6.15-11.30) Closed: 25 Dec
**Bar Meals** L served all wk 12-2 D served all wk 5.30-9.30 Av main course £10.95
**Restaurant** L served all wk 12-2 D served all wk 5.30-9.30 booking required Fixed menu price fr £22.95 Av 3 course à la carte fr £19.95 ⊕ FREE HOUSE ◖ John Smith's, Courage Directors, Black Sheep ales. ♟ 12
**Facilities** Children's menu Parking

## MYTHOLMROYD — Map 19 SE02

### Shoulder of Mutton ♥

**New Rd HX7 5DZ ☎ 01422 883165**
**e-mail:** shoulder@tesco.net
**dir:** *A646 Halifax to Todmorden, in Mytholmroyd on B6138, opposite rail station*

This award-winning Pennines' pub is the birthplace of Ted Hughes, Poet Laureate from 1984 to 1998, and has been under the same ownership for 34 years. It has a solid reputation for real ales, snacks and main meals of giant Yorkshire pudding; steak and onion pie; carvery roasts; beef chilli; and battered haddock; and a vegetarian blackboard. An interesting collection of counterfeit gold coins made by the Cragg Vale Coiners in the late-18th century is on display. There is a streamside beer garden for the warmer months which is popular walkers, cyclists and families.

**Open** Wed-Mon 11.30-3 (all wk 7-11) **Closed:** Tue L **Bar Meals** L served Wed-Mon 11.30-2 D served Wed-Sun 7-8.15 Av main course £4.50 ⊕ ENTERPRISE INNS ◀ Black Sheep, Copper Dragon, Timothy Taylor Landlord. ♥ 12 **Facilities** Children's portions Play area Family room Dogs allowed Garden Parking **Notes** ☺

## RIPPONDEN — Map 16 SE01

### Old Bridge Inn ♥

**Priest Ln HX6 4DF ☎ 01422 822595**
**dir:** *5m from Halifax in village centre by church, over a pack horse bridge*

An award-winning, whitewashed, traditional pub prettily situated by an ancient packhorse bridge in a Pennine conservation village. Three separate bars, with antique furniture and open fires, serve Timothy Taylor and three guest beers; outside, tranquil landscaped seating overlooks the River Ryburn. Good old-fashioned dishes like meat and potato pie should appeal, or maybe pan-roast duck breast with hash brown of braised duck leg, Savoy cabbage and red wine sauce; and the ever-popular weekday salad and cold meat carvery lunch.

**Open** all wk Fri-Sun open all day **Bar Meals** L served all wk 12-2 booking required D served Mon-Fri 6.30-9.30 booking required Av main course £9.50 ⊕ FREE HOUSE ◀ Timothy Taylor Landlord, Golden Best & Best Bitter, guest ales. ♥ 12 **Facilities** Children's portions Garden Parking

## SHELLEY — Map 16 SE21

### PICK OF THE PUBS

### The Three Acres Inn

*See Pick of the Pubs on page 548*

## SOWERBY — Map 16 SE02

### PICK OF THE PUBS

### The Travellers Rest ♥

**Steep Ln HX6 1PE**
**☎ 01422 832124  📠 01422 831365**
**dir:** *M62 junct 22 or 24*

The 17th-century former coaching inn sits high on a steep hillside with stunning views, a dining terrace for savouring the sunsets, a duck pond, space for camping, and a helipad. Restored and refurbished with style a decade ago by Caroline Lumley, it continues to draw the crowds despite its rural location. The appeal is the cosy stone-flagged bar, which boasts fresh flowers, a blazing winter log fire and Little Valley Brewery beers on tap, and the comfortable restaurant, with its exposed stone wall and beams, animal print sofas and eclectic pub menus. Dishes cooked to order from local produce are rooted in Yorkshire tradition yet refined with French flair, yielding an immaculate and happy mix of classic and contemporary cooking, overseen by head chef, Mark Lilley. Start with a warm salad of black pudding and bacon or chicken liver pâté, continue with minted lamb Henry with rosemary mash, beef bourguignon with parmesan risotto, or a classic beer battered cod and chips. Resist the rhubarb crumble if you can and don't miss the summer barbecues.

**Open** Wed-Sat (all day Sun) **Closed:** Mon-Tue **Bar Meals** L served Sat 12-2, Sun 12-7 D served Wed-Thu 5-9, Fri 5-9.30, Sat 5.30-9.30, Sun 12-7 Av main course £10 **Restaurant** L served Sat 12-2, Sun 12-7 D served Wed-Thu 5-9, Fri 5-9.30, Sat 5.30-9.30, Sun 12-7 Fixed menu price fr £17.50 Av 3 course à la carte fr £17.50 ⊕ FREE HOUSE ◀ Timothy Taylor Landlord, Timothy Taylor, Best Bitter, Little Valley Brewery. ♥ 10 **Facilities** Dogs allowed Garden Parking

## SOWERBY BRIDGE — Map 16 SE02

### The Alma Inn & Fresco Italian Restaurant

**Cotton Stones HX6 4NS ☎ 01422 823334**
**e-mail:** info@almainn.com
**dir:** *Exit A58 at Triangle between Sowerby Bridge & Ripponden. Follow signs for Cotton Stones*

This old stone inn is set in a dramatically beautiful location at Cotton Stones and enjoys stunning views of the Ryburn Valley. Inside there are stone-flagged floors and real fires, while the cosy bar serves Timothy Taylor Landlord and Golden Best plus Tetley Bitter, as well as a range of cool-serve lagers and over 50 Belgian bottled beers (each served with its own individual glass). Fresco Italian Restaurant features a wood-burning pizza oven and a fantastic fish display counter which is very popular with diners. Start with shell roasted queen scallops cooked in the wood-burning oven with fresh herbs, parmesan and parma ham; or mango and smoked chicken salad with mustard dressing, followed by a steak pasta or pizza from a wide selection. There's also a good choice of vegetarian dishes such as sun blushed tomato and leek capellini. A private function/dining room is available, and in fine weather there's outside seating for 200 people.

*The Alma Inn & Fresco Italian Restaurant*

**Open** all day all wk noon-10.30 **Bar Meals** L served Mon-Thu 12-10, Fri-Sat 12-10.30, Sun 12-9 D served Mon-Thu 12-10, Fri-Sat 12-10.30, Sun 12-9 food served all day **Restaurant** L served Mon-Thu 12-10, Fri-Sat 12-10.30, Sun 12-9 D served Mon-Thu 12-10, Fri-Sat 12-10.30, Sun 12-9 food served all day ⊕ FREE HOUSE ◀ Tetley Bitter, Timothy Taylor Landlord, Timothy Taylor Golden Best. **Facilities** Children's portions Dogs allowed Garden Parking

### PICK OF THE PUBS

### The Millbank ♥

**HX6 3DY ☎ 01422 825588**
**e-mail:** eat@themillbank.com
**dir:** *A58 from Sowerby Bridge to Ripponden, right at Triangle*

With the feel and function of a traditional village free house, the cosy stone-flagged tap room of this contemporary pub-restaurant contrasts with the wine bar atmosphere in the main wooden-floored drinking area. Since 1971, the conservation village of Mill Bank has been the home of writer and poet Glyn Hughes; and one of his sonnets — The Rock Rose — is engraved on a slate slab in the churchyard wall. Back in the pub, you'll find winter fires in the tap room, whilst the dining room chairs are recycled mill and chapel seats, complete with prayer-book racks. Expect lunchtime snacks and sandwiches like roast beef with horseradish onions, or look to the à la carte menu for main course options such as white bean and mushroom cassoulet with herb crust, and sea bass fillet with saffron mash, asparagus and potted shrimps. Enjoy stunning views from the spacious garden in warmer weather.

**Open** noon-3 5.30-11 (Sun noon-10.30) **Closed:** 1st 2 wks Oct & 1st wk Jan, Mon **Bar Meals** L served Tue-Sun 12-2.30 D served Tue-Sun 6-9.30 **Restaurant** L served Tue-Sun 12-2.30 D served Tue-Sun 6-9.30 booking required Fixed menu price fr £14.50 Av 3 course à la carte fr £21.50 ⊕ FREE HOUSE ◀ Timothy Taylor Landlord, Tetley Bitter, Erdinger. ♥ 20 **Facilities** Dogs allowed Garden

| THORNTON | Map 19 SE03 |
|---|---|

## PICK OF THE PUBS

### Ring O' Bells Country Pub & Restaurant ♥

*See Pick of the Pubs on page 549*

| WIDDOP | Map 18 SD93 |
|---|---|

### Pack Horse Inn ♥

X7 7AT ☎ 01422 842803   📠 01422 842803
dir: *Off A646 & A6033*

The Pack Horse is a converted Laithe farmhouse dating from the 1600s, complete with welcoming open fires. A beautiful location just 300 yards from the Pennine Way makes it popular with walkers, but equally attractive are the home-cooked meals, good range of real ales and fabulous choice of 130 single malt whiskies. Please note that from October to Easter the pub is only open in the evening.

Open Summer noon-3 7-11 Closed: Mon & Tue-Fri lunch (Oct-Etr) **Bar Meals** L served Tue-Sun summer only D served Tue-Sun Av main course £8.95 ⊕ FREE HOUSE ◀ Thwaites, Theakston XB, Black Sheep Bitter, Golden Pippin, Lancaster Bomber. ♥ 10 **Facilities** Dogs allowed Parking

## CHANNEL ISLANDS

## GUERNSEY

| CASTEL | Map 24 |
|---|---|

## PICK OF THE PUBS

### Fleur du Jardin ♥

Kings Mills GY5 7JT
☎ 01481 257996   📠 01481 256834
e-mail: info@fleurdujardin.com
dir: *2.5m from town centre*

This friendly hotel, bar and restaurant stands in a picturesque village, a short stroll from the island's finest sandy beaches. Dating from the 15th century, it has been restyled with contemporary shabby chic appeal, but historical features such as granite walls, solid wood beams and real fireplaces remain. The taller than average might have to stoop in the bar, but that needn't hamper the enjoyment of a pint of Guernsey Special. The watchwords in the kitchen are freshness and seasonality, underpinned by a deep-rooted respect for the surrounding waters and pastures. Expect superb Guernsey beef, scallops, and line caught seafood, in addition to classics in the gastro vein: Meadow Court bangers and mash; slow-roasted lamb shank; pan-fried calves' liver with crisp bacon; and the Fleur's individual fish pie topped with a cheese and potato crust. Desserts along traditional lines include Guernsey farmhouse ice creams and sorbets.

Open all day all wk **Bar Meals** L served all wk 12-2 D served all wk 6-9 booking required Av main course £8.95 food served all day **Restaurant** L served all wk 12-2 D served all wk 6-9 booking required Fixed menu price fr £15.95 Av 3 course à la carte fr £22.50 food served all day ⊕ FREE HOUSE ◀ Sunbeam, Guernsey Special, London Pride, Guest ales ♨ Roquette cider. ♥ 12 **Facilities** Children's menu Children's portions Dogs allowed Garden Parking

---

### Hotel Hougue du Pommier

Hougue du Pommier Rd GY5 7FQ
☎ 01481 256531   📠 01481 256260
e-mail: hotel@houguedupommier.guernsey.net
dir: *Telephone for directions*

An 18th-century Guernsey farmhouse with the only feu du bois (literally 'cooking on the fire') in the Channel Islands. Eat in the beamed Tudor Bar with its open fire or the more formal restaurant. Menu options may include dishes from the spit-roast menu, baked aubergine and Mediterranean vegetable ragout; chargrilled supreme of chicken; or chef's seafood fishcake. The 8-acre gardens have a swimming pool, barbecue and medieval area, where banquets are held the first Saturday of the month.

Open all day all wk **Bar Meals** L served all wk 12-2 booking required D served all wk 6.30-9 booking required ⊕ FREE HOUSE ◀ John Smith's, Guinness ♨ Roquette. **Facilities** Dogs allowed Garden Parking

| ST PETER PORT | Map 24 |
|---|---|

### The Admiral de Saumarez ★★ HL

Duke of Normandie Hotel, Lefebvre St GY1 2JP
☎ 01481 721431   📠 01481 711763
e-mail: dukeofnormandie@cwgsy.net
dir: *From harbour rdbt St Julians Ave, 3rd left into Anns Place, continue to right, up hill, then left into Lefebvre St, archway entrance on right*

Part of the Duke of Normandie Hotel, this thoughtfully restored bar is full of architectural salvage, including old timbers (now painted with well-known amusing sayings), and maritime memorabilia. Details of the great naval victories of the Admiral himself are engraved on the tables. On the menu are corned beef hash with free-range egg and meaty veal sauce; pavé of cod with buttered vegetables and cream white wine reduction; and pea and asparagus risotto.

Open all day all wk 11am-11.30pm **Bar Meals** L served all wk 12-2 D served all wk 6-9 ⊕ FREE HOUSE ◀ Guinness, John Smith's. **Facilities** Children's menu Garden Parking **Rooms** 37

## JERSEY

| GOREY | Map 24 |
|---|---|

### Castle Green Gastropub ♥

La Route de la Cote JE3 6DR
☎ 01534 840218   📠 01534 840229
e-mail: enquiries@jerseypottery.com
dir: *Opposite main entrance of Gorey Castle*

A superbly located pub overlooking Gorey harbour and, in turn, overlooked by dramatic Mont Orgueil Castle. The views from the wooden sun terrace are breathtaking. Genuine Jersey produce is used on the seasonally evolving menu. Naturally fish dishes feature strongly and fresh fish is purchased daily. The imaginative menu might include Jersey fish soup with rouille, garlic croutons and gruyère cheese; pan-fried local scallops with sauce vièrge, rocket and smoked pancetta salad; or Jersey classic herd sausage bean crock.

Open 11.30-3 6-11 Closed: Sun eve & Mon **Bar Meals** L served all wk 12-2.30 D served all wk 6-9 Av main course £9 **Restaurant** L served all wk 12-2.30 D served all wk 6-9 Av 3 course à la carte fr £25 ◀ Directors, John Smith's Extra Smooth, Theakstons. ♥ 8 **Facilities** Children's menu Children's portions

| ST AUBIN | Map 24 |
|---|---|

### Old Court House Inn

St Aubin's Harbour JE3 8AB
☎ 01534 746433   📠 01534 745103
e-mail: info@oldcourthousejersey.com
dir: *From Jersey Airport, right at exit, left at lights, 0.5m to St Aubin*

The original courthouse at the rear of the property dates from 1450 and was first restored in 1611. Beneath the front part are enormous cellars where privateers stored their plunder. Three bars offer food, and there are two restaurants, the Granite and the Mizzen, with terrific views over the harbour, plus an attractive courtyard. There's lots of locally caught fish on the menus of course, plus hand dived scallops, moules marinière and Jersey lobster. Real ales include some from the Jersey Brewery.

Open all wk Closed: 25 Dec, Mon Jan-Feb **Bar Meals** L served all wk 12.30-2.30 D served Mon-Sat 7.30-10 Av main course £8 **Restaurant** L served all wk 12.30-2.30 D served all wk 7.30-10 Fixed menu price fr £10 Av 3 course à la carte fr £20 ⊕ FREE HOUSE ◀ Directors, Theakstons, John Smith's, Jersey Brewery. **Facilities** Children's menu Children's portions Dogs allowed

## ST MARTIN — Map 24

### Royal Hotel ♀

**La Grande Route de Faldouet JE3 6UG**
☎ **01534 856289** 📄 **01534 857298**
e-mail: johnbarker@jerseymail.co.uk
dir: *2m from Five Oaks rdbt towards St Martyn. Pub on right next to St Martin's Church*

A friendly atmosphere, value for money, and great food and drink are the hallmarks of this friendly local in the heart of St Martin. John Barker, the landlord, has been extending a welcome for 23 years at this former coaching inn. Roaring log fires warm winter visitors, and there's a sunny beer garden to relax in during the summer months. Among the traditional home-made favourites are steak and ale pie, fresh grilled trout, monkfish and prawn Thai curry, and vegetarian lasagne. Ploughman's lunches, filled jacket potatoes, grills and children's choices are also on offer.

**Open** all day all wk ◀ John Smith's Smooth, Theakstons Cool, Guinness, Ringwood Real Ale. ♀ 9 **Facilities** Play area Garden Parking

## ISLE OF MAN

### PEEL — Map 24 SC28

### The Creek Inn ♀

**Station Place IM5 1AT**
☎ **01624 842216** 📄 **01624 843359**
e-mail: thecreekinn@manx.net
dir: *On quayside opposite House of Mannanan Museum*

On the quayside, overlooked by Peel Hill, the family-run Creek Inn is a real ale drinkers' paradise, with locally brewed Okell's ales and up to five changing guests. Bands play every weekend, and nightly during the TT and Manx Grand Prix, when the pub becomes the town's focal point. Fish, such as Manx kippers, smoked peppered mackerel and seafood platter, accounts for most of the main courses, alongside sandwiches, baguettes, tortilla wraps, toasties and burgers.

**Open** all day all wk **Bar Meals** L served all wk 11-9.30 D served all wk 11-9.30 Av main course £8 food served all day **Restaurant** L served all wk 11-9.30 D served all wk 11-9.30 food served all day ⊕ FREE HOUSE ◀ Okells Bitter, Okells Seasonal, Bushy's Bitter, 4 guest ales ♂ Green Goblin, St Heliers. ♀ 12 **Facilities** Children's menu Children's portions Dogs allowed Garden Parking

### PORT ERIN — Map 24 SC26

### Falcon's Nest Hotel ★★ HL

**The Promenade, Station Rd IM9 6AF**
☎ **01624 834077** 📄 **01624 835370**
e-mail: falconsnest@enterprise.net
dir: *Follow coast road, S from airport or ferry. Hotel on seafront, immediately after steam railway station*

A magnificent pub-hotel overlooking a beautiful sheltered harbour and beach. Head for the saloon bar, 'Ophidian's Lair', for the pool table, jukebox and live sports via satellite; alternatively the residents' lounge, also open to the public, serves the same local ales from Okells and Bushy's, among others, and over 80 whiskies. The former ballroom has been restored and turned into a Victorian-style dining room, where local seafood dishes include crab, prawns, sea bass, marlin, lobster and local scallops known as 'queenies'; the carvery here is also very popular.

**Open** all wk **Bar Meals** L served all wk 12-2 D served all wk 6-9 Av main course £9 **Restaurant** L served all wk 12-2 D served all wk 6-9 Fixed menu price fr £17.50 Av 3 course à la carte fr £17.50 ⊕ FREE HOUSE ◀ Manx guest ale, Guinness, John Smith's, Okells, Bushy's, guest ales. **Facilities** Children's menu Children's portions Family room Dogs allowed Parking **Rooms** 39

# Scotland

Glen Coe, Loch Leven, Highland

## SCOTLAND

## CITY OF ABERDEEN

### ABERDEEN                    Map 23 NJ90

## Old Blackfriars ♀

**52 Castle St AB11 5BB**
☎ 01224 581922    📠 01224 582153
e-mail: oldblackfriars.aberdeen@belhavenpubs.net
dir: *From train station down Deeside to Union St. Turn right. Pub at end on right*

Situated in Aberdeen's historic Castlegate, this traditional split-level city centre pub stands on the site of property owned by Blackfriars Dominican monks, hence the name. Inside you'll find stunning stained glass, plus well kept real ales (9 handpumps) and a large selection of malt whisky. The pub is also renowned for excellent food and an unobtrusive atmosphere (no background music and no television). There are monthy quiz nights.

**Open** all day all wk Mon-Thu 11am-mdnt (Fri-Sat 11am-1am Sun 12.30-11) Closed: 25 Dec, 1 Jan **Bar Meals** L served all wk 12-9.30 D served all wk 12-9.30 food served all day **Restaurant** L served all wk 12-9.30 D served all wk 12-9.30 food served all day ⊕ BELHAVEN ◀ Abbot Ale, Deuchars IPA, Landlord, Inveralmond, Ossian, Guest ales. ♀ 14 **Facilities** Children's menu Family room

## ABERDEENSHIRE

### BALMEDIE                    Map 23 NJ91

## The Cock & Bull Bar & Restaurant ◉

**Ellon Rd, Blairton AB23 8XY**
☎ 01358 743249    📠 01358 742466
e-mail: info@thecockandbull.co.uk
dir: *11m N of city centre, on left of A90 between Balmedie junct & Foveran*

What was once a coaching inn has been developed into a cosy gastro-pub. The bar area, warmed by a cast-iron range, has big sofas and a hotchpotch of hanging junk, from a ship's lifebelt to a trombone. The menu ranges from bar dishes of fish and chips, and cheese and bacon burger to restaurant fare like loin of monkfish wrapped in Parma ham with tarragon and chilli couscous and roasted red pepper reduction.

**Open** all day all wk 10-11.30 (Sun 12-6.30) Closed: 25-26 Dec, 1-2 Jan **Bar Meals** L served Mon-Sat 10-2.30, Sun 12-6.30 D served Mon-Sat 5.30-8.45, Sun 12-6.30 ⊕ FREE HOUSE ◀ Caledonian 80, Guinness. **Facilities** Children's menu Play area Garden Parking

### MARYCULTER                    Map 23 NO89

## Old Mill Inn

**South Deeside Rd AB12 5FX**
☎ 01224 733212    📠 01224 732884
e-mail: Info@oldmillinn.co.uk
dir: *5m W of Aberdeen on B9077*

This delightful family-run 200-year-old country inn stands on the edge of the River Dee, five miles from Aberdeen city centre. A former mill house, the 18th-century granite building has been tastefully modernised to include a restaurant where the finest Scottish ingredients feature on the menu: venison stovies, peppered carpaccio of beef, cullen skink, and chicken and venison terrine are typical. Food and drink can be enjoyed in the garden in warmer months.

**Open** all wk **Bar Meals** L served all wk 12-2 D served all wk 5.30-9 **Restaurant** L served all wk 12-2 D served all wk 5.30-9 ⊕ FREE HOUSE ◀ Caledonian Deuchars IPA, Timothy Taylor Landlord, London Pride. **Facilities** Children's menu Children's portions Garden Parking

### NETHERLEY                    Map 23 NO89

## PICK OF THE PUBS

### The Lairhillock Inn

**AB39 3QS** ☎ 01569 730001    📠 01569 731175
e-mail: info@lairhillock.co.uk
dir: *From Aberdeen take A90. Right towards Durris on B9077 then left onto B979 to Netherley*

Set in beautiful rural Deeside yet only 15 minutes drive from Aberdeen, this award-winning 200-year-old former coaching inn offers real ales in the bar and real fires in the lounge to keep out the winter chill. Dishes are robust and use a bounty of fresh, quality, local and regional produce such as langoustines from Gourdon, mussels from Shetland, scallops from Orkney, wild boar and venison from the Highlands and salmon from the Dee and Don, not forgetting certified Aberdeen Angus beef. In the bar and conservatory, try the Cullen skink; or peat smoked salmon with citrus dressing; followed by pan-fried duck breast on vanilla mash; or smoked haddock, pancetta and spring onion fishcakes. For a more formal dining option, the atmospheric Crynoch Restaurant menu might feature a starter of cauliflower pannacotta; or seared partridge breast with Stornoway black pudding; followed by main dishes such as seafood pot-au-feuille; or grilled saddle of venison with thyme jus. Quality also abounds on the children's menu.

**Open** all day all wk Closed: 25-26 Dec, 1-2 Jan **Bar Meals** L served all wk 12-2 booking required D served all wk 6-9.30 booking required Av main course £10.50 **Restaurant** L served Sun 12-2 booking required D served Tue-Sat 7-9.30 booking required Av 3 course à la carte fr £27 ⊕ FREE HOUSE ◀ Timothy Taylor Landlord, Deuchars IPA, Guest ales. **Facilities** Children's menu Children's portions Dogs allowed Garden Parking

### OLDMELDRUM                    Map 23 NJ82

## The Redgarth

**Kirk Brae AB51 0DJ** ☎ 01651 872353    📠 01651 873763
e-mail: redgarth1@aol.com
dir: *From A947 (Oldmeldrum bypass) follow signs to Golf Club/Pleasure Park. Establishment E of bypass*

Built as a house in 1928, this friendly family-run inn has been in the same hands for the past 20 years. It is situated in a small village with an attractive garden that offers magnificent views of Bennachie and the surrounding countryside. Cask-conditioned ales, such as Orkney Scapa and Inveralmond Thrappledouser, and interesting wines are served along with dishes prepared on the premises using fresh local produce. A typical selection might include duo of hot and cold salmon with horseradish mayonnaise, or pork fillet stuffed with black pudding served with red cabbage in pear cider gravy.

**Open** all wk 11-3 5-11 (Fri-Sat 11-3 5-11.45) Closed: 25-26 Dec, 1-3 Jan **Bar Meals** L served all wk 12-2 D served Sun-Thu 5-9, Fri-Sat 5-9.30 Av main course £10 **Restaurant** L served all wk 12-2 booking required D served Sun-Thu 5-9, Fri-Sat 5-9.30 booking required Av 3 course à la carte fr £18 ⊕ FREE HOUSE ◀ Inveralmond Thrappledouser, Timothy Taylor Landlord, Orkney Scapa & Best, Pivo Estivo. **Facilities** Children's menu Children's portions Garden Parking

### STRATHDON                    Map 23 NJ31

## PICK OF THE PUBS

## The Glenkindie Arms ★★★ INN ◉
## NEW

*See Pick of the Pubs on opposite page*

# PICK OF THE PUBS

## The Glenkindie Arms ★★★ INN ❀ NEW

**STRATHDON** Map 23 NJ31

**Glenkindie AB33 8SX** ☎ **01975 641288**
e-mail: iansimpson1873@live.co.uk
**dir:** *On A97 between Alford & Strathdon*

Set in Upper Donsdale, close to Balmoral and the Malt Whisky Trail, and enjoying breathtaking views of the Highlands, this 400-year-old traditional drovers' inn has been spruced-up with style and panache by chef/patron Ian Simpson and Aneta Olechno, who took over the inn in 2009, bringing with them a relaxed and friendly attitude. They injected their passion for good food and drink into the place, offering local real ales from Inveralmond, Cairngorm and Deeside breweries, 40 single malts and menus that bristle with meat, eggs and vegetables from local farms. Ian has an enviable culinary pedigree having served a stint at Gordon Ramsay's operation in Claridges.

Expect sound modern Scottish cooking, with dishes kept unfussy and put together with attention to detail and well balanced flavours. On the set dinner menu listing expect such starters as Wark Farm Black Spot pork terrine with spiced pear purée and home-baked bread, smoked ham hock and lentil soup, or pan-seared West Coast queen scallops with mint pea purée, bacon crisp and micro radish. Main course options may take in roast rump of Dexter beef with thyme Yorkshire pudding, roast potato, Cushlachie seasonal vegetables and beef jus, and poached Scrabster landed bream with cockle fricassée, saffron potato, baby spinach and sauce vièrge, with bitter chocolate tart or spiced rice pudding with apple compôte for pudding.

Book to avoid disappointment as The Glenkindie Arms is popular but not a large place. Even if you want to pop in for a drink, a quick call will avoid being turned away. For evening dining with children, there is a separate dining room. Comfortable accommodation is available.

**Open** all day all wk Closed: 3wks Nov **Bar Meals** Av main course £9.75 food served all day **Restaurant** Fixed menu price £19.95 or £23.95 (3 courses) food served all day ⊕ FREE HOUSE ◼ Inveralmond Brewery Ossian, Thrappledouser, Lia Fail, Houston Brewing Company Peters Well, Cairngorm Brewery Company Trade Winds. **Facilities** Children's menu Garden Parking **Rooms** 3

## ARGYLL & BUTE

### ARDUAINE                    Map 20 NM71

#### PICK OF THE PUBS

### Loch Melfort Hotel ★★★ HL ●●●

**PA34 4XG ☎ 01852 200233**
e-mail: reception@lochmelfort.co.uk
dir: *On A816, midway between Oban & Lochgilphead*

Standing in 26-acre grounds next to Arduaine Gardens, this is the perfect place for a relaxing holiday or short break. There's a uniquely informal and relaxed atmosphere as you step into the warmth and tranquility of this comfortable country house. Choose to dine in the formal Arduaine Restaurant, where poached pigeon breast, Stornoway black pudding, Puy lentils with apple and vanilla purée might introduce a main course of grilled Loch Duart salmon fillet, crushed potatoes and crab, tomato butter sauce. The more relaxed atmosphere of the modern Chartroom 2 bar and bistro is the place to enjoy all-day drinks and home baking, as well as light lunches and suppers. It has the finest views on the West Coast and serves home-made Scottish fare including plenty of locally landed seafood. You can sit outside and enjoy a drink in warmer weather or sit around the cosy fire in winter and watch the waves crashing against the rocks.

**Open** all wk 11-10 **Bar Meals** L served all wk 12-2.30 D served all wk 6-8.30 Av main course £8.50 ● FREE HOUSE ◀ 80/- Ale Belhaven, Fyne Ale. ♥ 8
**Facilities** Children's menu Children's portions Play area Dogs allowed Garden Parking **Rooms** 25

### CLACHAN-SEIL                Map 20 NM71

#### PICK OF THE PUBS

### Tigh an Truish Inn

**PA34 4QZ ☎ 01852 300242**
web: www.tighantruish.co.uk
dir: *12m S of Oban take A816. Onto B844 towards Atlantic Bridge*

Following the Battle of Culloden in 1746, kilts were outlawed on pain of death. The Seil islanders defied this edict at home but, on excursions to the mainland, they would stop at the Tigh an Truish – the 'house of trousers' – to change into the hated trews. Now popular with tourists and members of the yachting fraternity, the inn's waterfront beer garden is much in demand on summer days, where the tides can be watched as they

swirl around the famous Bridge over the Atlantic. Ales from local brewers stock the bar, along with a range of single malts, while an appetising menu is particularly well endowed with fresh seafood: salmon and mussels from Argyll producers, and salmon and prawns caught by local fishermen working the Firth of Lorne. If this all sounds rather sophisticated, families need not worry; a separate lounge off the main bar is furnished with children's books – another indication of the pub's genuinely warm welcome.

**Open** all wk 11-11 (Mon-Fri 11-2.30 5-11 Oct-Mar) Closed: 25 Dec & 1 Jan **Bar Meals** L served all wk 12-2 D served all wk 6-8.30 (Apr-Oct) Av main course £8.50 ● FREE HOUSE ◀ Local guest ales changing regularly.
**Facilities** Family room Dogs allowed Garden Parking

### CONNEL                      Map 20 NM93

#### PICK OF THE PUBS

### The Oyster Inn

**PA37 1PJ ☎ 01631 710666  ▤ 01631 710042**
e-mail: stay@oysterinn.co.uk
dir: *Telephone for directions*

A comfortable, informal hotel overlooking the tidal whirlpools and white water of the Falls of Lora, and enjoying glorious views of the mountains of Mull. It was built in the 18th century to serve ferry passengers, but the ferry has long since been superseded by the modern road bridge. Ferryman's Bar in the pub next door was, and still is, known as the Glue Pot. Years ago canny locals knew they could be 'stuck' here between ferries and evade Oban's Sunday licensing laws; additionally, a blacksmith's shop behind the pub melted down horses hooves for glue – the pots hang from the bar ceiling. Food is served all day, using locally-sourced quality produce, particularly from the sea and lochs: half a dozen West Coast oysters; chef's signature seafood chowder; and classic fish and chips. Meaty alternatives may include the home-made beef burger; or Ferryman's chicken Rob Roy (stuffed with haggis, in a whisky cream sauce).

**Open** all day all wk noon-mdnt **Bar Meals** L served all wk 12.30-5.30 D served all wk 6-9.30 Av main course £7.95 food served all day **Restaurant** L served all wk 12.30-3 D served all wk 6-9.30 Av 3 course à la carte fr £30 ● FREE HOUSE ◀ Guinness, John Smith's.
**Facilities** Children's menu Children's portions Family room Dogs allowed Garden Parking

### CRINAN                      Map 20 NR79

#### PICK OF THE PUBS

### Crinan Hotel

**PA31 8SR ☎ 01546 830261  ▤ 01546 830292**
e-mail: reservations@crinanhotel.com
dir: *From M8, at end of bridge take A82, at Tarbert left onto A83. At Inverary follow Campbeltown signs to Lochgilphead, follow signs for A816 to Oban. 2m, left to Crinan on B841*

At the north end of the Crinan Canal which connects Loch Fyne to the Atlantic Ocean, the Crinan is a romantic retreat enjoying fabulous views across the sound of Jura. It's a long-standing place of welcome at the heart of community life in this tiny fishing village. The hotel dates back some 200 years and has been run by owners Nick and Frances Ryan for nearly 40 of them. Eat in the Panther Arms or Mainbrace Bar, where you can sample Scottish beers or whiskies while chatting to the locals, or the Westward Restaurant. The cuisine is firmly based on the freshest of seafood – it's landed daily just 50 metres from the hotel. Bar dishes could include pickled herring with celeriac remoulade; Shetland crab and cream risotto; or Loch Crinan seafood chowder. From the dinner menu perhaps choose cauliflower velouté and sautéed cockles; roast fillet of Aberdeen Angus beef; roast saddle of Argyll venison; or pan-fried West Coast cod. Boat trips can be arranged to the islands, and there is a classic boats regatta in the summer.

**Open** all wk Closed: Xmas ◀ Belhaven, Interbrew, Worthington Bitter, Tennent's Velvet, Guinness, Loch Fyne Ales. **Facilities** Dogs allowed Garden Parking

### DUNOON                      Map 20 NS17

### Coylet Inn

**Loch Eck PA23 8SG ☎ 01369 840426**
e-mail: info@coyletinn.co.uk
dir: *9m N of Dunoon on A815*

A blissful hideaway with no television or games machines to disturb the peace, this beautifully refurbished 17th-century coaching inn overlooks the shores of Loch Eck and is famous for its ghost, the Blue Boy; a film was even made of the story, starring Emma Thompson. Unwind by one of three log fires with a pint of Pipers Gold or plunder the impressive menus, where choices range from salad of roll-mop herring to pan-seared pork loin with Stornoway black pudding and honey and mustard sauce. There is Wednesday steak deal and Friday fish supper to look forward to.

**Open** all day Closed: 3-26 Jan, Mon & Tue (Oct-Mar) **Bar Meals** L served all wk 12-2.30 D served all wk 6-8.30 Av main course £9.95 **Restaurant** L served all wk 12-2.30 D served all wk 6-8.30 ● FREE HOUSE ◀ Highlander, Pipers Gold, guest ales. **Facilities** Children's menu Children's portions Dogs allowed Garden Parking

# PICK OF THE PUBS

## Cairnbaan Hotel ★★★ HL

**LOCHGILPHEAD**          Map 20 NR88

**Cairnbaan PA31 8SJ**
☎ 01546 603668   📠 01546 606045
e-mail: info@cairnbaan.com
web: www.cairnbaan.com
dir: *2m N, take A816 from Lochgilphead, hotel off B841*

Once considered the wildest pub in Mid-Argyll, with goats and other animals sharing space at the bar, the Cairnbaan is now stylish, relaxed and particularly popular with the waterway-cruising fraternity. Originally a coaching inn, the hotel was built in the latter part of the 18th century during the construction of the Crinan Canal. Nowadays it's owned by ex-QE2 catering officer Darren Dobson and his wife Christine, a former teacher, who plans the menus and does all the baking.

Lighter meals are served from the bistro-style menu in the relaxed atmosphere of the bar, conservatory lounge, or al fresco. For a more formal occasion dine in the serene, AA Rosetted restaurant, where the carte specialises in the use of fresh local produce, notably seafood and game. Look for starters of twice baked lobster soufflé with langoustine sauce; fried halloumi cheese with sweet chilli jam and leaves; or Tarbet landed langoustine with bread, salad and mayo. Mains might include mushroom risotto cakes stuffed with mozzarella and served with herb truffle oil and salad; local seafood stew with chorizo and garlic bread; or roast breast of duck with Stornoway black pudding, white onion sauce and roast potatoes. Round off, perhaps, with lemon posset, passionfruit and langue de chat; profiteroles with chocolate sauce; or tiramisu with black cherries.

From nearby Oban there are sailings to the islands of Mull, Coll and Tiree. Inveraray Castle is also well worth a visit, as is Dunadd Fort where the ancient kings of Scotland were crowned. With so much to see and do in the area, the en suite bedrooms could be worth considering.

**Open** all wk **Bar Meals** L served all wk 12-2.30 D served all wk 6-9.30 **Restaurant** L served all wk 12-2.30 D served all wk 6-9.30 ⊕ FREE HOUSE ◖ Local ales. ⏚ 8 **Facilities** Children's menu Garden Parking **Rooms** 12

## KILFINAN
Map 20 NR97

### Kilfinan Hotel Bar

PA21 2EP ☎ 01700 821201 📠 01700 821205
e-mail: info@kilfinan.com
dir: 8m N of Tighnabruaich on B8000

On the eastern shore of Loch Fyne, set amid spectacular Highland scenery on a working estate, this hotel has been welcoming travellers since the 1760s. The bars are cosy with log fires in winter, and offer a fine selection of malts. There are two intimate dining rooms, with the Lamont room for larger parties. Menus change daily and offer the best of local produce: Loch Fyne langoustines grilled in garlic and butter; pan seared Loch Fyne scallops with crispy bacon and sage; or Isle of Bute venison steak. Enjoy the views from the garden on warmer days.

Open all wk Closed: winter Bar Meals L served all wk 12.30-4 D served all wk 6.30-9.30 Av main course £7.95 Restaurant L served all wk 12.30-4 booking required D served all wk 6.30-9.30 booking required Av 3 course à la carte fr £22 ⊕ FREE HOUSE ◀ McEwens 80/-, Fyne Ales. Facilities Children's menu Children's portions Family room Dogs allowed Garden Parking

## LOCHGILPHEAD
Map 20 NR88

### PICK OF THE PUBS

### Cairnbaan Hotel ★★★ HL ◉ ☻

See Pick of the Pubs on page 559

## LUSS
Map 20 NS39

### PICK OF THE PUBS

### The Inn at Inverbeg ★★★★ INN ☻

G83 8PD ☎ 01436 860678 📠 01436 860203
e-mail: inverbeg.reception@loch-lomond.co.uk
dir: 12m N of Balloch

Dating from 1814, but expensively remodelled and refurbished in contemporary style in 2008, the Inverbeg is an extremely popular venue for those living on or travelling the western shore of Loch Lomond. Set imposingly back from the main A82, you won't miss it – look for the flagpoles. In Mr C's Fish & Whisky Bar and Restaurant, swish leather furnishings and roaring log fires provide the ambience for West Coast steamed mussels; black pudding and haggis fritters; fresh Mallaig langoustines; penne pomodoro; chargrilled Buccleuch steak burgers; Thai-style chicken curry; and highly regarded fish and chips, as well as more than 200 malts and real ales, such as Deuchars IPA. Comfortable, individually styled rooms are split between the inn and, right by the loch, a sumptuous beach house featuring wooden floors, hand-crafted furniture, crisp linen, and a hot tub. There is traditional, live folk music every night throughout the summer. This was AA Pub of the Year for Scotland 2009-2010.

Open all day all wk 11-11 Bar Meals L served all wk 12-9 D served all wk 12-9 Av main course £9 food served all day Restaurant L served all wk 12-9 D served all wk 12-9 Av 3 course à la carte fr £19 food served all day ⊕ FREE HOUSE ◀ Killellan, Highlander, Deuchars IPA. ☻ 30 Facilities Children's menu Children's portions Parking Rooms 20

## PORT APPIN
Map 20 NM94

### PICK OF THE PUBS

### The Pierhouse Hotel & Seafood Restaurant ★★★ SHL ◉

PA38 4DE ☎ 01631 730302 📠 01631 730509
e-mail: reservations@pierhousehotel.co.uk
dir: A828 from Ballachulish to Oban. In Appin right at Port Appin & Lismore ferry sign. After 2.5m left after post office, hotel at end of road by pier

With breathtaking views to the islands of Lismore and Mull, it would be hard to imagine a more spectacular setting for this family-run 12-bedroom hotel and renowned seafood restaurant. Once home to the piermaster, the distinctive building now houses a popular bar, pool room, terrace and dining area, and offers a selection of menus featuring the finest seasonal Scottish seafood, meat, game and vegetables. Lunches in the Ferry bar range from freshly-filled ciabattas and baked potatoes to burgers, pastas and fish dishes. Meanwhile a typical three-course restaurant meal might start with velvet crab bisque, seafood medley and lemon oil; before progressing to roast loin of Kingairloch venison with truffle mashed potato, creamy Savoy cabbage and venison jus. The tempting desserts include Pierhouse sorbets and chocolate fondant with clotted cream. Twelve individually designed bedrooms include two with four-poster beds and superb loch views, and three triple family rooms.

Open all wk 11-11 Closed: 25-26 Dec Bar Meals L served all wk 12.30-2.30 D served all wk 6.30-7.30 Av main course £9.95 Restaurant L served all wk 12.30-2.30 booking required D served all wk 6.30-9.30 booking required Fixed menu price fr £30 Av 3 course à la carte fr £24.85 ⊕ FREE HOUSE ◀ Calders 80, Belhaven Best, Guinness. Facilities Family room Dogs allowed Garden Parking Rooms 12

## STRACHUR
Map 20 NN00

### PICK OF THE PUBS

### Creggans Inn ★★★ HL ◉◉

PA27 8BX ☎ 01369 860279 📠 01369 860637
e-mail: info@creggans-inn.co.uk
dir: A82 from Glasgow, at Tarbet take A83 towards Cairndow, left onto A815 to Strachur

From the hills above this informal family-friendly free house on the shores of Loch Fyne, you can gaze across the Mull of Kintyre to the Western Isles beyond. It has been a coaching inn since the days of Mary Queen of Scots. Current proprietors Archie and Gill MacLellan were preceded years ago by Sir Fitzroy Maclean, reputedly the man upon whom Ian Fleming based his most famous character. A good selection of real ales, wines by the glass and malt whiskies are all served at the bar. There's a formal terraced garden and patio for alfresco summer enjoyment. Regional produce plays a key role in the seasonal menus: the famed Loch Fyne oysters of course, but also salmon from the same waters, smoked or grilled. Robust main courses may feature cullen skink; fillet of Aberdeenshire beef; East Coast haddock in a crisp beer batter; Balagowan venison sausages; or thyme and lemon roast chicken. Apple and bramble tart with home-made cinnamon ice cream makes a fulfilling conclusion.

Open all day all wk 11am-mdnt Bar Meals L served all wk 12-2.30 D served all wk 6-8.30 Av main course £10 Restaurant D served all wk 7-8.30 booking required Fixed menu price fr £37 ⊕ FREE HOUSE ◀ Fyne Ales Highlander, Atlas Latitude, Deuchars IPA, Harvieston Bitter & Twisted. Facilities Children's menu Children's portions Dogs allowed Garden Parking Rooms 14

## TAYVALLICH
Map 20 NR78

### Tayvallich Inn ☻

PA31 8PL ☎ 01546 870282
dir: From Lochgilphead take A816 then B841/B8025

The inn stands by a natural harbour at the head of Loch Sween with stunning views over the anchorage, particularly from the outside area of decking, where food and drinks can be enjoyed. Not surprisingly given the location, fresh seafood features strongly, along with seasonally changing dishes. There's always lobster, crab and langoustine available in the summer and other typical dishes might be line-caught haddock served with chips; fish pie; beef and ale pie; and home-made burgers. Tayvallich Inn changed hands in late 2009.

Open all wk all day in Summer (closed 3-6 Mon-Fri in Winter) Closed: 25-26 Dec, Mon (Nov-Mar) Bar Meals L served all wk 12-2.30 D served all wk 6-9 Av main course £9.95 Restaurant L served all wk 12-2.30 booking required D served all wk 6-9 booking required Fixed menu price fr £18.95 Av 3 course à la carte fr £18.95 ⊕ FREE HOUSE ◀ Tennent's, Guinness, Loch Fyne Ales, Belhaven Best. ☻ 8 Facilities Children's menu Children's portions Garden Parking

# CLACKMANNANSHIRE

## DOLLAR
Map 21 NS99

### Castle Campbell Hotel ★★★ SHL ☻

11 Bridge St FK14 7DE
☎ 01259 742519 📠 01259 743742
e-mail: bookings@castle-campbell.co.uk
dir: A91 (Stirling to St Andrews road). In Dollar centre by bridge overlooking clock tower

Handy for Dollar Glen's spectacular gorges, this 19th-century coaching inn offers a real taste of Scotland. Built in 1821, pictures on the walls date back to that period. Recognised as a Whisky Ambassador, the hotel has over 50 malts; local ale is always on tap and the wine list runs to several pages. Prime Scottish produce features on the menus, with options ranging from fish and chips in the bar to seared rack of lamb with red wine and rosemary in the restaurant.

**Open** all wk **Bar Meals** L served all wk 12-2 D served all wk 5.30-9 **Restaurant** L served all wk 12-2 booking required D served all wk 5.30-9 booking required ⊕ FREE HOUSE ◀ Harviestoun Bitter & Twisted, Deuchars IPA (guest), McEwans 70'. ☙ 9 **Facilities** Children's menu Children's portions Dogs allowed Parking **Rooms** 9

## DUMFRIES & GALLOWAY

### ISLE OF WHITHORN    Map 20 NX43

## PICK OF THE PUBS

## The Steam Packet Inn ☙

Harbour Row DG8 8LL
☎ 01988 500334    📄 01988 500627
e-mail: steampacketinn@btconnect.com
dir: *From Newton Stewart take A714, then A746 to Whithorn, then Isle of Whithorn*

This lively quayside pub stands in a picturesque village at the tip of the Machars peninsula. Personally run by the Scoular family for over 20 years, it is the perfect place to escape from the pressures of modern living. Sit in one of the comfortable bars, undisturbed by television, fruit machines or piped music, and enjoy one of the real ales, a malt whisky from the great selection, or a glass of wine. Glance out of the picture windows and watch the fishermen at work, then look to the menu for a chance to sample the fruits of their labours. Extensive seafood choices - perhaps a kettle of mussels cooked in a cream and white wine sauce, isle-landed monkfish tail or fillet of bream - are supported by the likes of haggis-stuffed mushroom; and braised Galloway lamb shank.

**Open** all wk 11-11 (Sun noon-11) Closed: 25 Dec, winter Tue-Thu 2.30-6 **Bar Meals** L served all wk 12-2 D served all wk 6.30-9 ⊕ FREE HOUSE ◀ Timothy Taylor Landlord, Caledonian Deuchars IPA, Black Sheep Best Bitter, Houston Killellan. ☙ 12 **Facilities** Children's menu Children's portions Dogs allowed Garden Parking

### KIRKCUDBRIGHT    Map 20 NX65

## Selkirk Arms Hotel ★★★ HL ☙

Old High St DG6 4JG
☎ 01557 330402    📄 01557 331639
e-mail: reception@selkirkarmshotel.co.uk
web: www.selkirkarmshotel.co.uk
dir: *M74 & M6 to A75, halfway between Dumfries & Stranraer on A75*

Robert Burns is reputed to have written the Selkirk Grace at this privately owned hotel, and the proprietors have created their own real ale, The Selkirk Grace, in conjunction with Sulwath Brewers. There are two bars, and a great choice of dishes is offered in The Bistro or more intimate Artistas Restaurant, including pan-seared Kirkcudbright king scallops; slow roast lamb shank; and Eccelfechan butter tart. Accommodation is provided in 17 en suite bedrooms.

**Open** all wk ◀ Youngers Tartan, John Smith's Bitter, Criffel, Timothy Taylor Landlord, The Selkirk Grace. ☙ 8 **Facilities** Dogs allowed Garden Parking **Rooms** 17

### MOFFAT    Map 21 NT00

## Annandale Arms ★★★ HL ◉ NEW

High St DG10 9HF ☎ 01683 220013    📄 01683 221395
e-mail: reception@annandalearmshotel.co.uk
dir: *A74(M) junct 15. Take A701, Moffat 1m*

At the centre of Moffat's history for over 250 years, it used to be a matter of pride that this hostelry could change a coach and four in less than a minute, in which time the driver would down a pint of ale; today, Broughton's Merlin deserves much more time and appreciation. The menus, too, are worth pondering over: choose between 'wee balls of haggis' or goujons of sole on the bar menu, roast marinated chump of Dumfriesshire lamb from the restaurant carte, or specials such as duck and cherry pie.

**Open** all day all wk **Bar Meals** L served all wk 12-2.30 D served all wk 6-9 Av main course £8.50 **Restaurant** L served all wk 12-2.30 booking required D served all wk 6-9 Fixed menu price fr £25 Av 3 course à la carte fr £25 ⊕ FREE HOUSE ◀ Merlin, Reiver ◔ Westons First Quality, Westons Scrumpy. **Facilities** Children's menu Children's portions Dogs allowed Garden Parking **Rooms** 16

## Black Bull Hotel ☙

Churchgate DG10 9EG
☎ 01683 220206    📄 01683 220483
e-mail: hotel@blackbullmoffat.co.uk
dir: *Telephone for directions*

This historic pub was the headquarters of Graham of Claverhouse during the 17th-century Scottish rebellion, and was frequented by Robert Burns around 1790. The Railway Bar, in former stables across the courtyard, houses a collection of railway memorabilia and traditional pub games. Food is served in the lounge, Burns Room or restaurant. Dishes include Black Bull sizzlers (steak, chicken fillets, gammon) served on a cast iron platter; the daily roast, and deep-fried breaded haddock fillet. Recent change of hands.

**Open** all day all wk 11-11 (Thu-Sat 11-12 Sun 12-11) Closed: 25 Dec ⊕ FREE HOUSE ◀ McEwans, John Smith's. ☙ 10 **Facilities** Dogs allowed Garden Parking

### NEW ABBEY    Map 21 NX96

## Criffel Inn

2 The Square DG2 8BX
☎ 01387 850305 & 850244    📄 01387 850305
e-mail: criffelinn@btconnect.com
dir: *A74/A74(M) exit at Gretna, A75 to Dumfries, A710 to New Abbey*

On the Solway Coast in the historic conservation village of New Abbey, this former 18th-century coaching inn is ideal for touring Dumfries and Galloway. It sits close to the ruins of the 13th-century Sweetheart Abbey and has a lawned beer garden overlooking the cornmill and square. Expect a warm welcome, well kept beers and excellent home-cooked food using local produce, such as the chicken breast stuffed with haggis or the deep-fried breaded haddock.

**Open** all wk noon-2.30 5-11 (Sat noon-mdnt Sun noon-11) **Bar Meals** L served Wed-Sun 12-2 D served Wed-Sun 5-8 Av main course £7.50 **Restaurant** L served Wed-Sun 12-2 D served Wed-Sun 5-8 ⊕ FREE HOUSE ◀ Belhaven Best, McEwans 60-, Guinness. **Facilities** Children's menu Children's portions Family room Dogs allowed Garden Parking

### NEW GALLOWAY    Map 20 NX67

## Cross Keys Hotel ☙

High St DG7 3RN ☎ 01644 420494    📄 01644 701071
e-mail: enquiries@thecrosskeys-newgalloway.co.uk
dir: *At N end of Loch Ken, 10m from Castle Douglas on A712*

An 18th-century coaching inn with a beamed period bar, where food is served in restored, stone-walled cells (part of the hotel was once the police station). The à la carte restaurant offers hearty food with a Scottish accent, chicken stuffed with haggis and served with whisky sauce being a prime example. Real ales are a speciality, and there's a good choice of malts in the whisky bar.

*continued*

**NEW GALLOWAY** *continued*

**Open** all wk 6-11.30 Closed: Sun & Mon eve winter
**Bar Meals** L served all wk 6.30-8.30 ⊕ FREE HOUSE
◀ Houston, Sulwarth, guest ales ♂ Stowford Press. ♀ 9
**Facilities** Children's menu Dogs allowed Garden

### NEWTON STEWART     Map 20 NX46

## PICK OF THE PUBS

## Creebridge House Hotel

**Minnigaff DG8 6NP**
☎ 01671 402121    📄 01671 403258
e-mail: info@creebridge.co.uk
**dir:** *From A75 into Newton Stewart, turn right over river
bridge, hotel 200yds on left*

A listed building dating from 1760, this family-run,
country house hotel stands in three acres of tranquil
gardens and woodland at the foot of Kirroughtree
forest. Taking its name from the River Cree, the hotel
used to be the Earl of Galloway's shooting lodge and
the grounds part of his estate. The bar and brasserie
offer malt whiskies and real ales, including Creebridge
Golden Ale from the Houston Brewery. For lunch or
candlelit dinner in the restaurant, the well-filled menu
offers plenty of dishes with Scottish credentials, such
as grilled locally made haggis with melted Cheddar
and rich whisky cream sauce; pan-fried haunch of
Highland venison; Galloway wholetail scampi; and West
Coast prawn and salmon penne pasta. Home-made
desserts include pear and almond tart with custard,
and lemon posset with shortbread. If you're an outdoor
sort, this is the place to be as there is fishing, golf,
cycling, horse riding walking and deer stalking.

**Open** all wk noon-2 6-11.30 (Fri-Sat noon-2 6-1am)
**Bar Meals** L served all wk 12-2 D served all wk 6-9
⊕ FREE HOUSE ◀ Tennent's, Deuchars, Guinness,
guest ales. **Facilities** Dogs allowed Garden Parking

## The Galloway Arms Hotel ♀

**54-58 Victoria St DG8 6DB**
☎ 01671 402653    📄 01671 401202
e-mail: info@gallowayarmshotel.com
**dir:** *In town centre, opposite clock*

Established in 1750, the Galloway Arms Hotel is older
than the town of Newton Stewart, which was built around
it. The newly refurbished Earls Room lounge offers an
unrivalled range of over 100 malt whiskies, as well as
real ale and traditional Scottish beers. Local produce

from a 20-mile radius is the foundation of most dishes,
which might feature fresh Kirkcudbright scallops, beef
sourced from only five local farms or Galloway venison.

**Open** all day all wk 11am-mdnt (Fri-Sat 11am-1am)
**Bar Meals** L served all wk 12-2 D served all wk 6-9
**Restaurant** D served all wk 6-9 ⊕ FREE HOUSE
◀ Belhaven Best, Guinness, Caledonian Deuchars IPA.
♀ 11 **Facilities** Children's menu Children's portions Dogs
allowed Garden Parking

### PORTPATRICK     Map 20 NW95

## Crown Hotel ♀

**9 North Crescent DG9 8SX** ☎ 01776 810261
e-mail: info@crownportpatrick.com
**dir:** *Take A77 from ferry port at Stranraer*

Just a few yards from the water's edge in one of the
region's most picturesque villages, the Crown has
striking views across the Irish Sea. The rambling old bar
has seafaring displays and a warming winter fire.
Naturally seafood is a speciality: starters range from crab
and scallop fish soup, to fresh local crab claws in dill
sauce; main courses continue the briny celebration with a
hot seafood platter, or whole fresh pan-fried sea bass.

**Open** all wk ◀ John Smith's, McEwans 80/-, McEwans
70/-, Guinness. ♀ 8 **Facilities** Family room Garden
Parking

### SANDHEAD     Map 20 NX04

## Tigh Na Mara Hotel NEW

**Main St DG9 9JF** ☎ 01776 830210    📄 01776 830432
e-mail: tighnamara@btconnect.com
**dir:** *A75 from Dumfries towards Stranraer. Left onto
B7084 to Sandhead. Hotel in village centre*

Meaning 'house by the sea', this family-owned hotel and
restaurant stands within a stone's throw of a beautiful
stretch of unspoilt, sandy beach and breathtaking views.
Enjoy a drink in the bar with its warming fire or relax in
the comfortable lounge. From the extensive menu in the
popular restaurant choose fresh, local produce such as
succulent Scottish beef; seafood from the West Coast;
duo of pheasant and pigeon with Stornoway black
pudding and Arran mustard cream. This is the perfect
spot for walking, fishing or a game of golf.

**Open** all day all wk **Bar Meals** L served all wk 12-2.30 D
served all wk 6-9 **Restaurant** L served all wk 12-2.30 D
served all wk 6-9 booking required ⊕ BELHAVEN
◀ Belhaven Best, Morland Old Speckled Hen.
**Facilities** Children's menu Children's portions Family
room Dogs allowed Garden Parking

### DUNDEE, CITY OF

### BROUGHTY FERRY     Map 21 NO43

## The Royal Arch Bar ♀

**285 Brook St DD5 2DS**
☎ 01382 779741    📄 01382 739174
**dir:** *3m from Dundee. 0.5 min from Broughty Ferry rail
station*

In Victorian times, the jute industry made Broughty Ferry
the 'richest square mile in Europe'. Named after a
Masonic lodge which was demolished to make way for the
Tay Road Bridge, the pub dates from 1869. The deep, dry
cellars are ideal for conditioning ale so look forward to a
nice pint in the bar with its original hand-carved oak bar,
sideboard and counter. An extensive selection of meals at
this community pub range from light snacks to three-
course meals, served in the bar, lounge, restaurant or
pavement café.

**Open** all day all wk Closed: 1 Jan **Bar Meals** L served
Mon-Fri 12-2.15, Sat-Sun 12-5 booking required D served
all wk 5-7.30 booking required Av main course £7 food
served all day **Restaurant** Fixed menu price fr £8 ⊕ FREE
HOUSE ◀ McEwans 80/-, Belhaven Best, Caledonian,
Deuchars IPA, Angus Mashie Niblick Cask. ♀ 30
**Facilities** Children's portions Family room Dogs allowed
Garden

### DUNDEE     Map 21 NO43

## Speedwell Bar ♀

**165-167 Perth Rd DD2 1AS** ☎ 01382 667783
e-mail: jonathan_stewart@fsmail.net
**dir:** *From city centre along Perth Rd, pass university, last
bar on right*

This fine example of an unspoiled Edwardian bar is worth
visiting for its interior alone; all the fitments in the bar
and sitting rooms are beautifully crafted mahogany –
gantry, drink shelves, dado panelling and fireplace. The
same family owned it for 90 years, until the present
landlord's father bought it in 1995. As well as the cask-
conditioned ales, 157 whiskies and imported bottles are
offered. A kitchen would be good, but since the pub is
listed this is impossible. This community pub is home to
several clubs and has live Scottish music every Tuesday.

**Open** all day all wk ⊕ FREE HOUSE ◀ McEwans,
Belhaven Best, Caley Deuchars IPA. ♀ 18 **Facilities** Dogs
allowed **Notes** ⊛

## EAST AYRSHIRE

### DALRYMPLE Map 20 NS31

#### The Kirkton Inn

**1 Main St KA6 6DF ☎ 01292 560241**
**e-mail:** kirkton@cqm.co.uk
**dir:** *6m SE from centre of Ayr just off A77*

In the heart of the village of Dalrymple this inn was built in 1879 as a coaching inn and has been providing sustenance to travellers ever since; the welcoming atmosphere makes it easy to feel at home. It's a stoutly traditional setting, with open fires and polished brasses. Eat traditional and wholesome dishes in the Coach Room in the oldest part of the building, and perhaps choose haggis with Champit tatties, turnips and whisky cream; cullen skink; or smoked salmon from nearby Burns Country Smokehouse. Other favourites are steak and kidney pie, and haddock and chips.

**Open** all day all wk **Bar Meals** L served all wk 12-2.30 D served all wk 5-8 Av main course £8.75 **Restaurant** L served all wk 12-2.30 D served all wk 5-9 Fixed menu price fr £7.50 Av 3 course à la carte fr £15 ⊕ SCOTTISH & NEWCASTLE ◀ John Smith's, Guinness.
**Facilities** Children's menu Children's portions Play area Family room Dogs allowed Garden Parking

### GATEHEAD Map 20 NS33

#### The Cochrane Inn

**45 Main Rd KA2 0AP ☎ 01563 570122**
**dir:** *From Glasgow A77 to Kilmarnock, then A759 to Gatehead*

There's a friendly, bustling atmosphere inside this traditional village centre pub, which sits just a short drive from the Ayrshire coast. The menus combine British and international flavours. This might translate as borlotti bean casserole on toast with Italian sausage, coriander and tomatoes, or harissa spiced prawn cocktail to start; then lamb chops with garlic and rosemary, or Thai lamb curry. A lighter option might be one of the salads, perhaps Cajun spiced chicken, chilli apple coleslaw, mango and sour cream.

**Open** all wk noon-2.30 5.30 onwards (Sun noon-9)
**Bar Meals** food served all day **Restaurant** food served all day ⊕ FREE HOUSE ◀ John Smith's.
**Facilities** Children's menu Children's portions Garden Parking

### SORN Map 20 NS52

**PICK OF THE PUBS**

#### The Sorn Inn ★★★★ RR ◎◎ 🍷

**35 Main St KA5 6HU**
**☎ 01290 551305** 📠 **01290 553470**
**e-mail:** craig@sorninn.com
**dir:** *A70 from S; or A76 from N onto B743 to Sorn*

Dating back to the 18th century when it was a coaching inn on the old Edinburgh to Kilmarnock route, The Sorn is now a smart gastro-pub with rooms. Along with some great real ales, the menus in both the Chop House and Restaurant offer a fusion of fine dining and brasserie-style food using the best seasonal ingredients. From a dinner menu come starters of goat's cheese croquettes, cherry tomato compote; pan-fried mackerel, apple crushed new potatoes, horseradish foam; and smoked guinea fowl salad with 'bonbon' of confit leg and tarragon dressing. Main courses include pan-fried hake with chorizo, basil and tomato risotto; saddle of local rabbit wrapped in pancetta, creamed Savoy cabbage, potato pancake; and rib of beef, hickory smoked potatoes, honey roasted root vegetables. To follow, try Bramley apple crumble with vanilla ice cream or summer berry baked Alaska. The Sorn has held its two AA Rosettes for eight years. Four comfortable bedrooms are available.

**Open** noon-2.30 6-10 (Fri noon-2.30 6-mdnt Sat noon-mdnt Sun 12.30-10) Closed: 2wks Jan, Mon **Bar Meals** L served Tue-Fri 12-2.30, Sat 12-9, Sun 12-8 D served Tue-Fri 6-9, Sat 12-9, Sun 12.30-8 Av main course £10 **Restaurant** L served Tue-Fri 12-2.30, Sat 12-9, Sun 12-8 booking required D served Tue-Fri 6-9, Sat 12-9, Sun 12-8 booking required Fixed menu price fr £21 Av 3 course à la carte fr £20 ⊕ FREE HOUSE ◀ John Smith's, Reale Ale Texas, Houston Brewery, Guinness. 🍷 12 **Facilities** Children's menu Children's portions Dogs allowed Parking **Rooms** 4

## EAST LOTHIAN

### LONGNIDDRY Map 21 NT47

#### The Longniddry Inn NEW

**Main St EH32 0NF ☎ 01875 852401**
**e-mail:** info@longniddryinn.com
**dir:** *On A198 (Main St), near rail station*

Formerly a blacksmith's forge and four cottages on Longniddry's main street, this inviting looking pub is noted locally for good food and friendly service. From the extensive menu, start with haggis, neeps and tatties, deep-fried brie with redcurrant jelly, or pâté with Cumberland sauce, then follow with chicken and mushroom pie, lambs' liver, bacon and onion gravy, or a rib-eye steak from the grill. In warmer weather why not sit outside with a pint of Belhaven Best.

**Open** all day all wk **Bar Meals** L served Mon-Sat 12-2.30 booking required D served Mon-Sat 5-8.30 booking required **Restaurant** L served Sun 1-7.30 booking required ⊕ PUNCH TAVERNS ◀ Belhaven Best, Deuchars IPA. **Facilities** Children's menu Children's portions Garden Parking

## EDINBURGH, CITY OF

### EDINBURGH Map 21 NT27

#### Bennets Bar 🍷

**8 Leven St EH3 9LG ☎ 0131 229 5143**
**e-mail:** bennetsbar@hotmail.co.uk
**dir:** *Next to Kings Theatre. Please phone for more detailed directions*

Bennets is a friendly pub, popular with performers from the adjacent Kings Theatre, serving real ales, over 120 malt whiskies and a decent selection of wines. It's a listed property dating from 1839 with hand-painted tiles and murals on the walls, original stained glass windows and brass beer taps. Reasonably priced home-made food ranges from toasties, burgers and salads to stovies, steak pie, and macaroni cheese. There's also a daily roast and traditional puddings.

**Open** all day all wk 11am-1am Closed: 25 Dec
**Bar Meals** L served Mon-Sat 12-2 D served Mon-Sat 5-8.30 Av main course £6 ⊕ IONA PUB ◀ Caledonian Deuchars IPA, Guinness, Caledonian 80/-. 🍷 10 **Facilities** Children's menu Children's portions Family room

#### The Bow Bar 🍷

**80 The West Bow EH1 2HH ☎ 0131 226 7667**
**dir:** *Telephone for directions*

This free house in the heart of Edinburgh's old town reflects the history and traditions of the area. Tables from decommissioned railway carriages and a gantry from an old church used for the huge selection of whiskies create interest in the bar, where around 150 malts are on tap, and eight cask ales are dispensed from antique equipment. Bar snacks only are served, and there are no gaming machines or music to distract from conversation.

**Open** all wk Closed: 25-26 Dec, 1-2 Jan **Bar Meals** L served Mon-Sat 12-2 ⊕ FREE HOUSE ◀ Deuchars IPA, Stewarts 80/-, Timothy Taylor Landlord, Harviestown Bitter & Twisted, Atlas Latitude, Trade Winds, Stewarts Pentland IPA ♁ Stowford Press, Thistly Cross. 🍷 8
**Facilities** Dogs allowed

**PICK OF THE PUBS**

#### Doric Tavern

**15-16 Market St EH1 1DE ☎ 0131 225 1084**
**e-mail:** info@the-doric.com
**dir:** *In city centre opp Waverly Station & Edinburgh Dungeons*

The property dates from 1710, and claims to be Edinburgh's oldest gastro-pub. It became a pub in the mid-1800s and takes its name from a language that used to be spoken in north-east Scotland, mainly in Aberdeenshire. It's conveniently located for Waverley Station, just a short walk from Princes Street and Edinburgh Castle. Public rooms include a recently refurbished ground-floor bar, and a wine bar and bistro upstairs. In these pleasantly informal surroundings a

*continued*

## EDINBURGH continued

wide choice of fresh, locally sourced food is prepared by the chefs work on site. While sipping a pint of Deuchars or St Andrew's Ale, you can nibble on home-made roasted red pepper houmous served with warm pitta bread. Starter options include cullen skink; smoked venison and apple salad; and haggis filo parcels. Main dishes range from monkfish osso bucco with vegetable and potato casserole to fillet of salmon rolled in oatmeal and herbs. Haggis, neeps and tatties covered with a whisky jus will certainly satisfy traditionalists. Home-made puddings include warm chocolate tart; traditional Scottish cranachan; and sticky toffee pudding with butterscotch sauce.

**Open** all wk 11.30am-mdnt (Thu-Sat 11.30am-1am) Closed: 25-26 Dec, 1 Jan **Bar Meals** Av main course £7.50 food served all day **Restaurant** Fixed menu price fr £9.95 Av 3 course à la carte fr £22 food served all day ◀ Deuchars IPA, Tennent's, Guinness, Stewarts 80/, St Andrew's Ale. **Facilities** Children's portions Family room

## The Shore Bar & Restaurant ♀

**3 Shore, Leith EH6 6QW**
☎ **0131 553 5080** ▯ **0131 553 5080**
e-mail: info@theshore.biz
dir: Telephone for directions

Part of this historic pub was a 17th-century lighthouse and, befitting its location beside the Port of Leith, it has a fine reputation for fish and seafood. The carte changes at every sitting during the day to ensure the freshest produce is on offer. Typical dishes could be crab and prawn cakes, home smoked chilli, tomato and basil salsa; steak tartare with boiled quails' eggs; red mullet, caramelised chicory, fennel and green beans, red pepper and almond pesto; or a steak and kidney or game pie.

**Open** all wk noon-1am (Sun 12.30-1am) Closed: 25-26 Dec, 1 Jan **Bar Meals** L served all wk 12-2.30 booking required D served all wk 6-10.30 booking required Av main course £14 **Restaurant** L served all wk 12-2.30 booking required D served all wk 6-10.30 booking required Fixed menu price fr £18.95 Av 3 course à la carte fr £28 ⊕ FREE HOUSE ◀ Belhaven 80/-, Deuchars IPA, Guinness. ♀ 14 **Facilities** Dogs allowed

### RATHO                                    Map 21 NT17

#### PICK OF THE PUBS

## The Bridge Inn

**27 Baird Rd EH28 8RA** ☎ **0131 333 1320**
e-mail: info@bridgeinn.com
dir: From Newbridge at B7030 junct, follow signs for Ratho and Edinburgh Canal Centre

An 18th-century former farmhouse was converted to create this canal-side pub in 1820 with the opening of the Union Canal. It was once owned by the family of the last man to be hanged in public in Edinburgh, and his ghost is still reputed to haunt the building. In addition to the restaurant and two bars, The Bridge Inn also has

a restaurant barge on the canal, providing the perfect venue for wedding parties, dinner dances, birthdays and other special events. Dishes range from bar snacks and light bites, such as mushrooms stuffed with haggis and black pudding, battered, deep-fried and served with red onion marmalade, to main courses of smoked haddock fishcakes with lime and tarragon dressing, or pork and beef medallions with wholegrain mustard sauce and crushed potatoes. The canal's towpath is ideal for walkers and cyclists.

**Open** all day all wk 11-11 (Fri-Sat 11am-mdnt) Closed: 25-26 Dec, 1-2 Jan **Bar Meals** L served Mon-Sat 11-9, Sun 12-30-9 D served Mon-Sat 11-9, Sun 12-30-9 food served all day **Restaurant** L served Mon-Sat 12-2.30, Sun 12.30-8.30 booking required D served Mon-Sat 6.30-9.30, Sun 12.30-8.30 booking required ⊕ FREE HOUSE ◀ Belhaven, Deuchars IPA, Tennent's, Stewarts Pentland, guest ales. **Facilities** Family room Garden Parking

FIFE

### ANSTRUTHER                              Map 21 NO50

## The Dreel Tavern ♀

**16 High Street West KY10 3DL**
☎ **01333 310727** ▯ **01333 310577**
e-mail: thedreeltavern@btconnect.com
dir: From Anstruther centre take A917 towards Pittenweem

Complete with a local legend concerning an amorous encounter between James V and a local gypsy woman, the welcoming 17th-century Dreel Tavern has plenty of atmosphere. Its oak beams, open fire and stone walls retain much of the distant past, while home-cooked food and cask-conditioned ales are served to hungry visitors of the present. Peaceful gardens overlook Dreel Burn. Recent change of hands.

**Open** all day all wk 11am-mdnt (Sun 12.30-mdnt) **Bar Meals** L served Mon-Sat 12-9, Sun 12.30-9 ⊕ SCOTTISH & NEWCASTLE ◀ Deuchars IPA, 2 guest ales. ♀ 20 **Facilities** Family room Dogs allowed Garden Parking

### BURNTISLAND                             Map 21 NT28

## Burntisland Sands Hotel

**Lochies Rd KY3 9JX** ☎ **01592 872230** ▯ **01592 872230**
e-mail: mail@burntislandsands.co.uk
dir: Towards Kirkcaldy, Burntisland on A921. Hotel on right before Kinghorn

Just 50 yards from an award-winning sandy beach, this small, family-run hotel was once a highly regarded girls' boarding school. These days you can expect reasonably priced breakfasts, snacks, lunches and evening meals, including internationally themed evenings. Typical choices range from chicken curry to roast chicken breast with black pudding, wrapped in pancetta. Relax and enjoy a drink in the bar and lounge area or in the courtyard.

**Open** all day all wk **Bar Meals** L served Mon-Fri 12-2.30, Sat-Sun all day booking required D served Mon-Fri 5-8.30 booking required Av main course £8 **Restaurant** L served Mon-Fri 12-2.30, Sat-Sun all day booking required D served Mon-Fri 5-8.30 booking required Fixed menu price fr £12 Av 3 course à la carte fr £16.25 ⊕ FREE HOUSE ◀ Scottish Courage ales, Guinness, guest ales. **Facilities** Children's menu Children's portions Play area Garden Parking

### ELIE                                     Map 21 NO40

## The Ship Inn

**The Toft KY9 1DT** ☎ **01333 330246** ▯ **01333 330864**
e-mail: info@ship-elie.com
dir: Follow A915 & A917 to Elie. From High Street follow signs to Watersport Centre & The Toft

A pub since 1838, this lively free house sits right on the waterfront at Elie Bay. It has been and run by the enthusiastic Philip family for 20 years. The cricket team plays regular fixtures on the beach, live music is performed, and there is a regular programme of summer barbecues and events. The best of local produce features on the concise menu which offers the likes of steak and Guinness pie, and smoked haddock crêpe with salad.

**Open** all wk Closed: 25 Dec ⊕ FREE HOUSE ◀ Caledonian Deuchars IPA, Belhaven Best, Caledonian 801, Tartan Special. **Facilities** Play area Family room Dogs allowed Garden

### KINCARDINE                              Map 21 NS98

## The Unicorn

**15 Excise St FK10 4LN** ☎ **01259 739129**
e-mail: info@theunicorn.co.uk
dir: Exit M9 junct 7 towards Kincardine Bridge. Cross bridge, bear left. 1st left, then sharp left at rdbt

This 17th-century pub-restaurant in the heart of the historic port of Kincardine used to be a coaching inn. And it was where, in 1842, Sir James Dewar, inventor of the vacuum flask, was born. There is a comfortable lounge bar, a grillroom, and a more formal dining room upstairs. Leather sofas and modern decor blend in well with the older parts of the building; relax and enjoy a pint of Old Engine Oil by the open fire in the bar.

**Open** noon-2.30 5.30-mdnt (Sun 12.30-mdnt) Closed: 3rd wk Jul, Mon **Bar Meals** Av main course £14.95 **Restaurant** L served Tue-Sat 12-2.30, Sun 12.30-4 booking required D served Tue-Thu 5.30-11, Fri-Sat 5-11, Sun 4-7 booking required Fixed menu price fr £16.95 ⊕ FREE HOUSE ◀ Bitter & Twisted, Schiehavillion, Old Engine Oil. **Facilities** Children's menu Children's portions Parking

## LOWER LARGO | Map 21 NO40

### The Crusoe Hotel

**2 Main St KY8 6BT** ☎ **01333 320759** 📄 **01333 320865**
e-mail: relax@crusoehotel.co.uk
dir: *A92 to Kirkcaldy East, A915 to Lundin Links, then right to Lower Largo*

This historic inn is located on the sea wall in Lower Largo, the birthplace of Alexander Selkirk, the real-life castaway immortalised by Daniel Defoe in his novel, *Robinson Crusoe*. In the past the area was also the heart of the once-thriving herring fishing industry. Today it is a charming bay ideal for a golfing break. A typical menu may include 'freshly shot' haggis, Pittenweem haddock and a variety of steaks.

**Open** all day all wk 11am-mdnt (Fri-Sat 11am-1am) ◀ Belhaven 80/-, Best, Deuchars, Abbot Ale, Old Speckled Hen. **Facilities** Play area Dogs allowed Parking

## ST ANDREWS | Map 21 NO51

### PICK OF THE PUBS

### The Inn at
### Lathones ★★★★ INN ◉◉ ☗

**Largoward KY9 1JE**
☎ **01334 840494** 📄 **01334 840694**
e-mail: lathones@theinn.co.uk
dir: *5m from St Andrews on A915*

Ancient meets modern here at this 400 year old coaching inn at the heart of St Andrews. One long-time guest flatly refuses to leave; the stables, now converted into a stylish venue, is haunted by the spirit of The Grey Lady – and her horse. Today's guests can relax in deep sofas and leather chairs drawn around log-burners, enjoying classic beers and a generous selection of bottled ales from Orkney Brewery. For the past 12 years the chefs here have been awarded two AA Rosettes; their creative mettle can be judged from starters that include corn fed chicken and leek terrine or East Neuk fish bisque, whilst mains come up trumps with venison and mixed game steamed pudding with Stornoway black pudding and a port wine reduction, or baked turbot with hand-dived scallops, leek and potato crumble and fresh herb cream. The inn is an award-winning live music venue, hosting Lindisfarne and Curtis Stigers amongst many luminaries; the walls of the inn display one of the best collections of music memorabilia in the country. The Inn also offers stylish AA rated accommodation.

**Open** all wk Closed: 2wks Jan **Bar Meals** Av main course £15 food served all day **Restaurant** L served all wk 12-2.30 D served all wk 6-9.30 Av 3 course à la carte fr £36 ⊕ FREE HOUSE ◀ Dark Island, Three Sisters, Belhaven Best. ☗ 11 **Facilities** Dogs allowed Garden Parking **Rooms** 21

### PICK OF THE PUBS

### The Jigger Inn ☗

**The Old Course Hotel KY16 9SP**
☎ **01334 474371** 📄 **01334 477688**
e-mail: debbietaylor@oldcoursehotel.co.uk
dir: *Telephone for directions*

Once the stationmaster's lodge on a railway line that disappeared many years ago, The Jigger is in the grounds of the Old Course Hotel. St Andrew's is renowned, of course, throughout the world as the Home of Golf, so don't be surprised by the golfing memorabilia, or by sharing bar space with a caddy or two, fresh in from a long game. Even Tiger Woods has been seen here. Open-hearth fires are the backdrop for a selection of Scottish beers, including St Andrew's Ale from Belhaven Brewery in Dunbar. All-day availability is one advantage of a short, simple menu that lists soup, sandwiches and barbecued chicken salad wrap with honey mustard dressing as starters, and continues with beer-battered fish and chips; sausage and mash with onion gravy; warm sunblushed tomato with goat's cheese and rocket tart, and gremolata dressing; and grilled Speyside steak with seasoned fries and onion rings.

**Open** all day all wk 11-11 (Sun noon-11) Closed: 25 Dec **Bar Meals** L served all wk 12-9.30 food served all day **Restaurant** D served all wk 12-9.30 booking required ⊕ FREE HOUSE ◀ Guinness, St Andrews Best, Jigger Ale. ☗ 8 **Facilities** Garden Parking

## GLASGOW, CITY OF

## GLASGOW | Map 20 NS56

### Rab Ha's

**83 Hutchieson St G1 1SH**
☎ **0141 572 0400** 📄 **0141 572 0402**
e-mail: management@rabhas.com
dir: *Telephone for directions*

In the heart of Glasgow's revitalised Merchant City, Rab Ha's takes its name from Robert Hall, a local 19th-century character known as 'The Glasgow Glutton'. This hotel, restaurant and bar blend Victorian character with contemporary Scottish decor. Pre-theatre and set menus show extensive use of carefully sourced Scottish produce in starters like poached egg on grilled Stornoway black pudding, and pan-seared Oban scallops, followed by roast saddle of Rannoch Moor venison.

**Open** all day all wk noon-mdnt (Sun 12.30pm-mdnt) **Bar Meals** L served Mon-Thu 12-9, Fri-Sat 12-10, Sun 12.30-9 food served all day ⊕ FREE HOUSE ◀ Tennent's. **Facilities** Children's portions

### PICK OF THE PUBS

### Stravaigin ◉◉ ☗

**28 Gibson St G12 8NX**
☎ **0141 334 2665** 📄 **0141 334 4099**
e-mail: stravaigin@btinternet.com
dir: *Telephone for directions*

In a busy street close to the university, Stravaigin draws the crowds to its popular, recently extended café bar and its bright, modern basement restaurant below with its split-level seating. The style throughout is distinctly contemporary, with stone and leather-covered walls decorated with modern art and quirky antiques in the swish restaurant. Whether eating in the informal vibe of the bar or in the restaurant, it's the warm hospitality and service that makes Stravaigin the place to eat in Glasgow. The bar was intended to be where diners had pre-dinner drinks but for many years it has a life and clientele of its own, offering real ales like Deuchars IPA and Belhaven Best to casual drinkers. Expect imaginative and exciting fusion food cooked from top-notch Scottish ingredients. The wide range of eclectic dishes may include West Coast mussels with sweet chilli and coriander; hake with black bean and ginger sauce; roast guinea fowl with pan-fried Jerusalem artichoke and squash, pumpkin purée and port gravy; and apple and cinnamon crumble pie.

**Open** all day all wk 11-11 Closed: 25 Dec, 1 Jan **Bar Meals** L served all wk 11-5 D served all wk 5-11 Av main course £14 food served all day **Restaurant** L served Sat-Sun 12-11 D served all wk 5-11 Fixed menu price fr £12.95 Av 3 course à la carte fr £17 ⊕ FREE HOUSE ◀ Deuchars IPA, Belhaven Best, Chip 71 ♨ Westons Premium Organic. ☗ 18 **Facilities** Children's menu Children's portions Dogs allowed

### PICK OF THE PUBS

### Ubiquitous Chip ◉◉ ☗

**12 Ashton Ln G12 8SJ**
☎ **0141 334 5007** 📄 **0141 337 6417**
e-mail: mail@ubiquitouschip.co.uk
dir: *In West End of Glasgow, off Byres Rd. Beside Hillhead subway station*

Now 40 years old, the Ubiquitous Chip has acquired iconic status for its food and drink. The building is at the end of a cobbled mews; the main dining area opens into a beautiful, vine-covered courtyard, at mezzanine level is a new dining space for private dining, while upstairs is the brasserie-style, two-AA Rosette restaurant. There are three drinking areas: the traditional pub, serving real ales, 29 wines by the glass, more than 150 malt whiskies; the Wee Bar, which is indeed quite 'wee', possibly the wee-est in Scotland; and the Corner Bar, which serves cocktails across a granite slab reclaimed from a mortuary. Scotland's produce is prominent on the menu in the

*continued*

## GLASGOW *continued*

shape of pan-fried Mallaig-landed John Dory with orange and fennel salad; Argyllshire venison sausage with gin and juniper sauce; corn-fed chicken leg stuffed with skirlie (toasted oatmeal); pan-fried Scotch lamb's liver with Ayrshire bacon; and vegetarian haggis with neeps 'n' tatties.

**Open** all wk 11am-mdnt **Closed:** 25 Dec, 1 Jan **Bar Meals** L served all wk 12-11 D served all wk 12-11 Av main course £5.50 food served all day **Restaurant** L served Mon-Sat 12.30-2.30, Sun 12.30-3 booking required D served all wk 5.30-11 booking required Fixed menu price fr £23.85 Av 3 course à la carte fr £15 food served all day ⊕ FREE HOUSE ◀ Deuchars IPA, The Chip 71 Ale. ♥ 29 **Facilities** Children's menu Children's portions

### HIGHLAND

### ACHILTIBUIE        Map 22 NC00

### PICK OF THE PUBS

## Summer Isles Hotel & Bar ◉◉

IV26 2YG ☎ 01854 622282 📄 01854 622251
e-mail: info@summerisleshotel.com
dir: *Take A835 N from Ullapool for 10m, Achiltibuie signed on left, 15m to village. Hotel 1m on left*

Located in a stunningly wild and untouched landscape, the hotel is a favourite destination for food lovers, outdoor adventurers and for those simply looking for peace, tranquility and fresh air. It was developed over four decades by the Irvine family; in 2008 they sold it to Terry and Irina Mackay, who have pledged to maintain its style, traditions and ambience. The all-year bar at the side of the hotel was where the local crofters used to meet well over a century ago, but sadly unknown to them was the pleasure of eating from a bar menu strong on locally caught seafood – the famous Summer Isles seafood platter is a favourite – and Aberdeen Angus steaks. There are some fine beers to enjoy, also a huge selection of malt whiskies and more than 400 wines to choose from. Apart from the locally caught scallops, lobsters, langoustines, crabs, halibut, turbot and salmon, there's venison from local estates, brown bread fresh from the oven – the list is almost endless. Perhaps, then, it's not too surprising that Chris Firth-Bernard has won Scottish Chef of the Year, as well as many other titles. His short carte menu offers a light lunch specialising in the best of West Coast shellfish, and he prepares a five-course set meal in the evening.

**Open** all wk **Bar Meals** Av main course £9.50 food served all day **Restaurant** L served all wk 12.30-2.30 booking required D served all wk until 8 booking required Fixed menu price fr £56 ⊕ FREE HOUSE ◀ 40 Teallach, Suilven, Crofters Pale. **Facilities** Children's menu Children's portions Dogs allowed Garden Parking

### AVIEMORE        Map 23 NH81

## The Old Bridge Inn

Dalfaber Rd PH22 1PU ☎ 01479 811137
e-mail: sayhello@oldbridgeinn.co.uk
dir: *Exit A9 to Aviemore, 1st right to Ski Rd, then 1st left again 200mtrs*

Overlooking the River Spey, this friendly pub sits in the spectacular Scottish Highlands, in an area popular for outdoor pursuits. New owners are taking the pub in a new direction whilst retaining all of its old charm. Dine in the comfortable restaurant, the attractive riverside garden, or in the relaxing bars warmed by a roaring log fire. A tempting gastro-pub style menu includes a range of chargrilled steaks and whole sea bass, while other choices include ham and split pea broth and truffled cep risotto. Fine cask ales and large selection of malt whiskies available. There are now regular live music nights.

**Open** all wk Mon-Thu 11am-mdnt (Fri-Sat 11am-1am Sun 12.30-mdnt) **Bar Meals** L served Mon-Sat 12-3, Sun 12.30-3 D served Mon-Thu 6-9, Fri-Sat 6-10 Av main course £12 **Restaurant** L served Mon-Sat 12-3, Sun 12.30-3 booking required D served Mon-Sat 12-3, Fri-Sat 6-10 booking required Av 3 course à la carte fr £22 ⊕ FREE HOUSE ◀ Deuchars IPA, Cairngorm Trade Winds, Cairngorm Black Gold, Atlas Nimbus, Schiehallion. **Facilities** Children's portions Dogs allowed Garden Parking

### BADACHRO        Map 22 NG77

## The Badachro Inn ♥

IV21 2AA ☎ 01445 741255 📄 01445 741319
e-mail: Lesley@badachroinn.com
dir: *From Kinlochewe A832 towards Gairloch. Onto B8056, right to Badachro after 3.25m, towards quay*

Expect great views from one of Scotland's finest anchorages at this convivial waterside pub, which has two moorings for visitors. Decking, with nautical-style sails and rigging, runs right down to the water overlooking Loch Gairloch. Interesting photographs and collages adorn the bar walls, where there is a dining area by a log fire. Friendly staff serve beers from the An Teallach or Caledonian breweries and a farm cider. A further dining conservatory overlooks the bay. Excellent fresh fish is the speciality of the house, along with dishes such as local venison terrine and chicken breast on crushed haggis, neeps and tatties.

**Open** all wk **Closed:** 25-26 Dec **Bar Meals** L served all wk 12-3 D served all wk 6-9 **Restaurant** L served all wk 12-3 D served all wk 6-9 ⊕ FREE HOUSE ◀ Red Cullen, An Teallach, Blaven, 80/-, Guinness. ♥ 11 **Facilities** Children's portions Dogs allowed Garden Parking

### CARRBRIDGE        Map 23 NH92

## The Cairn ★★★ INN ♥

PH23 3AS ☎ 01479 841212 📄 01479 841362
e-mail: info@cairnhotel.co.uk
dir: *In village centre*

The Highland village of Carrbridge and this family-run inn make the perfect base for exploring the Cairngorms, the Moray coast and the Malt Whisky Trail. In the homely, tartan-carpeted bar, you'll find cracking Isle of Skye and Cairngorm ales on handpump, blazing winter log fires, all-day sandwiches, and hearty bar meals, including sweet marinated herring with oatcakes, venison sausage casserole, and sticky toffee pudding.

**Open** all day all wk 11-11 (Fri-Sat 11am-1am) **Bar Meals** L served all wk 12-2 D served all wk 6-8.30 Av main course £7 food served all day ⊕ FREE HOUSE ◀ Cairngorm, Orkney, Blackisle, Isle of Skye, Atlas. ♥ 9 **Facilities** Children's menu Children's portions Dogs allowed Garden Parking **Rooms** 7

### CAWDOR        Map 23 NH85

### PICK OF THE PUBS

## Cawdor Tavern ♥

The Lane IV12 5XP
☎ 01667 404777 📄 01667 493678
e-mail: enquiries@cawdortavern.co.uk
dir: *From A96 (Inverness-Aberdeen) take B9006 & follow Cawdor Castle signs. Tavern in village centre*

Standing close to the famous castle in a beautiful conservation village, the tavern was formerly a joinery workshop for the Cawdor Estate. Oak panelling from the castle, gifted by the late laird, is used to great effect in the lounge bar. Roaring log fires keep the place cosy and warm on long winter evenings, while the garden patio comes into its own in summer. A single menu is offered for both restaurant and bar, where refreshments include a choice of real ales such as Three Sisters, Nimbus and Red MacGregor, and 100 malt whiskies. The pub's reputation for seafood draws diners from some distance for dishes like fresh pan-seared Arisaig scallops. Other favourites include poached Shetland salmon salad; breast of Speyside pigeon breast with apple fritter, crispy bacon and red wine jus; and collops of Highland venison, turnip gratin with roasted garlic jus.

Save on Hotels. Book at **theAA**.com/hotel

**HIGHLAND** 567 **SCOTLAND**

Open all wk 11-3 5-11 (Sat 11am-mdnt Sun 12.30-11)
all day in Summer Closed: 25 Dec, 1 Jan, 2wks mid Jan
**Bar Meals** L served Mon-Sat 12-2, Sun 12.30-3 D
served all wk 5.30-9 Av main course £9.95
**Restaurant** L served Mon-Sat 12-2, Sun 12.30-3
booking required D served all wk 5.30-9 booking
required Av 3 course à la carte fr £22.50 ⊞ FREE
HOUSE ◀ Red MacGregor, Three Sisters, Orkney Dark
Island, Raven Ale, Latitude Highland Pilsner, Nimbus
♂ Thatchers Gold. ♀ 9 **Facilities** Children's menu
Children's portions Dogs allowed Garden Parking

---

### FORT WILLIAM     Map 22 NN17

## Moorings Hotel ★★★ HL ⊚

**Banavie PH33 7LY** ☎ 01397 772797   🖹 01397 772441
**e-mail:** reservations@moorings-fortwilliam.co.uk
**dir:** *From A82 in Fort William follow signs for Mallaig,
then left onto A830 for 1m. Cross canal bridge then 1st
right signed Banavie*

This modern hotel lies alongside Neptune's Staircase, on
the coast-to-coast Caledonian Canal. The canal is a
historic monument, its eight locks able to raise even sea-
going craft a total of 64 feet. Most hotel bedrooms and
the Upper Deck lounge bar have good views of Ben Nevis
(1344m) and Aonach Mor (1219m). A range of eating
options includes Mariners cellar bar, the Caledonian
split-level lounge bar overlooking the canal, plus the
fine-dining Jacobean Restaurant. Choose from cuisine
built on West Coast seafood and game - perhaps moules
marinière (Mallaig mussels); tournedos of Highland beef;
and a trio of home-made ice creams.

**Open** all day all wk Closed: 24-26 Dec **Bar Meals** Av main
course £8.95 food served all day **Restaurant** D served all
wk 7-9.30 Fixed menu price fr £28 Av 3 course à la carte
fr £30 ⊞ FREE HOUSE ◀ Calders 70/-, Tetley Bitter,
Guinness. **Facilities** Children's menu Dogs allowed
Garden Parking **Rooms** 27

---

### GAIRLOCH     Map 22 NG87

## PICK OF THE PUBS

### The Old Inn

**IV21 2BD** ☎ 01445 712006   🖹 01445 712933
**e-mail:** info@theoldinn.net
**dir:** *Just off A832, near harbour at south end of village*

Built in 1750 as a changing house for horses,
Gairloch's oldest hostelry enjoys a fabulous setting at
the foot of the Flowerdale valley. On a good day, you
might be able to spy the Outer Hebrides from this
attractive inn, which draws outdoor enthusiasts to the
many local activities. Long established as a real ale
pub, owner Alastair Pearson has recently supplemented
his offering with Erradale and Flowerdale beers from
his new on-site micro-brewery. Fresh local seafood
features prominently on the menu, which also includes
home-made pies, oven bakes and casseroles. Typical
choices include steamed hake fillet with Mediterranean
seafood broth; pheasant and game casserole with herb
dumpling; and vegetarian tagine with couscous. Picnic

tables on the large grassy area by the stream make an
attractive spot for eating and enjoying the views. Dogs
are welcomed with bowls, baskets and rugs to help
them feel at home.

**Open** all day all wk 11am-mdnt (Sun noon-mdnt)
**Bar Meals** L served all wk 12-2.30 (summer 12-4.30) D
served all wk 5-9.30 Av main course £9.50 food served
all day **Restaurant** D served all wk 6-9.30 booking
required Fixed menu price fr £25 Av 3 course à la carte
fr £17.50 ⊞ FREE HOUSE ◀ Adnams Bitter, Isle of Skye
Red Cullin, Blind Piper, An Teallach, Deuchars IPA,
Wildcat, Erradale, Flowerdale. **Facilities** Children's
menu Children's portions Play area Family room Dogs
allowed Garden Parking

---

### GARVE     Map 23 NH36

## Inchbae Lodge Guesthouse ★★ INN

**IV23 2PH** ☎ 01997 455269   🖹 01997 455207
**e-mail:** contact@inchbae.co.uk
**dir:** *30m from Inverness, 26m from Ullapool, A835 from
Tore rdbt*

Watch stags feeding in the garden of this 19th-century
hunting lodge in the heart of the Highlands. Residents
can fish for free in the river Blackwater, which flows just
outside. Inside there's a bistro and a conservatory dining
room with panoramic views, plus a large residents'
lounge warmed by a log fire. Food ranges from crab and
king prawn fishcakes to Arbroath smokies or chicken with
portobello mushrooms and Madeira sauce.
Accommodation and a good selection of local ales are
available.

**Open** all day all wk **Bar Meals** Av main course £6.99 food
served all day **Restaurant** food served all day ⊞ FREE
HOUSE ◀ Guinness, Isle of Skye Red Cullin, An Teallach
Brewhouse Special. **Facilities** Garden Parking **Rooms** 7

---

### GLENELG     Map 22 NG81

## Glenelg Inn

**IV40 8JR** ☎ 01599 522273   🖹 01599 522283
**e-mail:** info@glenelg-inn.com
**dir:** *From Shiel Bridge (A87) take unclassified road to
Glenelg*

The inn is a conversion of 200-year-old stables set in a
large garden stretching down to the sea, with stunning
views across the Sound of Sleat. Musicians are frequent
visitors to the bar, where at times a ceilidh atmosphere
prevails. Menus offer traditional Scottish fare based on
local produce, including plenty of fresh fish and seafood,
hill-bred lamb, venison and seasonal vegetables. In the
bar are seafood casserole and pies, while the dinner
menu offers West Coast turbot with fennel and new
potatoes.

**Open** all day all wk noon-mdnt ◀ Guest Ales.
**Facilities** Dogs allowed Garden Parking

---

### INVERGARRY     Map 22 NH30

## The Invergarry Inn ★★★★ INN **NEW**

**PH35 4HJ** ☎ 01809 501206   🖹 01809 501400
**e-mail:** info@invergarryhotel.co.uk
**dir:** *At junct of A82 & A87*

A real Highland atmosphere pervades this refurbished
roadside inn set in glorious mountain scenery between
Fort William and Fort Augustus. Spruced-up bars and
modern bedrooms make it a comfortable base from which
to explore Loch Ness, Glencoe and the West Coast. Relax
by the crackling log fire with a wee dram or a pint of
Garry Ale, then tuck into a good meal, following smoked
haddock chowder with duck confit with saffron and
celeriac mash and port wine jus, or rump of Highland
lamb with whisky jus. Good lunches and excellent walks
from the front door.

**Open** all day all wk Closed: 2 Jan-10 Feb **Bar Meals** Food
served all day 8am-9.30pm booking required for dinner
Av main course £14 **Restaurant** Food served all day 8am-
9.30pm booking required for dinner ⊞ FREE HOUSE
◀ Garry Ale, Timothy Taylor, Guinness.
**Facilities** Children's menu Children's portions Family
room Garden Parking **Rooms** 13

---

### INVERIE     Map 22 NG70

## The Old Forge

**PH41 4PL** ☎ 01687 462267   🖹 01687 462267
**e-mail:** info@theoldforge.co.uk
**dir:** *From Fort William take A830 (Road to the Isles)
towards Mallaig. Take ferry from Mallaig to Inverie (boat
details on website)*

Britain's most remote mainland pub, The Old Forge, is
accessible only by boat, and stands literally between
heaven and hell (Loch Nevis is Gaelic for heaven and
Loch Hourn is Gaelic for hell). It's popular with everyone
from locals to hill walkers, and is renowned for its
impromptu ceilidhs. It is also the ideal place to sample
local fish and seafood and there's no better way than
choosing the seafood platter of rope mussels,
langoustines, oak-smoked salmon, peppered mackerel
and smoked trout; other specialities include haunch of
estate venison and vegetarian haggis lasagne. There are
nine boat moorings and a daily ferry from Mallaig.

**Open** all day all wk **Bar Meals** L served all wk 12-3 D
served all wk 6-9.30 food served all day **Restaurant** L
served all wk 12-3 D served all wk 6-9.30 ⊞ FREE HOUSE
◀ Guinness, Calders 80, guest ales. **Facilities** Children's
menu Children's portions Play area Family room Dogs
allowed Garden Parking

### LYBSTER
Map 23 ND23

## Portland Arms ★★★★ INN ♥

KW3 6BS ☎ 01593 721721 📠 01593 721722
e-mail: manager.portlandarms@ohiml.com
dir: *Exit A9 signed Latheron, take A99 to Wick. Then 4m to Lybster*

Just half a mile from the North Sea coastline, this former coaching inn has evolved into a comfortable modern inn. The bar and dining areas serve fresh local produce and menus cater for all tastes, with everything from home-made soup with freshly baked baguette to flash-fried langoustine in garlic and brandy butter. Look out for delicious desserts and home baking with morning coffee and afternoon tea. Sunday lunch is a speciality. Take time for a nostalgic walk around this historic fishing town, or why not stay over in one of the bedrooms to explore the marvellous area further.

**Open** all day all wk 7am-11pm **Bar Meals** L served all wk 12-9 D served all wk 12-9 food served all day **Restaurant** L served all wk 12-9 booking required D served all wk 12-9 booking required food served all day ⊕ FREE HOUSE ◀ McEwans 70/-, Guinness, Belhaven Best, John Smith's. ♥ 18 **Facilities** Children's menu Children's portions Family room Garden Parking **Rooms** 23

### NORTH BALLACHULISH
Map 22 NN06

## Loch Leven Hotel

**Old Ferry Rd PH33 6SA**
☎ 01855 821236 📠 01855 821550
e-mail: reception@lochlevenhotel.co.uk
dir: *Off A82, N of Ballachulish Bridge*

Awesome views from the terrace and dining room encompass Britain's highest peaks (Glencoe and Ben Nevis are the hotel's neighbours) and the cobalt blue depths of Lochs Leven and Linnie. Travellers have rested awhile here for over 300 years; the hotel served one end of the Ballachulish Ferry until the bridge opened in 1975, nowadays discerning diners linger for the excellent dishes prepared from the best Scotland can offer. In season, locally grown mussels are a favourite, or perhaps roast haunch of venison or pan-seared sea bass fillet will detain.

**Open** all day all wk 11-11 (Thu-Sat 11am-mdnt Sun 12.30-11) **Bar Meals** L served all wk 12-3 D served all wk 6-9 Av main course £10 **Restaurant** L served all wk 12-3 D served all wk 6-9 Fixed menu price fr £20 Av 3 course à la carte fr £25 ⊕ FREE HOUSE ◀ Guinness, McEwans 80. **Facilities** Children's menu Children's portions Play area Family room Dogs allowed Garden Parking

*See advert below*

# PICK OF THE PUBS

## Kylesku Hotel

**KYLESKU**                           Map 22 NC23

**IV27 4HW** ☎ **01971 502231**
e-mail: info@kyleskuhotel.co.uk
web: www.kyleskuhotel.co.uk
dir: *A835, then A837 & A894 into Kylesku.
Hotel at end of road at Old Ferry Pier*

Legendary fell-walking writer Alfred
Wainwright once wrote of this village:
"Anyone with an eye for impressive
beauty will not regard time spent at
Kylesku as wasted." You can see why:
on the shores of Loch Glendhu and Loch
Glencoul, both arms of the sea, the
Kylesku Hotel is a delightful place with
truly memorable views. Now under new
ownership, it's at the centre of the North
West Highlands Global Geopark,
2,000-square kilometres of lochs,
mountains and wild coast. The hotel, a

former coaching inn dating from 1680,
stands by the old ferry slipway between
the two lochs, both of which are visible
from the restaurant and bar.

With local fishing boats landing their
catch on the slipway daily, seafood is
the mainstay – the langoustines,
spineys, lobster, crab, scallops, haddock
and mussels certainly don't have far to
travel far before ending up in the
kitchen. Salmon is hot- and cold-
smoked in-house, beef and lamb fillets
are from animals reared in the
Highlands, and all the venison is wild.
Changing on a monthly basis, the bar
menu offers starters of cullen skink
(smoked haddock, potato and chive
crème fraîche chowder); Strathdon Blue
cheese-stuffed button mushrooms with
confit garlic mayonnaise; and poached
egg with black pudding, curly endive
and mustard dressing.

Main courses include moules marinière
(also available as a starter); classic fish
pie of haddock, salmon, North Atlantic
prawns, white wine velouté, spring peas
and cheddar mash; venison burger with

iceberg lettuce, chutney, sliced cheese
and chunky chips; and mushroom
risotto with wilted rocket, white wine
and mascarpone. Puddings range from
lime cheesecake to sticky toffee pudding
to platters of Isle of Mull cheddar with
celery and spicy apricot sauce.

To drink, there's real ale from the Black
Isle brewery, bottled beers from the Isle
of Skye, 40 wines and 50 malt whiskies.

**Open** all day all wk Closed: Nov-Feb
**Bar Meals** L served all wk 12-6
D served all wk 6-9 Av main course
£12.95 food served all day
**Restaurant** D served all wk 7-9 booking
required Fixed menu price fr £24.50 Av 3
course à la carte fr £28.80 ⊕ FREE
HOUSE ◀ Tennents Ember 80/-,
Selection of Black Isle Brewery and Skye
Cuillin bottled ales. **Facilities** Children's
menu Garden

# PICK OF THE PUBS

## The Plockton Hotel ★★★ SHL

**PLOCKTON**      Map 22 NG83

**Harbour St IV52 8TN**
☎ **01599 544274**   📠 **01599 544475**
**e-mail:** info@plocktonhotel.co.uk
**web:** www.plocktonhotel.co.uk
**dir:** *On A87 to Kyle of Lochalsh take turn at Balmacara. Plockton 7m N*

The Pearson family – Dorothy, Tom, Alan and Ann-Mags – have been running this award-winning harbourside hotel for more than twenty years. It's easy to see why they stay (and indeed why so many guests return again and again) because as you walk down the main street a surprising panorama opens up: to one side the watchful mountains, to the other the deep blue waters of Loch Carron lapping at the edge of a sweep of whitewashed Highland cottages.

There are palm trees too, courtesy of the Gulf Stream. The building dates from 1827 and later became a ship's chandlery, from which it was converted into a hotel in 1913.

In the dining room and hotel bar the speciality is seafood, including locally caught langoustines and fresh fish landed at Gairloch and Kinlochbervie. Succulent Highland steaks and locally reared beef also add to the wealth of other tempting Scottish produce. Example starters from a recent menu are Talisker whisky pâté and Plockton mackerel smokies, while from among the mains there might be pan-fried medallions of pork with brandied apricots in cream sauce; casserole of venison in red wine, juniper berries and redcurrant jelly; supreme of chicken stuffed with Argyle smoked ham in sun-dried tomato, garlic and basil sauce; and chargrilled Plockton prawns. Vegetarian dishes are detailed on the blackboard. Basket meals, such as beer-battered fish and chips, and breaded scampi tails are served nightly.

A fine range of malts is available to round off that perfect Highland day.

All bedrooms are en suite and many look out across the loch to the mountains beyond. Two family suites are also available along with a cottage annexe nearby.

**Open** all day all wk 11am-mdnt (Sun 12.30pm-11pm) **Bar Meals** L served all wk 12-2.15 D served all wk 6-10 Av main course £9.75 **Restaurant** L served all wk 12-2.15 D served all wk 6-10 booking required Av 3 course à la carte fr £20 🍺 Caledonian Deuchars IPA, Hebridean Gold - Isle of Skye Brewery, Harvieston Blonde Ale, Crags Ale. 🍷 6 **Facilities** Family room Garden **Rooms** 15

# PICK OF THE PUBS

# Plockton Inn & Seafood Restaurant

**PLOCKTON**  Map 22 NG83

**Innes St IV52 8TW**
☎ **01599 544222** 📠 **01599 544487**
e-mail: info@plocktoninn.co.uk
dir: *On A87 to Kyle of Lochalsh take turn at Balmacara. Plockton 7m N*

Mary Gollan, her brother Kenny and his partner, Susan Trowbridge, bought this attractive stone-built free house, just 100 metres from the harbour, in 1997 and have built the business up to its current award-winning status. Mary and Kenny's great grandfather built it as a manse, and they themselves were born and bred in Plockton. The women do the cooking, while Kenny runs the bar. The atmosphere is relaxed and friendly, with winter fires in both bars, and a selection of more than 50 malt whiskies. With a wealth of freshly caught fish and shellfish, West Highland beef, lamb, game and home-made vegetarian dishes made from local produce on the set menu, plus mouth-watering daily specials, a meal in the dining room or lounge bar, is a must.

Martin, the barman, lands the Plockton prawns himself, while Kenny takes the finest seafood off to his smokehouse, for it to feature later as part of the seafood platter. Starters include fish-based soup of the day; gravadlax; vegetarian haggis with neeps, tatties and home-made pickled beetroot; and chicken liver pâté and toast. Among the main dishes are skate wing and black butter; halibut fillet with creamy smoked salmon sauce; venison in ale; fillet and sirloin steaks; chicken Caesar salad; and aubergine parmigiana. There are some truly tempting desserts like ice cream with raspberries, honey and whisky, as well as a selection of Scottish cheeses served with Orkney oatcakes.

The bar is alive on Tuesdays and Thursdays with music from local musicians, who are often joined by talented youngsters from the National Centre of Excellence in Traditional Music, which is based in the village. Incidentally, BBC Scotland's *Hamish Macbeth* series was filmed here in 1997.

**Open** all day all wk **Bar Meals** L served all wk 12-2.30 D served all wk 6-9 booking required Av main course £10 **Restaurant** D served all wk 6-9 booking required Av 3 course à la carte fr £18 ⊕ FREE HOUSE ◄ Greene King Abbot Ale, Fuller's London Pride, Young's Special, Plockton Crag Ale, Plockton Bay. **Facilities** Children's menu Play area Dogs allowed Garden Parking

# PICK OF THE PUBS

## Shieldaig Bar & Coastal Kitchen ★ SHL

**SHIELDAIG** Map 22 NG85

**IV54 8XN**
☎ **01520 755251** 📠 **01520 755321**
web: www.tighaneilean.co.uk
dir: *Off A896, in village centre*

Set in a charming, mostly 18th century fishing village and part of the two-AA Rosette Tigh an Eilean Hotel next door, the Shieldaig Bar positively jumps at weekends with live traditional Gaelic music. In fact, all over Wester Ross you are likely to find a ceilidh taking place somewhere.

Rustic and no-nonsense, this waterfront bar enjoys the most stunning views across Loch Torridon, which leads to the open sea, and it is from the first floor

eating area - The Coastal Kitchen and its balcony and open decks — that you will be most impressed by these views. Throughout the day a full range of alcoholic and non-alcoholic beverages is served to suit the hour, and there's always a ready supply of newspapers and magazines to read. Bar snacks include sandwiches, home-made soups, burgers and bangers and mash, but it's for fine seafood that the bar has earned its reputation. It's all caught locally, some from local prawn-fishing grounds that have won a sustainable fishery award. Daily menus ensure the freshest of catches; Loch Torridon spiny lobsters with lemongrass and coriander dressing, Shieldaig crab salad, and the speciality Shieldaig Bar seafood stew.

Alternatives to fish include steaks and pizzas from the Coastal Kitchen's wood-fired oven, local venison sausages with mash and red wine and onion gravy; and shallot and goats' cheese tart with salad and new potatoes. Food is served all day in summer, when you can also

dine in the lochside courtyard and outside on the balcony and decks. A good range of real ales is on tap from the Isle of Skye Brewery and Black Isle ales, plus malt whiskies and a choice of wines by the glass.

**Open** all wk **Bar Meals** L served all wk 12-2.30, Sum 12-9 D served all wk 6-8.30 Av main course £8.50 **Restaurant** L served all wk 12-2.30, Sum 12-9 D served all wk 6-8.30 🍺 **FREE HOUSE** 🛢 Isle of Skye Brewery Ales, Black Isle. 🍷 8 **Facilities** Children's menu Dogs allowed Garden Parking **Rooms** 11

# PICK OF THE PUBS

## The Torridon Inn ★★★ INN

**TORRIDON**  Map 22 NG95

**IV22 2EY**
☎ 01445 791242  📄 01445 712253
e-mail: inn@thetorridon.com
web: www.thetorridon.com/inn
**dir**: *From Inverness take A9 N, then follow signs to Ullapool. Take A835 then A832. In Kinlochewe take A896 to Annat. Pub 200yds on right after village*

Once a grand shooting lodge, The Torridon stands on the shores of the sea loch from which it takes its name. The inn itself results from the conversion of the stable block, buttery and farm buildings of the estate, which was created for the first Earl of Lovelace in 1887. In the convivial bar you can replay the day's adventures over one of the more than 60 malt whiskies, including local favourites Talisker and Glen Ord, or a pint of real ale from the An Teallach, Isle of Skye or Cairngorm breweries.

The inn has its own separate restaurant, where at any time you can sample the high quality, locally sourced food in which it specialises. During the day, hearty soups, sandwiches and bar meals are available, while in the evening there's a delicious choice of starters, main courses and desserts on menus likely to feature salmon and other local fish, venison, haggis and a variety of home-made specials. Dinner could therefore begin with fresh mussels and home-made beer bread and garlic sauce; double-baked Beauly wild boar belly glazed with honey, topped with Ewe scallops; or traditional bruschetta. Next, consider ordering Highland steak and real ale pie; Thai green chicken curry; game casserole; whole baked trout; or butternut pumpkin, ricotta and pine nut cappelletti (a type of stuffed pasta). Tea and coffee is available throughout the day. Live traditional music is laid on regularly.

All twelve bedrooms are en suite, and one is set aside for those guests who bring their dog, knowing that it will also enjoy the marvellous walking this remote location offers.

**Open** all day all wk Closed: Jan
**Bar Meals** food served all day
**Restaurant** food served all day
🛢 FREE HOUSE ◀ Isle of Skye Brewery - Red Cuillin, Torridon Ale, Cairngorm Brewery, Tradewinds, An Teallach, Crofters Pale Ale. **Facilities** Children's menu Play area Dogs allowed Garden Parking **Rooms** 12

| SHIELDAIG | Map 22 NG85 |

## PICK OF THE PUBS

### Shieldaig Bar & Coastal Kitchen ★ SHL ◉◉ ▼

*See Pick of the Pubs on page 572*

| TORRIDON | Map 22 NG95 |

## PICK OF THE PUBS

### The Torridon Inn ★★★ INN

*See Pick of the Pubs on page 573*

| ULLAPOOL | Map 22 NH19 |

## PICK OF THE PUBS

### The Ceilidh Place ▼

**14 West Argyle St IV26 2TY**
☎ **01854 612103** 📄 **01854 613773**
e-mail: stay@theceilidhplace.com
**dir:** *On entering Ullapool, along Shore St, pass pier, take 1st right. Hotel straight ahead at top of hill*

Developed over the last forty years from an old boatshed café, this unique free house has been transformed into an all-day bar, coffee shop, restaurant, bookshop and art gallery. The late founder Robert Urquhart had aspirations for a place for serious writing, eating, meeting, talking and singing. Today it's known mostly for live traditional Scottish music, although some jazz also slips in. The heart of the Ceilidh Place is the café/bar, with its big open fire and solid wooden furniture. It's a place to stay all day, and some do. Simple delights begin with a full breakfast menu featuring porridge; bacon or sausage rolls; and scrambled eggs with smoked salmon. Soups and sandwiches arrive at lunchtime and, as the day wears on, expect substantial choices like baked smoked hake with parmesan, cream and spinach mash; and wild venison casserole with clapshot.

**Open** all day all wk **Bar Meals** Av main course £8 food served all day **Restaurant** Av 3 course à la carte fr £20 food served all day ⊕ FREE HOUSE ◀ Belhaven Best, Guinness, Scottish ales. ▼ 12 **Facilities** Children's portions Garden Parking

| MIDLOTHIAN |

| DALKEITH | Map 21 NT36 |

## PICK OF THE PUBS

### The Sun Inn ★★★★ INN ◉ ▼ NEW

*See Pick of the Pubs on opposite page*

| PENICUIK | Map 21 NT25 |

### The Howgate Restaurant ▼

**Howgate EH26 8PY** ☎ **01968 670000** 📄 **01968 670000**
e-mail: peter@howgate.com
**dir:** *10m N of Peebles. 3m E of Penicuik on A6094 between Leadburn junct & Howgate*

Situated in a beautifully converted farm building, formerly the home of Howgate cheeses, the Howgate's fire-warmed bar offers bistro-style meals, while the candle-lit restaurant serves a full carte. Executive and head chefs, Steven Worth and Sean Blake, respectively, use the finest Scottish produce, especially beef and lamb; other options might include pan-fried trio of sea bass, salmon and king prawns; breast of Border pheasant stuffed with haggis; and mushroom and red pepper stroganoff. There are fine beers to enjoy and an impressively produced wine list roams the globe.

**Open** all wk Closed: 25-26 Dec, 1 Jan **Bar Meals** L served all wk 12-2 D served all wk 6-9.30 Av main course £11.95 **Restaurant** L served all wk 12-2 booking required D served all wk 6-9.30 booking required Fixed menu price fr £25 Av 3 course à la carte fr £25 ⊕ FREE HOUSE ◀ Belhaven Best, Hoegaarden Wheat Biere. ▼ 14 **Facilities** Children's portions Garden Parking

| MORAY |

| FOCHABERS | Map 23 NJ35 |

### Gordon Arms Hotel

**80 High St IV32 7DH**
☎ **01343 820508** 📄 **01343 829059**
e-mail: gordonarmsfochabers@live.co.uk
**dir:** *A96 approx halfway between Aberdeen & Inverness, 9m from Elgin*

This 200-year-old former coaching inn, close to the River Spey and within easy reach of Speyside's whisky distilleries, is understandably popular with salmon fishers, golfers and walkers. Its public rooms have been carefully refurbished, and the hotel makes an ideal base from which to explore this scenic corner of Scotland. The cuisine makes full use of local produce: venison, lamb and game from the uplands, fish and seafood from the Moray coast, beef from Aberdeenshire and salmon from the Spey - barely a stone's throw from the kitchen!

**Open** all day all wk 11-11 (Thu 11-mdnt Fri-Sat 11am-12.30am) ◀ Caledonian Deuchars IPA, John Smith's Smooth, Guest Ales. **Facilities** Dogs allowed Parking

| NORTH LANARKSHIRE |

| CUMBERNAULD | Map 21 NS77 |

### Castlecary House Hotel ▼

**Castlecary Rd G68 0HD**
☎ **01324 840233** 📄 **01324 841608**
e-mail: enquiries@castlecaryhotel.com
**dir:** *A80 onto B816 between Glasgow & Stirling. 7m from Falkirk, 9m from Stirling*

Run by the same family for over 30 years, this friendly hotel is located close to the historic Antonine Wall and Forth and Clyde Canal. Meals in the lounge bars plough a traditional furrow with options such as home-made steak pie; Scottish haddock in beer batter; and a range of flame-grilled steaks. There is an excellent selection of real ales on offer. More formal restaurant fare is available in Camerons Restaurant.

**Open** all day all wk Closed: 1 Jan **Bar Meals** Av main course £8 food served all day **Restaurant** L served Sun 12.30-3 D served Mon-Sat 6-9.30 booking required Fixed menu price fr £12.95 Av 3 course à la carte fr £15.95 ⊕ FREE HOUSE ◀ Arran Blonde, Harviestoun Brooker's Bitter & Twisted, Inveralmond Ossian's Ale, Housten Peter's Well, Caledonian Deuchars IPA. ▼ 8 **Facilities** Children's menu Children's portions Dogs allowed Garden Parking

| PERTH & KINROSS |

| GLENDEVON | Map 21 NN90 |

### An Lochan Tormaukin Country Inn and Restaurant ▼

**FK14 7JY** ☎ **01259 781252** 📄 **01259 781526**
e-mail: info@anlochan.co.uk
**dir:** *M90 junct 6 onto A977 to Kincardine, follow signs to Stirling. Exit at Yelts of Muckhard onto A823/Crieff*

As we went to press this attractive whitewashed building was about to change hands. Built in 1720 as a drovers' inn, at a time when Glendevon was frequented by cattlemen making their way from the Tryst of Crieff to the market place at Falkirk, the name Tormaukin is Gaelic for 'hill of the mountain hare', which reflects its serene, romantic location in the midst of the Ochil Hills. Sympathetically refurbished throughout, it still bristles with real Scottish character and charm. Original features like stone walls, exposed beams and blazing winter fires in the cosy public rooms ensure a warm and welcoming atmosphere.

**Open** all day all wk ◀ Bitter & Twisted, Thrappledouser Ö Aspall. ▼ 8 **Facilities** Dogs allowed Garden Parking

# PICK OF THE PUBS

# The Sun Inn ★★★★ INN ⊕ ♟ NEW

## AA PUB OF THE YEAR FOR SCOTLAND 2010-2011

### DALKEITH
Map 21 NT36

**Lothian Bridge EH22 4TR**
☎ **0131 663 2456**
e-mail: thesuninn@live.co.uk
dir: *On A7 towards Galashiels, opposite Newbattle Viaduct*

A recently refurbished gastro-pub with boutique rooms, rejoicing in its latest accolade - AA Pub of the Year for Scotland 2010-2011. Modern creature comforts sit comfortably alongside log fires, oak beams, exposed stone and wood panelling.

In the bar, local cask ales and Innis & Gunn's Edinburgh-brewed, oak-aged bottled beer have pride of place, while the wine list is put together by the combined brains and palates of host Bernie MacCarron, and chef and self-styled wine snob, Craig Minto. Food in the more formal, AA Rosetted restaurant is modern British, emphasised by seafood and pub classics. Lunch would get off to a great start with Pittenweem smoked haddock croquettes with Isle of Mull Cheddar sauce; braised skirt of beef with shallots, mushrooms and horseradish dumplings would be good to follow with. First and second courses at dinner could be an Indian tapas plate, followed by baked cod with potato pancake, seared king scallops, crispy leeks and chervil cream.

Other finds are game casserole with braised red cabbage and horseradish mash; milk-fed calves' liver with dry-cured bacon, caramelised shallots and creamy mash; whole roast partridge with honey-roast root vegetables, game chips and redcurrant and red wine jus; and Puy lentil and chestnut in puff pastry with champ potatoes, roast parsnips and peppercorn sauce. Modestly priced puddings include lemon posset with fresh raspberries and raspberry coulis; and Gavin's chocolate and Cointreau mousse with whipped cream. The pastries look pretty delectable too.

The wine list stabilises at around 50 bins; at least eight are served by the glass. Afternoon teas and 'yummy cakes' are served between 2pm and 5pm, every day except Sunday.

**Open** all day all wk Closed: 26 Dec, 1 Jan **Bar Meals** L served Mon-Sat 12-2 Sun 12-3.30 booking required D served Mon-Sat 6-9 Sun 5-7 booking required Av main course £10
**Restaurant** L served Mon-Sat 12-2 Sun 12-3.30 booking required D served Mon-Sat 6-9 Sun 5-7 booking required Fixed menu price fr £10 Av 3 course à la carte fr £25 ⊕ FREE HOUSE ◀ Deuchars, Timothy Taylor, Belhaven Best. ♟ 8 **Facilities** Children's menu Garden Parking

## GLENFARG        Map 21 NO11

### *The Famous Bein Inn* ★★ SHL ⊛

**PH2 9PY** ☎ **01577 830216**   📄 **01577 830211**
e-mail: enquiries@beininn.com
dir: *From S: M90 junct 8, A91 towards Cupar. Left onto B996 to Bein Inn. From N: M90 junct 9, A912 towards Gateside*

Situated in a wooded glen overlooking the river, the inn is now owned by a local farming family, well known for the quality of their beef, and maintains a nearly 150-year-old tradition of catering for travellers between Perth and Edinburgh. Locally sourced and freshly prepared food is served in the restaurant or bistro. Expect dishes such as North Sea mackerel fillet with Arran wholegrain mustard potato salad, or pan roast rump of black face Perthshire lamb with bacon and cabbage and sesame potatoes. Visitors might also enjoy coffee and a scone by a log fire or a refreshing pint of Belhaven Best on the sundeck.

**Open** all day all wk **Closed:** 25 Dec ◄ Belhaven Best, Inveralmond Ale, Guinness. **Facilities** Parking **Rooms** 11

## GUILDTOWN        Map 21 NO13

### PICK OF THE PUBS

### Anglers Inn   ★★★★★ INN ♀

**Main Rd PH2 6BS** ☎ **01821 640329**
e-mail: info@theanglersinn.co.uk
dir: *6m N of Perth on A93*

A contemporary gastro-pub completely renovated and refurbished by Shona and Jeremy Wares since they took it over in 2007. With its five en suite bedrooms, the Anglers is popular for small fishing and shooting parties; it's also only two miles from Perth racecourse. Comfortable leather chairs and a log fire induce a relaxed and homely atmosphere, ideal surroundings in which to sample one of the Inveralmond Brewery ales on offer at the bar. Expect food prepared to an award-winning standard: typical choices for a three-course dinner from the carte could include starters of potted Morecambe brown shrimps and Skye prawns, or fried herb and tomato risotto cake. Main courses could comprise roast herb marinated rump of lamb with haggis hack, or free-range chicken breast stuffed with black pudding. Banana and rum crème brûlée or sticky toffee pudding with butterscotch sauce are typical of the desserts.

**Open** 11-3 5.30-mdnt **Closed:** Mon **Bar Meals** L served all wk 12-2 D served all wk 6-9 Av main course £14.95 **Restaurant** L served all wk 12-2 booking required D served all wk 6-9 booking required ⊕ FREE HOUSE ◄ Ossian, Liafail, Boddingtons. ♀ 10 **Facilities** Children's menu Children's portions Dogs allowed Garden Parking **Rooms** 5

## KILLIECRANKIE        Map 23 NN96

### PICK OF THE PUBS

### Killiecrankie House Hotel ★★★ SHL ⊛⊛ ♀

**PH16 5LG** ☎ **01796 473220**   📄 **01796 472451**
e-mail: enquiries@killiecrankiehotel.co.uk
dir: *Take B8079 N from Pitlochry. Hotel in 3m after NT Visitor Centre*

Built in 1840 as a dower house, this small, friendly hotel is set in four sprawling acres of wooded grounds at the northern end of the historic Killiecrankie Pass, scene of the famous battle. The cosy, wood-panelled bar is a popular haunt of both locals and visitors, while the snug sitting room opens on to a small patio and a fine herbaceous border. At lunchtime options include open sandwiches and bar meals of deep-fried haddock with chips, and game pie. The restaurant gains ever-wider recognition for the quality of its food and not only retains two AA Rosettes, but is also recognised for its notable wine list. Grilled fillet of sea trout with roasted asparagus; roasted supreme of guinea fowl stuffed with walnut mousse; and leek, pea and Stilton risotto are typical of the restaurant menu. The Conservatory Bar also serves lunches and dinners.

**Open** all day all wk **Closed:** Jan & Feb **Bar Meals** L served all wk 12.30-2 D served all wk 6-8.30 **Restaurant** L served all wk 12.30-2 D served all wk 6-8.30 ⊕ FREE HOUSE ◄ Tennent's Velvet Ale, Red MacGregor, Deuchars IPA, Brooker's Bitter & Twisted. ♀ 8 **Facilities** Children's menu Dogs allowed Garden Parking **Rooms** 10

## KINNESSWOOD        Map 21 NO10

### PICK OF THE PUBS

### Lomond Country Inn ♀

**KY13 9HN** ☎ **01592 840253**   📄 **01592 840693**
e-mail: info@lomondcountryinn.co.uk
dir: *M90 junct 5, follow signs for Glenrothes then Scotlandwell. Kinnesswood next village*

The expanse of water you can see from this small, privately owned hotel is Loch Leven, and in a castle on one its islands Mary, Queen of Scots was imprisoned. The hotel's name comes not from another, perhaps more famous loch, but from its location on the slopes of the Lomond Hills. The friendly-feeling public areas offer log fires, real ales, including Orkney's Dark Island winter beer, and Harviestoun's Bitter & Twisted, as well as a fine collection of single malts. To enjoy the views,

choose the charming restaurant, a relaxing room freshly decorated country house style, where starters may feature pan-fried mushrooms with tarragon, brandy and cream in puff pastry, and prawn cocktail; and mains of chicken curry with basmati rice and naan; haddock in beer batter with hand-cut chips; and Cheddar-topped spicy five-bean chilli.

**Open** all day all wk 7am-1am **Bar Meals** L served all wk 7am-9pm D served all wk 5-9 Av main course £6.95 food served all day **Restaurant** L served all wk 7am-9pm D served all wk 5-9 Fixed menu price fr £10.95 Av 3 course à la carte fr £16.95 food served all day ⊕ FREE HOUSE ◄ Deuchars IPA, Calders Cream, Tetleys, Orkney Dark Island, Bitter & Twisted. ♀ 12 **Facilities** Children's menu Children's portions Play area Family room Dogs allowed Garden Parking

## PITLOCHRY        Map 23 NN95

### PICK OF THE PUBS

### Moulin Hotel ★★★ HL ♀

**11-13 Kirkmichael Rd, Moulin PH16 5EH**
☎ **01796 472196**   📄 **01796 474098**
e-mail: enquiries@moulinhotel.co.uk
web: www.moulinhotel.co.uk
dir: *From A924 at Pitlochry take A923. Moulin 0.75m*

Built in 1695 at the foot of Ben Vrackie on an old drovers' road, this great all-round inn is popular as a walking and touring base. Locals are drawn to the bar for the excellent home-brewed beers, with Ale of Atholl, Braveheart, Moulin Light, and Old Remedial served on handpump. The interior boasts beautiful stone walls and lots of cosy niches, with blazing log fires in winter; while the courtyard garden is lovely in summer. Menus offer the opportunity to try something local such as mince and tatties; Skye mussels; venison pan-fried in Braveheart beer; and Vrackie Grostel — sautéed potatoes with smoked bacon topped with a fried egg. You might then round off your meal with Highland honey sponge and custard, or raspberry crumble. A specials board broadens the choice further. Around 20 wines by the glass and more than 30 malt whiskies are available.

**Open** all day all wk 11-11 (Fri-Sat 11am-11.45pm Sun noon-11) **Bar Meals** L served all wk 12-9.30 D served all wk 12-9.30 Av main course £8.95 food served all day **Restaurant** D served all wk 6-9 booking required Fixed menu price fr £18 Av 3 course à la carte fr £23.50 ⊕ FREE HOUSE ◀ Moulin Braveheart, Old Remedial, Ale of Atholl, Moulin Light, Belhaven Best. ♀ 25 **Facilities** Children's menu Children's portions Dogs allowed Garden Parking **Rooms** 15

---

## RENFREWSHIRE

### HOUSTON                                    Map 20 NS46

## Fox & Hounds ♀

South St PA6 7EN
☎ 01505 612448 & 612991   🖹 01505 614133
**e-mail:** jonathon.wengel@btconnect.com
**dir:** A737, W from Glasgow. Take Johnstone Bridge off Weir exit, follow signs for Houston. Pub in village centre

Carl Wengel established the Houston Brewing Company in his parents' 18th-century, conservation village pub in 1997, putting the desire down to his German ancestry. Watch the ale being brewed from one of the three bars. His brother Jonathon ensures high culinary standards for dishes such as fresh Scottish scampi tails in ale batter; fillet of fresh halibut with citrus herb butter; and baked breast of chicken with black pudding and whisky cream. There is also an amazing whisky list and great wines. Look out for special food and music evenings.

**Open** all day all wk 11am-mdnt ( Fri-Sat 11am-1am Sun from 12.30) **Bar Meals** Av main course £8 food served all day **Restaurant** Fixed menu price fr £15 Av 3 course à la carte fr £25 food served all day ⊕ FREE HOUSE ◀ Killelan, Warlock Stout, Texas, Jock Frost, Peter's Well. ♀ 10 **Facilities** Children's menu Children's portions Dogs allowed Garden Parking

---

## SCOTTISH BORDERS

### ALLANTON                                   Map 21 NT85

## Allanton Inn

TD11 3JZ ☎ 01890 818260
**e-mail:** info@allantoninn.co.uk
**dir:** From A1 at Berwick take A6105 for Chirnside (5m). At Chirnside Inn take Coldstream Rd for 1m to Allanton

Now under new ownership, this 18th-century coaching inn is highly acclaimed for its well kept ales and excellent food; beef from the family farm, plus sea and river fish, game, dairy produce and vegetables are all sourced locally. Salmon is smoked in the garden smoke house. Try dishes such as wild boar and honey sausages with creamy mustard sauce and mash; Borders venison loin, parsnip and celeriac purée, fondant potatoes and juniper and blackberry gravy; or Galagate Farm rib eye steak, green pepper and Calvados sauce with home-made chips. Outside is a large lawned area with fruit trees overlooking open countryside.

**Open** all wk 11-3 5-11 Closed: Mon **Bar Meals** L served Mon-Sun 12-3 D served Mon-Sun 6-9 booking required Av main course £13.50 food served all day **Restaurant** L served Mon-Sun 12-3 D served Mon-Sun 6-9 booking required Av 3 course à la carte fr £22 ⊕ FREE HOUSE ◀ Ossian, Trade Winds, Pentland IPA. **Facilities** Children's menu Children's portions Dogs allowed Garden Parking

---

### ETTRICK                                    Map 21 NT21

## Tushielaw Inn

TD7 5HT ☎ 01750 62205   🖹 01750 62205
**e-mail:** robin@tushielaw-inn.co.uk
**dir:** At junct of B709 & B711(W of Hawick)

An 18th-century former toll house and drovers' halt on the banks of Ettrick Water, making a good base for touring the Borders, trout fishing (salmon fishing can be arranged) and those tackling the Southern Upland Way. An extensive menu is always available with daily-changing specials. Fresh produce is used according to season, with local lamb and Aberdeen Angus beef regular specialities. Local haggis, or steak and ale pie, are popular choices.

**Open** all wk ⊕ FREE HOUSE **Facilities** Dogs allowed Parking

---

### GALASHIELS                                 Map 21 NT43

## Kingsknowes Hotel ★★★ HL

1 Selkirk Rd TD1 3HY
☎ 01896 758375   🖹 01896 750377
**e-mail:** enquiries@kingsknowes.co.uk
**dir:** Off A7 at Galashiels/Selkirk rdbt

In over three acres of grounds on the banks of the Tweed, a splendid baronial mansion built in 1869 for a textile magnate. There are lovely views of the Eildon Hills and Abbotsford House, Sir Walter Scott's ancestral home. Meals are served in two restaurants and the Courtyard Bar, where fresh local or regional produce is used as much as possible. The impressive glass conservatory is the ideal place to enjoy a drink.

**Open** all day all wk Mon-Wed noon-11 (Thu-Sat noon-1pm Sun noon-11) **Bar Meals** L served Mon-Fri 12-2, Sat 12-9.30, Sun 12-8.30 D served Mon-Fri 5.45-9, Sat 12-9.30, Sun 12-8.30 ⊕ FREE HOUSE ◀ McEwans 70/-, John Smith's. **Facilities** Children's menu Play area Dogs allowed Garden Parking **Rooms** 12

---

### KIRK YETHOLM                               Map 21 NT82

## The Border Hotel ♀ NEW

The Green TD5 8PQ ☎ 01573 420237
**e-mail:** borderhotel@aol.com
**dir:** From A698 in Kelso take B6352 for 7m to Kirk Yetholm

A welcome sight for Pennine Way walkers, this 18th-century former coaching inn stands at the end of the famous long-distance trail and just a mile from the border between Scotland and England. Updated in recent years, it offers a warm, friendly welcome in the character bar, with its cosy log fire, Pennine Way Bitter on tap, and farmhouse ciders on draught through the summer months. A traditional British menu features local game and farm meats. Follow Cullen Skink with marinated Border lamb, peppered saddle of local venison, or Eyemouth haddock and chips, leaving room for a hearty pudding.

**Open** all day all wk Closed: 25 Dec **Bar Meals** L served all wk 12-2 booking required D served all wk 6-8.45 booking required Av main course £9.95 **Restaurant** L served all wk 12-2 booking required D served all wk 6-8.45 booking required Av 3 course à la carte fr £19.75 ⊕ FREE HOUSE ◀ Bramling Cross, Pennine Way Bitter Ŏ Westons Old Rosie, Thirsty Cross. ♀ 10 **Facilities** Children's menu Children's portions Play area Dogs allowed Garden Parking

---

### LAUDER                                     Map 21 NT54

## PICK OF THE PUBS

## The Black Bull ★★★★ INN ♀

*See Pick of the Pubs on page 578*

# PICK OF THE PUBS

## The Black Bull ★★★★ INN ♥

**LAUDER** Map 21 NT54

**Market Place TD2 6SR**
☎ 01578 722208 📄 01578 722419
e-mail:
enquiries@blackbull-lauder.com
dir: *In centre of Lauder on A68*

A whitewashed, three-storey coaching inn dating from 1750, in the centre of a Royal Burgh on the edge of the Lammermuir Hills. Under new ownership since mid-2009, it offers a choice of a drink and a gastro-pub-style lunch in the relaxed Harness Room bar, and the more formal lounge bar, where you can settle round a table after a day of walking in the hills, visiting Thirlestane Castle, playing golf or checking out the Princes Street bargains in nearby Edinburgh.

Whichever way you work up an appetite, the kitchen team will have prepared something seasonal to enjoy, made from the best quality local meats, game, fish and other produce. A light lunch menu of snacks and sandwiches is served from midday, while a typical supper menu might lead you to begin with a platter of Belhaven smoked salmon; deep-fried mushrooms in sweet potato and coriander batter with Thai sweet chilli sauce; or chicken liver and Cognac pâté with gooseberry jelly and Scottish oatcakes. You might follow with wholetail Whitby scampi with fries; chargrilled fillet of salmon with parsnip purée, chorizo and green beans; sauté of pheasant breast with Stilton, tomato, port, green peppercorn and cream sauce; or mushroom risotto cakes with sun-dried tomato, pine nuts, basil pesto, roast cherry tomatoes and parmesan shavings. Or something from the grill might appeal.

To finish, the menu might encourage you in the direction of banana meringue crush with caramelita ice cream, crushed meringue and cream; or a selection of Scottish cheeses - Isle of Mull Cheddar, Cooleeney, Gubbeens and Dunsyre Blue - with oatcakes and water biscuits.

If you have a successful day's fishing and you're staying in one of the inn's eight superb en suite rooms, the kitchen will happily prepare your catch for dinner.

**Open** all day all wk **Bar Meals** L served Mon-Fri 12-2.30, Sat-Sun 12-9 booking required D served Mon-Fri 5-9, Sat-Sun 12-9 Av main course £9.95
**Restaurant** L served Mon-Fri 12-2.30, Sat-Sun 12-9 D served Mon-Fri 5-9, Sat-Sun 12-9 🌐 PERTHSHIRE TAVERNS LTD ◀ Guinness, Timothy Taylor Landlord, Tetley, Deuchars IPA, Old Speckled Hen, Marstons Pedigree Ŏ Old English, Kopperberg. ♥ 27
**Facilities** Children's menu Dogs allowed Parking **Rooms** 8

Save on Hotels. Book at **theAA.com/hotel**

**SCOTTISH BORDERS** 579 | SCOTLAND

---

| **LEITHOLM** | **Map 21 NT74** |

## The Plough Hotel

**Main St TD12 4JN** ☎ **01890 840252** 🖷 **01890 840252**
e-mail: theplough@leitholm.wanadoo.co.uk
dir: *5m N of Coldstream on A697. Take B6461, Leitholm in 1m*

The only pub remaining in this small border village (there were originally two), the Plough dates from the 17th century and was once a coaching inn. Food is traditional pub fare, taking in crispy potato skins with cheese; moules marinière with crusty bread; rack of lamb served with jacket potato and vegetables with a rosemary gravy; plus a great choice of steaks.

**Open** all day all wk noon-mdnt **Bar Meals** food served all day **Restaurant** food served all day ⊕ FREE HOUSE ◀ Guinness, Real Ale. **Facilities** Garden Parking

---

| **MELROSE** | **Map 21 NT53** |

### PICK OF THE PUBS

## Burts Hotel ★★★ HL 🙂🙂 ♈

**Market Square TD6 9PL**
☎ **01896 822285** 🖷 **01896 822870**
e-mail: enquiries@burtshotel.co.uk
dir: *A6091, 2m from A68 3m S of Earlston*

Built in 1722 as a comfortable home for a local dignitary, Burts looks out over Melrose's picturesque 18th-century market square. This former temperance hotel offers a selection of real ales, 80 single malt whiskies and a good range of wines by the glass, suggesting a rather more liberal attitude nowadays. The Henderson family have run this award-winning business for almost forty years, and the food – which has earned two AA Rosettes since 1995 – reflects their personal commitment to the highest standards. For a true taste of the Borders, try starting with venison and pistachio nut terrine with green apple and grape dressing, followed by pan-fried fillet of salmon with shallot purée, buttered kale, new potatoes and a prawn and parsley sauce. To finish, the selection of Scottish and Border cheeses is served with biscuits and grape chutney. The bar menu also includes grills, vegetarian dishes and toasted foccacia sandwiches.

---

**Open** all wk noon-2.30 5-11 **Bar Meals** L served all wk 12-2 D served all wk 6-9.30 Av main course £10.95 **Restaurant** L served all wk 12-2 booking required D served all wk 7-9 booking required Fixed menu price fr £35 ⊕ FREE HOUSE ◀ Caledonian 80/-, Deuchars IPA, Timothy Taylor Landlord, Fuller's London Pride. ♈ 10 **Facilities** Children's portions Dogs allowed Garden Parking **Rooms** 20

---

| **ST BOSWELLS** | **Map 21 NT53** |

### PICK OF THE PUBS

## Buccleuch Arms Hotel ♈

**The Green TD6 0EW**
☎ **01835 822243** 🖷 **01835 823965**
e-mail: info@buccleucharms.com
dir: *On A68, 10m N of Jedburgh. Hotel on village green*

This smart and friendly country-house hotel, dating from the 16th century, sits next to the village cricket pitch. A large and comfortable lounge is warmed by a log fire in winter, while the spacious enclosed garden comes into its own during the warmer months. The bar serves one real ale at a time, but turnover is high so locals keep coming back to find out what's on offer – the Stewart Brewery, Broughton Ales, and the Hadrian and Border Brewery are just three of the regular suppliers. Food also plays a pivotal role, from breakfast through award-winning bar meals to dinner. Menus change seasonally, but the specials may well change twice daily to reflect the availability of ingredients from the Scottish Borders countryside. Enjoy a taste of Scotland with a starter of local haggis croquettes rolled in oatmeal, followed by a chargrilled organic veal and pork burger from Peelham Farm, Berwickshire.

**Open** all day all wk 7am-11pm Closed: 25 Dec **Bar Meals** L served all wk 12-2 D served all wk 6-9 Av main course £9.50 food served all day **Restaurant** D served all wk 6-9 booking required Fixed menu price fr £20 ⊕ FREE HOUSE ◀ John Smith's, Guinness, Broughton, guest ales. ♈ 12 **Facilities** Children's menu Children's portions Play area Dogs allowed Garden Parking

---

| **SWINTON** | **Map 21 NT84** |

### PICK OF THE PUBS

## The Wheatsheaf at Swinton ♈

**Main St TD11 3JJ** ☎ **01890 860257** 🖷 **01890 860688**
e-mail: reception@wheatsheaf-swinton.co.uk
dir: *From Edinburgh A697 onto B6461. From East Lothian A1 onto B6461*

In the past few years, the Wheatsheaf has built up an impressive reputation as a dining destination. Run by husband and wife team Chris and Jan Winson, this popular venue is tucked away in the picturesque village of Swinton. The Wheatsheaf's secret is to use carefully sourced local ingredients in imaginative combinations. In addition to wild mushrooms and

---

organic vegetables, wild salmon, venison, partridge, pheasant, woodcock and duck are all likely menu contenders subject to seasonal availability. Lunchtime offers the likes of sautéed Paris brown mushrooms and bacon in a tarragon crêpe with a Mull Cheddar glaze; and open omelette of Dunsyre Blue cheese and confit cherry tomatoes. In the evening settle back, enjoy the friendly service, and tuck into plates of seared scallops with a lemon and chive butter sauce; and braised shank of Border lamb, gratin dauphinoise and creamed Savoy.

**Open** Mon-Tue 5-11 (Wed-Thu 11-3 5-11 Fri-Sat 11-mdnt Sun noon-10) Closed: 25-27 & 31 Dec-1 Jan, Mon-Tue L **Bar Meals** L served Wed-Sun 12-2 D served Mon-Sat 5-9, Sun 5-8.30 **Restaurant** L served Wed-Sun 12-2 booking required D served Mon-Sat 5-9, Sun 5-8.30 booking required ⊕ FREE HOUSE ◀ Deuchars IPA, Broughton Greenmantle Ale, Belhaven Best, Guinness. ♈ 12 **Facilities** Parking

---

| **TIBBIE SHIELS INN** | **Map 21 NT22** |

### PICK OF THE PUBS

## Tibbie Shiels Inn

**St Mary's Loch TD7 5LH**
☎ **01750 42231** 🖷 **01750 42302**
dir: *From Moffat take A708. Inn 14m on right*

On the isthmus between St Mary's Loch and the Loch of the Lowes, this waterside hostelry is named after the woman who first opened it in 1826. Isabella 'Tibbie' Shiels expanded the inn from a small cottage to a hostelry which could sleep around 35 people – many of them on the floor! Famous visitors during her time included Walter Scott, Thomas Carlyle and Robert Louis Stevenson. Tibbie Shiels herself is rumoured to keep watch over the bar, where the selection of over 50 malt whiskies helps sustain long periods of ghost watching. Food from the traditional pub menu can be enjoyed in either the bar or the dining room. Sandwiches, salads, ploughman's, toasties, paninis, burgers and jackets are all on offer, while the straightforward carte may tempt with a plate of smoked salmon followed by Tibbie's pie (chef's chicken, bacon and haggis cooked in a creamy white sauce).

**Open** all day all wk 10am-mdnt **Bar Meals** Av main course £8 food served all day **Restaurant** food served all day ⊕ FREE HOUSE ◀ Broughton Greenmantle Ale, Belhaven 80/- Ò Stowford Press. **Facilities** Children's menu Children's portions Play area Dogs allowed Garden Parking

---

## WEST LINTON — Map 21 NT15

### The Gordon Arms

Dolphinton Rd EH46 7DR
☎ 01968 660208  📠 01968 661852
e-mail: info@thegordon.co.uk
dir: Telephone for directions

Set in the pretty village of West Linton but within easy reach of the M74, this 17th-century inn has a real log fire in the cosy lounge bar, and a lovely sun-trap beer garden. Enjoy a local ale alongside your meal, which may start with feta cheese and couscous fritters with a spicy red schoog, or cullen skink; continue with steak and ale pie, haggis, or collops of venison with a rustic butternut squash and sweet potato purée; and finish with sticky toffee pudding.

**Open** all day all wk 11-11 (Fri-Sat 11-1am Tue 11-mdnt) John Smith's, Guinness, real ales. **Facilities** Play area Dogs allowed Garden Parking

## SOUTH AYRSHIRE

### SYMINGTON — Map 20 NS33

### Wheatsheaf Inn

Main St KA1 5QB ☎ 01563 830307  📠 01563 830307
dir: Telephone for directions

This 17th-century inn lies in a lovely village setting close to the Royal Troon Golf Course, and there has been a hostelry here since the 1500s. Log fires burn in every room and the work of local artists adorns the walls. Seafood dominates the menu - maybe pan-fried scallops in lemon and chives - and alternatives include honey roasted lamb shank; haggis, tatties and neeps in Drambuie and onion cream, and the renowned steak pie.

**Open** all day all wk 11-11 (Fri-Sat 11am-mdnt) Closed: 25 Dec, 1 Jan Belhaven Best, Old Speckled Hen, Guinness. **Facilities** Garden Parking

## STIRLING

### ARDEONAIG — Map 20 NN63

### The Ardeonaig Hotel 🍷

South Loch Tay Side FK21 8SU
☎ 01567 820400  📠 01567 820282
e-mail: info@ardeonaighotel.co.uk
dir: In Kenmore take road to S of Loch Tay signed Acharn. 6m. Or from Killin, next Falls of Dochart, take South Rd through Achmore & on to Ardeonaig, 6m

A romantic retreat with a difference, on the south shore of Loch Tay with views of the Ben Lawers mountains. The difference is that chef/owner Pete Gottgens refurbished the inn and introduced many elements dear to his heart from his native Southern Africa. Developments included a new kitchen; five thatched colonial-style garden lodges (called rondawels); a fine dining wine cellar which houses Europe's largest collection of South African wines; a dining room called the Study, where light lunches or afternoon teas are served; and the landscaping of 13

acres of grounds. African influences notwithstanding, the Ardeonaig has a solid reputation for using the best of seasonal Scottish produce in the kitchen.

**Open** all day all wk 11-10 (Fri-Sat 11-11) Arran Blonde, Tusker, Castle Lager, Windhoek Lager. 🍷 10 **Facilities** Family room Dogs allowed Garden Parking

### CALLANDER — Map 20 NN60

### The Lade Inn 🍷

Kilmahog FK17 8HD ☎ 01877 330152
e-mail: info@theladeinn.com
dir: From Stirling take A84 to Callander. 1m N of Callander, left at Kilmahog Woollen Mills onto A821 towards Aberfoyle. Pub immediately on left

Built as a tea room in 1935, this family-run free house was first licensed in the 1960s. Today, it offers a friendly welcome and the highest standards of food and drink. Beside the usual range at the bar, the pub's own real ale shop stocks over 130 Scottish bottled beers from 30 micro-breweries, and ciders. Soak them up with pan-fried breast of Fife chicken or roasted Scottish salmon. There is a superb beer garden with three ponds and Scottish folk music is played every Friday and Saturday.

**Open** all day all wk noon-11 (Fri-Sat noon-1am Sun 12.30-10.30) **Bar Meals** L served Mon-Fri 12-3, Sat 12-9, Sun 12.30-9 D served Mon-Fri 5-9, Sat 12-9, Sun 12.30-9 booking required **Restaurant** L served Mon-Fri 12-3, Sat 12-9, Sun 12.30-9 D served Mon-Fri 5-9, Sat 12-9, Sun 12.30-9 booking required ⊕ FREE HOUSE Waylade, LadeBack, LadeOut, Belhaven Best, Tennent's ⊙ Thistly Cross. 🍷 9 **Facilities** Children's menu Children's portions Play area Family room Dogs allowed Garden Parking

### DRYMEN — Map 20 NS48

### The Clachan Inn

2 Main St G63 0BG ☎ 01360 660824
e-mail: info@clachaninndrymen.co.uk
dir: Telephone for directions

Believed to be the oldest licensed pub in Scotland, this quaint, white-painted cottage sits in a small village on the West Highland Way, and was once owned by Rob Roy's sister. In the bar, guest ales are changed often and there is a warming log fire to keep things cosy. Locate the appealing lounge bar for freshly-made food using the best of local produce, where the specials menu changes daily.

**Open** all day all wk Closed: 25 Dec & 1 Jan **Bar Meals** L served Mon-Sat 12-3.45 D served Mon-Sat 6-9.45 **Restaurant** L served Mon-Sat 12-3.45 D served Mon-Sat 6-9.45 ⊕ FREE HOUSE Guinness. **Facilities** Children's menu Children's portions Dogs allowed

### KIPPEN — Map 20 NS69

### Cross Keys Hotel

Main St FK8 3DN ☎ 01786 870293
e-mail: info@kippencrosskeys.co.uk
dir: 10m W of Stirling, 20m from Loch Lomond off A811

Refurbished by owners Debby and Brian, this cosy inn now serves food and drink all day. Nearby Burnside Wood is managed by a local community woodland group, and is perfect for walking and nature trails. The pub's interior, warmed by three log fires, is equally perfect for resting your feet afterwards. Regular events include a weekly Tuesday folk night.

**Open** all day noon-11 (Fri-Sat noon-1am Sun noon-11) Closed: 25 Dec, 1-2 Jan, Mon Belhaven Best, Harviestoun Bitter & Twisted, Guinness. **Facilities** Family room Dogs allowed Garden Parking

## WEST LOTHIAN

### LINLITHGOW — Map 21 NS97

## PICK OF THE PUBS

### Champany Inn - The Chop and Ale House ⊛⊛

Champany EH49 7LU
☎ 01506 834532  📠 01506 834302
e-mail: reception@champany.com
dir: 2m N.E of Linlithgow on corner of A904 & A803

Several 16th-century cottages and an ancient watermill comprise this unusual little hotel, which has two splendid restaurants. The more informal is the easy chair and couch-strewn Chop and Ale House, which occupies a converted farmer's cottage, where your eyes will alight on the rock pond, where you'll find fresh Loch Gruinart oysters and lobsters before preparation for the pot. The bistro-style menu offers starters of smoked trout with horseradish cream and lightly grilled home-smoked chorizo sausage with pickled red cabbage, followed by a classic Champany burger, deep-fried cod and chips, spit-roasted chicken, or an Aberdeen Angus rib-eye steak with all the trimmings. In the elegant, octagonal restaurant, the two-AA Rosette menu may deliver Highland black pudding with onion marmalade, triple-smoked rump of beef with single-vineyard olive oil and fresh oregano, and fillet of salmon hot smoked over woodchips.

Open all wk noon-2 6.30-10 (Fri-Sun noon-10) Closed: 25-26 Dec, 1 Jan **Bar Meals** L served 12-10 D served 6.30-10 food served all day **Restaurant** L served 12.30-10 D served 7-10 food served all day ⊕ FREE HOUSE ◀ Belhaven. **Facilities** Children's portions Garden Parking

## SCOTTISH ISLANDS
## COLL, ISLE OF

| ARINAGOUR | Map 22 NM25 |
|---|---|

### PICK OF THE PUBS

## Coll Hotel

**PA78 6SZ** ☎ **01879 230334**  📄 **01879 230317**
e-mail: info@collhotel.com
dir: *Ferry from Oban. Hotel at head of Arinagour Bay, 1m from Pier (collections by arrangement)*

The Coll is the only inn on the Isle of Coll, and commands stunning views over the sea to Jura and Mull. It's a popular rendezvous for the islands 170 locals, where pints of Loch Fyne ale are supped, malt whiskies are sipped, and the day's developments are digested. Food is served in the Gannet Restaurant, bar or garden. Fresh produce is landed and delivered from around the island every day and features on the specials board. As you would expect, seafood is a major component. You'll find it in openers such as Coll crab chowder, Connel mussels in garlic and cream, and seared scallops with crispy Parma ham; and in main courses too: home-made spaghetti with fresh Coll lobster in a lobster sauce; and fresh Coll langoustines, served either cold with mayo or hot and tossed in garlic butter with salad and new potatoes.

**Open** all day all wk **Bar Meals** L served all wk 12-2 D served all wk 6-9 Av main course £10 **Restaurant** L served all wk 12-2 D served all wk 6-9 booking required Fixed menu price fr £12 Av 3 course à la carte fr £20 ⊕ FREE HOUSE ◀ Loch Fyne Ale, Pipers Gold, Guinness. **Facilities** Children's menu Children's portions Play area Family room Garden Parking

| SKYE, ISLE OF | |
|---|---|
| **ARDVASAR** | Map 22 NG60 |

## Ardvasar Hotel ★★★ HL

**IV45 8RS** ☎ **01471 844223**  📄 **01471 844495**
e-mail: richard@ardvasar-hotel.demon.co.uk
web: www.ardvasarhotel.com
dir: *From ferry terminal, 50yds & turn left*

An early 1800s white-painted cottage-style inn, the second oldest on Skye, renowned for its genuinely friendly hospitality and informal service. Sea views over the Sound of Sleat reach the Knoydart Mountains beyond. Malt whiskies are plentiful, but beer drinkers will not be disappointed. Food is served in the informal lounge bar throughout the day and evening, with a sumptuous four-course dinner in the dining room during high season. Local produce figures prominently, particularly freshly-landed seafood, venison, and Aberdeen Angus beef.

**Open** all day all wk 11am-mdnt (Sun noon-11pm) **Bar Meals** L served all wk 12-2.30 D served all wk 5.30-9 ⊕ FREE HOUSE ◀ IPA, Isle of Skye Red Cuillin. **Facilities** Children's menu Dogs allowed Garden Parking **Rooms** 10

| CARBOST | Map 22 NG33 |
|---|---|

## The Old Inn

**IV47 8SR** ☎ **01478 640205**  📄 **01478 640205**
e-mail: reservations@oldinn.f9.co.uk
dir: *From Skye Bridge follow A87 north. Take A863, then B8009 to inn*

Two-hundred-year-old free house on the edge of Loch Harport with wonderful views of the Cuillin Hills from the waterside patio. Not surprisingly, the inn is popular with walkers and climbers. Open fires welcome winter visitors, and live music is a regular feature. With a great selection of real ales, the menu includes daily home-cooked specials, with numerous fresh fish dishes, including local prawns and oysters and mackerel from the loch.

**Open** all day all wk 11am-mdnt ◀ Red Cuillin, Black Cuillin, Hebridean ale, Cuillin Skye Ale, Pinnacle Ale. **Facilities** Family room Dogs allowed Garden Parking

| ISLEORNSAY | Map 22 NG71 |
|---|---|

### PICK OF THE PUBS

## Hotel Eilean Iarmain ★★★ SHL @@

**IV43 8QR** ☎ **01471 833332**  📄 **01471 833275**
e-mail: hotel@eileaniarmain.co.uk
dir: *A851, A852 right to Isleornsay harbour front*

An award-winning Hebridean hotel with its own pier, overlooking the Isle of Ornsay harbour and Sleat Sound. The old-fashioned character of the hotel remains intact, and decor is mainly cotton and linen chintzes with traditional furniture. More a small private hotel than a pub, the bar and restaurant ensure that the standards of food and drinks served here - personally chosen by the owner Sir Iain Noble - are exacting. The head chef declares: "We never accept second best, it shines through in the standard of food served in our restaurant." Here you can try dishes like Eilean Iarmain estate venison casserole, pan-seared sirloin steak, or grilled fillet of cod with hollandaise sauce. If you call in at lunchtime, a more humble range of baked potatoes, sandwiches and toasties is also available. Half portions are served for children.

**Open** all day all wk **Bar Meals** food served all day **Restaurant** food served all day ⊕ FREE HOUSE ◀ McEwans 80/-, Guinness, Isle of Skye real ale. **Facilities** Children's portions Dogs allowed Garden Parking **Rooms** 16

## STEIN — Map 22 NG25

### Stein Inn ♟

**Macleod's Ter IV55 8GA** ☎ **01470 592362**
**e-mail:** angus.teresa@steininn.co.uk
**dir:** *A87 from Portree. In 5m take A850 for 15m. Right onto B886, 3m to T-junct. Turn left*

The oldest inn on the island, set in a lovely hamlet right next to the sea, the Stein Inn provides a warm welcome, fine food, and an impressive selection of drinks: fine wines, real ales and no fewer than a hundred malt whiskies. Highland meat, game and local seafood feature strongly on daily-changing menus, ranging from fresh West Coast mussels marinière or Skye scallops in oatmeal, to Highland venison pie, Scottish salmon with vermouth and tarragon sauce, or pork chop with walnut and Achmore blue cheese butter.

**Open** all day all wk 11am-mdnt Closed: 25 Dec, 1 Jan **Bar Meals** L served all wk 12-4 D served all wk 6-9.30 **Restaurant** D served all wk 6-9.30 ⊕ FREE HOUSE ◀ Red Cuillin, Trade Winds, Reeling Deck, Deuchars IPA, Dark Island. ♟ 9 **Facilities** Family room Dogs allowed Garden Parking

## SOUTH UIST

### LOCHBOISDALE — Map 22 NF71

### The Polochar Inn

**Polochar HS8 5TT** ☎ **01878 700215** 📄 **01878 700768**
**e-mail:** polocharinn@aol.com
**dir:** *W from Lochboisdale, take B888. Hotel at end of road*

Overlooking the sea towards the islands of Eriskay and Barra, this superbly situated 18th-century inn enjoys beautiful sunsets. The bar menu offers fresh seafood dishes and steaks with various sauces, while restaurant fare includes venison, fresh scallops or steak pie. There is always a great choice of guest ales and food and drink can be enjoyed in the garden in warmer months.

**Open** all day all wk 11-11 (Fri-Sat 11am-1am Sun 12.30pm-1am) **Bar Meals** L served Mon-Sat 12.30-8.30, Sun 1-8.30 (winter all wk 12-2.30) D served Mon-Sat 12.30-8.30, Sun 1-8.30 (winter all wk 5-8.30) Av main course £8 food served all day **Restaurant** Av 3 course à la carte fr £25 ⊕ FREE HOUSE ◀ Hebridean ales, Guest Ales. **Facilities** Children's menu Children's portions Family room Garden Parking

Save on Hotels. Book at **theAA.com/hotel**

583 SCOTLAND

# Wales

Snowdon Mountain Railway, Snowdonia National Park

## WALES

## ANGLESEY, ISLE OF

### BEAUMARIS — Map 14 SH67

## PICK OF THE PUBS

### Ye Olde Bulls Head Inn ★★★★★ INN ⊚⊚♀

Castle St LL58 8AP
☎ 01248 810329 📠 01248 811294
e-mail: info@bullsheadinn.co.uk
web: www.bullsheadinn.co.uk
dir: From Britannia Road Bridge follow A545. Inn in town centre

Inextricably linked to Anglesey's history, the Bull was built in 1472 as a coaching inn and stands close to imposing Beaumaris Castle. Charles Dickens and Samuel Johnson were both visitors to this historic inn, which features antique weaponry, an ancient brass water clock and the town's ducking stool in the traditional beamed bar. Beyond is the popular brasserie, which offers modern European cuisine – perhaps fishcakes with mango and chilli salsa, followed by venison, mushroom and root vegetable casserole with braised red cabbage. Or it's up the stairs to the smartly modern, first-floor Loft restaurant which offers a more formal menu of modern British dishes (two AA Rosettes). Try pheasant and ham boudin with onion purée and truffle jus, followed by seared John Dory with seafood tartlet and a mustard and parsley potato cake. Delectable desserts like hazelnut praline soufflé with vanilla sauce, or coffee and orange brûlée will be hard to resist. If you'd like to stay and explore the area, there are richly decorated guest rooms available.

**Open** all day all wk Closed: 25 Dec **Bar Meals** L served Mon-Sat 12-2, Sun 12-3 D served Mon-Sat 6-9, Sun 6.30-9.30 Av main course £10.50 **Restaurant** D served Tue-Thu 7-9.30, Fri-Sat 6.30-9.30 booking required Av 3 course à la carte fr £39.50 ⊕ FREE HOUSE ◀ Bass, Hancocks, Worthingtons, guest ales. ♀ 20
**Facilities** Children's menu Children's portions Parking **Rooms** 26

### RED WHARF BAY — Map 14 SH58

## PICK OF THE PUBS

### The Ship Inn

LL75 8RJ ☎ 01248 852568 📠 01248 851013
dir: Telephone for directions

The pub faces east on the lee side of a hill, sheltered from prevailing winds and catching the morning and afternoon sun perfectly. Wading birds flock here to feed on the extensive sands of Red Wharf Bay, making The Ship's waterside beer garden a birdwatcher's paradise on warm days. Before the age of steam, sailing ships landed cargoes here from all over the world; now the boats bring fresh Conwy Bay fish and seafood to the kitchens of this traditional free house. In the Kenneally family's hands for nearly 40 years, real ales are carefully tended and a single menu, on which dishes are given refreshingly light-hearted titles, applies to both bars and restaurant; specials always include a catch of the day. So expect to see starters such as 'Over the Caws-way – locally produced Cwt Caws soft Welsh cheese gently melted over a reef of leeks…'; and main course titles like 'Walk the plank', featuring prime Welsh sirloin steak.

**Open** all wk **Bar Meals** L served all wk 12-2.30 D served all wk 6-9 booking required Av main course £10 **Restaurant** D served Sat-Sun booking required Fixed menu price fr £17.50 Av 3 course à la carte fr £20 ⊕ FREE HOUSE ◀ Brains SA, Adnams, guest ales. **Facilities** Children's menu Play area Family room Garden Parking

## BRIDGEND

### KENFIG — Map 9 SS88

### Prince of Wales Inn

CF33 4PR ☎ 01656 740356
e-mail: prince-of-wales@btconnect.com
dir: M4 junct 37 into North Cornelly. Left at x-rds, follow signs for Kenfig & Porthcaw. Pub 600yds on right

A 16th-century property, this stone-built inn has been many things in its time: a school, town hall and courtroom among others. The town hall, incorporated into the inn, has recently been restored and one of the landlord's family will happily show it to you. Local fare on the menu could include award-winning sausages, Welsh minted lamb chops and Welsh braised faggots. Also worth attention are the daily specials on the blackboard and traditional Sunday lunches.

**Open** all wk **Bar Meals** L served all wk 12-3 D served all wk 6-9 Av main course £8 **Restaurant** L served all wk 12-3 D served all wk 6-9 Fixed menu price fr £8 ⊕ FREE HOUSE ◀ Bass Triangle, Worthington Best, guest ales ♂ Taffy Apples. **Facilities** Children's menu Children's portions Dogs allowed Garden Parking

## CARDIFF

### CREIGIAU — Map 9 ST08

## PICK OF THE PUBS

### Caesars Arms

*See Pick of the Pubs on page 588*

### GWAELOD-Y-GARTH — Map 9 ST18

### Gwaelod y Garth Inn

Main Rd CF15 9HH ☎ 029 2081 0408 & 07855 313247
e-mail: gwaelo-dinn@btconnect.com
dir: From M4 junct 32, N on A470, left at next exit, at rdbt turn right 0.5m. Right into village

Meaning 'foot of the garth (mountain)', this welcoming pub was originally part of the Marquess of Bute's estate. Every window of the pub offers exceptional views, and it's a much favoured watering hole for ramblers, cyclists and hang-gliders as well as some colourful locals. Real ales change every week, and the pub offers Gwynt y Ddraig award-winning ciders. Starters might include provençale fish soup with rouille, and main courses like grilled sea bass with braised fennel, or vegetarian Glamorgan sausages with plum chutney.

**Open** all wk 11am-mdnt (Sun noon-11) **Bar Meals** Av main course £11 food served all day **Restaurant** L served Mon-Thu 12-2, Fri-Sat 11am-9pm, Sun 12-3 booking required D served Mon-Sat 6.30-9 booking required Av 3 course à la carte fr £25 ⊕ FREE HOUSE ◀ HPA (Wye Valley), Three Cliffs Gold, Gower, RCH Pitchfork, Vale of Glamorgan, Crouch Vale Brewers Gold ♂ Local cider. **Facilities** Children's menu Children's portions Family room Dogs allowed Garden Parking

*See advert on opposite page*

# Gwaelod y Garth Inn

It's just a short ride out of the city, but here, above the valley, in the shelter of the Garth, the pace of life is slower. The welcome at the Gwaelod y Garth Inn is a genuine one, so we're a much favoured watering-hole for walkers, cyclists, hang-gliders, and our colourful locals, too.

The village and the pub have exceptional views of the Taff Vale and the Bristol Channel beyond, and our terrace is a marvellous place just to meet and watch the world go by. Inside, in the cosy bar and in the pool-room, you'll find plenty of choice of drinks, including good real ales, tasty bar-food, friendly company and, when it's cold outside, open fires. Upstairs, Chef ensures that our comfortable award-winning restaurant serves a fine extensive menu with wines to match, and on Sundays there is always a traditional roast.

The pub has recently been given a Highly Commended Award from CAMRA. B&B is also available (awaiting rating - see website for up to date information). The rest is up to you.

Licenced restaurant

CAMRA Commended bar

Open fires

### Main Rd, Gwaelod y Garth, Cardiff, CF15 9HH

**Tel:** 029 20810408 **Email:** gwaelo-dinn@btconnect.com **Website:** www.gwaeloddinn.co.uk

# PICK OF THE PUBS

## Caesars Arms

**CREIGIAU**                          Map 9 ST08

**Cardiff Rd CF15 9NN**
☎ **029 2089 0486**    📄 **029 2089 2176**
e-mail: caesarsarms@btconnect.com
dir: *M4 junct 34, A4119 towards Llantrisant/
Rhondda. Approx 0.5m right at lights signed
Groesfaen. Through Groesfaen, past Dynevor
Arms pub. Next left, signed Creigiau. 1m,
left at T-junct, pass Creigiau Golf Course.
Pub in 1m on left*

Just ten miles outside Cardiff, Caesars
Arms sits tucked away down winding
lanes. A whitewashed building that is
probably older than it looks, it has an
appealing interior. With fine views over
extensive gardens and surrounding
countryside from its heated patio and
terrace, it attracts a well-heeled
clientele. And little wonder – there is so
much more here than simply excellent
ales from Llanelli's Felinfoel Brewery.
The award-winning wine list extends to
more than 100 bottles, probably one of

the best selections in Wales; it has its
own beehives and makes its own honey;
vegetables, herbs and salads from its
own gardens are raised organically and
used in the kitchen. There's an in-house
smokery, giving a truly local flavour; and
a farm shop is stocked with free-range
eggs, rare breed pork products, honey
from their hives, Welsh cheeses, home-
baked bread and chef's ready-prepared
meals to take away.

An award-winning restaurant has a vast
selection of fresh fish, seafood, with
meat and game taking pride of place
– locally sourced produce is displayed
on shaven ice. Fresh seafood is an
undoubted strength, with deliveries
taken twice daily. Pembrokeshire
dressed crab, hake, salmon, Dover sole,
John Dory, lobsters and crawfish are all
likely to be found here. A show-stopping
sea bass baked in rock salt is
theatrically cracked open and filleted at
your table. But it's not all about fish –
other choices include steak from slow-
reared, dry-aged pedigree Welsh Blacks,
plus mountain lamb and venison from
the Brecon Beacons; free-range
chickens come from the Wye Valley.
Bajan fishcakes, scallops with leek

julienne, or cherry-smoked duck breast
with organic beetroot give an indication
of the flavours that await in this much
favoured hostelry. There is private
parking for over 100 cars.

**Open** all wk noon-2.30 6-10 (Sun noon-
4) Closed: 25 Dec, 1 Jan, Sun eve
**Bar Meals** L served Mon-Sat 12-2.30 Av
main course £10 **Restaurant** L served
Mon-Sat 12-2.30, Sun 12-4 D served
Mon-Sat 6-10 Av 3 course à la carte fr
£24 ⊕ FREE HOUSE ◖ Felinfoel Double
Dragon, Guinness. **Facilities** Dogs
allowed Garden Parking

Save on Hotels. Book at **theAA.com/hotel**

**CARMARTHENSHIRE** 589    WALES

## CARMARTHENSHIRE

### ABERGORLECH    Map 8 SN53

## The Black Lion

**SA32 7SN** ☎ **01558 685271**
e-mail: georgerashbrook@hotmail.com
dir: A40 E from Carmarthen, then B4310 signed Brechfa & Abergorlech

The Black Lion sits in the middle of Abergorlech, a pretty village offering fabulous riverside woodland walks and the river Cothi which runs alongside this 16th-century former coaching inn. A family-run establishment with an award-winning beer garden overlooking an ancient stone-built Roman bridge, the bar has flagstone floors, settles and a grandfather clock, while the dining room is more modern. Lots of home-made food and puddings are served, with Welsh steaks, pies and bread and butter pudding proving firm favourites. The area is also popular for its mountain bike trails.

**Open** all day Closed: Mon (ex BH) **Bar Meals** L served Tue-Sun 12-2.30 D served Tue-Sun 7-9 booking required Av main course £7 **Restaurant** D served Tue-Sun 7-9 booking required Av 3 course à la carte fr £15 ⊕ FREE HOUSE ◀ Rhymney ♂ Stowford Press. **Facilities** Children's menu Children's portions Dogs allowed Garden Parking

### LLANDDAROG    Map 8 SN51

## PICK OF THE PUBS

## White Hart Thatched Inn & Brewery

**SA32 8NT** ☎ **01267 275395**
e-mail: bestpubinwales@aol.com
web: www.thebestpubinwales.co.uk
dir: 6m E of Carmarthen towards Swansea, just off A48 on B4310, signed Llanddarog

A family-run business that includes the micro-brewery adjoining this ancient thatched free house – Cwrw Blasus ('tasty ale') is always available, made from top quality ingredients including water from 300 feet beneath the inn. Built in 1371, thick stone walls, a cosy log fire and heavy beams bear witness to the pub's ancient origins. The restaurant in a converted barn has views to the open-plan kitchen where the chefs can be seen preparing your food. The menu uses the best of local produce together with a few exotic imports. Choose from the chalkboard the likes of minted Welsh lamb shank with mushy peas and mash; chicken fillet in spinach with a feta sauce; or a duck

breast in plum and ginger. In summer, the flower-filled patio garden is perfect for alfresco dining. Children will enjoy seeing the pigs, chickens, ducks and turkeys on the small home farm.

**Open** 11.30-3 6.30-11 (Sun noon-3 7-10.30) Closed: Jan, Wed **Bar Meals** L served all wk 11.30-3 D served all wk 6.30-11 Av main course £9 **Restaurant** L served all wk 11.30-3 D served all wk 6.30-11 Av 3 course à la carte fr £20 ⊕ FREE HOUSE ◀ Roasted Barley Stout, Llanddarog Ale, Bramling Cross, CWRW Blasus, Swn y Dail. **Facilities** Children's menu Children's portions Play area Garden Parking

### LLANDEILO    Map 8 SN62

## The Angel Hotel ☘

**Rhosmaen St SA19 6EN**
☎ **01558 822765**  📠 **01558 824346**
e-mail: capelbach@hotmail.com
dir: In town centre next to post office

This popular pub in the centre of Llandeilo has something for everyone. Real ales are available in the bar area, which hosts regular live music nights. Upstairs, the Yr Eglwys function room ceiling is decorated with soaring frescoes inspired by Michelangelo's Sistine Chapel, and at the rear is an intimate bistro with warm terracotta walls, where dishes might include fresh sardines with herb butter followed by slow roast pork and crackling. Leave room for whisky and white chocolate croissant butter pudding and mango couli. There are regular hot international buffet evenings.

**Open** 11.30-3 6-11 Closed: Sun **Bar Meals** L served Mon-Sat 11.30-2.30 D served Mon-Sat 6-9 Av main course £5.50 **Restaurant** L served Mon-Sat 11.30-2.30 booking required D served Mon-Sat 6-9 booking required Av 3 course à la carte fr £11.95 ⊕ FREE HOUSE ◀ Evan Evans Ales, Tetleys, Butty Bach. ☘ 10 **Facilities** Children's menu Children's portions Garden

## The Castle Hotel

**113 Rhosmaen St SA19 6EN** ☎ **01558 824714**
dir: Telephone for directions

A 19th-century hotel within easy reach of Dinefwr Castle and wonderful walks through classic parkland. A charming, tiled and partly green-painted back bar attracts plenty of locals, while the front bar and side area offer smart furnishings and the chance to relax in comfort over a drink. A good range of real ales is available and quality bar and restaurant food is prepared with the finest of fresh local ingredients.

**Open** all day all wk **Bar Meals** food served all day ⊕ ENTERPRISE INNS ◀ Hancocks HB, Courage Directors, Timothy Taylor Landlord, Exmoor Gold, Adnams Broadside. **Facilities** Children's portions Dogs allowed Garden Parking **Notes** ◉

### LLANLLWNI    Map 8 SN43

## Belle Vue Inn NEW

**SA40 9SQ** ☎ **01570 480495**
e-mail: mail@bellevueinn.co.uk
dir: Midway between Carmarthen & Lampeter on A485

Take the A485 between Carmarthen and Lampeter to locate this cosy and welcoming roadside inn, which certainly lives up to its name as the surrounding countryside and views are stunning. Head this way on a sunny day and dine alfresco in the garden, perhaps ordering braised beef with leek mash or gammon, egg and pineapple from the bar menu. There are two rotating ales here to enjoy along with local bottled Welsh ciders. In the dining room, follow chicken and venison terrine with whole bream with lime beurre blanc, and chocolate truffle torte, or, if you're feeling really peckish, tuck into the 9-course 'gastro' menu. There are monthly themed menus too.

**Open** 12-3 5.30-11 Closed: Mon (ex BHs) **Bar Meals** L served Tue-Sat 12-2 D served Tue-Sun 6-9 Av main course £9 **Restaurant** L served Sun 12-2 D served Tue-Sun 6-9 Av 3 course à la carte fr £22 ⊕ FREE HOUSE ◀ Guinness, Guest ales ♂ Stowford Press, Gwynt y Ddraig. **Facilities** Children's menu Children's portions Garden Parking

### LLANWRDA    Map 9 SN73

## The Brunant Arms ☘

**Caio SA19 8RD** ☎ **01558 650483**  📠 **01558 650832**
e-mail: thebrunantarms@yahoo.co.uk
dir: From A40 between Llandovery & Llandeilo take A482 at Llanwrda. 1.4m to Caio

Tucked away at the foot of a small valley, the village of Caio lies safely off the road from Lampeter to Llandovery. Here, the Brunant Arms offers a relaxed welcome with some unusual real ales, Taffy Apples cider and good food. The menu features soft floured baps and filled jacket potatoes, as well as daily choices that might include Welsh cawl with herb dumplings; locally sourced venison steaks; sweet potato and butternut korma; or home-cooked Carmarthen ham, egg and chips. There is an impressive 30 wines by the glass.

**Open** noon-3 6-11 (Fri-Sat noon-3 6-1am Sun noon-11) Closed: Mon ◀ Ramblers Ruin, Wolvers Ale, Cribyn, Jacobi Dark Ale ♂ Taffy Apples. ☘ 30 **Facilities** Dogs allowed Garden Parking

## NANTGAREDIG — Map 8 SN42

### PICK OF THE PUBS

### Y Polyn ⊛⊛ ❦

**SA32 7LH ☎ 01267 290000**
e-mail: ypolyn@hotmail.com
dir: *From A48 follow signs to National Botanic Garden of Wales. Then follow brown signs to Y Polyn*

Set in a lovely spot in the Towy Valley, this 250-year-old-inn was once a tollhouse – its name means 'pole' after the original barrier across the road. Conveniently placed by a fork in the roads between Aberglasney and the National Botanic Garden of Wales, Y Polyn is pretty much a restaurant in a pub setting but drinkers are undoubtedly welcome to call in for a quick pint by the fire. Everything is made on the premises, and there's an emphasis on buying locally. The fixed-price dinner menu could begin with Black Mountain smoked salmon with sweet pickled cucumber, before main course offerings like Welsh Black beef cheeks, parsnip mash and crispy ox tongue, or daube of Welsh lamb Provençale. Carmarthenshire yoghurt and cream pannacotta with honey roast plums and warm pear and almond tart are typical desserts.

**Open** all wk 12-4 7-11 Closed: Mon, Sun eve **Bar Meals** Av main course £12.50 **Restaurant** L served Tue-Sun 12-2 D served Tue-Sat 7-9 Fixed menu price fr £22.50 Av 3 course à la carte fr £28.50 ⊕ FREE HOUSE ◀ Otley 01, Tomos Watkin OSB. ❦ 12 **Facilities** Children's portions Garden Parking

## CEREDIGION

## ABERAERON — Map 8 SN46

### PICK OF THE PUBS

### The Harbourmaster
✫✫✫✫✫ INN ⊛ ❦

**Pen Cei SA46 0BA ☎ 01545 570755**
e-mail: info@harbour-master.com
dir: *From A487. In Aberaeron follow Tourist Information Centre signs. Pub next door*

Originally the harbourmaster's house, the inn has been the dominant building on Aberaeron's Georgian quayside since 1811. In 2008 the former grain store next door was converted into a relaxing bar overlooking the harbour – the perfect spot for a pint of Evan Evans Bitter. The cobalt blue interior is complemented by original features like the Welsh slate masonry and spiral staircase. Proud of its AA Rosette, the kitchen produces typical starters of Swansea Bay steamed mussels with Thai flavours; and devilled lamb's kidneys on sourdough toast; among the main courses are roast loin of rabbit in pancetta with mustard sauce and tagliatelle; fish stew with king prawns, mussels, chorizo and borlotti beans; and tart of organic baby leeks with Hafod cheese and caponata. On the first floor are four spacious bedrooms, two with terrace views of Cardigan Bay; the cottage along the quay houses additional rooms.

---

**Open** all day all wk 10am-11.30pm Closed: 25 Dec **Bar Meals** L served Mon-Sun 12-2.30 D served Mon-Sun 6-9 Av main course £12 **Restaurant** L served Mon-Sun 12-2.30 booking required D served Mon-Sun 6.30-9 booking required Fixed menu price fr £14.50 Av 3 course à la carte fr £30 ⊕ FREE HOUSE ◀ Evan Evans Best Bitter. ❦ 14 **Facilities** Children's menu Children's portions Parking **Rooms** 13

## LLWYNDAFYDD — Map 8 SN35

### The Crown Inn & Restaurant ❦

**SA44 6BU ☎ 01545 560396**
e-mail: thecrowninnandrestaurant@hotmail.co.uk
dir: *Off A487 NE of Cardigan*

A traditional Welsh longhouse dating from 1799, with original beams, open fireplaces and a pretty restaurant. Young owners Rob and Monique offer a carvery every Sunday and a varied menu with a good selection of dishes, including braised pork and apple sausages with garlic mash in a giant Yorkshire pudding with onion gravy and peas, or whole trout stuffed with pine nuts and bacon, with a rosemary and lemon butter and sautéed potatoes and roast root vegetables. Blackboard specials and bar meals are available lunchtimes and evenings. Outside is a delightful, award-winning garden, while an easy walk down the lane leads to a cove with caves and National Trust cliffs.

**Open** all day all wk **Bar Meals** L served all wk 12-3 D served all wk 6-9 Av main course £8.95 **Restaurant** L served all wk 12-3 D served all wk 6-9 ⊕ FREE HOUSE ◀ Flowers IPA, Old Speckled Hen, guest ale. ❦ 12 **Facilities** Children's menu Play area Family room Dogs allowed Garden Parking

## NEW CROSS — Map 8 SN67

### New Cross Inn

**SY23 4LY ☎ 01974 261526**
dir: *Left on A487 to Cardigan for 1.09m, left onto A4120 Devils Bridge, right onto B4340. Continue for 3.16m, New Cross Inn on right hand side*

The history of this small, family-run, rural Welsh free house goes back to the 1930s, and is documented in a collection of photos displayed in the bar. Along with a good selection of real ales, honest cooking uses the best of local produce. The menus might feature chicken liver pâté with endive and mango salsa; tiger prawns fried in garlic and ginger; roasted rack of Welsh lamb with redcurrant and rosemary jus; spinach and ricotta

---

cannelloni; or poached supreme of salmon with cucumber and dill sauce.

**Open** 12-3 6.30-11 Closed: 1 Jan, Mon **Bar Meals** food served all day **Restaurant** booking required Av 3 course à la carte fr £19.50 food served all day ⊕ FREE HOUSE ◀ Double Dragon, Cambria Ale, Worthington's ♂ Thatchers Gold. **Facilities** Children's menu Children's portions Parking

## CONWY

## BETWS-Y-COED — Map 14 SH75

### PICK OF THE PUBS

### Ty Gwyn Inn ✫✫✫✫ INN

**LL24 0SG**
**☎ 01690 710383 & 710787 📠 01690 710383**
e-mail: mratcl1050@aol.com
web: www.tygwynhotel.co.uk
dir: *At junct of A5 & A470, 100yds S of Waterloo Bridge*

A coaching inn on the old London to Holyhead road long before Thomas Telford built his impressive cast iron Waterloo Bridge over the River Conwy opposite in 1815. Much of the original 17th-century character is evident inside. The Ratcliffe family has owned and run it for the past 28 years, and now Martin (the chef for all that time) and his wife Nicola are in charge. Real ales come from as near as Conwy's Great Orme brewery, as well as from much further afield. Martin relies heavily on quality Welsh produce that results in breast of chicken, goat's cheese and asparagus marinated in Chardonnay, garlic and lime cream; rosemary-scented roast rack of Snowdon lamb with onion and peppercorn marmalade; and fresh fillet of line-caught wild sea bass with king prawns, saffron and garlic. Some of Nicola's own-designed en suite rooms have four-posters.

**Open** all wk noon-2 6.30-11 Closed: 1wk Jan **Bar Meals** L served all wk 12-2 D served all wk 6.30-9 booking required **Restaurant** L served all wk 12-2 D served all wk 6.30-9 booking required ⊕ FREE HOUSE ◀ Adnams Broadside, Reverend James, Old Speckled Hen, Bombardier, IPA, Orme Best. **Facilities** Children's menu Children's portions Parking **Rooms** 13

*See advert on opposite page*

Betws y Coed, Conwy LL24 0SG • **Ty Gwyn Inn** • **Tel:** +44 (0)1690 710383

**Email:** mratcl1050@aol.com    **Website:** www.tygwynhotel.co.uk

The *Ty Gwyn Hotel* situated in Betws-y-coed, at the heart of the Snowdonia National Park, is a former coaching Inn dating back to 1636. The *Ty Gwyn* has been owned and run by the Ratcliffe family for the past 28 years, and Martin (the chef for the 28 years) and his wife Nicola have now taken over the running of this centuries old, multi-award winning Inn.

*Ty Gwyn* has over the past 4 years undergone a refurbishment with all en suite bedrooms having new bath or shower rooms, and most having new carpets and some new beds and fittings. Two of them boast Spa Tubs in their bathrooms. The *Ty Gwyn* with its 3 four-poster rooms and a honeymoon suite, beamed ceilings, antiques, log fires (in winter) is one of the most traditional Inns you will visit in the beautiful Snowdonia National Park. The *Ty Gwyn* has a very good reputation for its food – *Ty Gwyn* local produce includes hand reared saddle back pork from Gelli farm, Capel Garmon (one mile away); local lamb from Penloyn Farm, Llanrwst (4 miles away); beef from Powys; local free range hens eggs from Happy Harrison in Betws-y-Coed; also included is fresh fish and shelve fish from Llandudno's Mermaid Seafoods, Conwy Estuary and the Llyn Peninsula. The owner also provides some home grown produce in his 40-foot poly Tunnel and two

acres of gardens – including New Potato's, Mixed Leaves, Fennel, Corn on the Cob, Pak Choi, Cucumbers, Marrow, Courgettes, Tomatoes, Peppers, Chilli's, Runner Beans, Sweet Peas, Apples, Pears, Gooseberries, Red Currants, Black Currants, Plums, Coriander, Basil, Parsley, Chives, Mint and many more fresh produce. The *Ty Gwyn* is also renowned for its international cuisine using the freshest of local produce. Bookings for dinner are recommended.

**BETWS-Y-COED** *continued*

## White Horse Inn

**Capel Garmon LL26 0RW**
☎ 01690 710271   📠 01690 710721
e-mail: r.alton@btconnect.com
dir: *Telephone for directions*

Picturesque Capel Garmon perches high above Betws-y-Coed, with spectacular views of the Snowdon Range, a good 20 kilometres away. To make a detour to find this cosy 400-year-old inn with its original exposed timbers, stone walls, and log fires, is to be rewarded by a menu featuring fresh local produce. Home-cooked food is available in the bars and cottage-style restaurant.

**Open** all wk 6-11pm Closed: 25 Dec ◀ Tetley Smoothflow, Rev James Ò Old English. **Facilities** Family room Dogs allowed Parking

---

| **BETWS-YN-RHOS** | Map 14 SH97 |
| --- | --- |

## The Wheatsheaf Inn

**LL22 8AW** ☎ 01492 680218   📠 01492 680666
e-mail: wheatsheafinn@hotmail.co.uk
dir: *A55 to Abergele, take A548 to Llanrwst from High Street. 2m turn right B5381, 1m to Betws-yn-Rhos*

The Wheatsheaf, licensed as a coaching inn during the 17th century, stands in the picturesque village of Betws-Yn-Rhos opposite the famous twin towered church of St Michael. The inn has plenty of historic character with splendid oak beams adorned with brasses, stone pillars and plenty of cosy, old world charm. Bar snacks are served in addition to the restaurant menu where choices range from local Welsh Black beef steaks; pork and leek sausages; home-made chicken korma or the house speciality: Welsh lamb joint slow roasted with rosemary and thyme.

**Open** all day all wk noon-11 (Fri-Sat noon-mdnt Winter closed 2.30-5 Mon-Fri) **Bar Meals** L served all wk 12-2 D served all wk 5-9 Av main course £5.95 food served all day **Restaurant** L served Mon-Thu 12-2 booking required D served all wk 6-9 booking required Fixed menu price fr £8.45 Av 3 course à la carte fr £13.45 ⊕ ENTERPRISE INNS ◀ Old Speckled Hen, Guinness, Deuchars, Black Sheep, Doom Bar Ò Kopparberg. **Facilities** Children's menu Children's portions Family room Dogs allowed Garden Parking

---

| **CAPEL CURIG** | Map 14 SH75 |
| --- | --- |

## Cobdens Hotel ★★ SHL

**LL24 0EE** ☎ 01690 720243   📠 01690 720354
e-mail: info@cobdens.co.uk
dir: *Telephone for directions*

Situated in a beautiful mountain village in the heart of Snowdonia, this 250-year-old inn offers wholesome, locally sourced food and real ales. Start with local rabbit and pancetta carbonara; or leek and potato terrine. Mains include roasted Welsh lamb with garlic and thyme mash; Welsh beef steaks; and pasta with roasted courgette,

blue cheese and chestnut. Children are welcome too, and have their own menu to choose from.

**Open** all day all wk noon-11pm (Sun noon-10.30pm) Closed: 6-26 Jan **Bar Meals** L served all wk 12-2 D served all wk 6-9 ⊕ FREE HOUSE ◀ Conwy Castle ale, Cobdens Ale, guest ales, Gunpowder. **Facilities** Children's menu Children's portions Dogs allowed Garden Parking **Rooms** 17

---

| **COLWYN BAY** | Map 14 SH87 |
| --- | --- |

### PICK OF THE PUBS

## Pen-y-Bryn ♥

**Pen-y-Bryn Rd LL29 6DD** ☎ 01492 533360
e-mail: pen.y.bryn@brunningandprice.co.uk
dir: *1m from A55. Follow signs to Welsh Mountain Zoo. Establishment at top of hill*

Behind the simple exterior of this 1970s building you'll find a friendly and chatty atmosphere with local ales, Taffy Apples cider, and good, straightforward food cooked and served throughout the day. The interior has character in spades, with oak floors, open fires, rugs and old furniture, whilst the stunning rear garden and terrace enjoy panoramic views over the sea and the Great Orme headland. The modern British menu offers a great choice of sandwiches and lighter meals: the steak open sandwich is served on toast with chutney and a few chips, for instance, or you might opt for Chinese chicken pancakes with hoi-sin sauce. Main course options range from lamb Wellington with fondant potatoes, red wine and rosemary sauce, to smoked haddock and salmon fishcakes with tomato and spring onion salad. Vanilla pannacotta with rhubarb compote is typical of the appetising pudding selection.

**Open** all day all wk noon-11pm (Sun noon-10.30pm) **Bar Meals** D served Mon-Sat 12-9.30, Sun 12-9 Av main course £10.95 food served all day **Restaurant** D served Mon-Sat 12-9.30, Sun 12-9 food served all day ⊕ BRUNNING & PRICE ◀ Timothy Taylor Landlord, Thwaites Original, Ormes Best, Flowers Original, Snowdonia Ale Ò Stowford Press, Taffy Apples. ♥ 14 **Facilities** Children's portions Garden Parking

---

| **CONWY** | Map 14 SH77 |
| --- | --- |

### PICK OF THE PUBS

## The Groes Inn ✩✩✩✩✩ INN ⊛

*See Pick of the Pubs on opposite page*

---

| **DOLWYDDELAN** | Map 14 SH75 |
| --- | --- |

## Elen's Castle

**LL25 0EJ** ☎ 01690 750207
e-mail: stay@hotelinsnowdonia.co.uk
dir: *5m S of Betws-Y-Coed, follow A470*

Once an 18th-century coaching inn and a part of the Earl of Ancaster's Welsh Estate, this family-run free house now boasts an old world bar with a wood-burning stove. The intimate restaurant offers breathtaking views of the mountains and Lledr River, which can also be enjoyed from the garden. Sample dishes include wild rice, spinach and honey roast with summer vegetable ratatouille; and Conwy valley lamb shank on mashed potato and leek with rosemary jus.

**Open** vary by season Closed: 2wks Jan, wk days in quiet winter periods ◀ Brains, Worthington, Black Sheep, Spitfire Ò Stowford Press. **Facilities** Play area Family room Dogs allowed Garden Parking

---

| **LLANDUDNO JUNCTION** | Map 14 SH77 |
| --- | --- |

### PICK OF THE PUBS

## The Queens Head ♥

**Glanwydden LL31 9JP**
☎ 01492 546570   📠 01492 546487
e-mail: enquiries@queensheadglanwydden.co.uk
dir: *From A55 take A470 towards Llandudno. At 3rd rdbt right towards Penrhyn Bay, then 2nd right into Glanwydden, pub on left*

Owners Rob and Sally Cureton have created this smart country pub with appealing menus, a good selection of wines and beers, and a team of attentive staff. Indeed, last year the pub was awarded AA Pub of the Year for Wales. The stylish terrace is great for summer evenings, whilst on colder nights the relaxed atmosphere in the bar is perfect for a pre-dinner drink by the log fire. The talented chefs make excellent use of local produce in varied menus that range from light lunchtime bites such as seafood medley with lemon and coriander mayonnaise; to more substantial fare that reflects the inn's surroundings. Try pot-roasted Anglesey pheasant with cranberry and orange port wine jus; or chargrilled halloumi with roasted red pepper, cherry tomatoes and dauphinoise potatoes. Just five minutes from the seaside at Llandudno, this charming free house is perfectly situated for country walks, cycling, or a day on the beach.

**Open** all wk 11.30-3 6-10.30 (Sat-Sun 11.30-10.30) **Bar Meals** L served Mon-Fri 12-2, Sat-Sun 12-9 D served Mon-Fri 6-9, Sat-Sun 12-9 Av main course £11 **Restaurant** L served Mon-Fri 12-2, Sat-Sun 12-9 D served Mon-Fri 6-9, Sat-Sun 12-9 ⊕ FREE HOUSE ◀ Carlsberg-Tetley, Weetwood Ales, Great Orme Brewery. ♥ 10 **Facilities** Children's portions Garden Parking

# PICK OF THE PUBS

## The Groes Inn ★★★★★ INN ⬢

CONWY         Map 14 SH77

**LL32 8TN**
☎ **01492 650545** 🖷 **01492 650855**
**e-mail:** reception@groesinn.com
**dir:** *Exit A55 to Conwy, left at mini rdbt by Conwy Castle onto B5106, 2.5m inn on right*

The Groes has kept the spirit of hospitality alive for more than four centuries. Built as a small two-storey house, it has flourished as an inn since 1573, making it the first licensed house in Wales; in 1889 the grandson of the Iron Duke witnessed its sale, an event now commemorated by the Wellington Room, where the deeds he signed are displayed. From the front of the inn are magnificent views of the River Conwy and surrounding hills; behind, the slopes rise towards Snowdonia.

Rambling rooms, beamed ceilings, historic settles, military hats, historic cooking utensils, a stag's head over an open fire - this inn has plenty to point out and even snigger over (namely, the saucy Victorian postcards) - but don't expect a jukebox, gaming machines or pool table.

Food is mainly traditional British, Welsh and European, which means visitors have a good choice, from the bar snacks and light snacks listed on the chalkboard, to the main menu in the AA Rosette restaurant, which regularly features sweet-tasting lamb from the salt marshes of the Conwy, fine Welsh beef, farm-cured hams, and fish and seafood from the river and the waters around Anglesey. As far as desserts are concerned, for some a home-made orange and Cointreau ice cream will justify a visit; others might plump for muscovado sugar and hazelnut tart; or cherry sundae. Fixed-price Sunday lunches might comprise the obvious roast beef and Yorkshire pudding, or grilled creamy garlic mushrooms on herb toast, followed by bread and butter pudding with fresh cream. A well-priced wine list includes several reds, whites and a rosé available in both 175ml and 250ml glasses.

Beneath a jaunty clock tower lie the guest rooms, some with private terrace or balcony from which to enjoy the afternoon and evening sun across open fields.

**Open** all wk 12-3 6-11 (Sun 12-11)
**Bar Meals** L served all wk 12-2 D served all wk 6.30-9 Av main course £11
**Restaurant** L served all wk 12-2 D served all wk 6.30-9 Fixed menu price fr £14.95 Av 3 course à la carte fr £17.95 ⊕ FREE HOUSE 🛢 Tetley's, Burton Ale, Groes Ale, Ormes Best, Great Orme, Welsh Black Ꝺ Stowford Press.
**Facilities** Children's menu Family room Dogs allowed Garden Parking **Rooms** 14

## LLANNEFYDD — Map 14 SH97

### The Hawk & Buckle Inn

**LL16 5ED ☎ 01745 540249**
e-mail: enquiries@hawkandbuckleinn.com
dir: *Telephone for directions*

A 17th-century coaching inn 200metres up in the hills, with wonderful views to the sea beyond. Traditional dishes using local produce - shoulder of Welsh lamb, chicken breast stuffed with Welsh cheese or Celtic loin of pork - sit comfortably alongside pub favourites like beer battered haddock, fish pie, or a mixed grill.

**Open** all wk winter 6-11, Sat-Sun noon-mdnt (summer 12-3 6-11 Sat-Sun noon-mdnt) **Bar Meals** L served winter Sat-Sun 12-9, summer Mon-Fri 12-3, Sat-Sun 12-9 booking required D served Mon-Fri 6-9, Sat-Sun 12-9 booking required ⊕ FREE HOUSE ◀ Glaslyn, Welsh Pride. **Facilities** Dogs allowed Parking

## DENBIGHSHIRE

### LLANGOLLEN — Map 15 SJ24

### The Corn Mill ♥

**Dee Ln LL20 8PN ☎ 01978 869555 📠 01978 869930**
e-mail: corn.mill@brunningandprice.co.uk
dir: *Telephone for directions*

The first two things to strike you as you walk through the door are the great jumble of old beams, and the waterwheel turning slowly behind the bar. The decks outside are built directly over the millrace and the rapids, and on the opposite bank of the river, steam trains huff and puff in the restored railway station: the perfect place to enjoy a pint. Mains include cold honey-roast ham; Cumberland sausage; lamb and vegetable suet pudding; and macaroni cheese.

**Open** all wk ◀ Boddingtons, Plassey ales ♂ Inch's Stonehouse. ♥ 12

### PRESTATYN — Map 15 SJ08

### Nant Hall Restaurant & Bar ♥

**Nant Hall Rd LL19 9LD**
**☎ 01745 886766 📠 01745 886998**
e-mail: mail@nanthall.com
dir: *E towards Chester, 1m on left opposite large car garage*

Nant Hall, a Grade II listed Victorian country house in seven acres of grounds, operates as a gastro-pub with a great variety of food, beers and wines. The menu offers local and regional dishes alongside recipes from around the world: Thai green chicken curry, pan-seared fillet of salmon with a creamy herb risotto, chargrilled steaks, Chinese chicken and vegetable satay, or creamy fish pie in a parsley sauce. The large outdoor eating area is great in summer.

**Open** all day noon-11pm Closed: Mon ◀ Bass Smooth, Boddingtons. ♥ 14 **Facilities** Family room Garden Parking

## RHEWL — Map 15 SJ16

### The Drovers Arms, Rhewl

**Denbigh Rd LL15 2UD**
**☎ 01824 703163 📠 01824 703163**
dir: *1.3m from Ruthin on A525*

A small village pub whose name recalls a past written up and illustrated on storyboards displayed inside. Main courses are divided on the menu into poultry, traditional meat, fish, grills and vegetarian; examples from each section are chicken tarragon; Welsh lamb's liver and onions; Vale of Clwyd sirloin steak; home-made fish pie; and mushroom stroganoff. Desserts include treacle sponge pudding.

**Open** all wk noon-3 5.30-11 (Sat noon-3 5.30-mdnt Sun noon-11pm all day Jun-Sep) Closed: Tue L ◀ J W Lees bitter. **Facilities** Play area Garden Parking

## RUTHIN — Map 15 SJ15

### PICK OF THE PUBS

### The Wynnstay Arms ★★★★ INN

**Well St LL15 1AN ☎ 01824 703147 📠 01824 705428**
e-mail: reservations@wynnstayarms.com
dir: *Telephone for directions*

It was in this 460-year-old, timber-framed inn that wandering 19th-century author George Borrow, after walking from Llangollen, treated his trusty guide, John Jones, to "the best duck he had ever tasted". Much of the food is sourced from within the Principality, while bread, pâtés and desserts are made in-house. The place for a quiet lunchtime pint of Conwy Welsh Pride and a read of the papers is Bar W, where still impressing travellers is the duck, these days pan-fried on buttered Savoy cabbage with crushed garlic potatoes and Cointreau and juniper sauce. Or settle perhaps for a panini. Typical in Fusions Brasserie are twice-roasted belly pork with grain mustard mash and red cabbage; lightly grilled black bream fillets with sauté potatoes and lemon and thyme sauce; and wild mushroom and mozzarella risotto with balsamic-glazed cherry tomatoes. En suite rooms offer high levels of comfort.

**Open** all day all wk **Bar Meals** L served all wk 12-2 booking required D served Mon-Sat 5.30-9.30, Sun 12-7 booking required Av main course £13.95 **Restaurant** L served Sun booking required D served Tue-Sat booking required Fixed menu price fr £16.95 Av 3 course à la carte fr £25 ⊕ FREE HOUSE ◀ Old Speckled Hen, Tetleys, Conwy Welsh Pride. **Facilities** Children's menu Children's portions Parking **Rooms** 7

### Ye Olde Anchor Inn

**Rhos St LL15 1DY ☎ 01824 702813 📠 01824 703050**
e-mail: info@anchorinn.co.uk
dir: *At junct of A525 and A494*

In the centre of town, this impressive-looking old inn has 16 windows at the front alone - all with award-winning window boxes. An extensive bar snack menu is available lunchtimes and evenings, while the main menu offers two types of lasagne, baked beef or Mediterranean vegetable; honey-spiced Welsh lamb shank; trinity of grilled fish; carpetbag fillet steak; and chestnut, mushroom and asparagus linguine; all eminently worth following with one of the freshly prepared desserts.

**Open** all wk ◀ Timothy Taylor, Worthington, guest ales. **Facilities** Dogs allowed Parking

## ST ASAPH — Map 15 SJ07

### The Plough Inn

**The Roe LL17 0LU ☎ 01745 585080 📠 01745 585363**
e-mail: ploughsa@gmail.com
dir: *Exit A55 at Rhyl/St Asaph signs, left at rdbt, pub 200yds on left*

An 18th-century former coaching inn, the Plough has been transformed. The ground floor retains the traditional pub concept, cosy with open fires and rustic furniture, while upstairs there are two very different restaurants: an up-market bistro and an Italian-themed art deco restaurant, divided by a wine shop. There's even a cocktail bar. All the kitchens are open so you can see the food being prepared – spaghetti carbonara, braised lamb shank, or salmon and king prawn skewers perhaps.

**Open** all day all wk **Bar Meals** Av main course £7.95 food served all day **Restaurant** Fixed menu price fr £14.95 Av 3 course à la carte fr £14.95 ⊕ FREE HOUSE ◀ Plassey brewery. **Facilities** Children's menu Children's portions Garden Parking

## FLINTSHIRE

### BABELL — Map 15 SJ17

### Black Lion Inn ♥

**CH8 8PZ ☎ 01352 720239**
e-mail: theblacklioninn@btinternet.com
dir: *A55 junct 31 to Caerwys turn left at crossroads signed Babell. Travel 3m turn right at fork*

Ancient inns spawn ghost stories, but the 13th-century Black Lion boasts more than its fair share. Ask about them when you visit, but don't be put off savouring a local real ale on the outside decking while the children enjoy the play area. Alternatively tuck into good home-cooked dishes like black pudding layered with crisp back bacon; and pork escalope with fresh asparagus sauce. Irish music keeps the spirits awake on the last Wednesday of the month.

**Open** 6pm-close (Sat-Sun noon-close) Closed: Mon, Tue **Bar Meals** L served Sat-Sun 12-9 D served Thu-Sun 6-9 Av main course £12.95 **Restaurant** L served Sat-Sun 12-9 D served Thu-Sun 6-9 Av 3 course à la carte fr £22 ⊕ FREE HOUSE ◀ Thwaites Smooth Bitter, Purple Moose Brewery - Traeth Mawr, Thirstquencher Spitting Feathers, Black Lion Bitter. ♀ 8 **Facilities** Children's menu Children's portions Play area Garden Parking

---

### CILCAIN　　　　　　　　　　Map 15 SJ16

## White Horse Inn

CH7 5NN ☎ 01352 740142 📄 01352 740142
e-mail: christine.jeory@btopenworld.com
dir: *From Mold take A541 towards Denbigh. After approx 6m turn left*

A 400-year-old pub, which is the last survivor of five originally to be found in this lovely hillside village - no doubt because it was the centre of the local gold-mining industry in the 19th century. Today the White Horse is popular with walkers, cyclists, and horse-riders. The dishes are home made by the landlord's wife using the best quality local ingredients, and be enjoyed with a good range of real ales.

**Open** all wk noon-3 6.30-11 (Sat noon-11 Sun noon-10.30) **Bar Meals** L served all wk 12-2 D served all wk 7-9 Av main course £8 ⊕ FREE HOUSE ◀ Marston's Pedigree, Bank's Bitter, Timothy Taylor Landlord, Draught Bass, Archers Golden. **Facilities** Dogs allowed Garden Parking

---

### MOLD　　　　　　　　　　　Map 15 SJ26

### PICK OF THE PUBS

## Glasfryn ♀

**Raikes Ln, Sychdyn CH7 6LR**
☎ 01352 750500 📄 01352 751923
e-mail: glasfryn@brunningandprice.co.uk
dir: *From Mold follow signs to Theatr Clwyd, 1m from town centre*

This busy North Wales free house attracts a varied clientele, from farmers and business people to holidaymakers. The building – a former Judge's residence dating from about 1900 – was rescued by the present owners at the end of the last century and transformed into a wonderful pub. Inside is a bright open space with lots of polished wooden tables and chairs, whilst outside the newly landscaped garden is maturing well. Along with a good choice of beer and ciders, the comprehensive daily menu runs from sandwiches like crayfish, pesto mayonnaise, bacon and gem lettuce; or Stilton, pear and cream cheese; through to full three course meals. Start, perhaps, with marinated artichoke, pea and mushroom salad with beetroot and horseradish; before moving on to duck leg with bacon, bean casserole and pickled cabbage; or sea bass fillet with fennel mayonnaise, spinach and fried new potatoes. Leave space for pudding - profiteroles with vanilla cream and chocolate sauce is a typical choice.

---

**Open** all day all wk noon-11 Closed: 25 Dec **Bar Meals** Food served all day 12-9.30 Av main course £11 food served all day **Restaurant** Food served all day 12-9.30 ⊕ BRUNNING & PRICE ◀ Timothy Taylor, Thwaites, Snowdonia Ale, Greene King IPA, Flowers Original Ò Organic Westons Vintage, Inch's Cider. ♀ 20 **Facilities** Children's portions Dogs allowed Garden Parking

---

### NORTHOP　　　　　　　　　Map 15 SJ26

## Stables Bar Restaurant ♀

CH7 6AB ☎ 01352 840577 📄 01352 840382
e-mail: info@soughtonhall.co.uk
dir: *From A55, take A119 through Northop*

Created from Soughton Hall's original stable block, this unusual free house dates from the 18th century. The magnificent main house was built as a bishop's palace, and original features like the cobbled floors and roof timbers remain intact. The selection of real ales includes Stables Bitter, and menu choices range from a simple sandwich lunch to an à la carte dinner menu featuring crispy potato wedges with sautéed chicken and bacon with tarragon cream and Cheddar cheese.

**Open** all day all wk **Bar Meals** L served all wk 12-9.30 D served all wk 12-9.30 Av main course £5.95 food served all day **Restaurant** L served Sun 1-3 booking required D served all wk 7-9.30 booking required Fixed menu price fr £14.95 ⊕ FREE HOUSE ◀ Coach House Honeypot, Dick Turpin, Plassey Bitter, Stables Bitter. ♀ 8 **Facilities** Children's menu Children's portions Family room Garden Parking

---

### GWYNEDD

### ABERDYFI　　　　　　　　　Map 14 SN69

### PICK OF THE PUBS

## Penhelig Arms Hotel & Restaurant ♀

**Terrace Rd LL35 0LT**
☎ 01654 767215 📄 01654 767690
e-mail: info@penheligarms.com
dir: *On A493 W of Machynlleth*

Step out of the front door of this late-18th century inn and the tidal Dyfi estuary is across the road. Indeed, in the summer months many customers sit on the sea wall opposite the pub. The wood-panelled and log-fire-warmed Fisherman's Bar, where Brains real ales, and bar meals such as chargrilled rib-eye steaks are served, is TV and music free. Or you might prefer a brasserie-style meal in the award-winning waterfront restaurant, where a strong dependency on local suppliers results in plenty of seafood and Welsh beef and lamb. A cosmopolitan menu offers cod and king prawns grilled with chilli, ginger and garlic butter; pan-fried chicken breast with creamy vegetable risotto, pancetta and herb dressing; and mushroom, brie, hazelnut and cranberry Wellington with salad and chips. The short wine list is attractively priced. Cader Idris, the Snowdonia National Park and historic castles are within easy reach.

---

**Open** all day all wk Closed: 25-26 Dec **Bar Meals** L served all wk 12-2 D served all wk 6-9 booking required Av main course £12.50 **Restaurant** L served all wk 12-2 booking required D served all wk 7-9 booking required Fixed menu price fr £24.50 Av 3 course à la carte fr £21 ⊕ S A BRAIN & CO LTD ◀ Brains Reverend James, Brains Bitter, Guest ale Ò Stowford Press, Thatchers Katy. ♀ 20 **Facilities** Children's portions Dogs allowed Parking

---

### BLAENAU FFESTINIOG　　　Map 14 SH74

## The Miners Arms

**Llechwedd Slate Caverns LL41 3NB**
☎ 01766 830306 📄 01766 831260
e-mail: quarrytours@aol.com
dir: *From Llandudno take A470 south. Through Betwys-y-Coed, 16m to Blaenau Ffestiniog*

Slate floors, open fires and staff in Victorian costume emphasise the heritage theme of this welcoming pub nestling in the centre of a Welsh village. On the site of Llechwedd Slate Caverns, one of the country's leading tourist attractions, it caters for all comers and tastes: expect steak and ale casserole, pork pie and salad, various ploughman's lunches, and hot apple pie, as well as afternoon tea with scones and cream.

**Open** all wk Closed: Oct-Etr **Facilities** Play area Family room Dogs allowed Garden Parking

---

### LLANBEDR　　　　　　　　　Map 14 SH52

## Victoria Inn ★★★★ INN ♀

LL45 2LD ☎ 01341 241213 📄 01341 241644
e-mail: junevicinn@aol.com
dir: *On A496 between Barmouth and Harlech*

Fascinating features for pub connoisseurs are the circular wooden settle, ancient stove, grandfather clock and flagged floors in the atmospheric bar of the Victoria. Home-made food is served in the lounge bar and restaurant, complemented by a range of Robinson's traditional ales. A children's play area has been incorporated into the well-kept garden, with a playhouse, slides and swings. The Rhinog mountain range and the famous Roman Steps are right on the doorstep. Newly redecorated bedrooms are all en suite.

**Open** all day all wk 11-11 (Sun noon-10.30) ◀ Robinson's Best Bitter, guest bitters Ò Stowford Press. ♀ 10 **Facilities** Play area Dogs allowed Garden Parking **Rooms** 5

## NANTGWYNANT                Map 14 SH65

### Pen-Y-Gwryd Hotel

**LL55 4NT ☎ 01286 870211**
**dir:** *A5 to Capel Curig, left on A4086 to T-junct*

This slate-roofed climbers' pub and rescue post in the
heart of Snowdonia has long been the home of British
mountaineering. The 1953 Everest team used it as their
training base, and etched their signatures on the ceiling.
The appetising and inexpensive menus make good use of
Welsh lamb and local pork; other options include home-
made pâté with pickles, salad and crusty bread; or ham
and cannellini bean spaghetti with home-made olive and
herb flatbread.

Closed: Nov-1 Jan & mid wk (Jan-Feb) ◀ Interbrew Bass,
Boddingtons, Bitter. **Facilities** Play area Family room Dogs
allowed Garden Parking

## TUDWEILIOG                 Map 14 SH23

### Lion Hotel

**LL53 8ND ☎ 01758 770244**
**e-mail:** martinlee1962@hotmail.com
**dir:** *A487 from Caernarfon onto A499 towards Pwllheli.
Right onto B4417 to Nefyn, onto Edern then onto
Tudweiliog*

The beach is only a mile away from this friendly inn, run
by the Lee family for over 30 years. The large garden and
children's play area makes the pub especially popular
with the cyclists, walkers and families who flock to the
Lleyn Peninsula. The bar features an extensive list of over
80 malt whiskies alongside ale from Purple Moose
Brewery. A typical menu might consist of country chicken
liver pâté; Pysgod Llyns crab and spinach cannelloni; and
home-made Bakewell tart.

**Open** all wk 11-3 6-11 (all day in Summer) **Bar Meals** L
served all wk 12-2 D served all wk 6-9 Av main course £9
⊕ FREE HOUSE ◀ Purple Moose Brewery Ale,
Boddingtons, Guinness. **Facilities** Children's
menu Children's portions Play area Family room Garden
Parking

## WAUNFAWR                   Map 14 SH55

### Snowdonia Parc Brewpub & Campsite

**LL55 4AQ ☎ 01286 650409  & 650218**
**e-mail:** info@snowdonia-park.co.uk
**dir:** *Telephone for directions*

This pub stands 400 feet above sea level at Waunfawr
Station on the Welsh Highland Railway. There are steam
trains on site (the building was originally the
stationmaster's house), plus a micro-brewery and
campsite. The foot of Mount Snowdon is four miles away.
Expect home-cooked food based on locally produced and
traditionally reared beef, lamb, chicken and pork. The Pub
serves its Welsh Highland Bitter along with other ales.
Children and dogs welcome.

**Open** all day all wk 11-11 (Fri-Sat 11am-11.30pm)
**Bar Meals** food served all day **Restaurant** food served
all day ⊕ FREE HOUSE ◀ Marston's Pedigree, Welsh
Highand Bitter (own brew). **Facilities** Children's menu
Play area Family room Dogs allowed Garden Parking

---

## MONMOUTHSHIRE

## ABERGAVENNY                 Map 9 SO21

## PICK OF THE PUBS

### Clytha Arms 🍷

**Clytha NP7 9BW ☎ 01873 840206**
**e-mail:** theclythaarms@tiscali.co.uk
**dir:** *From A449/A40 junction (E of Abergavenny) follow
signs for 'Old Road Abergavenny/Clytha'*

Andrew and Beverley Canning's converted dower house
stands in interesting gardens on top of a wooded hill,
just three miles from Raglan's famous castle. They are
still as enthusiastic as ever after 18 years at the helm
of this thriving dining pub, having recently refurbished
the kitchen and restaurant during the past year.
Drinkers who fill the traditional main bar, with its old
pews and posters and wood-burning stove, have an

---

impressive range of beers and ciders to choose from -
Rhymney Bitter, Felinfoel Double Dragon and Raglan
Perry – as well as gin and vodka from the Penderyn
Distillery just 20 miles away. As for the food, Andrew
sources local organic meat and poultry, fish from day
boats in Cornwall and West Wales, and some great
artisan cheeses for his imaginative bar and restaurant
menus, which give more that a nod to his own Welsh
roots. Take Black Mountain smoked salmon and
scrambled egg; rabbit and cider pie; bacon laverbread
and cockles; and excellent tapas dishes (Clytha ham
and chorizo) in the bar, with the likes of sand sole with
herb butter and roast Madgett's Farm duck with
parsnip brûlée on offer in the restaurant.

**Open** noon-3 6-mdnt (Fri-Sun noon-mdnt) Closed: 25
Dec, Mon L **Bar Meals** L served Tue-Sun 12.30-2.30 D
served Mon-Sat 7-9.30 Av main course £9
**Restaurant** L served Tue-Sun 12.30-2.30 D served
Mon-Sat 7-9.30 Fixed menu price fr £22 Av 3 course à
la carte fr £29 ⊕ FREE HOUSE ◀ Felinfoel Double
Dragon, Rhymney Bitter, 4 guest ales (300+ per year),
Wye Valley Bitter ♻ Black Dragon, Ragan Perry, Clytha
Perry. 🍷 12 **Facilities** Children's menu Children's
portions Play area Dogs allowed Garden Parking

## CHEPSTOW                    Map 4 ST59

### Castle View Hotel ★★★ HL

**16 Bridge St NP16 5EZ**
**☎ 01291 620349  🖷 01291 627397**
**e-mail:** castleviewhotel@btconnect.com
**dir:** *Opposite Chepstow Castle*

Standing opposite Chepstow Castle and built as a private
house in the 17th-century, the inn boasts walls that are
five feet thick and a delightful secluded walled garden.
Using quality ingredients from local suppliers the menus
may list moules marinière, braised lamb shank with
redcurrant and rosemary jus, wild mushrooms risotto,
and traditional bar snacks like sandwiches, ploughman's
lunches and omelettes.

**Open** all wk ◀ Wye Valley Real Ale, Double Dragon,
Felinfoel Best Bitter ♻ Stowford Press. **Facilities** Dogs
allowed Garden Parking **Rooms** 13

## LLANGYBI                    Map 9 ST39

## PICK OF THE PUBS

### The White Hart Village Inn

**NP15 1NP ☎ 01633 450258**
**e-mail:** enquiries@thewhitehartvillageinn.com
**dir:** *M4 junct 25 onto B4596 (Caerleon road) through
town centre on High St, straight over rdbt onto Usk Rd,
continue to Llangybi*

This historic inn was originally built in the 12th century
for Cistercian monks. Early in the 1500s it became the
property of Henry VIII as part of Jane Seymour's
wedding dowry and, a century later, Oliver Cromwell is
said to have used it as his headquarters in Gwent.
Today, the White Hart has been sensitively restored by

Save on Hotels. Book at **theAA.com/hotel**

MONMOUTHSHIRE 597 WALES

the Pell family, who have retained the exposed beams, original Tudor plasterwork and 16th-century fireplaces – just the place to enjoy a pint from the Wye Valley Brewery. There's crackling fires in winter and in summer the extensive outside seating area hosts barbecues and special events such as hog roasts and live jazz. Menus offer informal starters of curried sweetbreads; asparagus velouté with crispy quail's egg; or seared scallops, pork cheek, vanilla and apple; followed by mains of steak and chips; poached and roasted chicken, sweetcorn, kale and asparagus; or Jerusalem artichoke risotto with truffle and walnut. Tempting desserts might include chocolate tart, crème fraîche and pepper sorbet or lemon trifle.

**Open** all day 12–11 (Sun 12–6) Closed: Mon ⊕ FREE HOUSE ◀ Sharp's Doom Bar, Tribute, St Austell, Tomos Watkins Tomas Braf ♂ Taffy Apple, Stowford Press. **Facilities** Children's portions Garden Parking

### LLANTRISANT    Map 9 ST39

## PICK OF THE PUBS

# The Greyhound Inn ★★★ INN ♛

**NP15 1LE**
☎ 01291 672505  & 673447  📠 01291 673255
e-mail: enquiry@greyhound-inn.com
dir: *M4 junct 24, A449 towards Monmouth, exit at 1st junct signed Usk. 2nd left for Llantrisant. Or from Monmouth A40, A449 exit for Usk. In Usk left into Twyn Sq follow Llantrisant signs. 2.5m under A449 bridge. Inn on right*

A traditional 17th-century Welsh longhouse, once part of a 400-acre farm. In 1845 the milk parlour was converted into an inn, and over the years the land was sold off. By 1980, the whole complex was in a sorry state, as pictures hanging in the cocktail and Llangibby lounges bear witness. Today, approaching 30 years in the same family's hands, The Greyhound has two acres of award-winning gardens, a four-acre paddock, and an array of restored outbuildings. The lounges are served by one bar with a range of real ales including a monthly guest, and ciders such as Wales' own Gwynt y Ddraig. Owner Nick Davies heads the kitchen team, serving customers in the four eating areas, one of which is a candlelit dining room. Dishes, in traditional home-cooked style, range from old favourites such as steak and kidney pie, deep-fried whitebait, liver and bacon, and farmhouse sausages with fried egg, to lamb shank in red wine and rosemary, and pork Roberto – tenderloin in white wine, cream and mustard sauce.

**Open** all day 11–11 Closed: 25 & 31 Dec, 1 Jan, Sun eve **Bar Meals** L served all wk 12–2.15 D served Mon–Sat 6–10 Av main course £9.50 **Restaurant** L served all wk 12–2.15 booking required D served Mon–Sat 6–10 booking required Fixed menu price fr £12 ⊕ FREE HOUSE ◀ Interbrew Flowers Original & Bass, Greene King Abbot Ale, guest ale ♂ Gwynt y draig, Kingstone Press. ♛ 10 **Facilities** Children's menu Family room Dogs allowed Garden Parking **Rooms** 10

### LLANVAIR DISCOED    Map 9 ST49

## PICK OF THE PUBS

# The Woodlands Tavern Country Pub & Dining ♛

**NP16 6LX** ☎ 01633 400313  📠 01633 400313
e-mail: info@thewoodlandstavern.co.uk
dir: *5m from Caldicot & Magor*

At heart this is a friendly, family-run village free house, that's now been extended to accommodate the growing number of diners. It stands close to the Roman fortress town of Caerwent, as well as Wentwood forest and reservoir, which is popular with walkers, cyclists and fishermen. Ales come from Felinfoel, Butcombe and Bevans, and a decent range of wines is served by the glass. The modern British menu is supported by daily blackboard specials that might begin with Parma ham, pork, pheasant and apricot terrine, or deep-fried brie with spiced plum chutney. Main course options could include seared John Dory fillets on herby Puy lentils; or Usk valley fillet steak on horseradish mash with red onion marmalade and Welsh rarebit. A patio area with seating ensures that food and drink can be served outside in fine weather.

**Open** noon–3 6–mdnt Closed: 1 Jan, Sun eve, Mon **Bar Meals** L served Tue–Sat 12–2, Sun 12–3 D served Tue–Fri 6–9, Sat 6–9.30 **Restaurant** L served Tue–Sat 12–2, Sun 12–3 booking required D served Tue–Fri 6–9, Sat 6–9.30 booking required Fixed menu price fr £9.95 ⊕ FREE HOUSE ◀ Felinfoel, Butcombe, Bevans. ♛ 10 **Facilities** Children's menu Children's portions Dogs allowed Parking

### PANTYGELLI    Map 9 SO31

# The Crown

**Old Hereford Rd NP7 7HR** ☎ 01873 853314
e-mail: crown@pantygelli.com
dir: *Telephone for directions*

Dating from the 16th century, this charming, family-run free house with fine views of Skirrid Mountain, attracts its fair share of walkers and cyclists, but it's a genuine community pub too. Local real ales and ciders accompany a lunch/evening menu listing Welsh Black rib-eye steak with bubble and squeak; home-cooked ham platter; loin of local venison; pan-fried fillet of sea bass; and wild mushroom Mornay. Charity and fund-raising events are regularly held, along with jazz evenings, a country fair, a harvest auction and lots more.

**Open** noon–2.30, 6–11 (Sat-Sun noon–3, Sun 6–10.30) Closed: Mon L **Bar Meals** L served Tue–Sun 12–2 booking required D served Tue–Sat 7–9 booking required **Restaurant** L served Tue–Sun 12–2 booking required D served Tue–Sat 7–9 booking required ⊕ FREE HOUSE ◀ Rhymney Best, Wye Valley HPA, Bass, Guest ales ♂ Westons Stowford Press, Gwatkin Yarlington Mill. **Facilities** Children's portions Dogs allowed Garden Parking

### PENALLT    Map 4 SO51

# The Boat Inn

**Lone Ln NP25 4AJ** ☎ 01600 712615  📠 01600 719120
dir: *From Monmouth take A466. In Redbrook, pub car park signed. Access by foot across rail bridge over River Wye*

Dating back over 360 years, this riverside pub has served as a hostelry for quarry, mill, paper and tin mine workers, and even had a landlord operating a ferry across the Wye at shift times. The unspoilt slate floor is testament to the age of the place. The excellent selection of real ales and local ciders complements the menu well, with choices ranging from various ploughman's to lamb steffados or the charmingly-named pan haggerty. Ideal for walkers taking the Offa's Dyke or Wye Valley walks.

**Open** all wk Mon–Sat noon–11 (Sun 12–10.30, Summer all day) **Bar Meals** L served all wk 12–2.30 D served Tue–Sat 7–9 ⊕ FREE HOUSE ◀ Wye Valley Beers, guest ales ♂ Stowford Press. **Facilities** Dogs allowed Garden Parking

## RAGLAN
Map 9 SO40

### PICK OF THE PUBS

## The Beaufort Arms Coaching Inn & Brasserie ★★★ HL ◉ ☻

**High St NP15 2DY**
☎ 01291 690412 📠 01291 690935
**e-mail:** enquiries@beaufortraglan.co.uk
**dir:** 0.5m from junct of A40 & A449 Abergavenny/Monmouth

The Beaufort has been an inn since the time of the Civil War, when its proximity to Raglan Castle brought Roundhead soldiers to the bar during the siege of 1646. Later it became a coaching inn on the London to Fishguard route. The inn has been beautifully refurbished with many delightful design features, while holding strong to its traditional roots. A handsome display of fishing trophies dominates the country bar, where locals and visitors gather and chat over pints of Reverend James. Food is served in the lounge, with its carved bar, deep leather settees, and large stone fireplace ('lifted', some say, from the castle), as well as in the private dining room and brasserie with its modish shades of coffee and claret. Here skilfully presented modern British dishes are served, such as crispy Thai fishcakes with fresh chilli jam; beer-battered catch of the day; and specials such as marinated pork skewers with wild rice and mango salsa.

**Open** all day all wk **Bar Meals** L served Mon-Thu 12-3, Fri-Sat 12-5 D served all wk 6-9.30 Av main course £9.50 **Restaurant** L served Mon-Thu 12-3, Fri-Sat 12-5, Sun 12-4 booking required D served all wk 6-9.30 booking required Av 3 course à la carte fr £25 ⊕ FREE HOUSE ◀ London Pride, Reverend James, Old Speckled Hen ♂ Stowford Press, Thatchers Gold. ☻ 16 **Facilities** Children's menu Children's portions Garden Parking **Rooms** 15

## SHIRENEWTON
Map 9 ST49

## The Carpenters Arms

**Usk Rd NP16 6BU** ☎ 01291 641231 📠 01291 641231
**dir:** M48 junct 2, A48 to Chepstow then A4661, B4235. Village 3m on left

A 400-year-old traditional country pub in a wooded location in the valley of the Mounton Brook between the rivers Wye and Usk. Formerly a smithy and carpenter's shop, today's four bars have flagstone floors, open fires, church pew seating and lots of old chamber pots. Home-made food is typified by chilli and mint lamb; Ottoman stew; pheasant in red wine; variously filled pies in suet pastry; and a special vegetable and lentil shepherd's pie for vegetarians.

**Open** all wk Mon-Fri 12-3 5.30-mdnt (all day Sat & Sun) **Bar Meals** L served all wk 12-2.30 D served all wk 6.30-9.30 Av main course £4.95 **Restaurant** L served all wk 12-2.30 D served all wk 6.30-9.30 Fixed menu price fr £7.95 ⊕ PUNCH TAVERNS ◀ Fuller's London Pride, Bass, Spitfire. **Facilities** Children's menu Children's portions Family room Dogs allowed Parking

## SKENFRITH
Map 9 SO42

### PICK OF THE PUBS

## The Bell at Skenfrith ✩✩✩✩✩ RR ◉◉ ☻

**NP7 8UH** ☎ 01600 750235 📠 01600 750525
**e-mail:** enquiries@skenfrith.co.uk
**dir:** M4 junct 24 onto A449. Exit onto A40, through tunnel & lights. At rdbt take 1st exit, right at lights onto A466 towards Hereford road. Left onto B4521 towards Abergavenny, 3m on left

A fully restored 17th-century coaching inn with views of Skenfrith Castle, on the banks of the River Monnow. Character oozes from the oak bar, flagstone floors, comfortable sofas and old settles, while eleven individually decorated and well-equipped bedrooms, some with four-posters, provide high-quality accommodation. On draught are Wye Valley Bitter, Kingstone Gold, and Ty Gwyn cider. The two-Rosette restaurant uses produce from its organic kitchen garden in its regularly changing menus, from which a good lunch could be bouillabaisse made with Cornish fish, or roasted pumpkin and root vegetable crumble. For a thoroughly satisfying three-course dinner, perhaps confit salmon fillet with vanilla mayonnaise, baby leeks and pink grapefruit dressing; fillet of Brecon beef with a miniature steak and kidney pudding, horseradish bubble and squeak, and beef jus; and toffee soufflé, caramelised banana and brown bread ice cream. The walk-in wine cellar is home to a well-chosen world selection.

**Open** all day Closed: last wk Jan & 1st wk Feb, Tue Nov-Mar **Bar Meals** L served all wk 12-2.30 booking required D served Mon-Sat 7-9.30, Sun 7-9 booking required Av main course £14.50 **Restaurant** L served all wk 12-2.30 booking required D served Mon-Sat 7-9.30, Sun 7-9 booking required Fixed menu price fr £24 Av 3 course à la carte fr £32 ⊕ FREE HOUSE ◀ Wye Valley Bitter, Hereford Pale Ale, Kingstone Bitter ♂ Stowford Press, Local cider, Ty Gwyn. ☻ 13 **Facilities** Children's menu Dogs allowed Garden Parking **Rooms** 11

## TINTERN PARVA
Map 4 SO50

## Fountain Inn ☻

**Trellech Grange NP16 6QW** ☎ 01291 689303
**e-mail:** fountaininntintern@btconnect.com
**dir:** From M48 junct 2 follow Chepstow then Tintern signs. In Tintern turn by George Hotel for Raglan. Bear right, inn at top of hill

A fire failed to destroy this fine old early 17th-century inn, and its charming character remains unspoilt. It enjoys views of the Wye Valley from the garden, and is close to Tintern Abbey. Home-cooked food includes grilled sardines with balsamic vinegar and cherry tomatoes; leek and Caerphilly sausages with onion gravy; and beef and Guinness pie. Wash down a hearty meal with a pint of Spinning Dog!

**Open** all day all wk 6am-11pm **Bar Meals** L served Wed-Sun 12-2.30 D served all wk 6-9 Av main course £7.95 **Restaurant** L served Wed-Sun 12-2.30 D served all wk 6-9 ⊕ FREE HOUSE ◀ Hook Norton, Spinning Dog, Ring o' Bells, Interbrew Bass, Hobgoblin, Rev James, Kingstone Classic, Cats Whiskers, Butcombe, Mayfield, Rhymney ♂ Stowford Press. ☻ 9 **Facilities** Children's menu Children's portions Family room Dogs allowed Garden Parking

## TREDUNNOCK
Map 9 ST39

### PICK OF THE PUBS

## The Newbridge ★★★★ RR ◉ ☻

**NP15 1LY** ☎ 01633 451000 📠 01633 451001
**e-mail:** newbridge@evanspubs.co.uk
**dir:** M4 junct 24 follow Newport signs. Right at Toby Carvery, B4236 to Caerleon. Right over bridge, through Caerleon to mini rdbt. Straight ahead onto Llnagibby/Usk road

The Newbridge occupies an idyllic riverside location: to be there in the early morning and watch the mist over the river is magical. The decor is warm and welcoming, with comfortable sofas and subtle lighting. Head Chef Iain Sampson has worked in some of the country's finest kitchens and the quality and consistency of his modern British with Mediterranean-influenced food is well reflected in exciting seasonal menus, based extensively on local produce. Expect a typical meal of Welsh oak-smoked haddock risotto with parmesan wafer and herb oil; mustard-crusted rack of local Penperlleni lamb with fondant potatoes and carved vegetables; and banana Tatin with caramel ice cream. Dinner could be watercress, spinach and goat's cheese tart with beetroot coulis; Gloucestershire Old Spot pork loin with potato cake, baby vegetables and buttered tarragon jus; and home-made ice cream. The day's catch, purchased from the quayside in Cornwall, is displayed on the specials board.

**Open** all wk 11am-mdnt ◀ Brains Rev James, Hobby Horse, guest ale ♂ Aspall. ☻ 12 **Facilities** Garden Parking **Rooms** 6

## TRELLECH                                     Map 4 SO50

### PICK OF THE PUBS

## The Lion Inn

NP25 4PA ☎ 01600 860322  🖹 01600 860060
e-mail: debs@globalnet.co.uk
dir: *From A40 S of Monmouth take B4293, follow signs for Trellech. From M8 junct 2, straight across rdbt, 2nd left at 2nd rdbt, B4293 to Trellech*

Built by a naval captain in 1580 as a brew house and inn, the Lion's main structural beams are thought to have come from a tall ship. The former coaching inn has won many awards, and its growing reputation is soundly based on all that's best about a good British pub: a warm welcome, beams and winter log fires, as well as wholesome food, traditional ales (many from micro-breweries), ciders and games. For hearty appetites, the extensive menu embraces blackboard specials, bar snacks and basket meals. Other choices range from locally-made faggots with rich onion gravy; or salmon and mushroom tagliatelle in creamy Cheddar and dill sauce; to warm goat's cheese salad with roasted peppers and Melba toast. Children have plenty of favourites to choose from, while dogs are fussed over with biscuits and fresh water. The pub garden features a stream, a large aviary and views over fields.

**Open** 12-3 6-11 (Fri-Sat noon-mdnt Sun 12-4.30 Mon eve 7-11pm Thu eve 6-mdnt) Closed: Sun eve **Bar Meals** L served Mon-Fri 12-2, Sat-Sun 12-2.30 D served Mon 7-9.30, Tue-Sat 6-9.30 booking required Av main course £9 **Restaurant** L served Mon-Fri 12-2, Sat-Sun 12-2.30 D served Mon 7-9.30, Tue-Sat 6-9.30 booking required ⊕ FREE HOUSE ◀ Bath Ales, Wye Valley Butty Bach, Sharp's Cornish Coaster, Rhymney Best, Butcombe Gold. **Facilities** Children's portions Dogs allowed Garden Parking

## USK                                          Map 9 SO30

## The Nags Head Inn ♈

Twyn Square NP15 1BH
☎ 01291 672820  🖹 01291 672720
dir: *On A472*

Owned by the Key family for 40 years, this 15th-century coaching inn overlooks the square just a short stroll from the River Usk, and boasts magnificent hanging flower baskets. The traditional bar is furnished with polished tables and chairs, and decorated with collections of horse brasses, farming tools and lanterns hanging from exposed oak beams. Game in season figures strongly among the speciality dishes, including whole stuffed partridge, pheasant in port, home-made rabbit pie and brace of quails. There is a good choice for vegetarians and children's portions are also available.

**Open** all wk 10.30-2.30 5-11 Closed: 25 Dec **Bar Meals** L served all wk 11.45-1.45 D served all wk 5.30-9.30 Av main course £9.50 **Restaurant** L served all wk 11.45-1.45 D served all wk 5.30-9.30 ⊕ FREE HOUSE ◀ Brains Bitter, Dark, Buckleys Best, Reverend James, Bread of Heaven ♂ Thatchers Gold. ♈ 9 **Facilities** Children's portions Dogs allowed Garden Parking

### PICK OF THE PUBS

## Raglan Arms ◉ ♈

Llandenny NP15 1DL
☎ 01291 690800  🖹 01291 690155
e-mail: raglanarms@aol.com
dir: *From Monmouth take A449 to Raglan, left in village. From M4 take A449 exit. Signposted to Llandenny on right*

This mid 19th-century stone-built pub is tucked away in a small, attractive village. Its daily changing menu will prove easy to assimilate, with everything well chosen. Indeed, the restaurant holds an AA Rosette. Dine on mostly modern British dishes at rustic tables around the bar, where you'll find Wye Valley Bitter and Butty Bach, or in the conservatory. Some dishes, such as navarin of lamb, are French influenced; expect too, locally bred longhorn rib-eye of beef; Loch Fyne scallops; poached haddock with duck egg; and, in a category all of its own, a Middle Eastern dish called imam bayaldi, featuring spiced aubergine and tomato, a particular favourite with locals. Maybe to follow, a delicious zabaglione, or banoffee parfait and milk chocolate sauce, accompanied by one of the choice of dessert wines. A Raglan hallmark is its excellent selection of Welsh and English cheeses. In summer, head for the decked area and enjoy a crab platter with a glass of real ale, cider or one of the wines by the glass including champagne. Look out for the special events with tasting menus.

**Open** noon-2.30 6.30-9.30 (Sun noon-3) Closed: 25-27 Dec, last 2wks Feb, Sun eve & Mon **Bar Meals** L served Tue-Sat 12-2.30, Sun 12-3 D served Tue-Sat 6.30-9.30 Av main course £6 **Restaurant** L served Tue-Sat 12-2.30, Sun 12-3 booking required D served Tue-Sat 6.30-9.30 booking required Av 3 course à la carte fr £22.50 ⊕ FREE HOUSE ◀ Wye Valley Bitter, Butty Bach, Guinness ♂ Thatchers Gold. ♈ 12 **Facilities** Children's portions Dogs allowed Garden Parking

## PEMBROKESHIRE

## ABERCYCH                                     Map 8 SN24

## Nags Head Inn

SA37 0HJ ☎ 01239 841200
dir: *On B4332 (Carmarthen to Newcastle Emlyn road)*

This famous old inn, with its beamed bars and riverside gardens, is located at the entrance to an enchanted valley immortalised in Welsh folklore. Crossing into Pembrokeshire from the Teifi Falls at Cenarth, it is the first building you see over the county boundary. In one of the out-buildings the old forge still remains where the blacksmith crafted the first horse drawn ploughs to export to America. Old Emrys Ale is brewed on the premises and good food options include coracle caught Teifi sewin; hungry farmer's mixed grill; and home-made faggots.

**Open** Tue-Sun Closed: Mon **Bar Meals** L served Tue-Sun 12-2 D served Tue-Sun 6-9 **Restaurant** L served Tue-Sun 12-2 D served Tue-Sun 6-9 ⊕ FREE HOUSE ◀ Old Emrys. **Facilities** Play area Dogs allowed Garden Parking

## AMROTH                                       Map 8 SN10

## The New Inn

SA67 8NW ☎ 01834 812368
dir: *A48 to Carmarthen, A40 to St Clears, A477 to Llanteg then left*

A 400-year-old inn, originally a farmhouse, belonging to Amroth Castle Estate. It has old world charm with beamed ceilings, a Flemish chimney, a flagstone floor and an inglenook fireplace. It is close to the beach with views towards Saundersfoot and Tenby from the dining room upstairs. Locally caught fish, shellfish are specialities along with Welsh beef dishes; home-made dishes include soup, pies and curries. Enjoy food or drink outside on the large lawn complete with picnic benches.

**Open** all day all wk Mar-Oct 11am-11pm Closed: Oct-Mar **Bar Meals** food served all day **Restaurant** food served all day ⊕ FREE HOUSE ◀ Brains, Old Speckled Hen, Guinness, guest ales. **Facilities** Children's menu Children's portions Family room Dogs allowed Garden Parking

## CAREW — Map 8 SN00

### Carew Inn

**SA70 8SL ☎ 01646 651267**
**e-mail:** mandy@carewinn.co.uk
**dir:** *From A477 take A4075. Inn 400yds opp castle & Celtic cross*

A traditional stone-built country inn situated opposite the Carew Celtic cross and Norman castle. Enjoy the one-mile circular walk around the castle and millpond. A good range of bar meals includes Welsh Black steak and kidney pie; chilli con carne; Thai red chicken curry; and seafood pancakes. Fruit crumble and old favourite jam roly poly feature among the puddings. Live music every Thursday night under the marquee.

**Open** all day all wk Mon-Sat 11am-mdnt (Sun noon-12) Closed: 25 Dec **Bar Meals** L served all wk 12-2.30 D served all wk 6-9 ⊕ FREE HOUSE ◀ Worthington Best, SA Brains Reverend James, guest ales. **Facilities** Children's menu Children's portions Play area Dogs allowed Garden Parking

## CILGERRAN — Map 8 SN14

### Pendre Inn

**Pendre SA43 2SL ☎ 01239 614223**
**dir:** *Off A478, S of Cardigan*

Dating back to the 14th century, this is a pub full of memorabilia and featuring exposed interior walls, old beams, slate floors and an inglenook fireplace. An ancient ash tree grows through the pavement in front of the white stone, thick-walled building. Typical menu includes lamb steaks with red wine and cherries, rump and sirloin steaks, pork loin with honey and mustard glaze, and salmon with hollandaise.

**Open** Mon-Sun L Closed: Sun eve ◀ Tomos Watkins, OSB, Murphys, Worthington. **Facilities** Garden Parking

## LAMPHEY — Map 8 SN00

### The Dial Inn ▾

**Ridgeway Rd SA71 5NU**
**☎ 01646 672426 ▤ 01646 672426**
**dir:** *Just off A4139 (Tenby to Pembroke road)*

The Dial started life around 1830 as the Dower House for nearby Lamphey Court, and was converted into a pub in 1966. It immediately established itself as a popular village local, and in recent years the owners have extended the dining areas. Food is a real strength, and Pembrokeshire farm products are used whenever possible. You can choose from traditional bar food, the imaginative restaurant menu, or the daily blackboard.

**Open** all wk 11-2.30 6-11 (Summer all day) ◀ Rumney Bitter. ▾ 8 **Facilities** Children's menu Family room Garden Parking

## LETTERSTON — Map 8 SM92

### The Harp Inn

**31 Haverfordwest Rd SA62 5UA**
**☎ 01348 840061 ▤ 01348 840812**
**dir:** *On A40*

This 15th-century family-owned free house was once a working farm, as well as home to a weekly market. After remaining largely unchanged for 500 years, recent renovations have brought it completely up to date with the addition of the Conservatory Restaurant, where menu favourites include Welsh mussels; prime Welsh rib-eye steak; venison Roquefort; whole sea bass; and roast vegetable Wellington. Enjoy lunch with your children (and dog) in the fenced garden.

**Open** all day all wk Jul-Sep (ex Sun) **Bar Meals** Av main course £8 food served all day **Restaurant** Av 3 course à la carte fr £27.50 ⊕ FREE HOUSE ◀ Tetleys, Greene King, Abbot Ale. **Facilities** Play area Garden Parking

## LITTLE HAVEN — Map 8 SM81

### AA PUB OF THE YEAR FOR WALES

### PICK OF THE PUBS

### The Swan Inn

**Point Rd SA62 3UL**
**☎ 01437 781880 ▤ 04137 781880**
**e-mail:** enquiries@theswanlittlehaven.co.uk
**dir:** *From Haverfordwest take B4341 (Broad Haven road). In Broad Haven follow signs for seafront & Little Haven, 0.75m*

Follow the footpath to reach this unspoilt 200-year-old seaside gem perched above a rocky cove overlooking St Bride's Bay. The views across the water to Solva and Ramsay Island are spectacular, particularly from the terrace, the sea wall outside or even from the sought-after bay window in the beamed bar. A couple of years back The Swan was boarded up; now it buzzes with chatter and contented diners thanks to Paul and Tracey Morris. Expect well-kept real ales at the spectacular pewter-topped bar, a more than adequate wine choice, rustic old settles, polished oak tables, leather armchairs fronting a blazing log fire and an intimate dining room. Upstairs is an elegant contemporary-style restaurant. Cooking is modern British with a commitment to seasonal and local produce, so bag a table with a grand view and tuck into the bargain lunchtime table d'hôte menu, or dine on aqua pazza (a fiery Italian-style chunky mixed fish bisque), and roasted Long Lane lamb.

**Open** all day all wk **Bar Meals** L served all wk 12-2 D served Mon-Sun 6-9 **Restaurant** L served all wk 12-2 booking required D served Mon-Sun 6-9 booking required ⊕ FREE HOUSE ◀ Worthington Best Bitter, Old Speckled Hen, Guinness, S A Brains. **Facilities** Children's menu Children's portions Dogs allowed Garden

## NEWPORT — Map 8 SN03

### Salutation Inn ★★★ INN

**Felindre Farchog, Crymych SA41 3UY**
**☎ 01239 820564 ▤ 01239 820355**
**e-mail:** johndenley@aol.com
**web:** www.salutationcountryhotel.co.uk
**dir:** *On A487 between Cardigan & Fishguard*

Set right on the banks of the River Nevern, this 16th-century coaching inn stands in a quiet village in the heart of the Pembrokeshire Coast National Park. The oak-beamed bars are full of old world charm and country atmosphere. There is an emphasis on fresh local produce on the varied menu, including meat, poultry, fish, cheese and fruit and vegetables. Traditional roasts are served on Sundays. There are eight en suite bedrooms available.

**Open** all day all wk **Bar Meals** L served all wk 12.30-2.30 D served all wk 6.30-9 Av main course £8.50 **Restaurant** L served Sun 12.30-2.30 booking required D served Sat-Sun 7-9 booking required Fixed menu price fr £20 Av 3 course à la carte fr £25 ⊕ FREE HOUSE ◀ Felinfoel, Brains, Local guest ales ♂ Thatchers Gold. **Facilities** Children's menu Children's portions Dogs allowed Garden Parking **Rooms** 8

## PEMBROKE DOCK — Map 8 SM90

### Ferry Inn

**Pembroke Ferry SA72 6UD ☎ 01646 682947**
**dir:** *A477, off A48, right at garage, signs for Cleddau Bridge, left at rdbt*

There are fine views across the Cleddau estuary from the terrace of this 16th-century free house. Once the haunt of smugglers, the riverside inn has a nautical-themed bar with a 'great disaster' corner highlighting pictures of local catastrophes! The pub is also said to be haunted. Fresh fish features strongly on the menu: favourites include locally caught trout; salmon fillet with dill butter; and brill with cherry tomatoes and crème fraîche.

**Open** all wk noon-2.30 6.30-10.30 ◀ Worthington, Bass, Felinfoel Double Dragon, guest ale ♂ Stowford Press. **Facilities** Garden Parking

# PICK OF THE PUBS

## The Stackpole Inn ♟

**SA71 5DF**
☎ 01646 672324   📠 01646 672716
e-mail: info@stackpoleinn.co.uk
dir: *From Pembroke take B4319 & follow signs for Stackpole, approx 4m*

This traditional inn is a walker's delight, set in pristine gardens at the heart of the National Trust's Stackpole estate and close to the spectacular Pembrokeshire coastal path. There's a rare George V post box in the mellow stone wall outside, a survival from the time when one of the two original stone cottages was a post office. Nowadays the pub offers facilities for walkers, cyclists, fishermen and climbers, as well as those who simply prefer to relax and do nothing.

Once inside, you'll find a slate bar, ceiling beams made from ash trees grown on the estate, and a wood-burning stove set within the stone fireplace. The pub's free house status means that there's always a guest beer from around the UK to accompany three Welsh ales, a couple of real ciders and a varied wine list.

Local produce from the surrounding countryside and fish from the coast play a major part in the home-cooked menu. A lighter lunch menu offers freshly-baked Couronne loaves with an appetising selection of fillings that includes Welsh brie with locally cured bacon; and tuna with tarragon mayonnaise. Three-course appetites might begin with creamy Welsh blue cheese on bitter leaf salad with pickled walnuts and poached grapes, or smoked salmon on potato blini with herb crème fraîche. Main course options range from seared Welsh lamb with Moroccan cous cous and tomato jus with seasonal vegetables; to wild sea bass fillet with fennel and saffron risotto. Round things off with caramelised lemon tart and passionfruit sorbet, or creamy rice pudding with cinnamon and apple.

**Open** 12-3 6-11 Closed: Sun eve (winter) **Bar Meals** L served Mon-Sat 12-2, Sun 12-2.30 booking required D served all wk 6-9 booking required Av main course £11 **Restaurant** L served Mon-Sat 12-2, Sun 12-2.30 booking required D served all wk 6-9 booking required Av 3 course à la carte fr £25 ⊕ FREE HOUSE ◀ Brains Reverend James, Felinfoel, Double Dragon, Best Bitter, Guest ale ♻ Stowford Press, Westons Old Rosie. ♟ 12
**Facilities** Children's menu Dogs allowed Garden Parking

## PORTHGAIN
Map 8 SM83

### The Sloop Inn

**SA62 5BN** ☎ **01348 831449** 📄 **01348 831388**
**e-mail:** matthew@sloop-inn.freeserve.co.uk
**dir:** Take A487 NE from St David's for 6m. Left at
Croesgooch for 2m to Porthgain

Possibly the most famous pub on the North
Pembrokeshire Coast, the Sloop Inn is located in
beautiful quarrying village of Porthgain. The walls and
ceilings are packed with pictures and memorabilia from
nearby shipwrecks. The harbour is less than 100 metres
from the door and there is a village green to the front and
a large south-facing patio. With ales like Reverend James
on the pump, a long and varied menu includes
breakfasts, snacks, pub favourites, steaks from the grill
and as much home-caught fish as possible. The specials
board might offer home-made creamy leek and potato
soup; and pan fried red bream with Mediterranean
vegetables.

**Open** all day all wk 9.30am-11pm Closed: 25 Dec
**Bar Meals** L served all wk 12-2.30 D served all wk 6-9.30
booking required **Restaurant** L served all wk 12-2.30 D
served all wk 6-9.30 booking required ⊕ FREE HOUSE
◀ Reverend James, Brains Draught, Felinfoel, IPA.
**Facilities** Children's menu Garden Parking

## ROSEBUSH
Map 8 SN02

### Tafarn Sinc

**Preseli SA66 7QT** ☎ **01437 532214**
**dir:** Telephone for directions

The looming presence of this large red corrugated-iron
free house stands testament to its rapid construction in
1876. Now deserted by the railway it was built to serve,
this idiosyncratic establishment boasts wood-burning
stoves, a sawdusted floor, and a charming garden. Set
high in the Preseli Hills amid stunning scenery, it is
popular with walkers, who can stoke up on traditional
favourites like home-cooked Glamorgan sausage with
chutney, Welsh sirloin steak and chips, faggots and
Preseli lamb burgers.

**Open** all day noon-11 Closed: Mon (ex BH & summer)
**Bar Meals** L served Tue-Sat 12-2 D served Tue-Sat 6-9
**Restaurant** L served Tue-Sat 12-2 D served Tue-Sat 6-9
⊕ FREE HOUSE ◀ Worthington, Tafarn Sinc, guest ale.
**Facilities** Dogs allowed Garden Parking

## ST DOGMAELS
Map 8 SN14

### Webley Waterfront Inn & Hotel ♀

**Poppit Sands SA43 3LN** ☎ **01239 612085**
**e-mail:** enquiries@webleyhotel.co.uk
**web:** www.webleyhotel.co.uk
**dir:** A484 from Carmarthen to Cardigan, then to St
Dogmaels, right in village centre to Poppit Sands on
B4546

From its spectacular location at the start of the
Pembrokeshire Coast National Park, the inn offers
outstanding views across the River Teifi and Poppit
Sands to Cardigan Bay. Being where it is naturally means
fresh seafood, with specialities such as line-caught sea
bass, dressed crab and lobster, and Teifi sewin (sea
trout), while fresh lamb and beef comes from local farms,
and organic ice cream from Mary's Farmhouse in nearby
Crymych.

**Open** all wk ◀ Brains Buckleys Bitter, Worthington, Rev
James, DSB, guest ales. ♀ 8 **Facilities** Dogs allowed
Garden Parking

## SOLVA
Map 8 SM82

### The Cambrian Inn ♀

**Main St SA62 6UU** ☎ **01437 721210** 📄 **01437 720661**
**e-mail:** thecambrianinn@btconnect.com
**dir:** 13m from Haverfordwest on A487 towards St David's

This Grade II listed 17th-century inn is something of an
institution in this pretty fishing village, and attracts local
and returning visitors alike. A sample bar menu offers
local Welsh lamb cutlets, gammon steak or Welsh sirloin
steak, while the carte dinner menu offers lots of fresh
fish dishes. Sandwiches, jackets, salads and ploughmans
also available.

**Open** all day all wk **Bar Meals** Av main course £9 food
served all day **Restaurant** Fixed menu price fr £5 food
served all day ⊕ FREE HOUSE ◀ Tomos Watkins OSB &
Cwrw Braf/Haf, Butty Bach, guest ales. ♀ 15
**Facilities** Children's menu Children's portions Garden
Parking

## STACKPOLE
Map 8 SR99

### PICK OF THE PUBS

### The Stackpole Inn ♀

*See Pick of the Pubs on page 601*

## WOLF'S CASTLE
Map 8 SM92

### The Wolfe Inn

**SA62 5LS** ☎ **01437 741662** 📄 **01437 741676**
**dir:** On A40 between Haverfordwest & Fishguard. 7m from
both towns

The Wolfe, now under new ownership, is an oak-beamed,
stone-built property in a lovely village setting. The bar-
brasserie and restaurant comprise four interconnecting
but distinctly different rooms: the Victorian Parlour,
Hunters' Lodge, the Brasserie and a conservatory. There
is a bar menu and full à la carte, and dishes might
include braised lamb shank; lasagne; venison and
cranberry pie; beef brisket with horseradish mash.
Desserts could be raspberry crème brûlée or pear, toffee
and date crumble. Vegetarian options are available.

**Open** all wk all day in Summer **Bar Meals** L served all wk
12-2.30 D served all wk 6-9 booking required
**Restaurant** D served all wk 7-9 booking required
⊕ BRAINS ◀ Interbrew Worthington Bitter, guest ale.
**Facilities** Children's menu Garden Parking

### POWYS

## BERRIEW
Map 15 SJ10

### The Lion Hotel

**SY21 8PQ** ☎ **01686 640452** 📄 **01686 640604**
**e-mail:** trudi.jones@btconnect.com
**dir:** 5m from Welshpool on A483, right to Berriew. In
village centre next to church

Behind the black and white timbered exterior of this
17th-century family-run coaching inn lie bars and dining
areas where yet more old timbers testify to its age.
Menus, based on local produce, include whitebait with
sweet chilli mayo; parsnip fritters with blue cheese and
walnut dip; braised shoulder of Welsh lamb and honey
crushed root vegetables; or pork chop glazed with Welsh
rarebit, sautéed potatoes and caramelised onions with
cider gravy. There is a separate bar area where you can
enjoy a pint of real ale from the selection on tap including
Banks, Pedigree and Old Empire.

**Open** all wk noon-3 5-11 (Fri-Sat noon-11 Sun noon-3
6-10.30) **Bar Meals** L served all wk 12-2 D served all wk
6-9 **Restaurant** L served all wk 12-2 D served all wk 6-9
booking required ⊕ MARSTONS ◀ Banks Bitter, Pedigree,
Old Empire, guest ales. **Facilities** Parking

Save on Hotels. Book at theAA.com/hotel

POWYS 603 WALES

## BRECON
Map 9 SO02

### PICK OF THE PUBS

## The Felin Fach
## Griffin ★★★★ INN ☺☺ ♥

Felin Fach LD3 0UB ☎ 01874 620111
e-mail: enquiries@eatdrinksleep.ltd.uk
dir: 4.5m N of Brecon on A470 (Brecon to Hay-on-Wye road)

This much-feted country inn exemplifies owner Charles Inkin's passion for 'the simple things, done well'. The ethos is applied to food, wines, beers and en suite bedrooms. In the bar are deep leather sofas surrounding a newspaper-strewn table and open fire. Food is served in rambling bare-floored rooms where original features, including an Aga, are teamed with tasteful modern touches. Set on the edge of the Brecon Beacons, the Griffin draws much of its ingredients from the surrounding area, while the garden keeps up a steady flow of organic produce. The all important lunchtime menu includes Gorwydd Caerphilly ploughman's with home-made soda bread and pickles, or Welsh pork and leek sausages. The freshest seafood could feature wild halibut fillet with young spring vegetables and fresh creamed morels. Other mains include rack of Herdwick lamb, shepherd's pie and carrot purée, and oak roast salmon on crushed Witchill potato and spinach. Quality draught beers, 20 wines by the glass and beer tasting with the breweries complete the experience.

Open all day all wk 11-11 (Sun 11-10.30) Closed: 24-25 Dec Bar Meals L served Mon-Sat 12.30-2.30, Sun 12-2.30 booking required Av main course £15.50 Restaurant L served Mon-Sat 12.30-2.30, Sun 12-2.30 booking required D served Sun-Thu 6-9, Fri-Sat 6-9.30 Fixed menu price fr £28 Av 3 course à la carte fr £32.50 ⊕ FREE HOUSE ◀ Breconshire Breweries, Wye Valley Butty Bach, Pontypridd-Otley, Tomos Watkins ♂ Stowford Press, Ty Gwynn. ♥ 20 Facilities Children's menu Children's portions Dogs allowed Garden Parking Rooms 7

## The Old Ford Inn

Llanhamlach LD3 7YB
☎ 01874 665391 ◫ 01874 665391
e-mail: lynxcymru@aol.com
dir: 2.5m from Brecon on A40 towards Abergavenny

The family-run Old Ford is a 900-year-old inn set in the foothills of the Brecon Beacons, affording outstanding views over the mountains, the River Usk and the canal. There are cosy beamed bars and a cottage-style restaurant serving home-cooked food using local produce. Chef's specials might include Old Ford cow pie, with beef, vegetables and ale under a puffed pastry lid; and braised Welsh lamb shank with mint and rosemary sauce. There is a beer garden to relax in when the weather permits.

Open 12-3 6-11 Closed: 25 Dec, 3-6 months winter, Mon in winter Bar Meals L served all wk 12-3 booking required D served all wk 6-9 booking required Av main course £8.95 Restaurant L served all wk 12-3 booking required D served all wk 6-9 booking required Fixed menu price fr £8.95 ⊕ FREE HOUSE ◀ Worthington, Guinness. Facilities Children's menu Children's portions Garden Parking

### PICK OF THE PUBS

## The Usk Inn ★★★★ INN ♥

Talybont-on-Usk LD3 7JE
☎ 01874 676251 ◫ 01874 676392
e-mail: stay@uskinn.co.uk
dir: 6m E of Brecon, just off A40 towards Abergavenny & Crickhowell

The inn was established in the 1840s, just as the Brecon to Merthyr Railway arrived. In 1878 the locomotive Hercules failed to stop at the former station opposite and crashed into the street, seriously disrupting conversations and beer consumption in the bar. The owner Andrew Felix is making sure you can still partake of interesting food like fried haggis and chilli dressing. This haggis, by the way, is prefixed by the all-important word Celtic. Alternatively, opt for risotto of smoked garlic and porcini mushrooms, then half a honey-roast duck with apricot and tarragon, or a fish special, and home-made treacle tart to finish. The Brecon to Monmouth Canal runs through the village, in some places at rooftop level. Enjoy a stay in one of the en suite bedrooms; one room has a four-poster bed.

Open all day all wk 11am-11.30pm (Sun 11-10.30) Closed: 25-26 Dec Bar Meals D served all wk 12-2.30 Restaurant D served all wk 6.30-9.30 ⊕ FREE HOUSE ◀ Guinness, Guest ales ♂ Thatchers, Robinson. ♥ 11 Facilities Garden Parking Rooms 11

### PICK OF THE PUBS

## The White Swan Inn ♥

Llanfrynach LD3 7BZ
☎ 01874 665276 ◫ 01874 665362
e-mail: lee.harward@hotmail.co.uk
dir: 3m E of Brecon off A40, take B4558, follow Llanfrynach signs

The Brecon Beacons provide an awesome backdrop to this converted row of white-painted stone cottages, which stands opposite the ancient church of St Brynach. Originally a coaching inn in the 17th century,

it is now an unpretentious gastro-pub with character and atmosphere, featuring stone walls, exposed oak beams, stone-flagged floors, wooden furniture and bar counter, plus log fires, leather sofas, atmospheric lighting, and a warm and cosy feel. Eat in the spacious dining room, or more informally in the bar, which also offers a lighter snack menu and Brains Bitter on handpump. Enjoy crisp, honest dishes in the unpretentious gastro-pub mould, all freshly prepared using locally sourced produce - Welsh beef, lamb, pork and venison — with daily fish specials listed on the chalkboard. Dinner could include green tomato tart Tatin with red onion and fennel salad; rump of Welsh mountain lamb, leek and mutton steam pudding and minted sweet potato purée; orange and lemon crème brûlée with tequila and lime jelly.

Open 11.30-3 6.30-11.30 Closed: 25-26 Dec, 1st 2wks Jan, Mon & Tue (ex summer, Dec & BH) Bar Meals L served Wed-Sat 12-2, Sun 12-2.30 D served Wed-Sun 7-9 Restaurant L served Wed-Sat 12-2, Sun 12-2.30 D served Wed-Sun 7-9 ⊕ FREE HOUSE ◀ HB, Brains SA, Brains Smooth, Guinness, Rev James. ♥ 8 Facilities Children's menu Garden Parking

## COEDWAY
Map 15 SJ31

## The Old Hand and Diamond Inn

SY5 9AR ☎ 01743 884379 ◫ 01743 884379
e-mail: moz123@aol.com
web: www.oldhandanddiamond.co.uk
dir: 9m from Shrewsbury

This 17th-century inn retains much of its original character, with open winter fires to warm the beamed interior. This is the place to enjoy a pint of Woods Shropshire Lad, whilst choosing from an extensive menu that uses the best from local suppliers. Dishes might include creamy fish pie in rich thermidor sauce, and grilled lamb chops with Shrewsbury sauce. The beer garden has plenty of seating on the patio, and there's also a children's play area for summer days.

Open all day all wk 11am-1am Bar Meals L served Mon-Thu 12-2.30, Fri-Sun 12-9.30 D served Mon-Thu 6-9.30, Fri-Sun 12-9.30 Av main course £10.95 Restaurant L served Mon-Thu 12-2.30, Fri-Sun 12-9.30 D served Mon-Thu 6-9.30, Fri-Sun 12-9.30 Av 3 course à la carte fr £22 ⊕ FREE HOUSE ◀ Worthington, Shropshire Lad, guest ales. Facilities Children's portions Play area Dogs allowed Garden Parking

## CRICKHOWELL — Map 9 SO21

### PICK OF THE PUBS

### The Bear Hotel ★★★ HL ☺ ♀

**Brecon Rd NP8 1BW**
☎ 01873 810408  📠 01873 811696
e-mail: bearhotel@aol.com
dir: *On A40 between Abergavenny & Brecon*

Friendliness and charm are the keynotes of this 15th-century coaching inn. The Bear has been at the heart of the old market town of Crickhowell since the days of the London to Aberystwyth mail coach. Owned by the Hindmarsh family for more than 30 years, the front bars are resplendent with oak panelling, ornamental sideboards and welcoming log fires, whilst the more formal dining rooms are filled with candles, fresh flowers and linen-draped tables. The modern British menu leans towards the wholesome dishes of the past, using top-notch locally sourced ingredients. Dinner in the restaurant might take in venison terrine with apple and plum chutney, followed by baked salmon fillet with sun-dried tomato, crushed potato, chargrilled courgette and herb oil. The comfortable bedrooms are divided between the historic inn and the coach house facing the cobbled courtyard.

**Open** all wk 11-3 6-11 **Bar Meals** L served all wk 12-2 D served Mon-Sat 6-10, Sun 7-9.30 Av main course £10 **Restaurant** L served Sun 12-2 booking required Av 3 course à la carte fr £35 ⊕ FREE HOUSE ◀ Interbrew Bass, Ruddles Best, Brains Reverend James, John Smith's. ♀ 10 **Facilities** Children's menu Children's portions Family room Dogs allowed Garden Parking **Rooms** 34

### PICK OF THE PUBS

### Nantyffin Cider Mill Inn ♀

**Brecon Rd NP8 1SG**
☎ 01873 810775  📠 01873 810986
e-mail: info@cidermill.co.uk
dir: *At junct of A40 & A479, 1.5m W of Crickhowell*

Originally a drovers' inn, this family-run, 16th-century inn within the Brecon Beacons National Park, lies at the foot of the Black Mountains, an ideal spot for walking, cycling, canoeing and fishing. Until the mid-1960s, it was well known for its cider and the original press, still fully working, can be seen in the Mill Room Restaurant. The bars are full of character and offer a range of real ales, a selection ciders, and a comprehensive wine list. These days the Nantyffin is renowned for its British and European dishes, created by a kitchen that fully supports and develops its local suppliers. At lunchtime look for steamed Welsh mussels; confit shoulder of Welsh mountain lamb; and game pie; while in the evening, grilled Pant-Ysgawn goat's cheese; rack of Large White pork; Madgetts Farm free-range duck breast; and sweet potato, courgette and Welsh Cheddar terrine. Chalk boards list daily specials such as lobster risotto.

---

**Open** noon-3 6-11 Closed: Mon (ex BH), Sun eve Oct-Mar **Bar Meals** L served Tue-Sun 12-2.30 D served Tue-Sun 6.30-9.30 **Restaurant** L served Sun 12-2.30 booking required D served Fri-Sat 6.30-9.30 booking required ⊕ FREE HOUSE ◀ Reverend James, Rhymney Best Bitter ♂ Taffy Apples, Thatchers Gold, Thatchers Old Rascal. ♀ 10 **Facilities** Children's portions Dogs allowed Garden Parking

## DYLIFE — Map 14 SN89

### Star Inn

**SY19 7BW** ☎ 01650 521345  📠 01650 521345
e-mail: starinn365@aol.com
dir: *Between Llanidloes & Machynlleth on mountain road*

Dating from 1640 and set at 1300 feet amid breathtaking countryside, the Star Inn is in an area favoured by Dylan Thomas and Wynford Vaughn Thomas. Red kites swoop overhead, and the magnificent Clywedog reservoir is close by. This family-run inn is the perfect setting for getting away from it all. For a more active break, fishing, golf, sailing, walking and pony trekking are just some of the activities nearby. A varied choice of wholesome pub fare and great real ales complete the picture.

**Open** 12-2.30 6.30-11 Closed: Mon-Fri lunch (winter) **Bar Meals** L served Sun 12-2 D served all wk 6-9 ⊕ FREE HOUSE ◀ Brains Smooth, Rev James. **Facilities** Children's menu Children's portions Family room Dogs allowed Parking

## GLADESTRY — Map 9 SO25

### The Royal Oak Inn ♀

**HR5 3NR** ☎ 01544 370669  & 370342
e-mail: brianhall@btinternet.com
dir: *4m W of Kington, 10m from Hay-on-Wye on B4594*

This 400-year-old inn once welcomed drovers taking store cattle from Wales to England. The huge inglenook fireplace, heavily beamed ceilings and a flagstone floor set the scene for the home-made fare served in the lounge bar/dining area, including bar snacks, soups, jacket potatoes, sandwiches and salads. A roast is served every Sunday. Offa's Dyke footpath is nearby, and there's an exhilarating four-mile walk from Kington along Hergest Ridge with its breathtaking views.

---

**Open** all day all wk Etr-Aug (Oct-Mar reduced hrs) Closed Thu eve in winter **Bar Meals** L served all wk 12-2.30 D served all wk 7-9.30 booking required Av main course £7.50 **Restaurant** L served all wk 12-2.30 D served all wk 7-9.30 booking required Fixed menu price fr £9.45 Av 3 course à la carte fr £17 ⊕ FREE HOUSE ◀ Brains Reverend James, Butty Bach, Worthingtons, guest ales ♂ Stowford Press. ♀ 8 **Facilities** Children's portions Dogs allowed Garden Parking **Notes** ☺

## HAY-ON-WYE — Map 9 SO24

### Kilverts Inn ♀

**The Bullring HR3 5AG**
☎ 01497 821042  📠 01497 821580
e-mail: info@kilverts.co.uk
dir: *From A438 take B4351 to Hay. Turn right after bridge, left towards park & left again*

In the summer months, be sure to visit this pub's lovely garden, with its lawns, flower beds, pond and fountain. Indoors, there's a timber-framed, olde-worlde style bar offering a range of local beers. Expect robust, generous food, with worldwide influences – typical dishes include grilled goat's cheese with a pesto crust; Kilvert's famous home-made steak and pudding; home-made fisherman's pie and chilli con carne. At the bar there's an impressive selection of ales and ciders. There is an annual beer festival too.

**Open** all wk ◀ Wye Valley Butty Bach, The Reverend James, Pedigree, Guest Ales ♂ Westons Old Rosie. ♀ 8 **Facilities** Family room Dogs allowed Garden Parking

### PICK OF THE PUBS

### The Old Black Lion ★★★★ INN ☺ ♀

**HR3 5AD** ☎ 01497 820841  📠 01497 822960
e-mail: info@oldblacklion.co.uk
dir: *In town centre*

Parts of this charming whitewashed inn date from the 1300s, although structurally most of it is 17th century. It is situated close to what was known as the Lion Gate, one of the original entrances to the old walled town of Hay-on-Wye. The oak-timbered bar is furnished with scrubbed pine tables, comfy armchairs and a log-burning stove – perfect for savouring a pint of Old Black Lion Ale. The inn has a long-standing reputation for its food – witness the AA Rosette – and the pretty dining room overlooking the garden terrace is where to enjoy bar favourites of baked loin of cod with fennel, leeks and cheese sauce; and rice and pasta stir-fry with black beans. In the restaurant the menu typically offers supreme of guinea fowl with spinach, sun-blushed tomatoes and Madeira sauce; and herb-crusted rack of local lamb with sweet potatoes and rosemary and port jus. Guest rooms all accommodate a live-in teddy bear. Hay, of course, has bookshops at every turn, and it is also home to a renowned annual literary festival.

**Open** all day all wk Closed: 24-26 Dec **Bar Meals** L served Mon-Sat 12-2, Sun 12-2.30 D served Sun-Thu 6.30-9, Fri-Sat 6.30-9.30 Av main course £12.95 **Restaurant** D served all wk 6.30-9 Av 3 course à la carte fr £31.90 ⊕ FREE HOUSE ◀ Old Black Lion Ale, Reverend James ♂ Stowford Press. ♀ 8 **Facilities** Garden Parking **Rooms** 10

## LLANDRINDOD WELLS   Map 9 SO06

### The Bell Country Inn

Llanyre LD1 6DY ☎ 01597 823959 📠 01597 825618
e-mail: info@bellcountryinn.co.uk
dir: 1.5m NW of Llandrindod Wells on A4081

Sitting high in the hills above Llandrindod Wells, this
smartly refurbished former drovers' inn is now a pleasing
mix of old and new. Two bars and a restaurant serve a
range of beers and seasonally changing menus. Local
ingredients are used with meat coming from
neighbouring farms and woodland. A meal might include
seared scallops on cauliflower purée and black pudding
followed by breast of Gressingham duck with honey
glazed onions, minted pea purée, chateau potato and a
Madeira sauce. Finish with home-made lemon tart.

Open noon-3 6-11.30 Closed: Sun eve Bar Meals L served
all wk 12-2 D served Mon-Sat 6-9 Av main course £7
Restaurant D served Mon-Sat 6-9 booking required Fixed
menu price fr £8.95 Av 3 course à la carte fr £25 ⊕ FREE
HOUSE ◀ Guinness, Guest ales, HB. Facilities Children's
menu Children's portions Garden Parking

### The Laughing Dog NEW

Howey LD1 5PT ☎ 01597 822406
dir: From A483 between Builth Wells & Llandrindod Wells
follow Howey signs. Pub in village centre

A traditional country pub comprising a public bar, snug,
games room, restaurant and dog-friendly beer garden.
The original part of the building dates back to the 17th
century when it was used as a stop for drovers. Wye
Valley and Wood's Parish bitters are the resident real
ales, while Weston's provides the ciders. Locally sourced,
home-made British food, but sometimes with other
influences, includes grilled organic Welsh Black beef,
faggots in onion gravy with mushy peas and mashed
potato; or Poyning organic pork meatballs on linguine
with spicy tomato sauce.

Open Mon 6-11, Tue-Thu 11-2 6-11, Fri 11-2 5.30-1am,
Sat-Sun all day Closed: Mon until 6 Bar Meals L served
Tue-Sat 12-2 D served Tue-Sat 6.30-9 Av main course
£6.95 Restaurant L served Tue-Sun 12-2 booking
required D served Tue-Sat 6.30-9 booking required Av 3
course à la carte fr £16.85 ⊕ FREE HOUSE ◀ Wye Valley
Bitter, Newman's Wolver's Ale, Celt Experience Celt
Bronze, Felinfoel Double Dragon, Wood's Parish Bitter
Ö Westons First Quality, Westons Traditional Scrumpy,
Westons Country Perry. Facilities Children's
menu Children's portions Dogs allowed Garden

## LLANFYLLIN   Map 15 SJ11

### Cain Valley Hotel ★★ HL

High St SY22 5AQ ☎ 01691 648366 📠 01691 648307
e-mail: info@cainvalleyhotel.co.uk
dir: From Shrewsbury & Oswestry follow signs for Lake
Vyrnwy & onto A490 to Llanfyllin. Hotel on right

Family-run coaching inn dating from the 17th century,
with a stunning Jacobean staircase, oak-panelled lounge
bar and a heavily beamed restaurant with exposed hand-
made bricks. A full bar menu is available at lunchtime
and in the evening. Typical meals include Welsh lamb,
port, plum and ginger casserole or herb-crusted rainbow
trout with vegetables served in a white wine sauce.

Open all day all wk 11.30am-mdnt (Sun noon-11pm)
Closed: 25 Dec Bar Meals L served all wk 12-2 booking
required D served all wk 7-9 booking required Av main
course £8 Restaurant L served all wk 12-2 booking
required Av 3 course à la carte fr £18 ⊕ FREE HOUSE
◀ Worthington's, Ansells Mild, Guinness.
Facilities Children's menu Children's portions Dogs
allowed Parking Rooms 13

## LLANGATTOCK   Map 9 SO21

### The Vine Tree Inn ♥

The Legar NP8 1HG ☎ 01873 810514
dir: Take A40 W from Abergavenny then A4077 from
Crickhowell

A pretty pink pub on the River Usk, at the edge of the
National Park and within walking distance of Crickhowell.
The large garden overlooks the river, bridge and Table
Mountain. It is predominantly a dining pub serving a
comprehensive menu, with traditional roast lunches on
Sundays. Tuesdays now feature the weekly Mexican
evening, when authentic Latin dishes cooked to order
include nachos, spicy bean soup, a choice of fajitas and
enchiladas, and chilli con carne.

Open all wk noon-3 6-11 (Sun noon-8) ◀ Fuller's London
Pride, Worthington's, Golden Valley. ♥8 Facilities Garden
Parking

## LLANGYNIDR   Map 9 SO11

### The Coach & Horses

Cwmcrawnon Rd NP8 1LS ☎ 01874 730245
dir: A40 from Brecon to Abergavenny, 12m from Brecon.
Through Bwlch, pub after bend turn right

A free house just two minutes' walk from the nearby
canal moorings, and also a popular meeting place for car
club members – the car park can accommodate over 70
vehicles. Three real ales change more or less daily, while
the talented chefs prepare such dishes as fried potato
shells topped with chicken and melted brie; tempura
battered king prawns; grilled local venison sausages;
and home-made red Thai beef curry. August is the month
for live music and accompanying hog roast.

Open all day noon-mdnt Closed: Mon in winter
Bar Meals L served all wk 12-2 booking required D served
all wk 6-9 booking required Av main course £8
Restaurant L served Mon-Sat 12-2, Sun 12-4 booking
required D served Sun 6-9 booking required ⊕ FREE
HOUSE ◀ guest ales Ö Stowford Press.
Facilities Children's menu Children's portions Dogs
allowed Garden Parking

## MACHYNLLETH   Map 14 SH70

### PICK OF THE PUBS

### Wynnstay Hotel ♥

SY20 8AE ☎ 01654 702941 📠 01654 703884
e-mail: info@wynnstay-hotel.com
dir: At junct A487 & A489. 5m from A470

Draw a 50-mile radius from the door of this attractive
18th-century coaching inn and the resulting area, give
or take, is from where head chef Gareth Johns (a
contestant on TV's Iron Chef UK last May) draws the
ingredients for an alluring menu based firmly on good
Welsh produce, with European influences. The bars
stock real ales from all over Wales, as well as one or
two from across the English border. Drop in for tea,
coffee and cakes, or a pint of Celt Golden and
something to eat, perhaps Cefn Barhedyn lamb's liver
and bacon, or Cardigan Bay fish casserole. At dinner,
small plates include spiced Welsh beef tortellini, and
deep-fried Aberdyfi mullet, while among the large
plates are grilled Gaerwen pork loin with confit belly,
black pudding mash and treacle gravy; breast of
Barbary duck with Dulas whinberry gravy and potato
Florentine; and Welsh cheese cannelloni.

Open all wk 12-2.30 6-11 Closed: 1wk over New Year
Restaurant L served all wk 12-2 booking required D
served all wk 6.30-9 booking required Av 3 course à la
carte fr £20 ⊕ FREE HOUSE ◀ Greene King IPA, Celt
Golden, Guinness, Montys Moss. ♥10
Facilities Children's portions Dogs allowed Parking

## MONTGOMERY | Map 15 SO29

### PICK OF THE PUBS

## Dragon Hotel ★★ HL ●

SY15 6PA ☎ 01686 668359 📠 0870 011 8227
e-mail: reception@dragonhotel.com
web: www.dragonhotel.com
dir: *A483 towards Welshpool, right onto B4386 then B4385. Behind town hall*

In a small town amidst the stunning countryside of the Welsh Marches, this black and white timber-framed coaching inn dates back to the 1600s. An enclosed patio has been created from the former coach entrance, while the bar, lounge and most bedrooms contain beams and masonry allegedly removed from Montgomery Castle after its destruction by Oliver Cromwell. Ales from the Montgomery Brewery, wines from the Penarth Vineyard and whisky from the Penderyn Distillery are served at the bar. The hotel prides itself on its use of local produce in the kitchen. In addition to daily blackboard specials, ciabattas and soups in the bar, the carte may start with basil-coated Welsh brie with red onion chutney, and continue with slow-cooked Welsh lamb shank on spring onion mash with redcurrant gravy and braised leeks. Situated on Offa's Dyke, Montgomery provides an ideal base for touring and fishing on the Wye and the Severn.

**Open** all wk noon-2 6-11 **Bar Meals** L served all wk 12-2 D served all wk 7-9 Av main course £9 **Restaurant** L served all wk 12-2 booking required D served all wk 7-9 booking required Fixed menu price fr £25 Av 3 course à la carte fr £30 ⊕ FREE HOUSE ◀ Wood Special, Interbrew Bass, Montgomery Brew ⟳ Old Monty. **Facilities** Children's menu Children's portions Dogs allowed Garden Parking **Rooms** 20

## NEW RADNOR | Map 9 SO26

### PICK OF THE PUBS

## Red Lion Inn

Llanfihangel-nant-Melan LD8 2TN
☎ 01544 350220 📠 01544 350220
e-mail: theredlioninn@yahoo.co.uk
dir: *A483 to Crossgates then right onto A44, 6m to pub. 3m W of New Radnor on A44*

Here in the wild landscape of Mid-Wales is an ancient drover's inn that still provides water, though nowadays it's for hosing down muddy bikes, rather than for livestock to drink. There's a beamed lounge bar and a

locals' bar offering guest real ales, two small restaurants and a sun-trap garden. Traditional and modern cookery is based on fresh, local produce, some of the most popular dishes being Welsh Black sirloin steaks, Welsh lamb and organic salmon. Other main courses include game terrine with Cognac and grape preserve; and leek, wild mushroom and chestnut gâteau. Add imaginative vegetarian dishes, a children's menu and traditional Sunday roasts. Round off with Welsh cheeses and home-made walnut bread. Welsh cream teas are served during the afternoon. Next door is St Michael's church, one of four so named encircling the burial place of the last Welsh dragon. According to legend, should anything happen to them the dragon will rise again.

**Open** noon-11.30 (Sun noon-7.30) Closed: Tue **Bar Meals** L served Mon-Sat 12-3, Sun 12-7.30 D served Mon-Sat 6-11.30, Sun 12-7.30 ⊕ FREE HOUSE ◀ Guest Ales ⟳ Thatchers. **Facilities** Family room Dogs allowed Garden Parking

## OLD RADNOR | Map 9 SO25

### PICK OF THE PUBS

## The Harp

LD8 2RH ☎ 01544 350655 📠 01544 350655
e-mail: info@harpinnradnor.co.uk
dir: *Old Radnor signed off A44 (Kington to New Radnor)*

The Harp's website is billed as the 'first in its 600-year history', a tongue-in-cheek comment that amply underlines how old the pub is. A 15th-century Welsh longhouse, it's made from local stone and slate, and when you open the simple wooden door you step into a cosy lounge and bars with oak beams, log fires, semi-circular wooden settles and flagstone floors. Through the windows are glorious countryside views. Modern pub food includes starters of Parma ham with mango, wild rocket and honey mustard dressing; and salami and olives with ciabatta; follow with Welsh Black rump steak with hand-cut chips; roasted hake in tarragon butter with celeriac mash; or cassoulet de Languedoc, a hearty combination of duck confit, sausages and butterbeans. Deserts include apple and raspberry crumble, and marmalade bread and butter pudding. Two real ales, one Welsh and one English, are kept on hand-pump and when finished the next ale from around the country is available, ensuring a huge variety during the year; cider comes from Dunkertons of Leominster.

**Open** 6-11 (Sat-Sun noon-3 6-11) Closed: Mon **Bar Meals** L served Sat-Sun 12-2.30 booking required D served Tue-Sun 6-9 booking required Av main course £12.50 **Restaurant** L served Sat-Sun 12-2.30 required D served Tue-Sun 6-9 booking required Av 3 course à la carte fr £18.85 ⊕ FREE HOUSE ◀ Three Tuns, Hopback, Wye Valley, Hobsons, Ludlow ⟳ Kingston Rosie, Dunkertons, Stowford Press. **Facilities** Children's portions Dogs allowed Garden Parking

## TALGARTH | Map 9 SO13

## Castle Inn

Pengenffordd LD3 0EP
☎ 01874 711353 📠 01874 711353
e-mail: info@thecastleinn.co.uk
dir: *4m S of Talgarth on A479*

This welcoming inn enjoys a spectacular location in the heart of the Black Mountains, in the Brecon Beacons National Park. It is named after the Iron Age hill fort that tops the hill behind it – Castell Dinas. Numerous walks and mountain bike routes begin and end at its door, making it popular with outdoor enthusiasts. With a good selection of real local ales, substantial pub food includes sausage and mash and fisherman's pie. The pub also offers bunkhouse accommodation and a campsite. Look out for the Black Mountains' Beast – a large black cat that has been seen by several customers!

**Open** Wed-Fri 6-11 Sat-Sun noon-11 Closed: Mon-Tue **Bar Meals** L served Sat-Sun 12-2 D served Wed-Sun 6-9 Av main course £8.95 **Restaurant** L served Sat-Sun 12-2 D served Wed-Sun 6-9 ⊕ FREE HOUSE ◀ Butty Bach, Rhymney Bitter, Rev James, Hobby Horse, Guest ales ⟳ Stowford Press, Thatchers Gold, Westons Vintage Cider. **Facilities** Children's menu Children's portions Garden Parking

## TALYBONT-ON-USK | Map 9 SO12

## Star Inn

LD3 7YX ☎ 01874 676635
e-mail: anna@starinntalybont.co.uk
dir: *Telephone for directions*

With its pretty riverside garden, this traditional 250-year-old inn stands in a picturesque village within the Brecon Beacons National Park. The pub, unmodernised and with welcoming fireplace, is known for its constantly changing range of well-kept real ales, and hosts quiz nights on Monday and live bands on Wednesday. Hearty bar food with dishes such as chicken in leek and Stilton sauce, Hungarian pork goulash, traditional roasts, salmon fish cakes, and vegetarian chilli. Recent change of hands.

**Open** all wk 11.30-3 5-11 (Summer 11.30-11 Mon-Fri 11-11 Sat-Sun) **Bar Meals** L served all wk 12-2 D served all wk 6-9 ⊕ FREE HOUSE ◀ Felinfoel Double Dragon, Theakston Old Peculier, Hancock's HB, Bullmastiff Best, Wadworth 6X, regular guest ales. **Facilities** Children's menu Dogs allowed Garden

## TRECASTLE | Map 9 SN82

### PICK OF THE PUBS

## The Castle Coaching Inn

*See Pick of the Pubs on opposite page*

# PICK OF THE PUBS

## The Castle Coaching Inn

**TRECASTLE**     Map 9 SN82

**LD3 8UH**
☎ **01874 636354** 📠 **01874 636457**
**e-mail:**
enquiries@castle-coaching-inn.co.uk
**web:** www.castle-coaching-inn.co.uk
**dir:** *On A40 W of Brecon*

Owned and run by John and Val Porter and their son Andrew, this Georgian coaching inn on the old London to Carmarthen coaching route, in the northern part of the Brecon Beacons National Park, has been carefully restored in recent years. There are lovely old fireplaces and a remarkable bow-fronted bar window, and the inn also offers a peaceful terrace and garden. An open log fire burns in the bar throughout the winter, where with a pint of one of the weekly changing real ales or a glass of wine in your hand, you may savour the pub's great atmosphere.

Some guests prefer to stay in the bar to eat, where the menu is the same as in the restaurant, but which additionally offers fresh sandwiches, ploughman's, hot filled baguettes and filled jackets. Thus in both locations there might be minestrone or leek and potato soup; smoked haddock topped with ham and tomato in Cheddar cheese sauce; and Japanese-style prawns with sweet chilli dip as starters. Main courses typically include fillet steak with melted Stilton and roasted red onions; supreme of chicken with mushroom, Gruyère and white wine sauce; Welsh lamb chops with rosemary and redcurrant sauce; steak and Guinness pie; chilli con carne with rice and garlic bread; chicken curry served with rice; pan-fried salmon with orange and tarragon; and Mediterranean vegetable bake.

Finally, desserts include favourites like Dutch apple flan; cool mint fling; banana and amaretto cheesecake; and treacle sponge pudding and custard.

**Open** all wk noon-3 6-11 (Sun 7-10.30)
**Bar Meals** L served Sat-Sun 12-2
D served Mon-Sat 6.30-9, Sun 7-9 Av
main course £12 **Restaurant** L served
Sat-Sun 12-2 D served Mon-Sat 6.30-9,
Sun 7-9 🛢 FREE HOUSE 🛢 Fuller's
London Pride, Timothy Taylor Landlord,
Spitfire, Rhymney, Evan Evans.
**Facilities** Children's menu Dogs allowed
Garden Parking

## SWANSEA

### LLANGENNITH
Map 8 SS49

## Kings Head ★★★★ INN

SA3 1HX ☎ 01792 386212 📠 01792 386477
e-mail: info@kingsheadgower.co.uk
dir: M4 junct 47, follow signs for Gower A483, 2nd exit at rdbt, right at lights onto B495 towards Old Walls, left at fork to Llangennith, pub on right

The sands of Llangennith beach stretch to Rhosilli, almost four miles away. Take a stroll here before heading to the pub opposite the largest parish church on the Gower Peninsular. Originally a row of three 17th-century buildings, the interior retains its old beams, exposed stonework and a large winter fire. Real ales are carefully tended and include a local brew from the Felinfoel Brewery. The Stevens family are building something of a reputation for their Thai dishes, Indian curries, and British pies, like chicken, leek and asparagus; home-cooking of fresh Welsh produce is at the heart of it all. Comfortable accommodation is available.

Open all day all wk 9am-11pm (Sun 9am-10.30pm) Bar Meals L served all wk 9-9.30 D served all wk 9-9.30 Av main course £7.75 food served all day Restaurant L served all wk 12-2 D served all wk 7-9 ⊕ COORS ◄ Coors, Tomos Watkins, Guinness, Rhymney. Facilities Children's menu Children's portions Dogs allowed Parking Rooms 27

### REYNOLDSTON
Map 8 SS48

## King Arthur Hotel ♀

Higher Green SA3 1AD
☎ 01792 390775 📠 01792 391075
e-mail: info@kingarthurhotel.co.uk
dir: Just N of A4118 SW of Swansea

A traditional country inn, with real log fires, in a village lying at the heart of the beautiful Gower Peninsula. Eat in the restaurant, main bar or family room, choosing main menu or specials board dishes including seasonal game, Welsh Black beef, locally caught fish and vegetarian options. Enjoy the food with a choice of ales, or one of 11 wines served by the glass.

Open all day all wk Closed: 25 Dec Bar Meals food served all day Restaurant L served all wk 12-2.30 booking required D served Sun-Thu 6-9, Fri-Sat 6-9.30 booking required ⊕ FREE HOUSE ◄ Felinfoel Double Dragon, Worthington Bitter & Bass, Tomas Watkins OSB, King Arthur Ale. ♀ 11 Facilities Children's menu Children's portions Family room Garden Parking

## VALE OF GLAMORGAN

### COWBRIDGE
Map 9 SS97

## The Cross Inn NEW

Church Rd, Llanblethian CF71 7JF ☎ 01446 772995
dir: Telephone for directions

First licensed as a coaching inn in 1671, The Cross is tucked away in a peaceful corner of the Vale of Glamorgan just a few miles from the splendid Heritage Coast. The solid menu features several versions of mature Welsh Black steaks and an enticing pork chop cider reduction with butternut squash and coriander mash. Guest ales each week are promised, but a particular attraction is wines from Wales' longest established vineyard, with red, white and a sparkling from the nearby Glyndwr vineyard at Llanblethian.

Open all day all wk 10am-11pm Bar Meals L served Mon-Fri 12-2.30, Sat 12-9, Sun 12-3.30 D served Mon-Fri 5.30-9, Sat 12-9 Restaurant L served Mon-Fri 12-2.30, Sat 12-9, Sun 12-3.30 D served Mon-Fri 5.30-9, Sat 12-9 Fixed menu price fr £10.45 Av 3 course à la carte fr £22 ⊕ FREE HOUSE ◄ Hancocks HB, Wye Valley Butty Bach, Guest ales ♂ Westons, Stowford Press. Facilities Children's portions Dogs allowed Garden Parking

## PICK OF THE PUBS

## Hare & Hounds ♀

Aberthin CF71 7LG ☎ 01446 774892
e-mail: hare.hounds@hotmail.co.uk
dir: 1m from Cowbridge

Transformed from a run-down boozer to a popular dining pub, this 15th-century former mint stands in the pretty village of Aberthin. The bar remains traditional, a cosy haven for drinking pints of Oxford Gold or Pedigree by the open fire, while the dining room sports a fresh, contemporary look, with a warm decor and modern furnishings. Local diners now beat a path to the door for hearty food prepared from Welsh ingredients, local and organic where possible. At lunch, tuck into chicken liver parfait with plum chutney for starters or a light bite, or a main dish like cottage pie and gammon, egg and home-made chips. More imaginative evening dishes may take in pan-fried venison with fondant potato and roasted pear jus, or braised pork belly with cider apple jus. On fine days dine alfresco by the stream in the garden.

Open all wk Mon-Tue 4-12 (Wed-Sun noon-mdnt) Restaurant L served Wed-Sat 12-2.30, Sun 12-4 booking required D served Wed-Sat 6-9, Sun 12-4 booking required ⊕ MARSTONS ◄ Pedigree, Oxford Gold, Burton Bitter, guest ales ♂ Thatchers Gold. ♀ 11 Facilities Children's menu Family room Garden Parking Notes ☺

## Victoria Inn

Sigingstone CF71 7LP
☎ 01446 773943
dir: Off B4270 in Sigingstone

A quiet, attractively furnished old village inn with a fine reputation for good quality home-prepared food. The beamed interior, decorated with old photographs, prints and antiques, has a good feel about it. The daily menu is extensive, with some 40 different dishes on offer, including home-made pies and the famous fish pancake.

Open all wk ◄ Hancocks HB, Worthington Creamflow. Facilities Garden Parking

### EAST ABERTHAW
Map 9 ST06

## PICK OF THE PUBS

## Blue Anchor Inn

*See Pick of the Pubs on opposite page*

### MONKNASH
Map 9 SS97

## The Plough & Harrow

CF71 7QQ ☎ 01656 890209
e-mail: info@theploughmonknash.com
dir: M4 junct 35 take dual carriageway to Bridgend. At rdbt follow St Brides sign, then brown tourist signs. Pub 3m NW of Llantwit Major

This low, slate-roofed, 14th-century building was originally built as the chapter house of a monastery, although it has been a pub for 500 of its 600-year existence. Set in peaceful country on the edge of a small village with views across the fields to the Bristol Channel, this area is great for walkers. Expect an atmospheric interior, open fires, real ciders, up to eight guest ales on tap, and home-cooked food using fresh local ingredients.

Open all day all wk Bar Meals L served Mon-Fri 12-2.30, Sat-Sun 12-5 D served all wk 6-8.30 Av main course £7.50 Restaurant L served Mon-Fri 12-2.30, Sat-Sun 12-5 D served Mon-Sat 6-8.30 ⊕ FREE HOUSE ◄ Otley O1, Shepherd Neame Spitfire, Hereford Pale ale, Sharp's IPA, Bass, guest ales ♂ Happy Daze, Fiery Fox, Barnstormer. Facilities Children's menu Garden Parking

# PICK OF THE PUBS

## Blue Anchor Inn

**EAST ABERTHAW**  Map 9 ST06

**CF62 3DD**
☎ 01446 750329  📄 01446 750077
**web:** www.blueanchoraberthaw.com
**dir:** *From Barry take A4226, then B4265 towards Llantwit Major. Follow signs, turn left for East Aberthaw. 3m W of Cardiff Airport*

This pretty, stone-built and heavily thatched inn draws attention to its great age by informing us that it first opened its doors for business in 1380. The grandfather of the present owners, Jeremy and Andrew Coleman, acquired the property in 1941, when he bought it from a large local estate. Legend has it that an underground passage leading down to the seashore was used by wreckers and smugglers, who roamed a coastline that was once much wilder than it is today.

Inside, a warren of small rooms are separated by thick walls, low, beamed ceilings, and a number of open fires, including a large inglenook. A good selection of well kept real ales, including Brains and Wye Valley plus guests, is always on tap.

An enticing range of food is offered in both the bar and the upstairs restaurant. In the bar expect a starter such as poached jerk chicken Caesar salad; then follow with a main course of beef, mushroom and red wine stew; or deep-fried fillet of North Sea cod with minted mushy peas. In the restaurant, the first course might be steamed River Exe mussels with tomato and chilli sauce; followed by pan-roasted fillet of halibut with butterbean and vermouth creamed broth; grilled 10oz Welsh sirloin with watercress and pancetta salad; pan-fried rabbit loin with braised rabbit leg and wild mushrooms; or roasted beetroot and garlic risotto. A good choice is offered for Sunday lunch. Desserts are typified by Grand Marnier crème brûlée; and vanilla pannacotta with spiced poached figs.

**Open** all wk 11-11 (25 Dec noon-2) **Bar Meals** L served Mon-Sat 12-2 D served Mon-Sat 6-9 Av main course £8.95 **Restaurant** L served Sun 12.30-2.30 booking required D served Mon-Sat 7-9.30 booking required Av 3 course à la carte fr £22 ⊕ FREE HOUSE 🛢 Theakston Old Peculier, Wadworth 6X, Wye Valley Hereford Pale Ale, Brains Bitter. **Facilities** Dogs allowed Garden Parking

## WREXHAM

### GRESFORD — Map 15 SJ35

## PICK OF THE PUBS

### Pant-yr-Ochain ♥

**Old Wrexham Rd LL12 8TY**
☎ 01978 853525 ▤ 01978 853505
e-mail: pant.yr.ochain@brunningandprice.co.uk
dir: *From Chester take exit for Nantwich. Holt off A483. Take 2nd left, also signed Nantwich Holt. Turn left at 'The Flash' sign. Pub 500yds on right*

A sweeping drive lined by majestic trees leads to this 16th-century, decoratively gabled manor house overlooking a lake and award-winning gardens. The interior fulfils this initial promise, with an inglenook fireplace, wattle and daub walls, and a host of nooks and crannies. The bar dispenses well kept real ales such as Weetwood Cheshire Cat, with Weston's and Taffy Apples ciders in support. Wine lovers too will not be disappointed by having to choose between over two dozen options. A daily changing menu may offer a starter of trout and brown shrimp rillettes with cucumber pickle and Melba toast; a light bite such as a leek, bacon and gruyère quiche; and main courses such as whole grilled plaice with caper butter, or braised shoulder of lamb with new potatoes. Custard, clotted cream and ice cream are all to be found supporting desserts such as sticky toffee pudding, chocolate and hazelnut brownie, and syrup sponge pudding.

**Open** all wk noon-11.30 (Sun noon-11) Closed: 25 Dec **Bar Meals** Av main course £11.50 food served all day **Restaurant** food served all day ⊕ FREE HOUSE ◀ Timothy Taylor Landlord, Interbrew Flowers Original, Thwaites Original, Weetwood Cheshire Cat, Brunning & Price Original ⏾ Taffy Apples, Westons, Stowford Press. ♥ 22 **Facilities** Play area Garden Parking

### HANMER — Map 15 SJ43

### The Hanmer Arms ★★★★ INN ♥

**SY13 3DE** ☎ 01948 830532 ▤ 01948 830740
e-mail: hanmerarms@btconnect.com
dir: *Between Wrexham & Whitchurch on A539, off A525*

Locals fill the beamed and wooden floored bars of this traditional free house, set beside the parish church in a peaceful, rural location on the Welsh border. The daily set dinner for two includes a glass of house wine, whilst main menu options include Welsh beef fillet with a cabbage and shallot parcel, and asparagus and herb risotto with truffle oil and fresh parmesan. Contemporary en suite rooms make the Hanmer Arms a good touring base.

**Open** all day all wk **Bar Meals** L served all wk 12-2.30 D served all wk 6-9.30 Av main course £9.95 **Restaurant** L served Mon-Sat 12-2.30, Sun 12-9 D served all wk 6-9.30 Fixed menu price fr £14.50 Av 3 course à la carte fr £20 ⊕ FREE HOUSE ◀ Timothy Taylor, Adnams, Stonehouse ⏾ Stowford Press. ♥ 22 **Facilities** Dogs allowed Garden Parking **Rooms** 12

### LLANARMON DYFFRYN CEIRIOG — Map 15 SJ13

## PICK OF THE PUBS

### The Hand at Llanarmon ✕✕✕✕ INN ◉

**LL20 7LD** ☎ 01691 600666 ▤ 01691 600262
e-mail: reception@thehandhotel.co.uk
web: www.thehandhotel.co.uk
dir: *Exit A5 at Chirk follow B4500 for 11m. Through Ceiriog Valley to Llanarmon D C. Pub straight ahead*

Built beside the old drovers' road from London to Anglesey, this 16th-century farmhouse was a natural stopping place for drovers and their flocks. Yet The Hand only became a fully-fledged inn as recently as the late 1950s, and it still retains its original oak beams and large fireplaces. Make the journey up the remote Ceiriog Valley, and you'll find a classic country inn with a unique dining room and 13 comfortable en suite bedrooms. Chef Grant Mulholland has built a strong reputation for superb cuisine, and the pub menu includes traditional favourites such as traditional ploughman's with Welsh cheeses and home-made bread; as well as hot dishes like gammon, eggs and chips. Restaurant diners can expect starters like grilled red mullet with celeriac and ginger purée; followed, perhaps, by leg of Welsh lamb with cranberries and red wine. Desserts are just as inviting; try sticky date pudding, or honey and cranberry pannacotta.

**Open** all day all wk 11-11 (Sun 12-10.30) **Bar Meals** L served Mon-Sat 12-2.20, Sun 12.30-2.45 booking required D served all wk 6.30-8.45 booking required **Restaurant** L served Mon-Sat 12-2.20, Sun 12.30-2.45 booking required D served all wk 6.30-8.45 booking required ⊕ FREE HOUSE ◀ Worthington Cream Flow, Guinness, guest ale ⏾ Stowford Press. **Facilities** Dogs allowed Garden Parking **Rooms** 13

## PICK OF THE PUBS

### West Arms ★★★★ INN ◉◉ ♥

**LL20 7LD** ☎ 01691 600665 ▤ 01691 600622
e-mail: gowestarms@aol.com
dir: *Off A483/A5 at Chirk, take B4500 to Ceiriog Valley*

Centuries ago, cattle drovers coming down from the Welsh hills by way of three tracks (now passable roads) that converge on The West Arms refreshed themselves and their livestock here, before moving on to market. Attractive bedrooms have replaced the old cattle stalls, but nothing is likely to shift the original 16th-century

beams and other ancient timberwork, slate-flagged floors, inglenooks, and period furniture. Like the peripatetic drovers, award-winning chef Grant Williams has travelled too, working in kitchens around the world. His seafood dishes earn him tributes galore – one such dish is grilled fillets of witch (or Torbay) sole with wild River Dee smoked salmon and lemon, Champagne and crème fraîche sauce; or try his pan-fried fillet of Welsh lamb with a mint and rosemary crust. Maybe just relax outside with a pint, admire the distant Berwyn mountains, and lose track of time as the Ceiriog River burbles away below.

*West Arms*

**Open** all day all wk **Bar Meals** L served all wk 12-2 D served all wk 7-9 Av main course £12.95 **Restaurant** L served Sun 12-2 D served all wk 7-9 Fixed menu price fr £27.95 Av 3 course à la carte fr £29.95 ⊕ FREE HOUSE ◀ Flowers IPA, Guinness, guest ales. ♥ 11 **Facilities** Children's menu Children's portions Dogs allowed Garden Parking **Rooms** 15

### MARFORD — Map 15 SJ35

### Trevor Arms Hotel

**LL12 8TA** ☎ 01244 570436 ▤ 01244 570273
e-mail: thetrevorarmshotel@live.co.uk
dir: *Off A483 onto B5102 then right onto B5445 into Marford*

The early 19th-century coaching inn takes its name from Lord Trevor of Trevallin, who was killed in a duel; public executions, both by beheading and hanging, took place in the village. Grisly history notwithstanding, today's Trevor Arms is a charming hostelry, offering a selection of real ales and a varied menu of home cooked dishes. Starters may include chicken liver pâté or prawn cocktail; then a main course of a mixed grill; beer battered fish; or crispy Chinese glazed pork belly. Lite bites could be a duck wrap or salmon fish cakes.

**Open** all day all wk **Bar Meals** L served Mon-Thu 12-2.30, Fri-Sun all day D served all wk 5.30-9.30 Av main course £8 **Restaurant** L served Mon-Thu 12-2.30, Fri-Sun all day D served all wk 5.30-9.30 booking required ⊕ HEINEKEN ◀ John Smith's, Guinness, Guest Ales. **Facilities** Children's menu Children's portions Garden Parking

Save on Hotels. Book at **theAA.com/hotel**

611 WALES

# How to Find a Pub in the Atlas Section

Pubs are located in the gazetteer under the name of the nearest town or village. If a pub is in a small village or rural area, it may appear under a town within five miles of its actual location. The black dots and town names shown in the atlas refer to the gazetteer location in the guide. Please use the directions in the pub entry to find the pub on foot or by car. If directions are not given, or are not clear, please telephone the pub for details.

# Key to County Map

The county map shown here will help you identify the counties within each country. You can look up each county in the guide using the county names at the top of each page. Towns featured in the guide use the atlas pages and index following this map.

## England

1  Bedfordshire
2  Berkshire
3  Bristol
4  Buckinghamshire
5  Cambridgeshire
6  Greater Manchester
7  Herefordshire
8  Hertfordshire
9  Leicestershire
10  Northamptonshire
11  Nottinghamshire
12  Rutland
13  Staffordshire
14  Warwickshire
15  West Midlands
16  Worcestershire

## Scotland

17  City of Glasgow
18  Clackmannanshire
19  East Ayrshire
20  East Dunbartonshire
21  East Renfrewshire
22  Perth & Kinross
23  Renfrewshire
24  South Lanarkshire
25  West Dunbartonshire

## Wales

26  Blaenau Gwent
27  Bridgend
28  Caerphilly
29  Denbighshire
30  Flintshire
31  Merthyr Tydfil
32  Monmouthshire
33  Neath Port Talbot
34  Newport
35  Rhondda Cynon Taff
36  Torfaen
37  Vale of Glamorgan
38  Wrexham

Na h-Eileanan
an Iar

**Orkney Islands**

**Shetland Islands**

Highland

Moray

Aberdeenshire

City of
Aberdeen

Angus

Perth &
Kinross

City of
Dundee

SCOTLAND

Stirling

Fife

Argyll
& Bute

East
Lothian

Argyll
& Bute

Stirling

18

22

Fife

Inverclyde

25

20

Falkirk

North
Ayrshire

23

17

North
Lanarkshire

West
Lothian

City of
Edinburgh

North
Ayrshire

21

Midlothian

South
Ayrshire

19

South Lanarkshire

Scottish
Borders

24

Scottish
Borders

19

Northumberland

Dumfries &
Galloway

Tyne & Wear

Isle
of Man

Cumbria

Durham

North
Yorkshire

Isle of
Anglesey

Lancashire

West
Yorkshire

East Riding
of Yorkshire

Conwy

Merseyside

30

Cheshire

6

South
Yorkshire

Derbyshire

Lincolnshire

29

38

11

Gwynedd

ENGLAND

13

Norfolk

Shropshire

9

12

Ceredigion

Powys

15

14

10

5

Suffolk

WALES

16

1

Pembrokeshire

7

4

8

Essex

Carmarthenshire

Gloucestershire

2

Greater
London

Swansea

3

Oxfordshire

Kent

Wiltshire

Surrey

31

26

32

Hampshire

West
Sussex

East
Sussex

33

35

28

36

Somerset

27

34

Cardiff

Devon

Dorset

37

Isle of
Wight

Cornwall

Isles of
Scilly

**Guernsey**

**Jersey**

| 0 | 20 | 40 | 60 | 80 | 100 miles |

| 0 | 20 | 40 | 60 | 80 | 100 | 120 | 140 | 160 kilometres |

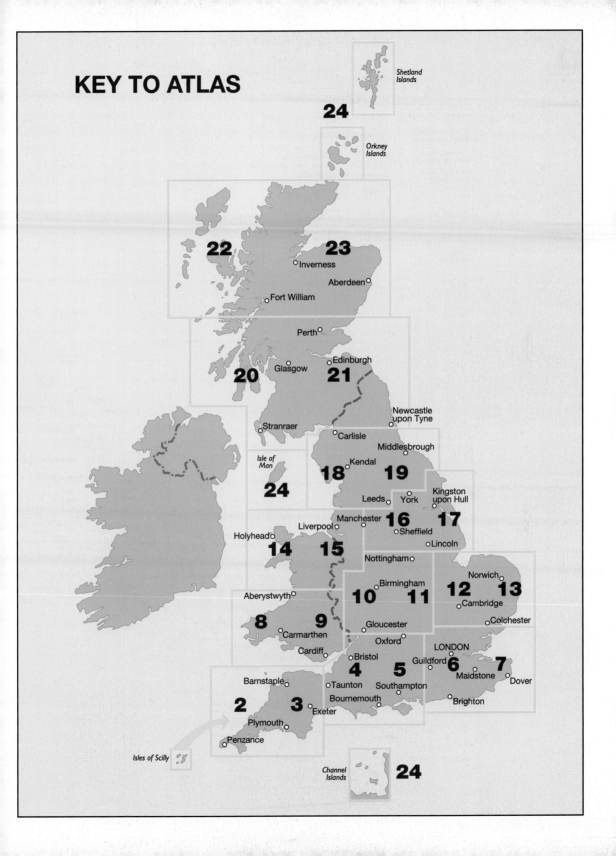

# KEY TO ATLAS

**2**

## Legend

| | |
|---|---|
| M6 | Motorway/toll motorway |
| | Motorway junction full/restricted. Service area |
| A35 | Primary route single/dual carriageway |
| A34 | Other A road single/dual carriageway |
| B3400 | B road |
| | Unclassified road |
| V | Vehicle ferry |
| C | Fast vehicle ferry or catamaran |

| | |
|---|---|
| ● Oundle | Pub/Inn |
| ◉ Oldstead | AA Pub of the Year |
| ○ King's Cliffe | Town/Village name |
| | National boundary |
| ESSEX | English county name & boundary |
| CONWY | Welsh county name & boundary |
| MORAY | Scottish county name & boundary |
| | National Park |

ISLES OF SCILLY

Bryher — Tresco — St Martin's · Higher Town
New Grimsby
TRESCO
Hugh Town — St Mary's
HUGH TOWN — ISLES OF SCILLY (ST MARY'S)
Middle Town — Old Town
St Agnes

**SV**

**SW**

Lundy

Hartland Point
Hartla

Morwenstow

Kilkhampto

Bude Bay · Bude
Widemouth Bay

Crackington Haven · Week St Mary

Boscastle
Tintagel
Trebarwith
Delabole · Camelford
Port Isaac · Port Gaverne
Polzeath · Pendoggett
Rock · St Tudy · St Breward · Bolventor
Harlyn · BODMIN MOOR
St Merryn · Padstow · Blisland
Porthcothan · Wadebridge · Dunmere · Bodmin · St Neot · St Cleer
Mawgan Porth · St Mawgan · St Columb Major · Lanivet · Dobwalls
Newquay · Roche · Bugle · Lanlivery · St Keyne
West Pentire · St Blazey · Lostwithiel · St Keyne
Cubert · Mitchell · Summercourt · St Austell · Tywardreath · Pelynt
Perranporth · Ladock · St Stephen · Polkerris · Bodinnick
St Agnes · Marazanvose · Polruan · Fowey · Polperro
Porthtowan · Grampound · Pentewan
Portreath · St Day · Truro · St Ewe · Mevagissey
Redruth · Carnon Downs · Malpas · Ruan Lanihorne · Tregony · Gorran Haven
St Ives Bay · Gwithian · Camborne · Feock · Veryan · Portloe
Zennor · St Ives · Lelant · Hayle · Mylor Bridge · St Just-in-Roseland · Portscatho
Ludgvan · Penryn · St Mawes
St Just · Marazion · Falmouth
Penzance · Goldsithney · Helston · Constantine · Mawnan Smith
Newlyn · Perranuthnoe · Gweek
Land's End · Sennen · St Buryan · Mousehole · Porthleven · Manaccan
Lamorna · Praa Sands · Gunwalloe · St Keverne
Porthcurno · Treen · Mullion
Coverack
Lizard · Cadgwith
Lizard Point

CORNWALL

For continuation pages refer to numbered arrows

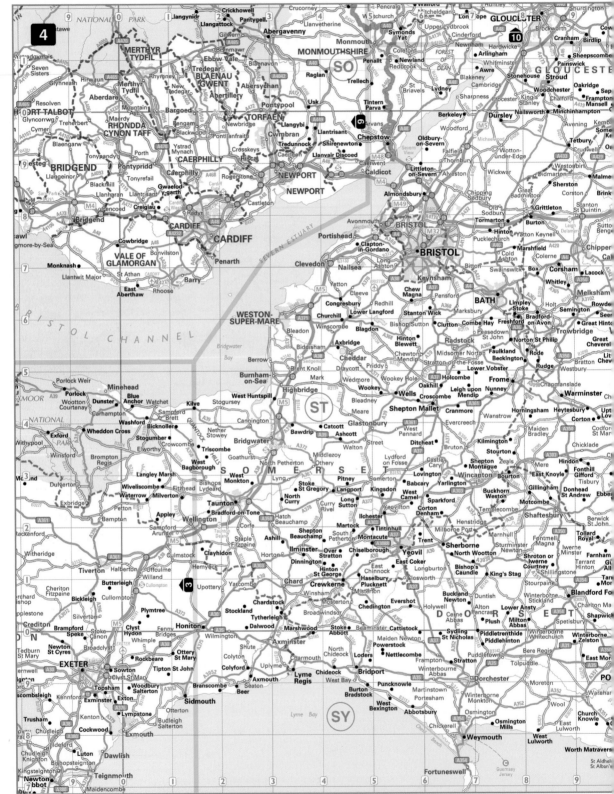

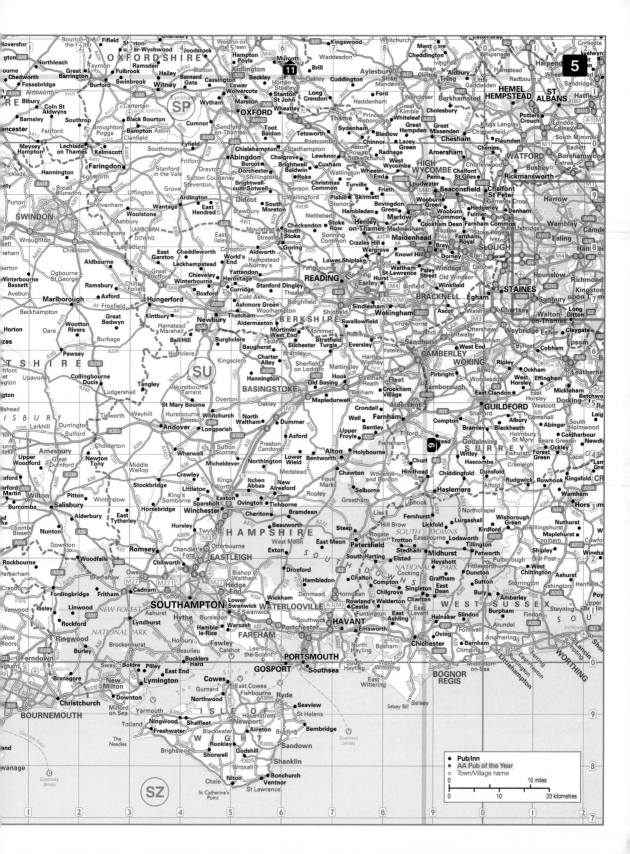

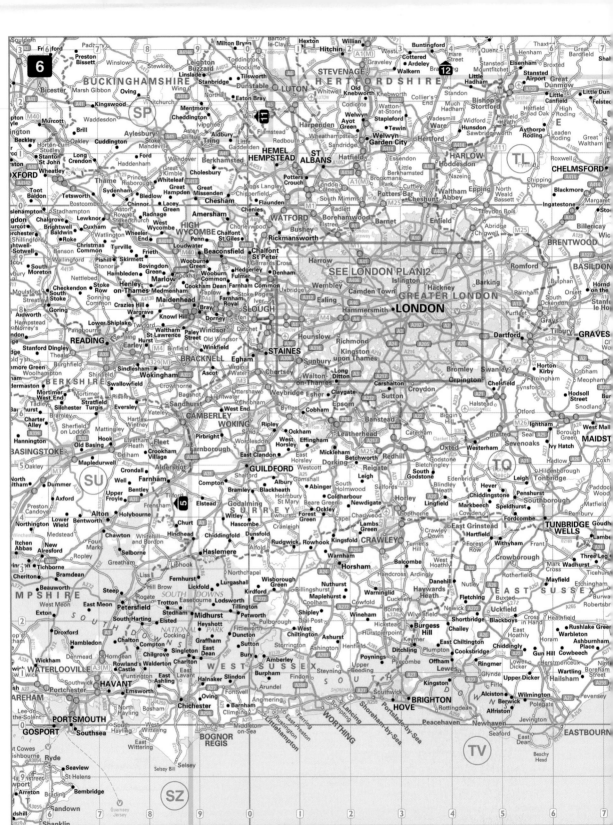

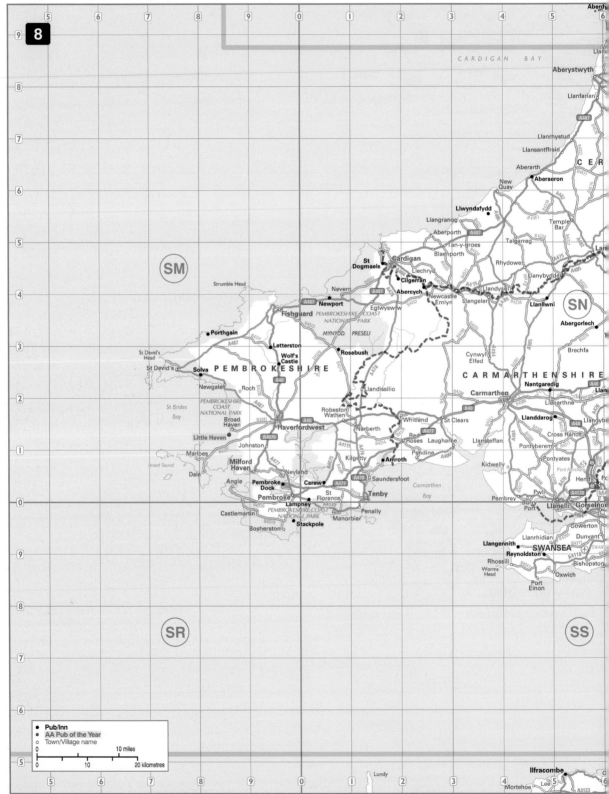

For continuation pages refer to numbered arrows

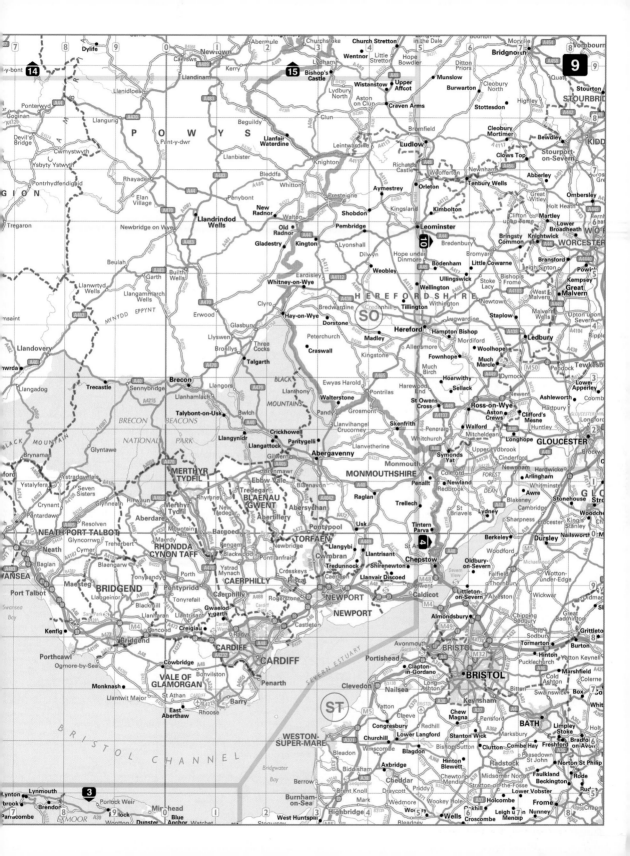

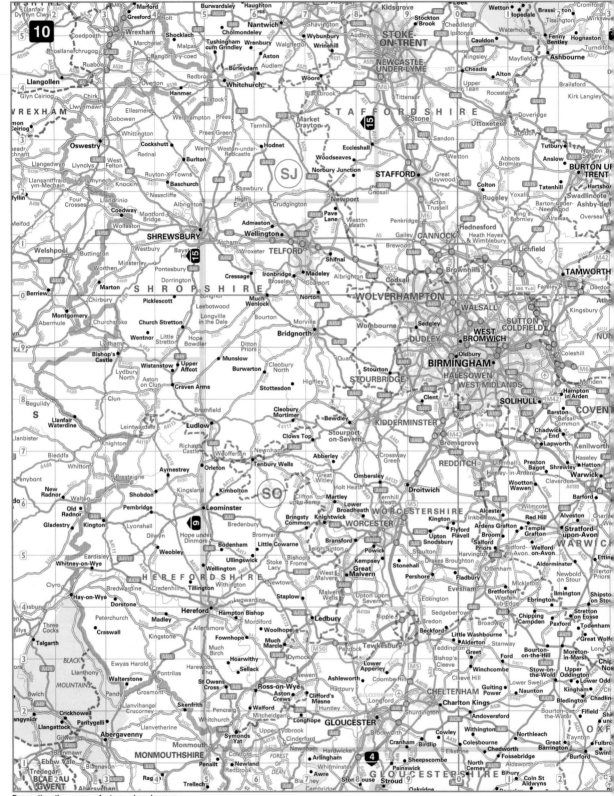

For continuation pages refer to numbered arrows

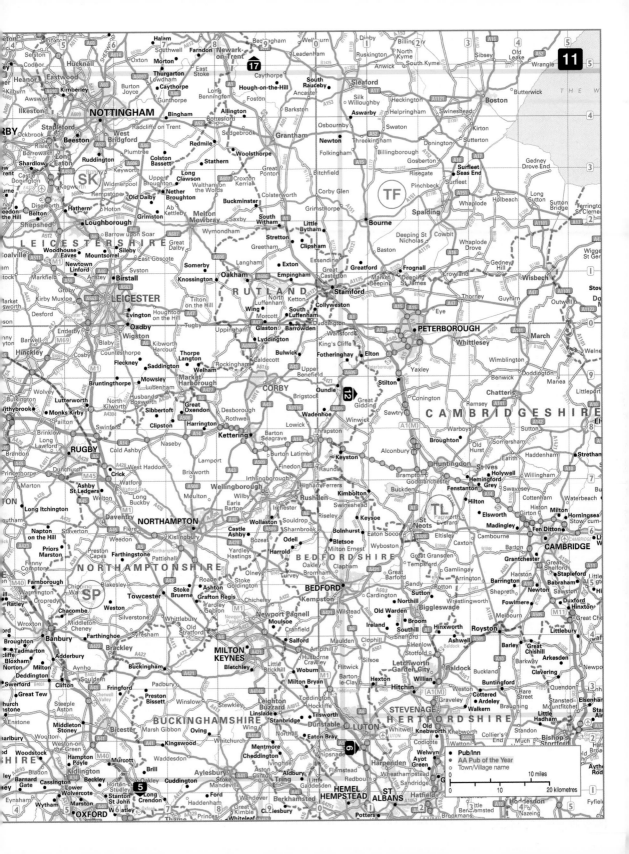

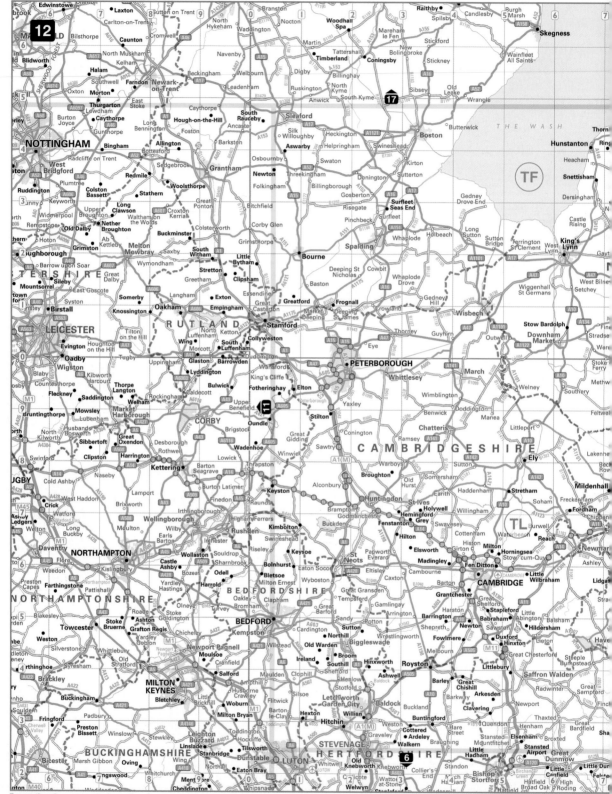

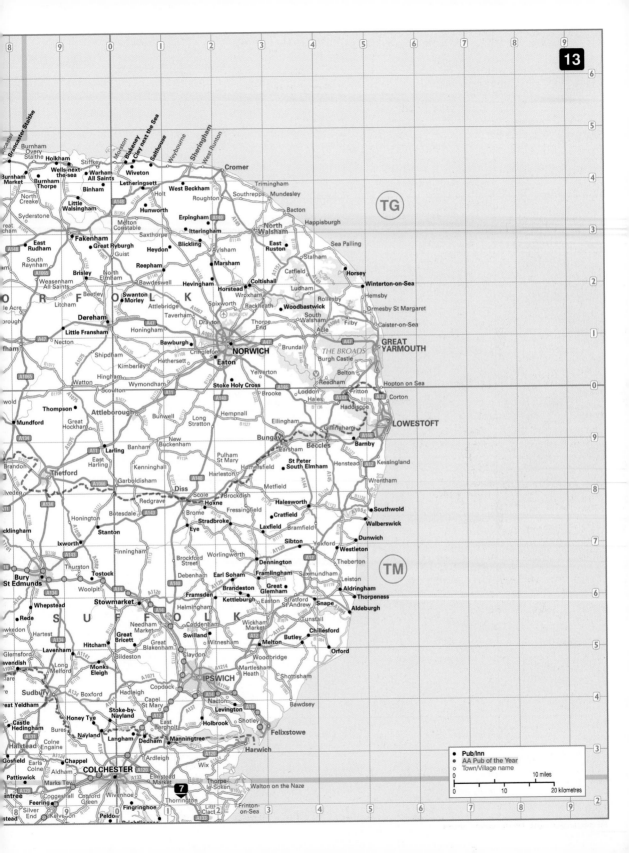

**14**

ISLE OF ANGLESEY

Cemaes
Amlwch
Llanerchymedd
Holyhead
Llanfachraeth
Benllech
Red Wharf Bay
Llandudno
Rhôs-on-Sea
Trearddur Bay
Pentraeth
Deganwy
Colwyn Bay
Holy Island
Llangefni
Llangoed
Penmaenmawr
Conwy
Llandudno Junction
Llanddulas
Rhosneigr
Menai Bridge
Beaumaris
Bangor
Llanfairfechan
Llansanffraid Glan Conwy
Llanfair P.G.
Llanfairfechan
Betws-yn-Rhos
Aberffraw
Y Felinheli
Llanllechid
Bethesda
Tal-y-Bont
Llanfair Talhaiarn
Newborough
Caernarfon
Llanrug
Llangernyw
Llansan
Bontnewydd
Llanberis
Trefriw
Llanrwst
Bylchau
Waunfawr
Capel Curig
CONWY
Caernarfon Bay
Llandwrog
Llanwnda
Betws-y-Coed
Clynnog-fawr
Penygroes
Dolwyddelan
Pentrefoelas
Rhyd-Ddu
Penmachno
Cerrigydrudion
Nantgwynant
SNOWDONIA
SH
Beddgelert
Blaenau Ffestiniog
Y M
Llanaelhaearn
Prenteg
Ffestiniog
Morfa Nefyn
Tremadog
Maentwrog
Nefyn
Llanystumdwy
Penrhyndeudraeth
NATIONAL
Bala
Bodfuan
Porthmadog
LLEYN
Criccieth
Borth-y-Gest
Talsarnau
Lland
Tudweiliog
PENINSULA
Trawsfynydd
GWYNEDD
Sarn
Pwllheli
Harlech
Llanuwchllyn
Llanbedrog
PARK
Y Rhiw
Abersoch
Llanbedr
Ganllwyd
Aberdaron
Dyffryn Ardudwy
Bardsey Island
Tal-y-bont
Dolgellau
Dinas-Mawddwy
Barmouth
Lla
Fairbourne
A470
Mallwyd
Llange
Llwyngwril
Corris
Cemmaes Road
Llanbrynmair
Bryncrug
Tywyn
Pennal
Machynlleth
Carno
Aberdyfi
SN
Dylife
Borth
Tal-y-bont
Llandre
Capel Bangor
Llanidloes
CARDIGAN BAY
Aberystwyth
Ponterwyd
9

● Pub/Inn
● AA Pub of the Year
○ Town/Village name

0          10 miles
0          10          20 kilometres

For continuation pages refer to numbered arrows

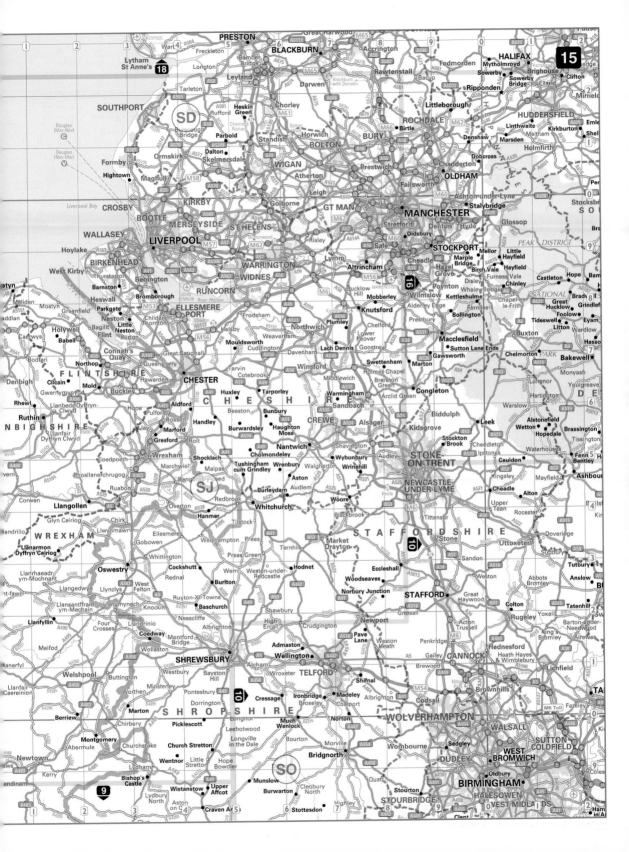

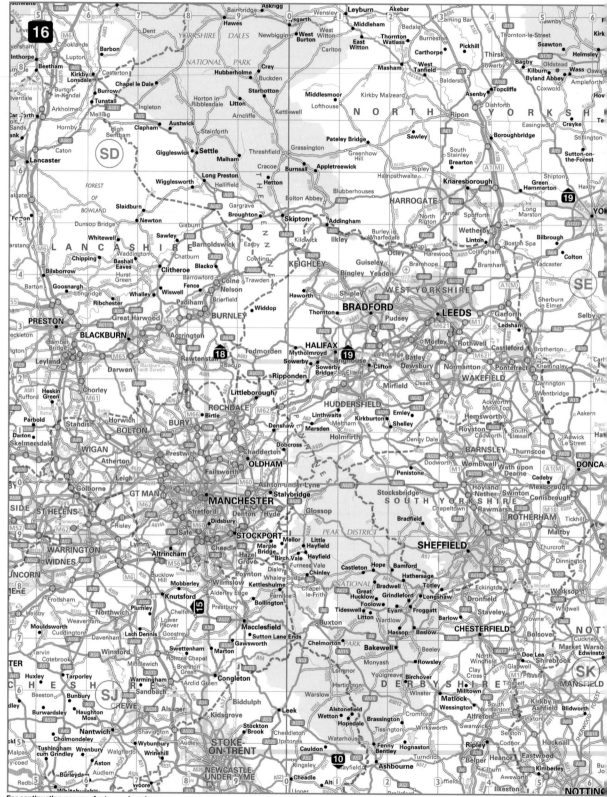

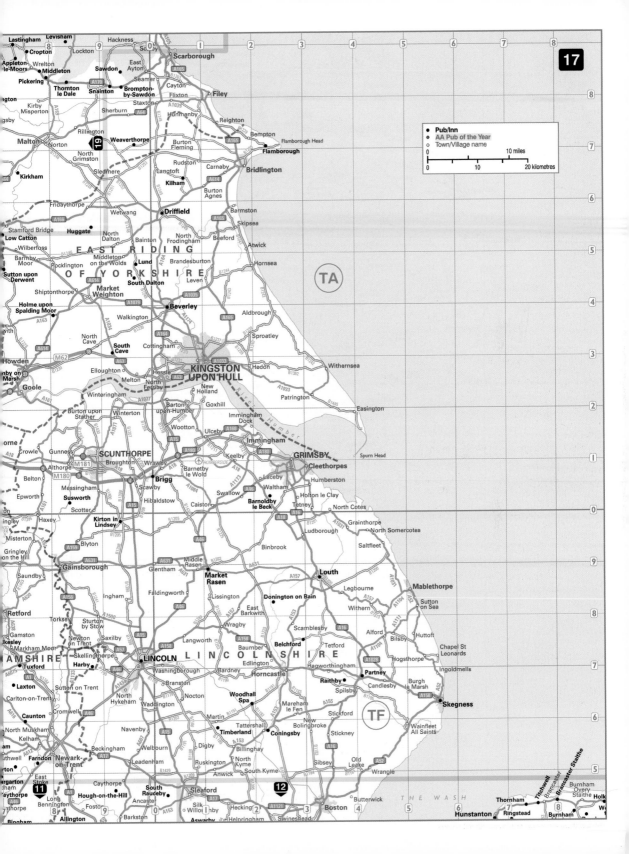

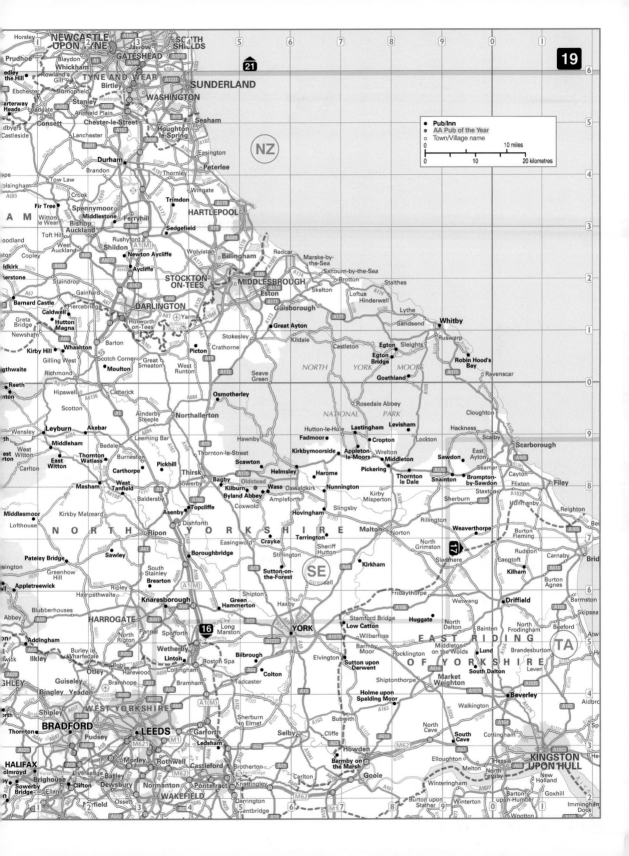

C EDIN — City of Edinburgh
C GLAS — City of Glasgow
CLACKS — Clackmannanshire
C DUND — City of Dundee
E DUNS — East Dunbartonshire
E RENS — East Renfrewshire
INVER — Inverclyde
MDLOTH — Midlothian
N LANS — North Lanarkshire
RENS — Renfrewshire
W DUNS — West Dunbartonshire
W LOTH — West Lothian

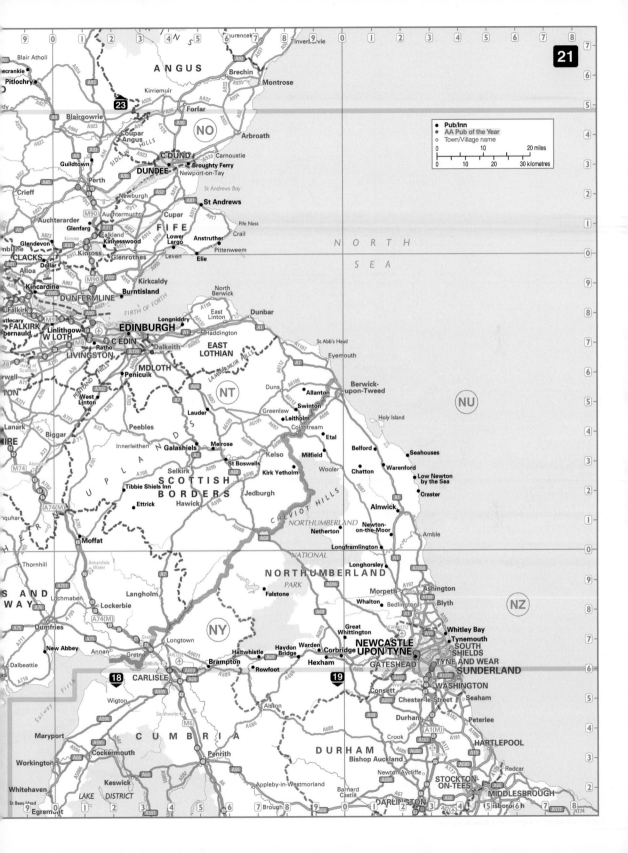

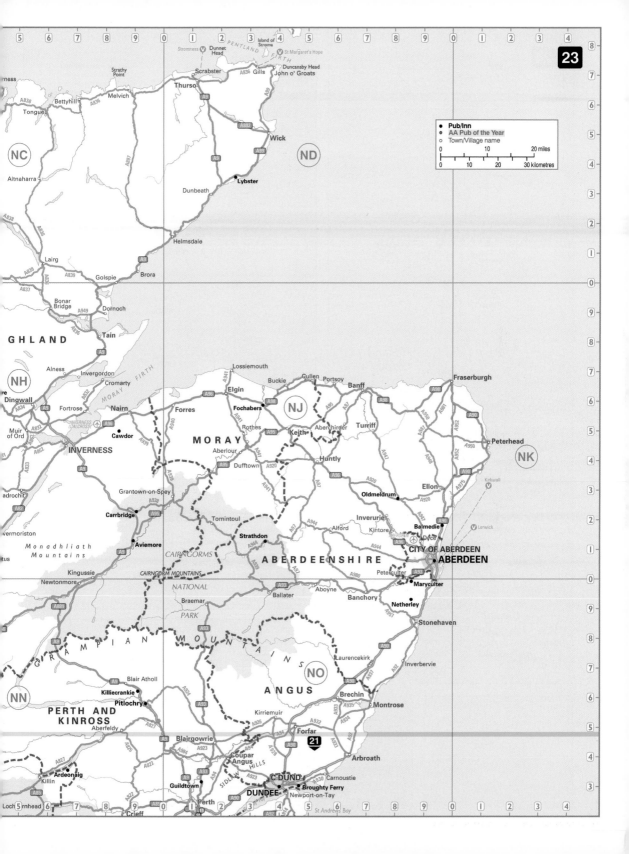

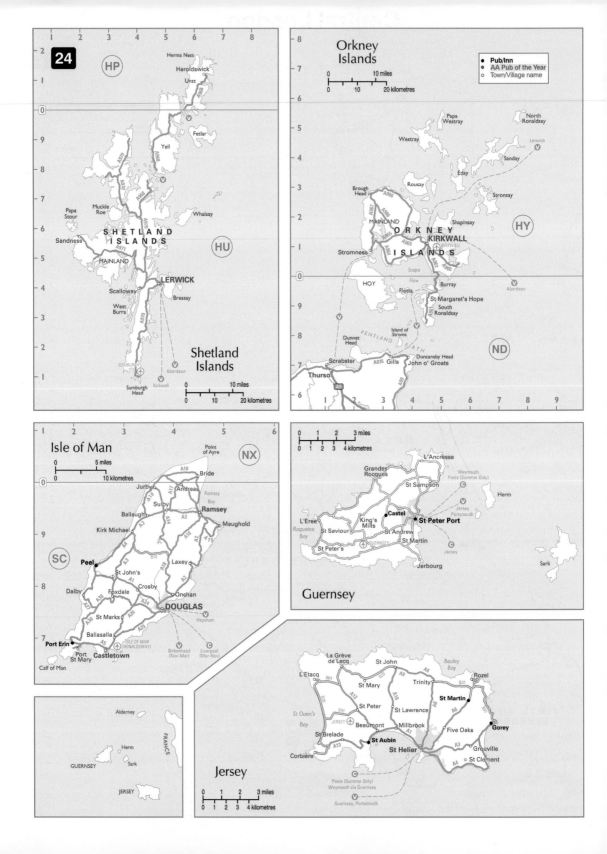

**24**

HP

Herma Ness
Haroldswick
Unst
A968

Fetlar

Yell
A970

Papa Stour
Muckle Roe
Whalsay

SHETLAND ISLANDS

Sandness
MAINLAND
A971

HU

LERWICK
Scalloway
Bressay
West Burra
A970
SUMBURGH
Aberdeen
Sumburgh Head
Kirkwall

0        10 miles
0    10    20 kilometres

Shetland Islands

## Orkney Islands

- ● **Pub/Inn**
- ● **AA Pub of the Year**
- ○ **Town/Village name**

0        10 miles
0    10    20 kilometres

Papa Westray
Westray
North Ronaldsay
Lerwick
Sanday
Eday
Brough Head
Rousay
Stronsay
Shapinsay
MAINLAND
A967
A966
ORKNEY
KIRKWALL
Stromness
ISLANDS
Scapa Flow
HOY
Burray
Aberdeen
Flotta
St Margaret's Hope
South Ronaldsay
HY

PENTLAND FIRTH
Dunnet Head
Island of Stroma
ND
Scrabster
Duncansby Head
Gills
John o' Groats
Thurso
A836
A9

## Isle of Man

0      5 miles
0    10 kilometres

Point of Ayre
NX
A10
Bride
Jurby
A17
Andreas
Ramsey Bay
Sulby
A14
Ramsey
Ballaugh
A3
Maughold
Kirk Michael
A18
A2
A15
A4
B10
Peel
Laxey
SC
St John's
A1
Crosby
A2
Dalby
Foxdale
Onchan
A36
A24
DOUGLAS
A27
St Marks
Heysham
Ballasalla
A23
ISLE OF MAN (RONALDSWAY)
Port Erin
A5
Birkenhead (Nov-Mar)
Liverpool (Mar-Nov)
Port St Mary
Castletown
Calf of Man

Alderney
Herm
FRANCE
GUERNSEY
Sark
JERSEY

0  1  2  3 miles
0  1  2  3  4 kilometres

L'Ancresse
Grandes Rocques
Weymouth Poole (Summer Only)
St Sampson
Herm
Castel
St Peter Port
L'Eree
King's Mills
Jersey Portsmouth
Roquaine Bay
St Saviour
St Andrew
St Peter's
St Martin
Sark
Jerbourg
Jersey

## Guernsey

La Grève de Lecq
St John
Bouley Bay
L'Etacq
B64
St Mary
A9
Trinity
Rozel
B33
St Peter
A10
St Lawrence
A8
St Martin
St Ouen's Bay
B41
JERSEY
Beaumont
Millbrook
Five Oaks
Gorey
St Brelade
St Aubin
A1
St Helier
A3
Grouville
Corbière
A13
A4
St Clement

Poole (Summer Only)
Weymouth via Guernsey
Guernsey, Portsmouth

## Jersey

0  1  2  3 miles
0  1  2  3  4 kilometres

# Central London

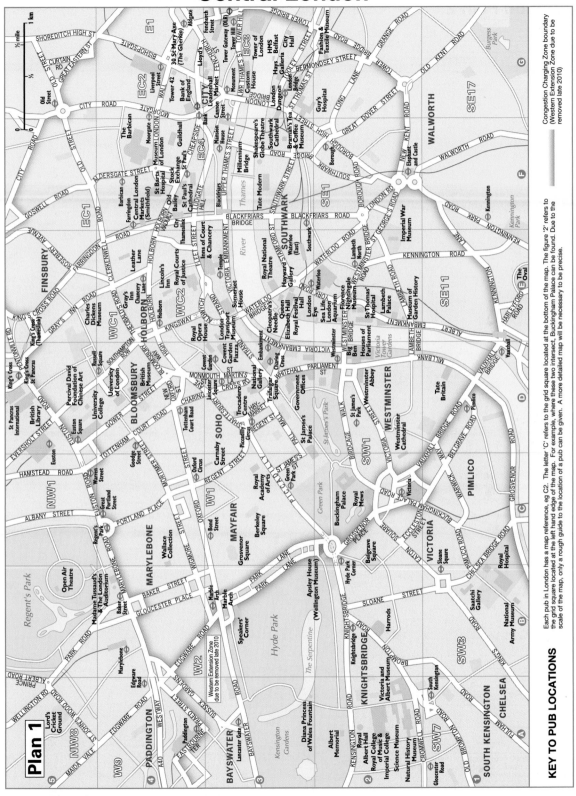

**Plan 1**

# London Plan 2

Central London Congestion Charging Zone
(The Western Extension Zone is due to be removed late 2010)

# Index

Red entries are Pick of the Pubs

AA Media Limited would like to thank the following photographers, companies and picture libraries for their assistance in the preparation of this book.

Abbreviations for the picture credits are as follows: (t) top; (b) bottom; (l) left; (r) right; (c) centre; (AA) AA World Travel Library

1 The Inn at Fossebridge; 2 The Red Lion, Shipston on Stour; 3 The Old Queens Head, Penn; 5 (t) Wiveton Bell, Wiveton; (b) The Masons Arms, Branscombe; 6 Royal Oak Inn, Chichester; 7 (t) The Horse & Groom Inn, Malmesbury (c) The Bush, Ovington (b) The Red Lion, Shipston on Stour; 8 The Black Swan at Oldstead; 9 (t) The Sun Inn, Dalkeith (b) The Swan Inn, Little Haven; 10 The Fox & Hounds, East Knoyle; 11 Hind's Head Hotel, Bray; 12 The One Elm, Stratford-upon-Avon; 14 The Walnut Tree, nr Abergavenny; 15 (l & r) Rose & Crown, Warwick; 16 Fever-Tree Tonic Water; 18 Hendrick's Gin; 19 No. 3 Gin, Berry Bros & Rudd; 20 Sipsmith Gin; 25 AA/C Sawyer; 26 AA/T Mackie; 552 lh page AA/W Voysey; 553 AA/P Trenchard; 554 AA/S Anderson; 583 AA/S Whitehorne; 580 AA/S Lewis; 611 AA/I Burgum; 614 AA/R Coulam

Every effort has been made to trace the copyright holders, and we apologise in advance for any accidental errors. We would be happy to apply the corrections in the following edition of this publication.

# Readers' Report Form

Please send this form to:–
Editor, The Pub Guide,
Lifestyle Guides,
AA Publishing,
13th Floor, Fanum House,
Basingstoke RG21 4EA

or fax: 01256 491647
or e-mail: lifestyleguides@theAA.com

Please use this form to tell us about any pub or inn you have visited, whether it is in the guide or not currently listed. We are interested in the quality of food, the selection of beers and the overall ambience of the establishment.

Feedback from readers helps us to keep our guide accurate and up to date. However, if you have a complaint to make during a visit, we do recommend that you discuss the matter with the pub management there and then, so that they have a chance to put things right before your visit is spoilt.

**Please note** that the AA does not undertake to arbitrate between you and the pub management, or to obtain compensation or engage in protracted correspondence.

Date

Your name (BLOCK CAPITALS)

Your address (BLOCK CAPITALS)

Post code

E-mail address

Name of pub

Location

Comments

(please attach a separate sheet if necessary)

Please tick here ☐ if you DO NOT wish to receive details of AA offers or products

PTO

# Readers' Report Form *continued*

Have you bought this guide before? ☐ YES ☐ NO

Do you regularly use any other pub, accommodation or food guides? ☐ YES ☐ NO
If YES, which ones?

_____

_____

What do you find most useful about The AA Pub Guide?

_____

_____

_____

_____

Do you read the editorial features in the guide? ☐ YES ☐ NO

Do you use the location atlas? ☐ YES ☐ NO

Is there any other information you would like to see added to this guide?

_____

_____

_____

_____

What are your main reasons for visiting pubs (tick all that apply)
food ☐    business ☐    accommodation ☐
beer ☐    celebrations ☐    entertainment ☐
atmosphere ☐    leisure ☐
other

How often do you visit a pub for a meal?
more than once a week ☐
once a week ☐
once a fortnight ☐
once a month ☐
once in six months ☐